The Granger Collection, New York

Drink

Coca-Cola

DELICIOUS and REFRESHING

Coca-Cola is a perfect answer to thirst that no imitation can satisfy.

Coca-Cola *quality*, recorded in the public taste, is what holds it above imitations.

Demand the genuine by full name— nicknames encourage substitution.

THE COCA-COLA CO.
ATLANTA, GA.

Sold Everywhere

The Granger Collection, New York

---

840   1850   1860   1870   1880   1890   1900

1863 National Banking Act creates a new banking system of federally chartered banks to eliminate the abuses of state-chartered banks.

1865 Civil War ends and subsequent improvements in rail and steamship transportation close the gap between producer and consumer.

1900 Coca-Cola establishes one of the first franchise operations by selling its syrup to franchised bottlers.

continued on inside back cover

LF

NIGGA WHAT?

for the

BUSINESS

21st

Century

BUSINESS

for the

21st Century

Steven J. Skinner
University of Kentucky

John M. Ivancevich
University of Houston

IRWIN

Homewood, IL 60430
Boston, MA 02116

About the Cover

The whole is greater than the sum of its parts. On the cover of this book, various individual images are combined to form a new picture. Similarly, the study of business is an overview of a number of individual functions, such as marketing and management, which work together to form an integrated system.

The types of businesses in this system (e.g., small, corporate, service, and manufacturing) vary as much as the shapes and colors in the picture on the cover. In the small, inset photos, a satellite view of the earth displays the new, global frontier of business. A green, organic border brackets the picture, signifying the fragile yet crucial connection between business and the environment. The combination of the organic border and the metallic shapes of the interior illustrates the range of business functions, from agriculture to industrial operations. Modern structural details point skyward, showing the path of business and technology into the future.

Cover photographs: © Chicago Photographic Company and courtesy of NASA
Part and chapter photographs: © Kenji Kerins

Sponsoring editor: Kurt L. Strand
Developmental editor: Laura Hurst Spell
Project editor: Jean Roberts
Production manager: Bette Ittersagen
Designer: Maureen McCutcheon
Photo researcher: Michael J. Hruby
Copyeditor: Charlotte Koelling
Compositor: Carlisle Communications, Ltd.
Typeface: 10/12 Times Roman
Printer: Von Hoffmann Press, Inc.

Library of Congress Cataloging–in–Publication Data

Skinner, Steven J.
  Business for the 21st Century / Steven J. Skinner, John M.
Ivancevich.
    p.   cm.
  Includes bibliographical references and indexes.
  ISBN 0-256-09222-2
  1. Business forecasting.   2. Twenty-first century—Forecasts.
I. Ivancevich, John M.   II. Title.   III. Title: Business for the
twenty-first century.
HD30.27.S57   1992
338.5'443—dc20   91–20643

Printed in the United States of America
1 2 3 4 5 6 7 8 9 0 VH 8 7 6 5 4 3 2 1

To Moira, Aaron, and Carrie Skinner

To my immediate family—Dan, Jill, Dana, Paul, and Pegi— and to all the people who are now experiencing free enterprise since the Iron Curtain and Berlin Wall have been torn down

Steven J. Skinner

Steven J. Skinner is the Rosenthal Professor in the College of Business and Economics at the University of Kentucky where he has taught Marketing and Management courses for nine years. He received a D.B.A. from the University of Kentucky. He was formerly a research administrator for State Farm Insurance. Dr. Skinner is the author of *Marketing*, a college textbook, and coauthor of *The New Banker*, a business trade book. He has published numerous refereed articles in the major journals in his field.

In addition to his academic pursuits, Dr. Skinner has consulted for several Fortune 500 companies as well as small businesses.

John M. Ivancevich

John M. Ivancevich has spent 17 years at the University of Houston teaching, conducting research, participating in professional associations, and consulting with many different enterprises in and outside the United States. In his academic career, which includes time spent earning a B.S. degree at Purdue University and master's and doctorate degrees at the University of Maryland, he has taught Introduction to Business, Human Resource Management, Management, and Organizational Behavior courses. He has written, coauthored, or coedited over 45 books and published over 130 refereed papers.

During his academic career, Dr. Ivancevich has consulted with over 100 firms on such topics as reward system implementation, performance appraisal plans, goal-setting programs, merging divergent organizational cultures, new business start-ups, team building, and leadership training. He is currently involved in a project of presenting free enterprise techniques, knowledge, and tools to Eastern European management trainees.

Contents in Brief

Contents

Preface

Our major goal in writing *Business for the 21st Century* has been to develop a text that blends basic business concepts with current business practice in a way that students and instructors will find interesting, exciting, and relevant. To prepare students for the challenges and opportunities that lie ahead, an instructor needs a book that takes a positive yet candid approach toward business, illustrating that business is *not* down and out in America. On the contrary, now is an exciting and challenging time to be entering the business world, whether in a small business or in a large corporation. Competitive conditions, work force changes, social trends, and technological advances mean that rewarding business careers await those individuals who are knowledgeable, skilled, and motivated. To motivate, excite, and educate students, a text should cover the basic concepts of business within the context of our changing world. This is that text.

As we move toward the 21st century, the business world is changing dramatically. Competition is becoming increasingly global. New markets are opening in Europe, Germany, and the Soviet Union. The American economy is leaning more toward services, and *quality* is the initiative of many firms. Social responsibility is becoming a major concern for business. Demographic and lifestyle shifts are changing the way we shop, where we work, and how we live. The changes taking place today are forming the business world of the future. Students who understand these changes will be more likely to succeed than those who do not. This is the business book that integrates these and many other current developments to prepare students for the 21st century.

INTRODUCING OUR TEXTBOOK

To accomplish the goals set forth above, we have organized *Business for the 21st Century* into seven parts that provide students with an integrated and practical approach to understanding current business practices. Every chapter fits logically into this integrated approach. No chapters are "left over" or "tacked on." Part One provides an overview of the core of business, the business enterprise, discussing the foundations of business, forms of business ownership, and small business, entrepreneurship, and franchising. Part Two presents the business environment that surrounds the core, including the social, legal, and international environment. The remaining parts form the outer circle, consisting of the various aspects of operating the business enterprise. Part Three focuses on managing and organizing the business, and on the management of production and operations. Part Four examines the management of human resources, as well as human relations and labor relations. Part Five covers marketing strategy, including product, price, distribution, and promotion decisions. Part Six explores the financial management of business firms. Part Seven is devoted to accounting and information systems.

FEATURES OF THE TEXTBOOK

Our textbook has several features that make it enjoyable to read and enjoyable to teach. Students can use the following learning tools to help them understand and retain the material in the text.

- *Learning objectives.* Each chapter begins with several clear, attainable learning objectives; questions in the test bank are keyed to these objectives.
- *Illustrations.* Numerous charts, graphs, diagrams, and photos reinforce and explain concepts in the text.
- *Margin notes.* Definitions of key terms are placed in the margins next to where the terms are introduced to facilitate learning.
- *Summary of learning objectives.* The chapter summary is concise yet complete. Each item in the summary is tied to the corresponding chapter opening learning objective to provide a cohesive, integrated chapter review.
- *Key terms.* A list of key terms at chapter end helps students identify and review important concepts.
- *Questions for discussion and review.* Students can use these questions to evaluate their understanding of the chapter.
- *Glossary.* Key terms and their definition may be quickly located in the comprehensive end-of-book glossary.
- *Name, subject, and company indexes.* Topics in the book can be easily located with the help of name, subject, and company indexes.

This textbook also offers several application features that will help students to relate the text material to their own experiences and to apply the concepts in the text to the real world of business.

- *Opening vignette.* The text of each chapter begins with a current news story that introduces students to the chapter's topics.
- *Business Action.* Each chapter features two additional news stories that focus on recognizable firms and contemporary topics, extending the concepts discussed in the text.
- *Connections.* Each chapter features a short self-assessment quiz that helps students evaluate their attitudes, orientations, and values, as they pertain to business.
- *You'll Know It's the 21st Century When. . . .* Each chapter concludes with a short feature presenting some interesting trend that will influence business activities in the 21st century.
- *Did You Know?* In each chapter, an interesting business-related sidebar appears next to one of the illustrations.
- *Real world examples.* Current examples of familiar organizations and business issues are used throughout each chapter to relate the text to the real world.

- *Cases.* Two current, realistic cases at the end of each chapter help students put business concepts into practice.
- *Career appendixes.* Each of the seven parts ends with a comprehensive and informative section on business careers.

SUPPORT FOR INSTRUCTORS AND STUDENTS

An integrated support system for both instructors and students accompanies *Business for the 21st Century*.

Integrated Teaching System

The integrator   The Integrator places all of the appropriate instructional materials for each chapter at the instructor's fingertips. The system consists of a sturdy file box containing a folder for each chapter. Each chapter folder holds appropriate instructor's manual pages, instructional strategies and activities pages, color acetates, and transparency masters. A three-ring binder is also provided for carrying the appropriate material to class.

Instructor's manual   The instructor's manual provides a master plan for implementing the various instructional tools provided with this textbook. Each chapter of the instructor's manual includes: (1) chapter overview, (2) list of resources, (3) learning objectives, (4) lecture outline, (5) Business Action notes, (6) answers to questions for discussion and review, (7) list of key terms with definitions, (8) case notes, (9) transparency master and color acetate notes, and (10) a list of recommended readings.

Computerized instructor's manual   The contents of the instructor's manual are also available on disk so that the instructor can customize his or her lesson plans.

Instructional strategies and activities   This handbook provides a variety of materials for expanding lectures and engaging students in classroom activities. Each chapter includes: (1) two current lecture supplements focusing on key concepts from the text; (2) two student activities, such as individual or small group classroom activities, individual homework, group projects, guest speakers, interviews, and class discussion tactics; and (3) one supplemental case, based on a student-oriented situation.

Test bank   The test bank includes more than 2,800 true-false, multiple-choice, and essay questions. Each question is categorized by level of learning and reflects one of the learning objectives.

Computerized Testing Software   The most recent version of Irwin's test-generation software, this program includes advanced features such as allowing the instructor to add and edit questions on-line, save and reload tests, create up to 99 versions of each test, attach graphics to questions, import and export

ASCII files, and select questions based on type, level of difficulty, or key word. The program allows password protection of saved tests and question databases, and is networkable.

Teletest   Those instructors without access to a microcomputer, or those who prefer not to use one to create tests, can use Irwin's Teletest service. The service provides a toll-free number for instructors to call in a test request. Tests and answer keys are printed on a laser printer according to the specifications provided. Requests are completed the same day they are called in and are shipped by first class mail. Please allow five business days for delivery.

Color acetates   These 150 full-color transparency acetates will help the instructor reinforce and extend the concepts presented in the text in classroom presentations. The acetates consist mainly of original materials, along with some of the key tables and figures from the text. Notes for using the acetates are provided in the instructor's manual.

Transparency masters   In addition to the acetates, all of the tables and figures from the text are reproduced as transparency masters.

Business videos   Eight hours of videos featuring timely business topics from a variety of organizations bring business concepts to life. To facilitate classroom use, videos are 10 to 15 minutes in length, and some videos are tied directly to cases and applications in the text. A guide to using the videos is also provided.

Business forms   In the search for a job, and on the job, students will encounter a multitude of forms. This packet of sample forms will help familiarize students with these vital tools of business.

Career implementation model   This supplement offers a series of lessons and activities designed to walk students through the process of deciding on a career and applying for and starting a new job. The lessons are linked to the career appendixes in the text.

Support for Students

Study guide   The study guide provides a variety of learning tools including a chapter overview; learning objectives; matching, true/false, and multiple-choice questions, and minicases. Students who use the study guide will be well prepared for class discussions and exams.

Tutorial software   With this interactive software, students can use their business knowledge and skills to manage their own firm. The questions in the tutorial are based on the concepts in the text and posed within the context of a realistic company. Answering these questions will help students to review the concepts from the text and to understand how they apply to managing an actual business.

Global trade game   This user-friendly computerized simulation/game reinforces many fundamental concepts from the text. Students start with a given amount of money and soybeans and make decisions to buy or sell soybeans. In making these decisions, students must take into consideration variables such as the forces affecting supply and demand, forms of transportation, methods of insurance, political and environmental conditions, and so forth.

ACKNOWLEDGMENTS

Many individuals have made valuable comments throughout the development of this book. We appreciate the helpful suggestions of the following reviewers.

Gaber A. Abou El Enein
Mankato State University

Jack F. Amyx
Cameron University

John J. Balek
Morton College

Kathryn C. Beebe
Salt Lake Community College

Robert J. Bielski
Dean Junior College

John S. Bowdidge
Southwest Missouri State University

Stephen C. Branz
Triton College

Robert A. Brechner
Miami-Dade Community College

Steven H. Brown
DeVry Institute

Carolyn Browning
Southwest Virginia Community College

John Bunnell
Broome Community College

Eugene J. Calvasina
Auburn University-Montgomery

Robert B. Carrel
Vincennes University

William A. Clarey
Bradley University

D. James Day
Shawnee State University

Parks B. Dimsdale
University of West Florida

W. Michael Gough
DeAnza College

Rita C. Griswold, Esq.
Saint Joseph College

John W. Hagen
California State University, Fresno

W. Eugene Hastings
Portland Community College

Steven E. Huntley
Florida Community College-Jacksonville

Paul F. Jenner
Missouri Western State College

Lynn J. Karowsky
University of Northern Colorado

Kenneth J. Lacho
University of New Orleans

Paul James Londrigan
Mott Community College

Michael B. Marker
Jacksonville State University

Alan Marks
DeVry Institute

Spencer P. Mehl
Coastal Carolina Community College

Randall D. Mertz
Mesa Community College

Charles C. Milliken
Siena Heights College

Warren E. Moeller
Midwestern State University

William Motz, Jr.
Lansing Community College

Gary R. Murray
Rose State College

Lee H. Neumann
Bucks County Community College

Henry Okleshen
Mankato State University

Ray Polchow
Muskingum Area Technical College

Mitchell Povsner
Moraine Valley Community College

David Reiter
Richard J. Daley College

Deborah Roebuck
Kennesaw State College

R. E. Schallert
Black Hawk College

James D. Sherriffs
Kankakee Community College

Lynette Klooster Shishido
Santa Monica College

Roger C. Shoenfeldt
Murray State University

Diana M. Skaff
*University of Toledo
Community and Technical College*

Carl J. Sonntag
Pikes Peak Community College

E. George Stook
Anne Arundel Community College

John F. Warner
The University of New Mexico

Rick Webb
Johnson County Community College-

Bernard L. Wolfe
Washington University

We are also grateful to those individuals who contributed to the text and ancillary package. We are thankful to Steve Huntley of Florida Community College for developing the instructional strategies and activities manual; to David Reiter of Richard J. Daley College for his work on the study guide and the instructor's manual; to Moira Skinner, Educational Consultant, for developing the test bank; and to Joyce Stockinger of Portland Community College for her work on the color acetates. We are also thankful to Marty Meloche of East Carolina University for helping with the development of the finance chapters, Joseph Carcello of the University of North Florida for his help with the accounting chapter, and Betty Westbrook for developing the content of the career appendixes.

Steven J. Skinner
John M. Ivancevich

The special features in *Business for the 21st Century* are designed to help you succeed in your study of business—and beyond. As you read each chapter, use the following tools to help you focus on, understand, and retain the terms and concepts in the text.

CHAPTER FIFTEEN

DISTRIBUTION

LEARNING OBJECTIVES

1. To define the term *marketing channel* and identify the two major types of marketing intermediaries.

2. To explain how marketing channels are integrated vertically.

3. To define *wholesaling* and describe the functions wholesalers perform.

4. To define *retailing* and outline the activities retailers perform.

5. To discuss the major considerations in retail planning.

6. To explain the role of physical distribution and identify its components.

Chapter Opening Photo

"Every picture tells a story." Each chapter begins with a unique photo consisting of objects that represent the topic of the chapter.

Learning Objectives

Accompanying the opening photo, a list of objectives identifies the major concepts and skills you will learn. Chapter summaries and test items are keyed to this list of learning objectives.

Technology is changing fast today. So are demographics. Markets are becoming global. Businesspeople may not realize that the ways goods and services get to customers are changing just as fast.

© Jonathan Selig 1986

In the United States, mutual funds that used to be sold only through brokerage houses now are sold also through regional banks, insurance agencies, and professional associations. In Japan most urban mom-and-pop shops have been converted to outlets of huge chains, such as 7-Eleven or Mister Donut. In Britain the bulk of consumer electronics products are now sold by four national chains carrying private brands.

Many U.S. department stores, especially those centered in urban downtown areas, are in trouble as workers and customers move increasingly to the suburbs. As consumers shop for the best price, big discount stores have flourished; category discounters that focus on one exhaustive line of goods are booming. Some manufacturers of clothing, luggage, and diverse other goods have opened outlets to

sell directly to consumers. Consumers are skipping stores altogether and using catalogs, television shopping networks, and buying clubs. This stiff competition, combined with poor customer service over the years and an aging and busier population less inclined to shop, may send many retail stores and regional malls into decline.

Nowadays customers do not always themselves buy the products they use. Hospitals often contract with independent firms for maintenance, billing, patient feeding, physical therapy, the pharmacy, or X ray. Many firms rely on computer management firms that design, buy, install, and run information systems for clients.

U.S. and foreign competition is

squeezing profits and reducing the number of distributors. The cost of holding inventory has doubled since the 1960s, the cost of labor has jumped, and the labor pool has dwindled. Manufacturing customers are demanding more service, especially as they adopt the just-in-time inventory approach in their operations (see Chapter Nine).

Large industrial producers are selling direct to customers. Foreign firms, competing on performance and price, are trying to gain a piece of the U.S. market through small distributing firms and catalog companies. Warehouse clubs selling office furniture and other merchandise are luring small-business and manufacturing customers from traditional industrial distributors.

Lines blur between manufacturers and distributors as firms merge, grow, and diversify. Kennemetal Inc., a maker of carbide cutting tools, bought a leading general-line firm and a national mail-order catalog distributor with four warehouses, and now distributes a broad range of industrial products nationally. New super distributorships, such as Sun Distributors of Philadelphia, carry many and varied product lines. Cooperatives such as ID ONE, a group of 30 large independent distributors, buy and promote together to compete with superdistributors and national chains.

As management expert Peter Drucker says, "Changes in distributive channels . . . should be a major concern of every business and every industry."[1]

522

After organizations devise marketing strategies, and produce products and price them, they must get the products to the marketplace. The distribution function is important to society because it enables goods and services to reach consumers. It is vital to firms' success. As the examples in the chapter opener show, firms use many different avenues to get products to consumers in a timely and efficient manner.

In this chapter, we examine the various activities involved in distributing goods and services. First we explain the concept of a marketing channel of distribution and describe the types of channels. Next we explore two major distribution activities: wholesaling and retailing. Finally we discuss the physical movement of products from producers to consumers.

MARKETING CHANNELS

A **marketing channel (channel of distribution)** is a group of interrelated organizations that directs the flow of products from producer to ultimate customers.[2] The channel organizations that provide the link between the producer and the consumer are called **marketing intermediaries**. Comp-U-Card is an example of a marketing intermediary.

The two major categories of marketing intermediaries are wholesalers and retailers. Wholesalers are individuals and organizations that sell primarily to other sellers or industrial users. Wholesale transactions generally involve large quantities of goods. Retailers specialize in selling products to consumers. They generally resell products that they obtain from wholesalers. We will discuss wholesalers and retailers later in the chapter.

Functions of Marketing Intermediaries

Consumers often wonder whether products would cost less if one or more marketing intermediaries could be eliminated from the distribution system. Would cars be less expensive if customers could simply buy them straight from the manufacturer? Perhaps, but think about the practical aspects involved. How many consumers would be willing or able to go to Detroit to buy a car? Or maybe Japan? If manufacturers offered cars for sale by mail order, how many consumers would buy one without seeing and test-driving it? Carmakers selling vehicles directly to buyers from around the United States or around the world would be impossible.

Marketing intermediaries are vital in creating place, time, and possession utilities. They ensure that products are available on a timely basis where they are needed. Eliminating intermediaries does not eliminate the need for their services, such as storage, record-keeping, delivery, and providing a product assortment. Either the manufacturer, the consumer, or some other organization has to perform these essential services. Without intermediaries, most consumer purchases would be much less efficient. Products probably would cost more, not less.

Marketing Channel
A group of interrelated organizations that directs the flow of products from producers to ultimate consumers; also called channel of distribution.

Marketing Intermediary
An individual or organization in a marketing channel that provides a link between producers, other channel members, and final consumers.

523

Opening Vignette

The text of each chapter begins with a current news story that introduces you to the topic of the chapter.

Margin Notes

For convenient reference, the terms and definitions in the margin mark the location of key terms within the text.

Chapter Map

Following the opening vignette, a verbal "map" indicates the main points that will be covered in the chapter.

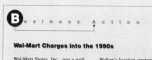

Wal-Mart Charges into the 1990s

Wal-Mart Stores, Inc., was a well-kept secret for years. Except for stories about the wealth of founder Sam Walton, Wal-Mart received little attention. This all changed in 1988, when Wal-Mart was named in *Fortune* magazine's survey as the ninth most admired corporation in America. It jumped to fourth place in 1991, and first place among retailers. Now the third-largest and fastest-growing retailer in the world—only Kmart and Sears are larger—is getting some attention.

Walton opened his first Wal-Mart in tiny Rogers, Arkansas, in 1962. His strategy was to focus on small towns. Conventional wisdom was that a discount store couldn't make it in a town smaller than 50,000. But Walton believed national discounters were ignoring rural towns, and he found that small towns were an excellent niche. By offering good prices, a local discount store could keep people shopping at home instead of traveling several hours to a larger city. Roughly 80 percent of Wal-Mart's 1,300 stores are located in towns of 15,000 or less. The stores sell nearly $20 billion worth of merchandise annually, including clothing, small appliances, cosmetics, and more than 50,000 other items.

Walton's location strategy was to build 30 or 40 stores within 600 miles of a distribution center. After the stores were opened in rural towns, Wal-Mart would expand to nearby metropolitan areas, such as Dallas, Kansas City, and St. Louis. When one geographic area reached its saturation point, Wal-Mart would expand into a new area. Wal-Mart currently has 14 distribution centers serving stores in 25 states, mostly in the Southwest, Midwest, and Southeast. Wal-Mart orders directly from manufacturers and uses its own trucks for delivery. By using its own distribution system and through quantity discounts, Wal-Mart realizes a tremendous cost savings, which it passes along to customers.

Wal-Mart Stores' image and atmosphere are consistent with its pledge to customer satisfaction. The physical facilities are plain, resembling a large warehouse. But the customer is number one. A sign reading "Satisfaction Guaranteed" hangs over the entrance to every store. Customers are often welcomed by an employee, called a "people greeter," eager to lend a helping hand. This customer orientation allows Wal-Mart to rely more on its reputation and less on advertising. Whereas Sears spends nearly $900 million each year for advertising and Kmart over $600 million, Wal-Mart spends only about $80 million.

Although the 1980s was not a prosperous decade for most retailers, Wal-Mart grew then by about 30 percent a year. On the average, 150 new stores are opened each year, and this trend is expected to continue. Experts predict that Wal-Mart will surpass Kmart as the number two retailer in the early 1990s, and that eventually it will surpass Sears and become number one.

Not everything has gone perfectly for Sam Walton. Wal-Mart's experiment with Hypermarkets U.S.A., 200,000 plus-square-foot stores selling everything from fresh vegetables to appliances, has been somewhat of a failure. Four hypermarkets have been opened, and Walton has no plans for future hypermarkets. Although Hypermarkets U.S.A. is the only hypermarket chain making a profit, the stores are too expensive to operate. Instead, Walton intends to push ahead with "SuperCenters," combinations of Wal-Mart discount stores and grocery stores in one 150,000-square-foot store.[12]

Business Action

Two current news stories in each chapter show the principles of business in action. These stories focus on recognizable firms and contemporary topics, extending the concepts discussed in the text.

Chapter 15 Distribution 531

A *commission merchant* receives goods from local sellers, establishes prices, and negotiates sales. For instance, in the agricultural industry, a commission merchant may take possession of a truckload of fertilizer and transport it to a central market for sale. A *manufacturers' agent* represents one or more manufacturers on a commission basis and offers noncompeting lines of products to customers. The relationship between the agent and the manufacturer is formalized by a written agreement. A *selling agent* is an independent wholesaler who sells a manufacturer's product for a commission, or fee. Manufacturers rely on selling agents to distribute canned foods, clothing, and furniture.

A **broker** is a wholesaler who brings together buyers and sellers on a temporary basis. Brokers are similar to agents, but they concentrate on specific commodities, such as insurance or real estate. A food broker, for example, markets food items to grocery chains, food processors, or other wholesalers. Brokers are paid a commission by the party that engages their services, such as a food manufacturer.

Broker
A wholesaler who brings together buyers and sellers on a temporary basis.

RETAILING

The side of distribution most familiar to consumers is retailing; most of us come in contact with retail stores almost daily. The marketing activity of **retailing** focuses on the sale of goods and services to the ultimate consumer for personal or household use.[7] Retailers, an essential link in the marketing channel, are often the only intermediary who deals directly with consumers. Retailers also are customers themselves, since they buy from producers and wholesalers.

Retailing is a significant part of the U.S. economy. Approximately 22 million people work in the retailing sector.[8] Nearly 2 million retail outlets are open for business in the United States. Who are America's largest retail companies? Table 15.1 lists the largest U.S. retailers according to sales, which amount to

Retailing
The marketing activities involved in selling products to final consumers for personal or household use.

TABLE 15.1
Ten Largest Retailers in the United States

DID YOU KNOW? *Sears, the largest retailer in the United States, has annual sales of nearly $56 billion.*

Rank	Name	Sales ($ in millions)
1	Sears Roebuck	$55,972
2	Wal-Mart Stores	32,602
3	Kmart	32,080
4	American Stores	22,156
5	Kroger	20,261
6	J. C. Penney	17,410
7	Safeway Stores	14,874
8	Dayton Hudson	14,739
9	Great Atlantic & Pacific Tea (A&P)	11,164
10	May Department Stores	11,027

Source: "The 50 Largest Retailing Companies," *FORTUNE*, June 3, 1991, p. 274. © The Time Magazine Company. All rights reserved.

---

524 Part Five Marketing

FIGURE 15.1
Typical Marketing Channels

Consumer products | Industrial products

A Producer / B Producer / C Producer / D Producer / E Producer / F Producer

Agent/broker

Wholesaler / Wholesaler / Wholesaler

Retailer / Retailer / Retailer

Consumer / Consumer / Consumer / Consumer / Industrial user / Industrial user

Types of Marketing Channels

Depending on the needs of the target market, firms utilize many different types of marketing channels to distribute products. Generally channels for consumer products are different than channels for industrial products.

Consumer products The four most commonly used channels for consumer products are shown in Figure 15.1. Channel A, the direct channel, shows the movement of products from producer to consumer. This channel is not typical for most consumer goods, although some products often are distributed this way, such as plants and flowers at nurseries, produce at farmers' markets, and arts and crafts items at fairs. Most services are distributed directly from service producers to the consumer, such as hair styling, dry cleaning, and auto repair.

Channel B reflects the movement of products from producer to retailer to consumer. This channel is commonly used for large, bulky products (automobiles, furniture), as well as perishable items (fresh seafood). Bringing in another intermediary, such as a wholesaler, would add delays or unnecessary costs to the distribution of these products.

Channel C, producer to wholesaler to retailer to consumer, is the traditional marketing channel. A wide range of products, including appliances, beverages, tobacco, and most convenience goods, is distributed through this channel.

The final channel (D) for consumer products—producer to agent/broker to wholesaler to retailer to consumer—is used to distribute small, inexpensive products purchased frequently. Several wholesalers are involved in the distri-

Did You Know?

Each chapter contains an interesting business-related sidebar to add to your store of knowledge about business.

Illustrations

Charts, graphs, diagrams, and photos reinforce and explain key concepts from the text.

● C o n n e c t i o n s

Retail Aptitude

Directions: The statements below reflect characteristics you would need to succeed in your own retail business. Circle the number that shows your level of agreement with each statement.

	Strongly Disagree					Strongly Agree
1. I am a self-starter who doesn't need a lot of guidance in getting the job done.	1	2	3	4	5	6
2. I wouldn't mind working long hours, even weekends, as long as I'm working for myself.	1	2	3	4	5	6
3. I like making my own decisions.	1	2	3	4	5	6
4. I would be willing to take a risk for the right opportunity.	1	2	3	4	5	6
5. I like to set my own schedule on a job—to be my own boss.	1	2	3	4	5	6
6. I like to perform a variety of tasks, the small stuff as well as the most visible duties.	1	2	3	4	5	6

	Strongly Disagree					Strongly Agree
7. I would enjoy being a leader and managing other people.	1	2	3	4	5	6
8. The potential for a high salary is important to me.	1	2	3	4	5	6
9. I like working with the public.	1	2	3	4	5	6
10. I am willing to stick with a job for several years if that's what it takes to succeed.	1	2	3	4	5	6

Feedback: Your answers should give you some feel for your potential as a retail store owner and operator. If you circled 1 or 2 for most items, you probably have little interest in owning a retail business. If you circled 5 or 6 for most statements, you just may possess many of the characteristics and skills needed to be a successful retailer. Retailing is a demanding field with no guarantees. The hours are long, the responsibilities great, and problems with employees or customers inevitable. But owning your own retail store also can be rewarding, both personally and financially.

---

cable hook-up.[14] In some instances, television shopping services employ as many as 400 to 500 operators in a room taking orders around the clock from a loyal following.

Direct Marketing
Nonstore retailing that uses nonpersonal media to introduce products to consumers, who then purchase the products by mail, telephone, or computer.

Direct marketing   Many firms promote products directly to buyers through a variety of techniques referred to as **direct marketing.** This type of nonstore retailing includes catalog sales, direct mail, telephone soliciting, and television or radio ads that include telephone numbers and instructions for ordering the items offered.

Direct marketing is one of the fastest-growing forms of retailing, with yearly sales in excess of $175 billion. The two major forms of direct marketing are telephone retailing and mail-order retailing. National companies such as American Express (credit cards), Time-Life (books), Merrill Lynch (investments), and Allstate (insurance) rely heavily on telephone retailing. Many firms generate telephone orders for their products by advertising them on cable television and including toll-free numbers. Thousands of firms use catalogs to sell a huge variety of items: clothing, books, records, household items, even specialty foods. Sears, L. L. Bean, and Spiegel exemplify firms that operate large mail-order businesses throughout the United States. Lands' End, a mail-order clothing company based in Wisconsin, has distinguished itself by providing services that range from helping callers determine sizes to an unconditional guarantee that customers can return any purchases.[15]

Vending machines   Candy, gum, snacks, soft drinks, coffee, newspapers, and other convenience goods are familiar items available in the self-service dispensers known as vending machines. In Japan even items like french fries and shrimp are sold in vending machines.[16] Firms place vending machines in high-traffic areas of office and classroom buildings, service stations, and shopping malls. Vending machines offer the advantages of 24-hour-a-day operation with no sales staff. Their main drawbacks include the costs of frequent servicing and needed repairs, as well as the threat of vandalism. Vending machines account for less than 2 percent of all retail sales.

Retail Planning

Owners, both individuals and large firms, must consider several factors when developing plans for a retail store. Major considerations include store location, atmosphere, scrambled merchandising, the wheel of retailing, and new technology.

Store location   Deciding where to locate the store is critical in retailing. Retailers usually prefer a location with a high level of pedestrian traffic or easy access from main thoroughfares. Owners must evaluate the cost to buy or rent space, the availability of parking spaces, and the nature and image of the area surrounding the store site.

Real World Examples

Current examples of familiar organizations and business issues appear throughout the text to relate the text to the real world.

Connections

Are you ready to run your own business? Do you have what it takes for sales? Explore your attitudes, opinions, and values as they pertain to these and other business issues by completing the self-assessment quiz in each chapter.

You'll Know It's the 21st Century When. . .

This feature concludes each chapter and gives you an idea of what business will face in the 21st century.

Summary of Learning Objectives

The summary of learning objectives allows you to review the main points covered in the chapter.

Key Terms List

A list of key terms, including page references, helps you identify and review important concepts.

Questions for Discussion and Review

These questions challenge you to recall and analyze what you learned in the chapter.

Left page mockups

Chapter 15 Distribution   545

Calling cards allow phone companies to distribute telephone services to consumers.

We can help you from the middle of anywhere.

Dial 10+ATT+0

AT&T The right choice.

AT&T. How can we help you?

Courtesy of AT&T

cars, insurance companies sell policies through vending machines at airports, entertainment firms sell tickets to concerts through computers in stores, and banks allow customers to have paychecks deposited directly into accounts and to pay bills by automatic withdrawal.

You'll Know It's the 21 Century When . . .

Hypermarkets Market Convenience

In the 21st century, today's supermarkets will look like the mom-'n'-pop stores of days gone by. Hypermarkets covering nearly 200,000 square feet will stock groceries, discount clothes, appliances, and housewares, plus videos, carryout meals, and other convenience services for harried people on the run. At the same time, small, quick-stop specialty stores and boutiques will flourish, while the

---

Chapter 15 Distribution   547

dards, selecting transportation modes, designing and operating warehouse facilities, processing orders, handling products, and managing inventory.

KEY TERMS

Marketing Channel (Channel of Distribution), p. 523
Marketing Intermediary, p. 523
Vertical Integration, p. 525
Vertical Marketing System (VMS), p. 526
Corporate VMS, p. 526
Administered VMS, p. 526
Contractual VMS, p. 526
Market Coverage, p. 526
Intensive Distribution, p. 526
Selective Distribution, p. 527
Exclusive Distribution, p. 527
Wholesaling, p. 527
Merchant Wholesaler, p. 529
Sales Branch, p. 530
Sales Office, p. 530
Agent, p. 530
Broker, p. 531
Retailing, p. 531
Department Store, p. 532
Discount Store, p. 532

Specialty Store, p. 532
Supermarket, p. 533
Superstore, p. 533
Convenience Store, p. 533
Warehouse Showroom, p. 533
Catalog Showroom, p. 533
Warehouse Club, p. 533
Nonstore Retailing, p. 535
In-Home Selling, p. 535
Direct Marketing, p. 536
Atmosphere, p. 538
Scrambled Merchandising, p. 539
Wheel of Retailing, p. 539
Physical Distribution, p. 540
Service Standard, p. 541
Transportation, p. 541
Warehousing, p. 543
Order Processing, p. 543
Materials Handling, p. 544
Inventory Management, p. 544

QUESTIONS FOR DISCUSSION AND REVIEW

1. What is a marketing channel?
2. Is it possible—or desirable—to eliminate the intermediary in the distribution of goods to consumers? Explain your answer.
3. What types of marketing channels are used to distribute consumer products? To distribute industrial products?
4. Have you ever purchased a product directly from a producer (channel A)? Name some products that manufacturers or producers sell directly to consumers.
5. Distinguish between intensive, selective, and exclusive distribution. Give examples of products distributed by each method.
6. Wholesalers perform a variety of services in product distribution. What are those services? Whom do they benefit?

---

546   Part Five Marketing

omnipresent mall declines as more women join the labor force and the number of young people decline. Some forecasters also predict that more and more convenience-minded consumers will shop by mail order, catalog, computer, and even TV—especially if prices include delivery.[23]

SUMMARY OF LEARNING OBJECTIVES

1. To define the term *marketing channel* and identify the two major types of marketing intermediaries.
   A marketing channel is a group of interrelated organizations that directs the flow of goods from producer to consumer. Marketing intermediaries, organizations that provide the link between producers and consumers, are vital because they create place, time, and possession utility. The major types of intermediaries are *wholesalers* and *retailers*.

2. To explain how marketing channels are integrated vertically.
   Vertical integration occurs when one organization takes control of another member of the marketing channel, often by purchasing it. Distribution efficiency may be improved with a vertical marketing system (VMS), a planned marketing channel in which one channel member manages all intermediaries. The three types of vertical marketing systems are corporate, administered, and contractual.

3. To define *wholesaling* and describe the functions wholesalers perform.
   Wholesaling consists of the activities of marketing intermediaries who sell to retailers, other wholesalers, or industrial users. Wholesalers provide several services, including ownership, financing, risk assumption, promotional assistance, information, product assortment, and transportation. The major types of wholesalers are merchant wholesalers, manufacturer-owned wholesalers, and agents and brokers.

4. To define *retailing* and outline the activities retailers perform.
   Retailing activities consist of the sale of goods and services to consumers for personal or household use. Retailing can take place in stores or through the nonstore retailing methods of in-home selling, direct marketing, and vending machines.

5. To discuss the major considerations in retail planning.
   Retail planning, crucial to success in the retail sector, involves several important considerations. Store *location* is a critical decision since it influences shopper traffic. The *atmosphere*, or design of the store's physical space, must be appealing to the target market. Retailers also must decide whether or not to use *scrambled merchandising*, which means adding unrelated products to a store's existing mix. Another consideration is the *wheel of retailing*, which suggests that new stores constantly emerge to replace established stores. Recent advancements in *technology* also have an impact on retail planning.

6. To explain the role of physical distribution and identify its components.
   Physical distribution activities accomplish the physical movement of products through marketing channels from manufacturer to customer. Physical distribution activities include establishing customer service stan-

CASE 15.1
Kmart Tries to Get Back on Track

Kmart, the pioneer discount retailer that experienced rapid growth in the 1970s, seems to have lost its momentum. The price of its stock has fallen, earnings are flat, and sales growth is slow. Trouble comes from stiff competition from Wal-Mart and newer retail outlets, changes in consumer buying habits, the chain's image, and its dated distribution system. Marketing expert Joseph E. Antonini, Kmart chairman since 1988, has been leading the drive to get the giant company back on track.

To compete with the increasingly popular specialty retailers that offer a huge selection of merchandise in one or two categories, Kmart has developed Builders Square, Office Square, and Sports Giant. To ward off the threat from hypermarkets and warehouse clubs, which force down the usual profit margins of discount stores, Kmart started American Fare (an Atlanta hypermarket) and purchased Pace Membership Warehouse Inc.

Such ventures may help Kmart compete in the 1990s, but Antonini and his management must also improve the 2,300 core Kmart stores, which produce 80 percent of the firm's sales. An important first step has been upgrading merchandise and image. Even in discount stores, shoppers increasingly want quality. So stores such as Kmart and Wal-Mart need to keep a delicate balance between convincing customers that prices are low and making people feel the stores are too cheap. Tactics like Kmart's "blue light special" may increase impulse buying but cheapen the store's image.

Experts say Wal-Mart excels at attending to the details that mold shoppers' attitudes. Some say Wal-Mart's simple logo in white letters on a brown background conveys a warm inviting message, which is carried out further by the "people greeters" inside the stores. Kmart followed suit by changing its logo and placing employees near the door to answer questions. Its highly recognizable logo of a bright red "K" and cool turquoise "mart" grabbed attention and signaled low prices but gave the impression the store hadn't changed in decades. So Kmart adopted a simpler logo with red letters on a gray background.

Antonini hired actress Jaclyn Smith and decorator Martha Stewart to design and promote better-quality apparel and housewares, and professional golfer Fuzzy Zoeller to promote sporting goods. The Martha Stewart promotion, heavily advertised, was especially successful, but almost a third of Kmart's stores were too small to properly carry the housewares line. Antonini earmarked $1.3 billion to enlarge and remodel 700 of the company's oldest outlets to feature wider aisles, bolder displays, and taller, deeper shelves. The roomy new design will make items available where customers can get them instead of in the stockroom.

Adapted from David Woodruff, "Will Kmart Ever Be a Silk Purse?" *Business Week*, January 22, 1990, p. 46; Francine Schwadel, "Little Touches Spur Wal-Mart's Rise," *The Wall Street Journal*, September 22, 1989, p. B1; "Lessons from Kmart's Very Tough Fight to Make It," *Boardroom Reports*, February 1, 1990, pp. 3–5.

Cases

Two current, realistic cases allow you to put business concepts into practice.

Career Appendixes

Each of the seven parts of the book ends with a comprehensive and informative section on business careers.

C a r e e r s   in

MARKETING

Marketing is everywhere. On a typical day, you see newspaper ads, TV commercials, and billboards advertising countless products. Flyers, catalogs, and brochures arrive in your mail daily. Each time you go to the supermarket, you look through hundreds of products packaged in myriad shapes and colors. In the mall, you're asked to fill out a questionnaire on which brand of toothpaste you use.

These are just some of the most obvious signs of the marketing effort. The field of marketing involves all of the steps that bring countless goods and services to consumers. These steps include marketing research, developing new products, advertising, packaging, distribution, and sales.

Marketing is a huge field employing millions of people. Opportunities in the field are vast and the demand for skilled, well-trained people continues to grow. While competition for entry-level positions is high, thousands of new jobs open in the field each year.

RETAILING

All of us are familiar with shopping in stores, but few actually understand what is involved in working in retailing. The field of retailing includes department stores, chain stores, supermarkets, specialty stores, franchise stores, mail-order businesses, and sidewalk vendors. Retailers buy their goods wholesale, display their wares, and sell them to individual consumers for a price higher than they initially paid.

Requirements: Retailing

Personal skills:
- Initiative
- Analytical ability
- Decision-making ability
Education:
- Bachelor's degree
- Any major

Because the field is very fast paced and involves constant change, careers in retailing can be exciting. Most follow one of two career paths, buying and store management.

Selected Employers of Marketing Personnel

Advertising agencies	International firms
Agents or brokers	Manufacturers
Computer service bureaus	Marketing research firms
Consulting firms	Marketing specialists
Credit bureaus	Media
Delivery firms	Nonprofit institutions
Entertainment firms	Public relations firms
Exporters	Real estate firms
Financial institutions	Retailers
Franchisees	Service firms
Franchisors	Shopping centers
Government	Sports teams
Health care providers	Transportation firms
Industrial firms	Wholesalers

Which path you first choose depends primarily on the employer. Many stores separate store management from buying at the entry level and you must choose which type of work you want to do. Other stores start all new trainees as assistant buyers. Smaller retailers often start people as salespeople or assistant managers. Most large department stores provide entry-level training programs for people first entering the field.

Buying

The buyer decides what goods to acquire and offer for sale in a store. Buyers purchase the goods directly from the manufacturers and set the price at which they will be sold in the store. A good buying decision results in profits for the store and advancement for the buyer. The buyer is also held responsible when a particular line does not sell.

Buyers need to understand customer preferences and anticipate trends, tastes, and styles months in advance. Careful analysis of previous sales, market research reports, and consumer trends are all important in making good buying decisions. A buyer must take calculated risks and have the courage to

Duties: Buying
- Ordering merchandise.
- Negotiating with suppliers.
- Pricing merchandise.
- Assisting with advertising.
- Analyzing sales.
- Overseeing sales promotions.
- Determining markdowns.

make decisions worth thousands or even millions of dollars.

Buyers often must travel a great deal of the time. They make frequent buying trips to manufacturers and wholesalers to purchase merchandise. The amount of travel time varies, but most buyers spend at least four or five days each month on the road.

In large stores, buyers specialize in one area or department; each department needs a buyer to select its stock. In small stores, all buying may be performed by only one or two people.

Store Management

Store management involves directing operations so that the store functions effectively and efficiently. Store managers have the

Career Ladder: Retail Buying Management

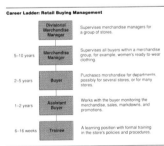

Divisional Merchandise Manager	Supervises merchandise managers for a group of stores.
5–10 years — **Merchandise Manager**	Supervises all buyers within a merchandise group, for example, women's ready-to-wear clothing.
2–5 years — **Buyer**	Purchases merchandise for departments, possibly for several stores, or for many stores.
1–2 years — **Assistant Buyer**	Works with the buyer monitoring the merchandise, sales, markdowns, and promotions.
6–16 weeks — **Trainee**	A learning position with formal training in the store's policies and procedures.

overall responsibility for ensuring the store operates at a profit.

Generally store management involves overseeing the flow of goods. This includes receiving and marking the goods, arranging and displaying them, and supervising the selling of the merchandise.

Duties: Store Management
- Hiring and training salespeople.
- Supervising the unpacking of merchandise.
- Handling customer complaints.
- Managing cash receipts.
- Displaying merchandise.
- Tracking inventory levels.

The duties of store managers depend on the size of the organization. In a small store, one manager may be responsible for all of the operations. Larger department

589

PART ONE •

THE BUSINESS ENTERPRISE

CHAPTER ONE

FOUNDATIONS OF BUSINESS AND ECONOMICS

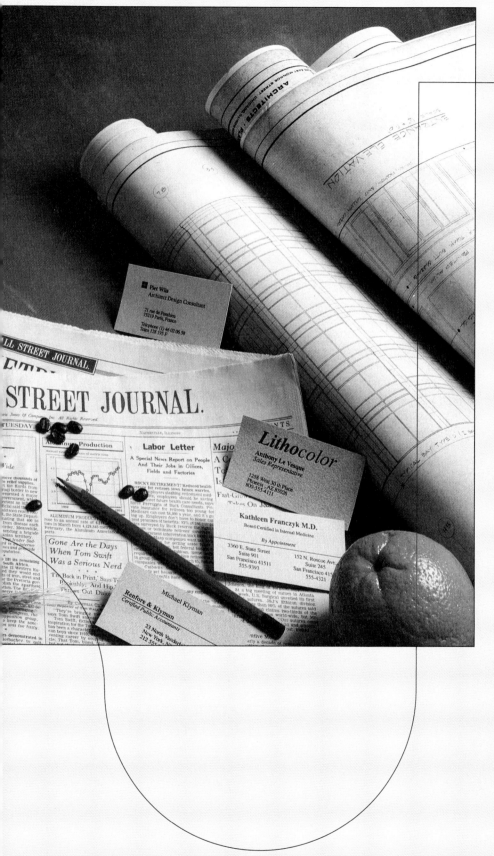

1. To define the term *business* and state why the study of business is important.

2. To explain how people form the core of business.

3. To identify four main objectives of business.

4. To explain two views of profit.

5. To define the term *economics* and discuss three types of economic resources.

6. To identify the characteristics of a free enterprise system.

7. To distinguish between planned and mixed economic systems.

8. To describe the stages of the historical development of the American economy.

9. To identify the challenges facing business in the 1990s.

A new product becomes a success in the marketplace. An overconfident business owner charges too much for his services as an accounting consultant. A joint venture between a small Ohio firm and a medium-sized Mexican firm turns a profit after only nine months. A recession strikes and destroys the business of Amy Lynch in San Diego. An exciting new job opportunity opens up for Don Carter, a college graduate in Laramie, Wyoming, after a yearlong search for a job in the computer industry.

Such successes and failures are the reality of being involved in business. The world of business is filled with ups and downs, hard knocks, challenges, competition, and excitement. Some of the most challenging and rewarding careers possible are found in business. A small firm, a large corporation, a company in New York, or one in Lyon, France: each can provide the opportunity for an exciting business career.

A brief look at a few true business stories will help set the tone for studying business. They demonstrate the meaning of ups and downs.

A few years ago, Motorola was faced with lagging sales, no profits, and cost overruns in the cellular telephone business. Japanese competitors were taking all the sales. Motorola had two business choices: (1) settle for second best or (2) retaliate with products so superb that nobody could challenge them. Motorola had surrendered to the Japanese in

Courtesy of Motorola, Inc.

televisions in 1974, stereos in 1980, and computer memory chips in 1985. It decided that enough was enough. The company picked itself up and has become an American business known for outstanding products and a large share of the cellular telephone market.

Donna Funk heard the audience applaud her at the Minnesota Entrepreneur of the Year awards ceremony. But she just couldn't look up. Donna felt like a fraud because she was almost bankrupt; her catering business was losing money. She decided to set high goals to generate more customers, to work harder, and to not let quality slip. Today, after a struggle, Donna's business is back on track because she dug deep inside for resources to turn the catering operation around.

Myron Berman is chairman of Keystone Camera Products Corporation in Clifton, New Jersey. His firm produces under-$50 cameras. Foreign competition has hit Keystone hard. However, Berman vows to fight back with more sales, better marketing, and careful control over production costs. He doesn't want to turn over his business to either a foreign or a domestic competitor without a fight.

King Camp Gillette founded his razor blade company in 1903. Since then the firm has had many successes and some failures. (In the 1950s, for example, Gillette lost some of its market and had to lay off loyal employees.) The latest innovation at Gillette is the Sensor razor, which the firm hopes will gain market share and keep employees working. The firm talked to over 10,000 shavers and tested the Sensor with a panel of 500 employees. The results are encouraging; the razor is being well received in the United States, Europe, and Japan as providing a smooth shave. The Sensor is a high-quality, technologically unique product. Competitors such as Schick will need time to catch up, to try to produce and sell a similar high-tech shaver.

As these four examples show, business is exciting, challenging, not always successful, and an important part of the fabric of American society. It is also a global phenomenon. In our internationally dependent world, competition in foreign locations, as well as across the street, is now an accepted part of doing business.[1]

The American business system has been copied, vilified, praised, misunderstood, and debated. Without question, the American way of business can be improved; however, to borrow from the words of Mark Twain, rumors of its death have been greatly exaggerated. Actually, it works exceptionally well, compared to other systems around the world. American business has helped provide Americans with a relatively high standard of living. The freedoms enjoyed by American businesses and consumers are typically not appreciated until they are compared with the lack of free enterprise freedoms in China, the Soviet Union, and Eastern Europe.

This chapter begins with a discussion of why the study of business is important. We explain how people—owners, managers, employees, and consumers—form the core of business. Next we discuss the business objectives of survival, growth, social responsibility, and profit. Our discussion of profit leads into a brief description of economics and economic systems. Then, a historical review of business shows how these economic principles have guided the course of American business to the present day. We also present the challenges and issues that must be addressed both today and in the future to ensure the continuing success of American business. The final section of this chapter explains how the organization and structure of the book will guide us through the study of business.

WHY WE STUDY BUSINESS

When you graduate from college, where will you work? Do you buy health food or traditional food when you shop? What price are you willing to pay for a compact disk, a ticket to a professional baseball game, a visit to the doctor because of a cold? Do you qualify for an automobile loan? Do international trade deficits have an impact on your standard of living? What caused the American stock market crash on "Black Monday"—October 19, 1987? Do you buy "Made in America" products only? None of these questions has a single, clear answer—249 million Americans have individual answers to them. The study of business will help you shape answers, sharpen your skills, and understand the business and economic links between the United States and other nations, in Europe, North America, the Third World (e.g., Pakistan, Peru), and the Pacific Rim (e.g., Japan, South Korea).

While studying business, you will learn about history, the free enterprise system, how changes in the environment affect businesses, and what skills are needed to have a good chance to be successful. You will also learn about business careers and what will be needed to succeed in a business career. There is no magic formula. However, the road to business success will be easier for those who understand how business works.

How much do you know about business? Try the Connections quiz on your business IQ. This quiz, as you start the course, will give you feedback regarding your current knowledge of business. We will have succeeded as authors, and you as students, if you know more about business by the end of the book.

● C o n n e c t i o n s

Check Your Business IQ

Directions: It is interesting to trace your progress as you learn about a subject. This quiz is designed to help you measure your business knowledge as you start the course.

Answer the questions; then turn to the Feedback section.

1. General Motors (not the Japanese) revolutionized automation by developing MAP. What does MAP stand for?
2. Name a successful U.S.–Japanese joint venture in the automobile industry.
3. What nation is the largest foreign investor in the United States?
4. Services have been the dominant component of gross national product (GNP) since 1950. What is services' current percentage share of GNP?
5. Female full-time workers' wages were what percentage of male full-time workers' wages in 1991?
6. What is a flextime work schedule?
7. What does the term *ESOP* mean?
8. The fourth-largest non-American multinational company is IRI. In what country is IRI headquartered?
9. What is the most powerful American brand name in the world?
10. Where is the European Community (EC) headquartered?

Feedback: How do you think you did on the quiz? The questions were not tricky, but you had to be knowledgeable about current events to score a perfect 10. Here are the answers:

Increasing Dependence on Others

Over the years, people have become more and more dependent on others. This book is about understanding mutual dependence, using the business system effectively, and being a part of business. **Business** is the exchange of goods, services, or money for mutual benefit or profit. Today, the business conducted in and among the United States, Canada, Great Britain, Germany, Japan, and other countries is more complicated than bartering shoes for corn. Years ago, our ancestors discovered that producing everything one needs occasionally requires doing some undesirable work. They also discovered that individuals have various traits, needs, and skills. If a person specialized in a particular job, such as making shoes or growing corn, the surpluses produced could be traded for other desirable goods. This early exchange of goods without using money was called **barter.** The most famous barter in American history was the purchase of Manhattan Island by Dutch traders for a few dollars' worth of colored glass beads.

Business
The exchange of goods, services, or money for mutual benefit or profit.

Barter
The exchange of goods without using money.

1. MAP stands for "Manufacturing Automation Protocol," a standardized communications network that allows diverse computers, robots, and controllers to communicate with one another in a common electronic language.

2. GM-Toyota, Ford-Mazda, and Chrysler-Mitsubishi are a few worth mentioning.

3. Great Britain (not Japan) is the largest foreign investor in the United States.

4. About 70 percent and increasing.

5. About 70 percent and improving each year. However, a gap still exists.

6. A work schedule that allows workers to vary their starting and quitting times. It is used by one in eight full-time workers.

7. Employee stock option plan. Nearly 10 million employees own ESOPs, which means they own part of their companies.

8. Italy. IRI is a metals manufacturer with over 400,000 employees.

9. Coca-Cola. It is found all over the world.

10. Brussels, Belgium.

How did you do?

0–5   You are not yet familiar with some business concepts or issues, but that's why we're here. Let's get to work.

6–8   Not a bad beginning. With some work, you can be really knowledgeable.

9   Outstanding. Not perfect, but really a great beginning.

10   Wow, you might be one in a thousand. Don't get too excited, because a lot of areas were not included in the quiz. Take a bow, and let's go to work and learn more.

No matter how independent we may be, almost everyone depends on others. Few people today produce everything they need or use; a complex division of labor has encouraged us to not be self-sufficient. For example, you buy food at the local supermarket. You drive a car manufactured in Dearborn, Michigan. You use fuel pumped from oil wells in west Texas. You go to schools built by carpenters, bricklayers, ironworkers, and cement workers. You watch news programs produced in Atlanta, Georgia. You wear clothing designed in Milan, Italy. You pitch baseballs manufactured in Haiti.

International Opportunities

For individuals educated in business, exciting opportunities will exist around the world as we move toward the 21st century. The new era of business performance in an international marketplace will require business leaders who know how to start, operate, and sustain businesses. Business negotiations,

With the changes taking place in eastern Europe, American businesses such as McDonald's can now be found in the Soviet Union.

Wojtek Laski/Sipa

joint ventures between companies in different countries, travel across borders, investment across geographical boundaries, and working for foreign-owned enterprises are becoming commonplace. To function in such a world, each of us must understand the principles of business.[2]

Standard of Living

Another reason to study business is to protect our way of life. Americans take great pride in being free and independent. Because of the independence, hard work, and values embodied in business institutions, Americans enjoy a comfortable standard of living:

- 96 percent of all American homes have at least one telephone.
- 96 percent of all American homes have at least one television.
- 50 percent of all Americans own at least one automobile.
- The United States provides half of the world's wheat.
- Agricultural output has increased 75 percent since 1940.[3]

Standard of Living
A measure of how well a person or family is doing in terms of satisfying needs and wants with goods and services.

Free Enterprise
A system in which private businesses are able to start and do business competitively to earn profits, with a minimal degree of government regulation.

Business has contributed to these and other success stories. We need to understand these contributions and also to learn how to maintain an acceptable standard of living for future generations. **Standard of living** describes the amount of goods and services that an average family or individual views as necessary. The standard of living of each generation of Americans has been better than the previous generation. How has this happened? We believe that a minimal amount of government interference and a free market business system have been the major reasons for perpetuating our way of living. This free market system, called **free enterprise,** means that private businesses are able to conduct business activities competitively with minimal government regulation. As a result of this system, the productive activities of people have been as free as possible. The powerful business system that has resulted should be understood, improved, and encouraged.

Economic Comparison of Four World Leaders (1987 data)   **TABLE 1.1**

	United States	Soviet Union	Japan	China
Population (in millions)	243.8	284.0	122.0	1,074.0
Gross national product (U.S. $ in billions)	$4,436.1	$2,375.0	$1,607.7	$293.5
GNP growth rate (annual averages)				
1976–80	3.3%	2.2%	5.0%	6.1%
1981–85	3.0	1.8	3.9	9.2
1987	2.9	0.5	4.2	9.4
Inflation (change in consumer prices)	3.7%	−0.9%	0.1%	9.2%
Total labor force (in millions)	121.6	154.8	60.3	512.8
Agricultural	3.4	33.9	4.6	313.1
Nonagricultural	118.2	120.9	55.7	199.7
Unemployment rate	6.1%	na	2.8%	na
Foreign trade (U.S. $ in millions)				
Exports	$250.4	$107.7	$231.2	$44.9
Imports	424.1	96.0	150.8	40.2
Balance	−173.7	11.7	80.4	4.7
Energy				
Consumption (barrels of oil equivalent per capita)	55.6	37.3	22.7	4.8
Oil reserves (barrels in billions)	33.4	59.0	0.1	18.4
Oil production (millions of barrels per day)	9.9	12.7	Negligible	2.7
Natural gas reserves (cubic feet in trillions)	186.7	1,450.0	1.0	30.7
Coal reserves (metric tons in billions)	263.8	244.7	1.0	170.0
Agriculture (kilograms per capita)				
Grain production	1,150	740	130	402
Meat production	109	65	31	18
Military: Active armed forces	2,163,200	5,096,000	245,000	3,200,000
Living standard				
Life expectancy (years)	75	69	78	68
Automobiles (registrations per thousand)	570	42	235	Negligible

Source: Organization of Economic Cooperation and Development Economic Outlook, 1988; "The 1990s and Beyond: The U.S. Stands to Return Its Global Leadership." Reprinted by permission of THE WALL STREET JOURNAL, © 1989 Dow Jones & Company, Inc. All Rights Reserved Worldwide.

Coping with Change

Business is dynamic—always changing. Coping with both predictable and unpredictable events can be easier, more efficient, and less traumatic if we understand business. Prices increase or decrease, products are added, needs change, services are created to meet needs, laws are passed, and unexpected events occur—for example, the October 19, 1987 (major), and October 13, 1989 (minor), stock market crashes; finding traces of benzene in bottles of Perrier water; and the war in the Persian Gulf. These all have been a part of the dynamic business system.

Preventing Misconceptions

Understanding business also prevents our accepting misconceptions, misinformation, and inaccurate data as truths. Many people still believe that Japan has the number one economy, that the average U.S. business earns 15 percent profit, that starting salaries for recent college graduates are usually $50,000 annually, and that most people work for large businesses. Each of these assumptions is inaccurate.[4] Table 1.1 enables us to compare four major nations on

TABLE 1.2

**Some Facts about
American Business**

New jobs created by U.S. economy
10.5 million between 1980 and 1986   2.5 million by Fortune 500 companies

Total U.S. franchise sales and services
$282.2 billion in 1978 $639.7 billion in 1988

Number of Apple Computer, Inc., employees
250 in 1978   10,000 in 1988

Number of U.S. millionaire households
832,000 in 1985   1.4 million in 1988

Number of fax machines sold in the United States
70,000 in 1983   1.5 million in 1988

Total number of personal computers in U.S. homes
2.4 million in 1982   22.8 million in 1988

New jobs created by manufacturers, 1980 to 1986
574,000 with fewer than 20 employees   1.7 million with more than 500 employees

Number of Japanese cars manufactured in the United States
0 in 1978   695,020 in 1988

Number of U.S. cars sold in Japan
13,947 in 1978   14,511 in 1988

**Percentage of U.S. high school students who picked the correct definition
of the term *profits* in a multiple-choice test**
34 in 1988

Source: Reprinted with permission, INC. magazine (April 1989). Copyright © 1989 by Goldhirsh Group, Inc., 38 Commercial Wharf, Boston, MA 02110-3883.

Gross National Product (GNP)
The market value of all final goods and services produced over a one-year period.

10 standard of living and other economic factors. The United States is number one in terms of the market value of all final goods and services produced over a one-year period, which is called the **gross national product (GNP)**. Also look at agricultural production and automobile registrations.

HOW WE ARE DOING IN BUSINESS

The GNP tells us how we are doing in business. It is calculated by adding expenditures on all goods and services for a one-year period. For example, if we spend about $11,000 on each of 8 million American cars, that $88 billion would go into GNP. We would add in 8 billion Big Macs at $2 each, for another $16 billion, and 1.5 million new homes at $80,000 each, for $120 billion. We would also include 4 billion doctor's office visits at $40 each, for $160 billion. Adding expenditures on all these types of products and services, we would get about $4.5 trillion.

Today in the United States, more than 14.5 million organizations, called **business enterprises,** contribute to the GNP by exchanging goods, services, or money to earn a profit. These business enterprises (such as Visible Changes hair salons, Olive Garden restaurants, and Fiesta supermarkets) intend to earn a fair or reasonable profit by selling goods and services through business transactions. When an organization such as Apple Computer exchanges a personal

Business Enterprise
An organization involved in exchanging goods, services, or money to earn a profit.

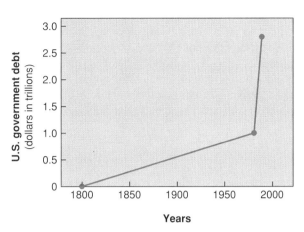

Years

Adapted from Earl H. Fry, "Is the United States a Declining Economic Power?" *Business in the Contemporary World,* Summer 1989, pp. 38–48.

FIGURE 1.1

Everything Is Not Perfect in the United States

DID YOU KNOW? *By the end of 1989, the cumulative debt of the U.S. government was about $2.8 trillion ($2,800,000,000,000)—up 300 percent since 1980. The United States took 191 years to reach the first trillion dollars in debt but only five years (1981–1986) to reach the second.*

computer for money, that is a business transaction. Apple hopes to earn a profit from its involvement in the transaction.

In the sense that business involves the exchange of goods, services, or money for *mutual benefit*, we are all involved in business. For example, Dana Vance, who bought a Macintosh SE computer through a business transaction with Apple Computer, hopes to benefit by becoming more organized and productive. For most of us, our food, clothing, automobile, telephone, airplane trip to Hawaii, golf clubs, and Spanish audio tapes were purchased, used, and enjoyed because we did business with an enterprise. We are all affected in some way by the activities of business enterprises.

Across the world, authoritarian governments and centralized or planned economies are on the run as free enterprise business gains strength. Table 1.2 presents some interesting statistics on the growth of American business. As we prepare this text, upheaval in Eastern Europe suggests that business power, not military power, will dominate the world. South Korea, Taiwan, Poland, and Chile are a few countries that have recently made substantial changes in how they conduct business.

As American business prospers, the U.S. government must manage more and more money, and more money can mean more debt. Figure 1.1 shows the size of the U.S. government debt in historical perspective.

PEOPLE FORM THE CORE OF BUSINESS

The human element is the core of business. Business needs people as owners, managers, employees, and consumers. People need business for the production of goods and services and the creation of jobs. Whether business is transacted in Mexico, Canada, or Nigeria does not matter. Businesses may be operated differently and the objectives of businesses may differ, but the universal element in all business activities is people.[5]

Owners

People who own a business, as well as those who invest money in one, do so because they expect to earn a profit. Most of the giant corporations, such as General Motors, Eastman Kodak, Dow Chemical, Du Pont, and Exxon, are owned by large numbers of people. General Motors has over 1.2 million shareholders (owners) and 820,000 employees. When making decisions, the professional managers in business organizations need to consider the owners and what they expect from the business.

Managers

The person responsible for operating the business may be the owner (an owner-manager, also called an entrepreneur) or a professional manager employed by the owner. Both types of managers seek to achieve profit, growth, survival, and social responsibility.

The owner-manager sets his or her own objectives, whereas a professional manager attempts to achieve objectives set by others. The professional manager is accountable to the owners of the business, who judge the manager's performance by how well their objectives have been accomplished over a period of time.

Many of these business owners are *entrepreneurs,* people who take the risks necessary to organize and manage a business and receive the financial profits and nonmonetary rewards. In Chapter 3, a more thorough discussion of entrepreneurs will be presented. The entrepreneur of the 1990s is expected to be innovative, practical, and strong willed. This view was actually established years ago by noted Austrian economist Joseph Schumpeter. He stated:

> The function of entrepreneurs is to reform or revolutionize the pattern of production by exploiting an invention or, more generally, an untried technological possibility for producing a new commodity or producing an old one in a new way, opening a new source of supply of materials or a new outlet for products, by reorganizing a new industry.[6]

The owner-managers who fit Schumpeter's description are too numerous to list. The list would include names like Ted Turner (CNN), Ken Olsen (Digital Equipment Corporation), Fred Smith (Federal Express), Bob Reis (Final Technology, Inc.), Frank Perdue (Perdue Chickens), John McCormack (Visible Changes), Bill McGovern (MCI Communications), Liz Claiborne (Liz Claiborne), Barbara LaMont (WCCL–TV), and Akoito Morita (Sony). Each of these entrepreneurs practices what Schumpeter described. They personify the term *entrepreneur.*

Employees

Employees supply the skills and abilities needed to provide a product or service and to earn a profit. Most employees expect to receive an equitable wage or salary and to be given gradual increases in the amount they are paid for the use of their skills and abilities. To compete with other businesses, a business enterprise needs a committed and effective team of employees.

Courtesy of the Bristol-Myers Squibb Company

Consumers

In the international marketplace, from Hong Kong to Monterrey to Los Angeles to Munich, the target of business activity is consumers. A **consumer** is a person or business who purchases a good or service for personal or organizational use. Consumers in economic systems such as those of Japan, Germany, Canada, and the United States want more and better products and services. They want better automobiles, better homes, more luxuries, and better leisure equipment. They want to pay a fair price for the goods and services they purchase. They also want the goods and services they purchase to be reliable.

A business enterprise attempts to satisfy consumer needs and desires while earning a profit. To do so, businesses must determine what those consumer needs and desires are. Because consumers continually want more and better things, new businesses are formed, and other businesses make adjustments to accommodate the demand. When a need or desire for products or services exists, a business can earn a profit by supplying it promptly and efficiently. The uncertainty and risk involved in assessing consumer needs and wants provide a challenge to the business decision maker attempting to earn a profit.

Consumer
A person who purchases a good or service for personal use.

BUSINESS OBJECTIVES

As we stated above, businesses must achieve their objectives to remain in operation. Lists of business objectives generally include such factors as profit, survival, growth, and social responsibility.

Survival, Growth, and Social Responsibility

Survival is an obvious objective. Other objectives can be accomplished only if the business enterprise survives.

Growth is an objective because business does not stand still. Market share increase, personal and individual development, and increased productivity are important growth objectives. The growth of Compaq Computer and Wal-Mart to multibillion-dollar enterprises is often used as an example of business success accomplished through growth.

In recent years, meeting social responsibilities has been recognized as an important objective. Businesses, like each person in society, must accept their responsibilities in areas such as pollution control, eliminating discriminatory practices, and energy conservation. Examples of new corporate acceptance of social responsibilities appear almost daily in the media, such as:

- Du Pont pulling out of a $750 million-a-year business because of some fear that it may harm the earth's atmosphere.
- McDonald's, which produces millions of pounds of paper and plastic waste annually, becoming a crusader for recycling. (In late 1990, the company announced that it would no longer use plastic containers.)
- 3M investing, beyond what the law requires, in pollution controls for its manufacturing facilities.

Profit: Two Views

Although survival, growth, and social responsibility are important objectives, the profit objective plays the major role in business. Profit, however, means different things to different people because of their values, attitudes, and perceptions.

Business profit   Typically, a businessperson calculates profit by subtracting all the costs, including taxes, from the revenue received for selling a product or service in the market. The difference is referred to as **business profit.** For example, the franchise owner of a Wendy's fast-food restaurant subtracts all expenses (for supplies, staff wages, property, advertising, and so on) from all income to determine the business profit.

Business Profit
The difference between business income (revenue) and business expenses (costs): selling price − all costs of making and selling a product, including taxes.

Successful business organizations earn a profit because their goods and services effectively meet customers' needs and demands. Basically, profits reward a business enterprise for effectively conducting a number of activities.

Risk-taking   The business may earn a profit when it takes risks by entering a new market or by competing head-on with another business. For example, Toyota invested millions of dollars in promoting and selling small cars in the United States. Today, this Japanese corporation is the largest small-car seller in the U.S. market.

Evaluation of demand Business organizations that evaluate consumer needs and demands and then move efficiently into a market can earn substantial profits. Xerox in the photoreproduction industry, Compaq Computers in personal computers, and Domino's in the pizza business are examples of companies whose accurate assessments of consumer demands resulted in good profits.

Efficient management A major cause of business failure is improper or inadequate management of people, technology, materials, and capital. Efficient planning, organizing, controlling, directing, and staffing can earn satisfactory profits. Some of the most profitable enterprises (e.g., Ethan Allen, Molly Maid, Blue Bell Ice Cream, H & R Block, and Coca-Cola) are also known as well-managed businesses. Such well-managed enterprises earn, on the average, around 5 percent profit a year on total sales. Of course, business profit rates vary greatly by industry, size of business, and location of the business, as well as managerial effectiveness.

Economic profit The economist, like the businessperson, subtracts expenses from income to find profit. But the economist also considers **opportunity cost,** the cost of choosing to use resources for one purpose while sacrificing the next-best alternative for the use of those resources. For example, Jana Neal, owner of a small florist shop in San Antonio, pays herself a salary of $9,000 for operating the business. But if she could earn $20,000 working for a large wholesale florist supply house, her opportunity cost is $11,000. The opportunity cost is a measure of everything a person sacrifices to attain an objective. **Economic profit**, then, is what remains after both actual expenses and opportunity costs are subtracted from revenue earned.

Opportunity Cost
The cost of choosing to use resources for a purpose, which results in sacrificing the next best alternative for the use of those resources.

One practical difficulty with the economist's view of profit involves calculating opportunity costs. In some cases, passed-up alternatives cannot be measured in dollars. Assigning a dollar value to a missed job opportunity, to refusing a promotion, or to not meeting with a potential customer because of another meeting is difficult. The businessperson's view of profits is easier to calculate. Therefore, in this book, we emphasize business profit.

Economic Profit
What remains after expenses and opportunity costs are subtracted from income.

ECONOMICS: THE FOUNDATION OF BUSINESS

Understanding economics is essential to understanding business.[7] No single definition of economics satisfies everyone, but let's look at one concise description: **Economics** is the study of how a society (people) chooses to use scarce resources to produce goods and services and to distribute them to people for consumption. This definition raises certain issues that are key to understanding economics: (1) resources, (2) goods and services, and (3) allocation of both resources and products. Let's discuss each of them.

Economics
The study of how a society chooses to use scarce resources to produce goods and services and to distribute them for consumption.

Resources

A nation's resources consist of three broad areas: natural, capital, and labor. **Natural resources** are provided by nature in limited amounts; they include crude oil, natural gas, minerals, timber, and water. Natural resources must be processed to become a product or to be used to produce other goods or services.

Natural Resources
Resources provided in limited amounts by nature, such as oil, coal, water, and timber.

For example, trees must be processed into lumber before they can be used to build homes, shopping malls, and schools.

Capital resources are goods produced for the purpose of making other types of goods and services. Some capital resources, called *current assets*, have a short life and are used up in the production process. These resources include fuel, raw materials, paper, and money. Long-lived capital resources, which can be used repeatedly in the production process, are called *fixed capital*. Examples include factory buildings, compact-disk machines, personal computers, and railroad cars.

Labor resources represent the human talent of a nation. To have value in the labor force, individuals must be trained to perform either skilled or semiskilled work. For example, the job of physicist requires extensive training, whereas only minimal training is needed to operate a service station's gas pumps. This collection of human talent is the most valuable national resource. Without human resources, no productive use of either natural or capital resources is possible.

Capital Resources
Goods produced for the purpose of making other types of goods and services.

Labor Resources
The human talent, skills and competence, available in a nation.

Goods and Services

A nation's resources are used to produce goods and services that will meet people's needs and wants. *Needs* are goods and services people must have simply to exist. *Wants,* on the other hand, are things they would like to have but do not absolutely need for survival. Such items as food, clothing, shelter, and medical care are needs; video recorders, cassettes, fashionable clothes, and luxury vacations are wants.

A person's wants can be unlimited: as soon as one want is satisfied, another is created. Even wealthy people tend to have unlimited wants. Henry Ford was

Taking a luxury vacation would be exciting. Most people want *to take a luxury vacation but do not* need *to do so.*

Courtesy of the Cunard Line Ltd.

once asked how much money it would take before a person would stop wanting more. He reportedly answered, "Just a little bit more."

Goods and services produced in the United States—each product manufactured, each service offered—are designed to meet needs and satisfy wants of consumers. Businesses start and operate hoping to produce some item or service that the public will like well enough or need badly enough to buy. Considering that people have many needs plus an almost unlimited list of wants, is it possible to satisfy all of the population's needs and wants? The answer is no.

Allocation

Resource allocation All countries face the age-old economic problem of limited resources and unlimited wants. We all know, for example, that the supply of oil and natural gas in the United States is a limited natural resource. Even the amount of capital resources, such as corporate stocks and bonds that can be raised during a specific period, is limited.

Because we live in a world in which the quantity of all resources is limited, we must make choices about how these scarce resources are to be used. To make these choices, we have to answer three fundamental economic questions:

- What goods and services will be produced, and in what quantities? What industrial goods and what consumer goods will be produced? Apartments or new houses? Railroad cars or large trucks?
- How will goods and services be produced, and by whom? For instance, will energy be produced from coal, natural gas, or nuclear power?
- Who will use the goods and services? When the goods and services are divided, who is to benefit from their use? Rich or poor? Families or single people? Old or young?

Once these questions are answered, we have a basis for choosing how our resources will be used, how they will be allocated to best satisfy consumers' wants and needs. In a free enterprise economy, **allocation** of resources also involves other issues. Should the need for business prosperity and success be a consideration? What priority should be given to government's need for resources? In our economy, allocating resources—especially scarce resources—involves all these questions. Allocation can be very complicated, indeed.

In the United States, answers to these questions differ from answers in Cuba, the Soviet Union, or Sweden. The different answers are the result of the economic systems used in various countries.

Allocation
The process of choosing how resources will be used to meet a society's needs and wants; includes the distribution of products to consumers.

Product distribution The issue of allocation is not limited to scarce resources. It also involves the distribution of goods and services to the consumer. In this context, allocation involves an exchange (e.g., money, goods, time, service) between a business and a consumer (e.g., client, customer, patron). In an ideal pattern of distribution in a free economy, the business earns a profit and the customer is satisfied with the good or service: the exchange provides mutual benefit. That is important in a free economy. A tailor able to earn a profit is likely to continue to work hard at the job. Likewise, a customer who likes the price and quality of the tailor's services will continue to use that tailor. When goods and services get to the customers who want or need them and mutual satisfaction occurs, both resources and products have been well allocated.

ECONOMIC SYSTEMS

Economic System
The accepted process by which labor, capital, and natural resources are organized to produce and distribute goods and services in a society.

An **economic system** is an accepted way of organizing production, establishing the rights and freedom of ownership, using productive resources, and governing business transactions in a society. There are three basic types of systems: (1) the government can produce almost all the goods and services (a planned economy); (2) private enterprise can produce almost everything (pure capitalism, found only in textbook examples); and (3) there can be some government production and some private production (a mixed economy).

No economy is entirely privately owned, but a few (e.g., the People's Republic of China and Cuba) are almost entirely government owned. The United States is a mixed economy, with about 90 percent of production provided by the private sector.

Private versus state ownership percentages for 18 countries are illustrated in Figure 1.2. Compare India, Austria, Canada, and the United States on degrees of ownership, and you will find some noticeable differences.

Planned Economy

Modern socialism has much of its roots in the ideas of Karl Marx (1818–1883), published in 1867 in *Das Kapital*. Marx believed that workers were being exploited by owners (capitalists) and forced to work for wages that barely allowed them to survive. Capitalists, who owned the means of production, were viewed as a separate, distinct class. According to Marx, capitalists made profits by paying workers less than the value of their production.

Planned Economy
An economy in which the government owns the productive resources, financial enterprises, retail stores, and banks.

Socialism The Union of Soviet Socialist Republics (USSR) was born with the Bolshevik Revolution of 1917. Marx's ideas helped shape the economic system adopted by the new nation. The communist leadership set up a centrally planned system that, until 1985, operated without the profit motive. It was a classic example of a planned economy.

Prior to major changes in 1989 and 1990, countries such as East Germany, Romania, Bulgaria, and the Soviet Union had **planned economies**. The governments owned productive resources, financial enterprises, retail stores, and banks. In a planned economy, the government is the owner because it speaks for the people. Personal property, such as autos, clothing, and furniture, is owned by private citizens; however, almost all housing and the means of production are owned by government.

In the Soviet planned economy, politically appointed committees planned production, set prices, and managed the economy.[8] Each factory received detailed instructions on how many goods to produce.

Perestroika In 1985 Mikhail Gorbachev, general secretary of the Communist party, began a new program called *perestroika*. *Perestroika* means economic restructuring. Gorbachev is promoting reduced government control, less direction, and fewer rules. On January 1, 1988, about 60 percent of Soviet enterprises were put on a self-financing basis. The managers of the businesses were asked to decide how much and what to produce. Workers' wages were tied to profits. Under *perestroika,* those firms not making a profit risk being shut down. This is a new pressure on enterprise managers in the Soviet Union.

The Scope of Government Ownership   **FIGURE 1.2**

Who Owns How Much?

Privately owned: ◯ All or nearly all

Publicly owned: ◔ 25%   ◑ 50%   ◕ 75%   ● All or nearly all

na = not applicable or negligible production.   * including Conrail

Source: *Economist*, December 30, 1978, p. 39. According to the *Economist* of December 21, 1985, the percentages stated in the figure were unchanged.

Perestroika has required the use of better management skills, teamwork, goal setting, and other practices typically unused in the Soviet Union. With *perestroika,* the prices of many products have increased and have resulted in a high inflation in the Soviet Union (e.g., a Big Mac cost $6.90 in April 1991). In the past, planners set prices so that Soviet citizens who make about $300 per month could afford food and other consumer goods. Under the new system, prices will rise based on supply and demand. In anticipation of the price and inflation problem, the Soviet state has postponed price decontrol until 1992.

A Bolshoi Makski (Big Mac), French Fries, and a Shake in the Land of Vladimir

Investment by a foreigner in a country's economy has always been regarded by Communists (Soviet Union, Hungary, China) as a form of capitalist exploitation. One of the first things new leaders in the Soviet Union and China did after the revolutions (1917 in the USSR, 1948 in China) was to rid their countries of foreign investors.

The times are changing, however. After 14 years of negotiations, the Soviets entered into a joint venture with McDonald's. On January 31, 1990, a 27–cash-register McDonald's opened its doors in Moscow. A total of 30,000 McDonald's hamburgers were served that first day to an eager stream of Soviet citizens. They typically wait 40 to 45 minutes in long lines. Over 630 Soviet workers, earning about $2.40 per hour, serve the hamburgers. McDonald's received 26,000 job applications after running a one-day classified ad.

The Soviets have found that joint ventures (working, cooperating, and sharing with investors from other countries) can be rewarding. McDonald's has made available good-quality, American-style hamburgers acceptable to Soviets. The McDonald's–USSR joint venture has forced the Soviets to create a new agricultural and food processing system in the Soviet Union. McDonald's does

not want to import all its food, so it is helping the Soviets develop sources. Few farms are currently capable of breeding the high-quality cattle or growing the russet potatoes that McDonald's demands. Thus McDonald's has had to find Soviet farmers willing to learn and do the job. McDonald's is demanding high standards, and the Soviets are responding with new systems, new methods, and a new appreciation for capitalism.

This venture is a form of *perestroika,* or economic restructuring, at the farm, fast-food, joint USA–USSR level. It provides McDonald's with access to a large, untapped market in the USSR. The Soviet citizens are learning first-hand new ways of doing business, while they become familiar with American fast food, eating out, and how to make milk shakes. If relations between the United States and the USSR remain cordial, you can expect to find more Soviets learning how to do business with Americans; you will also find more Americans wanting to do business in the USSR. The 284 million Soviet citizens are waiting for, are wanting, and eventually will be demanding more goods and services that businesses of all sizes can provide.[9]

The move to decontrol prices has caused Soviet citizens to fear future price increases. Their fear resulted in a stampede to buy everything in sight while government still controlled prices. Today there are shortages of many goods, such as meat, soap, and work clothing. The Soviet government believes that the postponement of price decontrol will reduce the fears of citizens about inflation and stop the panic buying.

Soviet citizens lack the opportunity to consume many of the goods and services that Americans, Canadians, and Japanese in all walks of life take for granted. However, Soviet citizens enjoy some advantages not obtainable in the United States. Medical care is available for everyone at no cost, and rents in government housing are subsidized; public transportation is relatively inexpensive, and most higher education is tuition free.

Perestroika also has given Soviets the opportunity to engage in joint ventures with partners in different countries. A **joint venture** is the formal cooperation of two or more businesses to share business decision making, investment risks, and profits. The Business Action tells how McDonald's learned to do business in the Soviet Union through a joint venture. Chapter Six will discuss joint ventures in more detail.

Joint Ventures
The formal cooperation of two or more businesses to share business decision making, investment risks, and profits.

The Soviet Union's economic system doesn't permit the freedoms found in the United States, Canada, Japan, and in the Western European nations. Even with the current (January 1991) version of *perestroika*, central planners set production goals on the basis of political goals rather than consumer needs and wants. The entire world is watching as the world's most powerful planned economy makes changes to improve its economic performance. (Return to Table 1.1 to see how far the Soviet Union has to travel to come even with the United States and Japan.) Most people around the world want Gorbachev's *perestroika* to succeed.

Mixed Economy

Most modern industrialized nations have mixed economies. In a **mixed economy,** both the government and private business enterprises produce and distribute goods and services. The government usually plays a role in supplying defense, roads, education, pensions, and some medical care. In the mixed economy, markets are generally free and competitive.

Mixed Economy
An economy in which both private and government production of goods and services occurs.

Capitalism and the mixed economy   The American brand of economic system, called *capitalism*, has created a mixed economy. **Capitalism** is characterized by private ownership of capital and by competition among businesses seeking a profit. Consumers play much more of a role under capitalism than they do in a planned economy. They have *freedom of choice* in purchasing goods and services, in selecting an occupation or a school, and in deciding how to use money that is earned. They are free to consume what they want and need. Their choices greatly influence decisions about production and use of resources.

Capitalism
Type of economic system characterized by private ownership of capital and by competition among businesses seeking a profit.

A mixed capitalist economy also allows the freedom to start a business.[10] *Freedom of enterprise* means that businesses and individuals with the capital may enter essentially any legal business venture they wish. This important feature of capitalism permits individuals to seek out profit-making business opportunities. Under capitalism, any business or individual can earn a profit by producing a useful good or service. However, businesses and individuals do not have an automatic right to profit. Profit is a reward to a business for using scarce economic resources efficiently. Consumers must consider a good or service reasonable in price, quality, and value before a profit can be made.

Competition is yet another important part of capitalism. In general, *competition* refers to the rivalry among businesses for consumer dollars. Because of competition for consumer dollars, businesses have to be aware of what consumers want to buy. If they ignore consumer wishes, they are likely to lose sales, which directly affect the level of profit. A business that consistently loses money and makes no profit will fail. Consequently competition among businesses generally provides consumers with lower prices, more services, and improved products. The 1980s fare wars in the airline industry illustrate how fierce competition among businesses can grow.

The American economic system is "mixed capitalism." It became mixed when government established operating guidelines and laws for businesses to follow. For example, one important federal law requires a variety of safety rules to be followed on construction jobs. An economic system also becomes mixed when government competes directly with business. This often happens in such areas as medical research, electric power generation, and communication. The U.S. Postal Service is an example of a government business that competes with private businesses such as Federal Express and United Parcel Service.

The U.S. economic system   The United States has developed the world's largest economic system.[11] The basic parts of the American economy are illustrated in Figure 1.3. This model, a simplification of our mixed economic system, includes only the broadest parts of the economy; it does not include the government.

FIGURE 1.3

Flow of Money and Products in the American Economy

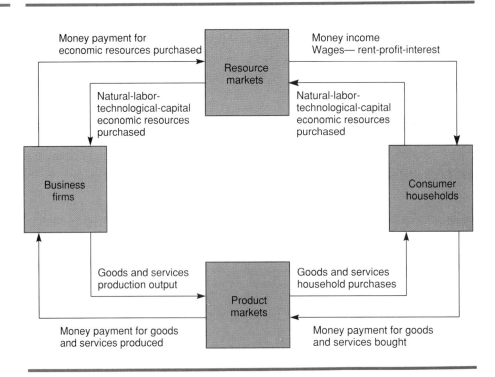

Note the differences between resource markets and product markets in the figure. *Resource markets* are places where economic resources—natural, labor, technological, and capital—are bought and sold. The New York Stock Exchange, where money is invested in companies, is a capital resource market. The employment ad in local newspapers is a resource market where labor is bought and sold. *Product markets* are the thousands of markets in America where business outputs—goods and services—are sold to consumers. Consumers pay for goods and services with money. This type of consumer expenditure is called retail sales. The money businesses receive from retail sales is business revenue.

Where do consumers get money to spend for goods and services? Figure 1.3 shows that consumer households supply economic resources to the resource markets. In return for money, people provide labor through work, invest in businesses (capital), and sell natural resources to businesses. The money received in payment for these economic resources is then used to purchase goods and services. Of course, businesses view money paid to suppliers of goods and services as an expense.

Two distinct types of economic resource flows are illustrated in Figure 1.3. The flow of economic resources and products is shown by the inner loop. It flows counterclockwise, showing that economic resources move from consumers to businesses and then return to consumers as finished goods and services. Money flow, on the other hand, is shown by the outer circle. This clockwise flow of money begins when firms pay consumers for the economic resource they purchase. Consumers use their money to purchase the goods and services produced by businesses. These two economic flows take place continuously and at the same time. As long as consumers spend all their money, the flow of money into and out of consumer households is equal. However, some money is diverted into savings, and the government needs to intervene to bring about a balance in the flows.

What economic system is best?   The most appropriate form of economic system for a nation depends on several things, including cultural factors and the availability of economic resources. For example, capitalism is unlikely to be appropriate for a nation that creates hurdles for individuals who want to organize their own businesses. The right of business owners to use economic resources for whatever purpose they want is the backbone of capitalism. Capitalism normally works best with people who are willing and able to make their own economic decisions. In fact, capitalism encourages people to take the initiative to become better educated and to make their own decisions.

A HISTORICAL REVIEW OF AMERICAN BUSINESS

As we mentioned previously, economics involves learning about a society's use of limited productive resources to satisfy the unlimited desires of its citizens. American economic success arises from the freedom to own property, freedom of choice, freedom to earn a reasonable profit, sufficient natural resources, hard-working and educated people, and outstanding business leadership. Throughout America's history, business leaders have displayed their talents in organizing businesses, managing human resources, financing business, marketing goods and services, and using information resources. However, Americans have no guarantee of being world leaders in business transactions, know-how, and success. Today their business leadership is being challenged by creative, hardworking, astute competitors throughout the world, especially in Japan, Germany, Italy, South Korea, and Hong Kong.

Historically, the influences of many societies and cultures have formed the business values that helped make the United States a worldwide economic power. Let's review the stages through which American business has reached its present position in the world.

Mercantilism

Mercantilism
A system of state power, with public authority controlling and directing the nation's economic life.

To understand the forces behind the founding of the American colonies, we must understand the economic thought of that time. The doctrine of mercantilism stressed the development of a strong economic state. **Mercantilism** is a system of state power, with public authority controlling and directing the nation's economic life. This economic philosophy led the governments of European nations—especially England, France, Spain, and Portugal—to do everything possible to increase the power and wealth of the country. According to the basic tenets of mercantilism, a nation should:

- Be as self-sufficient as possible.
- Sell more goods to foreigners than are purchased from foreigners, in order to increase the mother country's wealth.
- Accumulate gold and silver bullion because these serve as a measure of the country's wealth and power.
- Establish colonies, which serve as sources of raw materials or precious metals and as a market for finished goods.

Adam Smith: *The Wealth of Nations*

Adam Smith, a professor at the University of Edinburgh in Scotland in the late 1700s, was a prominent critic of mercantilism. Smith wanted to make individuals and their needs the focal point of the economy; he felt that individuals' pursuit of their own best interests would lead a nation to attain its goals. His book *The Wealth of Nations* (published in 1776) presented many of his views. Smith believed:

- People do their best when they reap the rewards of hard work and intelligence and suffer the penalties of laziness. (He favored the use of profits as a means of encouraging individual incentive and initiative.)
- People should be free to conduct business or seek work that provides them with the greatest reward for their efforts.
- What serves the individual also serves society. The pursuit of individual self-interest leads to the best allocation of the nation's resources and thus to the maximum satisfaction of people's needs.

Laissez-Faire
A policy that encourages government to leave business and the economy alone.

Smith assumed the enemy of human freedom at that time to be the state—the internationalist, mercantilistic government that imposed tariffs, granted monopolies, levied taxes, and above all sought to improve what was best left to itself. Smith argued for free competition among all producers. He felt that free competition can exist only if the government follows a policy of **laissez-faire,** which encourages government to leave business and the economy alone. (The

French word *laissez-faire* means to let people do as they choose.) Only on rare occasions, in order to prevent monopolies, should a laissez-faire government interfere with the operation of the economy. Instead, the economy is guided by the "invisible hand" of competition. This was the key to Smith's philosophy: if government stayed out of the economy and allowed businesses and consumers to pursue their own best interests, competition among producers would keep prices low while generating the goods demanded by consumers. The invisible hand that guides us, according to Smith, is the **profit motive.** Expected and actual profits motivate business leaders to do what must be done.

Profit Motive
Expected or actual returns that motivate business leaders to do what must be done.

The invisible hand works efficiently in the United States. It has even found its way to Eastern European economies. For example, as we prepare this book, about one third of the Soviet Union's food is produced on the 1 percent of land owned by private owners. The other 99 percent is in the form of collective farms, with centrally controlled farmers. The self-interested, motivated Soviet farmers work much harder on their own land than do the centrally controlled farmers who work the land owned by the Soviet government.

Though many of Adam Smith's suggestions have been practiced in the United States, the concept of laissez-faire has generally been rejected. Ignoring Smith's advice that the economy operates best when left alone, government officials have actively sought to improve its operation. Today, government involvement covers numerous areas, including:

Price regulation.

Truth in advertising.

Nonsmoking regulations.

Maintenance of product quality.

Personnel hiring decisions.

Highway construction.

Regulation of public utilities.

Automobile safety, emission, and mileage standards.

Pollution standards.

Many of these areas are covered in later chapters.

Photo courtesy of The Kroger Company

Kroger Food Store has Department of Commerce personnel check fresh and frozen fish before it is shipped to stores. The Kroger shopper knows that the assurance of quality is backed by U.S. government inspection.

The U.S. Industrial Revolution

Industrial Revolution
The development of modern technology and production processes, which began in England about 1769.

Although what we call the Industrial Revolution began in England about 1769, it made its appearance in America in 1790. The **Industrial Revolution,** characterized by extensive mechanization of production systems, caused the population to concentrate in cities and changed the nature of work for many people.

In 1790 a young apprentice mechanic, Samuel Slater, was able to construct the machinery necessary for the textile mill; his mill in Rhode Island was America's first true factory. After Eli Whitney invented the cotton gin in 1793, the great increase in cotton production meant that a number of cotton mills had to be constructed. The techniques of production were so improved that the sheer size of most enterprises dramatically increased.

Whitney made another significant contribution to the industrialization of America: interchangeable parts. In 1798 he won a contract to build 10,000 muskets for the American government. He immediately set out to build a plant and design the new musket. He first divided the work to be accomplished among his workers (each one specialized in a particular task). Next, he designed highly accurate machinery to make the parts. Because this machinery worked with such great accuracy, it enabled unskilled workers to do the work of skilled workers. Finally, by using templates, he was able to manufacture thousands of interchangeable pieces. In setting up his factory, he used the specialization of labor that Adam Smith had described and, through tight quality control, was able to use unskilled workers to make a product of high quality.

Industrial life in the United States changed drastically after the Civil War ended in 1865. Improvements in rail and steamship transportation closed the gap between producer and consumer. Products could be sold to a large market scattered over wide geographic areas rather than only in small, local markets. Also, the factory system expanded and began to influence all aspects of life. In fact, America began to shift from a predominantly rural society to an urban one.

To service the expanding markets, a new type of business was necessary. The general store or the small mill could not service a geographically dispersed market. Only a larger, more efficient business operation could deal with the demands of larger markets. Producers needed better distribution systems, transportation, warehouses, production capabilities, and managerial skills.

The Pre-Depression Years

The period from the end of the 19th century to the Great Depression in 1929 was one of growth in the oil, steel, and financial industries. Other industries, such as tobacco, meat, and copper, also grew. For example, in the early 19th century, meat processing had been quite primitive, done either at home or by local butchers. But around the turn of the century, a major industry based on hogs and cattle developed through the business spirit, risk-taking, and knowledge of leaders like Philip Armour, Gustavus Swift, and Michael Cudahy.

The prosperity of the 1920s resulted from a number of factors. One important cause was the profits made in stock market speculation. People were putting money into the stock market, often on credit. They would buy some stock and then use it as a security pledge to obtain a loan to buy even more stock. This method worked well when stock prices were increasing. But when prices dropped drastically, as they did following the Black Thursday of October

TABLE 1.3

Selected Stock Prices in the Depression Era

Company	1929 (High)	1932 (Low)
Consolidated Cigar	$115	$ 2–½
Erie Railroad	93–½	2
General Foods	82	20
General Motors	91	8
New York Central	256	9
Radio Corporation of America	115	2–½
Southern Railway	165	2–½
U.S. Steel	261	21
Wright Aeronautical	150	4

Source: Gordon V. Axon, *The Stock Market Crash of 1929* (New York: Mason & Lipscomb, 1974), pp. 93–94.

24, 1929, the bottom fell out.[12] The extent of the financial collapse is indicated in Table 1.3. Note, for instance, how Radio Corporation of America lost 98 percent of its stock market value in three years.

The Great Depression

A **depression** is a period of drastic decline in the national economy, characterized by decreasing business transactions, falling prices, and high rates of unemployment. The Depression of 1929–40 will be ingrained in the minds of Americans for generations to come. (Even today, many presidential decisions are affected by memories of and by reading and learning about the Great Depression.) The tragic poverty and unemployment of that time have had no equal. Between October 1929 and the early 1940s, unemployment hit 25 percent of the work force, or about 13 million people (this compares to about 34 million, using 1990 figures). The value of goods and services produced in the country was cut in half, and stock market prices fell about 90 percent. The hopes and dreams that marked the 1920s came to a sudden end.

Depression
A period of drastic decline in the national economy characterized by decreasing business transactions, falling prices, and high unemployment.

Although the 1929 stock market crash was a major factor leading to the Great Depression, other factors contributed. Some of the culprits included:

- The actions of the Federal Reserve System.
- Installment buying.
- Overproduction of consumer goods and a decline in investment.
- Speculation.

The crash of the stock market came early in the Depression, and its effects were less significant than the waves of bank failures that followed. The first wave came in October 1930, the second in March 1931, and the third in the last quarter of 1932. In each case, banks failed because savers panicked. Savers, fearful that the banks would collapse in the poor business climate, lined up to withdraw their funds. Banks did not (and still don't) keep on hand 100 percent

Unemployment lines circled city blocks during the Great Depression. Finding a job was a top priority for these out-of-work men. There were not enough jobs to go around.

UPI/Bettmann Newsphotos

of the cash deposited (they make loans to other people with their depositors' money); they could not pay back all their depositors at once and thus went bankrupt. Millions of Americans lost their life savings in the bank failures.

The New Deal Years

When Franklin D. Roosevelt became president of the United States in 1933, the country's economic system was paralyzed. One fourth of U.S. workers were unemployed, production of goods and services was down by half, and corporate profits were off by two thirds. Roosevelt made America's economic problems the focal point for both domestic and foreign policies. The policies of his New Deal centered in two areas: unemployment and banking reform.

Solving the unemployment problem proved very difficult. Roosevelt proposed, and Congress passed, a series of acts dubbed the alphabet acts because everyone referred to them by their initials. The National Industrial Recovery Act (NIRA), for example, brought labor, management, and consumers together to set prices and wages and to regulate output. The New Deal policies of Roosevelt seemed to work; but 20 percent of the work force, or almost 9 million Americans, was still unemployed in 1939.

World War II and the Postwar Period

The nation's economic troubles finally began to ease at the start of World War II. Unfortunately, economic problems were replaced by wartime fears.

War production meant Uncle Sam was the principal consumer of goods. Industries modified their facilities to produce tanks, weapons, tools, military clothing, airplanes, ships, and other wartime equipment. The government's total wartime expenditure (1941–45) was about $347 billion. As a result, such consumer goods as shoes, tires, clothing, gasoline, and meat became scarce and were rationed.

The end of World War II brought renewed fears of depression. But these fears were unfounded. The economy continued to expand because of:

- A pent-up demand for consumer goods, resulting from wartime limits on consumption.
- Built-up purchasing power resulting from individual savings during the war. Much of the wartime saving was forced on people by the government. At one point, the government deducted 10 percent of a person's wage and put it into Series E government bonds.
- Plant and equipment expansions created by the war.
- An efficient and ready-to-work labor force.
- The population explosion during the 10 years following the war.
- The emergence of new or modernized industries and processes: natural gas, plastics, electronics, data processing, aluminum, and aeronautics.

The Modern Era

In the 1950s, the economy continued to expand. Four recessions occurred during the 50s and 60s, but they were mild. When the level of economic activity declines for at least a six-month period, the economy is said to be in **recession.** Employment and the production of goods and services are generally down during a recession.

During the 1950–85 period, Americans became familiar with and enjoyed new shopping malls, high-technology consumer goods (such as microwave ovens), new educational opportunities, improved health care, and many other new commodities and services. At the same time, Americans became quite familiar with the term **inflation,** which refers to a period of rising prices, or a decline in the purchasing power of the dollar (the dollar buys less).

In the 60s and 70s, the government examined the inflation problems facing citizens and began to play a larger role in the economy. President John F. Kennedy's New Frontier and President Lyndon B. Johnson's Great Society meant more government involvement in business. A major part of the New Frontier concept was the cutting of personal income tax to stimulate consumption, investment, and employment and to hold inflation at a reasonable level. The Great Society programs included medical aid to older Americans, improved product safety, and improved housing.

The 1970s were highlighted by change. In 1974, following the oil price shock of 1973, a major recession hit the United States. The Organization of Petroleum Exporting Countries (OPEC) had quadrupled oil prices in fall 1973, right at a time of double-digit inflation. Our economic growth had stalled. Thus, Americans were faced with **stagflation,** a stalled economy (stagnation) with rising prices (inflation).

Recession
A cycle or period when the level of economic activity declines for at least a six-month period.

Inflation
The rise in the average level of prices for all goods and services in a particular time period.

Stagflation
A stalled economy faced with rising prices for goods and services.

TABLE 1.4

Main Economic Events (1929–1988)

Years of Presidency	President	Main Economic Events
1933–45	Franklin Roosevelt	Great Depression (1929–41), New Deal (1933–41), World War II (1941–45).
1945–53	Harry Truman	Recessions (1945, 1948–49), Fair Deal (1945–53), Korean War (1950–53).
1953–61	Dwight Eisenhower	Recessions (1953–54, 1957–58, 1960–61).
1961–63	John Kennedy	New Frontier (1961–63).
1963–69	Lyndon Johnson	Great Society (1964–68), Vietnamese War escalation (1965–68).
1969–74	Richard Nixon	Vietnamese War, recessions (1969–70, 1974–75).
1974–77	Gerald Ford	Recession (1974–75).
1977–81	Jimmy Carter	Recession (1980).
1981–88	Ronald Reagan	Recession (1981–82), tax cut (1981–83), tax reform (1987, 1988).
1989–present	George Bush	Mild recession, savings and loan crises, bank crisis, Persian Gulf War.

Source: Adapted from page 7 of ECONOMICS, by Stephen L. Slavin. Copyright © 1988 by John Wiley & Sons, Inc. Reprinted by permission of John Wiley & Sons, Inc.

Supply-Side Economics
Reducing government's role in business by decreasing taxes and government regulation.

In 1981 Ronald Reagan replaced Jimmy Carter as president, facing high interest rates, high inflation, high unemployment, and little productivity growth. He instituted **supply-side economics.** Supply-side economists believed the government had become too involved in business; they attempted to get the government out of the way by reducing taxes and government rules and regulations. The objective was to raise the total amount of goods and services produced. Supply-side economists believed high tax rates reduce a worker's incentive to work hard. A person faced with higher taxes is just not going to work hard to produce. President Reagan initiated tax cuts, which caused inflation to subside. Unemployment rates dropped from 11 percent to 6 percent. However, although inflation was brought under control, the supply-side approach did not lead to the rapid rate of economic growth its advocates had expected. A summary of the main economic events from President Roosevelt to President Bush appears in Table 1.4.

BUSINESS CHALLENGES FOR THE 1990S

The business and economic world of the 1990s faces many challenges. Much more will be involved than trade among 160 countries, entrepreneurs starting businesses, and Americans working hard to compete more effectively with the Japanese, South Koreans, and Germans. The average American will face many economic decisions in the 1990s, and learning how to do business will be very important. A number of statistics, trends, and data will significantly affect how business is conducted in the 1990s. A few of the most significant challenges that will influence our study of business are discussed in this section. First, the Business Action on page 34 looks at some good news about U.S. business.

An Aging Population

In 1991, 249 million Americans lived in a world of 5 billion people. The population of the United States increased about 11 percent between 1980 and 1990. Forecasts indicate that by the year 2000 there will be 272 million Americans; the country will be about 13 percent black, 9.5 percent Hispanic, 74.3 percent white non-Hispanic, and about 3.2 percent other.

The average American is getting older. In 1820 the median age of the population was only 16.7 years. Today the median age is about 32. An older population is not bad for business, but changes must be made in what products and services are produced. The aging of America also benefits those growing up and beginning their business careers in the 1990s. With fewer young workers available to provide goods and services, wages and salaries are expected to rise. The downside is the cost of caring for an aging America. With fewer and fewer workers bearing the tax burden to support programs for the care of the elderly, some difficult political decisions must be made. Social security and pension funds will have to be carefully managed to withstand the drain expected from an aging population.

The Changing Family

America has about 90 million households. There is really no average, close-knit, "Father Knows Best" (a television show during the 1950s) family. Rising divorce rates, working mothers, fewer children, and a changing world have altered the way many families live. For example, failed marriages mean more children are growing up in single-parent homes. There is also a mass migration of women into the labor market. Half of all mothers with children under the age of one year work outside the home. Today over 10 million children under the age of six have working mothers, yet only about 1,800 employers offer child-care benefits.

Parents are waiting longer to have children. In 1970 only 19 percent of all women had their children after the age of 25. In 1990 over 38 percent of the women having children were over 25. The parents who wait longer have more money to spend on children; today's $15 billion market in children's products is expected to grow to over $20 billion by 1999.

Jobs

Overall, employment will be about 135 million in 2000, according to Labor Department projections. The service economy will create more jobs (20 million) than any other part of the economy. *Services* are intangible products (e.g., insurance, airline travel, tax preparation advice) that are not physically

The Good News about U.S. Business

Some doomsayers have predicted the decline of business in the United States. In fact, the United States has slipped in some industries: there have been financial failures in the banking industry, there are trade deficits, and Americans spend beyond their means in some instances. On the other hand, in 1990 the United States admitted 630,000 legal immigrants—more than all other nations put together. Since 1970 the United States has allowed more legal immigration than the rest of the world's countries combined. These immigrants have added to the country's talent pool at a time when birthrates are down. Who are these immigrants? Most are from Asia and Hispanic countries. They are aggressive, entrepreneurial, and fighters who wanted to come to the United States.

Some observers have made negative comments about the decrease in America's share of world industrial production. It was 50 percent in the 1950s and is now 25 percent. However, the United States holds only about 4.8 percent of the world population. Why should one nation have or maintain 50 percent of the world's industrial production? Perhaps the sharing of wealth and the spread of economic power have helped human survival and world humanity.

While America has lost some of its share of world industrial production, the future looks bright. The United States remains the world leader in technological innovation, while Japan and Germany are also advancing. Researchers are currently applying new technologies to areas such as medicine, environmental safety and protection, communications, recreation, computers, and robotics. The end result—a world that is cleaner, safer, healthier, and more convenient. Products are available at affordable prices in stores that are conveniently located. It is rare that we have to wait to buy basics such as food and clothing, while individuals in some parts of the world wait in line for these products. Appliances, cars, stereos, and other luxury goods are also readily available for those able to purchase them. In short, the standard of living in America continues to be second to none. Isn't that why proud immigrants, like our own ancestors, continue to flock to the United States, bringing new dreams and new ambitions?

The United States also continues to make strides in the production of services—intangible products—and has been labeled the world's first service economy. McDonald's now has more employees than U.S. Steel, and continued growth is expected in the services sector of our economy,

with data processing and health care leading the way. This will mean more white-collar jobs in a variety of service industries.

As evidence of the United States' commitment to being a world industrial leader, consider the recent Deming Prize for quality received by Florida Power & Light Co. The award is named after American W. E. Deming, an 89-year-old statistician who pioneered ideas about quality control. Deming is more revered in Japan than in his native America, and Florida Power & Light Co. is the first non-Japanese company to win the prestigious award. More significantly, the award was created by the Japanese. Consider also the 1990 recipient of the Malcolm Baldrige National Quality Award, Cadillac. A car that was nearly written off as dead has come back to win this coveted award.

Make no mistake, the United States has its work cut out for it. Japan is gaining in several high-tech fields, including computers, telecommunications equipment, and medical equipment. But this competition is making giants like IBM work harder, and innovators like Bill Gates of Microsoft, who dominates the computer software industry, can still reach for the sky.[13]

A service business that is booming is the video store. This and hundreds of other Blockbuster video stores attract customers who want to rent movies and watch them at their own convenience.

Courtesy of Blockbluster Corporate Entertainment

possessed and that involve a performance or an effort. Examples of service industries include banking, transportation, retail trade, and entertainment.

An estimated 4 million jobs will be created between 1991 and 1996. About 10,000 new companies are formed each week. Women are the fastest-growing group of new-business owners (entrepreneurs). New job opportunities will probably continue in new businesses, in smaller businesses, and in the service industries.

Minorities in America

America has always been a country of minorities, a nation of immigrants and refugees. In 1920, of 105 million Americans 14 million were foreign born and 10.5 million were black. In 1990, of 249 million Americans 12 percent were foreign born. As the percentage of minorities and immigrants increases, they will play a more significant role in the American economy and workplace.

Like other Americans, minorities seek entrepreneurial opportunities. The number of nonwhite, self-employed persons increased by over 50 percent in the 1980s—faster than white self-employment, which grew by over 40 percent during the same period. Black entrepreneurs have made inroads in entertainment and media, led by long-established, black-owned firms such as Motown (entertainment) and Johnson Publishing (*Ebony* magazine).

Hispanic businesses grew significantly in the past decade and are likely to continue this growth in the 1990s; the Hispanic population is expanding at four times the national rate. As Hispanics begin to gain more affluence, they draw

Some top executives at Goya Foods, a very successful Hispanic-owned firm, taste some of the products. Goya products are bought by Hispanics and non-Hispanics because they are tasty and reasonably priced.

Courtesy of Goya Foods, Inc.

the attention of businesses. Hispanic-owned businesses such as Goya Foods, Inc., Banco Popular de Puerto Rico, E&G Trading, Inc., and Sedano's Supermarkets are already producing goods and services geared to the needs and wants of Hispanics.

An Wang (Wang Laboratories), Roberto Goizueta (Cuban-born chief executive officer of Coca-Cola), John Johnson (Johnson Publishing), and Barry Gordy (Motown) are examples of successful minority managers and excellent role models for all Americans. The talents of every American—black, Asian, Hispanic, white, male and female—are needed to conduct business in our globalizing economy.

The Global Boom

In past centuries, heads of state were all-important because the relationships between countries were primarily political. Today a country's business leaders are often as prominent as its political figures. H. Ross Perot (United States—Electronic Data Systems), Giovanni Agnelli (Italy—Fiat), Pehr Gyllenhammar (Sweden—Volvo), and Akio Morita (Japan) are as well known as the top political leaders in their countries.

Nations are now linked by telecommunications and trade (economics). Fiberoptic calls are faster and much clearer than calls using copper wire. Americans made over 5 billion minutes of overseas calls in 1990, up from 580 million in 1970. A fiberoptic cable across the Pacific went into service in April 1989, linking the United States and Japan. North America, Europe, Asia, and Australia are being strung with fiberoptic cable. In 1992 more than 16 million miles of fiberoptic cable will be in place. Why is that significant? The cable can carry 40,000 calls simultaneously, tripling the volume available in the 1980s.

Telecommunications will continue to link nations, people, and businesses. Just as we are becoming a global marketplace, we are moving toward a single worldwide information network. Businesses will soon have the capacity to communicate anything to anyone, anywhere in the world, by any form—voice, data, text, or image—at the speed of sound. Why do business students need the skills to work with computers and communications systems? Because their world of business will require these skills.

Another aspect of the global boom is exploding economies. Five hundred years ago, the world's trade center began moving from the Mediterranean to the Atlantic. It is now moving from the Atlantic toward the Pacific. Los Angeles, Tokyo, Sydney, and Hong Kong are becoming centers of business. Today Asia has half of the world's population. By the year 2000, it is expected to have two thirds, while Europe will have only 6 percent and the United States about 4.8 percent. Asia is a $3 trillion market growing at a rate of $3 billion a week.

The Pacific Rim stretches from the west coast of South America northward across the Bering Strait to the USSR, southward to Australia. It includes all countries touched by the Pacific Ocean. The lifeblood of Japan, a tiny group of islands that is far from self-sufficient, is trade with the United States, Europe, and other countries. Although Japan is the Pacific Rim's economic power today, South Korea, Taiwan, Hong Kong, and Singapore (called the "Four Tigers") are also major business centers.

The global boom has also touched communist countries and authoritarian regimes. Eastern Europe, the Soviet Union, Chile, and other Third World nations have caught the democracy "bug." The democratizing of these nations will have a significant impact on how business is conducted in the 1990s. To clean up the chaos and poor economies of Eastern Europe, more private ownership and free enterprise will be needed in the 1990s. Hungarians, Poles, Russians, Czechs, and Yugoslavs want more, better, and reliable goods and services. The opportunities for American businesspeople to conduct business in democratizing countries are constrained only by limits to their creativeness.

The Environment

The economically booming world of the 1990s will not be without environmental challenges. Business leaders must help solve the ozone layer depletion, acid rain, the greenhouse effect, and the destruction of rain forests. Some have called the 1990s the "Earth Decade."[14]

As the public becomes more concerned about the environment, business leaders take note. If a company's environmental reputation affects people's buying decisions, then business concern may be tied to survival of the enterprise. Business leaders in the 1990s will have to make environmental considerations (e.g., pollution, waste, recycling) a part of product decision making. Businesses will have to do the right thing routinely and by choice, not because some group or law forces them to do so. Chapter Four will discuss the environment further.

The changes in business concerns about the environment appear daily. At Wal-Mart, environmentalism is a cause; suppliers are asked to provide recycled or recyclable products. The London-based Body Shop, with 14 U.S. outlets, puts the environment at the center of its business. Its skin and hair care stores display literature on ozone depletion next to sunscreens and fill their display windows with information on issues like global warming. Each employee must

Firms like Amoco want to inform the public that they are environmentally responsible. Recycling to help clean up the environment is a top Amoco priority.

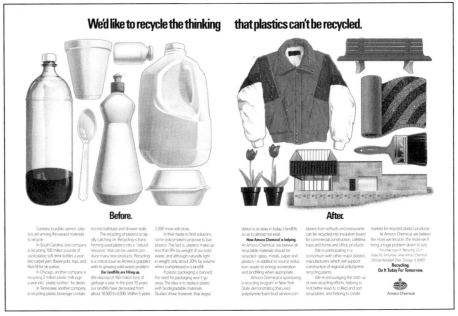

Courtesy of the Amoco Corporation

spend half a day each week on activist work. Customers get discounts if they bring their old bottles back for recycling. Sales are skyrocketing, the company gets frequent positive publicity, and the environmental theme excites Body Shop employees. They love to work for a responsible firm. More examples like Wal-Mart and Body Shop will be publicized in the 1990s, and their competitors will have to become environmentally active to stay in business.

THE SCOPE OF THIS BOOK

Some of these challenges will be covered in the remainder of Part One (The Business Enterprise) and in the next six parts. In Part Two, the environment of business will be presented. Part Three covers management and organization, while in Part Four, human resources are the focal point. Marketing is discussed and analyzed in Part Five. The concepts of financial management are presented in Part Six, and accounting and information systems are found in Part Seven. Figure 1.4 depicts the organization of the book.

Since finding a rewarding career is extremely important for a person's quality of life, we will also present career opportunities in business. A discussion about what careers are available, as well as many job descriptions, are presented in the career appendixes following each part. Tips on starting your own business are also featured.

FIGURE 1.4

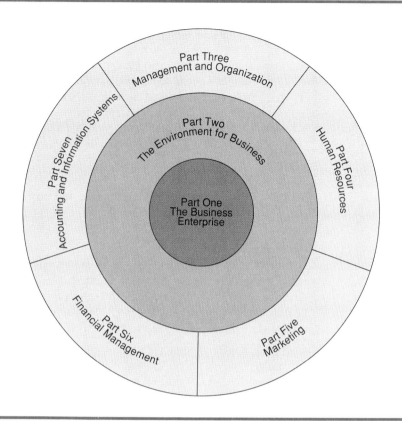

 You'll Know It's the **21**st **Century When . . .**

Everyone Belongs to a Minority Group

As the 20th century closes, white males are already less than half of the labor force. By 2010, married couples will no longer be a majority of households. Asians will outnumber Jews by a margin of two to one, and Hispanics will lead blacks as the nation's largest minority. But it will take until 2039, the year the youngest baby boomer turns age 75, for that generation to cease to dominate consumer markets.

By 2020, immigration will become more important to U.S. population growth than natural increase (the growth that occurs because births outnumber deaths). The population will diversify even more rapidly. Diversity creates opportunities for business, but targeting so many cultures, age groups, and lifestyles with the right products and messages will be an unprecedented challenge.

SUMMARY OF LEARNING OBJECTIVES

1. To define the term *business* and state why the study of business is important.
   Business involves the exchange of goods, services, or money for mutual benefit. We need to study business because (*a*) we have become so interdependent on others, both individually and as a nation, (*b*) increasing globalization of business will bring many opportunities, (*c*) we strive to maintain and improve our standard of living, (*d*) coping with unforeseen events will be easier and less traumatic, and (*e*) we will be able to separate fact from fiction in business issues.

2. To explain how people form the core of business.
   Business needs people as owners, managers, employees, and consumers. Businesses may be operated differently, and the objectives of business may differ, but the universal element in all business activities is people.

3. To identify four main objectives of business.
   A business must first *survive* if other objectives are to be accomplished. *Growth* is an objective because business does not stand still. Businesses must accept *social responsibility* in areas such as the environment and protection from discrimination. The *profit* objective plays a major role in business. Profits reward a business enterprise for effectively conducting a number of activities.

4. To explain two views of profit.
   Business profit is calculated by subtracting all costs, including taxes, from the revenue received from selling a product or service in the marketplace. *Economic profit* is calculated the same way, except opportunity costs are also deducted from revenues. Opportunity cost is the cost of choosing to use resources for one purpose while sacrificing the next best alternative use of those resources.

5. To define the term *economics* and discuss three types of economic resources.
   Economics is the study of how a society chooses to use scarce resources to produce goods and services and then distribute them to people for consumption. *Natural resources* are provided by nature in limited amounts (e.g., coal, oil, natural gas); *capital resources* are goods produced for the purpose of making other goods and services (e.g., fuel, money, factories); *labor resources* are the nation's human talent, the most valuable national resource.

6. To identify the characteristics of a free enterprise system.
   In the free enterprise system, business enterprises are free to do business competitively, with minimal government regulation. Consumers purchase those goods and services that satisfy their needs and wants. Resources are shifted into the production of these goods and services; things that do not satisfy consumers' needs and wants are not produced. Businesses are free to produce as much of whatever goods and services as consumers will buy.

7. To distinguish between planned and mixed economic systems.
   In *planned economies,* such as those in Cuba, China, and Vietnam, the government owns the means of production, financial enterprises, retail stores, and banks. Prior to 1985 in the Soviet Union, politically appointed

committees planned production (by telling factories how much of which goods to produce), set prices, and managed the economy. This is now slowly changing. In a *mixed economy,* such as operates in most industrialized nations, both the government and business enterprises produce and distribute goods and services. The government provides defense, roads, education, pensions, and some medical care. Markets are free and competitive.

8. To describe the stages of the historical development of the American economy.
The colonists settled in America during an era of mercantilism, a system of state power with public authority controlling and directing the nation's economic life. Then Adam Smith criticized mercantilism in his book *The Wealth of Nations*. Smith opposed the tariffs, granted monopolies, and taxes levied by the state. He argued for free competition among all producers. The Industrial Revolution caused the population to become concentrated in the cities and changed the nature of work for many people. In the pre-depression years, people began investing in the stock market, often on credit, until the bottom dropped out of the market, causing the Great Depression. The New Deal years of Franklin D. Roosevelt brought about reform in unemployment and banking. Later, during World War II and the postwar period, economic troubles began to ease. Economic expansion has continued in the modern era, troubled by periods of recession and inflation.

9. To identify the challenges facing business in the 1990s.
The challenges include aging populations, changes in family structure, the shift in emphasis from goods to services, the increasing importance of women and minorities in the business world, the trend toward globalization, and the need to protect the environment.

KEY TERMS

Business, p. 8

Barter, p. 8

Standard of Living, p. 10

Free Enterprise, p. 10

Gross National Product (GNP), p. 12

Business Enterprise, p. 12

Consumer, p. 15

Business Profit, p. 16

Opportunity Cost, p. 17

Economic Profit, p. 17

Economics, p. 17

Natural Resources, p. 17

Capital Resources, p. 18

Labor Resources, p. 18

Allocation, p. 19

Economic System, p. 20

Planned Economy, p. 20

Joint Venture, p. 23

Mixed Economy, p. 23

Capitalism, p. 23

Mercantilism, p. 26

Laissez-Faire, p. 26

Profit Motive, p. 27

Industrial Revolution, p. 28

Depression, p. 29

Recession, p. 31

Inflation, p. 31

Stagflation, p. 31

Supply-Side Economics, p. 32

QUESTIONS FOR DISCUSSION AND REVIEW

1. In a free enterprise system, should there be a limit placed on the amount of profit a business owner can earn? Explain.

2. Why will it be difficult for *perestroika* to be successful in the short run (three to five years) in the Soviet Union?

3. What features of the mercantilist philosophy still exist in the United States?

4. How would the incentive to produce high-quality goods be affected by a centrally planned (government) approach to quality control?

5. Why is the U.S. mixed economy called a free enterprise system?

6. Why should *you* study business, including its successes, failures, history, and principles?

7. What role does government play in the U.S. economic system?

8. Give some examples of government intervention in business practices?

9. What influence has Adam Smith had on the development of the free enterprise system in the United States?

10. Profits are presented as a reward for conducting a number of activities. What are these activities?

CASE 1.1
Dell Computer Corporation: An Example of Free Enterprise

Michael Dell. Do you know the name? His is an American success story that began in a University of Texas dormitory room in 1984. That year, at age 19, Michael Dell took $1,000 of his personal savings and started his firm, Dell Computer Corporation. He didn't finish his college education, but he does know business. He has built one of the 10 largest producers of personal computers in six years. The company now employs about 1,300 people, sells over $300 million of personal computers and accessories annually, and has plans for growth. Dell subsidiaries are now found in the United Kingdom, Germany, France, and Canada.

Dell had learned about computers as a boy in Houston and had become proficient in their technical aspects. He also possessed business sense. He reasoned that if a manufacturer receives $2,500 for a computer a customer buys for $4,000, there is a profit. The store owner keeps $1,500. Why? Dell asked himself. Did the owner add anything of value to the equipment? Dell concluded that the answer was no.

So Michael Dell came up with another way to sell computers. During the first few years of business, he sold directly to customers. He used direct advertising (tell the people about the computer with a flyer), telemarketing (call and tell people about the computer), and salespeople (go directly to large corporate clients).

Did Michael Dell learn how to be successful by studying business? Not in a formal sense. He was a good observer, a creative thinker, and a hard worker. He also was fortunate to be living in the United States, where everyone has the freedom to start a business. He decided to go into business, he had an idea about bypassing the retail store, and he took action. His inquisitive, fertile mind processed what he observed, and this led to action.

Early in the firm's history (in 1985), Dell made the decision not to clone IBMs. Wanting a more sophisticated machine than a stripped-down IBM, he decided to design and make his own Dell machine. He now has one.

Despite his market success, Dell has some critics. He is accused of being unable to delegate, of wanting to control, and of being difficult to work for. However, others quit high-paying, secure jobs just to work with him. To these individuals, Michael Dell has vision, is a hard worker, and is a world-class business leader.

Michael Dell was voted the Entrepreneur of the Year in January 1990 by *Inc.* magazine. He exemplifies what a person can do in a free enterprise system. Now that Dell has been successful in his first six years of business, he needs to keep paying attention to competition, employees, consumer needs and wants, and profit margins. His success in the first six years will not guarantee success in the next six. Business leaders such as Dell constantly face risks, changes, and uncertainty; the conduct of business and its dynamic nature pose challenges for them.

So far, so good. It has been a tremendous beginning for a young man who never was formally educated in business.

Questions for Discussion

1. How does an entrepreneur like Michael Dell view profit? From the point of view of an economist or from a business perspective? Explain.
2. How can competition alter the plans of successful business leaders such as Michael Dell?
3. What characteristics of the free enterprise system permitted Michael Dell to start and operate his business?

CASE 1.2
East Meets West: Business Joint Ventures

One of the shining examples of an East-West joint venture has been the case of Combustion Engineering and the Soviet Union. A firm from the Western world working with a Soviet partner is still big news. This example has been used to show how two different approaches to business could be integrated and blended. Lately, however, it has been rumored that this highly publicized joint venture is starting to unravel.

The internal bickering between the partners has centered on payment of money (hard currency) for services rendered, as well as on different management practices and manufacturing procedures. The partners are bickering, complaining about each other, and accusing each other of possessing poor business sense.

About 1,790 joint ventures are registered in the Soviet Union. Only about 445 have actually started operations. About 100 of the joint ventures are losing money. The reasons for the difficulties with Western–Eastern European business deals could fill a book. However, some clues suggest that business and the way it is conducted in New York or Tokyo are different from the way business is transacted in Warsaw and Leningrad. Western and Eastern economic systems have differed for decades. Under the Soviet system, the customer has been expected to be grateful for whatever he or she gets. Take it and don't complain. In the United States, this philosophy would get a business owner a severe case of "lost customers" and no "customer loyalty."

Customers under a mixed American-type economic system are kings and queens. The autocratic style of doing business will just not work in the West. Americans have numerous choices from which to select the company with whom they will do business or from whom they will purchase products or services.

Adapted from Rose Brady and Rosemarie Boyle, "Combustion Engineering's Dislocated Joint Venture," *Business Week,* October 22, 1990, pp. 49–50.

Improvement or education of Soviet managers in dealing with customers is what Combustion Engineering must accomplish. Even though the Soviet Union is slowly changing the way it conducts business, this will be a difficult task. More Western influences on joint ventures and how they operate will have to occur if profits are to be earned.

If the Soviets are going to attract more joint venture partners, they will need to change their management philosophy and their way of treating customers. They will need to place new emphasis on profit. Some Soviets claim that Americans are too impatient, wanting to earn a profit within five years. They estimate that some of the joint ventures will not earn a profit for 10 to 15 years.

Operating a joint venture like a business requires understanding the foundations of business. The Soviets and other Eastern Europeans are now learning that conducting business is challenging, and many plan to be successful in the near future. A Western joint venture partner can help in the learning process.

Questions for Discussion

1. Why would a joint venture partner from a planned economy have difficulty understanding that the consumer is king or queen?

2. Could a small business owner tolerate a business deal (joint venture) that had little probability of being profitable within the first 10 years?

3. Why have few Americans been willing to enter into joint ventures with Soviet partners today (it is now mid-1991)?

CHAPTER TWO

FORMS OF BUSINESS OWNERSHIP

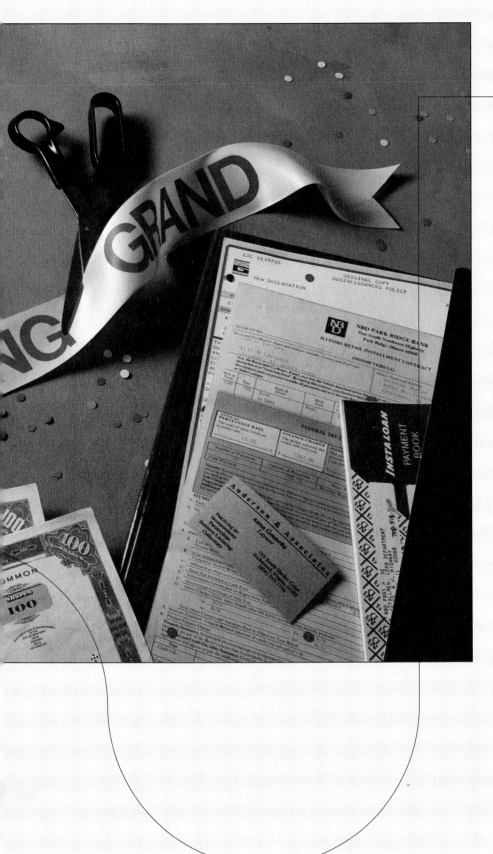

LEARNING OBJECTIVES

1. To discuss the advantages and disadvantages of sole proprietorships.

2. To discuss the advantages and disadvantages of partnerships.

3. To list the features that should be included in a written partnership contract.

4. To discuss the advantages and disadvantages of corporations.

5. To define the term *merger* and identify three types of mergers.

6. To identify other incorporated forms of business.

Courtesy of Thrislington Cubicles Inc.

Greg Braendel's (Bren-dell) accountants and consultants come from giant KPMG Peat Marwick, which advises him on a reduced-fee basis. His lawyers are with the Los Angeles branch of White & Case, an old-time New York City firm. They aren't charging him high fees either. In fact, a lot of people are helping him build his young company.

Greg, 44 years old, has been an actor for 20 years. He has no M.B.A., no Wall Street background, and no Mercedes-Benz in the driveway. His firm, Thrislington Cubicles, manufactures bathroom partitions.

Thrislington had been making and selling the cubicles in the United Kingdom and had a large share of the market there. The British firm asked Greg to think about finding a U.S. manufacturer for the product. After searching around, Greg decided to manufacture the product himself. He signed an agreement that gave him the North American manufacturing and marketing rights, with a royalty for every unit sold.

The Thrislington concept is simple enough. About 25 other companies sell ordinary, painted-metal bathroom stalls for about $175 apiece; the stalls are vulnerable to being scratched, written on, dented, and gouged. Thrislington's stalls, however, are fashion statements selling for about $700 apiece. They come in multiple colors and patterns instead of the typical gray or white plain metal enclosures found in most buildings.

Because the stalls are fiberglass or plastic-laminated, graffiti are easily washed off.

Greg had to line up sales representatives and distributors to sell his bathroom partitions, which are used in hotels, restaurants, airports, schools, offices—every building that has public bathrooms. In addition to sales and distribution teams, he had to set up at least one factory. Tapping his parents for some seed money, Greg took the step to become the owner of a business. It provides him with a lot of challenge, excitement, and autonomy. He works long, hard hours to make the business a success.

Greg hopes to have his young company (about three years old) reach sales of about $3 million in 1990. The goals he sets are based on the concept (high-quality, designer bathroom stalls) and the application of business tools. Whether he is successful in the short and long run will depend on the same factors that govern any business: how well he can manage his people and resources, how much the consumer likes and buys his product, how well he controls the costs and financial end of business, and how good he is at making decisions.[1]

As you read this chapter, think about Greg Braendel and others who have decided to go into business. They had to choose the type of business they wanted to enter. The environment in our mixed economy permits Greg and millions of others to form their own businesses, start partnerships, or work in other people's businesses. You, too, can make decisions about the type of business you want to be in, where you want to work, and how you want to spend your time.

Throughout this chapter, we will discuss the guidelines that can help you make a decision about which type of ownership is best for you. We will present the basic forms of business organizations and discuss the advantages and disadvantages of each. We begin with sole proprietorships, followed by partnerships (general, limited, and joint ventures) and other unincorporated forms of business (syndicates and business trusts). We then discuss corporations, deals, and mergers. We conclude by examining other incorporated forms of business (S corporations, cooperatives, savings and loan associations, and professional service organizations).

WHAT TYPE OF BUSINESS IS RIGHT FOR YOU?

In the United States today, there are about 12 million sole proprietorships (a business owned and managed by one person), 1.7 million partnerships (two or more co-owners of the business), and 3.4 million corporations (a legal entity created by the law).[2] Each form of business ownership has advantages and disadvantages. If you are planning to go into business, you need to review these pros and cons and determine which form of ownership meets your needs, style, and talents. Table 2.1 shows that many different types of people have achieved financial success.

A person thinking about owning a business should examine the following factors:

- *Capital requirements*—the amount of funds necessary to finance the operation.
- *Risk*—the amount of personal property a person is willing to lose by starting the business.

- The average age of the *Forbes* 400 is 63.
- Seven of the 400 did not finish high school; 40 finished high school only; 239 graduated from college; 46 held postgraduate degrees (M.B.A.'s) in business; 16 held law degrees; 17 held other postgraduate degrees.
- The states with the largest concentrations of the *Forbes* 400 are New York (87), California (71), Texas (38), Illinois (24), and Florida (20).
- Twenty-four members of the *Forbes* 400 are immigrants.
- Of the 124 members of the *Forbes* 400 age 70 or above, at least 54 are still working full-time.

Source: Adapted by permission of FORBES magazine, October 23, 1989. © Forbes Inc., 1989.

Some Words of Wisdom by Owners

Business owners' philosophies are usually captured in the type of creed that they live by in their firms. Their viewpoints and words of wisdom are often interesting and thought provoking.[3]

- **Brook Knapp,** president of a California private investment company: "Change is a constant. When you fly, location, weather, altitude, temperature alter minute by minute. I embrace chaos."
- **Craig Schechtman,** co-owner of Chicago Brothers Pizza: "Don't do anything special for one customer that you would not want other customers to know about."
- **Barbara Isenberg,** founder of North American Bear: (Advice from her brother.) "If you don't like problem solving, you shouldn't be in business, because every day is filled with problems."
- **Bill Zanker,** founder of The Learning Annex: "Don't quit! If you really believe in your con-

cept and your business, there will be light even in the darkest of days, and persistence and passion will rule."
- **Ben Cohen,** cofounder of Ben & Jerry's Ice Cream: "When somebody tells you that something can't be done, all it really means is that it hasn't been done before."
- **Al Copeland,** founder of Popeye's Famous Fried Chicken and Biscuits: "Plan for what happens when you succeed and plan for what happens when you fail. Planning is the most important thing."

Each of these business leaders emphasizes a main point. Some of the key points mentioned are change, problem solving, perseverance, and planning. They are good points to consider in any business.

- _Control_—the amount of authority the owner exercises.
- _Managerial abilities_—the skills needed to plan, organize, and control the business.
- _Time requirements_—the time needed to operate the business and provide guidance to the employees.
- _Tax liability_—what taxes a business must pay to various governments on earnings of the business.

Each of these factors should be considered along with your own personal values and philosophy. Do you have the character, work ethic, and style to succeed? The Business Action highlights some of the philosophies that have guided successful founders and owners.

SOLE PROPRIETORSHIPS

The oldest, most common form of private business ownership in the United States is the sole proprietorship.[4] A **sole proprietorship** is a business owned and managed by one individual. That person may receive help from others in operating the business but is the only boss; the sole proprietor _is_ the company.

Sole Proprietorship
A business owned and managed by one individual.

Typically the sole proprietor owns a small service or retail operation, such as a roadside produce stand, hardware store, bakery, or restaurant. The sole owner, often aided by one or two employees, operates a small shop that frequently caters to a group of regular customers. The capital (money) needed to start and operate the business is normally provided by the owner through personal wealth or borrowed money.

The sole proprietor is usually an active manager, working in the shop every day. He or she controls the operations, supervises the employees, and makes the decisions. The managerial ability of the owner usually accounts for the success or failure of the business.

D & D Cafe is owned by a sole proprietor, Gary Thompson. He is the person in charge, responsible, and accountable. There are 12 million other sole proprietors like Mr. Thompson operating their own businesses in the United States.

Courtesy of the D & D Cafe

TABLE 2.2

Forms of Business Ownership in Various Industries

Industry	Number of Businesses (000's)		
	Sole Proprietorships	Partnerships	Corporations
Agriculture, forestry, and fisheries	324	148	107
Mining	160	53	40
Construction	1,577	61	342
Manufacturing	329	28	285
Transportation, communication, and public utilities	576	21	138
Trade: Wholesale	304	23	314
Retail	1,886	151	621
Finance, insurance, and real estate	1,129	853	537
Services	5,758	325	1,012
All industries	12,394	1,703	3,429

Source: *Statistical Abstract of the United States, 1990* (Washington, D.C.: U.S. Department of Commerce, Bureau of the Census), p. 521.

As Table 2.2 indicates, approximately 12 million individuals operate sole proprietorships in the United States. The largest number are in retailing. Although sole proprietorships make up about 71 percent of all businesses in the United States, they account for only 6.1 percent of total sales, as Figure 2.1 shows. Corporations, on the other hand, account for just 19 percent of all businesses but about 90 percent of total sales.[5] Partnerships, about 9.7 percent of all businesses, account for 4.0 percent of total sales.

Advantages of a Sole Proprietorship

Many people desire to be their own boss. A sole proprietorship accomplishes this goal; it has other advantages as well.

Ease of starting   Sole proprietorship is the easiest way to start a business. It involves a minimum number of problems. For example, Jane Deleri wanted to start a delicatessen in Hammond, Indiana. She decided that a sole proprietorship was best for her needs. No general laws prohibited Jane from starting the deli, but she needed a food permit from the Hammond Health Department. She needed to check courthouse records to ensure that no other firm was using the name she wanted to use for the business. She also needed a $250 occupational license from the Indiana Department of Revenue.

Once Jane received the food permit and paid the license fee, she began operation. By contrast, a partnership usually must pay a legal fee for drawing up articles of partnership (a legally binding agreement). A corporation must pay an incorporation fee to the state in which it is chartered and legal fees for filing all the documents needed to incorporate.

Control   As the owner, Jane was the boss, who made final decisions; she worked as many hours as she wanted. Such freedom indicates the total control

FIGURE 2.1

Business Sales of U.S. Corporations

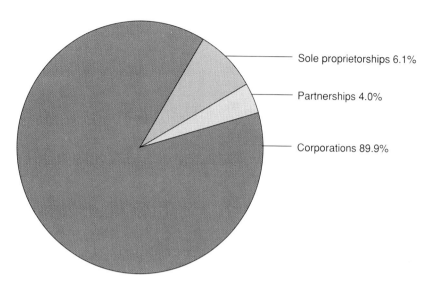

- Sole proprietorships 6.1%
- Partnerships 4.0%
- Corporations 89.9%

Source: *Statistical Abstract of the United States, 1990* (Washington, D.C.: U.S. Department of Commerce, Bureau of the Census).

she had over daily operations and decisions. Of course, if Jane decided to take every other afternoon off to go bowling, an employee would have to be present to operate the business or the doors would close.

Sole participation in profits and losses   All profits earned or losses incurred by operating the deli were Jane's. In contrast, partners share profits and losses. In states that permit one person to own a corporation, ownership of profits and losses in such cases compares to that in the sole proprietorship.

Use of owner's abilities   Jane had everything to lose or gain from her efforts. The chance of personal losses motivated her to devote time, energy, and expertise to the deli's operation, and success depended largely on the efficient use of her abilities. Jane had to use her own managerial abilities or pay someone else who had managerial expertise. Either way, full credit for success or blame for failure belonged to Jane.

Tax breaks   A major advantage of the proprietorship is that the business pays no income tax. A corporation pays taxes on profits; its owners, the shareholders, also pay taxes on their dividends. Jane, as a sole proprietor, paid no taxes on business profits. Instead, she paid taxes as an individual on all her income earned from the deli.

Secrecy   Jane filed information on income, expenses, hours worked, and other items required by income tax regulations. This information typically is not made available to the public. Information such as the special formula for her delicious Italian pastries or financial data does not have to be shared with the public because Jane is a sole proprietor.

Ease of dissolving   If Jane were to decide to dissolve her business for any reason, there would be no legal complications. If, after owning the deli for three years, she decided to close the business, she would be free to do so. As long as she had paid all the outstanding bills, her decision would be all that is needed to close the deli.

Disadvantages of a Sole Proprietorship

If the sole proprietorship had only advantages, a person organizing a business would have little to consider. But the realities of business are never so simple or certain. Sole proprietorships have disadvantages too.

Unlimited Liability
Obligation of investors to use personal assets, when necessary, to pay off debts to business creditors; a disadvantage of sole proprietorships and partnerships.

Unlimited liability   The law provides that Jane's total wealth may be used to satisfy the claims of the deli. This is called **unlimited liability.** For Jane this means almost everything she owns could be sold to pay any debts from operating the deli. For example, if Jane's deli failed, she might have to sell her personal jewelry or automobile to pay business debts that couldn't be paid by the liquidation or sale of such business assets as deli equipment (the computer, display cases) or inventory of canned products.

Difficulty in raising capital   Jane's investment in the deli was limited to personal wealth. The amount she could borrow to operate the business was also limited by her personal wealth; if she had a large estate, Jane would have little problem borrowing money. Generally, businesses requiring large amounts of capital are not formed as sole proprietorships. Few individuals can afford $500 million to build a gas pipeline or to operate a shuttle airline on the East Coast.

Limitations in managerial ability   Jane must have or must obtain all the know-how needed to manage the shop. Operating a deli requires planning, organizing, controlling, marketing, financial, motivational, and customer relations skills. Rarely does an individual have this range of needed expertise. However, many of these skills can be bought. For example, Jane could hire an accountant to keep the books and an advertising consultant to help promote her deli goods.

Lack of stability   Death, illness, bankruptcy, or retirement of the owner terminates the proprietorship. Jane's business could be sold to others, but the deli, as organized, would cease to exist.

Demands on time   Although Jane loves to bowl and attend major league baseball games, she will have trouble finding the time; the deli has to be open all day to develop a customer base. Owners such as Jane often work 60 to 80 hours a week, especially when the business is new.

Difficulty in hiring and keeping high-achievement employees   The sole proprietor is the business. Where can a self-motivated, high-energy employee go in the business? Workers with their own visions and goals and a high drive to succeed often have to quit the one-person business to find opportunities for personal growth.

PARTNERSHIPS

A business may have a small beginning as a sole proprietorship, later expand into a partnership, and finally become a corporation. Many corporate giants (e.g., Sears Roebuck, H. J. Heinz, and Ford) started as sole proprietorships. Section 6 of the Uniform Partnership Act defines **partnership** as "an association of two or more persons to carry on as co-owners of a business for profit." Other than the difference in the number of owners, a partnership is similar in many respects to a sole proprietorship.

Partnership
A business owned by two or more people.

A partnership can be based on a written contract or a voluntary and legal oral agreement. The law regards individuals as partners when they act in such a way as to make people believe they operate a business together.

Types of Partnerships

About 1.4 million partnerships of various types exist in the United States. Some, not all, types can be identified by name. The three major types are general partnership, limited partnership, and joint venture. A **general partnership** is a business with at least one general partner who has unlimited liability for the debts of the business. A **limited partnership** has at least one general partner and one or more limited partners (discussed below). The *joint venture* is a special type of partnership established to carry out a special project or to operate for a specific time period. Let's look at each type separately.

General Partnership
A partnership in which at least one partner has unlimited liability; a general partner has authority to act and make binding decisions as an owner.

General partnership   Regardless of the percentage of the business they own, general partners have authority to act and to make binding decisions as owners of the business. The general partner may be liable for all the debts of the business; by contrast, the sole proprietor is always liable for such debts. Partners generally share profits and losses according to a plan specified by agreement between them.

Limited Partnership
A partnership with at least one general partner, and one or more limited partners who are liable for loss only up to the amount of their investment.

With the authority to act as an owner, each general partner can engage the partnership in binding agreements. Unless a partnership agreement prevents a general partner from making such agreements, the partnership is responsible for all actions of each owner.

Limited partnership   All partnerships must have at least one general partner. A limited partnership includes one or more general partners and one or more limited partners. The general partners arrange and run the business, while the limited partners are investors only. Investors receive special tax advantages and protection from liability. Limited partners legally may have no say in managing the business. If this requirement is violated, the limited partnership status is dissolved.

Limited partnerships are usually found in real estate, dentistry, and various international arrangements. In some states, a special notice must be filed in the county or district where the limited partnership has its offices.

A limited partner has limited liability, being liable for loss only up to the amount of capital invested. Thus, a limited partner who invests $30,000 in the business is liable for only that amount. In contrast, general partners have unlimited liability in the partnership.

The Japanese have been masters at helping set up joint ventures. This American–Japanese joint venture produces engines that are then sent to four Honda plants in the United States and Canada. Both partners (American and Japanese) benefit if the venture is profitable. Of course, both partners suffer if the joint venture loses money.

Courtesy of Honda North America, Inc.

Master Limited Partnership (MLP)
A partnership that sells units traded on a recognized stock exchange.

The **master limited partnership (MLP),** used since 1981, is a partnership that sells units traded on a recognized stock exchange. The MLP has been popular in real estate and oil. It has many of the advantages of a corporation, such as unlimited life, limited liability, and transferable ownership. However, MLPs do not pay corporate taxes, because earnings are passed directly to unit holders. The unit holders then pay taxes at the individual rate. The highest average individual rate is now 28 percent, while for corporations the rate is 34 percent. The National Basketball Association's Boston Celtics organization is established as an MLP. A lot of limited partners hope the Celtics have a great season!

Joint venture   Sometimes a number of individuals and businesses join together in order to accomplish a specific purpose or objective or to complete a single transaction. For example, they may wish to purchase a building in downtown Boston and resell it for a profit. This would be called a joint venture. Wheeling-Pittsburgh Steel Corporation formed a joint venture with Japan's Nisshia Steel Co. for the purpose of manufacturing steel in the United States and selling it around the world. Hewlett-Packard (U.S.) and Samsung (South Korea) have also initiated a joint venture. Under the agreement, Samsung will manufacture both microprocessor chips and computer workstations, using Hewlett-Packard's technology and software. The firms are attempting to produce a $5,000 workstation that will compete with workstations costing twice as much.[6]

The Soviet government today encourages joint ventures between Soviet and Western firms. By the end of September 1990, about 400 Western firms had entered into joint ventures with the Soviets.[7] (We discussed McDonald's joint venture in a Business Action in Chapter One.) A new law was passed in 1990 that indicates that these partnerships can have less than 51 percent Soviet ownership, but firms operating in the Soviet Union will be subject to Soviet laws. Why would this be attractive to an American, Canadian, or French partner? Because of the virtually untapped market of 284 million Soviet citizens.[8]

A joint venture in the United States or abroad is something less than the ordinary partnership, which continues as a business. There is some confusion among the courts as to whether a joint venture is a partnership. We think there are enough similarities to categorize it as such. For instance, one of the joint venture partners acting within the scope of his or her authority may bind the other partner(s) in the joint venture. Also, the liabilities of the parties to a joint venture are similar to the liabilities of the partnership.

The Partnership Contract

Sound business practice dictates that a partnership agreement be written and signed, although that is not a legal requirement. Such a contractual agreement is called *articles of partnership*. Written articles of partnership can prevent or lessen misunderstandings at a later date. Oral partnership agreements, though quite legal, tend to be hard to recreate and are open to misunderstandings. Written articles of partnership provide proof of an agreement.

A written partnership agreement includes the following main features:

- Name of the business partnership.
- Type of business.
- Location of the business.
- Expected life of the partnership.
- Names of the partners and the amount of each one's investment.
- Procedures for distributing profits and covering losses.
- Amounts that partners will withdraw for services.
- Procedure for withdrawal of funds.
- Duties of each partner.
- Procedures for dissolving the partnership.

Complete the Connections quiz on partnership contracts; decide whether the contract presented is sound. Would you sign such an agreement? Why or why not?

Like the sole proprietorship, the partnership has both advantages and disadvantages. Any person considering a partnership should carefully weigh each of the following advantages and disadvantages before closing the deal. Do some of the pluses outweigh the minuses?

Advantages of a Partnership

More capital   In the sole proprietorship, the amount of capital is limited to the personal wealth and credit of the owner. In a partnership, the amount of capital may increase significantly. A person with a good idea but little capital can look for a partner with the capital and/or credit standing to develop and market the idea.

Combined managerial skills   In a partnership, people with different talents and skills may join together. One partner may be good at marketing; the other

---

● C o n n e c t i o n s

Is This a Sound Partnership Contract?

Directions: Carefully examine the following partnership agreement and decide if it is sound, complete, and accurate.

Agreement

This partnership agreement is entered into on January 8, 1991, between Mary Richards of Spring, Texas, and Niki Stutzman of Houston, Texas, both of Harris County.

We agree that:

One: We will become equal general partners in the women's cosmetics business.
Two: We will use the name "Yellow Rose" of 1818 Milam Street, Houston, Texas 77001.
Three: Each general partner will contribute $10,000 to the partnership on January 8, 1991.
Four: All profits earned from selling "Yellow Rose" cosmetics will be divided equally by the general partners, and all losses incurred by the business will be equally shared by them.
Five: Proper accounting books will be kept by the business; a public accounting audit will be conducted each year by a firm mutually agreed upon. Profits, inventories, and losses will be accurately accounted for each year.
Six: Each partner will earn no more than $750 per month, if earnings permit this amount to be taken out of the business. No more than $9,000 per partner per year will be drawn out during the first four years of the partnership.
Seven: No new partners can be added without the full written consent of both partners.
Eight: If grievances between partners cannot be resolved, an arbitrator will be hired that is acceptable to both partners. The decision reached after arbitration is binding.
Nine: In the event of the death or retirement of a partner, the remaining partner will pay the estate or retiring partner the full amount of the original investment ($10,000), plus 1.5 times the most recent year's gross sales for all "Yellow Rose" products. The payment will be made within one year of the death or retirement of the partner.
Ten: At the termination of the partnership, a full inventory and balance sheet will be prepared by an accounting firm. All debts will be paid, and all property will be divided between the partners.

---

may be expert at accounting and financial matters. Combining these skills could provide a greater chance of success.

Ease of starting   Because it involves a private contractual arrangement, a partnership is fairly easy to start. It is nearly as free from government regulation as a sole proprietorship. The cost of starting a partnership is low; it usually involves only a modest legal fee for drawing up a written agreement, which is highly desirable. An oral agreement is sufficient but not recommended.

Clear legal status   Over the years, legal precedents for partnerships have been established through court cases. The questions of rights, responsibilities, liabilities, and partner duties have been covered. Thus the legal status of the partnership is clearly understood; lawyers can provide sound legal advice about partnership issues.

Tax advantages   The partnership has some potential tax advantages over a corporation. In a partnership, as in a sole proprietorship, the owners pay taxes on their business earnings. But the partnership, as a business, does not pay income tax.

The parties have carefully reviewed the contract and have freely signed, in the presence of a witness, this document.

Witness _____   Partner _____
Date _____   Date _____
                                         Partner _____
                                         Date _____

Feedback: Well, what do you think? A fairly thorough contract? If you were Mary or Niki, would you sign the contract or would you make some modifications?

You should make some modifications. A review of the contract shows some key information is missing:

1. For how long will this partnership be doing business? There is no mention of the duration of the partnership.

2. Which partner is responsible for managing, marketing, handling complaints, ordering cosmetics, answering the telephone, using the word processor, paying bills, and so on? The duties of each partner need to be specifically spelled out. If a partner can't fulfill her duties, how will they be handled?

Other than these two major points, the contract is fairly thorough. It is not loaded with legalese, but it is descriptive enough to provide a clear understanding of each important point. You never want to be faced with a situation where you are in a partnership with a stranger or a friend and neither person knows the rules of the game. If you lack confidence in your ability to prepare a legal contract, spend the $100 to $500 needed to have a lawyer draw up this type of document. Be safe at the beginning.

Disadvantages of a Partnership

Unlimited liability   Each general partner is liable for a partnership's debts. Suppose Jack and Jill's partnership fails with outstanding bills of $25,000. This amount must be paid by someone. If Jack lacks the personal assets to pay the debt and Jill has the money, she has to pay off the debts. This is one reason for choosing partners carefully.

Potential disagreements   Decisions made by several people (partners) are often better than those made by one. However, having two or more people deciding on some aspect of the business can be dangerous. Power and authority are divided, and the partners will not always agree with each other. As a result, poor decisions may be made. Also, decision making becomes more time-consuming because agreement must be reached before action can be taken.

Investment withdrawal difficulty   A person who invests money in a partnership may have a hard time withdrawing the investment. It is much easier to invest in a partnership than to withdraw. The money, typically considered a "frozen investment," is tied up in the operation of the business.

Limited capital availability   The partnership may have an advantage over the sole proprietorship in the availability of capital, but it does not compare to a corporation in ability to raise capital. In most cases, partners have a limited capability and cannot compete in business requiring large outlays. The amount of capital a partnership can raise depends on the personal wealth of the partners and their credit ratings. It also depends on how much they are willing to invest in the partnership.

Instability   If a partner dies or withdraws from the business, the partnership is dissolved. A new partnership or some other form of business organization must be legally established.

OTHER UNINCORPORATED FORMS OF BUSINESS

Besides proprietorships and partnerships, several other forms of ownership do not require incorporation. These forms are used by people who want to join together to accomplish various objectives without going to the trouble of forming a corporation.

Syndicates

Syndicate
Two or more businesses joined together to accomplish specific business goals; a popular form in underwriting large amounts of corporation stocks.

An association of two or more businesses for a particular business purpose is a **syndicate.** In most cases, syndicates engage in financial transactions. Unlike a joint venture, a syndicate need not be dissolved after the transaction is completed. The members of a syndicate can sell their ownership interest to buyers of their choice. But in a partnership, the remaining partners can veto a new partner.

A common type of syndicate is the underwriting syndicate, a group of investment banking companies formed for the purpose of selling a large issue of corporation stocks. Managerial decisions are in the hands of the group that forms the syndicate.

Business Trusts

Business Trust
A business used to hold securities for investors; allows the transfer of legal title to a property of one person for the use and benefit of another.

A **business trust** is often used to hold securities for investors. In its simplest form, a trust allows the transfer of legal title to a property of one person for the use and benefit of another. The original name for this form of business was the Massachusetts trust, because it was created in that state when the laws did not allow corporations to buy and sell real estate.

Under the business trust, a trustee or group of trustees is legally permitted to do business. The trustees issue shares, called *trust certificates,* to investors. These shares show that the holder has transferred funds to a trustee and has the legal right to benefit from the success of the trust investments. Shareholders have no right to vote for trustees or to have a voice in management; they do have the right to sell their trust certificates to a buyer of their choice.

Courtesy of The Procter & Gamble Company

Procter & Gamble (P&G) is a large, Fortune 500 American Corporation headquartered in Cincinnati. P&G does business around the world and the United States.

CORPORATIONS

Some industries, such as automobile manufacturing, computer manufacturing, oil refining, and natural gas production, require millions of dollars to operate a business. Typically such vast sums of money are put together by attracting numerous investors. The unincorporated forms of business—the proprietorship and the partnership—do not attract investors who do not want to make decisions or to be actually involved in managing the firm. The **corporation,** by contrast, provides a form of business ownership in which owners spread over a wide geographical area can hire professional managers to operate the business. In the eyes of the law, the corporation is an artificial being, invisible and intangible.[9] It has the legal rights of an individual: it can own property, purchase goods and services, and sue other persons or corporations.

Corporation
A business that is a legal entity separate from its owners.

The corporate form of business organization accounts for 90 percent of the total sales (over $9,221 billion) of U.S. businesses. There are over 3.4 million profit-oriented corporations of all sizes. In addition, many corporations are not conducted for profit and do not have private owners or shareholders. These nonprofit corporations conduct their business in the areas of government (e.g., the U.S. Postal Service), education, health (e.g., a public-health clinic), religion, and charity (e.g., the Salvation Army).

FIGURE 2.2

Sample Articles of Incorporation

ARTICLES OF INCORPORATION
OF

_____
(name of corporation)

We, the undersigned, of full age, for the purpose of forming a corporation under and pursuant to the provisions of Chapter 301 Minn. Statutes, known as the Minnesota Business Corporation Act, and laws amendatory thereof and supplementary thereto, do hereby associate ourselves as a body corporate and adopt the following Articles of Incorporation:

ARTICLE I

The name of this corporation is: _____

Note: The corporate name must end with "Incorporated," "Inc.," or "Corporation," or contain "Company" or "Co." not immediately preceded by "and" or "&."

ARTICLE II

The purposes of this corporation are: _____

_____

_____

_____

ARTICLE III

The period of duration of corporate existence of this corporation shall be: _____

Note: The duration may be perpetual or for a specified period of time.

ARTICLE IV

The location of the registered office of this corporation in this state is: _____

Note: Give street or post office address, city or town, county, and Zip Code number.

ARTICLE VI

The amount of stated capital with which this corporation will begin business is: _____

Note: The stated capital must be at least $1,000.

ARTICLE VII

The total authorized number of shares of par value is: _____
and the par value of each share is: _____
The total authorized number of shares without par value is: _____

ARTICLE VIII

The description of the classes of shares, the number of shares in each class, and the relative rights, voting power, preferences, and restrictions are as follows: _____

Charter
A state's written agreement giving a corporation the right to operate as a business.

Domestic Corporation
An enterprise organized under the laws of one state or country and doing business within that state or country.

Forming a Corporation

The legal status of a corporation stems from a **charter**, which is a state-issued document authorizing its formation. The individuals forming the corporation are called its _incorporators_. In 1830, New York extended the use of the corporate form to businesses; by the early 1860s, most other states also granted corporate charters. A corporation that conducts business in the state in which it is chartered is known as a **domestic corporation**. A corporation doing business in a state

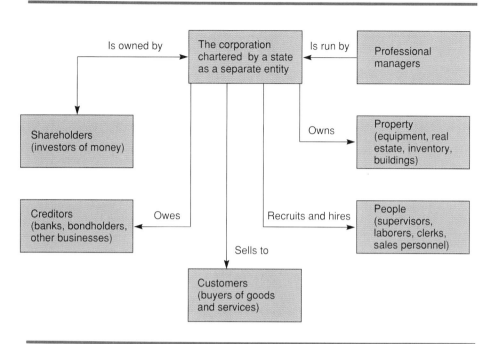

FIGURE 2.3

**The Range of a
Corporation's
Relationships**

other than the one in which it is incorporated is called a **foreign corporation** (e.g., a New Jersey–incorporated business doing business in Oregon).

Foreign Corporation
A business incorporated in one state or country and doing business in another state or country.

Most states require that at least three persons join together to form a corporation. The applicants fill out an application form for a charter (articles of incorporation); the form is then reviewed by the appropriate government officials. An example of such a form appears in Figure 2.2.

After the charter has been granted, the incorporators and all subscribers or the owners of the stock of the business meet and elect a board of directors. They also approve the bylaws of the corporation, if this is a state requirement. The board of directors then meets to select the professional managers and to make any other decisions needed to start the business.

The corporation has relationships with various groups. Included in the corporation's domain of operation are shareholders, creditors, customers, and employees. Figure 2.3 charts the corporation's range of relationships. The actual owners of the business are the shareholders, those who have invested their money. The corporation is run by professional managers who plan, organize, control, and direct the activities needed to sell goods and/or services to customers. The managers also decide what property to purchase, what employees to hire, and where to borrow needed funds.

Types of Corporations

When we think about business corporations, our attention usually centers on the giants listed annually in *Fortune*'s "Directory of the 500 Largest U.S. Industrial Corporations." This listing includes over 250 firms with assets of more than $1 billion.[10] Included are such well-known corporations as Procter &

TABLE 2.3 **Twenty-Five Largest U.S. Industrial Corporations**

Corporations	Sales ($ in millions)	Corporations	Sales ($ in millions)
1. GM (Detroit)	$126,017.0	14. Shell (Houston)	$24,423.0
2. Exxon (Irving, Tex.)	105,885.0	15. Procter & Gamble (Cincinnati)	24,376.0
3. Ford (Dearborn, Mich.)	98,274.7	16. Occidental Petroleum (Los Angeles)	21,947.0
4. IBM (Armonk, N.Y.)	69,018.0	17. United Technologies (Hartford)	21,783.2
6. Mobil (Fairfax, Va.)	58,770.0	18. Dow Chemical (Midland, Mich.)	20,005.0
5. GE (Fairfield, Conn.)	58,414.0	19. USX (Pittsburgh)	19,462.0
7. Philip Morris (New York)	44,323.0	20. Eastman Kodak (Rochester, N.Y.)	19,075.0
8. Texaco (White Plains, N.Y.)	41,235.0	21. Atlantic Richfield (Los Angeles)	18,819.0
9. Du Pont (Wilmington, Del.)	39,839.0	22. Xerox (Stamford, Conn.)	18,382.0
10. Chevron (San Francisco)	39,262.0	23. Pepsico (Purchase, N.Y.)	17,802.7
11. Chrysler (Highland Park, Mich.)	30,868.0	24. McDonnell Douglas (St. Louis)	16,351.0
12. Amoco (Chicago)	28,277.0	25. Conagra (Omaha)	15,517.7
13. Boeing (Seattle)	27,595.0		

Source: Adapted from "The Fortune 500," FORTUNE, April 22, 1991, p. 286. © 1991 The Time Magazine Company. All rights reserved.

TABLE 2.4

Types of Corporations

Type	Description	Examples
Private	Attempts to earn a satisfactory profit.	RJR Nabisco, Thrislington.
Public	Owned and run by the government.	NASA, Tennessee Valley Authority.
Closed	Stock held by only a few owners and not actively sold on the stock market.	Gallo Winery, Hallmark Cards, Weis Markets.
Open	Stock held by numerous people and actively sold on the stock market.	United Technologies, Ford.
Municipal	Cities and townships that carry out business.	Ft. Worth, Texas; Manitou Springs, Colorado.
Domestic	Incorporated in one state or country and doing business wtihin that state or country.	Georgia Pacific (Georgia) doing business in Georgia.
Foreign	Incorporated in one state or country and doing business in another state or country.	Compaq Computer (Texas) selling computers in New York.
Alien	Incorporated in one nation and operating in another nation.	Motorola (incorporated in Illinois) operating in Chiba Prefecture, Japan.
Nonprofit	Service organization incorporated for limited-liability status.	Harvard University, Boy Scouts of America.
Single-individual	Individually owned business incorporated to escape high personal income tax rate.	Johnny Carson Clothing, Inc.

Gamble, Exxon, AT&T, IBM, and Boeing. Each is profit oriented. The 25 largest U.S. industrial corporations in 1989 are listed in Table 2.3.

In reality, corporations come in many sizes and types (see Table 2.4). Many universities and religious organizations are **nonprofit corporations**; that is, they are not profit-seeking enterprises. The not-for-profit sector includes universities and other schools, charities, churches, volunteer associations, government organizations, country clubs, and a number of other kinds of organizations. The not-for-profit enterprise is prohibited by law from distributing any earnings (paying dividends) to owners. It exists because the founders believe that the firm provides something (e.g., help to the homeless, perpetuation of patriotism, education) of value that is not being provided well or at all by other enterprises. Not-for-profit firms provide jobs for millions of employees. Donations, collections, and the sale of goods or services provide the funds to pay employees and finance operations.

Nonprofit Corporation
An enterprise (e.g., university, charity, church) that is not driven by a profit-seeking motive.

Corporate Policymakers

A corporation's policy is established by a board of directors, which is elected by the shareholders, or owners. Directors are assumed to be free to make their own judgments on all matters presented to them. The directors do not make judgments for a single group or clique of owners—they make judgments in the best interest of *all* owners. Thus they are usually elected for their business ability. A growing number of shareholders are challenging the abilities and performance of board members. The Business Action discusses how serious the performance of the board is for owners.

Courtesy of Triton College

Triton Community College in River Grove, Illinois, is a nonprofit organization. It is not permitted, by law, to distribute earnings. However, like most universities, it must be efficiently operated in order to be supported by taxpayers in Illinois. The 20,000 students want their school to provide them with a good education.

Board Members Are Expected to Perform

A trustee for a shareholder sued the board of Occidental Petroleum for allocating $86 million to a museum named after Chief Executive Officer Armand Hammer. Shareholders sued Microsoft Corporation's board for failing to meet first-quarter earnings estimates, which caused its stock to drop eight points in one day. Because of these and other cases, being on the board of directors may mean you will be held accountable for decisions in a court of law. The pressure to perform has been building since 1985, when the Delaware Supreme Court stunned the corporate world by ruling that Trans Union Corporation's directors had used poor judgment and acted too quickly when they accepted a takeover bid. Of the $23.5 million settlement, the directors agreed to pay $13.5 million—the excess over the insurance.

Before the Trans Union ruling, boards of directors seemed immune to liability and claimed protection under the so-called business judgment rule. Now boards of directors' business judgments are being tested throughout the United States. Shareholder suits of interest include the following:

- *Northrup.* A shareholder's suit against the board is in the federal court in Los Angeles. The suit charges a wide range of illegal conduct, including payments to South Korean government officials to sell the F–20 Tigershark aircraft.
- *Data Point Corporation.* Shareholders sued for a variety of security violations. The company and directors settled before the trial and verdict was read. Instead of appealing, the company settled after a $21 million jury verdict was issued.
- *RJR Nabisco.* A class action suit pending in Delaware accuses the board of a breach of responsibility in conducting the auction of the company. Shareholders claim they received less than maximum value for their stock at the auction. The board is being held responsible.

These cases suggest that serving as a member of a board of directors is an important job that may require careful consideration of obligations. Directors are expected to perform and carry out their responsibilities in a serious manner. Companies across the United States are bracing for more assaults by aggressive investors. From Avon to Occidental Petroleum to USX, investors are challenging the board of directors at board meetings, in the press, and in the courts.[11]

A group of shareholders of Dow Chemical Co. discuss some of the topics of the annual meeting. Dow's meetings cover such topics as the firm's plans, strategies for growth, and environmental concerns. Dividend payouts are also a popular topic of discussion.

Courtesy of The Dow Chemical Company

Directors are elected by the shareholders. Usually, each share of common stock entitles the shareholder to one vote (see Chapter Eighteen for a discussion of stock). For example, Amanda Knight owns 10 shares of Amoco voting stock and therefore is eligible to cast 10 votes. In many cases, shareholders vote by proxy. A **proxy** is a written statement, signed by the shareholder, allowing someone else to cast his or her number of votes. Usually, the proxy permits a director to cast the votes.

Proxy
A written statement, signed by a shareholder of a corporation, allowing someone else to cast his or her number of votes.

The board, once elected, must put together the best possible team of managers to run the day-to-day operations. In governing the corporation, the board of directors decides for or against recommendations submitted by the officers of the corporation. Although the board is the final authority, it usually responds to requests and recommendations made by the professional managers.

More than 47 million Americans own stock in publicly traded companies. As shareholders they have the right to inspect the books and papers of the business, to attend shareholders' meetings, to vote on certain matters (such as mergers), and to share in the profits earned. Even if Amanda Knight owns only 10 shares of Amoco, she has all these rights. Many shareholders are uninterested in the rights of ownership except for the privilege of sharing in the profits by receiving dividends. This may be just as well because, if decisions had to be based on the opinions of all owners, the business would stand still. Of all U.S. corporations, AT&T has the largest number of shareholders (over 3 million). General Motors has about 1.2 million owners, and IBM has the third-largest number (about 740,000).

Advantages of a Corporation

The power and presence of corporations in American business suggest that this form has certain advantages over other forms of business ownership:

Limited liability   A person investing funds in a corporation receives shares of stock and becomes an owner. In a corporation, the liability for the shareholder equals the amount of funds invested. Thus, if the business is forced to liquidate, each owner loses only the amount of money he or she has invested.

Skilled management team   The board of directors has the duty of hiring professional managers, and the owners delegate their power of operating the business to these managers. Professional managers are trained and experienced career executives. They may own shares of stock in the business but usually not enough to control the corporation.

Transfer of ownership   Shareholders have the right to sell their shares of a corporation's stock to whomever they please, barring a legal restriction on some closed corporations. These shares of ownership can be sold whenever the shareholder desires and at the price the buyer is willing to pay. Thus, shareholders can freely buy and sell shares of stock. The investment flows easily and is not frozen. This right to sell shares of stock gives corporations the ability to attract large numbers of shareholders.

Greater capital base   As previously stated, the size of a proprietorship or partnership is limited to the amount of capital that one or several people have available and are willing to invest. Corporations, however, can attract capital from a large number of investors by selling shares of stock.

Stability   State law varies, but a corporation can usually be chartered to operate indefinitely. Shareholders' deaths, retirement, or sale of stock need not dissolve the business. The corporation's policies may be altered by the sale of large blocks of stock, but the business will go on. Nor will the death or retirement of the president of the board or the chief executive officer stop the corporation from doing business.

Legal-entity status   A corporation can purchase property, make contracts, or sue and be sued in its corporate name. These characteristics distinguish it most clearly from other forms of business organization. As Justice Thurgood Marshall of the U.S. Supreme Court stated, a corporation is "an artificial being." This legal status allows the shareholders to have limited liability.

Disadvantages of a Corporation

As was true with the other forms of business organization, the corporation has some disadvantages. Some of the more obvious ones follow.

Difficulty and expense of starting   Starting a corporation involves applying for a charter from a state. Each state has its own set of laws; these must be considered before deciding where to incorporate. An attorney should be hired to complete legal forms. Attorney fees and state charter fees must be paid. The chosen state then reviews the application and issues a charter that specifies various restrictions on operations.

Lack of control   The individual shareholder has little control over the operations of the corporation except to vote for a slate of individuals for the board of directors. The buying and selling of shares of stock is the only real control an owner has.

Multiple taxation   In addition to an annual franchise tax in the state of incorporation, an annual payment is required by most states for the right to operate as a corporation. No such fees are charged to a proprietorship or partnership. Some states levy a corporate income tax on those monies earned within the state. The taxes are at lower rates than federal taxes. At the federal level, the corporation has to pay taxes on its profits. The shareholders must also pay income tax on the dividends they receive through ownership. This practice of taxing corporate income and dividends is referred to as **double taxation**.

Double Taxation
Taxing a corporate owner's money twice by taxing it as income of a corporation and as dividends of the individual owner.

Government involvement   State and federal governments have the right by law to exercise certain controls on, and to require certain reports from, businesses. For example, a corporation cannot conduct its business in a state in which it is not registered. As mentioned previously, a corporation organized under the laws of one state or country is called, within that state or country, a domestic corporation. When such a business operates in another state or country, it is called a foreign corporation. Foreign corporations doing business in several states must obtain a certificate of authority from each. Some states require a foreign corporation to deposit bonds with the state treasurer to protect anyone who might suffer loss by reason of some action by the corporation.

Lack of secrecy   A corporation must provide each shareholder with an annual report. In a closed corporation, the few reports circulated usually won't get into the hands of nonowners. But when a large number of reports are issued, the reports become public knowledge. These reports present data on sales volume, profit, total assets, and other financial matters. Public disclosure of these data enables competitors and other outsiders to see the corporation's financial condition.

Lack of personal interest   In most corporations except the small ones, management and ownership are separate. This separation can result in a lack of personal interest in the success of the corporation. If the managers are also shareholders, the lack of personal interest is often minimized. It is assumed that employees who are also owners will work harder for the success of the business, but the accuracy of this assumption is an individual matter. Most managers have pride in their work and want any business they are involved with to succeed.

Credit limitations   Banks and other lenders have to consider the limited liability of corporations. If a corporation fails, its creditors can look only to the assets of the business to satisfy claims. For partnerships, the creditors can rely on personal assets of the partners to pay off business debts.

TABLE 2.5   **Comparison of Four Major Types of Business Organizations**

Characteristic	Type of Organization			
	Sole Proprietorship	General Partnership	Limited Partnership	Corporation
1. Start-up and operation	Simplest to establish and form.	Relatively easy but needs written contract.	Requires written agreement, filing of certificate, and compliance with limited partners' noninvolvement.	Laws and procedures vary from state to state; charter required; legal and charter fees can be expensive.
2. Liability for debts and taxes	Owner has unlimited liability.	General partners have unlimited liability.	Limited partner is liable only to the amount of investment.	Shareholders are liable only to extent of investment.
3. Federal taxes on profits	Taxed at individual rates, 15 to 28 percent.	Taxed at individual rates, 15 to 28 percent.	Taxed at individual rates, 15 to 28 percent.	Small corporations taxed at 15 percent for income up to $50,000; income $50,000–$75,000, 25 percent; income over $75,000, 34 percent. Companies earning over $100,000 pay 5 percent surcharge on income over that amount until the tax equals 34 percent.
4. Termination	Easy, after debts are paid.	May be complicated; depends on contract.	Same as general partnership.	Difficult and expensive.
5. Duration of business	Terminates at death of owner.	Terminates at death or withdrawal of partner.	Same as general partnership.	Indefinite.

Table 2.5 lists the characteristics of the four types of businesses we have discussed. It will help you summarize the main points discussed in the chapter so far.

MERGERS

Merger
Combining two or more business enterprises into a single entity.

As the 1990s progress, deal-making has subsided. The 1980s have been called the decade of the deals; a towering $1.3 trillion was spent in mergers.[12] **Mergers**, the joining together of two corporations, have always been a concern in government policy because of increased market share and reduced competition. Mergers that reduce market competition can result in government action under the Celler-Kefauver Act and review by the Justice Department and the

Federal Trade Commission (FTC). (Chapter Five will discuss further the laws that ensure competition.)

A **horizontal merger** occurs when competitive firms in the same market merge into one firm (e.g., Republic Steel and Jones & Laughlin Steel merged to form LTV Steel). A firm's merger with a supplier is called a **vertical merger** (e.g., General Motors purchased Electronic Data Systems). A **conglomerate merger** joins firms selling goods in unrelated markets (e.g., Xerox Corporation purchased an insurance firm, Crum and Foster).

In general, the government allows mergers when the market share of the largest firms in the industry is relatively low. It also does not intervene when new firms can enter the market easily. Government also has intervened less when mergers seem needed to meet foreign competition. Some people believe mergers bring cost and productivity advantages that can help reduce prices, making American products cheaper and more competitive on the world markets.

The desire to merge is not new. American industry also was caught up in merger mania at the turn of the 19th century. Between 1898 and 1902, over 2,653 companies disappeared in merger deals. What was behind the merger mania of the 1980s? A restructuring of the economy. Most of the mergers involved troubled parts of the economy—oil, manufacturing, and mining.

No person is more closely identified with the American merger frenzy of the past decade than Mesa Petroleum chairman T. Boone Pickens. His strategy was to gain 51 percent control of a corporation by buying a substantial block of stock and making offers that would interest enough shareholders to sell. Pickens typically never gained the 51 percent level of control. The specter of his taking over usually frightened management into a friendly takeover by a white knight. A **white knight** is a person or company considered more favorable by a target firm than the takeover it is facing. ''More favorable'' may mean that this white knight is inclined to keep all managers, to retain the way of doing business, or to be friendlier in dealing with employees. The white knights bought Pickens' stocks, usually leaving him with a profit. In his attempt to take over Gulf Oil, which forced the firm to sell out to Chevron, Pickens and his backers made about $760 million.

Pickens contends that his tactics force stock prices up to their real levels of value, help get rid of inefficient managers, and make firms more aware of shareholders' interests.

Horizontal Merger
A merger involving competitive firms in the same market.

Vertical Merger
A merger in which a firm joins with its supplier.

Conglomerate Merger
A merger involving firms selling goods in unrelated markets.

White Knight
A person or company considered more favorable by a target firm than the takeover it is facing.

OTHER INCORPORATED FORMS OF BUSINESS

The corporation is certainly the dominant form of incorporated ownership. However, a number of other widely used incorporated forms of business have unique advantages. Let's discuss four: S corporations, cooperatives, savings and loan associations, and professional service associations.

S Corporations

Special rules and regulations of the Internal Revenue Code of 1986 permit certain corporate entities (previously known as Subchapter S, now known as S corporation) to be set aside at the request of the shareholders. This is done for tax purposes only, to have the shareholders treated as individual taxpayers. In other words, the income or loss of the corporation passes through to the individual shareholders as if they were partners.[13]

S Corporation
A corporation with 35 or fewer owners that files an income tax return as a partnership to take advantage of lower tax rates.

To qualify as an **S corporation,** a business must meet the following requirements:

- It must be incorporated within the United States.
- All shareholders must be residents of the United States.
- Shareholders must be natural persons, estates, or trusts.
- No shareholder can be a partnership or a corporation.
- There cannot be more than 35 shareholders.

Like other forms of ownership, the S corporation has advantages and disadvantages. The primary advantage is that the shareholders' tax brackets can result in tax savings. If a corporation expects to lose money in the first years of operation and if the shareholders will have income from other sources, the S corporation is preferred. Here the losses "passed through" from the S corporation can shelter the shareholders from income tax. (Losses are limited to specific amounts.) The primary disadvantage is that the tax law governing the S corporation is very complex. Tax and legal advice is strongly recommended before and after making the S corporation choice. The best time to terminate S status is when the S corporation begins to produce very high levels of taxable income. Thus, an owner must be alert and up-to-date on the flow of taxable income.

Cooperatives

Cooperative (Co-Op)
An organization in which people collectively own and operate a business in order to compete with bigger competitors.

An organization in which a group of people collectively own and operate all or part of the business is a **cooperative (co-op)**. The first formal co-op, organized by Benjamin Franklin in 1752, is still in business today. Co-ops are often found where a large number of small producers can band together to become more competitive. Such well-known brands as OceanSpray juice, Sunkist oranges, and Sun-Maid raisins are the property of food producer cooperatives that formed to market the products grown by many members.

More than 5,500 producer co-ops do business in the United States, with annual sales of over $16 billion. In addition, approximately 7,500 farmer-owned, buying co-ops purchase machinery, fertilizer, seeds, materials, and so on, spending over $4 billion annually. Farm co-ops have increased their annual revenues from $25 billion in 1970 to over $60 billion today. Kansas City–based Farmland Co-op, owned by some 500,000 farmer members, had sales over $2.9 billion in 1989. Other billion-dollar co-ops are Associated Milk Producers, Grain Terminal Association, and Land O Lakes. Most farm co-ops are generally unknown to the public.

Dividends are paid to co-op members in proportion to the amount of goods that each member has bought or sold through the cooperative. These patronage dividends are considered a refund of overpayment rather than a distribution of profits.

A disadvantage of co-ops is that as they grow larger they become more visible to the public. And if the public questions their market power, they may lose their special status under the law.

Sun-Maid Raisin advertisement reprinted with permission of Sun-Maid Growers of California, copyright © 1990

Savings and Loan Associations

Savings and loan associations are corporations that operate in much the same manner as savings banks.[14] The owner of an account is given a passbook in which deposits and withdrawals are noted. About 30 percent of the 5,500 savings and loan associations (S&Ls) in the United States are incorporated under federal law. The remaining 70 percent have state charters. Over 40 million buyers own shares in S&Ls. These shares make up the assets of the associations.

In a mutually owned savings and loan association, both savers and borrowers are members. Members elect a board of directors to manage the association. Most S&L capital is invested in local home mortgages.

Savings and Loan Association
A corporation that operates in much the same manner as a savings bank. The owner of an account is given a passbook in which deposits and withdrawals are noted.

Professional Service Associations

Traditionally, the professional services of doctors, lawyers, dentists, and the like could be performed only by individuals, not by corporations. Impersonal corporate entities were not allowed to provide personal-care services. But in late 1969, the Internal Revenue Service agreed that organizations of professional people, structured under professional association laws, could be treated as corporations for tax purposes. Thus members could have the tax advantages of profit sharing and pension plans, not available to private persons and partnerships. Such organizations are called **professional service organizations.**

Entrepreneurship, franchising, and small business opportunities are discussed in the next chapter. Instead of considering only large firms and how they populate the landscape of business, business students need to learn about

Professional Service Organization
An organization of professional people, organized under professional association laws and treated as a corporation for tax purposes.

smaller business forms and their role in the world marketplace. In fact, in the United States, most new jobs and career opportunities in the 1990s will be found in smaller business organizations.

You'll Know It's the **21**ˢᵗ Century When . . .

Small Is Successful

In the 21st century, the race will often go to nimble, aggressive, smaller companies. Big business will still be around, it's true, but corporate downsizing, which began in the 1980s, will have left big companies trimmer and looking to small companies as models. Some experts even predict that corporations may act as holding companies with a bevy of small subsidiaries. By the 21st century, nearly 90 percent of jobs will be in the service sector, and small businesses—those with 100 employees or less—will have grown 200 percent to 32.5 million jobs. Some projections assert that 15 percent of the total work force in the 21st century will be owner-workers.[15]

SUMMARY OF LEARNING OBJECTIVES

1. To discuss the advantages and disadvantages of sole proprietorships.
   The advantages are (*a*) ease of starting, (*b*) owner's control over daily operations and decisions, (*c*) owner's sole right to profits, (*d*) use of owner's abilities, (*e*) secrecy about business information, (*f*) tax breaks, and (*g*) ease of dissolving. The disadvantages are (*a*) owner's unlimited liability, (*b*) difficulty in raising capital, (*c*) limitations of owner's abilities, (*d*) lack of stability, (*e*) demands on time, and (*f*) difficulty in hiring and keeping self-motivated employees.

2. To discuss the advantages and disadvantages of partnerships.
   Advantages include (*a*) more available capital, (*b*) combined managerial skills of the partners, (*c*) ease of starting, (*d*) clear legal status, and (*e*) tax advantages. Disadvantages include (*a*) general partners' unlimited liability, (*b*) potential for disagreements, (*c*) investment withdrawal difficulty, (*d*) more capital than the sole proprietorship but less than available to corporations, and (*e*) instability.

3. To list the features that should be included in a written partnership contract.
   The main features of a written partnership agreement include the name of the business partnership, type of business, location of the business, expected life of the partnership, names of the partners and the amount of each one's investment, procedures for distributing profits and covering losses, amounts that partners will withdraw for services, procedure for withdrawal of funds, each partner's duties, and procedures for dissolving the partnership.

4. To discuss the advantages and disadvantages of corporations.
   Advantages include (*a*) limitation of owners' liability to the amount of their investments, (*b*) use of skilled management team to run the corporation, (*c*) easy transfer of ownership, (*d*) greater availability of capital, (*e*) stability, and (*f*) status as legal entity. Disadvantages include

(*a*) difficulty and expense in starting, (*b*) individual owner's lack of control, (*c*) double taxation, (*d*) government involvement, (*e*) lack of secrecy, (*f*) managers' possible lack of personal interest in the corporation's success, and (*g*) credit limitations.

5. To define the term *merger* and identify three types of mergers.
   A merger takes place when two or more businesses combine to form a single enterprise. There are three types of mergers: horizontal, vertical, and conglomerate.

6. To identify other incorporated forms of business.
   The corporation is not the only incorporated form of business. Four other widely used incorporated forms of business are S corporations, cooperatives, savings and loan associations, and professional service associations.

KEY TERMS

Sole Proprietorship, p. 51

Unlimited Liability, p. 54

Partnership, p. 55

General Partnership, p. 55

Limited Partnership, p. 55

Master Limited Partnership (MLP), p. 56

Syndicate, p. 60

Business Trust, p. 60

Corporation, p. 61

Charter, p. 62

Domestic Corporation, p. 62

Foreign Corporation, p. 63

Nonprofit Corporation, p. 65

Proxy, p. 67

Double Taxation, p. 69

Merger, p. 70

Horizontal Merger, p. 71

Vertical Merger, p. 71

Conglomerate Merger, p. 71

White Knight, p. 71

S Corporation, p. 72

Cooperative (Co-op), p. 72

Savings and Loan Association, p. 73

Professional Service Organization, p. 73

QUESTIONS FOR DISCUSSION AND REVIEW

1. Describe some of the advantages and disadvantages of a sole proprietorship, partnership, and corporation.
2. What are the reasons for establishing an S corporation?
3. Explain the difference between an open and a closed corporation.
4. Of what value is a lawyer in drawing up partnership agreements?
5. Is what T. Boone Pickens does in attempting to take over firms ethical? Explain.
6. Why is the sole proprietorship the most popular form of business ownership?
7. What is a cooperative? What is a disadvantage of cooperatives?
8. What is meant by the term *double taxation*?
9. Are corporations managed directly by the owners? Explain.
10. How would you decide whether to team up with someone in a partnership form of business?

CASE 2.1
Manhattan Distributing: A Sole Proprietorship with Family Problems

Dozens of large corporations (e.g., Olympia & York Developments, Ltd., Toronto, Canada; value of business about $25 billion) and small businesses (e.g., Bradich Brothers Plumbing of Gary, Indiana; value of business about $200,000) have had to address issues about family businesses, that is, businesses operated by family members (husbands, wives, sons, daughters, sons-in-law, daughters-in-law, cousins, aunts, and uncles). Anheuser-Busch, Exxon, Caterpillar, and Hallmark Cards have all tackled the family-business problem because most of their dealerships are family run. And many training programs, pamphlets, and videos are available on this subject. The video titles point to the potential problems in family-run businesses: ''How In-Laws Become Out-Laws'' and ''Managing Nepotism Constructively.''

Increasingly, corporations recognize that members of family businesses are prone to feuding over everything from the size of a brother's office to who is in charge of the marketing campaign. Fights, arguments, and clashes that annoy family members mean that efficiency suffers and profits can be lost. In a family-run business, emotions can be extremely powerful.

Trouble within family-run businesses often brews below the surface for a long time before it finally explodes. Joseph Rothberg is the founder of a St. Louis–based wine and spirits business. Rothberg had no heir apparent. After thinking about selling out, he instead asked his son-in-law to join the business. Everything was fine at first, but the last six years have brought conflict, personality clashes, arguments, accusations, and a lot of pent-up emotions.

Joseph Rothberg is a self-made man. His firm, Manhattan Distributing Co., now has 90 employees and annual sales of over $30 million. Being a sole proprietor, Rothberg *was* the business. He hired and fired people, prepared the orders, sold the product, worked on payrolls, and purchased the delivery trucks needed to distribute the wine and spirits to St. Louis–area stores. As the business grew, it became apparent that Manhattan Distributing Co. was too big for one man to do everything.

In walked the son-in-law, Nolan. He had worked for 10 years in large corporations, and his motives for working were based on a different philosophy from Rothberg's. Nolan didn't plan to devote every waking hour to Manhattan Distributing, while Rothberg didn't have enough hours in the day to do everything he wanted to accomplish.

Adapted from Sharon Nelton, ''Earning One's Good Fortune,'' *Nation's Business,* January 1990, p. 63; John L. Ward and Gary E. Amoff, ''To Sell or Not to Sell,'' *Nation's Business,* January 1990, pp. 63–64; ''Inside the Reichman Empire,'' *Business Week,* January 29, 1990, pp. 32–36; Mark Robichaux, ''Family Business Isn't All in the Family,'' *The Wall Street Journal,* November 8, 1989, pp. B1–B2; Margaret Crane, ''How to Keep Families from Feuding,'' *Small Business Success Guide,* 1987, pp. 1–3.

Sensing their differences in philosophies, Rothberg began to isolate himself from Nolan. The elder man rarely shared major decisions or plans with his son-in-law. Nolan became frustrated, angry, irritable, cynical, and depressed. He attempted to have his spouse (Rothberg's daughter) talk to her father, but she really didn't want to become involved or take sides.

At a party, Nolan's wife overheard a friend, who works for his father in the construction business, commenting, ''I'll never have any say in our business unless they carry my father out feet first.'' He went on to mention an organization called Sons of Bosses (SOB).* Members included sons, daughters, sons-in-law, and daughters-in-law in family businesses. The friend said SOB had helped him deal with his father.

The SOB organization offers a set of practical guidelines to its members. These guidelines, which can be useful in preventing harsh, emotional conflict from bubbling over, include:

- Junior family members should acquire experience in the business elsewhere. Work for another enterprise first.
- Junior family members need to receive clear job responsibilities. Find out what your tasks are and what the founder expects you to do at work.
- Expect to work harder, longer hours in the first five years than you have ever worked.
- Discuss and reach agreement on salary and fringe benefits (perks) in advance. When will you vacation? When will discussions about raises and bonuses occur?
- Define the roles of other family members in the business. What will the relatives be doing?
- Establish a family council.
- Time is on the side of the SOB member. Be patient but firm. Be thoroughly prepared and in control of your emotions.

The family-run business can be a tremendous opportunity or a nightmare. Some families have shared success, challenge, and opportunity. Other families have split apart and don't even want to talk to each other. The SOB group hopes to improve relationships within families so that family members can enjoy the personal benefits of continuing a meaningful tradition.

Questions for Discussion

1. Why would a business's founder such as Joseph Rothberg be so emotional about how the company is run and operated?
2. Should Nolan work out a transfer-of-ownership plan with his father-in-law? Why is succession planning so important in a family-owned business?
3. Of what value to Nolan is a group like SOB?
4. Would it be informative for Joseph Rothberg to attend, as a guest, an SOB meeting? Why or why not?

---

* SOB was founded in 1969. In 1976 the national organization and some chapters were renamed the National Family Business Council; other chapters retained the original SOB name and are not affiliated with the national organization. For more information, contact the NFBC at 1000 Vermont Avenue, N.W., Washington, D.C. 20005.

CASE 2.2
Esprit Is No Longer "Little Utopia"

Esprit had been a very profitable, upbeat San Francisco sportswear company. Employees referred to the firm as "Little Utopia" or "Camp Esprit." They credited this good life to Doug and Susie Tompkins, the owners and soul of the company. The two had met in 1963 and then married. They became the inspiration and reason for the formation of Esprit. Doug and Susie introduced bright colors and chic style in a line of sport clothes and provided employees with unconventional benefits such as rafting vacations, foreign-language lessons, on-site aerobics classes, and tennis on the company courts.

Everything in "Utopia" was running smoothly, and business was great, until the relationship between Doug and Susie fractured. Their marriage began to split, the partnership began to sag, and business suffered. As the split between the owners widened, Esprit started to lose markets and profits. The normally productive Esprit management meetings became tense and filled with arguments and political maneuvering. The managers and employees began to choose sides—a "Doug" group and a "Susie" group.

Esprit's husband-and-wife partnership had run smoothly for almost two decades. Doug had always wanted to be in a business that had high standards and was very competitive. He was the business operations side of Esprit. In the period 1979–86, sales around the world soared from $120 million to $800 million. The Esprit line of clothes was sold in carefully selected shops, department stores, and catalogs.

In 1987 Esprit's earnings and sales went flat. The reasons cited include too much corporate spending, a declining dollar on the world market, and lack of management control over costs. The Tompkinses began to argue in public about business. Susie believed that Esprit's image was too youthful and had to change. She wanted to appeal to slightly older, stylish career women. Doug disagreed, and he promoted his idea to keep Esprit pointed toward the younger market. According to market experts, Doug's insistence cost the firm dearly. Esprit's customers were growing up, as Susie had suggested, and the firm didn't keep pace.

The setback in sales and marketing resulted in some drastic cost-cutting measures. Doug closed the company's San Francisco warehouse, laid off 700 employees, and even ended the employees' free telephone privileges. Doug and Susie also went public with their criticism of each other. Susie decried the company's image, and Doug found fault with the designs Susie was approving. Doug also started to take an active role in the design department—Susie's territory since the start of Esprit. Doug replaced the Esprit Kids' design team (which had won several awards) with a group from Japan. The Japanese team was a failure. Their designs clashed with American tastes.

The bickering, open criticisms, and tensions resulted in the design people backing Susie, while the graphics and advertising people supported Doug. The shouting matches between Doug and Susie at management meetings even included personal insults that had nothing to do with business. The lost sales,

Adapted from Ellen Rapp, "The War of the Bosses," *Working Woman*, June 1990, pp. 57–59.

arguments, personal insults, and choosing of sides increased employee anxiety; they resulted in an increased number of resignations from key people and delays in making important decisions. Doug and Susie also started spending more time away from Esprit. Finally they agreed to increase the number of members on the board of directors and give up operating control of the company.

Questions for Discussion

1. What advantages of the partnership between Doug and Susie helped Esprit grow to become a large business?

2. One of the disadvantages of a partnership is instability. Can personal problems ever be predicted and avoided in the kind of partnership that Doug and Susie had at Esprit?

3. If you were chairperson of the board of directors of Esprit, what course of action would you recommend to other members and to Susie and Doug?

CHAPTER THREE

ENTREPRENEURSHIP, FRANCHISING, AND SMALL BUSINESS

LEARNING OBJECTIVES

1. To define the term *entrepreneur*.

2. To identify the risks of entrepreneurship.

3. To explain the concept of franchising.

4. To compare the advantages and disadvantages of becoming a franchisee.

5. To identify services the Small Business Administration offers to small-business owners.

6. To describe a business plan and its purpose.

Al Copeland's career is the classic rags-to-riches story. He started with nothing; now his business does about $1 billion a year in sales. Copeland is chairman of the board and chief executive officer (CEO) of Al Copeland Enterprises, Inc., owner of 715 Popeye's Famous Fried Chicken restaurants around the country. In 1989 he

At age 18, Copeland bought his first business, a doughnut shop. He had his ups and downs. He kept the doughnut shop operating and bought a wig business. But he didn't know much about wigs and soon lost interest in them. The wig business taught him a good lesson: never get involved in something you don't understand.

too spicy, another batch was too dry, and so forth. Sinking deeper into debt, he decided to open a chicken restaurant he called Popeye's. Copeland came up with the name while watching the fast-moving film *The French Connection*. The scene in which actor Gene Hackman broke down a door and said, "Hit the wall—Popeye's here!" impressed him.

Courtesy of Al Copeland Enterprises, Inc./Photo by T. Michael Keza

bought the ailing Church's Fried Chicken chain for $394 million, adding 1,400 restaurants to his fast-food empire. His is the second-largest chicken chain, behind the number one chicken cooker, Kentucky Fried Chicken (over 8,000 restaurants).

Copeland, now 45 years old, has set some lofty goals for his firm and himself. He wants to be the number one chicken mogul in the world.

Copeland paid more attention to his doughnut shop after leaving the wig business. He observed how a Kentucky Fried Chicken (KFC) restaurant right down the block always had three times as much business as his shop. He decided that chicken was the food product of the future. He also decided that to compete he needed to develop something with a taste different from KFC's.

Copeland worked for six years trying to perfect a New Orleans–style spicy chicken. One batch was

The taste of Popeye's chicken caught the fancy of a lot of people. (The spicy recipe, a hit, is now safely stored in a New Orleans bank vault.) As Popeye's caught on, Copeland expanded the business by selling franchises. He didn't have the human resources or the money to expand in any other way. He wanted a billion-dollar company that would blanket the United States.

Al Copeland resembles a lot of other hardworking individuals. He is persistent, a risk-taker, a hard driver; he exudes confidence and puts in 12- to 15-hour workdays. He is also demanding and expects the people he hires to share his goals and drive.

Although he didn't achieve success overnight, Copeland knows that maintaining success is difficult. For example, in July 1991 Copeland ran into financial trouble as a result of the Church's purchase (owes banks over $279 million) and underwent a bankruptcy restructuring plan. Al Copeland is again attempting to work through a business problem.[1]

Not all businesses are large businesses. While the Fortune 500 corporations such as IBM and General Motors are the most visible, many individuals—like Al Copeland—start out with a small business. And small businesses can grow, like Copeland's Popeye's.

This chapter discusses the entrepreneurial and small-business spirit. First, we examine entrepreneurships and the risks that entrepreneurs take. Then we examine franchising, looking at both the advantages and disadvantages of franchising agreements. Finally, we discuss the important role of small business.

ENTREPRENEURSHIP

The debate about what makes an entrepreneur continues. However, some characteristics of entrepreneurs and entrepreneurship are worth discussing because they are consistently portrayed and studied.

The Entrepreneur

The entrepreneur, according to French economist J. B. Say, "is a person who shifts economic resources out of an area of lower and into an area of higher productivity and yield."[2] But Say's definition does not tell us who this entrepreneur is. Some define the entrepreneur simply as one who starts his or her own new and small business. For our purposes, we will define the **entrepreneur** as a person who takes the risks necessary to organize and manage a business and receives the financial profits and nonmonetary rewards.

Entrepreneur
A person who takes the risks necessary to organize and manage a business and receives the financial profits and nonmonetary rewards.

The man who opens a small pizza restaurant is in business, but is he an entrepreneur? He took a risk and did something, but did he shift resources or start the business? If the answer is yes, then he is considered an entrepreneur. Ray Kroc is an example of an entrepreneur because he founded and established McDonald's. His hamburgers were not a new idea, but he applied new techniques, resource allocations, and organizational methods in his venture. Ray Kroc *upgraded the productivity and yield from the resources applied* to create his fast-food chain. This is what entrepreneurs do; this is what entrepreneurship means.[3]

Many of the sharp, black-and-white contrasts between the entrepreneur and the professional have faded to a gray color. Formerly, professionals such as doctors, lawyers, dentists, and accountants were not supposed to be entrepreneurial, aggressive, or market oriented. They were "above" the market-driven world. Entrepreneurs, on the other hand, were the mavericks of society. They were risk-takers who aggressively sought to make something happen. Long hours were about all the two worlds had in common. However, increased competition, saturated markets, and a more price-conscious public have changed the world of the professionals. Today they need to market their skills, talents, and competencies: Lawyers advertise their services. Doctors specialize in one form of surgery. Accounting firms join with other businesses (e.g., consulting and law) to serve clients.

Entrepreneurs exhibit many different behaviors; searching for a specific personality pattern is very difficult. Some entrepreneurs are quiet, introverted, and analytical. On the other hand, some are brash, extroverted, and very

Arthur Fry may be the best example of an intrapreneur. The next time you use a Post-it™ note, think about Mr. Fry. He is the man who developed this product at 3M Corporation. He and other 3M employees are encouraged to spend time on pet projects and find new uses for old products or develop new products. Mr. Fry's discovery now earns 3M hundreds of millions of dollars annually.

Courtesy of 3M

emotional. Some qualities many of them share. Viewing change as the norm, entrepreneurs usually search for it, respond to it, and treat it as an opportunity. An entrepreneur such as Ray Kroc of McDonald's is able to take resources and shift them to meet a need. Making the decision to shift resources works better if a person is creative, experienced, and confident.

One example of how an entrepreneur operates is Polaroid's Edwin Land. One day, as he took pictures of his daughter, she asked impatiently why they had to wait for the pictures to be developed. Her question sparked her dad's imagination. Land worked, put his ideas together, and developed the first Polaroid instant camera. He combined his experience with cameras and films with his creativity to change history.

The Enterprise

An enterprise need not be small or new to be entrepreneurial. General Electric Co. (GE), a large multinational business, has a reputation of being entrepreneurial. GE organized the GE Credit Corporation and numerous new manufacturing businesses. These firms made money for GE; they also provided ideas and concepts that raised the company's overall level of performance.

Intrapreneur
An entrepreneurial person employed by a corporation and encouraged to be innovative and creative.

GE is one of a growing number of firms that employ and recognize intrapreneurs. An **intrapreneur** is a person with entrepreneurial characteristics who is employed within a large corporation. Companies such as 3M, Hewlett-Packard, Merck, and Rubbermaid encourage intrapreneurs. Post-it™ note pads were developed at 3M by an employee looking for a better paper for marking pages in a book. At Hewlett-Packard, researchers are urged to spend 10 percent of their workweek on personal pet projects. Intrapreneurs are usually found in enterprises that encourage experimentation, tolerate failure, recognize success, and share the wealth.

Another interesting example of experimentation in business is the case of Francis G. Okee of Minnesota Mining & Manufacturing (3M). He dreamed of ways to boost the sales of sandpaper, then (in 1922) the firm's top seller. Why not sell sandpaper to men as a replacement for razor blades? The idea (thankfully) never caught on. However, Okee, who continued to sand his own face, was still able to work for 3M. The company had a high tolerance for experimenting with creative ideas. It still does today.

Entrepreneurship is not applicable only to profit-making institutions. In health care, the traditional hospital—which appeared in Vienna in the late 1700s—has changed greatly. Today we have highly specialized centers, such as the Mayo Clinic and the Menninger Institute. Entrepreneurs in health care are introducing new methods of treatment delivery to serve patients' needs.

The Growth-Oriented Entrepreneur

Why do entrepreneurs continue to emerge when significant risks, time, and energy are needed to be successful? Researchers studying the entrepreneurial personality have made some interesting discoveries.

Researcher Donald Sexton compared founders of high-growth firms with founders of companies that exhibited little or no growth. Sexton's findings were similar to those in much earlier studies conducted by David McClelland, a noted social psychologist. High-growth–company founders appear to share a distinct cluster of personal characteristics (no single trait but a pattern, or cluster). As you review these characteristics, refer back to our discussions of Al Copeland, Ray Kroc, and Edwin Land. They personify these traits.

Need for achievement   Growth-oriented entrepreneurs have a high **need for achievement:** they need to succeed, to achieve, to accomplish challenging tasks. The strong desire for achievement leads to a desire for independence. Such entrepreneurs need to be free to set their own course, establish their own goals, and use their own style. The need for achievement may help explain why growth-oriented entrepreneurs are not satisfied with founding or working in one firm; they need to prove themselves again and again.

Need for Achievement
A strong desire to succeed, to grow, to accomplish challenging tasks.

Low need to conform   Growth-oriented entrepreneurs listen, but they are able to ignore others' advice. Also, handling skeptics is easy for entrepreneurs. Taking the unpopular course of action, if they consider it best, is the way they do business.

Persistence   Growth-oriented entrepreneurs are persistent, doggedly doing what is best for the business to succeed. They work hard on the details and relentlessly attempt to find ways to become more profitable.

High energy level   The capacity for sustained effort requires a high energy level. All the necessary work—planning, organizing, directing, creating strategy, and finding funds—can only be accomplished on a demanding schedule. The 60- to 80- hour workweek is common.

Risk-taking tendency   McClelland's findings suggest that people with a high need for achievement tend to take risks. Growth-oriented entrepreneurs

TABLE 3.1   **Business Failures in Nine Industries**

	Age of Company When It Failed			
	3 Years or Less	5 Years or Less	6 to 10 Years	Over 10 Years
Agriculture, forestry, and fishing	19.8%	29.5%	21.3%	49.2%
Mining	22.4	41.4	31.9	26.7
Construction	22.5	40.4	27.1	32.5
Manufacturing	34.0	51.3	22.4	26.3
Transportation and public utilities	30.0	49.2	24.2	26.6
Wholesale trade	31.0	48.8	24.9	26.3
Retail trade	38.1	57.1	22.3	20.6
Finance, insurance, and real estate	23.0	41.6	27.6	30.8
Services	31.4	50.6	25.0	24.4
Total	31.4	49.8	24.3	25.9

Source: 1989 data from Dun & Bradstreet's "Business Failures Record, 1990." Table reprinted by permission from *CHANGING TIMES*, the Kiplinger Magazine (January 1988 issue). Copyright 1988 by the Kiplinger Washington Editors, Inc.

believe so strongly in their ability to achieve that they do not see much possibility of failure. Thus they accept risk and find it motivating.

Risks of Entrepreneurship

In launching a business, the entrepreneur usually faces substantial business risk. Well over 3 million new businesses are started each year, and two out of three new jobs in the economy are in small businesses. The failure rate among these new ventures is disturbingly high. According to research by the Small Business Administration, from 25 to 33 percent of all independent small businesses fail during the first two years of operation. Eight of every 10 businesses end within 10 years. Table 3.1 shows the failure rates of businesses in nine industries.

Besides considerable business risk, entrepreneurs face significant financial risk, since they typically invest most—if not all—of their financial resources in the business. They may take a career risk by leaving a secure job for a venture with a highly uncertain future. They also incur family and social risks because the demands of starting and running a young business leave little time for attention to family and friends. The demands of entrepreneurship often strain marriages and friendships.

Nowhere is there a report listing the specific reasons why thousands of businesses fail each year. However experts, business practitioners, and consultants point again and again to three reasons. First, people fail because they jump into a business too quickly. They plunge into a new venture hastily, without doing their homework. They do not analyze their own strengths and weaknesses. Who am I? What do I want? What are my goals? Businesses also fail because they run out of money. If you cannot meet your payroll or pay your bills, you are out of business. Realistic planning for the money needed is critically important. Estimates of cash requirements are a top priority before starting the venture.

TABLE 3.2

Causes of Small-Business Failures

Cause	Characteristics
Planning oversights	Not able to detect market and competitive changes. Poor knowledge of economics. No plans for emergency situations. Inadequate financial planning.
Poor managerial qualities	Unwillingness to work hard, long hours. Lack of ability to deal with people. Failure to delegate responsibility and tasks. Unwillingness to learn the business from the ground up.
Use of inadequate business methods	Poor record-keeping. No credit controls. No inventory control system. Inability to hire help.
Underfinancing	Lack of funds to buy adequate stock and equipment. Lack of funds to buy merchandise. Lack of funds to hire personnel.

Third, failing to plan is an obvious mistake. A detailed business plan forces the entrepreneur to think ahead, to reflect, to decide on how to proceed. This business plan should be in writing.

These three reasons for business failure are not exhaustive. However, they are the most common and the most serious. Table 3.2 captures in a concise format the main reasons for small-business failure. These reasons need to be considered when starting or operating a business.[4] The four main categories (planning oversights, poor managerial qualities, inadequate business methods, and underfinancing), can undermine hard work, brilliant creativity, risk-taking, and distinctness.

FRANCHISING

An attractive business opportunity for many people is to obtain a franchise and become the owner of a restaurant, motel, service station, beauty salon, or other business. A **franchise** is the right to use a business name (e.g., Ramada Inn, Hickory Farms, Jiffy Lube, Putt-Putt Golf) and sell products or services in a specific geographical territory. In the United States, a new franchised business opens every 15 minutes. Numerous American franchises are also opening around the world.

Franchising is not only an American phenomenon. A visit to Hungary, Germany, Italy, Mexico, and over 70 other countries will indicate that franchises are found around the world.

Today approximately 600,000 franchise units operate in the United States. Franchising cuts across 40 industries, ranging from motels and automobile

Franchise
The right to use a specific business name (Pizza Hut, Subway, H & R Block, Blockbuster, Masterworks International) and sell its goods or services in a specific city, region, or country.

Courtesy of Putt-Putt® Golf Courses of America, Inc.

dealers to campgrounds. Franchise sales in 1990 were approximately $700 billion, nearly double the revenues earned in 1980.[5] Now, more than one third of the nation's retail revenue comes from franchised businesses, and over 8 million people are employed by franchises. The top 10 fields of franchising are presented in Table 3.3.

What exactly is a franchise system? The following explanation is accurate, informative, and concise:

Franchising
A system for selective distribution of goods and/or services under a brand name through outlets owned by independent business owners.

> **Franchising** is a system for the selective distribution of goods and/or services under a brand name through outlets owned by independent businessmen called "franchisees"; although the franchisor supplies the franchisee with know-how or brand identification on a continuing basis, the franchisee enjoys the rights to profit and runs the risk of loss. The franchisor controls the distribution of his goods and/or services through a contract which regulates the activities of franchisees, in order to achieve standardization.[6]

This description of a franchise system points out the crucial elements of a franchise business: (1) a contractual agreement between the **franchisee** (person) and **franchisor** (company), (2) a branded good or service (e.g., car mufflers), (3) operation by a businessperson for the purpose of earning a profit, and (4) monitoring by the franchisor so that standard procedures and a standardized product or service are used.

Franchisee
The independent owner of a franchise outlet who enters into an agreement with a franchisor.

Franchisor
The licensing company in the franchise arrangement.

The Changing European Scene

On December 31, 1992, the 12 European Community (EC) countries—Belgium, Germany, France, Italy, Luxembourg, the Netherlands, Denmark, Ireland, the United Kingdom, Greece, Spain, and Portugal—will dismantle internal regulations and barriers that have existed for 30 years. They will become a common

Franchise Sector	Projected 1990 Sales	Projected Annual Growth
Restaurants (all types)	$86.1	12.0%
Retailing (nonfood)	33.6	12.3
Hotels, motels, campgrounds	22.5	9.0
Business aids and services	21.3	12.0
Convenience stores	19.4	9.5
Auto products and services	15.9	8.5
Retailing (food other than convenience stores)	15.9	7.0
Rental services (auto, truck)	8.9	11.0
Construction and home services	9.2	20.0
Recreation, travel, entertainment	6.6	29.0

Source: *The Future of Franchising,* a study for the International Franchise Association by The Naisbitt Group, 1990.

market of 325 million consumers. The reduction of barriers (called EC 1992) should result in a franchising boom in Europe. Removing the barriers allows franchisors to protect their trademarks more readily, distribute goods more freely, and receive profit more easily. After 1992, setting up a Pizza Inn or a Putt-Putt Golf will be easier because instead of 12 different registration applications (one for each country) to get a trademark, only 1 will have to be filed.[7] American franchises may become a common sight in the 12 EC countries.

Franchising: A Brief History

Many people assume franchising is of recent origin, but this is not so. Two early franchise operations in the United States were Coca-Cola, which first supplied its syrup to franchised bottlers around 1900, and Rexall Drug Stores, which started around 1902. Other examples of early franchise pioneers included automobile dealerships and gasoline stations. Gasoline companies entered the franchising field around 1930:

> The stuff that makes the car go, namely gas, went in franchising sometime later, about 1930, to be precise. Up until then the oil companies had been operating their own stations. A few of them began to license dealers and in the period from 1930 to 1935, the practice spread until it became for all intents and purposes the sole method employed to distribute gasoline.[8]

In the 1950s, franchising spread across the United States. In fact, 90 percent of all franchise companies doing business today started in the early 1950s.

Franchise opportunities touch every type of business: motels, fast foods, drugstores, variety stores, repair shops, dry-cleaning services, laundromats, employment agencies, car rental services, pet shops, duplicating services, diet programs, home-cleaning services, and training programs. This list in no way exhausts all the possible areas of franchise opportunities.

Obvious signs of franchising's popularity are the numerous fast-food outlets lining the highways and littering shopping malls. Today there are over 75,000

John Patsch/Journalism Services

fast-food restaurants in the United States, many of them franchise operations. They serve everything from special flavors of ice cream to hot dogs. McDonald's has an international network of 11,100 restaurants that sell a billion hamburgers every five months. It is the biggest food franchise operation in the world, with sales of about $6.1 billion in 1989.

Kentucky Fried Chicken (KFC, a subsidiary of Pepsi-Cola) has over 8,000 outlets, which have total worldwide sales of about $5.4 billion. It serves about 2.7 trillion pieces of chicken a year—enough to provide 11 pieces for every man, woman, and child in the United States.

Pepsi-Cola for years sold franchises throughout the United States. However, for the last 20 years, no Pepsi franchises were made available. Earl Graves (*Black Enterprise* publisher) and Earvin Johnson ("Magic" Johnson of the Los Angeles Lakers basketball team) purchased the first available Pepsi Cola franchise in 1990 in Washington, D.C.[10] It covers 400 square miles of the District of Columbia and Prince Georges County. It is said to be worth $60 million.

The Franchising Agreement

Each franchise organization enters into a contractual agreement with each of its franchisees. These contracts may differ in a number of areas, such as capital needed, training provided, managerial assistance available, and size of the franchise territory. But most franchise contracts have points in common. The franchise buyer normally pays an initial fee to the company and agrees to pay the franchisor a monthly percentage of sales. In exchange, the franchisee has the right to sell a standard product or service.

In almost every franchise, the franchisee must invest some money. The amount can vary from a few thousand dollars to millions. Despite having to put money down, people still have to wait for certain franchises. Each year, more than 2,000 people apply for the approximately 150 franchises granted by McDonald's.

A McDonald's franchise can cost as much as $575,000. Although most of the fee can be borrowed from a bank, $66,000 would be the minimum cash down payment required. This money covers landscaping and opening costs, license fee, site development fee, equipment down payment, signs, and security deposit. McDonald's Corporation does not lend money or guarantee loans. The company will provide a site, build the restaurant, and develop the parking lot. In return, the franchisee must pay 12 percent of gross sales to McDonald's and put at least 4 percent of gross sales annually into marketing and advertising.

Most franchise purchasers enter the business to earn money; in fact, the owner and the company both want to earn money. Earnings are a measure of the franchise's success. To succeed, it must be well managed, provide good products or services, and obtain repeat customers.

The franchisor begins to earn money when the cash down payment is made. In some cases, a franchise fee must be paid before certain rights of operation are granted. The franchisor also requires some type of royalty payment on gross sales (the 12 percent franchisees pay to McDonald's, for example). The amount of royalty, or share of the proceeds, paid to the franchisor differs from company to company. Typically, a franchisee pays a royalty of between 3 and 15 percent on gross sales (total sales revenue).

No matter what the percentage of royalty, franchisees often dislike paying profits to someone else.

> Royalties have one negative aspect—a psychological one. It is only human nature for a man to feel some pain when he sees part of the fruit of his labor go to someone else. Paradoxically, this pain may become more intense as the franchise operation gets more successful. The franchisee may be making many thousands of dollars, but so is the franchisor. It may hurt.[11]

Being involved and working hard to make the franchise a success and then being required to share the earnings deflate the ego of some franchisees. If franchisees believe the sharing of profits is unfair, this perceived inequity is also a problem. The franchisee may believe that he or she does all the work, and the franchisor takes too big a share of the earnings.

Many people who consider entering into a franchise contract assume they will be their own boss. This assumption is only partially accurate. The franchisor exercises a significant amount of control over the franchisee in such areas as (1) real estate ownership, (2) territorial restrictions, (3) cancellation provisions, and (4) required exclusive handling.

Some franchise companies own the real estate, select the site of the business location, and build the facility. These companies then lease the facility to a franchisee. Exxon, Shell, Gulf, and Texaco, for example, often select the location for a service station and build it according to their specifications.

The **cancellation provision** in a contract is a powerful control device. For instance, gasoline companies often issue operators of service stations a one-year franchise. If the company does not consider the operator successful, the franchise agreement can be canceled after that time. This provision can force operators to run the business as directed by the franchisor.

Exclusive handling means that the franchisee will only sell items, products, or services that are acceptable to the franchisor. This means that the franchisor has control over what is sold directly to customers or clients.

Cancellation Provision
The contract provision giving a franchisor the power to cancel an arrangement with a franchisee.

Exclusive Handling
A form of control in which a franchisor requires the franchisee to purchase only supplies approved by the franchisor.

Franchising Benefits Both Sides

Dorian and Derrick Malloy, twin brothers in their mid-30s, are successful black businessmen in New York's north Bronx. They own two Wendy's International Inc. stores that do $2.5 million a year in sales. And now the Malloys are working with a partner to develop K-Sun Inc. automated suntan booths in Florida. Their route to business ownership: franchising.

Franchises enable many people to both own a business and get help running it. Franchisees do not have to develop a new product, create a new company, or test the market. They do have to invest their own money, give up some independence, and work hard. McDonald's, probably the best-known and most sought-after franchise, wants only owners who will personally manage their stores and who will commit to working 12- to 18-hour days, seven days a week. That's after a two-year training program that includes working without pay at a McDonald's restaurant. But the eventual payoff for McDonald's franchise owners is worth the sacrifices demanded; McDonald's has the highest average per store sales of the leading fast-food chains.

The Malloy twins have worked in the hamburger business since they were 17, much of that time at McDonald's restaurants. When buying their own Wendy's stores, they invested $200,000 per store,

with the chance to own the land and the building. They hope to be millionaires by age 40. "We're still looking for that money tree— where you don't have to put all that much time into it," says Dorian.

In addition to the highly visible national fast-foods chains, franchises are available in a wide variety of other fields. Some new companies offering franchises for $100,000 or less include Amerispec Home Inspection Service, Computertots (hands-on computer classes for preschool children), and Shampoo Chez (self-service dog washing facilities).

Franchising offers business firms of all sizes a way to grow with minimum investment. Joanne Kobar relies on franchising to expand TGIF Peopleworks, her Connecticut-based company that places in-home workers; she has sold about 20 franchises. Murry Evans, who got in on the ground floor of Burger King and now has 46 restaurants, is giving others a chance for a franchise—with his own company, Signs Now, which offers one-day service for computer-generated vinyl signs and lettering. After Rebecca Mathias established Mothers Work, a mail-order business selling sophisticated maternity clothes, she gained a national presence by franchising stores in major U.S. cities.

When sales took off, Mathhias started buying back stores to boost profits. Mothers Work now has 26 company-owned stores and 14 franchises.

Large corporations are franchising, too. Prudential Insurance Co. of America opened a nationwide chain of real estate agencies. "The franchiser doesn't have to spend money to open franchises," says Jerry Cole of Prudential. "On the contrary, somebody pays them to open it. It's immediately profitable." Prudential figured that opening its own agencies would have cost at least 10 times more. Ashland Oil used franchising to build its Valvoline quick-lube business quickly to avoid losing a promising new market to other firms. With plans to grow from around 200 outlets to 2,000 by the mid-1990s, Ashland realized that, at $500,000 each, company-owned locations were impractical.

Firms with their own large distribution networks in place also franchise. The investor who bought Days Inns of America converted the hotels into franchises to raise money to pay for the buyout. Some manufacturers grant franchises to the salespeople and distributors who sell the industrial parts they make. Consumer product companies also are franchising by selling routes to the truck drivers and other salespeople who deliver snacks and soft drinks to stores.[12]

Advantages of Owning a Franchise

Although the franchise business has its problems, there are reasons why it appeals to people. A person who has never owned or managed a business needs guidance to operate successfully. This guidance can be provided by a well-run franchise organization. Also, franchisors can provide a brand name, proven products or services, and financial assistance. The Business Action illustrates how franchising benefits firms and owners.

Guidance   A glaring weakness in small businesses is the lack of managerial ability. A person with limited managerial skills may be able to get by in a large organization because he or she is just one of many managers. But no one can cover up for or ''carry'' a franchise manager. Many franchisors try to overcome managerial deficiencies or inexperience by providing some form of training. Kentucky Fried Chicken operates Chicken University, a training school for improving management skills. A & W trainees study goology (preparation of burger dressings), thermal mixology (coffee and hot chocolate), and fryocracy (french frying).

Brand name   The investor who signs a franchise agreement acquires the right to use a nationally or regionally promoted brand name. This identifies the local unit with a recognized product or service. Travelers recognize the Holiday Inn sign, the colors of a Pizza Hut building, and Century 21 real estate signs. National promotion brings these features and characteristics to the attention of potential consumers.

Proven product   The franchisor can offer the franchisee a proven product and method of operating the business. The product or service is known and accepted by the public: customers will buy Baskin-Robbins ice cream, AAMCO transmissions, Athlete's Foot sneakers, and H & R Block income tax counseling.

Financial assistance   By joining a franchise company, the individual investor may be able to secure financial assistance. Start-up costs of any business are often high, and the prospective investor usually has limited funds. The sole owner generally has a limited credit rating, making it difficult to borrow needed funds. In some cases, association with a well-established franchisor—through its reputation and its financial controls—may enhance the investor's credit rating with local banks.

Disadvantages of Owning a Franchise

As does any business venture, franchising has some disadvantages. Many were mentioned briefly earlier in this chapter. Some of the more pressing negative features include costs, lack of control, and inadequate training programs offered by some unscrupulous promoters.

Costs   As already mentioned, franchisees must pay franchise fees. In return, the franchisor can provide training, guidance, and other forms of support that would otherwise cost money. Thus the franchisee pays for the opportunity to share in these forms of support. If it were possible to earn the same income independent of the franchisor, the investor could save the amount of these fees.

External control A person who signs a franchise agreement loses some independence. The franchisor, in order to operate all of the franchise outlets as a business, must exercise some control over promotional activities, financial records, hiring, service procedures, and managerial development. Although useful, these controls are unpleasant to the person who seeks independence. In the best of circumstances, the franchisee is semi-independent. In a sole proprietorship, by contrast, the owner is totally independent.

Weak training programs Some franchisors have developed excellent training programs. Even competitors concede that Kentucky Fried Chicken's training is outstanding. But some promoters promise sound training programs and never deliver. In other cases, the training programs are weak—too brief and staffed by trainers who do not have instructional skills. The facilities are sometimes unsuitable for proper learning and development.

Franchisor Disclosure

Because of the nature of franchising in the United States, evaluating an opportunity carefully before signing an agreement is important. The large number of franchise companies makes the task difficult. The Federal Trade Commission requires every franchise firm to provide buyers with a full disclosure form. The form has 20 categories of information, including a financial statement, company history review, fees, investment requirements, and a litigation history. The best investment a prospective franchisee can make is to have an attorney and an accountant review the document and provide opinions.[13]

SMALL BUSINESS

In projecting the future of small business, entrepreneurs, and entrepreneurship, management consultant Thomas Jones asserts that risk-takers and innovators will dominate the future. These individuals will continue to supply the lion's share of new jobs, growth, and innovation. Jones points to specific social trends that support his claim of increased small-business and entrepreneurial activity in the 1990s.

- Recent immigrants to the United States have demonstrated incredible talent, drive, and success in new business ventures and small businesses. Immigrants will continue to establish themselves in their new country.

- Advances in technology and access to information allow new ventures to begin with considerably less start-up costs and lower overhead expenses. The small business can compete with higher-cost firms by being efficient.

- A glut in the professions, such as law, has forced many educated professionals to seek other career paths. Many are choosing to go into business for themselves.

- Middle-managment cutbacks have put well-trained, educated men and women into the job market. Many of these managers have started their own businesses.

- Americans love their independence. This desire for freedom extends to the job one holds. The closest one can get to being independent is owning a business. Many people love to be their own boss.
- Entrepreneurship—being your own boss—is popular today. Success stories abound, and everyone wants to believe they can be a success.

The enthusiasm for small business and entrepreneurship is at an all-time high. This enthusiasm is a prerequisite for a healthy economy.

Many of the most publicized corporate giants began as small businesses and grew large through effective management.[14] For example, three engineers working out of a garage established the fastest-growing company in the United States, Compaq Computer; Coca-Cola began when a pharmacist brewed a batch of syrup that tasted good; a restaurant owner named Colonel Sanders owned a small cafe that served "finger-lickin' good" chicken; and a salesperson named Ray Kroc discovered a tasty hambuger in California that he turned into the McDonald's burger.

Characteristics

What characterizes small businesses? The Small Business Act of 1953 defines **small business** as "one which is independently owned and operated and not dominant in its field of operation." The act authorized the Small Business Administration (SBA) to use a number of yardsticks to identify a small business. For example, in lending money to small businesses, the SBA has established the following limits for qualifying:

Small Business
One that is independently owned and operated and is not dominant in its field of operation.

Dave Brown/Journalism Services

The United States without small businesses is almost unthinkable. There are small businesses everywhere, and, in fact, the majority of Americans in the work force (about 60 percent) are employed by small businesses. These employees of Merlin Andrew's dairy farm in Trenton, Utah, are part of the millions of small business workers that help make the United States a good business environment.

The Incubator Business Concept

Entrepreneurs attempt to find a market need and fill it; in doing so, they create jobs. The first business incubators were opened in the 1970s as private-public partnerships between Control Data and several cities and counties that wanted to create jobs in their communities. Since then, incubators have become popular among entrepreneurs. An estimated 350 operate today. Most are private, nonprofit operations sponsored by regional development organizations. They exist to create jobs and spark economic growth in the community.

In the incubator facility (usually a set of offices in the same building), different businesses share the cost of services such as photocopiers, fax machines, word processing, conference rooms, telephone services, and business consultants. The purpose is to help the businesses grow so they can graduate from the incubator to full-fledged independence.

Incubator businesses have requested specific management services. Ranked in order of importance were these needed services:

1. Business plan guidance.
2. Marketing advice/marketing plan development.
3. Information on government grants and loans.
4. Computer training.
5. Guidance in government procurement procedures.

To cut down on costs and help their tenants build business, many incubators specialize in certain types of businesses that either use similar services or provide each other with customers. The incubator manager needs to be skilled at working with creative, energetic, and often inexperienced entrepreneurs. The manager also must know when to move a business out of the incubator because of its growth and maturity. Graduating businesses from the incubator to the real world is the measure of an incubator manager's success.[15]

- *Retailing and service*. The amount varies depending on the industry. In some industries, the maximum amount of sales is $3.5 million. In other industries, the maximum amount may be as high as sales of $13.5 million.
- *Wholesaling*. The maximum number of employees cannot exceed 500.
- *Manufacturing*. The business must have 250 or fewer employees. If employment is more than 250 but less than 500, a size standard for a particular industry is used.
- *Special trade construction*. The maximum amount of sales is $7 million, regardless of industry.

These criteria suggest that smallness depends on your point of view. You may consider Marshall Field's (a department store company that started in Chicago) small in comparison to Sears. But compared to many other department store companies, Marshall Field's is large. Therefore, a small business is one that is not dominant (does not control a large market share) in its industry and that can be started with a moderate investment for that industry.[16]

The **incubator** is a facility, office, shop, or location in which fledgling businesses can share space, costs, services, and information to grow their firms and to become strong enough to leave and operate independently. The Business Action briefly explains some of the features of an incubator.

Smallness in business does not equate with a small contribution to the economy. Here are some facts about small businesses in the United States:

Incubator
A facility in which fledgling businesses can share space, costs, services, and information while their firms grow and become strong.

- They provide nearly 60 percent of the total employment in business.
- They account for about 43 percent of the gross national product of the United States.
- They account for nearly $8 of every $10 earned in the construction industry.
- More than 90 percent of all corporations are small, including farms.
- 50 percent of all American businesses employ fewer than 10 people.

Advantages and Disadvantages

Any business venture involves potential benefits and costs. For many people, one important benefit is the personal gratification gained from operating one's own business. Business owners can exercise all their talents and can do so with some degree of independence; some also can obtain power by operating their own business. Another benefit of starting a small business is financial gain. The financial return from a successful small business can be substantial, as Table 3.4 illustrates.

On the other hand, potential and actual costs can be important. The initial investment may be lost. Some risks are out of the entrepreneur's control; fashion changes, government regulations, competition, and labor problems may threaten the business. Some businesses also tend to produce irregular income; during the first six months of many potentially profitable firms, the owner may receive zero profits. Being in business for yourself also means long hours, generally leaving less time for recreation and the family. These important parts of life sometimes must be sacrificed to operate a business successfully.

TABLE 3.4

Small Businesses Can Produce Big Profits

Small Company	Three-Year Profit Increase (1988–1990)
T² Medical (provides in-home medical treatment)	190.3%
Rexhall Industries (motor homes)	204.4
DIGI International (software and hardware)	153.4
Handex Environmental Recovery (remediation techniques)	133.3
Quiksilver (surf and sporting clothes)	145.6
American Power Conversion (power systems for computers)	276.8
Catalina Lighting (light fixtures)	156.0

Source: Data from Small Business Administration.

The Small Business Administration (SBA)

Small Business Administration (SBA)
An independent agency of the federal government, created in 1953 to protect the interests of small-business owners.

The **Small Business Administration (SBA)**, an independent agency of the federal government, was created in 1953 to protect the interests of small-business owners. Big-business interests are promoted in Congress by well-organized lobbies, which work to create an atmosphere favorable for big business. Small businesses did not have this type of lobby power; for this and other reasons, the SBA was created.

SBA loans   One important SBA function is to provide loans. If a small-business owner needs more money, the agency can help. The SBA does not compete with banks. Generally it will lend money to entrepreneurs only after they have been turned down by private lenders.

   The SBA lends money on a term basis; that is, the money must be paid back within a specified number of years. *Direct loans* come from the agency's own funds. *Participating loans* supplement loans from banks. In another type of SBA loan, the *guaranteed loan,* the money comes from a bank, but the SBA guarantees to pay 80 percent of the loan if the owner defaults or can't pay. The SBA's guarantee cannot exceed $500,000. The process for applying for and securing an SBA loan is spelled out in Table 3.5. Banks often help the loan applicant fill out the right forms.

Managerial assistance   The SBA's Office of Management Assistance aids people who want to develop their managerial skills. In fact, SBA loan approvals often require applicants to take action to improve their abilities; the Office of Management Assistance offers such assistance.

   SBA management training courses stress the fundamentals of management. Typically the courses run for three or four weeks, one night a week. The agency also sponsors short, one-day updating courses covering the latest tax, investment, and legal developments.

Minority business and the SBA   The most popular minority-owned businesses are owner-operated restaurants, beauty parlors, barbershops, newspaper/magazine stores, and grocery stores. But in the United States, which has

TABLE 3.5

SBA Loan Application Procedure

1. Assemble the information outlined below.

2. Take it to your bank and ask your banker to review the information and loan proposal. (It will be necessary for you to locate a bank that is willing to participate with SBA and make the loan since direct loan funds from SBA are quite limited and an unreliable source of financing.)

3. If the bank is willing to participate, ask the bank to forward the information to us for our review, along with their comments.

Information Needed for Loan Review

1. Brief résumé of business.

2. Brief résumé of management, setting forth prior business experience, technical training, education, age, health, etc.

3. Itemized use of loan proceeds:

Working capital	$ _____
Land	$ _____
Building	$ _____
Furniture and fixtures	$ _____
Machinery and equipment	$ _____
Automotive equipment	$ _____
Other	$ _____
Total	$ _____

4. Current business balance sheet and profit/loss statement.

5. Year-ending balance sheets and profit/loss statements for the last three years or, if the business has been in existence less than three years, financial statements for each year it has been in operation. (Copies of the financial statements submitted with the income tax returns are adequate.)

6. If the business is not in existence but is proposed, furnish a projected balance sheet of the business, showing its proposed assets, liabilities, and net worth upon commencement of operations, together with projected annual operating statements for the first three years of operation.

7. Furnish a separate personal balance sheet showing all assets owned and liabilities owed outside of the business.

The above information is what SBA loan representatives need to properly analyze a loan proposal. They may request additional information.

about 45 million minority citizens, the number of black and Hispanic minority–owned businesses is disproportionately small. This may be due to lack of funds, inexperience, inability to obtain credit, or lack of interest in business. On the other hand, the number of Asian-owned businesses is large, possibly due to Asians' interest, experience, and skills in operating a business.

The business community, government, and a large portion of society are promoting minority ownership. Large corporations are attempting to buy from and support minority-owned businesses. In cooperation with the U.S. Department of Commerce, the SBA has instituted programs that assist small businesses owned and managed by the socially or economically disadvantaged. Such disadvantages may arise from cultural, social, or chronic economic

● C o n n e c t i o n s

Are You Ready to Run Your Own Business?

Directions: Are you ready to run your own business? An important starting point in making a decision is determining your goals in life. Then you must match these goals with the benefits offered by the type of business you are considering. Other important questions to ask yourself include:

- Are you a self-starter?
- Do you like other people?
- Can you lead others?
- Are you well organized?
- Are you a decisive decision maker?
- Do you enjoy hard work and long hours?
- Do you stick with a project?
- Can you handle pressure?
- Can you communicate well?

Small-Business Investment Company (SBIC)
A privately owned and operated company licensed by the SBA to furnish loans to small firms.

MESBIC
Minority-enterprise small-business investment company. Such a company is owned and operated by established industrial or financial concerns, private investors, or business-oriented economic development organizations.

circumstances or background. The category includes but is not restricted to blacks, Native Americans, Mexican Americans, Asian Americans, and Inuits (native Alaskans).

The Small Business Investment Act of 1958 allows small firms to more easily get needed long-term capital to finance their growth. This act authorized the SBA to license **small-business investment companies (SBICs)**, privately owned and operated companies that furnish loans to small firms.

SBICs dedicated to assisting small firms owned and operated by minority-group members are called **minority-enterprise small-business investment companies (MESBICs)**. A MESBIC is owned and operated by established industrial or financial concerns, private investors, or business-oriented economic development organizations. Minority owners can ask for financial and managerial support from a MESBIC.

In 1988 the SBA guaranteed $2.8 billion in loans to 17,135 businesses.[17] Here's how some of the money was distributed:

- Minorities—2,121 loans worth $392 million.
- Women—1,888 loans worth $280 million.
- Veterans—4,635 loans worth $853 million.

But the SBA does more than lend money. It offers a starter kit for owners, sponsors local college courses and workshops, puts clients in touch with volunteers, and helps owners secure contracts with the federal government.

Some growing and already large African-American–owned firms in the United States started as small businesses. A few of the biggest are TLC Beatrice International Inc. (foods, $1.51 billion in sales), Johnson Publishing

- Do you understand planning, organizing, and controlling?
- Do you learn from past mistakes?
- Are you in excellent health?

Feedback: Operating a small business can be both challenging and rewarding. But owning or running a small business is not for everyone. A small business can be a lot of pressure, long hours, and a test of management and leadership skills. The reward is the satisfaction in running your own show and succeeding both personally and financially.

If you answered no to some of these questions, you may want to think it over before attempting to operate a small business. Of course, this is only a checklist of questions, and is only meant to help you to do some soul searching. And even if you answered no, you can change—good communication skills can be developed, leadership skills can be acquired, and so on. If you answered yes to most of these questions, you seem to have what it takes to operate a small business.

Company (publishing and broadcasting, $241 million), H. J. Russell & Co. (construction, $133 million), and the Bing Group (steel processing and distribution, $74 million).[18]

Small-Business Opportunities

Many people imagine themselves running their own business, making the key decisions, and earning a profit. Becoming a small-business owner can provide these opportunities. The Connections quiz can help you decide if you are ready to operate your own business.

Three typical ways to become a small-business owner include taking over a family business, buying an existing business, or starting a new business. Children have often taken over the family business. In most cases, the employees in small bakeries, barbershops, grocery stores, and butcher shops were the owners' children. They learned the business by working with their parents. Sometimes the children learned well and wanted to continue the business. In other cases, the parents forced the business on the children, resulting in parent-child conflict and business failure.

Some people buy out an established business. The buyer and seller agree on terms involving the inventory, equipment, and price. The details of this purchase agreement should be spelled out in a legal contract between the buyer and seller.

The third method of becoming a small-business owner, starting a new business, requires hard work and careful planning. Without solid planning, a new owner is likely to be swamped by the first wave of problems. Because a new business has no previous customers or business records, as an established business does, getting all the information needed to do a good job will involve hard work. The new owner must study materials about products and markets, consult with professional and business experts, and perhaps attend seminars and workshops for a quick education about managing a small business. These activities are all very important.

Every industry has successful small businesses. Small-business owners operate manufacturing plants, salad bars, computer stores, yogurt stores, day-care centers, skating rinks, retail stores, computer production plants, construction firms, accounting offices, printing plants, record stores, and hundreds of other businesses. However, small business is more concentrated in some areas of the economy than in others.

Manufacturing   Small manufacturing businesses number in the thousands. In fact, about 30 percent of all manufacturing companies are considered small.[19] This category includes printing shops, steel fabricating shops, recreational equipment plants, clothing manufacturers, cabinet shops, furniture shops, and bakeries. The manufacturing business involves converting raw materials into products needed by society. Therefore the owner must understand production and marketing and how these business functions complement each other.

Service   The service sector is a diverse field; there are hundreds of service business opportunities. Around 60 percent of all private business jobs in the United States involve selling services to consumers. **Services** are intangible products that cannot be physically possessed and that involve performance or effort. Service businesses include:

Services
Intangible products that cannot be physically possessed and that involve performance or effort.

- *Business services*—businesses that provide service to other business organizations; include accounting firms, advertising agencies, software writers, computer programmers, systems analysts, blueprint service, tax consultants, collection agencies, and so on.
- *Personal services*—include barber and beauty shops, baby-sitting agencies, piano teachers, laundries, and travel agencies.
- *Repair services*—include automobile repair, jewelry repair, appliance repair, furniture repair, plumbing repair, and truck repair services.
- *Entertainment and recreation services*—include racetracks, motion picture theaters, amusement parks, golf courses, and bowling alleys.
- *Hotels and motels*—include the operation of hotels, motels, and recreational vehicle (RV) camps.

With increased leisure time and consumer spending power, individuals, families, and other businesses are expected to increase their use of service firms.

The wide array of service businesses suggests a number of common characteristics:

1. Most small service firms offer one or, at most, a few major services. The accountant specializes in taxes, the jewelry repair shop fixes watches, and the window washing company cleans windows.
2. The majority of small service businesses do not keep large amounts of supplies, or inventory, on hand; they purchase the materials or goods they need when there is a demand.
3. Because services are consumed immediately, suppliers operate on a cash-and-carry or partial-payment-in-advance basis: the plumber wants to be paid when the repair is made.

This accountant provides accounting services without having to leave her home. Home-based businesses are increasing in number every year because they are so convenient and because they permit the owner to stay close to home.

Cary Wolinsky/Stock Imagery

4. Service businesses rely on human ability. They sell such intangibles as income tax knowledge or the ability to care for children while parents work. This ability adds value to what the customer or client receives—a completed income tax form or quality care for children.

5. The majority of small service businesses are sole proprietorships. This is consistent with the other characteristics of small business, such as specialized expertise, little need for large inventory, and application of knowledge and craft ability.

Wholesaling Wholesaling involves selling to other sellers, such as retailers, other wholesalers, or industrial firms. Wholesale trade consists mainly of small businesses. Firms with fewer than 100 employees are responsible for more than 75 percent of the industry's paid employment. In fact, very small firms (those with fewer than 20 employees) have 41 percent of the total employment.

Merchant wholesalers sold over $1.3 trillion of goods in 1988. A merchant wholesaler is an independent business, such as Super Value Stores, Inc., that holds ownership to the goods it markets. Small wholesale firms also sell a wide range of products, including groceries, supplies, machinery, appliances, grain, and fruits and vegetables. These businesses serve as a link between manufacturers and retailers or industrial users. Wholesaling is discussed in detail in Chapter Fifteen.

Retailing Retailers are merchants who sell goods to ultimate consumers, that is, to us. The giants of retailing include Sears Roebuck, Kmart, Wal-Mart, and J. C. Penney. Small, local retail businesses sell many of the same products as these giant corporations. Corner drugstores, shoe stores, grocery stores, restaurants, jewelry stores, and hardware stores appear in almost every populated area in the United States. Chapter Fifteen explores retailing further.

Home-based businesses: another alternative About 27 million Americans—25 percent of the total work force—now work at home, either full- or part-time. By the end of 1992, an estimated 31 million Americans will be working out of their homes. The best chance of succeeding in a **home-based business** is to (1) start on a part-time base, (2) have enough start-up money, (3) do your research on the business idea, (4) select a business you truly enjoy, and (5) prepare a thorough business plan.

For most home-based businesses, the best business form is the sole proprietorship. In some cities, home-based businesses are covered by zoning laws. An operator may have to register the business name and may need to obtain a license to conduct business.

Some of the hottest home-based businesses today are auto detailing, desktop publishing, computer counseling, event planning, catering, day care, home/apartment cleaning, lawn care/landscaping, and pet services. Home-based franchise opportunities are available for those who do not want to start their own business. Molly Maid (maid service), Jani-King (cleaning services), Decorating Den (interior decorator service), and *Bingo Bugle* (a monthly publication for Bingo players) are some of the fastest-growing home-based franchises.[20]

Small-Business Start-Up

Starting any business requires careful investigation and planning. The SBA publishes valuable guides for those interested in starting a business. Some of the SBA's most popular publications are *Going into Business, Planning and Goal Setting for Small Business, Developing a Strategic Business Plan,* and *ABC's of Borrowing.*

A person can improve his or her chances of business success by taking the time to write a **business plan.** The business plan is an organized process of putting down on paper what the person is trying to accomplish with the business. It describes the business, the good or service, the customers, the competition, and the financing of all activities necessary to enter business and make or sell a good or service. It is the game plan of the proposed new venture. The business plan is also called a prospectus, proposal, or blue book.

Starting a business with no plan, goals, or direction is a good way to fail. Competition, personal skills, and a program of growth must be thought out carefully. Preparing a business plan forces a person to take a careful look at what the business will be, what resources will be needed, and how the business must be managed. The business plan also serves to show banks or investors that the individual is organized, serious about the business, and willing to discuss all aspects of the business, including motivation.

No business plan can be perfect. Unexpected market changes occur that cannot be controlled. However, a well-thought-out business plan provides the person, banks, investors, and others with a framework to analyze and evaluate the idea, prospects for success, and potential competition.

There is no specific formula for preparing a business plan. However, most business plans are brief, carefully prepared, accurate, and up-to-date. The

Home-Based Business
Business in which an individual works or conducts activities out of the home. About 22 percent of the total work force now works out of the home.

Business Plan
A written document that describes the business, the good or service, the customers, the competition, the financing, and all activities necessary to enter business and make or sell a good or service. It is the game plan of the new business.

Appendix to this chapter contains a business plan for a fictitious service business named Events Unlimited. We present it as an example of how to construct a business plan. It does not include information about research and development or about manufacturing, because the fictitious business deals with a service. We also have not included the financial documents because we have not yet covered this type of material in the text. Remember that a complete plan would typically include financial, accounting, and cost data.

You'll Know It's the **21ˢᵗ** **Century When . . .** _____

Your Pet's Nanny Is a Franchise

The International Franchise Association projects that by the year 2010 franchises will generate 50 percent of all retail dollars, up from about 33 percent in 1990, when they did over $600 billion of business. In a service economy where nearly 70 percent of women work, busy people will turn to franchises for home decorating, carpet dyeing, domestic help searches, letter writing, small repairs, emergency first aid, payroll services, party music—you name it. Others will open these small businesses, which they can run from home—even from a car or van. By the 21st century, hundreds of U.S. franchises will also be operating abroad, making the most of the global economy.[21]

SUMMARY OF LEARNING OBJECTIVES

1. To define the term *entrepreneur.*
   An entrepreneur is a person who takes the risks necessary to organize and manage a business and receives the financial profits and nonmonetary rewards.

2. To identify the risks of entrepreneurship.
   An entrepreneur faces substantial risks, including: personal risk of failure; financial risk; career risk; and family and social risks.

3. To explain the concept of franchising.
   Franchising is a system for the selective distribution of goods and services, under a brand name, through outlets owned by independent businessmen called franchisees. The franchisor (company) supplies the franchisee (person) with know-how and/or brand identification on a continuing basis; the franchisee enjoys the rights to profit and runs the risk of loss. The relationship between the franchisor and the franchisee is regulated by a contractual agreement.

4. To compare the advantages and disadvantages of becoming a franchisee.
   The advantages of owning a franchise include (*a*) managerial guidance from the franchisor, (*b*) the right to use a nationally promoted brand name, (*c*) use of a proven product and method of operating the business, and (*d*) financial assistance. The disadvantages of owning a franchise include (*a*) costs, in the form of franchise fees and also paying the franchisor a percentage of the franchise's profits; (*b*) loss of control over

promotional activities, financial records, hiring, service procedures, and managerial development; and (c) the weak training programs offered by some franchisors.

5. To identify services the Small Business Administration offers to small-business owners.

The SBA was created in 1953 to help, support, and encourage small business through a variety of services. The SBA provides direct, participating, and guaranteed loans to entrepreneurs. The SBA's Office of Management Assistance sponsors management training courses to aid people who want to develop their managerial skills. The SBA also helps small businesses owned and managed by the economically and socially disadvantaged. The SBA licenses small-business investment companies (SBICs) and minority-enterprise small-business investment companies (MESBICs), which provide financial and managerial support to small-business owners. It also offers a starter kit for owners, sponsors courses and workshops, and assists owners trying to secure government contracts.

6. To describe a business plan and its purpose.

A business plan is an organized process of analyzing and putting on paper what the business owner is attempting to accomplish. It is the overall game plan that describes the business, the good or service, and the competition. Not writing a formal business plan is a major cause of small-business failure.

KEY TERMS

Entrepreneur, p. 83

Intrapreneur, p. 84

Need for Achievement, p. 85

Franchise, p. 87

Franchising, p. 88

Franchisee, p. 88

Franchisor, p. 88

Cancellation Provision, p. 91

Exclusive Handling, p. 91

Small Business, p. 95

Incubator, p. 97

Small Business Administration (SBA), p. 98

Small-Business Investment Company (SBIC), p. 100

Minority-Enterprise Small-Business Investment Company (MESBIC), p. 100

Services, p. 102

Home-Based Business, p. 104

Business Plan, p. 104

QUESTIONS FOR DISCUSSION AND REVIEW

1. Why would a young person (21 to 45) start her own business? An older person (over 45) start his own business?

2. Why should a person hire a lawyer and an accountant to go over a franchise agreement?

3. How does the SBA help, support, and encourage small business?

4. If you were a franchise owner, would paying a royalty to the franchisor be a major issue and concern? Why or why not?

5. Does an organization have to be small to be considered entrepreneurial? Explain.

6. What have entrepreneurs contributed to America's standard of living?

7. Why do some small businesses typically fail to achieve their goals?

8. What does the future look like for entrepreneurs and entrepreneurship worldwide?

9. Why would a person want to own a franchise of a major, well-known franchisor?

10. What is an intrapreneur? Why do some firms encourage intrapreneurship?

CASE 3.1
Staying Put or Starting Over?

Jill Bradshaw, at age 29, was director of computer services for Micro-Network (MN) of Silver Spring, Maryland. As director, she was responsible for all planning, marketing, installation, and research of MN's computer services, which included programming, consulting, desktop publishing, and payroll preparation. The company's growth was exceptional, with sales of $15 million after only seven years of business. Jill was recognized as one of the key bright stars on the MN management team.

Jill occasionally became upset with Don Taylor, the president of MN. Her biggest complaint was that Don had no plan, direction, or idea of what he wanted the business to accomplish. One particular argument with Don involved a customer in Madrid, Spain, who wanted MN to provide extensive consulting services. Don refused to do business consulting in international settings. He believed that Americans should consult for Americans and that international markets were too difficult to penetrate. Jill, on the other hand, wanted MN to take the best projects available, whether they were next door in Washington, D.C., or in Madrid.

Don had hired a number of new managers, with some of his final choices based on the candidates' expressed opinions about international business. Jill believed that those who expressed strong interest in growth into international markets were not hired. This was an irritating point that she raised with Don, but he denied using international interest as a selection criterion.

Although young, Jill was a very articulate representative of the business. On a number of occasions, clients had asked her to quit MN and to become their vice president or director of computer services. At first, she was merely flattered by the attention and offers of the clients. She never thought about quitting MN. In five years, she had been promoted four times and now was the third-highest paid employee with an annual salary of $105,000, plus a company automobile, an expense account, a five-week vacation package, and a promise to be sent to the advanced management program at Harvard. However, Don Taylor's lack of vision, his disorganized way of conducting business, and the new influx of Taylor-like thinkers had become a burden.

Jill is an independent person, strong willed, self-confident, energetic, and competitive. She believed that as long as she was professionally challenged and had an opportunity to develop personally, MN was the place for her. But she also believed that Don Taylor's approach could turn MN into a failed business.

Jill saw tremendous opportunities in the computer service industry in the United States and internationally. But she recognized the difficulties of starting a new venture; she also knew that she was inexperienced in preparing a business plan, raising money, and putting a management team together. Computer services was not a new, distinct idea. It is a difficult industry in which to gain an edge and be profitable. These doubts were all that she thought about for a month.

While considering the possibility of starting her own computer services business, Jill heard from Arthur Andersen Consulting about a job. The Baltimore office was looking for a person for the computer services unit in their small-business division. Arthur Andersen is a prestigious national accounting firm with a major presence in international markets. They were hiring accountants and nonaccountants to service the tremendous domestic and international growth they had experienced in their consulting business.

Jill was now faced with several alternatives:

1. Attempt to change Don Taylor's thinking and style of management.
2. Quit working for MN and go to work immediately for Arthur Andersen.
3. Quit working for MN and attempt to start her own computer services business.
4. Keep quiet and continue doing the best she can under the circumstances at MN.

Questions for Discussion

1. Which alternative would you choose if you were Jill Bradshaw? Why?
2. What advice would you give Jill if she decided to start her own business? What are her chances for success?
3. Does Jill appear to have the entrepreneurial profile and spirit needed to be successful? Explain.

CASE 3.2
Franchising in the World of Corporate Giants

Union Carbide made a decision to find volunteers inside the firm to work in its intrapreneurial program. This involved establishing teams of volunteers to find new services or new goods to sell. One eager volunteer was Richard Broockman. His intrapreneurial group studied a number of possible markets for specialty chemicals. Someone in the group presented a need for restoring architectural marble. This seemed like a good market for Union Carbide, because the company already supplied industrial cleaning chemicals. However, Union Carbide was a product-driven company; marble care was a service business.

The intrapreneurial group, spurred on by Broockman, came up with an answer for marble care: franchising. The group developed an investment and franchising proposal for the chairman of Union Carbide. The proposal emphasized that if Union Carbide wanted the marble care market, it had to act now. Shortly after the presentation, Broockman was put in charge of Union Carbide Marble Care, Inc. He was instructed to build a national franchise network of marble restoration professionals consistent with Union Carbide's high standards of quality.

So far, 12 people have become franchisees. Each franchisee pays a fee of $20,000, makes a total investment that varies from $57,100 to $80,500, takes two weeks of training, and pays an advertising fee of 2 percent and a royalty of 6 percent.

Fortune 500 firms used to snub franchising as an inefficient way to grow a business. Today Ashland Oil, Prudential Insurance, and British Petroleum have started franchises. Hershey Foods exemplifies earlier reluctance to franchise. Hershey considered franchising a division of Friendly Ice Cream restaurants in the 1980s. The company saw itself then as unable to tolerate the energy and unconventional styles of freewheeling entrepreneurs. Hershey wanted to control from a centralized operation; there was no room for entrepreneurial input. The franchise idea was stopped because it violated the principle of centralized control.

Two firms that traditionally opposed franchising, White Castle System, Inc. (the original two-inch–square hamburger) and Krystal restaurants (a chain with 232 stores in the Southeast), have decided to franchise. For decades White Castle and Krystal opposed the McDonald's franchise model; they claimed it was a fad. Today White Castle is targeting Japan for franchising, and Krystal has just initiated a double-drive-through window franchise opportunity called Krystal Kwik.

British Petroleum (BP) also resisted franchising for years. BP simply supplied its product to licensed dealers and let them market the product any way they wanted to. When the firm wanted a new, hands-on approach with dealers selling their products, franchising was considered too unstructured. However, a new executive convinced BP that franchising doesn't mean no control, no contact, and no close relationships. The franchising method BP adopted has in fact meant more balanced control, increased company-franchisee contact, and a close working relationship.

For an increasing number of American corporations, franchising is becoming a respectable way to grow and invest. The Union Carbide, White Castle, Krystal, and British Petroleum cases are being closely examined by many other interested companies.

Questions for Discussion

1. Why would a manager like Union Carbide's Richard Broockman decide to volunteer for an intrapreneurial program?

2. Why would franchising have an image, or reputation, among some executives as being inefficient and encouraging little control?

3. When you purchase goods and services from franchisees versus a nonfranchised business, do you notice a difference in quality, price, or service? Explain.

BUSINESS PLAN

EVENTS UNLIMITED
Suite 1515
110 West C Street
San Diego, CA 92101
(619) 237-8899
July 5, 19XX

This business plan has been submitted on a confidential basis.

By accepting delivery of this plan, the recipient agrees to return this copy to the company at the address listed above.

Table of Contents

I. SUMMARY

Events Unlimited was formed in July of 19XX in San Diego, California by a highly knowledgeable and experienced team of three businesswomen in response to what they believe to be an attractive business opportunity created by the following conditions:

- The need for a facility equipped to cover the requirements of parties or receptions for large groups of people.
- The present competition (hotels and restaurants) cannot accommodate a large scale event without 18 months lead time.
- Hotels and restaurants require customers to use their catering services, which are substantially more costly.

Note: The concept and original draft of Events Unlimited were written by Janice Dehesh, Colleen Lily, and Victoria Ross.

Source: From the book *The Complete Handbook for the Entrepreneur,* by Gary Brenner, Joel Evan, and Henry Custer, © 1990. Used by permission of the publisher, Prentice Hall, a division of Simon & Schuster, Englewood Cliffs, N.J.

- Currently there are no companies that offer a party facility as well as consultation services.

Events Unlimited proposes to provide a facility where large corporations, small companies, and individuals could hold events, conventions and seminars. Events Unlimited would coordinate the caterer, florist, entertainment, invitations, and so on for the client at substantial savings in time, effort, and money. All aspects of the event would be subcontracted at various price ranges by Events Unlimited.

Events Unlimited's target market will be the companies and corporations of San Diego along with couples planning to wed. Our marketing plan will include advertisements in local papers and business journals. We will also utilize the radio and direct mail. The size of the market we are targeting is increasing with the rapid growth of San Diego. Potential individual clients will be from the middle and upper classes, which compose a high percentage of the households in our serving area. Because of the complexity and lack of information on industry trends at this time, it is difficult to estimate sales volume. Each function, depending on the size of the party, complexity of special requests, and season of the year will command a price directly related to the elements of the party itself. Because we are unique in our service business, we anticipate the market share to range from 6.0 to 6.5 percent in the San Diego area.

Pricing of our service will be reviewed on an individual party basis. If the particular request appears to be very time consuming or difficult, our fees would be based on an hourly basis plus costs. If the job appears to be relatively routine, a flat fee (which includes the subcontractor's fees) would be charged.

We at Events Unlimited believe we have a competitive advantage in that we are the only company in San Diego to offer both a facility and a full service consultation team. We will offer flexibility in pricing and quality currently not offered by our competition. Our clients will be able to select an event plan that fits into their budget; they can also choose to use only our facility.

Because of the varied types of services offered by our firm, gross margin may fluctuate between 20 and 30 percent depending upon the time involved in providing a particular service. Profits will experience a seasonal cycle. During the busiest periods, summer (weddings) and fall (office parties), profits should range between 5 and 10 percent. In the slower periods, profits should range between 3 and 5 percent. Based on the information we have gathered, we are anticipating attaining the breakeven point within 18 months. We project a positive cash flow within 12 months.

II. THE INDUSTRY, THE COMPANY, AND THE SERVICES

The Industry

The present catering and party consultation firms in the San Diego area do not have a business similar to Events Unlimited. Within San Diego County, there are 210 catering firms and 11 party planning firms. However, these firms are not full service consultation firms with a party facility.

The Company

The opportunity for a new party facility and consultation firm was perceived by a group of three businesswomen in July 19XX. The businesswomen collectively have more than 19 years of experience in finance, marketing and general management. After analysis of conditions in the industry, they are convinced there is a viable growth opportunity for a business of this type.

The customers of a business of this nature will be companies in need of a facility to hold company parties, seminars, and meetings. Another potential customer will be couples intending to be wed and in need of a facility to house their reception.

It will be Events Unlimited's philosophy to offer an attractive facility of adequate size to our clients. We will also provide them with a full service consulting team that will coordinate their needs without taking them away from the daily operation of their own businesses.

The Services

The following list represents the various services Events Unlimited will provide along with a facility capable of holding a maximum of 500 people.

Catering service A group of six caterers will be utilized to fill the varying needs of our clients. Each caterer will be in a different price range or specialty of food service. All prices will be contracted for 12 months.

Florists A group of at least three florists will be contracted to cover clients' needs at the florist's cost plus 15 percent. If the client chooses to contract the florists themselves, they would pay as much as 35 percent over cost.

Invitations Events Unlimited will act as distributor for the major invitation printers. This will enable us to sell the invitations to our clients at our cost plus 10 percent instead of the usual 25 percent over cost.

Decorations Utilizing our wholesale license in purchasing decorations and party favors, we can pass on the cost savings to our clients.

Along with these four services, we will negotiate contract pricing with limousine services, photographers, and bakers and pass those savings on to our clients.

Entry and Growth Strategy

In order to gain a foothold in the market place, we need to devote time to research the needs and growth potential of the San Diego market. Our competitive advantage is the full service nature of our firm in the arrangement of a party including the availability of a fully functional facility. The facility will provide us with the lure we require to entice clients to use our services. Our research of hotels, convention halls, and country clubs indicates that these facilities could be employed but that restrictions were often so severe that the planned party would exceed reasonable costs.

Advertising and promotional efforts will be concentrated in those areas that management experience has demonstrated to be the most effective. The use of local magazines and newspapers will tap the market we desire.

As is true of most new businesses, we expect growth during the first year to be slow. However, as more people become aware of our services through word of mouth and advertisement, we expect the sales volume to triple within five years.

III. THE MANAGEMENT TEAM

The following table lists the members of the management team of Events Unlimited and the responsibility of each member as well as employment prior to organization.

Team Members	Experience
V. L. Ross, Operations	Purchasing supervisor M/A COM
J. A. Dehesh, Marketing	Executive secretary M/A COM
C. F. Lily, Finance	Accountant Gabele & Oman, CPAs

Qualifications

Victoria L. Ross—Operations   Ms. Ross is currently enrolled at Chapman College in the undergraduate program seeking her degree in business administration. Her experience includes eight years of increasing responsibilities in purchasing management for a company generating $50 million in orders in the latest fiscal year. During her eight years as M/A COM, Ms. Ross has coordinated the day-to-day operations of a purchasing staff of 15 persons and currently has a staff of five buyers and two clerks. Along with her personnel management experience, she has gained experience in large dollar negotiations. Prior to working for M/A COM, Ms. Ross had two years experience working for a catering service and two years experience with a greeting card company handling orders for invitations and announcements.

Janice A. Dehesh—Marketing   Ms. Dehesh is presently attending Chapman College completing her degree in business administration. She has a vocational degree in sales, marketing, and management. Her experience includes eight years of management and administrative responsibilities. In 1979 she managed a boutique in which she supervised sales personnel and took care of all marketing and advertising, including newspaper layout, radio jingles, and so on. In recent years, Ms. Dehesh has broadened her experience to include bookkeeping, budget control, payroll, contract negotiations, and customer contact. She has also prepared major presentation materials for potential customers.

Colleen F. Lily—Finance   Ms. Lily is currently enrolled at Chapman College seeking her degree in accounting. Her initial experience was with Professional Copying, Inc. as an accountant and office administrator, where she implemented a new system in their accounting department. She was in charge of the entire financial operation as well as initiating administrative policies and procedures. In 1980, she joined the accounting firm of Gabele & Oman as an accountant. Her expertise with this firm includes preparation of financial statements and tax returns as well as financial planning for a variety of clientele. While with Gabele & Oman, Ms. Lily has been placed in charge of their information systems department and has supervised the personnel in this department.

IV. MARKET RESEARCH AND ANALYSIS

Customers

Events Unlimited's potential customer base is large and diverse. The following list represents the major groups we are targeting for our marketing plan.

Corporations   San Diego has experienced significant growth in the area of business, especially in the electronics field. The Sorrento Valley and the Golden Triangle areas are predicted to be the next Silicon Valley. Mission Valley continues to attract the professional service industry. The North Park area has several professional and production businesses. Our corporate clients will be our most important clients. Their interest in our services should be piqued by the availability of our facility for seminars, meetings, banquets, and parties. They will also appreciate our full range of consultation services. We are equipped to cater to any type of corporate event. It has been related to us that facilities currently equipped to handle the needs of corporate clients are limited. Events must be booked months in advance to accommodate all the special needs of an event. The availability of our facility within the first two years of operation will be very attractive to these clients. Our full service consulting team will be a must for most of our corporate clients. Most companies do not have a person designated solely for party consultation and therefore must take employees away from their designated tasks to coordinate their events. We would take care of all aspects of the event and significantly reduce the time requirements of corporate employees. All preliminary footwork would be handled by our staff and would require only final decisions from the corporate liaison.

Future brides and grooms   The needs of couples planning to be married vary with their family traditions, ethnic backgrounds, religious beliefs, and most importantly, their budgets. Events Unlimited will help them coordinate all the aspects of their wedding reception. We will present them with a comprehensive plan and price forecast for all the services they will require. They will then be able to select the plan that best serves their needs and budgets. We will also lease the facility to them at a flat rate and allow them to do their own preparation. The number of attractive facilities available for this type of function is limited and therefore difficult to book. Our availability and flexibility in pricing will be extremely attractive to these potential clients. As each couple comes in to book a reception with us, we will give them a presentation of our services and show them how we can save them time and money in coordinating their reception.

Charitable and political fund raisers   There are several political and charitable fundraisers in San Diego each year. A few of these are Las Patronas "Jewel Ball," La Jolla Museum of Contemporary Art "Night in Monte Carlo," and the Combo Gala. The main requirement for events of this type is a well-organized staff to attend to all the various aspects of the event. Events Unlimited is a professional and well-organized consulting firm that can handle any type of event. We maintain a selection of party themes complete with ideas for decorations, costumes, fireworks, and ice sculptures.

Quinceneras   Because of the large number of Hispanics in the San Diego area, there are hundreds of *quinceneras* each year. The *quinceneras* is an elaborate party given to celebrate the 15th birthday of a Mexican or Spanish girl. These parties require the same planning as a wedding reception. They are almost always formal. As with our other prospective clients, these parties would require expert coordination of all aspects of the event. We at Events Unlimited are capable of organizing an event of this scope.

Parties in general   Our remaining client base will require various types of parties, such as Bat and Bar Mitzvahs, birthdays, retirement, and over-the-hill, and 25th and 50th wedding anniversaries. We are expertly equipped to handle any theme or setting required for these types of parties. With our expert guidance, our clients' parties will not only be an event, they will be a memorable experience.

Market Size

The market size for the city of San Diego is estimated to be 10,000 parties per year. This figure represents a combination of both consultation engagements and facility rentals. This market is estimated to increase by 10 percent per year. Of this market, one-third is estimated to be party consultation while two-thirds is estimated to be facility rental. Since a consultation is estimated to be 15 hours at $30 per hour, the total consultation market appears to be approximately $1,500,000 per year. The facility market is estimated at the rate of $1,300 per rental or approximately $3,000,000 per year.

The sources of this data were newspapers, caterers, party consultants, and business consultants. The numbers above represent a consensus of all data received.

Competition

Our competition is limited. No one gives the complete service we provide. Hotels, restaurants, and caterers only provide part of the service we offer. We are the only company that will provide every party detail at our location. Following is a list of our competitors.

- Garden Creations of San Diego
- Conventions in San Diego, Inc.
- ESP (Executive Services Provided)
- Exclusive Coordinators of La Jolla, CA

- JRW Executive Service of Poway, CA
- Carole L. Mullen, On-Site coordinator of Solana Beach, CA
- San Diego in Style
- Host San Diego, Inc.
- Professional Meetings Unlimited of La Jolla, CA

This data was compiled from "Catering to You," a guide to entertaining in San Diego.

Compilation of our competitors' strengths is a difficult task since our business does not directly compete with any of these organizations. Party consultants provide the closest comparison to our firm. Their competitive advantage lies in the fact that they are established in San Diego. In the case of hotels and restaurants, we perceive their strength to be their visibility. The weaknesses that are consistent to all of our competitors are their lack of flexibility, their pricing, and failure to provide all the services required to put on a party. Pricing at hotels and restaurants for food, which is generally handled by an outside caterer, is at least $2 a head higher than we would charge. Facilities provided by these sources are limited in their configuration flexibility. We at Events Unlimited will overcome these strengths and take advantage of these weaknesses as follows: We plan to do a widespread advertising campaign including ads in *San Diego* magazine and through the radio media. In the area of flexibility, our primary philosophy is, and will continue to be, that the client's needs are our first priority. Further, our facility will be designed to provide maximum flexibility to conform with client requirements. We at Events Unlimited believe that these strategies will ensure a strong client base in a matter of months.

Events Unlimited is capable of handling in a professional manner every aspect of any type of social gathering. We have numerous creative ideas that will make our parties an event. M/A-COM Government Systems and Telecommunication Divisions have committed to a 20-plus party contract with Events Unlimited during the first year. This contract was committed based on the excellent performances of past employees, Janice Dehesh and Victoria Ross. In addition to this contract, contracts from General Instrument, Comstream, and Qualcom are out for final signature. These contracts will amount to another eight parties minimum. See attachments A and B for market data on the consulting and facilities phases of the business.

Ongoing Market Evaluation

To continue the process of ongoing evaluation of our target markets, Events Unlimited will mail questionnaires to previous customers asking pertinent questions regarding future customer needs. This questionnaire will serve both as a marketing tool and a quality control tool. In addition, we will send questionnaires and flyers to all corporations in the San Diego area inquiring as to services they might be interested in using. A sample questionnaire follows.

Questionnaire Number 1—The Business Survey
1. How many parties does your company sponsor per year?
2. What services do you require to put on a party?
3. Do you have a company party consultant?

4. If not, who coordinates your parties, meetings, etc.?

5. If you were to engage a professional party consultant, what would your expectations be?

6. Have you engaged a professional party consultant in the past? (If the answer is no, please skip to question 12.)

7. If you answered yes to question 6, was the service helpful?

8. If the service was inadequate, what were the major drawbacks?

9. Was the service charged at an hourly rate or a flat rate?

10. Do you feel the service was priced fairly?

11. Please circle the hourly rate:

$ 0–20

    21–40

    41–60

    61–80

    81 or higher

12. What service or services would encourage you to engage an event consultant?

Questionnaire Number 2—Client Survey

1. Were you satisfied with services provided by Events Unlimited?

2. If you were satisfied with our service, what were the best features?

3. What services could be improved?

4. If you were dissatisfied with any of our services, what improvements would you make?

5. Was our price reasonable?

6. Please add any additional comments you may have, or features you would like to see added.

V. MARKETING PLAN

Overall Market Strategy

The general marketing philosophy and strategy of Events Unlimited are to create excitingly original and unique events on or off site. Events Unlimited's target market is companies and corporations in San Diego County as well as couples preparing to wed. In the months after we open, we will extend that market to include charitable and political fund raisers, *quinceneras,* Bar and Bat Mitzvahs, birthdays, retirement and over-the-hill parties, and anniversary parties.

To reach our potential corporate clients, we will contact and solicit secretaries and human resource personnel who are normally responsible for planning and organizing corporate functions. Future brides will be contacted through newspaper advertisements and through bridal salons. Other potential clientele will be reached through appropriate ethnic and community newspapers. The objective of this advertising would be to make various ethnic groups such as Hispanics and Chinese Americans aware of our expertise in preparing for their special holidays.

Our total service concept will be emphasized in the generation of sales. Our flexible pricing, unique event themes, and captive facility will be extremely attractive to our potential clients. [Attachments would typically be indicated to show estimated total market and estimated market share of Events Unlimited.]

Events Unlimited will start as a regional business with our first facility located in the Mission Valley area, which we believe to be centrally located to our market area. Future growth includes sites in the Golden Triangle area and La Jolla.

Pricing

The pricing policy for services provided by Events Unlimited will of necessity be very flexible. We will establish standard rates for each service based on the fees and rates charged by competitors. Our consulting fees will be based on $30 per hour, which is slightly under market for comparable services. Events Unlimited predicts a gross margin of 20 to 30 percent which may fluctuate based on competitive factors. Gross margins on subcontracted caterer services will be closer to 20 percent, while margins on services such as invitations, flowers and decorations will be closer to 30 percent.

We project that our service will be accepted by consumers because we are very price competitive and provide a mix of unique services that no single competitor offers. Our sales ability will allow us to expand the extras we can sell to clients who wish to throw the truly unique party.

Sales Tactics

For the first year, the owners of Events Unlimited will be the sales force. With our knowledge and experience, we are also capable of managing the business aspects of Events Unlimited. After the initial one-year start-up period, we foresee hiring additional staff, which will include sales help, receptionist, and secretary.

Advertising and Promotion

Our advertising cost will be a significant part of our company's expenses and therefore must be monitored carefully. We feel that employment of an advertising agency will lead to the most efficient use of these funds. The agency will be responsible for establishing an advertising program, layout of business cards, brochures, and flyers, and design of the company logo. Its expertise will enable Events Unlimited to present a more professional and original image.

Newspapers will be the main advertising media. The use of community and ethnic newspapers will allow us to target our advertising dollars. We also anticipate the use of direct mailings from appropriate address lists targeting San Diego corporations of appropriate size. Initial phase advertising costs are estimated to be approximately $5,000.

VI. FINANCIAL DATA

Profit and Loss Forecasts   [Attachments would typically be included.]

Assumptions   Events Unlimited will require a deposit equal to 50 percent of the estimated job at contract signing with the balance due and payable on the day of the event. We do not foresee any bad debt loss since no terms will be extended beyond event date. This will guarantee cash flow for the payment of our vendors within a 10-day period.

Risks and sensitivity   We have taken into consideration seasonal trends and forecasted accordingly. By promoting unique nonholiday events, we have tried to reduce seasonal loss of revenue and smooth cash flows during nonseasonal periods.

Pro Forma Cash Flow Analysis   [Attachments would typically be included.]

Assumptions   As discussed previously all events and rental of facilities will be paid in full by the day of the event. Terms of payments to our vendors will be from day of event (caterers) to 30 days (stationers and florists). Wage increases will occur annually at approximately 10 percent per annum on employee's anniversary date.

Rent, insurance, and miscellaneous expense increases have been projected and accounted for in the three years of pro formas. Advertising will increase as a function of sales due to the importance of expanding our customer base.

Because of the expansion of projected sales, three party consultants and one full-time secretary will be hired by the end of the first year. Capital expenditures include a computer and appropriate software to provide bookkeeping capability. In the third year, we have planned a $15,000 enhancement to our facility to keep current clients and lure new clients.

Cash flow sensitivity   As projected, after the partners' initial investment for the business start-up, we should not need to borrow. Any other equipment or furniture for events requested or needed will be rented and in turn included in our contract to the client. Any repairs to facilities are included in our lease agreement and annual cost-of-living increases have been included in our pro formas.

Pro Forma Balance Sheets

With the initial capitalization contributed by each partner, Events Unlimited is able to start business without financing from a lending institution. In order to start business, Events Unlimited needs cash for advertising and promotional material, security deposit for rental of facility, and purchase of kitchen equipment and furnishings. Until year four, when expansion to a larger and more elegant facility is planned, we see no need for applying for a loan. [Attachment typically would be included.]

Breakeven Chart

Attachment [typically included] indicates that, based on our consulting service, we will reach breakeven in June of the first year. We forecast that we will reach breakeven for the rental of our facility by April 19XX.

If sales projections should fall short during the first nine months, and we do not reach our breakeven point, Events Unlimited will still be in a position to operate several months after this point. It is of the utmost importance that we continue to advertise our service and facility until Events Unlimited becomes well established in the market place.

Cost Control

Events Unlimited will use a peg board system to record cash receipts and disbursements on a daily basis. This information will be compiled at the end of each month for preparation of financial statements. Each month these financial statements will be reviewed and action taken to adjust costs or our budget. If we find that we are continually over budget, the first step will be to reevaluate our markup on contract services and our consulting fees. This will not cause a problem in the marketplace because our fees are somewhat below market at this point.

Since it is imperative that all outside services be charged to a particular contract, an accounts payable journal with ledger card for each contract will be used. Upon receipt of an invoice, quotation, or contract, the appropriate information will be matched with the correct party contract so as to maintain control of specific costs. Because she has 12 years of accounting experience, Colleen Lily will be responsible for controlling the finances of Events Unlimited.

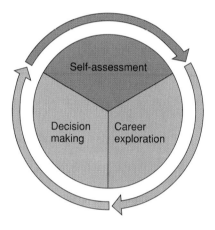

Careers in BUSINESS

CAREER CHOICES

Choose a job you love and you will
never have to work a day in your life.
Confucius

Trying to choose a career can appear to be an overwhelming task.
The number of career options is
staggering. Yet deciding on a career may be the most important
decision in your life. Your career
choice will affect your satisfaction
with life. It will have a significant
impact on who your friends are,
how much money you make,
where you live, and how much leisure time you have.

Many people simply fall into a
career and let things happen by
chance. They may wait for something to come along that sounds
interesting and fun. Others may
follow the advice of parents,
friends, or teachers. But some people take charge of their future and
actively plan for a career. The
odds of finding satisfying and challenging work are greatly increased
when you commit your time and
energy to planning for your career
instead of leaving things to chance.

CAREER PLANNING

Career planning is an ongoing process, one that occurs throughout
your working life. It involves
knowing what is important to you
and actually defining your interests
and skills. It involves exploring
and collecting information about a
wide range of opportunities. And it
includes evaluating options and
making informed decisions. Career
planning allows you control over
your working life.

Career Planning

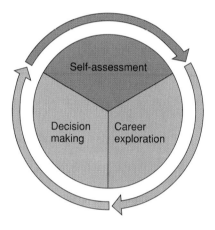

Self-Awareness

Before you can decide on a career,
you need to understand yourself
and what is important to you. You
want a career that will contribute
to your personal happiness, not
detract from it. To make a sound
career decision, you need to appreciate what you are good at, what
excites you, and what you find rewarding. Gaining an understanding
of your values, interests, and skills
will help you decide on a career
that is right for you.

Some people find taking a vocational test helpful in assessing their
interests or aptitudes. Most colleges have a center where they administer tests such as the Strong-
Campbell Interest Inventory or the
Myers-Briggs personality test.

Another helpful tool is working
through the self-assessment exercises found in career books and
magazines. An excellent resource

What Some Jobs Pay

	Accountant	Programmer	Secretary	Financial Analyst	Credit Representative
New England					
Entry	$22,800	$28,300	$17,800	$28,300	$22,600
Midlevel	36,300	43,400	19,800	44,300	25,500
Senior	55,700	58,100	22,300	57,300	37,000
South Central					
Entry	21,700	28,000	17,200	27,100	22,700
Midlevel	34,300	44,300	23,000	39,700	29,700
Senior	54,700	67,400	29,300	59,200	32,500
Mountain					
Entry	20,700	28,800	14,100	26,100	24,600
Midlevel	35,100	44,700	19,900	40,100	29,300
Senior	50,800	na	23,500	na	33,400
Pacific					
Entry	26,700	32,400	19,500	29,100	20,000
Midlevel	36,500	47,700	23,100	42,700	26,300
Senior	51,900	62,000	26,100	56,300	31,300

Myers-Briggs: Sample Questions

Is it harder for you to adapt to:
  A. Routine
  B. Constant change

If a teacher, would you rather teach:
  A. Courses involving theory
  B. Fact courses

Are you naturally:
  A. Rather quiet and reserved in company
  B. A good "mixer"

for self-assessment exercises is "What Color Is Your Parachute?" by Richard Bolles. Talking to parents, friends, and career advisers can also help you more clearly define your preferences and talents.

Career Exploration

Career exploration involves collecting information about the different types of work opportunities and career fields. It means sorting through alternatives and narrowing down the scope to work options that relate to your own interests and aptitudes. It is a process of identification and elimination.

The two best sources of information about careers are publications and people. The library, with hundreds of books on many different career fields, is a good place to start. The U.S. government publishes literature describing different occupations and providing the current outlook for different fields. The *Occupational Outlook Handbook* is an especially useful publication; it contains job descriptions and describes the qualifications and skills necessary for the job. A college placement office can also be

Sample Work Values

Travel	Status	Authority
Independence	Wealth	Social good
Variety	Security	Flexibility

very helpful in exploring career options. It maintains a complete library with books, directories, and brochures describing careers and job opportunities.

Talking with people who have worked in a field can also give you a good idea about what it is like to work in that field. Your friends, teachers, and relatives who have had different work experiences can be a valuable source of career information. Most people enjoy talking about their careers and work experiences. You should consult as many as possible.

Decision Making

In the end, planning for a career means making decisions. Once you thoroughly understand yourself and the available options, you can make an informed decision and establish a career goal. As with all decisions, career decision making requires information. By being well informed, you will improve the quality of your decisions.

Decision making is a skill that can be developed. Following a simple model can be helpful.

1. Clearly define the problem.
2. Determine the decision criteria.
3. Develop alternatives.
4. Evaluate each alternative.
5. Make a decision.

Sample Skill Types

People	Data	Things
Managing	Calculating	Operating
Communicating	Analyzing	Repairing
Coaching	Interpreting	Loading
Advising	Computing	Assembling
Negotiating	Classifying	Adjusting

Additional Resources for Career Exploration

Career Book, by Joyce Lain Kennedy and Darryl Laramore. Lincolnwood, Ill.: VGM Career Horizons, 1990.

Careers Encyclopedia, Lincolnwood, Ill.: VGM Career Horizons, 1989.

Occupational Outlook Handbook, by U.S. Department of Labor, Bureau of Labor Statistics. Washington, D.C.: Government Printing Office, annual.

Occupational Outlook Quarterly, by U.S. Department of Labor, Bureau of Labor Statistics. Washington, D.C.: Government Printing Office, quarterly.

What Color Is Your Parachute? by Richard Bolles. Berkeley, Calif.: Ten Speed Press, 1990.

Your career decision will be easier if you realize it does not have to mean deciding on a career for the rest of your life. Most people have several occupations over a lifetime. Changing careers does not mean you have made a bad decision. Values and interests may change; after a while, you might want to seek a new field of work. Today, as people look for more balance between personal life and work, career changes are more frequent than ever before.

WORLD OF WORK

Our free enterprise system provides, for millions of people, employment options in large corporations, government, and thousands of privately owned businesses. Sometimes trying to understand all of those options can be confusing. Understanding the different ways the world of work can be arranged is often helpful. One way to view the work world is to divide it into three major sectors: the private, or business, sector; the not-for-profit sector; and the public, or government, sector. Career choices may also be defined by industry or functional area.

Public Sector

The public sector includes opportunities in national, state, and local government. Government employs over 16 million people in various agencies. The public sector tends to be characterized by very structured work environments and promotion procedures; relatively low employee turnover, and a high degree of job security.

Sample Government Services (state and local)

Criminal justice
Education programs
Fire protection
Highway operations
Law enforcement
Parks and recreation
Prison operations
Roads and streets
Sanitation
Social welfare
Social work
Tax assessment
Tax collection
Transportation systems
Urban planning

Not-for-Profit Sector

The not-for-profit sector includes organizations that do not exist to make a profit for the owners. Nonprofit organizations return any earnings back into the organization for the benefit of their members or the public they serve. Job possibilities with these organizations are not numerous, and compensation tends to be relatively low.

Nonprofit Employers

Art museums
Consumer unions
Convention centers
Foundations
Hospitals
Industry trade groups
Labor organizations
Special-interest groups
Symphony orchestras
Trusts

Private Sector

The private sector consists of all businesses that operate for a profit. This sector offers the greatest number of job opportunities. Of the total U.S. employment of roughly 114 million, about 80 percent is within the private sector. Most people will probably work in the private sector at some point in their career. Generally speaking, it provides the opportunities for the greatest financial rewards. Businesses that are profitable are able to offer employees higher compensation than other types of organizations.

Industry Groups

Another way of categorizing career choices is by industry. Businesses

Sample Industries

Manufacturing

Aerospace	Metals
Automotive	Pharmaceuticals
Chemical	Oil
Construction	Textiles
Food and beverage	Tires
Machinery	

Service

Accounting	Entertainment
Advertising	Insurance
Banking	Real estate
Communications	Retailing
Computer	Utilities
Consulting	

Service Industries Keep Hiring

Number of jobs (in millions) in —

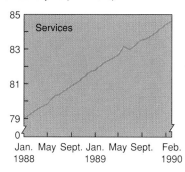

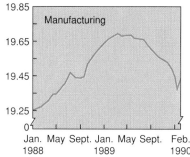

Source: "Economic Outlook," *U.S. News & World Report,* March 26, 1990, p. 51.

in the private sector may be viewed as either goods-producing (manufacturing) or service-producing organizations. In the United States today, most job opportunities are in service rather than manufacturing.

The U.S. Department of Labor classifies these two major groups further into major industry divisions based on the type of product or service. Within each industry are hundreds of large and small employers; within each organization, many different types of jobs exist.

Functional Areas

Finally, another way of organizing career choices is by functional area. All businesses—regardless of the industry they are in or whether they are in the private, not-for-

CAREER PROFILE: Anne Sweeney

ANNE SWEENEY

Age: 47
Undergraduate degree: Rosemont College, Rosemont, Pennsylvania
Major: English
First career: Flight attendant
Current career: Public relations consultant

When Anne Sweeney graduated from Pennsylvania's Rosemont College in 1964, she thought a career as a Pan Am stewardess (the term *flight attendant* hadn't been coined yet) sounded swell. Eleven years later, she had changed her mind. "Yes, I saw all the garden spots of the world. But I walked every step of the way—with a coffeepot in each hand."

Sweeney made her career change in stages, starting with a job switch within her own company. First she broke into management as a flight-service supervisor. Then she responded to an internal job search and became editor of the airline's employee newspaper. That job was in the public relations department, and she picked up a lot of knowledge about the field during her two years there. When her position was eliminated in a 1981 downsizing, Inter-Continental Hotels (which was affiliated with Pan Am at the time) promptly snapped her up as a manager for its own public relations department.

From there she went to a midtown-Manhattan publicity firm specializing in hotel and travel accounts. Finally, in early 1989, she resigned to launch her own public relations (PR) business. Handling travel industry accounts in the United States and abroad, Sweeney quadrupled her billings in the second year.

Source: Adapted from Anita Gates, "How to Come In from the Cold," *Working Woman,* July 1990, pp. 75–78.

Functional Areas

Marketing	Manufacturing	Finance	Administration
Sales	Purchasing	Accounting	Legal
Advertising	Distribution	Budgeting	Public Relations
Market research	Production	Info Systems	Personnel
	Engineering		

profit, or public sector—perform certain tasks. These tasks can then be organized by function, the work to be accomplished. Hundreds of

people or only one person may be employed in a functional area, depending on the size of the organization.

SMALL–BUSINESS OWNERSHIP

If you have ever dreamed of owning your own business, you are not alone. Thousands of new business ventures are started each year, and the trend toward entrepreneurship continues to grow. In fact, the 1990s have been labeled the decade of the entrepreneur. Some observers have predicted that half of all new jobs will be with businesses employing fewer than 100 employees. That could mean as many as 8 million new jobs with small businesses by the year 2000. The spirit of entrepreneurship is widespread. Yet starting a business is far from easy. It requires talent and hard work.

Owner-Manager

Most small businesses start with an owner who does it all. Usually the owner is the person who first conceived the idea for the business and does the planning, raises the capital, keeps the accounting records, does the purchasing and selling, and produces the good or service. If the business succeeds and grows, then the owner hires employees and manages the staff.

Running a small business requires knowledge and experience. Gaining business experience by working for another company is extremely useful before starting on your own. Many successful entrepreneurs worked in large corporations before they launched their own businesses.

To be successful, a small-business owner not only needs knowledge and experience but also should possess certain personality traits. Running your own business requires perseverance, the ability

126

CAREER PROFILE: Joanne Marlowe

Courtesy Double Sharp Garments, Inc.

JOANNE MARLOWE

Age: 23
Hometown: Chicago, Illinois
Business concept: Beach towels with weights in the corners so they won't flip in the wind
Financing: $750 of her own money
Source of idea: A gust of wind blew her towel and the sand underneath it all over her freshly oiled body
Critical hurdle: Maintaining quality control on a product she never handles
Expected sales: $4.5 million year one; $7 million–$8 million year two

Requirements: Small-Business Ownership

Personal skills	Education
High energy	Bachelor's degree
Persistence	Broad understanding
Self-confidence	of business
Initiative	Work experience
Risk-taking	Knowledge of a
	business area

to live with uncertainty and risk, and stamina. Many people think that having your own small business means having more free time. But the reverse is true. The owner-manager of a small business works twice as hard and puts in far more hours than do employees who work for others. The small-business owner also has all of the worries and responsibilities that go with trying to meet a payroll, pay suppliers, and pay the rent.

Arranging for financial backing to start or expand a small business is an important and difficult part of small-business ownership. Because the failure rate for new businesses is high, banks are often reluctant to lend money to entrepreneurs.

Rewards

While starting and running a small business takes effort, the rewards can be great. For many people, just being their own boss and having the freedom and flexibility to run things their own way is sufficient reward. For others, starting

In 10 years of self-employment, Joanne Marlowe has survived embezzlement, near bankruptcy, and life as a Chicago carriage driver. She has founded separate companies that made custom dresses, retailed clothes, and produced and telemarketed garments. Now she makes weighted beach towels and is expecting $4.5 million in towel sales.

Things haven't been easy. Six months after starting Double Sharp Garments, theft cost her about $450,000 in lost sales. She finally had to close down the plant and was seriously considering bankruptcy. An afternoon at the beach turned things around.

"I had just spent a lot of time putting on suntan oil. Just as I stretched out, a gust of wind picked up the towel and covered me in sand." So, instead of relaxing at the beach, she spent the day coming up with prototypes for a weighted beach towel. She developed the product within five weeks and had it to market within eight weeks.

"Developing the towel was extraordinarily easy for me. I had started out in fashion. I had learned how the larger retailers function, how the markets function, how the seasons sell—all with a much more difficult product.

"I took an odd job to pay the bills—driving a carriage for three months in downtown Chicago. I'd get up at 5:30 A.M., do all my office work, work with the couple of employees I kept on staff from 9 until about 3, then run downtown, clean my horse, get on the street by 6 P.M., and be out until 1 in the morning. I was sleeping about three hours a day from July until October.

"I've kept it very small this time. I have only two assistants and me. I work with five manufacturers, and all the towels are drop-shipped by the printer I'm working with without the overhead, which has been the key for getting this thing back together."

Source: Adapted from Leslie Brokaw, Jay Finegan, and Joshua Hyatt, "The Yearn for Start-Ups," *Inc.*, November 1989, pp. 66–67.

Entrepreneur: A high-rolling risk-taker who would rather be a spectacular failure than a dismal success.
Jim Fisk and Robert Barron

---

their own business may be the most promising way to make a great deal of money. Fortunes can be made by increasing profits over the long term and then either selling stock in the company or selling the company to another buyer.

Franchises

Another option for people interested in small-business ownership is investing in a franchise. Franchising can minimize the risk for a new business owner in several ways. First, people experienced in the business provide training and assistance. Instead of having to acquire business experience through years of work or by trial and error, the franchisee can be guided by the parent company. It provides assistance in setting up the business, choosing a location, estimating potential sales, and designing market strategies. Also, the franchisee does not have to develop a new product or conduct market studies. Instead the franchise offers a nationally known name and tested product. Savings can also be realized by getting supplies at lower cost through the volume buying power of the nationwide franchise. Some franchisors help arrange financing as well. With parent-company support, franchises often appeal more to bankers than do new start-ups; also, bankers know the success rate is higher for franchises than for independently owned small businesses.

Leading Franchises

Subway
McDonald's
Jani-King
Little Caesar's Pizza
Hardee's
Chem-Dry Carpet Cleaning
Arby's Inc.
Electronic Realty Associates (ERA)
Kentucky Fried Chicken
Jazzercise Inc.

Source: "The Top 10 Franchises for 1991," *Entrepreneur*, April 1991, p. 113.

The franchise option is not totally risk-free. Franchisees do not always get the expected training, guidance, and support. The Federal Trade Commission and some state laws require franchisors to provide prospective investors with a complete listing of what is involved in ownership of the franchise. Always check with the Better Business Bureau, the Small Business Administration, and an attorney before signing any agreement or paying a franchise fee.

Additional Small-Business Resources

National Association of Small Business Investment Companies
1156 Fifteenth Street, N.W.
Washington, D.C. 20005

U.S. Small Business Administration
1441 L Street, N.W.
Washington, D.C. 20416

International Franchise Association
1025 Connecticut Avenue, N.W.
Washington, D.C. 20036

PART TWO

THE ENVIRONMENT FOR BUSINESS

CHAPTER FOUR

SOCIAL RESPONSIBILITY AND BUSINESS ETHICS

LEARNING OBJECTIVES

1. To explain the meaning and importance of social responsibility.

2. To trace the evolution of the consumer movement and identify the rights of consumers.

3. To outline the responsibilities business firms have to employees.

4. To describe the impact of business decisions on the environment.

5. To explain the responsibility of firms to their investors.

6. To identify ways in which firms can advance social responsibility.

7. To list and describe factors influencing business ethics.

Until March 24, 1989, Prince William Sound represented Alaska at its finest—beautiful and unspoiled. But early that day, the oil tanker *Exxon Valdez* ran aground on a reef. It spilled nearly 11 million gallons of oil, the largest spill ever in North America. Within a week, the oily tide covered more

with barrier booms, which restrict oil from spreading (Alyeska's state-approved emergency containment plan requires that a spill be encircled within five hours). The Alyeska boom-deployment barge was docked for repairs. The required 15-member emergency crew was not on hand and took hours to

Environmentalists and area fishermen had predicted an oil spill there. Three tankers a day pass through the narrow waterway in Prince William Sound, with its hidden reefs, floating ice, and fast currents. In 1973, when the U.S. Senate approved the seaway oil route, many people argued against it—and the use of fragile oil tankers—favoring the construction of a pipeline through Canada to deliver oil directly to the Midwest. They believed the pipeline would have been safer and less expensive, although it would have taken longer to become operative. Oil firms said they needed the sea route, particularly to ship oil to Japan. They claimed state-of-the-art technology would prevent spills and enable them to clean up any spill quickly.

J. Schultz/Sipa

than 1,300 square miles. Its massive toll on wildlife included more than 36,000 birds (151 bald eagles), over 1,000 sea otters, unknown numbers of harbor seals and sea lions, and perhaps some killer whales. Experts say it will be years, perhaps generations, before the true effects of the oil spill can be assessed.

Exxon and the Alyeska Pipeline Service Co., the industry group operating the Alaskan pipeline, were soundly criticized for how they handled the spill in the critical first hours. Exxon took more than 35 hours to surround the tanker

assemble. (Until 1981, Alyeska had a round-the-clock emergency crew on location, but the team was disbanded to cut costs, with approval of Alaskan officials. When the city of Valdez twice offered to build and pay for a backup emergency spill system, the oil companies said that was unnecessary and a waste of taxpayer money.) Not until a full week after the spill did Exxon chairman Lawrence Raul make his first public statement, taking responsibility for the spill but blaming the U.S. Coast Guard and Alaskan officials for delaying cleanup efforts.

In the summer after the spill, Exxon employed more than 11,000 people and spent $2 billion to clean up the oil. The next summer Exxon returned for further cleanup efforts. More than 150 civil lawsuits were filed in state and federal courts on behalf of commercial fishermen, tour operators, kelp harvesters, and others who earn their living from Prince William Sound. On February 27, 1990, Exxon became the first company to be charged with criminal felony violations of two maritime safety and antipollution rules. The indictment is the government's most severe action ever in a pollution case. In May 1991, the state of Alaska rejected Exxon's offer of a $1 billion settlement, setting the stage for lengthy court battles in what was the nation's worst oil spill.[1]

The *Exxon Valdez* oil spill illustrates the sensitive balance between business and society. Our society expects firms to provide quality goods and services when they are needed and where they are needed, at acceptable prices. But we also expect business firms to do so in a manner that considers the good of society. Sometimes firms do not meet all of society's expectations, as was the case with Exxon's oil spill in Prince William Sound.

In this chapter, we discuss the concepts of social responsibility and business ethics. First we examine the meaning and importance of social responsibility. Next we describe the responsibility of business firms to customers, employees, investors, and the environment. We explore ways in which firms can advance social responsibility. Finally we examine business ethics, the factors that influence ethics, and ways to encourage ethical behavior.

SOCIAL RESPONSIBILITY

Business firms conduct activities to produce goods and services and to generate profits. These activities greatly affect our society. **Social responsibility** is the awareness that business activities have an impact on society, and the consideration of that impact by firms in decision making. Besides emphasizing profits, firms concerned with social responsibility voluntarily engage in activities that benefit society. Many, for instance, take an active role in rebuilding our public education system.[2] A socially responsible firm makes deliberate, regular efforts to increase its positive impact on society while reducing its negative impact.

Social Responsibility
The awareness that business activities have an impact on society, and the consideration of that impact by firms in decision making.

Jim Robinson, CEO of American Express, practices social responsibility by teaching a class at Chicago's Jobs for Youth Learning Center.

John S. Abbott

FIGURE 4.1

**Social Responsibility
Concerns of Business**

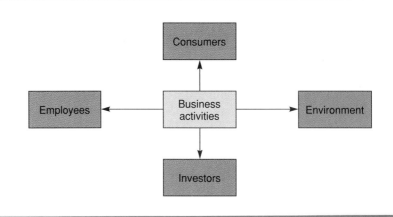

Today many firms practice social responsibility in various ways and to varying degrees. Newman's Own, Inc., a food company founded by actor Paul Newman, donates all profits to charities around the United States. The firm, which sells salad dressing, spaghetti sauce, popcorn, and lemonade, has donated more than $26 million since 1982.[3] Working Assets Money Fund offers investors a chance to invest in a mutual fund according to their beliefs; it screens companies and excludes any with a history of environmental or discrimination violations, military contracts, South African connections, or involvement in nuclear power plants. J. C. Penney sponsors awards for outstanding community volunteers in many areas where its retail stores are located. McDonald's has switched from disposable to reusable containers for delivering supplies to restaurants, reduced some packaging, and started using recycled paper for Happy Meal boxes, napkins, and paper towels.[4] The fast-food giant also stopped using cups and containers made of polystyrene, which is not biodegradable.

Practicing social responsibility costs money. But, as the *Exxon Valdez* oil spill demonstrates, failing to emphasize social responsibility also has its costs—whether in fines, increased regulation, negative publicity, public disfavor, or loss of customers. Consumers, special interest groups, and the general public are aware of business's impact on society and expect firms to do more than try to make profits. Most managers today regard social responsibility as a necessary part of doing business.

Social responsibility raises many challenging questions for business firms. To whom are we responsible? How far should we go to satisfy our customers and achieve organizational objectives? Will our decisions affect any segments of society that we have not considered? Decision makers in every type and size of firm must address many such questions, which rarely have simple answers. Business activities have an impact on consumers, employees, the environment, and those investing in the firm, as Figure 4.1 shows. Socially responsible firms weigh the consequences of their decisions on these different concerns. To understand how firms try to achieve an acceptable balance, let's look more closely at each of these concerns.

RESPONSIBILITY TO CONSUMERS

When you make a purchase, you cast a vote for a product and indicate your approval of the product and the company providing it. If you are satisfied with the product, you will buy and use it again and maybe recommend it to your friends.

Firms trying to succeed provide products that satisfy the needs of their customers, since dissatisfied customers eventually take their business elsewhere. But a company also needs to consider how customers view the firm itself. Increasingly customers are looking beyond a firm's goods and services, evaluating its policies and actions, and taking action in the marketplace. For instance, consumers can consult a book called *Shopping for a Better World,* which rates 168 companies and more than 1,800 products according to social responsibility issues. The guide is published by the Council on Economic Priorities, a 20-year-old research group. It includes categories such as environmental protection, involvement in weapons production (especially nuclear arms), promotion of women and minorities into upper management, availability of employee benefits such as corporate day-care centers, and charitable contributions.[5]

When firms engage in practices that individuals or special-interest groups oppose, consumers sometimes *boycott* products to convey their dissatisfaction with a product or one of the firm's activities. After the *Valdez* oil spill in Alaska, thousands of customers mailed their Exxon credit cards back to the company; many cards were covered with oil. Groups have organized boycotts of table grapes to protest the poor working conditions of migrant farmworkers; boycotts of coffee brands that include Salvadoran coffee beans, to protest Salvador's policies and violent events there; and boycotts of certain fruit and vegetables to protest pesticide use.[6]

Pressure from consumers and special-interest groups has prompted many business firms to adopt socially responsible policies. **Consumerism** includes the activities of individuals, groups, and organizations aimed at protecting consumer rights. Consumer groups perform many activities, including testing and reporting on the safety and performance of products and service firms, informing the public and government officials of consumer issues, and advocating legislation.

Consumerism
Activities of individuals, groups, and organizations aimed at protecting consumer rights.

Although many people think of the consumer movement as a 1960s phenomenon, consumerism actually originated with the Industrial Revolution. The rapid growth in the production of goods between 1870 and 1900 led to poor working conditions, the sale of harmful food and drugs, and false advertising. Shocking conditions in various industries were exposed in books such as Upton Sinclair's *The Jungle,* which chronicled dangerous working conditions and unhealthy practices in the meat packing industry. Subsequently the Consumers' League was formed in New York City, followed by several other consumer groups.

The consumer movement gained momentum during the 1920s and 1930s. During the Great Depression, many consumers blamed business firms for joblessness and difficult economic times. Concern with product safety grew, and independent testing groups such as Consumer Research formed. High school classes in home economics began to emphasize consumer rights.

Alar —Treated Apples Cause Consumer Reaction

Alar is a growth regulator made from daminozide, a chemical that has been linked to cancer. Vegetable and fruit growers have used Alar to achieve uniform color and ripening, especially on apples.

In spring 1989, the use of Alar came into question when the Natural Resources Defense Council, a consumer advocate group, reported that apples treated with Alar could cause cancer—especially in children, who eat more fresh fruit than do adults. The report led to the removal of apples from produce shelves and school cafeterias across America.

The Natural Resources Defense Council had released the report carefully, with the help of a public relations firm. Various national media picked it up, and the television show ''60 Minutes'' ran an exclusive story. Consumer reaction to the program was explosive. Worried consumers flocked to grocery stores that stocked organic fruit and vegetables. Many stores posted signs saying they did not sell produce treated with Alar. And the phone at the Environmental Protection Agency (EPA) rang constantly for days.

A few days after the council's report was released, the EPA contested its findings. The EPA claimed the study was based on outdated statistics that the council's own scientific advisory board had rejected. The EPA further noted that only about 5 percent of the nation's apple crop was being treated with Alar. (Several months later, the EPA revised the estimate to 15 percent of the crop. Some experts on pesticides claim Alar was used on as much as 38 percent of the crop.)

Consumers Union, an independent testing group, spot-checked apple juice shortly after the scare began. The consumer group reported that levels of Alar had dropped to one fourth of the levels found three years earlier. More than half of the apples tested by Consumers Union showed traces of Alar. Some of the apples showing traces of Alar came from stores claiming to carry only fruit and vegetables not treated with the chemical.

By May 1989, sales of apples had fallen dramatically—to levels 20 percent below those of previous years. Growers estimated the loss for the first five months of 1989 to be $50 million; they expected to lose at least another $50 million by

the end of the year. As a result, the International Apple Institute, an industry trade association, announced that apple growers would voluntarily stop treating apples with Alar by fall (use of Alar was not banned by the EPA). The institute continued to maintain that the chemical poses no hazard to human health. But because consumer response to Alar had caused a sharp drop in sales, the institute directed all member growers not to use Alar. If all the institute's members followed its directive, the nation's apple crop will have been virtually free of Alar beginning with the crop that matured in fall 1989.[7]

Interest in consumerism peaked again in the 1960s, when consumer advocates such as Ralph Nader called attention to abuses by business firms. During this time, President John F. Kennedy established the consumer "bill of rights," which includes the right to safety, the right to be informed, the right to choose, and the right to be heard. These four rights underlie many of the goals espoused by people and organizations active in consumerism today.

The Right to Safety

The most basic consumer right is the right to products that are safe to possess and use. To ensure safety of goods, manufacturers should test them and provide buyers with explicit directions for use. In 1972 the federal government created the Consumer Product Safety Commission (CPSC) to monitor the safety of thousands of products sold to consumers. Many state and local agencies also regulate product safety.

Industries in the United States have made great strides in product categories such as children's toys, mechanical equipment such as lawn mowers, and household appliances. But more progress is needed to ensure safe products. For instance, 70 million vehicles known to be defective but never recalled by auto manufacturers are still in use and have caused 20,000 accidents, 7,000 injuries, and 500 deaths.[8] Food producers have used pesticides found to pose health hazards. The Business Action explores public reaction to the use of a potentially dangerous chemical to treat apples.

The Right to Be Informed

Consumers have the right to receive information available about a product before they purchase it. Customers seeking a loan from a bank or other financial institution, for example, should be told of all costs and repayment terms associated with the loan. Necessary information for goods includes ingredients and detailed instructions for use. To aid shoppers making decisions in the supermarket, many food producers list nutritional information on product labels for certain foods even when not required to do so by law.

Consumers also have the right to know if the product has any limitations or problems. In one case, Missouri state officials found that 60,000 Chrysler vehicles sold as new between June 1985 and December 1986 had been driven—with odometers disconnected—on personal business by plant managers and Chrysler Motors executives. At least 40 of the vehicles presented as new had been involved in accidents. A St. Louis grand jury accused Chrysler Motors of "operating like Sleazy Lee's Used Car Lot—where the odometers always read zero no matter how far the car has been driven."[9] Although laws on odometer fraud apply only to used cars, auto manufacturers generally leave odometers connected during test drives of new cars and explain the mileage to prospective buyers.

The Right to Choose

Consumers have the right to choose and make purchases from a variety of products at competitive prices. They also have the right to expect quality service at a fair price. Consumer demand for pesticide-free foods, for example,

Consumers have a right to choose food that is free from chemicals.

Howard Dratch/The Image Works

has resulted in a movement to grow vegetables and fruits without chemicals. Thousands of farmers are experimenting with different methods of crop rotation and greater use of natural materials to control insects and increase productivity.[10] If the experiments are successful, consumers will have the choice they desire.

The Right to Be Heard

Consumers also have the right to have their opinions considered in the formation of government policies and in business firms' decisions that affect them. A number of large firms have established consumer affairs departments to address consumer concerns. Many, including Little Tykes (toys), General Electric (appliances), Nabisco (foods), and Beecham Inc. (toothpaste and other personal care products), provide toll-free telephone numbers as an easy way for consumers to ask questions, make comments, and register complaints. Small businesses may not have reason or resources to establish hotlines or hire personnel specifically for consumer relations. But small-business owners and managers can set up procedures and train employees to invite consumer comments, answer questions, and handle complaints.

Responsible firms of all sizes attempt to address customer complaints in a satisfactory manner. For instance, many consumers complained to telephone companies about huge bills racked up by their children and teenagers calling national numbers prefixed by 976 and 900. Such numbers reach party-line services, recorded sports scores or weather information, and even pornography (see Case 4.1 at the end of this chapter). In response to customer complaints, some telephone companies now offer an option called call blocking, which prevents a customer's phones from making a connection with any number beginning with 900 or 976.[11]

RESPONSIBILITY TO EMPLOYEES

Like consumers, employees hold certain expectations of business firms. They expect safe working conditions, fair compensation, equal opportunities, and adequate benefits (e.g., health insurance, vacation, and time off to care for sick children). Employees also want to know what is going on in the company and want managers to be responsive to problems or complaints. Firms aware of their responsibility to the people who work for them make every effort to meet these expectations.

Safety in the Workplace

In 1970 Congress passed the Occupational Safety and Health Act, which created the **Occupational Safety and Health Administration (OSHA).** Charged with the primary purpose of ensuring safe working conditions, OSHA has established many standards with which employers must comply. OSHA covers all employees except those working for government bodies and those covered by specific employment acts such as the Coal Mine Health and Safety Act. Under OSHA regulations, firms failing to protect the health of their employees can be held criminally liable.

Occupational Safety and Health Administration (OSHA)
A federal agency with the primary purpose of ensuring safe working conditions.

OSHA employs 1,000 field inspectors who make unannounced inspections of workplaces during normal working hours. Field inspectors concentrate their efforts in the most hazardous industries, such as construction and manufacturing. Firms with health or safety violations may be fined; the individuals responsible can receive prison terms. With more than 5 million workplaces to oversee, however, OSHA cannot identify every violation.

Many firms realize that responsibility for employee safety lies with them, not with a government agency. They adopt and carry out their own health and safety programs. Managers often face a balancing act to keep the workplace safe yet continually improve efficiency. At its Camry assembly plant in Georgetown, Kentucky, Toyota is striving to cut its injury and illness rate to half the national auto industry average. The company emphasizes safety training to avoid injuries and repetitive-motion illness, which results from performing the same stressful arm or hand motions over and over. Toyota tries to match workers physically to jobs so they do not work in areas for which they are too tall or too short. It has restructured workstations to eliminate awkward

As part of a safety program, workers at a Toyota plant in Georgetown, Kentucky, limber up before they begin their shift.

Courtesy of Toyota Motors Manufacturing

motions, improved job rotation so workers do not perform the same tasks all day, and analyzed every job in the plant to determine which ones are likely to produce injuries.[12]

Equality in the Workplace

Equal Employment Opportunity Commission (EEOC)
A federal agency whose purpose is to increase job opportunities for women and minorities.

Individuals also expect to be treated equally in the workplace. The Civil Rights Act of 1964 guarantees equal employment opportunities for all people regardless of age, race, sex, religion, or national origin. This act established the **Equal Employment Opportunity Commission (EEOC),** a federal agency whose purpose is to increase job opportunities for women and minorities, who are defined by the EEOC as blacks, Hispanics, Asian or Pacific Islanders, or American Indians or Alaskan natives. The EEOC can file legal charges against companies that discriminate in their hiring practices.

Nonetheless, some inequalities still exist. Although women and minority workers are being hired by more companies, they have generally been denied the needed experience to attain top-level positions. In some cases, women, minority workers, and handicapped people earn less than white men, even when they perform the same work. Such discrimination is against the law. A California woman turned down for a sales agent job with State Farm Insurance Company sued the company. The court found that the company imposed different requirements for women to become sales agents than for men. It awarded the woman $433,000 in back pay. About 1,100 other women in California could receive similar damages, which would cost State Farm hundreds of millions of dollars. The settlement also called for State Farm to hire women for 50 of its sales agent positions in California over the next 10 years.[13] To avoid similar lawsuits and meet their responsibility, many firms have begun *affirmative action programs* to increase job opportunities for women, minorities, and handicapped individuals at all levels of the organization.

The Hard-Core Unemployed

Some organizations also have taken active steps to train the hard-core unemployed. These are individuals with little training or few skills and a long history of unemployment. The National Alliance of Businessmen, for instance, works to train such individuals so they can find and keep jobs. This effort helps people to gain dignity and become productive members of society; it also reduces the burden on the nation's welfare system and adds trained individuals to the work force. Firms can take a progressive step by providing programs or extra training to qualify persons who want to work.

RESPONSIBILITY TO THE ENVIRONMENT

The public is concerned with the impact of business decisions and actions on ecology and the environment in the United States and around the world. Earth Day 1990 raised public concern for the environment to a new level and began what many people believe will be the decade of the environment. Socially responsible managers join consumers in this concern and take active measures to protect our environment. The Business Action illustrates how, for example, one firm is trying to slow the loss of valuable wetlands in Louisiana.

One vital environmental concern is **pollution,** the contamination of water, air, and land. As with other social concerns, laws and regulations play a critical part in environmental issues. The Environmental Protection Agency (EPA), created by the National Environmental Policy Act of 1970, is the federal agency charged with enforcing laws designed to protect the environment.

Pollution
Contamination of air, water, and land.

Water Pollution

Water pollution is caused by the dumping of toxic chemicals, sewage, and garbage into rivers and streams. Toxins and pollutants from buried industrial waste can also find their way into underground water supplies. A recent concern is the liberal use of agricultural fertilizers and pesticides, which drain into water supplies. Environmental laws such as the Water Quality Improvement Act of 1970 and the Water Pollution Control Act Amendment of 1972 regulate pesticides, but prosecutions are rare. Even in California, which the EPA considers the toughest state for pesticide regulation, growers and large agribusiness firms that break pesticide laws are rarely prosecuted. Critics attribute this to the fact that in most states pesticide regulation is handled by the state department of agriculture, whose main task is to help and protect farmers. The

Loss of Louisiana Wetlands

In the marshlands of Louisiana's Mississippi River Delta live and breed many species of fish, shrimp, and other marine life; animals; waterfowl; and songbirds. There, outdoor enthusiasts camp, wildlife photographers snap pictures, and people fish, harvest shrimp, and hunt and trap animals. Vitally important to Louisiana and the entire United States, the wetlands provide a third of the U.S. seafood crop, 40 percent of the fur harvest, and 40 percent of the alligators farmed.

But the wetlands are disappearing at an alarming rate—roughly 35 square miles each year. Of course, nature has been building and destroying marshlands for centuries. Over the last 7,000 years, 14,000 square miles of new land have been built and 7,000 square miles lost. But now the loss is much faster. At the current rate, much of the Louisiana wetlands will someday be buried in the Gulf of Mexico.

The problem can be traced to the days when settlers came to Louisiana in the early 1700s. Each spring, northern snows melted and poured water into the Mississippi. The river overflowed its banks and discharged large amounts of sediment-laden fresh water. The new sediment and renewed vegetation kept the land at about sea level. But the floods killed many people and damaged property. The settlers levied the river, which saved lives and property and made it easier to keep the mouth of the

Mississippi open to ocean-going vessels. Unfortunately, levying also caused most of the sediment to drain into deep gulf waters. As a result, no new soil is being added to the shoreline of the lower Mississippi Delta. Gulf tides cause erosion and add salt water to marsh streams and lagoons.

Several projects are aimed at conserving the Louisiana wetlands. The Louisiana Land and Exploration Company (LL&E), the largest private owner of U.S. coastal wetlands, has been practicing wet lands conservation since the early 1950s. The firm has built 400 water control structures to slow water flow, prevent drainage of marshes at low tides, and reduce erosion. When issuing oil and gas leases or canal and pipeline permits, LL&E restricts actions detrimental to the marshes. It has established a brown pelican rookery on its property, planted 700 black mangrove trees on an island hit by freezes and a hurricane, and made land available for studies and plant experiments. LL&E employees have adopted a beach that they help clean three times a year. In 1989 LL&E received the Conservation Award for Respecting the Environment (CARE) from the U.S. Department of the Interior. Other firms, plus government agencies, environmental groups, and private citizens, also need to increase efforts to save one of the nation's most valuable resources.[14]

Pesticides can work their way into water supplies, causing a major pollution problem.

Scott Berner/Stock Imagery

EPA estimates that, in 38 states, pesticides have contaminated the ground water used as the main source of drinking water by half of all Americans.[15] Citizens across the United States are calling for stricter regulation of pesticides.

Air Pollution

Air pollution is caused by carbon monoxide and hydrocarbons that come from motor vehicles and by smoke and other pollutants from manufacturing plants. The Clean Air Act of 1970 and the 1977 Clean Air Act Amendment provide stringent emission standards for automobiles, airplanes, and factories. Devices such as catalytic converters have been developed to help control air pollution.

Much progress has been made in fighting air pollution, but with air quality below federal standards in about 60 metropolitan areas and with the number of vehicles on the roads up 70 percent since 1970, environmentalists are calling for tougher regulation of auto emissions and better fuel efficiency.[16] Carmakers expect more emission controls to be required by both federal and state regulations.

Many scientists fear that the earth's ozone layer, which shields the planet from the sun's deadly ultraviolet rays, is being destroyed, with a *global warming trend* as a result. Scientists believe the major cause is chlorofluorocarbons (CFCs), used to cool refrigerators and air conditioners and to manufacture some plastic foam containers.[17] Congress has called for a 50 percent decrease in the production of CFCs by 1999. Additionally, 75 countries around the world have signed an agreement to eliminate within a decade the chemicals that destroy the ozone shield.[18]

Air pollution also has been attributed to *acid rain*. When sulphur dioxide is pumped into the air (often by manufacturing and power plants burning high-sulphur coal) and mixes with air, rain with a high acid content is created. Much of the damage to forests and lakes in the eastern United States and Canada has been blamed on acid rain.

Land Pollution

Land pollution results from strip mining of coal and minerals, forest fires, garbage disposal, and dumping of industrial wastes, including chemicals and medical supplies such as used hypodermic needles. Land pollution often results in water pollution because toxic wastes drain into water supplies. Congress created a $1.6 billion Superfund in 1980 to help cover the costs of cleaning up polluted land. And the Resource Conservation and Recovery Act of 1984 requires federal regulation of potentially dangerous solid-waste disposal. Solid waste—the term for trash and garbage discarded by homes, businesses, and factories—includes paper and cardboard, grass clippings and leaves, food wastes, metals, glass, plastics, textiles, leather, wood, and rubber.

Businesses and government organizations face the problems of where to dispose of solid waste and how to do so safely. Landfills are filling up at an ever-increasing rate, and many communities are opposed to locating additional ones near them. One recent concern is disposable diapers, a nearly $4 billion industry. Making up about 2 percent of total solid waste, disposable diapers may pose a health hazard to sanitation workers and may contaminate groundwater with bacteria and other pollutants, although this has not been proved conclusively.[19]

Recycling
Reusing materials such as paper, plastic, glass, and aluminum to make other products.

Many used products and containers do not have to go to the dump; they could be recycled. **Recycling** involves reusing materials to make other products. Newspapers, office paper, cardboard boxes, aluminum, tin cans, glass and plastic containers, and even motor oil can be recycled to reduce the drain on resources and the costs of producing new products and containers, and to slow the need for more and bigger landfills. Aluminum beverage cans are the most recycled containers in the United States, with more than 60 percent of all aluminum cans recycled.[20] Many firms conduct recycling programs within their organizations. They build the market for recycled materials by buying and using such products whenever possible. They also help educate consumers and encourage them to recycle.

Along with consumers and special-interest groups, many business firms and government bodies are trying to solve problems of garbage disposal and land and water pollution. Procter & Gamble, maker of Pampers and Luvs disposable diapers, is researching processes for recycling disposables. The paper part can be used to make cardboard and insulation; the plastic covering can be used to make plastic building materials and flowerpots.[21]

In New York City, as much as 50 percent of the garbage (32,000 tons a day) could be recycled. That includes millions of cans and bottles from soft drinks, beer, and bottled water. The We Can redemption center in New York helps the homeless convert empty bottles and cans into about $10,000 cash a day by accepting empties, paying cash on the spot, and arranging for beverage companies to collect the empties. Large firms are helping the We Can center in its

Courtesy of Du Pont

FIGURE 4.2

Du Pont's Plastics-Recycling Program: Largest in the United States

Du Pont is pioneering the largest plastics recycling program in the United States.

dual function of recycling and providing income for homeless persons. Manufacturers Hanover, for example, donates cans to the center from its employee cafeterias, which serve more than 60,000 lunches daily.[22] Figure 4.2 shows an advertisement explaining Du Pont's plastic-recycling program.

RESPONSIBILITY TO INVESTORS

Business firms also have a responsibility to the people who invest money in them. Many investment-related abuses have come to light in recent years. The public, government regulatory agencies, and many business leaders are concerned with problems such as the mishandling of investors' funds, insider trading of stocks, and excessive compensation of executives.

Proper Management of Funds

Firms have a responsibility to manage funds properly so as to return a fair profit to investors. Investment scams have probably existed since people started using money. The United States saw many during the California Gold Rush in the 1800s, when scores of hapless investors bought worthless mines. In recent years, some investors have been equally unfortunate. They have discovered that their money went for gold mines or oil wells that do not exist, resorts or hotels that were never built, or new business ventures that never got off the ground.

Unscrupulous firms today take advantage of computerized dialing and low telephone rates to reach unsuspecting consumers and trick them out of hundreds of millions of dollars each year. The Securities and Exchange Commission, which handles investors' complaints concerning stocks, bonds, and other investments, has received complaints of hundreds of *penny stock scams*. In these scams, operators offer stock in a company for only a few dollars a share or even less. But usually the companies are mere shells, with no operations or revenues. To sell the stock to clients, the scam operator employs telephone salespersons trained to be smooth-talking and persuasive. As sales of stock take off, its value skyrockets to several dollars a share. But when investors try to collect their money, they find their holdings are worthless.[23]

Mishandling of funds goes beyond penny stock scams. Managers have a responsibility to thoroughly investigate their investments and to clearly present all facts and risks to investors. When mismanagement causes investors to lose large sums of money, the results can be disastrous, especially for small investors who put their life savings into a risky venture on the advice of a trusted stockbroker or financial adviser. Prudential-Bache Securities, which uses the slogan, "rock solid, market wise," gained the confidence of numerous investors. But when the firm marketed real estate funds the managers and account executives knew little about and the funds lost millions of investors' dollars, Prudential-Bache lost many investors.[24] When investors lose confidence in a firm, they find another place to invest their money.

Access to Information

Insider Trading
The practice of buying and selling stock on the basis of information gained through positions or contacts with others that is not available to other investors or the general public.

Firms have the responsibility to make stock information available to all potential investors. **Insider trading** occurs when individuals buy and sell stock on the basis of information gained through their positions or contacts with others that is not available to other investors or the general public. Such information, known only to a few insiders, gives them an unfair advantage over typical investors. Stock purchases by officers of a corporation, for instance, often precede a merger or sale and lead to temporary increases in the value of the stock.[25]

Certain laws prohibit insider trading, and the Securities and Exchange Commission prosecutes individuals found violating them. Two recent widely publicized cases involve Wall Street traders Ivan Boesky and Michael Milken. Boesky, who used insider information to accumulate a fortune of $250 million, was fined $100 million and sentenced to three years in prison. Milken, after pleading guilty to felonies involving his dealings with Boesky and others, was sentenced to 10 years in prison and 3 years of full-time community work, the most severe penalty ever handed down for a white-collar-crime case. He was

TABLE 4.1

**The 10 Highest-Paid
Chief Executives**

DID YOU KNOW? *The
chief executives of America's
50 largest corporations
earned $124 million in 1990.*

Name	Company	Compensation*
1. Stephen M. Wolf	UAL	$18,301,000
2. John Sculley	Apple Computer	16,730,000
3. Paul B. Fireman	Reebok International	14,822,000
4. Dean L. Buntrock	Waste Management	12,290,000
5. Leon C. Hirsch	U.S. Surgical	11,676,000
6. Michael D. Eisner	Walt Disney Company	11,233,000
7. Joseph D. Williams	Warner-Lambert	8,483,000
8. David O. Maxwell	Federal National Mortgage	7,568,000
9. George V. Grune	Reader's Digest	7,463,000
10. P. Roy Vagelos	Merck	7,142,000

*Includes salary, bonuses, and stock options.

Source: Adapted from *Forbes,* May 13, 1991, p. 48.

fined $600 million by the government and also faces possible hundreds of millions of dollars in civil judgments. With Milken's harsh sentence, the judge wanted to raise the penalty for white-collar crime and deter others on Wall Street from insider trading and other violations.[26]

Executive Compensation

Executives who run firms carry tremendous responsibility and deserve to be compensated accordingly. But some people question whether executives of large corporations are now being paid too much. By orchestrating the turn-around of the Walt Disney Company, chairman Michael Eisner and president Frank Wells each earned more in one year than the founder of IBM (Tom Watson, Sr.) and the founder of General Motors (Alfred P. Sloan) earned in their careers.[27] Table 4.1 lists the 10 highest-paid chief executives in the United States.

According to a *Business Week* survey, the average salary and bonuses for a chief executive officer (CEO) in 1990 exceeded $1.2 million; the average total compensation approached $2 million. [28] The gap between executive pay and the pay others earn is widening dramatically and causing resentment. For instance, in 1960 a large-company CEO averaged annual pay of $190,383, 41 times that of a factory worker's average pay ($4,667) and 19 times that of an engineer's average pay ($9,828). But in 1988, the CEO's average pay had grown to $2,025,485, a figure 93 times an average factory worker's pay of $21,725 and 44 times an engineer's average pay of $45,680.[29] Some experts in the area of executive pay are predicting a revolt on the part of investors and consumers.

A fair compensation program should definitely reward executives for outstanding performance. In fact, some executives might be considered underpaid when you look at the performance of their companies. R. Lee Taylor II of Holly Farms Corp., a poultry producer, received relatively low pay—$816,000—for a

Lederle Laboratories have made $11 million in antibiotics available to homeless families and children.

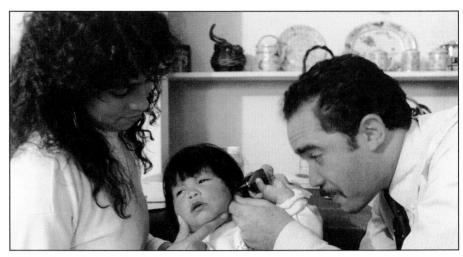

Photo courtesy of Lederle Laboratories

three-year period in which his company gave shareholders a 108 percent return on their investment.[30] But executive compensation is not always directly linked to performance, a fact that concerns many investors. For instance, of the chief executives included in the *Business Week* study, Chrysler Corp. chairman Lee Iacocca gave shareholders the lowest return relative to his pay for the third consecutive year; he has taken home $25.2 million in salary and stock options since 1987.[31] Although the problem has no easy solution, some suggest linking executive pay more closely to company performance and requiring full disclosure of executive earnings to investors.

ADVANCING SOCIAL RESPONSIBILITY

Many firms recognize the importance of social responsibility and take steps to see that their policies and activities make a positive impact on society. They practice social responsibility through programs of community support, self-regulation, and social audits.

Community Support

Business firms throughout the United States provide support for a wide variety of activities designed to improve their communities. Both large and small businesses contribute to the arts, build parks, donate equipment to schools, and sponsor academic scholarships. Some sponsor social programs to help the disadvantaged. For example, pharmaceutical manufacturer Lederle Laboratories has begun an $11 million health care program for America's homeless people. The program provides antibiotics for homeless individuals and funding to develop health care programs.[32] Many community activities could not start up or continue without the support of business.

TABLE 4.2

National Cable Television Association Standards

- Companies should state clearly on bills what services a customer is receiving and how much they cost.
- Customers should be given a month's notice when a company is going to raise rates.
- Telephone calls should be answered within 30 seconds.
- A customer should receive a busy signal less than 3 percent of the time a cable company office is open.
- A company should respond to service interruptions within 24 hours in situations not beyond its control, within 36 hours otherwise.
- If an installer or technician is running late, an attempt must be made to contact the customer to set up a new appointment.

Source: Associated Press, "Cable TV Industry Suggests Changes," *Herald-Leader* (Lexington, Ky.), February 16, 1990, p. A3.

Some firms enable employees to share their time and talent with their communities. IBM, for example, lends engineers to teach in schools for a year. Others provide company time, materials, or facilities for employees active in community organizations. Businesspeople also participate in the Rotary, Kiwanis, Junior Achievement, and other groups that raise money for local projects or help youngsters. Firms are major contributors to charities and encourage employees to donate to organizations such as United Way, which distributes donations among many diverse social agencies operating in an area. Through such activities, the business sector makes a significant contribution to society.

Self-Regulation

The business community can also advance social responsibility by establishing standards of conduct and ensuring that individuals follow them. One of the best-known self-regulatory agencies is the *Better Business Bureau,* a nationwide organization with local branches supported by local firms. The bureau's purpose is to help consumers settle problems with specific firms. Although the Better Business Bureau does not possess strong enforcement powers, it does maintain records of consumer complaints and warns consumers through local media when a firm is engaging in deceptive or questionable practices. More than 140 bureau branches operate today in the United States. Another active self-regulatory agency is called the *National Advertising Review Board (NARB).* NARB screens national advertisements for honesty and handles complaints about deceptive ads. If a firm refuses to comply with its directives, the NARB may publicize the incident or file a complaint with the Federal Trade Commission.

Many other industries, trade associations, and professional organizations establish self-regulatory programs. For example, the U.S. cable television industry, faced with complaints about service and prices, has established standards for cable companies to follow to guarantee better service. Table 4.2 lists the standards set by the National Cable Television Association.

Businesspeople generally prefer self-regulation to that imposed by the government. The guidelines established within an industry are often more realistic than those established by the government. Self-regulatory programs usually cost less to put into place than does government regulation. The main drawback of self-regulatory programs is that sometimes they are difficult or impossible to enforce. Complying with standards is often voluntary (as is the case with the cable TV industry). When firms comply with the standards, self-regulation can be an effective way to foster social responsibility.

The Social Audit

Social Audit
A systematic review of an organization's performance of social responsibility activities.

Some firms conduct a systematic review of their performance of social responsibility activities through a **social audit.** A social audit looks at the firm's short- and long-run contributions to society. Activities reviewed might include community involvement, product safety, and the impact of business practices on the environment.

With information from a social audit, managers can evaluate how effective the current programs are and decide whether they should initiate new courses of action. Some firms spend millions of dollars each year on social responsibility activities; they need to determine whether they are spending their money wisely. Although a social audit is more informal than an accounting audit, it can be a useful tool in assessing social responsibility.

BUSINESS ETHICS

Ethics
The principles of behavior that distinguish between right and wrong.

Business Ethics
The evaluation of business activities and behavior as right or wrong.

Social responsibility requires individuals engaging in business endeavors to behave in an ethical manner. **Ethics** are principles of behavior that distinguish between right and wrong. Ethical conduct conforms with what a group or society as a whole considers right behavior. People working in business frequently face ethical questions. **Business ethics** is the evaluation of business activities and behavior as right or wrong. Ethical standards in business are based on commonly accepted principles of behavior established by the expectations of society, the firm, the industry, and an individual's personal values.

With unethical business practices often receiving publicity, the public sometimes believes that people in business are less ethical than others in society. But ethical problems challenge all segments of our society, including government, churches, and higher education. For instance, college basketball players bring in millions of dollars every year for universities, coaches, television networks, and sports announcers; yet many of those athletes do not even receive an education.[33] Also, universities and professors have been accused of abandoning the undergraduate student while professors pursue grants, conduct research, and participate in academic politics to further their careers and promote their universities.[34] Such situations could destroy the trust society holds for higher education and may lead to close scrutiny of university policies and practices.

Most business leaders realize their firms cannot succeed without the trust of customers and the goodwill of society. A violation of ethics makes trust and goodwill difficult to maintain. In thousands of companies, executives and employees act according to the highest ethical standards. Unfortunately managers

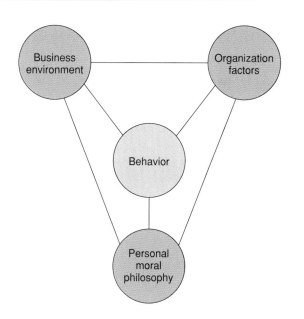

FIGURE 4.3

Factors Influencing Behavior in Business

in some firms behave unethically, and these instances are often highly publicized. Personnel executives say the major reason managers behave unethically is to obtain power and money.[35] In this section, we examine the various factors influencing ethical behavior and discuss how firms can encourage ethical behavior.

Factors Influencing Ethical Behavior

To encourage ethical behavior, executives, managers, and owners of firms must understand what influences behavior in the first place. Figure 4.3 presents several factors that affect individuals' behavior in business: the business environment, organizational factors, and an individual's personal moral philosophy.

The business environment Almost daily, business managers face ethical dilemmas resulting from the pressures of the business environment. They are challenged to meet sales quotas, cut costs, increase efficiency, or overtake competitors. Managers and employees may sometimes think the only way to survive in the competitive world of business is by deception or cheating. In some instances, an organization may use someone else's successful work without the permission of the owner or originator. For example, the U.S. importer of Swedish-produced Absolut vodka sued Brown-Forman of Louisville for advertising Icy, a new vodka from Iceland, as an "absolute improvement." The ad for Icy also features Absolut's signature, a clear bottle against a blue-black background.[36]

Conflict of interest is another common ethical problem stemming from the business environment. Often an individual has a chance to further selfish interests rather than the interests of the organization or society. To gain favor with people who make purchasing decisions for their companies, a seller may

● C o n n e c t i o n s

Evaluating Ethical Behavior

Directions: Below are a number of statements that involve ethical decisions you may have to make when conducting business. Circle the number that represents your level of agreement with each statement.

	Strongly Disagree				Strongly Agree	
1. It is OK to take supplies such as pencils and paper home from a company office.	1	2	3	4	5	6
2. I would break a company rule if my co-workers did.	1	2	3	4	5	6
3. If it meant getting ahead, I would take credit for someone else's work.	1	2	3	4	5	6
4. I would not turn in a fellow employee for breaking a company policy.	1	2	3	4	5	6
5. If I made a mistake that could hurt the company, I would cover it up to avoid being reprimanded.	1	2	3	4	5	6
6. I would not mind breaking a law to get a promotion, as long as I did not get caught.	1	2	3	4	5	6

offer special favors or gifts, ranging from a meal to clothing to trips. Some offer cash—a kickback—for putting through a contract or placing orders with a company. Others offer bribes. Such illegal conduct will damage the organization in the long run. In order to limit unethical behavior, business firms must begin by expecting their employees to obey all laws and regulations.

The international business environment presents further ethical dilemmas. Businesspeople and government officials in other countries and cultures often operate according to different standards than those held in the United States. Firms doing business internationally sometimes have separate ethical standards for domestic and international operations.

The organization   The organization itself also influences behavior. Individuals often learn ethical or unethical behaviors by interacting with others in the organization. An employee who sees a superior or co-worker behaving unethically may follow suit. In the Iran-Contra trial, Oliver North defended himself by saying that his actions (including shredding documents and withholding information from investigators), although unethical, were expected by his superiors. A simply stated directive from the person at the top can set the tone in an organization, as is the case for purchasers who work for Robert J. Bretz of

7. I would be willing to provide customers false information to make a sale.	1	2	3	4	5	6
8. I see no problem with taking longer than necessary to do a job and then billing a client for the extra time.	1	2	3	4	5	6
9. It is OK to take care of personal business on company time.	1	2	3	4	5	6
10. I would call in sick to take a day off work.	1	2	3	4	5	6

Feedback: How are your ethical standards? Although the situations are hypothetical, they present typical business decisions. For items circled 1 or 2, you considered these behaviors unacceptable; 3 or 4 indicates you are uncertain or indifferent; and 5 or 6 suggests you believe these activities are acceptable.

Some people view the activities listed as common practices. Doesn't everyone take pens and paper home from the office? Yet many companies prohibit such actions. Some of the activities, such as misleading customers or covering up mistakes, can result in serious penalties. If you believe most of the activities are unacceptable, you have a solid ethical base from which to work. If you found most of these activities acceptable, think about them again. It may seem as though people must do such things to succeed in business. We hope that is not true.

Pitney Bowes Inc. Says Bretz, "I don't allow them to take anything—no lunch, no dinner, golfing only if they can reciprocate."[37]

An organization can also use rewards to influence the behavior of its members. If an individual is rewarded or is not punished for behaving unethically, the behavior will probably be repeated. Likewise the threat of punishment and the lack of reward for unethical activities encourage ethical behavior. The severity of punishment also sends a message to other individuals who might be considering similar activities. For example, the National Collegiate Athletic Association (NCAA) has placed member institutions on probation for violating recruiting rules. Teams on probation have been barred from tournament games and from having games televised and have had limits placed on scholarships. These penalties should discourage other university athletic programs from violating NCAA rules.

The individual   A person's own moral philosophy also influences his or her ethical behavior. A **moral philosophy** is the set of principles that dictate acceptable behavior. These principles are learned from family, friends, co-workers, and other social groups and through formal education. The Connections quiz will help you evaluate your moral philosophy.

Moral Philosophy
The set of principles that dictate acceptable behavior.

Humanistic Philosophy
A set of moral principles focusing on individual rights and values.

In developing a moral philosophy, individuals can follow two approaches: humanistic and utilitarian. The **humanistic philosophy** focuses on individual rights and values. Individuals and organizations adopting this philosophy would honor their moral duties to customers and workers. For instance, when senior management at Hertz Corporation found that the company had over-billed car renters and insurance companies $13 million for repairs to its cars, Hertz repaid $3 million before the government took action. Hertz was fined $6.85 million and agreed to return an additional $12.7 million to those it over-billed.[38]

Utilitarian Philosophy
A set of moral principles focusing on the greatest good for the largest number of people.

Individuals and organizations following the **utilitarian philosophy** seek the greatest good for the largest number of people. Pharmaceutical manufacturers who make vaccine for pertussis, the deadly disease of whooping cough, adhere to this philosophy. Some children react to the killed bacteria in the vaccine, administered three times in the first two years of life. Reactions include fevers, persistent crying, and temporary unresponsiveness. The vaccine has been blamed for severe brain damage in a few children, although several studies disproved this. Despite these problems, because so many children benefit from the vaccine, doctors continue to administer the current version while researchers work on new pertussis vaccines. And some states require children to receive it before attending school, to prevent outbreaks of whooping cough and resulting deaths.[39]

Encouraging Ethical Behavior

Many organizations take positive steps to encourage ethical behavior. Some offer courses in ethics and include ethics in training programs. (For instance, Boeing Company line managers lead ethics training seminars.)[40] Most courses and training seminars focus on how to analyze ethical dilemmas. The emphasis is on understanding why individuals make the decisions they do rather than on teaching ethics or moral principles.

Code of Ethics
A statement spelling out exactly what an organization considers ethical behavior.

A basic way for an organization to encourage ethical behavior is to establish a code of ethics. A **code of ethics** is a statement specifying exactly what the organization considers ethical behavior. Many firms, as well as trade and professional associations, have established codes of ethics. For instance, the American Medical Association has its own code of ethics that limits the amount and types of advertising used by doctors. By enforcing codes of ethics, rewarding ethical behavior, and punishing unethical behavior, a firm limits opportunities to behave unethically. Figure 4.4 shows the code of ethics established by Johnson & Johnson.

Whistle-Blower
An employee who informs superiors, the media, or a government regulatory agency about unethical behavior within an organization.

Employees of an organization can also encourage ethical behavior by reporting unethical practices. **Whistle-blowers** are employees who inform their superiors, the media, or a government regulatory agency about unethical behavior within their organization. Whistle-blowers often risk great professional and personal danger by reporting the unethical behavior of others. They may be harassed by co-workers or supervisors, passed up for promotions, fired, or even threatened with damage to their property or harm to themselves or their families. Nonetheless, some organizations have developed plans that encourage employees to report unethical conduct and that provide protection for whistle-blowers.

Our Credo

We believe our first responsibility is to the doctors, nurses and patients,
to mothers and fathers and all others who use our products and services.
In meeting their needs everything we do must be of high quality.
We must constantly strive to reduce our costs
in order to maintain reasonable prices.
Customers' orders must be serviced promptly and accurately.
Our suppliers and distributors must have an opportunity
to make a fair profit.

We are responsible to our employees,
the men and women who work with us throughout the world.
Everyone must be considered as an individual.
We must respect their dignity and recognize their merit.
They must have a sense of security in their jobs.
Compensation must be fair and adequate,
and working conditions clean, orderly and safe.
We must be mindful of ways to help our employees fulfill
their family responsibilities.
Employees must feel free to make suggestions and complaints.
There must be equal opportunity for employment, development
and advancement for those qualified.
We must provide competent management,
and their actions must be just and ethical.

We are responsible to the communities in which we live and work
and to the world community as well.
We must be good citizens — support good works and charities
and bear our fair share of taxes.
We must encourage civic improvements and better health and education.
We must maintain in good order
the property we are privileged to use,
protecting the environment and natural resources.

Our final responsibility is to our stockholders.
Business must make a sound profit.
We must experiment with new ideas.
Research must be carried on, innovative programs developed
and mistakes paid for.
New equipment must be purchased, new facilities provided
and new products launched.
Reserves must be created to provide for adverse times.
When we operate according to these principles,
the stockholders should realize a fair return.

Johnson & Johnson

Courtesy of Johnson & Johnson

FIGURE 4.4

Code of Ethics

Johnson & Johnson encourages ethical behavior in its organization through its code of ethics, or "credo."

Efforts to encourage ethical behavior will be effective only with the support of top-level management. Employees base their decisions on the guidelines and examples set by their superiors. Management must set the proper tone by never compromising ethical behavior in its dealings with customers, employees, and competitors.

You'll Know It's the (21ˢᵗ) **Century When . . .**

All of the Sierra Club's Wishes Come True

By 2010, the generation born after Earth Day 1970 will be in control of the country. Nearly all 21st-century Americans will consider themselves environmentalists. Yet most consumers won't voluntarily switch to green products: instead, green products will be mandated by environmental legislation. Before the U.S. population hits 300 million, in 2029, strict national laws will govern recycling, packaging standards, and waste disposal.[41]

SUMMARY OF LEARNING OBJECTIVES

1. To explain the meaning and importance of social responsibility.
   Social responsibility is the deliberate effort of a firm to increase its positive impact on society while reducing its negative impact. In light of many publicized instances of corruption and illegal behavior, the public, special interest groups, and consumers are making increasing demands that business firms demonstrate social responsibility.

2. To trace the evolution of the consumer movement and identify the rights of consumers.
   The consumer movement began with the Industrial Revolution, when many workers faced unsafe conditions and consumers were exposed to harmful products. The movement gained momentum during the 1930s, the time of the Great Depression, and peaked again in the 1960s. During this time, President Kennedy established the consumer ''bill of rights,'' including the right to safety, the right to be informed, the right to choose, and the right to be heard.

3. To outline the responsibilities business firms have to employees.
   Firms have a responsibility to provide safe working conditions, fair compensation, equal opportunities, and adequate benefits for employees. The Occupational Safety and Health Administration monitors conditions in the workplace. The Equal Employment Opportunity Commission works toward increasing job opportunities for women, minorities, and handicapped people.

4. To describe the impact of business decisions on the environment.
   Business decisions have a profound impact on the environment. Business activities can cause pollution, the contamination of the environment—water, air, and land. The Environmental Protection Agency sets standards and monitors compliance among business firms and industry. Socially responsible firms and consumers take active measures to reduce pollution.

5. To explain the responsibility of firms to their investors.
   Firms have a responsibility to provide information to investors and to act prudently in managing funds, as well as to compensate executives fairly.

Recent problems, including the mishandling of investors' funds, insider trading, and excessive compensation for executives, have contributed to a loss of money and trust on the part of investors.

6. To identify ways in which firms can advance social responsibility.
   Firms can advance social responsibility in many ways, such as supporting programs to improve communities where they are located. Some firms and industries participate in self-regulation to encourage good business practices. Others review their performance of social responsibility activities through periodic social audits.

7. To list and describe factors influencing business ethics.
   Socially responsible businesspeople behave in an ethical manner. The business environment, the organization, and an individual's own moral philosophy influence ethical and unethical behavior. Firms can encourage ethical behavior through education and by developing and enforcing codes of ethics.

KEY TERMS

Social Responsibility, p. 133

Consumerism, p. 135

Occupational Safety and Health Administration (OSHA), p. 139

Equal Employment Opportunity Commission (EEOC), p. 140

Pollution, p. 141

Recycling, p. 144

Insider Trading, p. 146

Social Audit, p. 150

Ethics, p. 150

Business Ethics, p. 150

Moral Philosophy, p. 153

Humanistic Philosophy, p. 154

Utilitarian Philosophy, p. 154

Code of Ethics, p. 154

Whistle-Blower, p. 154

QUESTIONS FOR DISCUSSION AND REVIEW

1. What is social responsibility? Why is it important for businesses to act in a socially responsible manner?
2. Do you think social responsibility is worth the cost?
3. What is consumerism? How does consumerism benefit society?
4. What rights are guaranteed in the consumer "bill of rights"? Give an example of each.
5. What responsibilities do business firms have to their employees?
6. What is the purpose of OSHA?
7. What is affirmative action? Why are affirmative action programs necessary?
8. Describe the three major types of pollution. What can business firms do to help reduce each type of pollution?
9. Why is insider trading illegal?

10. Do you think executives generally are paid too much? Why or why not?

11. Describe several ways in which business firms can advance social responsibility. Find three examples of firms demonstrating social responsibility in your community.

12. What factors help determine whether a business manager will behave ethically or unethically? Give an example of how each factor might influence ethical behavior.

13. How might a firm encourage its employees to behave ethically?

CASE 4.1
Dialing 900 Numbers

Imagine coming home from work to a $2,000 phone bill. First you place an angry call to your telephone company to say there's something wrong with your bill. Then the person at the phone company informs you that your bill is indeed correct; there really is a 900–666–PORN. When you get off the phone, you find the guilty party: your 12-year-old child.

This scenario has actually happened, over and over again. Every day more than 1 million people dial numbers prefixed by 900 and 976 to hear jokes, sports news, stock reports, and much more. Estimates of annual revenue from such dial-up services exceed $330 million a year. More than $50 million dollars is spent on dial-a-porn services offering sexually explicit messages. Many of the callers are children and teens.

Parents and other concerned groups, the Federal Trade Commission, and Congress are proposing regulation of dial-a-porn services. Conveying pornographic messages to minors or nonconsenting adults over telephone lines is already prohibited by the Federal Communications Act. But many observers believe that banning dial-a-porn may be unconstitutional. Therefore lawmakers are considering a plan that requires phone companies to offer a free service that would allow customers to block their phones from access to 900 or 976 exchanges.

Independent of Congress, several local phone companies have introduced plans to block calls to porn lines because of complaints by consumers. In many instances, phone companies have been accused of promoting pornography since they provide the 900 and 976 dial-up exchanges for companies to use. Bell Atlantic Corp. plans to block all porn lines in Pennsylvania and Maryland. Customers could unblock the services by writing to the phone company. New York Telephone plans to offer call blocking for a one-time charge of $5. Most local companies are dealing with customer complaints by enabling them to block access to 900 and 976 numbers. But blocking can also hurt firms offering legitimate services.

American Telephone & Telegraph Company has threatened to drop its 900 exchange if Congress requires call blocking. AT&T claims it does not have the computer software to handle such a task. Antipornography advocates do not believe blocking will be effective, since kids can simply find another telephone. Some argue that the telephone companies should refuse to carry dial-a-porn services.

The law governing dial-a-porn services is unclear and varies by state. A federal appeals court in Atlanta upheld a decision by Southern Bell to disconnect dial-a-porn services in Atlanta and Miami. However, a federal district

Adapted from Bob Davis, ''Proposed Curbs on Dial-a-Porn Are Seen Reducing Access to All Dial-Up Services,'' *The Wall Street Journal,* March 30, 1988, p. 21; Christopher Elias, ''Dialing for Cash and Controversy,'' *Insight,* August 15, 1988, pp. 44–45; ''Get Off the Telephone,'' *Time,* August 1, 1988, p. 25.

court in California stopped Pacific Bell from disconnecting porn services. Because of the large sums of money involved, this issue will not be resolved without a lengthy fight.

Questions for Discussion

1. Should the government be involved in the regulation of dial-a-porn services?
2. If they can do so legally, should telephone companies refuse to carry dial-a-porn services?
3. Should telephone companies be required to block dial-a-porn or other services upon request from customers? If so, should the consumer pay a fee for blocking or should the telephone company pick up the expense?
4. Do you think it is the responsibility of the firms involved to keep children from accessing dial-a-porn services? Why or why not?

CASE 4.2
Perrier Taints Its Pure Reputation

Perrier sparkling water has a long-standing reputation for purity that can be traced back to the time when the Caesars ruled. But this reputation was damaged severely when lab workers in North Carolina found that some bottles of Perrier contained traces of benzene, a potentially harmful chemical used in cleaning fluids.

Although Perrier officials assured the public that the benzene had tainted only a few bottles shipped from France to the United States, distributors in Denmark, the Netherlands, and Japan recalled the product. Then company president Gustave Leven announced a worldwide recall to protect Perrier's "pure" image. Unfortunately the damage may have been done already.

Confusion surrounded the initial contamination. Company officials first said that the benzene had been accidentally applied to some of the machinery that bottles the water. Later they said the real cause was failure to clean filters that remove benzene and other naturally occurring impurities from the water.

The product recall cost Perrier an estimated $30 million after taxes. Worse, the product image may be tainted forever. The company spent years developing an image of water that is naturally pure; the advertising slogan in the United States proclaimed, "It's perfect. It's Perrier." After the discovery, the firm admitted that benzene appears in its spring and must be filtered out before consumers can drink the water. Now Perrier has to convince consumers that its product, again safe, is worth the high price.

Adapted from Patricia Sellers, "Perrier Plots Its Comeback," *Fortune,* April 23, 1990, pp. 277–78; Stewart Toy and Lisa Driscoll, "Can Perrier Purify Its Reputation?" *Business Week,* February 26, 1990, p. 45; E. S. Browning, Alix M. Freedman, and Thomas R. King, "Perrier Expands North American Recall to Rest of Globe," *The Wall Street Journal,* February 15, 1990, pp. B1–B8.

Although Perrier faces a tough road back—some say it may never recover—many observers applauded the way in which the firm handled the crisis. Many experts believe consumers are more willing to forgive a company that is honest about its mistakes and makes an effort to correct them. In the meantime, Perrier has to fight for the business it lost to a host of competitors.

Questions for Discussion

1. Did Perrier make the right decision when it decided to remove the product from the market?

2. What consumer rights did Perrier violate when it sold water containing a chemical that had to be removed by a filtering process?

3. Does it pay for firms like Perrier to act in a socially responsible manner?

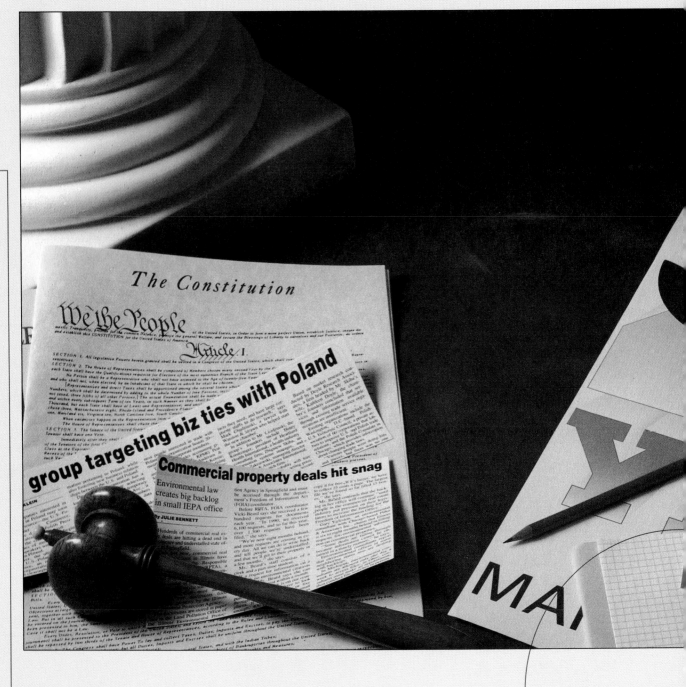

CHAPTER FIVE

BUSINESS, LAW, AND GOVERNMENT

LEARNING OBJECTIVES

1. To list the sources from which laws are derived.

2. To outline the court system in the United States.

3. To identify the various categories of business law.

4. To describe how government regulates business activities to encourage competition.

5. To explain the effects of deregulation on business.

6. To describe how taxation supports the activities of government.

163

Each summer, across the United States, millions of sun worshippers cover their bodies with a variety of sunscreens so they can enjoy the sun while blocking out harmful rays. The suntan lotion business has swelled into a $500 million industry. But the Food and Drug Administration (FDA) is concerned

tion of America, based on research conducted by scientists at the George Washington Medical Center, reported that sunscreen lotions containing urocanic acid may increase the likelihood of skin cancer.

Sunscreens are among several products to come under recent

Other food marketers face accusations of outlandish health claims. Quaker Oats promises that its oat products can help lower cholesterol. Kellogg's All-Bran cereal is said to reduce the risk of cancer. General Mills' Total supposedly helps resist infection, promotes healing, and helps in digestion. The FDA and Congress are both investigating these claims and are putting together new food labeling laws.

States are also becoming involved; 34 state attorneys general have urged the FDA to outlaw any kind of health claims in food product labels. Firms counting on the health trend to carry them into the 21st century may face serious obstacles if health claims are disallowed. Many food producers, especially those who make cereals, have spent millions of dollars developing new products that appeal to health-conscious consumers.

Robert E. Daemmrich/TSW

that some sun-care companies mislead the public about the protection their products provide. Most sunscreens block shorter-wavelength radiation that causes sunburn and some forms of skin cancer. Claims that these products block the longer UV–A rays may not be true, however. The longer rays, once thought to be safe, have now been linked to aging, cancer, and cataracts. So far, only a single product—Photoplex—has won FDA approval for UV–A coverage. Ironically, the Consumer Federa-

government scrutiny. Several food manufacturers have been questioned for the health claims they make about their products. The Federal Trade Commission (FTC) has charged Campbell Soup Company with making deceptive claims about soup. Campbell has advertised that some of its soups are low in fat and cholesterol and therefore help fight heart disease. But Campbell fails to point out that the soups are high in sodium, which can increase the risk of a heart attack.

A study published in the *Journal of the American Medical Association* in April 1991 counters these criticisms. The research found that two ounces of oat bran daily reduced cholesterol. The study also found that if a person stops eating oat bran, his or her cholesterol goes back up. This research is likely to fuel the heated controversy over health claims.[1]

Business firms must operate within the boundaries of laws and government regulation. Laws have been developed not only to protect consumers but also to preserve competition. Government agencies enforce these laws at the federal, state, and local levels. Business firms that do not comply with the laws face fines and other penalties.

In this chapter, we examine the important roles of law and government in business. First we discuss business law, the sources of law, and the court system. We describe the various types of law and specific laws affecting business. Then we examine government regulation of business, with emphasis on the laws designed to encourage competition. We discuss the trend toward deregulation. Finally we explain how the government uses various taxes to support its activities.

INTRODUCTION TO LAW

A **law** is a standard or rule established by a society to govern the behavior of its members. Federal, state, and local governments, constitutions, and treaties all establish laws. So do court decisions. Laws have a direct and substantial impact on how business firms conduct various activities. In this section, we discuss some of the basic concepts of law, including the sources of law, the U.S. court system, and laws affecting business.

Law
A standard or rule established by a society to govern the behavior of its members.

Sources of Law

The United States Constitution specifies how the U.S. government must operate, and it is the foundation of law. Federal and state constitutions provide the framework for the various levels of government, which derive laws from three major sources: common law, statutory law, and administrative law.

Common law The body of law created by judges through their court decisions is known as **common law.** Based on custom, usage, and court rulings of early England, common law came to America when the first colonies were established and has become a major body of law in the United States. Judicial decisions establish precedents, or standards, that later are used in similar cases. Following precedents gives certainty and stability to many areas of law.

Common Law
The body of law created by judges through their court decisions.

Statutory law A law created by a federal, state, or local legislature, constitution, or treaty is called a **statute**. Most laws created today are statutes. Together the laws enacted by various legislative bodies make up **statutory law.** A statute must be drawn up in a precise manner to be constitutional. However, courts often must interpret a law's meaning. Court decisions sometimes lead to statutes being changed, clarified, or even dismissed entirely.

Many statutes pertain to the business environment or business practices. Congress, for example, passes laws establishing tax regulations for individuals and businesses. State legislatures and city councils also pass laws regulating general and specific business practices. For instance, a toxic substances law

Statute
A law created by a federal, state, or local legislature, treaty, or constitution.

Statutory Law
As a body, the laws enacted by federal, state, and local governments, constitutions, or treaties.

Tobacco companies are required by law to place warnings like these on their products. The New York Lung Association uses their warning to make a point about the dangers of smoking.

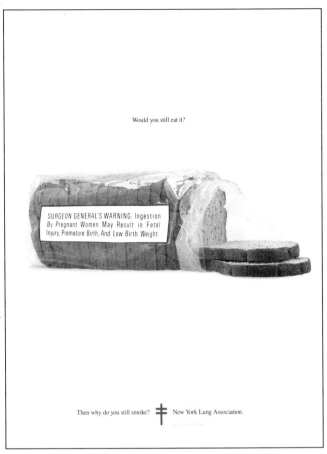

Would you still eat it?

SURGEON GENERAL'S WARNING: Ingestion By Pregnant Women May Result in Fetal Injury, Premature Birth, And Low Birth Weight.

Then why do you still smoke?   New York Lung Association.

Courtesy of New York Lung Association

Uniform Commercial Code (UCC)
Comprehensive statutory laws designed to eliminate differences between state laws governing business.

Administrative Law
Regulation affecting business, passed by state and federal administrative agencies.

passed in California requires that the public be warned about the dangers of any products containing toxic substances that could cause cancer or birth defects.[2]

An important part of statutory law is the **Uniform Commercial Code (UCC),** a group of statutory laws designed to simplify interstate commerce by eliminating differences between state laws governing business. The UCC, consisting of 10 articles, covers the rights of buyers and sellers in transactions. Originally drafted in 1952, the UCC has been adopted in its entirety by every state except Louisiana (which has adopted about half of the code).

Administrative law   Regulations passed by state and federal administrative agencies are included in **administrative law.** Numerous administrative agencies enforce laws affecting business. Federal agencies with extensive powers include the Federal Trade Commission, the Consumer Product Safety Commission, the Federal Communications Commission, and the Food and Drug Administration. Table 5.1 lists the major federal agencies and their responsibilities. Agencies on the state level include public utility commissions, licensing boards for various professions and trades, and other regulatory bodies. Some

TABLE 5.1

Major Government Agencies

Government Agency	Responsibility
Federal Trade Commission (FTC)	Antitrust, deceptive advertising.
Interstate Commerce Commission (ICC)	Interstate rail, bus, truck, and water carriers.
Environmental Protection Agency (EPA)	Pollution standards and control.
Food and Drug Administration (FDA)	Consumer protection from hazardous products.
Occupational Safety and Health Administration (OSHA)	Safety in the workplace.
Federal Communications Commission (FCC)	Radio, television, and telephone communications.
Securities and Exchange Commission (SEC)	Stocks and bonds.
Consumer Product Safety Commission	Consumer safety.
Federal Power Commission (FPC)	Rates and sales of natural gas.
Nuclear Regulatory Commission (NRC)	Nuclear power.

examples of local agencies are planning commissions, zoning boards, and boards of appeal.

The Court System

The court system, or judiciary, is the branch of government responsible for applying laws to settle disputes between parties. Courts possess **jurisdiction,** the legal right and power to interpret and apply laws and make binding decisions. The major method of taking disputes to court is by filing a lawsuit. Singer Bette Midler filed lawsuits against Ford Motor Co. and its advertising agency, Young & Rubicam, for advertisements featuring one of her backup vocalists singing a song for which Midler is well known. In the lawsuits, Midler charged that her voice had been imitated.[3] Although the judge ruled there was insufficient evidence to proceed against Ford, Midler was awarded $400,000 from Young & Rubicam.[4] Because of the considerable time and expense involved in going to court, many firms try to resolve their legal disputes outside the courtroom.[5]

Jurisdiction
The right and power of a court to interpret and apply laws and make binding decisions.

A dual court system operates in the United States. The federal government and each of the 50 state governments have separate court systems, as Figure 5.1 illustrates. The federal court system includes district courts established by Congress, federal courts of appeals, and the Supreme Court (created by the U.S. Constitution). The systems established by the states include circuit courts, courts of appeals, and state supreme courts.

Federal court system   Federal courts primarily hear cases involving questions of constitutional law; federal crimes; disputes between citizens of different states (or between an American citizen and a citizen of another country) over property valued at $10,000 or more; bankruptcy, tax, postal, copyright, patent, or trademark laws; and maritime cases.

FIGURE 5.1

The U.S. Court System

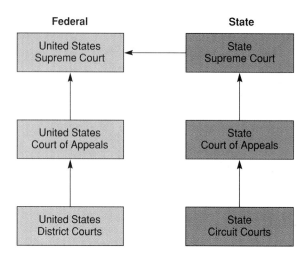

A U.S. district court is the first to hear a federal case (see Figure 5.1). At least one district court is located in each state. The decision resolving the case is made by a jury, or by the judge if each party waives the right to a jury trial. The losing party can appeal the case to the U.S. court of appeals for that region, one of 13 federal courts of appeals. Finally, a party may appeal the decision of a U.S. court of appeals to the U.S. Supreme Court.

The highest court of the land, the U.S. Supreme Court is composed of nine justices appointed by the president and confirmed by the Senate. Justices are appointed to the Supreme Court for life. The Court's major function is to hear cases appealed from the U.S. courts of appeals or state supreme courts. The Supreme Court decides which cases to hear; roughly 4 percent of all appeals are heard each year.[6]

State courts   Most state court systems are similar to the federal system (see Figure 5.1). Cases originate in a circuit court; each county generally has a circuit court. Most states also have courts of appeals. Decisions of a court of appeals can be appealed to the state supreme court. Finally, decisions made by a state supreme court that involve a question of constitutional or federal law can be appealed to the U.S. Supreme Court.

Specialized courts   Several specialized courts have been created to hear certain types of cases. Some states have small-claims courts to hear cases involving disputes over small amounts of money, usually below $1,500. States also commonly have divorce courts, juvenile courts, and traffic courts. At the federal level, specialized courts include the U.S. Tax Court (for tax cases) and the U.S. Court of Claims (for claims against the government).

Rock bands like Mötley Crüe may be liable if concertgoers suffer hearing loss.

Helmut Werb/Shooting Star

LAWS AFFECTING BUSINESS

Numerous and varied laws regulate the activities of all businesses and everyone involved in the business, from owner to manager to employee. In this section, we discuss the major business law categories, which involve torts, contracts, sales, agency, property, bankruptcy, and negotiable instruments.

The Law of Torts

While criminal law deals with crimes against society or the state, tort law is concerned with compensating the victims of noncriminal wrongs. Derived from the French word for wrong, a **tort** is a noncriminal (civil) injury to other persons or their property or reputation. Torts can be intentional or they may result from negligence. *Intentional torts* are deliberate acts by a person or business firm. For example, slander (spoken defamation of character) and libel (written defamation of character) are intentional torts. A tort results from *negligence* when one party fails to exercise reasonable care and causes injury to another. Negligence torts arise from carelessness rather than intentional behavior. A hotel, for example, may be held responsible for injuries to a guest who trips on loose or worn carpeting on the premises.

Product liability is an important part of tort law. **Product liability** involves the responsibility of business firms for negligence in design, manufacture, sale, and operation of their products. A Florida woman sued the heavy-metal rock band Mötley Crüe and Beach Club Promotions Inc. after attending a concert by the group. She experienced a severe hearing loss and claimed the musicians and concert promoters knew that the volume of the music posed a danger and that they failed to warn ticket holders. Her attorney noted that the performers wore

Tort
A noncriminal (civil) injury to other persons or their property or reputation; results from intentional acts or negligence.

Product Liability
Area of tort law that holds business firms responsible for negligence in design, manufacture, sale, and operation of their products.

Clearing the Air: Product Liability in the Tobacco Industry

Since the 1960s, only four tobacco product liability cases have ever reached juries. Large tobacco companies use persuasive means and vast resources to avoid paying damages in suits, as the case of *Horton* v. *American Brands* shows. Nathan H. Horton, a carpenter, smoked two packs of Pall Malls daily for more than 30 years. After he died of lung cancer, his family sued American Brands. Horton was black, and the trial was in the small, predominantly black community of Lexington, Mississippi. Under the state's negligence law, 9 of the 12 jurors could find the company at fault by only 1 percent and still establish liability. It looked like a product liability case the tobacco industry would lose—for the first time.

Determined to win, American Brands hired respected local trial lawyers and spent $10 million on its defense. The judge declared a mistrial after the jury was deadlocked 7–5. The strategy appeared to pay off. But officials are investigating allegations that American Brands improperly attempted to influence the jury. Attorneys for the Horton family claim that a group of area residents were

paid $50 an hour to help influence the trial. Ordering an investigation, the judge said, "There's enough smoke. I want to see if there's some fire."

Horton v. *American Brands* put the tobacco companies on notice, but it was *Cipollone* v. *Liggett, Philip Morris, and Lorillard* that shocked the industry. Antonio Cipollone's wife, Rose, died of lung cancer in 1984. Cipollone claimed that the Liggett Group, Inc. implied in advertisements run before 1966 that cigarette smoking was safe; the federal jury agreed and awarded $400,000 to Cipollone. The jury maintained that Liggett's ads should have warned customers about the dangers of smoking. Analysts predict the *Cipollone* case will lead to many lawsuits using the same argument: failure to warn. Litigation expert Calvert Crary believes that this complaint could be made against every tobacco company, since at one time or another they all implied their products were safe. For instance, in the 1940s, R. J. Reynolds stated in an ad that "more doctors smoke Camels."

Tobacco companies have maintained for many years that smokers must take personal responsibility for their actions and that no conclusive evidence links smoking to lung cancer. Their stance is not

expected to change, but the Horton case put the courtroom tactics of tobacco companies under close watch. And the Cipollone case proved a jury will award damages in a tobacco product liability case.

The future of product liability for the tobacco industry remains cloudy. Giants Philip Morris and Batus Inc. are backing a bill that would put a 15-year limit on lawsuits and allow as a defense the fact that products met government standards at the time they were manufactured. Many large manufacturers, armed with lobbying funds from the tobacco industry, are joining it to support the bill. In the meantime, the Supreme Court has said that it will decide whether warning labels on cigarette packs protect tobacco companies from product liability suits. The case will be argued in the Court's fall 1991 term. If the Court decides against tobacco companies, antismoking groups predict the industry could face ruinous lawsuits.[7]

earplugs on stage.[8] This case is one of several such product liability complaints against rock bands in recent years. The Business Action examines some product liability cases in the tobacco industry. (Product liability will be discussed further in Chapter Twenty.)

In certain instances, product liability laws have been expanded to cases in which the producer or marketer of the product is not proved negligent. Under **strict product liability**, the manufacturer is responsible if the injured party can show that the product was defective, that the defect caused the injury, and that the defect caused the product to be dangerous.

Strict Product Liability
Legal concept that holds manufacturers responsible for injuries caused by products regardless of whether negligence was involved.

The Law of Contracts

A **contract** is a legally enforceable, voluntary agreement between two or more parties. A contract is like a private statute, in which the parties define the considerations they owe each other. Contracts are generally part of most business transactions. They can be either express or implied. An *express contract* is one in which the words are actually put forth, either orally or in writing. Generally, oral contracts are just as legally enforceable as written contracts. (Some types of contracts must be in writing to be valid, such as for the sale of an interest in land.) But since the words used in an oral contract may be difficult to prove at a later time when parties are in dispute, the best policy for business firms to follow is to put all contracts in writing. An *implied contract* results from the actions of the parties rather than from an explicit promise. For example, when a passenger boards a train, it is implied that the passenger will have a ticket when the agent collects them and that the train will provide safe transportation to the destination. Again, since actions can be misunderstood, the best policy in business situations is for the contract to be expressed in words and written down.

Contract
A legally enforceable, voluntary agreement between two or more parties.

To be enforceable, a contract must meet several requirements:

- *Voluntary agreement.* Both parties must accept the terms of the agreement voluntarily, free of coercion, fraud, and the like.
- *Consideration.* Each party must provide something of value to the other, such as money, a product, or a promise to do or not do something.
- *Contractual capacity.* Each party must have the legal ability to enter into a binding agreement. (Generally, minors, persons with mental handicaps, and intoxicated persons do not have contractual capacity.)
- *Legality.* A contract must not involve any unlawful act.

The failure of one party to live up to a contractual agreement is called **breach of contract.** For example, failure to make payments on a car loan would be considered breach of contract. The bank or other lending institution could bring legal action against the breaking party—the car owner who signed the loan— and recover damages.

Breach of Contract
The failure of one party to live up to a contractual agreement.

The Law of Sales

Sales law, which grew out of contract law, involves products sold for money or credit. Sales agreements are contracts subject to the requirements discussed above. Article 2 of the Uniform Commercial Code provides that some sales contracts are binding even if all the requirements for a contract are not met. For

Sales Law
Body of law involving the sale of products for money or on credit.

Ford's Lifetime Service Guarantee is an express warranty.

What many other car repair guarantees cover after 90 days.

The Lifetime Service Guarantee lasts for as long as you own your Ford, Lincoln or Mercury. That's Peace of Mind."

Most car repair guarantees last for only 90 days or 4,000 miles. Ours lasts a lifetime.
A lifetime means you only pay for a covered repair once. If it ever needs to be fixed again, just hand a copy of the bill to your dealer. He'll fix it free. Free parts. Free labor. For as long as you own your vehicle.
A lifetime means it doesn't matter how many miles you drive. Or if your car is new or used. And that means LSG covers more parts and labor longer than anyone else. Which makes it **QUALITY CARE** America's best car **FOR QUALITY CARS** repair guarantee.
Ask a participating Ford or Lincoln-Mercury dealer for LSG. Because Peace of Mind is having a guarantee that won't disappear.

© 1990 Ford Motor Company

Courtesy of the Ford Motor Company

instance, a sales agreement is legally binding even if the selling price is left out of the agreement; the buyer must pay the reasonable value of the goods.

Article 2 also establishes the law of warranty for sales transactions. An **express warranty** is any statement of fact or promise made by the seller to the buyer relating to the products sold, and which becomes an important part of the sales agreement. A warranty is in the nature of a guarantee, although no formal words such as *warrant* or *guarantee* need be used. If the products in fact are not as represented by the seller, the seller can be held responsible either to make the products as warranted or to give the buyer the money back. The law also imposes an **implied warranty,** not specifically expressed by the parties, ensuring that the business firm has clear title of the products it sells and that the products will serve the purpose for which they are sold.

The Law of Agency

An **agency** is a business relationship in which a principal (the person or business entity who wants a task performed) appoints an agent (the person or business entity who performs the task) to act on his or her behalf. The actions of the agent, authorized by the principal, are legally recognized as though they were

Express Warranty
Oral or written assurances made by the seller regarding a product.

Implied Warranty
Warranty legally imposed on the seller; ensures that the seller owns the products and that they will serve the purpose for which they are sold.

Agency
A legal relationship between two parties who agree that the agent will act on behalf of the principal.

performed by the principal. For example, a talent agent can enter into a contract for a client as though the client signed the contract him- or herself. Agents are used in many diverse industries, including insurance, sports, entertainment, and real estate. Generally, agents are paid a fee or commission for their services.

Because the principal is bound by the actions of the agent, it is important to put the agency agreement in writing. Generally, a legal document called a **power of attorney** is granted to authorize the agent to act on behalf of the principal. For instance, a person may grant an accountant power of attorney to act as his or her agent during a tax audit. It is the agent's duty to act in a professional manner and to exercise good judgment. The agency relationship can be terminated when the task is completed or by mutual agreement of the parties.

Power of Attorney
A legal document authorizing an agent to act on behalf of the principal.

The Law of Property

Anything that can be owned is considered property. Property is something for which a person or business entity has unrestricted right of possession or use. There are several categories of property. **Real property** is real estate, land, and anything permanently attached to it, such as houses, buildings, and parking lots. **Tangible personal property** means physical items such as a store's inventory of goods, equipment, and automobiles. **Intangible personal property** is that shown by documents or other written instruments, such as checks, money orders, receipts, stocks, and bonds.

Three forms of intangible personal property provide legal protection for individuals or business firms. A **trademark** is a name or symbol registered with the U.S. Patent and Trademark Office. It guarantees the owner exclusive rights for 20 years and can be renewed as many times as the owner wishes. **Patents**, granted by the U.S. Patent and Trademark Office, give inventors the exclusive right to make, use, or sell their products for 17 years. Patents cannot be renewed. In patent disputes during the 1980s, the courts ruled increasingly in favor of the rights of patent owners.[9] A **copyright**, filed with the U.S. Copyright Office, gives the creator exclusive right to publish and sell an original written work. Copyrights last for the lifetime of the author plus 50 years. Hal David and a group of songwriters and music publishers filed a suit against Sony to protect their music from being copied on recorders that can make perfect copies of compact disks. Sony's defense was that people have been taping music at home for years.[10]

Real Property
Real estate (land and anything permanently attached to it, such as houses, buildings, and parking lots).

Tangible Personal Property
Physical items, such as goods and equipment.

Intangible Personal Property
Property represented by a document or other written statement.

Trademark
A name or symbol, registered with the U.S. Patent and Trademark Office, that guarantees the owner exclusive rights to its use.

Patent
The exclusive right of an inventor to make, use, or sell the registered product.

Copyright
Protection of an individual's exclusive right to publish and sell original written materials.

The Law of Bankruptcy

Bankruptcy is a legal procedure for individuals and firms that cannot pay their debts. By declaring bankruptcy, the individual or firm asks the court to be declared unable to satisfy creditors and to be released from financial obligations. The debtor's assets are usually sold to pay off as much of the debt as possible.

Three types of bankruptcy are possible: Chapter 7, Chapter 11, and Chapter 13. Under *Chapter 7* bankruptcy, the business firm is dissolved, and the assets are sold to pay off debt. Individuals filing Chapter 7 are allowed to keep a limited amount of assets, determined by federal or state law. *Chapter 11*

Bankruptcy
The legal procedure for nonpayment of debts.

FIGURE 5.2

Types of Endorsements

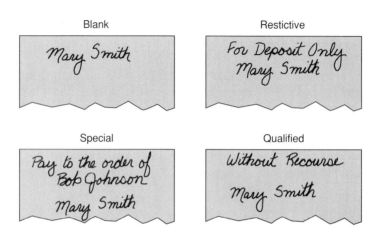

Blank

Mary Smith

Restictive

For Deposit Only
Mary Smith

Special

Pay to the order of
Bob Johnson
Mary Smith

Qualified

Without Recourse

Mary Smith

bankruptcy temporarily relieves a company from its debts while it reorganizes and works out a payment plan with its creditors. *Chapter 13* bankruptcy allows an individual to establish a plan for repaying debts within three to five years.

The Law of Negotiable Instruments

Negotiable Instrument
A written promise to pay a specified sum of money; it can be transferred from one person or firm to another.

A **negotiable instrument** is a substitute for money. It is a written promise to pay a specified sum of money; it can be transferred from one person or business firm to another. Examples of negotiable instruments include checks, drafts, and certificates of deposit. The Uniform Commercial Code specifies that negotiable instruments must meet the following requirements:

- They must be in writing and signed by the maker or drawer (the party who orders the payment of the money).
- They must contain an unconditional promise to pay a certain sum of money.
- They must be payable on demand or at a specific date.
- They must be payable to a specific person or business firm or to the bearer (the party who possesses the instrument).

Endorsement
A person's signature on the back of a negotiable instrument, making it transferable.

The payee (the one to whom the instrument is written) must endorse a negotiable instrument before it is transferred. An **endorsement** is a person's signature on the back of a negotiable instrument (see Figure 5.2). A *blank* endorsement is accomplished when the payee signs the back of the instrument. This type of endorsement can be unsafe because anyone can cash the instrument once it is endorsed. Using the words *for deposit only* along with the signature constitutes a *restrictive* endorsement; it states what the instrument is for and is much safer than a blank endorsement. A *special* endorsement specifies to whom the instrument is payable by including the person's or firm's name on the back of the instrument along with the signature. Restrictive and special endorsements protect the negotiable instrument should it be lost or stolen. Finally, a *qualified* endorsement—usually the words *without recourse*—means

TABLE 5.2

Major Laws Designed to Preserve Competition

Law	Purpose
Sherman Antitrust Act (1890)	Prohibits contacts or conspiracies that attempt to reduce competition.
Clayton Act (1914)	Prohibits specific acts that reduce competition: price discrimination, tying agreements, binding contracts, and community of interest.
Federal Trade Commission Act (1914)	Prohibits unfair trade practices and deceptive advertising.
Robinson-Patman Act (1936)	Prohibits price discrimination that reduces competition.
Celler-Kefauver Act (1950)	Prohibits mergers that reduce competition.
Antitrust Improvement Act (1976)	Provides additional time for the Federal Trade Commission and the Justice Department to evaluate proposed mergers.
Gramm-Rudman Act (1985)	Requires Congress to meet annual deficit targets and to balance the federal budget by 1993.

the person who originally signed the instrument, not the endorser, is responsible for payment. The endorser does not guarantee payment if the instrument is not backed by sufficient funds.

GOVERNMENT REGULATION OF BUSINESS

The federal and state governments have enacted substantial legislation to encourage competition among business firms. Many laws, such as those outlawing monopolies, price-fixing, and other practices that restrain trade, are intended to help ensure that consumers have a choice in the marketplace and that firms have the freedom to compete. In this section, we discuss federal laws designed to regulate competition among American business firms. Table 5.2 summarizes these laws.

Sherman Antitrust Act

One of the first laws passed to regulate competition, the Sherman Antitrust Act (1890) declared that two or more business firms could not agree to the prices to be charged for goods. It also prohibited business firms from dividing markets among themselves and from deciding not to sell to or buy from a particular company.

The Sherman Antitrust Act was not used for more than a decade. But in the early 1900s, with Teddy Roosevelt in the White House, the act was used to break up J. P. Morgan's railroad monopoly, John D. Rockefeller's Standard Oil, and Buck Duke's tobacco trust.[11] Today the Sherman Act is still the basis for legal action. For example, in one case the Justice Department charged three Arizona dentists with criminal price-fixing in setting patient fees.[12]

Clayton Act

Congress enacted the Clayton Act in 1914 to strengthen the Sherman Antitrust Act. Specifically, the Clayton Act outlawed five practices that reduce competition. These are:

- *Price discrimination*—charging one firm (usually a large one) a lower price for goods than the price other (usually smaller) firms are charged.
- *Tying agreements*—requiring a buyer to purchase unwanted products for the right to purchase desired products.
- *Binding contracts*—requiring a buyer to purchase products from a specific supplier.
- *Interlocking directorates*—a member of the board of directors of one firm serving on the board of a competing firm when the total combined capital of the two firms is more than $1 million.
- *Community of interest*—a business buying stock in a competing firm to reduce competition between the two.

Federal Trade Commission Act

The Federal Trade Commission Act (1914) established the Federal Trade Commission (FTC), a five-member committee empowered to investigate illegal trade practices. This act prohibits all unfair methods of competition. The Wheeler-Lea Amendment (1938) expanded the FTC's power to eliminate deceptive business practices, including those affecting consumers as well as competitors.

The FTC acts on its own accord to investigate a firm's business practices or on complaints made by other firms or individuals. Recent targets have included fly-by-night telemarketers who use television to help sell fraudulent products. One firm, Twin Star Productions, produced commercials that used a talk show format and lasted as long as 30 minutes to sell diet aids and baldness cures.[13]

Robinson-Patman Act

The Robinson-Patman Act, passed in 1936, outlaws price discrimination that substantially reduces competition. Price discounts are legal, however, if they are based on actual lower selling costs, such as discounts for large orders. The act also prohibits advertising and promotional allowances unless they are offered to all retailers regardless of size.

Celler-Kefauver Act

The Celler-Kefauver Act (1950) outlaws mergers through the purchase of assets, when the mergers tend to reduce competition. The act also makes it mandatory that all mergers be approved by the FTC and the Justice Department. The FTC denied a proposal by McKesson, the largest U.S. drug wholesaler, to take over number four, Alco Health Services Corp. The merger would have given McKesson 90 percent of the market in some states.[14]

Antitrust Improvement Act

The Antitrust Improvement Act of 1976 strengthens previous antitrust laws. The act gives the FTC and the Justice Department a longer period of time to evaluate proposed mergers. It also allows state attorneys general to prosecute firms accused of price-fixing.

Gramm-Rudman Act

The Gramm-Rudman Act was passed in 1985 to force politicians to meet annual deficit targets, thereby balancing the budget by 1991. In a 1987 rewrite, the date for achieving a balanced budget was postponed to 1993. To reduce the deficit, the government has cut spending on defense and other goods and services, impacting many industries. Gramm-Rudman could also result in higher corporate taxes because corporate taxation is one of the major means of reducing the deficit.

DEREGULATION

Since the 1970s, a trend toward deregulation of business has been evident. **Deregulation** is the process of reducing the involvement of government in the regulation of business, by eliminating legal restraints on competition. The goal of deregulation is to make business regulations less complex and to lower the costs of complying with them. Industries that have been most affected by the movement toward deregulation include airlines, railroads, and banking (see Table 5.3).

Deregulation
The process of reducing government involvement in the regulation of business, by eliminating legal restraints on competition.

TABLE 5.3

Major Deregulation Laws

Law	Purpose
Natural Gas Policy Act (1978)	Requires pipeline firms to transport natural gas owned by other companies.
Airline Deregulation Act (1978)	Eliminates regulation of airline rates and schedules.
Motor Carrier Act (1980)	Allows trucks to travel more freely and change prices more quickly.
Staggers Rail Act (1980)	Gives railroads more flexibility to raise and lower rates without government approval.
Depository Institutions Deregulatory Committee Act (1981) Depository Institutions Act (1982)	Permit financial institutions to compete on a more even basis for deposit accounts by paying higher interest rates and to broaden investments beyond homes and small commercial mortgages.
Drug Price Competition and Patent Term Restoration Act (1984)	Allows generic drugs to reach the market sooner by awarding patents for shorter periods of time.

● C o n n e c t i o n s

How Do You Feel about Regulation?

Directions: For each statement, circle the number that shows your level of agreement.

	Strongly Disagree					Strongly Agree
1. The government should let business regulate itself.	1	2	3	4	5	6
2. It is up to consumers to make sure the products they use are safe.	1	2	3	4	5	6
3. Firms should be able to advertise in the manner they desire.	1	2	3	4	5	6
4. Regulations and the paperwork they require cost businesses too much money.	1	2	3	4	5	6

Deregulation of business results in several benefits for business firms and consumers. Regulation costs firms and consumers billions of dollars each year; deregulation eliminates or reduces some of the costs, and the savings can be passed on to consumers. Deregulation can also increase competition, resulting in lower prices for consumers. After the airline industry was deregulated, for example, air fares dropped to the lowest levels in many years. Increased competition can also lead to better service. Since the government deregulated the banking industry, many banks are providing more services, such as discount brokerages (for purchasing stocks, bonds, and other securities) and money market accounts.

TABLE 5.4

Regulation of Business: Is the Government Doing Enough?

DID YOU KNOW? *In an era of deregulation, one survey shows that a majority of Americans wants more government control in several important areas.*

Area	"No" Answers
Toxic waste disposal	73% surveyed
Exposure to hazardous substances	60
Honesty/accuracy in advertising	56
Use of pesticides and herbicides	52
Manufacture/sale of barbiturates	51

Source: Roper Reports (reported by Julie Stacey, *USA Today,* July 17, 1988, p. A1). Copyright, USA TODAY. Reprinted with permission.

5. The public and business firms, not
   the government, need to control
   pollution.   1   2   3   4   5   6

Feedback: Government regulation of business is a sensitive issue. It does indeed
increase the amount of paperwork firms must do. It may limit business activities.
Yet, without regulation, firms may not act in the interest of consumers or the public.
In short, someone usually needs to police the activities of business firms, whether
it be the government, businesses themselves, or another alternative.

Do you think government is the best source of regulation? If you circled 1 or 2
for most statements, you strongly think so. In which business sectors would you
like to see more regulation? If you chose 3 or 4, you are neutral. Finally, if you circled 5 or 6, you strongly support less government regulation. In what realms of
business should the government regulate less?

Opponents of deregulation fear that this trend could actually reduce competition. For example, since the airline industry has been deregulated, many
major carriers have gone out of business, while others continue to lose money.
Many politicians and consumers believe that further deregulation will lead to
some of the same problems that led to government regulation in the first
place—pollution, poor working conditions, and low-quality products. As
shown in Table 5.4, many Americans think greater regulation is needed. The
future of deregulation is uncertain, but it will depend to a large extent on the
conduct of business organizations. Do you think U.S. business needs more
regulation or less? The Connections quiz will help you determine your attitude
toward regulation.

GOVERNMENT TAXATION

Citizens of a country must pay for the services the government provides. This
is accomplished through taxation. A **tax** is a payment for the support of government activities, required of organizations and individuals within the domain
of the government. Revenues from taxes pay for national defense, roads,
schools, social programs, medical care, regulation of business, and for government itself.

The U.S. government obtains about 95 percent of the money it needs to
operate through taxes, including corporate and personal income taxes and
other federal taxes. State and local governments are also financed through
taxation. Taxation can be viewed as another form of government regulation,
because virtually all business firms and individuals pay taxes.

Tax
A payment for the support of
government activities, required of organizations and
individuals within the domain
of the government.

Do Foreign—Owned Companies in the United States Pay Taxes?

Foreign-owned companies operating in the United States make a lot of money. From 1979 to 1987, the assets of foreign corporations grew 368 percent, to $959 billion. During that same period, the receipts of these firms grew 183 percent, to $685 billion. Yet in 1986 these same companies reported a net loss of $1.5 billion. Most foreign corporations operating in the United States pay little or no tax to Washington; the loss is estimated at $20 to $30 billion.

How can firms that show such growth be losing money? That is what the IRS wants to know. In 1990 it began investigating the 1989 income tax returns of foreign-owned firms. The IRS believes that if foreign companies were losing so much money, they would pull out of the U.S. market. Instead, the firms were increasing their investments.

Japanese firms are thought to be major offenders. Easily the most successful foreign investors in the United States during the past decade, the Japanese have nevertheless reported decreasing income during that time. That fact prompted the IRS to launch investigations of 18 Japanese companies.

IRS officials think foreign companies are overcharging their U.S.–based firms. This strategy is sometimes referred to as *transfer of payments*. The corporation gains an advantage by shifting costs to a high-tax country and income to low-tax countries. For instance, a product is manufactured in Germany at a cost of $80, and then sold to an Irish subsidiary for $80. The tax rate is 48 percent, but no taxes are paid because there was no profit. The Irish subsidiary then sells the item to a U.S. subsidiary for $150, earning a $70 profit. The tax rate in Ireland is 4 percent, so $2.80 is paid in taxes. The U.S. subsidiary then sells the item at cost for $150. The U.S. tax rate is 34 percent, but no profit is earned. The Irish subsidiary then lends money to the U.S. company for future expansion. Such transfer of payments is illegal but extremely difficult to prove.

The IRS runs into several obstacles when investigating a suspected corporate tax evader. First, the agency is understaffed; in 1990 it was just beginning to examine 1987 tax returns. If the IRS does decide to audit a company, investigators are often outmatched by the troop of accountants that represents the corporation. When the IRS does decide to prosecute a case, six to eight years may pass before it reaches court.

No one knows exactly how to solve the problem. Congress may end up writing some form of legislation to enable the IRS to conduct effective global audits. But many observers fear that as long as firms devote large sums of money to the illegal practice of shifting, the IRS stands little chance of catching them.[15]

Courtesy of Ingersoll-Rand Company

Revenues from taxes are needed to build and maintain highways.

Corporate Income Tax

Corporations are required to pay federal tax on their income, after deducting allowable business expenses. Corporations pay a **progressive tax,** meaning the percentage of income paid in taxes increases as income increases. The federal tax rate for corporations is:

Progressive Tax
Form of taxation in which the percentage of income paid in taxes increases as income increases.

- 15 percent on the first $50,000 of pretax profit.
- 25 percent of the next $25,000.
- 34 percent on profits over $75,000.
- 39 percent on profits between $100,000 and $335,000.
- A flat federal rate of 34 percent on profits over $335,000.

As noted in Chapter Two, some corporate profits are actually taxed twice. The corporation must first pay a federal income tax on its profits. Then, if the corporation distributes profits to shareholders by declaring dividends, the shareholders must pay a personal income tax on the dividends they receive. The Business Action examines how the profits of some foreign-owned companies operating in the United States go untaxed.

Individual Income Tax

Individuals are subject to a personal income tax. In 1991, three tax rates were used for individuals: 15 percent for single individuals with a yearly income of $20,350 or less; 28 percent for those with an annual income from $20,350 to $49,300; and 31 percent for individuals earning over $49,300 a year.[16] For employees, most income tax is withheld from paychecks by employers and paid to the Internal Revenue Service (IRS). Individuals who own a sole proprietorship or a partnership pay income taxes to the IRS in four quarterly payments.

Every individual paying income taxes must file a return with the IRS on or before April 15 each year (unless an extension is requested and granted). If too much money was deducted from an individual's paycheck, he or she is entitled to a refund. A person may owe additional taxes if insufficient taxes were withheld. Individuals also pay state and, in many cases, local (city) income taxes.

Other Taxes

Federal, state, and local governments use several taxes other than income taxes as sources of funds. The second largest source of federal revenue is *social security tax,* which both employers and employees pay. This tax provides retirement, disability, hospital insurance, and death benefits for participants. In 1991 the annual social security tax was 15.30 percent of the first $51,300 earned; the employee pays half and the employer pays half. Employers also pay an annual *unemployment tax* of 6.2 percent of the first $7,000 of each employee's wages. This tax is used to fund unemployed workers.

The government taxes products to help pay for services directed at those who use the products and sometimes to discourage the use of harmful products. An *excise tax* is a tax on the manufacture or sale of a domestic product. For instance, Americans pay an excise tax on gasoline to help finance the construction of roads and bridges. The government has also set an excise tax on tobacco and alcohol products to discourage their use. Before his retirement, then Surgeon General C. Everett Koop urged the government to increase the excise tax on alcoholic beverages to discourage consumption of alcohol.[17] The government also places an *import tax* on certain foreign products entering the United States.

The majority of states obtain most of their revenues through a *sales tax* on the merchandise consumers buy; some cities levy additional sales taxes on the same products. Some states have no sales tax, while others exempt certain items such as food from being taxed. Local governments raise the majority of their operating revenues through a *property tax* on both commercial and residential property, such as land, buildings, machinery, houses, and automobiles.

You'll Know It's the Century When . . .

The Good Ol' Boys Are History

Women, blacks, Hispanics, and other minorities will drive politics in the 21st century. As new personalities enter government, the way government regulates business is likely to be affected. By 2000, minorities will be mayors in most of the nation's largest cities. Blacks and Hispanics will win more elections for two reasons: because of their growing numbers, and because minority voter participation rates will increase relative to white voter participation. Racial crossover voting will be more common.

At the turn of the century, women will make up more than half of all college students and almost half of all workers. But long before substantial numbers of women take their place as leaders in industry, they will win the popular vote for political office. In the first presidential election of the 21st century, 53 percent of voters will be women. Even though women may not be making the majority of executive decisions on the inside, women in government will have their say in how businesses are operated.[18]

SUMMARY OF LEARNING OBJECTIVES

1. To list the sources from which laws are derived.
   Laws have a substantial impact on how business firms conduct activities. The various levels of government derive laws from three sources: common law, created by judges through court decisions; statutory laws, passed by federal, state, and local legislatures; and administrative laws, enacted by federal and state administrative agencies.

2. To outline the court system in the United States.
   The U.S. judicial system is charged with the application of law to settle disputes between parties. The United States has a dual court system. The federal court system includes district courts, courts of appeals, and the Supreme Court. The state court system includes circuit courts, courts of appeals, and state supreme courts. Specialized state courts include small-claims, divorce, juvenile, and traffic courts.

3. To identify the various categories of business law.
   Several types of laws regulate business activities. These include tort law (which includes product liability) and laws governing contractual agreements, sales agreements, use of agents, property transactions, bankruptcy proceedings, and negotiable instruments.

4. To describe how government regulates business activities to encourage competition.
   The most important laws designed to preserve competition are the Sherman Antitrust Act (1890), which prohibits price-fixing, firms dividing markets among themselves, and boycotting certain firms; the Clayton Act (1914), which prevents price discrimination, tying agreements, binding contracts, interlocking directorates, and community of interest; the Federal Trade Commission Act (1914), which prohibits all unfair methods of competition; the Robinson-Patman Act (1936), which outlaws price discrimination that reduces competition; the Celler-Kefauver Act (1950), which outlaws mergers through the purchase of assets; the Antitrust Improvement Act (1976), which strengthens the previous laws; and the Gramm-Rudman Act (1985), passed to force politicians to meet annual deficit targets.

5. To explain the effects of deregulation on business.
   Since the 1970s, the United States has experienced a trend toward deregulation—reducing government involvement in the regulation of business. Deregulation can lower the costs of regulating business and can lead to increased competition, better service, and lower prices.

6. To describe how taxation supports the activities of government.
   Citizens pay for the work of government through taxation. Corporations and individuals are subject to federal, state, and local taxes, including

taxes on the money they earn, the property they own, and the products they purchase.

KEY TERMS

Law, p. 165

Common Law, p. 165

Statute, p. 165

Statutory Law, p. 165

Uniform Commercial Code (UCC), p. 166

Administrative Law, p. 166

Jurisdiction, p. 167

Tort, p. 169

Product Liability, p. 169

Strict Product Liability, p. 171

Contract, p. 171

Breach of Contract, p. 171

Sales Law, p. 171

Express Warranty, p. 172

Implied Warranty, p. 172

Agency, p. 172

Power of Attorney, p. 173

Real Property, p. 173

Tangible Personal Property, p. 173

Intangible Personal Property, p. 173

Trademark, p. 173

Patent, p. 173

Copyright, p. 173

Bankruptcy, p. 173

Negotiable Instrument, p. 174

Endorsement, p. 174

Deregulation, p. 177

Tax, p. 179

Progressive Tax, p. 181

QUESTIONS FOR DISCUSSION AND REVIEW

1. Why are there three separate sources of law in our government? How do these sources of law relate with one another?

2. Explain the relationship between the state court system and the federal court system?

3. What is a tort? Give an example of a tort.

4. Why is product liability a concern of business firms?

5. What requirements must a contract meet to be enforceable? Have you ever entered into a contract?

6. What is the difference between an express warranty and an implied warranty? Give an example of each.

7. Explain the requirements of a negotiable instrument.

8. In a free enterprise system such as we have in the United States, why does government regulate business?

9. In our free enterprise system, why is it important to limit the size of an individual company?

10. List the specific practices the Clayton Act outlaws, and describe how each practice limits competition.

11. What has the movement toward deregulation been intended to accomplish?

12. How can government establish social policy through the use of taxes?

CASE 5.1
Name Brands versus Counterfeits:
A Tough Battle with High Stakes

We have all heard of counterfeiting before. Usually it refers to people making money—printing it instead of earning it. But counterfeiting also can involve all sorts of consumer goods and manufactured products. From well-known brand names such as Calvin Klein jeans to auto parts, counterfeiters have found ways to produce goods that look authentic. In some instances, counterfeit products look better than the original!

The demand for brand-name products has helped counterfeiting grow into a very profitable business throughout the world and into a serious problem for legitimate manufacturers and consumers alike. Faulty counterfeit parts have caused more than two dozen plane crashes. Most counterfeit auto parts do not meet federal safety standards.

Counterfeiting hurts manufacturers in many ways. Analysts estimate that, in the United States alone, annual revenue lost runs from $6 billion to $8 billion. Perhaps even worse, consumers blame the innocent manufacturer when they unknowingly buy a counterfeit product and find it doesn't perform as expected. Sometimes entire economies can suffer. For instance, when farmers in Kenya and Zaire used counterfeit fertilizers, both countries lost most of their crops.

In 1984 the U.S. government enacted the Trademark Counterfeiting Act and made counterfeiting of products a criminal offense punishable by fines and stiff jail terms. Unfortunately counterfeiting does not receive top priority from law enforcement officers and prosecutors. Legitimate firms therefore have the burden of finding their own ways to fight the problem. IBM, with a court order, conducted its own raids and found keyboards, displays, and boxes with its logo. The fake parts were used to create counterfeits of IBM's personal computer XT™.

Some companies have developed secret product codes to identify the genuine article. They must change the codes periodically because counterfeiters learn the codes and duplicate them. Perhaps the most effective way for manufacturers to fight counterfeiting is to monitor the distribution network and make sure counterfeit products are not getting into the network. Some companies even hire investigators to track counterfeit products.

By copying other firms' products, counterfeiters avoid research and development costs and most marketing costs. High-tech products such as computers are especially vulnerable. As long as counterfeiting is profitable, an abundance of products are available to copy, and the laws are difficult to enforce, counterfeiters can be expected to prosper for a long time.

Adapted from Ronald F. Bush, "Product Counterfeiting Self-Defense Strategies," *Boardroom Reports,* January 15, 1990, pp. 9–10; Celia F. McAllister, "Using Stool Pigeons to Clip Software Pirates' Wings," *Business Week,* March 19, 1990, p. 122; Chris Brown, "IBM Crackdown Uncovers Signs of Counterfeiting Ring," *Computerworld,* July 10, 1989, p. 95.

Questions for Discussion

1. What type of law does counterfeiting violate?
2. Why isn't the Trademark Counterfeiting Act of 1984 effective in controlling counterfeiting?
3. What part can manufacturers play in seeing that their products are not copied?
4. Can you suggest any other remedies for the counterfeiting situation?

CASE 5.2
Government Regulation of Advertising

During the Reagan administration in the 1980s, the government relaxed many controls over business practices. After Reagan left office, however, regulatory groups began to target several industries, including advertising. With the Senate and the House of Representatives considering more than 30 proposals concerning advertising, it looks like the days of deregulation of advertising are over. Advertisers of numerous products will feel the effects.

Senator Albert Gore of Tennessee and Representative Joseph Kennedy of Massachusetts are pushing for mandatory health warnings in all alcoholic beverage ads. Whether or not the Kennedy-Gore bill passes, the liquor industry expects more restrictions on its advertisements.

Congress is considering one of the most comprehensive antitobacco bills ever. Sponsored by Rep. Henry Waxman of California, the bill contains very restrictive provisions that would have the effect of eliminating most tobacco advertising. For example, ads could not use human or cartoon figures or even brand names or logos; they could show only a package against a white background. The bill would also ban tobacco companies from sponsoring auto, musical, or other special events and would eliminate merchandise such as T-shirts that promote tobacco. Additionally the Waxman bill would allow individual states to regulate tobacco advertising. Tobacco and liquor advertisements are faring no better in other parts of the world. The French government, for example, has approved the draft of a law banning all cigarette ads and most alcoholic beverage ads.

Sen. Edward Kennedy of Massachusetts chairs the Senate Labor and Human Resources Committee, which is investigating promotional practices in the prescription drug industry. Although the committee has remained tight-lipped, the investigation is rumored to center on practices such as giving doctors gifts and sending them on trips to encourage them to prescribe a firm's products.

Adapted from Steven W. Colford, "Ad-Bashing Is Back in Style," *Advertising Age,* April 30, 1990, pp. 4, 58; Teresa Y. Wiltz, "It's Enough to Drive the Distillers to Drink," *Business Week,* June 25, 1990, pp. 98–99; Patricia Winters and Laurie Freeman, "Sen. Kennedy Aims at Drug Marketing," *Advertising Age,* August 6, 1990, pp. 1, 36; Steven W. Colford, "Anti-Cig Bill Packs It All In,"*Advertising Age,* May 21, 1990, pp. 1, 60.

The industries in question claim the potential regulations are unfair. Citing basic freedoms, industry officials argue that the government is attempting to regulate what the public can hear. Government agencies and investigators do not agree. Federal Trade Commission (FTC) chairperson Janet Steiger declared one of her top priorities to be investigating the marketing of tobacco and alcohol products. Transportation secretary Samuel Skinner has agreed that alcohol ads may need greater regulation.

Questions for Discussion
1. Why do government agencies regulate the advertising of products such as tobacco and alcohol?
2. Should the government increase the regulation of advertising by the alcohol, tobacco, and prescription drug industries? Why or why not? How about advertising by other industries?
3. Is the government violating consumers' rights by regulating what they see and hear? Why or why not?

CHAPTER SIX

INTERNATIONAL BUSINESS

LEARNING OBJECTIVES

1. To understand the meaning and scope of international business.

2. To explain why firms become involved in international business.

3. To define the basic concepts of international business.

4. To list the various barriers to international business.

5. To identify the ways in which international business is regulated.

6. To list and describe the different approaches firms take to conduct business internationally.

7. To explain how a firm can adapt to foreign markets.

Fortuna Sports International/Shooting Star

The National Basketball Association (NBA) is on the offensive. Arenas throughout the United States are sold out; expansion teams have been added in Miami, Charlotte, Minnesota, and Orlando; television ratings are up. NBC paid a record $600 million for the broadcast rights to NBA games starting with the 1990 season. With all the success at home, NBA commissioner David Stern is looking toward international markets.

Sports are not new to international business. Tennis and golf have long been successful internationally. Major league baseball and National Football League games are televised in foreign countries. But basketball may have the greatest global potential of all American sports. The fastest-growing sport in the world, it is played by more than 200 million men and women around the globe, which makes it more popular than soccer.

Foreign countries also have their share of basketball fans. More than 50 countries broadcast NBA games. Pictures of NBA stars can be found on the covers of foreign basketball magazines, while inside are advertisements for sporting goods endorsed by Michael Jordan, Larry Bird, and other American superstars.

The NBA is taking advantage of basketball's global popularity. Revenues from overseas broadcasts for the 1988–89 season reached about $5 million, up 30 percent from the previous year, and are expected to exceed $25 million by 1995. Commissioner Stern also plans to expand the league into Europe. Some experts say at least six European cities will have NBA franchises by the end of the 1990s.

Expanding into Europe presents problems for the NBA. The talent pool of athletes will be spread out, perhaps creating weak expansion teams. Seating capacity requirements exceed the size of some cities' arenas. Certain aspects of the game may have to be adapted to European preferences. Europeans are used to international rules, which differ somewhat from NBA rules. They also prefer a multicolored ball over the standard ball. Nonetheless, many basketball insiders expect to see a true world championship played in the near future.[1]

L ike the NBA, more and more American firms are conducting business across national boundaries. The world is changing rapidly, and opportunities in foreign markets will play a critical role in the future of many U.S. firms.

In this chapter, we examine some of the unique aspects of international business. First we discuss the nature and scope of international business. Then we present the reasons why firms start to do business internationally. Next we introduce several concepts important to understanding international business. We explain some barriers to international business and discuss its regulation. Finally we describe different approaches to international business and discuss how a firm can adapt to foreign markets.

THE NATURE AND SCOPE OF INTERNATIONAL BUSINESS

Nearly 64 percent of the real estate in downtown Los Angeles and 39 percent in downtown Houston are owned by foreign investors. During the 1980s, foreign investment in the United States increased 636 percent.[2] Many U.S. corporations, such as Purina Mills and Standard Oil of Ohio, are controlled by foreign interests. The British, Canadians, and Japanese are the leading owners of U.S. assets.[3] Table 6.1 lists the states in which foreign companies and individuals own the most manufacturing plants, property, and equipment. The boundaries dividing the business world into separate nations have truly disappeared.

Dave Brown/Journalism Services

DID YOU KNOW? *Nearly 64 percent of the real estate in downtown Los Angeles is owned by foreign investors.*

Foreign Business in the United States

Directions: For each statement, circle the number that shows your level of agreement.

	Strongly Disagree					Strongly Agree
1. Foreign individuals and firms should be restricted from purchasing assets, such as banks, farmland, and hotels, in the United States.	1	2	3	4	5	6
2. Americans should purchase American-made products whenever possible.	1	2	3	4	5	6
3. The United States should limit the amount of foreign goods it imports.	1	2	3	4	5	6
4. Foreign companies should not be allowed to build factories in American cities.	1	2	3	4	5	6

TABLE 6.1

Foreign Investment in the United States

State	Foreign holdings ($ in billions)	State	Foreign holdings ($ in billions)
Texas	$40,324	Illinois	$11,057
California	37,017	New Jersey	10,608
New York	18,016	Ohio	9,530
Alaska	15,134	Florida	9,487
Louisiana	13,563	Pennsylvania	9,293

Source: Washington/Baltimore Regional Association, from Jack Anderson, "Who Owns America?" Reprinted with permission from PARADE, copyright © 1989.

As the 1990s progress, changes are sweeping the world at a record pace. In February 1990, the Soviet Communist party's Central Committee agreed to permit new, competing political parties, thereby ending 72 years of total communist rule.[4] As Russia inches closer to democracy, new opportunities open up for U.S. firms to enter Soviet markets; one study indicated that top priorities

5. The United States should put a
   high tax on all foreign goods en-
   tering the country.   1   2   3   4   5   6

Feedback: Americans often have strong feelings about foreign companies selling products in our country and competing with American firms. If you strongly disagreed with most of the statements, you favor foreign firms being able to do business in the United States. If you strongly agreed with the statements, you tend to be against such business. You may echo a popular phrase of the last several years, "Buy American!"

Some Americans fear foreign competitors because we do not fully understand them—in language, culture, or social values. Some American companies have been hurt by foreign competition; you may know people who lost jobs after U.S. firms closed or moved operations overseas. Conversely some Americans have few qualms about foreign companies conducting business on U.S. soil. They, and you, may think that international business is exciting and that competition from all manufacturers of a product, regardless of country of origin, is fair to businesses and beneficial to consumers. Regardless of your position on this issue, you as a student of business have already realized that international business will continue to expand in the United States and throughout the world.

for the Soviet people are better food and housing and a larger selection of clothing and household goods.[5] On March 18, 1990, East Germany voted for unity with West Germany. A unified Germany is expected to be the world's fastest-growing importer of foreign goods.[6] The Pacific Rim countries— markets such as Malaysia, Japan, Taiwan, Singapore, and Korea—are also removing barriers to foreign goods. Asia is the world's hottest market for cars, paint, telecommunications equipment, and many other products.[7]

International business is the performance of business activities across national boundaries. Every nation in the world participates in international business to some extent. Large companies (e.g., Coca-Cola, Exxon, and IBM) as well as smaller firms (e.g., Prime Computer) sell their products throughout the world.

International Business
The performance of business activities across national boundaries.

Involvement in international business has increased steadily since World War II. It is expected to continue growing as we move into the 21st century. More than $2 trillion is spent annually on trade between nations. By the year 2000, one of the key requirements for chief executives of American firms will be experience in international business. And worldwide employment will increase in nearly 75 percent of American firms.[8]

As more and more firms begin to conduct business with foreign countries, the significance of international business will increase. Connections will help you assess your thoughts about foreign firms doing business in the United States.

WHY FIRMS CONDUCT INTERNATIONAL BUSINESS

A country with a surplus of some product may decide to sell this surplus to other nations. Such sales will enable the country to purchase other products that it may not have the ability to produce. Thus scarcity of resources is perhaps the major reason why nations trade with each other.[9]

No nation has every raw material or resource; no nation can produce everything it needs. Most nations specialize in producing particular goods or services. The United States, for example, has developed a specialty in producing agricultural products efficiently; thus it sells food to many nations of the world. But the United States purchases much of its oil from other countries, such as Saudi Arabia, that specialize in the production of crude oil.

Absolute Advantage
When a country can produce a product more efficiently than any other nation.

A nation has an **absolute advantage** if it can produce a product more efficiently than any other nation. South Africa has an absolute advantage in the production of diamonds. Absolute advantages are rare because usually at least two countries can efficiently supply a specific product.

Comparative Advantage
When a country can produce one product more efficiently and at a lower cost than other products, in comparison to other nations.

A country has a **comparative advantage** if it can produce one product more efficiently than other products, in comparison to other nations. For instance, countries with low labor costs, such as China and South American countries, have a comparative advantage in producing labor-intensive products such as shoes and clothing. Many nations become involved in international business because they have a comparative advantage. Firms sell those goods for which they have the greatest comparative advantage over other countries. The United States has its greatest comparative advantages in food products, aircraft, and coal.

Comparative advantages shift frequently. For many years, the United States held a comparative advantage in manufacturing a variety of products, such as automobiles, television sets, and appliances. Today many of these products are

Chrysler exports Jeep Wrangler and Cherokee models to Japan.

Courtesy of The Goodyear Tire & Rubber Company

made in Japan, Germany, and South Korea. The United States experienced a dramatic loss of comparative advantage in manufacturing televisions. Within five years, from 1982 to 1987, U.S. sales of imported TVs jumped from 25 percent of all U.S. sales to 80 percent.[10] One reason for shifts in comparative advantages is competition.

Some nations want to become self-sufficient and thus do not specialize in the production and sale of particular products. The choice of specialization or self-sufficiency is generally a political and economic issue. For instance, communist nations traditionally have strived for self-sufficiency because they feared economic dependency on other countries. Some nations also view self-sufficiency as necessary for achieving military supremacy. Of course, no country is completely self-sufficient.

BASIC CONCEPTS OF INTERNATIONAL BUSINESS

Several basic concepts are important for an understanding of international business. In this section, we discuss the concepts of exporting and importing, balance of trade, balance of payments, and exchange rates.

Exporting and Importing

The United States is one of the world's largest exporters and importers. **Exporting** is selling domestic-made goods in another country. **Importing** is purchasing goods made in another country. Most of the video recorders purchased in the United States are imported from Japan.

No doubt you realize that the United States imports a wide variety of products: oil, automobiles, electronic equipment, clothing and shoes, iron and steel, and paper products, to name a few. But American exports are on the rise. In addition to grain and computers, U.S. firms export such products as escalators to Taiwan, machine tools to Germany, and shoes to Italy.[11] Table 6.2 contains a list of the leading U.S. exports and imports.

Exporting
Selling domestic-made goods in another country.

Importing
Purchasing goods made in another country.

TABLE 6.2

Top U.S. Exports and Imports

Exports	Value ($ in billions)	Imports	Value ($ in billions)
Chemicals	$32,300	Electrical machinery	$31,009
Motor vehicles	25,178	Crude petroleum	25,844
Office machinery and computers	23,128	Office machinery and computers	22,601
Electrical machinery	21,602	Telecommunications machinery	22,278
Aircraft and parts	20,004	Clothing	21,518

Source: *Statistical Abstracts of the United States, 1990* (Washington, D.C.: U.S. Department of Commerce, Bureau of the Census), p. 805.

Balance of Trade

Balance of Trade
The difference (in dollars) between the amount a country exports and the amount it imports.

Balance of trade is the result of importing and exporting. A country's **balance of trade** is the difference (in monetary terms) between the amount it exports and the amount it imports. A nation that exports more than it imports maintains a favorable balance of trade, or a *trade surplus*. Japan and Taiwan have a favorable balance of trade. Japan's trade surplus rose from $55 billion in 1985 to about $100 billion within the next three years.[12] A nation that imports more than it exports has an unfavorable balance of trade, or a *trade deficit*. The United States continues to struggle with an annual trade deficit of more than $100 billion.[13]

Balance of Payments

Balance of Payments
The total flow of money into and out of a country.

A country's **balance of payments** is the total flow of money into and out of the country. The balance of payments is determined by a country's balance of trade, foreign aid, foreign investments, military spending, and money spent by tourists in other countries. A country has a favorable balance of payments if more money is flowing in than is flowing out; an unfavorable balance of payments exists when more money is flowing out of the country than in. For many years, the United States enjoyed a favorable balance of payments. But in recent years, more money has been leaving the country than has been flowing in.

Exchange Rates

Exchange Rate
The rate at which one country's currency can be exchanged for that of another country.

The rate at which one country's currency can be exchanged for that of another country is called the **exchange rate.** For instance, on April 23, 1991, one U.S. dollar exchanged for 1.15 Canadian dollars, for .59 British pounds, and for 139.50 Japanese yen.

Governments and market conditions determine exchange rates. *Devaluation* by its government reduces the value of a nation's currency in relation to currencies of other nations. If the United States were to devalue its currency, for example, the cost of American goods in foreign countries would decrease. *Revaluation* increases the value of a country's currency in relation to that of other countries. Revaluation of the dollar would increase the cost of American goods purchased in foreign countries.

Fixed Exchange Rate
An unvarying exchange rate set by government policy.

After World War II, during a meeting in Bretton Woods, New Hampshire, the major industrialized nations of the world established a **fixed exchange rate.** Known as the *Bretton Woods Accord,* this agreement mandated that a nation pay its debts by transferring gold reserves to the reserves of creditor nations. As the U.S. balance of payments deficit began to exceed its gold reserves, President Richard Nixon took the United States off the gold standard. This led to a **floating exchange rate,** which allows the exchange rate to fluctuate with market conditions. For instance, when Americans spend U.S. dollars to buy automobiles and other products from Japan, the value of the dollars relative to the Japanese yen goes down. Today, many nations use a floating exchange rate.

Floating Exchange Rate
An exchange rate that fluctuates with market conditions.

The exchange rate for the dollar is posted at a currency exchange in Germany.

R. Drechsler/Journalism Services

BARRIERS TO INTERNATIONAL BUSINESS

Firms desiring to enter international business face several obstacles, some much more severe than others. In this section, we examine the most common barriers to effective international business: cultural, social, and political barriers, and tariffs and trade restrictions.

Cultural and Social Barriers

A nation's culture and social forces can restrict international business activities. *Culture* consists of a country's general concepts and values and tangible items such as food, clothing, and buildings. *Social forces* include family, education, religion, and customs. Selling products from one country to another is sometimes difficult when the cultures of the two countries differ significantly. For example, when McDonald's opened its first restaurant in Rome, it was met with protest. The people of Rome objected to the smell of hamburgers frying. McDonald's overcame this objection by changing the exhaust system of the restaurant.[14] Other products, such as soft drinks, are less likely to encounter such cultural resistance.

Some countries also have different values about spending than do Americans. The Japanese have long been a nation that believes in paying cash for the products they buy, although the use of credit cards has soared in Japan over the last few years. In 1982, outstanding credit on all consumer purchases was less than 10 trillion yen; by 1988, it was nearly 50 trillion yen.[15] The more the Japanese borrow and spend, the more they import—meaning increased trade

The use of credit cards is growing in Japan, meaning increased trade for the United States and other countries.

Courtesy of VISA USA, Inc.

for countries such as the United States. Yet the Japanese as a nation still save nearly 20 percent of individual income, compared to about 4 percent saved by people in the United States.

Social forces can create obstacles to international trade. In China, for instance, a firm cannot claim in its advertisements to be number one, since the moral system there holds that everyone is equal.[16] In some countries, purchasing items as basic as food and clothing can be influenced by religion. In many nations, individuals do not have the choices in food, clothing, and health care that we do in the United States. And some societies simply do not value material possessions to the same degree that Americans do.

Most firms know the importance of understanding the cultural and social differences between selling and buying countries. However, executives still make costly mistakes when conducting business internationally simply because they do not understand such differences. For instance, a business deal in Japan can fall through if a foreign executive refuses a cup of green tea during a visit to a native Japanese firm. As one official at a major Tokyo trading company put it, "Why don't they just take it? It's so simple, but refusing can throw off the whole pace of the meeting."[17]

Political Barriers

The political climate of a country can have a major impact on international business. Nations experiencing intense political unrest may change their attitude toward foreign firms at any time; this instability creates an unfavorable atmosphere for international trade. The greatest risk for international firms is in politically unstable areas of the world such as Africa, Central America, and the Middle East. Countries such as the United States and Japan are more attractive because of their political stability.

Tariffs and Trade Restrictions

Tariffs and trade restrictions are also barriers to international business. A nation can restrict trade through import tariffs, quotas and embargoes, and exchange controls.

Import tariffs   A duty, or tax, levied against goods brought into a country is an **import tariff.** Tariffs can be used to discourage foreign competitors from entering a domestic market. Some Americans have called for high tariffs on Japanese products such as cars and stereos. The risk in imposing tariffs is that the other country could take the same action against U.S. products.

Import Tariff
A duty, or tax, levied against goods brought into a country.

Quotas and embargoes   A **quota** is a limit on the amount of a product that can leave or enter a country. For many years, Japan placed strict quotas on beef and citrus imports. When Japan began to lift the quotas in 1988, with all scheduled to be eliminated over three years, it opened one of the world's wealthiest consumer markets to beef and citrus producers in countries such as the United States and Australia.[18]

Quota
A limit on the amount of a product that can leave or enter a country.

Some quotas are established on a voluntary basis. Generally, a *voluntary quota* fosters goodwill and protects a country from foreign competition. For instance, Japanese automobile manufacturers have voluntarily reduced the number of cars shipped to the United States to give automakers here the time they need to modernize their factories.[19]

An **embargo** is a total ban on certain imports and exports. Many embargoes are politically motivated, such as the United Nations' embargo of goods to Iraq after that nation invaded Kuwait in 1990. Often, if a country places an embargo on products imported from or exported to another country, the second country retaliates with embargoes of its own.

Embargo
A total ban on certain imports and exports.

Exchange controls   Restrictions on the amount of a certain currency that can be bought or sold are called **exchange controls.** A government can use exchange controls to limit the amount of products that importers can purchase with a particular currency. In 1985, for example, China placed strict restrictions on foreign exchange spending.

Exchange Controls
Restrictions on the amount of a certain currency that can be bought or sold in a nation.

REGULATION OF INTERNATIONAL BUSINESS

As business between nations has grown, so has the number of laws and organizations involved in the regulation of international trade. In this section, we look at major legislation and organizations that have been developed to regulate international business.

TABLE 6.3

**U.S. Laws Affecting
International Business**

Law	Purpose
Webb-Pomerene Export Trade Act (1918)	Exempts U.S. firms from antitrust laws if they are acting together to develop international trade.
Foreign Corrupt Practices Act (1978)	Makes bribing foreign officials to obtain sales illegal for American firms.
Export Trading Companies Act (1982)	Encourages the formation of export trading companies by eliminating antitrust barriers and allowing banks to participate in such ventures.

Legislation

The major U.S. laws affecting American firms engaged in international business are summarized in Table 6.3. The *Webb-Pomerene Export Trade Act* of 1918 exempts U.S. firms from certain antitrust laws if they are working together to develop export markets. The Webb-Pomerene Act does not allow companies to reduce competition in the United States or to use unfair methods of competition. The *Foreign Corrupt Practices Act,* passed in 1978, prohibits American firms from making bribes to foreign officials. This law spells out the penalties for companies and individuals who are in violation: companies may be fined up to $1 million, and individuals may receive a fine up to $10,000 and a prison sentence of up to five years. The *Export Trading Companies Act* of 1982 eliminates some antitrust barriers and allows banks to participate in joint ventures. An export trading company is an organization that attempts to create exports.

International Organizations

Several international organizations exist to facilitate world trade. We will now examine the major ones, summarized in Table 6.4.

GATT
An international organization formed to reduce or eliminate tariffs and other barriers to international trade.

GATT   Signed in 1947, the **General Agreement on Tariffs and Trade (GATT)** formed an international organization of 23 nations, including the United States. GATT works to reduce or eliminate tariffs and other barriers to international trade. Today nearly 100 countries agree to the guidelines established by GATT.

Since it was organized, GATT has sponsored several "rounds" of negotiations to reduce trade barriers. President John F. Kennedy, through authority granted by the Trade Expansion Act of 1962, called for the reduction of tariffs through GATT. The Kennedy Round, which began in 1964, led to a nearly 40 percent reduction in tariffs. The Tokyo Round, held from 1973 to 1979, led to a reduction of over 30 percent. Other nontariff restrictions, such as import quotas and unnecessary red tape in customs procedures, were also removed. In 1989 more than 100 countries agreed to halt farm subsidies and to institute a new system of arbitration for handling disputes between countries. Known as the Uruguay Round, this most recent set of talks is expected to change dramatically the way nations trade.[20]

TABLE 6.4

Organizations that Facilitate International Business

General Agreement on Tariffs and Trade (GATT)

Formed in 1947 by 23 nations to reduce or eliminate tariffs and other barriers to international trade.

Members: 96 countries, including the United States and the USSR.

European Community (EC)

Founded in 1957 to reduce trade barriers among members.

Members: Belgium, Denmark, France, Germany, Greece, Ireland, Italy, Luxembourg, the Netherlands, Portugal, Spain, and the United Kingdom.

Latin American Free Trade Association (LAFTA)

Founded in 1960 to develop free trade among member nations.

Members: Argentina, Brazil, Chile, Colombia, Ecuador, Mexico, Paraguay, Peru, and Uruguay.

European Free Trade Association (EFTA)

Founded in 1960 to eliminate trade restrictions among members and develop common trade policies.

Members: Austria, Iceland, Norway, Portugal, Sweden, Switzerland, and Finland (associate member).

Organization of Petroleum Exporting Countries (OPEC)

Established in 1960 to provide oil-producing nations control over prices and reduce the oversupply of oil.

Members: Algeria, Ecuador, Gabon, Indonesia, Iran, Iraq, Kuwait, Libya, Nigeria, Qatar, Saudi Arabia, United Arab Emirates, and Venezuela.

International Monetary Fund (IMF)

Founded in 1944 to promote trade among member nations by eliminating trade barriers and increasing cooperation on financial issues.

Members: 149 industrial and developing countries.

World Bank

Founded in 1946 to lend money to underdeveloped and developing countries for a variety of projects.

Members: 149 industrial and developing countries.

Economic communities   An organization formed to facilitate the movement of products among member nations through the creation of common economic policies is called an **economic community.** One of the largest is the European Community (EC), formed in 1957. The purpose of the EC is to reduce trade barriers among the 12 member nations: Belgium, Denmark, France, Germany, Greece, Ireland, Italy, Luxembourg, the Netherlands, Portugal, Spain, and the United Kingdom. The European Community is in the process of eliminating all trade barriers among member nations. The Business Action examines the significance of a unified Europe.

Another economic community, the Latin American Free Trade Association (LAFTA), was organized in 1960. Its purpose was to develop free trade among members, a goal yet to be achieved. The European Free Trade Association (EFTA), organized in 1960 in response to the European Community, has eliminated many trade barriers among members. Two original members of EFTA,

Economic Community
An organization that facilitates the movement of products among member nations through the creation of common economic policies.

Europe 1992: What Unification Means

When the Treaties of Rome, signed in 1957, created the European Community (EC), the member countries dreamed of an economically unified Europe. They continued, however, to operate as separate markets for three more decades and found it difficult to compete with the United States and Japan. Now, the EC is working to eliminate most trade barriers between member nations.

With barriers removed, European industry should be more competitive in the world market. If western Europe can succeed in ending trade barriers, the result could be one, unified European market of 323 million people. This market would provide a big boost to American firms, whose current sales in Europe exceed $500 billion. As European demand for American products increases, opportunities for U.S. firms to increase sales could be unlimited.

The top five exports to the European Community are petroleum products, office equipment, apparel and accessories, road vehicles (including cars), and electrical machinery and parts. New markets should also open in 1992. Ending barriers should lead to the cross-border sales of service and information such as insurance, mutual funds and other financial products, and television programs. Industries that were closed to foreigners, such as telecommunications, will present more new opportunities.

U.S. firms, however, should not count on easy access to Europe in the 1990s and beyond. The EC fears that large American and Japanese firms may try to dominate the new European market. So it is considering new trade barriers aimed at non-European companies. Such trade barriers present a serious concern to the United States. Competition will also grow more intense for U.S. firms as their counterparts throughout the world struggle for a share in the unified Europe's marketplace.

Some firms already have taken action to ensure that they are not locked out of Europe. Acquisitions, such as Campbell Soup Co.'s purchase of German foods manufacturer Beeck-Feinkost, are one method. Other firms, such as Digital Equipment Corporation, moved part of their operations to Europe. But the message sent from Europe needed no translation: if any EC country is denied from doing business in your country because of some trade restriction, you won't be doing business in Europe.

European officials are confident that EC members can successfully eliminate trade barriers among themselves and make Europe into the largest single market in the world. And the EC's commission for trade is making it clear that full access to unified Europe will be expensive.[21]

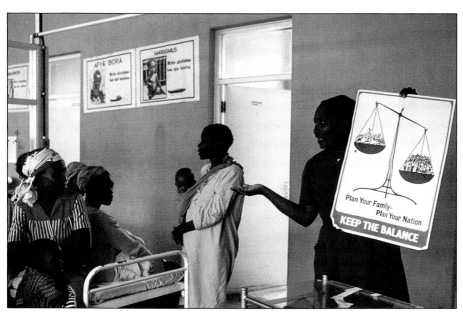

The World Bank helped provide funding for a family planning center at the Machakos Hospital in Kenya.

Courtesy of Information & Public Affairs Division, The World Bank

the United Kingdom and Denmark, dropped out to join the EC. Another well-known economic community is the Organization of Petroleum Exporting Countries (OPEC). Established in 1960, OPEC exists to give oil-producing nations some control over the price and supply of oil. OPEC has been fairly successful in controlling both.

IMF and World Bank   Two international organizations have been established to help finance international trade. The **International Monetary Fund (IMF)** was founded in 1944 to promote cooperation among member nations by eliminating trade barriers. IMF lends money to countries that need short-term loans to conduct international trade. The **World Bank** was formed in 1946 to lend money to underdeveloped and developing countries for various projects. The World Bank makes loans to member nations to fund the development of roads, factories, and medical facilities.

IMF
An international financial organization that lends money to countries to conduct international trade.

World Bank
An international organization that lends money to underdeveloped and developing countries for development.

APPROACHES TO INTERNATIONAL BUSINESS

A firm that decides to enter international trade must select an approach. It can be done in a number of ways; some require relatively low levels of commitment, while others require much higher levels. Approaches to international business include exporting, licensing, joint ventures, trading companies, countertrading, direct ownership, and multinational corporations.

Exporting

The simplest way to enter international business is *exporting,* selling domestic goods to a foreign country. It requires the lowest level of resources and commitment. More than half of the U.S. firms involved in international trade do so through exporting.[22] In many cases, a firm can locate an exporting firm that can provide assistance in selling products to foreign countries.

American exports are making a strong comeback. Many products once considered in serious trouble domestically are selling well in foreign markets. For instance, Chrysler exported $750 million worth of Jeeps and minivans to Europe and Asia in 1988. In Japan, Schick razor blades have 70 percent of the safety-blade market, Pampers has 20 to 22 percent of the disposable-diaper market, and Kodak amateur color film has 12 to 15 percent of the market.[23] The fastest-growing U.S. exports are music, video, and computer tapes; cigarettes and tobacco products; meat; pulp and wastepaper; and synthetic resins, rubber, and plastics.[24]

Licensing

Licensing
An agreement in which one firm allows another firm to sell its product and use its brand name in return for a commission or royalty.

In a **licensing** agreement, one firm (the licensor) agrees to allow another firm (the licensee) to sell the licensor's product and use its brand name. In return, the licensee pays the licensor a commission or royalty. For example, a beverage company such as Pepsico might enter into a licensing agreement with a firm in Taiwan. The Taiwanese firm would have the right to sell Pepsi products in Taiwan and would pay Pepsico a specified percentage of the income from sales of the product.

Licensing offers advantages for both the licensor and the licensee. The licensor can become involved in international trade with little financial risk. The licensee gains products and technology that may otherwise be too costly to produce. However, licensing does not result in a large payoff for the licensor, usually only about 5 percent of sales. Some American executives and managers believe that licensing agreements result in giving away trade secrets for a meager 5 percent of sales; after the agreement expires (usually in less than 10 years), the licensee may continue to market the product without paying the licensor.

Joint Ventures

Firms may also conduct international business through a *joint venture,* in this case a partnership between a domestic firm and a firm in a foreign country. Because of government restrictions on foreign ownership of corporations, joint ventures are often the only way a firm can purchase facilities in another country. For instance, after 14 years of negotiations, McDonald's of Canada opened a restaurant in the Soviet Union in 1990. Eventually McDonald's will open 20 restaurants in Moscow. The Moscow City Council's Food Service will own 51 percent of the enterprise, a requirement under Soviet joint venture laws.[25]

One major drawback to international joint ventures is that organizations may lose control of their operations. For example, because India does not allow foreign companies to own industries, Coca-Cola once entered into a joint venture with the Indian government. Despite the huge soft drink market in India,

Coca-Cola pulled out over a decade ago rather than risk giving up majority control and its secret formula.[26]

Trading Companies

Another approach to international business is to use or form a trading company to provide a link between buyers and sellers in different countries. A **trading company** buys products in one country and sells them in another without being involved in manufacturing. Trading companies take title to products and move them from one country to another. Trading companies can simplify entrance into foreign markets because they are usually favored by the foreign governments. Many major corporations such as General Electric Co. and Sears Roebuck have developed trading companies.

Trading Company
A firm that buys products in one country and sells in another without being involved in manufacturing.

Countertrading

Complex bartering agreements between two or more countries are involved in **countertrading.** (*Bartering* refers to the exchange of merchandise between countries.) Countertrading allows a nation with limited cash to participate in international trade. The country wishing to trade requires the exporting country to purchase products from it before allowing its products to be sold there. For instance, a nation with little cash but a strong comparative advantage for producing shoes might require an exporter of rubber to buy shoes before it can sell rubber products in that country. The use of countertrade agreements is expected to grow during the 1990s, especially between Western and Communist-bloc countries.

Countertrading
Bartering agreements between two or more countries.

Direct Ownership

A much more involved approach to international business is **direct ownership**— purchasing one or more business operations in a foreign country. Direct ownership requires a large investment in production facilities, research, personnel, and marketing activities. General Electric, for example, invested $150 million to purchase 12 light-bulb plants in Hungary that were once owned by the Hungarian government. GE planned to spend at least $140 million over five years to modernize the plants and did not expect to get back its investment for some time.[27] Many large companies, such as Ford, Polaroid, and 3M, own facilities outside the United States. Through direct ownership, a firm has greater control over a foreign subsidiary. However, owning facilities in another country can be extremely risky; governments sometimes decide to take over certain industries or facilities.

Direct Ownership
The purchase of one or more business operations in a foreign country.

Multinational Corporations

Some corporations operate as if the world were a **global market.** This approach represents a total commitment to international business, and is used by **multinational corporations** who have assets committed to operations or subsidiaries in foreign countries. Large organizations such as Exxon, General Motors, IBM, Grand Metropolitan (a British company), and Nestlé (a Swiss company) are multinational corporations.

Global Market
The entire world viewed as a large market.

Multinational Corporation
A firm that operates on a global basis, committing assets to operations or subsidiaries in foreign countries.

Boeing Revives the 737

Boeing is one of the world's top international firms. With 54 percent of the commercial aircraft business, Boeing dominates the industry. The company has more than $4 billion in cash, little debt, and a $91 billion backlog in orders, enough to keep factories busy for years. One reason for Boeing's global success is its ability to develop quality products such as the 737 aircraft.

The Boeing 737 is the best-selling commercial jet of all time. Introduced more than 20 years ago to compete with McDonnell Douglas's DC–9, the 737 was initially a flop. The DC–9 had reached the market three years earlier, it flew a little faster, and it was the preferred plane. The 737 won few orders, and Boeing considered killing the product.

That's when Boeing called on company engineer Bob Norton. In an effort to save the 737, Norton began to look for new markets for the plane. Norton thought the future looked bright in underdeveloped parts of the world such as Africa, South America, and the Mideast. Although nations in these areas did not purchase a large number of planes, Norton believed they would one day. And Boeing would be there with a strong customer base.

For the idea to work, Boeing had to adapt the plane to the aviation conditions of underdeveloped and developing countries. First, the runways were too short to accommodate the large jet. The runways were also too soft; they were made of asphalt rather than cement. And finally, the pilots in Africa tended to come in for hard landings. When they hit the runway, the 737 bounced, causing the brakes to fail. As a result, the pilots would run out of runway on landings—obviously a serious problem. Norton's only option was to adapt the 737 to these conditions.

Thus Boeing redesigned the 737's wings to allow shorter landings. The company added more power to the engine so the big plane could take off more quickly. To help the plane stay on the ground on hard landings, Boeing redesigned the landing gear and installed low-pressure tires. The 737 then held the runway much better when it touched down.

The adaptation was a huge success. At first Boeing sold a few 737s throughout the developing world. These orders were much smaller than the 20 or 30 planes that U.S. airlines customarily order. But the plane was well received. As small Third World airlines grew, they began to place orders for Boeing's larger planes. The new long-haul 747 has already been purchased by 18 world airlines. Even though it takes five years to get a new 747, orders keep coming in from all over the world.

Boeing's plans call for more global business; its dreams hinge on the 777. A new long-distance, 350-seat airplane, the 777 would compete for business in the fastest-growing market of the 1990s. Boeing will spend at least $4 billion to develop the plane and will need a few large orders to justify production. Five of Boeing's eight target customers are foreign airlines.[28]

Courtesy of The Coca-Cola Company

Coca-Cola can be spoken in any language.

Products most suitable for this approach include airlines, automobiles, heavy equipment, machine tools, computers, petroleum, cosmetics, and soft drinks. Coca-Cola is a multinational corporation. According to one spokesperson, the company's objective is to have "one sight, one sound, one sell around the world."[29]

ADAPTING TO FOREIGN MARKETS

Because of differences from country to country, a firm engaged in international trade must generally adapt to foreign markets. In this section, we examine how a firm gears its product offerings, prices, distribution systems, and methods of promotion to foreign countries.

Product

In some cases, the same product developed for the U.S. market can be sold in a foreign country. Coca-Cola and Pepsico have successfully taken their soft drinks to foreign markets without changing them. But usually products have to be altered to meet conditions in a foreign market. General Electric faced problems selling refrigerators in Japan because they were too large to fit into most Japanese homes.[30] The Business Action shows how Boeing adapted one of its planes, the 737, to conditions in underdeveloped and developing countries.

In some cases, companies cannot modify existing products to fit the needs of a foreign country. They then can either develop a new product for that country or try to sell the current product in other countries. Developing new products

Colgate-Palmolive developed Axion, a dishwashing paste, for consumers in South America who like to use leftover soap chips in a bowl to wash dishes. The product became a market leader, and today it is sold in countries such as Malaysia, Pakistan, and Costa Rica.

Courtesy of Colgate-Palmolive Company

is a costly alternative but may provide a large payoff. The Colgate-Palmolive Co., for example, developed Axion, a dishwashing paste packaged in a plastic cup, for consumers in South America who traditionally used leftover soap chips in a bowl to wash their dishes.

Price

The price of a product is usually different in domestic and foreign markets. The costs of foreign trade, such as taxes, tariffs, and transportation, often result in higher prices in the foreign country. Exchange rates can also influence the price of foreign goods.

In some instances, firms intentionally establish lower prices in foreign markets. The practice of selling surplus products in a foreign country at a lower price than that in the country of origin is called **dumping.** This practice is illegal in the United States and many other countries. U.S. flower growers have accused firms in Colombia, the Netherlands, and South America of dumping flowers in the United States at below production and distribution costs.[31]

Dumping
Selling surplus products in a foreign country at a lower price than in the country of origin.

Distribution

The task of providing products in foreign nations often presents challenges and problems. Many international business firms attempt to move and sell goods and provide services through existing transportation systems, stores, and suppliers. In some countries, however, adequate distribution systems do not exist. Then a firm must develop ways to get its products to the customers. In

China, for example, manufacturers typically do not make deliveries to stores and other outlets. Both Coca-Cola and Pepsico have invested heavily in trucks and refrigeration for store owners to use to obtain and sell Coke and Pepsi products in China.[32]

Promotion

Many companies use the same message worldwide to inform customers about products and persuade them to buy. Uniform promotion, including advertising and publicity, enables firms to gain recognition throughout the world. But promotion often must be modified because language, laws, and culture differ from country to country. For instance, Japanese advertisements commonly use ideas that people elsewhere would consider sexist. Household appliances have been promoted with the phrase "So simple a woman can operate it." Japanese companies have issued wall calendars featuring nude women.[33] In many countries, such promotional methods would not be acceptable.

Decisions concerning which media to use for advertising or publicity must also be adapted to different countries. Some nations do not have commercial television. Others do not have advertising space in newspapers. The circulation of magazines and newspapers also varies greatly from one country to another. In nations with a low literacy rate, radio and television advertising, if available, is more effective than print media.

You'll Know It's the Century When . . .

Managers Hablan Español

And perhaps Japanese and French, too. In the 21st century, the "typical CEO will be a global operator," according to author Joseph E. Pattison. Foreign leaders will sit on company boards; foreign employees will collect paychecks along with domestic staffs; and thinking globally will be an integral part of a winning firm's every move—from research to sales—enabling it to compete and win market shares in Asia, Europe, and beyond.

Multilingual and multicultural skills will also yield results at home, where America will have become a "world nation." By the year 2000, America's work force will be 10.2 percent Hispanic, 11.8 percent black, and 4.1 percent Asian; and large Hispanic and Asian communities will assert their tastes, needs, and values. The best managers will be able to teach and coach their multicultural staffs, to provide services and products to new, lucrative multicultural markets. The growth of America's minorities, in fact, will have primed American business to succeed on the larger, international stage. [34]

SUMMARY OF LEARNING OBJECTIVES

1. To understand the meaning and scope of international business.
   International business is the performance of business activities across national boundaries. Involvement in international business is increasing, with growth expected to continue into the 21st century.

2. **To explain why firms become involved in international business.**
   Countries cannot produce everything for themselves. Most nations specialize in the production of certain goods and services and sell any surplus to other nations. A country has an absolute advantage if it can produce a product more efficiently than any other nation. A country that can produce one product more efficiently than other products, in comparison to other nations, has a comparative advantage.

3. **To define the basic concepts of international business.**
   Exporting is selling domestic goods to a foreign country; *importing* is purchasing goods from another country. A country's *balance of trade* is the difference between the amount it exports and the amount it imports. The total flow of money in and out of a country is its *balance of payments*. The *exchange rate* is the rate at which one country's currency can be exchanged for another's currency.

4. **To list the various barriers to international business.**
   A nation's culture and social forces can create obstacles to international trade. The political climate of a country also influences international trade. A nation can also restrict trade through import tariffs, quotas and embargoes, and exchange controls.

5. **To identify the ways in which international business is regulated.**
   Several laws affect American firms doing business in foreign countries. These laws generally exempt U.S. firms from certain antitrust laws, prohibit bribing of foreign officials, and allow banks to participate in joint ventures. Several organizations also exist to facilitate world trade, including the General Agreement on Tariffs and Trade (GATT), the International Monetary Fund (IMF), the World Bank, and economic communities such as the European Community (EC) and the Organization of Petroleum Exporting Countries (OPEC).

6. **To list and describe the different approaches firms take to conduct business internationally.**
   A firm can take several approaches to international trade. Some require little commitment on the part of the firm, while others require a great deal of involvement. The approaches to international business are exporting, licensing, joint ventures, trading companies, countertrading, direct ownership, and multinational corporations.

7. **To explain how a firm can adapt to foreign markets.**
   A firm engaged in international business must generally adapt to foreign markets. Some products have to be changed to be suitable to another country. Prices of products may be set differently in various countries. In some cases, products can be distributed through existing systems, but if appropriate distribution systems do not exist, firms must develop them. Advertising and publicity often must be modified because of differences in language, laws, and culture.

KEY TERMS

International Business, p. 193

Absolute Advantage, p. 194

Comparative Advantage, p. 194

Exporting, p. 195

Importing, p. 195

Balance of Trade, p. 196

Balance of Payments, p. 196

Exchange Rate, p. 196

Fixed Exchange Rate, p. 196

Floating Exchange Rate, p. 196

Import Tariff, p. 199

Quota, p. 199

Embargo, p. 199

Exchange Controls, p. 199

General Agreement on Tariffs and Trade (GATT), p. 200

Economic Community, p. 201

International Monetary Fund (IMF), p. 203

World Bank, p. 203

Licensing, p. 204

Trading Company, p. 205

Countertrading, p. 205

Direct Ownership, p. 205

Global Market, p. 205

Multinational Corporation, p. 205

Dumping, p. 208

QUESTIONS FOR DISCUSSION AND REVIEW

1. Why do firms become involved in international business?

2. In what areas does the United States have a comparative advantage? Would you expect this to change in the future?

3. Explain the difference between exporting and importing. Give examples of products that the United States exports and those it imports.

4. Why is the United States' balance of trade considered unfavorable?

5. How is a country's balance of payments determined?

6. Explain the meaning of exchange rate. How are exchange rates determined?

7. Describe three barriers to international business.

8. How does a country use import tariffs to restrict international trade?

9. What is the difference between a quota and an embargo?

10. What is the purpose of the Foreign Corrupt Practices Act?

11. What is an economic community? Give two examples.

12. Name and explain three different approaches to international business. Under what conditions should each of these approaches be used?

13. Why do firms engaged in international business often have to adapt to foreign markets? Give an example of how products, prices, distribution methods, and promotion methods might have to be adapted to a foreign country.

14. What is dumping? Why is it illegal in many countries?

CASE 6.1
Nestlé Expands Internationally

The Switzerland-based Nestlé corporation, once a Swiss chocolate maker, now is the world's largest food company and the largest producer of coffee, powdered milk, and frozen dinners. The company also became number one in candy after passing Mars. Nestlé achieved its success through intensive global expansion.

One of the first multinational corporations, Nestlé has production facilities in more than 60 countries. Its products can be found almost everywhere around the globe. In Europe, where Nestlé has experienced the greatest success, sales of instant coffee, mineral water, yogurt, frozen foods, cold cuts, candy, and cereal bars are roughly $10.2 billion. The company's sales in North America are approximately $6.7 billion, for products such as Nescafé instant coffee, Carnation Coffee-mate nondairy creamer, Friskies pet food, Nestlé Crunch chocolates, and Stouffer frozen foods. Other big markets for Nestlé have been Asia, $3.1 billion; Latin America, $2.4 billion; and Oceania (Australia, New Zealand, and other islands of the Pacific Ocean), $.6 billion.

One secret to Nestlé's success is that many of its products, especially instant coffee, chocolates, and frozen foods, appeal to consumers all over the world. For example, coffee is closing in on tea as the favorite drink in Japan. Frozen dinners, long a hit in the United States, are catching on in Europe. And of course, chocolate tastes the same in any language. Although these products have to be adapted slightly to local tastes, they generally can be sold worldwide. Because of high research and development costs, Nestlé benefits greatly by offering products with global appeal. After making large investments in its products, the company has been able to move brands from one country to another with relative ease.

Nestlé's Lean Cuisine dinners illustrate well how the company expands internationally. Lean Cuisine was introduced in the United States in 1981 and became a huge success. In 1985 Nestlé chief executive Helmut Maucher endorsed a plan to sell Lean Cuisine in Britain. In the beginning, before the company's British frozen-food plant reached full production, products were imported from a plant in Canada. The cost of shipping frozen dinners in refrigerated ships, in addition to paying customs taxes, was extremely high. But Maucher was patient, and the venture has paid off. In 1989, sales of frozen dinners in Britain reached $100 million, and Nestlé has a 33 percent share of the market. Lean Cuisine has also been successfully introduced in France.

Now Nestlé is looking to what Maucher thinks is the market of the future, the Third World. Currently, 20 percent of the world's population consumes 80 percent of Nestlé's products. Maucher thinks his company's products will soon be seen in more parts of the world. The company also will look to what Maucher considers the food of the future—pasta. As he puts it, "We can't feed the world on beefsteak. So noodles will conquer the world."

Most industry experts agree that Nestlé is in the best position of any food company to expand internationally. Most of its competitors, which have been concentrating on their domestic markets, are scrambling to become involved in the profitable international trade.

Questions for Discussion

1. Would you classify Nestlé as a multinational corporation? Why or why not?

2. Does Nestlé have to adapt its products for foreign markets?

3. Why is it so expensive for Nestlé to sell a product like Lean Cuisine in other countries?

4. Will competitors be able to follow Nestlé into foreign markets with the same degree of success?

CASE 6.2
Europe Presents Business Opportunities

Many industries see Europe as the land of opportunity, with its strong economic growth and steady deregulation as the European Community becomes a single market and with the fall of communism and the opening of Eastern Europe. As Europeans' incomes rise and they discover the joy of spending, firms will see numerous opportunities to sell their wares to eager new customers. Deregulation of radio and television will create demand for new programs, advertising, and privately owned networks. The construction industry will boom, with billions spent to develop roads, telecommunications systems, and modern cities.

U.S. companies do not want to miss their chance in Europe. Through exporting, joint ventures, acquisitions, and the opening of manufacturing plants, American firms are investing heavily in Europe. Intel Corporation, for instance, has built its first plant in Europe, a $400 million computer facility in Ireland. Motorola expanded its operations in Europe by selecting Scotland as an export base for the rest of the European Community. Pfizer bought Medinvent, a manufacturer of medical equipment in Switzerland.

U.S. firms are not alone, however. They face great competition for the prime European markets. Japan's business interest in Europe is small but growing. Japanese automakers are challenging the European franchises of Ford and GM.

Adapted from Blanca Riemer, Peter Elliott, and Dinah Lee, "Overseas, the Buzzword for the 1990s Is 'Europe,'" *Business Week,* May 21, 1990, pp. 124–25; Shawn Tully, "What Eastern Europe Offers," *Fortune,* March 12, 1990, pp. 52–55; Blanca Riemer, Jonathan Kapstein, Mark Maremont, John Rossant, and Stanley Reed, "America's New Rush to Europe," *Business Week,* March 26, 1990, pp. 48–49.

Japan is also the major supplier of components to Europe's largest computer manufacturer. U.S. firms believe they must take quick action in Europe or lose to Japanese companies.

As a result of unification and new political direction, Germany seems to be the most promising country. Growth in unified Germany is expected to average 4 percent from 1990 to 1995. Meanwhile the flow of immigrants from east to west in Germany is increasing the demand for consumer goods. Additionally a huge construction effort means increased sales of everything from housing to transportation. Czechoslovakia also offers excellent business prospects. The industrial heart of the Eastern bloc, it has 32 million relatively affluent consumers. The least promising countries are Romania (where chaos and bloodshed still loom) and Yugoslavia (where reforms are slow).

Business firms are finding Europe fairly receptive to foreign investors. For instance, Italy paid half of the $1.2 billion that Texas Instruments spent to build calculator and semiconductor plants there. Scotland and Ireland compete vigorously for foreign investors by providing tax incentives, help with training, facilities, and capital. However, U.S. firms believe they may encounter some resistance in Europe if they invest too rapidly.

Questions for Discussion

1. Why does Europe offer new opportunities for business firms?
2. What are some of the approaches firms have used to become involved in European markets?
3. What barriers will firms face to investing in Europe?

The world of business is expanding daily. No longer confined within their own borders, businesses compete in markets around the globe. Each day, more companies move into international activities—joint ventures, imports-exports, overseas investments, expansion into foreign markets. In almost every industry, thousands of different companies are trying to compete in the international arena.

The growth in the global marketplace means exciting career opportunities in international business. Increased global competition opens more and more opportunities for people interested in international careers.

Many people are attracted to international organizations because of the appeal of international travel. Traveling abroad and exploring new cultures can be an exciting prospect. However, having an international career does not necessarily mean working abroad. An international career could involve working in the international division of a U.S. firm or working for the Department of State and seldom traveling overseas.

Opportunities for developing an international career exist in all of the main employment sectors: business, government, and non-profit.

BUSINESS

One of the fastest-growing areas for international careers is in the field of foreign, or international, trade. Thousands of organizations are involved with exporting and importing products or services between countries, which creates the need for specialists in a variety of areas. International trade requires many different kinds of specialists. Brief descriptions of a few very specialized jobs appear here:

Foreign traffic managers are responsible for getting things from one location to another. They determine the best methods and routes for shipping cargo. The job requires extensive knowledge of cargo-handling and claims procedures and of packaging requirements.

Foreign branch managers direct foreign offices or factories overseas for U.S.-based firms. Because they supervise the foreign nationals on the staff, they need to be aware of the customs, laws, and business regulations of the host country.

Many small companies use *export brokers* to sell their products

---

Is an International Career for You?

- Do you find change stimulating?
- Do you enjoy reading about events in other countries?
- Do you look for places that are away from the normal tourist spots?
- When you travel, do you prefer small, local restaurants instead of the hotel's dining room?
- Do you like to try new and different foods?
- Do you enjoy people who are very different from you?

in global markets. Export brokers act as foreign sales representatives overseas for smaller companies. The job usually involves extensive international travel.

Import merchants purchase merchandise abroad and then try to find domestic buyers for the goods.

No nation was ever ruined by trade.

Benjamin Franklin

Generally speaking, the major types of business activities or specializations are the same in both domestic and international business. However, in international business, specializing in areas such as accounting, marketing, and management is more complex and involves making adjustments to different cultural and political environments. Americans interested in international business typically build a specialty in a domestic business function before moving into an international area.

Starting an international career can be difficult; getting an overseas assignment in business is not always easy. Often companies doing business overseas rely primarily on personnel from the host countries. Many employers fill overseas positions with nationals who have been educated in the United States and who want to live in their home countries. Overseas assignments for Americans are frequently given

CAREER PROFILE: Tracy Steinmetz

Thomas Iannuzzi

TRACY STEINMETZ

Undergraduate degree: Cornell University
Major: Asian studies
Big break: A fellowship in Japan
Career turning point: Moving back to the States

Tracy Steinmetz had no particular interest in Japan until, as a high school junior, she received a scholarship from the American Field Service to go there. She spent a summer in Gifu, a small town where no one spoke any English. Despite the language barrier, Steinmetz fell in love with her Japanese "family" and with the country itself.

After graduating from Cornell, where she focused on Japanese language and culture, she landed a position as a Mombusho English Fellow in a program sponsored by the Japanese government. During that year, she lectured at 160 schools throughout Japan. "It was sort of a media ambassador's job," she says. "I was their Miss America, telling them what it means to be American."

When her tenure was up, Steinmetz stayed on in Japan. She moved to Tokyo and, over the next three years, took jobs ranging from student exchange program development to singing in a band called Club Taboo.

"At the end of my fourth year in Japan, I realized I wanted to get started on a career, so I went home. I started out looking at the banking industry, but when I heard about a job at Fujisankei in New York, I knew it was more up my alley." From the international headquarters of Japan's largest media conglomerate, Steinmetz scouts for American films, theater productions, and sporting events to bring to Japan; in addition, she produces a radio show.

"Working at Fujisankei has given me a new area of expertise—the entertainment industry. I'd like to keep going with it and to continue speaking Japanese. If that means staying at Fujisankei, fine. I'm very happy where I am."

Source: Adapted from Marin Gazzaniga, "Speaking in Tongues," *In View*, January–February 1990, pp. 4–5.

Requirements: International Business

Personal skills:
- Self-confidence
- Patience
- Open-mindedness
- Adaptability

Education:
- Bachelor's degree
- Master of business administration degree
- Mastery of foreign language
- International business courses

to managers who have many years of experience and expertise in a particular area. Highly skilled and experienced personnel are often the ones sent abroad to help solve specific problems or build a new office.

GOVERNMENT

The U.S. government offers international job opportunities through several organizations, such as the Peace Corps, the International Trade Administration, and the U.S. Agency for International Development. Most people interested in gaining international experience, however, think of the Foreign Service. Approximately 7,000 Americans work overseas as members of the Foreign Service, which is part of the State Department. Foreign Service jobs exist both in Washington and in U.S. embassies and consulates abroad.

Consular officers provide aid to Americans living, traveling, and working abroad. They help in emergencies and find doctors for Americans who are sick. They also grant visas to foreigners requesting to come to the United States, issue

Selected Government Agencies Dealing with International Matters

U.S. Information Agency (USIA)

International Development Cooperation Agency (IDCA)

U.S. Agency for International Development (USAID)

Central Intelligence Agency (CIA)

Defense Intelligence Agency (DIA)

Office of the United States Trade Representative

International Trade Administration (ITA)

U.S. Department of Commerce (USDOC)

U.S. Travel and Tourism Administration (USTTA)

Foreign Commercial Services (FCS)

passports, register absentee voters, and issue birth certificates to Americans born abroad.

Political officers deal with political issues and developments between the United States and other countries. They maintain contact with foreign officials, prepare analyses and reports, and negotiate agreements.

Commercial officers analyze and report on economic trends and events that affect U.S. interests. They work to find new markets abroad for American products and help American investors abroad. They work closely with American businesses, providing help in setting economic policy in trade, economic development, energy, and transportation.

Administrative officers provide the support operations of U.S. embassies and consulates. These operations include handling communications, planning budgets, purchasing supplies, and meeting the personal needs of Foreign Service officers and their families.

All applicants for the Foreign Service must take the written examination, which is given in December. Each year about 13,000 people take the exam, about 2,000 pass, and of these only about 300 are selected as officers. Candidates for the Foreign Service must be U.S. citizens, 21 years of age, and at least a high school graduate. The length of time between applying and getting a job offer (if you're lucky) is at least nine months. It frequently is longer because of all of the detailed steps required.

NONPROFIT

A number of organizations with international interests are not run for profit. Many are active around the world, involved in areas such as economic assistance programs, educational programs, human rights research and causes, refugee assistance, family planning, student exchange programs, and community development.

Nonprofit organizations hire people in many different areas. Knowledgeable people in various fields such as health, business, nutrition, and agriculture work as

Selected International Nonprofit Organizations

CARE

Volunteers in Technical Assistance (VITA)

American Red Cross

International Volunteer Services (IVS)

American Field Service

United Nations Volunteers

staff members. They handle administrative tasks and run research projects. Most positions require a bachelor's degree; some may require proficiency in a second language. Entry-level salaries tend to be at the low end of the international pay scale, but most people attracted to nonprofit organizations find increased job satisfaction from working on behalf of people and worthwhile ideas.

Additional International Business Resources

AISEC—US
14 West 23rd Street
New York, NY 10010

International Trade Administration
Commerce Department Building
Washington, DC 20230–0002

World Trade Centers Association
One World Trade Center, 63W
New York, NY 10048

U.S. Student Travel Service
801 Second Avenue
New York, NY 10017

PART THREE

MANAGEMENT AND ORGANIZATION

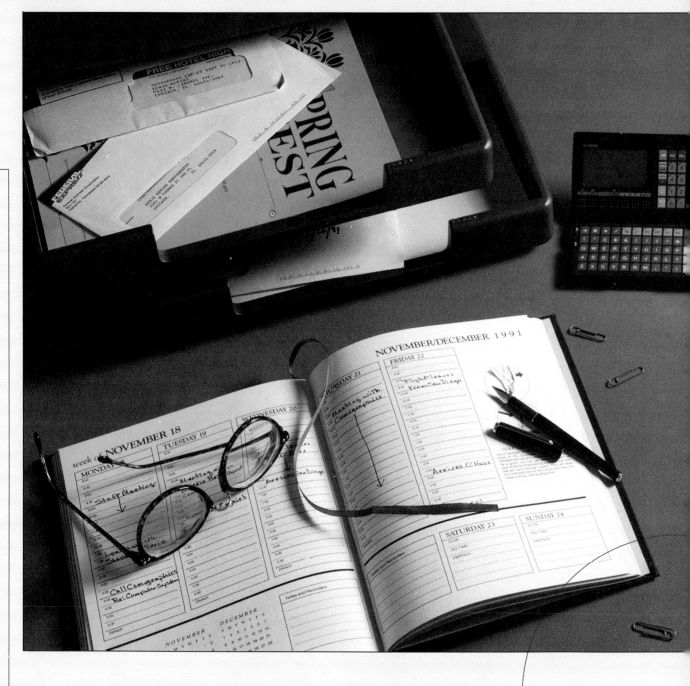

FUNDAMENTALS OF MANAGEMENT

LEARNING OBJECTIVES

1. To define the term *manage-ment*.

2. To explain what is meant by the term *organizational objectives*.

3. To discuss the five functions that successful managers must perform.

4. To compare the three levels of management in terms of authority, responsibility, and accountability.

5. To explain the three types of managerial roles.

6. To identify the four core skills that managers need to acquire and practice.

Jan Carlzon, the president of Scandinavian Airline System (SAS), stated that "all business is show business." We heartily agree. In fact, all management is show business. That doesn't mean standing up on stage entertaining an audience like Robin Williams or Arsenio Hall does; it means shaping the values of others, being passionate about what one is attempting to accomplish, showing enthusiasm when helping others, and paying attention to detail. The actor in a Broadway play, like the manager of a small machine shop in Salem, Oregon, displays these attributes. Individuals such as Willard Marriott, Jr., of the Marriott Corporation, Frank Perdue of Perdue Farms, Sam Walton of the Wal-Mart Corporation, and Chuck Knight of Emerson Electric recognize these kinds of attributes as the ingredients necessary to succeed in business.

Chuck Knight, chief executive officer (CEO) of Emerson Electric, has his own formula for successful

Gerd Ludwig

management. These ideas, his personal fundamentals of management, are put to the test each day. Knight believes planning is a line job, one that must be done by the operating managers. If a plan fails, it is usually not a failure in planning but a failure in implementing. To find the best planners and implementers, Knight spends a lot of time going over personnel files. He looks at the names, photos, and experience of his top 700 managers. Data on the managers are arrayed on magnetic boards, by division and business.

The St. Louis–based company is committed to developing new products and expanding to overseas markets with Emerson's lines of motors, switches, and electric tools. Knight has planned and organized a focused research and engineering effort to produce the needed state-of-the-art, high-quality products.

Chuck Knight believes managers must pay attention to detail, implement and monitor plans, and be enthusiastic. If managers stay aggressive and pay attention, they will succeed. This is how Chuck Knight helped Emerson Electric succeed and become a major competitor of the giant of the industry, General Electric.

Coaching, passion, enthusiasm, and attention to details are so important to successful management that entire sections are devoted to them in books such as *In Search of Excellence, A Passion for Excellence, Thriving on Chaos, Swim with the Sharks without Being Eaten Alive, The Renewal Factor,* and *The One-Minute Manager.* These characteristics represent what managers must do to help their firms attain organizational goals. They are so important that we will discuss them throughout this section of the book.[1]

There are 14.5 million businesses in the United States. Of those, about 160,000 are large organizations that are in the news frequently, such as IBM, General Motors, Exxon, Procter & Gamble, and General Foods. About 4.5 million are medium-sized businesses, with annual sales of $500,000 to $10 million. Finally, the majority of businesses are the 10 million mom-and-pop operations, with an owner (manager) and one to three employees.

Every size firm—large, medium, and small—employs managers. There are managers in the Fortune 500 company and managers in the family-owned corner delicatessen. This means that millions of managers (some estimate over 30 million) perform the types of roles and responsibilities spelled out in this chapter. Managers are a vital cog in the 14.5 million American businesses trying to compete effectively in an increasingly complex global marketplace.[2]

In this chapter, we begin by defining management and indicating its importance to the pursuit of various organizational and individual objectives. We present the managerial functions—planning, organizing, staffing, directing, and controlling—as ways managers try to obtain these objectives. We then discuss the three levels of management and the various roles managers play. The chapter concludes with a presentation of four core management skills needed by managers at each level and in each role.

WHAT IS MANAGEMENT?

Everyone seems to have an opinion about the meaning of management. Unfortunately, the opinions are usually stated in complex terms and shed little light on what management is. Perhaps the most succinct description of management was offered by early management scholar and theorist Mary Parker Follett. She stated that management is the "art of getting things done through people." In other words, the manager coordinates the work of others to accomplish goals that might not be achievable by an individual. Thus **management** will be defined as the application of planning, organizing, staffing, directing, and controlling functions in the most efficient manner possible to accomplish meaningful organizational objectives.

Management
The application of planning, organizing, staffing, directing, and controlling functions in the most efficient manner possible to accomplish objectives.

The theme of our definition of management is that a central person (a manager such as Chuck Knight at Emerson Electric or Chuck Daly, coach of the Detroit Pistons basketball team) must—by using such skills as decision making, communication, and objective setting—coordinate the work activities of others to achieve organizational objectives. Research has highlighted a direct relationship between the clarity of organizational objectives and business success. The successful management team develops clear objectives and enthusiastically undertakes programs and projects to accomplish them.

Objectives
Specific results or targets to be reached by a certain time.

A VARIETY OF OBJECTIVES

Objectives are desired results or targets to be reached by a certain time. Objectives are specific, state what is to be accomplished, and indicate when it will be achieved. On the other hand, **goals** are broadly stated general guidelines that an organization or individual seeks to achieve. A college student's goal may be

Goal
A broadly stated guideline that an organization or an individual is attempting to achieve.

FIGURE 7.1

Cascade Approach

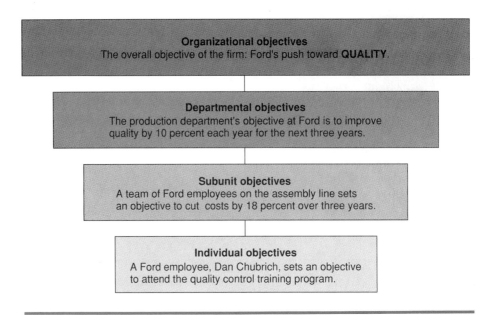

Organizational objectives
The overall objective of the firm: Ford's push toward **QUALITY**.

Departmental objectives
The production department's objective at Ford is to improve quality by 10 percent each year for the next three years.

Subunit objectives
A team of Ford employees on the assembly line sets an objective to cut costs by 18 percent over three years.

Individual objectives
A Ford employee, Dan Chubrich, sets an objective to attend the quality control training program.

Cascade Approach
A procedure for setting objectives in which the objectives are set from the top level of management down.

to earn a degree in business administration. An objective would be to earn a bachelor's degree in business administration by June 1994 with an overall grade point average of at least 3.5.

One procedure for setting objectives is called the **cascade approach,** in which objectives are set from the top level of management down (see Figure 7.1). (The "cascade" analogy emphasizes flowing from the top to the bottom.) This process provides direction to lower-level managers as the goals are converted to objectives from the top down:

1. A clear statement of organizational purpose is issued. The mission statement identifies the scope and uniqueness of the organization. (A unique mission statement—that of BBA Group, a $1.6 billion, 25,000-employee British firm—is presented in Figure 7.2. The firm builds a range of products, including industrial textiles and automotive components.)

2. Long-range goals are developed from this statement.

3. The long-range goals are converted into specific performance objectives.

4. Objectives are then developed for each subunit in each department.

5. Within the subunits, challenging but attainable personal objectives are set.

Most organizations pursue multiple objectives. Some are short-run targets, while others are based on a longer time span. The manager developing a strategy or a program for maximizing objectives must set priorities among sometimes conflicting objectives. Retail firms such as Wal-Mart, Kmart, Sears Roebuck, and Eckerd Drug Stores emphasize shorter-run objectives, while organizations such as the Edison public utility, Eli Lilly Research, and development laboratory teams aim at longer-term results.

FIGURE 7.2

Mission Statement: BBA Group

BBA—A CORPORATE PHILOSOPHY

The inertia of history is a powerful influence on corporate philosophy. BBA, in its 103 years of existence, has strayed little from:

    i. Yorkshire paternalism.
    ii. Weaving of heavy textiles.
    iii. Friction technology via woven or pressed resin media.

The philosophy of BBA for the next few years will be to adapt rather than abandon the inert.

Management
(a) Grit and gumption are preferable to inertia and intellect.
(b) The Victorian work ethic is not an antique.
(c) One man can only serve one master, to whom he is responsible for a minimum number of succinctly defined tasks.
(d) Most companies owned or yet to be acquired possess adequate people waiting to be transformed by dedicated leadership.
(e) The effectiveness of an organization is in inverse proportion to the number of hierarchical layers.

Markets We shall concentrate in markets where:
(a) The products are in a state of maturity or decline, "Sunset Industries."
(b) The scale of our presence in a market segment will allow price leadership.
(c) The capital cost of market entry is high.
(d) Fragmentation of ownership on the supply side facilitates rapid earnings growth by acquisition of contribution flows.

Money
(a) The longer run belongs to Oscar Wilde, who is dead.
(b) The key macro and micro variables of our business are so dynamic that poker becomes more predictable than planning and reactivity more profitable than rumination.
(c) Budgets are personal commitments made by management to their superiors, subordinates, shareholders, and their self-respect.
(d) The cheapest producer will win.
(e) The investment of money on average return of less than three points above market should be restricted to Ascot.
(f) Gearing should not exceed 40 percent. The location from which funds emanate should be matched to the location from which the profit stream permits their service.
(g) We are not currency speculators, even when we win.
(h) Tax is a direct cost to the business and, accordingly, should be eschewed.
(i) Victorian thrift is not an antique.
(j) Nothing comes free; cheap assets are often expensive utilities.

Monday Our tactic is to:
(a) Increase the metabolic rate of BBA through directed endeavour.
(b) Increase profit margins by drastic cost reduction.
(c) Massage and thereby extend the life cycle of the products in which we are engaged.
(d) Become market dominant in our market niches by:
    i. Outproducing the competition.
    ii. Transforming general markets where we are nobody to market niches where we are somebody.
    iii. Buying competitors.
(e) Use less money in total and keep more money away from the tax man and the usurer.
(f) Avoid the belief that dealing is preferable to working.
(g) Go home tired.

Maybe
(a) The replication of our day-to-day tactic provides long-term growth.
(b) We need to address "Monday" this week and what our reaction will be to what may be on "Monday" for the next three years.
(c) Three years is, in the current environment, the limit of man's comprehension of what may be.
(d) Long-term growth necessitates:
    i Resource– notably men and money.
    ii. Sustained performance rather than superficial genius.

Source: Reprinted by permission of HARVARD BUSINESS REVIEW. An exhibit from "Mirrors and Windows . . . (from The Gray Area)," by Andrew Campbell, July–August 1989. Copyright © 1989 by the President and Fellows of Harvard College; all rights reserved.

Objectives are important for several reasons:

- *To focus attention on the organization's mission.* Objectives give specific purpose to the organization. Managers initiate actions designed to bring an organization's resources to bear on the objectives.

- *To help integrate the work of the organization.* Objectives provide a means for setting priorities and resolving conflict between departments and subunits.
- *To help measure an organization's performance.* Objectives provide a target to be achieved and a benchmark of how well the firm is doing.

Organizations have multiple sets of objectives. Four important levels of objectives are organizational, departmental, subunit, and individual.

Organizational Objectives

The overall objectives of a firm are the responsibility of the top management group—typically the chief executive officer and staff, with the assistance and concurrence of the board of directors. In short, they represent the thinking of the executive level of management. Top managers, however, cannot act without having a great deal of information and intelligence passed up the line from the levels below.

Ford Motor Co. provides a good example of the role played by organizational objectives. After losing over $3 billion early in the decade, Ford became the comeback story of the 1980s, the world's most profitable car company. Ford established the highest quality objectives in the industry and pushed the responsibility for meeting these objectives down into the ranks of workers. The

Ford has established and communicated that its organizational objective is QUALITY. As one Ford executive stated, the top three objectives in the company are QUALITY, QUALITY, and QUALITY.

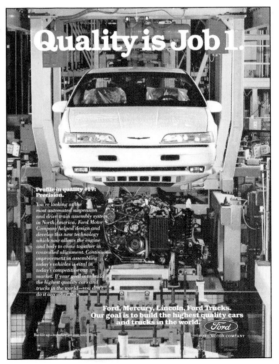

Courtesy of the Ford Motor Company

objective set in 1980 was to increase Ford's market share during the decade by at least 5 percent. This objective for market share was specific and clearly communicated.[3] By January 1, 1991, Ford had increased its share by three percentage points to 23 percent, while General Motors had shrunk nine percentage points to 35 percent. The push for quality in all Ford products has earned the firm a solid reputation in the marketplace.

Departmental Objectives

The Northeast Insurance Company relies on its sales force to sell policies. In 1990 the sales team decided to set an objective of capturing at least 8 percent of the Chicago-Calumet regional market by 1995. The ambitious five-year objective means the sales department will have to increase its market share from 3.6 percent to 8 percent in only five years. An increase in market share means that someone else's business must be taken away, a hard task in the insurance industry.

Subunit Objectives

The operations department of Scott Manufacturing, Inc., is divided into three teams. Each team, which includes technicians, operators, and material-handling personnel, has an informal leader and a team nickname—Wildcats, Pirates, and Copperheads. These teams compete to be the most productive group in the department without sacrificing product quality.

Each team sets objectives for specific quantities and quality, and it outlines a plan for achieving the objectives and a set of target dates. At Scott the subunit sets objectives; the organizational and departmental objectives described above are usually first set within the framework of a formal organization.

Individual Objectives

Dan Chubrich (see Figure 7.1) has been employed at Ford's Chicago assembly plant for 15 years. Dan's boss wants him to become certified as a quality control inspector. Dan wants to attend the quality control training program but has put it off for six years in a row. Whenever he planned to attend the program, some personal problem (such as too much unfinished work or a family crisis) prevented him from taking the course.

After one of his closest friends attended the program, Dan finally began to outline a set of objectives. He has established July as the starting date to enroll in the program. He will also have to help his boss find someone to operate his spot on the line while he attends the program. Dan's individual objectives are somewhat different than Ford's overarching organizational objective. However, they are just as important and challenging.

Objectives serve as targets for both managers at the top of an organization and those who work with operating employees. They are the specific guideposts around which the entire management group focuses. If the objectives are clear, challenging, meaningful, and measurable, the organization will have the standards to judge whether managers are efficiently performing the functions of management.

Chaparral Steel: A Mini-Mill that Practices Effective Management

Chaparral Steel is a success story that shows what can be done by planning carefully and by setting realistic organizational objectives. Chaparral is a young firm. The original plant was built in 1975 on a cow pasture about 30 miles south of Dallas. Within three years, Chaparral had established itself as a leader in mini-mill steelmaking technology. Chaparral employs just over 900 employees who produce over 1.1 million tons of bar and structural steel products.

The Chaparral plan was to:

- Choose a site where population growth is higher than average, energy costs are lower, and the business climate is favorable. In 1975 this meant Dallas.
- Use the most advanced steelmaking technology.
- Keep the business small and specialized.
- Set up an organization with few layers of management so that quick, informed decisions could be made.
- Establish a system so that a key player is the first-line supervisor.

First-line supervisors at Chaparral are expected to plan, organize, staff, direct, and control. They are involved in planning, which is usually not true at this level of management. They hire and fire. They're responsible for quality. They are responsible for establishing and meeting rigorous cost and preventive maintenance objectives. They are expected to schedule, organize, and direct the crews that run the equipment. When Chaparral talks about management, the spotlight is on the first-line supervisors.

Instead of using highly paid research and development scientists to find the technology needed to compete, Chaparral insists that all managers, especially the first-level supervisors, be responsible for keeping the firm up-to-date. So far this formula has resulted in objectives being achieved, profits being earned, and long-range plans for continued success being enthusiastically embraced by each employee.[4]

MANAGEMENT FUNCTIONS

Given our definition of management, exactly how do managers go about managing in an office, on a shop floor, or in a committee meeting? What do they do to help accomplish objectives? Management theorists (e.g., Henri Fayol, Mary Parker Follett, and Chester Barnard) have identified five primary functions of managers.[5] These functions (planning, organizing, staffing, directing, and controlling), first formally discussed over 80 years ago, still characterize the activities of most managers. Although the amount of time spent on each varies, these five categories pinpoint the variety of work performed by managers. Let's look at each one.

Planning

Former President Dwight Eisenhower once said, "Plans are nothing, planning is everything." When managers plan, they project a course of action for the future. They will attempt to perform a systematic set of business actions aimed at achieving objectives. Thus **planning** essentially means deciding in advance what is to be done. Of course, plans alone do not bring about desired results; but without a plan and a set of objectives, managerial actions are likely to produce confusion. Planning is a task that each manager must do every day.

Planning
The management function of establishing objectives and developing plans to accomplish them.

The work of planning is basically mental. It requires thinking things through logically. Managers should think before acting and act in light of facts rather than best guesses. For example, experts analyzing the decline in the quality and competence of the work of NASA point to excessive guessing and poor planning.[6] The space agency has been accused of exaggerating promises, guessing about costs, and not correcting flawed designs. The *Challenger* disaster, the flawed mirror in the $1.5 billion Hubble telescope, and design problems with the $37 billion space station point to such problems as faulty planning.

One reason for such business failures as the Ford Edsel (Ford lost over $350 million), the Penn Central Railroad, and Daniel Boone Chicken was faulty planning, or no planning at all. In the early 1970s, the Daniel Boone Chicken franchise tried to compete head-on with Kentucky Fried Chicken but failed to secure proper sites or to train store managers. In addition, the business couldn't secure the money needed to properly operate the fast-food stores over the long haul. The managers at Daniel Boone made incorrect assumptions, failed to properly scan the environment, and did not spend enough time on planning. On the other hand, the management team of Chaparral Steel spent a lot of time on planning, as the Business Action relates.

There are many reasons why a manager must plan. Planning helps provide the coordination needed to do the job. It helps ensure that things will get done; it can also show the manager when things may not get done and why they were not done right. Planning also helps the manager determine who will do what job, how long the job will take, and what resources are needed to get the job done.

Despite its numerous advantages, some managers still do not plan. Some reasons managers have given for not planning include:

- *"It is risky."* Developing a plan involves setting targets. When targets or objectives are stated, a manager's performance can be monitored and evaluated.

- *"It is costly."* Planning takes time, energy, and creative thinking. Some managers are not willing to absorb these expenses.
- *"It is difficult."* Planning involves complex decisions, having people from different backgrounds develop a common and interdependent approach, patience to wait for results, and a commitment to a program of often new and untested activities.

Although these reasons are often valid, intense competition forces firms to plan. They must because companies can no longer count on having a solid lead over their competitors. Too much is changing in the business environment for any manager to put off planning.

Organizing

Organizing
The management function of grouping people and assignments to carry out job tasks and the mission.

The **organizing** function of management consists of grouping people and assigning activities so that the job tasks and the mission can be properly carried out. The establishment of the managerial hierarchy, which we discuss later, is the foundation of the organizing function. Specific details of organizing will be discussed in the next chapter.

Staffing

Staffing
The management function of selecting, placing, training, developing, and compensating subordinates.

Selection, placement, training, development, and compensation of subordinates make up the **staffing** function. A manager's staffing activities also include the evaluation and appraisal of performance. Specific details about this function are covered in Chapter Eleven.

Some managers see staffing activities as the sole responsibility of the personnel/human resource department. But because managers are directly affected by staffing decisions, they should become involved. Line managers can be aided by the personnel/human resource department but typically should not give up the final responsibility for staffing.

Directing

Directing
The management function of initiating action: issuing directives, assignments, and instructions.

Leadership
The process of influencing the activities of an individual or group toward accomplishing objectives. Leadership may be autocratic, democratic, or laissez-faire.

As the managerial function that initiates action, **directing** means issuing directives, assignments, and instructions. Directing also means building an effective group of subordinates who are motivated to perform. It means getting subordinates to work to accomplish objectives. Directing can be accomplished through **leadership,** the process of influencing the activities of an individual or group toward the accomplishment of an objective.

The directing function is a part of any manager's job, but the time and effort managers spend in directing vary with their position in the managerial hierarchy, the number of assigned subordinates, and the type of job activities being performed. For example, the supervisor in a McKesson's distribution center in Milwaukee spends most of the day directing subordinates, whereas the president of McKesson's spends significantly greater time in more abstract and general activities.

Generally speaking, managers may choose from many directing styles. Two such styles of direction are autocratic and democratic leadership.

Autocratic leadership, the close style of supervision, means providing subordinates with detailed job instructions. The manager structures or specifies exactly what is to be done and when the work is due. Managers using this style delegate as little authority as possible. Autocratic managers assume they should do the planning and make the necessary decisions.

Some employees respond positively to the autocratic style. Others tend to lose interest and lack initiative when working for an autocratic manager. In some cases, individuals or even groups of subordinates may actively resist and develop hostilities toward the autocratic manager.

Under certain circumstances and with specific employees, autocratic direction may be necessary. Employees with skill deficiencies, lack of experience, or certain personality traits want firm and structured direction. For example, the new employee who is unsure of the job, his or her skills, and the manager's expectations would probably respond positively to an autocratic style. Some employees feel that general supervision is no supervision at all.

The opposite of autocratic direction is **democratic leadership,** or general supervision (also referred to as participative). In this style, the manager consults with subordinates about job activities, problems, and corrective actions. Managers using the general approach seek help and ideas. Democratic leadership does not lessen managers' formal authority; decision-making power still rests with them. With an experienced, skilled, and intelligent group of employees, a manager would likely benefit from using a democratic style that encourages participation.

For democratic management to be successful, the manager must be enthusiastic and honest in using it, and the employees must want it. If a worker believes a boss "knows best," the person is not likely to be motivated to perform better under the general supervision style.

Probably the best reason for considering the democratic style is that subordinates who participate in a job-related decision are apt to be more enthused about performing the job. Those allowed to take part in decision making generally support the final decisions enacted. They try hard to make the decision a success.

With **laissez-faire leadership,** the supervisor avoids power and responsibility. He or she exists as a contact person who provides information and guidance that can be helpful in accomplishing objectives. The laissez-faire, or free-rein, supervisor may give task assignments and offer support when requested but stays out of the group's way. Such a style may be appropriate when, for example, a person who is a liberal arts or business graduate (i.e., has minimum technical knowledge) is managing a group of engineers.

Controlling

The managerial function of checking to determine whether employees are following plans and progress is being made, and of taking action to reduce discrepancies, is called **controlling.** The core idea of control is to modify behavior and performance when deviations from plans are discovered.

Planning, organizing, staffing, and directing are the initial steps for getting the job done. Controlling is concerned with making certain that plans are correctly implemented. Supervisors who delegate their responsibility should

Autocratic Leadership
A type of close supervision in which the manager delegates as little authority as possible.

Democratic Leadership
A type of general supervision in which the manager consults with subordinates about job-related issues.

Laissez-Faire Leadership
A type of supervision in which the manager avoids power and responsibility by giving assignments and support but staying out of the group's way.

Controlling
The management function of checking to determine whether employees are following plans and progress is being made, and of taking action to reduce discrepancies.

Ernestina Galindo operates a small tortilla factory in Austin, Texas. She is involved in planning, organizing, staffing, directing, and controlling. She knows a lot about making tortillas, and she is a hands-on manager who carries out each function.

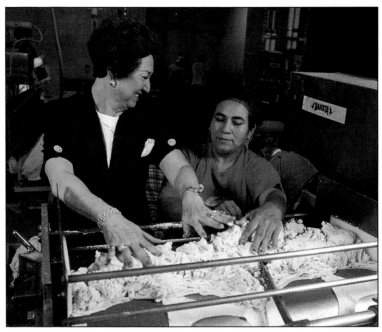

Daemrich/The Image Works

take care to control because the ultimate responsibility for the delegated work is theirs. The process of control has four basic steps:

1. Set standards for time, quality, quantity, and so on.
2. Measure performance (results).
3. Compare performance to standards.
4. Make necessary modifications.

A standard indicates to employees what is expected. Ideally standards are measurable and easy to understand. For example, a management team may set a standard for producing two acceptable units a day or for achieving industrial sales of $50,000 a month. But how are standards set for an accountant or personnel manager? Standards in these and other staff areas often are somewhat fuzzy attempts to determine the important functions in the departments.

An important part of a manager's job is to monitor performance so that problems can be pinpointed. Once managers assess performance and compare it to the standards set earlier, they can begin a course of action. Of course, too much measurement can be expensive and can alienate the people being monitored. Each person involved in the control checks needs to understand his or her importance.

The Japanese pride themselves on having sound quality control monitoring systems. Yet, in 1990, Matsushita, Sony, Isuzu, and Yamaha all had recalls. The Japanese quality edge could be seriously damaged in the international

FIGURE 7.3

**Del Ray Electronics'
Control Process**

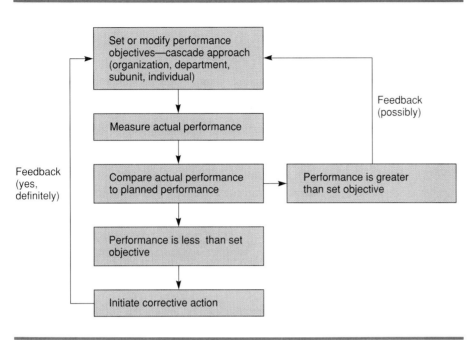

marketplace if the control system of these firms is not put back into top working order.[7]

Managers often develop clear standards and monitor results, yet fail to make the necessary corrections. If standards are not being met, the manager must search for the problem, find it, and correct it. In the centralized planning systems now being dismantled in Eastern Europe, managers failed to search for problems and correct them. An old Soviet story associated with the five-year plans tells of the plant manager who needed an accountant. He asked each applicant for the position, "How much is two and two?" He gave the job to the applicant who answered, "How much do you need it to be, Comrade Manager?"[8] Adapting a result to fit the standards is the complete opposite of using control to improve performance.

The control process at Del Ray Electronics (a small firm in Florida) is spelled out in Figure 7.3. An important phase of organizational control is the feedback that occurs. If performance is acceptable, no modification may be needed; if performance is unacceptable, objectives will not be met, so modifications are needed.

Planning, organizing, staffing, directing, and controlling—these five functions must be carried out in all firms, large or small, in the United States or in Europe, profit or nonprofit. The Boston Celtics basketball team, Procter & Gamble, Ben & Jerry's Ice Cream, and Nick's Shoe Hospital all have managers who plan, organize, staff, direct, and control. As firms grow in size, they tend to have layers, or levels, of managers. At each level, these functions are carried out to some degree.

LEVELS OF MANAGEMENT

As enterprises grow from an owner to a group to a corporation, a number of managerial levels are created and they begin to take on a shape. Three distinct levels of management—executive, middle, and first-line—are usually portrayed as a **managerial hierarchy.** This hierarchy depicts what is called a **chain of command,** or simply a channel of communication, coordination, and control. The first-line manager reports to a middle-level manager, who reports to an executive-level manager.

Figure 7.4 is a pyramid diagram of a managerial hierarchy. The pyramid is used for many medium- and large-sized businesses because it can show the number of managers at each level and the authority relationships among them.

Three levels of management are shown in the pyramid: executive, middle, and first-line. Executive-level managers have more authority in decision making than middle-line managers; middle managers have more authority in decision making than first-line managers. Some titles typically associated with the various levels are also shown in Figure 7.4.

Managerial Hierarchy
The levels of management in an organization, typically three distinct levels: executive, middle, and first-line.

Chain of Command
The channel in which communication, coordination, and control flow through the various levels of management to subordinates.

Executive

At the top of the management pyramid sits the president or chief executive officer (Sam Walton, Chuck Knight) and other managers engaged primarily in charting the overall mission, strategy, and objectives of the business. The executive management team must be skilled in planning product distribution, recruiting key personnel, and developing plans. In addition, executive-level managers often are asked to represent the organization in community activities, dealings with the government, and seminars and the like at educational institutions. They function externally for the business and are important spokespersons for everything the company is attempting to accomplish.

FIGURE 7.4

Levels of Management: The Managerial Hierarchy

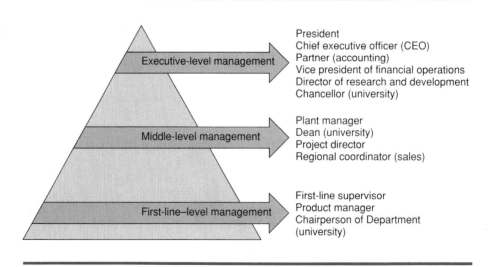

The obligations and responsibilities of executive managers in large organizations are many. Consequently, the monetary rewards are often relatively large. The pay of executive-level managers—including base salary, bonus, and other monetary considerations—is often in six figures. The effective executive is usually very mobile; each year at least one out of five moves to a new geographic location. Many executive-level managers move from one company to another. Thus the question is not *whether* the executive-level manager will move but where and when.

Middle

The middle level of the management hierarchy includes plant supervisors, college deans, project directors, and regional sales coordinators. These managers receive the broad overall strategies, missions, and objectives from executive-level managers and translate them into specific action programs. The emphasis is on implementing the broad organizational plans. Basically the middle manager is a conduit between the top policymakers (executive management) and the supervisory personnel responsible for producing products and/or services so that the company achieves its objectives.

First-Line

The third level of management, the first-line or supervisory level, is directly responsible for the minute details needed to coordinate the work of nonmanagers. Supervisors must work directly with employees and motivate them to perform satisfactorily. The supervisor in a factory, the departmental chairperson in a college, and the product manager in a marketing department must translate overall corporate goals into action plans. This management level is the link between managers and nonmanagers. Organizational objectives eventually meet the test of reality at the supervisory level.

The cornerstone that separates the three levels of managers from nonmanagers is decision making. Managers at any level, performing any managerial function and applying any management principle, must make decisions. Executive-level managers must determine the overall direction of the company. The middle manager must decide how to implement the overall plan at the supervisory level: How should the plan be communicated? How should supervisors be motivated? When should the supervisor be informed about the overall plans? The first-line supervisor must decide how to motivate employees and reward the best performers.

Operating Employees

The managerial hierarchy in Figure 7.4 shows only managers. The majority of employees (the **operating employees**) in medium- and large-sized business organizations do nonmanagerial work. The bank teller waits on customers, the salesperson sells dresses to a customer, and the machinist works on equipment that produces the units the company sells. Therefore, the organization pyramid is complete only with a base that shows all the employees who are not performing managerial duties.

Operating Employees
The nonmanagers in an organization, who perform specific tasks and usually manufacture a product or provide a service for customers.

FIGURE 7.5   **How Managers Spend Their Time**

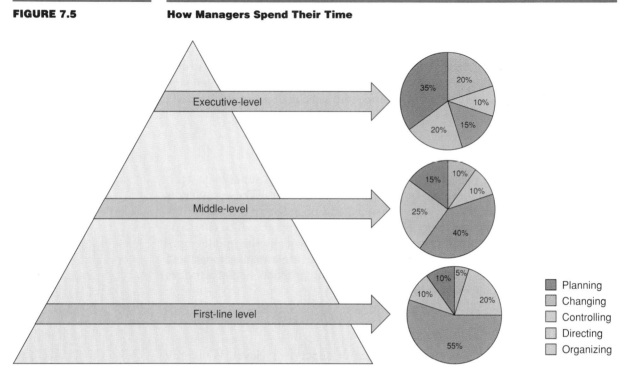

Source: Derived from *The Nature of Management Work* by Henry J. Mintzberg. Copyright © 1973 by Henry J. Mintzberg. Reprinted by permission of Harper Collins Publishers.

WHAT DO MANAGERS DO WITH THEIR TIME?

Once we understand the management hierarchy, we can examine what managers do with their time. As shown in Figure 7.5, managers at different levels generally focus on different tasks. One study found that executive managers concentrate a significant portion of their workday on planning, managing and coping with change, and organizing; first-line managers focus primarily on directing operating employees. They spend far less time in such conceptually oriented areas as planning and in developing change programs.[9]

Another study of managerial time examined how time was used by middle-level managers in various departments.[10] Four departments were examined: production, marketing, finance, and personnel/human resource management. Four management functions were used, including planning, organizing, controlling, and a miscellaneous "other" category. The study found distinct uses of time across functions, as illustrated in Table 7.1. Production, marketing, and finance managers all spend the greatest percentage of their time in controlling activities. Personnel/human resource managers, however, spend the largest proportion of their time on planning activities. The diversity in time use between level of management and function of management has been confirmed by different researchers over the years.

TABLE 7.1

Middle-Level Managers' Allocation of Time

Department	Management Functions			
	Planning	**Organizing**	**Controlling**	**Other**
Production	17%	19%	46%	18%
Marketing	14	17	53	16
Finance	15	12	60	13
Personnel/human resources	33	26	20	21

Source: Adapted from J. Horne and T. Lupton, "The Work Activities of Middle Managers: An Exploratory Study," *Journal of Management Studies,* 1965, pp. 14–33. Reprinted with the permission of Basil Blackwell Ltd.

TABLE 7.2

The High Price of a Manager's Time

DID YOU KNOW? *Consider that a manager works approximately 2,000 hours, or 50 weeks, a year (simply an estimate). Suppose managers waste about five hours a week on trivial tasks. If 10 $30,000-per-year managers waste about five hours a week, the cost is 10 × 5 × $21.00 = $1,050 per week. Thus, wasting time can be very costly.*

Annual Salary	Weekly Salary	Benefits*	Total per Week	Value per Hour†	Value per Minute
$ 30,000	$ 600	$240	$ 840	$21	$0.35
40,000	800	320	1,120	28	0.47
50,000	1,000	400	1,400	35	0.58
75,000	1,500	600	2,100	52	0.88
100,000	2,000	800	2,800	70	1.17

*Approximately 40 percent of weekly salary.
†Assume a 40-hour week.

In discussing how time is spent, a less formal portrait of time use also can give us insights. The Business Action about "the 24-hour day" discusses CEOs and their quest to develop time management tactics. In most cases, the day is just not long enough for everything to be done and for everyone to visit with the CEO. Time management is important to managers not only because they have so much to do but also because wasting time can be very costly, as Table 7.2 shows.

MANAGEMENT ROLES

In carrying out the five major management functions, managers perform various roles. A **role** is a set of expected behaviors. For example, a man may play the role of a father. As such he serves as a role model; he is expected to be kind, understanding, helpful, and a good example to his child. Similarly a manager is expected to serve a number of roles and to be a good role model.

Role
A set of expected behaviors. A manager has three major roles to perform: interpersonal, informational, and decision-making.

The 24—Hour Day Is Not Enough Time

As you read this chapter and attend to other parts of your life, you may think you're really busy. Telephone interruptions, a lack of clear objectives, drop-in visitors, and meetings seem to plague managers and nonmanagers alike. However, take a peek at the fully packed schedules kept by chief executive officers of various organizations. What sets the CEO's job apart from others on the management team is not the amount of time worked but the number of people and the variety of tasks that must be dealt with every day. Time demands on CEOs come from every direction—subordinates, the board of directors, customers, lawyers, consultants, civic leaders, and suppliers. Donald Schuenke, CEO at Northwestern Mutual Life Insurance, estimates that he would need to work at least 24 hours a day if he were to accept all the requests he receives from people wishing just a little of his time. In fact, he devotes about 60 hours a week to the job.

Since flying is such a frequently used mode of transportation, CEOs learn how to use time in an airplane efficiently. Peter Grace, CEO of W. R. Grace, uses the airplane like his office (however, he refuses to take telephone calls). Robert Crandall, CEO of American Airlines, puts a trash bag on the seat next to him and goes through all his paperwork.

The ability to delegate work to others is one of the CEO's most important tools for managing time efficiently. Allen Rosenshine, CEO at the Omnicom Group (a holding company that controls two of the three largest U.S. advertising agencies), states, "For me, the first decision is, do I handle it or do I delegate it to somebody else and forget about it?" Delegation means giving jobs to others without always checking on them. It is tough for CEOs to give up important, crucial jobs.

Secretaries and staff assistants are an important weapon in the CEO's time management program. CEOs vary widely in the degree to which they allow secretaries to screen people, requests, and information. Most often the secretary is not an arbiter of access but rather an assistant who helps screen and schedule the bidders for the CEO's time—subject to later approval or rearrangement. Allen Rosenshine, like a growing number of CEOs, has two secretaries. One handles typing, filing, and other clerical chores. The other helps him better manage his time, by both keeping the appointment book straight and serving as a go-between when Rosenshine can't immediately get in touch with someone.

Because CEOs must so often play important roles outside their firms, many designate special assistants to take up some of these responsibilities. Barry Sullivan, CEO at First Chicago Bank, is a trustee to the University of Chicago, a trustee of the Art Institute of Chicago, a cochairperson of the financial advisory committee for the city, and a participant in many other civic endeavors. He assigned Michael Leyden of First Chicago to help him with these demands. Now Barry and Michael share the civic responsibilities.

In the busy world of CEOs, there is concern about establishing objectives, applying the functions of management, performing multiple roles, and learning relevant management skills. However, there is also a lot of concern about stretching time, using it wisely, and establishing tactics to make the most of each minute.[11]

Chuck Keeler/TSW

Managers are important to firms, but so are operating employees. This punch press operator is the key to output. If he is not up to par or is absent, this machine's output will be affected. Operating employees perform tasks that result in the product or service being made ready to sell.

First, managers perform a number of interpersonal activities by virtue of their position in the managerial hierarchy. Second, the communications that flow to and from managers make it necessary for them to process information. Third, the fact that a manager is a conduit and communicator means decisions must be made; managers are the key decision makers in organizations. These aspects of managing are referred to as roles, or behaviors associated with the position.

Interpersonal Roles

The manager must be in frequent contact with others to fulfill the organization's objectives. Part of these activities requires the manager to lead subordinates. Leadership is essential for influencing employees' behavior and performance. Each time a manager influences an employee to work a little harder, to have confidence in the organization, or to report minor problems before they become major ones, he or she is acting as a conduit from management to the operating employee. An important feature of influencing others is, of course, the ability to communicate confidence and mutual respect.

Information Roles

The manager is the nerve center, or focal point, of a group. He or she should have a total picture of the group, its strengths and weaknesses and its needs. With this knowledge, managers process information flowing to and from the group, feeding it the relevant information. For example, the manager may receive word that a community action group will file a legal suit against the company for polluting the environment. This information may be considered

TABLE 7.3

**The Katz and Mintzberg
Skill Categories**

Katz	Mintzberg
Technical (having the required knowledge to perform job).	Technical (especially required at first-line management due to closeness to the operation).
Human relations (listening to, observing, and working effectively with people).	Human relations: Peer Leadership Conflict resolution
Conceptual (understanding the organization as a whole, and its future).	Conceptual: Information processing Decision making Resource allocation Entrepreneurial Introspection

premature or inaccurate by the organization's executives, who may ask managers to discuss this with their subordinates. Managers would need to assure the subordinates that, to date, no legal action had been taken and that the problem would be handled by top management. The manager also would inform the group of the organization's official position on the rumor.

Decision Roles

Managers must accept responsibility for decision making. The manager must take bits of information from various sources, interject a personal opinion, consider the present situation, analyze the resources available, and then tie this all together before reaching a decision. The exact mix of factors that must be considered before reaching a decision differs for every situation.

CORE MANAGEMENT SKILLS

Management Skill
The ability to use knowledge, behaviors, and aptitudes to perform a task.

Technical Skills
Skills involved in making a product or providing a service.

Human Relations Skills
The ability to relate and interact with subordinates, peers, superiors, and customers or clients.

Conceptual Skills
The ability to organize and integrate information to better understand the organization as a whole.

Management skill is the ability to use knowledge, behaviors, and aptitudes to perform a task. Skills are learned and developed with experience, training, and practice. Management writers have attempted to define the skills used by successful managers. Robert Katz classified management skills as technical, human relations, and conceptual.[12] **Technical skills** are those involved in making a product or providing a service. Katz points out that technical skills are especially important at the first-line management level. **Human relations skills** involve relating and interacting with subordinates, peers, superiors, and customers or clients. **Conceptual skills** are the manager's ability to organize and integrate information to better understand the organization as a whole. Conceptual skills are especially important at the executive level of management.

Henry Mintzberg provided a broader classification. He expanded the human relations skill to include three categories and the conceptual skills to include five categories. Table 7.3 provides a comparison of the Katz and Mintzberg classification systems.

TABLE 7.4

Needed Managerial Skills at Sohio

Skill, Ranked by Relation to Success	Description
1. Problem solving	Looks beyond the obvious; takes practical concerns into account; determines accuracy of information and effects of alternatives.
2. Initiative	Makes up mind quickly; recognizes when decision is needed, takes charge quickly, presses for a decision; independently identifies problem areas.
3. Adaptability	Copes with change; adapts to new assignments, switches strategies rapidly, revises plans.
4. Planning	Formulates plans; imposes order in ambiguous situations; identifies key tasks and critical steps.
5. Reasoning	Organizes information; handles abstract concepts; extracts important data; identifies subtle relationships.
6. Thoroughness	Pays careful attention to detail; checks and rechecks accuracy; produces accurate work; notices even minor problems.
7. Interpersonal sensitivity	Varies his or her approach to others; adapts communication style to the audience; shows sensitivity to others; delegates when appropriate; gives recognition to the accomplishments of others.
8. Impact	Commands attention and respect; influences events; takes charge in groups; presents convincing arguments.
9. Discussion participation	Participates actively in group discussions; speaks up without being called on; expresses ideas in one-on-one meetings.
10. Quantitative analysis	Utilizes quantitative data effectively; applies extensive knowledge of quantitative techniques to work; tackles problems by using quantitative techniques.
11. Written communications	Writes concise, organized, easy-to-read reports; edits others' work substantively; writes clear and meaningful technical reports.
12. Oral communications	Makes effective formal presentations; presents oral material in an interesting way; speaks with a polished style.

Source: Adapted from V. R. Boehm and Larry M. King, "What Do Managers Really Do?" (Paper presented by V. R. Boehm at the Annual Meeting of the AACSB Graduate Admissions Council, Toronto, June 1981).

Studies of Management Skills

Virginia Boehm conducted an extensive study of managerial skills by assessing 1,000 managers from all levels at Sohio Corporation.[13] She wanted to determine which skills should be emphasized in selection and training at Sohio. Boehm asked each manager to describe what skills and abilities he or she used to accomplish the job objectives. In addition each manager was rated on overall job performance. The results are summarized in Table 7.4, with those skills most related to success listed first (e.g., problem solving, initiative, adaptability).

Boehm's results show that interpersonal skills were only of moderate importance in this sample. Six of the top 10 skills relate to problem solving and change. When the study was conducted, however, the company was growing

TABLE 7.5   **Core Management Skills and Their Characteristics**

Decision-Making/ Problem-Solving	Communication	Interpersonal	Objective/ Goal–Setting
Identifies problems.	Writes clearly and concisely.	Shows empathy.	Establishes meaningful, challenging, and clear objectives.
Creates feasible alternatives.	Speaks effectively.	Uses power and influence fairly.	Sets priorities.
Selects an optimal alternative.	Listens carefully.	Projects a positive image to others.	Evaluates success of objectives/goals approach.
Delegates.	Has computer skills.	Leads effectively.	Uses objectives/goals as standards to establish reward program.
Makes decisions under risk and/or uncertainty.		Behaves ethically.	
Evaluates alternatives used to solve problem.		Resolves conflict.	

rapidly. Change was therefore a fact of everyday life for managers. Under these conditions, successful managers had to possess skills to cope with managing uncertainty.

Robert Burnaska conducted a number of studies at General Electric.[14] He attempted to determine which early career experiences led to managers' success. Four early-career factors were found to be associated with success: (1) technical ability, (2) realistic job expectations, (3) having a mentor, and (4) challenging work assignments. New employees tend to overestimate their skills, abilities, and knowledge; they also assume they will be given challenging job tasks. However, assignments for new employees are often rather routine. Thus Burnaska recommends career counseling so that unrealistic assumptions and expectations are kept to a minimum. An astute, knowledgeable manager can serve as a **mentor,** a role model who provides orientation, emotional support, coaching, and insight to new employees. The mentor can also provide technical help and organizational hints to minimize improper behavior and unacceptable performance. Finally, receiving challenging work assignments early in a career—being exposed to challenging work and successfully accomplishing it—results in recognition, enriched confidence, and the establishment of challenging objectives.

The Katz and Mintzberg classifications and the Boehm and Burnaska research results point to four core management skills that you will have to learn, practice, and become proficient in to be a successful manager. These skills, highlighted in Table 7.5, are decision-making/problem-solving skills, communication skills, interpersonal skills, and objective/goal-setting skills. Whether we discuss a small convenience shopping store (e.g., 7–Eleven, Circle K) or an organization with thousands of employees (e.g., J. C. Penney), these skills are important.

Mentor
A role model who provides orientation, emotional support, coaching, and insight to new employees.

Talking, listening, and observing are communication skills that are vital to business success. These Hewlett-Packard (HP) employees are exchanging information. Being able to communicate clearly and concisely is important as HP attempts to service customers 24 hours a day, 365 days a year.

Courtesy of Hewlett-Packard

Decision-Making/Problem-Solving Skills

Tony Vallone owns and manages a seafood restaurant in Baltimore. He has to solve price, customer complaint, personnel, staffing, supplier delivery, maintenance, and advertising problems almost every day. If there were no problems to solve, there would be no need for Tony to manage. Decision making and problem solving involve the type of activities listed in Table 7.5: identifying problems, creatively generating alternative solutions, selecting a specific alternative, delegating authority to implement a solution, making decisions under uncertain and risky circumstances, and evaluating the success or failure of the alternative selected. These specific skill activities must be applied by managers at all levels in the management hierarchy.

Communication Skills

Surveys show consistently that both managers and nonmanagers must possess communication skills.[15] The majority of time a manager spends applying the functions of management is spent communicating with others via memo, speaking, listening, or use of the computer. Managers in the 1990s are expected to give speeches, make inspirational talks to employees, and write clear memos, letters, and reports. Computers are here to stay, so managers will also have to use the computer efficiently. They don't have to be computer programmers, but they will have to know how to use computer software to make their job easier.

According to Madelyn Burley-Allen, author of *Listening: The Forgotten Skill,* a survey of Fortune 1,000 company presidents indicated that listening is a major problem for most people.[16] For example, managers report that subordinates' failure to receive critical information and to accept and/or carry out

● C o n n e c t i o n s

Listening Skills

Directions: Place an X on the number that indicates how important you think the specific skill is for good listening. Then place a circle around the number to indicate your estimation of your present skill level in listening to people.

Skill areas	High/ excellent				Low/ poor
1. Regarding what the other person says as important—at least to the speaker.	5	4	3	2	1
2. Listening without interrupting.	5	4	3	2	1
3. Not rushing the other person.	5	4	3	2	1
4. Giving full attention to the other person.	5	4	3	2	1
5. Not responding judgmentally.	5	4	3	2	1
6. Adjusting to the other person's pace of speaking.	5	4	3	2	1
7. Listening objectively.	5	4	3	2	1
8. Responding both to what is said and to what is left unsaid.	5	4	3	2	1
9. Checking to be sure that the other person heard correctly.	5	4	3	2	1
10. Maintaining confidentiality.	5	4	3	2	1

responsibilities is a major problem in business. Both of these failures imply deficient listening skills. With regard to all communications, listening takes about 40 percent of a manager's time (speaking is 35 percent, reading is 16 percent, and writing is 9 percent).

We tend to equate listening with hearing, but this is not correct. Good listening means being aware of what you hear, accurately receiving the information you hear, and combining the information you hear in a way that is useful to you. Connections will help you determine your current level of listening skills. You're probably like most people, good in some areas but need to improve in others.

Interpersonal Skills

Interpersonal relations in the work environment are the primary glue in a successful organization.[17] Talking, listening, cajoling, facilitating, and showing concern are all important in developing relationships with people. Using power and influence skillfully and serving as a referee are also crucial parts of the manager's network of interpersonal relationships. A manager's ability to

Give your overall rating of the quality of your listening skills (circle one):
Very high—10 9 8 7 6 5 4 3 2 1—very low

Feedback: Both students and managers have completed the Listening Skills quiz. Based on many responses, the two skill areas in which respondents seem to be the weakest are (2) listening without interrupting and (4) giving full attention to the other person. People seem to have a knack for interrupting others and of not listening to what is being said. Any item that has an X on the 1 or 2 rating may require attention on your part. Also, an X–O gap of two or more numbers indicates a discrepancy between importance and skill level. Each of these 10 areas is extremely important.

Listening skills can be improved by:

- Talking less.
- Avoiding hasty judgments.
- Taking notes.
- Letting the person finish talking.
- Asking questions.
- Paying attention.

Students need to practice good listening skills in all of their classes. Without listening ability, learning is difficult.

empathize affects subordinates' behavior and attitudes significantly. Empathy is a skill with two main characteristics: accurately perceiving the content of another person's message and giving attention to the message's emotional components. Positive changes in behavior and attitude and interpersonal growth are associated with the superior's show of empathy in an interaction.

The act of managing isn't the simple process of sitting down to plan, thinking about actions, allocating resources, and controlling through monitoring. Because people are involved, it is interpersonal, one-on-one, a person talking to a group, a person watching someone's eyes or gathering cues to form an impression. Whenever people are involved, managers must use their interpersonal skills.

Jerre Stead, president of Square D, the Illinois-based electric product company, knows how important interpersonal skills are in managing.[18] He has worked at listening, talking, and observing. Yet he feels that many of his subordinates still do not open up and provide the complete story. Until he is able to win their total confidence, Mr. Stead has to work extra hard to develop a more trusting interaction pattern. In a fragmented, action-packed day, he still tries to improve his interpersonal style.

Objective/Goal—Setting Skills

The fourth skill area—setting objectives and goals—is concerned with establishing organizational, departmental, subunit, and individual objectives. Carefully set and attended-to objectives (specific targets) and goals (general targets) can affect individuals' motivation and performance. Carefully set objectives/goals are meaningful, challenging, and clearly established. Priorities must be set and an evaluation program developed. The evaluation program must then be used as the basis for creating an equitable, timely, and clearly communicated reward system.

The four core management skills apply to managers at each level in the management hierarchy. These skills are used to perform the planning, organizing, staffing, directing, and controlling functions of management. How well managers do their jobs depends on how proficient they are in these skills; deficiency in any area diminishes the manager's chance of success. Learning, practicing, receiving feedback on, and observing (through videotaping in training programs) these skills will help shape and refine them so that optimal results are achieved.

Managers can make a difference in organizational performance. The way they work, use their skills, and apply the functions of management affects the actions of others and the accomplishments of businesses. Since managers are human, they may make mistakes, err in judgment, act unethically, and behave selfishly or insensitively. When this happens, people on the receiving end of such behavior get hurt, and objectives may be jeopardized. At other times, managerial behavior is very positive. Managers anticipate errors, help a floundering employee, create career opportunities for others, behave ethically, and act decisively. When this happens, people working with a manager blossom and gain self-confidence, and organizational objectives are accomplished.

You'll Know It's the Century When . . .

The Boss Learns to Nurture

Retaining good workers will be a top corporate priority in the 21st century. Slow population growth will make skilled entry-level workers more difficult to find. Turnover will be even more expensive, because many new workers will have to be trained in-house for highly specialized jobs. Relocating skilled personnel will be more difficult, because people in two-career marriages won't move unless their spouse can also find work. In the year 2000, one employee in four will come from a minority group. Many will not speak English. Most larger corporations will have special offices that deal with minority concerns.

Today, nearly all major corporations have job training programs. In the 21st century, most workers will have access to company-sponsored support networks that include mental health programs, drug and alcohol counseling, and fitness programs.[19]

SUMMARY OF LEARNING OBJECTIVES

1. To define the term *management.*
   Management is the application of planning, organizing, staffing, directing, and controlling functions in the most efficient manner possible in order to

accomplish meaningful organizational objectives. Management is carried out by one or more managers to get things done through other people.

2. To explain what is meant by the term *organizational objectives.*
Objectives are desired results or targets to be reached by a certain time. They are specific, state what is to be accomplished, and indicate when it will be achieved. Objectives are tailored to four important levels: organizational, departmental, subunit, and individual.

3. To discuss the five functions that successful managers must perform.
Planning involves developing a set of actions to achieve objectives. Organizing consists of grouping people and assigning activities so that job tasks and the mission can be carried out. Staffing involves the selection, placement, training, development, and compensation of subordinates. Directing involves taking charge, initiating action, and directly motivating employees. Controlling is monitoring, or checking, employees and objectives and taking action to correct discrepancies between objectives and performance.

4. To compare the three levels of management in terms of authority, responsibility, and accountability.
Executive-level managers are engaged primarily in charting the overall mission, strategy, and objectives of the business. These managers must be skilled in planning product distribution, recruiting key personnel, and developing plans. They often represent the company in the community and in dealing with the government. Middle-level managers receive the overall strategies, missions, and objectives from the executive managers and translate them into specific action programs. They function as a conduit between executive managers and supervisory personnel. First-line managers are directly responsible for coordinating the work of nonmanagers. They work directly with employees and motivate them to perform satisfactorily.

5. To explain the three types of managerial roles.
Because managers constantly interact with others to fulfill the organization's objectives, they assume interpersonal roles. They lead, inspire, motivate, and encourage employees. They communicate confidence and mutual respect. Managers also play informational roles by being the group's focal point. Managers play decision roles by accepting responsibility for decision making.

6. To identify the four core skills that managers need to acquire and practice.
The core skills are decision-making/problem-solving, communication, interpersonal, and objective/goal–setting skills.

KEY TERMS

Management, p. 225

Objectives, p. 225

Goals, p. 225

Cascade Approach, p. 226

Planning, p. 231

Organizing, p. 232

Staffing, p. 232

Directing, p. 232

Leadership, p. 232

Autocratic Leadership, p. 233

QUESTIONS FOR DISCUSSION AND REVIEW

1. What is challenging about being a middle-level manager? Try to locate such a manager and ask him or her this question.

2. What did Dwight Eisenhower mean when he stated, "Plans are nothing, planning is everything"?

3. Can female and male managers apply each of the skills discussed in this chapter with equal effectiveness? Explain.

4. In theory, a pyramid type of management hierarchy indicates a top-down management atmosphere. Describe what you think a bottom-up management atmosphere would mean.

5. Why are communication skills so necessary for success in the field of management?

6. How could a manager develop and improve his or her decision-making/problem-solving skills?

7. The need to practice good or efficient time management seems to apply to everyone. Why is it so important to managers? How do you rate yourself in terms of being a time manager?

8. Do you set individual objectives? Describe how you can improve upon the establishment of objectives and the monitoring of your progress.

9. Tom Peters (coauthor of *In Search of Excellence* and consultant) claims that there are no excellently managed companies. He states, "If it isn't broke, you just haven't looked hard enough." He is speaking to managers. What is he talking about in terms of the practice of management?

10. Why would a manager have to be physically and mentally healthy to be successful in today's organizations?

CASE 7.1
Body Shop International: Practicing
Management Differently

Managers are involved in objective setting, carrying out management functions, and serving as role models to operating employees. Anita Roddick is a manager, leader, and role model for not only employees but also society in general. She and her husband started her business, "Body Shop International," in Britain in 1976, with a $6,400 loan. One objective, now becoming reality, is to make the Body Shop a $1 billion company by 1995. Anita Roddick's company sells cosmetics. However, she has become an inspirational role model because much of her time is devoted to passionate environmentalism—including offering only biodegradable products and providing refillable containers.

Anita is an environmentalist who has instilled an activism about ecology throughout her management hierarchy and among nonmanagers. Although many people still suspect firms that profess devotion to social causes, her leadership is convincing; she also practices astute management. Body Shop is not just another chain of stores that sells shampoo, skin lotion, and hair conditioners. The firm is now pushing into the United States, with Japan the next target. Then it will be other parts of the world.

Body Shop's growth and expansion is a result of sound planning, organizing, control, and Anita's leadership. Her product line includes Rhassoul Mud Shampoo, White Grape Skin Tonic, and Peppermint Foot Lotion. The names are odd, but the packaging is simple; there are rows of shampoos and lotions in identical plastic bottles with black caps and green labels. Simplicity, no push to sell, pleasant sales personnel, and refillable containers characterize the business. Anita wanted to manage a simple, no-fantasy, creative cosmetic business. She decided to sell cosmetics without any hype and without damaging the environment.

Anita decided to not spend money on advertising. Can you imagine a manager making such a decision in the cosmetics business, one of the most advertising-oriented industries around? Apparently customers are buying from a company whose values they respect. They become promoters of the business by word of mouth, telling their friends about Body Shop.

Anita has carefully organized the firm's employee motivation programs. Body Shop employees receive newsletters, videos, brochures, posters, and other information. Communicating with employees is the most important skill emphasized at Body Shop. Not only does Anita communicate about business, she also devotes much energy to talking about the company's campaigns to save the rain forest and ban ozone-depleting chemicals.

Anita is passionate about managing her business in a way that is exciting, is profitable, and has a social consciousness. The effect of her management style is electric. As a role model, she wants every employee to feel the same excitement she does. She wants her employees to try to be remarkable, to all be role models, to not damage the environment, and to treat customers as family. All the little details of the practice of management are important at Body Shop.

At the time this text is being written, Anita Roddick's corporate activism is probably considered bold by U.S. standards. However, a time may come in the United States when this form of management is considered a true inspiration for society. The global community may be leaning toward introducing a new core management skill called environmentalism. It would be added to the traditional decision-making, communication, interpersonal, and objective-setting skills. Anita Roddick appears to be proficient in these traditional skills along with her special environmentalism skill.

Questions for Discussion

1. Most managers would balk at the prospect of being asked to become a social activist like Anita Roddick. Do you agree? Why?

2. How did Anita Roddick become a role model for her employees?

3. Should companies be managed like Body Shop International? Why?

CASE 7.2
Ethical Dilemma: A Manager's Daily Concern

Managers face ethical dilemmas every single day. How they spend their time is discussed in terms of planning, organizing, and controlling. However, no category exists for decision making with an ethical orientation. Certainly planning, organizing, and controlling are important, but so is making ethical decisions that are in the best interests of people, the firm's objectives, and one's own value system. Who should be promoted? Who should be sent to the executive development seminar? Should the company hire a woman who is extremely intelligent but can't speak English very well? What about Mary's attendance record, which has been poor since her son was diagnosed as having a life-threatening disease? Each of these questions involves making decisions that managers know have an ethical overtone. Making the right decisions is not easy for any manager.

The news media give the impression that ethics is only a managerial or business-related issue. But ethics and breaches of it are a societal issue. Ethical decision making is extremely important for any manager, employee, parent, lawyer, doctor, or person who must weigh the facts and take action; each individual must decide what is ethical and what is right. Family upbringing, laws, experiences, pressures, and self-imposed anxiety all play a role in how a person deals with the ethical aspect of a decision, event, or situation.

Ethical dilemmas arise in many everyday situations. A sample of dilemmas that can be used to discuss ethical decision making can be found in Andrew S. Grove, "What's the Right Thing? Everyday Ethical Dilemmas," *Working Woman,* June 1990, pp. 16–18.

Here are three ethical issues a manager might face. In reading them and answering the end-of-case questions, consider your own style, needs, values, and perspectives.

Nick is a district sales manager of a firm that sells men's hygiene and sports products (e.g., jock itch cream, sprays, hernia belts, athletic supporters). This successful firm has never employed a woman as a sales specialist. Now three qualified women are applying for the few vacancies in the sales force. Nick believes that legally and morally the women must be thoroughly considered for the positions. His fellow district managers believe that Nick is off-base on this issue. There are male candidates, and they can do the job well. Nick is concerned. He wants to make a good business decision, one that is best for the company and that is ethical.

Mark is a department manager. He invited four office employees out to lunch to celebrate Joyce's promotion to office manager. Each employee chipped in $15 for the lunch. The bill was paid by Mark, who placed it on his credit card.

About one week after the lunch, Don, one of the luncheon participants, found out that, after collecting the money, Mark had billed the company for the entire lunch. Now Don is trying to decide how to handle this discovery.

Dana is a new account specialist working for Anders, Welboldt, and Daneke, a certified public accounting group. She has been teamed up with Rudy, an experienced CPA consultant in charge of a project. Rudy informed Carrie, the partner in charge, that a new business plan had been submitted to the client. Dana knows that Rudy did not submit the business plan. Dana does not want to be part of any project that misleads the partner. She also does not want to get Rudy into trouble. He has been a tremendous mentor and has supported her in every way possible. Deciding how to handle this dilemma is creating a lot of anxiety for Dana.

Questions for Discussion

1. Is Nick involved in an ethical dilemma, a legal dilemma, or both? Explain.
2. What should Don do to resolve his ethical quandary?
3. How can Dana keep Rudy as a friend and mentor and still solve her ethical problem?
4. Why is it said that the way daily dilemmas of a firm are handled shape the overall ethical climate of an organization?

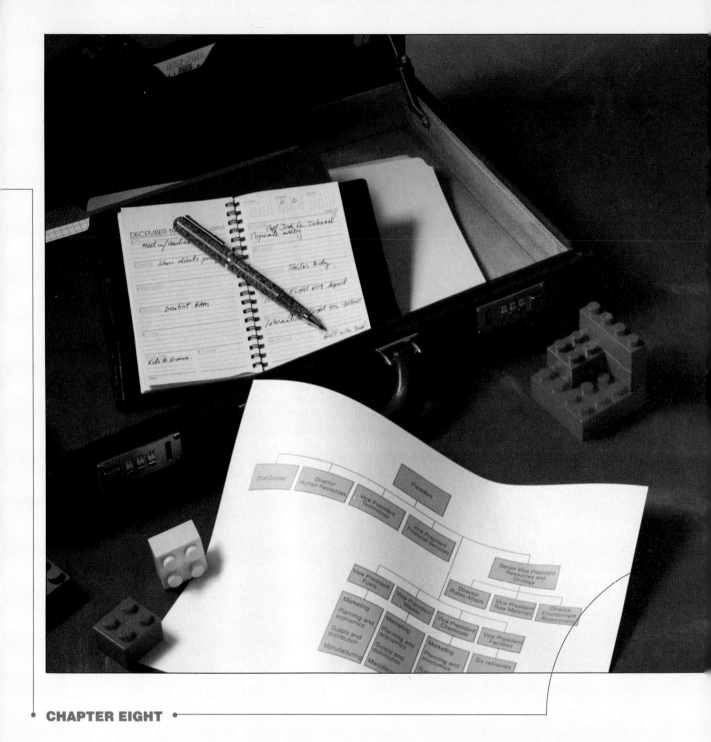

ORGANIZING THE BUSINESS

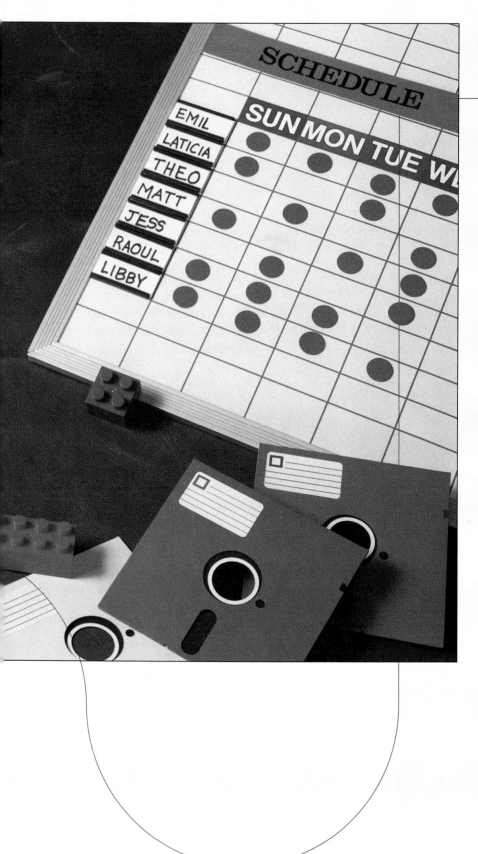

Arrow Dynamics, Inc. was founded over 40 years ago. It rapidly became a leader in the amusement industry. In the 1950s, the company collaborated with Walt Disney Company to design and produce many of the breathtaking rides found at Disneyland and Disney World. Arrow management is

necessary to achieve the desired capacity. Fast, upside-down, rail-hugging, quick-turning, and exhilarating, gasping for air, and search for your "heart" rides are Arrow's goal. The Texas Giant roller coaster at Six Flags over Texas provides a 62 mph, 137-feet incline, 90-second, orchestrated for

In 1985, because of large debts, Arrow was forced into Chapter 11 bankruptcy. The term *bankruptcy* applies to the process of settling a firm's debts, or obligations. Chapter 11 gives a company like Arrow a chance to make good on its financial obligations by staying in business and making payments to creditors. A number of employees filed an opposing plan, which the creditors accepted. Thus 12 employees took ownership of the company and began to restructure the management and employee hierarchy.

Arrow, prior to the Chapter 11 threat, employed about 200 workers. Downsizing and lost business resulted in the layoff of almost everyone; at its lowest point, Arrow had 20 employees. By September 1990, however, Arrow had approximately 135 employees.

Arrow decided its new organization structure would not include a track fabrication unit. Arrow decided to spin off the track fabricating unit into a new firm called Fabriweld. Arrow now subcontracts its construction and fabrication work to Fabriweld.

The result has been a leaner Arrow Dynamics both in departments and in number of full-time employees. The new organizational design has made Arrow a streamlined business that can respond more quickly to customer demands. The increased efficiency and flexibility have resulted in more exciting rides being developed and in increased sales, from $4 million at the time of the 1986 reorganization to over $20 million four years later.[1]

Courtesy of Arrow Dynamics, Inc.

proud of the firm's reputation as a trendsetter. The custom-engineered rides have provided unparalleled fun to millions of amusement park customers.

Arrow's engineers are famous for custom-designing a roller coaster system to fit the customer's specifications. Once Arrow understands what is wanted, they design a preliminary layout, considering the terrain that will be used for ride placement, length of track, number and kind of looping elements desired, height and number of lifts, and number of trains

screaming and gasping ride. This is what Arrow can produce.

Despite the white-knuckle outcome of moving up, down, and around, Arrow Dynamics needs to be managed effectively. Ron Toomer (who ironically is prone to motion sickness) is now Arrow's president and chief executive officer (CEO). He became president in 1986 after a significant reorganization of the firm. The original owners sold the firm to Rio Grande Industries, which then sold it to a German company, Huss, in 1981. Arrow lost money designing and producing rides for the New Orleans World's Fair.

More and more firms are looking closely at their organization structures. The decision to change an organization's structure requires an understanding of various principles of organization. The next time you visit a restaurant, a service station, or a movie theatre, think about how well or poorly it is organized. This little exercise of thinking through "the organizing question" will be more meaningful after you complete this chapter.

The issues and choices involved in organizational structure decisions are the subject of this chapter. First, we will discuss why businesses organize, and then we will examine some basic decisions made in organizing a business. Next, we will review the principles of organizing, followed by a discussion of the management practice of downsizing. Finally, we will present the various structures for organizing a business.

WHY ORGANIZE?

Arrow Dynamics, Inc. had to restructure, change its system, and downsize (eliminate some jobs) to survive and stay in the roller coaster business. That is, Arrow's management decided to reorganize the firm. *Organizing* is the management function of assigning activities and grouping people (designing and developing a blueprint or structure) so that the firm's objectives can be accomplished.

When a business grows from a one-person operation to one with employees, organization becomes necessary. Increased size requires specialization, more personal interactions, and the need to integrate differing viewpoints. Rather than having a single owner do everything, the growing business has employees with assigned tasks. Some type of organization structure is needed for things to run smoothly. Managers must plan and implement the way a business will be organized.

Tuan Huynh arrived in Dallas in 1980, speaking very little English, and found work as an auto mechanic. His wife also worked. After five years, the family

By being a good manager, Tuan Huynh, owner of H & A fashions in Dallas, started the firm and helped it grow to a point where sales are over $35 million.

Mark Perlstein

had saved $50,000. He decided to start his own company, H&A Fashions, and hired a general manager, a designer, a salesperson, and a secretary. As the business grew, he had to have people to meet the demand for his skirts, dresses, and jumpers. The company's sales are now over $35 million, and Huynh must make organizing decisions for a business that continues to grow. The next five-year goal is $100 million in sales, and this growth will require still more organizing decisions.[2]

Organization Structure
The arrangement of work to be done in a business.

In organizing a business, management (an individual or a group) usually decides what each person will do and how much authority each will have. The **organization structure** is intended to help the business accomplish its objectives by arranging the work to be done. There is really no one best way to organize.[3] The "how to organize" decision for a particular business depends on many different factors, including size, market, personnel, competition, history, and available financial resources. Each firm believes that a particular organizational structure works best. What works for Arrow Dynamics is not what is best for its spun-off company, Fabriweld. Similarly the Sears structural arrangement differs from that of Montgomery Ward, which differs from Kmart's. If there is a sound lesson about organizing, it would be: "Observe what your competitors are doing, but arrange your structure in a way that is best for your firm, its employees, and the objectives the enterprise seeks to accomplish."

ORGANIZING DECISIONS

Although differences in objectives, resources, and markets mean that different organizing strategies should be used, a knowledgeable manager will proceed with caution. Understanding some basic features of organizing can be helpful in earning a reasonable profit or operating a business efficiently. All managers need to keep the following issues in mind when organizing the business.

Clear Objectives

In Chapter Seven, we said that objectives are desired results or targets. To have clearly stated, meaningful, specific, and challenging objectives is important. They give meaning to the business and what it is attempting to accomplish. The multiple objectives (e.g., profit, market share, human resource development) of a business provide the direction for those organizing the firm. Objectives provide the framework for hiring the type of human resources needed.

Coordination

Organizational, departmental, subunit, and individual objectives must fit together. This means the efforts of individual employees must be coordinated, or interwoven.

Coordination requires everyday, informal communication among employees. When Lee Iacocca took over Chrysler Corporation in 1978, he found little communication between the engineers and manufacturing departments. Nobody seemed to be interested in coordination. Iacocca conducted meetings in which the engineers and manufacturing technicians were required to talk and work with each other.

Any organization structure, no matter how complicated, requires someone or some group to work continually on coordinating the activities of others. Managers and leaders can be the coordinators if they are respected and skilled in integrating the efforts of their subordinates or followers. Managers should not underestimate the effort that must go into coordination.

Formal and Informal Organizations

Two distinct organizations influence a company's employees. The **formal organization** is the one put together by management, created by those who have authority, responsibility, and accountability. At Arrow Dynamics, it was CEO Ron Toomer and his associates. At Sears Roebuck, CEO Ed Brennan developed the formal reorganization plan. The formal organization is displayed in the organization chart, the graphical representation of the formal structure of the business. (We will talk more about the *organization chart* later.)

Formal Organization
The management-designed, official structure of the business.

Informal organizations exist in every business. Not planned or shown on an organization chart, the **informal organization** is the network of personal and social relationships that emerges when people work together.

Informal Organization
The network of personal and social relationships that emerges when people work together.

Informal organizations develop because people who work together form relationships. In the past, managers tried hard—and unsuccessfully—to abolish them. Informal organization networks serve a purpose for employees. For example, a group of preretirement employees may be concerned about the pension program revision. They represent different units and are in various jobs (e.g., manager, technical, sales). Because of their common interest, they form an informal group to share information and opinions. Other informal groups

©Steve Niedorf 1989

DID YOU KNOW? *This 3M facility was actually built to encourage informal gatherings and discussions. These research and marketing employees share ideas and conversations in a leisurely and informal way. A lot of good information exchange results in friendship and network building.*

begin when employees bowl, golf, play cards, or perform charity work together. These informal associations provide chances for communication between individuals from many different units of the firm. This kind of communication improves group members' understanding of each other.

Formal Authority

Formal Authority
The right to give orders.

Delegation
Giving an employee at a lower level in the organization the responsibility for a given task as well as the authority to carry it out.

The right to give orders constitutes **formal authority.** In effective organizations, managers delegate authority. **Delegation** is the process by which authority is distributed or pushed downward in an organization. The organization structure can provide the framework for such delegation. Managers who do not have the time to perform their jobs often have failed to delegate authority properly. And subordinates who become frustrated in meeting their responsibilities may not be clear about what authority has been delegated to them.

Organization structure determines the pattern for delegation of authority. It establishes common understanding between the manager and the employee about the degree and type of authority delegated. Two major types of authority used in organization structural arrangements are line and staff. Managers should understand these distinctions to know how much decision-making freedom they have.

Line Authority
Unquestioned, direct authority to make decisions and take action.

Line authority   Each position in the managerial hierarchy has **line authority,** or direct authority over lower positions in the hierarchy. A manager with line authority is the unquestioned superior for all activities of his or her employees. At a McDonald's restaurant, the manager has authority over the salesclerks and the cooks. At the DSX electronics firm in Plano, Texas, the quality control director has authority over 15 quality inspectors. He instructs, commands, and coordinates all quality inspection activities. He is in a line authority position.

Staff Authority
An advisory authority in which a person studies a situation and makes recommendations but has no authority to take action.

Staff authority   A person with **staff authority,** which is advisory authority, studies a situation and makes recommendations but has no authority to take action. For example, EuroDisney is a new theme park located on the outskirts of Paris, France. Walt Disney Company owns 49 percent of the joint American-French business. The French partners in this joint venture can make recommendations to Walt Disney Company, but they do not have the authority to add attractions, change prices, or alter any of the Disney characters.[4]

The backbone of most organization structures is line authority. Staff authority is narrower because staff expertise comes as advice, which may not be used by the line manager. In structuring a business, managers may use both line and staff authority. Table 8.1 summarizes some of the advantages and disadvantages of each of these forms of authority.

Centralization and Decentralization

Centralized Business
An organization in which all, or nearly all, authority to make decisions is retained by a small group of managers.

Another important organization consideration is the amount of authority to delegate. In a **centralized business,** only a small amount of authority is delegated. A relatively small number of managers make the decisions and hold most of the power and authority. At Marie Vianett's aerobic exercise studio in Quebec, Canada, she makes all the decisions. She is the centralized and only source of authority. She hires employees and instructors, establishes the budget, provides the aerobic regimen schedule, and conducts all negotiations with the building landlord and suppliers of the aerobic exercise outfits sold in the studio.

Advantages	Disadvantages
Line Authority	
Everything kept simple.	Neglects advisers.
Authority relationship graphically illustrated by hierarchy.	Too many decisions to make in short time period.
Close to employees so decisions can be made quickly.	Requires very skilled line managers.
Staff Authority	
Uses the best experts.	Confusing to some employees.
Frees line managers for day-to-day activities.	Creates line-staff conflicts.
Can be used as screening and training arena for future line managers.	Places staff in subservient role.

TABLE 8.1

Advantages and Disadvantages of Line and Staff Authority

TABLE 8.2

The Decentralized-Centralized Continuum of Authority

Advantages	Disadvantages
Centralized	
Increases uniformity of policies, rules, and procedures.	Places demands and pressure on a few managers.
Helps avoid duplication of effort and use of resources.	Reduces sense of involvement.
Increases uniformity of decisions.	Gives large amount of power to a few managers.
Decentralized	
Places decision making closer to the action.	Makes coordination more difficult.
Gives individual decision makers more responsibility for their actions.	Limits availability of capable managers.
Helps develop managers for the future.	Lacks uniform policies.

←———————|————————|————————|————————→
Maximum delegation   Little or no delegation
of authority   of authority

←———————|————————|————————|————————→
Decentralized   Centralized
operation   operation

In a **decentralized business,** the opposite of a centralized business, authority is delegated to more (lower) levels of management rather than held by a small management group. The authority continuum in centralized and decentralized business is presented in Table 8.2. The table includes a comparison of some advantages and disadvantages of each type of delegation.

Decentralized Business
An organization in which a significant amount of the authority to make decisions is delegated to lower-level managers.

● **C o n n e c t i o n s**

Delegation Ability

Directions: Place an X on the number that indicates how important you think the skill is for delegating job assignments or decision-making power. Circle the number that indicates how much of the skill you now possess.

Skill Areas	Very important/ significant				Not important/ little
1. Trusting the ability of other people.	5	4	3	2	1
2. Delegating meaningful, not just routine, jobs to others.	5	4	3	2	1
3. Coaching and helping others with a new job.	5	4	3	2	1
4. Sharing power and authority.	5	4	3	2	1
5. Following up to let individuals know how they are doing.	5	4	3	2	1
6. Setting reasonable goals on what is to be accomplished.	5	4	3	2	1
7. Determining others' ability to make decisions.	5	4	3	2	1
8. The challenges of the delegated job are motivational.	5	4	3	2	1

The consulting firm McKinsey & Co. reported that Toyota, which has a decentralized structure, can introduce a new car, get market feedback, and introduce three new cars in the same amount of time it takes General Motors (GM) to introduce one car. Three cars versus one car. GM managers recognized this plodding reaction time and gave the Cadillac Division more autonomy to make decisions. GM decentralized decision-making power.[5]

Organizations move back and forth along the continuum. For years Sears was a centralized business; but in the 1950s and 60s, it changed to a more decentralized business. Then, around 1980, Sears executives declared they wanted closer control of decision making; in other words, management wanted authority centralized. In the 1990s, Sears has moved again toward a decentralized organization structure.

Feedback: A person with a strong orientation toward delegation would score between 33 and 40. A score of 40 would result from placing an X on the number 5 for all eight items. Being a good delegator has several payoffs for a manager. First, delegating regular, routine tasks frees the manager's time for more important tasks. Second, employees develop and become more involved with the job because they have added responsibility. Third, having more varied tasks can break the monotony for the employee of doing the same job over and over again.

Although delegation seems simple, it requires the manager to look closely at these factors:

1. Can the employee handle delegation?
2. What will be delegated? Is it clearly stated?
3. How will the person know he or she is doing a good job, especially in terms of the delegated tasks? Are there standards of performance?
4. Is the delegator available to answer questions, coach, and provide feedback?
5. Does the employee feel good after completing the delegated task?

Instead of rushing into delegation, the manager must carefully think these factors through. The quiz points to such managerial concerns as trust, coaching, sharing of power, and building in job challenge. The quiz also highlights points that managers need to address before deciding whether delegation is a useful organizing strategy for them.

An important management skill in a decentralized operation is delegation. This skill is the ability to pass on to an employee the responsibility for a given task, as well as the authority to carry it out. Can you delegate? Complete Connections and learn about your delegation skills.

Organization Chart

A graphical presentation of the formal structure of a business is the **organization chart.** It is similar to the blueprint of a new home. It maps positions, people, and their authority relationships. The organization chart shows authority, the location of responsibility, and to whom subordinates report. Figure 8.1 illustrates a simple line authority chart. Each position is represented by a box

Organization Chart
A graphic blueprint, or map, of positions, people, and formal authority relationships in the organization.

FIGURE 8.1   **Organization Chart: Line Authority**

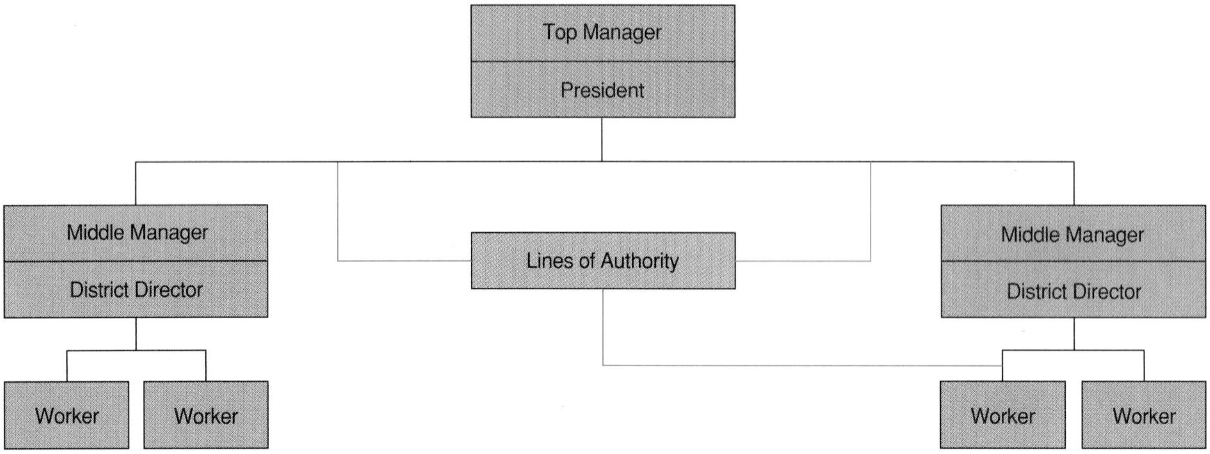

Lines of authority are pointed out as they would appear on a real organization chart.

FIGURE 8.2   **Organization Chart: Line and Staff Authority**

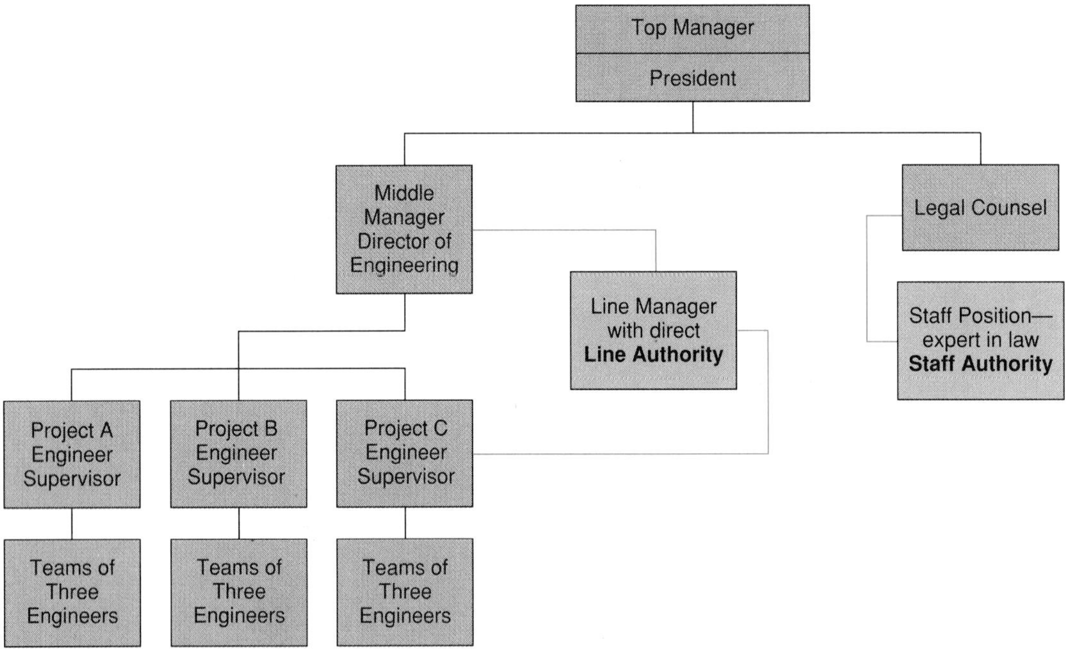

(with a title), and the flow of authority is represented by straight lines. Figure 8.2 shows a chart expanded to include staff authority. The legal counsel is a staff position advising the president on legal matters. The director of engineering exercises line authority over three project engineer supervisors.

Because it cannot picture informal relationships, the chart does not show exact communication patterns. A worker communicating directly with the president, for example, would represent an informal-organization activity.

Organization charts offer only a general view of the formal structure at a specific time. Every chart needs continual updating. Changes in the environment, personnel, resources, size, and technology necessitate the updating.

The Business Action describes the origin of the organization chart. As you will see, a railroad executive was the first manager to draw up and use such a chart.

PRINCIPLES OF ORGANIZING

Are delegation of authority, organization charts, and formal and informal organizations all there is to organizing? No, some principles of organizing have been found through practice and experimentation. These principles have been considered in organizing large businesses (Sara Lee, Scott Paper, and Boeing), medium-sized businesses (Allied Champion and Castle Metals), and small businesses (Champion Forest Roofing Co. and Mayo's Pharmacy).

Principles are guidelines for decision making; they are not laws etched in stone. Sometimes principles are used exactly as they are stated; other times they are modified or completely ignored. In general, those responsible for organizing keep a number of organizational principles in mind. Many principles are available to consider, but we have selected just a few of the more popular ones as illustrations.

Principle
A guideline that managers can use in making decisions.

Division of Labor

Organizations of all sizes perform a wide variety of tasks. A basic principle of organizing is that a job can be performed more efficiently if the jobholder is allowed to specialize. This principle, called the **division of labor,** involves dividing a major task into separate smaller tasks. The major task of manufacturing textiles is divided into smaller tasks of weaving, finishing, and needling.

Division of Labor
A principle of organization that a job can be performed more efficiently if the jobholder is allowed to specialize.

The efficiency achieved by becoming an expert in a small task can be significant. However, breaking a job into smaller and smaller tasks can be overdone. Dividing labor into small, boring jobs that offer no challenge can result in employees feeling frustrated, having low levels of job satisfaction, and seeking employment elsewhere.

Unity of Command

The principle of **unity of command** states that no member of an organization should report to more than one superior. Subordinates need to know from whom they receive the authority to make decisions and do the job. Conflicting orders from different superiors should be avoided; they can cause confusion, result in contradictory instructions, and create frustration about which order to follow. This principle can be followed in an organization having only line authority. However, when a staff and line authority structure is used, the unity of command is often violated.

Unity of Command
The principle of organization that no employee should report to more than one superior.

The Birth of Organization Charts

In 1854 David McCallum became general superintendent of the New York and Erie railroad. It stretched for nearly 500 miles from Jersey City through Pennsylvania and New York to the shores of the Great Lakes. The railroad lacked a blueprint of the organization and operation. McCallum solved the problem by drawing the first organization chart.

According to accounts of those who saw the first chart, it resembled a tree. Its roots represented the president and the board of directors. The chart's branches were the five operating divisions and the passenger and freight departments. Its leaves represented the new freight agents, first-line supervisors, and so on.

The history of the organization chart outside the United States highlights differences among countries. In Great Britain, Nobel Industries used a chart in 1919. Families owned the main British companies; there was much secrecy and a desire not to show others anything about the company. So, if these companies used organization charts, they were not made available to the public.

The Germans combined organization charts with thick operations manuals that documented the functions of every office and the persons in charge. The manual also described how employee replacements would be handled in the event of travel, sickness, or death.

The Japanese in 1908 used clearly presented organization charts to illustrate business units. Mitsubishi Co. relies on these charts to portray its functional structure arrangements.

The organization chart symbolizes the evolution of business from simple enterprises such as the mom-and-pop business to multinational conglomerates such as Tenneco, Nestlé, TRW Systems, and RJR Nabisco.[6]

Scalar Principle

That authority and responsibility should flow in a clear, unbroken line from the highest to the lowest manager is called the **scalar principle.** Because managerial levels are arranged in a hierarchy, the importance of the scalar chain from top to bottom is obvious. Breaking the chain results in uncertainty, frustration, and confusion.

An extension of the scalar principle is the notion that authority should equal responsibility. For example, suppose a production supervisor at Rockwell International has been assigned the responsibility to purchase new plant equipment. It would be important for this supervisor to have the authority to determine what price should be paid for the new equipment. Without this authority, how could the supervisor be held responsible for the decision?

Scalar Principle
The principle of organization that authority and responsibility should flow in a clear, unbroken line from the highest to the lowest manager.

Span of Control

Span of control is the number of subordinates reporting to a supervisor, or boss. The **span of control** principle says there is a limit to the number of subordinates one superior should supervise. Managers using that principle often specify an exact number of subordinates. This is unrealistic, however, because some supervisors can handle more subordinates than others. The optimum span of control depends on many factors, such as the type of skill and the experience levels of subordinates, the nature of the job, the supervisor's skill in handling subordinates, the situation, and the time available to do the job.

In general, highly skilled employees require less supervision than the less skilled. This permits the manager to have a wide span of control—that is, a larger group of employees reporting to him or her. For example, a large group of highly skilled technicians in a Du Pont research and development unit can be supervised by a single manager. On the other hand, an open-heart surgery team at St. Joseph Hospital in Chicago involves highly skilled employees but a narrow (also called tall or small) span of control.

Span of Control
The principle of organization that limits the number of subordinates reporting to a supervisor.

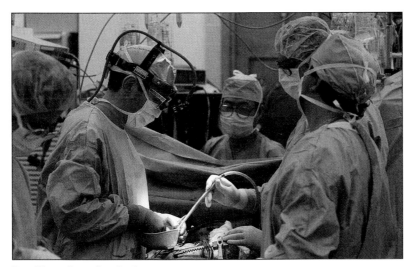

Scott Wanner/Journalism Services

An open heart surgery team at St. Joseph's Hospital in Chicago illustrates the span of control. The chief surgeon with all the headgear is in charge, but he is just one member of this important team. The patient, of course, doesn't care who is in charge. He just wants the best care possible from the team.

Downsizing the Organization

Some firms believe efficiency can be improved by reducing the number of advisers in the organization. This view is in the forefront of what is called "downsizing" the corporate staff. How many lawyers, accountants, purchasing agents, real estate managers, and futurologists does an organization really need? This question is being asked more and more by chief executive officers. Some firms have hacked away at key staff positions, while others are carefully analyzing what kind of staff is needed to compete. The list of downsizers includes diverse firms such as Eastman Kodak, Grumman, Levi Strauss, Merrill Lynch, US West Communicating, and Bank of New England.

Nucor, the mini-steel company in North Carolina, has sales of around $1 billion annually and a corporate staff of 17. Each division manager runs the business almost as an autonomous unit.

Mobil formerly employed 175 to 200 planners, human resource experts, and systems specialists. Each division had its own staff resembling Mobil's New York corporate staff. These "clone" staffs were cut back to save money, reduce duplication, and create a more aggressive program for responding to environmental changes. Baker Hughes fired 6,000 employees and shut down several plants to become more focused and leaner in the oil-field drilling and services industry.

AT&T eliminated over 12,000 staff jobs and decentralized decision making. Its traditional bureaucratic structure just didn't work well after deregulation; with increased and fierce competition, the line manager had to respond more quickly. The bloated AT&T structure was too inflexible. Thus, cutbacks enabled AT&T to be more responsive to changes, customer needs and complaints, and competitive forces.

Changing a structure by reducing staff must be done carefully. Simply hacking away and eliminating people has risks. Loss of control, the lack of timely data and information, and not having managerial talent to succeed retiring managers may be costly side effects of staff cuts. These costs must be weighed against the benefits: reduced expenses (salaries are eliminated), faster decision making, and closer contact with customers or clients. If the benefits outweigh the costs, downsizing may prove beneficial.[7]

Thus the optimum span of control depends on many factors. Rather than a universal set of numbers, managers have only general suggestions to examine the total picture—the managers, subordinates, job, resources, and time available. For example, millions of individuals are employed under the U.S. civil service to help run the country. The British, however, ran the Indian subcontinent for 200 years (from the middle of the 18th century through World War II) with a flat, or pancake, organization structure. Only 1,000 Indian civil servants administered the vast and densely populated subcontinent. The system worked well; it was purposely designed to ensure that each civil servant had the information needed to do the job.[8]

Downsizing

The procedure of keeping levels in a managerial hierarchy to a minimum often means that **downsizing,** or cutting out entire layers of managers, is necessary. Arrow Dynamics had to cut 180 jobs and almost the entire management hierarchy to meet its financial obligations. Communication, message distortion, personal contact, and feeling like a part of a team are factors addressed by this principle. As the levels, or layers, of management increase, so do a number of problems. The more levels of management, the longer the communication chain. This means more potential for message distortion. Moreover, top management and the lower levels have less contact as the distance from top to bottom increases. Finally, people feel more isolated as this distance increases, and there is a loss of team spirit, of pulling and working together.

Downsizing
Cutting out entire layers of management in the organization.

Downsizing has become a popular management practice. The Business Action explains why more firms are in the mood to downsize.

These five principles of organizing are by no means the only ones.[9] They are but a sample of guiding principles that enable managers to build an organization that can compete and adapt. The principles help managers assemble specific organization structures to meet their particular needs. The principles of organization are the building blocks for constructing a formal organization structure.

HOW TO ORGANIZE A BUSINESS

A person involved in organizing a business should identify the business objectives, the types of people working for the business, the technology, and the environment in which the business operates. If you've ever been in a house in which the rooms are too small or poorly arranged, you know the importance of the notion that "form follows function." That principle is also important in making organization structure decisions. People making decisions about structure need to examine the functions before selecting a form (that is, the structure).

Numerous forms, or designs, of structure are available to managers. Each way of organizing a business has advantages and disadvantages. A manager has to weigh all of these in making a selection. When the decision is made without considering disadvantages, the resulting choice may be the least effective or least suitable structure. The ones we present here are the most popular and widely used in business organizations.

FIGURE 8.3   **Functional Structure in a Hospital**

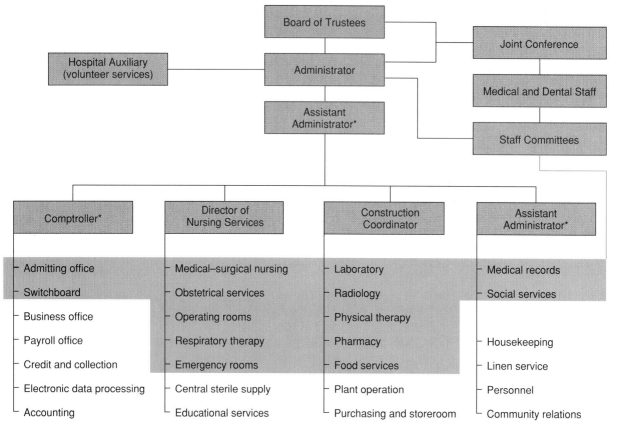

This chart reflects the line responsibility and authority in the hospital organization. However, a great part of the work of the hospital is accomplished through informal interaction between the identified services and functions. These functional working relationships are encouraged. Where there is difference in understanding or changes in procedure are required, the line organization should be carefully observed.
*Area directors.

Functional Structure

Functional Structure
A structure in which each unit or department has a different set of activities and responsibilities.

Each unit or department in the **functional structure** has a different set of activities and responsibilities. In a manufacturing firm, this means that engineering, manufacturing, and marketing would be separate departments. In a hospital, functional structure would include departments of nursing, housekeeping, medical records, radiology, and so forth. A functional structure for a county hospital is shown in Figure 8.3.

Advantages   The functional structure orients workers toward a specific set of activities. The engineer focuses on product design and improvement, and the salesperson works on selling. These functional experts become even more skilled in their areas. Research shows that the functional structure works well

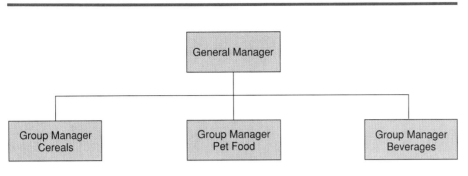

FIGURE 8.4

Outline of General Foods' Post Division: Product Structure

for a firm operating in a relatively stable (unchanging or slowly changing) environment.[10] Glass and building material companies such as Corning Glass Works, PPG Industries, and Owens-Illinois operate in a normally stable environment. Product lines change little from year to year, so the arrangement used is a functional structure.

Disadvantages The functional structure de-emphasizes the exchange of ideas and cooperation with other departments. The boundary between, say, marketing and engineering is imaginary, but it seems like the Great Wall of China. This happens because each department is evaluated on the basis of its own performance. Knowing they will be evaluated this way, managers concentrate on departmental matters instead of overall organizational objectives.

If the business's objectives and environment require coordination across departments, the functional structure becomes an obstruction. Problems arise that have no single departmental solution. As a result, the problems go unresolved, the buck is passed, or problems are pushed up to top management.

In summary, functional structures are best suited for businesses with a relatively stable environment, such as Corning Glass Works. At Corning the organization structure takes advantage of technical expertise. On the other hand, in an environment with numerous style changes (such as that of Liz Claiborne), a functional structure would lack flexibility and be slow in reacting. Liz Claiborne has to react quickly to fashion changes.

Product Structure

Businesses producing a wide variety of products often establish a **product structure.** The product structure was used as early as 1927 by Procter & Gamble (P&G). A new soap product, Camay, was not selling. A young executive, Neil McElroy (who later became the president of P&G), was told to give his exclusive attention to increasing the sales of Camay. This he did by using product managers. Soon afterward P&G added other product managers.

Today many firms, especially those in the food (Pillsbury), toiletries (Gillette), and chemical (W. R. Grace) industries, use product structures. General Foods uses a product structure in its Post Division, in which separate product managers are in charge of cereals, pet foods, and beverages. Figure 8.4 presents an outline of General Foods' Post Division.

Product Structure
An organization structure in which a manager is placed in charge of and has responsibility for a product or product line.

Advantages   The product structure places responsibility for a product or product line with the managers. The success or failure of Post Toasties is the responsibility of the general manager of cereals. This means product managers devote all their energy and skill toward the objectives of containing product costs, meeting schedules, and earning a profit. Instead of a department orientation, as with the functional structure, the focus is on product.

In addition the product structure encourages creativity. One study found that businesses with product structures were more successful in creating and selling new products than were businesses without product structures.[11] The product structure also is flexible enough to cope with changing environments. People have to cooperate so that the product will perform well.

Disadvantages   The price of the product structure can be high. Product managers often are not given enough authority to carry out responsibilities. They have to spend a lot of time coordinating activities so that people work together efficiently. This means less time for planning. Often they are told that they are like presidents in their product area, but in fact they are usually only referees and low-level coordinators.

Managers have also found that, compared to employees in functional structures, employees in product structures are more insecure and anxious about unemployment and personal development.[12] Perhaps this results from using product structures in relatively unstable, unpredictable environments. (Such environments reject products, even certain kinds of packages and names of products.) This unpredictability sometimes is stressful and produces anxiety because people's success depends on their product's success.

Territorial Structure

Territorial Structure
An organization structure in which units are divided on the basis of territory or geographical region.

Businesses that divide units on the basis of location are using **territorial structure.** When adjustments to local conditions, markets, or resources are important, responsibility affixed on the basis of territory has advantages.

Merchandising organizations such as Macy's, J. C. Penney, and Federated Department Stores have found territorial structure attractive. A&P, Safeway, and Kroger also use territorial division structures, coupled with centralization of certain functions (e.g., purchasing and distribution). Figure 8.5 charts the territorial structure of Macy's department stores. Each division operates like an independent business. Division managers have authority to take advantage of regional cost, resource, and competitive conditions.

Transportation companies may also be structured by territory. Low-cost airline prices have eaten into long-distance bus travel. Today the average bus trip has decreased from about 500 miles to slightly over 200 miles. This type of competition encouraged Greyhound Lines' management to change the company from a functional to a territorial structure. Greyhound now has four territorial divisions: eastern, central, southern, and western. Customer needs in Phoenix are monitored and then met by the western division, while customer needs in Chicago are observed and handled by the central division. The territorial structure helps Greyhound be more responsive to consumer needs and better able to coordinate schedules, maintenance, replacement, and employee preferences in each region.[13]

R. H. Macy., Inc.   **FIGURE 8.5**

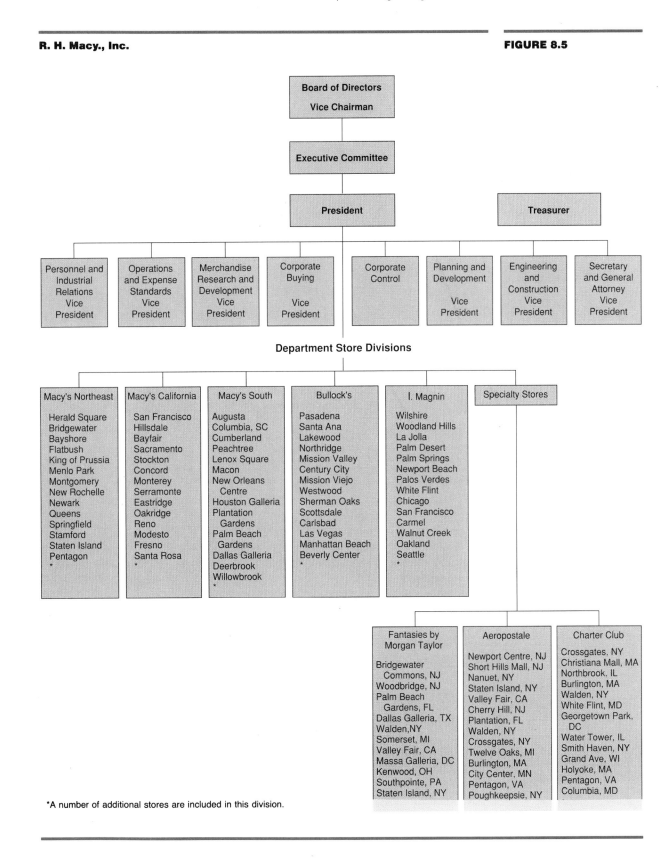

Board of Directors
Vice Chairman

Executive Committee

President   Treasurer

| Personnel and Industrial Relations Vice President | Operations and Expense Standards Vice President | Merchandise Research and Development Vice President | Corporate Buying Vice President | Corporate Control | Planning and Development Vice President | Engineering and Construction Vice President | Secretary and General Attorney Vice President |

Department Store Divisions

Macy's Northeast

Herald Square
Bridgewater
Bayshore
Flatbush
King of Prussia
Menlo Park
Montgomery
New Rochelle
Newark
Queens
Springfield
Stamford
Staten Island
Pentagon
*

Macy's California

San Francisco
Hillsdale
Bayfair
Sacramento
Stockton
Concord
Monterey
Serramonte
Eastridge
Oakridge
Reno
Modesto
Fresno
Santa Rosa
*

Macy's South

Augusta
Columbia, SC
Cumberland
Peachtree
Lenox Square
Macon
New Orleans
 Centre
Houston Galleria
Plantation
 Gardens
Palm Beach
 Gardens
Dallas Galleria
Deerbrook
Willowbrook
*

Bullock's

Pasadena
Santa Ana
Lakewood
Northridge
Mission Valley
Century City
Mission Viejo
Westwood
Sherman Oaks
Scottsdale
Carlsbad
Las Vegas
Manhattan Beach
Beverly Center
*

I. Magnin

Wilshire
Woodland Hills
La Jolla
Palm Desert
Palm Springs
Newport Beach
Palos Verdes
White Flint
Chicago
San Francisco
Carmel
Walnut Creek
Oakland
Seattle
*

Specialty Stores

Fantasies by Morgan Taylor

Bridgewater
 Commons, NJ
Woodbridge, NJ
Palm Beach
 Gardens, FL
Dallas Galleria, TX
Walden,NY
Somerset, MI
Valley Fair, CA
Massa Galleria, DC
Kenwood, OH
Southpointe, PA
Staten Island, NY

Aeropostale

Newport Centre, NJ
Short Hills Mall, NJ
Nanuet, NY
Staten Island, NY
Valley Fair, CA
Cherry Hill, NJ
Plantation, FL
Walden, NY
Crossgates, NY
Twelve Oaks, MI
Burlington, MA
City Center, MN
Pentagon, VA
Poughkeepsie, NY

Charter Club

Crossgates, NY
Christiana Mall, MA
Northbrook, IL
Burlington, MA
Walden, NY
White Flint, MD
Georgetown Park,
 DC
Water Tower, IL
Smith Haven, NY
Grand Ave, WI
Holyoke, MA
Pentagon, VA
Columbia, MD

*A number of additional stores are included in this division.

The territories of firms like United Parcel Service (UPS) have no limits. Eastern Europe is now on UPS's map. Adjusting to local conditions in Warsaw and Moscow will become old hat as UPS uses the structure that gets the job done.

They're wearing a new uniform in Moscow this winter.

UPS is delighted to announce delivery service to the places everyone is talking about.

Now you have a fast, efficient way to send international letters and packages to Moscow, East Berlin, Warsaw, Cracow, and Budapest. More destinations in Eastern Europe will be added soon.

Best of all, UPS will be controlling your delivery every step of the way. Thanks to exclusive new joint ventures and service partnerships, UPS is managing the entire delivery process inside of Eastern Europe, with UPS vehicles on the job and personnel trained to UPS standards.

So if you've got a parcel or document headed East (or to over 180 other countries and territories, for that matter), you know who to look for.

We're the ones wearing those snappy brown uniforms.

We run the tightest ship in the shipping business.

Courtesy of United Parcel Service

Advantages   The main advantage of the territorial structure is that it allows coordination at the point of sale. This coordination can lead to more personalized and speedier service. In a territorial arrangement, customer needs can be better addressed.

Disadvantages   Some duplication of effort occurs in the territorial structure. Also, the corporation needs to hire, train, and develop managers with the broad-based ability and technical knowledge required to manage multiple functions such as sales, production, and marketing.

Matrix Structure

Matrix Structure
A functional structure combined with either a product or a project structural arrangement.

Occasionally a company utilizes a functional structure and either a product or a project structure simultaneously; that is, it combines functional structure and a second management arrangement into a **matrix structure.** The result violates the unity-of-command principle of organizing because a person works for more than one boss. The employee is assigned to both a functional department (permanent home) and a particular product or project (temporary home). Figure 8.6 shows a matrix structure with five functional departments and three projects staffed by employees from the departments.

Matrix Structure   **FIGURE 8.6**

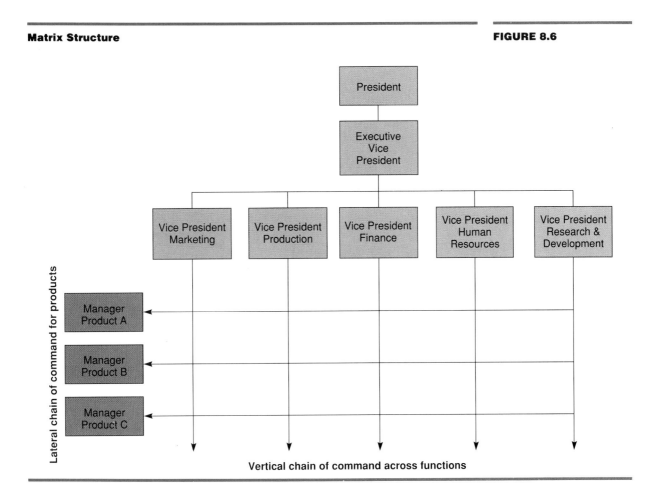

Why have the matrix, when it obviously violates the principle of unity of command? Recall the weaknesses of functional and product structures. The functional structure de-emphasizes the exchange of ideas and cooperation, although it does permit specialists to interact and strive for technical excellence. The product structure is weaker at encouraging job security, although it is strong at inducing cooperation, adhering to schedules, and controlling costs. The matrix design gains the strengths of both while avoiding the disadvantages of either. Matrix structures have been used in diverse organizational types:

- Manufacturing—aerospace, chemicals, electronics.
- Service—banking, insurance, retailing.
- Professional—accounting, consulting, law.
- Nonprofit—hospitals, United Nations, universities.

Advantages   The matrix structure responds effectively to three conditions. First, a matrix can handle a dual focus. For example, the company may need to respond to two equally important environmental pressures. Aerospace firms such as Lockheed and McDonnell Douglas must meet both technical requirements and customer cost constraints. While the manager argues for more

To develop, manufacture, and market the MD-11, McDonnell Douglas used the matrix organization structure. Each phase had to use the best talent available to produce the safest, most efficient, and most profitable aircraft.

Courtesy of McDonnell Douglas Corporation

money to improve the product technically, the product manager argues for meeting budget constraints. The dual focus of technical and cost interests is possible in the matrix structure.

Second, requirements for communication among employees may exceed the capacity of a traditional functional structure. Environmental uncertainty, work complexity, and interdependence of departments increase as a business grows and diversifies its products and markets. The functional structure does not encourage cooperation and a total team spirit. What is needed is a structure that encourages the sharing of information. The matrix gives the cross-functional benefits of a product structure while keeping the administrative controls of the functional structure.

Third, performance, cost, and time pressures require greater sharing and use of resources. Placing limited resources in only one department results in a monopolization of the resources. When talented engineers, physicists, computer specialists, and other skilled professionals are in scarce supply, several groups, projects, or units must share the talent and resources. In the matrix structure, talent and resources can be moved from project to project. Priorities for the use of the limited resources are measured against the overall business objectives and interests. The matrix makes this shifting of resources easier.

Disadvantages   If the matrix always worked for every business, it would always be used. There are, however, problems with the matrix. Some of the most frequently cited include:[14]

- Confusion about who reports to whom, and when.
- Power struggles between functional and product managers.
- Groupthink, or too much group decision making.
- ''Meetingitis,'' or just too much time wasted in one meeting after another.
- The tendency to become ''papermills.'' To ensure cooperation and coordination, everyone puts everything in writing. The result is a seemingly endless paper output.
- Excessive costs of having more managers to compensate.

Sun Petroleum's Business-Line Multiple Organization Structure   **FIGURE 8.7**

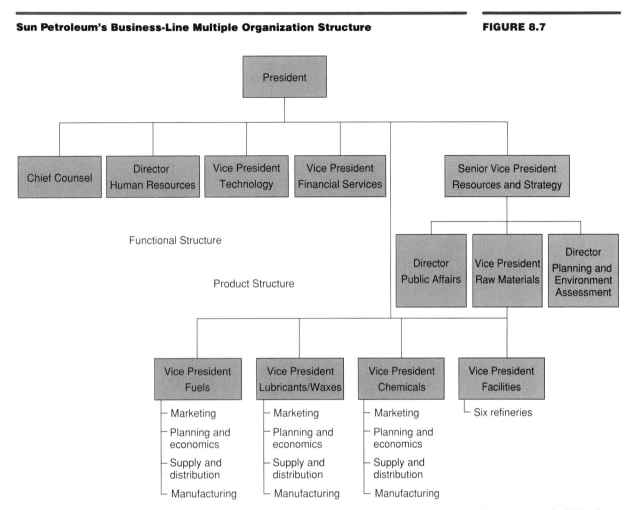

The advantages of the matrix structure seem to outweigh its problems. Nevertheless, this type of organization structure is not for everyone. The manager with two bosses must work very well with people. Would you be able to work with two bosses—one functional and one product? Think about some of the conflicts you might face. Suppose each wanted you to attend a different important meeting at 10 A.M. or to attend training seminars, one in Los Angeles and one in Boston, on the same date. Having more than one boss contradicts the principle of unity of command.

Multiple Structures

We have been discussing forms of structure as if they were an either/or choice. In fact a business is free to use any form or combination of structures. An example of a *multiple structure* appears in Figure 8.7. Sun Petroleum Products' structure shows three product divisions: fuels, lubricants/waxes, and chemicals. Each division has its own functional departments of marketing, planning and economics, supply and distribution, and manufacturing. Sun also has a number of centralized functions, such as human resources, technology, public affairs, and facilities. The multiple organization structure enables the refineries to produce products for the three product divisions.

Advantages   Companies use multiple structures to gain the benefits of each arrangement. Perhaps the biggest advantage of the multiple structure is that it encourages management to look at the total picture of organizing. This overall view stimulates a total-company enthusiasm and a realization that each part or unit is important in accomplishing corporate objectives.[15]

Disadvantages   Potential drawbacks to multiple structures, such as the one used by Sun Petroleum, are increased management overhead expenses, duplication of resources, and conflict between headquarters and product divisions. Problems in coordination of policies, programs, and resources arise often. Finally, a successful move from a single-structure arrangement to a multiple-structure system may take significant time and resources.

You'll Know It's the Century When . . .

→ There's Nowhere to go but Sideways

In the year 2000, one fifth of the labor force will be 45 to 54 years old. Many will expect to move into top management jobs, but the number of opportunities will be limited. Some companies will offset this structural change by creating positions with top-level pay but without top-level authority. Other companies will offer alternative rewards, including long paid vacations and free education. But many employees will leave their firms to begin their own small businesses. Job specialization will increase, and competition will intensify.[16]

SUMMARY OF LEARNING OBJECTIVES

1. To define the term *organizing*.
   Organizing is the management function of grouping people and assigning activities so that the company's objectives can be accomplished.

2. To describe formal and informal organizations.
   The formal organization is put together by management, created by individuals who have authority, responsibility, and accountability. The formal organization is depicted in the organization chart. The informal organization is the network of personal and social relationships that emerges when people work together.

3. To distinguish between line and staff authority.
   Managers with line authority have direct control over lower positions in the management hierarchy. Managers with staff authority can study a situation and make recommendations, but they have no authority to take action.

4. **To discuss centralized versus decentralized decision-making authority.**
   In a centralized business, a relatively small number of managers make the decisions and hold most of the power and authority. Advantages of centralization include uniformity of policies, rules, and procedures; avoiding duplication of effort and use of resources; and uniform decisions. The disadvantages include greater pressure and demands on a few people, a reduced sense of involvement, and large amounts of power concentrated in a few people. In a decentralized business, authority is delegated to more levels of management. Decentralization places decision making closer to the action, gives decision makers more responsibility for their actions, and develops managers of the future—all advantages. The disadvantages include more difficult coordination, possible lack of capable managers, and lack of uniformity in policies.

5. **To identify what a manager can learn about an organization by reviewing an organization chart.**
   An organization chart is a graphical presentation, or blueprint, of the formal structure of an enterprise. The chart shows people, their positions, and their authority relationships.

6. **To identify the principles of organizing.**
   Division of labor involves dividing a major task into separate, smaller tasks to achieve greater efficiency. Unity of command means subordinates report to no more than one supervisor. The scalar principle states that authority and responsibility should flow in a clear, unbroken line from the highest to the lowest manager. An extension of this principle states that authority should equal responsibility. Under span of control, the number of subordinates who should report to a supervisor is limited.

7. **To compare the advantages and disadvantages of functional, product, and territorial structures.**
   The functional structure orients people toward a specific set of activities. As a result, they become more skilled in their areas. It works well in a relatively stable environment. However, the exchange of ideas and cooperation with other departments is lessened, and problems may arise that cannot be solved by one department. In the product structure, managers are responsible for one product or product line. They devote all their energy and skill to containing product costs, meeting schedules, and earning a profit. This structure encourages creativity. Its disadvantages include managers not having enough authority to carry out their responsibilities, the extra time required for planning, employees more insecure and anxious, and more stressful environments. The territorial structure's main advantage is coordination at the point of sale, leading to more personalized and speedier service. Disadvantages include some duplication of effort and the need to have managers who are able to perform multiple functions within their territories.

8. **To explain what types of structures combine to form a matrix organization.**
   The matrix organization is a combination of the functional structure and either a product or project structure. As a result, subordinates have a functional boss (their permanent home is in the functional unit) and a product/project boss (a temporary home).

KEY TERMS

Organization Structure, p. 258

Formal Organization, p. 259

Informal Organization, p. 259

Formal Authority, p. 260

Delegation, p. 260

Line Authority, p. 260

Staff Authority, p. 260

Centralized Business, p. 260

Decentralized Business, p. 261

Organization Chart, p. 263

Principle, p. 265

Division of Labor, p. 265

Unity of Command, p. 265

Scalar Principle, p. 267

Span of Control, p. 267

Downsizing, p. 269

Functional Structure, p. 270

Product Structure, p. 271

Territorial Structure, p. 272

Matrix Structure, p. 274

QUESTIONS FOR DISCUSSION AND REVIEW

1. Why would a large organization such as Du Pont, Teledyne, or Shell be likely to use multiple structures?

2. What skills should a manager in a matrix structure possess to overcome the matrix's violation of the unity-of-command principle?

3. Nino Kazurkus owns a small ethnic restaurant in Baltimore. He claims that because he only employs 12 people, he doesn't need to worry about the organizing principles of management. Is Nino correct? Explain.

4. Why would a middle-level manager be reluctant to work within a highly centralized organization structure?

5. How is the scalar principle applied to the U.S. government?

6. Why do informal organizations emerge within even the most efficiently managed organizations?

7. Are actual communications networks and flows shown in a formal organization chart?

8. List some significant disadvantages of the product structure.

9. Is the chain of command in a matrix structure based primarily on line or staff authority? Explain.

10. What questions should a manager ask before deciding to restructure an organization?

CASE 8.1
IBM's Restructuring Strategy

For years International Business Machines Corp. (IBM) has been blessed with top-of-the-line senior executives and chief executive officers—Thomas Watson, T. Vincent Learson, Frank Cary, and John Opel. Now it is John Akers' turn to keep IBM at the top of the industry.

When Akers took over, IBM was a $50 billion company that had grown to such a size that it was slow in responding to market signals, customer demands, and competitors. Even its image as a firm that provides job security and has never had a layoff was threatened. "Big Blue," as IBM is referred to by friend and foe, had become bloated: too many staff managers, duplication of jobs, excessive layers of management, and too much distance between the company's designers of state-of-the-art computers and its customers. IBM's structure, with its imperfections, was hampering, not helping business.

IBM realized it had no guarantee of continued success. Competition in mainframes, minicomputers, PCs, software, and systems integration is constant. Strong domestic and international competitors challenge IBM in each of these areas. The days of a Big Blue fun feast and easy profits are over.

The traditional IBM model of organization structure (a select group of top managers made the decisions) was not doing the job. So Akers moved into restructuring with a vengeance. Courageously he put IBM through a series of structural reorganizations.

However, merely shuffling the organization chart would not likely be enough for IBM to be successful. Akers knew that changing the chart had to be combined with action. Thus he delegated main responsibilities to six general managers. These managers were instructed to introduce an entrepreneurial, risk-taking spirit into their lines of business.

Akers' restructuring philosophy was based on the premise of giving managers a greater sense of "ownership." This meant decentralization. The six general managers were told to act and behave as though they had their own companies. Each has his own markets, each a different set of competitors. Each heads a product unit that employs tens of thousands of workers and generates billions of dollars in total revenue.

Four years of slumping sales, the success of rival Digital Equipment Corp. (DEC), and PC clones led to Akers' decision to push down and decentralize some of the decision-making power at IBM. (Gordon Bell, CEO at DEC, sees IBM as a bloated company that is still building dull machines based on the past, doing nothing that the user wants.) The new structural arrangement, Akers hoped, would open IBM up as never before. Instead of designing products in secret and then surprising the market, IBM began talking and listening to

This case was developed from multiple sources but primarily "The Downsizing of IBM and DEC," *Fortune,* March 26, 1990, pp. 26–27; Easther Dyson, "Dear John Akers," *Forbes,* January 8, 1990, p. 300; "IBM," *Barron's,* May 28, 1990, pp. 24–25; Kenneth Labich, "The Shootout in Supercomputers," *Fortune,* February 29, 1988, pp. 67–70.

customers. Divisions started listening hard to help improve their products, service, and prospects for the future.

The six general managers are faced with a major challenge. Can they inspire their subordinates to act, think, and behave like entrepreneurs? Will the new, leaner structure permit this kind of change? Can restructuring be totally accomplished without laying people off?

Before the company could turn itself around, from a flabby giant to a quickstepping, proud leader, IBM had to wrestle with these tough questions. Increased competition, decreasing net profits, and the loss of some key executives and engineers forced the company to take a close look at how it is organized. Principles of organizing had to be applied to stem the downward trend.

New structures are now in place. The market will vote and tell IBM whether Akers' leadership will be as successful as that of his predecessors.

Questions for Discussion

1. How should the Akers restructuring plan at IBM be evaluated? What needs to happen before it is considered a success?

2. Do you feel that a leader such as Akers can instill an entrepreneurial spirit in IBM? Why?

3. What was Akers attempting to accomplish by decentralizing decision making?

CASE 8.2
Ford and Honda Reaching to Become "Learning" Organization Structures

Reorganizing. Downsizing. Coordination. Delegating. These are all attempts to organize a business to perform better, to produce more efficiently, to develop human resources. Despite these activities, some claim that even proactive steps to improve will not be enough to meet environmental demands. The command-and-control, top-down structures will not be fast enough to meet product development advances of foreign competitors, close enough to the customer to provide high-quality service, or tuned in enough to manage effectively the polyglot work force of the 21st century.

The evidence indicates that in the 1980s over half of the Fortune 500 engaged in significant restructuring. The process goes on and on at General Motors, Sears Roebuck, and Kodak. They, along with other firms, continue to search for the "one best" way to structure, when in fact there is no such arrangement.

A growing group of firms is attempting to put together a structural arrangement with what is called a "learning" orientation. The learning organization listens to customers, suppliers, competitors, and employees. It then automatically takes action to meet changes quickly and responsibly. In the learning

Adapted from Walter Kiechel III, "The Organization that Learns," *Fortune*, March 12, 1990, pp. 133–34; Peter M. Senge, *The Fifth Discipline* (New York: Doubleday, 1990); Robert H. Waterman, Jr., *The Renewal Factor* (New York: Bantam Books, 1987).

organization, people continually expand their capacity to create desired re-sults, and they are continually learning how to learn together. The learning organization, for example, would not anticipate the events in Eastern Europe (which no one did but many claimed they did) but would view the changes as opportunities to seize.

A few firms have some of the qualifications of a learning organization. Ford has designed a middle-manager training program to help managers become learning organization oriented. In the course of a 5½-day session, managers are grouped by their specialties (marketing, manufacturing, finance, etc.). They are asked to think about how their area works within the firm, how others perceive and relate to it, and how it should work. Only when colleagues from other units level with them do they find out how they come across. Groups review each other to make sure each sees clearly how it is viewed by others. Cross-department learning results from the training debates, arguments, and atten-tion. Ford uses the term *chimney breaking* to describe the process of getting people to think beyond their own discipline.

Robert H. Waterman, Jr., in his book *Renewal Factor,* cites other means of deliberate bureaucracy busting (a form of chimney breaking): moving people from function to function; letting people roam to areas in which they have an interest; recognizing and encouraging product champions; forming teams made up of employees drawn from different disciplines. In other words, loosen up the structure, move people around, and let people do some things on their own. Keep a laissez-faire distance to permit free thoughts to surface.

At Honda, top managers set tough strategic objectives. There is little room for lazy, slow-thinking managers. On the shop floor, however, Honda wants everyone to learn. They want middle managers to work on multifunctional teams, to integrate what's coming from the top and lower levels, and to seize opportunities to improve production and quality. Honda wants everyone to learn so that the company can use the creative talents of each. The monster bureaucracy with 22 layers—till now the American automobile company ideal—is not suited for the five managerial layers of the learning ideal that Honda believes it will need to remain competitive.

Questions for Discussion

1. So far, the learning organization exists only as an ideal. What is the role of the middle manager in this ideal organization?

2. Would a learning organization be structured as a tall, "programmed" or a short, flat arrangement? Explain.

3. What features of the Ford and the Honda examples make the two companies more like ideal learning organizations than bureaucratically structured ones?

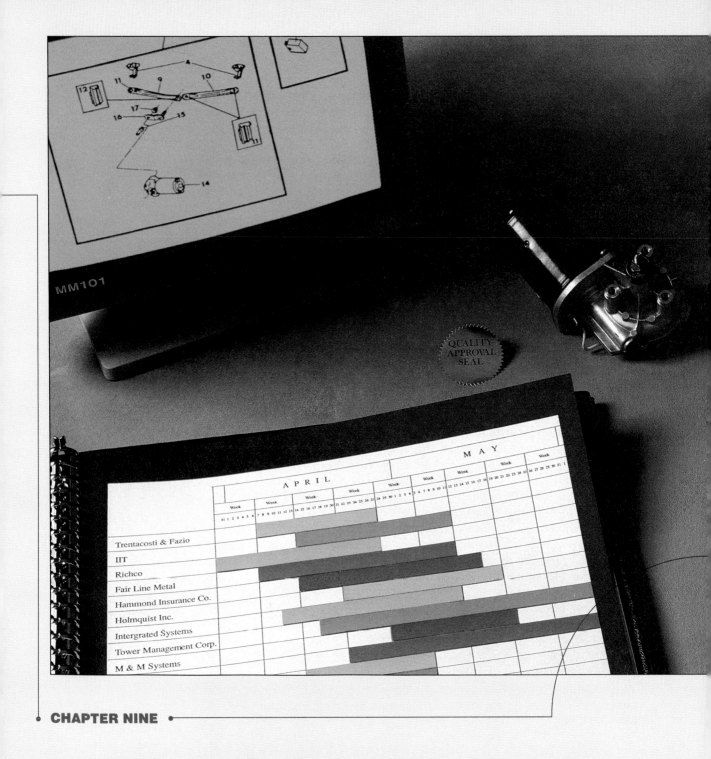

CHAPTER NINE

MANAGING PRODUCTION AND OPERATIONS

Quality remains long after price is forgotten.

QUALITY APPROVAL SEAL

QUALITY APPROVAL SEAL

A blank computer circuit board moves down an assembly line at the Next computer factory. Suddenly a robot starts placing tiny parts on its surface. Just as rapidly, a laser zaps each new electrical connection. Two robot arms work together, one choosing the

Ed Kashi

parts from a bin, the other swiftly and precisely placing them on the board. Pick, place, zap! Pick, place, zap!

When 20 minutes have passed, robot-laser combinations will have attached hundreds of tiny components with 1,700 bits of solder. A robot will have checked each joint, measuring its height and skew to within 1/10,000 inch. Moving at speeds of up to 150 parts per minute, robots will have completed

the circuit board entirely without human beings.

Speed is only one amazing aspect of this operation. The circuit board will have a defect rate of only 15 to 17 parts per million—less than a 10th of the industry's usual rate.

This efficient computer factory is the brainchild of Steve Jobs, a former whiz kid and cofounder of Apple Computer. But Steve Jobs is not a whiz only at technical aspects. He is a superb manager. He has created a factory in which employees are free from the tedium of repetitious, physically demanding tasks. In this plant, the machines do the tiring work, and the humans are in charge. Thus, they are free to examine the product, check the process for defects, troubleshoot, and improve an already excellent production process.

Steve Jobs has helped create a production operation in which machines build machines. His Next company attempts to combine proper organization and high-tech production methods with the best possible results. The company is able to produce enough to meet its current market demands as well as multiply production 10 times over for future demands, all without sacrificing quality or speed.[1]

B usinesses strive for the perfect blend of management and machine. Creating and maintaining that balance is the task of the production and operations manager. The job has not been easy. In the 1970s, double-digit inflation plus a recession dealt heavy blows to industry in the United States, along with the rest of the industrial world. Consumers could no longer afford to buy as much, so they wanted goods that would last. The cost of money soared, and financing the growth of companies became very expensive. Millions of employees lost their jobs. Vulnerable in key areas such as automotive textiles, machine tools, and steel, the United States gradually lost its number one position in those markets to the competition—Japan, Germany, Korea, and other nations.

In order to recapture markets, top management asked production and operations managers to increase production, improve quality, and cut costs. There is much work to be done to complete a turnaround. And technology, competition, products, and worker skills have changed so much in the last 20 years that the job of the production and operations manager requires a wide range of analytical and communication skills. These managers must understand sophisticated technology, delegate more, and forfeit some decision-making power. Everything used to be mechanical: now it is more sophisticated, computerized, and modern.[2]

This chapter will portray how production and operations managers do their job. We start with a description of production and operations, followed by a brief history of manufacturing. We then discuss the various responsibilities of the production and operations manager, including organizing the production process, planning site location and layout, controlling materials, purchasing, inventory, and production scheduling. Other topics covered include using technology such as computers and robots, increasing productivity while maintaining quality control, and maintaining safety for employees, consumers, and the environment. Finally, we examine some critical issues and their implications for the future.

WHAT ARE PRODUCTION AND OPERATIONS?

Many people confuse the terms *production, operations,* and *manufacturing.* **Production** is the total process by which a company produces finished goods or services. This process might involve the work, ideas, and plans of the design engineers; the production manager, the plant manager, the plant superintendent, and their crews; and any other department actually involved with bringing forth the product. Table 9.1 illustrates different types of businesses, products, and the processes involved. Production is not limited to the manufacture of goods; it applies to both the service and the manufacturing sectors of the economy. For example, a company might produce shampoo and cream rinse for hair, which are manufactured goods; another company might operate a chain of hair salons, which provide a service. The word *production* can also be used to name the total amount of product brought forth, as in the statement "Total production increased by 20 percent in 1990."

Manufacturing refers only to the physical process of producing goods; services are not manufactured. The word *manufacturing* comes from the ancient

Production
The total process by which a company produces finished goods or services.

Manufacturing
The actual processes of making products out of materials and parts: literally, creating something by the work of one's hands.

TABLE 9.1   **Several Types of Production**

Organization	Inputs	Production Processes	Outputs or Products (Type)
Magazine publisher	Information in various forms: written, verbal, and photo or art pictorials. Labor, energy, capital, ink, paper, tools, equipment, technology.	Planning, budgeting, scheduling, design and layout, writing, editing, typesetting, art and photo preparation, management control, printing, folding, cutting, binding, shipping on time.	Magazines (nondurable goods).
Hair styling salon	Clients, hair knowledge, skills, information. Hair care supplies, tools, technology, equipment, labor, energy, capital, water.	Planning, budgeting, scheduling, materials ordering and handling, design, hair preparation, washing, conditioning, coloring, styling, meeting schedules, maintaining customer satisfaction (quality control).	Personal hair care (service).
Steel conduit manufacturer	Steel, chemicals, labor, energy, capital, tools, technology, equipment, water, location.	Planning, budgeting, scheduling, materials ordering and handling, metal processing, labor organization, employee relations and safety, quality control, forming, cooling, storage and distribution, meeting schedules.	Steel wire and pipe products (durable goods).

Latin words *manu* (hand) and *facto* (create, or make)—in other words, hand-made. In ancient Rome, distinguishing between machine made and handmade was not an issue; all goods were handmade. If someone sang for the Romans, it was a service; if someone crafted a brand-new jar for storing olive oil, it was a manufactured good, something created by the work of hands.

Operations are the functions needed to keep the company producing, literally any function or series of functions enacted to carry out a strategic plan. In a firm such as Ford Motor Co., operations will usually include purchasing, materials management, production, inventory and quality control, maintenance and manufacturing engineering, and plant management. See Figure 9.1 for the activities managed by operations in the traditional plant.

Operations
Any function(s) needed to carry out a strategic plan, to keep the company producing.

A SHORT HISTORY OF MANUFACTURING

Until the 19th century, manufacturing was done largely by hand, using only hand-operated tools. Modern industry began with (1) the use of fuel energy in manufacturing and (2) the development of mass production.

The Traditional Plant   **FIGURE 9.1**

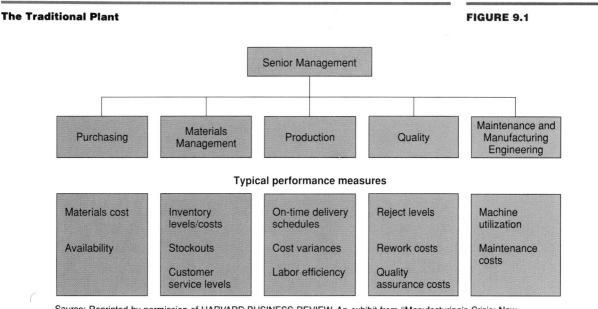

Source: Reprinted by permission of HARVARD BUSINESS REVIEW. An exhibit from "Manufacturing's Crisis: New Technologies, Obsolete Organizations," by Robert H. Hayes and Ramchandran Jaikumar, September–October 1988. Copyright © 1988 by the President and Fellows of Harvard College; all rights reserved.

Early and Crucial Innovations

The use of fuel energy   Fuel energy made it possible to use large machinery in factories; the use of large machinery made mass production possible. In the United States, the steam-powered mills of the 19th century were the first indication of the growth of industry that would follow.

Scientific management   As the 20th century began, managers became very interested in improving production of individuals and of the total organization. Frederick Taylor, the "father of scientific management," pioneered the use of scientific methods to improve productivity.[3] The essence of his philosophy was that scientific laws govern how much a person can produce per day and that it is the function of management to discover and use these laws in the operation of productive systems.

Taylor's approach was not greeted with universal approval. Some unions feared scientific management because it was rigid, unions played almost no role in Taylor's setup of jobs, and they had little idea of Taylor's ultimate goal. In some cases, managers embraced Taylor's time study and incentive plans but ignored the need to organize and standardize the work to be done. The result was poorly designed production operations and overworked employees.[4] Despite critics and inept use, Taylor's philosophy and work helped shape workflow systems, incentive packages, and the design and arrangement of jobs. His principles of scientific management are still a part of the procedures used in production and operations.

In 1914, the Ford assembly line in Highland Park, Michigan, was the first moving assembly line in automobile history. Those are car radiators coming down the chute.

The Bettmann Archive

Mass Production
Rapid manufacture of large quantities of goods accomplished through division of labor, specialization, and standardization.

Assembly Line
A production line made up of workers who each perform one specific task as the product moves past, toward completion.

Form Utility
The value added to materials by changing them into products, giving them useful form.

Mass production   The use of assembly lines and the division of labor—each worker does one small, specialized part of the work—brought about **mass production,** which permits the manufacture of goods in large quantities.

The assembly line   Around 1913 a significant breakthrough occurred with the establishment of the moving assembly line for the manufacture of Ford automobiles. In the mass production of the early Ford cars, one worker attached the headlamps, another attached the hood, and so on. Each worker performed one function on each and every car as its chassis came down a moving conveyor belt, or **assembly line.** The belt carried work from one workstation to the next. Ford's assembly line began at the entrance to a long shed-like factory building and emerged bearing finished cars at the other end. When a finished automobile emerged at the end of the assembly line, workers had given **form utility** to the materials used. Form utility is the value added by giving useful form to materials, and a formed car is indeed more useful than a pile of parts!

Standardized parts   Standardization of parts was another essential factor in the development of mass production. At Ford each headlamp was exactly the same size and was connected to the same spot on identical car frames as they came down the assembly line. Thus one worker could attach headlamps over and over rather quickly and easily with a standard level of quality because the parts were standardized.

   Some workers and social critics complained about the "human machines" who moved their arms and hands over and over again, in the same motions, to the rhythms of the inescapable assembly line. Comedian Charlie Chaplin even imitated and mocked them. But mass production and the assembly line were

This Ford Mustang convertible is an example of a finished product that has form utility. The automobile was assembled with precision equipment and tools by highly trained workers.

Courtesy of the Ford Motor Company

here to stay. No significant business operation could afford to ignore the technological advances they represented. Their tremendous production capacity would eventually make the United States the most productive and richest nation in the world.

Industrialization and America's Postwar Supremacy

During the 1920s, the nations of the world became increasingly industrialized and some of them increasingly competitive. By World War II, Japan and Germany were well-developed industrial nations, but they needed raw materials and markets. With its superior production and manufacturing achievements and the fact that its production capacity was not destroyed or badly damaged, the United States emerged from World War II the leader in production and manufacturing.

During the 50s, 60s, and most of the 70s, American goods and services were the most sought after in the world. The holds of cargo planes and ships carried American cars and trucks, mechanical and electrical parts, chemicals, commodities, wearing apparel, medicines, food products, toys, soft drinks, and recordings to every major port in the world. In the passenger compartments of the planes and ships, American services and technical know-how were being exported as well. Doctors, nurses, dentists, X-ray technicians, teachers, broadcasters, engineers, agricultural advisers, and hundreds of other specialists carried their know-how to foreign markets. Soon the workers, entrepreneurs, and governments of those markets began to respond in kind. As Europe and Japan recovered from the devastation of war, they began to rebuild their industries. They began to export goods and services, competed with each other, and created an industrial and marketing basis for competing in world markets.

The U.S. World Market Share

Directions: The MIT Commission on Industrial Productivity published a book in 1989 entitled *Made in America*. The book emphasized that some U.S. industries and products have lost 50 percent or more of their share of world markets since 1960. Which of these industries do you think have lost this share?

	Yes	No
Automobiles	_____	_____
Cameras	_____	_____
Microwave ovens	_____	_____
Machine tools	_____	_____
Optical equipment	_____	_____

Consumerism and Planned Obsolescence

In the expansion of the late 50s and the 60s, the pace of life—and the pace of production and consumption—escalated to unimagined speed. Salaries rose, prices increased, production rates climbed. By the 70s, new and unexpected pressures appeared. An uneasiness and dissatisfaction began to spread. Americans became disillusioned with leadership at national, local, and even trade and labor union levels. With disillusionment came cynicism. Manufacturers talked of planned obsolescence—goods made to last only a short period of time so consumers would have to buy again. Consumers began to question the quality of products and services and the prices charged for them. Critics also questioned the facilities being used for manufacturing; many factories were old, outdated, inefficient, and dirty.

In addition to leadership, quality, and facility problems, the pressures to produce more and faster made pride of accomplishment all but impossible. Goods and services were needed so fast that the prevailing cry was, "Never mind about the details—it's got to get out!" And, "If there's anything wrong with it, they can send it back!" And they did. In the 1940s, products might be returned once in a while; by the mid-70s, corporations maintained whole departments solely to handle returns of defective items.[5]

"Made in the U.S.A.": Trying for a Comeback

The decline in confidence in once invincible "Made in the U.S.A." products became a crucial issue. The manufacturing community developed a new interest in what production and operations managers do and how to improve it. Today American firms are searching for new ways of manufacturing goods and delivering services.

The book *Made in America* starts with the statement "To live well, a nation must produce well."[6] In the United States, fears of economic decline have been

	Yes	No
Color TV sets	_____	_____
Stereo equipment	_____	_____
Steel	_____	_____
Copiers	_____	_____
Commercial aircraft manufacturing	_____	_____

Feedback: Every check mark should be yes, except for the manufacturers of commercial aircraft. Each of the other U.S. industries or products listed has lost 50 percent or more of the world market since 1960. The decline of the manufacturing or production part of business has been one reason why market share has dwindled.

linked to the nation's inability to manage production and operations efficiently over the past two decades. Critics claim that America does not produce as well as it should or as well as some other nations (e.g., Germany, Japan, and Korea) do. Check your understanding by completing the Connections quiz.

Why does the United States need to find new manufacturing methods? Traditional mass-production methods have been changing as other countries, such as Germany and Japan, have used alternatives successfully. For example, the success of the Japanese auto industry is based on a system different from Detroit's. The Japanese make products that are different (in color, shape, weight) for each segment of the market. They have had to develop manufacturing technologies, job designs, and workflows that allow them to reduce production volume yet increase the speed with which new products are brought to market. The Japanese emphasize quality, service, and cost.

American industry today is competing globally, as companies worldwide are eyeing global markets rather than relying on domestic markets. The United States must sell abroad to pay for the goods and services it purchases abroad and for the money it has borrowed from abroad. To compete successfully for foreign markets, it must explore foreign innovations such as the Japanese auto industry's, as well as manufacturing technologies being developed in other countries.

For decades, American businesses largely ignored technological innovations coming from foreign laboratories and companies. Most production and operations experts scoffed at Korean steel-processing procedures, Japanese inventory systems, Swedish assembly-line team concepts, and Taiwanese electronics procedures. But today more and more U.S. managers are scanning foreign projects, activities, and innovations. Importing ideas and methods of potential benefit is becoming an accepted practice. At Xerox, for example, every department is expected to conduct a global search for the firm or organizational unit that performs its function the best. This performance level then becomes the target for Xerox.

How to speed product development is a top priority of all managers, especially those in production and operations. Compaq, Boeing, Merck, Microsoft, Honda, 3M, and Toyota are known for their ability to develop, manufacture, and market what consumers want, when they want it, and at an affordable price for a specific group of customers. Typically these cutting-edge product developers are global, and 35–70 percent of their sales come from outside their home market.[7]

In the search for new and better manufacturing methods, production and operations managers are playing more significant roles in their organizations. As markets and technologies globalize, these managers will increasingly need to understand foreign customers' needs, preferences, and price limitations. The basis for successful global competition lies in the successful adaptation of the production and operations functions of American business. Unless production and operations can restore the stature of "Made in the U.S.A." goods and services, the economic quality of life of Americans is likely to suffer. Products that cannot compete in the global market in terms of quality and price are unacceptable for the future of business in the United States.

WHAT DOES THE PRODUCTION AND OPERATIONS MANAGER DO?

Production and operations managers are responsible for producing the goods that business needs to sell. There are many kinds of production and operations systems, just as there are many kinds of products—goods and services—wanted by people in the marketplace. Production and operations can vary in size from a single person in a very small company (e.g., a family-owned bakery

The production and operations manager doesn't have to produce machines or turbines. The owner of this bakery in Courbevoie, France, also performs the role of a production (bakery) and operations (selling) manager.

Cameramann International, Ltd.

such as L'Madiellenes) to thousands of employees in a huge, multinational corporation such as Procter & Gamble.

Every business's production goals focus on producing products—and producing the best, the fastest, and at the least cost. Thus the production and operations manager must produce with effectiveness and efficiency while maintaining quality control. Richard Bodine, president of Bodine Corporation, knows about speed, efficiency, and effectiveness. He manufactures assembly lines for organizations.[8] His firm is now working on an electromechanical system that will assemble 2,400 alkaline batteries an hour. Bodine manufactures about 30 machines a year at a rate that is fast, efficient, and maintains high quality.

A production and operations manager's job is to see that the operations necessary to achieve the company's production goals are carried out. To do this, these managers oversee a number of company operations. The following functions are typical:

Product planning	Manufacturing and production
Site location and layout	Production control
Inventory control	Quality control
Purchasing and materials management	Plant management

In moderate-sized firms, the production and operations manager is often a vice president who reports directly to top management; managers or supervisors representing the functions listed above report to the production and operations manager.

Production and operations managers have *product planning* responsibilities, such as preparing forecasts, schedules, and budgets in collaboration with top management, finance, and marketing. In start-up operations, they oversee site location and layout. They also oversee the hiring, training, and development of personnel for departments involved with production and operations. Working with all other departments in the company—especially marketing, physical distribution, warehousing, and shipping—is important as well.

Organizing the Production Process

Chapter Eight presented different ways to organize businesses, depending on needs, types of production, strengths and weaknesses of company managers, and the like. Titles vary also. The inventory control manager in one company may be called the purchasing and inventory control manager in another company. Knowing the exact titles and type of organization in place enables managers to have appropriate expectations and communicate effectively. Production and operations managers must fit into different types of organizations.

Traditional organization   The organization chart shown in Figure 9.2 follows the most traditional form. It gives each manager a specific area of authority and responsibility; however, it also sometimes pits managers against each other. For example, if a purchasing manager has budgeted $50,000 for a quantity of a specific part and the inventory control manager must order them on a rush basis for $60,000, the purchasing manager's responsibility and authority are subordinated to the inventory manager's needs.

FIGURE 9.2   **Traditional Organization: Manufacturing Firm**

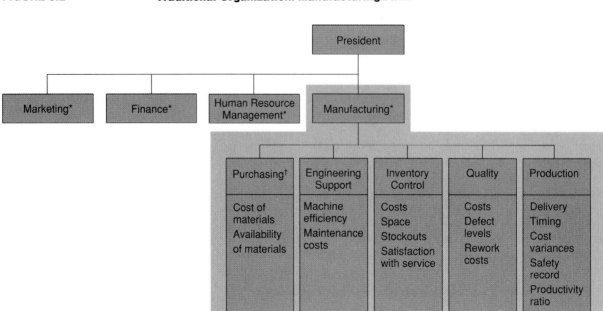

*Each function would have a complete structure if chart were presented in full.
†Examples of performance measures are shown below each departmental grouping.

Figure 9.2 shows typical departments in this type of organization and some common measures used in judging departmental performance. For example, the quality manager's performance would be appraised on the basis of costs, defect levels, and rework costs.

Cellular organization   In the past decade, more and more companies have begun to use a cellular organization. In this type, workers cooperate in teams, or cells, to manufacture total products or subassemblies. Each cell is responsible for the quality and quantity of its products. Each has the authority to make adjustments to improve performance and product quality. Figure 9.3 illustrates how, in the cellular arrangement, machines are arranged to handle all of the operations needed to assemble the products. The parts follow a path through each cell to final assembly.

The basic difference between the cellular and the traditional organization is that workers in the cells are all responsible for their output. The linear competitiveness of the traditional structure is avoided. Instead each individual is pressured to perform so that the group will succeed. Cells tend to be tightly self-monitoring and self-correcting. In a cellular organization, companies tend to have much smaller staffs overall, with middle management positions reduced and lean management numbers at the top.

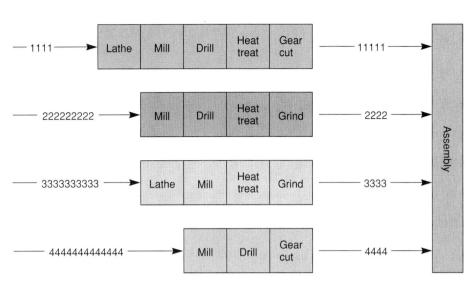

FIGURE 9.3

Cellular Manufacturing Layout

Process and project manufacturing   The way a company organizes may be related to the type of manufacturing carried on. *Process manufacturing,* for example, is carried on in various forms. This type of manufacturing applies various processes, or methods, to change materials into finished goods.

- The *assembly process* puts parts together to form whole products, such as automobiles and trucks.
- The *continuous process* uses mass-production techniques to make many items of one kind, such as roller bearings, nuts, or bolts.
- *Intermittent processing* uses one process for a batch of goods, and then changes processes to produce goods having some differences from the earlier batches, such as in stainless steel restaurant kitchen drainboards or fitted metal cabinets.
- The *analytic process* breaks down materials into components to extract the parts needed, as in oil refining or ore smelting.
- The *synthetic process* brings items together to create an entirely different product. For example, in the synthetic fabric industry and the rubber industry, materials are changed by chemical and heat processes before being formed.
- The *extractive process* removes a product from raw material, as in coal mining.

Project manufacturing usually involves very large projects to which materials and workers must be moved. There is no assembly-line or workstation layout within a factory or shop; the product is built in place. Examples include the building of large ships, large printing presses, and buildings.

The Forces of Globalization

Not only does international competition between companies force changes in the outlook for production and operations managers but the growth of international joint ventures and international entrepreneurship is making sweeping changes in many markets.

With the political changes in the Communist nations of the Eastern bloc, the tearing down of the Berlin Wall, and the reunification of Germany have come new opportunities for investment and manufacturing, with expected savings in labor, energy, and other basic costs of industry. By 1995, Volkswagen expects to make 250,000 cars in Zuorckan, which is in eastern Germany. Japan has invested heavily in joint ventures in automobile production and has also announced a $1 billion economic aid program to Poland and Hungary, similar to programs being provided by Germany and the United States.

Automobile production, telecommunications, cable television, aluminum, and petrochemical products are slated for production by American and European firms in the Soviet Union and eastern Europe, among others. Billions of dollars are expected to be invested, primarily because production costs are less—for the time being—in these countries and markets for goods are large and mostly untapped. Central and eastern Europe constitute a market of over 425 million consumers who have not experienced a choice of goods and services.

Just a short time ago, goods brought home by Soviet citizens who traveled abroad on business or those taken into the USSR by tourists could be purchased only on the black market or in special tourist shops. These deals were illegal under Soviet law. Now there is a demand for these goods and an interest in producing them in joint ventures or independently. The market is large, and production and operations expertise and tools are needed to provide the volume of goods being demanded. Of course, until the ruble becomes a medium of international exchange and has some value, production facilities will not be operated at anywhere near capacity.[9]

Planning Site Location and Layout

When a company starts up or opens a new branch, the production and operations manager is heavily involved in planning the site location and layout. Company officers, engineers, and heads of departments add their ideas and lists of requirements.

Site selection   A site may be bought or leased, with or without a building already in place. If the site is to be leased, all managers involved will make their plans and submit their needs to a commercial or industrial real estate broker. The broker will then submit a list of properties available in the area within the price range required. Sites may come with a "build to suit" lease or may be a turnkey location, in which the building and interior facilities are already completed.

The type of business dictates the kind of facility. Service sector businesses will often require small office facilities in heavy traffic areas convenient to customers or to the electronic communications and other services the business itself requires. Heavy industry, on the other hand, requires vast space near ship or rail transportation, often beside bodies of water that can be used for cooling operations as well as transportation to market. Most if not all of the factors in the following list will be considered in the production and operations manager's plan for site location.

- Economies of cost or other economic advantages for land, buildings or units, taxes, insurance, and so on.
- Nearness to related industries and suppliers, warehouses, or service operations.
- Availability of appropriate labor force, considering such factors as quality or low cost.
- Availability of economical transportation for materials and supplies as well as for finished goods.
- Nearness to market for goods.
- Air and water conditions.
- Nearness to plentiful and economical energy sources.
- Climate and environment in line with needs for the kind of industry and amenable for employees' lifestyle.
- Ample space for planned needs of business and for later expansion.
- Nearness to such employee needs as housing, schools, mass transportation, religious facilities, day care, shopping, and recreational facilities.
- Community receptiveness.

Some site choices may be based on the overriding advantages of one factor, such as availability of labor or market, or the low cost of land. In recent years, for example, many American companies have chosen to locate in Mexico because of the low costs of facilities, land, and labor. Clothing manufacturers have settled in Korea and Taiwan because of the abundant supply of cheap labor. Another production site growing in popularity is eastern Europe. Major changes in the business climate and a large untapped market have made the Soviet Union, Poland, Hungary, and other central and eastern European countries intriguing options for joint ventures and new plants. The Business Action discusses a few issues involved in locating plants in eastern Europe. Perhaps the most significant is the need for a convertible and usable currency.

The site and layout of the Commonwealth Edison plant near Joliet, Illinois, are important factors in the production of electric power. This plant is capable of producing 2,240,000 kilowatts of electric power for customers.

Courtesy of Commonwealth Edison

Site layout Just as it dictates the kind and location of facility, the type of business will determine the layout of the site selected. For each kind of business, production and operations managers must meet different needs. Different kinds of production require varying space for assembly lines, workstations, or other specific arrangements for the work layouts.

The manager must plan the layout in detail before the site is chosen. The plan must account for the needed square footage, work areas, office and conference areas, storage, and shipping needs. To draw up specific plans, managers use templates, models, drawings, and the latest computer techniques.

The case of a small manufacturer in a Chicago suburb illustrates how site layout decisions are made. After carefully considering a number of sites, management decided on the suburban Chicago location. It had around 100,000 square feet of interior space plus three recessed loading docks and one enclosed loading dock. The company distributes finished goods by direct mail, at party sales, and in private-label batches for other companies. All finished goods are transported by truck from the facility. The interior layout required office space for top management, finance, marketing, design and pattern making, conferences, order handling, customer service, billing, accounting, and personnel management. In addition, the firm needed work areas for cutting, assembling, sewing, finishing, labeling, storing, and packing and shipping. Because of the humidity and extreme temperatures, all interior work and storage areas required heating and air-conditioning. At least one enclosed loading dock was required for shipping in subzero temperatures or heavy rain and snow. The shape and layout of the building chosen was well suited to the particular kind of assembly process that the company uses.

Photo courtesy of the Hewlett-Packard Company

The Hewlett-Packard PC is manufactured using a just-in-time (JIT) approach. Only the parts needed for one day's assembly are kept on hand. This cuts inventory carrying costs.

Managing Materials, Purchasing, and Inventory

Materials management, purchasing, and inventory control cover the planning, ordering, and internal storage and distribution of the supplies and materials needed for production. Other names used for these areas include material handling, procurement, supply room management, and inventory management. You will encounter many variations.

Some variations also occur in the way authority and responsibility are organized. In some companies, the purchasing department purchases every good or service bought from outside sources. In others the purchasing function covers only those materials and supplies used in the actual production process.

In large companies, the materials manager may oversee the functions of purchasing and inventory control, or inventory control may be part of production control, depending on its scope. Inventory control may handle only inventory of components and subassemblies, or it may cover all inventories—of supplies, raw materials, components and subassemblies, and even finished products.

In recent years, two important systems have been created to handle materials management and inventory control. Just-in-time (JIT) inventory control and materials requirements planning (MRP) have greatly refined the degree to which materials and inventory control can be managed and scheduled.

The **just-in-time (JIT)** inventory control approach was developed by Taiichi Ohno at Toyota Motor Company of Japan.[10] ''Just-in-time'' aptly names a production system in which operations (purchase orders, movement of materials, etc.) occur just at the time they are needed. As a result, very little

JIT
A system for decreasing inventory by using suppliers who agree to deliver the fewest possible items at the latest possible moment to keep production moving smoothly.

inventory is carried. Under Ohno's JIT system, Toyota factories carry very little inventory. When parts are needed they are delivered from other Toyota plants or from outside suppliers.

The Toyota system is called *kanban*. Kanban is the Japanese word for the piece of paper enclosed in clear plastic that accompanies each bin of parts. When a worker on the line takes a part from a new bin, the kanban is removed and routed back to the supplier. This signals the need to place a new order for a bin of parts.[11]

An efficient JIT system can result in low inventories of purchased parts and raw materials, work in process, and finished goods. It saves warehouse and work area space as well as lowering the costs of carrying large inventories. Reducing inventory can also expose other production problems. A sometimes tardy supplier can be covered if the firm carries a large inventory. Smaller inventories spotlight the efficiency of all sources. A delinquent supplier will be replaced.

Since JIT systems have little finished-goods inventory, machine breakdowns are very costly. Thus careful attention to maintaining efficient equipment becomes a top priority. Machines must be in tip-top working order to fulfill the JIT demands. A top-quality repair team that can move into immediate action must be available if JIT is to work effectively.

MRP
A computerized forecasting system used to plan ordering of parts and materials for manufacturing.

Materials requirements planning (MRP) is a computer-driven system for analyzing and projecting materials needs and then scheduling their arrival at the work site at the right time. MRP works closely with the master production schedule (see below) and takes into account such variables as lead time in ordering.

MRP focuses on "getting the right materials to the right place at the right time." In most cases, making "right" decisions requires a computer to handle all of the materials and components involved. The MRP program analyzes data from inventory, the master production schedule, and the bill of materials. The output includes inventory status, planned order timing, and changes in due dates because of rescheduling.

MRP is used in companies involved in assembly operations. Firms that produce large volumes of tools, generators, turbines, appliances, and motors are particularly attracted to MRP. It is also very useful in companies that order a high number of units.

Together JIT and MRP provide a system that saves time and dollars. They have helped managers control the amount of inventory required to keep production moving smoothly. With JIT and MRP, suppliers of parts and subassemblies can plan in much closer time tolerances. In very large operations, such as the Detroit automobile assemblies, nearby suppliers are actually hooked up by computer to follow the progress of assembly-line work. From this vantage point, their trucks can arrive very nearly at the moment the materials are needed. Lead times on orders are greatly reduced, and costs of storing inventory drop sharply.

Controlling Production: Scheduling

The production, or manufacturing, manager is responsible for the main goal of the company: producing goods in the amounts and sequence planned and on schedule. This function is critical to the success of the company. Three elements of management—planning, organizing, and controlling—can be clearly seen in the tasks of the production manager. Planning the use of labor, facilities, and materials for fulfilling the production schedule is a complex, ongoing task. The manager will usually have more than one product to plan for, with the resultant needs for changes in materials, production processes, energy, and labor.

A *master production schedule* must be created. It will show when the manager plans to produce each product and in what quantities. The production manager is responsible for meeting the dates, quantities, and cost commitments on the schedule. The master schedule will affect the efforts and success of every department in the company. Therefore it should also reflect the needs of the finance, marketing, shipping, and all other departments.

Production managers must plan for flexibility in order to be able to change from one process to another on short notice. They may use a number of tactics to meet emergencies or make changes in the plan. Requesting overtime, hiring temporary workers, cross-training workers so they can do more than one job, and many other methods are available.

PERT charts   Flexibility as well as adherence to schedule can be achieved with the use of the **program evaluation and review technique (PERT) chart.** PERT developed in the 1950s from the joint efforts of Lockheed Aircraft, the U.S. Navy Special Projects Office, and the consulting firm of Booz Allen & Hamilton. They were working on the Polaris missile project and wanted to provide the United States with an advantage over the Soviet Union in time of completion.

PERT Chart
Program evaluation and review technique that tracks a project's progress and enables management to make optimal allocation of resources.

An important part of PERT is the construction of a chart, a graphical system for tracking the events that must take place in order to accomplish a task. A PERT chart is one of the most effective tools of modern management. To create one, five steps are followed:

1. Break the project to be accomplished into events, or completed actions; label each with the amount of time needed to do it.
2. List the first event of the task.
3. List the event that follows the first one; draw a line with an arrow from the first event to the next one, showing the sequence. (If two events follow, draw arrows to both events to show that one event leads to two—or more—events.)
4. Chart all the events needed to complete the project in the same way, to completion.
5. Label the arrows with the amount of time it takes to complete each activity.

Figure 9.4 presents a PERT chart for the assembly of an engine. The interdependency of the events is spelled out in the column of prerequisites. That is, the development of the production plan, circle 5, requires that activities 1, 2, and 3 be completed. To reach the final assembly event, all seven other events must be completed.

When the chart is completed, the longest path from start to completion of the project (in time needed to complete the activities) is called the *critical path*. Path 1–2–3–5–6–7–8 will require 12 weeks, while path 1–2–4–6–7–8 will require 10 weeks. Thus path 1–2–3–5–6–7–8, as the longest, is called the critical path.

FIGURE 9.4

PERT Chart

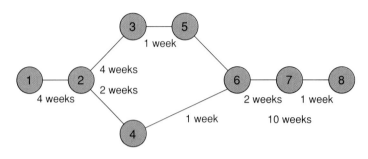

	Activity			Event	
Arrow	**Description**	**Prerequisite**		**Circle**	**Description**
1–2	Develop engineering specifications			2	Specifications completed
2–3	Obtain test models	1–2		3	Test models obtained
2–4	Locate suppliers of component parts	1–2		4	Suppliers located
3–5	Develop production plans	2–3		5	Plans completed
5–6	Begin subassembly 1	3–5		6	Subassembly 1 completed
4–6	Place orders for component parts	2–4		6	Component parts received
6–7	Begin subassembly 2	5–6 and 4–6		7	Subassembly 2 completed
7–8	Begin final subassembly	6–7		8	Engine completed

Source: Adapted from James H. Donnelly, Jr., James L. Gibson, and John M. Ivancevich, *Fundamentals of Management,* 7th ed. (Homewood, Ill.: Richard D. Irwin, 1990), pp. 601–2.

The PERT chart can be used to track exactly where a product is in its development and what needs to be done next to keep it on its path. Bottlenecks can be identified and corrected. For example, if the third event in a sequence always involves a delay, the production manager can identify the problem and make changes as needed.

The PERT chart is only as good in planning as the ability of its users to identify all of the steps in a chain of events. Because it helps break down the production tasks into clearly separate segments, PERT also helps to identify needs and uses for computerized manufacturing programs, temporary workers, and overtime techniques. This breakdown is very helpful in the current climate of rapid change in production techniques, numbers of products, and kinds of new products. The public presents an ever ready market for newer, more appealing products; getting the products to the consumer is up to the production staff. In the recent past, companies could expect to bring out a new product line or new models in the line no more frequently than every year. Now, in many industries, new products are inserted into the master schedule—

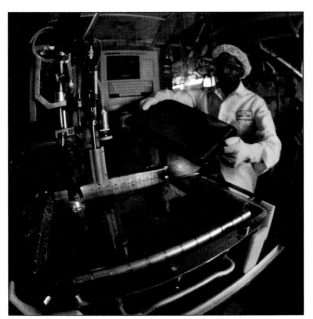

The assembly line at this Zenith picture tube facility in Melrose Park, Illinois, uses computer-aided manufacturing procedures. This ensures precision alignment and high-quality output.

Courtesy of Zenith Electronics Corporation

and from there into the marketplace—as fast as they can be designed. With the increased capability offered by computerized design and engineering, that is very fast indeed.

USING TECHNOLOGY: CAD, CAE, CAM

Increased production is not achieved only through efficient planning. Computers have added flexibility and speed to the production process. **Computer-aided design (CAD)** and **computer-aided engineering (CAE)** have made possible the development of millions of new designs. Designs can be drawn, extended, contracted, added to, or taken from—all within the computer. Engineers can test designs for function and stress and try out variations without the cost or risk of building models or samples. Drafters using CAD can perform many of these tasks once the initial design has been developed. The computer does much of the calculation and the drawing, in two or three dimensions as needed.

CAD
The use of computers to draw plans for a product.

CAE
The use of computers to plan engineering processes and test designs.

CAD has been used to design buildings, ships, and even potato chips. Frito-Lay used CAD to design its O'Grady's double-density ruffled potato chip. An improperly designed chip is not attractive, may be too brittle and break into small pieces, or may not be suitable for using with dips.[12]

Computer-aided manufacturing (CAM) includes the use of computers for controlling the operation of traditional, modified, and electronic machines, including robots. In Japan the Fujitsu plant in Akashi was using robots effectively in the 1980s. The plant specializes in sheet-metal manufacture, producing more than 100,000 parts each month for 1,500 different products. The produc-

CAM
The use of computers to guide or control the actual production of goods.

tion order, specifying the parts, the number, and the materials to be used, is given to the main computer. The computer then selects the most efficient way to make the parts and creates a layout for the automated shear machines and punch presses to follow. The Fujitsu plant is estimated to be 40 percent more productive with the CAM system, saving approximately $10,000 worth of material a month.

Robotics

Robot
A computerized, reprogrammable, and multifunctional machine that can manipulate materials and objects in the performance of particular tasks.

In the United States, the automotive industry is the best-known user of **robots** for manufacture. Robots paint, sand, test, and weld car parts; robots track individual cars on the assembly line and perform dozens of repetitive, exacting, unwieldy, or dangerous tasks.[13]

In 1988 approximately 51 percent of robots in operation in the United States were used in the automotive industry. By 1995 that percentage is expected to drop to about 26 percent as the use of robots increases in the service sector and in other areas. However, robots play a significant role in automotive production and will probably continue to do so.

The ability to manipulate other objects makes a robot unique compared to other kinds of computerized machinery. Robots also can perform the same tasks, such as welding a piece in place over and over again, hundreds and hundreds of times, without becoming tired or being endangered, as the human worker would be in the same function. Robots are therefore used especially in situations that are too repetitive or dangerous for human beings. For example, a robot can be more efficient, consistent, and cost effective than its human

Robots are used to greet visitors at a microchip exhibition in a Ginza department store in Japan.

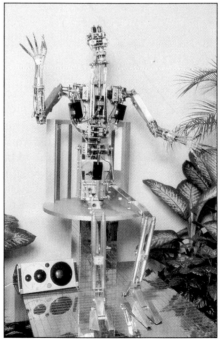

Sipa

counterpart in the task of opening and closing a car door thousands of times. In applying acid to the surface of metal parts, a robot can perform at a constant pace for thousands of hours without danger or exhaustion.

From the early, simple machines (e.g., automated mail delivery carts) to the sensor-monitored "intelligent" machines of today, robotics has made a rapid ascent indeed. An estimated 33,000 robots are currently at work in American industry, most of them in the automotive, appliance, aerospace, chemical, electronics, food processing, home furnishings, pharmaceuticals, and textiles manufacturing areas. Technologies such as machine vision and tactile sensing promise to expand robot use in service industries such as education, health care, security, and training and development.

Flexible Manufacturing Systems

Robots and other computerized machines programmed to switch fairly easily from producing one kind of product to another can be grouped in **flexible manufacturing systems (FMS).** Parts and materials flow to the operation by automated equipment, and finished products are removed automatically. Their flexibility allows FMS to be used in just-in-time inventory control projects as well as for small batches of customized parts or products without raising costs drastically.

FMS
The use of computers to change from one production process to another in order to produce different goods.

The National Bicycle Industrial Co., a subsidiary of Japanese electronics giant Matsushita, has used FMS with great success. Robots, computers, and people work together to turn production on a dime.[14] With 20 employees and a design-smart computer, the firm can produce any of 11,231,862 variations of 18 models of racing, road, and mountain bikes in 199 different color patterns and about as many sizes as there are people. Production doesn't start until an order is placed. But within two weeks, the customer is riding his or her personalized bike.

National Bicycle designs and manufactures the bicycle to fit the size, shape, and strength of the customer. The bicycle store sends the specifications, by mail or fax, to the firm. A computer operator punches the data into a microcomputer. The bicycle is bar coded for *one* customer. The bar code is fed into the computer that instructs a robot where on the frame to build or what color the bicycle should be painted. The customer's name is imprinted on the frame. A custom-made, personalized bike brings many smiles to a happy customer. The personalized, flexibly manufactured bicycles sell for $545 to $3,200, compared with $250 to $510 for standard bicycles.

IMPROVING QUALITY

Computers, JIT systems, production schedules, and robots are all used in production and operations to improve quality, cost, service, and productivity. Improvements in productivity and quality have long-term effects on the success of business.

The term *quality* and its implications are now very important throughout the industrialized world. Germans brag about the quality of their automobiles. The Swiss praise the quality of their watches. The quality of Italian marble and tile work sets the standard for everyone in that industry. At times quality refers to

TABLE 9.2

Dimensions of Quality

Dimension	Example
Performance: Good/service's primary operating characteristics.	Sony TV's richness of color, clarity of sound.
Features: Secondary, "extra" characteristics.	Hyatt Regency's complimentary breakfasts.
Reliability: Consistent performance within a specific period.	Honda Acura's rate of repair in the first year of purchase.
Conformance: Degree to which design and characteristics meet specific standards.	Apple computer's compatibility with IBM software.
Durability: Length of a good/service's useful life.	Average 17-year life of Kirby vacuum cleaners.
Serviceability: Speed, courtesy, competence, and ease of repair.	Caterpillar Tractor's worldwide guarantee of 48-hour delivery of replacement parts.
Aesthetics: Look, taste, feel, sound, smell of a good/service.	Flavor, texture of Baskin-Robbins ice cream.
Perceived quality: Quality conveyed via marketing, brand name, reputation.	Bose's reputation in stereo speakers.

Source: James H. Donnelly, Jr., James L. Gibson, and John M. Ivancevich, *Fundamentals of Management,* 7/E (Homewood, Ill.: Richard D. Irwin, 1990), p. 512.

workmanship or an evaluation (e.g., the "Good Housekeeping seal of approval"). From the consumer's perspective, quality is best defined as "perceived excellence." It is how a person views the product or service.

The perception of quality generally depends on how well the product or service meets the evaluator's specifications and requirements. A consumer makes decisions about quality by evaluating one or more of its dimensions. Table 9.2 illustrates eight such dimensions, including performance, features, durability, and aesthetics. In judging the quality of a Honda Accord or a Pontiac Bonneville, a car buyer may compare the vehicles on performance, features, serviceability, aesthetics, and perceived quality before making the purchase decision. Whether the buyer purchases a second Honda or Pontiac three years later will depend on how well the first car meets his or her expectations of quality.

As we discussed earlier in this chapter, the quality of American goods— unquestioned before and just after World War II—slipped in the 60s, 70s, and 80s. Many reasons have been advanced for this. The postwar economic boom created a seemingly ever expanding market as demand for goods and services rose. Consumers, looking for the latest models in cars, cameras, tape recorders, and televisions, bought more and faster. Technological change accelerated and business hurried to keep pace, while workers complained they had no time or authority to maintain quality. In the midst of plenty, imperfections in the production process began to erode the confidence of consumers and the optimism of industry.

As American-made goods no longer were seen as top quality, foreign competitors' products began to gain acceptance as meeting top-quality standards. In major markets (automobiles, steel, electronics), this loss of sales cut deeply into the U.S. economy.

TABLE 9.3

Deming's 14 Principles of Quality

1. Drive out fear.
2. Eliminate quotas and numerical goals.
3. Break down all barriers between departments.
4. Eliminate inspection. Learn to build products right the first time.
5. Institute a vigorous program of education and self-improvement.
6. Remove barriers that rob workers of their right to pride of workmanship.
7. Institute leadership. The aim of leadership should be to help people do a better job.
8. Eliminate slogans, exhortations, and production targets.
9. Adopt a new philosophy. This is a new economic age. Western managers must awaken to the challenge, learn their responsibilities, and take on leadership for change.
10. End the practice of awarding business based on the price tag. Move toward a single supplier for any one item. Base this long-term relationship on loyalty and trust.
11. Improve constantly and forever the system of production and service.
12. Put everybody to work to accomplish the transformation.
13. Institute job training.
14. Create constancy of purpose toward improvement of product and service to become competitive and to stay in business and to provide jobs.

Source: John Hillkirk, "On Mission to Revamp Workplace," *USA Today,* October 15, 1990, p. 4B. Copyright, USA TODAY. Reprinted with permission.

Greater pressure from competitors increases the importance of high quality in products. For example, foreign competitors—the Japanese, BMW, Daimler-Benz, and Volvo—have stimulated the improvements in quality now taking place in the American automobile industry. Meanwhile the Japanese are again redefining and expanding the notion of quality. Their newest concept is called *miryokuteki hindshitsu:* making cars that are more than reliable, that fascinate, bewitch, and delight.[15] Japanese engineers are now working to give each car a special look, sound, and feel without sacrificing reliability. They call this the "second phase of quality." (The first phase of Japanese quality was inspired by American engineer W. Edwards Deming. Table 9.3 highlights Deming's 14 principles of quality.)

Chrysler chairman Lee Iacocca isn't surrendering the auto market to the Japanese—or to the Germans, French, Italians, or Swedes. He claims that "our cars are every bit as good as the Japanese." And recent recalls of Japanese products, including cars, do raise questions about consistency of quality. Four electronics giants—Sony, Matsushita Electric, Pioneer Electronics, and Toshiba—recalled hundreds of thousands of color TV sets in 1990.[16] Seiko Epson recalled laptop computers that smoked. Toyota had to recall thousands of luxury Lexus cars in the United States because of defects in the cruise control mechanism and in a brake light. Nissan recalled nearly 38,000 cars in Japan. These recalls underscore the principle that working on quality is a continual process.

Consumer pressure, lost market share, good business thinking, and competition, then, all motivate companies (whatever their nationality) to focus on quality. The unit in the company that controls quality is often called *quality assurance (QA)*.

In printing, as in most industries, quality is an important concern. This customer and press operator work together to review and monitor the quality of a book as it is printed.

Managing Quality Control

The quality control manager may be responsible for defining standards with exact specifications or for issuing guidelines regarding exact specifications set by an outside agency. Standards are set by agencies such as the federal Food and Drug Administration (FDA), the Bureau of Standards, and hundreds of other regulating groups. These standards affect the color, size, shape, taste, texture, durability, and many other properties of goods produced in the United States. From toothpaste to rocket fuel, American products are tested and standardized to a greater degree than any others in the world. Government contracts can be lost and consumer purchasing can fall rapidly if standards are not met.

The quality control manager must select or devise procedures to test the quality of products, establish troubleshooting procedures, pinpoint causes of any defects in products, and correct any problems rapidly to minimize losses. Customer complaints or returns of defective products must also be analyzed so that necessary corrections can be made.

Complaints and returns from customers can build up and result in lost customers and sales. Therefore a quality control expert must develop a system that reduces the chances that low-quality products or services get to the customers. A four-step program can help keep the perception of poor quality from being associated with the company.

Step 1: Define quality characteristics   The first step involves defining the quality characteristics desired by the customer or client. Examining customer preferences, technical specifications, marketing suggestions, and competitive products provides necessary information. Customer preferences are extremely

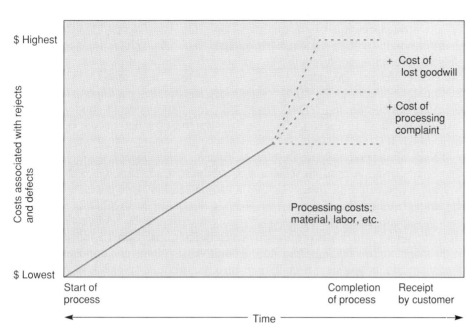

Source: Adapted from David Bain, *The Productivity Prescription: The Manager's Guide to Improving Productivity and Profits,* © 1982 McGraw-Hill, Inc. Reproduced by permission of the publisher.

FIGURE 9.5

The Quality Funnel Principle

significant, since repeat sales will likely depend on a reasonable degree of customer satisfaction. A Rolex customer wants accuracy, a long service life, and a stylish watch. But a Timex watch customer has other quality standards and preferences. The Timex keeps reasonably accurate time and sells at a much lower price than the Rolex. The exact quality characteristics for the Rolex and Timex watches meet, and depend on, different customer preferences.

Step 2: Establish quality standards   Once the quality characteristics have been defined (e.g., a Rolex or Timex), the next step is to establish the desired quality levels. Quality standards serve as the reference point for comparing the ideal to what actually is. Standards for factors such as size, color, weight, texture, accuracy, reliability, time of delivery, and support are set by management.

The cost of achieving and sustaining a specific level of quality must be estimated and compared to the cost of potential rejections. Figure 9.5 represents what is often called the *quality funnel principle:* the closer to the start of the production process, the lower the cost of rejection. As the product or service progresses through the process, more resources are invested; the greater the amount of resources invested, the higher the cost of rejection. The greatest cost is incurred when the customer or client is the source of rejection. In that case, the cost of processing the complaint and the cost of lost goodwill are added to the cost of resources. For example, complaints about Ford's Pinto were costly in the form of lost repeat sales, customer lawsuits, and recalls to repair defective parts.

Step 3: Develop the quality review program   The methods for quality review, where and by whom reviews will be reported and analyzed, and other review procedures must be formalized. One important decision involves how many products will be checked for quality. Will all products be inspected or only a representative sampling? The greater the number of products inspected, the greater the costs associated with quality review. Representative sampling is less costly but creates (1) the risk that more low-quality products will get into the hands of customers, (2) a greater likelihood that customer goodwill can be tarnished, and (3) the need to decide on what number of defects or poor-quality products will be acceptable.

Sampling procedures can take many forms. Some organizations use a random spot check. A random selection of products (e.g., cars, generators, computers) is inspected for quality. When a formal random spot check is used, the results can be meaningful and can provide adequate control. Other forms of sampling plans using statistical analysis are also available.[17] In each case, the decision about which plan to use involves making inferences about the entire production, based on samples. Representative sampling presupposes that defective products will occasionally slip through the quality check network.

Step 4: Build quality commitment   A commitment to quality among the work force within an organization has three ingredients:

- *Quality focus.* There must be a sincere belief by employees, from top management to operating employees, that quality of all outputs is the accepted practice. Satisfying customer or client quality needs must be a goal of all employees.
- *Quality intelligence.* Employees must be aware of the acceptable quality standards and how the standards can be met.
- *Quality skills.* Employees must have the skills and abilities to achieve the quality standards set by management.

The employees' commitment to producing high-quality output is imperative.[18] It can be obtained with motivational programs; numerous approaches are available. Job enrichment, goal setting, positive reinforcement, and team development are just a few. An approach with many adherents, participative management, involves employees in important management decisions.

Quality Circles

Quality Circles
A method of grouping employees in small units that work together to improve quality and processes to further the company's goals.

Quality circles are based on the belief that the people who work with the process are the best able to identify, analyze, and correct the problems in any given production situation. They are said to have begun in the United States but were expanded into a highly developed system by Japanese firms. **Quality circles** usually consist of 7 to 11 people working in a related area. They meet about once a week and discuss the flow of work, its problems, and potential solutions. Participation in the circle is voluntary, and the workers establish a moderator or team leader to lead discussions. Findings and proposals of the group are forwarded to management.

Experience with quality circles suggests that several preconditions are required for success. First, those involved must be intelligent. They must know how to use statistics and work design analyses. They must know the technical aspects of the job. Second, management must trust the participants enough to provide them with confidential cost information (from competition). Third, the participants must be dedicated to working together as a team. They must have a team spirit, since groups, not individuals, are rewarded for success. Fourth, quality circles work best as part of what is called total quality control. This philosophy follows three principles: (1) The goal is to achieve a constant and continual improvement in quality year after year. (2) The focus extends beyond the actual product or service that a firm provides, to every process in the organization (e.g., finance, accounting, research and development). (3) Every employee bears the responsibility for quality improvement.

The implementation of total quality control involves the same steps used to develop the quality control system. However, the breadth of the quality focus—that every employee is responsible—and the challenge of continual improvement require extra effort.

The extra effort has paid off in the Metal Stamping Division of Irvin Industries, Inc., of Richmond, Kentucky. After receiving quality improvement training, the firm declared that quality was a must and that each quality circle would set, as a goal, zero defects. Each Irvin employee has accepted the goal and is working to achieve zero defects.[19] The quality circle improvements have resulted in many cost savings, a reduced injury rate, and increased morale.

Quality is also important in services. A plastic surgeon who performs a poor-quality surgical procedure on a patient's face can have it result in permanent disfiguration. Businesses trying to provide quality services need to use every single step of the process applied to product quality control.

Service quality is of concern at the Soviet Union's Aeroflot Airlines.[20] It has been described as the world's biggest airline. The company carries about 5 million passengers annually. Statistics and glossy promotion booklets boast of

An Aeroflot jetliner in the sky may look like any other successful airline operation. Passengers, however, continually complain about the lack of service received from Aeroflot. If this giant airline is to ever compete with airlines such as Singapore, KLM, United, or SAS, it will have to significantly increase the quality of its passenger services.

Tass/Sovfoto

"excellent" services to and from 99 countries. In reality Aeroflot's reputation among most Soviet and Western passengers is that it provides the poorest service of any world-class airline: overbooked flights, long lines to make reservations, poor or no food service, shortages of trained flight attendants, and old equipment. The airline, to compete in the international marketplace, must totally overhaul its view of service quality and delivery.

IMPROVING PRODUCTIVITY

Productivity
The rate at which goods and services are created.

The rate at which goods and services are created is called **productivity.** In a healthy economy, productivity must be high and also steadily increasing. One common measure of productivity, labor productivity, is expressed in dollars of output (adjusted for inflation) per hour worked. Another important factor in output is technology and how it is being used by employees. Labor and technology combined generate the outputs that are priced and sold to consumers.

In the presence of increasing labor, material, and opportunity costs, uncertain world events, fast technological change, and shifting investment policies, the productivity of a company must continually increase in order for the company to stay in business. The challenge facing managers and nonmanagers in firms of all sizes is immense. Ignoring either quality or productivity improvements is likely to result in lost markets, layoffs, foreclosures, and general business decay. Consumers are demanding more quality, and companies need to improve the output per labor and technological input.

From a manager's perspective, a motivated employee works hard, sustains that pace, and is self-directed toward meeting challenging goals. Productivity improvement can only occur through such motivated employees. Thomas J. Peters and Robert H. Waterman, Jr., authors of the well-known book *In Search of Excellence,* warn against falling for "the gimmicks." A quality circle program, a total quality control system, and a productivity improvement strategy all need motivated employees to implement and sustain them.

Peters and Waterman aptly point to the success of companies who have put the responsibility for quality on every employee and backed it up with management commitment to job security and meaningful profit sharing and recognition. They cite companies such as Dana Corporation, a midwestern manufacturer of propeller blades and gearboxes. Through the leadership of then chairman Rene McPherson, Dana Corporation became the number two Fortune 500 company in returns to investors. McPherson points out:

> Until we believe that the expert in any particular job is most often the person performing it, we shall forever limit the potential of that person, in terms of both his own contributions to the organization and his own development. Consider a manufacturing setting: Within their 25-foot-square area, nobody knows more about how to operate a machine, maximize its output, improve its quality, optimize the material flow, and keep it operating efficiently than do the machine operators, materials handlers, and maintenance people responsible for it. Nobody.[21]

This attitude, according to Peters and Waterman, is expressed in one way or another by the best of the American corporations: at Delta it's the "Family

Feeling," at Hewlett-Packard the "HP Way," and "Management by Wandering Around."[22] The authors define the attitude as "tough-minded respect for the individual and the willingness to train him, to set reasonable and clear expectations . . . and to grant him practical autonomy to step out and contribute directly to his job."[23]

In this age of automation, computerization, and rapid change, there are firms such as Volvo and Rolls-Royce that believe human resources may be as important as technology in improving productivity. The Business Action provides a view of what these two firms are doing to place people in the spotlight when attempting to personalize productivity.

MAINTAINING SAFETY: FOR EMPLOYEES, PRODUCTS, AND THE ENVIRONMENT

A productivity and quality improvement strategy and motivated workers are key ingredients for business success. However, these can be diminished if the company shows little regard for the environment or sacrifices safety. It is important to improve productivity and quality without jeopardizing the well-being and future of the employees or the environment.

Employee and Product Safety

Chapter Four has a detailed discussion of safety and social responsibility. Here we will view these issues in relation to the operations and production areas, where many of the most potentially hazardous materials, processes, and products are found. Although safety is a part of the responsibility of every employee in the work force, corporate responsibility for safety is most often delegated to the production and operations manager. Employee safety is mandated by a number of government regulations and laws; the production and operations manager is responsible for the implementation of these regulations in the plant. Compliance costs time, work, and money that must be provided for in schedules and budgets. Production and operations managers should realize that unsafe practices and contamination of the environment can implicate them and their failure to practice sound management.

Johnson & Johnson, maker of bandages and other health care products, is intent on being known as the number one firm in safety.[24] When any workplace accident causes death or a fracture, injury, or burn resulting in at least one lost day of work, the head of the company unit involved must file a written report to top management within 24 hours. The head must then travel to company headquarters in New Brunswick, New Jersey, and personally explain to a top-level committee what went wrong. Johnson & Johnson slashed its annual lost workday incidence per 100 workers from 1.81 to 0.14 in eight years (1981–89). Corporate workers' compensation expenses now average about $50 billion annually.[25] It pays to be as safe as possible.

Not only must employees have safe working conditions, the goods produced must be safe for the consumers who ultimately buy them. Product safety is the specific responsibility of the quality control department. Growing consumer

Employees: The Key to Productivity at Volvo and Rolls-Royce

Volvo has concluded that mass production will be out of vogue in the future manufacture and assembly of automobiles. Management contends that craftsmanship, personal input, and care will be needed to produce what the customer wants.

A societal warning signal helped Volvo decide to redesign their factory floors and to incorporate "team car building." Swedes are highly educated and well trained. However, they do not like the Henry Ford–inspired assembly-line factory. Their displeasure showed in absenteeism rates of 28 percent, compared with 4 percent per day in Belgian plants. The high absenteeism rate combined with a small, 1 percent unemployment rate meant that if Volvo wanted its employees to show up it had to improve the job environment.

An offer to increase wages rarely entices the Swedes, since taxes take about 70 percent of each paycheck. So Volvo Group head Pehr Gyllenhammar decided to radically redesign the company's Uddevalla plant in Sweden. The firm instituted a teamwork system in which all employees (team members) are trained to handle all assembly jobs. There are eight assembly teams. Each has a spokesperson who reports to one of six plant managers, who report to the president of the Uddevalla Complex. Instead of supervisors and engineers, ordinary employees manage the shop floor. Each team member works an average of three hours before repeating the same task. The teams manage themselves, including production scheduling, quality control, and other duties normally handled by a supervisor.

The new, non-assembly-line approach seems to be successful. Morale is high, absenteeism is around 8 percent, and Volvo says that Uddevalla produces cars with fewer hours of labor and better quality than its other three Swedish plants.

Rolls-Royce, a unit of Britain's Vickas PLC, doesn't use a team approach. But instead of assembly lines, it focuses on handcrafting and care. In an era of significant change in manufacturing, Rolls-Royce still emphasizes that it makes the "best" handcrafted automobile. In 1989 only 3,243 Rolls-Royces were sold; each was handcrafted. How long Rolls-Royce can keep workers handcrafting the elegant veneer panels and plush upholstering is uncertain. However, Rolls sees the future as keeping their customers and workers happier. The Rolls worker takes pride in each unit that is produced because it is he or she who has assembled and cared for the car. In this age of mass-produced food, autos, and televisions, it is interesting to find a firm such as Rolls-Royce, that is resisting mass production.[26]

TABLE 9.4

The Monsanto Pledge

- Reduce all toxic releases, working toward a goal of zero.
- Ensure that no Monsanto operation poses undue risk to employees and communities.
- Work to achieve sustainable agriculture through new technology and practices.
- Ensure groundwater safety—making our technical resources available to farmers dealing with contamination, even if our products are not involved.
- Keep our plants open to our communities, bringing the community into plant operations. Inform people of any significant hazard.
- Manage all corporate real estate to benefit nature.
- Search worldwide for technology to reduce and eliminate waste from our operations, with the top priority being not making it in the first place.

Source: *Business and Society Review,* Spring 1990, p. 66.

consciousness of the issue has increased efforts to make products that are accident-proof. Automatic testing devices tug and pull plastic eyes and noses on toy rabbits to make sure they will not come off in the mouths of eager two-year-olds. Medicine bottles are made tamperproof, and sharp products such as paring knives bear brightly colored labels to prevent consumers from cutting themselves accidentally.

Production in the United States is the most highly regulated in the world. Compliance, a production cost, has become increasingly expensive; research and development, testing, and fulfillment functions also add to the cost of production. The increased expenditures show that most companies and employees at all levels have begun to take safety issues seriously: consumer accidents receive greater attention and investigation today than they did a decade ago.

Monsanto, the United States' fourth largest chemical producer, has developed a program to help clean up the environment. Their pledge is reproduced in Table 9.4.

Globalization of Environmental Pollution

A 1990 summit meeting between President Bush and the Soviet Union's Mikhail Gorbachev focused international concern on some alarming issues. The atmosphere's ozone layer is thinning. World climate is changing as a result of deforestation of large areas such as the Amazon rain forest. The Chernobyl nuclear accident released radiation on people hundreds of miles from its source, which is now enclosed in a giant sarcophagus-like enclosure.[27] In addition to workers and consumers, our very environment is at risk from the dangers of industry. Major corporate safety issues are chemical casualties, air/water/land pollution, waste disposal, site location and maintenance, and general environmental protection from products or by-products of industry.

Industry will continue to come under pressure to produce more, yet do it safely, cleanly, and efficiently. As globalization in all areas emphasizes the limitations and the vulnerability of our ecosystem, production managers all over the world will continue to be challenged to find new and better ways to produce.

THE CHALLENGE FOR PRODUCTION MANAGERS

If the problems of and pressures on production and operations management are unprecedented, perhaps so too are the opportunities for positive solutions. Most of these solutions have become possible as a result of the electronics revolution. It has been said that if the first Industrial Revolution multiplied the power of production 100 times, the second Industrial Revolution—empowered by the microcomputer—has increased it thousands of times.

Today, with the aid of CAD, CAE, CAM, and a wealth of other computer-based management tools, managers can plan, project, design, research, and modify an infinite number of systems and products with complete safety from the old expense of trial and error. The expansion or contraction of schedules, the addition of a different wing to an experimental plan, the modification of a chemical coating for a 300-foot antenna that must last 20 years can all be planned and tested on the computer, with great accuracy. The computer is the single most important technological change to occur in industry in the 20th century, and the change has only begun.

Microelectronics represents not only the most powerful avenue of positive change for industry but also the greatest potential arena for error. As with all forms of power, the test is in how the power is used. Already in the last two decades, we have witnessed major problems caused by error or misuse of microelectronics—from the space shuttle disaster to the failure of AT&T's electronic programs, which tied up half the country's telephone lines for nearly an entire day. A high degree of skill is needed to use the new technology well. Keeping up with technological change is, therefore, the primary challenge to the production managers of today and tomorrow.

You'll Know It's the **Century When . . .**

The Workplace Shrinks

In the 21st century, the number of manufacturing jobs will continue to decline as the number of service jobs grows. Because service businesses are generally small, local operations, the size of the average workplace will shrink—both in the number of employees and in the total square footage of space. Increased specialization will also make manufacturing plants smaller; the size of wholesale and retail outlets will shrink along with them. Businesses no longer will need to stock large inventories.

Working won't always mean going to the office, either. With advanced communications equipment, employees on the road or in smaller satellite offices will be able to work closely with the main office. Many others will work at home. The workweek will be shorter, but flexible work schedules will keep offices and shops open longer. As a result, customer service will improve.[28]

SUMMARY OF LEARNING OBJECTIVES

1. To define the production and operations management function.
   Production refers to the total process by which a business brings forth

finished goods or services. *Operations* refers to the functions needed to keep the company producing. Functions such as purchasing, materials management, production, inventory and quality control, and maintenance are included. The process and functions needed to produce and/or deliver goods or services make up the production and operations management function.

2. To discuss two or three critical issues facing production and operations management in the 1990s.
The concept that to live well a nation must produce well is a critical issue. The United States must find a way to improve the stature, performance, and quality of manufacturing firms. Another crucial issue involves finding the skilled workers needed to work with more sophisticated production techniques and processes.

3. To compare traditional company organization with cellular organization.
The traditional organization emphasizes specialists in areas linked to manufacturing. Cellular organizations have a layout in which machines are grouped into what is called a cell. Groupings are determined by the operations needed to perform work for a set of similar items. In the cellular arrangement, units are completed by a team. The layout speeds up the assembly from start to finish.

4. To describe the effects of globalization on competition and productivity.
Globalization and interdependence have spurred competition. Competition not only within a country but between countries is now at a fever pitch. This competition has resulted in improved productivity. Better technology, more strategic planning, and improved management methods have contributed to increased productivity in many countries. The United States is faced with small productivity gains and must work more on skills improvement, better management, and improved quality to increase productivity more.

5. To evaluate the effects of computerization on production and operations management functions.
The effects have been significant in terms of speed, efficiency, and productivity. CAD and CAE have made possible tremendous flexibility and experimentation. The computer has become a major tool that must be understood by all production and operations employees.

6. To explain the importance of productivity and quality to business.
Improvements in productivity and quality have long-term effects on the success of business. Ignoring either quality or productivity improvements is likely to result in lost markets, layoffs, foreclosures, and general business decay. Consumers are demanding more quality, and companies need to improve the output per labor and technological input.

7. To review the role of the production and operations unit in employee and product safety and environmental concerns.
Corporate responsibility for employee safety is often delegated to the production and operations manager. Product safety is the specific responsibility of the quality control department. Concerns about pollution, global warming, toxic wastes, and preserving the earth's forests have made these topics of debate. The production and operations unit is expected by the corporation to oversee environmental matters. Environment-friendly technologies are needed in all areas, especially manufacturing. Production

and operations units will be asked to work more on minimizing pollution at the same time they are expected to contribute to a firm's profit margins.

KEY TERMS

Production, p. 287

Manufacturing, p. 287

Operations, p. 288

Mass Production, p. 290

Assembly Line, p. 290

Form Utility, p. 290

Just-in-Time (JIT), p. 301

Materials Requirements Planning (MRP), p. 302

Program Evaluation and Review Technique (PERT) Chart, p. 303

Computer-Aided Design (CAD), p. 305

Computer-Aided Engineering (CAE), p. 305

Computer-Aided Manufacturing (CAM), p. 305

Robot, p. 306

Flexible Manufacturing Systems (FMS), p. 307

Quality Circles, p. 312

Productivity, p. 314

QUESTIONS FOR DISCUSSION AND REVIEW

1. What is the function of production in business? What is its importance?

2. When you look at a good (an automobile) or a service (help from an accountant at tax time), what features of quality are important?

3. Review a daily newspaper for one week. Cite examples of American businesses concerned about environmental pollution and safety. Also cite examples of concerned non-American firms.

4. If you were going to open a fast-food chicken restaurant (e.g., Kentucky Fried Chicken), what factors would be important in choosing a site and a site layout?

5. Develop a PERT chart that depicts your plans for a college education. What events should be noted?

6. Write out the terms the following abbreviations stand for. In a sentence or two, describe how each is used in manufacturing: CAD, CAE, CAM, FMS.

7. Will robots eliminate the need for human workers? Explain.

8. Describe some advantages and disadvantages of just-in-time inventory control. How would you, as a manager in a large firm with many plants, implement a JIT system?

9. Give some of the reasons why the ''Made in the U.S.A.'' label doesn't carry as much weight with consumers today as it did in the 1960s.

10. What is the meaning of the notion that quality is ''perceived excellence''?

CASE 9.1
Motorola: Rising to Compete against the Japanese

Toyota has been proclaimed the best carmaker in the world. The firm's dedication to *kaizen* (continuous improvement) is interesting. It continually refines an already elegant manufacturing process. Some Americans, however, are getting tired of hearing about the Japanese and their product quality. The "land of the rising sun" stories are getting stale. The claims of Japanese superiority rub some managers and employees the wrong way.

Is any product or firm as good or better than its Japanese counterpart? Where is our American model of superiority? It just might be found in Shaumburg, Illinois, at the headquarters of Motorola.

Motorola, like other American firms, was having problems with quality. They had two choices: lose market share in communications, automotive electronics, defense systems, and microcomputer systems or adopt a new "quality must be superior" approach. Motorola managers chose the "superior approach." It became a crusade.

As more and more employees bought into and adopted a pledge of quality, Motorola began to make a comeback. The corporate goal became a tenfold reduction in all defects. Motorola sent teams on worldwide missions to see what other manufacturers were doing. They observed over 75 plants around the world, focusing on defects and defect reduction approaches. Quality audits were conducted to determine exactly what defects were occurring in Motorola plants. What Motorola called Six Sigma quality was initiated. Six Sigma is a statistical term for near-perfect production (3.4 defects per million units). The hourly workers, responsible for identifying defects, were rewarded under Six Sigma for finding quality flaws. The Six Sigma quality program in the cellular phone division resulted in a 90 percent reduction in defects. By 1992 the division plans to reach that almost-zero state of 3.4 defects per million parts.

From the cellular phone division, Six Sigma traveled across all Motorola units. Wallet-sized cards stating quality goals in 11 languages were given to all employees.

That Motorola is serious is shown by a notice to all 10,000 of their suppliers in which quality is emphasized. Motorola wants each supplier to apply for and earn quality awards such as the Malcolm Baldrige award (issued by the U.S. Commerce Department) or lose Motorola as a customer.

The Motorola success story has been contagious. A growing number of U.S. firms, led by IBM and Digital Equipment Corp., have adopted Six Sigma programs. At IBM Six Sigma is being used in all divisions. Since 1988, Motorola has taught Six Sigma to more than 7,000 managers and government agencies. If

Adapted from Alex Taylor III, "Why Toyota Keeps Getting Better and Better and Better," *Fortune*, November 19, 1990, pp. 66–79; John Hillkirk, "Quality-Conscious Firms Set Sights on Perfection," *USA Today*, September 4, 1990, p. B1; John Hillkirk, "Top Quality Is behind Comeback," *USA Today*, March 28, 1989, p. B1.

U.S. firms lose their competitive base, Motorola will lose its suppliers. Cooperation and sharing are stressed because Motorola needs reliable suppliers to compete internationally.

Questions for Discussion
1. Why can a firm such as Motorola compete with the Japanese on quality, yet other American firms are just not up to the competition?
2. Is Motorola's logic concerning cooperating with their suppliers and sharing their quality improvement ideas a sound approach? Why?
3. Is zero-defects quality possible for any firm? Explain.

CASE 9.2
Profile of Corning Glass: How to Survive

Competition from international firms has whittled the number of American television set makers down to one—Zenith. U.S. suppliers of TV set makers had to either give up or learn how to survive in a market dominated by foreign manufacturers. American suppliers had grown up in an era in which quality was not a top priority. The U.S. market became hungry for high-quality TV sets.

Corning Glass closed plant after plant. Once a major supplier to American TV manufacturers, by 1985 Corning Glass was down to one color-video-glass plant in State College, Pennsylvania. The global market for video glass was about $3 billion annually. One of the early developers, Corning decided that the market was attractive enough to try to regain a foothold. The firm worked on improving quality, controlling manufacturing costs, and improving inventory control systems. Corning concluded that better management, marketing, and manufacturing would lead to survival and profitability in a highly competitive market.

Corning initiated a number of offshore joint-venture activities with Samsung in South Korea and Thompson in Europe. The firm also formed a new marketing approach, a joint venture with Asahi Glass Co. Ltd., Tokyo. The Corning-Asahi venture emphasized the importance of quality. Corning Asahi Video Products Co. (CAV) is a model venture where computers, quality control, and production engineering are each considered important. Asahi is famous in Japan for manufacturing and marketing a top-quality product. This theme has carried over to CAV.

The manufacturing process at CAV combines continuous and discrete parts manufacturing. At the beginning, the process is continuous as raw materials are fed into three furnaces capable of producing about 650 tons of molten glass each day. Process variables are continuously monitored to prevent "blisters," gas bubbles that cause quality problems in producing video glass.

CAV has been successful in reducing product-development time and improving manufacturability. One example of this success is the knowledge-based

Adapted from John Teresko, "Corning's Rebirth of the American Dream," *Industry Week*, January 7, 1991, pp. 44–47.

software that helps design molds for the glass parts. With this software, a designer can encode into the system rules about how the shape of a mold and plunger must relate to the dimensions and property of the video glass. CAV claims the software has reduced mold-design time from 10 weeks to 1.

Corning wanted to remain in the video-glass business and decided that a joint venture was important if they were to maintain a position in the industry. The CAV joint venture has been a success. At CAV, quality, improved manufacturability, and reduced product-development time are strong competitive weapons. There is much more work to be done, but so far Corning has survived international competition and flourished.

Questions for Discussion
1. Why have most American firms failed to survive international competition in an array of industries such as steel, machine tools, and TV set manufacturing?
2. What is meant by the concept that better manufacturing is needed to be successful? Use this case as an example in preparing your response.
3. What did Corning gain by joining with Asahi Glass Co. Ltd.?

Nearly everything needs to be managed—money, people, property, children, and of course businesses. All organizations—large corporations, small businesses, government agencies, and non-profit organizations—operate within some kind of management structure. Managers appear in all areas, including accounting, marketing, engineering, teaching, and other professional and technical fields. Managers are the backbone of the organization.

Management is one of the most widespread career areas. Because managers are found in all organizations and functions, opportunities for working in a management capacity are endless. People in all types of organizations aspire to management positions. Many seek higher status, greater salaries, and authority. The most high-paying, high-status positions in any organization are usually management positions.

ing, and controlling. Specific activities may differ, but all management involves these same functions.

Supervision is one aspect of management. Supervisors oversee the work being done by others. They train workers, motivate employees, communicate policies and procedures, evaluate performance, and assist workers with work and personal problems.

All managers supervise, but not all supervisors are managers. Supervisors usually do not make major organizational decisions or exercise strategic planning. Supervisors follow policies and guidelines developed by managers.

Sometimes new hires are trained by supervisors or may start in a supervisory position. If they perform well, they can advance to management positions. Conversely the supervisor position may be as far as an individual advances because of limited skills or educational background.

Duties: Management

- Setting goals.
- Providing employee assignments.
- Motivating employees to achieve goals.
- Monitoring performance.
- Providing performance feedback.
- Determining resources needed.

RESPONSIBILITIES

Regardless of the industry, organization, or functional area, all managers perform the same key functions: planning, organizing, direct-

SPECIALIZATION

The management function crosses all areas and industries. Broadly speaking, management positions represent advancement in any area. However, to break into management, a level of technical competence or an area of specialization often is very important. People with a specialty get hired for their first job more easily than generalists. When firms hire new, entry-level people, they usually look for someone who can do a particular job such as accounting, sales, or computer progamming.

At high levels of management, a broad generalist who can understand all aspects of the business is highly desirable. In some specialty areas, managers need a high degree of expertise in the field. Hospital administration, hotel and restaurant management, and city management are a few examples.

Requirements: Management

Personal skills:
- Communication
- Writing
- Decision-making
- Motivational

Education:
- Bachelor's degree
- Master of business administration degree

CAREER PATHS

Many large businesses and government agencies hire entry-level professionals with the idea of grooming them for management. Most enter straight out of college, or perhaps they are starting over in a

---

Characteristics of Successful Managers

Ability to communicate
Integrity
Organizational ability
Creativity
Ability to delegate
Courtesy
Decisiveness
Ambition
Respect for others
Optimism

CAREER PROFILE: Nolan D. Archibald

Katherine Lambert

NOLAN D. ARCHIBALD

Age: 47
Undergraduate degree: Weber State College
Graduate degree: Master of business administration, Harvard Business School
Current position: Chairman and chief executive officer, Black & Decker

Today Nolan Archibald, as chairman and CEO of Black & Decker Corp., runs the largest public corporation of any of his 1970 classmates at Harvard. But Archibald often wondered whether a professional basketball career might have suited him better than his grueling days at Harvard Business School. The star forward from Utah's Weber State College felt humbled by the long nights of study, demanding teachers, and quick-minded classmates. "There was something carved on one of the restroom stalls that characterized how we all felt," says Archibald. "It said: 'This is the only place at Harvard where I really know what I'm doing.' "

Archibald learned a thing or two at Harvard, though. The school taught him to make quick decisions, establish priorities, and handle pressure. He came well prepared for the pressure at Harvard. Archibald, the second of an electrician's five children, pulled mostly C's in high school and was cut from the basketball team three times. After getting his act together in junior college, 6-foot, 5-inch Nolan considered going pro. But after a few lackluster tryouts, he opted for Harvard and the corporate route.

Lucky thing. After earning his degree, Nolan rose rapidly through the ranks in seven years at Conroy Inc., handling operations as diverse as snowmobiles and textiles. Then he moved to Beatrice Co., where he rose to president of its nonfood businesses and gained a reputation as a turnaround artist, something that led headhunters (executive search firms) to lure him to Black & Decker.

At 47, still Archibald can't resist a challenge. "Are there better jobs in corporate America? Yes, I think there are," he says. But he'd be content to spend his career building Black & Decker into a major industry powerhouse.

Source: Adapted from Joseph Weber, "Class Reunion" and "Black & Decker's Master Builder," *Business Week,* June 18, 1990, pp. 160–68.

"This is management trainee Timmy Scott. Timmy has come up through the ranks from our daycare program."

Generally, after one to three years, strong performers may move into a junior management position, where they directly supervise workers. First-level managers are concerned with the planning and scheduling of day-to-day employee operations. They are responsible for the work of several employees in a particular unit, such as data entry, shipping, or security. A key function is to train and oversee workers to ensure that all tasks are performed properly.

As a manager moves up in rank, responsibility and authority increase. Those in middle management positions have lower-level managers reporting to them; they

new career. Firms must develop managerial talent for leading the organization in the future, so they seek people with high potential for management. Entry-level positions provide the opportunity for training and practical experience.

Promotion into management is not guaranteed. Advancement depends on merit and performance. Nonperformers do not get promoted. They either leave, get terminated, or remain at low-level assignments.

Some organizations design programs specifically to train new hires for management roles. People in the programs generally rotate through several different departments to gain experience in a variety of functional areas. In recent years, a number of employers have discontinued their management training programs. Placing entry-level hires directly in a functional

area, such as finance or marketing, is more common today.

Degrees of authority and rank vary in management. The level of management rank is determined by how much authority and responsibility the position has. In large companies, each management level contains dozens of ranks.

> The most difficult part of getting to the top of the ladder is getting through the crowd at the bottom.
>
> *Arch Ward*

Advancement through the various levels of management takes time and requires experience. How much time differs widely among individuals and organizations. Some employers take a slow, methodical approach to advancement; others prefer to put capable individuals on a fast track for promotions.

Management Levels

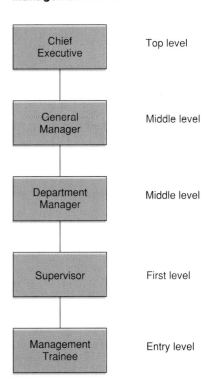

Chief Executive	Top level
General Manager	Middle level
Department Manager	Middle level
Supervisor	First level
Management Trainee	Entry level

in turn report to top management. At the middle level, the ability to see the "big picture" and demonstrate leadership skills becomes important. Generally speaking, middle management comprises department managers, general managers, regional managers, and plant managers. Movement between functional areas and even between organizations commonly occurs at this level.

Only a very small number of people reach the top, or executive, level of management. As the management pyramid gets smaller and smaller toward the top, fewer and fewer positions are available. While a company has only one chief executive officer, it may have hundreds of middle managers. At the executive level, managers spend a good deal of their time dealing with the conceptual issues of the organization. They direct significant effort toward setting overall goals and policies.

Additional Management Resources

American Management Associations
135 West 50th Street
New York, NY 10020

Institute of Management Sciences
146 Westminster Street
Providence, RI 02903

National Management Association
2210 Arbor Boulevard
Dayton, OH 45439

PART FOUR

HUMAN RESOURCES

CHAPTER TEN

HUMAN RELATIONS AND MOTIVATION

LEARNING OBJECTIVES

1. To define the term *scientific management*.

2. To explain what the Hawthorne studies revealed about the role that groups play in motivating employees.

3. To define the term *motivation*.

4. To discuss Maslow's view of needs and motivation.

5. To compare and contrast the Theory X, Theory Y, and Theory Z approaches to motivating employees.

6. To explain why Herzberg's view of motivation is so popular with practicing managers.

7. To describe the principles of goal setting.

The 1990s are fast becoming the motivation decade. Strengthening a trend already evident in the 80s, radio stations, newspapers, and company training programs are using a variety of methods in an attempt to create a "motivation generation" of hard-working, happy, positive-thinking employees.

Courtesy of Colorado Outward Bound

Capitalizing on this trend toward motivation, Joe Nichols founded the Winner's News Network, a 24-hour motivational radio station in Fort Lauderdale, Florida. The tiny AM station broadcasts positive messages about achievement, self-esteem, inspiration, and dedication.

Frank, who works for Pacific Gas & Electric Co., is experiencing the current fad in management training and self-motivation: an outdoor executive program. He is 30 feet up in the trees on a

"ropes" course, a grid of ropes, logs, and cables that looks more like an airborne training tower at an army boot camp than a management training and self-motivation program. The challenges, risks, and fear Frank faces on the ropes course are designed to get him to look closely at himself, his self-confidence, and his coping ability. Hundreds of managers at Pacific Gas & Electric have experienced the ropes course.

The original idea of using ropes and conducting training in an outdoor setting far from the office, the shop floor, or wherever the job is usually located began with the Outward Bound programs of the 1940s. Modeled on British wartime survival courses, the training is designed to improve self-motivation, self-confidence, self-reliance, and teamwork. The emphasis is on personal growth and development.

Not everyone agrees that motivational speeches and other programs are beneficial. However, while the debate continues about the success of these and other unusual motivational techniques, motivation remains a primary concern for modern business.[1]

Today people all around the world—managers and nonmanagers alike—have their own definitions of motivation. Usually the definitions include one or more of the following words: *needs*, *drives*, *motives*, *goods*, *incentives*, *desires*, and *wants*. The term *motivation* can be traced to the Latin word *movere* (to move). In terms of the work to be performed in an organization, moving employees to accomplish desired goals is extremely important. Thus this chapter will focus on moving people to perform.

The difficulties involved in motivation have not lessened the enthusiasm or creativity of attempts to find ways to motivate employees. Each year, for example, the Premium Incentive Show displays various motivational techniques, materials, and activities. In 1990, 1,800 exhibitors showed their wares to 34,000 potential customers in New York. There were prizes for quota-busting salespeople, awards for quality and service contests, and giveaways for customers. One of the more novel items was the "congratulator." When a person pulls a string on the shoulder-mounted contraption, a wooden hand pats him or her on the back. "To that special employee," a brochure explains, "the congratulator says, 'thank you.' "[2]

Devices such as the congratulator are interesting, but this chapter focuses on how managers specifically look at human resource management and motivation. We begin by defining scientific management and motivation and then present several need and management theories. The chapter concludes with a discussion of various ways managers can motivate their employees.

MOTIVATION AND PERFORMANCE

In any attempt to motivate, the psychology of individuals—why they behave the way they do—is important. Motivation attempts to influence or cause certain behaviors. In fact many people equate the causes of behavior with motivation. The importance of the behavior concept is spelled out in advice Ross Perot gave to General Motors. Some of it is repeated in the Business Action.

One of the major problems of *perestroika* in the Soviet Union will be motivation of the work force. The work force in that country has been uninspired and unmotivated. The culture of the society and years of central planning have depressed individual motivation.[3] Even Russian fairy tales indicate a nonmotivational fabric. For example, one hero is the crafty peasant Yemela, whose central ambition is to be atop a warm oven and get what he wants by magic. The Soviet citizen asks, "Why should I work hard when my wages are the same as my colleagues, who are lazy and, like Yemela, not very motivated?" Motivating Soviet workers under perestroika will be challenging, a long, hard road for managers.

One of the most difficult tasks facing managers at Pacific Gas & Electric or Motorola or any other company is motivating employees. Managers are responsible and accountable for meeting important organizational objectives. Therefore they must be concerned about the performance of employees in such important tasks as answering a customer complaint, interpreting a computer printout, or selling a graphic computer disk player to a customer. Successful business managers must create an atmosphere that motivates employees to use

Listen Up, General Motors: A Few Words of Advice

Ross Perot, Jr., is an entrepreneur, a businessman, and one who forcefully expresses his opinions. He believes that the United States needs to wake up and take international competition seriously.

Perot was president of Electronic Data Systems when General Motors (GM) acquired the company. Perot served on the GM board, which at the suggestion of GM chairman Roger Smith bought him out for over $700 million. Perot believed GM has a number of problems that must be corrected. Among these problems are some motivation issues that need to be addressed immediately. Here are some of Perot's suggestions for GM, which could be modified to fit most companies of any size. Even 10-employee Morgan's Restaurant in Chevy Chase, Maryland, could apply these concepts in creating a motivation program.

- Starting today, every person on the GM team will be dealt with as an individual. Every person will be treated with dignity and respect.

- As of today, all people who manage in an authoritarian way will be fired. The full potential and capability of people cannot be accomplished with the authoritarian style.
- Immediately send senior leaders to the field for several weeks to visit and listen to people, learn how they see the world, and communicate to them about issues, problems, and solutions.
- Reward excellence and publicize the rewards.
- From this day forward, everyone is a GMer. Everyone will be a full member of a tightly knit, unified GM team.

Perot's ideas indicate that motivation eventually must address the worker's self-concept. Building self-confidence, self-respect, self-esteem, and self-motivation is the key.[4]

their skills and abilities. When a skilled employee does not perform up to his capabilities, is this a motivation problem? Yes, it probably is.

Here are some statistics about how sagging motivation has affected American workers' productivity:

- U.S. worker productivity has slowed to a crawl. From 1973 to 1989, it was .5 percent per employee.
- Productivity growth per employee in the service sector has been almost zero since 1980.
- The United States ranks sixth in productivity among developed nations.
- Japanese productivity has grown six times faster than American productivity in the past 15 years; productivity in England grew almost three times faster.

HUMAN RESOURCE MANAGEMENT AND RELATIONS

Frederick Winslow Taylor's principles of scientific management introduced the importance of managing human resources and relations. Taylor studied workers in the Midvale and Bethlehem steel plants in 1885. His most famous experiment involved a pig iron shoveler he called Schmidt (his real name was Henry Noll). Using a time-and-motion approach and a stopwatch, Taylor studied Schmidt's every move and work activity. He presented improvements in how to handle pig iron. Schmidt increased his productivity from 12.5 long tons (a long ton equals 2,240 pounds) to 47.5 long tons per day!

This is **scientific management**—the systematic study and breakdown of work into its smallest mechanical elements, and then rearrangement of these elements into their most efficient combination. The application of the principles of scientific management has resulted in many cases of increased or improved productivity.

Scientific Management
The scientific study and breakdown of work into its smallest mechanical elements, and then rearrangement into their most efficient combination.

The Hawthorne Studies

The **Hawthorne studies** were conducted from 1927 to 1932 at a Western Electric plant in Cicero, a suburb of Chicago.[5] The team of Harvard University researchers included Elton Mayo, Fritz Roethlisberger, and William Dickson. This series of experiments is the single most important event in the historical foundation of the behavioral study of employees.

In an illumination experiment, employees were divided into two groups. One group worked in a test room where the intensity of lighting was varied, and the other group worked in a room with constant lighting over the time of the experiment. When light levels were raised in the test room, production increased; when light levels were lowered, production still increased. Puzzled, the researchers decided to change working conditions. They introduced shorter rest periods, longer but fewer rest periods, and other changes. Once again, no matter what change was introduced, production still improved.

The researchers next interviewed many of the employees involved in the study, asking questions about their reactions to working conditions. The researchers found that a change in morale occurred because the employees felt

Hawthorne Studies
A series of experiments that found that work groups significantly affected the way workers behave and perform.

The famous Western Electric plant in Cicero, Illinois, where the Hawthorne studies were conducted in 1924–1932. This is the most cited and quoted behavioral study ever conducted.

Courtesy of AT&T Archives

more responsible. They also did not want to let down co-workers. This was a form of self-imposed pressure. They also felt good about being a part of the experiment. Labor turnover stopped, and absences were drastically reduced. An employee who had been absent 85 times in the 32 months before the experiment went for 16 months without an absence.

A second experiment, which lasted for only 16 weeks, was designed to measure the effect of group incentive plans on productivity. Although economic incentives were offered for increased productivity, the members of the group set informal production quotas that would allow most group members to work at a comfortable pace. The power of the informal group, not the economic incentive, controlled production.

The Hawthorne findings offered no perfect answers or specific motivation programs for managers. But the studies did show that informal groups can influence productivity. Productivity increased through self-imposed pressure in the first experiment, but it was restricted by group pressure in the second. Both experiments used highly cohesive, or tightly knit, groups.

The major difference in the two experiments was the supervisory style used. The first used general supervision. The employees stated that they had freedom and were treated well. They felt special and good about themselves. The self was recognized, and employees liked this kind of recognition. In the second experiment, a closer supervisory style was used.

There were other dissimilarities. The employees were women in the first experiment, men in the second. In the second experiment, the room in which the employees worked was set up just for the experiment and involved no researcher-introduced changes. In the first experiment, the researchers changed lighting and rest periods.

Regardless of the differences, the Hawthorne studies showed how group characteristics and type of supervision, among other things, influence motivation and productivity. The studies have been interpreted in different ways, but one message is clear. Managers attempting to create a favorable climate for motivation need to consider (1) the group, (2) helping employees improve their self-esteem, and (3) style of supervision.

The importance of helping people to feel good about themselves, to feel special, is captured in Roethlisberger's own words: "If one experiments on a stone, the stone does not know it is being experimented upon"—all of which makes it simple for people experimenting on stones. But a human being experimented upon is likely to know it. Therefore, attitudes toward the experiment and toward the experimenter become very important factors in determining his or her responses to the situation. This phenomenon is known as the "Hawthorne effect."[6]

Scientific management and the Hawthorne studies contributed insights, methodologies, and ideas to the area of human relations; that is, the study of how organizations manage their employees individually and within groups to improve productivity. The Hawthorne studies are so important in understanding motivation, groups, and productivity that the original readings are now considered classics and are required reading for scholars and researchers around the world.

MOTIVATION: WHAT IS IT?

Motivation is the way in which drives or needs direct a person's behavior toward a goal. It concerns the level of effort put forth to pursue specific goals. Managers cannot observe the motivation process directly since it occurs internally. So they observe behaviors and then reach conclusions about a person's motivation. For example, Gina knows that Jose and Mike have similar skills and work experience. Jose completes his work, but Mike recently has begun to slip. She concludes that Jose is motivated but Mike is not. Why? That's the motivation puzzle Gina must solve.

Gina and other managers become concerned about motivation when employees exhibit a lack of success, productivity problems, reduced commitment to quality, and resistance to management programs. Managers know it is not simple to motivate employees. In fact, managers realize they must understand how to use an array of tools (e.g., techniques, programs, rewards) to create the best motivational atmosphere possible.

Generally speaking, rewards and punishments are the tools managers use to motivate employees. Rewards can be extrinsic or intrinsic. **Extrinsic rewards** are external to the work itself; they are administered by someone else, such as a manager. Examples include pay, fringe benefits, recognition, and praise. **Intrinsic rewards** are related directly to performing the job. In this sense, they are often described as self-administered. Intrinsic rewards include feeling good about accomplishing an objective and about being able to make job-related

Motivation
The way drives or needs direct a person's behavior toward a specific goal; involves the level of effort put forth to pursue the goal.

Extrinsic Reward
Reward external to the work itself and administered by someone else, such as a manager.

Intrinsic Reward
A sense of gratification directly related to performing the job.

There are many different kinds of rewards. As a reward for good performance, this Limited Store sales manager was one of 23 managers selected by Executive Vice President of Sales Andy Guerriero to attend a special management seminar at The Limited Support Center in Columbus, Ohio.

Courtesy of The Limited Stores

Punishment
An undesirable consequence of a particular behavior.

decisions without consulting a supervisor. On the other hand, **punishment** involves taking something away from a person or administering an undesirable consequence for a particular behavior. For example, a frequently tardy worker would be punished by having his pay docked for the time missed.

Communicating and administering rewards and punishments are part of the manager's job in creating the best motivational atmosphere. Both types of rewards appear to produce higher levels of performance than punishment does.

Motivation is goal oriented. It can work this way: First, the person experiences tension created by unfulfilled needs. A need indicates a deficiency; for example, when you are hungry, you have a need for food. Second, the person starts a search to find a reasonable way to satisfy these unfulfilled needs. Third, when some of the needs are fulfilled and some of the goals are accomplished, the process begins again. Figure 10.1 illustrates the goal-oriented process of motivation.

To create the atmosphere their subordinates need to perform efficiently, managers must have some grasp of the motivation process. As recognized management educator and consultant Peter Drucker stated: "No matter how authoritarian the institution, it has to satisfy the ambitions and needs of its members and do so in their capacity as individuals."[7] The rest of this chapter discusses various types of needs and how they can be used to motivate and manage employees.

FIGURE 10.1

**The Process of
Motivation in the
Individual**

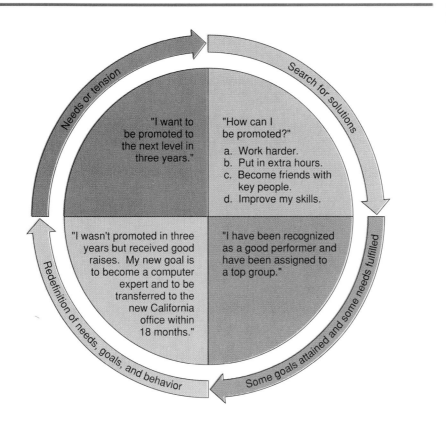

"I want to
be promoted to
the next level in
three years."

"How can I
be promoted?"

a. Work harder.
b. Put in extra hours.
c. Become friends with
   key people.
d. Improve my skills.

"I wasn't promoted in three
years but received good
raises. My new goal is
to become a computer
expert and to be
transferred to the
new California
office within
18 months."

"I have been recognized
as a good performer and
have been assigned to
a top group."

Needs or tension

Search for solutions

Some goals attained and some needs fulfilled

Redefinition of needs, goals, and behavior

Some goals attained and some needs fulfilled

THEORIES OF MANAGEMENT AND NEEDS

Maslow's Needs Hierarchy

A popular theory of human needs that helps us understand motivation is psychologist Abraham Maslow's **needs hierarchy.** He identified five basic needs that explain the internal motivation process: physiological, safety, social, esteem, and self-actualization needs.[8]

Five need levels   The needs Maslow identified fall into a hierarchy, or arrangement, of power to motivate behavior, as illustrated in Figure 10.2. Each higher-order need becomes active and motivates a person only when lower-level needs have been fulfilled. Each person is assumed to have needs in each category. Examples of job satisfiers that can fulfill the needs are also included in Figure 10.2.

The starting point for understanding motivation is **physiological needs.** The person who is hungry or tired is thinking about food or sleep, not work. But once physiological needs are fulfilled, they lose their power to motivate. Then **safety needs** become important. For instance, workers are concerned about keeping their jobs and about being financially secure when they retire. "How safe is my job?" is a question being asked around the United States. In 1990

Needs Hierarchy
A motivational theory, offered by Maslow, that people have five needs arranged in a hierarchy from physiological to self-realization.

Physiological Need
Biological need, such as for food, air, water.

Safety Need
Security need, such as the need to be financially secure and protected against job loss.

FIGURE 10.2

The Maslow Needs Hierarchy and Job Satisfiers

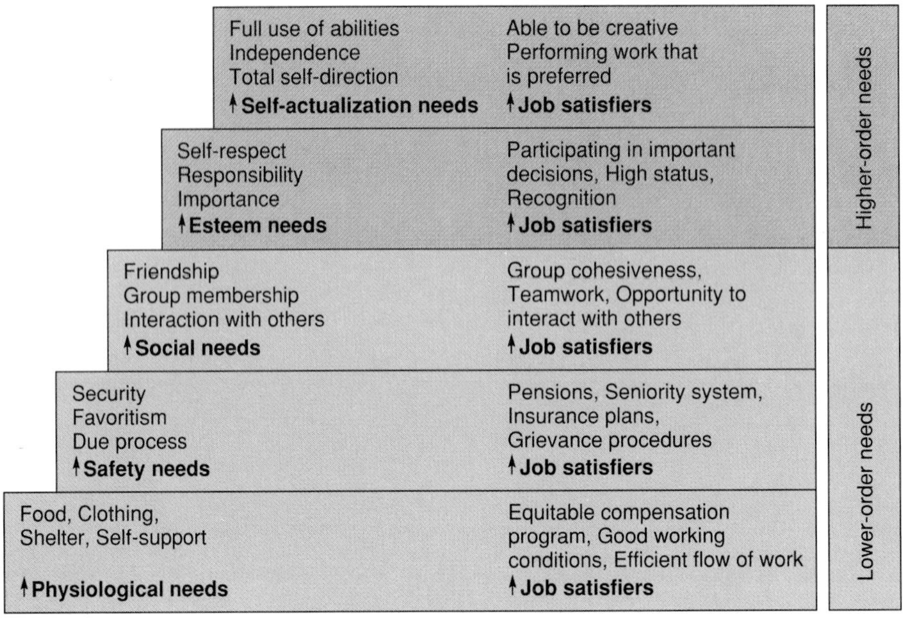

Full use of abilities Independence Total self-direction ↑ **Self-actualization needs**	Able to be creative Performing work that is preferred ↑ **Job satisfiers**	Higher-order needs
Self-respect Responsibility Importance ↑ **Esteem needs**	Participating in important decisions, High status, Recognition ↑ **Job satisfiers**	
Friendship Group membership Interaction with others ↑ **Social needs**	Group cohesiveness, Teamwork, Opportunity to interact with others ↑ **Job satisfiers**	
Security Favoritism Due process ↑ **Safety needs**	Pensions, Seniority system, Insurance plans, Grievance procedures ↑ **Job satisfiers**	Lower-order needs
Food, Clothing, Shelter, Self-support ↑ **Physiological needs**	Equitable compensation program, Good working conditions, Efficient flow of work ↑ **Job satisfiers**	

about 30,000 positions a month were trimmed from company payrolls. At American Telephone & Telegraph, 6,000 positions were cut at its long-distance unit.[9] Such cutbacks threaten an employee's sense of job security. Safety needs can be satisfied by the creation of seniority systems, pensions, and insurance plans. As with physiological needs, once most of the safety needs have been satisfied, the next level of needs becomes more important.

Employees want to belong, to interact with other employees. Thus the friendly behavior of individuals in small groups within organizations is a major source of satisfaction for **social needs.** In a small group, individuals support and encourage one another; as a by-product, they get a sense of being an accepted member of the group. Once social needs have been largely satisfied, they also begin to lose their power to motivate.

The **esteem needs** are needs for self-respect and respect from others. An important part of this area is that an employee's work efforts and output be recognized and appreciated by others. When the need for esteem is strong, the individual will often set difficult goals, work hard to achieve the goals, and expect to receive recognition for these efforts. Goal accomplishment and the resulting recognition lead to feelings of self-esteem and self-confidence.

The top of the needs hierarchy is **self-actualization,** the ability to display and use one's full potential. This need takes over when an adequate level of satisfaction has been reached in the other four need levels. A person who reaches self-actualization has come close to using his or her full set of skills. Maslow noted that self-actualizing people display certain characteristics:

- They tend to be serious and thoughtful.

Social Need
The need to belong and to interact with other people.

Esteem Need
The need for self-respect and for respect from others.

Self-Actualization Need
The need to use and display one's full range of skills and competence.

- They focus on problems outside themselves.
- Their behavior is unaffected and natural.
- They are strongly ethical.

Most people think of artists, composers, and scientists as seeking self-actualization. Because people work to satisfy the more basic needs, managers often overlook employees' self-actualization need.

Reaching a level of complete self-actualization rarely occurs. Certainly it is hard to achieve if other needs are not being adequately satisfied. But everyone is capable of partially satisfying the self-actualization need. Richard Nicolosi, a general manager at Procter & Gamble, was able to create a self-actualizing environment. His approach is briefly described in the Business Action on motivating people.

Of course employees differ in the intensity of their needs. Some have an intense security need that will dominate their behavior no matter what managers do. Others are more strongly influenced by esteem needs. Managers have no standard program to follow when attempting to encourage a high level of motivation. Differences in personal background, experience, and education are powerful; conditions that work for one individual may not work for another.

McGregor's Theory X and Theory Y

Although managers should try to understand needs, they often don't. Douglas McGregor, a professor of management, introduced a theory of managerial style, referred to as Theory X and Theory Y, to explain this phenomenon.[10]

Theory X managers are assumed to view the average employee as:

- Disliking work and finding ways to avoid it as much as possible.
- Responding to threats of punishment or control because of the dislike of work.
- Avoiding responsibility because of a lack of ambition.
- Wanting to be directed and have security.

Theory X
Managerial assumptions that employees dislike work, responsibility, and accountability and must be closely directed and controlled to be motivated to perform.

A problem with making such assumptions about people is that they can become self-fulfilling. A manager with a Theory X view of workers will probably focus on creating conditions to satisfy physiological and safety needs, closely controlling and supervising subordinates. Of course some employees respond favorably to this style, but others feel frustrated, anxious, and very much in conflict. Their goals for self-esteem and self-actualization cannot be achieved.

Theory Y, on the other hand, is a set of managerial assumptions that results in looser control and more delegation of authority. The Theory Y manager assumes that the average employee:

Theory Y
Managerial assumptions that employees want to be challenged, like to display creativity, and can be highly motivated to perform well if given some freedom to direct or manage their own behavior.

- Enjoys work and does not want to avoid it.
- Wants to achieve organizational goals through self-directed behavior.
- Responds to rewards associated with accomplishing goals.
- Will accept responsibility.
- Has initiative and can be creative in solving organizational problems.
- Is intellectually underutilized.

Motivating People: A Self-Actualizing Environment

When Richard Nicolosi became the associate general manager of paper products at Procter & Gamble (P&G), he made things happen. He is a motivator of people. He was so successful in improving productivity that he soon became the head of the paper products division.

Nicolosi stressed teamwork and taking the initiative. He also stressed a training regimen that is often called the boot camp of consumer marketing. Noncreative, slow, and less-than-stellar performers are weeded out of the P&G training programs quickly. Nicolosi wants his paper products division to be filled with creative, hard-working, take-charge people.

What Nicolosi did was manage in such a way that an entrepreneurial environment had a chance to evolve. He talked about his vision and goals, which became the goals of some of the paper products division employees from the top to the bottom. The innovations that the division needed to gain market share came from motivated employees. For example, Ultra Pampers were developed within the unit and swept the market by storm. Luvs Deluxe, another diaper product, took its market in short order.

Even most of the secretaries in Nicolosi's division felt empowered and wanted to be a part of the team. They pitched in to help develop training and recognition programs and became part of an exciting team.

From the secretaries to the chief in charge, the paper products division became a highly motivated environment. Although competition was tough, Nicolosi was able to help create and nurture a motivated work force. The division's employees wanted to work hard and enjoyed the entire set of challenges they faced.

No manager can directly create a self-actualization atmosphere. The job, the colleagues, and the style and behavior of a manager such as Richard Nicolosi all help create self-actualization opportunities for employees. Nicolosi couldn't observe what motivated each employee. However, he was creative enough to help establish an environment in which each employee was able to enjoy a degree of need satisfaction, goal accomplishment, and an improved self-concept.[11]

According to McGregor, Theory Y assumptions reflect a managerial emphasis on human growth and development instead of coercive authority.

Theory X and Theory Y represent two extremely different positions—an autocratic management style and a democratic management style. Many workers now demand Theory Y behavior from managers. They want to satisfy some of their social, esteem, and self-actualization needs on the job, and Theory X–oriented management behavior only produces frustration and anxiety. Because of our democratic political heritage, the idea of Theory Y is more appealing to most people. On the other hand, some workers don't respond well in a Theory Y–oriented organization; some job situations call for autocratic controls. The key is the manager. He or she must review the people involved and the situation and then determine if a Theory X or a Theory Y management style will work.

Ouchi's Theory Z

The economic growth and power of Japan has garnered a lot of publicity. In the past decade, it outperformed other countries in a number of industries. This performance miracle is attributed to many factors, such as business-government cooperation, operating with relatively new (post–World War II) plants and equipment, a homogeneous ethnic population, a group-oriented culture, and even a rigorous educational system (see Table 10.1).

Another factor in the successes achieved by a highly motivated work force is called the **Theory Z** style of management. William Ouchi's Theory Z approach draws on characteristics of successful U.S. and Japanese management styles and organizational practices. Ouchi, a management researcher, emphasizes these characteristics of Theory Z practices:[12]

Theory Z
Management theory that draws on the characteristics of successful Japanese and American managers; emphasizes consensus management practices.

- Lifetime employment (to help satisfy physiological and safety needs).
- Consensus decision making (to help satisfy social needs).
- Individual responsibility (to help satisfy self-esteem needs).
- Careful evaluation and promotion (to build confidence and self-esteem).
- Opportunity to use skills (to help satisfy self-actualization needs).

TABLE 10.1

The Beginning of Self-Motivation

DID YOU KNOW? *Does self-motivation start in elementary school in the U.S.? Perhaps this issue should be investigated. Look at these 1990 data. Is the U.S. education system preparing students for the achievement and self-motivation world of the 21st century?*

	Elementary and Secondary Schools	
	United States	Japan
Days of school per week	5	5.5
Days per year	180	240
Weeks per year	36	46
Average hours of homework per school day	0.5	2

TABLE 10.2

Blending American and Japanese Styles into Theory Z

| Characteristic | Management Style | | |
	American	Japanese	Theory Z
Length of employment	Relatively short-term; layoffs when business is slow.	Long-term; lifetime when possible.	Retain employees in good and bad times.
Evaluation and promotion	Short-term and rapid promotions.	Longer-term and moderate promotion schedule.	Evaluate skills and promotions based on contributions, not tenure.
Decision making	Individual.	Collective, with input from all parties.	Use of a democratic process that strives for consensus.
Responsibility	Individual.	Shared by group.	Responsibility remains with key individuals.
Control	Control by use of policies and rules.	Self-control.	Informal but with an emphasis on objective facts and data.
Concern for workers	Emphasis on work itself.	Focus on entire life of worker.	Concerned with worker's life and family.

Source: A. Paarasuraman, *MARKETING RESEARCH*, © 1991 by Addison-Wesley Publishing Co., p. 20. Reprinted by permission of the Addison-Wesley Publishing Co., Reading, MA.

A comparison of American, Japanese, and Theory Z styles (see Table 10.2) illustrates the blending of the first two approaches into the third.

Theory Z places a special emphasis on participative management. Employees participate in goal setting, decision making, problem solving, and designing and implementing changes. Participation, or being involved, is thought to improve employee motivation. Of course, some workers may prefer not to participate in these areas. This point should be kept in mind when an enthusiastic advocate of Theory Z and participation attempts to get everyone involved. Some people simply want to do their job and go home. Likewise some firms or jobs have a culture or atmosphere in which participation would not work. For example, the head of a police SWAT team doesn't want other police officers to be involved in quick decisions about a dangerous and trapped criminal. Also, the pilot who has lost radio contact with a control tower has to solve landing problems without the help of others.

As with Theory X and Theory Y, the Theory Z assumptions and suggestions have not been scientifically tested or evaluated. There is no solid evidence to support any of these explanations. However, each offers a perspective on the behavior of employees in organizations. And managers are interested in each perspective to help explain the differences they observe daily among their employees.

Building the Saturn automobile to compete in international markets relied on participation. These five team members are happy about their participation, the car they helped produce, and the good feeling they have about their company. (Photos courtesy of the Saturn Corporation)

"You better be ready for change. You better be ready for commitment and high intensity. If this is more than you want to give, it's not for you."

"Saturn is not Disneyland. Saturn is reality. Saturn is people working very, very hard to produce a product that will sell and ensure their livelihoods. And that's a tough reality sometimes."

WHAT IT'S LIKE WORKING AT SATURN . . .

"We all have a vision here at Saturn, but it's gonna take a lot of hard-earned effort. And, in a lot of ways, a lot of blood, sweat, and tears."

"People are trying to fulfill a vision of what Saturn should be. And every day is a challenge to keep that vision in front of us. We don't always necessarily meet that vision, but the challenge is to always keep trying."

Herzberg's Two-Factor Model of Motivation

In the 1950s, Frederick Herzberg, a social psychologist and consultant, proposed a **work motivation model** that is still very popular among business managers.[13] Herzberg surveyed accountants and engineers, asking them to describe when they felt good or bad about their jobs. He found that one set of job and personal factors produced good feelings and that another created bad feelings.

One set of factors Herzberg called **hygiene factors** (also called maintenance factors). These factors, if present and available, are essential to job satisfaction, although they cannot motivate an employee. They include:

Salary	Working conditions	Technical supervision
Job security	Status	Company policies
Personal life	Interpersonal relations	

Work Motivation Model
An explanation of motivation that defines hygiene factors and motivator factors, and how they affect job satisfaction and dissatisfaction.

Hygiene Factor
External characteristic essential to avoiding job dissatisfaction.

Hygiene factors, if absent or inadequate, cause job dissatisfaction. Herzberg believes that by providing these factors, managers can prevent job dissatisfaction but cannot motivate employees to perform any better.

The second set of factors was described by Herzberg as **motivators** of on-the-job behavior. They include:

Motivator
Content–oriented characteristic that contributes to job satisfaction.

Achievement	Advancement	Growth opportunities
Recognition	The job itself	Responsibility

While hygiene factors deal with external features of the job, motivators are job content oriented, or tied to the job itself.

The employee appreciates the hygiene and motivator factors at different times. For example, the employee takes a paycheck (hygiene factor) to a bank, cashes it, and receives some satisfaction when the money is received. While actually performing the work, the employee can receive and enjoy such motivators as responsibility, recognition, and growth opportunities. These and other motivator factors make up the fabric of the job.

Omni Hotels has established a motivator-based program for its hardworking employees.[14] The Omni Service Champion (OSC) program recognizes employees who go beyond the call of duty to ensure guest satisfaction. Employees observed doing something extra to help a guest are given OSC commendations on the spot. Commendations are given for packing luggage for a guest with a broken hand, saving someone's life at the hotel pool, or taking a taxi to another location to get something fixed for a customer. On the 1st, 5th, 10th, 15th, and 20th days of each month, the recognized employees receive the OSC medal that is worn on the uniform. At the end of the year, the three employees from each Omni hotel who received the most medals are awarded medals and cash prizes, and they attend a gala celebration to culminate the program for the year.

Hygiene factors can result in not being dissatisfied, but they are not motivational. Managers need to know this because the elimination of job dissatisfaction will not necessarily motivate employees. Figure 10.3 presents Herzberg's

FIGURE 10.3

The Dissatisfaction-Satisfaction Relationship: An Application

Job factors	Worker dissatisfaction with the job	Neutral about the job	Satisfaction with the job
Motivators		Little or no satisfaction → with motivators "I'm not being challenged by my job."	→ Satisfaction "My job is now really challenging me."
Hygienes	Dissatisfaction with the hygiene factors. "I am dissatisfied with my working conditions."	Little or no dissatisfaction "My job is OK, I guess."	

thinking on this issue. If motivation is what the manager wants to achieve, then he or she must emphasize recognition, achievement, and growth—the motivators.

Maslow and Herzberg: A Comparison

Maslow's needs hierarchy and Herzberg's work motivation model have many similarities, as Figure 10.4 shows. The lower-level needs are similar to the hygiene factors. These needs are satisfied for many employees, but some have not adequately fulfilled their lower-level needs. Then hygiene factors may be motivators. Today managers pay more attention to the higher-level needs, or motivator factors, than they did previously.

Although Herzberg's model is popular and makes sense, it has been criticized. Some critics remind us that the original study group from which the model was developed included only engineers and accountants. These two occupational groups do not represent most employees (salesclerks, computer operators, teachers, police officers, scientists, nurses) in organizations. In response Herzberg cites studies that used nurses, supervisors, scientists, food handlers, and assemblers and found results similar to his original study. Other critics question the manner in which Herzberg collected his information. They believe that his method of asking questions influenced the way the accountants and engineers responded.

Despite these criticisms, the work motivation model is used by many managers, as it is logical and uses language that managers understand. However, it was not Maslow, McGregor, or Herzberg who really stimulated management thinking about motivation at work. It was the Hawthorne studies.

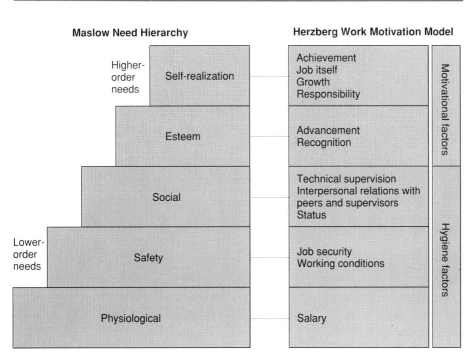

FIGURE 10.4

Similarities in the Needs Hierarchy and Work Motivation Model

● C o n n e c t i o n s

What Motivates You?

Directions: Circle the number under the response that best describes your own feelings about the statement. There are no right or wrong answers; the purpose of this questionnaire is simply to organize your own thoughts about your personal preferences.

	Strongly Agree	Agree	Neither	Disagree	Strongly Disagree
1. I value friendship more than almost anything else.	5	4	3	2	1
2. Just knowing I've done something well gives me satisfaction; I don't need praise from others.	1	2	3	4	5
3. Being happy is more important to me than making money.	5	4	3	2	1
4. I need a lot of time by myself.	1	2	3	4	5
5. My first priority is high income and job security.	5	4	3	2	1
6. I don't believe people should waste their time pursuing dreams.	1	2	3	4	5

We have discussed types of needs that employees have. The Connections quiz examines the Maslow needs hierarchy. Take a few minutes and complete the scale. Maslow's needs hierarchy provides a useful framework for managers.[15] Now let's talk about how managers can use their knowledge of these needs to motivate their employees and thus increase their production.

MOTIVATING EMPLOYEES

The group incentive plan in the Hawthorne studies did not motivate the employees as expected. Those and other studies show that there is no magic formula for providing employees with the interest and desire to perform well—although some programs work better than others. The manager's job is to find the best motivational trigger for his or her group and situation. For some, money is a key, whereas others prefer more job authority, and still others like to have clear objectives to use as targets.

7. I feel disgusted if someone
   else gets credit for my accom-
   plishments.   5   4   3   2   1

8. I'm more concerned with
   whether or not I enjoy my work
   than what I get paid for doing it.   1   2   3   4   5

Feedback: This quiz measures one's current motivational interests. This insight will help you understand why you view the interests of others to be similar or different.

Score your answers by filling in the numbers you have circled in the form below. Your scores will range from 2 to 10 on each of the four need scales. The four need scores correspond to the four higher-order categories of needs (or motives) identified by Abraham Maslow. The lowest-level need category, physiological needs (food, shelter, water, etc.) is not included.

High-scale scores are 8, 9, or 10. Did you score high on more than one scale? Which ones? Do you think your scores accurately describe your own predominant motives?

Items	Scores	Need Scale
5 + 8	_____ + _____ = _____	Safety/security
1 + 4	_____ + _____ = _____	Belongingness/social
2 + 7	_____ + _____ = _____	Self-esteem
3 + 6	_____ + _____ = _____	Self-actualization

Goal Setting

The notion that employees' motivation and performance may be enhanced by setting specific job performance goals has gained popularity in the past 20 years. As a result of research, some specific principles of goal setting have been established.[16] **Goal setting** is the process of identifying specific levels of performance that a person seeks to accomplish in a certain time frame.

Probably the best-established goal-setting principle is that workers perform at higher levels when asked to meet a specific challenging goal than they do when simply asked to "do your best" or when no goal at all is assigned. This principle relates the effectiveness of goal setting not only to *specific* goals but also to *challenging* goals. However, when goals become too difficult, performance drops because the goals are seen as unrealistic. For example, a usually average student setting a goal to be the number 1 person in the class might be unrealistic.

Another interesting goal-setting concept is to involve workers in the process. Meaningful goals that employees have helped to set may enhance performance

Goal Setting
The process of identifying specific levels of performance to be achieved in a certain time frame.

more than goals that are simply assigned by a manager. The logic is that, by participating, a person becomes more committed and develops a stronger drive to accomplish the goal.

Feedback on goal accomplishments is also important.[17] People want to know how they are doing. Whether the accomplishment concerns schoolwork, hitting a baseball, or drawing a picture, people value feedback. A study of different units in the U.S. Air Force showed that feedback and goal setting together helped improve performance for work groups as opposed to individuals.[18]

Managers can use goal setting to motivate employees. Setting specific, challenging goals and providing feedback about goal accomplishment enhance motivation and performance. Management by objectives (MBO), discussed in Chapter Seven, involves the use of goal setting either throughout an organization or within units.

One excellent goal setter and goal accomplisher is Harvey Cook, the author of *Scientific Success*. He sells insurance only two days a week for seven months out of the year. He sells $4 million of insurance in the first eight days.[19] His advice: "Don't compete for number 1; compete with yourself." Cook uses a 15-minute time guide for his goals; he breaks his day into 15-minute increments.

According to Cook, a person must decide what to accomplish in each 15-minute period of the day. A salesperson's game plan might be:

- Every 15 minutes, make the three telephone calls you'll need to get one qualified appointment.
- Spend 35 minutes of selective canvassing with potential clients to get one appointment.
- Line up 16 appointments to make the 11 client presentations you need in order to close at least 10 sales every two days.

Don't just set goals to increase numbers. Use tools of motivation to improve effectiveness. Novelists such as Irving Wallace and Ernest Hemingway used reinforcement systems and goals to increase their writing productivity. Day by day they would chart the number of words they had written. That number compared to a goal scolded or encouraged the author. Hemingway accumulated words he'd written over his goal so he could reward himself with a day off. Goal setting is a powerful technique that, when combined with rewards, sanctions, and self-discipline, can be a powerful motivating force.

Job Enrichment

Job Enrichment
A motivational technique that involves incorporating variety, feedback, and autonomy in the job.

In his work motivation model, Herzberg introduced **job enrichment,** a method intended to increase the motivation and satisfaction of employees and to improve production through job design. By adding more motivators to the job, job enrichment can make work meaningful, stimulating, and challenging. The employee comes to view the job a lot like play. Don Ritcher owns an Arby's Restaurant in Chicago. He did not use authority, commands, and directives to motivate his employees to be courteous to customers, show up for work on time, help keep the restaurant immaculate, and work hard. Instead he created an achievement-oriented franchise. He permitted his workers to establish flexible work schedules to fit their needs, he instituted an "employee of the week" reward program, he held discussion meetings and allowed each employee to present opinions on how to improve business and service, and he let employees attend development seminars to improve their skills. He made working at Arby's more meaningful and interesting.

The first step in job enrichment is to determine which characteristics of a job increase motivation. Picture the golfer hitting a bag of practice balls. Such practice is meaningful because the hitting skill can be improved. The golfer is in charge of every shot attempted. Once a shot is made, the golfer receives immediate feedback on how well the ball was hit. The sense of hitting the ball well is important in determining the golfer's "psychological feelings" about practicing; it serves to motivate him or her to continue or to come back for another practice session.

The same is true for an employee doing a job. Motivational jobs contain the following characteristics:

- *Meaningfulness.* The work must be perceived as worthwhile.
- *Responsibility.* The employee must be personally responsible for any effort expended.
- *Knowledge of results.* The employee must receive, on a regular basis, feedback about how well he or she is performing.

When these conditions are present, jobholders usually feel good about the job and their contribution. These good feelings motivate employees to continue to do well. But if one of these three conditions is missing, the internal feeling (motivation) drops off dramatically.

Studies indicate that five job characteristics create good psychological feelings about a job.[20] These characteristics can be enriched by a manager. Three of the five characteristics contribute to the meaningfulness of a job:

- *Skill variety*—the degree to which a job requires activities that are challenging.
- *Task identity*—the degree to which the job requires the completion of a "whole" piece of work. For example, building an entire generator has more tasks than just placing a flywheel on the generator as it passes by on a conveyer belt.
- *Task significance*—the degree to which the job is significant to the organization or other individuals.

A fourth job characteristic leads an employee to experience more responsibility: *Autonomy* is the degree to which the job gives the worker freedom, independence, and leeway to carry out what is required. The fifth job characteristic, *feedback,* is the degree to which a worker gets information on his or her effectiveness in carrying out the job.

Such organizations as AT&T, Saab-Scania, Volvo, and General Foods have used job enrichment to motivate employees; they have redesigned or changed job characteristics for various employees or groups. But like all sound motivation programs, job enrichment must be used selectively. Management must also provide enough time for the approach to be understood. The user must consider the situation, the job, and the people involved (see Figure 10.5). Job characteristics that can be enriched are especially important for employees

FIGURE 10.5

Job Characteristics, Individual Differences, and Reactions

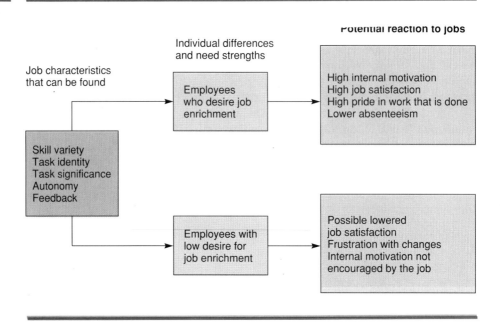

who desire enrichment. The potential consequences for these workers are spelled out in the figure. Usually, if the organization supports enrichment, more employees desire the job changes.

Quality of Work Life

QWL
Managerial programs that increase outcomes such as productivity or performance by better management of jobs, people, and working conditions.

The term **quality of work life (QWL)** describes a wide variety of approaches to improve the quality of human experience in the workplace. The work experience is improved to help individuals satisfy needs and accomplish goals and to give more relevance to a person's work-related contributions.[21] QWL approaches are designed to help employees feel good about themselves, their jobs, and their organizations. As such they are considered motivational.

The following dimensions have been associated with QWL:

- Adequate and fair compensation.
- Safe and healthy working conditions.
- Opportunities to develop human capacities.
- Opportunities for continued growth and job security.
- More flexible work scheduling and job assignments.
- Careful attention to work flow and job design, and worker participation in designing work.
- Attempts to achieve more and better union-management cooperation.
- Less structural supervision and more development of effective work teams.

These and other QWL approaches have been used by such firms as Xerox, Nabisco, Weyerhaeuser, and Procter & Gamble. These firms have recognized

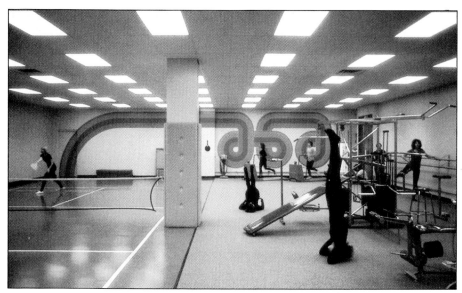

Weyerhaeuser provides a company gym for its employees. "A happy, healthy worker is more productive." This is a motto used by such firms as Xerox, Nabisco, Weyerhaeuser, and Procter & Gamble.

Courtesy of the Weyerhaeuser Company

that managers attempting to motivate employees need to be aware of the kinds of factors involved in the eight dimensions listed. The commitment to employee needs, goals, and satisfaction must be continual.

Despite the humanistic orientation of QWL programs, there has been some resistance. First, some managers are not convinced that the QWL programs have lasting effects on motivation or productivity. Second, the changeover to a QWL program often costs money in terms of time, people, and equipment resources; in tight economic times, such costs become threatening and unacceptable. Third, some unions have resisted QWL programs; they view these programs as weakening the power of the union in its adversarial relationship with management.

The pro and con arguments about QWL programs will continue. However, the potential benefits suggested by QWL advocates—such as improved motivation, increased productivity, and reduced costs—convince more and more managers that QWL improvements may be worthwhile in the organization.

Behavior Modification

The application of a set of learning principles called operant conditioning, developed by psychologist B. F. Skinner (1904–1990), is called **behavior modification.**[22] Behavior modification grew out of the idea that changing the attitude of a person does not necessarily improve performance. Instead the person's behavior must be changed. This is done by changing the environment in which the person behaves.

Behavior Modification
Application of learning principles called operant conditioning.

Skinner believed that the way people behave is a function of heredity, past experiences, and the present situation. Managers can control only the present situation. Therefore Skinner recommends that managers consider these two

Reinforcer
A consequence of behavior that improves the chances it will or will not reoccur.

Positive Reinforcer
A consequence of behavior, such as praise or other rewards, that when administered increases the chances that the behavior will be repeated.

Negative Reinforcer
A consequence of behavior, such as a reprimand, that when administered encourages employee to adapt more desirable behavior to avoid the unpleasant consequence.

points: (1) if an act (behavior) is followed by a pleasant consequence (say, a pat on the back), it probably will be repeated; (2) if an act is followed by an unpleasant consequence (a reprimand, a harsh glare), it probably will not be repeated. The manager's job is to design the present situation so that good performance will result.

The manager can shape the behavior of subordinates by controlling the reinforcers. A **reinforcer** is a consequence of behavior, one that can improve the likelihood that the behavior will or will not occur again. For example, praise—a **positive reinforcer**—given immediately after an employee completes a job on time may increase the occurrence of finishing work on time. Or a reprimand—a **negative reinforcer**—given immediately for not finishing on time may also increase the likelihood of work being done on time. By finishing on time, the employee creates a situation in which the supervisor will not issue a reprimand.

An interesting reinforcer-based program is used by a Chicago firm, Mediatech. Each week the firm contributes $250 to the Mediatech Employee Lottery (MEL).[23] All of the 350 full-time and 25 part-time employees in the firm's offices in New York, Los Angeles, and Chicago are eligible for the MEL. Their hopes of winning rest on the employees' last four digits of their payroll identification number. Every Monday, a different employee spins a wheel at Mediatech's headquarters. Depending on where the wheel lands, there is either a Friday afternoon drawing or the prize money rolls over until the next week. The money accumulates. The biggest winnings on a Friday so far have been $1,000. Other prizes are also given for $600, $300, and $100. Attendance on Friday has improved significantly in all of Mediatech's offices. The reinforcer (winning the lottery) increases the likelihood of coming to work.

Punishment influences behavior by presenting something distasteful or withdrawing something that is liked. For example, a manager says something rude to an employee and receives disapproval (punishment) from other managers. If the disapproval is unpleasant enough, the manager's rudeness is less likely to occur in the future. Another kind of punishment takes something pleasant away. Suppose Nick Rodman, a project engineer, is assigned temporarily to a group that is important to him. Because Nick frequently arrives late to work for the new assignment, he is placed back in a regular work group. Nick is not able to work with the group he likes because of his tardiness. He has been punished.

Punishment and negative reinforcement are not the same. In negative reinforcement, an act (completing work on time) that allows the person to avoid some unpleasant event (supervisor's reprimand) is reinforced when the unpleasant event is removed. In punishment, one of two things happens: (1) an unpleasant event (group disapproval) follows a behavior (rude remark) or (2) a pleasant event (being a member of a group) is taken away after a behavior (tardiness).

Managers applying behavior modification on the job must:

1. Identify the elements of a job that are observable and measurable.
2. Measure how frequently behaviors occur.
3. Positively reinforce the person when a correct behavior occurs.

These procedures have met with some success at Emery Worldwide, the air freight carrier. Emery personnel load containers with packages and ship them by air. Management had assumed that containers were always being loaded to

Emery has applied behavior modification to improve productivity. This type of container is almost always fully loaded since the Emery behavior modification program has been used.

Courtesy of Emery Worldwide

capacity, but a check found that containers were being fully loaded only 45 percent of the time. A list of employee activities and goals for filling containers was developed. Results were recorded in terms of container use so that team results could be compared. By correcting deficiencies and providing feedback and recognition for good performance, management increased container capacity.

Like other motivation programs, behavior modification has its critics. Some view it as a technique that Skinner transferred to humans after conducting trial experiments with animals such as pigeons. They claim that employees are not pigeons and do not respond like pigeons. Another criticism is that behavior modification is too artificial. The employee who receives reinforcement should know why he or she receives a reward. In most behavior modification programs, positive reinforcers are provided without an explanation. The complexity of the work environment often leaves no time to explain their use. Finally, behavior modification has a manipulative aspect. Behavioral consequences are controlled, and people are forced to change behavior instead of changing behavior on their own initiative. This approach is not consistent with the theme that people should act freely. The need for self-actualization is not recognized, which is considered dehumanizing.

You'll Know It's the **Century When . . .**

Full-Time Homemakers Approach Extinction

As the new century begins, more than 80 percent of women aged 25 to 54 will be in the labor force. Most of the rest will be out of work only temporarily. Women will account for nearly half of the total labor force, and businesses will be heavily dependent on their skills.

But women will still be the family's principal caretakers. Businesses will have to adapt to keep them on the job. Parental leave and flexible working hours will be the rule for all but the smallest businesses.[23]

SUMMARY OF LEARNING OBJECTIVES

1. To define the term *scientific management.*
   Scientific management is the scientific study and breakdown of work into its smallest mechanical elements, and then rearrangement into their most efficient combination.

2. To explain what the Hawthorne studies revealed about the role that groups play in motivating employees.
   The Hawthorne studies at the Western Electric plant showed the importance of informal work groups as motivators of employees. Work groups can affect individual behavior. The studies also showed that the employees felt they were special because they were involved in the experiment. This feeling of specialness causes their work performance to improve.

3. To define the term *motivation.*
   Motivation is the way in which drives or needs direct a person's behavior toward a specific goal. It determines the level of effort a person puts forth to achieve the goal. It is an unobservable phenomenon that takes place inside everyone. Managers can readily observe a person's behavior, but they can only make assumptions about what causes the person to behave in that way.

4. To discuss Maslow's view of needs and motivation.
   Maslow believed that people's behavior was motivated by their desire to fulfill needs. These needs were arranged in a hierarchy from the most basic survival needs at the bottom to self-fulfilling needs at the top. The need levels are physiological, safety, social, esteem, and self-actualization. After needs on the lowest level have been satisfied, people are motivated to fulfill needs at the next highest level.

5. To compare and contrast the Theory X, Theory Y, and Theory Z approaches to motivating employees.
   Managers have the challenging task of identifying their employees' needs in order to motivate them to perform better. They can also determine how their style of managing influences employee behavior. McGregor's *Theory X* manager is concerned with helping employees satisfy lower-level physiological and safety needs; such managers are more autocratic and controlling. *Theory Y* managers are concerned with fulfilling their employees' higher-level needs; their managerial style results in looser control and more delegation of authority. *Theory Z* managers emphasize lifetime employment, consensus decision making, and giving employees the opportunity to use their skills.

6. To explain why Herzberg's view of motivation is so popular with practicing managers.

   Herzberg's theory of motivation uses understandable managerial language and instructs managers that motivators should be used to create a more positive work environment. Motivators are conditions such as employees having increased responsibility, more advancement opportunities, and more recognition for good work.

7. To describe the principles of goal setting.

   Goal setting is a way to motivate employees. One principle holds that employees perform better when given specific, challenging goals than when they are given no goals at all or simply told to do their best. Workers also should be involved in the goal-setting process and should be given timely, meaningful feedback on their performance.

KEY TERMS

Scientific Management, p. 335

Hawthorne Studies, p. 335

Motivation, p. 337

Extrinsic Reward, p. 337

Intrinsic Reward, p. 337

Punishment, p. 338

Needs Hierarchy, p. 339

Physiological Need, p. 339

Safety Need, p. 339

Social Need, p. 340

Esteem Need, p. 340

Self-Actualization Need, p. 340

Theory X, p. 341

Theory Y, p. 341

Theory Z, p. 343

Work Motivation Model, p. 345

Hygiene Factor, p. 345

Motivator, p. 346

Goal Setting, p. 349

Job Enrichment, p. 350

Quality of Work Life (QWL), p. 352

Behavior Modification, p. 353

Reinforcer, p. 354

Positive Reinforcer, p. 354

Negative Reinforcer, p. 354

QUESTIONS FOR DISCUSSION AND REVIEW

1. Can job enrichment be used by all managers? Why or why not?

2. Theory Z, like Theories X and Y, has not been proved scientifically. Why has Theory Z had an impact on management practices when it has not been scientifically verified?

3. Can the principles of goal setting be applied to nonwork settings such as school, family, or leisure activities? Explain.

4. Who on the management team would be responsible for implementing a quality of work life program?

5. Can the Hawthorne effect influence motivation negatively? Explain.

6. Why would behavior modification appeal to some managers?

7. What limitations of punishment should be considered before using it?

8. Could Herzberg's model of motivation be used to explain the motivational techniques used by teachers? Why or why not?

9. Do the principles of scientific management still apply to 1990 managerial situations? Explain.

10. How can managers improve their ability to motivate employees?

CASE 10.1
Pay for Performance: An Application

The merit pay increases people receive are the most specific information they are given as to how well they are performing. The motivating potential of a merit pay increase is especially important if employees equate pay with performance. A pay raise can be interpreted as a reward or as a punishment.

Managers never have enough raise money to go around. Someone is always left out or believes that the system is unfair. In this case, you will serve as a manager who has a raise pool of $14,000 and must grant raises to six subordinates, all of whom have worked less than one year in the firm. You are the sole decision maker. Write down how much each person would receive and explain your decisions.

B. Nostocke: Is having adjustment problems. Performance has become worse. Nostocke is always on time, is eager to please, and works hard. Tries to serve as a resource person for a poorly trained group. Complains often about the company and its policies.

Present salary $26,300. Raise: _____

Comments: _____

_____

A. Calero: Hard worker, good team player, has trouble correcting others. Has good background but lacks line management experience. Volunteers for tough projects.

Present salary $24,000. Raise: _____

Comments:_____

_____

C. Babcock: Wastes time and is a big spender. Careless in comments and style. Not willing to compromise. Loses temper occasionally. Is highly skilled but doesn't seem to want to be a part of a team. Likes to needle colleagues.

Present salary $22,000. Raise: _____

Comments: _____

_____

R. Cisneros: Has trouble communicating ideas and problems. Is likable, willing to learn. Needs some training in computer skills and also in preparation of business plans. Hard worker who puts in long hours and works in miserably hot, dirty working conditions.

Present salary $24,000. Raise: _____

Comments: _____

_____

P. Karsner: Lots of experience. Occasionally is a loafer and drags feet on projects not interested in. Creative, would like to be promoted as soon as possible. Has appeal to brighter and more skilled workers. Is not tolerant of unskilled workers.

Present salary $22,700. Raise: _____

Comments: _____

_____

J. Webber: Is one of the most competent managers ever hired. Knows how to manage people. Every project worked on has been a success. Has ability to influence people. Is a good listener and is self-motivated.

Present salary $25,400. Raise: _____

Comments: _____

_____

Questions for Discussion

1. Which person is the most difficult to judge in terms of allocating a merit-based raise?
2. What kind of information is provided here that gives some indication of the motivation level of these employees?
3. Should a manager discuss performance issues with the employee before making a raise decision? Explain.

CASE 10.2
The Motivation Crisis: Hitting the Wall

Many people have achieved great fame and fortune before turning 40. Mozart died five years before reaching 40. Alexander the Great conquered Asia Minor and died at 34. Steve Jobs (co-founder of Apple Computer) is just turning 35. When Jack Benny was in his 60s and 70s, he used to get laughs by claiming to be 39 instead of what he really was, say 74. Why did Benny pick 39?

Some consider 39 to be the last-gasp outpost of youth. In business, the goal to be president or the ambition to invent a world-renowned product may run smack into reality at 40. A 40-year-old often has a long history of work experience, including a few scars from failures.

Many 39-year-olds and even younger men and women have accomplished a lot. They may have been promoted every three or four years, and their compensation packages may be in six figures. They may also have realized that the corporate program or the management hierarchy is becoming narrow and that their opportunities are decreasing. The first 15 years in the work force are often

Adapted from "Hitting the Wall at 40," *Business Month*, September 1990, pp. 52–58.

years of advancement, recognition, autonomy, and high expectations. Motivational inspiration is all around. However, reality, burnout, fatigue, long hours, and travel are also common. By 40, motivational inspiration may be harder to find.

A few examples will highlight how self-motivation becomes a very serious concern for many people around 40 years old. Tim hit the wall at about 38 years old. He was a senior product manager at Borden's Consumer Products Division in Columbus, Ohio. He had always wanted to be president of a company. At 38 he realized that, at Borden, this wouldn't happen. His goals were being stalled. He left Borden and joined a manufacturing firm in Dayton. Today, at 44, as vice president for sales, marketing, and engineering applications for Freund Precision, he is happier and more realistic. He wants to be financially independent at 55, but he is not going to drive himself to exhaustion.

Juanita was a fast tracker when the birth of her son made her rethink her goals. The Princeton graduate had been only 34 when she stepped up to the top rung of the management ladder as president of telemarketing for Time-Life Libraries. At 36 she started to assess her life, the dizzying schedules and the frequent travel. She concluded that a person *can* have it all—but not all at the same time. By all, she meant success, power, money, recognition, time, energy, and influence. Juanita is now enjoying motherhood. When she wants to go back to managing, she will go back to work. She is confident, satisfied, and very aware of the costs and benefits of being a mother, wife, and management superstar.

About 4 million Americans turn 40 each year. Forty is the age at which reality, pyramid narrowing, and self-assessment become crucial. However, success can be measured in many ways. How a person copes depends on many things. Self-confidence, talent, resourcefulness, goals, and adaptability all count. People who love their work, have strong work ethics, and know themselves well will not be stymied by the ''40'' wall. The over-40 successes are the ones who, like Jack Benny, have a passion to accomplish, to achieve, and to be creative well into old age without feeling a day over 39.

Questions for Discussion

1. Can a person like Tim achieve a sense of self-actualization even though he hasn't achieved one of his major goals (becoming a president of a firm)? Explain.

2. What role does self-confidence play in terms of motivation for Juanita?

3. How did Tim and Juanita use self-assessment to their advantage in maintaining a strong degree of self-motivation?

4. What type of motivational self-assessment do you perform?

CHAPTER ELEVEN

MANAGING HUMAN RESOURCES

LEARNING OBJECTIVES

1. To define the term *human resource management (HRM)*.

2. To explain why human resource planning, recruiting, and selecting are important.

3. To describe job analysis, job descriptions, and job specifications.

4. To explain the role of the federal government in providing equal opportunities for employment to all Americans.

5. To discuss training and development programs for hourly and salaried employees.

6. To identify examples of direct and indirect compensation.

7. To discuss comparable worth.

Merck & Co., a pharmaceutical company based in Rahway, New Jersey, has been honored in *Fortune*'s 1990 annual survey as "America's Most-Admired Corporation." In terms of human resource decisions, Merck is tuned in

Courtesy of Merck & Co., Inc.

to people needs, demographic shifts, and the importance of human resources. The company has a 5- to 10-year strategic plan for human resources that identifies individual and organizational roles and needs. New hires at Merck are treated like first-class citizens. An atmosphere of sharing and trust is immediately established for the spouse and family of the new hiree. Merck also has a reputation

for recruitment from within. The firm wants to be viewed as providing a career opportunity instead of simply a job.

Merck aggressively pursues its affirmative action program; it has made significant progress in hiring and promoting females and minorities. Training for employees involved in affirmative action planning has become widespread.

In a people-oriented program called "Face to Face," employees meet with their bosses to discuss important work-related issues. Another Merck program offers daycare services for employees' children. Wellness programs are also available at no cost.

Merck's management has concluded that to be globally competitive, human resource issues, concerns, and problems must have top priority. (Today 20 percent of Merck's sales and profits come from Europe.)

To meet the challenges of managing human resource issues, managers must place human resources at the top of their priority list. The activities of the unit, department, or group that makes people its top priority are called human resource management (HRM). At Merck, this department works to put people's needs, feelings, and skills in the spotlight.[1]

The fundamental key to business survival is people who are skilled to perform jobs. Nevertheless most human resource issues and problems have played second fiddle to other business decisions. Financial, production, and marketing judgments are usually made first, before people-related decisions. This second-class status is changing fast, though, as people—workers and managers—are recognized as a delicate, scarce commodity.

As many as 90 percent of all jobs in American organizations will be candidates for change in the early part of the 21st century. The population and, thus, the work force are growing more slowly than at any time since the 1930s. The average age of the population and work force is rising, and the pool of young workers entering the labor market is shrinking. Minorities represent a larger share of new entrants into the labor market, and more women are entering the work force. These rapidly changing demographics mean that human resource experts are going to be asked to work harder and longer to solve problems. In business organizations of any size—large, medium, or small—human resources must be recruited, compensated, developed, and motivated. Small organizations typically cannot afford to have a separate HRM department that continually follows the progress of individuals and reviews the accomplishment of goals. Larger firms, such as Merck & Co., usually have an HRM department that can be a source of help to line managers. In large or small firms, with or without HRM departments, however, each manager is responsible for using the skills and talents of employees. And in either case, much of the work in recruitment, compensation, and performance appraisal must be finalized and implemented by managers.

In this chapter, we discuss the human resource management function's importance to business. We begin with human resource planning, recruitment, and selection. Laws governing recruitment and recruitment sources are discussed, as are drug and AIDS testing. We explain how a company arrives at a decision to hire a candidate for a job. In the section on training and development, we cover orientation, training, and management development, including performance appraisals. The next topic, compensation and benefits, includes direct and indirect compensation, individual and group incentives, comparable worth, benefits and services, and protection programs. The chapter concludes with a discussion of safe work environments.

THE WORK OF HRM

Human resource management (HRM) can be defined as the process of accomplishing organizational objectives by acquiring, retaining, terminating, developing, and properly using the human resources in an organization. Accomplishing objectives is a major focus of any form of management. Unless objectives are met, the organization ceases to exist.

The success of any HRM program requires the cooperation of managers, who must interpret and implement policies and procedures. Line managers must translate into action what an HRM department provides. Without man-

Human Resource Management (HRM)
The process of acquiring, retaining, terminating, developing, and properly using the human resources in an organization.

agerial support at the top, middle, and lower levels, HRM programs cannot succeed. Therefore, managers need to understand clearly how to mesh their responsibilities with those of the HRM department.

The human resource program at IBM serves the needs of the organization and facilitates the accomplishment of IBM's objectives. But this program would probably not be well suited for Apple or Compaq without modifications. Each company develops its own HRM program after considering such factors as size, type of skills needed, number of employees required, unionization, clients and customers, financial posture, and geographic location.

Acquiring skilled, talented, and motivated employees is an important part of HRM. The acquisition phase involves recruiting, screening, selecting, and properly placing personnel. Merck and other firms are finding that acquiring the talent needed to survive in the 21st century is becoming more difficult; talented candidates are in short supply. If qualified individuals regularly leave a company, then that company must continually seek new personnel. This costs money and is time-consuming. Thus retention of productive people has become a major objective.

The opposite of retention is, of course, termination, an unpleasant part of any manager's job. Employees occasionally must be terminated for breaking rules, for failing to perform adequately, and/or when job cutbacks occur. The procedures for such terminations are usually specified by an HRM staff expert or in a labor-management contract.

Developing human resources involves training, educating, appraising, and generally preparing personnel for present or future jobs. These activities are important for the employee's economic and psychological growth. Self-realization needs cannot be satisfied in an organization that does not have an efficient set of development activities.

The proper use of people involves understanding both individual and organizational needs so that the full potential of human resources can be employed. This aspect of personnel management suggests the importance of matching individuals over time to shifts in organizational and human needs. Figure 11.1 is an example of a human resource department in an organization large enough (usually over 1,000 employees) to have such a unit. In smaller firms, all the jobs shown in the figure are performed but usually by only one or two people. The objectives of HRM are to clarify the firm's human resource problems and develop solutions to them. HRM focuses on action, satisfying individual needs, and the future. The contribution of HRM to an organization's effectiveness is so important that managers must use the knowledge and skills of HRM specialists.

Preston Trucking of Preston, Maryland, exemplifies companies that emphasize human resource development. At Preston, people—human resources, not tractors, trailers, or management systems—are the most important assets. A quotation from German philosopher Goethe summarizes Preston's regard for people: "Treat people as though they were what they ought to be and you help them become what they are capable of being." This is the philosophy the firm attempts to instill in both managers and nonmanagers. In simple terms, Preston people—everyone who works for the company—are regarded as partners rather than adversaries.[2]

Sample of Human Resource Department   **FIGURE 11.1**

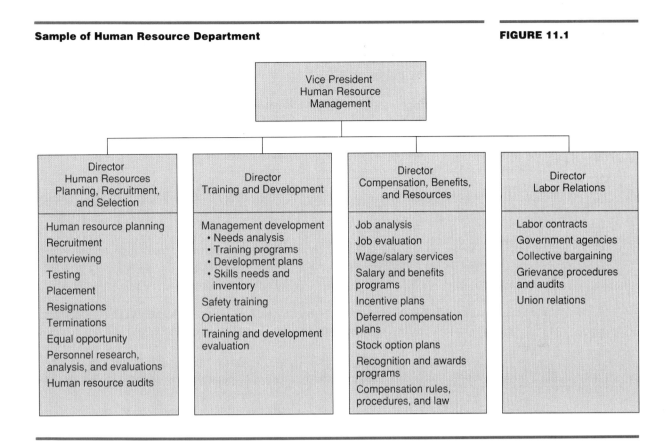

HUMAN RESOURCE PLANNING, RECRUITMENT, AND SELECTION

An organization can only be as effective as the people who operate the business. Thus, acquiring the people necessary to operate the business is the first step in any HRM program. This step is carried out by the employment division.

In conducting the activities of the employment division, managers throughout the organization need to establish human resource plans. Recruitment, selection, placement, and other employment actions stem from this planning.

Planning

Human resource planning involves estimating the size and makeup of the future work force. This process helps the firm acquire the right number and kinds of people when they are needed. Experience indicates that the longer the period predicted, the less accurate the prediction. Complicating factors include changes in economic conditions, in the labor supply, and in the political environment.

Human Resource Planning
The steps taken in estimating the size and makeup of the future work force.

Formal and informal approaches to human resource planning are used. For example, some organizations use mathematical projections. Data are collected on such topics as the supply of resources, labor market composition, demand for products, and competitive wage and salary programs. From these data and previous records, statistical procedures are used to make predictions. Of course, unforeseen events can alter past trends, but somewhat reliable forecasts can still be made.

Estimating from experience is a more informal forecasting procedure. Department managers may be asked for opinions about future human resource needs. Some managers are confident about planning, whereas others hesitate to offer an opinion or are just not reliable forecasters.

Consider the importance of human resource planning to a large firm such as Xerox, which employs over 100,000 people. Every day some new people begin jobs there, while others retire or leave for other jobs. This inflow and outflow is constant. Paying attention to inflow, outflow, future plans, and competitors is vital to the effective operation of Xerox Corporation.

A small firm such as Kent Electronics of Houston, Texas, also must pay attention to human resource planning. The firm employs about 300 people and plans to expand its sales by exporting to markets in Germany, Italy, Portugal, and Spain. The expansion means more employees must be hired.

Although the inflow and outflow at Kent is not as frequent or as large as that at Xerox, it still must be monitored. To have the right number and type of people in the right place at the right time, a firm must engage in human resource planning. By having a sound human resource planning system, a firm can translate its objectives and plans into the number of employees needed to do the job.

Recruitment

Recruitment
Steps taken to staff an organization with the best-qualified people.

Job Analysis
The process of determining the tasks that make up a job and the skills, abilities, and responsibilities needed to perform the job.

Job Description
A statement that furnishes information about a job's duties, technology, conditions, and hazards; based on data from job analysis.

Job Specification
A statement of the human qualifications needed to perform a job; derived from the job analysis.

Recruitment is an essential step in staffing. Virtually every company has to perform this function.[3] The primary objective of **recruitment** is to find and attract the best-qualified applicants to fill vacancies. However, before that can be done, those involved in the recruiting process must clearly understand the position to be filled. The methods and procedure used to acquire an understanding about jobs are called job analysis.

Job analysis is the process of determining the tasks that make up the job and the knowledge, skills, and abilities (KSAs) an employee needs to successfully accomplish the job. *Knowledge* relates to the body of information in a subject area that is needed to adequately perform a job (e.g., knowledge of Lotus® 1–2–3® spreadsheet; knowledge of joint venture loans in Canada). The terms *skills* and *abilities*, used interchangeably, describe observable capabilities to perform a learned behavior (e.g., operating a wood lathe).

From the data gathered through job analysis, job descriptions are generated. A **job description** outlines the activities involved in performing the work and the conditions under which the jobholder will work. A statement of the qualifications, education, and experience needed for a job is called a **job specification.** Both job descriptions and job specifications must be in written form.

An efficient job analysis program provides information used to make important decisions. For example, to recruit and select effectively, qualified personnel

FIGURE 11.2

Job Description of an HRM Manager

Job Title: Human Resource Manager   Department: HRM
                                                       Date: January 2, 1992

General Description of the Job

Performs responsible administrative work managing personnel activities of a large state
agency or institution. Work involves responsibility for the planning and administration of an
HRM program that includes recruitment, examination, selection, evaluation, appointment,
promotion, transfer, and recommended change of status of agency employees, and a system of
communication for disseminating necessary information to workers. Works under general
supervision, exercising initiative and independent judgment in the performance of assigned
tasks.

Job Activities

Participates in overall planning and policymaking to provide effective and uniform personnel
    services.
Communicates policy through organization levels by bulletins, meetings, and personal contact.
Interviews applicants, evaluates qualifications, and classifies applications.
Recruits and screens applicants to fill vacancies and reviews applications of qualified persons.
Confers with supervisors on personnel matters, including placement problems, retention or
    release of probationary employees, transfers, demotions, and dismissals of permanent
    employees.
Supervises administration of test.
Initiates personnel training activities and coordinates these activities with work of officials and
    supervisors.
Establishes effective service rating system, trains unit supervisors in making employee
    evaluations.
Maintains employee personnel files.
Supervises a group of employees directly and through subordinates.
Performs related work as assigned.

---

must be matched with job requirements. The job description and job specification provide full job information. Another example involves the establishment
of proper rates of pay. For equitable pay systems, complete job descriptions are
needed. A job description for an HRM manager appears in Figure 11.2.

Laws governing recruitment   Individuals responsible for recruiting must
comply with legal requirements. For example, a certain percentage of minority
group members and women must be recruited for positions that have seldom
been filled by minorities. These requirements are enforced by laws administered by the Equal Employment Opportunity Commission (EEOC), as Chapter
Four mentioned. Through Title VII of the **Civil Rights Act of 1964** and the
Equal Employment Opportunity Act of 1972, the federal government attempts
to provide equal opportunities for employment without regard to race, religion,
age, creed, sex, national origin, or disability. These laws have broad coverage
and apply to any activity, business, or industry in which labor disputes would

Civil Rights Act of 1964
An act that makes various
forms of discrimination illegal.
Title VII of the act spells out
the forms of illegal discrimination.

**Equal Employment
Opportunity Act of 1972**
A law that has specific provisions about equal opportunities for employment.

Leadership: Room for Men and Women at the Top.

Are women's leadership styles different from men's? Is the ideal leader a John Wayne-type character? Or is there room for Kay Unger, an owner of a women's clothing company in New York? We believe there is room for both the John Waynes and the Kay Ungers. Some believe that women are more consensus-building and less hierarchical or quasi military than men. We are not so sure that the best way to define leaders is to say that men are quasi military and that women are consensus builders.

As never before, the United States is witnessing the emergence of the female leader. It's happening most quickly in businesses started by women (more than 4 million of them). But the smart companies are not just woman-friendly; they are people-, talent-, and performance-friendly. Some women are suited to lead, and some men are suited to lead. Using the strengths and talents of men and women as individuals is what is needed. Leadership qualities should not be separated into male and female traits or characteristics.

The labor shortages facing the United States suggest that organizations will need increasingly more female leaders. What seems disturbing is that we are starting to label female leaders as consensus builders. A new stereotype is emerging based on labeling leaders as predominantly male or predominantly female. In a nation hungry for good leaders, it is unfortunate that gender is the issue and not performance, results, and respect.

Don't management styles develop out of personalities and life experience? This is a question that is going to be debated and studied more in the next decade. No matter what the answer, more women and minorities will be needed and will achieve leadership positions. When consumers say that they are looking for the best *person* for the job, it will mean that the "glass ceiling" has been penetrated. The best person may be a 72-year-old white male, a 36-year-old Hispanic woman, or a 29-year-old black man. This philosophy and practice would be tremendously encouraging. Too many talented women, minorities, and men have been bypassed or overlooked because of stereotyping. Americans do not need another form of stereotyping and discrimination.[4]

hinder commerce.[5] The laws also cover state and local governments, government agencies, and agencies of the District of Columbia.

Specific provisions of the Equal Employment Opportunity Act of 1972 include the following:

> It is unlawful for an employer to fail or to refuse to hire, or to discharge, any individual or otherwise to discriminate against any individual with respect to compensation, conditions, or privileges of employment because of race, color, religion, sex, age, or national origin. This applies to applicants for employment as well as current employees.
>
> Employers may not limit, segregate, or classify employees in such a way that would deprive them of employment opportunities because of race, color, age, religion, sex, or national origin.
>
> The EEOC has the power to file action in a federal district court if it is unable to eliminate alleged unlawful employment practices by the informal methods of conference, conciliation, and persuasion.
>
> Employment tests may be used if they can be proved to be related to the job or promotion sought by the individual. Tests should be validated for each company. No discriminatory statements may be included in any advertisements for job opportunities.

The EEOC first attempted to encourage employers to follow the guidelines of the law. Now the EEOC is more aggressive and asks employers to prepare **affirmative action programs.** This means the employer must spell out how the company plans to increase the number of minority and female employees. If EEOC investigators believe the distribution of employees reflects discriminatory hiring policies, they can propose adjustments. The employer may then state why these adjustments can or cannot be made.

Affirmative Action Program
A program in which an employer spells out plans to increase the number of minority and female employees.

Business Week (August 6, 1990) conducted a study that attempted to identify woman-friendly companies. They classified as pacesetters the firms making strides in hiring, promoting, and rewarding women; those firms showing good progress in making their firms woman-friendly were referred to as up-and-comers; finally, those firms making some progress were called late bloomers. *Business Week* used several criteria: number of women in key executive positions and on the board of directors, programs to help women advance, and programs to help with work and family issues. The Business Action emphasizes that some progress is being made in utilizing the knowledge, talent, and skills of women. Smart companies are finding places for a diversity of styles, men and women, and just plain hardworking employees.

The **Immigration Reform and Control Act (IRCA)** of 1986 places on employers a major responsibility for stopping the flow of illegal immigrants into the United States.[6] The employer must:

Immigration Reform and Control Act
A 1986 law that places on employers the major responsibility for stopping the flow of illegal immigrants into the United States.

1. Not recruit, hire, or continue to employ unauthorized aliens.
2. Verify the identity or work authorization of every new employee.
3. Not discriminate on the basis of citizenship or national origin.

The initial penalties for employers who violate the IRCA entail a cease-and-desist order along with a fine of $250–$2,000 for each unauthorized alien. Second violations result in a fine of $2,000–$5,000 per unauthorized alien. Additional violations can result in imprisonment for the employer. The IRCA requires every individual who is recruited and hired to provide acceptable documentation of his or her status.

**Americans with
Disabilities Act**
A comprehensive act, passed
in 1990, aimed at integrating
the disabled into the American work force.

An estimated 43 million Americans have some type of disability. Although many would like to work, they can't because of discrimination. In May 1990, the **Americans with Disabilities Act (ADA)** was passed.[7] This comprehensive antidiscrimination law aimed at integrating the disabled into the American work force. The ADA prohibits all employers, including privately owned businesses and local governments, from discriminating against disabled employees or job applicants when making selection decisions.

Typically, discrimination against disabled applicants takes the form of application forms and preemployment interviews that inquire into the existence of a disability rather than the ability to perform the required job activities. Title I of the ADA prohibits these and other practices that may prevent a disabled person from obtaining and maintaining employment.

To be in compliance with the ADA, business owners must make their premises accessible to the disabled by removing architectural and communication barriers. Any business undergoing renovation must give disabled persons access to rest rooms, telephone, water fountains, and altered areas. Businesses that fail to comply face civil penalties of as much as $50,000 for the first violation and $100,000 for subsequent violations. Also, a disabled person can obtain an injunction against the business. Additionally, courts can award monetary damages to disabled persons victimized by discrimination.

Recruitment sources   Internal sources of recruitment include present employees, friends of employees, former employees, and previous applicants. Firms such as Bristol-Myers, CBS, Borden, and Boise Cascade keep files on previous employment applicants. Even though these applicants were not hired, they often maintain an interest in working for a company with a good reputation

Staffing an organization with talented people is important. A recruitment fair for finding and attracting black M.B.A.s is set up in Philadelphia. Firms come to the fair prepared to recruit the M.B.A.s looking for jobs.

The Image Works

and image. By carefully screening these files, some good applicants can be added to the pool of candidates.

If needed human resources are not available within the company, outside sources must be tapped. New applicants can be found through advertisements in newspapers, trade journals, and magazines. Responses to ads come from both qualified and unqualified individuals. Occasionally a company will list a post office box number and not provide the company name. This is called a *blind advertisement*. (Such an ad appears in Figure 11.3.) Blind ads eliminate the need to contact every applicant, even the unqualified ones. However, a blind ad does not permit the company to use its name or logo, which is a form of promotion.

One important source for lower-level or entry-level (e.g., supervisors, management trainees) management recruits is the college campus. Many colleges and universities have placement centers that work with organizational recruiters. The applicants read advertisements and information provided by the companies and then are interviewed. The most promising students are invited to visit the company, where other interviews are conducted. The college recruit-

---

FIGURE 11.3

Blind Advertisement

The company is not identified in the ad. This means that the applicant is impressed with the job description and that the company can look at who applies without even acknowledging receipt of the inquiry.

TRAINING AND DEVELOPMENT MANAGER

A large profit-oriented company with headquarters in Houston is currently expanding its management development and training program. We seek a manager whose responsibilities will include the overall planning, development, and direction of the corporate training and development program. The qualified candidate for this position will report directly to the Vice President of Personnel Services.

The qualified candidate must have a Bachelor's degree with a minimum of 8 years directly related experience in training and development, with a demonstrated record of results in private industry. The individual must communicate effectively with different organizational levels to include working directly with high-level management and company officers.

Initial selection of qualified candidates will be based on detailed resume and any other material the candidate wishes to submit, along with salary history and salary requirements. For prompt confidential reply, send resume to:

Confidential Reply Service
Nationwide Advertising Service Inc.
Dept. 6-GC-28
5805 Richmond Ave.
Houston, TX 77057

Our client is an equal opportunity employer. M/F.

Nationwide Advertising Service, Inc. is a full-service recruitment advertising agency with 36 offices throughout the United States and Canada.

FIGURE 11.4

The College Recruiting Process

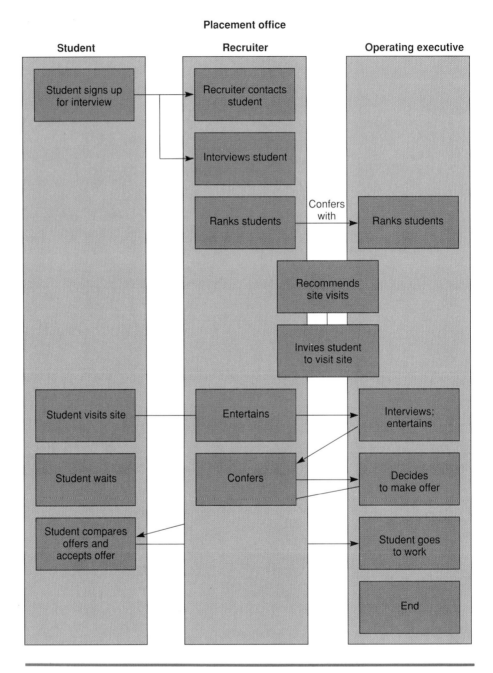

ing process is outlined in Figure 11.4. Applicants might be eliminated from further consideration after any step.

To locate experienced employees, organizations can use private employment agencies, executive search firms, or state employment agencies. Some are no-fee agencies, which means the employer rather than the applicant pays the fee (if there is one). An organization is not obligated to hire any person referred by an agency, but the agency is usually notified when an applicant is hired.

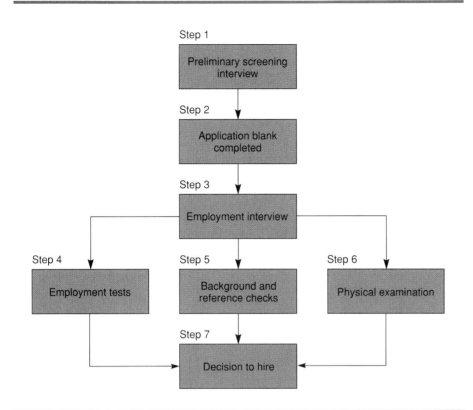

FIGURE 11.5

Typical Selection Decision Using All Possible Steps

Selection

The selection and placement of employees begin with a need for human resources but must comply with legal requirements. Discriminatory practices in recruiting, testing, and hiring are illegal, as stated in the Civil Rights Act of 1964 and the Equal Employment Opportunity Act of 1972.

The **selection** process is a series of steps that starts with the initial screening and ends with a decision to hire the person. Figure 11.5 is a flow diagram showing each step in the process. Preliminary interviews screen out unqualified applicants. This screening is often the first personal contact an applicant has with a company.

Applicants who pass the preliminary screening usually complete an application blank. The form asks for information that can be used in reaching an employment decision. Answers to the questions can even, in a general sense, *predict* job success. The appropriate questions are usually developed after a careful job analysis is completed. The application should provide all necessary information and yet be concise enough not to give a jumbled mass of unnecessary information.

Interviews occur throughout the selection process, but each includes three basic steps: (1) interviewers must acquaint themselves with the job analysis; (2) they must analyze the information on the application; (3) they need to ask questions that will add to information on the application. Every question must also be legal. Connections will help you determine what is and is not lawful.

Selection
A series of steps that starts with the initial screening and ends with a hiring decision.

● C o n n e c t i o n s

Do You Know What Questions Can Be Asked?

Directions: Here is a description from a preemployment interview guide. The description includes a number of unlawful inquiries made by the firm's interviewer. How many illegal inquiries can you find?

> Hi, my name is Jim. What is your name? Can you tell me a little about your background? Where were you born? We operate a very high-energy firm and like our employees to be well rested and ethical. Do you attend religious services? How frequently? We will need a complete record on your spouse. Are you married? Fine. Does your wife read and write English? Are you a citizen of the United States? Do you read or write English or any other language fluently? Have you or your wife ever been convicted of a homicide? We will need to have a name and address of a person to be notified in case of an accident. How is this person related to you? Have you ever collected workers' compensation for a previous work injury? Is there any illness that you have that may interfere with your job duties? Thank you for answering my questions.

Feedback: Well, our interviewer violated the Equal Employment Opportunity Act in several areas by making a number of unlawful inquiries. These questions should not and do not have to be answered.

Let's go through the unlawful inquiries. You should have found seven problem questions.

Japanese recruiters interviewing and selecting American workers for plants operated in the United States sometimes appear puzzled by the illegality of certain questions. For example, not asking a job applicant about his or her religion, upbringing, or home life is questioned by the Japanese. "How can you learn about the applicant?" the Japanese ask. The Japanese and any other foreign employer hiring in the United States will have to comply with the law or risk being sued.[8]

In interviews, the interviewer must be courteous, create a favorable atmosphere, and provide the applicant with information and a positive image of the organization. Interviewees acquire their first impression of a firm by observing the interviewer. First impressions are often recalled when job applicants finalize decisions about joining a particular firm.

Testing   For years selection tests have been widely used to screen applicants. Frequent use started with World War I, when the Army Alpha test was used to measure intelligence. Installing a sound testing program is costly and time-consuming, and it must be done by experts. Just because a test was useful for selecting sales personnel in one company does not mean it will be just as useful

1. *Where were you born?* After the person is employed, you can ask if he or she can show proof of U.S. citizenship. You cannot ask the birthplace of an applicant.

2. *Do you attend religious services?* Don't even inquire about any aspect of religion.

3. *How frequently?* (Attendance at religious services: see item 2.)

4. *Does your wife read or write English?* Ask the applicant about what he or she can read or write, but ask nothing about the spouse's ability.

5. *Have you or your wife ever been convicted of a homicide?* Unless the conviction is substantially related to the job responsibilities, you shouldn't ask the question.

6. *How is this person* [the outside person to notify in case of an accident or emergency] *related to you?* You can't ask about relationship.

7. *Have you ever collected workers' compensation for a previous work injury?* You can't ask this question.

How did you do? If you only found six or less of the unlawful inquiries, you need to brush up on the law. The EEOC compliance manual published by the Bureau of National Affairs in Washington, D.C., can help you conduct, and be a part of, the interviewing process legally.

in another. Table 11.1 (see page 378) presents the results of a study of 437 firms involved in making selection decisions. The study results indicate which procedures are often used (reference checks and unstructured interviews) and which procedures are not (personality tests and polygraph tests).

The advantages of a sound testing program include:

- *Improved accuracy in selecting employees.* Individuals differ in skills, intelligence, motivation, interests, and goals. If these differences can be measured and if they are related to job success, then performance can be predicted to some extent by test scores.

- *An objective means for judging.* Applicants answer the same questions under the same test conditions, so one applicant's score can be compared to the scores of other applicants.

- *Information for current employee needs.* Tests given to current employees can provide information about training, development, or counseling needs. Thus they can objectively uncover needs.

Despite these advantages, tests have become controversial in recent years. Important legal rulings and fair-employment codes have resulted in strict pro-

378

TABLE 11.1

Selection Procedures Used in Hiring and Promoting

Procedure	Companies Using* For Outside Applicants		For Candidates for Promotion	
Reference/record check	97%	(426)	67%	(292)
Unstructured interview	81	(355)	70	(305)
Skill performance test/work sample	75	(329)	40	(176)
Medical examination	52	(229)	8	(34)
Structured interview	47	(206)	32	(142)
Investigation by outside agency	26	(112)	3	(14)
Job knowledge test	22	(94)	15	(64)
Mental ability test	20	(89)	10	(44)
Weighted application blank	11	(49)	7	(30)
Personality test	9	(39)	4	(18)
Assessment center	6	(28)	7	(30)
Physical abilities test	6	(27)	4	(16)
Polygraph test/written honesty test	6	(27)	1	(4)
Other	3	(13)	2	(9)

*n = 437. Actual number using procedure is given in parentheses.

Source: Reprinted with permission from *Bulletin to Management (BNA Policy and Practice Series)*, ASPA-BNA Survey No. 45, Employee Selection Procedures, p. 2 (May 5, 1983). Copyright 1983 by the Bureau of National Affairs.

cedures for developing tests. The following criticisms have been directed at testing programs:

- *Tests are not infallible*. Tests may reveal what people *can* do but not what they *will* do.
- *Tests are given too much weight*. Tests cannot measure everything about a person. They can never be a complete substitute for good judgment.
- *Tests discriminate against minorities*. Ethnic minorities, such as blacks and Mexican-Americans, may score lower on certain paper-and-pencil tests than whites. Title VII of the Civil Rights Act of 1964 prohibits employment practices that artificially discriminate against individuals on the basis of test scores.

Drug testing   One highly controversial form of testing is drug testing. Based on a survey by the Senate Judiciary Committee, an estimated 2.2 million Americans are hooked on cocaine.[9] Substance abuse by employees costs the business community an estimated $160 billion per year and is responsible for productivity decreases, industrial accidents, absenteeism and tardiness, inflated health care costs, employee theft to support drug habits, and drug sales to other employees on company time.[10]

Criticisms of drug testing should be carefully weighed. The issue of accuracy is crucial. No drug-screening test can predict with 100 percent accuracy. Employees who fail a company's drug test may be given a second test. However, a job applicant usually has no second chance.

The issue of privacy also bears scrutiny. When a testee must provide a urine sample, someone from the company has to be present to ensure that no deceit occurs in "filling the bottle."

Thus drug testing is not an easy topic to discuss, defend, or reject. However, evidence suggests that it will increase as a method of selection. An increasing number of firms—including about 150 Fortune 500 companies—have begun testing recruits and current employees.[11] The growing list of firms that provide drug-testing services will probably attract even more businesses to the use of drug tests.

AIDS testing   The human costs of acquired immune deficiency syndrome (AIDS) are incalculable. For those who suffer from AIDS and for their families, the emotional toll is terribly high. For employers AIDS presents the specter of a major economic drain. Benefits paid out for an employee with AIDS typically exceed $100,000. The average expenditure per afflicted worker includes $47,702 for health care costs, $11,285 for long-term disability, and $44,363 for death benefits.

The spiraling costs of caring for AIDS patients require the immediate attention of employers and insurers. Since the law states that an employer cannot discharge or refuse to hire someone with AIDS, employers need to check their health, life, and disability insurance coverage. In many federal and state courts, AIDS sufferers have been extended the protection of laws for the handicapped. A handicap can be a reason for dismissal or refusal to hire only if it prevents the person from doing the job.[12]

AIDS victims are protected by the Rehabilitation Act of 1973. Section 504 of the act states:

> No otherwise qualified individual with handicaps . . . shall, solely by reason of his handicap, be excluded from the participation in . . . or be subjected to discrimination under the program or activity receiving federal financial assistance.

There are now over 171,876 confirmed cases of AIDS in the United States, with 151,000 to 225,000 new cases expected by the end of 1993.[13] Because AIDS is a major challenge and a serious problem, organizations are now establishing guidelines for dealing with it. Some of the guidelines found in policies at IBM, Johnson & Johnson, and Bank of America include:

- People with AIDS or who are infected with HIV, the AIDS-causing virus, are entitled to the same rights and opportunities as people with other serious illnesses.
- Employment policies should be based on the scientific evidence that people with AIDS or HIV infection do not pose a risk of transmitting the virus through ordinary workplace contact.
- Employers should provide workers with sensitive and up-to-date education about AIDS and risk reduction in their personal lives.
- Employers have the duty to protect the confidentiality of employees' medical information.

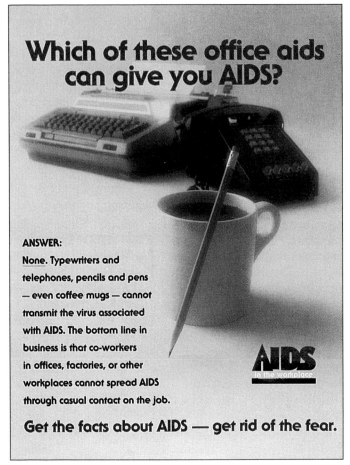

Courtesy of the Dartnell Corporation

Knowledge and information in the form of a policy document can be helpful in alleviating fear and correcting misinformation about AIDS. The devastation of AIDS is well documented. It is a disease caused by a virus that breaks down part of the body's immune system. A firm's policy can't help the body fight the disease, but it provides useful information to help employees understand that AIDS victims will be treated with human dignity and concern. This important message to those suffering from AIDS, as well as to their colleagues, says that the firm cares and wants to help.

Decision to Hire

After preliminary screening, evaluating the application, interviewing, and testing, the company may decide to make an offer. If so, a background check is usually made. The background check verifies information by consulting references. This information may be obtained by letter, by telephone, or in person. One important group of references is previous employers; the company tries to gather information about the applicant's previous job performance. Under the Fair Credit and Reporting Act, the prospective employer must secure the applicant's permission before checking references.

When the reference check yields favorable information, the line manager and an HRM representative meet to decide what the offer will be. The offer is usually made subject to successful completion of a physical examination, which can be conducted by a company physician or by a doctor outside the organization. The objective is to screen out people whose physical deficiencies might be expensive liabilities and to place people on jobs they are physically able to handle.

TRAINING AND DEVELOPMENT

Training and development programs include orientation activities that *inform* employees of policies and procedures, *educate* them in job skills, and *develop* them for future advancement. The importance of the training and development program to the organization cannot be overemphasized. Through recruitment and placement, good employees can be brought into the company. They then need continual education and development so that both their needs and the objectives of the firm can be achieved.

Orientation

Most large companies have a formal orientation program for new employees. Although new hires usually know something about the firm, they often lack specific information about working hours, pay, parking, rules, facilities, and so on. The HRM department usually coordinates the orientation, but the immediate supervisor is the key to the process. He or she and the new employee must eventually establish a cordial relationship that will encourage communication.

Training

Training is a continual process of helping employees perform at a high level. It begins on the person's first day at work. It may occur in the workplace or at a special training facility, but it should always be supervised by training experts.

Training
A continual process of helping employees to perform at a high level.

To be effective, a training program must accomplish a number of objectives. First, it must be based on both organizational and individual needs; training for training's sake is not the objective. Second, the objectives of training should spell out what problems will be solved. Third, all training should be based on sound theories of learning. This is the major reason why training and management development are not for amateurs. Finally, a training program must be evaluated to determine whether it is working.

Before a training program can be developed, problem areas must be pinpointed. Companies use a number of techniques to identify problems, including reviewing safety records, absenteeism data, job descriptions, and attitude surveys to see what employees think about their jobs, bosses, and the company.

Betty Gray, a marketing representative of USA Today, works in a training program with other USA Today employees. The team had one hour to devise a direct mail campaign for a potential client. Betty, Zygmunt Wozniak, and Pete Donohue are putting together their campaign.

Scott Maclay/Gannett Co., Inc.

Once training needs have been identified, objectives need to be stated in writing. They provide a framework for the program. Objectives need to be concise, accurate, meaningful, and challenging. There are usually two major categories of objectives—skills and knowledge. *Skill objectives* focus on developing physical abilities; *knowledge objectives* are concerned with understanding, attitudes, and concepts.

Various methods are available for reaching the skill and knowledge objectives. Such factors as cost, available time, number of persons to be trained, background of trainees, and skill of the trainees determine the method used. Some of the more widely used training methods are:

On-the-job training. A supervisor or other worker may show a new employee how to perform the job.

Vestibule training. This is training in a mock-up or facsimile of the actual work area.

Classroom training. Numerous classroom methods are used by business organizations. The lecture—a formal, organized presentation—is one method. A conference or small discussion group gets the student more involved than the lecture method. Interactive video (IAV) lecturing is becoming a popular technique. In IAV training, employees communicate with a computer to acquire knowledge and skills.

Management Development

Training is generally associated with operating, or nonmanagerial, employees; management development is associated with managerial personnel. **Management development** refers to the process of educating and developing selected personnel so that they have the knowledge, skills, attitudes, and understanding needed to manage in future positions. The process starts with the selection of a qualified individual and continues throughout that individual's career.

Management Development
The process of developing and educating selected personnel in the knowledge, skills, and attitudes needed to manage in future positions.

Companies use management development to ensure the long-run success of the organization, to furnish competent replacements, to create an efficient team that works well together, and to enable managers to reach their potential. Management development may also be needed because of high executive turnover, a shortage of management talent, and our society's emphasis on lifelong education and development.

Employees can acquire the knowledge, skills, attitudes, and understanding necessary to become successful managers through two types of programs: on-the-job training and formal development. On-the-job programs include:

Understudy programs. A person works as a subordinate partner with a boss, with the goal of eventually assuming the full responsibilities and duties of the job.

Job rotation. Managers are transferred from job to job on a systematic basis. Job assignments can last from two weeks (Caterpillar Tractor) to six months (General Electric).

Coaching. A supervisor teaches job knowledge and skills to a subordinate. The supervisor instructs, directs, corrects, and evaluates the subordinate.

On-the-job development programs emphasize actual job experience. They are designed to increase the employee's skill, knowledge, and confidence.

Formal management development programs are often conducted by training units within organizations or by consultants in universities and specialized training facilities around the country. In very large corporations, full-time training units conduct regular management development courses. For example, General Electric's Advanced Management Course, designed for the four highest levels of management, lasts 13 weeks. It covers business policy, economics, social issues, and management principles. Many smaller firms send managers to development programs at universities. Publicized and well-attended programs are found at the University of Michigan, Columbia University, Duke University, the University of Houston, and Indiana University.

Performance Appraisals

Training and development also involve performance appraisals. Managers use appraisal programs to communicate expectations and to help subordinates improve personal deficiencies. Most employees want to know how well they are performing, and appraisals provide a basis for reviewing their performance. Appraisals also give employees a chance to discuss their career plans with their supervisor.

Properly handled, formal performance appraisals can help supervisors and subordinates develop mutual trust, respect, and understanding. But to do that, managers must divorce performance appraisals from the review of salary.

TABLE 11.2

Typical Graphic Rating Scale

Name _____ Dept. _____ Date _____					
	Out-standing	Good	Satis-factory	Fair	Unsatis-factory
Quantity of work: volume of acceptable work under normal conditions Comments:	☐	☐	☐	☐	☐
Quality of work: thoroughness, neatness and accuracy of work Comments:	☐	☐	☐	☐	☐
Knowledge of job: clear understanding of the facts or factors pertinent to the job Comments:	☐	☐	☐	☐	☐
Personal qualities: personality, appearance, sociability, leadership, integrity Comments:	☐	☐	☐	☐	☐
Cooperation: ability and willingness to work with associates, supervisors, and subordinates toward common goals Comments:	☐	☐	☐	☐	☐
Dependability: conscientious, thorough, accurate, reliable with respect to attendance, lunch periods, reliefs, etc. Comments:	☐	☐	☐	☐	☐
Initiative: earnestness in seeking increased responsibilities. Self-starting, unafraid to proceed alone Comments:	☐	☐	☐	☐	☐

Perhaps the oldest performance appraisal technique is the graphic rating plan. Usually the supervisor is supplied with a printed form for each person to be rated and is asked to circle or check the phrase that best describes the individual on the particular trait. Table 11.2 shows a sample rating scale.

This type of scale is easy to use but has serious disadvantages. First, scoring is difficult. Second, it doesn't tell which traits are most important. For example, is quality more important than cooperation? Third, ratings usually cluster around the more positive statements. Finally, this system doesn't tell a manager how to help subordinates correct identified deficiencies.

The perfect system would be accurate, reliable, fair, informative, and designed for each key feature of a job. Furthermore, the supervisor and subordinate would know exactly what is expected in the job and that performance results are linked to preestablished criteria. Such a perfect system simply is not available. But the search has gone on for years.[14]

Pepsico has a dual performance appraisal system to evaluate managers (see the Business Action). Although other firms may not consider Pepsico's system ideal, the company is comfortable with making promotion and career opportunity decisions based on it.

COMPENSATION AND BENEFITS

In modern society, money is important both economically and psychologically. Without it a person can't buy necessary goods and services or those that make life more comfortable; also it is equated with status and recognition. Because money is so important, employees are quite sensitive about the amount of pay they receive and how it compares to what others in the company and in society are earning. Employees need to believe they are being compensated fairly for the time, effort, and results they provide the employer.

A compensation system has one objective: to create a system of rewards that is equitable to both employer and employee. The system must motivate the employee to work hard and accomplish goals. An employer views compensation in terms of cost effectiveness, fairness, and adequacy. An employee views compensation in terms of equity, security, motivation, and meaningfulness.

Compensation is direct or indirect. **Direct compensation** includes an employee's base pay (wages or salary) and performance-based pay (incentives). **Indirect compensation** consists of federally required and state-mandated protection programs, private protection programs, paid leave, and miscellaneous benefits. (We discuss protection programs and benefits later in the chapter.) The total (direct and indirect) compensation package is used to:

- Attract potential job applicants.
- Retain good employees.
- Motivate employees.
- Administer pay within legal regulations.
- Gain a competitive edge.

Many people take part in compensation decisions. Top management determines the total amount of the budget that goes to pay, the pay form to be used (wages versus incentive plans), and pay policies. The manager working with employees makes inputs into the pay decision. An HRM unit advises management (top and operating) on pay strategy, legal issues (regular pay, overtime pay), competition, and market conditions.

Wages

The most common system for compensating operating or nonmanagerial employees is **wages**, based on time increments or number of units produced. Blue-collar workers have traditionally been paid at an hourly or daily rate,

Direct Compensation
An employee's base pay and performance-based pay.

Indirect Compensation
Federally required and state-mandated protection programs, private protection programs, paid leave, and miscellaneous benefits.

Wages
Compensation based on time worked or number of units produced.

Performance Appraisal at Pepsico

There is no such thing as one ideal performance appraisal system. Pepsico has developed two distinct types of managerial performance appraisal; the company believes they are pretty good. Are these ideal?

The first appraisal is the annual performance review. A manager sits one-on-one with each subordinate to discuss results. Were sales targets in Des Moines met? Was the soap opera commercial effective? Were the four new district managers trained in the new reporting system? The review focuses on results—not effort, hopes, or dreams.

The second Pepsico appraisal system is called human resource planning (HRP). It focuses on the careers of Pepsico's 20,000 managers. The managers are placed in one of four groups. The bottom group is considered out of the running for promotions. The middle includes a group who need more time to develop and a group of those who are promotable when vacancies occur. The top group are the "fast trackers," the stars.

In HRP analysis and discussions, individuals from the HRM unit sit in to listen and present their views. The HRM participants learn firsthand where the firm is going and who is moving up. Thus HRM is in on the ground-level discussions about growth plans, profits, margins, and competition.

The Pepsico dual performance appraisal program is tough. Not everyone makes it through the system. Some managers are told that they do not have the skill, talent, or drive to make it up the promotion ladder. The company wants to be honest, timely, and in control. This type of company atmosphere and results-oriented system is not for everyone. Pepsico rewards results, risk-taking, and dedication. It seeks to promote those who can withstand the pressure. To all its employees, Pepsico also provides annual options equal to 10 percent of their compensation, including bonuses and overtime for the previous fiscal year.

Pepsico believes its fringe benefits for those who make it up the ladder are excellent. The top 550 Pepsico managers travel by air first class, stay in luxury hotels on the road, receive a company car every two years or $11,000 a year, and receive an annual bonus of 25 percent to 90 percent of their salaries. If you are good and are able to show good results in the performance appraisal system, Pepsico may be the place to work.[15]

The textile workers at Levi Strauss & Co. are paid on an individual incentive basis. They receive compensation based on the number of pieces they sew in a regular eight-hour shift.

Oscar Williams/Journalism Services

although some are now being paid biweekly or monthly. Hewlett-Packard has eliminated the daily rate of pay and now considers all personnel at all levels to be salaried employees—paid by the week or some longer time period.

Individual incentives The oldest form of compensation is the individual incentive plan, which by definition pays for performance. Individual incentive plans take several forms: piecework, production bonuses, and commissions.

Straight *piecework* means the employee is paid a certain rate for each piece produced, with no other form of compensation. A modified piecework plan works like this. The employer guarantees the employee an hourly rate for performing the expected minimum output. For production over the standard (set through work measurement studies), the employer pays so much per extra piece produced. For example, suppose the hourly rate is $5.00 and the standard of production is 10 units per hour. Management determines that paying $.50 per unit produced above the standard level is fair. Thus an employee who produces 15 units per hour (rather than the standard 10 units) would earn $2.50 more per hour, or a total of $7.50 per hour ($5.00 hourly rate + $2.50 incentive for being above standard).

Production bonus systems pay an hourly rate. A bonus—something extra—is paid when the employee, or the total output, exceeds the standard. Ruth Manufacturing Co. in Janesville, Wisconsin, has a popular bonus system. Every Friday workers get a bonus added to their paychecks.[16] The bonus is based on how much stainless-steel tubing they shipped the previous week. During the past year, an extra $1.56 an hour was tacked onto their average $10.37 hourly wage. At Ruth, the employees work together and have high morale because they like the firm and certainly appreciate their bonus.

Du Pont's fibers department in Wilmington, Delaware, has implemented a program in which employees receive lower than usual merit increases. In exchange for accepting lower salaries and wages, they have the opportunity to earn bonuses as high as 18 percent of their salaries. The bonus is based on outstanding performance as measured by quantitative results.[17]

Sales employees often receive *commissions*. A commission is payment tied directly to performance standards. Straight commission, the equivalent of straight piecework, is typically a percentage of net sales.

Group incentives   To provide broader motivation than that furnished by individual incentive plans, several group-based approaches are used. Their aim is to increase productivity and improve morale. Group incentive plans give each group member a chance to receive a bonus based on the output or performance of the group.

Scanlon plans   A combination group incentive, suggestion, and employee participation arrangement, the Scanlon plan, has been popular in small and medium-sized manufacturing firms.[18] Such plans require management and employee involvement, interaction, and cooperation. In a Scanlon plan, named after its designer, Joseph Scanlon, each department of the firm has a production committee. Members include the supervisor and employee representatives elected by co-workers or appointed by the union. The committee receives and reviews employees' and managers' suggestions for improving work practices and procedures. The number of suggestions in a Scanlon plan company is usually double the typical suggestion-plan rate.

A Scanlon plan formula is used to calculate productivity gains resulting from the suggestions. Workers typically receive about 75 percent of the cost savings from improvements resulting from the suggestions, while the remainder goes to the firm. The savings are distributed to employees based on their wage levels.

Profit-sharing plans   The Gallatin glassworks factory in New Geneva, Pennsylvania, used the first recorded profit-sharing plan in 1794. Today over 430,000 such plans are used by American businesses.[19] In profit sharing, an employer pays or makes available to regular employees special current or deferred sums based on profits earned in addition to their regular pay. There are three types of profit-sharing plans:

- *Case, or current, payment*. Profits are immediately distributed quarterly or annually.
- *Deferred*. A portion of profits is credited to employee accounts, with payment made at the time of retirement, disability, or severance (when an employee leaves the company). This is the most popular plan because of the tax advantages of deferring income.
- *Combined*. This plan incorporates features of the current payment and deferred plans.

In the United States, profit sharing is the most common method firms use to provide retirement income for their employees. Advocates contend that the plans encourage better performance by employees. However, profit sharing has some potential problems. What does management do in down years, when there are no profits? Even though employees have worked hard, an ineffective advertising program or a new product from a competitor may wipe out any profits. After several difficult and lean years, employees may begin to wonder whether hard work is worth the effort. Even in good years, it is often difficult to see how hard work is significant to profits received a year away or, worse, at retirement many years later.

Lincoln Electric plan   The majority of group incentive plans are customized to fit a particular organization. The most publicized and successful has been the Lincoln Electric plan. Lincoln Electric employees are rewarded for good performance. At Lincoln Electric, all jobs are compensated on the bonus system. The year-end bonus is intended as a sharing of the results of efficient operation based on each individual's initiative, quality, and teamwork. Lincoln has used this effective merit-rating system since 1934.[20] Needless to say, Lincoln Electric jobs are in great demand.

Wage determination   In many organizations, the relative worth of a job and the wage adjustments for it are determined by using **job evaluation systems** in which a job is compared with others within the organization. Under the ranking method, all jobs are ranked from highest to lowest on the basis of skill, difficulty, working conditions, and importance to the success of the organization. The work attitudes or personalities of the current jobholders often distort rankings. In most cases, unions are not enthusiastic about job evaluation. With such a system, the union negotiator has almost no role to play.

Job Evaluation System
A process by which the relative values of jobs within the organization are determined.

Unions generally prefer the daily rate of pay over systems that involve piecework or incentive payments. Because time standards and records of the employee's output are not needed, a daily rate of pay is easier to understand and use than are piece rates, bonuses, or commissions. Unions also believe that a piecework system reduces the group orientation, the need for union solidarity; a worker paid on the basis of individual effort can produce at any level he or she wants to. Unions prefer to encourage group solidarity and a united front.

Many factors help determine the wage rate for a nonmanagerial job. Wages for certain jobs are affected by the supply of and demand for qualified personnel, although unions and the government may hinder these effects. Unions, for example, using strike threats and contract agreements, can prevent employers from lowering wage rates even when qualified personnel abound.

Existing wage rates in competing companies or in the community also influence wage determination. Organizations typically conduct wage surveys to assess hourly rates, piecework or other incentive rates, and fringe benefits offered by other organizations. If the wage rates of a firm are too low, it may be difficult to attract qualified personnel.

Wage and salary administration, like other areas of HRM management, has been the target of various laws. For instance, full-time employees must be paid at least $3.35 per hour. Since the first minimum wage law was enacted in 1938, the rate has risen over 1,000 percent, from $.25 to $3.35 as of January 1, 1981. In 1990 the minimum wage was increased to $3.80 for experienced workers and $3.30 for employees in training.[21] In addition the Fair Labor Standards Act of 1938 forbids the employment of minors between 16 and 18 years of age in such hazardous occupations as coal mining, logging, and woodworking. And the Equal Pay Act of 1963 forbids employers to pay employees differently on the basis of sex.

Until recently, female iron-workers, the "sky-walkers" of construction, would be difficult to find. This female iron-worker is sent out from the union hall and is paid a wage comparable to that paid to men.

Maxwell MacKenzie/TSW

Comparable Worth
The concept of equal pay for jobs that require similar levels of skills, training, and experience.

Comparable worth   In 1991 American women working full-time earned only about 65 percent of what men earn.[22] In an effort to close this earnings gap, a growing movement has worked to have the widely accepted concept of equal pay for equal jobs expanded to include equal pay for comparable jobs. The issue is known as **comparable worth**. In *Gunther* v. *Washington*, the Supreme Court ruled five to four that a sex discrimination suit can be brought under the 1964 Civil Rights Act on the basis of "equal or substantially equal work."[23] In that case, male prison guards received significantly higher pay than female prison guards doing similar work. The county had evaluated the male prison guard's jobs and found them to have 5 percent more job content than the female jobs. However, the males were paid 35 percent more.

Using comparable worth principles requires a sound job evaluation system, regular comparison of pay across jobs, and a documented pay system. A job evaluation point system is widely used. It requires the evaluator to quantify the value of the elements of a job. For example, job knowledge may receive 20 points, quality of work 30 points, and so forth. The points are then added up and are used to rank jobs.

Comparable worth is likely to continue to be controversial because job evaluation is not a perfectly valid technique; also the labor market must always be considered, in terms of supply and demand. Suppose the jobs of electrician (male-dominated field) and librarian (female-dominated field) are evaluated to be comparable. Should there still be a pay differential because of labor market conditions? Nurses and pastry chefs or electricians and librarians may not seem to know much in common. But because of the law and legal precedent, firms have to compare diverse jobs.[24] Table 11.3 shows differences in pay for jobs that have received similar job evaluation scores. How do you think the pay system should be applied?

TABLE 11.3

Inequalities in Point-to-Dollar Relationships

Location and Job Title	Monthly Salary	Difference	Number of Points
A. Pay Inequality in Relation to Job Evaluation Points			
Minnesota			
Registered nurse (F)	$1,723	$537	275
Vocational education teacher (M)	2,260		275
San Jose, California			
Senior legal secretary (F)	665	375	226
Senior carpenter (M)	1,040		226
Senior librarian (F)	898	221	493
Senior chemist (M)	1,119		493
Washington State			
Administrative services manager A (F)	1,211	500	506
Systems analyst III (M)	1,711		426
Dental assistant I (F)	608	208	120
Stockroom attendant II (M)	816		120
Food service worker (F)	637	332	93
Truck driver (M)	969		94
B. Job Evaluation Points Inequality in Relation to Pay			
Minnesota			
Health program representative (F)	$1,590	82 points	238
Steam boiler attendant (M)	1,611		156
Data processing coordinator (F)	1,423	65	199
General repair work (M)	1,564		134
San Jose, California			
Librarian I (F)	750	104	228
Street sweeper operator (M)	758		124

Note: F = Female; M = Male.

Source: Ronnie J. Steinberg, "Identifying Wage Discrimination and Implementing Pay Equity Adjustments," in *Comparable Worth: Issue for the 80's*, vol. 1 (Washington, D.C.: U.S. Commission on Civil Rights, 1985).

DID YOU KNOW? *The number of points earned for the job may be the same, but the monthly salary is different. How can this be explained?*

Salaries

Employees compensated on a weekly or longer schedule are paid **salaries.** Salaried employees are assumed to be able to influence the way they perform their jobs more than can employees who are paid wages. But the approach to developing an equitable compensation system for executives is similar to that for hourly workers. Companies make comparisons, conduct surveys, and analyze supply and demand, job duties, and job responsibilities.

Hay Associates developed one method specifically for evaluating middle- and top-management positions. First, analysts evaluate each position from information provided in the job description. They consider three factors: job know-how, problem solving, and accountability. Then, through a statistical procedure, they convert evaluations for the jobs in a particular company to the Hay control standards, a special ranking system. Hay Associates publishes annual surveys showing the compensation practices of a number of companies for jobs of similar control standards. All Hay clients use the same evaluation method, so they can compare management salaries.

Salaries
Compensation based on a longer time period—a week, a month, or longer.

Benefits and Services

Benefits
Forms of indirect compensation that are financial in nature.

Services
Forms of indirect compensation that are programs supplied by employers for employees' use.

Benefits and services are forms of indirect compensation. They are monetary and nonmonetary payments over and above wage and salary rates. **Benefits** are financial in nature (e.g., health insurance payment, contributions to a pension fund), whereas **services** are employer-supplied programs, facilities, or activities (e.g., parks, gymnasiums, housing, transportation, child care, company cafeterias) useful to employees.

To yield a return to the employer and provide something positive to employees, benefits and services must be developed and used systematically. Too often, the so-called benefits are improperly installed. The company must first determine what benefits and services employees prefer and what resources are available and then select the best package the company can afford. In developing a benefit and service package, the employer must consider two important Internal Revenue Service issues:

- Passed in 1985, the Consolidated Omnibus Budget Reconciliation Act (COBRA) ensures that terminated or laid-off employees have the option to maintain health care insurance by personally paying the premiums.
- The Tax Reform Act of 1986 has two provisions that affect indirect compensation. Essentially it caps at $7,313 the amount of tax-exempt deferred contributions (to be paid out at a later date) employees can make into a deferred pay plan. Also the average benefits to employees not highly compensated must be at least 75 percent of the average benefits provided to highly compensated employees (top 20 percent).

The benefits and services offered to employees are significant. The average firm pays between 30 and 50 percent of its payroll to benefits. A breakdown of this payment appears in Table 11.4. Indirect compensation tends to be greater on average in the manufacturing industries than it is in the nonmanufacturing industries and greater for blue-collar than it is for white-collar and service workers.

Linda Taylor, six months pregnant, talks to her Pepsico benefits specialist on a weekly basis. She is manager of a Pepsico-owned Pizza Hut restaurant. Pepsi has a flexible benefits plan that permits employees to select benefits from a menu, or list.[25] The flexible program is based on a $1,500–$3,500 subsidy that Pepsico employees have. The amount is based on age, dependents, and length of service.

The company's prenatal specialist, a benefit Linda selected, asks her not to smoke. He also asks whether Linda knows that smoking could be harmful to the baby. He sends her some pamphlets about smoking and pregnancy. Pepsico believes that the benefit menu and services promoting education will lower the firm's benefit expenses for its 92,000 employees.

Protection Programs
Programs that assist employees and families when direct compensation is terminated and with health care expenses.

Protection programs   **Protection programs** are designed to assist employees and their families if direct compensation is terminated and to alleviate the burden of health care expenses. Public protection programs grew out of the Social Security Act of 1935. They include social security benefits, unemployment compensation, and workers' compensation.

Funding of the *social security* system is provided by equal contributions from the employer and employee under terms of the Federal Insurance Contribution Act (FICA). The average social security benefit per year for a single person is $6,444 (for a married couple, $11,052), with adjustments periodically for increases in the consumer price index.

TABLE 11.4

Employee Benefits as a Percentage of Payroll by Type of Benefit

Type of Benefit	Overall	Manu-facturing	Nonmanu-facturing
1. *Legally required payments* Social security Unemployment compensation Workers' compensation	8.9%	8.7%	9.0%
2. *Retirement and savings plan payments* Defined pension plan Defined contribution plan	6.7	7.2	6.3
3. *Life insurance and death benefits*	.5	.5	.5
4. *Medical benefits* Hospital, medical premiums Short-term disability Long-term disability Dental insurance	8.3	10.2	6.7
5. *Paid rest periods* Lunch breaks Wash-up time Travel time	3.4	3.3	3.4
6. *Payment for time not worked* Vacation Holidays Sick leave Parental leave	10.2	10.2	10.1
7. *Miscellaneous benefits* Discount on goods and services Employee meals Education expenses	1.3	1.9	.8
Total benefits	39.3	42.0	36.8

Source: Reprinted with permission from *Bulletin to Management (BNA Policy and Practice Series)*, Vol. 39, No. 5 Datagraph, p. 37 (February 4, 1988). Published by The Bureau of National Affairs, Inc.

The Social Security Act dictates that *unemployment compensation* (given when a person loses a job) be jointly administered by the federal and state governments. Because income levels vary from state to state, unemployment compensation also varies by state. With the exception of Alabama, Alaska, and New Jersey, only employers contribute to the unemployment fund. All profit-making firms pay tax on the first $7,000 to $10,000 of wages earned by each employee. Their contribution rate, however, varies based on the number of unemployed people drawing from the fund.

To be eligible for unemployment compensation benefits, a person must:

- Have worked a set number of weeks (established by the state).
- Be available and ready to work.
- Be actively searching for a job.
- Not be unemployed due to a labor dispute (except in New York and Rhode Island).
- Not have been terminated for gross misconduct.
- Not have terminated voluntarily.

The time period that the employee receives benefits is a function of how long the person worked prior to termination; in general the standard maximum period is 26 weeks. Benefits can be extended up to 13 weeks during periods of high unemployment or when jobs are lost due to foreign competition. The benefits vary across states but are around $225 per week.

Workers' compensation benefits are provided for temporary and permanent disability, disfigurement, medical expenses, and medical rehabilitation. Several benefits, the terms of which vary by state, are provided following fatal injuries.

Private protection programs are provided by firms but are not required by law. They include such benefits as health care, income after retirement, insurance against loss of life or limb, and, in some firms, guaranteed work and pay programs.

Another category of indirect compensation includes programs for elder care, child care, and employee services. The U.S. population 80 years old and older is expected to grow from 5 million in 1980 to over 23 million in 2040. The Traveler's Company in Hartford, Connecticut, has established an *elder care* program to help employees with the cost of care for aging parents or dependents. Travelers has established a flexible spending account, which allows employees to deduct up to $5,000 per year in pretax dollars from their paycheck. This money can be used to cover costs of the necessary care.[26]

Until recently America's work force was largely composed of traditional family heads—the husbands who work as the employed breadwinner. Increasingly both spouses are working for pay; dual-career couples now account for over 40 percent of the work force. One problem faced by dual-career couples

Hiring and retaining the top talent means that child care must be addressed by organizations. Susan Kramer, Ph.D., picks up her daughter Kelly at Genentech's new child-care center. Genentech has concluded that child care is so important that it has built one of the most comprehensive centers of its kind in the United States.

Courtesy of Genentech, Inc.

is *child care*. Organizations, now aware of the child-care problem, address it in a number of ways. Over 3,000 firms provide day-care services, financial assistance, or referral services for child care. A growing number of firms have on-site or near-site centers.[27] Other firms allow flexible work schedules; employees can use the time to care for sick children or for special child activities (e.g., dentist appointments or meetings with school counselors). Some observers claim that the key fringe benefit of the 1990s will be child care.

Golden parachutes   One executive-level benefit is called the **golden parachute.** It provides financial protection in the event the company's ownership changes. It can be in the form of either guaranteed employment or severance pay on termination or resignation. Because mergers or acquisitions can sometimes help companies and shareholders, the parachutes were initiated to help reduce top-management resistance to takeover attempts.

Some organizations have what is referred to as **golden handcuffs**. This benefit program makes it too costly for an executive to leave an organization. The stock options and the retirement packages (or portions of them) are forfeited if a person leaves before a certain time period or age.

> **Golden Parachute**
> An executive termination package that guarantees employment or severance pay even when another firm takes over.

> **Golden Handcuffs**
> A benefit program that makes it too costly for an executive to leave a company, because of benefits that would be forfeited.

WORKPLACE SAFETY

Another important benefit for any person is a safe work environment, as discussed in Chapter Four. The December 1984 disaster in Bhopal, India, which resulted in the deaths of 3,000 people and injury to another 300,000, emphasizes the importance of safety. Americans are also familiar with the nuclear accident at Three Mile Island (1979) and the 1986 space shuttle *Challenger* disaster. Such incidents emphasize that safe equipment, practices, and procedures are crucial benefits. Annually over 1.8 million American workers suffer crippling injuries, and over 6,000 are killed on the job.[28]

Due to the efforts of unions, employees, the government, insurance companies, and society in general, the **Occupational Safety and Health Act (OSHA)** became law on April 28, 1970. The act directs the secretary of labor to enforce safety and health standards in over 4 million businesses and for over 57 million employees. The core of the act is the system of standards that must be met. For example, OSHA has set an industrial noise limit of 90 decibels where workers are exposed eight hours per day. OSHA puts special emphasis on improving safety in the five industries with injury rates more than double the national average, which is 15.2 disabling injuries per million employee-hours worked. These industries are longshoring (69.9 injuries per million employee-hours), meat and meat products (43.1), roofing and sheet metal (43.0), lumber and wood products (34.1), and miscellaneous transportation equipment (33.3).[29]

OSHA enforces standards through a system of inspectors, citations, and penalties. To inspect health and safety conditions, Labor Department representatives may enter any business at a reasonable time. (OSHA inspectors denied entry must obtain a search warrant before conducting an inspection.) They may also question the employer, employees, or employee representatives. Criminal penalties for violations can go as high as $20,000 and/or one year in prison. Four categories of violations may result from an inspector's visit:

> **OSHA**
> Acronym both for the Occupational Health and Safety Act of 1970, which mandates safety and health standards for U.S. businesses, and for the agency that administers the law.

Coal mining is still a dangerous business, even with OSHA codes and regulations. This miner is working in a narrow coal seam, busting off coal that will be collected, placed on a conveyor, and sent to the surface. How would you like to be a coal miner?

Mike Abrams/TSW

De minimis—a minor violation not directly job related.

Nonserious—a minor violation that is job related; can result in a penalty up to $1,000.

Serious—one in which a chance of serious injury or death exists; can result in a penalty of over $1,000.

Imminent danger—one that threatens serious injury or death; penalty is assessed by the federal courts.

This chapter emphasizes the importance of people and people-related issues. Increasingly organizations such as Federal Express, Liz Claiborne, American Brands, Dreyer's, and 3M are indicating that managing human resources is now mandatory in business. The recruitment, selection, development, health, and safety of employees are all part of the strategic plans of more and more organizations. Kathryn Conners, vice president of human resources at Liz Claiborne, captured the importance of people in doing business:

> Human resources is part of the strategic planning process. It's part of policy development, live extension planning, and the merger and acquisition process.[30]

Little can be done in any organization without a motivated work force. The people doing the work, carrying out the plans, meeting the customer, finalizing the sale, working on a project theme, reviewing the purchase order, and training the recently hired engineer must be motivated. Thus, understanding people is a requirement for developing programs to encourage and sustain employee motivation, which will be covered in the next chapter.

You'll Know It's the **Century When . . .**

•Parents No Longer Dream of Better Lives for Their Children

In 2000, most new jobs will require schooling beyond high school. This will drive unemployment rates up among less educated workers, and low-income parents will find themselves unable to send their children to college. If there is no attempt to stop current trends, half of all children born in New York City this year will be on welfare by 2010. Other big cities will face the same problem. Businesses will have to work harder than ever to recruit skilled employees and to retain customers.[31]

SUMMARY OF LEARNING OBJECTIVES

1. To define the term *human resource management*.
   Human resource management (HRM) is the process of accomplishing organizational objectives by acquiring, retaining, terminating, developing, and properly using the human resources (people) in an organization.

2. To explain why human resource planning, recruiting, and selecting are important.
   Planning is an important activity that involves estimating the size and makeup of the future work force. Planning of human resources is the lifeblood of the firm. Without the right people in the right place at the right time, the firm could go out of business. Recruiting is important because the best-qualified applicants must be found to fill vacancies. The company wants to have the best possible pool of applicants from which to choose. Selecting is the series of steps beginning with initial screening of candidates and ending with the decision to hire one candidate. Selecting must be done in compliance with federal laws regulating employment discrimination.

3. To describe job analysis, job descriptions, and job specifications.
   Job analysis is the process of determining what knowledge, skills, and abilities (KSAs) an employee needs to successfully accomplish the job. Job descriptions use the data gathered from job analysis to outline the activities involved in the job and the work conditions. Job specifications state the qualifications necessary for a job.

4. To explain the role of the federal government in providing equal opportunities for employment to all Americans.
   Through Title VII of the Civil Rights Act of 1964 and the Equal Employment Opportunity Act of 1972, the federal government attempts to provide equal opportunities for employment without regard to race, religion, age, creed, sex, national origin, or disability. These laws are administered by the Equal Employment Opportunity Commission (EEOC). In addition, the Immigration Reform and Control Act of 1986 (IRCA) has made employers responsible for prohibiting the recruitment and employment of unauthorized foreign-born individuals.

5. To discuss training and development programs for hourly and salaried employees.

   Training programs inform hourly employees of company policies and procedures, educate them in job skills, and develop them for future advancement. Management development programs for salaried employees are used to educate and develop selected personnel so that they have the knowledge, skills, attitudes, and understanding needed to manage in future positions.

6. To identify examples of direct and indirect compensation.

   Direct compensation includes an employee's base pay (salary or wages) and performance-based pay (incentives). Wages are compensation based on time increments or number of units produced. Salaries are compensation based on a weekly or longer schedule. Individual incentives include piecework, production bonuses, and commissions. Examples of group incentives include Scanlon plans, profit-sharing plans, and the Lincoln Electric plan. Indirect compensation includes federal- and state-mandated protection programs, private protection programs, paid leave, and miscellaneous benefits. Benefits are financial in nature (e.g., insurance programs), and services are employer-supplied programs, facilities, or activities useful to employees (e.g., child-care services). Public protection programs include social security benefits, unemployment compensation, and workers' compensation. Private protection programs include health care benefits, income after retirement, insurance, and guaranteed work and pay programs (e.g., golden parachutes).

7. To discuss comparable worth.

   The concept of comparable worth is an expansion of the concept of equal pay for equal work. This has become an issue because American women working full-time earn only about 65 percent of what men earn. The idea is to rank occupations typically held by men and those typically held by women, and then assign the same pay for jobs with the same rank. Comparable worth is controversial, and its principles are difficult to practice.

KEY TERMS

QUESTIONS FOR DISCUSSION AND REVIEW

1. What is the argument against drug testing used by those who claim that it is an invasion of privacy? Do you agree? Why or why not?

2. Why is it impossible to find the ideal or perfect performance appraisal system?

3. What activities does a human resource management department conduct in a business firm?

4. How have affirmative action programs influenced recruitment programs of businesses?

5. Why is it important to develop an accurate and reliable job analysis program?

6. Explain the difference between direct and indirect compensation plans.

7. Why would a pay-for-performance plan such as the Scanlon plan or the Lincoln Electric plan be attractive to employees?

8. Before developing a training program, what should an organization do to identify problems?

9. What is the responsibility of the employer with regard to the Immigration Reform and Control Act of 1986?

10. Should safety in the workplace be classified as a benefit? Why or why not?

Cases

CASE 11.1
You're Darned If You Do and Darned If You Don't

Sally Yuen, director of HRM for Dough Pineapple's Maui cannery, returned to her office deep in thought. She'd just spent the last hour and a half in a lengthy and somewhat heated discussion with cannery manager Danny Sackos regarding the latest turnover crisis among cannery employees. Shrugging her shoulders, Sally wondered if Sackos was right. Maybe the current turnover problem was her fault—well, the fault of her department anyway. According to Sackos, if she'd done a better job in selecting employees in the first place, Dough Pineapple (DP) would not be in the current mess. "You hired quitters," he argued, pointing to the high turnover among temporary *and* permanent full-time employees. But then Sally questioned whether it really was her fault.

DP maintained a regular work force of 200 employees. Depending on the harvest, as many as 150 temporary employees were also hired. Temporary workers received higher base salaries than regular employees ($6.25 per hour). However, they were not eligible for any benefits, including vacation leave, day care, and sick leave. If they were sick, they had to take time off without pay. They also could not participate in DP's highly successful profit-sharing program and matching pension fund.

Full-time, regular cannery workers were paid $5.00 per hour ($10,400 annually). While DP's hourly rate was below the industry average of $6.00 per hour ($12,480 annually), employees more than recouped this amount in performance bonuses. To date, DP was the only canner on the islands to have a state-of-the-art incentive pay program. In fact, it was the only canner that shared organizational profits with employees at all.

Last year employees received approximately $2,000 each in bonuses. This amount was lower than usual due to a hurricane that destroyed almost all of one harvest. Since the program was implemented in 1986, bonuses have averaged $8,000 per employee. And this year they were expected to be back on target. Sally anticipated handing out bonuses in the range of $10,000 each. Employees had the option of taking the money in one lump sum, in quarterly installments, or in even distributions throughout the next year. According to company policy, employee bonuses would be announced at the semiannual employee's meeting, to be held in six weeks.

Sally also was proud of DP's benefits. Employee benefits as a percentage of payroll averaged 30 percent in the industry. DP's percentage was 45 percent. All full-time employees with one year's seniority (tenured) were eligible to participate in DP's extensive benefit program, which included such innovations as an on-site day-care center (Sally's brainchild, which took her two years to get approved) and an employee assistance program, including free legal assistance. The company also matched, dollar for dollar, employee contributions to a retirement fund and offered two college scholarships annually to employees' children. Sally was particularly proud of DP's fitness center, which could be used by tenured employees and their families. Swimming lessons were provided free of charge to family members.

Vacation days also were above the industry average. Employees with one to two years of seniority earned one-half day of paid vacation per month, three-fourths day per month with three to five years' seniority, and one day per month with more than five years' service. Personal days accrued at the same rate for tenured employees. To prevent abuse, employees calling in absent before or after a holiday or after a payday are charged with an absence of 1.5 days. Employees with less than one year's service and temporary employees are not reimbursed for absences. The failure of any employee to call in to report an absence at least four hours before his or her shift starts is grounds for disciplinary procedures.

By having a core of permanent, tenured employees, DP is assured of having enough employees to meet average production demands. By paying temporary employees base salaries slightly above the labor market average, DP has traditionally had its pick of new employees. The system was cost effective because the salaries of temporary employees were only 18 percent over the base pay for cannery employees and well under the estimated hourly rate (with benefits) for permanent tenured employees (estimated at $7.98 per hour).

With all this going for DP, Sally wondered where things had gone wrong. Maybe Sackos was right, and she just hadn't picked the right kind of employees. Bewildered, she had her assistant, Mark George, interview some employees to see what was going on. He also prepared a report on causes of turnover at DP (see Exhibit 1).

According to Mark, the following comments are typical of the feelings of full-time permanent employees:

- "Sure, it's a great place to work, but I'm tired of those young kids walking in off the street and making more than I do."

Turnover among DP Employees   **EXHIBIT 1**

Group	Higher Pay	Better Benefits	Supervision	Moving	Better Job	Job Security	Fired
Permanent							
Less than 1 year	40	22	1	2	3	1	2
1–2 years	10	0	3	3	2	4	1
Over 2 years	1	0	5	4	4	2	0
Temporary							
Less than 6 months	10	45	4	3	10	17	3
6–12 months	12	23	1	0	2	32	2
Over 1 year	5	15	2	3	15	19	0

Note: An employee could list more than one reason for leaving.

EXHIBIT 2

Results of the Employee Attitude Survey: Levels of Satisfaction*

	Permanent			
	Less than 1 year	**1–2 years**	**Over 2 years**	**Temporary**
Pay level	2.1	2.3	2.4	3.4
Pay system	1.5	2.4	3.2	3.3
Benefits	1.0	3.2	4.1	1.1
Supervision	3.4	4.1	3.7	3.3
Job	2.4	2.7	3.1	2.3
Co-workers	3.3	4.0	4.7	2.3
Work environment	3.4	4.1	3.6	2.7

*Based on a scale of 1 to 5: 1 = Very dissatisfied; 5 = Very satisfied.

- "I know, I know, we're eligible to get bonuses, but they just can't make up for a weekly salary—at least not when you have three kids to support."
- "I worry that things are going to be the same as last year. I hung in there and look what I got, a lousy $2,500. The bottom line is that I still made less than temporary employees and those at the other canneries. I don't like it one bit."

The following comments were typical of the views of permanent untenured workers (two years' seniority):

- "I got really steamed last month when they docked my pay for being sick. I mean, I was really sick. I hadn't gone out with the girls or anything. I was down flat in bed with the flu. Why should I work hard here if I can't even get a lousy day off when I'm sick?"
- "I've worked here seven months already, and I'm pulling my own weight around here. Know what I mean? Well, it doesn't seem right that I should be paid less than those part-timers."

Among temporary workers, the view was:

- "Yeah, we make a good rate of pay but that's not everything. My wife had to have a C-section last month. Without insurance, it cost me a bundle."
- "I work just as hard as everyone else, so why shouldn't I have the same benefits? I'm getting up there in years. It'd be nice to have a little bit set aside."

Sally, reading these comments, felt she couldn't win for losing. Maybe the most current employee attitude survey would be of help. At least it was worth a try (see Exhibit 2). All she knew was that if they didn't come up with a strategy soon, DP would not meet its canning quotas, and the employee bonuses would be lost forever.

Questions for Discussion
1. What do you think about a firm that pays below-industry hourly wages and uses a bonus to make up the difference?
2. Review the DP employee attitude survey results and explain why there is a turnover problem.
3. If you were Sally, how would you solve the current HRM crisis?

CASE 11.2
The Delayed Drug Test

Most of the paper mill's employees thought one of their co-workers got off easy when, after being convicted of cocaine possession, the company took him back with the understanding that for the next year he would be subjected to "spot drug testing." It was also understood, of course, that if such testing disclosed use of an illegal substance, he would be fired.

Shortly thereafter the employee was injured in an automobile accident and placed on the sick list for two months. When he returned, management thought it the right time for a urine test. A security guard escorted the man to the office of a physician, who asked him to provide a sample under supervision. The employee did not refuse; he just insisted that he was unable to provide the sample. He was offered water and other liquids to drink but nothing helped. After several hours, the doctor threatened to obtain a sample by medication or catheterization. Still the employee refused, and nothing more was said because the doctor did not believe it was legal to use intrusive methods to get a sample.

The next day, the doctor and the personnel manager discussed the possibility that the employee might truly be unable to provide a sample because of embarrassment or a medical disorder. The doctor said this was possible but unlikely and later expressed this opinion in writing. Armed with the letter, management fired the man, and the union protested the company's action.

Questions for Discussion
1. Who has the burden of proof in any discharge case, the employee or the employer? Explain.
2. What are some problems with drug testing accuracy?
3. Would you have upheld the discharge? Why?

Adapted from "Right or Wrong in Employee Relations," *The Office*, March 1990, p. 66. Permission provided to use the actual grievance.

CHAPTER TWELVE

LABOR–MANAGEMENT RELATIONS

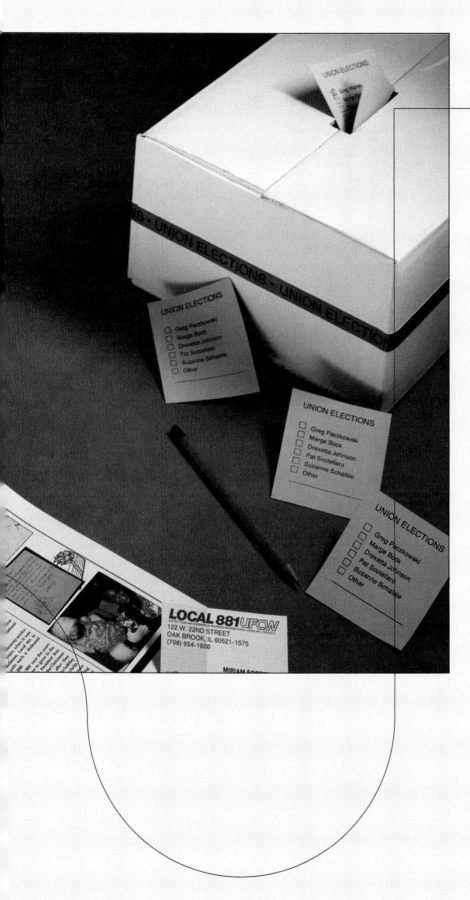

LEARNING OBJECTIVES

1. To define the term *labor union*.

2. To identify the significant trends facing the labor movement today.

3. To explain why employees decide to organize unions.

4. To compare the main features of the major labor legislation.

5. To list the steps in both organizing and decertifying a union.

6. To define the term *collective bargaining*.

7. To discuss what is included in a union-management contract.

8. To explain how a strike, boycott, and lockout differ.

Although labor-management history includes many laws, rituals, and procedures, there is also an emotional quotient not found in textbooks or television appearances. Emotions still surround some labor-management situations. In 1980, 187 major work stoppages, strikes, and lockouts involving 1,000 workers or more took place.

The Image Works

In 1989 fewer than 51 major work stoppages resulted in 17 million lost workdays.

Eastern Air Lines machinists went out on strike on March 4, 1989. Usually strikes have a clear economic objective. But the Eastern strike also involved what some refer to as the "Lorenzo factor." Although Frank Lorenzo sold his business interest in Eastern in August 1990, his legacy and the emotions he stirred up lingered until the airline shut down in early 1991.

Lorenzo, head of Texas Air, had taken over Eastern when it was failing financially. At that time, every American airline was struggling to slash costs and increase competitiveness following deregulation of the industry. Lorenzo was the biggest slasher, the most committed belt tightener, the ultimate final decision maker who asked Eastern Air Lines employees to take pay cuts, to hold costs in line, and to work harder. Finally, in a highly unusual move, federal bankruptcy judge Burton Lifland removed Lorenzo, saying that Lorenzo and his management were not competent to reorganize this estate: "It is time to change the captain of Eastern's crew."

Isn't this how a chairman is supposed to turn a company around? Yes, it is. But Lorenzo's management style had caused employees' emotions to reach the boiling point. Critics claim he is an intimidator. The union members believed Lorenzo created a restrictive work atmosphere in which he watched them too closely and treated them like children. This atmosphere was a major problem, according to the striking machinists and the pilots who joined them in a strike that grounded 27,000 employees.

The Eastern strike was loaded with emotion, hostility, and anger. Behind the rage was distrust of Lorenzo's mission and plan for the airline. In reading this chapter and learning about the history, structure, legislation, and procedures concerning labor-management relationships, consider the emotions, feelings, needs, and backgrounds of both labor and management. There are some major differences.[1]

Labor unions are organizations of employees who formally join together to protect, maintain, and improve their economic, social, and political power and well-being. For centuries people have formed labor organizations known as clubs, guilds, associations, and unions. In America, labor organizations existed before the Revolutionary War. They evolved as a way to combat inhumane working conditions and practices, which were commonplace during the early stages of the Industrial Revolution.

The term *unions* has historically referred to organizations of men and women in the same trade. Today, however, some groups of professionals who formally join together may call themselves associations. For example, the American Association of University Professors and the American Nurses Association are labor organizations.

In this chapter, we first provide a brief history of the American labor movement. Next we consider trends in unionization and reasons for people to join unions. Then we examine the structure of unions and the federal regulations governing their operations. We also explore the processes of organizing and decertifying a union and of collective bargaining. Finally, we look at nonunion organizations.

Labor Union
Organization of employees who join together to protect, maintain, and improve their economic, social, and political power and well-being.

A BRIEF HISTORY OF THE AMERICAN LABOR MOVEMENT

Unions are of two general types: industrial and craft. **Industrial union** members are all employed in a company or industry (e.g., workers in the steel industry or the auto industry), regardless of occupation. **Craft union** members belong to one craft (e.g., carpenters, bricklayers, ironworkers) or to a closely related group of occupations.

Today approximately 17 million workers belong to unions. This means that about 16 percent of all employed people are in unions. To understand unions in the 1990s, let us briefly trace how they evolved.[2]

Industrial Union
A union in which all members are employed in a company or industry, regardless of occupation.

Craft Union
A union in which all members belong to one craft or to a closely related group of occupations.

Works Projects Administration in the National Archives

Dark, cluttered, dusty, smelly working conditions were common in the early 1900s. Here some steelworkers are pouring steel without any protective gear. Today someone would be fined or sent to jail for having workers perform this type of task.

As early as 1790, skilled shoemakers, printers, and tailors organized themselves into trade unions. They made demands about minimum wages and pressured fellow workers to not accept a lesser wage. Employers did not sit idly by as craftsmen attempted to unionize employees. An 1806 court ruling made it a "conspiracy in restraint of trade" for workers to combine or exert pressure on management. In effect, then, unions were illegal until 1842 when the Massachusetts Supreme Court, in *Commonwealth* v. *Hunt,* decided that criminal conspiracy did not apply if unions did not use illegal tactics to achieve goals.

Even then employers still resisted by discharging employees who joined unions. They also forced employees to sign a **yellow-dog contract,** a statement in which the employee promised not to form or join a union. If employees who signed such contracts later joined a union, they were discharged. Employers also obtained court injunctions against strikes.

Early unions promoted social reform and free public education. Some of the more militant groups—such as the Molly Maguires from the Pennsylvania coal mines—were considered socialist or anarchist. They were involved in rioting and bloodshed, initiated by both employers and union members.

The turbulent 1870s and 1880s brought growing recognition of the labor union approach to social and economic problems. These experiences helped solidify the union movement and encouraged the development of a nationwide organization.

The first union federation to achieve significant size and influence was the **Knights of Labor,** formed around 1869. This group attracted employees and local unions from all crafts and occupational areas. The strength of the Knights

Yellow-Dog Contract
A statement signed by an employee promising not to form or join a union.

Knights of Labor
The first union federation that attracted members from local unions from all crafts and occupational areas.

The AFL–CIO merger is celebrated in a December 1955 ceremony. Today over 85 percent of all union members are part of the AFL–CIO.

The George Meany Memorial Archives

was diluted because it failed to integrate the needs and interests of skilled and unskilled, industrial, and craft members. Also, many workers left the Knights of Labor because they thought it was too radical.

A group of national craft unions cut their relationships with the Knights of Labor around 1886. They formed the American Federation of Labor (A.F. of L., later changed to AFL). Samuel Gompers of the Cigar-Makers' International Union was elected president. The AFL restricted its membership to skilled tradespeople. In 1935 the Committee (later changed to Congress) for Industrial Organizations (CIO) was formed by John L. Lewis, president of the United Mine Workers, in cooperation with a number of presidents of unions expelled from the AFL. The CIO was formed to organize industrial and mass-production employees. At this time, the AFL began offering membership to unskilled employees also.

As shown in Figure 12.1, the union movement grew slowly from 1900 to 1930. The federal government's attitude toward union organizing was at different times neutral, indifferent, or opposed. But with the passage of federal laws in the 1920s and 30s that gave protection to the union organizing process, union membership began to climb. (We will discuss some of this legislation later in the chapter.) Thus, formal law helped unions grow during their formative years. From 1930 to 1947, union membership increased from 3 million to 14 million.

Competition for new union members led to bitter conflicts between the AFL and the CIO, but in 1955 they merged. The structure of the present **AFL–CIO**

AFL–CIO
The merged body of the American Federation of Labor (craft union members) and the Congress of Industrial Organizations (industrial union members).

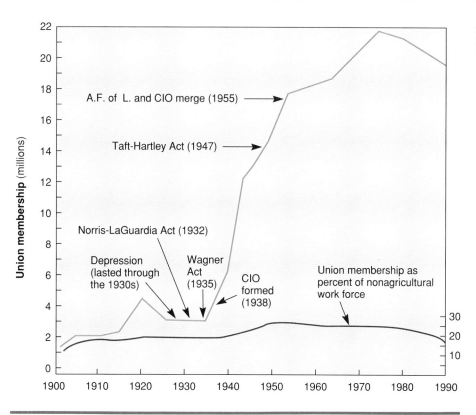

FIGURE 12.1

20th Century Union Membership in the United States

FIGURE 12.2   **Structure of the AFL–CIO**

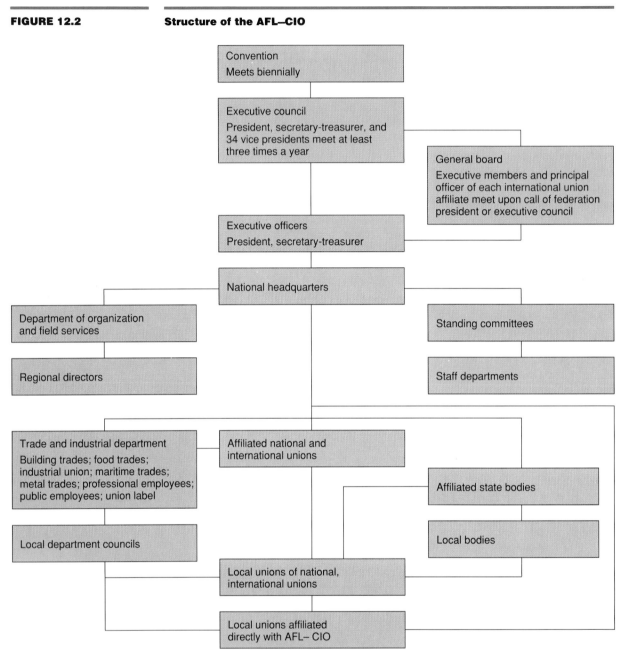

Source: From *Directory of U.S. Labor Organizations,* 1990–1991 Edition, by Courtney D. Gifford, ed., p. 2. Copyright 1990 by the Bureau of National Affairs, Inc., Washington, D.C.

is shown in Figure 12.2. Most national and international labor unions now belong to the AFL–CIO, although a number of unions, representing over 4 million members, are unaffiliated. Such large and powerful unions as the Teamsters and the United Automobile Workers at one time broke away from the AFL–CIO, but they have now rejoined the group.

TABLE 12.1

Ten Largest Unions in the United States

Union	Affiliation	Membership
International Brotherhood of Teamsters, Chauffeurs, Warehousemen and Helpers of America	AFL–CIO	1,161,000
American Federation of State, County and Municipal Employees (AFSCME)	AFL–CIO	1,090,000
United Food and Commercial Workers*	AFL–CIO	1,000,000
United Automobile, Aerospace and Agricultural Implement Workers of America, International Union (UAW)	AFL–CIO	917,000
Service Employees' International Union	AFL–CIO	762,000
International Brotherhood of Electrical Workers (IBEW)	AFL–CIO	744,000
United Brotherhood of Carpenters and Joiners of America	AFL–CIO	613,000
International Association of Machinists and Aerospace Workers	AFL–CIO	517,000
United Steelworkers of America	AFL–CIO	481,000
Laborers' International Union of North America	AFL–CIO	406,000

*The Retail Clerks and Meatcutters unions merged in 1979 to form this union.

Source: AFL–CIO Executive Council, telephone interview, September 1990. These figures are based on conversations with union officials. Other sources show slightly higher figures which conversations did not substantiate.

President John F. Kennedy's 1962 executive order (10988), which was strengthened by amendments in 1969 and 1971, set up a form of collective bargaining (union and management representatives meeting to work out an agreement) for federal government employees.

UNIONIZATION TRENDS

The 10 largest U.S. unions and their memberships are listed in Table 12.1. The two largest unions, with memberships of more than a million each, are the Teamsters and the American Federation of State, County, and Municipal Employees. Figure 12.3 shows the degree of unionization by industry type. For example, at least 75 percent of the blue-collar employees in transportation are unionized, whereas fewer than 25 percent of local government employees are unionized.

Union membership has dropped over the past decade. Why? Several factors have contributed to the decline.

FIGURE 12.3   **Degree of Union Organization in Selected Industries**

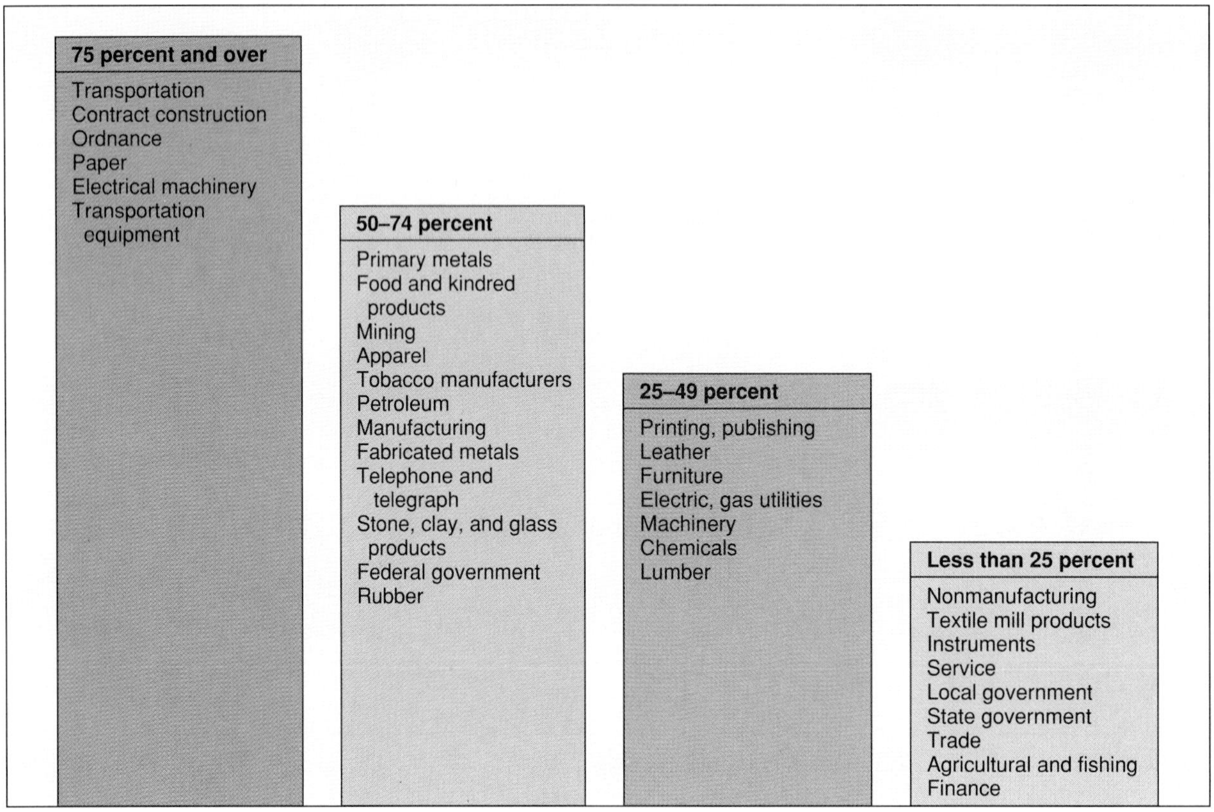

75 percent and over		
Transportation		
Contract construction		
Ordnance		
Paper		
Electrical machinery	**50–74 percent**	
Transportation equipment	Primary metals	
	Food and kindred products	
	Mining	
	Apparel	
	Tobacco manufacturers	**25–49 percent**
	Petroleum	Printing, publishing
	Manufacturing	Leather
	Fabricated metals	Furniture
	Telephone and telegraph	Electric, gas utilities
	Stone, clay, and glass products	Machinery
	Federal government	Chemicals
	Rubber	Lumber

Less than 25 percent

Nonmanufacturing
Textile mill products
Instruments
Service
Local government
State government
Trade
Agricultural and fishing
Finance

Adapted from U.S. Department of Labor, Bureau of Labor Statistics (Washington, D.C.: U.S. Government Printing Office, 1987), pp. 65–73.

First, the public has been bombarded with news of irresponsible union strikes, unreasonable wage or salary demands, some union leaders' criminal activities, and featherbedding (make-work) situations. These stories are poor publicity for unions. One study indicated that the monopolistic practices of unions cost the U.S. economy $5 billion to $10 billion annually. (In their democratic role, however, unions increase the efficiency of the economy by the same amount. How? By reducing training expenses, job search costs, and worker turnover.) The American public's confidence in unions as an institution has dropped more than in any other enterprise in the past two decades. Only 22 percent of the public holds unions in high regard. And union leaders are rated last in ethical conduct and moral practices, behind lawyers, advertising executives, government officials, and stockbrokers.[3]

Second, several economic factors, including intense international competition, poorly equipped factories, poor management, new technologies, and government regulations, have struck hardest at unionized industries—steel, autos, oil and gas, and mining. The deregulation of trucking, airlines, and communications has contributed to the erosion of union membership. Economic conditions and deregulation have caused the layoff of millions of union members, the permanent closing of unionized plants, and the relocation of plants and offices to nonunion locations. Mergers and acquisitions have eliminated union and nonunion jobs throughout the country. The reduction in union jobs has been felt the most in the states where unionization is strongest—New York, Illinois, Michigan, Ohio, California, and Pennsylvania.

Third, management in the 1970s began to resist union organizing efforts and large wage demands. They developed programs and strategies to fight back against unions. They also built new facilities in areas with less union strength—the South and the Sunbelt.[4]

Finally, since the proportion of blue-collar jobs in the work force has decreased and the labor force is now predominantly white-collar, unions have had to redirect organizing efforts to recruit more nurses, teachers, engineers, and professionals. Results have been spotty. White-collar employees have for years felt superior to their blue-collar counterparts. Perhaps many believe that by joining a union they would lose status, prestige, and esteem. Educational achievements, mode of dress, language, and job locations within businesses typically give the white-collar employee a more common base with management than with the blue-collar employees. Also, a higher proportion of women work in white-collar jobs, and women generally have been more resistant to unionization.

To sound the death knell for labor unions would be premature. Unionized workers across all industries on average earn 15 to 30 percent more than comparable nonunion workers.[5] Union advocates claim this significant difference resulted from union bargaining. Also, unionism has increased among government employees. The increasing numbers of better-educated, higher-status civil servants and state employees have helped improve the union's image. How much impact the image improvement will have on union membership is uncertain. But aggressive, imaginative, and fair union leadership could be effective in organizing significantly more white-collar workers. The increase in the unionization of government employees indicates that white-collar workers are listening to and watching the union message.

Organizational and recruiting efforts of unions have always varied according to changes in economic, social, and political conditions. Membership drives continue in the public sector (which includes military personnel, police, and firefighters), among professionals (teachers, medical personnel, athletes, lawyers), among employees in service industries, and among agricultural workers. For the reasons discussed above, unions are very interested in attracting public employees.

WHY DO PEOPLE JOIN UNIONS?

Many people ask, ''Why do people unionize?'' Of course, this question has no single answer. People join for different reasons. Research shows that people are attracted to unions because they are dissatisfied with the Herzberg type of hygiene factors: (1) pay and benefits, (2) supervision, and (3) job security. Recognizing the importance of job security, a growing group of companies have either contract specifications or a tradition to not lay off employees. Some of these companies believe that no-layoff policies mean higher productivity, in-

The "Steelworkers Guarantee" highlights some of the reasons workers join unions and some interesting facts and data about union membership.

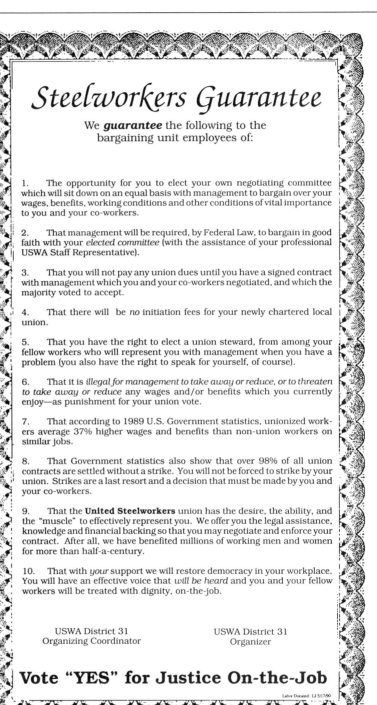

Steelworkers Guarantee

We **guarantee** the following to the bargaining unit employees of:

1.   The opportunity for you to elect your own negotiating committee which will sit down on an equal basis with management to bargain over your wages, benefits, working conditions and other conditions of vital importance to you and your co-workers.

2.   That management will be required, by Federal Law, to bargain in good faith with your *elected committee* (with the assistance of your professional USWA Staff Representative).

3.   That you will not pay any union dues until you have a signed contract with management which you and your co-workers negotiated, and which the majority voted to accept.

4.   That there will be *no* initiation fees for your newly chartered local union.

5.   That you have the right to elect a union steward, from among your fellow workers who will represent you with management when you have a problem (you also have the right to speak for yourself, of course).

6.   That it is *illegal for management to take away or reduce, or to threaten to take away or reduce* any wages and/or benefits which you currently enjoy—as punishment for your union vote.

7.   That according to 1989 U.S. Government statistics, unionized workers average 37% higher wages and benefits than non-union workers on similar jobs.

8.   That Government statistics also show that over 98% of all union contracts are settled without a strike. You will not be forced to strike by your union. Strikes are a last resort and a decision that must be made by you and your co-workers.

9.   That the **United Steelworkers** union has the desire, the ability, and the "muscle" to effectively represent you. We offer you the legal assistance, knowledge and financial backing so that you may negotiate and enforce your contract. After all, we have benefited millions of working men and women for more than half-a-century.

10.   That with *your* support we will restore democracy in your workplace. You will have an effective voice that *will be heard* and you and your fellow workers will be treated with dignity, on-the-job.

USWA District 31
Organizing Coordinator

USWA District 31
Organizer

Vote "YES" for Justice On-the-Job

Labor Donated: LJ 5/17/90

Courtesy USSW District 31 Education Department

TABLE 12.2

Factors that Determine Subordinates' Satisfaction with Supervisors

Subordinates are more satisfied with a supervisor who:
- Displays technical competence.
- Sets clear work goals for subordinates.
- Gives clear instructions.
- Clearly defines subordinates' job responsibilities.
- Backs subordinates with other managers.
- Fairly appraises subordinates' performances.
- Allows subordinates adequate time to do the job right.
- Allows subordinates adequate time to learn the job's tasks.
- Informs subordinates of work changes before they are to take place.
- Displays consistent behavior toward subordinates.
- Helps subordinates to get the job done.
- Gives subordinates credit for their ideas.
- Listens to and understands subordinates' job-related problems.
- Follows through to get the job's problems solved.
- Treats subordinates fairly when they make mistakes.
- Shows concern for subordinates' career progress.
- Congratulates subordinates for doing a good job.

DID YOU KNOW? *Subordinates are more satisfied with a competent supervisor who provides clear directions.*

Source: Adapted from V. Scarpello and R. J. Vandenberg, "The Satisfaction with My Supervisor Scale: Its Utility in Research and Practice," *Journal of Management,* Fall 1987, pp. 447–66.

creased loyalty, and retention of skilled workers. They cite research findings, especially reports issued by the Work in America Institute. The leaders in practicing no layoffs are Bank of America, Delta Airlines, Eli Lilly, Federal Express, R. J. Reynolds, Hallmark Cards, Materials Research Corp., Wm. Wrigley, and many public utilities.

One study of nearly 88,000 clerical, sales, and technical employees at Sears Roebuck found that the strongest predictor of unionization attempts was the employees' dissatisfaction with the supervisor.[6] What does that really mean? Is the supervisor not being fair, not being a good listener, or not being supportive? Table 12.2 lists the qualities found to be important in the bond between managers and workers. They suggest that workers are satisfied with managers who possess three specific skills: technical (they know the job), administrative (they know the system), and interpersonal (they know people).

The Maslow needs hierarchy covered in Chapter Ten provides a framework for tying research findings together. Maslow portrayed humans as driven to put forth effort by the desire to satisfy needs. As research suggests, employees try to gratify important needs and wants because they are dissatisfied with how well these needs and desires are being met. When needs are unsatisfied, the union becomes an attractive alternative to doing nothing or agreeing with management. Unionization will continue to be an alternative as long as some employees fail to satisfy their economic, interpersonal, and job security needs. Connections will help you to discover your feelings about unions and management.

● C o n n e c t i o n s

My Union-Management Attitude

Directions: Complete this quiz to determine your general feelings about labor (unions) and management (organizational managers). There are no correct or incorrect answers; only general impressions that you hold are of interest.

1. Do you trust management to give a fair deal on grievances, if no union (within the firm) exists?

   Yes _____   No _____

2. Do you believe that unions have been responsible for improved working conditions in the United States over the past 40 years?

   Yes _____   No _____

3. Do you believe that unions are democratically run?

   Yes _____   No _____

4. Do you believe that management has fairly treated nonmanagerial personnel?

   Yes _____   No _____

5. Do you believe that a union representative should be placed on the board of directors of a unionized company?

   Yes _____   No _____

6. Do you believe that police officers should have the right to strike?

   Yes _____   No _____

7. Do you believe that management would have raised wages and fringe benefits to generally high levels without union pressure?

   Yes _____   No _____

8. Do you believe that union busting or decertification should be permitted in the United States?

   Yes _____   No _____

THE STRUCTURE AND MANAGEMENT OF UNIONS

Many unions are large organizations. They have management, leadership, and financial control problems similar to those faced by business firms. Unions' national headquarters employ staff economists, engineers, attorneys, accountants, wage and salary experts, and professional managers.

Local Union Structure

The labor movement has its foundation in the local craft union. The local directly influences the membership. Through the local, members exercise their complaints and pay the dues that support the national union.

9. Do you believe that management should be permitted to make promotion decisions without having to pay attention to seniority clauses (those with longer job tenure are given some preference) in a union contract?

   Yes _____   No _____

10. Do you believe that unions treat minority employees more fairly than management treats them?

   Yes _____   No _____

Feedback: Now assess your attitudes toward unions and management. The following answers indicate a union or management bias or attitude.

1. Yes—Management   No —Union
2. No —Management   Yes—Union
3. No —Management   Yes—Union
4. Yes—Management   No —Union
5. No —Management   Yes—Union
6. No —Management   Yes—Union
7. Yes—Management   No —Union
8. Yes—Management   No —Union
9. Yes—Management   No —Union
10. No —Management   Yes—Union

If you answered 8 of the 10 questions from either the management orientation or the union orientation, you lean in favor of that particular group. For example, if you answered all 10 questions as shown on the left (management key), the indication is that you have a strong management bias.

This is not a scientific quiz, but is used for information purposes only. Did you know that you had a bias or that you are generally neutral? Have you ever been a union member?

Local union activities are conducted by officials elected by the members. Elected officers include the president, vice president, secretary-treasurer, business representative, and committee chairpersons. Elected officials of local unions often have full-time jobs in addition to their regular union duties.

In many local unions, the **business representative** is the dominant person. The major responsibilities of the business representative are to negotiate and administer the labor agreement and to settle problems that may arise in connection with the contract. The business representative also collects dues, recruits new members, coordinates social activities, and arranges union meetings.

The **union steward** (sometimes called the *shop steward*) represents the interests of local union members in their relations with managers on the job. In

Business Representative
A union official who negotiates and administers the labor agreement and settles contract problems.

Union Steward
A person who represents the interests of local union members in their on-the-job relations with managers.

the auto industry, the steward (called a *committee person*) devotes full time to solving disputes that arise in connection with the union-management labor contract.

National-Local Relationship

The constitution of the national union establishes the rules, policies, and procedures under which the local unions may be chartered and become members. Each national union exercises some control over the local unions. These controls usually deal with the collection of dues, the admission of new members by the local, and the use of union funds. The national also provides the local unions with support for organizing campaigns and strikes and for the administration of contracts. Over 100 national union organizations support about 80,000 local unions.

Managing in the Union

The job of managing a union is challenging and time-consuming. Union officials need to be dedicated, willing to work long hours, able to counsel members on personal problems, and skilled in influencing people. Officers must periodically run for reelection.

The Teamsters are a powerful union organization. They hold a national convention every five years. At this convention delegates will deal with union business, changes in regulations, and election of national union leaders.

Eli Reed/Magnum

Unions finance themselves through dues, fines, and initiation fees collected at the local level. But members resist high assessments. Union officials have to convince them that the union needs a sound financial base to have the power to secure favorable labor agreements. Most union members pay dues that come out to roughly two hours' wages per month; two major unions—the Steelworkers and Automobile Workers—have set their monthly dues at exactly this two-hours level. Initiation fees, paid once, tend to be in the $50–$150 range.

FEDERAL REGULATION OF LABOR–MANAGEMENT RELATIONS

State and federal laws govern union-management interaction. These laws have evolved through common law and rulings by the National Labor Relations Board and the courts. They have swung back and forth like a pendulum, at one time favoring management and at another time favoring unions. Table 12.3 contains a summary of the major labor-management regulations discussed in this section.

Major Labor-Management Regulations   **TABLE 12.3**

Legislation	Provisions	Coverage
Railway Labor Act (1926)	Gave employees the right to organize and bargain collectively.	Railroads. Airlines.
Norris-LaGuardia Act (1932)	Prohibited federal courts from enjoining strikes and from enforcing yellow-dog contracts.	Private-sector employment.
Wagner Act (1935)	Established the right to organize and engage in other concerted activities; declared certain employer actions to be unfair labor practices; established procedures for employees to elect a union; regulated collective bargaining; established the National Labor Relations Board (NLRB).	Private-sector employment: • Businesses. • Nonprofit hospitals and nursing homes. • Private colleges and universities. • Performing arts.
Taft-Hartley Act (1947)	Established the right to refrain from the activities protected in the Wagner Act; declared certain union actions to be unfair labor practices; provided for passage of state right-to-work laws; established the Federal Mediation and Conciliation Service (FMCS); outlawed closed shops.	Same as Wagner Act.
Landrum-Griffin Act (1959)	Established standards for union treatment of union members; regulated internal union affairs.	Same as Wagner Act and Taft-Hartley Act.
Title VII, Civil Service Reform Act (1978)	Established the right to form and assist labor union; bargaining; required arbitration of impasses and grievances; prohibited strikes and other disruptions.	Federal employment (excludes some agencies, such as FBI, CIA).
The Workers' Adjustment and Retraining Notification Act (1989)	Employers with 100 or more employees or who have 100 or more employees who together work at least 4,000 hours per week excluding overtime must give employees 60 days' written notice of anticipated plant closings or other mass layoffs.	Private-sector employment.

Early Labor Legislation: Prolabor

Railway Labor Act   The first labor legislation passed by Congress since the Clayton Act of 1914 excluded unions from the Sherman Antitrust Act of 1890 was the **Railway Labor Act** of 1926. It established the process of collective bargaining as a means for resolving labor-management disputes.

Norris-LaGuardia Act   In the 1930s, the federal government became involved in labor disputes outside the railroad industry. **Injunctions,** court decrees to stop union activities, gave employers an easy way to hinder union activities. However, in 1932 came the **Norris-LaGuardia Act** as a response to the Great Depression. This act, also called the Anti-Injunction Act, limited the power of federal courts to stop union picketing, boycotts, and strikes. The Norris-LaGuardia Act also made the yellow-dog contract (a contract, mentioned earlier, in which employees agree not to join any union) unenforceable.

Wagner Act   The National Labor Relations Act, better known as the **Wagner Act,** was passed in 1935. It encouraged the growth of trade unions by restraining management from interfering with them. By restricting the activities of management, this act forced the government to take an active role in union-management relationships. Five unfair management practices specified in the Wagner Act are summarized in Table 12.4.

The power to implement the Wagner Act was given to a three-person **National Labor Relations Board (NLRB)** and a staff of lawyers and other personnel responsible to the board. The board sets up elections, on request, to determine if a given group of workers wishes to have a union as a bargaining representative. The board also investigates complaints of unfair labor practices.

Postwar Labor Laws: Restoring a Balance

Taft-Hartley Act   The Wagner Act was considered prolabor. To swing the pendulum back, to equalize labor and management, Congress passed the **Taft-Hartley Act** (also called the Labor-Management Relations Act) in 1947. It amended and supplemented the Wagner Act and increased the size of the National Labor Relations Board to five persons (allegedly to get rid of the NLRB's pro-union bias). Taft-Hartley guaranteed employee bargaining rights and specifically forbade the five unfair employer labor practices first established in the Wagner Act. But the act also specified unfair union labor practices; the union was restrained from the practices shown in Table 12.4. Finally, the act established the Federal Mediation and Conciliation Service (FMCS).

Landrum-Griffin Act   In view of the corruption found in some unions, Congress assumed that the individual union member was still not adequately protected by the labor laws in existence. So in 1959 Congress passed the **Landrum-Griffin Act,** which is officially designated the Labor-Management Reporting and Disclosure Act. It was designed to regulate the internal affairs of unions.

This act, called the bill of rights of union members, gave every union member the right to (1) nominate candidates for union office, (2) vote in union elections, and (3) attend union meetings. Union members also gained the right to examine union accounts and records, while the union was required to submit an annual financial report to the secretary of labor. Employers had to report any payments or loans made to unions, their officers, or their members. This

---

Railway Labor Act
A 1926 law that established collective bargaining as a means for resolving labor-management disputes.

Injunction
Court order that prohibits the defendant from engaging in certain activities, such as striking.

Norris-LaGuardia Act
A 1932 law that limited the power of federal courts to stop union picketing, boycotts, and strikes; also made the yellow-dog contract unenforceable.

Wagner Act
A law that made collective bargaining legal and required employers to bargain with the representatives of the employees. The law is also referred to as the National Labor Relations Act.

NLRB
A group that investigates cases of alleged unfair labor practices by employers and unions and holds elections to determine whether groups of employees want to be unionized.

Taft-Hartley Act
A 1947 labor law that prohibits the closed shop, requires unions to bargain in good faith, and makes it illegal for a union to discriminate against employees who don't join the union.

Landrum-Griffin Act
A 1959 labor law that requires unions and employees to file financial reports with the secretary of labor and that specifies certain activities to ensure democratic operation of the union.

TABLE 12.4

Unfair Labor Practices

By management:

To interfere with, restrain, or coerce employees in the exercise of their rights to organize.

To dominate or interfere with the affairs of a union.

To discriminate in regard to hiring, tenure, or any employment condition for the purpose of encouraging or discouraging membership in any union organization.

To discriminate against or discharge an employee because he or she has filed charges or given testimony under the Wagner Act.

To refuse to bargain collectively with representatives of the employees—that is, to refuse to bargain in good faith.

By unions:

To restrain or coerce employees in the exercise of their right to join or not to join a union except when an agreement is made by the employer and union that a condition of employment will be joining the union, called a union security clause authorizing a union shop.

To cause an employer to discriminate against an employee other than for nonpayment of dues or initiation fees.

To refuse to bargain with an employer in good faith.

To engage, induce, encourage, threaten, or coerce any individual to engage in strikes, refusal to work, or boycott where the objective is to:

- Force or require any employer or self-employed person to recognize or join any labor organization or employer organization.
- Force or require an employer or self-employed person to cease using the products of or doing business with another person, or force any other employer to recognize or bargain with the union unless it has been certified by the NLRB.
- Force an employer to apply pressure to another employer to recognize a union. Examples include picketing a hospital so that it will apply pressure on a subcontractor (food service, maintenance, emergency department) to recognize a union; forcing an employer to do business only with others, such as suppliers, who have a union; picketing by another union for recognition when a different one is already certified.

To charge excessive or discriminatory membership fees.

To cause an employer to give payment for services not performed (featherbedding).

---

portion of the act was to end **sweetheart contracts,** under which the union leaders and management agree to terms that work to their mutual benefit but maintain poor working conditions for other employees.

The Issue of Job Security

Without members the union ceases to exist. Thus job security is a requirement. Unions have fought and continue to fight for job security. To establish security, unions focus on gaining the right to represent an enterprise's workers and, where possible, to be the exclusive bargaining agent for all employees of the unit. Union job security takes several forms:

- **Union shop.** The company can hire nonunion people, but they must join the union after a prescribed period of time and pay the union dues. (Failure to join means they could be fired.)

Sweetheart Contract
Agreement between union leaders and management to terms that work to their mutual benefit but maintain poor working conditions for other employees.

Union Shop
A company that requires employees to join the union after being hired.

Agency Shop
A company where all employees pay union dues, whether or not they are union members.

Open Shop
A company in which employees don't have to join a union or pay dues but can decide without pressure whether to become union members.

Maintenance of Membership Agreement
Agreement that, although employees do not have to join a union, union members must maintain membership in the union over the length of the contract.

- **Agency shop.** Employees who do not belong to the union still must pay the full union dues (assuming that the union's bargaining and agreement efforts benefit all the workers).
- **Open shop.** The workers decide whether or not to join the union. Those not joining pay no dues.
- **Maintenance of membership agreement.** Employees do not have to join a union. However, union members must maintain membership in the union over the length of the contract.

An interesting example of union job security is the case of Nordstrom, a corporation with 59 retail establishments and over $2.6 billion in annual sales. Of Nordstrom's 30,000-person work force, approximately 2,000 salespeople are union members of the United Food and Commercial Workers (UFCW) union.[7] Nordstrom had offered the union an unusual contract proposal: optional union membership at its six stores in the Seattle and Tacoma area.

The union saw this open shop arrangement as a management tactic to weaken the union. It claimed that Nordstrom was having sales personnel work without pay, attending store meetings, writing thank you notes to customers, and delivering merchandise to customers' houses and offices. The union began an aggressive campaign to gain public sympathy for its position.[8] On February 15, 1990, the state of Washington's Department of Labor and Industries ordered Nordstrom to change its compensation and record-keeping procedures and retroactively compensate current and former Washington State sales employees.

FIGURE 12.4

Right-to-Work States

Legend

■ States with right-to-work laws

□ States without right-to-work laws

For years the Nordstrom name conjured visions of tremendous service, quality merchandise, and accommodating salespeople eager to help. But union-management bickering and the state's order may have a long-lasting impact on sales, image, and goodwill. Labor disputes can be resolved, but the long-term effects may hurt both the union and the company.

Although unions have encouraged legislation to protect their security, a number of concerns remain. First, a labor organization has no guarantee that it will not be replaced by a rival union at a later date. Second, employees still have a number of channels through which to voice their anti-union feelings and can use these to get rid of unions. Third, no government guarantee protects unions from "free riders." A free rider is an employee who decides not to be a part of the union but still gains the benefit of unionization.

The Taft-Hartley Act allows states to forbid union shops by passing **right-to-work laws.** Under these laws, two persons doing the same job must be paid the same wages, whether they belong to the union or not. Unions see this as unfair because the nonunionized employees pay no dues but share in the benefits won by the union. Twenty-one states have right-to-work laws, as shown in Figure 12.4.

A **closed shop,** prohibited by the Taft-Hartley Act, requires that a new employee be a union member when hired. The union itself provides labor to the

Right-to-Work Laws
State laws requiring that two people doing the same job be paid the same wages, whether or not they belong to the union.

Closed Shop
A company that hires only workers who are members of the union; illegal under the Taft-Hartley Act.

Bob Daemmrich/The Image Works

Ironworkers are sent from a union hall to a job site. How many nonunion members do you think will be sent out to these types of jobs? This is why ironworkers' union halls are called modified closed shops.

organization. Although this type of shop is illegal, modified closed shops are still found in the construction, printing, and maritime industries. For example, an ironworkers' union hall sends out union members to construction sites on request. A nonunion worker has little chance to be sent from a union hall to a job because the union's business agent makes the assignments. Union members elect the business agent, while the nonunion members have no vote.

Recent Legislation

Title VII
Part of the Civil Service Reform Act of 1978; outlawed certain unfair labor practices and created the Federal Labor Relations Authority (FLRA); granted covered employees the right to form, join, or assist any labor organization or to refrain from such activity, freely and without reprisals.

Title VII   **Title VII** of the Civil Service Reform Act of 1978, also referred to as the Federal Service Labor-Management Relations Act, did for the federal government sector what the Wagner and the Taft-Hartley acts did for employment in the private sector. Title VII outlawed certain unfair labor practices and created the Federal Labor Relations Authority (FLRA), with powers similar to the National Labor Relations Board (NLRB).

Employees covered by Title VII are granted the right to form, join, or assist any labor organization or to refrain from such activity, freely and without reprisals. Employees of some federal agencies (e.g., Federal Bureau of Investigation, Central Intelligence Agency, National Security Agency, Tennessee Valley Authority) are exempted. Noncitizens working outside of the United States for federal agencies are also excluded.

WARN Act
A 1989 law that requires employers with 100 or more full-time employees to give affected employees 60 days' written notice of plant or office closing or other mass layoffs. The law is commonly known as the Plant Closing Bill.

WARN   The employee's right to notice of plant/office closing or relocation became a major issue in the 1980s. A growing number of workers in the steel, automobile, and general manufacturing industries lost their jobs because of competition, mergers, or relocation of facilities. The **Worker Adjustment and Retraining Notification Act (WARN),** commonly referred to as the Plant Closing Bill, was passed and went into effect in 1989. The act requires employers with 100 or more full-time employees to give affected employees 60 days' written notice of plant or office closing or other mass layoffs. WARN covers nonprofit organizations but not federal, state, or local governments. "Affected employees" are all workers, including managerial and supervisory personnel, who may suffer some employment loss as the result of a plant closing or mass layoff.

Employers violating WARN may be required to provide back pay and benefits for up to 60 days to workers laid off without proper notification. In some cases, employers may also be required to pay fines of $500 per day, up to $30,000. However, WARN allows some exceptions. A failing company actively seeking capital to prevent the plant closing or layoff is exempt, if giving notice to employees would reasonably have prevented the firm from receiving the financing. Closings due to natural disasters, such as earthquakes or floods, are also exempt from the 60-day notice requirement.

There are also humanitarian arguments to support WARN. Victims of plant closures show higher rates of alcoholism, child abuse, ulcers, heart attacks, and suicides. Before WARN was passed, General Motors shut down its Fremont, California, plant and gave the 4,000 employees only three weeks' notice. Ford Motor Co. closed its San Jose, California, plant, idling 2,300 workers but giving them six months' advance notice. There were eight suicides among the laid-off General Motors employees and none among the displaced Ford workers.[9]

Critics of WARN argue that turnover, pilferage, destruction of property, and other negative behavior may occur between the time of notice and the layoff. However, research conducted in Europe and other countries with advance notice requirements reveals no evidence to support that claim.

ORGANIZING AND DECERTIFYING A UNION

The organizing drive is the process through which a group of employees attempts to establish a legally binding relationship with the employer. The process involves three steps: (1) petition for union representation, (2) determination of appropriate bargaining unit, and (3) union representation election.

The organizing drive officially begins when employees sign authorization cards that empower the union to petition the NLRB for union representation. Thirty percent of the employees must sign, per NLRB rules. But most unions will not petition the NLRB unless a majority of the workers in the group sign the authorization cards. The union must receive 50 percent plus two of the votes cast in the election that takes place later.

After they receive the petition for union representation and check its accuracy, the NLRB notifies the employer that a particular union is seeking to be the representative of a group of employees. If 30 percent of the firm's employees are on the petition list, the NLRB notifies both the employer and the employees. The employer can then recognize the union as the representative. However, if the employer does not, a formal unit determination hearing is scheduled by the NLRB. Employer and employees present facts and arguments about representation. The hearing enables the NLRB to determine (1) the employees' interest in being represented, (2) eligibility of employees to belong to the proposed unit, and (3) desires of employees as to who should or should not be a member of the proposed unit.

NLRB regional directors are empowered to decide the composition and appropriateness of the bargaining unit. After this is decided, the NLRB informs the employer and union that a bargaining unit has been formed. The NLRB then supervises a representation election. Again, the union must receive 50 percent plus two of the votes cast to win the election. When this happens, the NLRB certifies the union as the exclusive representative of the employees within the bargaining unit. If the union loses the election, the union must wait one year before trying again.

The NLRB is the referee, the guiding arm of organizing drives and elections. Its chief concern is to provide an atmosphere that permits employees to make a clear choice. The employer and union are not permitted to use threats, promises, or any means of influencing each person's free choice in the process. Table 12.5 outlines employer behaviors permitted and not permitted by the NLRB.

Just as unions can be voted in and become the representative of employees, they can also be voted out by the same employees. The law that grants employees the right to organize also allows them to terminate the union's right to

TABLE 12.5

Permitted and Not Permitted Employer Behaviors in Union Organizing Drives

Yes: The employer may
- Discharge and discipline employees for violation of employment rules, provided the rules apply uniformly to all employees.
- Forbid the union to solicit workers during working hours and on the employer's property.
- Forbid employees to distribute union literature in working areas.
- Make speeches and speak against the union and also write letters to employees giving its position with respect to the union, as long as the speeches and letters are noncoercive and not perceived as potentially benefiting the employee if he or she does not join the union.

No: The employer may not
- Prohibit union solicitation by employees during their nonworking time in work areas or nonwork areas.
- Question employees about the union or its activities, even though the questions are nonthreatening and the employees are willing to answer those questions.
- Circulate anti-union petitions or engage in any attempts to get the employees to withdraw from the union.
- Engage in any activities that change the wages, hours, terms, and conditions of employment during the term of the organizing drive.

Decertification
The process, guided by the NLRB, that results in voting out a union that has been representing employees.

represent them. The process of voting out a union is called **decertification.** A petition must be submitted showing 30 percent employee support for the action. If there is support, the NLRB will conduct a secret ballot election to determine whether a majority of employees in the unit wish to decertify. In 1990, 587 decertification elections were held. In 170 of these elections, the employees voted to decertify the union.[10]

Employers use "union busting" consultants to help keep unions out in the first place or to decertify them when they are the representatives of employees. The consultants help managers comply with the law and use persuasive procedures to communicate better with employees. Programs guided by such consultants are usually designed to win the attention and loyalty of employees.

COLLECTIVE BARGAINING

A union certified by the NLRB becomes the collective bargaining representative of the employees. According to the Wagner Act, it is an unfair labor practice for the employer to refuse to bargain collectively with chosen representatives of a duly certified labor union. The Taft-Hartley Act states that it is an unfair practice for the representatives of a labor union to not bargain in good faith with an employer. The current national policy, then, is that employees and employers must bargain in good faith to work out employment issues and disputes.

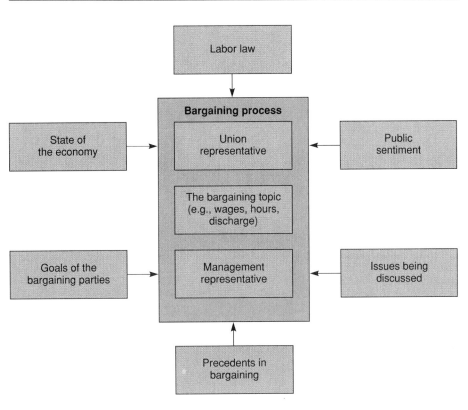

FIGURE 12.5

Forces Influencing the Bargaining Process

Collective bargaining is a process by which the representatives of the firm meet and attempt to work out a contract with union representatives. Through this process, contractual agreements are established, managed, and enforced. *Collective* means only that representatives join in the attempt to negotiate an agreement. *Bargaining* is the process of cajoling, debating, discussing, and threatening to bring about a favorable agreement for those being represented.

Bargaining *in good faith* is the cornerstone of effective labor-management relations. It means that both sides must communicate and negotiate. Proposals are matched with counterproposals, and reasonable efforts are made to reach an agreement.

The collective bargaining process and the final agreement reached are influenced by many variables. Figure 12.5 identifies some of the variables influencing union and management representatives. For example, the state of the economy affects collective bargaining. The firm's representative must consider whether, based on current and expected economic conditions, the company can pay an increased wage.

The actual process of collective bargaining involves a number of steps: (1) prenegotiation, (2) selecting negotiators, (3) developing a bargaining strategy, (4) using the best tactics, and (5) reaching a formal contractual agreement.

Collective Bargaining
Negotiation of a labor contract by union and management.

TABLE 12.6

Major Sections Found in Typical Labor-Management Contracts

Purpose and intent of the parties	Seniority
Scope of the agreement	Safety and health
Management	Military service
Responsibilities of the parties	Severance allowance
Union membership and checkoff*	Savings and vacation plan
Adjustment of grievance	Supplemental unemployment benefits (SUB) program
Arbitration	
Suspension and discharge cases	SUB and insurance grievances
Rates of pay	Prior agreements
Hours of work	Termination date
Overtime—holidays	Appendixes
Vacations	

*In a checkoff arrangement, the employer deducts monthly union dues from the employee's pay. The dues are then transmitted to the union.

THE RESULT OF COLLECTIVE BARGAINING: THE CONTRACT

The union-management contract designates the formal terms of agreement reached in collective bargaining. The average contract covers two or three years and varies from a few typewritten pages to well over a hundred pages, depending on the issues covered, the size of the organization, and the union. It must be in compliance with federal, state, and local laws.

The labor contract is divided into sections and appendixes. The sections covered in some labor agreements are listed in Table 12.6. A major part of the contract is concerned with such employment issues as wages, hours, fringe benefits, and overtime.

A major task of labor and management is to jointly administer the contract. Contracts are difficult to administer perfectly because contract language requires interpretation—it is not perfect. Day-to-day compliance with contract provisions becomes an important responsibility of the first-line manager, who works closely with union members. As the representative of management, the first-line manager must discipline workers, handle grievances, and prepare for such actions as strikes.

Discipline

Most contracts state that management has a right to discipline workers. But any discipline in a unionized firm must follow legal due process. If an employee or a union challenges a disciplinary action, the burden of proof rests on the company. Often management will lose a case that is arbitrated (settled by an impartial third party), because improper disciplinary procedures have been followed.

Contracts usually specify the types of discipline and the offenses for which corrective action will be taken. Some of the infractions typically spelled out include:

Incompetence—failure to perform the assigned job.

Misconduct—insubordination, dishonesty, or violating a rule such as smoking in a restricted area.

Violations of the contract—initiating a strike, for example, when there is a no-strike clause.

The contract should list penalties for infractions. Violators must be disciplined similarly, but inconsistent application of discipline is sometimes a problem. When one employee is reprimanded for regularly arriving at work late but another with a similar tardiness problem is discharged, discipline is being applied inconsistently.

Consistent, prompt, and reasonable discipline programs are what union and management representatives attempt to spell out in the contract. One strategy is to use a progressive program in which repeated or more serious violations result in penalties of increasing severity. The sequence of progressive discipline might be:

1. An oral caution and a note in the personnel file of the employee.
2. A written reprimand that becomes a part of the file.
3. A short, two-day to one-week suspension.
4. Demotion to the next-lower job position.
5. A long, one- to three-month suspension.
6. Discharge.

The emphasis in a progressive discipline approach should be on developing within the total work force a willingness to obey and follow rules and regulations. The goal is to encourage employees to follow rules because they want to, not because they are afraid of the progressively severe penalties. In one classic example of progressive discipline, an employee had broken many rules, but none so serious as to justify her discharge. This microfilm operator was finally fired by an Illinois firm for a hostile work attitude. Her record contained frequent notations for absenteeism, insubordination, smoking at her desk, and being absent from her workstation. A third-party judge acting as an arbitrator (see page 433 for discussion of arbitrator) ruled that this action violated a progressive discipline program. The employer cannot abruptly discharge the worker for a minor fault unless preliminary steps, such as reprimands and suspensions, have been administered in a timely manner.[11]

Grievances

A complaint about a job that creates dissatisfaction or discomfort, whether it is valid or not, is a **grievance.** The complaint may be made by a single employee or by the union. Even a grievance of questionable validity should be handled correctly. Even if it seems absolutely without support, management should still handle it according to formal contractual provisions.

Grievance procedures are usually followed in unionized companies, but they are also important channels of communication in nonunionized organizations.

Grievance
Complaint made by an employee or the union about a job, person, or condition that creates dissatisfaction or discomfort.

FIGURE 12.6

Steps in the Grievance Process

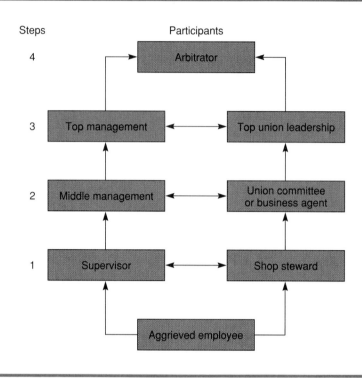

In the unionized organization, the contract contains a clause covering the steps to be followed and how the grievance will be handled. The number of steps varies from contract to contract.

Figure 12.6 illustrates a four-step grievance procedure used in a unionized company.

1. The employee meets with the supervisor and the union steward and presents the grievance. Most grievances are settled at this point.
2. If the grievance is not settled at step 1, a conference takes place between middle management and union officials (a business agent or union committee).
3. If the grievance cannot be settled at step 2, then a top management representative and top union officials attempt to settle the grievance.
4. If the grievance cannot be settled at step 3, both parties (union and management) turn the grievance over to an arbitrator, who makes a decision. Arbitration is usually handled by a mutually agreed upon individual or a panel of an odd number.

Although most grievances are handled at step 1, managers should follow a number of important principles: (*a*) take every grievance seriously; (*b*) work with the union representative; (*c*) gather all information available on the grievance; (*d*) after weighing all the facts, provide an answer to the employee voicing the grievance; and (*e*) after the grievance is settled, attempt to move on to other matters.

Wide World Photos

Strikes occur throughout the world. This is a crowd of Solidarity strikers in Poland. Their union leader, Lech Walesa, was elected president of Poland in December 1990. In Poland, a union leader like Walesa has now become a politician.

Strikes

A **strike** is an effort to withhold employee services so that the employer will make greater concessions at the bargaining table. The strike, or a threatened one, is a major bargaining force used by the unions. However, the total amount of work time lost to strikes has been decreasing. As of October 1990, there had been 43 work stoppages (in 1990) that involved 195,000 workers, and 6.1 days were lost because of strikes.

A union planning to strike needs to consider the legality of striking, the members' willingness to endure the hardships of a long strike, and the employer's ability to operate the organization without union members. The greater the employer's ability to operate the organization, the less chance the union will have of gaining its demands.

When a strike occurs, management must be able to function during the work stoppage and protect the company from strike sabotage. Employers sometimes bring in strike replacement employees to keep the firm operating. The union refers to these replacements as **scabs.** An emotional description that captures how union members felt about scabs in 1947 is presented in the Business Action.

Management should also be aware of picketing procedures. Hoping to shut down the company during a strike, the union may place members at plant entrances to advertise the dispute and discourage people from entering or

Strike
A union weapon that involves withholding employees' services to get management to make concessions.

Scab
The union label for a strike replacement hired by management.

A Scab Is the Lowest Form

After God had finished the rattle-snake, the toad, and the vampire, he had some awful substance left with which He made a *scab*. A *scab* is a two-legged animal with a corkscrew soul, a water-logged brain, and a combination backbone made of jelly and glue. Where others have hearts, he carries a tumor of rotten principles.

When a *scab* comes down the street, men turn their backs, and angels weep in heaven, and the devil shuts the gates of hell to keep him out. No man has a right to *scab* as long as there is a pool of water deep enough to drown his body in, or a rope long enough to hang his carcass with. Judas Iscariot was a gentleman compared with a *scab*. For betraying his Master, he had character enough to hang himself. A *scab hasn't!*

Esau sold his birthright for a mess of pottage. Judas Iscariot sold his Savior for thirty pieces of silver. Benedict Arnold sold his country for a promise of a commission in the British Army. The modern strikebreaker sells his birthright, his country, his wife, his children, and his fellow men for an unfulfilled promise from his employer, trust, or corporation.

Esau was a traitor to himself, Judas Iscariot was a traitor to his God. Benedict Arnold was a traitor to his country.

A strikebreaker is a traitor to his God, his country, his family, and his class![12]

leaving. Peaceful persuasion through the formation of a picket line is legal, but violence is not. Picketing may also take place without a strike to publicize union viewpoints about an employer.

Another type of union pressure is the **boycott.** In a primary boycott, union members do not patronize the boycotted firm. A secondary boycott occurs when a supplier of a boycotted firm is threatened with a union strike unless it stops doing business with the boycotted company. According to a 1988 Supreme Court decision, secondary boycotts are legal if they do not involve coercive tactics or picketing by the union. A special type of boycott is the **hot-cargo agreement.** Under this agreement, the employer permits union members to avoid working with materials that come from employers who have been struck by a union. This type of boycott is illegal except in the construction and clothing industries.

Boycott
A bargaining tactic in which the union refuses to do business with a firm or attempts to get people or other organizations to refuse to deal with the firm.

Hot-Cargo Agreement
A boycott agreement between management and union that workers may avoid working with materials that come from employers that have been struck by a union.

Management's response to these union pressures may be to continue operations with a skeleton crew of managerial personnel, to shut down the plant, or to lock the employees out. **Lockouts** are used by management to keep employees from their jobs, prevent union work slowdowns, prevent damage to property, or eliminate violence related to a labor dispute. Many states allow locked-out employees to draw unemployment benefits, thereby weakening the lockout. In practice, lockouts are more often threatened than used.

Lockout
Management pressure tactic that involves denying employees access to their jobs.

The Racketeer Influenced and Corrupt Organizations Act (RICO) was intended to be used to help keep organized crime out of labor-management business. However, a number of firms have attempted to use RICO as the basis of lawsuits to prevent or stop some union activities.[13] Desperate to end the strike violence that had engulfed Greyhound Lines, the bus firm filed a $30 million civil RICO suit accusing the striking Amalgamated Transit Union of using "coordinated criminal and extortion means" to injure the firm financially. Eastern Air Lines filed a massive $1.5 billion RICO suit accusing its machinists and pilots unions of attempting to destroy the company through racketeering, extortion, fraud, and defamation. RICO-based suits by management usually result in lengthy litigation that would seem to favor companies.

Occasionally, serious disputes between union and management do not reach the strike or lockout stages. Instead a third party becomes involved. The third party may be a fact-finding group appointed by the government or the two parties. A fact-finding group investigates the issues and makes a public report; the public statement often causes the parties to become less antagonistic or extreme. Or the third party may be a mediator or an arbitrator.

A **mediator** tries to get the two parties to reason and works at improving communication between them. Typically, mediators are full-time employees of the Federal Mediation and Conciliation Service (FMCS), a division of the U.S. Department of Labor. Under the Taft-Hartley Act, employers are required to notify the FMCS 30 days before the expiration of a contract or when new negotiating has begun. The FMCS provides experienced mediators at no cost to help the parties reach a contract agreement. The mediator does not make a decision but attempts to stimulate the parties to reach an agreement. Mediators have no power to impose a solution to the bargaining impasse.

Mediator
Third party to a labor dispute who tries to get union and management to reason and works at improving communication between them.

An **arbitrator** is a third party who collects information, listens to the positions taken, and (unlike the mediator) makes a binding decision. Union and management must comply with the decision. Most labor contracts provide for

Arbitrator
Third party to a labor dispute who makes the final, binding decision about some disputed issue.

True or False: Unions and Management Cooperate More Today than a Decade Ago?

The answer to the title question is both true and false. As the chapter's opening comments about mechanics, pilots, and management at Eastern Air Lines suggest, cooperation is scarce. Other union-management conflicts have also made the news. For example, at GM's engine and assembly plant in Pontiac, Michigan, distrust and anger have developed into a fight. Hard hit by layoffs and concessions, or givebacks, on contracts, UAW dissidents are telling workers to not sell out to management. The dissidents inform the rank and file that cooperative labor-management work teams often result in the elimination of jobs and in fewer worker grievances because employees fear further job cutbacks.

If cooperation doesn't work, what is the alternative? The UAW dissidents want to argue for job security, wage increases, and better working conditions. They want to move back to the old militant style. Their campaign to gain supporters includes an interesting statistic: 43,000 GM workers have been laid off since the cooperative teamwork plans have been in place.

Donald Ephlin, retired UAW vice president, has some candid opinions about cooperation. He believes that companies need to see unions more as partners than as the enemy. For many years, unions only reacted to what management did. Today unions must participate more in company operations.

USX Corporation in Pittsburgh is moving from the old iron-fist management approach to a more cooperative style. The steelmaker paid $20,000 so that 4,000 union and managerial employees at its Pittsburgh mills could have a day at the Kenningwood Amusement Park. Company management has begun to set up worker-management teams to study and solve quality problems. USX is convinced that cooperation with the workers is important. The USX approach does not depend on the union leadership. In fact, the company has gone around the union leadership and formed alliances with the workers. Of course the union leaders are skeptical and believe that management is on a risky course. But to date, the program is showing results.

Quality programs are popping up at other USX facilities. The plants are posting profit gains, and customer rejection rates for products have been slashed. Quality teams, training, and better profits are the first results of the cooperative programs. Unless USX can improve relationships with labor and enter joint ventures with South Korea (Pohany Steel) and Japan (Kobe Steel) to become more profitable, the firm may have difficulty surviving.

The jury is still out on cooperative programs. However, more are being attempted today than a decade ago. The need to compete in world markets has a way of encouraging some managers and union leaders to team up to save jobs, be competitive, and increase profits. Union dissidents, however, are not at all convinced that being cozy with management will be good for the membership. Keep tuned. We are probably going to see more arguments within the union movement.[14]

use of an arbitrator in grievance procedures, as shown in Table 12.6. In arbitration, each party tries to persuade the arbitrator that its position is ethical, fair, accurate, and in the best interest of everyone involved. Following an arbitration hearing, the arbitrator considers the evidence and renders a decision on the case that is legally binding unless one or both parties decide to appeal the arbitrator's decision in a court of law. This rarely occurs.

The written contract usually specifies the arbitrator's selection method and scope of authority. Most contracts state that the parties shall select a mutually acceptable arbitrator from a list of available arbitrators provided by either the American Arbitration Association (AAA) or the FMCS, or from both lists.

Are unions and management cooperating more or less today than a decade ago? At the General Motors Saturn plant in Spring Hill, Tennessee, cooperation is high. Workers have willingly spent 16 to 17 hours a day on the job building test versions of the Saturn.[15] The workers have been working closely with management to prove they can produce cars as efficiently as nonunion workers at Japanese-owned U.S. plants. The Business Action, however, indicates that while cooperation is greater in some cases, in others conflict, problems, and distrust still are prominent.

National Emergencies

A widespread strike or lockout or one that occurs in a crucial industry could pose a threat to the nation's economy and security. For example, if the airline, trucking, or rail industries were shut down for any length of time, such vital services as food distribution, the movement of medical supplies, or the delivery of military repair parts could be threatened.

The president of the United States can take action to resolve such strikes and lockouts. The Railway Labor Act and the Taft-Hartley Act provide the mechanisms employed in national emergency situations. For example, if there is no contract agreement and a strike or lockout could threaten the nation's welfare or security, the president can (1) direct the attorney general to obtain a court order (an injunction) preventing the strike or lockout for 80 days; (2) appoint a board of inquiry to study the impasse and make recommendations; and (3) order the FMCS to attempt to mediate the dispute.

If the impasse is still not settled by the 60th day, the inquiry board is reconvened. After the board reports the employer's final offer, the National Labor Relations Board conducts a secret ballot election among the employees. If the employees vote not to accept the offer, the attorney general must ask the federal court to dissolve the injunction. The union has a legal right to strike after this 80-day cooling-off period.

By 1989 the national emergency provisions of the law had been invoked 35 times (only twice, however, since 1972). Thirty injunctions have been issued.

NONUNION ORGANIZATIONS

Most business firms in the United States are nonunion, or unorganized. One of the largest union-free firms is IBM. In most cases, union-free firms are small and are found in right-to-work states. Union penetration is highest in the Northeast and Midwest and lowest in the South and in rural areas.

An increasing number of firms have specific union-avoidance policies and, to support these goals, develop employee relations practices: participation programs, profit-sharing plans, formal grievance systems, and all-salaried (that is, everyone is paid a salary instead of hourly wages) compensation systems.[16]

Another study of nonunion organizations concluded that two types of firms—doctrinaire and philosophy-laden—can operate effectively without unions.[17] The *doctrinaire* firm wants to continue to be nonunion. It develops policies that mimic what unions have won in similar organizations. The belief is that, since the firm has good human resource policies, employees will resist union organizing efforts. The *philosophy-laden* firm has no unions because its climate of labor-management relations is excellent. Management has adopted policies on compensation, staffing, grievance handling, and discipline that it believes are correct and equitable.

You'll Know It's the **Century When . . .**

Labor Unions Are Rare

By the year 2000, union membership will have plunged from 33 percent of all nonfarm workers in 1955 to 13 percent or less. Even public sector unions, which boomed in the 1970s and 80s, will have lost some steam. Why the decline? Automated factories and the shift to service jobs played a part in the private sector, and increased fiscal responsibility will have affected the government side. But union successes and failures contributed to the slide, too—success at winning better wages and working conditions, and the failure to accept women and minorities and successfully court service workers. Some predict that unions, much changed, will survive, but will work more closely with management for the good of both union members and the company.[18]

SUMMARY OF LEARNING OBJECTIVES

1. To define the term *labor union.*
   Labor unions are organizations of employees who formally join together to protect, maintain, and improve their economic, social, and political power and well-being. They may also be called guilds or associations.

2. To identify the significant trends facing the labor movement today.
   Unions are facing declining memberships due to bad publicity surrounding union activities and union officials; economic factors, including deregulation of certain industries, plant closings, and mergers and acquisitions; management resistance; and the reduced number of blue-collar workers in the labor force. Some success in organizing white-collar workers and government employees has helped improve the image of unions.

3. To explain why employees decide to organize unions.

   Employees organize unions for different reasons. They may organize to try to satisfy needs for such things as pay and benefits, supervision, and job security. They may also be experiencing dissatisfaction with work-related conditions.

4. To compare the main features of the major labor legislation.

   The *Railway Labor Act* gave employees the right to organize and bargain collectively. The *Norris-LaGuardia Act* limited the courts' injunction power and made yellow-dog contracts unenforceable. The *Wagner Act* spelled out the right of employees to organize and elect a union, regulated collective bargaining, and listed unfair employer labor practices. It established the National Labor Relations Board (NLRB). The *Taft-Hartley Act* guaranteed employee bargaining rights, provided for passage of right-to-work laws, listed unfair union labor practices, and established the Federal Mediation and Conciliation Service (FMCS). The *Landrum-Griffin Act* specified rules for how unions were to conduct their affairs and eliminated sweetheart contracts. *Title VII* did for public-sector employees what the Wagner and Taft-Hartley acts had done for the private sector. The *Worker Adjustment and Retraining Act (WARN)* requires employers to give 60 days' written notice of plant closings or layoffs.

5. To list the steps in both organizing and decertifying a union.

   Organizing a union involves petitioning for union representation, determining the appropriate bargaining unit, and conducting a union representation election. To decertify a union, employees must petition the NLRB, which then conducts a secret ballot election.

6. To define the term *collective bargaining.*

   Collective bargaining is the process that establishes, manages, and enforces contractual agreements between labor and management. Representatives of both sides debate, discuss, and demand better solutions for their groups. The process includes several steps: prenegotiation, selecting negotiators, developing a strategy, using negotiation tactics, and reaching a formal agreement.

7. To discuss what is included in a union-management contract.

   The contract represents the formal terms of agreement reached through collective bargaining by labor and management. Various sections cover the responsibilities of the parties, adjustment of grievances, rates of pay, savings and vacation plans, and arbitration procedures.

8. To explain how a strike, boycott, and lockout differ.

   A *strike* is an effort by employees to withhold their labor so that the employer will make greater concessions at the bargaining table. The strike—or the threat of one—is the union's strongest bargaining tool. In a *boycott,* unions try to get management to concede by not patronizing the firm. A *lockout* occurs when management closes the doors to prevent union work slowdowns, violence, or damage to property.

KEY TERMS

Labor Union, p. 407

Industrial Union, p. 407

Craft Union, p. 407

Yellow-Dog Contract, p. 408

Knights of Labor, p. 408

AFL–CIO, p. 409

Business Representative, p. 417

Union Steward, p. 417

Railway Labor Act, p. 420

Injunction, p. 420

Norris-LaGuardia Act, p. 420

Wagner Act, p. 420

National Labor Relations Board (NLRB), p. 420

Taft-Hartley Act, p. 420

Landrum-Griffin Act, p. 420

Sweetheart Contract, p. 421

Union Shop, p. 421

Agency Shop, p. 422

Open Shop, p. 422

Maintenance of Membership Agreement, p. 422

Right-to-Work Laws, p. 423

Closed Shop, p. 423

Title VII, p. 424

Worker Adjustment and Retraining Notification Act (WARN), p. 424

Decertification, p. 426

Collective Bargaining, p. 427

Grievance, p. 429

Strike, p. 431

Scab, p. 431

Boycott, p. 433

Hot-Cargo Agreement, p. 433

Lockout, p. 433

Mediator, p. 433

Arbitrator, p. 433

QUESTIONS FOR DISCUSSION AND REVIEW

1. Trace and discuss the history of labor unions in the United States.
2. How does a worker file a grievance and win a grievance dispute?
3. What labor laws have had the greatest impact on the growth of unions?
4. What power does the union possess to acquire what it wants in the form of better pay, working conditions, and fairness in treatment from management?
5. Why have many women been reluctant to join unions?
6. What was the objective of the Landrum-Griffin Act?
7. To discipline an employee, how must management prepare the case against the person?
8. What is your opinion about the national emergency power of the president?
9. Why do employees join a union?
10. Give some of the reasons for the decline in union membership.

CASE 12.1
An Edgy UAW Eyes the Japanese and *Kaizen*

In rural Ohio, the Japanese have a plant with more than 25,000 employees. Another plant is under construction nearby. Honda will produce 500,000 cars a year at these two facilities. Honda and the American factories of Nissan, Toyota, Mazda, Mitsubishi Motors, Suzuki, Subaru, and Isuzu will be making over 2 million cars and light trucks a year by 1992 or 1993.

Japanese managers talk about family, pride, dignity, and teamwork. The United Automobile Workers union listens, watches, and is starting to ask questions. Some of the union leaders, as indicated in the chapter, are now feeling rebellious. There is the joke about the vacationing American, French, and Japanese autoworkers who found themselves captured by cannibals. Before they were to be dropped into a kettle of boiling water, they were given a last request.

"Let me taste an exquisite French wine before I go," said the Frenchman.

"Let me give my lecture on *kaizen*," said the Japanese.

"Eat me first," said the American. "I can't stand to hear another word about *kaizen*."

The Japanese approach at these transplanted plants in Ohio, Indiana, Tennessee, and Kentucky centers on *kaizen*—or constant improvement. What does constant improvement mean? Union dissidents, once enthusiastic supporters of the Japanese coming to America, say that it means constant speedup.

Speedups, even if they are called constant improvements, mean more stress for workers. The UAW also is not happy with their agreement to permit Mazda to have only two classifications of workers—maintenance and production. This permits Mazda management to assign workers to the jobs and rotate them. The result is a reduction in the total number of employees. Another problem plant is the one in Fremont, California (GM and Toyota). In organizing the plant, the union accepted Toyota's unique production system, which included *kaizen*.

The UAW is fearful of losing more members. Its membership, which peaked at 1.5 million in 1979, is now about 1 million. The Japanese have brought in new techniques and are now increasing their share of the U.S. market by selling the assembled American models. This hasn't stopped the loss of members in the union.

The UAW is attempting to gain a foothold in some of these plants. It has targeted American-Japanese joint ventures, such as the Fremont plant, for organizing drives. The union has not been able to win recognition at a U.S. plant that is owned and operated solely by the Japanese. Whether such plants will ever be unionized is a question both labor and management experts are asking.

Adapted from Terry Maxon, "GM/Toyota," *American Way,* March 1990, pp. 28–34; Kirk Victor, "Tensions over Teamwork," *National Journal,* May 20, 1989, pp. 1128–31; "Constant Improvement? Or Speedup?" *Forbes,* May 17, 1989, pp. 92–94.

The Fremont plant has been successful using the production system featuring *kaizen*. Absenteeism is low, production is up, and workers freely express their opinions. The plant also has a reputation for producing high-quality cars. Is the Fremont plant a model for union-management cooperation? There are complaints, as we have seen, but it is a start. *Kaizen* apparently can work even in unionized plants. If there are no layoffs, the union is likely to accept *kaizen*. If layoffs occur, however, confrontations are probable. Whether it involves speedups, improvements, or quality, the key to maintaining peace seems to be workers keeping their jobs.

Questions for Discussion

1. Why haven't workers in Japanese-run auto plants voted to unionize?
2. What does *kaizen* have to do with maintaining the competitive edge in the marketplace?
3. How can a selection (hiring) system be used to screen out potential job candidates who would be opposed to Japanese production techniques?

CASE 12.2
Correcting a Tardiness Problem: The Internal Revenue Service

Working in a midwestern office of the Internal Revenue Service was a clerk who had established a very bad record of tardiness. During May and June of one year alone, she was late 14 times for periods ranging from 15 to 90 minutes. On several occasions, in an attempt to avoid tardiness, she parked in restricted areas and was warned for that infraction as well. Finally, when it appeared to the office manager that she was not likely to mend her ways, the clerk was discharged.

The office manager did not take this action lightly. He knew the clerk was a single parent and that her poor attendance was often caused by problems with arranging day care for her young children. But things had reached the point, he believed, where management simply could not tolerate the intrusion of her personal problems.

During a grievance procedure, the union offered a novel solution. "Add up all the absences and charge them against her annual leave," the chief steward suggested.

The office manager refused. "There is nothing in the union contract that requires us to do anything like that."

"Right or Wrong in Employee Relations," *Office,* August 1990, p. 43.

When the matter came before an arbitrator, the union also argued that management was partly to blame in that timely action was not taken earlier—before the poor attendance record became fully established. Said the steward: "If we had had these discussions earlier, we might have done something."

Questions for Discussion
1. Should the clerk be reinstated? Why?
2. How valid is the union claim that management is partly to blame for not taking earlier action? Why?
3. Should this situation be handled by mediation or arbitration? Why?

HR MANAGEMENT

At one time, human resource managers were very low on the corporate organization chart. They were thought of as paperpushers who took job applications, kept salary records, and enforced workplace rules. Today, as more and more companies recognize the importance of managing their most valuable asset—people—human resource managers have moved into the executive suite and into the boardroom. Their higher status reflects the increasingly difficult task of keeping employees content and productive. Today's human resource manager must deal with challenging issues such as affirmative action, child care, incentive plans, benefits programs, flexible work schedules, and labor shortages.

The human resource field offers challenges and a promising career. Jobs in the field are expected to grow as more and more employers recognize the importance of employee morale and productivity. Almost half a million people are employed in human resources, and the number is expected to increase.

Personnel selection is decisive. People are our most valuable capital.
Joseph Stalin

The field has become increasingly technical and offers a number of specialty areas.

TRAINING

Training specialists develop and coordinate programs to meet specific training needs for the firm's employees and managers. They are usually involved in orientation for new employees, training manual preparation, development programs for new managers and supervisors, and provision of educational opportunities for employees.

Specialists in this area may develop course materials and teach classes in general areas. In most cases, however, they coordinate educational programs by bringing in experts to teach specific subjects. To instruct employees in technical areas related to their jobs, speakers may come from outside the firm or from within the firm.

In most organizations, training is a coordinating function. The department brings together employees needing training with individuals capable of providing it.

COMPENSATION

The compensation administrator works to establish fair and equitable pay policies and practices. Job analysts evaluate job duties, write job descriptions, and develop job specifications. Wage and salary specialists determine proper pay ranges. Compensation experts conduct compensation surveys, maintain pay records, and devise pay

Human Resources Departments

Director
Human Resources

Employment	College Recruiting	Training and Development	Compensation	Benefits	Labor Relations	Equal Opportunity

plans. They are concerned with the company's pay range and keeping the organization competitive with similar jobs in other companies.

EMPLOYMENT AND RECRUITING

The employment manager has overall responsibility for identifying and selecting qualified personnel for factory, office, sales, technical, and professional positions. College recruiters conduct on-campus interviews to find prospects for professional employment. Personnel interviewers interview applicants to fill job vacancies and evaluate their qualifications.

Employment professionals refer selected applicants for specific job openings. They seldom make the actual hiring decision but might recommend candidates to the managers making the final decision. They are also involved in employee transfers, promotions, terminations, layoffs, exit interviews, and outplacement activities.

Duties: Human Resources

- Interviewing employment candidates.
- Maintaining employment records.
- Handling employee grievances.
- Conducting wage and salary surveys.
- Preparing payroll reports.
- Developing and coordinating new-employee orientation.
- Writing job descriptions.

BENEFITS

Company benefits programs for employees are administered by benefits managers. They handle the company medical and dental insurance, disability, pension, and retirement programs. They may be involved in designing and developing additional programs and services related to employee welfare, such as child care, carpooling, fitness programs, counseling, and personal financial planning.

Benefits specialists must understand social security regulations and administer pension plans in accord with government requirements. They may be involved in

negotiating insurance plans for thousands of employees and must be knowledgeable of the tax implications of various benefit plans.

LABOR RELATIONS

Labor relations specialists are experts on labor laws and collective bargaining. They assist in union-management negotiations and provide background and analysis on topics such as labor market conditions, wages, employee benefit programs, and labor legislation.

Labor relations experts analyze and interpret labor contracts and

Requirements: Human Resources

Personal skills:
- Strong communication skills
- Ability to deal with people
- Fair-mindedness
- Sensitivity

Education:
- Bachelor's degree
- Master's degree
- Major in human resource management

443

CAREER PROFILE: Madelyn Jennings

Elizabeth Naples

MADELYN JENNINGS

Undergraduate degree: Texas Woman's University
Major: English and business economics
Current position: Senior vice president, human resources,
Gannett Co.

Golf and curiosity about becoming a pro like her father are probably most responsible for starting Madelyn Jennings' three-decade climb through the steep corporate ranks. Her sports ambition took her to a southern college, where she could play year-round. She chose Texas Woman's University, a school dedicated to training women for the business world. There she learned that golfing was destined to be recreational only and that a degree in business economics "certainly wouldn't hurt you."

Jennings began her career by turning down a dull air force job at $100 a week. She chose a lesser-paying slot as assistant director of public relations for Slick Airways, in Dallas, Texas. Soon she tired of only writing press releases. She wanted to try something different—like Europe. "So I became a stewardess," she says. "I proposed a deal that I would do public relations abroad, and I would pay for my way by working the trips over."

Jennings stayed with public relations and advertising for several companies until 1960. Then she joined General Electric, spending the next 16 years in a variety of jobs that led to employee relations. At one point in her career at GE, she gave herself a four-level demotion to get valuable labor relations experience.

After 16 years with GE, Jennings moved to Standard Brands, where there was plenty of room to grow. She eventually became vice president of human resources. After four years, she was qualified to walk into the top human resources position at Gannett. There Jennings has been responsible for not only judging talent and contribution but also nurturing people and attracting talent to the company of more than 37,000 employees. "I'm concerned with who we are hiring, who we are promoting, who we are firing, and how we are training. They're the ones who are going to run this place in 1995," she says.

Jennings' career-climbing philosophy is that the ambitious should not look at the next rung of the career ladder, it will come soon enough. "I really think you have to do the very best you can in the job you have and not be thinking about the next job, or the job after that," she says. "First off, you're probably wrong about what those next jobs are going to be. Secondly, you may divert yourself from the job at hand and not take it seriously enough."

Source: Adapted from "Building the HR Network," by Martha I. Finney (December 1988). Reprinted with permission from HRMagazine (formerly Personnel Administrator), published by the Society for Human Resource Management, Alexandria, VA.

monitor company practices. They are involved in all aspects of settling labor disputes. They follow the company's grievance procedures, arranging meetings with complaint-initiating workers, managers, and union representatives.

EQUAL EMPLOYMENT OPPORTUNITY/ AFFIRMATIVE ACTION

The equal employment opportunity (EEO) manager is responsible for developing and implementing employment programs to conform with equal opportunity and affirmative action laws and regulations. Under the direction of the EEO manager, specialists in the area help develop and write the company's affirmative action plan and communicate affirmative action policies and plans to employees, top management, and government agencies. They interface with minority employees and investigate employee complaints and charges of discrimination, as well as compiling and submitting required equal opportunity and affirmative action statistical reports.

Additional Human Resources Information

American Society for Personnel Administration
606 North Washington Street
Alexandria, VA 22314

International Personnel Management Association
1313 East 60th Street
Chicago, IL 60637

National Employment Association
1850 K Street, N.W., Suite 870
Washington, DC 20006

Personnel Accreditation Institute
P.O. Box 19648
Alexandria, VA 22320

PART FIVE

MARKETING

CHAPTER THIRTEEN

MARKETING STRATEGY

LEARNING OBJECTIVES

1. To explain the purpose and importance of marketing.

2. To trace the evolution of marketing.

3. To define the term *market* and distinguish between the two major types of markets.

4. To describe the steps involved in developing a marketing strategy.

5. To identify the four elements of the marketing mix.

6. To define the term *marketing environment* and list the environmental forces.

7. To describe how consumers make purchase decisions, and compare consumer buying behavior to industrial buying behavior.

8. To explain the value of marketing research and outline the research process.

Speedy service, a simple menu, consistent quality, good value. With that formula, McDonald's revolutionized the fast-food market and grew to be the world's largest food service company. The giant chain of 11,000-plus outlets still earns healthy profits. But growth has slowed and now comes mainly from overseas. The average number of customers per U.S. restaurant hasn't increased in five years.

McDonald's introduced new items like fish, pasta, and pizza to attract families, couples, and groups of teenagers for dinner—the slowest part of the day. With pizza now the most popular evening meal in U.S. restaurants, McDonald's offers its own 14-inch version after 4 P.M. In four varieties prepared from frozen crusts, the pizza is baked in special ovens in 5½ minutes. Costs range from about

town of Hartsville, McDonald's Golden Arch Cafe is a 1950s-style diner offering plate dinners and Coke floats in real glasses.

With about 41 items on the menu, McDonald's has veered from its devotion to hamburgers, begun by founder Ray Kroc. According to one observer, the outlets "are turning themselves into the very kind of restaurant they used to run out of business."

Some wonder if McDonald's will cloud its clear identity with fast food. But the firm is known for wise marketing strategy. Its 1981 "Build a Big Mac" game popularized game card promotions, used so often today. Chicken McNuggets led the growth of finger foods. Constructing the McDonald's Olympic Swim Stadium for the 1984 Olympic games in Los Angeles pioneered sports sponsorship. The Ronald McDonald Children's Charities is a model for corporate community involvement. McDonald's television ads have featured deaf actors using sign language. McDonald's can be found in hospital cafeterias and airport terminals. Outlets in Hungary and Yugoslavia opened in 1988, before Eastern Europe's political barriers fell; the world's largest McDonald's (seating 900) opened in 1990 in Moscow. And to keep its name in consumers' minds, McDonald's spends more than $1 billion a year for advertising and other promotion, which makes it the single most advertised brand in the United States.[1]

Mike Clemmer/Picture Group

These days, McDonald's faces fierce competition from major chains (e.g., Burger King, KFC, Wendy's) and also from small, independent restaurants, convenience stores, the supermarket deli, and the microwave. Consumers are eating less red meat, fried foods, cholesterol, and salt. They are staying home for dinner more. To spur growth in the 1990s, McDonald's is trying new ways to reach new customers.

$6 for plain cheese and tomato to $10 for the deluxe. It takes longer than typical fast food, but it is still fast for pizza and competitively priced.

McDonald's customers may also find a smiling, coffee-serving hostess, dimmer lights, music, and meals in baskets instead of paper wrappings. The chain has tested hot dogs in its Toronto Skydome restaurant, breakfast burritos in Toledo, and spicy omelets elsewhere. In the small Tennessee

McDonald's offers a prime example of how marketing can help a firm achieve its goals. Effective marketing strategy contributes greatly to success; the lack of it can doom a business to failure. Marketing firmly links the company to customers, their needs, and their desires. McDonald's has devised new products, revised old ones, and explored new ways to reach potential customers. Those activities, all part of marketing, are based on a tried-and-true idea: give people what they want.

In this chapter, we provide an overview of basic marketing concepts. First we define marketing and discuss the benefits and costs of marketing activities. After briefly tracing the evolution of marketing, we introduce the marketing concept. Next we explain the steps involved in developing a marketing strategy: (1) selecting a target market and (2) designing a marketing mix (product, price, promotion, distribution) that will satisfy the needs of the target market. We also discuss the importance of understanding buyer behavior and the value of marketing research. Finally, we look at what the future holds for marketing.

AN OVERVIEW OF MARKETING

Each of you has been involved in marketing activities at one time or another. Perhaps you have tried to sell a used textbook back to the campus bookstore or to convince your parents to finance a spring vacation. You may not have known it at the time, but you were performing marketing activities.

What Is Marketing?

When people hear the term *marketing,* many think of advertising or selling. Although those are part of marketing, the part we see most, marketing is much more. As the American Marketing Association defines it, "**Marketing** is the process of planning and executing the conception, pricing, promotion, and distribution of ideas, goods, and services to create exchanges that satisfy individual and organizational objectives."[2] This definition emphasizes the diverse activities marketers perform: deciding what products to offer, setting prices, developing sales promotions and advertising campaigns, and making products readily available to customers. Table 13.1 lists several activities usually found in the marketing domain.

Marketing
The process of planning and executing the conception, pricing, promotion, and distribution of ideas, goods, and services to create exchanges that satisfy individual and organizational objectives.

Typical Marketing Activities

TABLE 13.1

Product	Pricing	Promotion	Distribution
Develop new products.	Establish price objectives.	Determine type of promotion (advertising, personal selling, sales promotion, publicity).	Select wholesalers and retailers.
Modify existing products.	Conduct cost analysis.	Design the advertising message.	Establish procedures for handling and moving products (transportation, storage, inventory control).
Test-market products.	Analyze competitors' prices.	Select the advertising media (print, radio, television, billboard, specialty items).	Find the best locations for plants, warehouses, and retail outlets.
Select brand names.	Set actual prices.	Schedule the advertisements.	
Package products.			

Marketing activities are required for many different kinds of products. The term *product* often brings to mind tangible goods—those that can be held or touched, such as compact-disk players or soft drinks. But products also can be services or ideas. Hospitals offer products: health care services. The American Cancer Society offers an idea, quitting smoking, as a product. Like firms that produce goods, nonprofit and service organizations and even individuals rely heavily on marketing. The Los Angeles Mission, for example, used mailers and advertisements to raise money to save the financially troubled mission.[3]

Exchange
The process by which parties provide something of value to one another to satisfy the needs of each.

Ultimately the purpose of marketing activities is to bring about exchanges between buyers and sellers. **Exchange** consists of one party providing something of value to another party, who gives something in return.[4] Just as the "something of value" is not always a physical good, the "something in return" is not always money, as Figure 13.1 shows. The American Cancer Society's

FIGURE 13.1

The Exchange Process

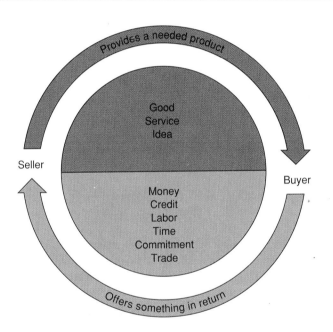

FIGURE 13.2

Types of Utility

Form utility:	Time utility:
Manufacturers use petroleum to produce gasoline.	Gas stations are open during peak traffic times, with many open 24 hours a day.
Place utility:	Possession utility:
Gas stations are located in numerous places convenient to drivers.	Customers pump gasoline into their vehicles and pay for the gasoline.

notion of quitting smoking to live a longer, healthier life is an intangible product, one that cannot be physically touched. For smokers who "buy" that idea, the price is the effort required to break a habit that they have found pleasurable.

Marketing Adds Value

Through activities that enable exchanges to take place, marketing adds value to products. This value is known as **utility,** the ability of a product to satisfy a consumer need. There are four types of utility: form, time, place, and possession (see Figure 13.2).

As Chapter 9 discussed, *form utility* is created when a firm's production function yields a product. For example, through the use of raw materials, labor, and other inputs, publishers produce newspapers and magazines. Marketing indirectly affects form utility, since an organization may depend on its marketing people to find out which products consumers would welcome in the marketplace.

Marketing directly creates the other three types of utility. By making products available when consumers want and need them, marketing creates *time utility.* Publishing companies print and distribute morning newspapers early so readers can read them at breakfast or while commuting to work. Making products available where consumers need or want to obtain them creates *place utility.* Newspapers are delivered to homes and businesses; sold in vending machines, supermarkets, convenience marts, drugstores, and bookstores; and placed in libraries. Marketing creates *possession utility* when the ownership of a product is transferred from seller to buyer. To obtain newspapers, customers pay the publishing company for home delivery, drop money into vending machines, or pay clerks in stores.

Utility
The ability of a product to satisfy consumers' needs.

New York Newsday *outlets such as this one near Times Square create place utility.*

Courtesy of Times Mirror

● C o n n e c t i o n s

How Do You Feel about Marketing Activities?

Directions: Circle the number that represents your level of agreement with each statement.

	Strongly Agree					Strongly Disagree
1. Marketing helps improve the quality of goods and services.	1	2	3	4	5	6
2. The number of commercials on TV is about right.	1	2	3	4	5	6
3. I would be proud to have a job in marketing.	1	2	3	4	5	6
4. Marketing people are concerned with product safety.	1	2	3	4	5	6
5. Most marketing activities are conducted ethically.	1	2	3	4	5	6
6. Advertisements portray women and minorities realistically, without stereotypes.	1	2	3	4	5	6
7. The benefits of marketing justify the costs.	1	2	3	4	5	6

Marketing Affects Everyone

Marketing is important to organizations and consumers alike. It touches the lives of all members of society. First, through the cost of what we purchase, each of us supports the costs of marketing. By estimate, nearly half of every dollar spent on goods and services pays for marketing activities. Most people

DID YOU KNOW? *Nearly half of every dollar spent on goods and services goes to pay the costs of marketing.*

	Strongly Agree					Strongly Disagree
8. Marketing doesn't increase materialism in our society.	1	2	3	4	5	6
9. Marketing doesn't encourage people to buy things they don't really need.	1	2	3	4	5	6
10. Marketing doesn't make people too concerned with how they look and dress.	1	2	3	4	5	6

Feedback: Now let's assess your attitudes toward marketing. Items circled 1 or 2 show a positive attitude; 3 or 4 suggests a middle-of-the road or neutral position; and 5 or 6 identifies a negative feeling.

Anyone considering a marketing career would want to feel positive about the different activities marketers perform. But, like consumers in general, students usually have mixed feelings about marketing. It is the most visible side of business and often one of the most controversial. Why? Are consumers generally skeptical of the purpose, methods, and results of marketing activities? Are they unfamiliar with the benefits marketing brings? To build positive attitudes toward marketing, do marketers and their organizations need to make changes in the ways goods, services, and ideas are developed, promoted, and sold?

would agree that marketing costs are worth it because the many and varied marketing activities enable us to satisfy our needs and wants. To review earlier discussions, a *need* is something required for human survival, such as food, water, shelter, and clothing; a *want* is something desired but not necessary for basic survival. Without marketing, many needs and wants would go unsatisfied because exchanges would be much harder to accomplish.

Marketing often has special importance for students. Many of you will work in marketing—whether in sales, retailing, advertising, or another field—in a for-profit firm or a nonprofit organization. The career appendix that follows this part of the book explores various marketing careers, some of which may be new to you. How do you feel about marketing activities? Use Connections to explore your attitudes; then compare your attitudes to your classmates'.

HOW MARKETING EVOLVED

When organizations and individuals conduct marketing activities today, they usually have consumers' needs and desires clearly in mind. But they have not always done so. Beginning with the Industrial Revolution in the 19th century and the capability of mass production that resulted, most businesses had a *production orientation*. Demand for new manufactured goods was so great that producers were concerned with increased production and operating efficiency rather than with consumer preferences. As goods rolled off the production line, marketing consisted of taking orders and shipping products.

By the mid-1920s, manufacturers discovered that supplies of basic consumer goods had caught up to demand; they were now producing an abundance of goods. Needing to move their products, firms developed a *sales orientation*. Marketing began to emphasize advertising and sales. Companies started using sophisticated sales techniques to increase demand for existing products, but they still did not look to the marketplace to ensure that consumers' needs and desires were met.

Not until the early 1950s did firms begin to develop a *consumer orientation*. With soldiers returning from World War II, reentering the workplace, and starting families, demand for consumer goods and services surged. So did competition among firms to meet that demand. They began to focus on satisfying consumers. One of the first companies to state a policy of customer satisfaction was General Electric. GE said that marketing should be integrated into each phase of business. The policy of customer satisfaction has become known as the marketing concept.

The Marketing Concept

With the U.S. population becoming older and people drinking more soft drinks, the average person's consumption of milk has dropped 15 percent over the last 20 years. Americans also are drinking more low-fat milk as they become more health conscious. In response the dairy industry has improved the taste of low-fat milk and is working to develop a no-cholesterol milk. Dairy firms are also trying to back up their product with improved packaging. In short, the milk industry is practicing the marketing concept.[5]

Marketing Concept
A managerial philosophy of customer orientation with the goal of achieving long-term success.

The **marketing concept** is a management philosophy stating that an organization should strive to satisfy the needs of consumers through a coordinated set of activities that also allows the organization to achieve its objectives.[6] Thus customer satisfaction is the major force underlying the marketing concept and driving the entire company. The marketing concept calls for all departments and all members to be committed to satisfying customers. The firm must determine consumer needs and wants, develop quality products that satisfy them, make products readily available at prices acceptable to buyers (and that will allow a profit), and provide service and after-sales support.

Firms benefit from practicing the marketing concept. They do not waste money on developments in which customers are not interested. Also, customers pay more for products they believe will provide greater value and satisfaction, they come back, and they refer business. Repeat business lowers sales costs and boosts profits; holding on to current customers is about one fifth the cost of acquiring new ones.[7] Some marketers say the marketing concept helps set up a cycle of success: Customer satisfaction leads to loyal customers, which produces higher profits that make employees want to stay with the firm, which in turn makes for better customer service and satisfaction.

Focusing on the customer sounds like an obvious, commonsense way to run a successful business, but not all firms gear their marketing activities closely to

In a world of the flighty and fly by night,   a label like this can be a wonderful thing.

1-800-356-4444

Lands' End demonstrates a commitment to customer satisfaction with its unlimited guarantee on all merchandise.

the customer. The marketing concept is not always easy to put into practice. Top-level managers must be committed to it and must gain the commitment of other members of the organization. An organization may need to restructure departments or functions to better coordinate activities. Often a firm must be willing to forgo short-term profits for long-term customer satisfaction. And because consumer tastes and preferences constantly change, the firm must continually obtain information about customers and their needs and tailor its products to meet changing consumer preferences. The Business Action illustrates how several firms, large and small, practice the marketing concept.

Beyond the Marketing Concept

Does giving consumers what they want and need serve the long-term interests of society? As we move through the 1990s, the traditional marketing concept, with its consumer focus, is taking on more meaning. Besides satisfying customers to meet company goals, many firms today also take into consideration how marketing affects society. This broader *societal orientation* means that firms are concerned with the welfare of society as well as their own interests and those of consumers.

As Chapter Four pointed out, many firms and nonprofit organizations alike take active roles in dealing with issues such as scarce resources, environmental destruction, hunger, housing shortages, and illiteracy. Forward-thinking firms and their employees are involved in programs to work on such problems, as

Putting Customers First

Visitors might be surprised when they walk into the headquarters of MBNA America, a Baltimore-based credit card company. Woven into the plush carpet at all four entrances are the words *The Customer First*. Above all 350 doorways are signs: THINK OF YOURSELF AS THE CUSTOMER.

Those are much more than nice-sounding slogans. MBNA found that credit cardholders' satisfaction is greatly influenced by how quickly telephone or written inquiries are answered and whether billing statements are error free. So managers have set performance standards. When a department meets 97 percent of the standards, MBNA puts a portion of its profits toward employee bonuses, plus it offers individual incentives. Phone service agents call customers who want to close an account and try to win them back, even waiving annual fees at times. In the collection department, senior vice president Craig Smith tells his 380 employees that customers late in making payments "need a hugging, not a mugging." More than 95 percent of the delinquent customers say MBNA service people are polite. Its emphasis on customers helps the firm retain 95 percent of its customers each year, while competitors keep about 88 percent; it holds em-

ployee turnover to 7 percent, compared to an average 21 percent for competing credit card operations.

Like MBNA, many firms try to find out what customers want and how to serve them better. Technimetrics, a computer database supplier in Houston, regularly interviews customers to determine needs before developing new products. Once it develops a product, a ready group of interested buyers already exists. Embassy Suites Hotels interviews at least five customers each day and posts their comments for the entire staff to see. Du Pont technicians now spend a significant time in customers' plants to figure out new applications for Du Pont products. A Du Pont salesman in Korea once asked Reebok International managers how his company could better serve them. As a result, Du Pont flexible plastic tubes (developed for the auto industry) are built into the soles of Reebok's ERS sneakers to give them more bounce.

Some firms change production and distribution processes to help customers. Everex Systems Inc., a small computer firm in Fremont, California, uses a system called "zero response time." It reviews phone orders every two hours so the factory can adjust assembly of its personal computers to match demand. Another example: After buying Detroit Diesel Corp., which makes truck engines, former race-car driver Roger Penske invited 40

independent distributors to visit the firm's Canton, Ohio, warehouse. Based on their suggestions, Detroit Diesel made 250 changes to cut delivery time for engine parts from five days to three and allow the warehouse to fill emergency orders in less than 24 hours.

Customer-minded firms know that pleasing customers depends heavily on employees. Many firms train employees to give good service and reward them for it. Before opening the Warsaw Marriott, Poland's first Western-owned hotel, Marriott hired 20 Polish managers and brought them to Boston for discussions and role-playing to teach them to think like customers. The managers went back and trained 1,000 employees, who have helped the Warsaw Marriott earn higher customer satisfaction ratings than the firm's U.S. hotels. Montgomery Ward has authorized 7,700 salesclerks to approve checks and handle merchandise return problems on the spot instead of calling for the manager. Some MasterCare auto service centers base wages partly on how many customers come back. Xerox, Ameritech, and BMW also link some part of annual bonuses to customer satisfaction. American Express uses more than 100 programs to recognize and reward employees for taking unusual care of customers.[8]

Courtesy of The Dow Chemical Company

Dow contributes to the wel-fare of society by creating a science museum for children.

well as to help their communities, improve education, support the arts, and provide job training and opportunities for disadvantaged children and adults.

The marketing activities we discuss throughout this chapter focus on satisfying consumer needs and wants. In the next section, we look at how firms can design marketing strategies to satisfy consumers.

DEVELOPING A MARKETING STRATEGY

To put the marketing concept into action, a firm must decide on the appropriate marketing activities to satisfy customer needs and achieve its goals. A **marketing strategy** is an overall plan for conducting marketing activities that enables an organization to use its resources and strengths to meet the needs of the marketplace. For instance, the marketing strategy at Aluminum Co. of America (Alcoa) is to use its knowledge of aluminum production and its financial resources to meet the needs of such markets as autos, trucks, and railcars.[9] Firms developing a marketing strategy follow two basic steps: (1) select a target market and (2) design a marketing mix (a combination of product, price, promotion, and distribution) that will satisfy the needs of the target market.

Marketing Strategy
A plan for selecting and analyzing a target market and developing and maintaining a marketing mix that will satisfy this target market.

FIGURE 13.3

Approaches to Selecting a Target Market

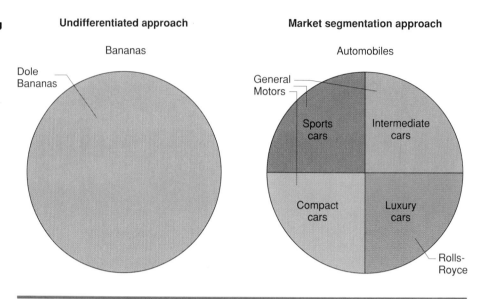

Undifferentiated approach

Bananas

Dole Bananas

Market segmentation approach

Automobiles

General Motors

Sports cars

Intermediate cars

Compact cars

Luxury cars

Rolls-Royce

Selecting a Target Market

Market
People with the authority, financial ability, and willingness to purchase a product.

Consumer Market
People who purchase products for personal use.

Industrial Market
Those who purchase products to use in the production of other products or to resell.

Market Segment
A group of individuals with one or more similar product needs.

Target Market
A group to which a firm directs its marketing activities.

Organizations gear their marketing activities to reach certain customers—a market. A **market** is a group of people who need and want a product and have the ability, willingness, and authority to purchase it. Markets are divided into two broad, overall categories: consumer and industrial. **Consumer markets** are made up of individuals who purchase products for personal use. **Industrial markets** consist of individuals or organizations that purchase goods and services so they can produce products to supply to others. Examples include manufacturers, governments, hospitals, nonprofit organizations, and stores.

One firm often sells products to both types of markets. Rossi Pasta, a family-owned business in Ohio, sells hand-rolled pasta through catalogs mailed to households (consumer) and also supplies the pasta to restaurants, supermarkets, and businesses (industrial).

Consumer or industrial, most markets include numerous customers with many different needs. Businesses, rarely able to satisfy the needs of all customers in a market, divide a market into **market segments,** groups of individuals with one or more similar product needs. Then they decide which segment or segments to serve. Bain de Soleil Suncare lotion offers three shades of tans to appeal to the tanning preferences of different market segments.[10]

The segment to which a firm directs its marketing activities is called a **target market.** In a recent survey conducted for *Working Woman* magazine, 75 percent of female executives polled said they were involved in buying office computers. Now women are a target market for many computer makers, including IBM, Apple, and Hewlett-Packard.[11]

Selecting a target market is crucial in developing an effective marketing strategy. Trying to sell a product to a group of customers who do not want or need it is bound to fail. To select a target market, firms use either the undifferentiated approach or the market segmentation approach, as Figure 13.3 illustrates.

Undifferentiated approach A firm using the **undifferentiated approach** develops one marketing mix for the total market for a product. It offers one type of product with little or no variation, sets one price, establishes one distribution system, and conducts one promotional program. Producers commonly use this approach to sell staple food items like salt or sugar, many fruits and vegetables, and other products that most customers regard as equal to similar offerings.

For this approach to work, the firm must be able to determine that most customers in the total market have the same needs. Putting together and maintaining a single marketing mix that satisfies customers' needs must be feasible.

The firm may turn to advertising or packaging to distinguish its product from those of competitors and to convince customers that its product is superior. This technique is called **product differentiation.** The makers of Puffs facial tissues, for example, advertise that Puffs are softer than other tissues on the market. Through product differentiation, an organization emphasizes a product characteristic it believes important to most consumers and encourages consumers to establish preferences. Many oil companies promote their gasolines as being different and better than competing brands: Gulf with detergent additives "keeps engines clean," Shell "boosts mileage," and Union 76 "eliminates engine knock."

Market segmentation approach Customers in a market may have many different needs that cannot be satisfied by a single marketing mix. Then a **market segmentation approach** proves crucial. The firm divides the total market into segments and creates a marketing mix for one smaller market segment rather than for the total market (see Figure 13.3).

Segmenting enables a firm to apply its strengths and resources to satisfy the needs and wants of consumers. For instance, to sell cars with an undifferentiated approach—one type of vehicle for all drivers—would be difficult if not impossible. Some drivers want luxury vehicles, others prefer economy models; some crave sports cars, and others can get by only with a station wagon or minivan. Therefore automakers divide the total vehicle market into several segments.

Firms segment markets in one of two ways. An auto company could specialize in vehicles for one group of consumers with the _concentration approach,_ as Rolls-Royce Motor Cars does with its top-of-the-line luxury vehicles. The concentration approach allows a firm to use all its knowledge, experience, and resources to meet the needs of a distinct customer group. In this way, firms with limited resources often can compete with larger firms. However, a company using this approach is dependent on a single market segment, with sales and profits tied closely to that segment's demand for the product. A drop in demand will cause a drop in sales and profits.

A firm with considerable resources and expertise may use a _multisegment approach,_ directing its efforts at two or more groups by developing a marketing mix for each. General Motors produces several different vehicles intended for different groups of customers. The multisegment approach can help an organization reach more customers and increase sales in the total market. But it also can push up a company's costs, since the firm often must use more production processes, materials, and labor, as well as several different promotion, pricing, or distribution methods.

To divide a market into segments, marketers use **segmentation bases** to define characteristics of individuals or groups of customers. Marketers can

Undifferentiated Approach
The tactic of developing one marketing mix for the total market for a product.

Product Differentiation
The use of advertising, packaging, or other product characteristics to establish the superiority of a product.

Market Segmentation Approach
The division of the total market into segments, with a marketing mix directed to one of the segments.

Segmentation Base
The individual or group characteristics that marketing managers use to divide a total market into segments.

Rolls-Royce uses the concentration approach to segment the auto market.

"Live all you can; it's a mistake not to."
—Henry James

Dealer Logo

THE NAME "ROLLS-ROYCE" AND THE MASCOT, BADGE AND RADIATOR GRILLE ARE REGISTERED TRADEMARKS. ©ROLLS-ROYCE MOTOR CARS, INC., 1988.

Reprinted by permission of Rolls-Royce Motor Cars, Inc.

segment consumer markets according to geographic, demographic, psychographic, or product-related bases.

Geographic segmentation bases include city, state, region, and zip code, as well as characteristics such as climate, terrain, and population density. A heating and air-conditioning manufacturer marketing to the entire United States, for instance, could divide the country into several regions: northeast, southeast, midwest, north, northwest, southwest, and west. Property owners living in different regions—and climates—may require different heating and cooling systems.

Demographic segmentation bases divide a market in terms of personal characteristics such as age, income, education, occupation, sex, race, social class, marital status, or family size. Such vital statistics determine in large part a person's product needs. For instance, the increasing number of women in the work force has prompted growth in child care, elderly parent care, convenience foods, time-saving appliances, and home cleaning services. Likewise many firms are developing products for older consumers, the fastest-growing age group in the United States.[12]

Today many firms target products to the Hispanic population, the fastest-growing ethnic group in the country. Hispanics in the United States number nearly 20 million and will contribute 47 percent of the U.S. population growth

FIGURE 13.4

Targeting the U.S. Hispanic Market

Courtesy of *Ser Padres* Magazine

during the 1990s.[13] Businesses are trying to tap the huge potential of this market through new products or special promotional activities, as Figure 13.4 illustrates. The publishers of *Parents Magazine* now distribute three Spanish-language family magazines to hospitals and doctors' offices.[14] Firms as diverse as Taco Bell, Acme Boot Co., Chief Auto Parts, MasterCard, Procter & Gamble, Pillsbury, McDonald's, and Southeast Bank in Miami use Spanish-language print, television, or radio ads and sweepstakes in California, South Florida, San Antonio, and Chicago. Recording groups such as Gloria Estefan and the Miami Sound Machine are releasing both English and Spanish versions of their songs.[15]

Psychographic segmentation bases are a person's attitudes, personality, opinions, lifestyle, interests, and motives. In recent years, many consumers have grown more health conscious and fitness oriented. Products from athletic footwear and clothing to exercise equipment to "light foods" have cropped up to appeal to those leading active or health-conscious lifestyles.

Product-related segmentation bases divide the total market according to aspects of product use, including volume of use (heavy or light, frequent or infrequent), brand loyalty, and expected benefits. For instance, bankers have segmented customers according to the benefits they're looking for. There are loan seekers, one-stop customers wanting convenience, value seekers searching for the lowest loan interest rates and no-charge checking accounts, and major investors who bank only at big-name institutions.

Many marketers believe that segmentation will become increasingly important as firms attempt to identify and reach their markets. For many products, the U.S. market, once considered fairly uniform, is slowly breaking up along regional and demographic lines, such as location, ethnic heritage, or age. Firms also segment industrial markets. Common bases include geographic location, size of customer firms, type of organization, and product usage.

Designing a Marketing Mix

Marketing Mix
The combination of four elements—product, price, promotion, and distribution—used to satisfy the needs of the target market.

Once a firm has selected a target market, it must decide how to satisfy the needs of the target through the **marketing mix,** the combination of four elements: product, price, promotion, and distribution. The marketing mix of Curtis Mathes, for example, consists of state-of-the-art television sets priced higher than most other brands, available through selected dealers, and promoted through print and television advertisements emphasizing the product's quality and dependability. Curtis Mathes targets its televisions to consumers who are willing and able to pay extra for a television and who want a strong warranty. Now let's look more closely at the marketing mix elements.

Product   As we said earlier, a product can be a good, a service, or an idea. Manufacturing a product (creating form utility) is a production function. But marketing managers have the responsibility to inform the production people about products consumers would find appealing and about existing products that need to be changed or that are no longer needed. Marketers also develop brand names, packaging, and warranties. You'll read more about developing products in Chapter Fourteen.

Price   Once a firm develops a product, it must set a price. Pricing requires crucial decision making because price is very visible to the consumer and is closely tied to a company's profit. Customers may not accept products priced too high; a firm may not recover its costs when products are priced too low. Chapter Fourteen discusses price in more detail.

Distribution   Even a terrific product, priced right, can fail if it is not available where and when the customer wants it. Distribution of products, a complex process, involves decisions about transportation, storage, and store selection. Chapter Fifteen gives a detailed look at distribution.

Promotion   Before they can purchase a product, consumers must know about its availability, its characteristics or benefits, and where it can be purchased. Promotion, consisting of advertising, personal selling, sales promotion, and publicity, informs or reminds the target market about a product and tries to persuade consumers to buy or adopt it. We examine aspects of promotion in Chapter Sixteen.

The Marketing Environment

Marketing Environment
All the forces outside an organization that directly or indirectly influence its marketing activities.

Marketing does not take place in a vacuum. Several forces outside the firm influence its marketing decisions. Economic conditions, regulation by government and industries, politics, the attitudes of society, technology, and competition from other firms combine to form the **marketing environment** (see Figure

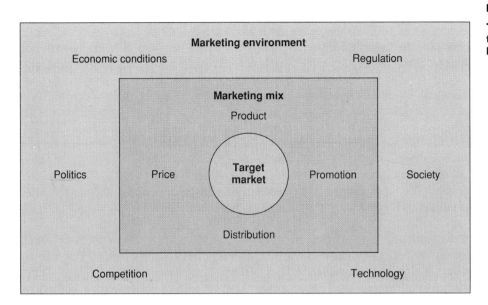

FIGURE 13.5

The Marketing Mix and the Marketing Environment

13.5). These forces continually change. An organization often must adjust its marketing mix or focus on a new target market to meet changes in the marketing environment.

Economic conditions   Economic forces in the United States and throughout the world can fluctuate rapidly and greatly influence marketing activities. Periods of slow economic growth, inflation, high interest rates for borrowers, or high unemployment may decrease consumers' ability or willingness to spend. Depending on their products and target markets, some organizations are more vulnerable than others to changes in economic conditions.

Regulation   As Chapter Five discussed, laws and regulatory agencies bear directly on marketing decisions. Numerous federal, state, and local laws have been enacted to preserve competition and to protect consumers. For example, many states have pressured the Food and Drug Administration to enforce a federal law that restricts disease-related health claims on food labels; some labels claim the products reduce cholesterol and the risk of cancer.[16] In addition to government agencies that enforce laws, industry associations impose self-regulation. For instance, the American Marketing Association has written a code of ethics and encourages its members to follow it. Consumer groups also serve as watchdogs. Consumers Union (CU) tests hundreds of products each year and publishes ratings in its monthly *Consumer Reports*. Low ratings have prompted firms to redesign products to meet CU's stringent standards. Other independent groups analyze the way medical charities and other fund-raising organizations obtain and spend contributions; they then release information to potential donors.

Politics   Laws and government policies are determined by elected officials, who can create legislation having a favorable or an unfavorable impact on for-profit and nonprofit organizations alike. Organizations and entire industries often use lobbying to inform politicians and elected officials about issues of concern and to obtain support for favorable legislation. Legislators or federal officials who believe automobile manufacturers are trying to comply with pollution standards, for example, are less likely to impose additional restrictions.

Society   Individuals and groups in our society raise questions about business practices that they believe go against the wishes of society, as we discussed in Chapter Four. When marketing activities have the potential to harm society, special-interest groups may raise objections through publicity, consumer protests, or boycotts—refusals to buy certain products. In recent years, consumer groups who object to certain television programs have boycotted products of firms that advertise on those shows; in response some companies have pulled their advertising from the programs in question.

Competition   The actions of competitors have a big impact on a firm's marketing activities. When one organization identifies a target market and introduces a successful product, others often follow with similar offerings. When competing firms raise or lower prices, improve packaging, launch innovative promotional programs, or rewrite service policies, a firm evaluates and usually adjusts its marketing strategy.

Technology   The explosion of technological innovations has deeply affected marketing mix decisions for many organizations. Dramatic developments such as the microchip, robotics, laser technology, and satellite communications offer great potential for the design, production, distribution, and promotion of products.

The Walgreen Company uses the latest in satellite communications technology to make customer prescription records available at any Walgreens pharmacy in seconds.

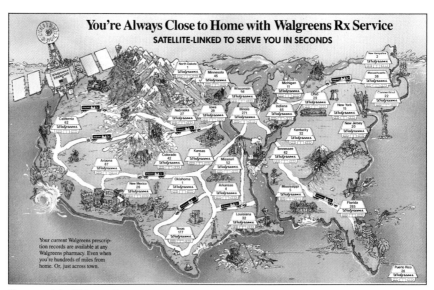

Courtesy of the Walgreen Company

While they cannot control environmental forces, marketers can influence them. They can shape the political environment to some extent through lobbying, as mentioned earlier. They can use a strong promotional program of advertising, news coverage, or sponsoring a sports event to color society's attitude toward a firm or product or to minimize a controversy. A firm that can anticipate and quickly respond to the actions of society, competitors, or other environmental forces can more effectively control its destiny.

UNDERSTANDING BUYER BEHAVIOR

What makes buyers choose one brand of soft drink over another? Why do some shoppers looking for video recorders consult *Consumer Reports* and poll all their friends, while others simply go to an electronics store and pick one out? Marketing managers study consumer behavior and consult with experts to answer such questions. Understanding buyer behavior helps firms bring about satisfying exchanges. Since purchase decisions in consumer markets differ from those in industrial markets, we will discuss those two types of buying decisions separately.

Consumer Buying Behavior

The actions and decisions of individuals who purchase products for their personal use constitute **consumer buying behavior**.[17] The process involved in purchasing products can differ from buyer to buyer and from product to product. Figure 13.6 shows a decision-making continuum. Product cost and frequency of purchase influence consumer decisions. Choosing low-cost, often-used products requires little thought and quickly becomes *routine* decision making. Buyers often use *limited* decision making for products they purchase occasionally and that require some consideration. To choose expensive, infrequently purchased products that involve complex thought, consumers use *extensive* decision making.

Consumer Buying Behavior
The decisions and actions of individuals who purchase products for personal use.

FIGURE 13.6

Types of Consumer Decision Making

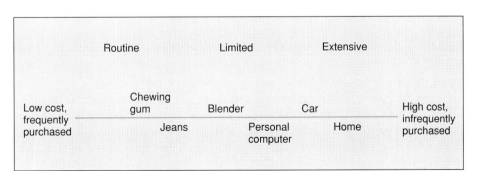

FIGURE 13.7

The Consumer Buying Process

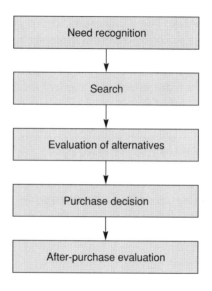

Regardless of how simple or complex the decision, consumers making purchase decisions follow a series of steps, shown in Figure 13.7. The buying process begins when a consumer recognizes a product need or want. An advertisement, a free sample, or a product display can trigger need recognition. The buyer then searches for information about and compares alternative products. After evaluating the different options, the consumer decides on a product, uses it, and determines how well it performs or meets expectations. The consumer's level of satisfaction or dissatisfaction determines future purchases.

After buying a product, especially something expensive, consumers sometimes worry that they bought the wrong brand or that they should not have bought the product at all. The conflict buyers experience when they have doubts about a purchase is called *cognitive dissonance*. Often firms try to reduce buyers' doubts through advertising or by providing follow-up information or service.

Several factors, some within individuals and some external, affect the buying decisions of consumers. People are influenced by social factors (e.g., family members, peers), psychological factors (attitudes, personality), personal characteristics (age, education), and specific conditions that exist at the time of a purchase decision. Table 13.2 explains and gives examples of factors influencing buying behavior.

Consumer attitudes toward a firm and its products certainly affect the success or failure of its marketing strategy. If enough consumers have strong negative attitudes toward some part of a firm's marketing mix, the firm may try to change consumer attitudes to make them more favorable. Changing negative consumer attitudes to positive ones is usually a long, difficult, expensive task. The Business Action explores how two meat industries have tried to change consumer attitudes toward their products.

TABLE 13.2

**Influences on Consumer
Purchase Decisions**

Influence	Examples
Social	
Family: parents, siblings, children, grandparents.	A woman buys the same brand of dishwasher her mother always had.
Roles: as parent, spouse, child, student, employee, club member.	A young man orders flowers to send his mother on Mother's Day.
Reference groups: people such as co-workers or friends with whom a person identifies and shares attitudes and behaviors.	An accountant chooses the same kind of computer her associates use.
Social class: group of people with similar values, lifestyles, and behaviors, often classified by income, occupation, education, religion, or ethnic background.	Wealthy art lovers from all over the world come to auctions at Sotheby's in New York.
Culture: values, behaviors, and ways of doing things shared by a society and passed down from generation to generation.	Americans like soft drinks colder than Europeans do.
Subculture: group that shares values and behaviors different from those of the broader culture to which it belongs.	An American woman of Oriental background shops at a specialty food store.
Psychological	
Motive: reason or internal force that drives a person toward a goal.	A student gets a haircut before a job interview.
Perception: the way people select, organize, and give meaning to the things they see, hear, taste, smell, and touch.	A mall shopper smells cookies and stops at the cookie shop to buy some.
Attitude: a person's overall feeling about something.	A family donates money to an animal rights organization.
Learning: changes in an individual's behavior caused by experiences and information.	After a high cholesterol reading, a man cuts down on the amount of meat and fats he eats.
Personality: traits, experiences, and behaviors that make up a person.	An outgoing young woman with many friends racks up huge long-distance phone bills.
Demographic	
Personal characteristics such as age, sex, marital status, family size, race, income, education, and occupation.	A working couple take their young children to a day-care center.
Situational	
Conditions that exist when a person is making a purchase decision, such as unexpected circumstances, amount of time for the decision, or expectations for future employment.	A man who is laid off from his job puts off buying a new car.

Changing Consumers' Minds about Meat

Since the health and fitness trend began in the 1980s, consumers have been eating less red meat and more chicken and fish. Feeling the impact, the meat industry is trying to change consumer preferences to put more beef and pork on dinner tables.

First the pork industry improved its product. Pork used to be fatty and high in cholesterol; many consumers thought it came from dirty animals and could transmit disease. Today the threat of trichinosis is gone. Improved feeding and breeding methods now produce pork that is 50 percent leaner than it was 20 years ago.

Then the industry tackled pork's image problem. In 1986 the National Pork Producers Council—a trade group representing 100,000 hog farmers—launched its $12 million-a-year advertising campaign to make pork "the other white meat," like chicken in appearance and nutrition. Ads show stylish entrees normally prepared with chicken, such as pork au vin and pork cacciatore, and give recipes and nutritional information. Most ads feature fresh pork tenderloin, the leanest cut, which is similar in fat and calories to chicken breast. And to keep pork's reputation for hearty, satisfying taste—one of the good qualities consumers identified with it—the industry trademarked a thick cut of pork loin called America's Cut and advertised it as "a new kind of steak."

Changing hog farmers' attitudes proved as challenging as changing consumers' attitudes. But the results have been encouraging. People are eating more pork and buying more expensive cuts like fresh tenderloin. Sales increased to almost $30 billion in 1989. The council has worked to put pork on more restaurant menus. It persuaded McDonald's to try the McRib sandwich again and convinced some International House of Pancake outlets to feature a roast pork dinner and Shoney's family restaurants to serve a breakfast chop. Now 35 percent of all pork is eaten outside the home, up from 12 percent in 1982.

The "other white meat" campaign has met other resistance. The Center for Science in the Public Interest, a consumer trade group, filed a petition with the Federal Trade Commission challenging the advertising claims that pork is low in fat, cholesterol, and calories. It says tenderloin represents only about 5 percent of all pork consumed, while the average cut of fresh pork actually has twice as much fat and more calories than an equivalent serving of chicken. And most pork is found in fatty foods such as sausage and bacon.

Still, the pork industry has had more success in changing consumers' eating habits than has the beef industry, which has been spending more than twice as much per year on advertising. Like pork, beef has a bad image—even though U.S. government tests show that lean, cooked beef is nearly identical in fat, cholesterol, and calories to skinless, roasted chicken.

The industry has tried offering leaner products and using brand names and better packaging, including Laura's Lean Beef, a Kentucky brand introduced in 1984; Coleman Natural Beef, a no-additive Colorado meat; Certified Angus Beef, used in stores and restaurants; Sun Land Beef of Arizona, a lean, vacuum-packed product; and Excel vacuum-packed beef, part of Cargill Inc. None has had great success so far.

Besides image, other problems plague beef. It is generally priced higher than chicken or pork and is a complex product sold in several cuts. Many consumers don't understand or remember the differences between the three grades: prime, choice, and select. Beef lasts only three or four days in the meat counter and darkens when frozen. Chicken, in contrast, comes in just a few parts and one grade and doesn't change color when frozen so that it can be shipped on ice for an extended shelf life.[18]

Industrial Buying Behavior

The purchase decision making of organizations such as manufacturers, service providers, government agencies, institutions, and nonprofit groups is referred to as **industrial buying behavior.** Buying decisions by organizations typically differ from consumer purchases in several ways. First, organizational transactions are usually much larger and less frequent than typical consumer purchases. Organizational buyers, who must meet exact product specifications, tend to be more concerned than consumers about quality and the services offered by sellers. Buyers usually seek more information and base decisions less on emotional factors than consumers do. In small companies, one person (usually the owner) is responsible for purchase decisions; in large firms, the responsibility for buying decisions rests with several individuals who make up a buying center.

Industrial Buying Behavior
The decisions and actions of buyers in organizations.

MARKETING RESEARCH

Throughout this chapter, we have emphasized that marketing activities should focus on customer satisfaction. No matter what its size or objectives, a firm cannot implement the marketing concept without information about customer needs. Are customers' lifestyles or preferences changing? Do some market segments still need to be reached? Who are the competitors? What product, price, distribution system, and promotional activities would enable satisfying exchanges to take place with people in the target market? To answer such critical questions, marketers must continually look at buying trends, talk to customers, and establish ways to receive feedback. Much of this communication with consumers takes place through marketing research. **Marketing research** is the systematic gathering, recording, and analyzing of information relating to the marketing of goods and services.[19]

Marketing Research
The systematic gathering, recording, and analyzing of information for guiding marketing decisions.

The Need for Marketing Research

Years ago, the attitudes of many businesspeople toward marketing research could be summarized as "If it's not broken, don't fix it." Firms conducted research in response to problems, such as decreasing profits, failure to reach sales quotas, or customers lost to a competitor. But today many firms realize that research should be ongoing. Successful firms, regardless of size, continually talk to customers and study the market. As Table 13.3 shows, marketing

TABLE 13.3

Proactive and Reactive Research Questions

Proactive	Reactive
Are we attracting new customers?	Why are we losing customers?
How do we maintain and increase sales?	Who has surpassed us in our sales?
Are we satisfying our current customers?	How do we get lost customers back?
What new products are needed by our target market?	Can we develop a new product to keep up with our major competitor?

research can be proactive to prevent "breakdowns" or reactive to respond to a problem and try to fix it. Unfortunately marketing research conducted after serious problems emerge may be too late. Forward-looking companies take a proactive stand to help keep ahead of the competition.

The Research Process

Marketing Research Process
Series of steps consisting of problem definition, research design, data collection, data analysis, interpretation, and conclusions.

The **marketing research process** consists of six steps: problem definition, research design, data collection, data analysis, interpretation, and conclusions.

Forming the research question   Marketing researchers must first define what they want to find out—the research question. A research study should address a specific topic or problem rather than several different issues at once. Researchers need to clearly state their purpose and their plan for using the information they gather. For example, Frito-Lay, which sells several varieties of snack foods, decided to do a research study to identify individual supermarkets where customers prefer Frito's "Light" snacks. The company wanted to increase promotional spending in stores where customers are more likely to buy the light snacks.[20]

Research design   After defining the research question, marketers formulate a plan for collecting information essential to the study. Depending on the type and amount of information already available, the researcher will choose one of several alternative designs.

If little is known about the question being investigated, marketers engage in *exploratory research*. They may look at company records and government or industry publications or talk to knowledgeable people inside or outside their organization. Focus group interviews, in which a researcher informally discusses an idea or issue with a small group of employees, consumers, or others, can provide helpful insights.

Sometimes organizations conduct *experimental research* to determine whether one event, circumstance, or situation causes another. For example, a publisher may distribute an issue of a magazine with different covers in different parts of the country. After a trial period, researchers investigate which cover resulted in the highest sales.

Marketers often want to know the age, sex, education, income, lifestyle, buying habits, or buying intentions of consumers. To obtain such information, they conduct *descriptive research*.

Data collection   After settling on a research design, marketers accumulate the information that will answer the research question. Researchers sometimes rely on *secondary data*—published information available inside the firm or from government, industry, or other sources. Secondary data offer tremendous advantages. They usually can be obtained quickly at relatively little cost, which may be especially important to small firms and nonprofit organizations. Marketers generally start all research projects by looking for secondary data. Table 13.4 lists common sources of secondary data.

Often secondary data are unavailable or inadequate. In such cases, marketers obtain *primary data*—information collected for the first time and specific to

TABLE 13.4

Sources of Secondary Data

Internal Sources

Company reports

Sales and cost data from accounting

Reports from the sales staff

Cash register receipts

External Sources

Private publications

Editor and Publisher Market Guide

Guide to Consumer Markets

Moody's manuals

Poor's registers

Sales & Marketing Management Survey of Buying Power

Chamber of Commerce publications

Industry reports and publications

Computer databases available through industry associations or research organizations

University business and economic research centers

Census data

Census of Population

Census of Retail trade

Census of Service Industries

Government publications

County and City Statistics

Economic Indicators

Statistical Abstract of the United States

Survey of Current Business

the study. Researchers use experiments, observation, or surveys to collect primary data.

Researchers conduct experiments either in a controlled, isolated setting (laboratory experiments) or in actual marketplace settings such as a store (field experiments). *Observation* involves watching a situation and recording relevant facts. A marketer may observe supermarket shoppers and record the purchases made. Through *surveys,* researchers question respondents to obtain needed information. Mail, telephone, and in-person surveys are becoming more and more common; you yourself probably have taken part in a consumer survey.

Because reaching all consumers in the target market (e.g., all television viewers) is often impossible or impractical, researchers collect data from a sample. A *sample* is a portion of a larger group and accurately represents the characteristics of the larger group. Companies that provide ratings for television shows may survey 1,200 viewers throughout the United States. With a sufficient sample, the researcher can use the data collected to infer important facts about the larger group.

Data analysis   To determine what all the information means, researchers analyze the data they collect. Usually they enter the data into a computer and run special programs to find the frequency of responses and how different items of information are related. While extremely valuable, computer analysis is costly because of the equipment, programs, and skills required. Businesses sometimes hire research consulting firms to conduct the data analysis.

*Nielsen helps businesses an-
alyze data to identify problems and determine what can
be done to solve them.*

Courtesy Nielsen Marketing Research

Interpretation and conclusions   A stack of data isn't worth much unless it
provides a workable answer to the research question. In the final research step,
marketers determine what the information means and draw conclusions. Business owners and managers concern themselves most with this part of the study;
they use the interpretations and conclusions as the yardstick for measuring the
value of the research.

Firms of all types and sizes use research to tackle marketing challenges or
problems. Some have their own marketing research departments, while others
use outside consultants or research firms from time to time. Either way, marketing research often requires considerable time and money, as well as a commitment to act on the findings.

MARKETING IN THE FUTURE

Through the 1990s and beyond, marketing will no doubt undergo many
changes. It seems to be headed into a new era marked by intense global
competition. This does not mean marketers will abandon the marketing
concept. Satisfying customers will be even more important than before, as

BO KNOWS SCHOOL!

Courtesy of Nike, Inc./Photography by Dave Lamont

In the highly competitive sneaker market, firms use well-known athletes like Bo Jackson to fight for market share.

will developing sound marketing strategies. What the changes do mean is that as the size of many markets remains constant or even decreases, competition will grow more fierce.

Already we can see the effects of heavy competition in many industries. In many cases, firms trying to grow must do so at another firm's expense. "Marketing warfare"—the battle for market share held by a competitor—rages in several different markets. Nike, Reebok, and L.A. Gear have been skirmishing for market share among consumers buying sneakers. Four years after falling from the number one position in the sneaker industry, Nike returned with its "Bo Knows" campaign, featuring professional baseball and football player Bo Jackson. In the meantime, Reebok signed Atlanta Hawks star Dominique Wilkins to go head-to-head with Nike's Michael Jordan in advertising basketball shoes. And L.A. Gear signed a deal with pop star Michael Jackson to help design a line of L.A. Gear clothes and shoes.[21] In the orange juice market, leader Minute Maid and major competitors Tropicana and Citrus Hill are fighting for market share.[22] In another intense battle, Goodyear Tire & Rubber Co., with a 17.2 percent share of the $46 billion tire market, has been overtaken by the Michelin Group, with a 17.6 percent share.[23]

The field of marketing promises to be challenging and exciting as businesses strive to deliver quality products to consumers in the midst of tremendous worldwide competition. In the next three chapters, we take a closer look at how companies can develop a marketing mix that will enable them to withstand fierce competition.

You'll Know It's the **Century When . . .**

Consumers Have It All

Many 21st-century products will be "smart" versions of products that now exist.
Smart cards will carry magnetic strips containing your financial or medical
information. Smart TVs will know what you want to watch before you turn them on.
They will even record programs you forget to watch. Smart houses will allow you
to control all of your appliances with one device. Smart pill bottles will beep when
it's time to take the pill, then automatically record time and dosage.

But some things won't change. Though consumers will have an abundance of
products to choose from, they won't buy those that don't fit their lifestyles.
Targeting consumer niches will be the only way for businesses to increase sales.[24]

SUMMARY OF LEARNING OBJECTIVES

1. To explain the purpose and importance of marketing.
    Through marketing, firms plan and execute decisions on what products to
    offer, what prices to charge, how to distribute them, and how to inform
    customers about them. Marketing enables firms to create exchanges that
    satisfy consumer needs and organizational objectives. Marketing is valu-
    able because it creates time, place, and possession utility and indirectly
    affects form utility.

2. To trace the evolution of marketing.
    Marketing's emphasis on satisfying customers is a relatively recent occur-
    rence. Beginning with the Industrial Revolution, most firms focused solely
    on producing enough needed consumer goods. With basic goods available in
    sufficient quantities in the 1920s, firms tried primarily to sell their products.
    Only in the early 1950s did companies embrace the marketing concept, a
    philosophy that they can achieve their goals by satisfying customers. Many
    firms today also consider society's welfare.

3. To define the term *market* and distinguish between the two major types of
    markets.
    Firms decide to offer products to a *market,* a group of people who need a
    product and who have the ability to purchase it. *Consumer markets* con-
    sist of individuals who purchase products for personal use. *Industrial
    markets* include buyers who purchase products in order to make other
    products.

4. To describe the steps involved in developing a marketing strategy.
    To develop a marketing strategy, a firm (1) selects a *target market* and (2)
    designs a *marketing mix* to meet the needs of that group of people. Depend-
    ing on the product and the firm's goals and resources, a firm may sell to the
    total market for a product or divide the total market into segments based on
    customers' geographic area, demographic characteristics, or psychographic
    aspects (such as attitudes), or on product characteristics.

5. To identify the four elements of the marketing mix.
   Product decisions require marketers to determine what would satisfy customers' needs and wants. *Price* affects a customer's purchase decisions and the seller's profits. *Promotion* communicates product information to the target market. *Distribution* makes products available when and where people in the target market want them.

6. To define the term *marketing environment* and list the environmental forces.
   The marketing environment is the combined outside forces that influence business firms' marketing decisions. Economic conditions, regulation by government and industry, societal attitudes, political policies, actions of competitors, and technological advancements have tremendous impact on marketing activities.

7. To describe how consumers make purchase decisions, and compare consumer buying behavior to industrial buying behavior.
   Considering buyer behavior helps firms conduct activities that will bring about more exchanges. Consumers go through a decision-making process of recognizing a need, seeking information about a product, comparing alternatives, deciding on a product, and evaluating the product. Purchase decisions for industrial markets differ from consumer decisions because transactions are larger and less frequent and require more information.

8. To explain the value of marketing research and outline the research process.
   Ongoing, systematic research gives firms information they need to satisfy customers and achieve their objectives. To conduct effective and accurate studies, marketers (1) define the specific purpose of the research, (2) design a plan to collect information, (3) gather needed information, (4) analyze the information, usually by computer, and (5) interpret the information and draw conclusions to use in marketing decisions.

KEY TERMS

Marketing, p. 451

Exchange, p. 452

Utility, p. 453

Marketing Concept, p. 456

Marketing Strategy, p. 459

Market, p. 460

Consumer Market, p. 460

Industrial Market, p. 460

Market Segment, p. 460

Target Market, p. 460

Undifferentiated Approach, p. 461

Product Differentiation, p. 461

Market Segmentation Approach, p. 461

Segmentation Base, p. 461

Marketing Mix, p. 464

Marketing Environment, p. 464

Consumer Buying Behavior, p. 467

Industrial Buying Behavior, p. 471

Marketing Research, p. 471

Marketing Research Process, p. 471

QUESTIONS FOR DISCUSSION AND REVIEW

1. What are some typical activities performed by marketers?
2. How does marketing add value to products?
3. In today's business environment, why is it essential for companies to practice the marketing concept?
4. Some cattle growers have formed a company to sell a new type of extra lean beef. How would the company develop a marketing strategy?
5. Give an example of a firm using the undifferentiated approach for a product and one using the market segmentation approach.
6. Select a firm and describe the marketing mix for one of its products.
7. What is the marketing environment? How does it affect a firm's marketing decisions?
8. Trace one of your recent purchase decisions through the stages of the buying process.
9. What are some of the differences between consumer purchases and industrial purchases?
10. How do organizations benefit from marketing research?

CASE 13.1
Disney Makes a Comeback

For decades Walt Disney reigned as king of family entertainment, with well-loved animated classics, family movies, a weekly TV show, and Disneyland and Walt Disney World—fantasy come to life. But his empire faded after his death in 1966. The movie studio turned out box office duds. The TV show disappeared. Only the theme parks were profitable. By 1984 the Magic Kingdom had had years of declining earnings and faced threats by raiders.

Then Michael D. Eisner became chairman and chief executive officer of the Walt Disney Company, and Frank G. Wells became president. These former Hollywood executives developed a marketing strategy to take Disney to the forefront of modern entertainment.

They brought the "Disney Sunday Movie" back to network TV and developed new children's cartoon series and new adult shows such as "Golden Girls." The Disney Channel became available to cable subscribers. Disney reissued classics such as *Snow White and the Seven Dwarfs* and *Bambi* for a new generation of children to see in theaters. The movie studio created new children's movies, such as the critically acclaimed *The Little Mermaid*. It also started producing films for new audiences—teens and adults. Box office hits like *Down and Out in Beverly Hills, Three Men and a Baby, Good Morning, Vietnam,* and *Dick Tracy* also became big video hits. Disney began releasing its classics on cassettes for the huge home video market. (One million copies of *Sleeping Beauty* sold in one year.) Disney moved into international broadcasting, too. Mickey Mouse and Donald Duck are prime-time stars on Chinese television. "Adventures of the Gummi Bears," "Ducktails," and "The Disney Club" air weekly in seven European countries. Videocassette sales are high in Britain, Spain, and Israel.

Disney expanded the merchandising of its famous mouse and his pals, with 8,000 products now sold in 50 countries. Besides stuffed toys, books, and clothes, fans can find skis, a $175 Seiko Mickey Mouse watch, or a $3,200 diamond-studded Dumbo brooch. Disney sells its products through 8 million catalogs mailed each year or in new mall stores that offer a touch of Disneyland coast to coast.

At the theme parks, the company raised admission prices and added new attractions, including a "Star Tours" spaceship ride and Indiana Jones adventure at Disneyland, Big Thunder Mountain at Tokyo Disneyland, and the MGM movie studio in Florida. To keep visitors pouring into the parks, Disney launched big advertising campaigns. Disney's goal is to make every customer feel like a guest. The company makes sure it knows who its customers are and what they expect from a family vacation, then tries to exceed their expectations. Employees attend Disney University to learn how to provide superior

Adapted from Stewart Toy, Robert Neff, et al., "An American in Paris," *Business Week,* March 12, 1990, pp. 60–61, 64; Jeanne Meister, "Disney Approach Typifies Quality Service," *Marketing News,* January 8, 1990, pp. 38–39; Ronald Grover, "Disney's Magic," *Business Week,* March 9, 1987, pp. 62–69.

service, such as solving customer problems on the spot. The Disney approach to satisfying customers is so successful that the company holds seminars for executives in other industries. Since 1986 more than 3,000 executives from 1,200 companies have attended three-day seminars.

Eisner firmly believes in the Disney tradition of providing high-quality family entertainment. "I must maintain the company, the quality, the image," he says. Effective marketing contributed to a dramatic turnaround for the company. Disney profits increased 35 percent for the year ending September 30, 1989, on revenues of $4.6 billion.

Still, some people believe Disney's growth years in U.S. markets are over. Executives are looking to Europe for growth in the 1990s. Their largest new venture is the $2.6 billion Euro Disneyland on 4,500 acres near Paris. The park is within two hours' driving distance for 17 million people and two hours' flying time for 310 million. Disney also plans to open a $1 billion studio tour next to the theme park in 1996. (MCA, Inc. plans to build a similar studio two years sooner and only 20 miles away.)

Tokyo Disneyland is a big hit with the Japanese, who are enjoying new affluence and who seem to love American culture, the Disney characters, and the park's cleanliness, order, outstanding service, and technology. But Disney may face problems in Europe, with its diverse languages and tastes as well as France's chilly winter weather. Many French see Disney as the height of foreign arrogance and are critical because their government has spent $350 million on park-related infrastructure (roads, utilities, etc.) and has condemned farmers' land for sale to Disney.

Questions for Discussion

1. Would you say that the Walt Disney Company practices the marketing concept? Why or why not?

2. Which approach to selecting a target market has Disney taken? Name some of the market segments Disney wants to reach.

3. What are some factors of the marketing environment that have an influence on Disney's marketing decisions? Explain.

CASE 13.2
The Downfall of Uptown

For its new Uptown cigarette, the R. J. Reynolds Tobacco Company followed basic marketing strategy: define your target market and develop a marketing mix for it. The strategy had every indication of being a winner. Reynolds selected black smokers as its target. As a group, blacks smoke in greater numbers than other population segments. According to the U.S. Office of Smoking and Health, 34 percent of blacks smoke, compared to 28.8 percent of whites and 29.1 percent of the total U.S. population. And while the number of U.S. smokers is dropping 2 percent a year, the number of black smokers is on the rise.

Adapted from Associated Press, "Flawed Strategy Doomed Cigarette," *Herald-Leader* (Lexington, Ky.), January 28, 1990, p. E1; Judann Dagnoli, "RJR's Uptown Targets Blacks," *Advertising Age*, December 18, 1989, pp. 4, 44; Michael Quinn, "Don't Aim that Pack at Us," *Time*, January 29, 1990, p. 60.

Reynolds carefully designed Uptown for the tastes of the black consumer. Since 65 percent of all black smokers smoke menthols, Reynolds made Uptown a menthol cigarette, with a lighter menthol flavor than its major menthol, Salem. Although Salem is the number five cigarette in the industry and the best-selling menthol, it never succeeded with black smokers, who saw it as a "white-bread brand." Uptown would compete with Lorillard Inc.'s Newport, the fastest-growing menthol, which is advertised using black models and in black publications but also is advertised to whites and Hispanics.

Reynolds packaged Uptown in a glitzy black-and-gold box. Its advertising agency developed ads featuring blacks enjoying nightlife and suggesting glamour and high fashion. Reynolds planned a market test of Uptown beginning in Philadelphia, where blacks make up 40 percent of the population.

But then the wrong people got a whiff of the new cigarette. Shortly after Reynolds announced plans for the Philadelphia market test, the American Cancer Society there started making plans to block it. Within a week, nearly 30 religious, health, and black community groups joined the Coalition against Uptown. Said the Rev. Jesse Brown, president of the Philadelphia-based Committee to Prevent Cancer among Blacks, "The protest was designed to say to R. J. Reynolds . . . we do not need another instrument of destruction to come into the African-American community." The uproar caused U.S. Health and Human Services Secretary Louis W. Sullivan to ask Reynolds to halt the campaign of "slick and sinister advertising." Reynolds did stop the market test; the company denounced the "unfair and biased" attention that had been focused on the product by a "small coalition of antismoking zealots."

Targeting tobacco products to specific market segments is not new; 398 brands and brand styles are sold in the United States. Since Philip Morris USA introduced Virginia Slims, companies commonly target women. (In 1986 lung cancer surpassed breast cancer as the most common cancer in women.) But an organized protest against cigarettes designed for women has never occurred. After the defeat of Uptown, however, Sullivan and others now plan to approach cigarette makers that target women.

Protesters of the new cigarette aimed so obviously toward blacks argued that the black community is already overburdened with smoking-related diseases. Black men have a 58 percent higher incidence of lung cancer than white men. And blacks lose twice as many years of life because of smoking-related diseases. But many people, blacks included, disagreed with the protest. Civil rights activist Benjamin Hooks said that "buried in this line of thinking is the rationale that blacks are not capable of making their own free choices." Still, a concern exists that big corporations have targeted minorities as markets for tobacco, liquor, and even junk food. A survey in Baltimore found that only 20 percent of the billboard advertising in white communities featured smoking and drinking while in black neighborhoods 76 percent promoted those habits.

Questions for Discussion

1. What consumer trends determined Reynolds' marketing strategy for Uptown cigarettes?

2. Do you think Reynolds' marketing strategy for Uptown was flawed in some way?

3. What marketing environment factors influenced Reynolds' decision to cancel the market test of Uptown?

4. Did Reynolds demonstrate social responsibility in this incident? Explain.

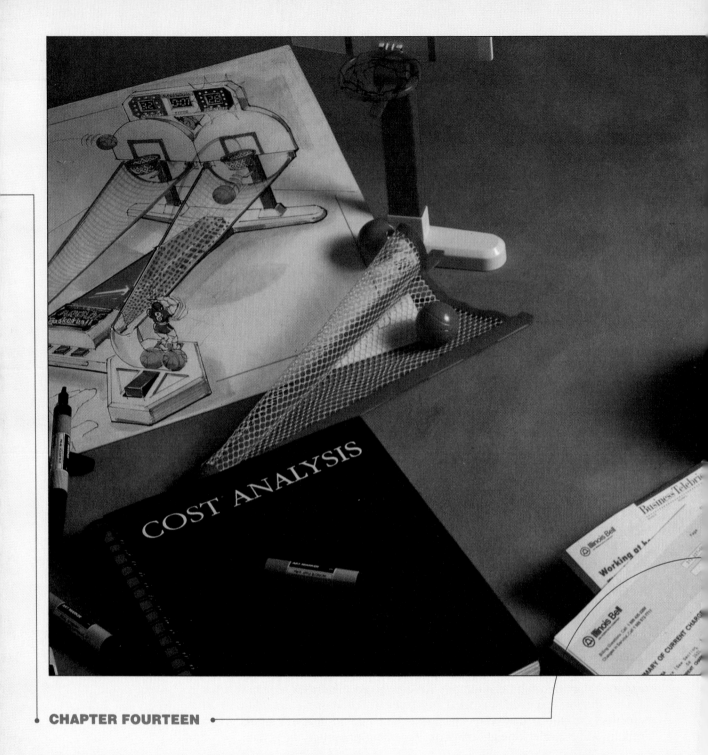

CHAPTER FOURTEEN

PRODUCT AND PRICE

LEARNING OBJECTIVES

1. To define the term *product* and distinguish between consumer and industrial products.

2. To differentiate between product line and product mix.

3. To trace the process of developing new products.

4. To describe the stages of the product life cycle and explain how firms can extend the product life cycle.

5. To explain the purposes of branding, packaging, and labeling.

6. To list four pricing objectives and identify three factors to consider when making pricing decisions.

7. To distinguish between cost-oriented, demand-oriented, and competition-oriented pricing methods.

8. To list and explain four pricing strategies.

483

Black & Decker is now the fastest-growing firm in the power tool industry. But not always. In the mid-1980s, it lost business to competitors such as Makita of Japan, Bosch of West Germany, and Emerson Electric's Skil. Then Black & Decker restructured to emphasize product quality and develop new products that can be sold the world over.

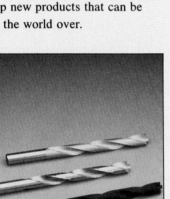

Courtesy of Black & Decker Corporation

An overhaul was overdue for B&D's power tool business, which included only high-priced professional tools and low-priced tools for consumers. Construction-industry professionals complained that B&D products lacked continuity and the tools didn't hold up. The company's British, French, German, and U.S. factories each developed and sold their own products. Worldwide it made 100 different motors (the most expensive component of power tools).

Black & Decker cut the number of motors to under 20, with plans for just 5. The firm tackled its quality problem with a little help

from the Japanese, as B&D engineers tore apart Makita tools and analyzed them. In two years, Black & Decker brought out 60 new or redesigned products. Most involve the convenient and popular cordless tools—the fastest-growing aspect of the industry and half of Black & Decker's power tool sales. Its new midpriced tools meet the needs of a rapidly growing

market segment: consumers who like to do things themselves and construction semiprofessionals.

Black & Decker also has become a leader in household products. After purchasing General Electric's small-appliance line (without the GE name), B&D renamed the brand and spent $100 million to advertise it. It brought out scores of new products and updated existing ones: irons with an automatic shut-off feature, cordless blenders, more powerful Dustbusters, and an entire line of stylish, scaled-down Spacemaker Plus appliances that won an Industrial Designers Society of America award. About 40 percent of Black & Decker's household appliance

sales come from products three years old or less.

With its clear new marketing strategy, Black & Decker could use its excellent capabilities in manufacturing, engineering, and research to develop products quickly. One of the company's stars is Peter Chaconas, a design engineer who invented the Piranha circular saw blade, one of the best-selling tool accessories in company history, and the Bullet power drill bit, a major innovation in the industry-standard product. "Once you identify a problem, it's easy to fix it," says Chaconas, a former auto mechanic with a degree in mechanical engineering technology. He devotes all his time to designing new products and loves his job. "I sit down, see what's wrong with products, and redesign them," Chaconas says.

The Bullet bit drills clean holes, bites into wood or metal without skating, and doesn't lock up in a hole. Black & Decker says it drills four times faster, stays sharp seven times longer, and produces six times as many holes per battery charge as other drill bits. That's not a bad piece of work for something Chaconas wasn't even supposed to be doing. He was told to choose 1 of nearly 40 designs submitted by outside suppliers. When none met his standards, he went to the drawing board and created a product that buyers would welcome. Such innovative products, plus quality and a famous brand name, have helped Black & Decker boost annual sales to $2.3 billion.[1]

Black & Decker's Bullet drill bit is more than a piece of grooved steel that makes holes. People who purchase the physical item expect a range of benefits:

- A perfect fit with their Black & Decker drills.
- Ease of use.
- Savings of time.
- Less waste of material because of mistakes.
- The convenience of longer use from a charge.
- The prestige of owning state-of-the-art tools.
- A warranty to help ensure satisfaction.

For this, consumers pay a price that allows Black & Decker to profit for producing and marketing Bullet drill bits. In this chapter, we discuss two of the marketing mix elements: product and price. First we define what products are and list ways to classify them. We introduce the concepts of product line and product mix. We explore the ways in which firms manage their products, including developing new ones. We describe how firms create product identification. Then we cover price by discussing pricing objectives, factors involved in pricing decisions, and methods and strategies used to price products.

WHAT ARE PRODUCTS?

A **product** consists of all the tangible and intangible characteristics provided in an exchange between a seller and a buyer. People buy a product for the benefits and satisfaction it gives. A product's characteristics include not only its physical aspects but also its function, brand name, image, packaging, warranty, and price, as well as the provider's reputation and customer service policy.

Product
A good, service, or idea, including all the tangibles and intangibles provided in an exchange between buyer and seller.

As we noted in Chapter Thirteen, a product can be a good (an actual physical entity such as a drill bit), a service (your checking account at the bank), or an idea (the American Heart Association's advice to follow a diet low in fat and cholesterol). Sometimes a product is a blend of all three. Dinner at a fine restaurant, for example, consists not only of tangible items—food and beverages— but also preparation, service, and the appeal of dining in that special setting.

Because different products are designed for different target markets, they require various pricing, distribution, and promotion decisions. To help plan effective marketing strategies, marketers classify goods and services according to the manner in which they are purchased and used. Marketers generally divide products into two broad categories: consumer and industrial products.

Consumer Products

Products used by individuals for personal and family consumption are **consumer products.** Marketers classify consumer products according to customers' buying behavior, as Figure 14.1 shows.

Consumer Product
A good or service used for personal or family consumption.

Convenience Product
A frequently purchased, inexpensive item that buyers spend little effort to find and purchase.

Convenience products   Inexpensive goods and services that consumers buy often, without much thought or effort, are **convenience products.** Milk, bread,

FIGURE 14.1   **Convenience, Shopping, and Specialty Products**

Courtesy of White Hen Pantry, Inc., Sony Corporation of America, and Maserati Automobiles Incorporated

magazines, soft drinks, and gasoline are examples. So are the routine services offered by dry cleaners and automatic teller machines. People make such purchases or go to such service providers because of habit and closeness of the outlet: they've always bought that brand; the store is nearby.

Shopping products   Consumers will expend time, effort, and energy to find and obtain some goods and services. Buyers comparison shop for these; thus they are known as **shopping products.** Consumers gather information about different brands and styles, visit different stores, note prices, read advertise-

Shopping Product
An item that buyers will expend time and effort to find and purchase.

ments and consumer guides, and consult family or friends. This category includes goods such as TV sets, VCRs, major appliances, and furniture and services such as dental care, legal advice, and tax preparation.

Specialty products   Goods and services that have specific attributes desired by a particular group of consumers are known as **specialty products.** Buyers go to considerable trouble to obtain a specialty product, no matter what the price or location, and will rarely accept a substitute. Specialty products can be expensive and unique, such as a Maserati sports car or Adolfo designer dress, or less costly but still fairly uncommon, such as a certain breed of dog or tickets to a Broadway show.

Specialty Product
A product with one or more unique features that a group of buyers will spend considerable time and effort to purchase.

Because consumers differ in their purchasing behaviors, the convenience-shopping-specialty distinction is not absolute. One customer may order food from a pizza parlor strictly because of its delivery service (convenience). Another may choose to eat there after comparing the pizza and prices all over town (shopping). Other customers may go out of their way for the super deluxe, 10-topping pan pizza available only at that restaurant (specialty). Therefore marketers classify products according to the buying patterns of the majority of consumers. Pizza thus would fall in the convenience category.

Industrial Products

Products used by organizations in producing goods and services or in carrying out their operations are **industrial products.**[2] Manufacturers, contractors, mining companies, utilities, government agencies, wholesalers, retailers, and institutions such as hospitals and schools buy and use a great array of goods and services to carry out their operations and produce products of their own. Industrial products often require substantial investment but have a long, useful life span, such as a robotics system in an automobile plant or a computer network for the government. Other industrial products cost much less and are purchased regularly, such as office equipment or the printing of an annual report.

Industrial Product
A good or service used by an organization in producing other goods or services or in carrying out its operations.

Marketers sometimes find it useful to categorize industrial products into more specific classifications, such as:

- Installations, such as large storage and distribution centers or factories.
- Major equipment, including machinery and large tools essential to the production process.
- Accessory equipment, such as forklifts and small tools or office computers and furniture.
- Component parts, usually prefinished items put into a physical product, such as cassette players installed in cars.
- Raw materials, such as minerals, sand, coal, and petroleum, which become part of physical products.
- Supplies, such as pens and paper and cleaners, which do not become part of the item produced.
- Services, either provided in-house or hired from outside the organization, such as accounting, advertising, printing, legal, and janitorial.

TABLE 14.1

Classification of Services

Category	Examples
Type of market	
Consumer	Life insurance, car repairs.
Industrial	Lawn care, management consulting.
Degree of labor intensiveness	
Labor based	Repairs, executive recruiting.
Equipment based	Public transportation, air travel.
Degree of customer contact	
High contact	Hotels, health care.
Low contact	Dry cleaning, motion pictures.
Skill of the service provider	
Professional	Legal counsel, accounting services.
Nonprofessional	Taxi, janitorial.
Goal of the service provider	
Profit	Financial services, overnight delivery.
Nonprofit	Government, education.

Classifying Services

While services are classified as consumer or industrial, other classifications are also important because of the unique characteristics of many services. Table 14.1 shows the classifications marketers use for services.

Marketers often find it useful to categorize services by degree of *labor intensiveness*. Services such as hair styling, education, and health care require a great amount of human labor while others, such as automatic car washes, rely heavily on machines and equipment. Labor-intense services are especially difficult to standardize.

Another way to classify services is by degree of *customer contact*. High-contact services, such as real estate agencies, involve frequent interactions with customers. The consumer must be present for such services to be performed. Low-contact services involve much less participation on the part of the customer. The consumer may need to be present only to initiate the contact but not for the service to be performed. A customer goes to the dry cleaner to drop off clothes, for example, but does not have to stay while they are being cleaned.

A fourth way to classify services is by *skill of the service provider*. Some services require professionals, such as lawyers, physicians, or accountants. Other services can be offered by individuals with lower levels of skills. Consumers are more selective when choosing providers for services that require higher levels of skills.

Finally, services can be classified by the *goal of the service provider*. Not all service organizations are profit oriented. Universities, charities, libraries, and some clinics are a few examples of nonprofit service organizations.

FIGURE 14.2

Boeing's Line of Jetliners

Courtesy of The Boeing Company

PRODUCT LINE AND PRODUCT MIX

Decisions concerning what products to offer—the type, number, and variety—are fundamental to any organization. Often firms manufacture and sell goods or offer services that are similar in design, production, or use and are targeted to similar market segments. A group of related goods or services marketed by a firm is called a **product line.** A firm's product line can be shallow, with only one or two products, or deep, including many products. T. J. Cinnamon's product line is shallow, with a few types of sweet rolls. Boeing has a deep product line, as Figure 14.2 illustrates.

Product Line
A group of related products that are considered a unit because of marketing, technical, or use similarities.

Firms realize distinct advantages in offering related products and introducing new products within an established product line: They can use their know-how, resources, and experience to effectively produce and market new products. Similar products help promote each other. Marketers can stretch advertising dollars by emphasizing an entire product line in an advertising campaign.

While many firms expand existing product lines by introducing new, similar items, others decide to add completely different product lines. The collection of items and services a firm offers for sale make up its **product mix.** Marketers refer to product mixes as narrow or wide, depending on how many product lines are carried.

Product Mix
The total group of products a firm offers for sale, or all of the firm's product lines.

FIGURE 14.3   **General Foods' Product Mix**

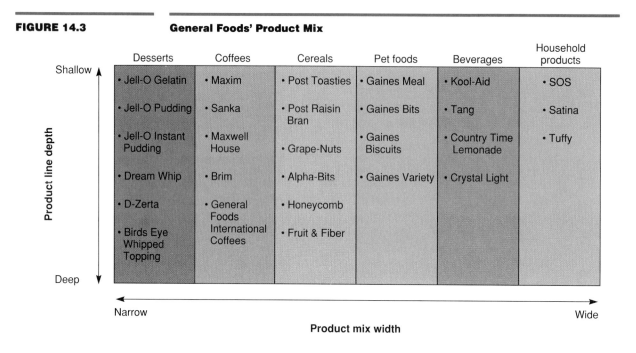

Some companies opt for a narrow product mix, such as Mita, which has advertised that it makes only photocopiers. Others develop several product lines targeted to the same or similar markets. Fisher-Price, well known for years for its popular toys, added a line of baby furniture and equipment including high chairs, portable cribs, and car seats. Still other firms develop an extremely wide product mix consisting of multiple product lines aimed at different markets. General Foods' many and diverse product offerings, shown in Figure 14.3, illustrate a wide product mix.

The decision to offer a single line of related products or many and varied product lines depends on an organization's knowledge, goals, and resources. Developing new product lines often allows a company to expand into different markets, achieve growth, and increase stability. Firms with multiple product lines often find themselves in a better position to adapt to changes in economic conditions, technology, or consumer needs.

MANAGING THE PRODUCT MIX

Whether they offer a few similar products or many diverse ones, firms face numerous decisions in developing and managing their products. They must determine which to offer and must continue to develop new ones. They may need to modify products in response to competition and changing consumer preferences. Firms also must determine when to stop offering certain products.

FIGURE 14.4

**The New-Product
Development Process**

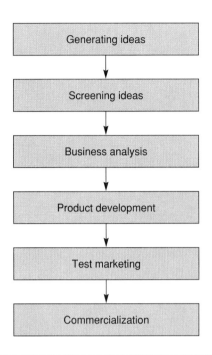

Developing New Products

New products are vital for a firm's long-term success. For instance, 3M's Post-it™ Notes, invented in 1974 but not introduced nationally until 1980, bring the company annual sales of $11 billion.[3] Businesses that fail to develop new products may limit their potential for growth and eventually become vulnerable to competitors. In this text, we consider a new product to be one that a particular firm offers for the first time, whether or not similar products exist in the marketplace.

Developing new products with high growth potential is no simple task. Around 10,000 new products are brought to the marketplace each year, but many of them fail.[4] Estimates range from as low as 10 percent to as high as 90 percent. A realistic average failure rate is 30 to 35 percent.[5] Because of the high failure rate and the $30 million average cost of introducing a new product to the marketplace, many firms are reluctant to develop new products.[6]

Products fail for many reasons, including lack of research, design problems, or poor timing in the product's introduction.[7] Firms cannot eliminate the risks inherent in introducing new products, but they can reduce risks through a well-planned, thorough product development process (see Figure 14.4). Let's examine how a firm uses a six-step process to develop new products. The process is expensive and time-consuming but it is helpful in avoiding costly mistakes.

Advanced features developed by Zenith engineers helped the company expand its leadership in digital TVs. New interactive, multicolor on-screen menus provide instant reference for picture, sound, signal source, picture-in-picture, and other functions.

Courtesy Zenith Electronics Corporation

Generating ideas   The road to a new product offering begins with finding ideas that fit with the organization's goals and objectives. Ideas emerge from within the firm through engineers and researchers or from outside sources such as customers, competitors, or consultants. Fewer than 10 percent of all new ideas make it into the later stages of product development.[8]

Screening ideas   The many ideas born in the initial step must be screened to select the ones the firm will pursue. An idea may not match a firm's objectives. Others may require resources and knowledge that the firm does not have and cannot easily obtain. Such ideas will be rejected, while others are evaluated further.

Business analysis   During this phase, the firm estimates the market potential of the product: what are the expected costs, sales, and profits? If management believes the product will make enough profit to justify the costs, the idea will advance to the product development phase.

Product development   Here firms develop a working model of the product. In this way, they can examine the feasibility of making and offering the product on a large scale. Some ideas are rejected at this stage because the production costs are too high to bring the product to market.

The Most Popular Test Market Cities in the United States   **TABLE 14.2**

DID YOU KNOW? *Your city may be one often selected by firms to test sales of new products.*

Akron	Fort Wayne, Indiana	Phoenix
Albany–Schenectady–Troy	Fresno	Pittsburgh
Albuquerque	Grand Rapids–Kalamazoo–Battle	Portland, Maine
Ann Arbor	Creek	Portland, Oregon
Atlanta	Green Bay–Appleton, Wisconsin	Poughkeepsie
Augusta, Georgia	Greensboro–Winston-Salem–High	Providence, Rhode Island
Austin	Point, North Carolina	Quad Cities: Rock Island–Moline,
Bakersfield, California	Greenville–Spartanburg, South	Illinois–Davenport–Bettendorf, Iowa
Baltimore-Washington, D.C.	Carolina–Asheville, North Carolina	Raleigh–Durham
Bangor, Maine	Harrisburg	Reading, Pennsylvania
Baton Rouge	Hartford, Connecticut	Reno–Carson City
Beaumont–Port Arthur, Texas	Houston	Roanoke–Lynchburg
Binghamton, New York	Huntsville, Alabama	Rochester, New York
Birmingham–Anniston, Alabama	Indianapolis	Rockford, Illinois
Boise	Jacksonville, Florida	Sacramento–Stockton
Boston	Kansas City, Missouri	St. Louis
Buffalo	Knoxville	Salem, Oregon
Canton, Ohio	Lansing, Michigan	Salinas–Monterey
Cedar Rapids–Waterloo, Iowa	Las Vegas	Salt Lake City
Charleston, South Carolina	Lexington, Kentucky	San Antonio
Charleston, West Virginia	Lincoln, Nebraska	San Diego
Charlotte, North Carolina	Little Rock	San Francisco–Oakland
Chattanooga, Tennessee	Los Angeles	Savannah
Chicago	Louisville	Seattle–Tacoma
Cincinnati	Lubbock, Texas	Shreveport
Cleveland	Macon, Georgia	Sioux Falls, South Dakota
Colorado Springs	Madison	South Bend–Elkhart, Indiana
Columbia, South Carolina	Memphis	Spokane
Columbus, Georgia	Miami	Springfield, Massachusetts
Columbus, Ohio	Milwaukee	Springfield, Missouri
Corpus Christi	Minneapolis–St. Paul	Springfield–Decatur–Champaign,
Dallas–Fort Worth	Modesto	Illinois
Dayton	Nashville	Syracuse
Denver-Boulder	New Haven, Connecticut	Tallahassee
Des Moines	New Orleans	Tampa–St. Petersburg
Detroit	Newport News	Toledo
Duluth–Superior, Minnesota	New York	Topeka
El Paso	Oklahoma City	Tucson
Erie, Pennsylvania	Omaha–Council Bluffs	Tulsa
Eugene, Oregon	Orlando–Daytona Beach	West Palm Beach
Evansville, Indiana	Pensacola	Wichita–Hutchinson, Kansas
Flint, Michigan	Peoria	Youngstown, Ohio
Fort Lauderdale	Philadelphia	
Fort Smith, Arkansas		

Source: "The Nation's Most Popular Test Markets," *Sales & Marketing Management,* March 1987, pp. 65–66. Reprinted by permission of Sales & Marketing Management. Copyright March 1987.

Test marketing   Before full-scale introduction of a new product, a firm introduces it in selected areas to a part of the market that represents the entire market. Test marketing can be used to monitor consumer reaction to the product and to refine the marketing mix if needed. Sometimes test marketing uncovers a weakness in the product, price, promotion, or distribution that can be adjusted before introduction to the entire market. Marketers carefully select locations to test market a product. Table 14.2 lists cities often chosen as test market sites.

Commercialization   When a product shows promise in test marketing, the firm generally begins the process of production and distribution to the entire market. In some cases, the firm introduces the product in a selected geographic region (e.g., Cajun-style foods in the Southwest) and eventually moves it into other regions. Because the firm has invested so much money in its development, failure of a new product at this stage costs dearly. Thus marketers monitor commercialization carefully and attempt to make any necessary adjustments in the product itself, the price, advertising or other promotional methods, or distribution system. The commercialization of a new product begins its life cycle.

A firm that can bring out a product faster than can its competitors enjoys a huge advantage. Several companies have taken steps to speed up the new-product development process. For instance, Japanese producers of projection televisions can develop a new television in one third the time required by U.S. firms.[9] It is becoming increasingly important that firms get it right the first time when developing products.

The Product Life Cycle

Product Life Cycle
The theoretical life of a product, consisting of four stages: introduction, growth, maturity, and decline.

Like living things, products go through several stages of life, known as the **product life cycle.**[10] New products enter the market during their introduction stage, they gain momentum and begin to bring a profit during the growth stage, they stabilize during the maturity stage, and finally they fade away in the decline stage. Figure 14.5 illustrates the four stages of the product life cycle.

As you can see from the figure, products pass through these stages over time. For some products, the life cycle may be very short. Fad items such as cartoon-cat Garfield stick-ons placed on car windows may last for only a few years. Other products, such as black-and-white television sets and microwave ovens, enjoy a life cycle of several decades. Let's examine what generally occurs at each stage of the product life cycle.

FIGURE 14.5

Stages in the Product Life Cycle

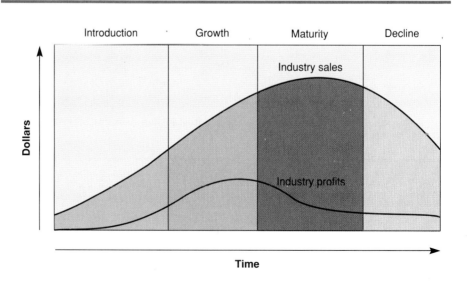

Introduction   In the first stage of the product life cycle, a firm makes the new product available to customers, who gradually become aware of it. Sales rise slowly. Profits are low during this stage because the firm must recover the costs of developing and marketing the product. In some cases, firms suffer losses. Examples of products in the introduction stage include liquid crystal television screens, low-calorie fat substitutes, and iced coffee.

Marketers face several challenges during a product's introduction. They must develop and carry out promotional programs to inform potential customers about the product's availability and its features. Marketing managers must monitor sales, which may be slow, and make early adjustments in the product or in promotional efforts if needed. Many products don't survive the introduction stage. Have you ever heard of Campbell's Red Kettle Soups, Listerine Toothpaste, or Scott's Baby Scott Diapers? How about a graphics compact-disk player? All were brought to the marketplace, but none made it past the first stage of the product life cycle. In contrast, sales of Dow Brands' new premoistened, disposable cleaning towels called Spiffits topped $100 million the first year.[11]

Growth   Sales increase more rapidly during the growth stage, and the product begins to generate a profit. Competitors, seeing an opportunity, are likely to enter the market with similar products during this stage. The firm that originated the product may reduce its price as a result of new competition and decreased production costs. For instance, the prices of such growth products as compact-disk players, video cameras, and personal computers fell after manufacturers recovered their initial development costs and other firms began to introduce competing products. As prices fall, profits peak and begin to decline.

A product in the growth stage usually faces intense competition from similar offerings. Firms must rely heavily on repeat purchases for continued sales growth. Marketers therefore attempt to establish consumer loyalty to their products. They often create fresh promotional programs to emphasize the product's benefits and to encourage loyal customers to continue buying the same brand. Growth-stage products include facsimile (fax) machines.

Maturity   During the maturity stage of the product life cycle, sales peak as profits continue to decline. As other products are introduced with new features and improvements, the product may become somewhat outdated. Color television sets and video recorders are examples of products in the maturity stage.

Intense competition from many different firms forces some products out of the market. Companies may cut prices further and increase their promotion budgets to compete for customers. They also may try product improvements, new package designs, and changes in style to encourage consumers to keep buying the product.

Decline   Sales fall rapidly during the decline stage of the product life cycle. Profits also continue to fall, and sometimes additional price-cutting leads to losses. Consumers often start to prefer new products in earlier stages of their life cycles that provide greater satisfaction or meet different needs or wants. Electric typewriters, for example, are in decline as people increasingly use personal computers.

Managers must decide at which point to eliminate a product nearing the end of its life cycle. Some products in the decline stage, such as black-and-white televisions, are not immediately eliminated. Sometimes firms generate a profit from decline-stage products by reducing promotional costs and selling to only the most profitable markets.

Extending the Product Life Cycle

Ideally firms would like their products to remain forever in the growth stage, when profits are highest. Although products eventually reach the decline stage, that some survive for decades is no accident. Firms can extend the life cycle of a product in several ways.

Increasing the frequency of use   Marketers commonly try to keep their product sales growing by encouraging consumers to use their goods and services more. Telephone companies, for example, run advertisements using emotional appeals to spur people to call relatives and friends more often. In some markets, Coca-Cola has promoted Coke as a morning drink to replace coffee or tea. Toothbrush ads, citing dentists' recommendations, have advised consumers to buy a new toothbrush more often, every two or three months.

Identifying new users   Another way to extend a product's growth stage is to identify new target markets and promote the product to them. Oreo cookies and Frosted Flakes cereal, usually kids' fare, have been targeted to adults. Nintendo has promoted its video systems to adults to expand beyond its major category of users, teenage boys.

Finding new uses   Marketers sometimes maintain and increase sales by showing consumers other ways to use the product. For instance, with the popularity of microwave ovens, Campbell Soup is promoting several of its soups as toppings for baked potatoes. Figure 14.6 shows how Heinz advertises its vinegar as a multipurpose household product.

Product Modification
The changing of one or more of a product's features as a strategy to extend its life cycle.

Product modification   As products encounter fierce competition and reach the maturity stage, firms may need to modify products to compete more effectively. **Product modification** is a life-cycle extension strategy that involves changing a product's quality, features, or style to attract new users or increase usage.

Quality modification means altering the materials used to make the product or changing the production process. Adding longer life to a battery is a quality modification. *Functional modification* is achieved by redesigning a product to provide additional features or benefits. With microcomputer technology, Toshiba enabled its microwave oven to select a power level for cooking based on the weight and density of the food. Changing how a product looks, sounds, smells, or feels results in *style modification*. Denim jeans have been prewashed, stonewashed, and acid-washed to alter color and reduce their characteristic stiffness.

Deleting Products

Products in the decline stage of the product life cycle may become too costly for a firm to continue offering. A company may decide the money would be better spent on developing new products or modifying existing ones that are

FIGURE 14.6

**New Uses: Extending
the Product Life Cycle**

*Showing customers new
ways to use products helps
extend the product life cycle.*

Courtesy of Heinz USA

still profitable. For example, as consumers started buying cassettes and compact disks more and more, many music companies stopped making vinyl records.

A firm can delete a product in one of several ways. A *phaseout* approach gradually eliminates the product without any change in the marketing strategy. When using a *runout* strategy, firms may increase distribution and promotion and try to exploit any strengths left in the product. If a product is very unprofitable, a firm often makes an *immediate-drop* decision.

CREATING PRODUCT IDENTIFICATION

Firms could not succeed in developing and managing products without effectively identifying their products. Consumers must be able to distinguish one product from another. Organizations identify their offerings in three important ways: branding, packaging, and labeling.

Branding

A name, sign, symbol, design, or combination of these used to identify a product and distinguish it from competitors' offerings is called a **brand.** The part of the brand that can be spoken is the **brand name.** The AT&T brand

Brand
A name, sign, symbol, or design a company uses to distinguish its product from others.

Brand Name
The part of a product's brand that can be spoken.

Are All the Good Names Taken?

A rose by any other name may smell as sweet, but it's different for products. Inappropriate or unappealing names can hinder sales. Aware of the power in a name, firms try hard to come up with clever, catchy, memorable ones. But the job is getting harder. The U.S. Patent and Trademark Office registers nearly 70,000 new product names a year now. It has 680,000 active trademark registrations on file, 100,000 more than in 1984. When a trademarked product is in use, its brand name can be renewed indefinitely.

"Any word or name a company thinks of, three quarters of the time it will be unavailable because someone's claimed it," says Frank Delano, head of the product-naming firm of Delano Goldman & Young Inc. He and his partners have named products such as Honda's Fourtrax off-road vehicle and Bristol-Myers' Bran Tabs laxative. "Flashy names like Mustang and Sting Ray are all gone," he says. "In the animal kingdom, you're pretty much down to skunk and opossum."

Manufacturers, who may risk as much as $20 million introducing a new retail product, are turning more to outside consultants to find the perfect name. Consultants often use computers, which link word fragments into new combinations with high-tech sounds. Just

eight letters can create 11 billion new "words" that can be pronounced in English. One Chicago naming expert offers clients a list of 5,000 computer-generated names for $5,000. At that price, the names are not guaranteed to be original.

A legal search is required to make sure a name isn't already taken. When Parfums International introduced Elizabeth Taylor's Passion perfume, it was sued by Annick Goutal Inc., which already had its own Passion fragrance on the market. A judge ruled that Ms. Taylor's product couldn't be sold in 55 "first-tier" stores that carry the original Passion.

Consultants who guarantee a name's originality charge hefty fees of up to $75,000. Delano's firm creates new product names through old-fashioned brainstorming—talking about the product, image, and target market and thinking up possibilities. To name an expensive new perfume, Delano visited perfume counters and talked to manufacturers' representatives about what kind of woman buys $200-an-ounce perfume. The name had to look at home on the shelves of classy stores and appeal to elegant, affluent women who want an exclusive brand.

Companies consider names so important that they start searching for a name long before the new product is ready. A Japanese carmaker once asked Delano to name

its new car without having even a picture to go by. The car was still being designed.

With product naming so tough, firms benefit from existing brands. After General Electric bought RCA Corporation, it used the RCA name for a new, low-priced line of microwaves, stoves, dishwashers, refrigerators, washers, and dryers. The RCA name offered the advantage of instant recognition and a reputation for quality, even though consumers did not identify RCA with appliances. "It takes far too much money to build a brand with the inherent awareness of a well-established brand name like RCA," says Victor Alcott, manager of industrial design for GE Appliances. Other firms resurrect old names. General Motors, which owns 360 trademark registrations, may bring back Cadillac's LaSalle brand for a new model, four-door luxury car with all-wheel drive and a computerized highway navigation system. Hills Bros. Coffee, Inc. brought back Chase & Sanborn coffee, a brand it got in an acquisition. The company discovered that almost 9 out of 10 people fondly remembered Chase & Sanborn coffee from the 1940s and 1950s, when it was advertised on radio. With little advertising, Chase & Sanborn has captured 3 percent of the $4 billion coffee business—a small but profitable share.[12]

Product Identity: Brands   **FIGURE 14.7**

QUALITY NEVER GOES OUT OF STYLE.

toys that last.

Courtesy of AT&T; Chicago Cubs; Chrysler Corporation; Fuji Photo Film U.S.A., Inc.; General Mills, Inc.; LEGO Systems, Inc.; Levi Strauss & Co.; The Little Tikes Company; New York Life Insurance Company; and Texas Instruments Incorporated

includes the brand name and a design, its stylized globe. Figure 14.7 shows some well-known brands.

Firms usually want exclusive use of their brands and take steps to prevent others from using them. A brand registered with the U.S. Patent and Trademark Office is called a *trademark*. A trademark, legally protected, can be used only by its owner. People sometimes identify a brand so closely with a product that they use it for the product itself. Xerox Corporation has run advertisements pointing out that the name Xerox refers only to its products, not to all copy machines. Many brand names, including aspirin, celluloid, lanolin, zipper, and escalator, have become generic terms because their owners failed to protect them.

Firms are acutely aware of the importance of brand names. Good names sell products. Firms often search for short names that are easy to pronounce and easy to remember, such as Sprite, Tide, or Prell. Names can suggest the product's function (L'Eggs pantyhose) or its performance (SupraLife, Energizer, and Duracell batteries). Brand names must also fit the image the company desires for its product, like the Jaguar car or Joy perfume. The Business Action discusses some tactics of naming products. The process takes considerable care, time, research, and often money.

Types of brands   Brands are classified as manufacturer, private, or generic. A *manufacturer* (or producer) *brand* is owned and used by the manufacturer or service provider. Firms often use manufacturer brands to market products throughout the United States and abroad in many stores and outlets. Such brands identify who makes the products and provide the consumer with a

---

● C o n n e c t i o n s

Are You a Brand Loyal Consumer?

Directions: Test your brand loyalty to the toothpaste you use. Answer the following questions; then discuss your classmates' responses.

1. The last time you bought toothpaste, what brand did you buy?

   _____

2. Was price a major factor in your most recent toothpaste purchase?

   _____ Yes   _____ No

3. Do you ever buy other brands of toothpaste?

   _____ Yes   _____ No

4. Would you switch brands for a lower price?

   _____ Yes   _____ No

5. If the store were out of the brand you bought most recently, would you buy a different brand?

   _____ Yes   _____ No

---

nationally known, uniform, and widely available product such as Butternut bread, Lee jeans, or Chevrolet trucks.

A *private* (or store) *brand* is owned by a wholesaler or retailer. Examples of private brands include Sears' Die Hard and J. C. Penney's Penncraft. A firm offering private brands often can sell them at lower prices, achieve higher profits, and encourage customer loyalty. Most products sold under private brands are produced by companies that also market products under manufacturer brands. These firms find this practice profitable because they can use any excess production capacity and greatly reduce their marketing costs. For example, Whirlpool makes the refrigerators Sears sells under its Kenmore brand.

Some products have no brand name at all. These are *generic products,* usually sold in simple, no-frill packages that identify only the contents. Many grocery items such as canned vegetables, cereals, crackers, and paper goods are available as generics. Generic products offer consumers an alternative to manufacturer and private brands. By using plain packages and keeping advertising to a minimum, producers and stores can sell generics at reduced prices. Sometimes, but not always, products sold as generics are not uniform in size or appearance or are of lower quality than branded goods.

Brand loyalty   Consumers frequently buy only their favorite brands of certain products. They will not switch brands even if an alternative is offered at a lower price. *Brand loyalty* is the extent to which a consumer prefers a particular brand.

Marketers measure consumers' brand loyalty at three stages. The first, *brand recognition,* means consumers are familiar with a manufacturer's prod-

6. Would you consider buying a new brand of toothpaste being introduced to
   the market?

   _____ Yes   _____ No

Feedback: Although the quiz considered only one product, it should help you see
how brand loyalty pertains to one consumer—you. If you said yes to all the questions, you are not at all brand loyal about toothpaste. If you answered no every
time, you are extremely loyal. You would insist on one brand whenever you buy
toothpaste. If you answered some questions yes and others no, you prefer one
brand but would consider switching. You would be the target of competitors looking
for customers!

Discuss with your classmates how they answered the quiz. Give possible reasons why some people are brand loyal to toothpaste while others are not. How
important are differences between individuals, such as when and where they shop,
financial situations, interest in finding a bargain, family shopping patterns, or willingness to try new things? Answer the questions again for other products—soft
drinks, shampoo, fast food, shoes. You may find your brand loyalty varies from one
product to another.

uct. Buyers are more likely to choose a brand they recognize than an unfamiliar
one. At the second stage of brand loyalty, *brand preference,* consumers will
buy the product if it is available. At the third stage, *brand insistence,* buyers
will not accept a substitute for their favorite brand.

The degree of brand loyalty varies from customer to customer and from
product to product. But all firms that brand products attempt to establish brand
loyalty through the product's performance, packaging, price, and advertising
and other promotional efforts. Loyalty keeps consumers coming back for
more. Are you a brand-loyal consumer? Connections will help you find out.

Brand strategies   A company can use either individual branding or family
branding when developing brands for its products. *Individual branding* requires
creating a different brand for every product. It establishes separate identities
for different products and thus helps target products to different market segments. Also, with individual branding, problems with one product seldom influence the success of other products in the line.

With *family branding,* a firm uses the same brand for most or all of its
products. Many companies adopt this strategy to develop a product mix with a
recognized brand name. Pepperidge Farm, for example, employs family branding. All of its breads, cookies, crackers, and desserts bear the Pepperidge Farm
brand name. A company using the same brand for most or all of its products
often uses similar packaging for all the products, too.

In some cases, family branding can be a liability. When Clorox introduced a
new detergent, many consumers associated the product with Clorox Bleach
and were afraid the detergent would not be color safe.[13]

Packaging

Packaging
The development of a container and a graphic design for a product.

Packaging involves designing a product container that will identify the product, protect it, and attract the attention of buyers. It is important to both consumers and manufacturers. The food and beverage industries alone spend $35 billion each year to package products; that sum represents 9 cents of every dollar spent on those products.[14]

Originally, packages were designed mostly for their functional value; they protected products from damage or spoilage. Today packaging also has significance as a marketing tool. To develop an appealing package that will catch the buyer's eye, marketers consider not only function but also shape, color, size, and graphic design.

Firms work to create innovative packages to meet the needs of the consumers they want to reach. For example, after a scientific study reported that taking an aspirin a day can ward off first heart attacks, Bayer promptly designed "calendar paks"—packages of 28 aspirins in separate blister compartments—to help buyers keep track of whether they took their daily aspirin tablet.[15] Other innovations are Clorox's no-splash spouts on bleach containers, Armour's Golden Star Fresh Packs with deli meats individually wrapped in two-slice servings,[16] and Wella's So Fine Shampoo Mist in a self-pressurized spray applicator that eliminates spills.[17]

For consumers who want convenience and small portions, the Dannon Company offers 4.4-ounce, individual cups of its light yogurt in a six-pack, as Figure 14.8 shows. The label pictured in the Dannon ad shows the brand, package and serving size, type of yogurt, ingredients, and number of calories. Such packaging adds to a product's function, safety, and appeal.

Packaging has become an important aspect of product safety. Since 1982, when eight Chicago-area people died from Tylenol capsules injected with cyanide, manufacturers have developed tamper proof packages for products such as medicines, foods (peanut butter, catsup), and personal care items (toothpaste). Products available in safety-sealed packages satisfy an additional consumer need.

The impact of packaging on the environment has become another critical issue many industries are facing. Packages from foods and consumer goods make up much of the tons of waste dumped into landfills each day in the United States. In response, some firms are changing packaging and products. Kellogg Co. puts its cereals into boxes made from recycled paper, while manufacturers now make disposable diapers such as Pampers and Luvs with half the amount of material as before.[18] In spite of such efforts, groups such as the Environmental Action Foundation and the U.S. Public Interest Research Group continue to criticize companies for developing wasteful packages.

Labeling

Labeling
The display of important information on a product package.

Manufacturers communicate with buyers through **labeling.** The label is the part of the package that identifies the brand and provides essential product information regarding contents, size, weight, quantity, ingredients, directions for use, shelf life, and any health hazards or dangers of improper use.

Labels also provide the means for automatic checkout and inventory monitoring. The universal product code (UPC), an electronic bar code on labels that identifies manufacturers and products, enables supermarkets and other stores to use computerized scanners at the checkout counter. Not only do scanners

Courtesy of The Dannon Company, Inc.

FIGURE 14.8

Product Identity: Packaging

The packaging for Dannon yogurt adds to the product's function, safety, and appeal. Note that the label gives the brand, package size, and serving size, and identifies the product as lowfat yogurt containing NutraSweet. It also prominently displays the number of calories.

save time and help keep down costs, they also compile complete sales records valuable to both stores and manufacturers.

The Consumer Product Safety Commission and the Food and Drug Administration require that labels indicate warnings, instructions, and manufacturer's identification. Federal laws mandate that labels include content information and potential hazards. Manufacturers are required to be truthful in listing product ingredients on labels. Ingredients must be listed in order, beginning with the ingredient that constitutes the largest percentage of the product down to the ingredient that makes up the smallest percentage. Snack chips that contain more vegetable oil than potatoes, for example, must be labeled to show oil as the first ingredient. Congress is considering stricter labeling laws to address the increase in labels containing health claims, such as low cholesterol, diet, light, or high fiber.[19]

PRICING

The price of a product is one of its most important aspects for both sellers and buyers. Many terms are used to represent price: taxi *fare,* insurance *premium,* parking *fine,* apartment *rent,* and—let's not forget—income *tax.* No matter how it is expressed, **price** is the value consumers exchange in a marketing transaction.

Price
The value that buyers exchange for a product in the marketing transaction.

Money usually is the value exchanged for a product that satisfies a consumer need. But sometimes money isn't involved at all; the parties exchange goods or services instead. Children trade baseball cards. Teenagers may do yard work to earn use of the family car. A retail store and a radio station may work out a deal to trade merchandise for free radio ads. Such trading, called *bartering,* is the oldest form of exchange and is used in all societies.

Although price does not always mean money, its purpose is always the same: to assign value to items involved in a marketing exchange. The price of a product generally reflects the level of satisfaction a buyer receives from the product. A Japanese collector purchased a stereo copy of the Beatles' 1966 album *Yesterday and Today* for $15,000, the most ever paid for an album. The price represents the satisfaction the collector receives from owning one of three known copies of the album still in its shrinkwrap and never played.[20]

The pricing decision is crucial for marketers because price is highly visible to consumers and greatly affects purchase decisions. After noticing a product, buyers generally look at the price tag. Prices that consumers perceive as too high will prevent them from buying.

PRICING OBJECTIVES

Before establishing prices, marketing managers must decide their pricing objectives. Survival is the most fundamental one; firms will tolerate financial losses and other difficulties if needed for survival. Besides survival, firms use price to increase sales and market share, boost profits, achieve a return on their investment, and maintain their present position in the industry.

Market Share

A firm's *market share* is its percentage of the total industry sales in the geographical area where it sells its products. Maintaining or increasing market share is a common pricing objective. Many firms use market share figures to assess their performance. An increase in sales may help a company reduce production costs and achieve higher profits since it is cheaper on a per unit basis to produce more goods or offer more services. Firms sometimes lower prices to try to capture a larger share of the market. Canon, for instance, attempted to increase market share by offering basic copiers in the $1,000 to $1,200 range when the low-end copier on the market was priced around $2,000.

Profit

Of course the objective of many companies is to maximize profit. But in practice, defining "maximum profit" is difficult. No matter how profitable a firm becomes, it still may not have reached a point of maximum profit. Most firms express this pricing objective as a percentage increase over current profits. A company's pricing objective may be to increase profit by 10 percent in one year.

Return on Investment

Return on investment (ROI) is the amount of profit earned, expressed as a percent of the total investment. ROI is sometimes more desirable as a pricing objective than is profit maximization, because it is a better measure of a firm's operating performance. For instance, the typical ROI in the automobile industry is 20 percent per year.

Status Quo

Firms wishing to maintain their present situation in the industry may establish status quo pricing objectives. A company that wants to meet (but not beat) competitors' prices, develop a favorable public image, or maintain its market share would favor status quo pricing objectives. By maintaining price stability, a firm reduces the risk it could face in a climate of price competition. For instance, when several airlines planned price hikes in the late 1980s, a few airlines lowered their fares. Most competitors then matched the price cuts, and all the airlines lost revenues from the resulting lack of price stability.

FACTORS IN PRICING DECISIONS

A firm cannot determine a product's price without considering several factors that affect price. Managers must take into account the use of price and nonprice competition, supply and demand, and consumer perceptions of price.

Price and Nonprice Competition

The pricing decision is influenced by the extent to which firms decide to use price as a competitive tool. Some rely heavily on price competition while others compete on aspects other than price. Firms competing based on **price competition** generally set prices equal to or lower than competitors' prices. Car rental companies often compete based on price competition by emphasizing economy rates, as the "Alamo" Business Action demonstrates.

> **Price Competition**
> Policy of using price to differentiate a product in the marketplace.

A firm competing based on price must be prepared to change prices quickly and frequently in response to competitors' price changes. One drawback to this strategy is that competitors can easily reduce their prices to counter it. Price competition is practiced by firms in many different industries, such as hotels, electronics component manufacturers, and automakers.

Nonprice competition involves competing based on factors other than price, such as quality or service. This strategy is useful in building brand loyalty. Customers who prefer a brand for reasons other than price are less likely to switch to a brand that costs less. For instance, consumers who pay thousands of dollars for a Rolex watch are not likely to switch brands because of a lower price. Several firms in the athletic shoe industry use nonprice competition and emphasize the benefits and styling of their brands.

> **Nonprice Competition**
> A policy of emphasizing aspects other than price, such as quality, service, or promotion, to sell products.

Supply and Demand

The price of a product is also influenced by the economic forces of supply and demand. The penny you pull out of your pocket is worth just that—a penny. But a coin collector may pay a great deal for a rare penny. That's the principle of supply and demand at work. **Supply** refers to the quantity of a product that producers will sell at various prices; the **demand** for a product is the quantity that consumers will purchase at different prices. For most products, the

> **Supply**
> The quantity of a product that producers will sell at various prices.
>
> **Demand**
> The quantity of a product that consumers will purchase at various prices.

Alamo Aims for Lowest Prices

Low prices. That's what vacation travelers want when they rent a car, and that's what Alamo Rent A Car promises. Competing on price has helped Alamo become one of the fastest-growing and most profitable firms in the highly competitive rental car industry.

Headquartered in Fort Lauderdale, Florida, Alamo began in 1974. Founders chose the name because it begins with "A" and would appear first in rental car listings in the Yellow Pages. Alamo decided to compete with the bigger, longer-established car rental companies by being a price-cutter. The firm advertises rental prices as much as 20 percent lower than its competitors and does not include an extra charge for mileage. For instance, in May 1990, a driver in Los Angeles could rent a Chevy Beretta with no extras from Alamo for $38 a day with free mileage. The same car from Hertz cost $51.93 a day plus 32 cents for every mile driven over 100 miles, unless the driver reserved the car three days in advance.

Alamo's strategy has been to target a specific but large market segment—leisure travelers who generally value low prices more than convenience. The leisure rent-a-car market has grown 10 to 15 percent a year compared to about 5 percent for the commercial market. Car rental industry ana-

lysts estimate the leisure market to be worth $2.3 billion.

Alamo's managers keep prices down by keeping costs down. They carefully choose rental locations and limit the number and types of cars they offer. Rather than locating in airport terminals, where space is very expensive, they choose rental offices outside airport gates and provide buses to transport customers from the airport terminal to the Alamo site. Alamo has about 75,000 cars at 90 of the most highly trafficked locations in the United States and the United Kingdom, far fewer than the approximately 300,000 cars Hertz rents from 5,400 sites.

Alamo has been criticized in the past for its advertising and customer service. The Federal Trade Commission and the National Association of Attorneys General charged that the company's advertising misled customers by concealing a variety of surcharges that boosted the final bill. In 1988–89 Alamo resolved the disputes and agreed to change its advertising. The rental firm used to have telephone and counter agents try to get customers to trade up to more expensive cars and sign on for collision insurance at what were the highest rates in the industry, $11.99 a day for a midsized car; now Alamo offers three collision damage policies ranging from $3 to $9 per day. And after the July 1989 *Consumer Reports* ranked Alamo

last in customer satisfaction among 11 rental car companies, management started a program called "Best Friends" to retrain all 4,000 employees in providing friendly, courteous service. "Phantom shoppers" monitor the program, which has helped Alamo cut customer complaints in half.

Alamo's strategy has helped boost its sales an average 20 percent a year since 1984, to number five in the industry, behind the big four rental agencies—Hertz, Avis, National, and Budget. Targeting leisure travelers has proved so effective for Alamo that its competitors have also gone after that segment, which many people believe offers the biggest growth for the 1990s. To compete with Alamo, Avis and Hertz also began to advertise unlimited mileage (with some restrictions). Alamo, which spends about $20 million a year for advertising, responded with ads promising free mileage for "every car, every day, everywhere" with no restrictions. "No wonder the other car rental companies are trying to copy our style," the ad said.

To keep growing, Alamo has begun to target another segment: the budget-minded business traveler. With airport desks in nearly one fourth of its locations, including Atlanta, Philadelphia, and Boston, Alamo wants to add convenience along with low prices.[21]

FIGURE 14.9

Supply and Demand Curve: VCRs

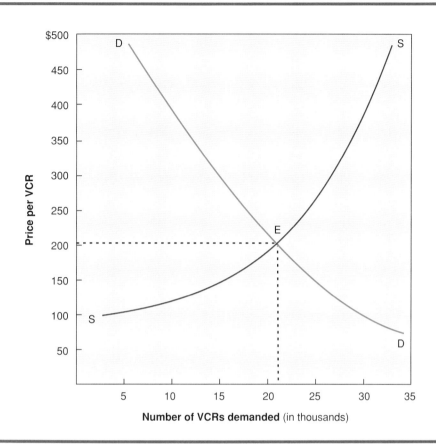

quantity demanded goes up as the price goes down; demand goes down as the price goes up.

Figure 14.9 shows a supply and demand curve for video recorders. The curve marked S is a typical supply curve. The supply curve slopes upward to the right, which means manufacturers are willing to offer more VCRs for sale when they can receive higher prices. The number of items supplied increases as price increases. The demand curve, labeled D, slopes downward to the right. This means that consumers are willing to buy more VCRs at lower prices; the number of items demanded goes up as price goes down.

The point at which the two curves intersect is called the equilibrium point, E on the graph. At this point, the quantity supplied equals the quantity demanded. In our example, a manufacturer is willing to produce 20,000 VCRs priced at $200, and consumers will buy 20,000 VCRs at $200 each. If the manufacturer makes more than 20,000 VCRs and prices them higher than $200, not all VCRs will be sold.

Consumer Perceptions of Price

Pricing decisions also require firms to consider consumers' perceptions of price. Price may be the top consideration in the buying decision of some consumers, while to others it may be much less important. The importance of price varies a great deal for different products and different target markets.

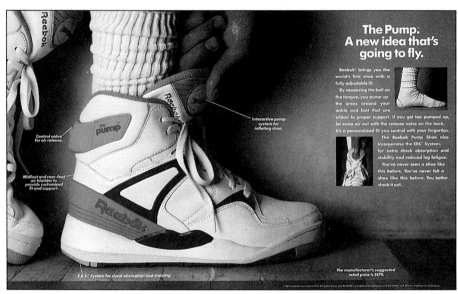

The Reebok Pump was intro-duced at a price of $170, establishing an image of a high-quality shoe.

Buyers generally believe price is closely related to quality. For products such as wine, jewelry, and perfume, a higher price signals higher quality to the target market. In such cases, firms can use price to establish an image of product superiority. A person shopping for a diamond ring may expect a high price and be skeptical of lower-priced gems.

PRICING METHODS

Pricing Method
A systematic procedure for determining prices on a regular basis; considers costs, product demand, or competitors' prices.

After establishing pricing objectives and considering various factors that influence price, a firm decides on a **pricing method,** a procedure used to determine prices on a regular basis. When selecting a pricing method, a company takes into account the product, the market, and sales volume. The method used to price products in a hardware store carrying thousands of items must be fairly simple. On the other hand, calculating the price of a bridge or a dam would be complex. In this section, we examine three common pricing methods: cost-oriented, demand-oriented, and competition-oriented pricing.

Cost-Oriented Pricing

Cost-Oriented Pricing
A method whereby a firm determines a product's total cost, then adds a markup to that cost to achieve the desired profit margin.

Firms such as supermarkets, department stores, and discount stores that sell numerous products often use a **cost-oriented pricing** method. They calculate prices by determining a product's total cost and adding on a percentage called the **markup.** The markup covers additional expenses incurred in marketing a product and allows the store to make a profit.

The percentage of the markup varies substantially from one product category to another but is often standardized across an industry. For instance, the markup for hardware is around 35 percent, while the markup for greeting cards is about 100 percent. How would you determine the price of a greeting card? Suppose that the total cost of producing one greeting card is 50 cents and the markup is 100 percent above costs. The price of the greeting card would be $1 (50 cents + 100 percent of 50 cents).

The major difficulty in using a cost-oriented pricing method is determining the actual markup percentage. If a firm uses a markup percentage that is too low, it underprices the product and loses potential profit. If the markup percentage is too high, the product is overpriced, and the firm may not sell enough units to cover costs.

Markup
In cost-oriented pricing, a percentage added to the total cost of the product to cover marketing expenses and allow a profit.

Demand-Oriented Pricing

Incorporating the level of demand for the product into the pricing decision is **demand-oriented pricing.** Strong product demand means prices are high. Where demand is weak, prices are lower. The price of houses, for example, fluctuates with demand (as well as interest rates). Home prices in the San Francisco Bay area are extremely high because of the great demand for houses in a relatively small area.

In using demand-oriented pricing, firms estimate the quantities of a product that consumers will demand at various prices. A technique called **breakeven analysis** can help a manager determine how many product units must be sold at various prices for a firm to break even—to recover the costs of production and marketing and to begin making a profit. The **breakeven quantity,** the point beyond which profits occur, is reached when the total revenue for all units sold is equal to the total cost of all units sold. Total revenue, or all income from product sales, is obtained by multiplying the number of units sold by the selling price.

Besides total revenue, marketers must consider various business costs to calculate the breakeven quantity. *Fixed costs* are expenses that remain constant regardless of the number of units produced. Insurance, rent, and equipment are fixed costs. *Variable costs* are those that change depending on the number of units produced. Costs for raw materials and labor, for example, rise when more units are produced and fall when fewer units are produced. Fixed costs plus variable costs equal the total cost of producing a specific number of units.

Figure 14.10 shows how the breakeven quantity is calculated for college textbooks. A publishing company has fixed production costs of $100,000. The variable costs are $20 per book, meaning the company incurs a cost of $20 for every book produced. Suppose the textbook sells for $40. The breakeven quantity is calculated as follows:

Demand-Oriented Pricing
A method based on the level of demand for the product.

Breakeven Analysis
A determination of how many product units must be sold at various prices for a firm to recover costs and begin making a profit.

Breakeven Quantity
The point at which the cost of making a product equals the revenue made from selling the product.

$$\text{Breakeven quantity} = \frac{\text{Fixed costs}}{\text{Price} - \text{Variable costs}}$$

In our example, the breakeven quantity is:

$$\frac{\$100,000}{\$40 - \$20} = \frac{\$100,000}{\$20} = 5,000 \text{ textbooks}$$

FIGURE 14.10

Breakeven Analysis for Textbooks

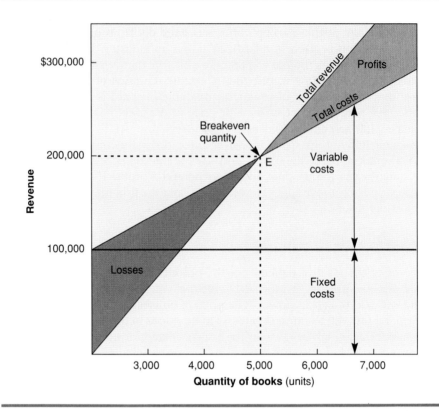

If 5,000 textbooks are sold, the publisher's total costs (both fixed and variable) will be recovered. Take another look at the graph in Figure 14.10. The breakeven quantity can be found where the total-revenue line and the total-cost line intersect. If more than 5,000 books are sold at $40, the publisher will generate a profit. Sales below 5,000 books will result in a loss.

A firm can use breakeven analysis to figure the profits and losses that would result from several different possible prices by calculating the breakeven quantity for each price. In our example, if the publishing firm reduces the price to $32, it would need to sell 8,333 books to break even. Raising the price to $48 would lower the breakeven quantity to 3,571 books. Marketers must rely on their research and experience to estimate how many units could be sold at each potential price. Then they can compare their estimated sales with the breakeven quantities to find the most appropriate price, the one at which sales will exceed the breakeven point and result in a profitable venture.

Competition-Oriented Pricing

Competition-Oriented Pricing
A method whereby a firm sets prices on the basis of its competitors' prices rather than its own costs and revenues.

In the two pricing methods we have discussed, costs and demand are the major considerations in setting a price. In **competition-oriented pricing,** firms consider the prices charged by competitors as the major factor in setting their own prices. Competition-oriented pricing is appealing, especially to retailers, because it is simple. It involves no complex calculations; prices are simply set close to (preferably below) competitors' prices. This method is useful when a firm's pricing objective is to increase sales or market share.

Courtesy of the Sharp Electronics Corporation

Sharp used price skimming to introduce Sharp Vision. The product initially sold for $5,299, but the price fell below $4,000 within six months.

Firms find competition-based pricing especially important when fierce price competition exists in the market or when competing products show little difference. Customers often use price to select a service provider, especially when services are quite similar. If students perceive all copy shops to do work of similar quality, they are likely to select the one that charges the lowest price per copy. Likewise, if customers view all banks as similar, they will probably select the one that charges the lowest checking account fee.

PRICING STRATEGIES

Once a firm selects a pricing method, it develops a strategy for setting and adjusting prices. We will examine four common pricing strategies: pioneer pricing, psychological pricing, professional pricing, and price discounting.

Pioneer Pricing

A firm setting a price for a new product may use **pioneer pricing.** There are two pioneer pricing strategies: price skimming and penetration pricing.

Price skimming   Firms using price skimming charge the highest price possible during the introduction stage of the product life cycle. The purpose of this

Pioneer Pricing
New-product pricing strategy of charging the highest possible price to regain costs quickly (price skimming) or setting the price below competitors' prices to build sales quickly (penetration pricing).

strategy is to "skim" the best buyers from the top of the market—those willing to pay a high price. When manufacturers introduced compact-disk players, they priced them fairly high. However, prices of CD players have dropped substantially since their introduction. Price skimming helps firms recover development costs more quickly and also may help to keep demand down during product introduction, when production capacities may be limited.

Penetration pricing   Some firms prefer to set prices low when offering a product for the first time. Penetration pricing, used to generate a large sales volume and gain a substantial market share quickly, establishes prices for new products below what competitors charge. Firms introducing consumer goods such as cosmetics, soups, or cleansers often use this strategy. One drawback is less flexibility than price skimming; raising a penetration price is more difficult than lowering a skimming price.

Psychological Pricing

Psychological Pricing
A policy that encourages purchase decisions based on emotion rather than reason; includes odd-even pricing, customary pricing, prestige pricing, and price lining.

Psychological pricing strategies encourage consumers to make purchase decisions on an emotional rather than a rational basis. Such strategies include odd-even pricing, customary pricing, prestige pricing, and price lining.

Odd-even pricing   Marketers sometimes try to influence buyers' perceptions of price by using certain numbers. In *odd pricing,* prices end with odd numbers, such as $98.99. This strategy assumes that buyers will perceive the product as a bargain—less than $100. The opposite strategy, *even pricing,* is used to give a product an exclusive image. Consumers may perceive a pair of slacks priced at $44 to be of higher quality than a pair priced at $43.95.

Customary pricing   When firms price products based on tradition, they use customary pricing. Products such as candy bars, gum, magazines, and mass transit are priced according to this strategy. A company introducing a new candy bar probably would charge the same price that consumers already pay for other candy bars.

Prestige pricing   An organization that sets an unusually high price to provide a quality image for a product uses prestige pricing. This strategy is most useful when buyers perceive a relationship between the item's price and its quality; indeed they may have second thoughts about purchasing the product if it does not cost enough. Prestige pricing is used for products such as furs, jewelry, and perfume.

Price lining   In price lining, sellers set a limited number of prices for selected lines of merchandise. These prices reflect various ranges in which consumers concentrate their purchases. For instance, a clothing store may sell a line of men's shirts for $22, $30, and $36. By holding prices constant within a certain range, price lining simplifies pricing decisions of sellers and purchasing decisions of consumers.

Professional Pricing

People with great amounts of training and skill in different fields use **profes-sional pricing.** Doctors, lawyers, accountants, and many other professionals charge standard fees that reflect the expertise required to perform their jobs. For instance, a doctor may charge $30 for an office visit and $100 for a physical examination.

Professional Pricing
A policy—practiced by doctors, lawyers, and others with skills or experience in a particular field—of charging a standard fee for a particular service.

Price Discounting

Many types of sellers engage in **price discounting,** offering customers deductions from the price of a product. Sellers often give cash discounts for prompt payment. A seller may specify a *cash discount* of "2/10 net 30," which means that a 2 percent discount is offered if the account is paid in 10 days and that the full balance is due in 30 days. *Quantity discounts* are provided to customers who buy on a large basis. Producers offer *trade discounts* to other sellers for performing various functions such as transporting, storing, and selling goods.

Price Discounting
A policy of offering buyers deductions from the price of a product.

Discounts during times of lower demand are common. Because of the perishable nature of services (unused capacity cannot be stored), service providers often use price to increase demand during slow periods. Movie theaters, for instance, charge less for morning and afternoon shows than for evening shows. Some health clubs drop prices during the summer. Telephone companies reduce rates for late night or weekend long-distance calls.

Another pricing practice growing among service firms is *bundling,* which involves selling two or more services in one package for a special price.[22] An example of bundling is an airline package that includes air travel, car rental, and hotel accommodations.

You'll Know It's the 21ˢᵗ Century When . . .

You Can Expect the Unexpected

Twenty-first–century consumers will want high quality and service at low prices. But innovators will be able to name their price if they spot new opportunities before the competition does. Don't expect a slump in the toy market as the baby boom ages out of its childbearing years, for example. As the new century begins, the baby boomers will swell the ranks of grandparents. The 21st century's fortunes will be made by businesses that look for markets where no one else expects to find them.[23]

SUMMARY OF LEARNING OBJECTIVES

1. To define the term *product* and distinguish between consumer and industrial products.
   A product consists of all the tangible and intangible characteristics provided in an exchange between a seller and a buyer. The products people

use for personal or family use are consumer products, classified as convenience, shopping, or specialty products. Organizations use industrial products in producing goods and services and in carrying out their operations.

2. **To differentiate between product line and product mix.**
Firms often market a group of related products and services known as a product line. A product line of only one or two products is shallow; a deep product line contains many items. A firm's product mix is the entire collection of products it offers. Product mix width (narrow or wide) refers to the number of product lines a firm carries.

3. **To trace the process of developing new products.**
To be successful, firms try to develop new products to satisfy consumers. New-product development consists of (*a*) generating ideas that fit a firm's objectives; (*b*) screening ideas to determine which are feasible to pursue; (*c*) analyzing the costs, sales, and profits of the proposed product; (*d*) developing a working model of the product; (*e*) test marketing the product in selected areas; and (*f*) distributing the new product to the entire market during commercialization.

4. **To describe the stages of the product life cycle and explain how firms can extend the product life cycle.**
A product enters the market during the *introduction* stage, in which sales rise slowly and profits are low. In the *growth* stage, sales increase rapidly and the product begins to generate a profit. In the *maturity* stage, sales peak as profits decline. Sales volume falls rapidly during a product's *decline* stage. To extend a product's life cycle, a firm can modify the product's quality, functions, or style. It can find new uses for the product, identify new users, or encourage more frequent use. A product that becomes too costly for a firm is deleted from the product mix.

5. **To explain the purposes of branding, packaging, and labeling.**
Firms identify their products through branding, packaging, and labeling. In *branding,* products are named and sometimes represented with a design called a brand. Unbranded products, called generics, also are often available. *Packaging* protects products, adds to their functions, helps ensure product safety, and attracts consumer attention. *Labeling* identifies the product and brand and provides information about contents and use.

6. **To list four pricing objectives and identify three factors to consider when making pricing decisions.**
Price, the value consumers exchange for a product in a marketing transaction, is important to both buyers and sellers. Besides mere survival, a firm can use price to increase market share, increase profit, increase return on investment, or maintain the industry status quo. When making pricing decisions, a firm determines whether to compete based on price and nonprice competition and considers the forces of supply and demand and consumer perceptions of price.

7. **To distinguish between cost-oriented, demand-oriented, and competition-oriented pricing methods.**
A firm can use any of several methods to set prices. *Cost-oriented* pricing bases price on total cost of a product plus a predetermined percentage

amount called the markup. *Demand-oriented* pricing, using breakeven analysis, considers the level of demand for the product at various possible prices in order to find out how many products must be sold for the firm to recover its costs. *Competition-oriented* pricing uses prices charged by competitors as the major factor in selecting prices.

8. To list and explain four pricing strategies.
   Various pricing strategies enable a firm to adjust the price of a product at certain times. *Pioneer pricing,* used in pricing new products, can mean setting the price high during a product's introduction to recover costs quickly (price skimming) or setting the price low during introduction to build sales and market share quickly (penetration pricing). A firm may use *psychological pricing* (odd-even pricing, customary pricing, prestige pricing, or price lining) to encourage consumers to make purchase decisions on some emotional basis. People with great amounts of training and skill use *professional pricing* to set standard fees. *Price discounting* means offering customers reductions from a product's price.

KEY TERMS

Product, p. 485
Consumer Product, p. 485
Convenience Product, p. 485
Shopping Product, p. 486
Specialty Product, p. 487
Industrial Product, p. 487
Product Line, p. 489
Product Mix, p. 489
Product Life Cycle, p. 494
Product Modification, p. 496
Brand, p. 497
Brand Name, p. 497
Packaging, p. 502
Labeling, p. 502
Price, p. 503

Price Competition, p. 505
Nonprice Competition, p. 505
Supply, p. 505
Demand, p. 505
Pricing Method, p. 508
Cost-Oriented Pricing, p. 508
Markup, p. 509
Demand-Oriented Pricing, p. 509
Breakeven Analysis, p. 509
Breakeven Quantity, p. 509
Competition-Oriented Pricing, p. 510
Pioneer Pricing, p. 511
Psychological Pricing, p. 512
Professional Pricing, p. 513
Price Discounting, p. 513

QUESTIONS FOR DISCUSSION AND REVIEW

1. What do marketers mean when they refer to a convenience product? A shopping product? A specialty product? Name a product for each category.
2. Explain the difference between product line and product mix.
3. Are the following product lines shallow or deep—Dr Pepper soft drinks, Levi's jeans, Reebok athletic shoes? Discuss. Would you consider the

following companies to have a narrow or wide product mix? McDonald's, Rolls-Royce, IBM.

4. A new product doesn't jump from the drawing board to the marketplace. What phases must it go through first?

5. Why do many new products fail? Can you name a new consumer product that failed? What are some possible reasons for its failure?

6. Products we see and use every day are in different phases of the product life cycle. Name two products in each phase.

7. Choose one of the products you named in the maturity stage. What are some ways its life cycle could be extended?

8. Distinguish between manufacturer brands, private brands, and generic brands.

9. What is the difference between packaging and labeling?

10. Name and describe three factors that influence pricing decisions.

11. What objectives might a firm have in mind when setting prices?

12. A clothing store uses a 50 percent markup to price most of its items. What pricing method is the store using? Explain what 50 percent markup means.

13. How does a company know when it breaks even on one of its products?

14. A company that manufactures umbrellas has fixed costs of $30,000 and variable costs of $5 for each umbrella it makes. The umbrellas sell for $10 each. What is the quantity that must be sold for the company to break even?

15. Which pioneer pricing strategy is a firm likely to use when introducing an innovative new medication that stops heart attacks instantly? Why?

CASE 14.1
Gillette Wants the Edge with Sensor

To consumers all over the world, the Gillette Co. means shaving. Its founder, King C. Gillette, invented the first safety razor in 1903. The Gillette Blue Blade (1932) and the Trac II twin-blade razor (1971) were pioneering products. With about 65 percent of the U.S. market, Gillette is by far the most powerful brand in the shaving business. Razors and blades represent one third of the firm's sales but two thirds of its profits. "Nothing is as good as the razor business," says Derwin Phillips, a vice chairman.

Aiming to make the razor business even better, Gillette developed the Sensor. This high-tech razor, introduced in 1990, uses cartridges with twin blades mounted on tiny springs so they can move separately along the contours of the face almost like tiny independent shock absorbers. Gillette designed the Sensor to give a smoother, closer, more comfortable shave than other razors—a quality it hopes will be important enough to prompt men throughout the world to change their shaving habits.

The people at Gillette knew that getting men to switch to the Sensor would be a challenge. Men seem to get firmly entrenched in their grooming habits, especially shaving. Those who use Gillette's Trac II, for example, keep their razors from 7 to 10 years. And a new cartridge system would go against the trend toward inexpensive disposable razors, introduced in the mid-70s and used by two thirds of American shavers. The Sensor, priced around $3.50 for a razor and three cartridges, costs about 25 percent more than Atra cartridge razors and double the cost of shaving with disposables. But Gillette officials believed consumers would pay more for a new cartridge razor providing a better, easier shave. Gillette wanted to reverse the trend toward disposables (which cost more to make, yet sell for less than cartridges for permanent razors); in 1989 it stopped advertising them in the United States.

The firm spent more than $200 million and took 10 years to develop the Sensor. After a model was first developed in 1979, the firm hoped to introduce the razor in 1984 or 1985 but faced obstacles in mass-producing the cartridges. Gillette had to develop lasers that could operate fast enough to attach the springs to the blades on a high-speed assembly line that makes two and a half cartridges per second. In 1986 a test assembly line showed the technology would work. During the next two years, Gillette spent $150 million to build manufacturing equipment to mass-produce the razor system. Now that Gillette has the technology, it may have the market for the Sensor to itself, since the high cost and complex nature of the manufacturing facilities may prevent competitors like Wilkinson, Bic, and Schick from developing similar products.

Gillette tested the Sensor by asking employees at its Boston factory to come to work early each morning and shave there. Researchers measured their whiskers

Adapted from Joshua Levine, "Global Lather," *Forbes,* February 5, 1990, p. 146; Keith Hammonds, "It's One Sharp Ad Campaign, but Where's the Blade?" *Business Week,* March 5, 1990, p. 30; Lawrence Ingrassia, "A Recovering Gillette Hopes for Vindication in a High-Tech Razor," *The Wall Street Journal,* September 29, 1989, pp. A1, A4.

with a microscopic camera mounted on the razor and collected cut whiskers and measured them with a microscope.

In January 1990, after shipping 4.5 million of the new razors to U.S. stores, Gillette introduced the Sensor to American consumers during $3 million worth of Super Bowl commercials. The ads featured the theme "The best a man can get" and showed smiling, confident "regular guys." Gillette planned a 1990 worldwide promotional campaign at a cost of $110 million to launch the Sensor in 19 countries in Europe and North America. The firm chose a global approach, with little change in ads from country to country, to save packaging, advertising, and other production and marketing costs.

In the United States, Gillette's promotion of the Sensor was highly effective. But there was a hitch. Gillette had not made enough of the product. Many large drugstore chains did not receive their orders in full or on time. The razors sold out immediately, and replacement cartridges were scarce or not available for several months. Said Gillette executive vice president John W. Symons, "This is one of the hottest items in health and beauty aids . . . and the trade knows it." Symons said he and other executives simply underestimated the effect of the media hype that surrounded the Sensor's launch. To resolve the problem, Gillette stopped advertising the razor for a few months, delayed launching it in Spain, Portugal, and Italy, and used razors intended for European markets to fill orders from U.S. stores. The firm also rushed to install manufacturing lines in its West Berlin factory eight months earlier than planned.

Questions for Discussion

1. In which product category would you classify the Sensor shaving system?

2. Classify twin-blade razors, disposable razors, and Sensor razors according to product life-cycle stage. How does the product life-cycle stage influence marketing decisions for each product?

3. Why does the Gillette Co. use family branding for its products? What degree of brand loyalty does the Gillette brand enjoy?

4. What pricing strategy is Gillette using for Sensor? How does Sensor's pricing relate to the price-quality relationship?

CASE 14.2
Rising Prices Leave French Winemakers' Glass Half-Empty

Daniel Johnnes, wine manager at Montrachet, a top French restaurant in New York, was shocked when he placed an order for Côte-Rotie, a red wine from France's Rhone region. The wine was priced at $250 for a 12-bottle case, up from $140 a case 18 months earlier. Said Johnnes, "This time I just refused to pay the price."

Instead Johnnes is doing what many other restaurateurs and importers are—buying more California wines. That spells trouble for France's $10 billion wine

Adapted from Christopher Elias, "No Whines over '89's Great Grapes," *Insight,* May 28, 1990, p. 38; Joshua Levine, "Pride Goeth before a Fall?" *Forbes,* May 29, 1989, p. 306; John Rossant, "For French Winemakers the Glass Is Half Empty," *Business Week,* February 15, 1988, p. 50.

industry, which employs 700,000 people. The United States is one of the largest importers of French wines. But steady price hikes since 1985 have contributed to a dramatic drop in exports of French table wine to the United States; 1987 alone saw a 27 percent decrease, to 18 million gallons. In contrast, sales of California wines have doubled since 1970. And while sales of jug wines and wine coolers are dropping, sales of midpriced and expensive California wines (costing $5 and up) doubled between 1984 and 1989. These better vintages, called varietals because they are identified by the main variety of grape, are competing with the French imports. Many wine retailers believe California wines offer good value for the money, but fewer see French wines that way.

Prices of French wines rose through the 1980s and are continuing to rise, often substantially. One reason is the exchange rate. The franc has been strong compared to the dollar, which increases the price U.S. buyers pay for French wine. Another reason may be that the French wine industry wants to make the highest possible profits, especially for wines made from outstanding grape crops, such as the 1989 Bordeaux wines. Demand is expected to be high for these wines, which were bottled and delivered late in 1991. Price hikes are also high. For example, the price of one red Margaux wine surged from $185 a case for the 1988 vintage to about $300 a case for the 1989 vintage—an increase of 62 percent. One of the Bordeaux region's most highly prized wines, $600 a case for the 1988 vintage, was priced at about $799 for the 1989.

One New York wine merchant attributes such sharp price increases to the greed of growers, winemakers, and distributors. While some growers have taken a reasonable 10 percent increase, most have increased prices 18 percent, and one chateau boosted its prices 25 percent. On top of that, 2 to 3 percent is added for the agents who represent the growers to the distributors. Then the distributors mark up prices another 10 to 25 percent. For superior vintages in much demand, such as the 1989 Bordeaux wines, distributors were marking up prices 30 to 50 percent. To avoid paying top prices yet still trade in French wines, some U.S. buyers look for bargains and lesser-known wines of good quality.

Some French winemakers are reluctantly considering price cuts. One has been cutting his profits on exports, which are 80 percent of his sales. But most producers of fine French wines are maintaining their prices; they believe the market will eventually turn around. Wine exports have dropped before, but this time the French could lose some market share permanently. The stature of premium French wine is changing. Says one top U.S. wine importer, "For an older generation of Americans, France was the standard by which to judge all wine, just as it was with high fashion and perfume. For the younger generation, that is no longer the case."

Questions for Discussion

1. When consumers purchase a product such as wine, what, other than the wine itself, are they buying?
2. Is the wine market characterized by price competition or nonprice competition?
3. Do you think consumers believe that the more a French wine costs, the better it is? If so, why do you think the French winemakers are losing their market share?
4. Which pricing objective do the French wine producers seem to have established?

CHAPTER FIFTEEN

DISTRIBUTION

LEARNING OBJECTIVES

1. To define the term *marketing channel* and identify the two major types of marketing intermediaries.

2. To explain how marketing channels are integrated vertically.

3. To define *wholesaling* and describe the functions wholesalers perform.

4. To define *retailing* and outline the activities retailers perform.

5. To discuss the major considerations in retail planning.

6. To explain the role of physical distribution and identify its components.

Technology is changing fast today. So are demographics. Markets are becoming global. Businesspeople may not realize that the ways goods and services get to customers are changing just as fast.

© Jonathan Selig 1986

In the United States, mutual funds that used to be sold only through brokerage houses now are sold also through regional banks, insurance agencies, and professional associations. In Japan most urban mom-and-pop shops have been converted to outlets of huge chains, such as 7–Eleven or Mister Donut. In Britain the bulk of consumer electronics products are now sold by four national chains carrying private brands.

Many U.S. department stores, especially those centered in urban downtown areas, are in trouble as workers and customers move increasingly to the suburbs. As consumers shop for the best price, big discount stores have flourished; category discounters that focus on one exhaustive line of goods are booming. Some manufacturers of clothing, luggage, and diverse other goods have opened outlets to sell directly to consumers. Consumers are skipping stores altogether and using catalogs, television shopping networks, and buying clubs. This stiff competition, combined with poor customer service over the years and an aging and busier population less inclined to shop, may send many retail stores and regional malls into decline.

Nowadays customers do not always themselves buy the products they use. Hospitals often contract with independent firms for maintenance, billing, patient feeding, physical therapy, the pharmacy, or X ray. Many firms rely on computer management firms that design, buy, install, and run information systems for clients.

U.S. and foreign competition is squeezing profits and reducing the number of distributors. The cost of holding inventory has doubled since the 1960s, the cost of labor has jumped, and the labor pool has dwindled. Manufacturing customers are demanding more service, especially as they adopt the just-in-time inventory approach in their operations (see Chapter Nine).

Large industrial producers are selling direct to customers. Foreign firms, competing on performance and price, are trying to gain a piece of the U.S. market through small distributing firms and catalog companies. Warehouse clubs selling office furniture and other merchandise are luring small-business and manufacturing customers from traditional industrial distributors.

Lines blur between manufacturers and distributors as firms merge, grow, and diversify. Kennemetal Inc., a maker of carbide cutting tools, bought a leading general-line firm and a national mail-order catalog distributor with four warehouses, and now distributes a broad range of industrial products nationally. New super distributorships, such as Sun Distributors of Philadelphia, carry many and varied product lines. Cooperatives such as ID ONE, a group of 30 large independent distributors, buy and promote together to compete with superdistributors and national chains.

As management expert Peter Drucker says, "Changes in distributive channels . . . should be a major concern of every business and every industry."[1]

A fter organizations devise marketing strategies, and produce products and price them, they must get the products to the marketplace. The distribution function is important to society because it enables goods and services to reach consumers. It is vital to firms' success. As the examples in the chapter opener show, firms use many different avenues to get products to consumers in a timely and efficient manner.

In this chapter, we examine the various activities involved in distributing goods and services. First we explain the concept of a marketing channel of distribution and describe the types of channels. Next we explore two major distribution activities: wholesaling and retailing. Finally we discuss the physical movement of products from producers to consumers.

MARKETING CHANNELS

A **marketing channel (channel of distribution)** is a group of interrelated organizations that directs the flow of products from producer to ultimate customers.[2] The channel organizations that provide the link between the producer and the consumer are called **marketing intermediaries.** Comp-U-Card is an example of a marketing intermediary.

The two major categories of marketing intermediaries are wholesalers and retailers. Wholesalers are individuals and organizations that sell primarily to other sellers or industrial users. Wholesale transactions generally involve large quantities of goods. Retailers specialize in selling products to consumers. They generally resell products that they obtain from wholesalers. We will discuss wholesalers and retailers later in the chapter.

Marketing Channel
A group of interrelated organizations that directs the flow of products from producers to ultimate consumers; also called channel of distribution.

Marketing Intermediary
An individual or organization in a marketing channel that provides a link between producers, other channel members, and final consumers.

Functions of Marketing Intermediaries

Consumers often wonder whether products would cost less if one or more marketing intermediaries could be eliminated from the distribution system. Would cars be less expensive if customers could simply buy them straight from the manufacturer? Perhaps, but think about the practical aspects involved. How many consumers would be willing or able to go to Detroit to buy a car? Or maybe Japan? If manufacturers offered cars for sale by mail order, how many consumers would buy one without seeing and test-driving it? Carmakers selling vehicles directly to buyers from around the United States or around the world would be impossible.

Marketing intermediaries are vital in creating place, time, and possession utilities. They ensure that products are available on a timely basis where they are needed. Eliminating intermediaries does not eliminate the need for their services, such as storage, record-keeping, delivery, and providing a product assortment. Either the manufacturer, the consumer, or some other organization has to perform these essential services. Without intermediaries, most consumer purchases would be much less efficient. Products probably would cost more, not less.

FIGURE 15.1

Typical Marketing Channels

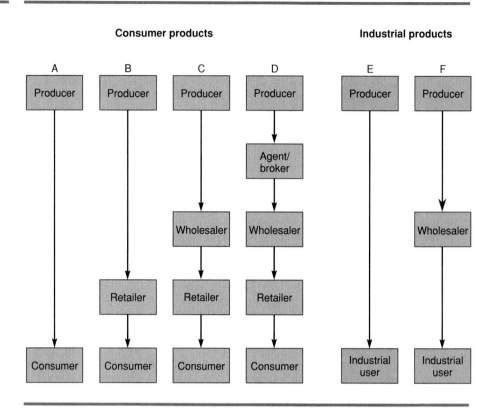

Types of Marketing Channels

Depending on the needs of the target market, firms utilize many different types of marketing channels to distribute products. Generally channels for consumer products are different than channels for industrial products.

Consumer products   The four most commonly used channels for consumer products are shown in Figure 15.1. Channel A, the direct channel, shows the movement of products from producer to consumer. This channel is not typical for most consumer goods, although some products often are distributed this way, such as plants and flowers at nurseries, produce at farmers' markets, and arts and crafts items at fairs. Most services are distributed directly from service producers to the consumer, such as hair styling, dry cleaning, and auto repair.

Channel B reflects the movement of products from producer to retailer to consumer. This channel is commonly used for large, bulky products (automobiles, furniture), as well as perishable items (fresh seafood). Bringing in another intermediary, such as a wholesaler, would add delays or unnecessary costs to the distribution of these products.

Channel C, producer to wholesaler to retailer to consumer, is the traditional marketing channel. A wide range of products, including appliances, beverages, tobacco, and most convenience goods, is distributed through this channel.

The final channel (D) for consumer products—producer to agent/broker to wholesaler to retailer to consumer—is used to distribute small, inexpensive products purchased frequently. Several wholesalers are involved in the distri-

Products like plants and flowers are often distributed through direct marketing channels.

Russell Lincoln/Stock Boston

bution of items, such as gum and candy bars, that are purchased daily by millions of consumers at thousands of outlets.

Industrial products   The common channels employed to distribute industrial products also appear in Figure 15.1. These channels are much shorter than the consumer channels. Most industrial products are distributed through the direct channel, producer to industrial user (channel E). For industrial products such as heavy equipment and machinery, the producer can communicate directly with the customer and provide needed and timely services such as training and repairs.

Some industrial products are distributed to customers through wholesalers (channel F). This channel is most common for accessory (smaller) equipment and supplies that are produced in large quantities but sold in small quantities. Tools and automotive parts, for instance, are sold to industrial users through wholesalers.

Vertical Integration

When one organization in the marketing channel assumes control of another, **vertical integration** takes place. For instance, Zenchiku Co. Ltd., the largest meat distributor in Japan, purchased a 77,000-acre cattle ranch in Montana, a move that enables the firm to control the product from the U.S. pasture to the dinner plate in Japan.[3] Total vertical integration occurs when one organization controls all of the channel functions, from producer to consumer. Some oil companies, for example, own the oil wells, refineries, terminals, trucks and tankers, and service stations.

Traditionally marketing intermediaries have operated independently. However, vertical integration has led to the concept of a planned marketing channel.

Vertical Integration
Combining two or more functions of a marketing channel under one management.

The Sherwin-Williams Company is an example of a corporate vertical marketing system. Sherwin-Williams distributes paint and other products through its own retail stores.

Courtesy of The Sherwin-Williams Company 1990

VMS
A marketing channel in which all intermediaries are under one manager to improve distribution.

Corporate VMS
A marketing channel in which one organization owns all stages of the channel.

Administered VMS
A marketing channel in which independent organizations use informal coordination, usually dominated by one channel organization.

Contractual VMS
A marketing channel in which organizations' relationships are formalized through legal agreements.

Market Coverage
The number of outlets in which a product is sold.

Intensive Distribution
Market coverage in which all available outlets are used for distributing a product.

A **vertical marketing system (VMS)** is a planned marketing channel in which a single channel member manages the different intermediaries to improve distribution efficiency. Vertical marketing systems have become increasingly popular in recent years.

Vertical marketing systems can be one of three types: corporate, administered, or contractual. Under a **corporate VMS,** marketing intermediaries are owned by one organization. The Sherwin-Williams Company, which makes paint and sells it in its own retail stores, uses a corporate VMS. In an **administered VMS,** channel organizations remain independent, but one member dominates the others. This organization, usually large and powerful, greatly influences the decisions of all organizations in the channel. Manufacturers such as Campbell Soup Company and Kellogg Co., for example, have extensive influence in distributing their products, including the ability to obtain adequate shelf space in supermarkets, and promotional cooperation. The third type, **contractual VMS,** ties channel organizations together through legal agreements. This arrangement is popular among franchises such as McDonald's and Hallmark stores.

Intensity of Market Coverage

The characteristics of the product and the needs of the target market determine how many outlets a manufacturer will employ to cover the market. **Market coverage** refers to the number of outlets in which a product is sold.

The level of market coverage that uses all available outlets for distributing a product is called **intensive distribution.** Many convenience goods such as gum, candy bars, newspapers, bread, and soft drinks are distributed in a wide variety of locations convenient to consumers. Availability is a major factor in the sale of these items.

In **selective distribution,** only some of the available outlets are used to distribute a product. Goods such as furniture and electrical appliances are distributed selectively. Because these products are much more expensive and are purchased much less frequently than convenience goods, consumers will spend more time and travel greater distances to shop for them.

The type of market coverage in which only a single outlet is used in a specific geographic area is called **exclusive distribution.** Infrequently purchased, expensive products are often distributed in this manner. Consumers wishing to buy a Rolls-Royce, for example, would find only one dealership selling the car in their area.

Selective Distribution
Market coverage in which only some of the available outlets are used for distributing a product.

Exclusive Distribution
Market coverage in which one outlet is used in a specific geographic area for distributing a product.

WHOLESALING

Wholesaling involves the activities of marketing intermediaries—called wholesalers—who sell to retailers, other wholesalers, or industrial users. (Wholesalers generally do not sell directly to consumers.) Wholesaling is a crucial component of distribution: about 60 percent of all products move through wholesalers. They account for $1.6 trillion in sales annually—30 percent of the U.S. gross national product.[4] Wholesaling is growing and offers many opportunities to persons who want to establish their own businesses (see the Business Action). It provides several essential services in the distribution of goods and services.

Wholesaling
The marketing activities of intermediaries who sell to retailers, industrial users, and other wholesalers.

Services Wholesalers Perform

Wholesalers exist because of the services they offer. They provide many services of value to both their suppliers and their customers (retailers and other sellers).

Ownership   By purchasing large amounts of goods, taking title to them, and storing them for resale, wholesalers absorb inventory costs for manufacturers.

Financing   Wholesalers invest large amounts of money in inventory, extend credit to retailers, and collect payment from retailers.

Risk Assumption   Wholesalers take possession and ownership of products that may become obsolete or deteriorate before they are sold. In that way, wholesalers assume a great deal of risk. They also face the risk of nonpayment from retailers.

Promotional assistance   Wholesalers often help promote the products they sell. They may provide retailers with displays or ideas for special promotions.

Information   Wholesalers commonly employ their own sales forces, publish catalogs, and sponsor trade journals. By those means, they provide both retailers and producers with valuable information about product demand, buying trends, and prices.

Getting It Wholesale

Wholesaling is one way to sell a popular product without getting into manufacturing. That makes it one of the hottest opportunities around. Two entrepreneurs taking advantage of that opportunity are cousins Asta Baskauskas and Margaret Kyle Petraits. Konceptual Design, their $1 million business, distributes top-of-the-line door hardware to designers, architects, and manufacturers.

The two women started Konceptual Design in 1984 with less than $2,000 and little knowledge of wholesaling. Baskauskas was a former dental student, Petraits an interior designer. They faced many challenges. Wholesaling is traditionally a male-dominated business; distributorships often are handed down from father to son. Wholesalers have little control over the quality, volume, and design of the products they represent. They must work out complex legal issues with manufacturers about how many wholesalers handle the products, how much of the product wholesalers must sell, when products will be delivered, and whether contracts will be renewed.

Baskauskas and Petraits took good first steps toward success. (1) They chose the right product: high-quality doorknobs, latches, cabinet handles, and door plates made from brass, bronze, or even 24-carat gold plate. (2) They chose

the right manufacturer: Vervloet-Faes, a Belgian, family-run company in business since 1905 that was looking for a distributor for the U.S. market. The two women visited Belgium to meet the owners of Vervloet-Faes and learn as much as possible about the company. "You're really picking a partner," says Baskauskas.

They also did their homework to pick the 39 other manufacturers they now represent. They found out how each company has treated other wholesalers, the kind of advertising support it provides, and what its sales history has been—valuable information for success.

Besides choosing products and manufacturers carefully, Baskauskas and Petraits take care in providing customer service. (Some say service is the heart of the business in distribution.) Because Konceptual Design deals in expensive, high-quality items, customer expectations are high. The two owners advise architects and interior designers on which of 45,000 different items will best suit their clients. They also handle special orders. Once they arranged for Vervloet-Faes to custom-make door handles for an air terminal for King Fahd of Saudi Arabia; Konceptual Design received a $100,000 order for 790 handles with the royal seal (two crossed swords and a palm tree). And Baskauskas and Petraits try to make sure their service to customers is not hampered

by problems in the distribution channel. When the importer for one manufacturer's line wasn't delivering orders on time or returning calls, they persuaded the manufacturer to find another importer.

The two partners recognize that they are vulnerable, because manufacturers can replace them. As their business has grown, they have tried to build in control by gaining exclusive distribution rights to a product line and by adding new lines. In 1987 they worked out a deal with Vervloet-Faes to be the sole American distributor—a position that brings more clout with the Belgian manufacturer and the chance to sign up other wholesalers and thus increase sales and earnings. Konceptual Design since has earned exclusive New England distribution rights for two U.S. manufacturers of door hardware.

Baskauskas and Petraits have expanded their wholesaling base and now are offering a new product to a new target market—a computer software package, custom-made for people in their business, that maintains accounting, inventory, and other management records. They hope that selling the package and looking for more growth opportunities in wholesaling will keep Konceptual Design growing in an increasingly competitive business climate.[5]

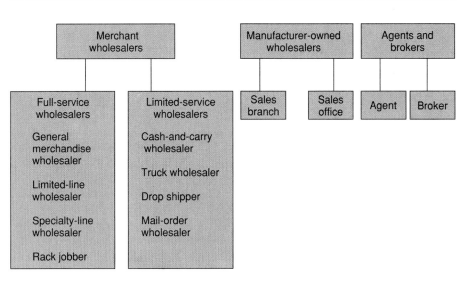

FIGURE 15.2

Types of Wholesalers

Product assortment   Because wholesalers usually carry an assortment of products, customers are able to order from a single source.

Transportation   Wholesalers generally arrange local and long-distance shipments to customers.

Types of Wholesalers

Many different types of wholesalers offer numerous channel alternatives. Wholesalers commonly are grouped into three categories: merchant wholesalers, manufacturer-owned wholesalers, and agents and brokers (refer to Figure 15.2).

Merchant wholesalers   A wholesaler who takes title to products and resells them to retailers, other wholesalers, or industrial users is a **merchant wholesaler.** The majority of all wholesalers fall into this category. They account for nearly 60 percent of total wholesale sales.[6] Merchant wholesalers can be either full-service wholesalers or limited-service wholesalers.

Merchant Wholesaler
A marketing intermediary that takes ownership of goods and the risks associated with ownership.

As their name implies, full-service wholesalers provide the widest range of services that wholesalers can offer, such as ownership, financing, and risk assumption. Full-service wholesalers who carry a very wide product mix are called *general merchandise wholesalers*. Those who carry only a few product lines are called *limited-line wholesalers*. For example, a general merchandise wholesaler may supply a supermarket with cosmetics, hardware, drugs, and tobacco and food items. A limited-line wholesaler may carry only a few product lines, such as tools and lighting fixtures. A *specialty-line wholesaler* usually carries a single product line, such as exotic flowers or fresh seafood. A *rack jobber* provides display units and places products on shelves. Rack jobbers serve a certain section of a store, such as bakery products, magazines, hardware, or cosmetics.

Limited-service wholesalers provide only a few of the services offered by wholesalers. Thus they leave some of the functions for producers or retailers to perform. *Cash-and-carry wholesalers* sell products such as construction materials to customers for cash, with the customers providing transportation of the goods. *Truck wholesalers* deliver products directly to customers but offer limited services and require cash payments. They often handle perishable items such as fresh fruit and vegetables. *Drop shippers* do not physically handle products but simply take title and negotiate sales. They commonly work in the lumber and coal industries. *Mail-order wholesalers* use catalogs to sell products such as jewelry and automobile parts to retailers and industrial customers.

Manufacturer-owned wholesalers   In some cases, the manufacturer owns the wholesale business. Except that the manufacturer owns them, **sales branches** resemble merchant wholesalers, taking title to products and reselling them. Sales branches provide services such as carrying inventory, extending credit, providing delivery, and assisting with promotion. They commonly are found in the chemical and electrical supplies industries.

A **sales office** is basically a sales force owned by the manufacturer. Although they do not maintain inventories, sales offices sell the manufacturer's products. Sales offices also may sell other products that complement the manufacturer's product line.

Agents and brokers   A wholesaler hired permanently on a commission basis by a buyer or a seller is an **agent**. Agents can take possession of goods, but they do not accept legal title. By concentrating on a few products, they can provide a high level of selling effort. The major types of agents are commission merchants, manufacturers' agents, and selling agents.

Sales Branch
A manufacturer-owned wholesaler that takes title to products, assumes the risks of ownership, and provides services.

Sales Office
A manufacturer-owned sales force that sells products without maintaining an inventory.

Agent
A wholesaler hired by a buyer or seller on a permanent basis and paid commissions.

Real estate brokers represent home buyers and sellers on a temporary basis.

Courtesy of RE/MAX International, Inc.

A *commission merchant* receives goods from local sellers, establishes prices, and negotiates sales. For instance, in the agricultural industry, a commission merchant may take possession of a truckload of fertilizer and transport it to a central market for sale. A *manufacturers' agent* represents one or more manufacturers on a commission basis and offers noncompeting lines of products to customers. The relationship between the agent and the manufacturer is formalized by a written agreement. A *selling agent* is an independent wholesaler who sells a manufacturer's product for a commission, or fee. Manufacturers rely on selling agents to distribute canned foods, clothing, and furniture.

A **broker** is a wholesaler who brings together buyers and sellers on a temporary basis. Brokers are similar to agents, but they concentrate on specific commodities, such as insurance or real estate. A food broker, for example, markets food items to grocery chains, food processors, or other wholesalers. Brokers are paid a commission by the party that engages their services, such as a food manufacturer.

Broker
A wholesaler who brings together buyers and sellers on a temporary basis.

RETAILING

The side of distribution most familiar to consumers is retailing; most of us come in contact with retail stores almost daily. The marketing activity of **retailing** focuses on the sale of goods and services to the ultimate consumer for personal or household use.[7] Retailers, an essential link in the marketing channel, are often the only intermediary who deals directly with consumers. Retailers also are customers themselves, since they buy from producers and wholesalers.

Retailing
The marketing activities involved in selling products to final consumers for personal or household use.

Retailing is a significant part of the U.S. economy. Approximately 22 million people work in the retailing sector.[8] Nearly 2 million retail outlets are open for business in the United States. Who are America's largest retail companies? Table 15.1 lists the largest U.S. retailers according to sales, which amount to

TABLE 15.1

Ten Largest Retailers in the United States

DID YOU KNOW? *Sears, the largest retailer in the United States, has annual sales of nearly $56 billion.*

Rank	Name	Sales ($ in millions)
1	Sears Roebuck	$55,972
2	Wal-Mart Stores	32,602
3	Kmart	32,080
4	American Stores	22,156
5	Kroger	20,261
6	J. C. Penney	17,410
7	Safeway Stores	14,874
8	Dayton Hudson	14,739
9	Great Atlantic & Pacific Tea (A&P)	11,164
10	May Department Stores	11,027

Source: "The 50 Largest Retailing Companies," *FORTUNE*, June 3, 1991, p. 274. © The Time Magazine Company.

FIGURE 15.3

**Retail Sales for Major
Store Types** ($ in Millions)

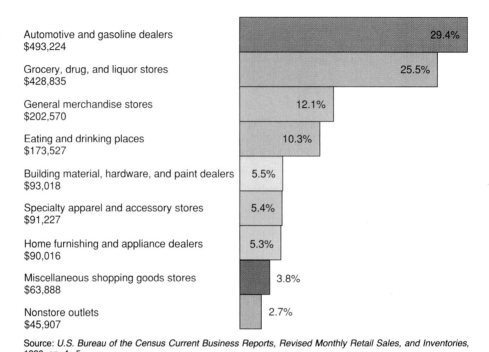

Automotive and gasoline dealers $493,224	29.4%
Grocery, drug, and liquor stores $428,835	25.5%
General merchandise stores $202,570	12.1%
Eating and drinking places $173,527	10.3%
Building material, hardware, and paint dealers $93,018	5.5%
Specialty apparel and accessory stores $91,227	5.4%
Home furnishing and appliance dealers $90,016	5.3%
Miscellaneous shopping goods stores $63,888	3.8%
Nonstore outlets $45,907	2.7%

Source: *U.S. Bureau of the Census Current Business Reports, Revised Monthly Retail Sales, and Inventories,* 1990, pp. 4–5.

billions of dollars each year. Figure 15.3 shows retail sales for major store types in the United States.

Types of Retail Stores

Most retail sales take place within stores. The diverse types of retail stores include department stores, discount stores, specialty stores, supermarkets, superstores, convenience stores, warehouse showrooms, catalog showrooms, and warehouse clubs.

Department stores   Retail stores such as Nordstrom's, Hudson's and Macy's carry a wide variety of products. These **department stores** are organized into separate departments for such items as apparel, housewares, furniture, sporting goods, and appliances. Department stores generally offer a full line of services, including credit, delivery, and personal assistance.

Discount stores   Stores such as Wal-Mart and Target that offer general merchandise at low prices are called **discount stores.** They carry a wide assortment of products but keep services to a minimum. For example, Home Depot, the largest home-repair chain in the United States, stocks 30,000 separate items; its prices are 30 percent below those of a typical hardware store.[9]

Specialty stores   Retailers who offer a narrow mix of products with deep product lines are called **specialty stores**. The Foot Locker, for example, offers

Department Store
A large retailer organized into separate departments and offering a full line of services and a wide product mix.

Discount Store
A retailer offering a wide variety of general merchandise at low prices and with minimum services.

Specialty Store
A retailer that carries only particular lines of products.

athletic shoes, Gap Kids features clothes for children, and Talbot's specializes in traditional clothing and accessories for women.

Supermarkets   Known for their large size, self-service, wide variety of food products, and limited assortment of household goods, **supermarkets** usually offer convenient locations, adequate parking, and lower prices than those at neighborhood grocery stores. Kroger, Winn-Dixie, A&P, and Jewel are large supermarket chains.

Supermarket
A large, self-service retailer that stocks a wide variety of groceries and a limited assortment of nonfood products.

Superstores and hypermarkets   A giant retail outlet that carries food and nonfood items plus a wide assortment of other routinely purchased products is a **superstore.** Larger than supermarkets, superstores emphasize low prices and one-stop shopping. Many supermarkets are turning to this concept. Today the typical supermarket is 50 percent larger than 10 years ago and stocks 20,000 items, double the number offered in 1976.[10] An even larger retail store is the *hypermarket,* which combines the one-stop supermarket and the discount store. Hypermarkets offer more than 50,000 items, including groceries, clothing, building materials, and furniture. Several retail giants such as Kmart and Wal-Mart have developed hypermarkets but with little success. The hypermarket concept has not caught on in the United States; many shoppers think they are too big and too remote.[11] The Business Action examines the success of Wal-Mart's discount stores, and looks at some of the problems the retail firm encountered with hypermarkets.

Superstore
A giant retail outlet that stocks food and nonfood items as well as most other products purchased routinely.

Convenience stores   Small retail stores characterized by convenient locations and long hours open for business are called **convenience stores**. Convenient Food Mart and 7–Eleven fall into this category. At convenience stores, the variety of food and nonfood items is limited, with prices generally higher than at supermarkets.

Convenience Store
A small retail store in a convenient location and open for long hours.

Warehouse showrooms   Retail stores with sizable inventories housed in large buildings, **warehouse showrooms** deal in volume and provide limited service. Warehouse showrooms commonly are operated by large furniture retailers.

Warehouse Showroom
Retail store carrying a large inventory that deals in volume and provides limited service.

Catalog showrooms   A combination of catalog shopping and a warehouse showroom is found in the **catalog showroom**. Catalogs are sent to customers' homes and are also available in the store. Sample items are displayed in the store, with the merchandise kept in the warehouse. Customers can examine display items, then place orders with clerks. Customers are responsible for transporting their purchases. Service Merchandise, Zale, and Best Products are well-known catalog showrooms.

Catalog Showroom
A form of warehouse showroom where customers select products from catalogs sent to customers' homes or available in the store.

Warehouse clubs   Among the newest retail stores are **warehouse clubs**—large-scale, discount operations open to members only. Membership fees typically are around $25. These huge outlets, often located in industrial districts, carry a broad range of brand-name merchandise, including appliances, tires, clothing, food, and beverages. Warehouse clubs usually sell items at 20 to 40 percent below prices at supermarkets and other discount stores. Prices are held down by keeping services to a minimum. Transactions often are cash only. PACE Membership Warehouse, Price Club, Sam's Wholesale Club, and Costco Wholesale Club are warehouse clubs. Some experts predict that by the early

Warehouse Club
A large discount retail store offering members a broad range of name-brand merchandise at low prices.

Wal-Mart Charges into the 1990s

Wal-Mart Stores, Inc., was a well-kept secret for years. Except for stories about the wealth of founder Sam Walton, Wal-Mart received little attention. This all changed in 1988, when Wal-Mart was named in *Fortune* magazine's survey as the ninth most admired corporation in America. It jumped to fourth place in 1991, and first place among retailers. Now the third-largest and fastest-growing retailer in the world—only Kmart and Sears are larger—is getting some attention.

Walton opened his first Wal-Mart in tiny Rogers, Arkansas, in 1962. His strategy was to focus on small towns. Conventional wisdom was that a discount store couldn't make it in a town smaller than 50,000. But Walton believed national discounters were ignoring rural towns, and he found that small towns were an excellent niche. By offering good prices, a local discount store could keep people shopping at home instead of traveling several hours to a larger city. Roughly 80 percent of Wal-Mart's 1,300 stores are located in towns of 15,000 or less. The stores sell nearly $20 billion worth of merchandise annually, including clothing, small appliances, cosmetics, and more than 50,000 other items.

Walton's location strategy was to build 30 or 40 stores within 600 miles of a distribution center. After the stores were opened in rural towns, Wal-Mart would expand to nearby metropolitan areas, such as Dallas, Kansas City, and St. Louis. When one geographic area reached its saturation point, Wal-Mart would expand into a new area. Wal-Mart currently has 14 distribution centers serving stores in 25 states, mostly in the Southwest, Midwest, and Southeast. Wal-Mart orders directly from manufacturers and uses its own trucks for delivery. By using its own distribution system and through quantity discounts, Wal-Mart realizes a tremendous cost savings, which it passes along to customers.

Wal-Mart Stores' image and atmosphere are consistent with its pledge to customer satisfaction. The physical facilities are plain, resembling a large warehouse. But the customer is number one. A sign reading "Satisfaction Guaranteed" hangs over the entrance to every store. Customers are often welcomed by an employee, called a "people greeter," eager to lend a helping hand. This customer orientation allows Wal-Mart to rely more on its reputation and less on advertising. Whereas Sears spends nearly $900 million each year for advertising and Kmart over $600 million, Wal-Mart spends only about $80 million.

Although the 1980s was not a prosperous decade for most retailers, Wal-Mart grew then by about 30 percent a year. On the average, 150 new stores are opened each year, and this trend is expected to continue. Experts predict that Wal-Mart will surpass Kmart as the number two retailer in the early 1990s, and that eventually it will surpass Sears and become number one.

Not everything has gone perfectly for Sam Walton. Wal-Mart's experiment with Hypermarkets U.S.A., 200,000 plus-square-foot stores selling everything from fresh vegetables to appliances, has been somewhat of a failure. Four hypermarkets have been opened, and Walton has no plans for future hypermarkets. Although Hypermarkets U.S.A. is the only hypermarket chain making a profit, the stores are too expensive to operate. Instead, Walton intends to push ahead with "SuperCenters," combinations of Wal-Mart discount stores and grocery stores in one 150,000-square-foot store.[12]

Tupperware sells its products through demonstrations in homes and offices.

Courtesy of Tupperware Home Parties

1990s, warehouse clubs will be a $30 billion industry with more than 400 outlets.[13] Successful retailers often expand and diversify by opening up more than one type of store. For example, the discount chain Wal-Mart operates Sam's, the warehouse club industry leader.

With retailing making up a major part of the U.S. economy, business students frequently pursue careers in the retailing sector. Many Americans dream of one day owning and running their own retail store; some make it a reality. Take Connections (page 536) to help you assess your potential as a retailer.

Nonstore Retailing

As you know if you have ever bought merchandise from a catalog and had it delivered to your home, not all retailing takes place within stores. **Nonstore retailing** includes in-home selling, direct marketing, and vending machines.

In-home selling   Personal contact with consumers in their homes is the essence of **in-home selling.** Salespeople may go door-to-door or may telephone potential customers in advance and make appointments. Avon, Fuller Brush, and Encyclopaedia Britannica are a few of the many firms that sell products to consumers in their homes. Sales representatives of firms such as Tupperware or Mary Kay Cosmetics sell products at demonstrations given in homes or offices.

The newest method of in-home selling is television home shopping, which has grown into a billion-dollar industry. Televised home shopping services, such as the Home Shopping Network, are available 24 hours a day on some cable stations. They potentially can reach every home with a television and a

Nonstore Retailing
Retailing that takes place outside of stores; can be in-home selling, direct marketing, and vending machines.

In-Home Selling
Nonstore retailing activities that involve personal contact with consumers in their homes.

Retail Aptitude

Directions: The statements below reflect characteristics you would need to succeed in your own retail business. Circle the number that shows your level of agreement with each statement.

	Strongly Disagree				Strongly Agree	
1. I am a self-starter who doesn't need a lot of guidance in getting the job done.	1	2	3	4	5	6
2. I wouldn't mind working long hours, even weekends, as long as I'm working for myself.	1	2	3	4	5	6
3. I like making my own decisions.	1	2	3	4	5	6
4. I would be willing to take a risk for the right opportunity.	1	2	3	4	5	6
5. I like to set my own schedule on a job—to be my own boss.	1	2	3	4	5	6
6. I like to perform a variety of tasks, the small stuff as well as the most visible duties.	1	2	3	4	5	6

cable hook-up.[14] In some instances, television shopping services employ as many as 400 to 500 operators in a room taking orders around the clock from a loyal following.

Direct Marketing
Nonstore retailing that uses nonpersonal media to introduce products to consumers, who then purchase the products by mail, telephone, or computer.

Direct marketing Many firms promote products directly to buyers through a variety of techniques referred to as **direct marketing.** This type of nonstore retailing includes catalog sales, direct mail, telephone soliciting, and television or radio ads that include telephone numbers and instructions for ordering the items offered.

Direct marketing is one of the fastest-growing forms of retailing, with yearly sales in excess of $175 billion. The two major forms of direct marketing are telephone retailing and mail-order retailing. National companies such as American Express (credit cards), Time-Life (books), Merrill Lynch (investments), and Allstate (insurance) rely heavily on telephone retailing. Many firms generate telephone orders for their products by advertising them on cable television and including toll-free numbers. Thousands of firms use catalogs to sell a huge variety of items: clothing, books, records, household items, even specialty foods. Sears, L. L. Bean, and Spiegel exemplify firms that operate large mail-order businesses throughout the United States. Lands' End, a mail-order clothing company based in Wisconsin, has distinguished itself by providing services that range from helping callers determine sizes to an unconditional guarantee that customers can return any purchases.[15]

	Strongly Disagree				Strongly Agree	
7. I would enjoy being a leader and managing other people.	1	2	3	4	5	6
8. The potential for a high salary is important to me.	1	2	3	4	5	6
9. I like working with the public.	1	2	3	4	5	6
10. I am willing to stick with a job for several years if that's what it takes to succeed.	1	2	3	4	5	6

Feedback: Your answers should give you some feel for your potential as a retail store owner and operator. If you circled 1 or 2 for most items, you probably have little interest in owning a retail business. If you circled 5 or 6 for most statements, you just may possess many of the characteristics and skills needed to be a successful retailer. Retailing is a demanding field with no guarantees. The hours are long, the responsibilities great, and problems with employees or customers inevitable. But owning your own retail store also can be rewarding, both personally and financially.

Vending machines   Candy, gum, snacks, soft drinks, coffee, newspapers, and other convenience goods are familiar items available in the self-service dispensers known as vending machines. In Japan even items like french fries and shrimp are sold in vending machines.[16] Firms place vending machines in high-traffic areas of office and classroom buildings, service stations, and shopping malls. Vending machines offer the advantages of 24-hour-a-day operation with no sales staff. Their main drawbacks include the costs of frequent servicing and needed repairs, as well as the threat of vandalism. Vending machines account for less than 2 percent of all retail sales.

Retail Planning

Owners, both individuals and large firms, must consider several factors when developing plans for a retail store. Major considerations include store location, atmosphere, scrambled merchandising, the wheel of retailing, and new technology.

Store location   Deciding where to locate the store is critical in retailing. Retailers usually prefer a location with a high level of pedestrian traffic or easy access from main thoroughfares. Owners must evaluate the cost to buy or rent space, the availability of parking spaces, and the nature and image of the area surrounding the store site.

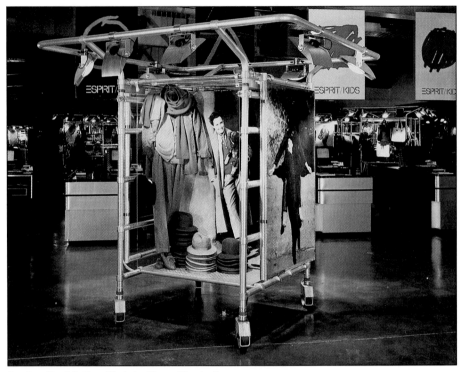

Courtesy Esprit DeCorp./Photo by Sharon Risedorph

Retailers also need to consider the type of store best suited for their business. Retailers able to attract many customers often prefer a *free-standing store,* a building not attached to another. Because this store stands alone, a retailer locating there cannot rely on other stores to generate traffic.

In an *unplanned business district,* stores are located close to one another without any prior planning by retailers. Business districts in the downtown areas of cities are typical examples. Unplanned business districts also are located in suburbs and residential areas. Central business districts are located in the downtown areas of cities. Secondary business districts are bounded by at least two major streets. Neighborhood business districts are located in residential areas.

A third type of store location, the *planned shopping center,* is a privately developed facility consisting of several complementary stores. Through landscaping, parking facilities, and special events, shopping centers create an environment designed to attract a broad mix of consumers. Neighborhood shopping centers are made up of several small stores serving a residential district. Community shopping centers include larger department stores and specialty stores. Regional shopping centers, with several large department stores as well as specialty stores, serve consumers in a wide geographic area.

Atmosphere
The design of a store's physical space.

Atmosphere   The design of a store's physical space is called the store's **atmosphere.** Retailers try to develop an atmosphere that appeals to the target

TABLE 15.2

Components of a Store's Atmosphere

Exterior	General Interior	Store Layout	Interior
Storefront	Flooring	Floor plan	Displays
Entrances	Colors	Product groupings	Merchandise display
Windows	Lighting	Department locations	Racks
Marquee	Fixtures		In-store advertising
Traffic	Scents		Mannequins
Store visibility	Aisle width		
Surrounding area	Dressing facilities		

market. Waterfalls and plants in shopping centers, music in record stores, bright colors in toy stores, or crowded aisles in discount stores all create different atmospheres to draw customers and influence their shopping moods. Some banks have begun designing their branches with bright colors, moving stock tickers, and "boutiques" that offer everything from home loans to travel services in an effort to liven up their atmosphere.[17] Table 15.2 lists the major components of a store's atmosphere.

Scrambled merchandising   To maintain or increase their sales volume, many retailers use **scrambled merchandising,** which involves adding unrelated products to a firm's existing product mix. Scrambling merchandise is rapidly gaining popularity. Gas stations, for instance, have added convenience items such as bread, ice, candy, and even grocery items. Many supermarkets, such as certain Kroger stores, now offer pharmacies, floral departments, bank branches, insurance, and photo processing.

Scrambled Merchandising
Adding unrelated products to a firm's existing product mix.

The wheel of retailing   As they strive to succeed, retailers face constant changes as new stores replace established ones. A popular explanation for how retail stores originate and develop is called the **wheel of retailing,** illustrated in Figure 15.4. This theoretical depiction suggests that a retail business enters the market as a low-priced, low-profit, low-status store. Gradually it moves up by improving facilities and adding new services, thus increasing business costs. Over time it becomes a high-cost establishment that is vulnerable to new competitors entering the market—and the wheel turns.

Wheel of Retailing
A depiction of the cycle retailers begin as they enter the market, evolve, and become vulnerable to new competitors.

The wheel of retailing can be illustrated by off-price retail chains such as T. J. Maxx and Clothestime. They attract customers by offering brand-name merchandise discounted as much as 60 percent below department store prices. In the past, the outlets were plain and offered limited services. Spurred by weak performance, department stores began to discount their prices up to 50 percent and started taking business from the off-price stores. Now some off-price retailers are imitating department stores—redesigning stores to be more attractive, conducting advertising campaigns that emphasize quality, and promoting specific products rather than focusing on discount prices.[18]

FIGURE 15.4

The Wheel of Retailing

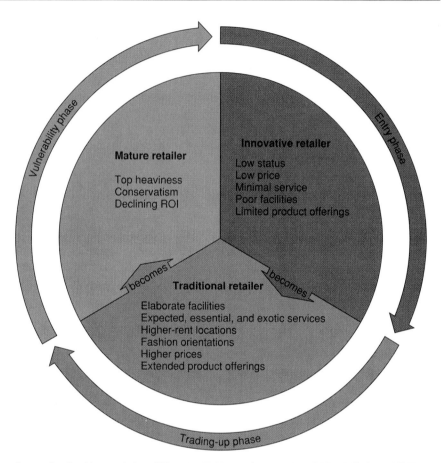

Source: Reprinted by permission of Macmillan Publishing Company from *RETAILING,* Second Edition, by Dale M. Lewison and M. Wayne Delozier, p. 94. Copyright © 1986.

Technology   Recent advances in technology also have affected retailing. Cable television and video ordering systems are changing the retail environment. Antishoplifting tags attached to merchandise reduce thefts. Computerized checking systems speed up checkouts, reduce cashier errors, and provide valuable data for inventory planning. New developments in computerized site selection programs enable firms to make better location decisions. Such technological advances help retailers improve efficiency, reduce labor costs, minimize loss, and obtain accurate and timely information.

PHYSICAL DISTRIBUTION

Physical Distribution
Those activities that involve the movement of products through marketing channels from manufacturer to customer.

Physical distribution includes the activities that enable the movement of products through marketing channels from manufacturer to customer. Physical distribution activities, which are essential marketing functions providing customers with the goods they want, where and when they want them, include

Courtesy Norfolk Southern Corporation. Created by J. Walter Thompson, USA

Norfolk Southern is a carrier that offers its customers a variety of transportation alternatives.

establishing customer service standards, selecting transportation modes, designing and operating warehouse facilities, handling products, and managing inventory. These activities are strongly interrelated. For instance, a modern warehouse facility may reduce handling costs. However, if it is not properly located, it can increase transportation costs. Firms thus need to plan and integrate their physical distribution activities.

Customer Service Standards

Physical distribution begins with a consideration of customers' needs. One survey found that improving customer service is a major priority in the distribution industry.[19] Some marketers examine the activities performed by competing firms and develop service standards that meet or exceed those of competitors. **Service standards** are specific, measurable goals relating to physical distribution activities. Because on-time delivery is important to customers, for example, a company may set a service standard to "deliver all orders within 24 hours." When a firm such as Federal Express guarantees overnight delivery, it must develop physical distribution activities that will achieve this service standard. Federal Express transports packages via airplane in many cases, since shipping by truck or railroad could not meet the overnight deadline.

Service Standard
A specific, measurable goal relating to physical distribution activities.

Transportation

Transportation, shipping goods to customers, is a critical physical distribution activity. To ship goods, firms generally choose one of the five major modes of transportation: rail, air, truck, water, and pipeline. Firms that transport products, through any means, are called *carriers*.

When selecting a transportation mode for products, marketing managers look at important factors such as cost, delivery speed, number of locations served, reliability, range of products carried, loss and damage records, and fuel

Transportation
Shipping goods to customers by rail, air, truck, water, and pipeline.

TABLE 15.3

Ranking the Transportation Modes

	1*	2	3	4	5
Lowest cost	Water	Pipeline	Rail	Truck	Air
Delivery speed	Air	Truck	Rail	Water	Pipeline
Number of locations served	Truck	Rail	Air	Water	Pipeline
Dependability	Pipeline	Truck	Air	Rail	Water
Range of products carried	Rail	Truck	Water	Air	Pipeline
Losses and damages	Pipeline	Water	Air	Truck	Rail
Fuel efficiency	Pipeline	Water	Rail	Truck	Air

*1 = Highest ranking.

Source: Donald J. Bowersox, David J. Closs, and Omar K. Helferich, *Logistical Management,* 3rd ed. (New York: Macmillan, 1986), p. 166; Carl M. Guelzo, *Introduction to Logistics Management* (Englewood Cliffs, N.J.: Prentice Hall, 1986), p. 46.

efficiency. Table 15.3 ranks the different transportation modes according to these factors. Figure 15.5 compares the share of shipping mileage and shipping revenue for each transportation mode.

Rail Railroads carry about 37 percent of all products and account for 10 percent of shipping revenue. Railroads are fairly cost and fuel efficient and can reach a large number of locations. A wide range of products such as coal, grain, chemicals, lumber, and automobiles can be transported by rail.

Air Air transport, the most expensive means of transportation, accounts for only 1 percent of all products transported. Yet the use of air transportation is growing rapidly. The need to deliver some items quickly, such as fresh flowers, perishable foods, technical instruments, and emergency parts, justifies the high cost.

Truck Trucking dominates the transportation industry, with a 78 percent share of shipping revenue. Although trucks account for only a 25 percent share of ton miles shipped, they often carry the most profitable products, such as clothing, paper goods, computers, fresh fruit and vegetables, and livestock. Trucks are the most flexible mode of transportation. They can travel anywhere there are roads and can provide door-to-door service.

Water Barges and cargo ships are the least costly means of transportation; they also are among the slowest and least dependable. Another limitation is , of course, that only cities with ports can be served. In spite of these drawbacks, water transport accounts for about 15 percent of ton miles shipped. Products commonly transported on waterways include petroleum, chemicals, and iron ore.

Pipeline The major products shipped via pipelines are oil, processed coal, and natural gas. Pipelines have increased in importance as the demand for oil and natural gas has increased. Pipelines account for 22 percent of ton miles shipped and 2.5 percent of shipping revenues.

Shipping Mileage and Revenue of Transportation Modes

FIGURE 15.5

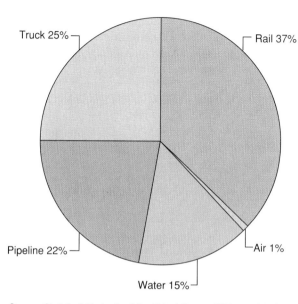

Share of ton miles shipped

Truck 25%
Rail 37%
Pipeline 22%
Air 1%
Water 15%

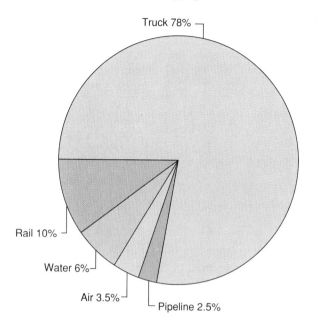

Share of shipping revenue

Truck 78%
Rail 10%
Water 6%
Air 3.5%
Pipeline 2.5%

Source: *Statistical Abstracts of the United States,* 1990, pp. 596–97.

Warehousing

Another important aspect of distribution is the design and operation of storage facilities. **Warehousing** includes various responsibilities involved in receiving, storing, and shipping goods. Warehouses accept delivered goods, record the quantities received, store them, coordinate shipments, and dispatch orders.

Private warehouses are owned and operated by firms who wish to distribute their own products. Usually these are companies that carry large inventories. For example, Spec's Music, a Miami-based firm with music and video outlets throughout Florida, has its own warehouses. It carries huge inventories and can quickly process orders and deliver fast-selling items to the stores.[20] *Public warehouses* provide storage on a rental basis. Firms that do not wish to own warehouses or that need extra space on a temporary basis often use public warehouses.

Warehousing
The receiving, storing, and shipping activities involved in the physical distribution of goods.

Order Processing

Order processing refers to the receipt and preparation of an order for shipment. Efficient order processing procedures can reduce the time needed for delivery and thus help firms to satisfy their customers.

Processing begins as soon as a customer places an order by mail, telephone, or computer. Typically the order is forwarded to the warehouse and the credit department. Clerks can fill an order quickly if the item is in stock and the

Order Processing
The receipt and preparation of an order for shipment.

customer's credit rating is approved. For items not in stock, an order is placed at the factory. Finally the product is packaged and shipped.

Materials Handling

Materials Handling
The physical handling of products during transportation and warehousing.

The physical handling of a product during transportation and while it is in the warehouse is termed **materials handling.** Firms institute materials handling procedures that make maximum use of warehouse space, minimize the number of times a product is handled, and reduce damage to merchandise.

The use of containerization and freight forwarders has improved the ability of organizations to handle materials. *Containerization* is packing goods within a strong container that is easy to transport by train, truck, ship, or airplane. Containerization reduces damage, theft, insurance costs, and materials handling time, thereby reducing the cost of distribution. *Freight forwarders* combine small shipments from several firms. They arrange for the merchandise to be picked up from the shipper and delivered to the buyer.

Inventory Management

Inventory Management
The process of developing and maintaining stocks of products that customers need and want.

Inventory management is the process of developing and maintaining products that are in demand by customers. Efficient inventory management, an important aspect of physical distribution, can help a firm achieve its profit goals. For instance, Hanes Hoisery Inc. developed a computerized inventory management system to drastically reduce the time needed to restock a store carrying Hanes products. Orders that once took seven days to reach a store now arrive in one.[21]

Good inventory management balances the cost of holding a large inventory with the cost of losing sales because of shortages, or stockouts, of certain products. One inventory management technique used to achieve this balance is *just-in-time (JIT) inventory,* popularized in Japan. As Chapter Nine discussed, companies using JIT maintain smaller inventories by ordering more often and in smaller quantities, just in time for production. Fireplace Manufacturers, which makes metal fireplaces in Santa Ana, California, trimmed its inventory from $1.1 million to $75,000 using JIT. In the meantime, sales doubled because the firm was able to respond to customers' orders much faster.[22]

Distributing Services

Service firms are generally limited in their channels of distribution since services are produced and consumed at the same time and the customer is present to initiate the contact. Through employees, service providers usually perform services directly for customers with no use of intermediaries. Health care professionals at clinics, for instance, perform physical examinations and medical tests for clients.

Distribution can separate a service from the seller, however. Bank credit cards allow the intangible service of credit to be separated from the financial institution. Through bank credit cards, organizations such as restaurants, gas stations, retailers, supermarkets, and even fast-food restaurants can distribute credit to consumers. Some service businesses have developed innovative methods of distribution. The communications industry offers cellular phones for

Courtesy of AT&T

Calling cards allow phone companies to distribute telephone services to consumers.

cars, insurance companies sell policies through vending machines at airports, entertainment firms sell tickets to concerts through computers in stores, and banks allow customers to have paychecks deposited directly into accounts and to pay bills by automatic withdrawal.

You'll Know It's the Century When . . . .

Hypermarkets Market Convenience

In the 21st century, today's supermarkets will look like the mom-'n'-pop stores of days gone by. Hypermarkets covering nearly 200,000 square feet will stock groceries, discount clothes, appliances, and housewares, plus videos, carryout meals, and other convenience services for harried people on the run. At the same time, small, quick-stop specialty stores and boutiques will flourish, while the omnipresent mall declines as more women join the labor force and the number of young people decline. Some forecasters also predict that more and more convenience-minded consumers will shop by mail order, catalog, computer, and even TV—especially if prices include delivery.[23]

SUMMARY OF LEARNING OBJECTIVES

1. To define the term *marketing channel* and identify the two major types of marketing intermediaries.
    A marketing channel is a group of interrelated organizations that directs the flow of goods from producer to consumer. Marketing intermediaries, organizations that provide the link between producers and consumers, are vital because they create place, time, and possession utility. The major types of intermediaries are *wholesalers* and *retailers*.

2. To explain how marketing channels are integrated vertically.
    Vertical integration occurs when one organization takes control of another member of the marketing channel, often by purchasing it. Distribution efficiency may be improved with a vertical marketing system (VMS), a planned marketing channel in which one channel member manages all intermediaries. The three types of vertical marketing systems are corporate, administered, and contractual.

3. To define *wholesaling* and describe the functions wholesalers perform.
    Wholesaling consists of the activities of marketing intermediaries who sell to retailers, other wholesalers, or industrial users. Wholesalers provide several services, including ownership, financing, risk assumption, promotional assistance, information, product assortment, and transportation. The major types of wholesalers are merchant wholesalers, manufacturer-owned wholesalers, and agents and brokers.

4. To define *retailing* and outline the activities retailers perform.
    Retailing activities consist of the sale of goods and services to consumers for personal or household use. Retailing can take place in stores or through the nonstore retailing methods of in-home selling, direct marketing, and vending machines.

5. To discuss the major considerations in retail planning.
    Retail planning, crucial to success in the retail sector, involves several important considerations. Store *location* is a critical decision since it influences shopper traffic. The *atmosphere*, or design of the store's physical space, must be appealing to the target market. Retailers also must decide whether or not to use *scrambled merchandising*, which means adding unrelated products to a store's existing mix. Another consideration is the *wheel of retailing*, which suggests that new stores constantly emerge to replace established stores. Recent advancements in *technology* also have an impact on retail planning.

6. To explain the role of physical distribution and identify its components.
    Physical distribution activities accomplish the physical movement of products through marketing channels from manufacturer to customer. Physical distribution activities include establishing customer service stan-

dards, selecting transportation modes, designing and operating warehouse facilities, processing orders, handling products, and managing inventory.

KEY TERMS

Marketing Channel (Channel of Distribution), p. 523

Marketing Intermediary, p. 523

Vertical Integration, p. 525

Vertical Marketing System (VMS), p. 526

Corporate VMS, p. 526

Administered VMS, p. 526

Contractual VMS, p. 526

Market Coverage, p. 526

Intensive Distribution, p. 526

Selective Distribution, p. 527

Exclusive Distribution, p. 527

Wholesaling, p. 527

Merchant Wholesaler, p. 529

Sales Branch, p. 530

Sales Office, p. 530

Agent, p. 530

Broker, p. 531

Retailing, p. 531

Department Store, p. 532

Discount Store, p. 532

Specialty Store, p. 532

Supermarket, p. 533

Superstore, p. 533

Convenience Store, p. 533

Warehouse Showroom, p. 533

Catalog Showroom, p. 533

Warehouse Club, p. 533

Nonstore Retailing, p. 535

In-Home Selling, p. 535

Direct Marketing, p. 536

Atmosphere, p. 538

Scrambled Merchandising, p. 539

Wheel of Retailing, p. 539

Physical Distribution, p. 540

Service Standard, p. 541

Transportation, p. 541

Warehousing, p. 543

Order Processing, p. 543

Materials Handling, p. 544

Inventory Management, p. 544

QUESTIONS FOR DISCUSSION AND REVIEW

1. What is a marketing channel?

2. Is it possible—or desirable—to eliminate the intermediary in the distribution of goods to consumers? Explain your answer.

3. What types of marketing channels are used to distribute consumer products? To distribute industrial products?

4. Have you ever purchased a product directly from a producer (channel A)? Name some products that manufacturers or producers sell directly to consumers.

5. Distinguish between intensive, selective, and exclusive distribution. Give examples of products distributed by each method.

6. Wholesalers perform a variety of services in product distribution. What are those services? Whom do they benefit?

7. How do full-service wholesalers and limited-service wholesalers differ? Give two examples of each type.

8. Name three different types of retail stores and give examples of each.

9. Give some examples of instances when you've made purchases through nonstore retailing. What advantages does nonstore retailing offer sellers? Buyers?

10. Choose one of your favorite retail stores and describe its atmosphere. Why is store atmosphere important in retail planning?

11. What can the wheel of retailing teach someone who is starting a retail business?

12. List the various forms of transportation and the advantages and disadvantages of each.

13. Why should managers be concerned about materials handling?

14. What is the purpose of inventory management?

CASE 15.1
Kmart Tries to Get Back on Track

Kmart, the pioneer discount retailer that experienced rapid growth in the 1970s, seems to have lost its momentum. The price of its stock has fallen, earnings are flat, and sales growth is slow. Trouble comes from stiff competition from Wal-Mart and newer retail outlets, changes in consumer buying habits, the chain's image, and its dated distribution system. Marketing expert Joseph E. Antonini, Kmart chairman since 1988, has been leading the drive to get the giant company back on track.

To compete with the increasingly popular specialty retailers that offer a huge selection of merchandise in one or two categories, Kmart has developed Builders Square, Office Square, and Sports Giant. To ward off the threat from hypermarkets and warehouse clubs, which force down the usual profit margins of discount stores, Kmart started American Fare (an Atlanta hypermarket) and purchased Pace Membership Warehouse Inc.

Such ventures may help Kmart compete in the 1990s, but Antonini and his management must also improve the 2,300 core Kmart stores, which produce 80 percent of the firm's sales. An important first step has been upgrading merchandise and image. Even in discount stores, shoppers increasingly want quality. So stores such as Kmart and Wal-Mart need to keep a delicate balance between convincing customers that prices are low and making people feel the stores are too cheap. Tactics like Kmart's "blue light special" may increase impulse buying but cheapen the store's image.

Experts say Wal-Mart excels at attending to the details that mold shoppers' attitudes. Some say Wal-Mart's simple logo in white letters on a brown background conveys a warm inviting message, which is carried out further by the "people greeters" inside the stores. Kmart followed suit by changing its logo and placing employees near the door to answer questions. Its highly recognizable logo of a bright red "K" and cool turquoise "mart" grabbed attention and signaled low prices but gave the impression the store hadn't changed in decades. So Kmart adopted a simpler logo with red letters on a gray background.

Antonini hired actress Jaclyn Smith and decorator Martha Stewart to design and promote better-quality apparel and housewares, and professional golfer Fuzzy Zoeller to promote sporting goods. The Martha Stewart promotion, heavily advertised, was especially successful, but almost a third of Kmart's stores were too small to properly carry the housewares line. Antonini earmarked $1.3 billion to enlarge and remodel 700 of the company's oldest outlets to feature wider aisles, bolder displays, and taller, deeper shelves. The roomy new design will make items available where customers can get them instead of in the stockroom.

Adapted from David Woodruff, "Will Kmart Ever Be a Silk Purse?" *Business Week,* January 22, 1990, p. 46; Francine Schwadel, "Little Touches Spur Wal-Mart's Rise," *The Wall Street Journal,* September 22, 1989, p. B1; "Lessons from Kmart's Very Tough Fight to Make It," *Boardroom Reports,* February 1, 1990, pp. 3–5.

Kmart officials also lowered prices on 8,000 items to be more competitive. But lower prices reduced Kmart's profit margins and made some goods, such as health and beauty aids, so popular that the chain's distribution system couldn't keep them in stock. A flawed distribution system has hampered Kmart outlets. Even when inventory is piled high in warehouses, stores are not always able to keep popular items on the shelves—a serious failing that can lose customers. In response, Kmart has installed a $1 billion computer system that monitors store sales and automatically reorders fast-selling merchandise. Antonini expects the computer system—similar to Wal-Mart's—to greatly improve Kmart's distribution.

Kmart has had other distribution problems. Like many U.S. retailers, the giant discounter's dealings with suppliers have often resulted in misunderstanding and mistrust between the two parties. For example, when vendors called on Kmart buyers, the buyers would make demands about delivery dates, advertising assistance, or buying back unsold merchandise. The result was that the buyer and seller could not agree on the true cost of the goods. In contrast, some U.S. retailers (including Wal-Mart) are now trying to be more straightforward and cooperative with vendors. Their buyers go to a manufacturer with specifications, quantities, and shipment dates; payment is made when the manufacturer ships the goods.

Questions for Discussion

1. What type of retailer is Kmart? What types of retailers are its major competitors?
2. Discuss some factors that contributed to Kmart's decline in sales, growth, and profit.
3. What is Kmart's strategy to regain its market position?

CASE 15.2
Moving Hazardous Materials

Each day in the United States, 500,000 shipments of hazardous materials take place. Thousands of federal, state, and local regulations govern the movement of the more than 33,000 commodities classified as hazardous. In recent years, citizens' groups and the general public have expressed growing concerns about such shipments passing through their states. As a result, the job of moving hazardous materials safely and legally is becoming more difficult.

Firms involved in moving hazardous materials face increased regulations covering nearly every aspect, from the move itself to cleaning equipment afterward. Recent regulatory changes have addressed three areas in particular: documentation, uniform standards, and packaging.

Under new documentation rules, firms must provide emergency response information with every hazardous shipment. That includes information on potential hazards, first-aid measures, and instructions for those on the scene of an

Adapted from Peter Bradley, "Facing the Hazards of Moving Hazardous Materials," *Purchasing*, April 5, 1990, pp. 66–69.

accident, plus a 24-hour telephone number for emergencies. Many chemical manufacturers already comply with these regulations, but other companies that move hazardous materials may face additional paperwork to meet the requirements.

It has been nearly impossible for many trucking companies to keep up with all the regulations, since what is legal in one city or state may be illegal in another. "The biggest problem is not complying itself, but finding out what the rules are," says Jack Lewis, president of hazardous waste hauler Transtec Environmental. Shippers are hopeful that new federal regulations will give them one set of uniform standards to follow rather than numerous, inconsistent rules that boost costs.

New regulations on packaging of hazardous materials are designed to bring the U.S. packaging standards in line with international standards. Kirt Pinney, director of dangerous goods sales for Burlington Air Express, says the rest of the world will demand compliance now that the United States is no longer the globe's dominant economic power. Some shipping firms already working internationally conform to overseas standards, but others will have to make expensive changes to comply.

Many shippers are taking it upon themselves to increase safety. Also, various industries are joining together to develop safety standards. For instance, people in the railroad, chemical, and rail equipment industries recognized the need to increase safety in rail transportation of hazardous materials. Representatives therefore designed a joint program that calls for employee training, involvement of communities along key routes in emergency planning, train speed limits, improved track maintenance, and derailment safeguards.

Buyers of transportation services also are becoming more and more concerned about the safety of hazardous materials shipments. Carrier performance reflects back on the buyers, says Transtec's Lewis. "So it behooves the shipper to pick the best-quality carrier for his purpose. It's not a low-bid deal."

The push from customers for higher quality and the growth in regulations will boost costs. This may force many smaller shipping companies out of business. The cost of regulation is a big concern of carriers, especially tank truck operators. (A large part of their business is hazardous materials transportation.) Survivors will likely be large, sophisticated firms with the skills and resources needed to meet the increased regulation.

Questions for Discussion

1. Personnel involved in which transportation modes should be concerned with the regulation of hazardous materials shipments?
2. What effects might increased regulation of the transporting of hazardous materials have on firms in the shipping industry?
3. Why should transportation customers be concerned with safety in the shipment of hazardous materials?

CHAPTER SIXTEEN

PROMOTION

LEARNING OBJECTIVES

1. To explain the role of promotion in marketing and list five promotional objectives.

2. To describe the major types of advertising and the purpose of each.

3. To list the steps involved in planning an advertising campaign.

4. To differentiate among the three types of salespeople and their functions.

5. To outline the personal selling process and describe each step.

6. To explain the purpose of sales promotion and list common activities of consumer sales promotion and trade sales promotion.

7. To describe how firms use publicity.

8. To identify factors that influence a firm's promotion mix.

Commercial boats casting their nets for tuna often pull in dolphins traveling with the schools of fish. The dolphins drown underwater in nets or are killed with the catch. But when environmental groups and consumers began to strongly protest the killing of dolphins, several U.S. tuna companies responded. The canners of Starkist, Chicken of the Sea, and Bumblebee announced that they would

C. Allan Morgan/Peter Arnold, Inc.

refuse to purchase tuna caught in gill or drift nets, which catch dolphins along with tuna.

The next task was to inform consumers of the new "dolphin-safe" tuna. Publicity was the first vehicle. Newspapers, magazines, and television and radio broadcasts throughout the country reported the firms' announcements. Starkist also advertised its commitment to dolphin safety in national network television commercials and print advertisements.

Then the firms took their message to the places where consumers buy tuna. All three companies changed their labels to include pictures of dolphins and the words *dolphin safe*. Starkist and Chicken of the Sea began a rash of sales promotions, or "theme events" as one marketer called them.

To retailers who bought a pallet of tuna, Starkist gave a free color dolphin poster and display. The firm placed shelf-talkers (in-store advertisements on tuna shelves), distributed cents-off coupons, and joined with Home Pride bread to give consumers a rebate for free mayonnaise if they bought both Starkist tuna and the bread. The company also offered consumers a tuna cookbook, and a T-shirt bearing the dolphin-safe logo and the words *Thanks Starkist*. Response to the T-shirt was especially high. The aim of Starkist's dolphin-safe promotional campaign was to increase awareness and distinguish the brand from others, says Erik

Bloemendaal, general manager of quality and communications. "We planned a balanced approach."

Chicken of the Sea conducted a six-month campaign with the theme "The Mermaid Cares." The program relied on sales promotion. "It's a simple, quick way for consumers to understand where we stand," explains Norty Cohen, vice president of the firm that markets Chicken of the Sea for Van Camp Seafood Company. "Tuna tends to be a staple. We need to convince consumers there's a difference. Our hope is that the customer will walk in and say they want to buy only dolphin-safe tuna." The company's techniques included a merchandising kit for stores to use and for consumers; tear-off pads in stores to explain the firm's dolphin-safe policy and give tuna recipes; rebates for Chicken of the Sea tuna and salmon; a free "Sea Mammals and Mermaids" poster for product proofs of purchase; and a 10-inch mermaid doll for $4.95 and a proof of purchase. For every doll purchased, Chicken of the Sea donated $1 to the Humane Society of the United States.

For their commitment and promotional efforts, Chicken of the Sea and Starkist were recognized by Greenpeace and by the Earth Island Institute, both environmental activist organizations, as being dolphin safe.[1]

The communication of positive, persuasive information about an organization or its products with the intent of directly or indirectly influencing exchanges is called **promotion.**[2] As the example of dolphin-safe tuna illustrates, firms use advertising and other methods to communicate favorable messages to consumers or other audiences. Promotional messages can inform consumers about organizations and products and influence them to make a purchase or adopt a special cause or belief.

Promotion
The communication of favorable, persuasive information about a firm or product in order to influence potential buyers.

In this chapter, we discuss the role of promotion and promotional objectives and introduce the concept of promotion mix. Next we discuss several types of advertising, major advertising media, and advertising campaign planning. Then we discuss personal selling, the roles of salespeople, and the personal selling process. We explain the use of sales promotion and various sales promotion activities. We provide an overview of publicity. Finally we describe the strategies and other factors that go into promotion planning.

THE ROLE OF PROMOTION

The fourth element in the marketing mix, promotion supports product, pricing, and distribution decisions. It is crucial to the success of any firm. Before deciding what type of promotional program to conduct, a firm needs to establish its objectives.

Promotional Objectives

Firms set promotional objectives that will help meet their broader marketing and organizational objectives. Promotional programs can be built around a single objective or multiple objectives.

Informing The basic objective underlying all promotion is providing information. Firms want to tell potential customers about themselves as well as

Mike Mazzaschi/Stock Boston

Doubleday Book Shop uses a flyer to inform potential customers about their products.

what products are available, where they can be purchased, and for what price. A new restaurant, for example, may advertise in local newspapers or magazines and on radio and television stations, distribute coupons in the mail, invite the newspaper restaurant critic to review and publicize it, rent billboards, and buy a listing in the telephone directory.

Increasing sales   Aside from providing information, encouraging prospective customers to purchase products is the most common promotional objective, since sales mean survival and success for firms. Using advertisements, coupons, and other promotional methods, firms attempt to persuade customers to try new products, remind them of the benefits of products that have been on the market awhile, and reinforce their choice of particular brands.

Stabilizing sales   Firms also rely on promotional activities to reduce or eliminate substantial variations in demand throughout the year. Companies marketing seasonal products may step up promotional efforts during slow times of the year to use production facilities and distribution systems most effectively.

Positioning the product   Often a firm uses promotion to position a product as different or superior to competing products. Positioning means emphasizing certain product features to create a specific image for the product and add to its appeal. Firms often rely on advertising to position products.

Building a public image   Sometimes a company wants to develop a certain image through promotion. Publicity and, to a lesser extent, advertising provide effective vehicles for image building. Mobil, for example, sponsors programs on public television stations to provide quality entertainment for viewers and to foster goodwill toward the corporation.

The Promotion Mix

Promotion Mix
The combination of advertising, personal selling, sales promotion, and publicity used to promote a specific product.

To inform, influence, and remind customers in their target markets or the general public, firms use personal selling (person-to-person approach) and advertising, sales promotion, and publicity (nonpersonal approaches). How these four elements are combined to promote a specific product is called the **promotion mix** (see Figure 16.1).

A promotion mix may contain any or all of the four elements, depending on the firm's objectives, promotional strategy, product characteristics, and target market characteristics. Later in the chapter, we explore how the promotion mix is developed; now let's examine the four promotion mix elements.

ADVERTISING

Advertising
A paid form of nonpersonal communication to a target audience through a mass medium such as television, newspapers, or magazines.

Any paid form of nonpersonal communication to a target audience through a mass medium such as television, newspapers, or magazines is **advertising**. Of all promotional activities, consumers are most familiar with advertising. We see and hear many advertisements every day. Organizations and individuals spend

The Promotion Mix   **FIGURE 16.1**

Advertising

Sales promotion

Publicity

Personal selling

Photos courtesy of The Pepsi-Cola Company and Scott Wanner/Journalism Services

nearly $130 billion dollars on advertising in the United States each year.[3] Table 16.1 will give you an idea of how much money some large companies spend to advertise their products to consumers.

Advertising can be quite expensive, especially using national media with immense audiences. But firms often find advertising to be cost effective. It can reach a vast number of people at a low cost per person. It is also quite flexible, since advertisers can choose outlets to reach audiences of any size or demographic makeup. Ads can be repeated as often as sponsors wish.

DID YOU KNOW? *Philip Morris spends over $2 billion annually on advertising, more than any other firm.*

Company	Annual Advertising Expenditures ($ in millions)
Philip Morris	$2,072.0
Procter & Gamble	1,779.3
Sears Roebuck	1,432.1
General Motors	1,363.8
Grand Metropolitan PLC	823.3
Pepsico	786.1
McDonald's	774.4
Eastman Kodak	718.8
RJR Nabisco	703.5
Kellogg	611.6

Source: Reprinted with permission from *ADVERTISING AGE,* September 26, 1990, p. 1. Copyright Crain Communications, Inc. All Rights Reserved.

Types of Advertising

An advertiser can use any of several different types of advertising, depending on its promotional objectives. Companies advertise brands, industries advertise products, and firms or individuals advertise themselves, their activities, and their beliefs. One Omaha businessman personally placed and paid for full-page ads in *The Wall Street Journal,* the *New York Times,* and other major newspapers, asking fast-food chains and consumer products firms to reduce the amount of animal fats in their products.[4] We will examine three major categories of advertising: primary-demand, selective (brand), and institutional.

Primary-Demand Advertising
Advertising used to create demand for all products in a product group.

Primary-demand advertising　At times organizations want to create or increase demand for all products in a product group. In this case, they use **primary-demand advertising.** The Florida Grapefruit Growers, for instance, sponsored the advertisement shown in Figure 16.2 to persuade consumers to buy and drink more grapefruit juice. The ad promotes the product without mentioning any particular brand or producer.

Selective (Brand) Advertising
Advertising used to sell a specific product or brand.

Selective advertising　Most often a firm wants to create selective demand, or demand for a specific brand of product rather than for other, competing products. **Selective (brand) advertising** makes up the majority of advertising; marketers of virtually all goods and services use it in their promotion mixes. The manufacturer of Oil of Olay, for example, spends more than $21 million each year to persuade women to choose that skin lotion.[5]

Sometimes a firm compares its brand of product to another in advertisements. *Comparative advertising* identifies competitors and claims the superiority of the sponsor's brand. This form of selective advertising has grown in popularity during the last decade. Libby's used the advertisement in Figure 16.3 to compare its Juicy Juice with seven competing products.

FIGURE 16.2

An Example of Primary-Demand Advertising

Courtesy of State of Florida Department of Citrus

FIGURE 16.2

An Example of Primary-Demand Advertising

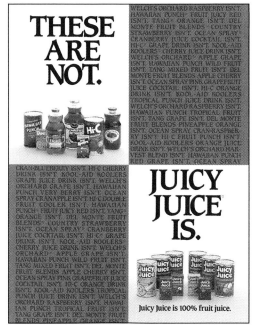

Courtesy of the Nestlé Foods Corporation

FIGURE 16.3

An Example of Comparative Advertising

FIGURE 16.4

**An Example of
Institutional Advertising**

Courtesy of Du Pont

Institutional Advertising
Advertising used to build goodwill and create a favorable public image.

Institutional advertising When an organization desires primarily to build goodwill and create a favorable public image rather than promote specific products, it employs **institutional advertising.** Consider the advertisement in Figure 16.4. In an understated manner, the ad shows how a unique plastic manufactured by Du Pont helps disabled people such as Vietnam veteran Bill Demby get on with their lives. Advertisements like these can be inspirational to readers and viewers and enhance the public image of the sponsoring company.

A form of institutional advertising used to address a public issue is called *advocacy advertising.* Firms, industry groups, nonprofit organizations, and even individuals use advocacy advertising to explain controversial topics and influence public opinion. For example, several women's magazines ran a full-page advocacy advertisement about birth control pills.

Advertising Media

Advertising Media
Advertising outlets, including newspapers, television, direct mail, radio, magazines, and outdoor displays.

The different outlets that present advertisements are called **advertising media.** The most commonly used are newspapers, television, direct mail, radio, magazines, and outdoor displays. Table 16.2 shows the advertising dollars spent for each medium and the percent of total advertising dollars each expenditure represents.

TABLE 16.2

**Annual Advertising
Media Expenditures**

Medium	Expenditure	
	Millions of Dollars	**Percent of Total**
Newspapers		
National	$ 3,720	3.0%
Local	28,648	23.1
Total	32,368	26.1
Magazines		
Weeklies	2,813	2.2
Women's	1,710	1.4
Monthlies	2,193	1.8
Total	6,716	5.4
Farm publications	212	0.2
Television		
Network	9,110	7.4
Cable (national)	1,197	1.0
Syndication	1,288	1.0
Spot (national)	7,354	5.9
Spot (local)	7,612	6.1
Cable (non-network)	330	0.3
Total	26,891	21.7
Radio		
Network	476	0.4
Spot (national)	1,547	1.3
Spot (local)	6,300	5.1
Total	8,323	6.8
Yellow Pages		
National	1,011	0.8
Local	7,319	5.9
Total	8,330	6.7
Direct mail	21,945	17.7
Business papers	2,763	2.2
Outdoor		
National	653	0.5
Local	458	0.4
Total	1,111	0.9
Miscellaneous		
National	10,998	8.9
Local	4,273	3.4
Total	15,271	12.3
Total		
National	68,990	55.7
Local	54,940	44.3
Grand total	$123,930	100.0%

Source: Reprinted with permission from *ADVERTISING AGE,* May 14, 1990, p. 12. Copyright 1990 Crain Communications, Inc. All Rights Reserved.

Newspapers   Newspapers make up the largest category of the advertising media. Spending for newspaper advertising exceeds $32 billion each year, with more than half of that amount purchased by retailers.[6] Firms can advertise in newspapers distributed locally, regionally, nationally, or internationally. Newspapers offer good coverage for firms of any size, because there is at least one newspaper in every local market and many people read the newspaper every day. Newspapers are well suited for immediate needs since they can run advertisements with little lead time. Advertisers can choose ads of any size, from a few lines in the classified section to full pages or separate supplements.

Because they reach diverse audiences, newspapers do not always allow advertisers to target their audience precisely. The life span of newspapers is very short since readers usually discard them quickly, although readers can clip or refer back to ads if they wish. Also, the quality of the paper is generally low, and the use of color is limited.

Television   Another large medium, television accounts for almost 22 percent of advertising expenditures. Advertisers spend in excess of $26 billion each year on television commercials.[7] Automobile manufacturers alone spend a total of $2 billion to advertise their vehicles on television; General Motors, spending more than $500 million a year, is the largest network television advertiser.[8]

Perhaps television's greatest advantage is that it allows creative use of action, color, and sound to an extent not possible in any other medium. Television advertising also offers the capability of reaching vast audiences, since 98 percent of U.S. homes have at least one TV set. Firms can advertise nationally on a major network, regionally through cable networks, or locally through local stations.

The major drawback of network television advertising is the high cost. A 30-second commercial can cost as much as $300,000, or even more than $800,000 for broadcast during a special event such as the Super Bowl, which can draw half of the people in the United States.[9] To keep costs down, many advertisers now use 15-second ads, with networks running more of these shorter ads during a commercial break. When so many air during a program, they may not have much impact on viewers. At any rate, TV ads have an extremely short life, which prompts creators to use special effects, unusual sounds, music, humor, and distinctive characters to encourage viewers to remember advertisements and products.

Television advertisers face difficulty in determining the audience that actually sees the commercials. Viewers in public places such as hotels, airports, restaurants, or stores are not counted. In homes, commercials play to empty rooms when viewers take breaks. Many viewers change channels when commercials begin, a habit called "zapping" that is made easier by today's remote controls and cable systems with 80 or more channels. Some rating systems estimate that zapping cuts a prime-time commercial's audience by 10 percent or more. Viewers in almost 20 percent of U.S. homes are heavy zappers, switching to a new channel an average of one zap every two minutes.[10] A Roper poll of 1,994 television viewers reported the top five activities of people when a commercial plays: get annoyed, 58 percent; get up, 45 percent; talk to others, 42 percent; watch, 33 percent; and switch channels, 28 percent.[11]

Empty rooms and zapping can mean that television advertisers do not get the audience they pay for. Commercials during TV sports, for example, get zapped heavily on weekends, when viewers switch between two or more games; such ads have lost up to 53 percent of the audience. Sometimes advertisers get more than they pay for. The ads ending one "CBS Evening News" program, for instance, were viewed by twice as many people as the show's first commercial because thousands of viewers had tuned in for the next show, "Wheel of Fortune."

Direct mail Thousands of organizations send catalogs, advertisements, flyers, brochures, and fund-raising materials to homes, offices, or stores of target individuals. Nearly 18 percent of all advertising expenditures—almost $22 billion—goes for direct mail, the third-largest advertising medium in the United States.

For direct mail to be effective, the material must reach the target group through up-to-date mailing lists. Advertisers can develop or purchase mailing lists that will reach nearly any target market imaginable, although selective mailing lists are expensive to buy. Direct mail's effectiveness is easily determined by the response: customers' orders or donations to fund-raising organizations. Even banks use direct mail. Targeting certain neighborhoods or high-income customers, some banks now mail catalogs explaining brokerage services, credit cards and loan offers along with applications, toll-free numbers, and even coupons for free checks. Direct mail, traditionally considered one of the less expensive forms of advertising, is becoming more costly as postal rates rise. Many firms are trimming mailing lists to include only their best customers or prospects.

Radio About 7 percent of all money spent on advertising goes for radio ads. Radio serves a large and varied audience. Homes in the United States have nearly 500 million radio sets! Because of the wide variety of programming that caters to numerous interests—such as talk shows, all news, hard rock, classical music, jazz, oldies, easy listening, or Spanish language broadcasts—advertisers can easily pinpoint target audiences. Spending on radio advertising has grown significantly because of its low cost and its ability to reach precisely defined target audiences.[12]

Radio advertisements have the disadvantage of an extremely short life. Messages are limited because radio relies only on the sense of hearing. Listeners may keep radios turned on for background music or mere noise and ignore the advertisements.

Magazines The last decade has seen a dramatic increase in the number of magazines being published. More than 11,000 magazines were published in 1989; of these, 491 were new publications.[13] Expenditures for magazine advertising also have grown in the last several years. They now account for about 6 percent of total advertising volume. The top five magazines, by total advertising revenues, are *Time, Sports Illustrated, People, TV Guide,* and *Parade.*[14]

The sheer number and tremendous variety of magazines give advertisers the opportunity to target nearly any audience. Publications with huge circulations (*Reader's Digest, Time, Good Housekeeping*) allow advertisers to reach huge general audiences. National magazines now can offer more local advertising by publishing several regional editions. Smaller, specialized magazines such as *Golf Digest, Apartment Life,* or *Cincinnati Magazine* reach more precise market segments.

Advertising: Here, There, and Everywhere

When Richard Kent wanted to advertise his company's new product, Orval Kent Salad Singles, he found a way to make a big impact: full-color ads mounted on trailer trucks. These mobile billboards, 9 feet high by 48 feet long, show people enjoying shrimp, chicken, and macaroni salads. Kent figures it costs 21 cents for every 1,000 people who see the ads. And people do see ads on trucks—about 90 percent, according to one survey. "Since we had limited ad dollars to spend," says Kent, "we had to do something different to get attention."

Advertisers believe consumers will look at and remember messages conveyed in unexpected ways. They are using traditional media in new ways. Some billboards now sport elaborate lights and music. One for a Southern California hospital featured a huge, inflatable heart with fans inside simulating beating motions. On television, both General Electric and Shearson Lehman Hutton have experimented with different sounds—buzzes, hums, and weird music—to catch the public's ear. Magazines feature gatefolds (fold-out ads attached to front or back covers), pop-ups, and even computer chips that play Christmas carols. Newspapers offer ads in red ink with a strawberry scent; other scents, such as coffee, are being developed.

Then there are alternative media, everything from matchbook covers to blimps. Use of nontraditional media represents a tiny share of the advertising dollar but is growing fast. Human billboards—people wearing huge popcorn bags—hand out samples of Smartfood cheese popcorn in Chicago. Jeep and Hardee's advertise on Baltimore parking meters. Ski lifts carry lip balm and tanning lotion ads. Campbell Soup once put fish recipes calling for its soups on the back of Roman Catholic church bulletins during Lent.

In high schools, Channel One television plays commercials along with newscasts. Televisions in doctors' offices feature a magazine show, with ads of course. Bank customers with personal computers will see three "infomercials" if they use a certain diskette on home banking. Theatergoers and people who buy or rent videotapes sometimes get commercials along with the movie.

At supermarkets and drugstores, shoppers are bombarded with electric signs, closed-circuit radios playing commercials in aisles, and video recorders showing how to use products. Video screens mounted on shopping carts play ads as customers make their way through stores.

"Everywhere there's space, they're slapping something on it," says one marketer. Even in restrooms in restaurants and elsewhere. TWA planes have had restroom ads for Samsonite, American Tourister, Rubbermaid, Ramada, and Best Western. With restroom ads, notes the ad company president, passengers "can't turn the pages."[15]

Expenditures for magazine advertising have increased in recent years.

Charles Gupton/Stock Boston

Magazines offer the unique capability of high-quality color reproduction, a valuable asset in promoting many products. Magazines provide a more permanent message than do the other media, since subscribers often keep their favorites in their homes or workplaces for weeks or months and pass them along to friends. Magazine ads are not suited for immediate messages; they take a long time to produce and may be dated by printing time. Also, advertising in a widely circulated publication can be quite expensive.

Outdoor displays   Billboards, posters, and other outdoor displays account for about 1 percent of advertising expenditures. Outdoor displays are inexpensive and useful in high-traffic areas. Their main disadvantage is that only a brief message can be communicated. Many people criticize outdoor displays along highways and roads for detracting from the beauty of the natural scenery.

The advertising media expose consumers to thousands of commercial messages each day. Advertising experts say that with the rapid growth of ads—ad "clutter"—consumers may actually remember only a fraction of these messages, perhaps only 1 percent. To grab consumers' attention, advertisers are turning to alternative media and are using traditional advertising media in new ways, as the Business Action illustrates.

Developing Advertising Campaigns

Firms go to considerable effort and expense to design, create, and evaluate advertisements that will accomplish their promotional goals. To develop an effective advertising campaign, they generally must take these steps:

- Identify the target audience of the advertisements.
- State the objectives to be accomplished (increase sales, build awareness, etc.).
- Determine how much money to spend to achieve the advertising objectives.
- Develop an *advertising platform* consisting of the points to be emphasized to consumers (such as Maytag's dependability, Budget Rent A Car's low prices).
- Outline a media plan, indicating specific media in which advertisements will be run and when they will be run to reach the target markets.
- Create the actual advertisement.
- Place the advertisements with the media.
- Through sales or research, evaluate the effectiveness of the ads (see if the objectives were met).

Some firms handle their own advertising through an employee or an in-house department that plans, designs, and creates advertisements and places them with the media. Others use specialists outside the organization. An *advertising agency* is a business that specializes in planning, producing, and placing advertising and offers other promotional services for clients. Agencies, ranging from small firms handling local and regional advertising to large firms with national and international clients, can offer expertise and production facilities unavailable in many firms. Newspaper, radio, and television companies also offer advertising assistance, as do freelance writers, artists, and producers. Small firms often find that these sources can provide needed assistance at a reasonable cost.

PERSONAL SELLING

Personal Selling
Person-to-person communication with one or more prospective customers in order to make a sale.

The oldest form of promotion, personal selling is unique among the promotion mix elements because, as its name says, it is personal. **Personal selling** is communicating person to person with one or more prospective customers for the purpose of making a sale. At one time or another, all of us have encountered personal selling. Has a car salesperson ever taken you on a test drive? Or maybe a salesperson helped you during a recent clothing purchase. These activities are highly visible because they are aimed at consumers. Yet they represent only a fraction of the situations involving personal selling. More than four times as many personal selling activities are directed toward industrial customers than toward consumers.

For many firms, personal selling is a critical element in the promotion mix. In the United States, companies spend more than $140 billion each year on personal selling, more than they spend on any other single promotion method.[16] The average cost of a sales call to an industrial customer is about $210.[17]

Salespeople play an important role in the success of many firms. The best are highly trained professionals who before and after the sale help buyers satisfy their wants and needs. They know the product and effectively communicate their knowledge to buyers face-to-face. They also keep track of new products and competitors' activities. Sales representatives often can reap substantial financial rewards; a highly skilled salesperson may earn more than $100,000 a year.

Types of Salespeople

Firms employ different types of salespeople for various selling situations, depending on such factors as type of product, price, number of customers, and channels of distribution used. We will examine three common types of salespeople: order getters, order takers, and support salespeople.

Order getters   A salesperson responsible for selling products to new customers and increasing sales to current customers is an **order getter.** Order getters engage in *creative selling.* They size up a customer's needs and convey product information in a thorough and persuasive manner. Creative selling is especially important when customers are carefully weighing alternatives in making their purchase, when they are not aware of product features and benefits, or when the product is a new one. Many industries, including insurance, computers, appliances, and heavy machinery, employ order getters.

Order Getter
A salesperson who recruits new customers and increases sales to current customers.

Order takers   The person who receives and processes orders for repeat sales, with the objective of maintaining positive relationships with customers, is an **order taker.** The major function of order takers is to ensure that customers have the right amount of products they need when and where they need them. Order takers include salespeople who handle telephone and mail orders in a sales office and salespeople in retail stores. Other order takers handle route sales of products such as milk, potato chips, bread, and beverages. They call on stores to check stock, inform managers of inventories, and make deliveries.

Order Taker
A salesperson who processes repeat sales and maintains positive relationships with customers.

Support personnel   Firms commonly employ **support salespeople** to assist in selling but primarily to locate potential customers, educate them about products, build goodwill, and provide service after sales. Support people most often help sell industrial products.

Producers of technical industrial products such as computers, chemicals, steel, and heavy equipment rely on *technical salespeople* to provide information

Support Salespeople
Salespeople who assist in selling by locating potential customers, educating them about products, building goodwill, and providing after-sale service.

IBM relies on technical salespeople to help employees set up new computer systems.

Courtesy of the International Business Machines Corporation.

● Connections

Do You Have What It Takes for Sales?

Directions: Circle the number that represents your level of agreement with each statement.

	Strongly Disagree					Strongly Agree
1. If I didn't have direct supervision in my job, I would work just as hard anyway.	1	2	3	4	5	6
2. I am willing to work long hours.	1	2	3	4	5	6
3. I enjoy trying hard to please people.	1	2	3	4	5	6
4. I am organized and plan my daily schedule to make the most of my time.	1	2	3	4	5	6
5. I can be flexible if the situation requires it.	1	2	3	4	5	6
6. When under pressure, I try to remain calm and solve the problem.	1	2	3	4	5	6
7. I can speak to groups of people.	1	2	3	4	5	6
8. I don't think being late for appointments is a good idea.	1	2	3	4	5	6
9. I listen carefully to others in conversations and ask them questions about themselves.	1	2	3	4	5	6

and service to current customers. Technical salespeople usually need formal education in engineering or science because they instruct customers in how a product is designed or made, how to install it, or how to use it.

Manufacturers often employ *missionary salespeople* to encourage retailers and other sellers to purchase their products. Missionary salespeople commonly represent pharmaceutical and medical supply companies to promote their products to physicians, hospitals, clinics, and pharmacies.

Trade salespeople help customers, especially retail stores, promote products to their own customers. They may set up displays of a manufacturer's product, demonstrate products to customers, give out samples, and restock shelves. Trade salespeople often work for food producers.

Chances are good that some of you reading this book will become salespeople. In the United States, roughly 1 of every 15 workers performs a sales-

	Strongly Disagree				Strongly Agree	
10. I think solving a problem or completing a task I'm interested in is exciting.	1	2	3	4	5	6

Feedback: Pinpointing the sort of person who's destined for success in sales is impossible; after all, there are as many styles of selling as there are products to be sold. But those who succeed in the field share certain characteristics. If you think those qualities include being pushy, manipulative, or sneaky, think again. In fact these stereotypes generally come from salespeople who are failing.

Sales achievement requires three basic qualities. The first is *ego drive*, the desire to succeed, to win a yes, that keeps people doing the hard work required to get there. Ego drive also helps salespeople, who are largely independent, motivate and manage themselves. The second quality is *empathy*, the ability to listen and understand what someone else is thinking and feeling. Top salespeople know what questions to ask and how to interpret answers. Third, salespeople need to possess *ego strength*, the ability to take rejection and to persevere during slumps. If you find it painful when someone tells you no, don't go into sales!

How you answered the quiz questions should give you an idea of whether you have the qualities needed by effective salespeople. If you circled 1 or 2 to most of the questions, you probably don't have the interest or characteristics for sales. If you circled mostly 3s or 4s, you may make a good salesperson if you really want to work at it and learn. If you circled 5 or 6 to most questions, you have many of the qualities shared by successful salespeople. You are hard working, emotionally mature, dependable, independent, and knowledgeable.

related job. Did you ever wonder what makes a successful salesperson and whether you might share some of those characteristics? Connections can help you find out whether you have what it takes to sell.

The Selling Process

A salesperson's work is outlined in the steps that take place in the **selling process** (see Figure 16.5). Of course, not all salespeople perform their jobs in exactly the same way, and an individual salesperson may alter tactics for different situations. But the ultimate goal of the selling process is a long-term relationship with the customer. Customer loyalty is invaluable to a firm's long-range success.

Selling Process
A series of steps salespeople perform, consisting of prospecting, preparing, approaching, presenting, answering objections, closing, and following up.

FIGURE 16.5

Steps in the Selling Process

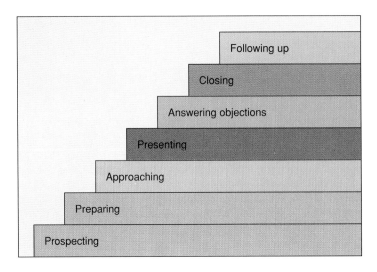

Prospecting   Locating potential customers is called prospecting. Salespeople find prospects through many sources, including current customers, trade directories, business associates, telephone directories, newspaper or magazine articles, or public records. At this stage in the selling process, the salesperson tries to identify as possible customers those who have a need for the product and the financial ability and authority to purchase it.

Preparing   Sales calls require some preparatory research. A salesperson attempts to find out about the prospect's needs, attitudes about available products and brands, and personal characteristics, as well as the products and brands currently used. Knowing as much as possible about the prospect allows a salesperson to tailor the approach and presentation specifically for that prospect and that situation.

Approaching   The third step involves making the initial contact with, or approaching, a prospect. A salesperson's approach makes the all-important first impression with a potential customer. Adequate preparation and knowledge increase a salesperson's chances of making a good first impression. In approaching the prospect, a salesperson may mention a referral from an acquaintance or business associate or remind the prospect of a previous meeting. Salespeople may make the call "cold"—without the prospect's prior knowledge or an appointment.

Presenting   The next step is actually presenting the promotional message to the potential customer. During the presentation, a salesperson points out the product's features and benefits and emphasizes any advantages the product offers over competitors' products. When possible, salespeople encourage potential customers to hold, touch, or use products to experience them personally and reinforce significant points of the presentation. A salesperson also needs to ask the client questions and listen carefully to determine the client's needs and focus the presentation on those needs.

Answering objections   After presenting, the salesperson gives a prospect sufficient opportunity to ask questions or raise objections. By answering objections, the salesperson increases the likelihood of a sale. This step gives the salesperson a second chance to tell the major benefits of the good or service and point out additional features, guarantees, service, and so forth.

Closing   In closing the sale, the salesperson asks the prospect to buy the product. Some salespeople ask directly if the prospect is ready to make a purchase. Others use trial closings to imply that the customer will buy the product. A salesperson can ask questions such as, Would you like us to finance the car for you? or, When would you like delivery? to encourage customers to finalize the purchase. Sometimes salespeople offer prospects a chance to try the product for a period of time with no obligation to buy.

Following up   A salesperson would make a critical mistake to assume that the selling process ends after the sale. To follow up, a salesperson contacts the customer to make sure that the product was delivered and installed properly (if needed) and to ask if it is performing as expected. When a problem exists, an effective salesperson assists the customer in resolving it. Providing service after a purchase encourages future sales and helps build a long-term relationship.

SALES PROMOTION

Sales promotion is a paid form of nonpersonal communication that provides direct incentives to customers, salespeople, and marketing intermediaries for purchasing a product. Methods such as coupons, contests, and displays can get consumers excited about a product, motivate salespeople to be enthusiastic, and stimulate dealers to be interested and involved in distributing it. Sales promotion activities, generally short-term, offer the advantage of immediacy; firms can implement them and obtain results quickly. Firms use sales promotion occasionally or year-round to support their personal selling, advertising, and publicity programs.

> **Sales Promotion**
> An activity that offers customers or marketing intermediaries direct incentives for purchasing a product.

Sales promotion is big business in the United States. Companies spend more than $85 billion each year on sales promotion activities. In this section, we will examine the major categories of sales promotion: consumer and trade.

Consumer Sales Promotion

Firms that market consumer products frequently use **consumer sales promotion,** activities that encourage customers to buy certain brands or to shop at a particular store. Companies are increasing their expenditures for consumer promotion, which now accounts for more than a fourth of promotional budgets.[18] The most common consumer sales promotion methods are coupons,

> **Consumer Sales Promotion**
> Activities—including coupons, rebates, samples, gifts, premiums, trading stamps, contests, and sweepstakes—directed to consumers to increase sales.

rebates, samples, gifts, premiums, trading stamps, contests, and sweepstakes. Firms may use one or more of these methods in a promotional campaign. For example, Texaco offered a coupon, a rebate, and a sweepstakes in a single-page ad in a campaign for Havoline motor oil.

Coupons Manufacturers and retailers provide special price reductions for consumers through **coupons.** The reduction may be a specified amount ranging from a few cents to several dollars, or a certain percentage to be deducted from the price of a product. Manufacturers and retailers often use coupons to encourage consumers to try new products. Some try coupons to reverse a decline in sales of a product. Sometimes a firm will distribute coupons as a defensive tactic when a competitor introduces a new product or begins a new sales promotion program. Firms distribute more than 200 billion coupons every year in the United States through newspapers, magazines, direct mail, store displays, and other methods. But customers redeem less than 5 percent of these. Many firms are reducing their use of coupons because they believe clutter has made this type of sales promotion less effective.[19] Table 16.3 shows where consumers obtain coupons.

Rebates Firms may offer customers who buy a product and send in proof of their purchase an extra discount or refund in the form of a **rebate.** Rebates range from a small percentage of the purchase price to the full purchase price. Firms typically use rebates both to motivate consumers to try new products and to provide incentives for purchasing established products. Manufacturers offer rebates for all types of products, from convenience items such as toothpaste to big-ticket goods such as cars.

Free samples An effective way to encourage consumers to get familiar with a product is to provide them with a **free sample** of the merchandise. Companies may mail or deliver samples to homes, give them out in stores, or distribute coupons for free products. While providing samples is the most expensive method of consumer sales promotion, it generally works best to induce buyers to try new products.

Coupon
A sales promotion technique which reduces the price of a product by a stated amount at the time of purchase.

Rebate
An extra discount or refund given to consumers who buy a product and supply proofs of purchase.

Free Sample
A free package or container of a product given as a sales promotion technique.

TABLE 16.3

Where Consumers Find Coupons

Source	Percentage of Total Respondents
Newspapers	73.0%
Product packages	5.5
Weekday newspapers	5.5
Magazines	4.0
Other	1.9
Don't use them	10.5

Source: *USA Today,* April 21, 1988, p. 1D (data from a Good Housekeeping Institute poll). Copyright *USA TODAY.* Reprinted with permission.

Premiums and trading stamps Many firms offer a **premium,** or gift, to customers as a bonus for purchasing a certain product. Banks, for example, often offer household items to customers who open new accounts. To attract customers to a particular store, retailers sometimes give customers **trading stamps** based on the dollar amount spent. Customers can save the stamps and exchange them for merchandise. Trading stamps such as S&H Green Stamps were once widely distributed by grocery stores but have been losing their popularity. In 1969, 77 percent of U.S. supermarkets gave out Green Stamps; this figure had dropped to 7 percent by 1989.[20]

Premium
A gift given to customers for purchasing a certain product.

Trading Stamps
Tokens given out by retailers based on the amount of purchase; redeemable for gifts.

Contests and sweepstakes Contests and sweepstakes probably generate more excitement than do other promotional methods. To stimulate sales, firms offer consumers the chance to win free trips, vacation dream houses, cars, cash, and merchandise. In a **contest,** consumers compete for prizes based on some skill. Food manufacturers, for example, often sponsor cooking contests in which contestants use certain products to create new recipes. In a **sweepstakes,** consumers send in their names to enter a drawing for prizes. Sweepstakes cost considerably less than contests and attract many more participants.

Contest
A sales promotion method in which consumers compete for prizes on the basis of some skill.

Sweepstakes
A sales promotion method in which consumers enter a drawing for prizes.

Trade Sales Promotion

A manufacturer often uses **trade sales promotion** activities to encourage wholesalers and retailers to stock and promote its products or salespeople to increase sales. Common methods of trade sales promotion are point-of-purchase displays, trade shows, trade allowances, premium or push money, and sales contests.

Trade Sales Promotion
Activities a firm directs to wholesalers, retailers, or salespeople to encourage them to stock or sell its products.

Point-of-purchase displays Manufacturers or wholesalers provide and set up signs, posters, freestanding shelves, and other specialized materials to use as **point-of-purchase displays** in retail stores. For example, a large, inflatable

Point-of-Purchase Displays
Promotional materials such as signs, posters, and freestanding shelves used in retail stores.

Courtesy of the Point-of-Purchase Advertising Institute, Inc.

Gillette used its point-of-purchase display in retail stores to introduce the "Sensor."

plastic Green Giant may stand atop the frozen vegetable case in a supermarket to grab attention and promote that brand. A display may contain the product being promoted. For example, Pepsico has supplied refrigerators bearing the Pepsi name to retailers carrying its products.

Video players with videotapes provided by manufacturers are among the newest point-of-purchase displays. Department stores, for instance, play videos on how to tie scarves and how to put together clothing separates for a complete outfit.

Trade Show
A temporary exhibit where manufacturers display products to potential customers and gather names for a list of prospects.

Trade shows   Sellers in an industry gather at **trade shows** to exhibit their merchandise. There manufacturers display and demonstrate products to potential customers and gather names of prospects. Industries representing food, fashion, furniture, computers, toys, and many other products hold trade shows each year, usually in large cities. While most trade shows are conducted by manufacturers for retailers, some also are designed for a consumer audience, such as shows featuring home building and interior decorating products or boats and recreational vehicles.

Trade Allowance
A discount a manufacturer gives for performing certain functions or making purchases during a specified time period.

Trade allowances   A manufacturer may give retailers and wholesalers a **trade allowance,** a discount for performing certain functions or for making purchases during a specified time period. For instance, a firm could offer price reductions to retailers to encourage them to stock a product and pass the savings on to consumers. A retailer also may earn a discount for setting up a special display to promote a manufacturer's products.

Premium or Push Money
Additional compensation provided to salespeople to encourage them to sell a product.

Premium or push money   Firms often conduct sales promotion activities for their own salespeople and those representing distributors and other sellers. To encourage salespeople to push a product, a firm may provide additional compensation in the form of **premium** or **push money.** While expensive, using premium or push money can boost commitment from salespeople when personal selling is a major part of the promotion mix.

Sales Contest
A competition designed to stimulate sales efforts by salespeople, distributors, or retailers.

Sales contests   Conducting a contest for the people who sell and distribute its products is another method a firm could use to increase involvement and create excitement. In a **sales contest,** a firm may offer prizes to salespeople, distributors, and retailers who meet certain sales goals in a specific time period. A sales contest with a desirable prize, such as a trip to an exotic vacation spot, can increase participation and sales throughout the channel of distribution. The results may be only temporary, however, and the cost of prizes may be high.

Publicity
A nonpersonal form of communication transmitted in news story form and not paid for directly by a sponsor.

Public Relations
A set of communications activities designed to create and maintain a favorable public image for a firm.

PUBLICITY

Like advertising and sales promotion, **publicity** is a nonpersonal form of communication. But it is transmitted by a mass medium in news story form and is not paid for directly by a sponsor. Publicity is actually part of **public relations,** a set of communications activities designed to create and maintain a favorable public image for a firm. Many organizations, industries, and individuals conduct ongoing public relations campaigns to demonstrate social responsibility.

Courtesy of the Los Angeles Marathon/Photo by D. Gifford

Sponsorship of sporting events like the Los Angeles Marathon is another way firms promote their goods and services.

Publicity Approaches

Firms attempt to gain publicity for several purposes. They may want to increase awareness of their products, to build a positive image with the general public, to gain recognition for employees and their accomplishments, to encourage others to participate in community projects, or at times to counter negative events or news stories.

Companies use several vehicles to obtain publicity. The *news release* is a brief report—a page or two—that announces an organization's national, regional, or local events. Firms distribute news releases widely and include the names of people within the firm for media representatives to contact for more information. A *feature article* is a longer, more detailed story about a firm, its products, or its people. It may run as long as 3,000 words and include photographs or illustrations. Firms usually submit a feature article to a specific magazine or newspaper. A *captioned photograph,* a picture along with a short explanation, can be effective in informing consumers about new products or stores. Another option is sending an *editorial film or tape* to broadcast media for inclusion in news programs. To release important or timely news, a firm may invite media representatives to a *news conference* to make announcements, hand out supplemental materials, and answer questions.

Another approach gaining use is *sponsorship* of events, programs, or even people such as amateur athletes or teams. Besides publicity, sponsorship can

Sponsorship: Sports, Special Events, and Spring Break

The last thing firms want to achieve through promotion is a low profile. Many sponsor various events to gain recognition, target specific segments, and increase sales with a "soft sell" that associates the product with something customers like.

When it comes to sports marketing, businesses want to play. More than 3,400 U.S. companies spend around $1.5 billion a year on national and local events. Some firms buy the right to name events after themselves, like the Coors International Bicycle Classic and the Sunkist Fiesta Bowl. Others contribute prize money in return for associating their names with events, such as the Ironman Triathlon in Hawaii, sponsored since 1981 by Anheuser-Busch Inc., or the Iditarod sled-dog race in Alaska, financed by the bootmaker Timberland Co.

Stock-car racing has long been boosted by business. Procter & Gamble spends $5 million for a Tide car, a Crisco car, a Folger's car, and others. There's even an Underalls car—driver Sterling Marlin's Oldsmobile Delta 88—sponsored by Hanes Hosiery Inc. to appeal to women, who make up 43 percent of the stock-car racing audience.

Besides backing sports, firms spend about $560 million yearly to sponsor events such as the Super Bowl halftime show, the Kool Jazz Festivals, and thousands of annual festivals and fairs across the country. Visa U.S.A. sponsored Paul McCartney's 1990 world tour. The charge card company contributed to the multimillion-dollar advertising campaign for the tour and agreed to help the international environmental group Friends of the Earth, with which McCartney was involved; concertgoers could charge the purchase of tickets and tour merchandise only with Visa credit cards.

Large consumer products companies view event sponsorship as an effective marketing method that is less expensive than advertising. Events can cost from $100,000 for a small, local music festival to $3 million for Chicago's elaborate food fest "Taste of Chicago." The field is not yet cluttered, and the public enjoys live drama and spectacle. While people watch events on television or attend in person, firms can advertise heavily or give away products or prizes.

Sponsorship helps marketers reach audiences that are difficult to reach through traditional media, such as the 350,000 students who spend spring break from Daytona Beach, Florida, to South Padre Island, Texas. To get their attention, firms pass out free samples and hold sporting events and parties. The maker of Coast soap lets students sing in a simulated shower (complete with background music) and take home a cassette. Zenith Data Systems gives prizes to students who try their color-screen personal computers, and Clairol gives away 200 hairstyle makeovers a day with its Pazazz mousse. Nestlé's Quik and the U.S. Marine Corps cosponsor the National Collegiate Sports Festival. And for students who want to call the folks back home, AT&T gives away three minutes of free long-distance phone time.

Some marketers are unsure that the expense of sponsorship—especially the high price tag for sports—pays off in sales. Volvo North America spends nearly $5 million a year to sponsor professional, college, and amateur tennis tournaments. Says president and CEO Bjorn Ahlstrom, "I know from market research that our tennis program has increased the awareness of Volvo. But how that translates into more business is anybody's guess." Despite the uncertain results, firms line up for the chance to link their names with big sports events such as the Olympic Games.[21]

involve advertising and sales promotion activities (e.g., samples and contests). Each year thousands of firms sponsor sporting events, festivals of the arts, public radio and television programs, and public interest advertisements. At least 400 large U.S. corporations have developed event marketing departments with separate budgets; others hire consultants to manage sponsorship for them. Smaller firms often work with local government and community organizations to sponsor events. The Business Action explores why and how firms invest sponsorship dollars.

Using Publicity Effectively

Positive publicity provides many benefits for an organization. A newspaper or magazine article or television or radio broadcast can reach large and diverse audiences at no direct cost to the firm. News and feature stories can reach people who pay no attention to advertisements. Since publicity is provided by independent media, it has a great deal of credibility. Are you not more likely to believe a news story about a new product than an advertisement paid for by the seller?

Publicity also poses several limitations. A firm exerts little or no control over a message—its content, placement, timing, or whether the media transmits it at all. News editors may have different ideas of what is news than do members of an organization seeking publicity. A news story may run on the late news show and reach only a fraction of potential viewers. Or it may be cut to a line or two in a newspaper column full of corporate news. Publicity does not always enhance a firm's image. At times the media report negative events and criticize a firm's activities, policies, or products.

To foster positive and effective publicity, a firm must conduct well-planned, regular efforts. Many firms employ individuals or departments to handle ongoing publicity efforts, while others rely on advertising or public relations firms or freelance writers or consultants. Personnel trained in communications can supply the media with newsworthy, well-written publicity releases, handle media requests, and build cooperative relationships with reporters, editors, news directors, and other media "gatekeepers."

DEVELOPING THE PROMOTION MIX

A firm marketing several products often uses several promotion mixes simultaneously. When designing the promotion mix for a product, marketers first consider their promotional objectives (discussed earlier in the chapter). They also consider promotional techniques known as push and pull strategies, as well as product characteristics, including type of product, stage of product life cycle, and target market characteristics.

Promotional Strategies

In developing promotional programs, marketers decide whether they want to use a push strategy or a pull strategy. With a **push strategy,** the firm promotes a product to wholesalers or retailers in the marketing channel, who in turn

Push Strategy
Promotion of a product to wholesalers or retailers in the marketing channel, who in turn promote the product to consumers.

FIGURE 16.6

Push and Pull Strategies

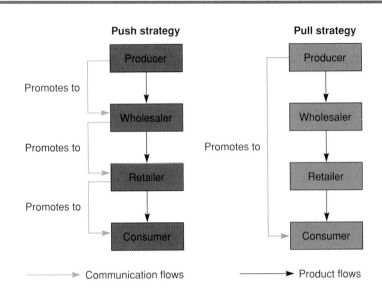

promote the product to consumers (see Figure 16.6). Personal selling often is used with this strategy to "push" the product to wholesalers and retailers.

In the **pull strategy** (also shown in Figure 16.6), by contrast, a firm promotes a product directly to consumers so that they will seek the product in retail stores and ask managers to stock it. In effect, customer demand "pulls" the product into stores. To implement a pull strategy, marketers usually use advertising and sales promotion to stimulate consumer demand for the product. While a firm often focuses on either a push or a pull strategy, it could use both at the same time.

Pull Strategy
Promotion of a product directly to consumers to stimulate strong consumer demand.

Product Characteristics

Various aspects of a product influence a firm's selection of promotion mix elements. Consumer and industrial products require different promotion mixes to meet the needs of those markets. Services often require unique considerations. For all products, firms must take into account the current product life-cycle stage and numerous characteristics of the targeted customers.

Type of product   Firms selling industrial products generally emphasize personal selling in their promotion mixes and use advertising, sales promotion, and publicity to support personal selling efforts. For consumer products, advertising is the primary element. Firms offering consumer convenience products promote them heavily with advertising and sales promotion. Those selling consumer shopping and specialty products add personal selling to the mix so that salespeople can provide information and advice about higher-priced or unfamiliar products such as appliances, cars, or computers.

Marketers of services face specific considerations when planning promotional activities. As intangible products, services cannot generally be defined in

FIGURE 16.7

Promoting Services with Physical Symbols

Physical symbols help make services like insurance more tangible to consumers and also build an image for the provider.

OUR CLIENT LIST INCLUDES 50% OF THE FORTUNE 500.

THE BOTTOM LINE IS YOUR FINANCIAL PEACE OF MIND.

When the leaders of America's most important companies seek expertise in insurance and financial services, they turn to the company that can help them the most. The Travelers.

We tailor our broad range of products and services to fit the specific needs of our diverse clients.

This flexibility is backed by the power of our $50+ billion in assets and 125 years of experience. As a result, our clients are better equipped to meet the growing demands of the business world. With confidence and financial peace of mind.

The Travelers Companies, Hartford, Connecticut 06183

The Travelers
You're better off under the Umbrella.®   © 1989 The Travelers Corporation

Courtesy of The Travelers Companies

terms of physical attributes. Therefore, when service firms advertise, they use cues that provide physical representation of the service offered. Common cues are the physical facility or the employees. Carnival Cruise Lines portrays its ships as resorts on water, complete with pools, casinos, and restaurants. As Figure 16.7 shows, insurance companies use cues—Allstate's good hands, State Farm's good neighbors, The Travelers' umbrella, and Prudential's rock—as physical representations of their protection, stability, and concern. Such symbols make the service more tangible to consumers and build an image of the provider that the consumer will, it is hoped, retain.

Services also are based on human performances—as in rock concerts, legal advice, or dental care—which are even more difficult to define in tangible terms. Marketers need to emphasize not only the actual service but all the benefits the customer is buying.[22] For many services, personal selling becomes especially useful; it provides the interaction between service personnel and consumers that is so valuable in marketing intangible products.

Publicity, with its lower cost and generally higher credibility compared to advertising, is an important promotion element for service firms. Health providers often receive publicity by sponsoring fairs in which medical personnel perform cholesterol screening, blood pressure checks, and vision and hearing tests free for the public. Service firms may also use sales promotion, such as coupons, rebates, and free first-time visits. Some sales promotion activities are not feasible for service providers; many services cannot be displayed, and providing a free sample requires giving away the entire product.

Product life cycle   A firm introducing a new product, either industrial or consumer, usually advertises heavily to make potential customers aware of it and encourage them to try it. Personal selling and sales promotion also prove valuable for many products in the introduction stage. For consumer convenience products in the growth and maturity stages, advertising usually continues to dominate the promotion mix. For industrial products in the growth and maturity stages, however, firms often concentrate on personal selling supported by sales promotion activities. When a product reaches the decline stage, marketers cut back on promotion, especially advertising. Instead they rely on personal selling and sales promotion to obtain a few more sales.

Target markets   The size, geographic distribution, and demographic characteristics of a firm's target market greatly influence the choice of promotion elements. Personal selling will likely be an important element for the target market that has a limited number of potential customers, while advertising and sales promotion usually dominate the promotion mix designed to reach millions of people at a low cost per person. Similarly, personal selling is generally more practical when a firm's customers are concentrated in a small area; advertising and sales promotion, which are much more flexible, can be easily geared to markets in any geographic region whether small and precisely defined or large.

A target market's demographics—age, income, education, social class, occupation—also influence the promotion mix. A firm marketing to teenagers would emphasize advertising, especially on television, but rely less on personal selling, sales promotion, or publicity. A firm targeting educated, financially well off consumers aged 35 and older would use personal selling, advertising, and perhaps publicity but not consumer sales promotion activities, since coupons, refunds, and sweepstakes are more important to lower- and middle-income families.

You'll Know It's the **21**st Century When . . .

The Family Must Be Redefined

Advertisers will need to be tactful when depicting 21st-century home life. By the year 2000, more than half of all children will spend part of their lives in single-parent homes. Though divorce rates will be stable, an increasing number of babies will be born to unmarried mothers. By 2010, about one in three married couples with children will have a stepchild or an adopted child. Interracial marriage and adoption will increase, encouraged by increasing immigration and growing social tolerance. Most children will never know a time when their mothers did not work outside the home.

In the 21st century, alternatives to marriage will be sought not just by young singles, but also by older people. Households that the Census Bureau now defines as "nonfamilies," including unmarried heterosexual couples, homosexual couples, and friends who live together, eventually will receive legal recognition as families in all 52 states.[23]

SUMMARY OF LEARNING OBJECTIVES

1. To explain the role of promotion in marketing and list five promotional objectives.
Organizations use promotion to communicate favorable, persuasive information about themselves or their products, to influence buyers to make a purchase, or to foster goodwill. Promotional objectives may include informing, increasing sales, stabilizing sales, product positioning, or building a public image. To meet these objectives, a firm develops a combination of advertising, personal selling, sales promotion, and publicity—called the promotion mix.

2. To describe the major types of advertising and the purpose of each.
Virtually all organizations use advertising to present messages to target markets. *Primary-demand advertising* helps create demand for a product group; *selective, or brand, advertising* builds demand for a specific brand; *institutional advertising* helps create a favorable public image. The media used most often are newspapers, television, direct mail, radio, magazines, and outdoor displays.

3. To list the steps involved in planning an advertising campaign.
When firms plan their advertising, they identify the target market, define their objectives, determine the budget, develop a platform, establish a media plan, create the advertisement, and evaluate the effectiveness of the campaign. Some companies have employees to handle their advertising, while others use advertising agencies or other specialists.

4. To differentiate among the three types of salespeople and their functions.
Personal selling involves person-to-person communication with one or more prospective buyers. Firms employ *order getters* to sell products to new and current customers, *order takers* to process repeat sales and maintain good relationships with customers, and *support salespeople* to sell, educate customers, and provide service.

5. To outline the personal selling process and describe each step.
Salespeople perform a series of steps in the selling process: prospecting (locating potential customers); preparing (learning about prospects and their needs); approaching (making the first contact and a good first impression); presenting (explaining product benefits and demonstrating the product); answering objections (encouraging questions and emphasizing product benefits); closing the sale (asking the prospect to buy); and

following up (finding out if the product satisfies the customer's needs and providing service).

6. To explain the purpose of sales promotion and list common activities of consumer sales promotion and trade sales promotion.

Sales promotion encourages sales through direct inducements to customers, salespeople, and marketing intermediaries. Coupons, refunds, samples, premiums, trading stamps, contests, and sweepstakes can get consumers interested in a product. Trade sales promotion methods—point-of-purchase displays, trade shows, trade allowances, premium or push money, and sales contests—help motivate salespeople and distributors and increase their involvement in product sales.

7. To describe how firms use publicity.

Publicity can increase awareness of products and help build a positive image with target markets or the general public. Sponsors do not pay directly for publicity, which is transmitted through mass media. News releases, feature articles, captioned photographs, editorial films or tapes, and press conferences facilitate publicity. Many firms sponsor events, programs, and public interest advertising to gain recognition, target specific markets, and increase sales.

8. To identify factors that influence a firm's promotion mix.

When planning a promotion mix, a marketer considers the firm's promotional objectives, whether to use a push or pull strategy, the characteristics of the product and target market, and the stage of product life cycle.

KEY TERMS

Promotion, p. 555

Promotion Mix, p. 556

Advertising, p. 556

Primary-Demand Advertising, p. 558

Selective (Brand) Advertising, p. 558

Institutional Advertising, p. 560

Advertising Media, p. 560

Personal Selling, p. 566

Order Getter, p. 567

Order Taker, p. 567

Support Salespeople, p. 567

Selling Process, p. 569

Sales Promotion, p. 571

Consumer Sales Promotion, p. 571

Coupon, p. 572

Rebate, p. 572

Free Sample, p. 572

Premium, p. 573

Trading Stamps, p. 573

Contest, p. 573

Sweepstakes, p. 573

Trade Sales Promotion, p. 573

Point-of-Purchase Displays, p. 573

Trade Show, p. 574

Trade Allowance, p. 574

Premium or Push Money, p. 574

Sales Contest, p. 574

Publicity, p. 574

Public Relations, p. 574

Push Strategy, p. 577

Pull Strategy, p. 578

QUESTIONS FOR DISCUSSION AND REVIEW

1. What do firms aim to accomplish through promotion?
2. What four elements could a promotion mix include?
3. Distinguish between the three major types of advertising.
4. Why would a firm use institutional advertising? Give an example of a recent institutional advertisement—its sponsor, its message, and where it appeared.
5. Identify two strengths and two weaknesses of each major advertising medium: newspapers, television, direct mail, radio, magazines, and outdoor displays.
6. How would a firm go about conducting an advertising campaign?
7. What is an advertising platform? Select two current advertising campaigns for two products and describe the platform of each.
8. Name the different types of salespeople. How do their jobs differ?
9. Consider a recent purchase you made in which a salesperson assisted you a great deal. Describe the interaction in terms of the steps of the selling process.
10. Why do companies engage in sales promotion activities?
11. Distinguish between consumer sales promotion and trade sales promotion. What consumer sales promotion methods influence *you* to purchase products?
12. Tell some of the advantages and disadvantages of publicity. Give a recent example of a firm receiving favorable publicity and an example of one receiving unfavorable publicity.
13. Why does the promotion mix vary considerably from one firm to another?
14. Distinguish between a push strategy and a pull strategy.

CASE 16.1
Ski Resorts Try to Give Business a Lift

For ski buffs, getting to Steamboat Springs used to be a hassle. To reach this remote Colorado ski resort, skiers first landed at the crowded Denver airport, walked for blocks to catch a shuttle bus, then rode for four hours through mountains. Not anymore. Steamboat Springs arranged with an airline to fly skiers straight into a nearby town, where a shuttle bus picks them up and takes them to the lodge. As one skier said of the shorter journey: "Instead of worn out, I felt rested. It was a new experience."

That's just one special deal ski resorts are sponsoring to boost the flat $1.5 billion market. The boom in skiing has been fading since the late 1970s; since 1980, 25 percent of U.S. ski resorts have closed. To lure customers, resort areas such as Jackson Hole, Crested Butte, Vail, and Aspen offer bargain packages, discount tickets, hot air balloon rides, fireworks, and even seminars. They have built children's slopes, spas, and fancy restaurants.

Sales had stalled at Vail, the second-largest U.S. ski resort, with annual revenues of $80 million, when Nashville businessman George N. Gillett, Jr., bought Vail Associates Inc. in 1985. Gillett increased marketing expenditures by 20 percent, began advertising on his 12 television stations, and started aggressive programs to capture business from competitors. He sent buses to nearby resorts to give skiers free rides to Vail if they bought a $25 lift ticket. Another resort countered with the same deal. An avalanche of packages and discounts followed. Vail once offered 33 different ticket prices.

Some industry experts say the promotional activities may backfire, with the flashy promotions bringing only inexperienced skiers who make a single trip to the slopes. Meanwhile people who ski regularly may be turned off. So far the costly programs have succeeded in attracting skiers, but profits still are down. Ski resort marketers are rethinking their promotional mixes.

At Sunday River Skiway in Bethel, Maine, president Leslie B. Otten conducts simple promotional programs with a clear aim: to bring in first-time customers and turn them into lifetime buyers. Service begins in the parking lot where attendants hand out maps and direct newcomers to an orientation center. Then Otten gives his product away. For $33 a lesson, first-time skiers receive two hours on the slopes with an instructor plus free use of skis, poles, and boots ($18 otherwise), a free lift ticket (worth $33), and the chance to sign up for two more lessons at the same rate. Students who complete three lessons get a coupon for a fourth day of free skiing. They also can buy poles, skis, and boots at Otten's cost.

Sunday River's learn-to-ski program doesn't itself make any money, but it does bring skiers back. Before the promotion started in 1985, only 20 percent

Adapted from Mark Ivey, Corie Brown, and Alice Z. Cuneo, "Hi, I'm Goofy. Come Ski with Me," *Business Week,* February 15, 1988, pp. 58–60; Paul B. Brown, "Return Engagements," *Inc.,* July 1990, pp. 99–100.

of the resort's first-time visitors returned. Now more than 75 percent do. Gross revenues have increased from $6 million to $18.3 million. Otten uses other promotional methods to keep skiers coming back. He created a frequent-skier program that gives customers a free day of skiing after as few as five visits. Customers also receive mailings describing other special deals.

"We want to stay top of mind," Otten says. "When we started here (in 1980), we tried to grow by stealing customers from other ski slopes by featuring lower prices, longer hours, or more services. That works for a while, but this is better."

Questions for Discussion

1. If you were advising a ski resort about its promotion mix, what are some questions you would ask?

2. Do you think the ski resorts are following a plan for their promotional programs or are they taking a shotgun approach? Which would bring more long-term benefits?

3. Could ski resorts direct some of their promotional messages to nonskiers in an effort to tap this market? What would be some of the problems with this strategy?

4. Could personal selling be used in this market? If so, how?

CASE 16.2
Does Sex Still Sell?

When an *Advertising Age* survey asked college students to rank print ads, a favorite was one for Calvin Klein's Obsession cologne that showed a nude couple, the man standing with his back to the camera and the woman draped over him. "Sexy ads always do well on the college level," says the president of a firm called College Market Consultants. "They grab attention on two levels, the conscious level as a consumer and on a subconscious level as well."

Like Calvin Klein, many advertisers use sex to pitch products. Sexy ads attract the attention of consumers who may otherwise never look at a product. They give consumers the impression the product is daring or sensual. Advertisers believe many consumers purchase clothing, cosmetics, and fragrances in hopes of becoming more sexually appealing. Firms with smaller advertising budgets sometimes use attention-grabbing, sexy ads to compete with larger competitors.

Using sex in advertising is an old idea that has varied according to media standards and public acceptance. Magazines have run more risqué ads, while network television has been more cautious. But barriers are constantly falling. In 1986, Fruit of the Loom television commercials showed men's underwear—but not with men wearing them. Three years later, TV celebrities Ed Marinaro,

Adapted from "Jovan's Steamy New Ads Pick Up Where Its Other Sizzlers Left Off," *Marketing News,* June 20, 1988, pp. 1–2; Michael Perreca, "Key to 'Successex'," *Product Marketing,* June 1988, p. 19; "Sandinistas Lure Youth Vote with Sex, Not Marx," *Herald-Leader* (Lexington, Ky.), February 20, 1990, p. A5; Joshua Levine, "Fantasy, Not Flesh," *Forbes,* January 22, 1990, pp. 118–20.

Patrick Duffy, and James DePaiva appeared in network commercials wearing only their Fruit of the Looms.

Some advertisers stretch the boundaries beyond previous limits. For its Jovan Musk ads in 1988, Beecham used footage by Adrian Lyne, who directed the movies *Fatal Attraction* and *9 1/2 Weeks.* Network censors twice ordered cuts before approving the ads. Beecham made use of the resulting publicity and actually placed ads in *TV Guide* and *USA Today* so viewers would know when the commercials would air. The firm's marketers appeared on talk shows to discuss the Musk ads and Beecham products. One executive said the publicity was worth about $13 million, equal to the company's advertising expenditure. He claimed that Jovan's commercials are just images on the screen and do not promote sex but simply reflect typical intimate relationships. Although Beecham advertises heavily on MTV, with its audience of mostly 18- to 24-year-olds, Zast says the company has acted responsibly.

With the U.S. population getting older, baby boomers settling down with families, and the threat of AIDS, advertising reflects contemporary attitudes toward sex roles. Ads now show women as equal sexual partners rather than sex objects. Print and television ads for Revlon's Charlie cologne, for example, featured a fashionable woman patting her male companion's rump. Other firms now use advertisements that suggest sensuality rather than show explicit images. For Iron cologne for men, Coty TV commercials show an attractive man pulling on a T-shirt and spraying on the cologne and a woman in a simple dress coming into the room and kissing his neck.

Even political advertising has exploited sex. Nicaragua's Sandinista Youth party used sexy ads to enlist young people to join the party and vote. Posters directed to first-time voters showed two pairs of naked legs pressed together and jeans and a crumpled rose on the floor, with the slogan, "It's beautiful the first time when you do it with love."

Using sex in advertising can pose drawbacks. Consumers may become so obsessed with the fantasy the ad creates that they forget about the product. Also, many consumers are turned off by sensual ads. Americans do not always accept the amount of nudity that appears in European advertising. After the German firm that markets Nivea moisturizing lotion featured a naked woman profiled against the sky in ads appearing in *Vogue, Harper's Bazaar,* and *Ladies Home Journal,* U.S. readers objected; the firm substituted a more demure photograph. And Chicago stores refused to be identified at the end of a commercial for Sansabelt pants in which a woman says, "I always lower my eyes when a man passes, to see if he's worth following."

Questions for Discussion
1. What promotional objectives do you think firms may have when they use sex in advertising?
2. Why have the ways in which advertisers use sex in ads changed?
3. What are some of the problems with using sex in advertising?

Careers in MARKETING

Marketing is everywhere. On a typical day, you see newspaper ads, TV commercials, and billboards advertising countless products. Flyers, catalogs, and brochures arrive in your mail daily. Each time you go to the supermarket, you look through hundreds of products packaged in myriad shapes and colors. In the mall, you're asked to fill out a questionnaire on which brand of toothpaste you use.

These are just some of the most obvious signs of the marketing effort. The field of marketing involves all of the steps that bring countless goods and services to consumers. These steps include marketing research, developing new products, advertising, packaging, distribution, and sales.

Marketing is a huge field employing millions of people. Opportunities in the field are vast and the demand for skilled, well-trained people continues to grow. While competition for entry-level positions is high, thousands of new jobs open in the field each year.

RETAILING

All of us are familiar with shopping in stores, but few actually understand what is involved in working in retailing. The field of retailing includes department stores, chain stores, supermarkets, specialty stores, franchise stores, mail-order businesses, and sidewalk vendors. Retailers buy their goods wholesale, display their wares, and sell them to individual consumers for a price higher than they initially paid.

Requirements: Retailing

Personal skills:
- Initiative
- Analytical ability
- Decision-making ability

Education:
- Bachelor's degree
- Any major

Because the field is very fast paced and involves constant change, careers in retailing can be exciting. Most follow one of two career paths, buying and store management.

Selected Employers of Marketing Personnel

Advertising agencies	International firms
Agents or brokers	Manufacturers
Computer service bureaus	Marketing research firms
Consulting firms	Marketing specialists
Credit bureaus	Media
Delivery firms	Nonprofit institutions
Entertainment firms	Public relations firms
Exporters	Real estate firms
Financial institutions	Retailers
Franchisees	Service firms
Franchisors	Shopping centers
Government	Sports teams
Health care providers	Transportation firms
Industrial firms	Wholesalers

Source: Reprinted from *CAREERS IN MARKETING*, 1985, published by the American Marketing Association.

Which path you first choose depends primarily on the employer. Many stores separate store management from buying at the entry level and you must choose which type of work you want to do. Other stores start all new trainees as assistant buyers. Smaller retailers often start people as salespeople or assistant managers. Most large department stores provide entry-level training programs for people first entering the field.

Buying

The buyer decides what goods to acquire and offer for sale in a store. Buyers purchase the goods directly from the manufacturers and set the price at which they will be sold in the store. A good buying decision results in profits for the store and advancement for the buyer. The buyer is also held responsible when a particular line does not sell.

Buyers need to understand customer preferences and anticipate trends, tastes, and styles months in advance. Careful analysis of previous sales, market research reports, and consumer trends are all important in making good buying decisions. A buyer must take calculated risks and have the courage to

Duties: Buying

- Ordering merchandise.
- Negotiating with suppliers.
- Pricing merchandise.
- Assisting with advertising.
- Analyzing sales.
- Overseeing sales promotions.
- Determining markdowns.

Career Ladder: Retail Buying Management

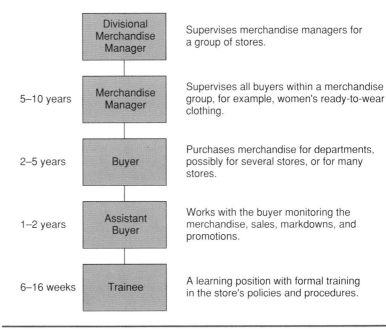

	Divisional Merchandise Manager	Supervises merchandise managers for a group of stores.
5–10 years	Merchandise Manager	Supervises all buyers within a merchandise group, for example, women's ready-to-wear clothing.
2–5 years	Buyer	Purchases merchandise for departments, possibly for several stores, or for many stores.
1–2 years	Assistant Buyer	Works with the buyer monitoring the merchandise, sales, markdowns, and promotions.
6–16 weeks	Trainee	A learning position with formal training in the store's policies and procedures.

make decisions worth thousands or even millions of dollars.

Buyers often must travel a great deal of the time. They make frequent buying trips to manufacturers and wholesalers to purchase merchandise. The amount of travel time varies, but most buyers spend at least four or five days each month on the road.

In large stores, buyers specialize in one area or department; each department needs a buyer to select its stock. In small stores, all buying may be performed by only one or two people.

Store Management

Store management involves directing operations so that the store functions effectively and efficiently. Store managers have the overall responsibility for ensuring the store operates at a profit.

Generally store management involves overseeing the flow of goods. This includes receiving and marking the goods, arranging and displaying them, and supervising the selling of the merchandise.

Duties: Store Management

- Hiring and training salespeople.
- Supervising the unpacking of merchandise.
- Handling customer complaints.
- Managing cash receipts.
- Displaying merchandise.
- Tracking inventory levels.

The duties of store managers depend on the size of the organization. In a small store, one manager may be responsible for all of the operations. Larger department

CAREER PROFILE: Paul Davis

Chris Wright/Gamma-Liaison

PAUL DAVIS

Age: 30
Current position: Regional retail manager, Gillette Company
Education: Bachelor of science Prairie View
Major: Agriculture/animal science
Best advice ever received: "Take a Dale Carnegie course."
Ambition: "To be a national sales manager or a corporate sales training manager."

Paul Davis was headed toward being a veterinarian or a farm agent when corporate recruiters talked to him about entering sales after college. Sizing up such things as the opportunity for advancement, travel, and benefits, he decided that "even though I'll always be an animal lover, I'd try my luck at sales."

Selling agricultural chemicals for Monsanto, he slogged through soybean fields in blue jeans and listened to farmers despair of pulling through the 1980s. He figured it was time to find another industry, and he signed on with Johnson & Johnson to sell baby products in Houston.

"At J&J, I learned to be a professional: how to look, how to dress, how to make a presentation," says Davis. His new assignment required him to call on higher-ups in the buying offices of food and drug chains, and despite his abundant enthusiasm, Davis had a problem approaching people with impressive titles. His superiors sent him off to take a Dale Carnegie course, which became the turning point of his career. "It helped me to see those executives as people."

Now at Gillette, Davis has gradually been handed management and training responsibilities that have broadened his views on the profession. "I don't think everybody can be in sales," he says. "For example, although it's a people business, just getting along with people isn't enough. You've got to have tact along with persuasiveness and know the right time to interject your opinion.

"It's up to you to coordinate everything in your territory," says Davis, emphasizing the need for continual follow-up. "Buyers see a lot of people, and sometimes things fall in the cracks, so you have to make sure that your product is being pulled through. It's not just selling. In the end, you're doing it all."

Source: Reprinted by permission of *Sales & Marketing Management.* Copyright October 1989.

stores distribute the responsibilities among several managers. In chain operations, managers are usually supervised by the central office.

Large retail operations have structured training programs for new hires. Most start as assistant department managers and begin to supervise salespeople very quickly.

Additional Retailing Resources

National Retail Merchants Association
100 West 31st Street
New York, NY 10001

National Association of Retail Grocers of the U.S.
200 Spring Road, Suite 620
Oak Brook, IL 60521

National Association of Wholesalers and Distributors
1725 K Street, N.W.
Washington, DC 20006

SALES

Career opportunities in sales are vast. Today the selling function is found in some form within every business; without sales, companies cannot stay in business. Every retail company, large or small, needs people to sell its wares. And all manufacturing and service businesses require effective sales forces to sell their goods and services.

A salesman is an optimist who finds the world full of promising potential.

Jerry Dashkin

Working in sales can be one of the most lucrative and attractive careers. Advancement and earnings are directly related to your

Requirements: Sales

Personal skills:
- Communication
- Self-discipline
- Poise
- Enthusiasm

Education:
- Bachelor's degree
- Any major

performance. Salespeople earn annual salaries but receive extra compensation based on their sales. Some companies provide year-end performance bonuses; others offer sales commissions. Some firms offer automobiles and expense accounts as an extra benefit. A sales career can provide the opportunity for substantial earnings.

Sales representatives may have only a few accounts or the responsibility for hundreds of customers. They call on potential and existing customers to present the features and benefits of the company's products. They must understand the needs of each customer and see that orders are filled properly.

Most entry-level salespeople receive some type of training. Some companies will use the term *sales trainee*, while others may use *sales representative*. Training periods generally last from one week to a year.

Advancement comes in the form of increased responsibility for larger and larger territories and larger sales forces. After one to

three years, sales representatives may begin to take on management responsibilities. Sales managers are responsible for preparing budgets, meeting sales goals, and supervising and training lower-level salespeople.

Additional Sales Resources

Direct Selling Association
1730 M Street, N.W., Suite 610
Washington, DC 20006

Sales & Marketing Executives,
  International
330 West 42nd Street
New York, NY 10036

National Association of Professional
  Saleswomen
600 Valetta Way
Sacramento, CA 95800

Manufacturers' Agents National
  Association
23016 Mill Creek Road
Laguna Hills, CA 92653

If you are successful at managing sales representatives, you may be given increased management responsibility by actually managing the regional managers as well as the sales force under them. Training for top management positions usually includes assignments in other marketing areas, such as advertising, marketing research, and product management. The top-level position is vice president of marketing or sales.

Salespeople have a very unstructured job. They have a good deal of flexibility and control over their time. Days are filled with calling on customers, and many hours are spent on preparing sales reports, writing up orders, and drafting correspondence.

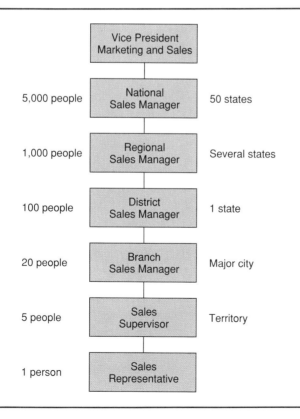

	Vice President Marketing and Sales	
5,000 people	National Sales Manager	50 states
1,000 people	Regional Sales Manager	Several states
100 people	District Sales Manager	1 state
20 people	Branch Sales Manager	Major city
5 people	Sales Supervisor	Territory
1 person	Sales Representative	

Duties: Sales

- Contacting customers.
- Developing new customers.
- Documenting contacts made.
- Arranging delivery dates.
- Taking orders.
- Settling customer complaints.
- Preparing expense reports.
- Presenting at trade shows.
- Providing product feedback.
- Assisting in advertising.
- Preparing sales reports.

Marketing Starting Salaries: Bachelor's Degree Candidates

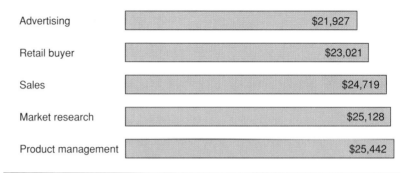

Advertising	$21,927
Retail buyer	$23,021
Sales	$24,719
Market research	$25,128
Product management	$25,442

Source: Salary survey, College Placement Council, Inc., September 1990.

ADVERTISING

Every day, we see commercials and advertising messages on television and radio, in newspapers and magazines, on billboards, and in our mail. Most of what we see and hear is prepared by advertising agencies.

If I were starting life over again, I am inclined to think that I would go into the advertising business in preference to almost any other. The general raising of the standards of modern civilization among all groups of people during the past half-century would have been impossible without that spreading of the knowledge of higher standards by means of advertising.

Franklin D. Roosevelt

Agencies are hired to plan, design, and produce an advertising campaign to reach potential customers. The field is highly competitive. Agencies compete with one another to be able to handle a company's advertising program.

An advertising agency has specialists in writing and creating ads, market research, public relations, media selection, and managing client accounts. The advertising account executive is the primary link between the agency and the client.

Selling is a major part of the job. The account executive makes presentations about the agency to prospective clients.

Account executives direct the advertising program. They oversee the development of the concept and work with the client to gain approval of the overall plan. They also see that the campaign stays on schedule and within budget.

Requirements: Advertising

Personal skills:
- Creativity
- Communication skills
- Organizational ability
- Ability to deal with people

Education:
- Bachelor's degree
- Master of business administration
- Major in marketing
- Major in communications

Advertising is a very fast-paced field. People in the field must work under a great deal of pressure. Their work hours may be long and unpredictable.

Competition for jobs in advertising is intense. The field is considered quite "glamorous" by

many, and large numbers of people want to get into the field. Most have some degree of specialization to offer, such as photography, copywriting, graphic art, market research, or marketing sales.

Additional Advertising Resources

American Advertising Federation
1400 K Street N.W., Suite 1000
Washington, DC 20005

American Association of Advertising
  Agencies
666 Third Avenue
New York, NY 10017

Association of National Advertisers
155 East 44th Street
New York, NY 10017

MARKETING RESEARCH

Before spending millions of dollars on a new product or advertising campaign, companies want answers to some questions. How big is the market? Will my customer like the package? Is the price too high? How does the consumer decide what to buy?

Marketing research specialists help provide the answers to these kinds of questions. They plan, design, conduct, and analyze results of surveys. They may conduct research by interviewing shoppers, asking questions by telephone, sending out questionnaires, and conducting group interviews. Analysts interpret many kinds of data from surveys, economic studies, and sales records. Computers and statistical techniques are used extensively to analyze the data. Reports are prepared summarizing their findings.

Most large companies have their own marketing research department. Advertising agencies also often have their own marketing research staff. Job opportunities can also be found in independent market research firms.

Requirements: Marketing Research

Personal skills:
- Communication
- Organizational
- Problem-solving

Education:
- Bachelor's degree
- Master of business administration
- Major in marketing
- Major in communications
- Familiarity with statistics
- Familiarity with computers

PRODUCT MANAGEMENT

Every new product on the market needs to be introduced to the public through a marketing campaign. The person responsible for planning, developing, and directing the marketing effort of a particular product is the product manager. Some firms use the term *brand manager* rather than product manager.

The product manager will oversee the research and development, packaging, manufacturing, pricing, distribution, advertising, promotion, and sales of the product. He or she has the full responsibility for success or failure of the product.

Because millions of dollars are often at stake with the introduction of a new product, companies do a good deal of test marketing. Market research provides feedback about the product's price, its packaging, and its features long before the product is introduced to the public. The product manager decides whether to modify the product to make it more appealing, or to cancel the product altogether.

Product management requires knowledge and expertise in all areas of the marketing process. Because of the great responsibility in the hands of product managers, most people are required to work as assistants for several years before being promoted to manager. Many firms require several years of sales experience before even starting as an assistant product manager.

Additional Marketing Resources

American Marketing Association
250 South Wacker Drive
Chicago, IL 60606

Marketing Research Association
111 East Wacker Drive, Suite 600
Chicago, IL 60601

PART SIX

FINANCIAL MANAGEMENT

CHAPTER SEVENTEEN

MONEY AND BANKING

1. To define *money* and state its functions and characteristics.

2. To identify the elements that make up both the M_1 and M_2 money supplies.

3. To compare the different types of financial institutions.

4. To explain how the federal government is involved in money and banking in the United States.

5. To discuss how the Federal Reserve System controls the supply of money and credit.

6. To identify the major changes occurring in banking and the impact of technology.

On the third floor of the Bank-America headquarters in San Francisco hangs a cartoonlike painting of BankAmerica executives riding in a military tank and waving a banner reading "Annihilate the

Courtesy of Bank of America

Competition"—certainly an indication that BankAmerica has become an aggressive competitor in the bank business. But this aggressiveness was necessary. A little more than two years ago, BankAmerica's survival was in doubt. Today—largely because of its aggressive posture in retail banking (bank services for consumers as opposed to businesses)—BankAmerica is back on profitable ground and moving forward at a rapid rate. BankAmerica now considers itself to be a consumer-oriented bank, not simply a money center bank.

Since deregulation of the U.S. banking business in the 1980s, the very nature of banking has changed. Prior to deregulation, banks were often seen as cold stone buildings full of stodgy, stiff executives with little concern for their customers. Not that this was true, but, to a great extent, the image stuck. Following deregulation, banks faced much broader competition. Services, such as checking accounts, once solely the domain of banks, were now offered by brokers, savings and loans, and credit unions. Banks had to react by becoming more aware of their customers' needs and by beginning to market their products.

BankAmerica began to offer what it calls "Alpha," a package linking checking and savings accounts with a credit line that kicks in when customers' accounts are overdrawn. In addition, BankAmerica has offered free checking accounts, credit lines with no up-front charges, and $5 to any customer who has to wait in line for more than five minutes. All of this was promoted with a multimedia, multimillion-dollar promotional blitz. Alpha was pitched as the "first step in simplified banking"—one-stop shopping for bank customers.

Certainly the nature of banking in this country is still undergoing rapid change and likely will continue to do so. Banks will promote and develop new services and packages, and consumers will demand more. Not all bankers are happy with the changing image, but most see the need for change. As one BankAmerica executive put it, "A lot of this stuff is hokey, but hokey works."[1]

The healthy functioning of a modern mixed economic system—whether it will have economic growth or decline, prosperity or recession, employment or mass unemployment—depends largely on what is happening with money. Money is an important commodity to all of us. With it, we can purchase many of the things that we need to survive. In the United States and other great industrial and economic powers such as Japan and Germany, we associate money with banks; therefore banks and other banklike institutions (e.g., credit unions, savings and loans) are also very important to us. We depend on them to keep our savings safe, to make it possible for us to pay our bills with a check, and to lend us money for the major purchases we need to make. We also depend on banks to keep our economy healthy by serving the financial needs of business.

In this chapter, we study money and banking. First we discuss the need for a common element for exchanges and how money serves as this common element, or *medium*. Then we consider the functions and characteristics of money. Next we discuss financial institutions: commercial banks, other banking institutions, and nonbanking institutions. A discussion follows on the government's role in the monetary system and banking, including the Federal Reserve System and government regulation. Finally we look at the future of banking and discuss the technological changes we see already.

MONEY AND EXCHANGE SYSTEMS

One of the things taught in economics is that individuals cannot efficiently produce for themselves everything they need to survive. You cannot grow all your own food, sew your own clothes, construct your own home, build your own car, or teach yourself a business. You depend on others to provide some of these things for you. As we noted previously, one way you can get these things is through bartering, that is, exchanging something you have (other than money) with someone else to get the other things you need. For example, if you were a carpenter, you might build something for a tailor if he would make you a suit.

You might think that this type of exchange does not occur anymore, but actually bartering does still occur. For example, many radio stations and television stations exchange commercial time with companies for merchandise: one may offer commercial time to a car dealer in exchange for an automobile to give away as part of a radio station listener sweepstakes. As we prepared this book, bartering was still used when Eastern European countries transacted business with international partners. Because the economic isolation of these countries causes a lack of sufficient hard currency in their central banks, a significant amount of bartering still takes place: Florida phosphate for Polish sulfur, Soviet merchant ships for Pepsi Cola extract, and Rumanian glass and textiles for General Electric turbines.[2]

While bartering works, it is not very efficient. If you are a carpenter, you cannot build something for everyone you want something from. You could not, for example, go build a step for a grocer every time you needed a carton of milk. After a while, the grocer wouldn't need any more steps, and you would be tired

FIGURE 17.1

Functions and Characteristics of Money

Functions	Characteristics
Medium of exchange	Acceptance
Measure of relative value	Divisibility
Store of value	Portability
	Durability
	Stability
	Scarcity

of building steps. And, if everytime you wanted to get a carton of milk you had to find a grocer who needed a step built, you would waste a great deal of time looking for one. It would be better if you could receive some common item for building steps and the grocer could receive a similar common item for selling milk.

Money
Anything commonly accepted as a means of paying for goods and services.

Money is this item. **Money** is anything that is commonly accepted as a means of paying for the goods and services individuals need and want. Money enables us to function in society and to have the things we need to survive—things such as housing, food, clothing, transportation, heat, and water.

Money has not always been the coins and paper bills known to us. Throughout history various things of value have been used as money. For example, in many parts of the ancient world, salt was used as money because it was rare and necessary to life. Among many early American cultures, furs or pelts were used as money. Eventually valuable metals became the most common type of money; in fact, gold coins were used as money in the United States as recently as 1933.

Currency, which is dollar bills and coins, fits most of the definition of money. However, checks are accepted payment for purchases, and checking account deposits are considered money and not currency. To define money as currency would be considered too narrow for most economists.

Functions of Money

Money has three basic functions. It serves as a medium of exchange, as a measure of relative value, and as a store of value (see Figure 17.1).

As a *medium of exchange,* money enables two individuals to exchange without having to barter; that is, the carpenter doesn't have to build a step for the grocer every time he wants a carton of milk. The carpenter can build steps or anything else for anybody, receive money for his services, and use the money to purchase milk from the grocer. The grocer can in turn use the money received from the carpenter and others to purchase a suit from the tailor.

As a *measure of relative value,* money allows two dissimilar items to be purchased on a similar basis. It is in terms of money that we think of value. How many cartons of milk should the grocer pay for a suit? If asked that question, you might ask, How much is a carton of milk worth? and, How much is the suit worth? You would want to define the exchange in terms of the relative value of the two items and would use the value in dollars (money) to determine how many cartons of milk it should take to buy a suit. Money helps us think of different things in terms of a common value base.

As a *store of value,* money makes it possible for us to hold onto the value over time. If the grocer would have to hold the value of his milk in milk, he could not hold it for long because it would spoil. However, if he sells the milk and gets money for it, he can hold the money until he wishes to purchase something.

Of course, other things can serve as stores of value. Some people collect antiques, stamps, or baseball cards and keep these things as stores of value because they will likely increase in value over time.

While the earning power of these and other items is important, money has one distinct advantage over them: it is highly liquid. That is, it can be obtained and disposed of quickly and easily. You don't have to find someone to buy it first. We will cover liquidity in more detail in our discussion of the money supply.

Characteristics of Money

As noted before, a number of significant problems surface when we try to exchange steps for milk. Some forms of money also cause problems. For example, the inhabitants of one South Pacific Island used huge stones, weighing as much as 90 pounds, for money. This certainly made everyone aware of how much money each of them had, since these stones were very visible. But if one of the inhabitants wanted to purchase something really only worth one fourth of a stone, how could they divide the stone? And if they decided to buy something from an individual on the other side of the island, how did they get the stone to that individual? Clearly, to be useful as a medium of exchange, money needs to have certain characteristics: acceptance, divisibility, portability, durability, stability, and scarcity.

Acceptance   To be useful, money must be accepted by the general population it is meant to serve. You may have heard the expression "That isn't worth a continental dollar." The expression refers to the continental currency issued during the American Revolution. This currency was issued in such large amounts and with so little backing that it was virtually useless for purchasing goods. These dollars were not an effective medium of exchange.

Divisibility   If you wanted to buy a single candy bar for 25 cents, you would pay the grocer with a quarter or give her a dollar and receive three quarters as change. If the dollar was not divisible, you would have to buy four candy bars or allow the grocer to make a large profit from the exchange. The American dollar is easily divisible. It can be divided into pennies (100), nickels (20), dimes (10), quarters (4), or half dollars (2). This ability makes it an easily used medium of exchange, since it can be used to purchase items of any monetary value. All money needs this characteristic of divisibility.

Portability   Not surprisingly, paper currency and coins are the most common forms of money throughout the world. They are easily transported from one location to another. Dollar bills fold easily and store in a wallet, and coins are easily carried in a pocket or change purse. This makes money easy to take with us and use when we want to make an exchange. Those natives in the South Pacific could not fold their 90-pound rocks and tuck them into their pockets to go shopping.

Durability   Money must be durable. It cannot act effectively as a store of value if it does not last. If a society used milk as money, a lot of sour money would appear in a short period of time. Paper money and coins are very durable; they last a long time. The average dollar is in circulation for 18 months and may be folded several thousand times. While it is true that coins are more durable, they are not as portable as paper money, and so both are used. Paper money maximizes portability, and coins make the paper money easily divisible.

Stability   To maintain acceptability, money needs to be relatively stable. People lose faith in money when its value is not stable. Inflation is a major concern for governments. When inflation runs extremely high, people begin to lose faith in their currency as a medium for exchange and as a store of value. They begin to abandon their currency and demand gold coins, or they may begin to store their wealth in items such as real estate and precious metals. Furthermore, when inflation runs extremely high, as it has in recent years in many Latin American countries, people abandon their currency and return to the barter system or use another country's money. (The U.S. dollar, the German mark, and the Japanese yen enjoy wide use.) Neither of these solutions benefits the economy of the affected country. The barter system is not economically efficient and therefore tends to stunt economic growth, and other currencies are usually not available in sufficient quantities to allow for a normal, healthy economy.

Scarcity   By scarce we do not mean that money needs to be rare or in very limited supply, like rare stamps. Rather we mean that the supply cannot be unlimited. Money cannot grow on trees and everyone cannot have all they want, or it would have little value. For this reason, governments go to great lengths to prevent counterfeiting of their currency. Currency in the United States is produced by the U.S. Treasury Department; production of money by anyone else is a serious crime. Governments also go to great lengths to make duplication of currency difficult. Some countries use highly colored paper, while others use highly watermarked paper. The United States uses special paper with small red and blue silk threads imbedded in it. This makes counterfeiting the currency difficult and avoids the watering down of its value.

The Bettmann Archive

THE SUPPLY OF MONEY

To measure the money supply, we measure the amount of money in the economy. However, what to measure is a problem. Should someone's home be considered money? After all, it can be sold for cash. An individual's car? Boat? Or should the money supply include only cash?

To understand the money supply in the United States, you have to first understand the concept of liquidity. **Liquidity** is simply a measure of how quickly an item can be converted to cash. Obviously the most liquid item is cash itself, since it does not need to be converted. However, many other items approach cash in liquidity because they function as cash in many transactions. These items include demand deposits, against which checks can be written or from which funds can be withdrawn; time deposits, from which funds can be withdrawn; and money market funds, which can be immediately sold for cash.

When measuring the U.S. money supply, we look at it at various levels, each including items that are less liquid than the items included in the previous level

Liquidity
A measure of how quickly an item can be converted to cash.

FIGURE 17.2

The Total Money Supply

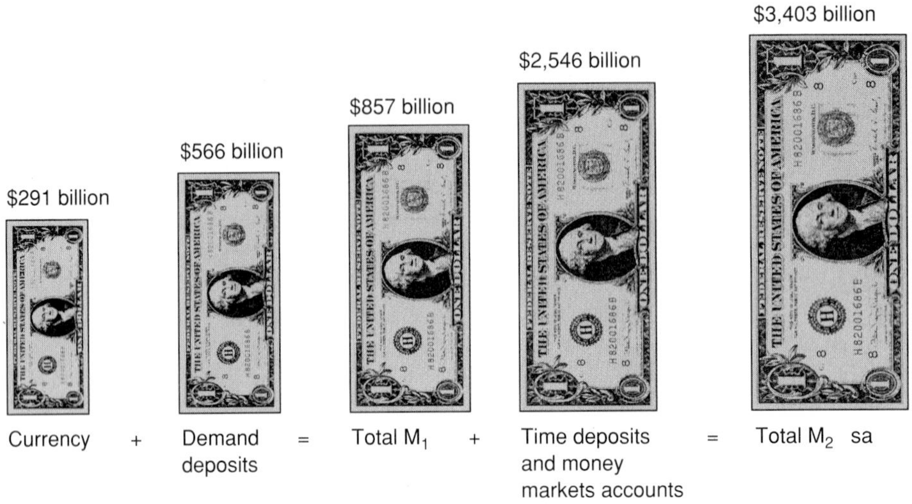

$3,403 billion

$2,546 billion

$857 billion

$566 billion

$291 billion

Currency + Demand = Total M$_1$ + Time deposits = Total M$_2$ sa
deposits and money
markets accounts

sa = Seasonally adjusted

Source: *The Wall Street Journal,* June 21, 1991, p. C10.

of the money supply. For our purposes, the first two levels of the money supply are the most important. These two levels are referred to as M$_1$ and M$_2$ (see Figure 17.2).

M$_1$

M$_1$, the first level of money supply measurement, includes the most highly liquid forms of money: currency and demand deposits.

Currency **Currency** includes the coins and paper money spent to purchase things. Actually, even though most of us think of currency when we think of money, it represents only a small part of the total M$_1$ money supply, about 20–25 percent. Cashier's checks, money orders, and traveler's checks are also considered currency, since they can be used even in situations where the individual cashing them is not personally known.

Demand deposits Deposits at banks against which an account holder can write checks, withdrawing money immediately and without prior notice, are **demand deposits.** The holder can require the bank to pay another person or business (called the payee) the amount written on the check. Of course, the bank does not have to honor the demand if the holder's account doesn't have enough money to cover the amount of the check. This situation is referred to as insufficient funds.

Checks are used in about three fourths of the financial transactions conducted in the United States. They are popular due to a number of factors. First, checks are more secure than currency. A person carrying checks does not have to worry about the loss of currency. Checks cannot be spent by anyone other

M$_1$
The first level of money supply measurement; includes the most highly liquid forms of money: currency and demand deposits.

Currency
The coins and paper money spent to purchase things. Cashier's checks, money orders, and traveler's checks are also considered currency.

Demand Deposits
Bank accounts against which an account holder can write checks, withdrawing money immediately and without prior notice.

than the account holder; they require the account holder's signature to be cashed. Second, they may be more convenient for paying odd amounts or large amounts. Writing one check for $187.85 is easier than counting out nine 20s, a five, two ones, three quarters, and a dime. It is also safer, since carrying large amounts of cash invites crime. Finally, checks make payment by mail easier and safer, and the canceled check gives the person making the payment a record of the transaction.

Deregulation of the banking industry has brought about additional types of demand deposits, which go by such names as NOW (negotiable orders of withdrawal) and share draft accounts. In 1972, after two years of litigation, mutual savings banks in Massachusetts were allowed to issue NOW accounts that could pay interest on checking accounts. NOW accounts were an immediate success because the mutual savings banks, able to attract more funds that could be loaned out, could earn higher profits. In 1980, legislation was passed that authorized NOW accounts nationwide for savings and loans, mutual savings banks, and commercial banks and provided for similar accounts (called share draft accounts) at credit unions.[3]

M$_2$

M$_2$, the second level of money supply measurement, includes time deposits and money market accounts in addition to currency and demand deposits.

Time deposits   Savings accounts that allow the financial institution to require notice—prior notification by the account holder—before withdrawal or that allow the financial institution to assess a penalty for early withdrawal are called **time deposits.** Time deposits, while not used for transactions or as a medium of exchange, are extremely liquid. Money can be moved from time deposit accounts to checking accounts, or cash can be withdrawn to make purchases.

Money market accounts   Accounts that pay interest rates very competitive with the interest rates paid on other short-term investments, such as short-term U.S. Treasury bills, are called **money market accounts.** Typically handled through banks, money market accounts pay interest based on investments in such things as U.S. Treasury bills. Banks limit the number of checks that a holder can write each month from a money market account, and checks must be written in minimum amounts of $500.

Credit cards   Not officially considered money, credit cards represent an individual's approval for credit. Since they can be used to draw directly against that credit, they in a sense are a medium of exchange. They represent a special credit arrangement between the cardholder and the financial institution issuing the card. Each time the cardholder uses the card, he or she in effect takes out a loan for the amount of the charge. This loan can be repaid at the end of the billing period, or (in the case of bank cards and retail credit cards) a stated minimum amount can be paid each month, with interest charged on the outstanding balance until it is repaid.

Over 300 million credit cards are in circulation. In fact they are becoming a more and more popular medium of exchange in the industrial world (i.e., Japan,

M$_2$
The second level of money supply measurement; includes time deposits and money market accounts in addition to currency and demand deposits.

Time Deposits
Savings accounts that allow the financial institution to require notice before withdrawal or to assess a penalty for early withdrawal.

Money Market Accounts
Deposits that pay interest rates very competitive with those paid on other short-term investments; some allow a limited number of checks to be written in amounts over $500.

A consumer can use his or her credit card to purchase this 10-speed bike. The Visa card is accepted in millions of businesses around the world, from Leningrad to Sydney to Miami.

Europe). This is due in part to the increased willingness of merchants to accept credit cards and the increased desire of banks and other financial institutions to issue credit cards.

Banks and other financial institutions want to issue credit cards because they are profitable. Credit card issuers earn money three ways: fees charged to customers, interest from outstanding credit balances, and the "discount" charge they assess merchants on each purchase. [4] In many cases, cardholders pay an annual membership fee, and interest charges on unpaid balances typically range between 15 and 20 percent annually. As a result, credit cards generate profits three times as great as other bank services.

FINANCIAL INSTITUTIONS: THEIR ROLE IN BUSINESS

Financial institutions that serve business include banking institutions—commercial banks, thrifts, credit unions, and others—and nonbanking institutions, such as insurance companies and commercial and consumer finance companies. Before 1863 all commercial banks in the United States were char-

Rank	Bank and Head Office	Assets ($ in millions)
1	Citibank, New York	$164,413,000
2	Bank of America, San Francisco	94,127,000
3	Chase Manhattan, New York	83,028,964
4	Morgan Guaranty of NY, New York	75,051,648
5	Bankers Trust, New York	59,937,000
6	Manufacturers Hanover, New York	58,783,000
7	Security Pacific, Los Angeles	58,460,658
8	Chemical Bank, New York	51,195,000
9	Wells Fargo Bank, San Francisco	48,520,543
10	Bank of New York, New York	44,709,711
11	First National Bank of Chicago, Chicago	37,099,251
12	NCNB Texas, Dallas	35,606,501
13	First National Bank of Boston, Boston	29,841,244
14	Continental Bank, Chicago	25,859,126
15	Republic of New York, New York	22,339,051

Note: Based on figures as of September 30, 1990.

Source: *The Bank Quarterly, Ratings & Analysis*, Sheshunoff Information Services, Inc., 1991, p. I.45.

tered by banking commissions of the states in which they operated. To eliminate the abuses of some of the state-chartered banks, the National Banking Act of 1863 created a new banking system of federally chartered banks, supervised by the Office of the Comptroller of Currency, a department of the U.S. Treasury.[5] Today the United States has a dual banking system in which banks supervised by the federal government and by the states operate side by side. Insurance companies and consumer finance companies are regulated by the states in which they operate.

Commercial Banks

About 14,000 commercial banks do business in the United States. A **commercial bank** is a profit-making institution that holds the deposits of individuals and businesses in checking and savings accounts and then uses these funds to make loans to individuals, businesses, and the government. Commercial banks in the United States are chartered by either the state or the federal government. While bank charters issued by states and the federal government do differ, the differences are not noticeable to the individual depositor. Table 17.1 shows the top 15 commercial banks in the United States, based on their assets.

Commercial banks are sometimes called full-service banks. Certainly most offer an extensive range of services. In addition to checking and savings accounts and personal and business loans, commercial banks offer bank credit

Commercial Bank
A profit-making institution that holds the deposits of individuals and businesses in checking and savings accounts and then uses these funds to make loans.

Seed Money for Small Fry

Like many entrepreneurs, Adam Fingersh started his small designer sweatshirt business at home, where his living room table doubled as a workstation. The business grew, and before long Fingersh cried out for an infusion of working capital. He created a business plan, approached a loan officer at his bank, offered his Apple computer as collateral, and shrewdly negotiated a set of terms. Within four months, he had not only paid off his loan but also received a revolving line of credit from the bank. An impressive small-business success story, especially considering just how small a businessman Adam Fingersh is. At age 11, he is only one of the young capitalists who have lined up for money at a Denver financial institution catering exclusively to children.

Young Americans Bank has clients who stand no taller than T. Boone Pickens' belt buckle. The bank makes MasterCards available to customers as young as 12. To qualify for the $95-a-year plastic credit card, the applicant must have an account at the bank and, if under 18, an adult cosigner. When the bank opened, it amused locals. But the bank is proving itself. It opened an impressive 5,000 accounts in the first seven months of business, has $1.3 million in capital, and plans to break even this year, even though the typical new bank takes three years to make a profit.

Junior patrons can open a checking account with as little as $10 and take out loans. The bank has lent money to buy a horse, to cut a record, and to start and sustain young businesses. "We get some incredibly ambitious kids here," says Leanne Cadman, Young Americans' loan administrator. "They're 15, 16 years old, and they're ready to make a million dollars." The bank accommodates even the most pint-sized entrepreneur. It features steps to the teller windows and multilevel loan desks.

The bank was started by Denver cable TV magnate Bill Daniels as a way to teach money management skills to kids. He spent two years convincing the Colorado banking board to issue a state charter and contributed $2 million of his own money toward the project. He also enlisted 20 founding sponsors, who agreed to deposit $50,000 to $100,000 each for at least a year without collecting interest.

Some skeptics ask if "buy now, pay later" is a lesson we want to teach our youth. But despite skeptics, young bank customers keep coming. Cadman sees six to eight loan applicants a week—some of whom have already launched successful business ventures. Fourteen-year-old Lee Nicholson saw his snow removal business take off after borrowing $700 for a snowblower. With a $1,500 loan, University of Colorado junior Greg Phelps began marketing a software program for Shaklee distributors.

The bank has had little trouble with its borrowers, and Daniels promises to treat junior deadbeats the same as their adult counterparts. He states, "The kids will learn that, if they default on a bicycle, we're going to repossess it." Indeed, the only snags have been in the 18- to 22-year-old age group, where giddy checking account customers abused their overdraft privileges.[6]

cards, safe-deposit boxes, discount brokerage services, wire transfers of funds between banks, financial advice, overdraft protection (for checking accounts), traveler's checks, and trusts.

Trusts are legal entities set up to hold and manage assets for a designated beneficiary. Funds in a trust are typically invested in stocks, bonds, real estate, and other investments (to be discussed in the next few chapters). Parents often use trusts to protect their children in the event of their death, especially when the children are too young to manage their own financial affairs.

Automatic teller machines have become a very popular service of commercial banks. Automatic teller machines (ATMs) enable customers to make deposits and withdraw cash 24 hours a day. Furthermore, through ATM networks such as CIRRUS, customers are able to use ATMs all over the country and, in some cases, all over the world. (We will discuss them in more detail later in the chapter.)

Young Americans Bank has an interesting approach to banking. It offers services to customers as young as 11 years old; these are explained in the Business Action.

Thrifts and Credit Unions

Institutions other than commercial banks can accept deposits from customers or members and provide some form of checking account. These other banking institutions include thrifts (savings and loan associations and savings banks), credit unions, and limited-service banks.

Savings and loan associations (S&Ls) and savings banks are sometimes referred to as thrifts. **Savings and loans** offer both savings and checking accounts and use the majority of their funds to make home mortgage loans to consumers. They and savings banks are often referred to as thrifts because they were created with the primary purpose of encouraging family thrift. Individual households could regularly place small amounts of money in these institutions and earn higher interest on their savings than they could in banks. (With deregulation this is no longer true.) The S&Ls would in turn lend this money to individual households for the purchase of homes. At one time, over 60 percent of all residential mortgages were originated by thrifts. Today, however, thrifts face serious financial problems.

Savings banks are also called mutual savings banks because they are depositor owned. They are almost identical to savings and loan associations in their operation and are chartered by the individual states. These banks originated in New England at the beginning of the 19th century. They were originally created to provide for the savings of households in New England and to pay interest on those savings (early U.S. banks did not provide interest-earning savings accounts). Often these banks were opened by members of a particular trade or guild, such as fishermen. While savings banks have existed for nearly 200 years in New England, they have not really caught on in other parts of the country. Today the 600 existing savings banks are primarily concentrated in the New England states, New York, and New Jersey.

A form of savings cooperative because they are member owned, **credit unions** are typically sponsored by a union, company, or professional or religious group. While credit unions have over 50 million members in the United

Trust
A legal entity set up to hold and manage assets for a designated beneficiary.

Savings and Loans
Institutions that now offer both checking and savings accounts and use the majority of their funds to finance home mortgages; sometimes called thrifts.

Savings Banks
Depositor-owned, banklike institutions that began in New England in the early 19th century with the purpose of paying interest on deposits.

Credit Unions
Member-owned savings cooperatives, normally sponsored by a union, company, or professional or religious group; typically concentrate on small, short-term consumer loans.

States, individual credit unions tend to be rather small. They have typically concentrated on savings and short-term consumer loans such as auto loans. However, with deregulation they have been able to expand their services and today offer share draft accounts (similar to checking accounts) and even provide some long-term mortgage loans.

Limited-Service Banks

Limited-service banks offer some services of banks, such as commercial loans and demand deposits; however, they cannot do both within the same organization. Perhaps the most recognizable of the limited-service banks is the Sears Roebuck Financial Network. Through acquisitions, Sears has developed a complete financial supermarket offering insurance, securities brokerage, and real estate services. With the addition of the Discover Card, it has also developed a significant consumer credit base. Sears expects this card to generate between $2 billion and $3 billion in additional revenues.[7]

Pushed by concerns expressed by commercial banks, Congress decided in 1987 to ban the formation of new limited-service banks and limit the growth of the existing ones. However, the trend toward their formation had already slowed by that time, as many did not achieve sufficient volume and consumers did not show the expected enthusiasm about "financial supermarkets."[8]

Nonbanking Financial Institutions

Financial institutions act as sources and users of funds. Given this fact, many institutions that do not provide banking services qualify as financial institutions. These include insurance companies, pension funds, large brokerage houses, and commercial and consumer finance companies.

Insurance companies Insurance companies were originally created by groups (such as trade unions and religious groups) who pooled their resources to provide some financial protection for members and families should the member become disabled or die. The first life insurance company in the United States, Presbyterian Ministers' Fund in Philadelphia, was established in 1759.

Today insurance companies accept premium payments from policyholders and provide various types of protection. (Insurance will be discussed in greater detail in Chapter Twenty.) Insurance companies use the funds generated through premium payments to provide long-term loans to corporations, to provide commercial real estate loans, and to purchase government bonds. Property and casualty insurance companies are regulated by states and operate in a similar fashion to life insurance companies.

Pension funds Pension funds can be set up by a company, union, or nonprofit organization to provide for the retirement needs of its members or employees. To meet these needs, the fund uses a pool of money created by contributions of the members, the employer, or both. They invest these funds in long-term mortgages on commercial property, business loans, government bonds, and common stock in major firms. In addition, company pension funds will typically invest a portion of the fund in the company's own stock.

State, local, and federal governments have set up pension funds for their employees. A very important public pension plan is social security (Old Age and Survivors Insurance Fund), which covers virtually all individuals employed in the private sector as well as disabled persons and children under 18 whose parents are deceased. The fund was originally set up to supplement individual savings and other pension funds as a means of support for retired persons. It is administered through the federal government and applies to most employees. The federal government collects social security funds from employers and deducts them from employee checks. These funds are used to pay benefits to the retired, the disabled, and young children of deceased parents.

The social security system recently faced a serious crisis. Concerned that the fund would not be sufficient to pay current benefits, the government increased social security taxes for both employees and employers. This action appears to have solved the immediate problem, as the fund now has a sizable surplus. However, many experts fear there will not be sufficient funds to pay future benefits.

The reason for this concern is the change in the makeup of the American work force. The average age of U.S. citizens is increasing and, with the current low birth rate, will continue to increase. As a result, the number of people requiring benefits (especially retirement benefits) is increasing, while the number of people contributing to the fund (working) is decreasing. This means that in the future fewer people will be paying into the social security fund and more people will be withdrawing funds from it. The result could be a serious shortfall.

Large brokerage houses   Brokerage firms buy and sell stocks, bonds, and other assets for their customers. They have also started to provide other financial services. Many brokerages have created accounts for their customers, such as Merrill Lynch's Cash Management Account and Paine Webber's Cash-Fund, which pay interest on deposits and allow clients to write checks, borrow money, and withdraw cash.

Commercial and consumer finance companies   By issuing commercial paper (large corporate promissory notes) or stocks and bonds, **finance companies** acquire funds. They use the funds to make loans appropriate to consumer and business needs. Finance companies typically charge a higher rate of interest because of the higher risk of the loans that they make. These companies also frequently require some sort of collateral for loans. Businesses may be required to pledge their inventory as security for the loan, and an individual may have to put up an automobile or some interest in stocks as security.

Finance Companies
Institutions that offer short-term loans, typically at a higher interest rate, to businesses and individuals unable to obtain loans elsewhere.

Commercial and consumer finance companies get the money they lend by selling bonds in their corporation and through loans from other corporations. In recent years, finance companies, such as Household Finance Corporation and General Motors Acceptance Corporation, have become increasingly competitive with commercial banks. They are now often able to offer attractive loans with longer-term paybacks.

As you can see, consumers have more choices for financial services than ever, and the choices are harder to make. Test your choice of bank and banking services with Connections.

● C o n n e c t i o n s

How Do Your Banking Choices Measure Up?

Directions: Assess your financial services by answering the following questions.[9] If you cannot answer them, ask your banker. Then review the feedback to determine what changes you might make in your banking practices.

Checking account:

1. What are the fees?
2. Must you maintain a minimum balance to avoid fees or to qualify for free services?
3. What does the monthly statement look like?
4. What does the bank charge for money orders or certified checks?

Interest-paying accounts:

1. How is interest calculated?
2. Are there any restrictions on withdrawals, such as only a certain number allowed each month or a fee after a certain number?
3. Can you write checks on the account? How many per month?

Credit cards:

1. What are the annual percentage rate and the annual fee?
2. What is the grace period on the card?
3. Does the card also function as a debit card?

Feedback: After reviewing the information that follows, think about changes you might consider in your banking choices. How will these changes benefit you?

Checking accounts:

Fees vary. If no minimum balance is required, you should pay no more than 20 cents a check and $5 per month. With a required-minimum-balance account, first figure how much interest you would earn if the minimum balance were invested. If

GOVERNMENT INVOLVEMENT IN MONEY AND BANKING

The federal government is very involved in money and banking in this country. It insures deposits in commercial banks and other banking institutions, regulates commercial banks and other banking and financial institutions, and through the Federal Reserve System controls the money supply and the flow of money through the banking system.

the interest you would earn is equal to or greater than the fees you would have to pay if you did not have the balance tied up, you may be better off paying the fees.

Balancing the checkbook at the end of every month is easier if the statement lists checks in numeric order rather than by date of receipt. Statements that summarize types of transactions are also helpful.

While the cost of money orders or certified checks may vary, money orders should not cost any more than you would have to pay at the currency exchange or the post office. Certified checks should run $3 to $6.

Interest-paying accounts:

For the saver, the best method for calculating interest is day of deposit to day of withdrawal. And the more often your interest is compounded, the higher the yield. Daily compounding is ideal.

Withdrawal restrictions can cause a problem for small savings accounts used as a backup to bill payments. Check for required minimum balances to avoid fees, and make sure the fees are reasonable.

Many more savings or interest-bearing accounts give checkwriting privileges. If the restrictions are not too great and your volume is not too high, many of these accounts make excellent alternatives to simple checking accounts.

Credit cards:

If you use your card a great deal and let your unpaid balance build up, you need a card with a lower rate of interest and no transaction fees. If you pay off your card every month, look for minimum annual fees and don't worry about the interest rate. Most banks allow a 25-day grace period before any interest is charged. Some charge interest from the day of purchase on the card. If you pay off your balance every month, look for a card with a grace period.

Debit cards, similar to credit cards, deduct funds directly from the customer's account rather than creating a loan. Once heralded as the new generation of plastic, they have not caught on nearly as well as expected. Part of the reason is the loss of the float, or the period between the time you write a check and the time the check clears your account. However, debit cards are accepted in many cases where checks would not be.

Insuring Bank Deposits

Before the creation of insurance funds, any bank failure resulted in almost all of the depositors losing whatever savings they had deposited with the bank. This problem was most apparent during the early years of the Depression. In 1933 nearly 4,000 banks collapsed, leaving hundreds of thousands of depositors without any way of recovering their savings. In many cases, this spelled financial ruin both for individuals and for businesses.

This sign, posted by the Federal Deposit Insurance Corporation, tells customers that the bank has failed and is now in the hands of the government. The bank will be closed until further notice. The FDIC took control of savings and loans and banks at an alarming rate during 1988–1990.

Dan Ford Connolly/Picture Group

On January 2, 1991, Governor Bruce Sundlum of Rhode Island closed 45 banks and credit unions covered by a private insurance fund. He decided that depositors would not be adequately protected from insolvency. The banks will not be able to be reopened until protected by federal deposit insurance.[10]

The Federal Deposit Insurance Corporation (FDIC) is responsible for protecting the deposits in banks. The FDIC provides $100,000 worth of insurance for depositor accounts and, perhaps more important, sets requirements for sound banking practices and regularly checks on banks to make sure these practices are being followed. Any commercial bank that is a member of the Federal Reserve System must also subscribe to the FDIC; most other banks have joined voluntarily. About 98 percent of all commercial banks are now insured by the FDIC. Up until 1989, similar protection was provided for depositors of most savings and loans by the Federal Savings and Loan Insurance Corporation (FSLIC). However, the responsibilities for protecting savings and loans have now passed to the FDIC, as Table 17.2 explains.

Certainly, as Table 17.2 outlines, the United States faces a huge cost from the 1980s savings and loan disaster. Some refer to the debacle as the case of the missing "megabillions." One expert believes that comments about the money being stolen or fraudulently invested are wrong; instead, the reasons for the insolvency of so many savings and loans are bad judgment, stupid decisions, and desperate dealing.[11] The events presented in Table 17.2 suggest that, although complaints about government involvement in financial institutions abound, there apparently was not enough supervision to prevent the massive losses. The lack of proper supervision, plus poor decision making, occasional fraud, and economic collapses, all add up to problems that must be solved as soon as possible.[12]

TABLE 17.2

The Savings and Loan Disaster

For nearly a century, risk was a four-letter word at savings and loans. The business consisted mostly of taking deposits at low, fixed rates and making mortgages to homeowners. Losses were rare. But all that changed in the 1980s.

1980–1982   Congress begins phasing out interest rate limits, allowing banks and S&Ls to offer new savings accounts that compete with market interest rates. Federal deposit insurance is boosted to $100,000 from $40,000. Money that flowed out of S&Ls in 1980, when deposit rates were capped at 5.5 percent, begins flowing back. But paying higher interest rates on the new deposits costs more than S&Ls can earn on old, fixed-rate mortgages made in the 60s and 70s at rates as low as 5 percent. Result: billions of dollars in losses.

As the losses spread, hundreds of S&Ls fail in the first wave of industry trouble. Congress passes the landmark Garn–St Germain deregulation bill, allowing S&Ls to enter new lending areas and make adjustable-rate loans.

Mid–1980s   S&Ls lend billions of dollars for office buildings, apartments, and other projects in the booming Southwest. Many S&Ls are after profits to make up for the low rates on old 30-year mortgages they're still stuck with. Many other S&Ls are bought or started by unscrupulous operators. Now that interest rate controls are gone, operators discover they can use federal deposit insurance to attract billions of dollars in deposits at high rates. Once they get the money, S&L owners invest much of it recklessly.

1986   Texas's economy collapses as oil prices plunge. Wild lending that resulted in overbuilding adds to the problem. Developers can't rent finished office towers and apartment buildings, and they default on their loans. S&Ls take over the properties, which now are worth only a fraction of what they cost to build. The soured deals drag S&Ls into insolvency. The FSLIC, its capital depleted by earlier S&L failures, is forced to allow broke S&Ls to stay open.

1988   Regulators begin to tackle the crisis and realize a federal bailout of massive proportions is needed. And bailout costs will be heavy. Estimates indicate costs to taxpayers could run as high as $250 billion, or about $1,000 for every man, woman, and child in this country.

1989   The FSLIC loses solvency, and its functions are taken over by the FDIC. The bill for cleaning up the S&L mess is turned over to Resolution Trust Corporation and will be primarily paid by taxpayers.

1990   Estimates of the bailout run as high as $500 billion, or about $2,000 for every man, woman, and child in the United States. Money needed to cover losses is estimated to be $140 billion to $180 billion. Interest expense and the extra cost of a recession can add another $300 billion–plus.

Source: *USA Today,* February 14, 1989, p. 4B; May 29, 1990, p. 2B. Copyright, USA TODAY. Reprinted with permission.

As mentioned above, FDIC insurance is limited to $100,000 for any depositor. However, accounts in different banks are separately and fully protected; so the number of $100,000 deposits that can be fully protected in different banks is unlimited. Joint accounts, opened by one person in combination with another person or persons, are all eligible for insurance coverage, even when opened in the same bank.

The National Credit Union Association (NCUA) insures deposits for federally chartered credit unions. In addition to providing insurance, the FDIC and NCUA also set requirements for sound banking practices. Compliance is controlled through the use of *bank examiners*. These trained representatives of the enforcement agency regularly inspect the financial records and management practices of the financial institutions. Inspections are unannounced and occur at least once a year. Examinations almost always take at least a week to complete and may take up to several months.

Key Bank of Central New York has met any bank examiner's criteria of success. No giant, it ranks only 184th in assets among American banks.[13] Key grew in size by buying up failed or failing savings and loan banks in Wyoming, Idaho, Washington, and Alaska. Key imposed rigorous financial controls over the banks it bought; it avoided making loans to corporations involved in large real estate development deals; and it is a well-managed bank. These characteristics have resulted in a profitable bank that is able to pay managers bonuses because they are linked to earnings, which are improving each year.

Examiners look at the ability of the bank's management, level of earnings, sources of earnings, adequacy of loan security, capital, and the current level of liquidity. A bank with serious problems in one or more of these areas will be included on a "problem list." These banks are seen as candidates for failure unless problems are corrected. Examiners discuss the nature of the problems and potential actions with the management of the bank, and more frequent examinations are scheduled to ensure compliance with the examiners' recommendations.

While bank and thrift failures have been rare events since the institution of bank regulations in the 1930s, the number of failures has been rising in recent years at an alarming rate (see Table 17.3). The potential failure of a bank or savings and loan is a serious matter. It requires a swift, direct response by the appropriate government agencies. Figure 17.3 outlines the steps followed in the case of a potential bank failure.

TABLE 17.3

Bank Failures Are Increasing

Year	Failed Banks	
	Total Number	**Total Assets ($ in millions)**
1989	207	na
1988	221	na
1987	184	$6,900
1986	138	7,000
1985	116	2,800
1984	78	2,800
1983	48	4,100

Note: na = Not available.

Source: FDIC reports, 1988; *USA Today*, May 29, 1990, p. 1B. Copyright, USA TODAY. Reprinted with permission.

Often depositors will not even be aware of the bank failure. It used to take a whole week to shut down a bank. Now a federal team armed with computers can go in on a Thursday night, work feverishly through the night, and reopen the bank under new management on Friday with no interruption in service.[14]

The downturns in the economies in several states, especially those with a heavy dependence on oil (e.g., Texas, Oklahoma), have increased the number of banks that are candidates for failure. Based on recent data, a total of 540 banks nationally could fail—249 in Texas alone.[15]

In the past, many state-chartered thrifts opted for private insurance programs; these offered more freedom from federal regulation and an opportunity to grow more rapidly. However, the near-collapse in 1985 of Home State Savings Bank of Cincinnati and 102 savings and loan associations insured by the private Maryland-Share Insurance Corporation and the resulting actions taken by the governors of the two states resulted in thousands of depositors withdrawing their funds from privately insured thrifts. As a result, many of the privately insured thrifts have chosen to seek federal insurance.

Deregulation of the Banking Industry

Prior to 1981, the banking industry was highly regulated. The role played by each of the financial institutions within the system was clearly defined. Commercial banks were the only institutions allowed to offer demand deposit accounts. Savings banks and savings and loan associations offered home mortgage loans, and credit unions offered their members savings accounts and

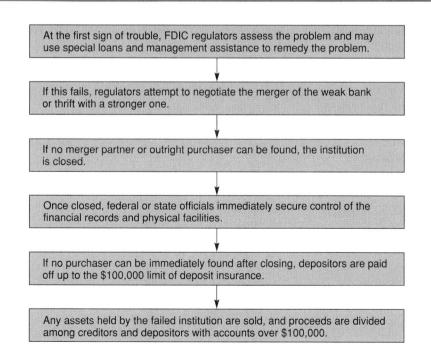

FIGURE 17.3

Steps Taken in Potential Bank Failure

At the first sign of trouble, FDIC regulators assess the problem and may use special loans and management assistance to remedy the problem.

If this fails, regulators attempt to negotiate the merger of the weak bank or thrift with a stronger one.

If no merger partner or outright purchaser can be found, the institution is closed.

Once closed, federal or state officials immediately secure control of the financial records and physical facilities.

If no purchaser can be immediately found after closing, depositors are paid off up to the $100,000 limit of deposit insurance.

Any assets held by the failed institution are sold, and proceeds are divided among creditors and depositors with accounts over $100,000.

short-term consumer loans. The government even regulated the amount of interest each institution could pay on savings accounts.

With the high inflation of the late 1970s, this system began to fall apart. Depositors, seeking higher interest rates, began to move their deposits to money market mutual funds and other higher-yielding investments. Since the government dictated interest rates, banks could not respond to this threat. Pressure brought by the banks and thrifts resulted in a deregulation of the banking industry, and, while this did increase the competition among different types of financial institutions, it also blurred the differences between them.

The primary deregulation legislation was the Depository Institution Deregulation and Monetary Control Act (DIDMCA) of 1980. It permitted all deposit institutions to offer checking accounts; expanded the lending powers of thrifts to nonmortgage loans, increasing the competition between commercial banks and thrifts; allowed credit unions to make mortgage loans; and eliminated the interest ceilings on all types of deposits.

The intent of DIDMCA was to increase competition among financial institutions. It did throw many of the small thrifts into a competitive environment. The number of savings and loans declined from 4,600 in 1980 to less than 3,000 in 1989. DIDMCA also increased the amount of control the Federal Reserve System had over all financial institutions.

Federal Reserve System

Federal Reserve System
Term used to refer to the Federal Reserve Bank, the central bank of the United States. Generally referred to as the Fed.

The base of the commercial banking system in the United States is the *Federal Reserve System* (generally referred to as simply the Fed). The **Federal Reserve System**—the central bank of the United States—was established by Congress in the Federal Reserve Act of 1913 to control the nation's money supply.

The Fed was originally created to help eliminate the problems brought on the economy by bank panics.[16] Since banks do not hold the deposits of their customers but rather lend these deposits out to other customers of the bank in order to earn interest, the banks are capable of giving only a small percentage of their depositors the funds in their account at any given time. When a number of depositors demand their money at one time, it creates a problem for the bank. The bank has to borrow the needed funds from other banks.

If the depositors of many banks demand their money, the bank faces a panic. That is, the bank would have to close its doors until the needed funds could be collected from the borrowers. Panics can result in the failure of commercial banks and can have devastating effects on the national economy. Between the Civil War and 1907, four economic depressions in the United States began with bank panics. After the depression of 1907, Congress appointed a commission to study the problems of the banking system and recommend changes. The result of this study was the foundation of the Federal Reserve System in 1913.

The Federal Reserve System is a network of 12 district banks (Figure 17.4) supervised by a board of governors. This board, the Federal Reserve Board, has seven members, appointed by the president of the United States with the advice and consent of the Senate. Because members serve 14-year terms, with one member's term expiring every two years, political control is minimized. Theoretically no president should control the appointment of more than a few members of the board (although retirements and deaths can change this). The president does, however, appoint the chairman of the Federal Reserve Board

Federal Reserve Bank Districts and Branches   **FIGURE 17.4**

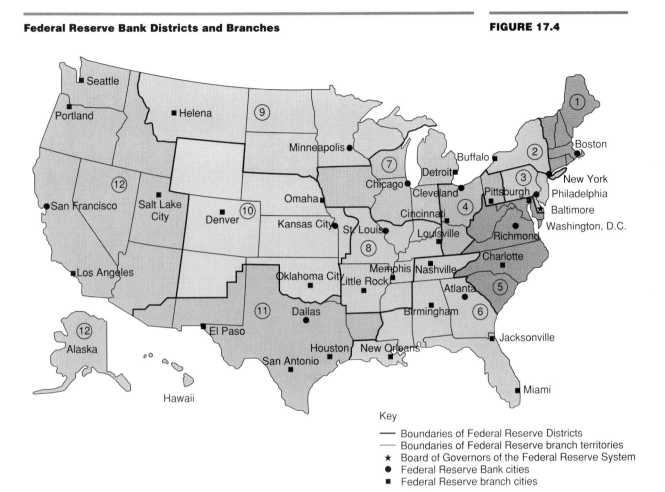

Key

— Boundaries of Federal Reserve Districts
— Boundaries of Federal Reserve branch territories
★ Board of Governors of the Federal Reserve System
● Federal Reserve Bank cities
■ Federal Reserve branch cities

every four years. Therefore the president controls the appointment of the most influential member of the board.

The Fed provides general direction to the 12 Federal Reserve district banks, and it has the power to audit district bank books and coordinate their operations in the public interest. In addition, the Fed has considerable power to control the money supply. This power is discussed in the section on monetary policies later in this chapter.

The organization of the Federal Reserve revolves around the 12 bank districts, each with a Federal Reserve Bank (FRB). These banks are owned by the member commercial banks in that district. Each FRB has nine directors. Three are appointed by the board of governors; the member commercial banks elect three to represent banks and three to represent businesses.

In addition to the board of governors, the Fed has a Federal Advisory Council. This council is comprised of 12 members, 1 from each of the Federal Reserve banks. The council advises the board of governors on policies of the Fed.

The headquarters of the Federal Reserve Bank system is in Washington, D.C. Inside the Federal Reserve Building the policies, procedures, and programs of all Federal Reserve districts are reviewed, monitored, and supervised.

Courtesy of the Board of Governors of the Federal Reserve System

Another element of the Fed is the Federal Open Market Committee (FOMC). The FOMC consists of the seven members of the board of governors plus five Federal Reserve Bank representatives. This committee sets the Fed's open market policies, which are discussed later in this chapter.

The Federal Reserve performs several major functions: it manages regional and national check clearing procedures; it controls the money supply through control of the reserve requirement, open market operations, and control of the discount rate; it regulates commercial banks; it supervises the federal deposit insurance of financial institutions belonging to the Federal Reserve System; and it provides services to the U.S. Treasury.

Check clearing   The Federal Reserve provides national check clearing. The Federal Reserve clearinghouse handles almost all checks drawn on a bank in one city and presented for deposit to a bank in another city. Not all checks, however, are cleared through the Fed. Small banks in rural areas pay larger banks to provide the check clearing service for them. Also, commercial banks have their own system for clearing checks written and deposited within the same city. However, checks that involve more than one Federal Reserve district are handled by the Fed. Figure 17.5 illustrates how a check is cleared through the Federal Reserve System.

Monetary policies   The Fed controls the size of the money supply, both M_1 (currency and demand deposits) and M_2 (time deposits and money market accounts). Though the primary focus traditionally has been on M_1, the Fed has

The Path of a Check in the Fed

FIGURE 17.5

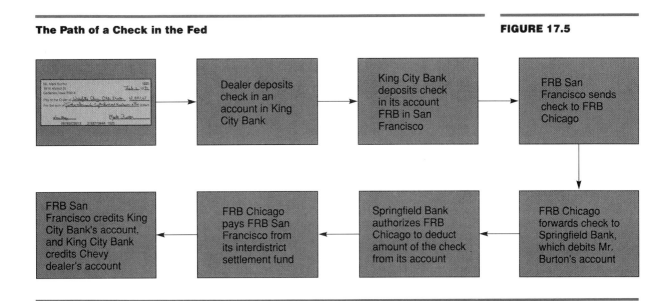

recently found that the size of M_2 and its effect on the money supply are more predictable.[17] The tools the Fed uses to control the money supply include control of the reserve requirement, open market operations, and control of the discount rate.

Reserve requirement   Each time you deposit money in your account at the bank, the bank is allowed to lend that money out to someone else. The amount lent out, however, does not equal the amount you deposited. The bank must keep a prescribed amount on hand as **reserve.** The Federal Reserve dictates the reserve requirement. Lowering or raising it can very significantly affect the money supply.

If you deposit $100 in your bank and the reserve requirement is 10 percent, your bank holds $10 in reserve and lends out the rest. If the $90 lent out is deposited in another bank, that bank keeps $9 as reserve and lends out $81. This continues until all the funds are used. If full expansion were reached, the $100 you deposited would expand the money supply by $1,000. We compute this effect by dividing new deposit dollars by reserve requirement. So, if the reserve requirement were 5 percent, a new deposit of $100 would expand the money supply by $2,000 ($100 ÷ 5 percent).

Because of its dramatic effect on the money supply and because such a dramatic move will be discussed in the news and may send shock waves through corporations and Wall Street, the Fed rarely uses adjustments in the reserve requirement to regulate the money supply.

Open market operations   Open market operations are conducted by the Federal Open Market Committee. The FOMC consists of the seven members of the board of governors, plus five federal bank presidents. The FOMC uses savings bonds, Treasury notes, and Treasury bills—the financial obligations of

Reserve
The percentage of money from deposits that a bank must keep on hand or on deposit in the Federal Reserve Bank. Funds above this amount can be loaned out.

the federal government—to expand or contract the money supply. Open market operations involve the sale or purchase of these securities.

If the FOMC decides to purchase Treasury bills, Treasury notes, or savings bonds on the open market, the cash used to purchase these is a new infusion of cash; it expands the money supply. If the FOMC decides to sell these securities on the open market, the money used by individual investors to purchase these is removed from the money supply and held by the Fed. The actual buying and selling of securities takes place between the Federal Reserve Bank of New York, on behalf of the system, and a few dozen large dealers in bonds. Open market operations are the most widely and most regularly used of the three methods for controlling money supply.

Discount Rate
The rate of interest charged to member banks when they borrow money from the Fed.

Discount rate   The rate of interest charged to member banks to borrow funds from the Fed is called the **discount rate.** Each FRB sets its own discount rate, with the approval of the board of governors. Raising the discount rate makes member banks less willing to borrow and causes them to increase the interest rate they charge their borrowers. This in turn reduces the tendency of bank customers to borrow and results in a reduction in the money supply. Lowering the discount rate has the opposite effect.

Perhaps the most important impact of the discount rate, however, is that changes in it gain a great deal of national attention. It signals how the Fed feels about the economy in general and what its future policy is likely to be relative to the money supply. Many businesspeople consider the discount rate as a strong indicator of economic conditions.[18]

Supervising banks   The Fed is responsible for regulating commercial banks. It approves requests to open a branch or merge with another bank, enforces regulations, and admits banks to membership within the system. Each of the 12 Federal Reserve Banks examines member banks in its district.

Depository insurance   The Federal Reserve Board also supervises the three federal depository insurance agencies: the Federal Deposit Insurance Corporation, the Federal Savings and Loan Insurance Corporation, and the National Credit Union Administration. As indicated earlier in this chapter, recent occurrences in the savings and loan industry have made this an extremely important function of the Fed.

Services to the Treasury   The Fed is really the U.S. government bank. In addition to its other functions, it provides a number of services to the U.S. Treasury and to the public:

- The FRBs physically house much of the coins and paper money in circulation. They provide for the movement of paper money and coins throughout the nation and also remove worn and damaged currency from the system.
- The Fed takes care of all paperwork involved when the government sells securities such as savings bonds, Treasury bills, and other government securities.
- The Fed holds the legally required reserve accounts of member banks and acts generally as a bank for banks.
- The Fed makes sure that state member banks comply with consumer protection regulations.

THE FUTURE OF BANKING

The future of banking will develop around three important areas: (1) technological innovation and its impact on banking, (2) the further development of interstate, regional, and possibly national banks in this country, and (3) the changing impact of the world banking community.

Technological Impacts: Electronic Funds Transfer

The impact of technology on banking will be far-reaching. Some key areas developing very rapidly involve electronic funds transfer. **Electronic funds transfer (EFT)** is the transfer of funds by means of an electronic terminal, telephone, computer, or magnetic tape that orders a bank or other financial institution to debit (reduce) or credit (increase) an account. Areas showing the most promise for EFT use include automatic teller machines (ATMs), automated clearinghouses (ACHs), point-of-sale (POS) systems with the use of debit cards, and in-home banking.

Automated teller machines (ATMs) were relatively slow to catch on. Early ATMs broke down frequently, and customers were reluctant to trust the machines. They worried that their account would get charged but the money wouldn't come out, or that a deposit they made wouldn't get credited. However, because of their convenience and improved reliability and because we are growing more accustomed to dealing with machines, ATMs have become extremely popular (see Figure 17.6). There are about 75,000 ATMs in the United States.

ATMs dispense cash, accept deposits, transfer funds from one account to another, and display a customer's account balance. They provide 24-hour service, and with the expansion of ATM networks, customers of member banks

Electronic Funds Transfer (EFT)
The transfer of funds by means of an electronic terminal, telephone, computer, or magnetic tape that orders a bank or other financial institution to debit or credit an account.

Automated Teller Machine (ATM)
Machine that dispenses cash from a customer's account, accepts deposits to the account, or performs other banking functions.

FIGURE 17.6

Increases in ATM Usage

The ATM explosion

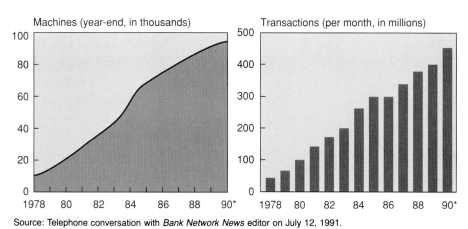

Machines (year-end, in thousands)

Transactions (per month, in millions)

Source: Telephone conversation with *Bank Network News* editor on July 12, 1991.

The automatic teller machine (ATM) provides instant money to these customers. As people become more comfortable with ATMs, they are using this system of obtaining cash more often. Of course, the person's account must have a balance sufficient to provide the money that is requested.

The Image Works

can use ATMs nationwide, always having access to their bank funds. About three quarters of America's ATMs are linked into a single network. Any of the 300 million cards issued by banks belonging to the network work at member banks' ATMs.[19]

To use an ATM, the customer inserts a plastic card supplied by the bank and then punches in a personal identification number (PIN). To access the account, the customer needs both the card and the PIN. This helps protect the customer who loses the card.

ATMs help reduce transaction costs for banks as well as providing convenience for bank customers. Each teller transaction costs a bank an estimated 50 cents; each ATM transaction only costs about 20 cents.[20] ATMs are now available in shopping malls, supermarkets, student centers, airports, and just about every other public place.

Automated clearinghouses (ACHs) allow payments or withdrawals to and from a bank account by magnetic computer tape. Employers use ACHs to

Automated Clearinghouse (ACH)
An automated clearinghouse allows payments or withdrawals to and from a bank account by magnetic computer tape.

make payroll withdrawals and to transfer employee pay directly to employee accounts. ACHs are also becoming popular with utilities such as telephone and electric companies, who sign customers up to have their bills deducted directly from their checking accounts. The federal government is the largest ACH system user; over 50 percent of all social security payments are made through this system. However, ACH systems are expensive to implement and therefore are only efficient for large batch processing.

Point-of-sale (POS) systems, along with electronic fund transfers, allow merchants to draw money directly from a customer's bank account at the time a purchase is made. These systems work through the use of a debit card. The **debit card** is very similar to a credit card except that the card does not create a loan but rather transfers funds from the customer's account to the merchant's account. Both the customer and the retail store must belong to the same bank or bank network, and the retailer must have a POS terminal.

Point-of-Sale (POS) System
Point-of-sale system, along with EFT, allows merchants to draw money directly from a customer's bank account at the time a purchase is made.

When the customer makes a purchase using this system, the cashier enters the debit card on the POS terminal. If sufficient funds are in the customer's account, the money automatically transfers to the retailer's account through an EFT. The transaction is then complete.

Debit Card
A plastic card, similar to a credit card, that deducts funds directly from the customer's account rather than creating a loan.

POS systems help reduce check processing costs and the problem of bad checks. They also help with security, since less funds need to be kept on hand in the store.

In-home banking is gradually developing in this country as more and more homes become equipped with computers. To this point in time, the consumer response has not been overwhelming. Bank customers have been reluctant to pay a monthly charge for a service that cannot accept deposits or dispense cash. Primary interest has been shown by business travelers and businesses.[21] However, as more innovative services become available, and with the possible tie-in with cable shopping networks, home banking may take hold in the future.

Interstate Banking

The 1927 Pepper-McFadden Act prohibited banks from having offices in more than one state unless authorized by state law. It also required that banks adhere to the branch banking laws of the states in which they operate. Since some states do not even permit branch banking within the same city, this law greatly restricted bank growth.

In June 1985, the U.S. Supreme Court ruled that interstate banking within regions (e.g., New England, the Southeast) should be allowed. This would be controlled by the states themselves, which would have to make mutually acceptable agreements that let banks in each region merge across state lines. Today, 45 of the 50 states, plus the District of Columbia, have enacted laws permitting some form of interstate banking. Furthermore, the problems faced by banks in certain economically depressed areas have caused the FDIC to allow banks from other regions to buy weakened banks in order to protect the troubled banks' depositors.[22]

As a result, a number of *superregionals* have developed in different regions of the country. Banks such as Banc One in Ohio, NCNB in North Carolina, and PNC Financial in Pennsylvania are operating across state lines. NCNB has

NCNB: Superregional and Growing

The Federal Deposit Insurance Corporation auctioned off First Republic Bank in 1988. NCNB (a Charlotte, North Carolina, bank) offered $700 million more than the next bidder. The FDIC agreed to take responsibility for most of First Republic's bad loans, and NCNB was in business. Hugh McColl, president of NCNB, then proceeded to buy 18 other Texas savings and loans and banks. Now NCNB is the largest bank in Texas and the seventh largest in the United States.

NCNB is a superregional bank that is buying assets at bargain prices. McColl has a reputation of being a bargain hunter and a bold, aggressive banker. Seeing growth as the only way to survive, he has adopted a motto, "Buy or be bought." NCNB's strategy is to become dominant in the South, especially in the Sunbelt states.

In Texas there has been a backlash to McColl and NCNB. Texas businesspeople have pegged the man and his bank as out-of-state interlopers; they claim NCNB stands for "No Cash for Nobody." However, McColl believes NCNB is on the right track in Texas, that NCNB Texas is just a prudent and cautious lender. The bank made over $2.2 billion in new loans in 1989.

The superregional bank hasn't stopped growing and overcoming complaints. One idea bouncing around is that NCNB will merge with another giant bank or a company with special talents in investment banking. Hugh McColl sees takeovers, mergers, and bold growth as the course for NCNB. So far, North Carolina, South Carolina, Florida, and Texas know that when Hugh McColl speaks, everyone listens.

This banker does not sit around waiting for someone to help him do the job. His go-go attitude and behavior have made NCNB a strong superregional bank, a growth company in a sluggish industry.[23]

NCNB Statistics

Headquarters: Charlotte, North Carolina
Assets: $66.2 billion
Employees: 27,000
Coverage: 800 banking offices in seven states
Services: Consumer banking, corporate banking, investment banking, real estate loans, securities brokerage, trust and investment management

---

acquired a reputation as a growth-oriented superregional. As the Business Action suggests, the driving force behind NCNB's growth is Hugh McColl, the bank's president. He is an aggressive and bold banker who plans to beat competitors.

With regional banking possible, national commercial banking may not be too far in the future. A number of factors point to this. First, firms such as American Express and Merrill Lynch are not subject to the same restrictions as the commercial banks. Since deregulation has enabled these companies to offer checking accounts and banking services on a nationwide basis, we currently have the equivalent of national banking. Second, as a nation, we are still very mobile. On average, one out of every six families will move in any year. National banking would provide greater convenience to these customers. Finally, the disasters in the banking industry in Texas and Oklahoma brought about by the drop in the oil business indicate the need to have banks less concentrated in areas where a single industry dominates. A broader base would have helped many of the Texas and Oklahoma banks.

World Banking Community

As indicated in Table 17.4, of the 15 largest banks in the world, only 1—Citicorp—is a U.S. bank. In fact, the top 10 banks in the world (based on value of assets) are Japanese. While our focus has been on banking in this country, banking and finance obviously are global, not local, issues.

TABLE 17.4

Fifteen Largest Banks in the World

Rank	Bank	City	1990 Assets ($ in billions)
1	Dai-Ichi Kangyo Bank	Tokyo	$428.2
2	Sumitomo Bank	Osaka	409.2
3	Mitsui Taiyo Kobe Bank	Tokyo	408.8
4	Sanwa Bank	Osaka	402.7
5	Fuji Bank	Tokyo	399.5
6	Mitsubishi Bank	Tokyo	391.5
7	Credit Agricole Mutuel	Paris	305.2
8	Banque Nationale de Paris	Paris	291.9
9	Industrial Bank of Japan	Tokyo	290.1
10	Credit Lyonnais	Paris	287.3
11	Deutsche Bank	Frankfurt	266.3
12	Barclays PLC	London	259.0
13	Tokai Bank	Nagoya	249.8
14	Norinchukin Bank	Tokyo	249.7
15	Mitsubishi Trust	Tokyo	237.7

Source: *American Banker,* July 17, 1991; reprinted with permission from *American Banker.*

Sanwa Bank focuses its advertising on helping customers achieve their goals. The Japanese banking community has become a powerful force around the world.

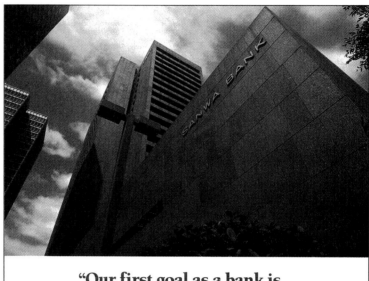

"Our first goal as a bank is to help our customers meet theirs."

New products, markets, and opportunities
The world of finance is changing as never before. Each day brings new products. New markets. New opportunities.
But can you harness these changes to meet *your* evolving needs?

Our multimarket capabilities can help
The Sanwa Bank can help.

With our vast resources, global presence, and comprehensive financial services, we can create the products you need. Uncover opportunities you overlook.
And put you on top of the world's financial markets as never before.

Visit Sanwa today. You'll be one step closer to your business goals.

The Sanwa Bank, Limited
Sanwa Bank California

Courtesy of Sanwa Bank

Any decisions made within the U.S. economy have an impact on the world economy. If the Fed decides to lower the interest rate, foreign investors can withdraw their money and invest it in banks in other countries with higher rates. Bankers look for the maximum return on their money. For this reason, they do not tend to be nationalistic in their business decisions, which causes the banking market to become more and more global.

Many of the financial difficulties faced by major banks in this country arose in part from international occurrences. First, the large U.S. banks' investments in Third World economies for the development of oil and natural resources went sour; the oil markets fell, and many of the nations were unable to pay off these debts. Second, aggressive foreign lenders have lured away many U.S. corporate borrowers; they now lend about $4 to U.S. companies for every $10 lent by U.S. banks.[24]

Certainly, as detente continues and as previously unopened markets such as the Soviet Union, China, and Eastern Europe open up, global financing will expand even more. The formalization and lifting of trade restrictions in the European Community in 1992 will lead to more intense competition. We now face a world economy financed by international banks. American banks are just one more player in this arena—an important player, but one that must more completely understand its role in a world economy and the importance of consumers. American bankers need to compete with international banks and to win more business with smarter marketing, packages of products, and service.[25]

You'll Know It's the 21st **Century When . . .**

You Buy Insurance at Your Bank

L. William Seidman, chairman of the Federal Deposit Insurance Corporation, predicted in *Fortune* that by 2000, S&Ls may have vanished as a breed along with large numbers of commercial banks. Where to get a home mortgage or business loan? At the "universal" bank that offers traditional banking services, but also sells insurance and securities. The forces driving this dramatic change from the old world of banking are—no surprise—global: Europe 1992 will operate on the basis of universal banking, and so will Japan, where the trend to deregulation and fewer, more all-purpose banks gathered force in the early 1990s.[26]

SUMMARY OF LEARNING OBJECTIVES

1. To define *money* and state its functions and characteristics.
   Money is anything that is commonly accepted as a means of paying for the goods and services individuals need and want. The three basic functions of money are that it serves as a medium of exchange, making it possible for two individuals to exchange without having to barter; as a measure of relative value, allowing two dissimilar items to be purchased on a similar basis; and as a store of value, making it possible for us to hold the value over time. The desirable characteristics of money are acceptance, divisibility, portability, durability, stability, and scarcity.

2. To identify the elements that make up both the M_1 and M_2 money supplies.
   The M_1 money supply consists of the most liquid forms of money. M_1 includes currency (including cashier's checks, traveler's checks, and money orders) and demand deposits. The M_2 money supply consists of all of the elements of M_1 plus time deposits and money market accounts.

3. To compare the different types of financial institutions.
   The primary types of financial institutions are *banking institutions,* consisting of commercial banks, savings and loans, savings banks, and credit unions, and *nonbanking institutions,* such as insurance companies, pension funds, brokerage houses, and commercial and consumer finance

companies. Before deregulation, the differences between the banking institutions were clear and their functions distinct; now the differences are not as significant. All of them offer some type of demand deposits, and all can handle most types of loans. Nonbanking institutions, while acting as sources and users of funds, do not perform major banking services.

4. To explain how the federal government is involved in money and banking in the United States.
The federal government insures bank deposits for up to $100,000 through the Federal Deposit Insurance Corporation; the National Credit Union Association insures deposits for federally chartered credit unions. The federal government has also regulated the types of accounts financial institutions can offer and the amount of interest institutions could pay in savings accounts. Deregulation has eliminated the interest ceilings on all types of deposits and has permitted all deposit institutions to offer checking accounts. Finally, the Federal Reserve System was established by Congress in 1913 to manage regional and national check clearing procedures, to control the money supply with monetary policy, to regulate commercial banks, to supervise the federal deposit insurance of institutions belonging to the Federal Reserve System, and to provide services for the U.S. Treasury.

5. To discuss how the Federal Reserve System controls the supply of money and credit.
The Fed controls the money supply and credit primarily through control of the reserve requirement, open market operations, and control of the discount rate. The *reserve requirement* is the percentage of deposits a bank must keep on hand. Due to the deposit multiplier effect, changes in the reserve requirement can have extreme effects on the money supply; therefore the Fed rarely uses this tool. It does use *open market operations*—that is, buying or selling government securities on the open market to expand or contract the money supply. The final tool of the Fed is the *discount rate,* the rate banks must pay to borrow money from the Fed. By raising the discount rate, the Fed can discourage banks from borrowing and therefore from lending money, thus slowing the rate of expansion. By lowering the discount rate, the Fed can have the opposite effect. This tool, like changes in the reserve requirement, is rarely used to conduct money policy.

6. To identify the major changes occurring in banking and the impact of technology.
Deregulation has enabled a broad range of financial institutions to provide banking services. Technology is impacting banking through electronic funds transfers in the form of automatic teller machines, automated clearinghouses, point-of-sale systems, and in-home banking. Banks have been given the right to expand across state borders within regions, and national banking may occur in the near future. Finally, the role of foreign banks is becoming more significant, not only on the world market but also on the domestic market in the United States.

KEY TERMS

Money, p. 600

Liquidity, p. 603

M_1, p. 604

Currency, p. 604

Demand Deposit, p. 604

M_2, p. 605

Time Deposit, p. 605

Money Market Accounts, p. 605

Commercial Bank, p. 607

Trust, p. 609

Savings and Loans, p. 609

Savings Banks, p. 609

Credit Union, p. 609

Finance Companies, p. 611

Federal Reserve System, p. 618

Reserve, p. 621

Discount Rate, p. 622

Electronic Funds Transfer (EFT), p. 623

Automated Teller Machine (ATM), p. 623

Automated Clearinghouse (ACH), p. 624

Point-of-Sale (POS) System, p. 625

Debit Card, p. 625

QUESTIONS FOR DISCUSSION AND REVIEW

1. What is money? Why is it important for an efficient economic system? Give an example of how exchanges would occur if money were not available.

2. Explain how money functions as a medium of exchange and a measure of relative value. What are the advantages and disadvantages of using money as a store of value?

3. List the desirable characteristics of money. Why is each important to the usefulness of money within an economic system?

4. Many small governments have been overturned because they were unable to maintain a stable value for their money. Why is stable value so important? How could the lack of stability cause a revolt?

5. What is the difference between demand deposits and time deposits? Why are checks the most used method of paying for exchanges? Do you think they will remain as the most useful and frequently used method of payment?

6. What are limited-service banks, and why were commercial banks concerned about these institutions?

7. Explain how the various deposit insurance funds work. If a bank were in trouble, would the Fed immediately go to payment out of the insurance funds? If not, what steps would the Fed first take?

8. What were the primary provisions of the banking act of 1980? What effect have these had on commercial banking?

9. You have been elected as chairman of the Federal Reserve board of governors. Recently you have noticed that inflation is rising; you fear that the money supply might be expanding too fast. What actions might you take to alleviate this problem? Which actions would be most appropriate to take first?

10. Identify the major changes occurring in banking at this time. How will these changes affect the future of banking? How do you think a bank will operate in A.D. 2010? Do you think that U.S. banks need to become more active in the world financial market?

CASE 17.1
Monday Morning Quarterbacking: How to Regulate?

Oh, the loans that tiny Republic Bank for Savings made—at your expense! Like lending $650,000 of federally insured deposits to the owners of a $22-a-night motel and bingo parlor in Longview, Texas—two states away from Mississippi. Republic Bank president Philip Shunk never visited the property. And not a dime was repaid.

"They probably shouldn't have made the loan," admits one of the owners of the motel in an interview. "They should have stayed closer to home."

Instead, Republic Bank lent the motel another $25,000 three months later. That was not repaid either.

Bad loans such as these—thousands of them across the United States—have dragged the savings and loan industry into an estimated $500 billion hole that the Federal Savings and Loan Insurance Corporation doesn't have the money to fill. Loans suffering from insufficient analyses, shoddy reference checking, and poor decisions can accumulate, and suddenly an S&L finds itself in trouble. This has happened much too frequently across the United States.

Republic Bank was the typical S&L failure: a sleepy little S&L turned into a freewheeling lender making loans far beyond its management's experience. Republic, headquartered in Iuka, Mississippi (population 2,800), had just $15 million in deposits until Louisiana investor John Martin Marron bought it in 1984. Marron moved the S&L to the state capitol in Jackson, Mississippi, and, like many S&Ls in those go-go years, began offering high interest rates to attract money. Deposits swelled to $85 million. The S&L built a fancy new headquarters with Greek pillars and an electric sign. Employees conducted business on antique furniture acquired, ironically, from a failed Texas bank. Foolish loans quickly mounted. In its first three months in Jackson, Republic Bank loaned $11 million—an extraordinary amount for an S&L its size.

"We ordered them not to do things," says regulator George Barclay, head of the Federal Home Loan Bank of Dallas. "They boldly defied our instructions."

Last July, regulators seized Republic Bank. A bailout will cost at least $36 million. Marron and Shunk couldn't be reached for comment.

By the way, the motel was repossessed by another creditor, who had been smart enough to get the motel as collateral, something Republic Bank failed to do. The owners of the motel are being sued by the FSLIC.

Questions for Discussion
1. What steps should the regulating agencies have taken to avoid this failure and the hundreds of others like it?

Adapted from Gary Hector, "S&Ls: Where Did All Those Billions Go?" *Fortune,* September 10, 1990, pp. 82–88; "Broke S&L Gave Away More than a Toaster," *USA Today,* February 13, 1989, p. 2A.

2. Much of the problem was originally created by regulation; that is, the savings and loans were locked into providing low-interest mortgage loans but, during the high-interest period of the early 1980s, were forced to pay high interest rates on savings in order to attract funds. Deregulation changed this, but many tried to make up for lost profits quickly. Should deregulation have occurred? What amount of control should the government have maintained to avoid the problems?

3. When the oil industry in Texas and Oklahoma collapsed, so did the real estate markets in these states, which resulted in S&Ls and banks losing much of the money they had invested in these states. What changes could be made to avoid the occurrence of this kind of regional catastrophe?

4. How do you see the role of deposit insurance in the failure of this S&L? Do you feel that deposits should be insured against loss? For how much?

CASE 17.2
Debit Cards: A Way to Restrain Credit

Some observers say that since the 1980s, an era of debt, Americans have sobered from their fling with credit, the hangover is subsiding, and we are becoming a cash society again. If this is true, then we will depend more on checks and cash than we have in the past, and credit cards will be used less. But remember, Americans still love those credit cards. Each American owns an average of three plastic credit cards. Citibank made $3.6 billion just in credit card interest in 1989.

In recent years, a special type of card, called a debit card, has been developed. The debit card differs from a credit card in that a debit card transaction actually transfers money from your bank account instead of creating a loan that you must repay.

The automatic teller machine card you have from your bank is a form of debit card. When you use it to get cash, you reduce the balance in your demand deposit account by the amount of cash you get from the ATM. If you have ever forgotten to record some of your ATM cash withdrawals, your next account statement certainly proved this is true. Hopefully, you saw that surprising balance and caught your error before you issued any checks your account could not cover.

Debit cards are also now being used for retail sales. The high-tech systems, such as the one at Lucky Stores, a California supermarket chain, require you to enter your debit card by sliding it into a terminal at the checkout. The clerk pushes buttons to enter the amount of the sale; then you punch in your personal identification number, and the funds are transferred from your account to that of Lucky Stores. You, of course, get a receipt to remind you to enter the withdrawal in your checkbook.

Adapted from Bill Saporito, "Who's Winning the Credit Card War?" *Fortune,* July 2, 1990, pp. 66–71; Jane Bryant Quinn, "The Era of Debit Cards," *Newsweek,* January 2, 1989, p. 51.

While a number of these high-tech systems are in operation, some low-tech uses also hold promise. No special terminals are necessary. Your bank simply issues your debit (ATM) card with a VISA or MasterCard logo on the corner, and the card is accepted by any merchant who accepts VISA and MasterCard. The procedure for use is the same as if you were paying with a credit card, but the transaction transfers money from your account rather than creating a loan.

Debit cards present some problems. Banks and merchants debate who should pay for the system; retailers worry that use of debit cards will reduce impulse buying; and the costs of the system still outweigh the benefits, such as cutting down on check processing. Consumers have not rushed to adopt them, either. If you want to pay cash, consumers figure, you can do so or write a check. And if you want to use a card, you can use your MasterCard or VISA and pay it off at the end of the month. Furthermore, with instant transfer, you lose the float you have when you use a check or credit card.

Doubters feel the debit card will go the way of the Edsel. However, the industry is growing by more than 50 percent a year.

The safeguards for debit cardholders differ from the protection given to those who pay in other ways:

Checks   If a thief cashes one of your checks and you sign an affidavit of forgery, the bank will pay, says First Atlanta Corp.'s Boris F. Melnikoff. If you write a check for a shirt and it turns out to be torn, the check can be stopped.

Credit cards   If your credit card is stolen and used, you pay no more than $50; and the bank will often waive even that. If you buy a torn shirt and the store won't replace it, the bank that issued your card can wipe it off your charge.

Most debit cards   If a debit card is stolen and used, you lose only $50 as long as you report the loss within two or four days, but up to $500 if you wait longer. If you let more than 60 or 90 days pass after getting the bank statement showing the fraudulent charges, all subsequent losses are yours. It's entirely up to you to get that shirt replaced.

VISA and MasterCard debit cards   You can get your money back on the shirt. You are given the same protection against shoddy products that you have with a credit card.

Questions for Discussion

1. Do you think debit cards will catch on with consumers? If so, what advantages do you think will cause them to catch on? If not, why do you think people will avoid using them?
2. How do you think banks should go about promoting debit cards? Who should foot the bill for the costs of the system: banks, retailers, or consumers? Why?
3. If debit cards catch on, what do you think retail transactions will look like in the future?

CHAPTER EIGHTEEN

FINANCIAL MANAGEMENT

LEARNING OBJECTIVES

1. To define *finance* and explain its role within the firm.

2. To identify the reasons firms need cash and why financial management is important.

3. To discuss the different sources of funds available to a firm.

4. To compare the different types of short- and long-term financing.

5. To identify the specific duties of the financial manager.

6. To explain the role of working capital management and capital budgeting in the ongoing success of the firm.

Tom Sears couldn't believe he had stayed up most of the night for this. Having gone after bankers, venture capitalists, and friends, and failing to get the needed

tions were precise, penetrating, and to the point. Sears was stunned. Their informality belied the intelligence of these investors, and he quickly began to think

preneurs and, of course, make a profit in the process. They typically provide their personal capital for high-risk, early-stage deals and help the entrepreneur get started.

This is not a new phenomenon. Wealthy families have provided private capital for start-up businesses for many years. In fact, Lotus Development, Compaq Computer, Pronet, and Landmark Graphics started with such investments. The New York firm Sevin-Rosen Management Co. has provided money to 45 new entities.

Tom was asking for $300,000 to start his business and will likely get it. Others also are going to this special group for funds. Marc Holtzman had an idea for a device that would automate the sample-preparation stage in biochemical research laboratories. He brought his idea to the breakfast club after being rejected by 30 venture capital firms. Linda Pfeiffer had started Grandma Pfeiffer's Products Inc. on her own. The company, which made a cake in a jar, was unable to expand without further capital. Linda went to Richard Sears (no relative of Tom), who provided about $150,000.

If you think you have a winning idea, don't go to the yellow pages to locate these investors. You won't find them. Many of them prefer to keep their investment interests private; as one of the breakfast club members notes, this elusive nature is a necessary hurdle. "If an investor is not willing to turn over every rock to find capital, then I don't want to meet him."[1]

Lou Jones

money to start his educational software company, Tom now stood before an obviously disinterested group of potential investors. When Sears proudly passed out his business plan, none of them even looked at it. Disregarding their obvious disinterest, Tom pressed on, pointing to his 10-year reputation in the industry, his exclusive contracts, and the relative vacuum in the market he had identified. But as he completed his presentation, he was sure he had lost them. Tom slumped in his chair and began to sip his coffee.

But Tom was in for a surprise. No sooner did he pick up the coffee cup than the group began questioning him rapid-fire. The ques-

maybe he was in the right place after all.

What Tom had encountered was "the breakfast club," a group of middle-aged entrepreneurs who meet for breakfast about seven times a year to hear presentations, hash over business plans, and decide which start-ups to back with their time, energy, and capital.

These entrepreneurs are members of an ever growing group of investors in the future of small businesses. Because they are outside the mainstream of venture capital investors, they are sometimes called *ad*venture capitalists. They do not represent large finance corporations; they are entrepreneurs who want to provide seed money for other upcoming entre-

Every business needs capital to start, run, maintain itself, and grow. Money fuels business. If businesses are successful, they will make money. But, successful or not, they will use it. They need money to purchase equipment, inventory, land, and buildings, as well as to pay the utilities, employees' wages, taxes, and rent. Without the necessary cash, a business cannot survive. A well-funded business can lose money for a long time and hold on; but without the cash needed to pay its bills and creditors, it will not last long. It will be forced into bankruptcy.

In this chapter, first we define finance and the role of the financial manager. Then we look at the uses of money for a firm—what the specific costs of running a firm are. Next we discuss the sources of money—where firms can go to get the funds they will use. Finally we examine the management of the firm's finances, including the management of working capital, capital budgeting, and the use of financial controls.

DEFINING FINANCE

Since a firm must have a sufficient supply of cash, the area of cash management requires special attention. Management must determine the firm's cash needs for both the short and the long term and then find sources to provide the necessary cash. This responsibility for cash management within the firm is management's finance responsibility.

Finance is the study of money within the firm. It is the functional area with the responsibility for finding funds for the firm, managing those funds, and determining their best uses. The financial manager is the individual responsible for the finance function. While some firms do not formally appoint a financial manager, the financial management tasks must still be performed, and one of the managers or owners will handle these tasks. In this text, when we refer to the financial manager, we are referring to the individual who is responsible for the finance function, regardless of whether that individual is actually called a financial manager.

To be effective, the financial manager has to develop and follow a financial plan. In order to accomplish this, the financial manager must perform a number of tasks:

1. Project the month-by-month flow of funds out of the business.
2. Project the month-by-month flow of funds into the business.
3. Compare the monthly inflows to the monthly outflows and
   a. If excess funds exist, find ways to generate revenue from these.
   b. If funds are short, adjust inflows or outflows if possible and/or look for other sources of funding.
4. If other funding sources are needed, analyze the alternative sources of these funds to find the most efficient source.
5. Establish a system to monitor and evaluate the results of this process.

The importance of effective cash management makes finance a crucial subject for all business managers. Connections will help you see how effective you might be as a financial manager.

Finance
The study of money within the firm; the business function responsible for finding funds, managing them, and determining their best use.

Look before Leaping

Directions: Assume that you are interested in buying a business. You believe that you have the intelligence, energy, and skills to be successful. Review the following list of points. Then write down what things you will do to be sure that the business is right for you.

- Profits
- Cash flow
- Business records
- Financial statements
- Industry trends
- Inventories
- Supplier relationships
- Employees
- Customers

   Check your steps or ideas with the feedback report, which just wants you to be cautious. The list, compiled by Western States Business Consultants, Inc., is not intended to be negative; it encourages caution. How many points that you raised correlate with the feedback pointers?

Feedback: When buying a small business:

1. *Determine exactly why the company is for sale.* People sell businesses for a lot of reasons, many of them good. But if you are buying, you need to know why they are selling. Avoid getting stuck with someone else's lemon.

2. *Ensure that a seller hasn't made a business look more attractive than it is.* You not only want to know what the owner says profits and cash flow are

PLANNING FOR CASH FLOW

One common mistake made by new businesses is failure to plan for sufficient start-up capital (the money needed to start a business). As a result, these businesses start with little chance of success. Insufficient capital can also be a problem for long-established firms. Cash needs change over time, and having sufficient capital for continued operations is a concern even for these firms. For example, Chrysler Corp. had to seek federal loan guarantees in 1979 to stay in business, and Braniff Airlines declared Chapter 11 bankruptcy in 1989, asking for court protection from the creditors they were unable to pay due to insufficient funds.[2] The Business Action shows some of the problems a firm can have when it does not properly plan for its cash needs.

   To avoid the problems faced by Carnes Enterprises, a firm must plan its cash flow; it has to know what its cash needs will be. By developing a detailed financial plan, management helps ensure the long-run success of the firm. We discuss details of the financial planning framework in this section.

like, but you should also take the time to do estimates of these yourself. Survey the area, look at competition, check payroll and expense numbers, and talk to suppliers. Be happy with your projection—not the seller's.

3. *Hire an experienced lawyer to review all business records.* You can't do it all. An experienced lawyer can review records, check on unusual liabilities, and advise you on how to write the sales contract to protect yourself against past or hidden costs or liabilities.

4. *Tie financial statements to historical tax returns to spot deviations.* This is another opportunity to check what is being said against reality. If an individual will not give you tax records for the business, be suspicious.

5. *Analyze major developments and trends within the company and the industry.* This serves two purposes: it helps you to make some kind of long-term forecast for the business and forces you to familiarize yourself with the nature of the business and competition. If long-range prospects are not good or you cannot understand the nature of the business, back out.

6. *Verify inventories and supplier relationships.* Take a physical inventory of goods and make sure it matches reported inventories. Spot-check invoices to verify costs. Call some suppliers, at random, to determine potential credit problems or past-due bills.

7. *Check key personnel to determine if the sale will trigger employee benefits or loss of major customers or contracts.* In a lot of selling firms, the customers are loyal to the salesperson they work with rather than to the company they are buying from. If a key salesperson would leave because of the sale, you may lose significant accounts. Also, severance agreements, golden parachutes, and the like may be activated by the sale. Explicitly inquire about these.

Projecting Month-by-Month Outward Flow of Funds

The month-by-month flow of funds out of the business represents the firm's use of funds. A financial manager sitting down to project the firm's use of funds needs to consider such areas as the cost of daily operations, the cost of the firm's credit service, the purchase of inventory, the purchase of major assets, debt repayment, and dividend payments.

Cost of daily operations When a new business is formed, the owners generally have considered the cost of purchasing land, building a building, buying a cash register, purchasing a delivery van, or paying state and federal licensing fees. However, many of the costs of daily operation are not considered as start-up costs. The costs of payroll, utilities, rent, taxes, and interest on loans all have to be paid. In a new business, which has little if any revenue at first, these costs have to be paid out of a cash reserve (extra cash held to pay debts). If this cash reserve, needed to cover daily expenses until revenues are sufficient

Success Comes Too Late

"You don't know what pressure is until you go to bed with $200 in the bank and you have a $4,000 payroll in the morning," says Julian H. Carnes, Jr. As owner of a troubled Red Bank, New Jersey, concrete drilling and cutting concern, he had plenty of days like that. "I'd decide who was the debtor with the greatest chance of paying, and when he opened in the morning, I'd be there. I wouldn't leave until I had a check."

Such is the life of a small-business owner trying to salvage a failing business. Carnes says he is about to dissolve his concern, Carnes Enterprises, Inc. A look at his experience shows how a company can fail even while its sales rise steadily. It also shows how seemingly small mistakes, especially in the start-up process, can later make the difference between success and failure.

Carnes says, "I had a burning desire to run a business." In 1981 he signed a technical-licensing agreement with Concrete Coring Co., a Hawthorne, California, company that developed diamond-edged tools to drill and cut concrete. "My wife was worried," he says. "But I said, 'Don't worry, honey. In three years, we will need people to help us carry the money.'" But by now, Carnes says, he has borrowed from his parents, borrowed against his life insurance, and used the $20,000 he had set aside for his son's college education. Both he and his business have filed for protection from creditors under Chapter 11 of the Federal Bankruptcy Code. Now, Carnes is fighting to save his house.

The seeds of disaster go back to the heady start-up days. To finance his new concrete-drilling business, Carnes invested $50,000 of his own money—all he had besides his son's college money. He applied for a $250,000 bank loan guaranteed by the Small Business Administration. The SBA approved only $200,000, with the loan ultimately backed by a personal guarantee. Carnes says, "I would never go in undercapitalized if I were doing it again."

Compounding this, Carnes fully staffed and equipped the young business immediately. Then an exceptionally severe winter set in, and construction work collapsed. As a result, expenses in the first four months of operation totaled $25,000 a month, while revenue was only $8,000 a month. "If I had to do it again, I would do everything I could to preserve capital in the early stages," Carnes says.

In spring 1982, Carnes started attracting more business, and sales began rising sharply. Revenues for the first year (a short year) were $28,000; 1982 revenues were $314,000; and sales climbed to $960,000 by 1986.

The company, however, lost money every year except 1983.

The problem was cash. "By the time we had the business, we had run out of cash," Carnes says. Given the losses, the bank rejected his plea for an extra $50,000.

Meanwhile a contractor that awarded Carnes Enterprises a $106,000 contract canceled the deal in the middle of work. Carnes sued, but the contractor filed for protection under Chapter 11 of the Bankruptcy Code and Carnes was never able to recover any money.

Desperate to stay afloat, the company also took on jobs from small, undercapitalized contractors that a stronger firm might have avoided. Collections on receivables, which had averaged 45 days, started taking 60, even 100, days.

Finally, in October 1986, a New Zealand company agreed to take over the company's operations and most of its obligations. But the deal with the New Zealand company didn't absolve Carnes of the original bank debt (now $297,000 with back interest, according to the bank), which he had personally guaranteed with his home. To protect his house, Carnes filed a personal Chapter 11 petition. He is now trying to resolve the problem by refinancing the house.

For all his traumas, however, Julian Carnes is far from sour on small business. "I never would have been happy if I hadn't tried it," he says. "I'd go back to owning a business in a minute."[3]

Salaries, furniture, lighting, rent, and utilities are expenses that must be paid to operate a business. Each of these items is a cost of operations.

Bob Daemmrich/The Image Works

to cover them, is not figured into the start-up capital, the firm will run out of funds as soon as its first bills come due.

So the firm must plan to have sufficient cash reserves to pay rent, utilities, wages, interest expense, taxes, and the other short-term expenses of doing business.

Cost of credit service   Most firms cannot do business on a strictly cash basis. Typically they provide customers with some form of credit to gain new customers and to encourage larger purchases.

A firm that provides credit must maintain accounts receivable (the amount of money owed to a business from customers who purchased its goods or services). As long as the credit remains outstanding, as long as the receivable has not been received, it cannot be counted as part of the firm's cash flow. The firm does not have the use of those funds to purchase the goods and services it needs to remain in business.

Since much of the firm's assets can be tied up in accounts receivable at any given time, customers who are slow to pay greatly impact the short-term cash needs of the firm. For this reason, most firms "date" their accounts receivable; that is, they keep track of how many days a particular receivable has been outstanding. Accounts that have been outstanding for the longest period of time get special attention from the financial manager.

The financial manager may follow a policy of sending a friendly reminder to customers whose accounts are over 30 days past due and a more stern reminder to customers whose accounts are over 60 days past due. Finally, a strong reminder with a threat of ending all credit privileges may be sent to accounts over 90 days past due.

Such measures may seem harsh; but if the firm does not receive the money owed by customers, it may have to go to outside sources for the needed funds. These outside sources may charge interest. Therefore the firm loses in one of two ways: either it has to pay interest for the funds it needs, or it cannot earn the interest it might have earned if the timely payment of the receivables had

FIGURE 18.1

Effect of Varying Demand Cycles on Cash Flow

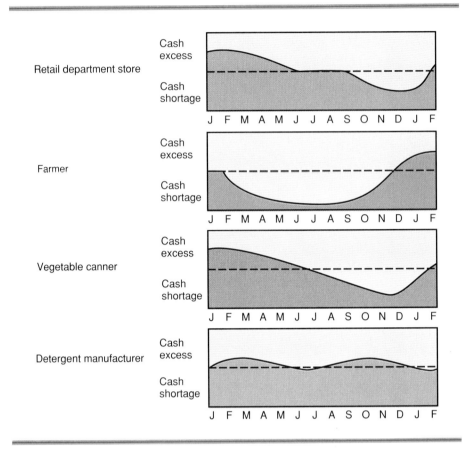

generated excess funds. Many of these problems can be avoided if the firm performs careful credit checks prior to granting customers credit.

✴Cost of inventory   A firm that hopes to survive in a competitive environment has to provide for its customers' needs. It cannot afford to be out of products that its customers demand. If it does not maintain sufficient inventory, it may eventually find itself out of customers. Maintaining sufficient inventory to satisfy your customers' needs requires a considerable expenditure of funds.

Inventory needs are further complicated by the fluctuations in demand that occur in various businesses. A retail business such as Wal-Mart will have to build up its inventory for the Christmas season, when sales are the highest, and then hold down inventory levels in January and February, when sales are much lower. A farmer must purchase his inventory of seed and fertilizer all at one time but can expect no income from his crops until they are harvested. A vegetable canner will have to purchase the vegetables for canning when the vegetables are harvested; yet while the inventory will have to be purchased and canned all at one time of the year, sales of that inventory will be stretched over the entire year. A detergent manufacturer, on the other hand, will experience a relatively stable product demand and material supply and therefore will experience much less fluctuation in inventory needs than the other firms mentioned. Figure 18.1 shows the different demand cycles discussed above and their effect on cash flow.

✗Purchase of major assets   While major assets such as land, buildings, and equipment have to be purchased by a firm when it first opens, these same assets must be periodically replaced and upgraded. And as business increases, additional assets may be required. A firm may need to open a second plant, purchase another delivery truck, or buy additional machinery. The company may also want to plan for the future by purchasing land for future expansion, when the real estate market is most favorable. All of these represent major expenditures and therefore major uses of company funds. If these expenditures are not planned for, the company may have to borrow unnecessarily or at high rates of interest to get the needed funds. Or the firm may have to forgo the purchase of new equipment, expansion of the plant, or purchase of delivery equipment.

One factor cited in businesses from Japan and other nations taking over so much of the United States' steel business was the failure of U.S. steel corporations to recapitalize. That is, they did not upgrade their plants and machinery, and the older equipment became obsolete and inefficient. With new plants and equipment, manufacturers from other countries were able to produce steel more efficiently and therefore sell it at lower prices than U.S. steel manufacturers.[4] Obviously it is important for companies to plan for the replacement of equipment as better equipment becomes available and to plan for growth.

Payment of debt   Most firms need to borrow money at some time or another. They may borrow to make major purchases or to get over a particularly tight cash period during the year. The use of debt will be discussed in the next section; however, the financial manager has to consider the payment of interest and principal on any outstanding debt as a use of funds and needs to add this debt service into the calculation for funds usage.

Payment of dividends   Dividends are payments made to the shareholders of the firm as a form of earnings on their stocks. While stock usually does not require the payment of dividends, most firms pay dividends in order to keep their stock attractive to potential investors and to show that the firm is financially sound. As a use of funds, the payment of dividends must be planned for.

The firm needs funds for many reasons. However, the firm is also able to get funds from many different sources. Some of these sources are internal and therefore have no interest cost or repayment. Others are external and therefore cost interest and require repayment. In the next section, we examine where a firm can get money and look at the advantages and disadvantages of the various sources of funds.

Projecting Month-by-Month Flow of Funds into the Business

The finance function in a business is responsible for acquiring the funds needed by the business. Sound financial management involves determining how much money is needed for various time periods and the most appropriate sources of these funds. Obviously the most appropriate place to get funds for the daily running of the business—that is, for expenses such as payroll, taxes, utilities, and rent—is from the revenue generated by the business. To determine the amount of outside financing needed, financial managers project the internal revenues the firm can expect on a month-to-month basis. They do this by estimating sales volume. If credit sales are involved, then the rate of payment on accounts receivable must also be estimated, since the company will not receive the cash from a credit sale until the receivable is paid. Managers should also consider any interest income expected from the investment of cash reserves and other excess funds.

Comparing Monthly Inflows to Monthly Outflows

Comparing expected income to expected expenditures will yield three possible outcomes. First, the two can match perfectly, and no action need be taken (highly unlikely). Second, expected expenditures for the month can exceed expected income, and additional funds must be found to cover the shortfall (discussed in a later section). Third, expected income for the month can exceed expected expenditures, and the company will have excess funds. The next section examines how firms generate revenue from excess funds.

GENERATING REVENUE FROM EXCESS FUNDS

If expected income for the month exceeds expected expenditures, the firm must decide how to use the extra funds. Firms may decide to expand the business, or may use the funds to make highly liquid investments.

Expansion

A company with substantial excess funds may want to consider expansion of current operations through an increase in production capacity, the addition of new sales outlets, or some other form of expansion. The firm might want to look at acquiring another firm.

In the 1970s and early 1980s, R. J. Reynolds Tobacco Company underwent considerable expansion through acquisition.[5] They had excess funds and felt the acquisitions would produce good long-term revenues; also they needed to reduce their dependency on the tobacco industry, since tobacco sales were declining. However, a company that uses its excess funds in this way has to be aware that it is hurting its *liquidity*, or the ability to generate cash quickly from internal sources. In 1987 RJR was bought by Kohlberg Kravis Roberts & Co. for $29.6 billion and now finds itself mired in debt and unable to challenge Philip Morris, which has gone on the attack to increase market share.[6]

Not all acquisitions involve large firms. In fact one half of all acquisitions reported in 1988 involved firms worth less than $25 million.[7]

High-Liquidity Investments

To protect liquidity, a company has alternatives that will produce interest income and still allow the firm access to its cash almost immediately. The first of these is an interest-bearing checking account. While this does give some interest income, the yield is typically low compared with other liquid market alternatives.

The most popular placement for excess funds is in marketable securities. These securities can easily be converted into cash, giving a high level of liquidity. They pay relatively high rates of interest for a liquid investment. The three most commonly used marketable securities are U.S. Treasury bills, commercial paper, and certificates of deposit.

Treasury bills are issued each week to the highest bidder. These loans to the U.S. Treasury typically have maturity dates of three or six months. The *maturity date* is the date on which the principal must be repaid to the purchaser. Treasury bills (often called T-bills) are considered to be virtually risk free and therefore are one of the most popular marketable securities. However, since they are only issued in amounts of $10,000 or more, they are not for the small investor.

Commercial paper is a short-term note that represents a loan to a major corporation with a high credit standing. The maturity date on commercial paper may run from three days to nine months. While commercial paper carries more risk than T-bills and is not as liquid, it does pay the purchaser a higher rate of interest. Commercial paper is normally issued in amounts of $25,000 to $100,000.

Certificates of deposit (CDs) are notes issued by a commercial bank or brokerage firm. The size of CDs runs from $100 to $100,000. The smaller CDs are usually available with very long maturity dates (generally 10 years); the larger CDs ($100,000) can be purchased for periods as short as 24 hours. The more common CDs are issued for 7 to 31 days, 3 months, 6 months, 18 months, and 42 months. CDs issued by banks can be redeemed early; however, early redemption results in a substantial interest penalty.

Treasury Bill
A loan to the U.S. Treasury that typically has a maturity date of three or six months. Often called a T-bill.

Commercial Paper
A short-term loan to a major corporation with a high credit standing.

Certificate of Deposit
Interest-bearing note issued by a commercial bank or brokerage firm.

FINDING EFFICIENT SOURCES OF FUNDS

Often the firm will find that projected expenditures exceed projected revenues for a given period, making it necessary to seek funds from other sources. The financial manager must determine the most efficient source, given the firm's needs at that time. Generally managers match the source of funds to the type of need. That is, for a short-term need, short-term sources should be used. If the need is long-term, then long-term sources should be used.

The two major categories of funds sources for a business are debt capital and equity capital. **Debt capital** is simply funds obtained through borrowing. **Equity capital**, on the other hand, does not require repayment. These funds come from the current owners of the firm or from outsiders who provide capital in exchange for some ownership in the firm. Sources of equity capital include *retained earnings*, or earnings that the owners do not pay to themselves but rather leave in the firm as an additional investment; additional contributions of the owners, additional money from the owners' personal sources; investments by outsiders in a privately owned firm, adding new partners to bring in new capital; and stock issues to the general public, stock sold to the public for capital. Table 18.1, on the next page, compares debt and equity capital.

Debt Capital
Funds obtained through borrowing.

Equity Capital
Funds provided in exchange for some ownership in the firm.

Short-Term Financing: Debt Capital

Short-term financing is used to obtain money to finance current operations, with repayment required within one year. The finance manager spends the most time obtaining short-term financing, generally when funds needed for day-to-day operations are not sufficient. Short-term financing can come from several

TABLE 18.1

Characteristics of Debt and Equity Capital

Debt Capital	Equity Capital
Repayment is designated.	No repayment required.
Interest is an expense.	Dividends can be an expense but are optional.
Interest paid may be deductible.	Dividends are not a deductible expense.
Can place claim against firm's assets.	Has only secondary claim against assets.
Does not directly affect management power.	Can challenge corporate control.
Lenders may constrain management.	Shareholders typically will not block management.

different sources: trade credit, family and friends, commercial banks, commercial paper, and internal funds management.

Trade credit   The most widely used source of short-term financing is trade credit. **Trade credit** is credit given to a firm by the trade—that is, by the suppliers the company deals with. For example, when Kroger purchases a carload of green beans from Del Monte, Kroger does not pay for the green beans at the time that they receive them. Del Monte gives the beans to Kroger on credit, with the understanding that Kroger will pay for the beans according to the terms of the invoice.

Invoice terms are usually stated in numbers, such as ''2/10 net 30'' (as Chapter Fourteen noted). Interpretation: The buyer can take a 2 percent discount if the invoice is payed within 10 days; if the discount is not taken, the full bill is due in 30 days. The financial manager pays close attention to such discount terms, as they represent considerable savings.

You might see 2 percent as not very much, but think about it. If the firm pays the bill 20 days before the bill is due, it saves 2 percent of its cost. Twenty days is about 1/18 of a year (365 ÷ 20). If the buyer were to save 2 percent every 20 days, he or she would save 2 percent about 18 times in a year, for an annual return of just over 36 percent. So, if the financial manager needs to borrow money for 20 days in order to pay the bill and take the discount, he or she should do so as long as the annual interest rate on the loan is less than 36 percent.

Family and friends   When funds are only needed for a short time, friends and family will often help a small business. However, such borrowed funds bring an extra risk: if things do not work out and the business goes sour, you may not only lose your business but your friend or the family relationship, as well. If you do borrow from family or friends, handle it the same as any other loan. Write an agreement at agreed-upon terms of interest and payment and then pay it back just as you would a bank loan.

Trade Credit
Credit given by suppliers for the purchases the firm makes from these suppliers.

Most likely, these Samsung televisions, imported from Korea, will not be paid for at the time they are delivered to this firm in Laredo, Texas. Instead, Samsung will give the Texas firm trade credit.

The Image Works

Commercial banks   As an alternative source for short-term funds, commercial banks generally make more sense than relatives or friends. The commercial banker can better help with any cash flow problems and give sound advice. Developing a close relationship with a local banker is a good idea. Once you select one, send him or her your financial statements and meet regularly to discuss your business. Establishing a close and open relationship with the bank will pay off in the long run because the banker will pay closer attention to your business and alert you to potential problems. Also, when you need emergency funds, the banker will be more willing to lend these, since you have developed a trusting relationship.[8]

Bank loans come in many different forms. Unsecured loans are the most difficult loans to get from a bank or other financial institution. **Unsecured loans** are loans on the good credit of the borrower. They require no collateral. New businesses have great difficulty getting unsecured loans. Generally banks will require some form of collateral to guarantee the loan.

Secured loans are backed by collateral, by something valuable. Collateral reduces the risk for the banker. If the borrower fails to pay the loan, the lender may take possession of the collateral. It may be property, equipment, inventory, or accounts receivable. Using accounts receivable as collateral for a loan is called *pledging*. The cash received for the accounts receivable goes to the banker instead of being retained in the company.

A borrower who has a good relationship with the bank may be able to open a **line of credit**. The bank preapproves the borrower for a specified amount of credit, usually unsecured; provided the bank has the funds available, the borrower may borrow up to that amount without having to apply for a loan each time

Unsecured Loan
A loan issued on the good credit of the borrower and requiring no collateral.

Secured Loan
A loan backed with some form of collateral.

Line of Credit
A preapproved amount the holder may borrow in whole or in part, provided that the bank has sufficient funds.

In Venezuela, a banker meets with a businessperson to discuss a loan. The businessperson requesting the loan has to present the needed documentation to support the request.

Courtesy of UNISYS Corporation

Revolving Credit Agreement
A line of credit guaranteed by the bank.

Factoring
The sale of accounts receivable to a bank or other lender, generally at a considerable discount.

funds are needed. As the customer's credit record with the bank lengthens and the business matures, this line of credit is often increased. However, a line of credit does not guarantee that the loan will be available. A **revolving credit agreement** guarantees that the bank will honor your line of credit up to the stated amount. A revolving credit agreement generally requires payment of a fee.

Another, relatively expensive form of short-term credit is **factoring**. Rather than pledging its accounts receivable to a financial institution as collateral, a firm actually sells the accounts receivable to the institution—at a discount. The seller receives less than the full value of the accounts receivable. For example, a bank may only pay $7 for each $10 of receivables. This protects the bank from any uncollectible accounts and allows it to make a tidy profit. Firms do not generally like to use factoring; it is expensive and sends a message to suppliers and creditors that the company may be in financial trouble.[9]

Floor planning is another option in bank financing. In some industries, such as automobiles and major appliances, borrowers will assign the title to their inventory to the bank as collateral for short-term loans. As the inventory is sold, borrowers pay off the loan, plus interest, to the lender.

Internal funds management   Whenever possible, a firm should attempt to get its needed funds from internal sources. Frequently a close review of the balance sheet and accounting ratios will reveal possible sources of funds that have been overlooked. For example, overdue accounts receivable may be collected more quickly, or a discount may be offered for earlier payment. Inventory may be reduced, since every dollar of excess inventory that is reduced represents one less dollar needed from outside sources. (Of course the manager always has to remember the need to provide adequate inventory for customer demand.) Costs may also be cut and expenses reduced to free up more dollars. A good financial manager will work hand in hand with accountants to ensure that funds are not tied up in noncash assets.

Grand Opening Monday Oct. 1
Matteson
21410 South Cicero Avenue

Courtesy of Wal-Mart Stores, Inc.

As a result of careful long-term financial planning, Wal-Mart has always had the necessary capital available to add new stores.

Long-Term Financing

A firm planning its finances should plan for long-term needs as well as short-term needs. Successful companies constantly refocus on their long-term goals and objectives. If the firm has an objective to maintain a certain level of growth, it must provide the funds to pay for that growth.

Wal-Mart had a 40 percent growth rate over the last decade. Although the growth rate has slowed, the company still adds about 150 stores a year.[10] Because Wal-Mart has always planned for this growth, the needed capital has always been available, mostly from internal sources. Forward planning has helped make Wal-Mart one of the 10 most admired corporations in America in 1988 and 1989.[11]

If a company knows its objectives, it needs to look at possible sources of long-term capital to help it accomplish those objectives. The principal questions are, What sources of capital are available? and What sources best fit the company's needs?

Because they involve the purchase of fixed assets and the expansion of the organization, decisions involving long-term financing usually take place at the highest company levels. In large firms, this may involve the chief executive officer (CEO) and the financial vice president as well as the board of directors. In smaller firms, it generally involves the owners.

Debt capital   Debt capital can also be used for long-term financing. The interest rates are generally higher than for short-term financing because the lender has to incur the risk of loss for a longer period of time.

Loans   Long-term debt financing can often be used once a firm has established a rapport with a bank or other financial institution, such as an insurance company or pension fund. For a smaller business, the Small Business Administration (SBA) can often be a good source of loans. The SBA actually participates in two types of loans: direct loans and guaranteed loans. *Direct loans* are generally given to higher-risk businesses, usually at lower interest rates than banks would charge. However, these loans are gradually being phased out. The more frequent method of loan support used by the SBA is the *guaranteed loan*. In this case, the loan actually comes from a private lender, and the SBA guarantees 90 percent of the loan value. This guarantee enables many small-businessowners, who might not otherwise be able to get loans, to borrow the funds needed for their business.

Most long-term loans have 3- to 7-year terms, though some may extend to 15 or 20 years. For these loans, the business signs a *term loan agreement*. This agreement is a **promissory note**, which requires the borrower to repay the loan according to a schedule of specified installments and at either a fixed (remains constant) or flexible (changes as market conditions change) rate of interest.

Most long-term loans require some form of collateral, such as real estate, machinery, equipment, or stock. Typically, when determining the interest rate for such loans, the bank looks at the length of time the loan is for, the type of collateral, the firm's credit rating, and the general level of market interest.

Promissory Note
A legally binding promise of payment that spells out the terms of the loan agreement.

Bond
An agreement between a firm and an investor with specific terms spelled out in an indenture.

Bonds   Another form of long-term debt financing is a **bond** issue. This IOU with an investor stipulates periodic interest payments (usually every six months) and payment of the principal at maturity (usually 10 years or more). Bonds almost always are issued in $1,000 amounts or multiples. The details are spelled out in an agreement called an *indenture* (see Figure 18.2).

Bonds, just like loans, can be secured or unsecured. A *secured bond* is backed by some form of collateral—specific property such as real estate, inventory, or long-term assets that will pass to the bondholders should the company not live up to the terms of the agreement. *Unsecured bonds*, or *debenture bonds*, are backed by the good name of the issuing company. Holders can make claims against the assets of a failed company only after the creditors with specific collateral have been paid.

Bonds pay interest to the bondholders, at specified intervals or on specified dates. For example, the holder of a $1,000 bond that pays 10 percent interest due April 1 and October 1 could expect to receive $50 on each of these two dates.

Generally, the lower the quality of the bonds (higher risk of loss due to the heavy debt of the issuing corporation or a poor credit record), the higher the interest paid to bondholders. This only makes sense, since no one would buy a low-quality bond without receiving a sufficient premium over the normal amount paid on higher-quality bonds. The term **junk bonds** designates a low-grade bond issued by financially weak companies with no solid collateral, to fund internal expansion or corporate acquisitions and buyouts. These bonds, with a very high interest rate, have become popular in financing takeovers and leveraged buyouts.[12] Junk bonds became big business largely because of one

Junk Bond
A low-grade bond that carries a very high risk.

FIGURE 18.2

Corporate Bond

Courtesy of Mobil Corporation

firm, Drexel Burnham Lambert. Michael Milken, a senior vice president, pushed junk bonds, and they accounted for over $14.5 billion of the $500 billion in corporate bonds outstanding. Milken, involved in an insider trading scandal, was convicted and began serving a 10-year prison sentence in March 1991.

A firm that sells bonds must repay its debt to the bondholders. The point at which payment is due is known as maturity. The amount due at maturity can be huge, since bonds usually fund major expansions or asset purchases. To ease their payment burden, companies sometimes issue *serial bonds*, which mature at different intervals from the date of issue. This way, the company pays off the debt in portions. A *sinking fund* may also be used. The sinking fund requires that the company set aside a certain sum of money each year to "sink" the bond debt. The company may then pay off a portion of the bonds each year or accumulate the funds until the bonds mature.

Two special types of bonds sometimes issued by corporations are callable bonds and convertible bonds. *Callable bonds* give the company the right to purchase back its bonds early. This might be desirable if the interest rates have fallen since the bonds were issued and the company wants to issue new bonds at a lower rate of interest. Callable bonds generally carry a slightly higher rate of interest than noncallable bonds, and the company usually pays a premium (an amount over the normal interest rate) to the holder when the bonds are called.

Convertible bonds may be paid off with stock in the company. The amount of stock is indicated in the indenture terms. The decision to accept stock or money is left up to the individual bondholder.

Leverage The use of long-term debt to raise needed cash is sometimes referred to as **leverage.** The borrowed cash acts like a lever to increase the

Leverage
The use of long-term debt to raise needed cash.

Campeau's Empire: A Crumbled Dream

In mid-1988 Robert Campeau toasted his purchase of Federated, a large retail conglomerate that owns such well-known stores as Bloomingdale's, Abraham & Straus, and I. Magnin with Dom Perignon. Campeau had purchased the Federated stores to go with his previously purchased Allied Cos., which owned Jordan Marsh, Bonwit Teller, and Brooks Brothers, among others. The purchase of the Federated stores cost $6.6 billion.

Why make such a large purchase in an area that has been questionable in recent years? To a great extent, it seems to have been pride. Campeau spoke of creating a vast retailing and shopping center empire across the United States. People who know him say he took particular pride in his ownership of Bloomingdale's and the access to New York society the glittering store provided him. The former Ontario factory hand who had made his fortune in real estate was a beaming host at elegant store openings and charity dinners. His wife, Ilse, would sometimes phone Bloomingdale's chairman Marvin Traub to offer suggestions on merchandise the store should carry.

Campeau's problems seem to have been classic: overextended debt, overestimated sales, underestimated expenses, and all of a sudden you have a major cash crunch. With the purchase of Federated and Allied, Campeau had taken on a combined debt of $10 billion. Always a risk-taker, he figured he could confound the skeptics with a bold program of asset sales, cost-cutting, and expansion of such chains as Bloomingdale's. A glamorous new Bloomingdale's did open in Chicago in 1988. But much of the rest just did not work out.

Sales of such chains as Ann Taylor and Gold Circle brought less than projected. Caught in an industrywide slump in women's apparel sales, Campeau's retail operation failed to meet the ambitious revenue projections that were crucial to servicing the debt. The Allied unit, for example, reported a cash flow of $40.6 million for the first fiscal quarter ended April 30, while its interest costs were an overwhelming $65.3 million.

The shortages were compounded when, in November 1988, Campeau found himself unable to tap previous lenders. Since that time, Federated bonds have dropped about 20 points, or $200 for each $1,000 of face value; and Allied's have seen a decline of nearly 50 points, or $500 per $1,000 face amount.

As a result, Campeau faced losing control of his company, if not worse. If a $400 million bridge loan from PaineWebber, Dillion Read, and First Boston could not be refinanced, the lenders would obtain a 7 percent equity stake in Federated. In addition, strapped for cash going into the critical Christmas season, Campeau had to turn to Olympia and York Developments Ltd. for a $250 million loan to help purchase needed inventory. The loan was convertible into Campeau stock and, if taken, would increase the stake of O&Y in Federated to 35 percent and, more important, would reduce Campeau's controlling position below 50 percent.

The news does not get any better. Going into the 1989 Christmas season, many competitors of Federated's numerous chains were circling, fully expecting to gain some market share against the wounded company. As one industry expert put it, "Unless he can arrange a lot more financing, he won't be able to order and receive enough goods to make holiday sales." The possibility of low shelves, plus the fact that nervous Federated executives were looking for work elsewhere and, therefore, may not have been paying attention to business, indicated that the Federated chains might go into the Christmas season shabbily dressed.

In January 1990, the corporation's directors banished Robert Campeau from all U.S. operations; he said he would confine himself to developing Canadian real estate. In late January, the Federated chain filed for protection under Chapter 11 of the Bankruptcy Law.[13]

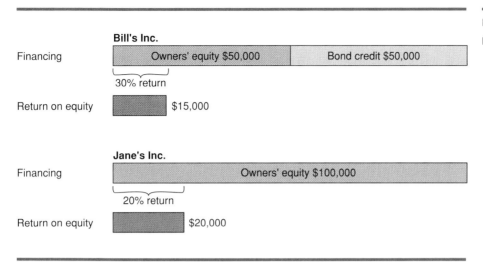

FIGURE 18.3

Effect of Leverage

purchasing power of the owner's investment. Figure 18.3 shows the different rate of return on the owner's investment generated when leverage is used versus when leverage is not used. Bill's Inc. used a $50,000 owner's investment and a $50,000 bond issue to raise $100,000. Jane's Inc. sold 10,000 shares of common stock at $10 per share to raise $100,000. Both companies earned $20,000 before interest and taxes. After Bill pays the $5,000 in interest on the bond issue, he makes a 30 percent return (15,000 ÷ 50,000) on his investment of $50,000. Jane, however, returns only 20 percent (20,000 ÷ 100,000) to her shareholders.

Leverage works to maintain higher rates of return on owners' investments and allows the owners to create a larger firm for the same investment. As long as earnings exceed interest payments on borrowed funds, the firm should be all right. However, leverage also means a continued obligation to service the debt, and any significant downturn in sales could threaten survival. The ability to generate additional cash through debt would be limited, leaving few outside sources of funds. Continuing interest payments would represent a larger percentage of total sales. Current creditors and suppliers may become worried if the balance sheet does not look healthy, and suppliers may demand cash payment for merchandise, increasing the size of any cash flow shortages. The judicious use of leverage can help increase owners' returns. However, too much debt can create massive problems for a company. The Business Action shows risks involved in the use of leverage as it tells the story of Robert Campeau.

Equity capital   As we discussed earlier, equity capital is funds from owners of the firm. The funds can be contributed by current owners or by outsiders who receive some share of ownership in the company in return. The five forms of equity capital are retained earnings, additional contributions by the current owners, the sale of partnerships in a privately held firm, venture capital, and the sale of stock issues to the general public.

Retained earnings   Retained earnings are profits the owners have chosen to leave in the company rather than pay them out in the form of dividends to shareholders. While this method of financing growth is extremely safe, it limits

FIGURE 18.4

A Mobil Corporation stock certificate that is issued to those individuals who purchase stock. It is something tangible that the shareholder possesses to indicate his or her ownership in the company.

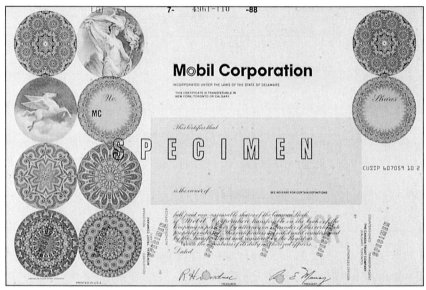

Courtesy of Mobil Corporation

the amount of cash that will be available and may cause long delays before expansion can occur.

Contributions   The current owners of the firm can increase their contributions to the firm. While this also tends to be a safe method for financing growth, the funds of current owners are often limited, which means slower growth. Outside investors may have more funds to spend, but they may require some control over the operations of the company.

Sale of partnerships   If the current owners of the firm do not have extra funds to contribute to the firm, additional partners can be sought. The additional partners contribute funds to the firm and in return receive a share of the ownership.

Venture Capital
Funds provided by individuals or organizations to new firms with high potential for growth; the investor receives a share of the ownership and frequently a share of control.

Venture capital   One popular form of financing for new, small, or struggling businesses is **venture capital**. Venture capitalists provide funds for such a firm (provided they see potential for rapid growth) and in exchange receive a share of the ownership and frequently a share of control. This chapter's opening vignette shows a special group of these investors who have chosen to take on higher-risk investments than even typical venture capitalists. (The article calls these individuals *ad*venture capitalists.)

Public sale of stock   As a company grows, its need for funds also grows; typically, at some point, debt financing, retained earnings, and owner contributions no longer meet these needs. Then the owners have to consider selling shares of ownership in their company. These shares of ownership are called *stocks*. As evidence of ownership, a shareholder receives a stock certificate (see Figure 18.4). Each certificate shows the name of the shareholder, the

Wide World Photos, Inc.

DID YOU KNOW? *On September 13, 1989, Walt Disney Company unveiled plans to offer European Community residents nearly 51 percent of the shares in its "Euro Disneyland."*

4,800 acres of sugar-beet farmland about 20 miles east of Paris are being transformed into a gigantic $3 billion theme park and resort. Set to open in 1992, the park will join similar parks in Anaheim, California; Orlando, Florida; and Tokyo, Japan.

The stock issue represents the first public offering of shares in all European Common Market countries simultaneously. It also marks the first time that investors have had a chance to own a stake in a Disney theme park.[14]

number of shares of stock owned, and the special characteristics of the stock. Many stocks will also show a *par value,* a small, arbitrary value bearing no relation to the market value of the stock.

After making a request to the secretary of state (in some states, to the attorney general), the original incorporators and the board of directors of the corporation set a maximum number of shares into which the company can be divided. This represents all the shares of stock that can be sold at any time and is called the *authorized stock.* Typically a company does not place all the authorized stock up for sale at one time but rather sells only a portion of the shares. The shares sold are called *issued stock,* and unsold shares are *unissued stock.*

When a company sells stock, it gives a portion of the ownership of the firm to outsiders. However, shareholders do not directly run a firm. They elect a board of directors to represent them. Each shareholder has a number of votes equal to the number of shares owned and uses these votes to elect the members to the board of directors. Shareholders may also vote on mergers, acquisitions, and takeovers.

The company also may pay *dividends* to shareholders. Dividends are a distributed portion of the firm's earnings. The company is not required to pay dividends; many do not, or they distribute only a small portion of the earnings in dividends in order to conserve cash for growth, research, and similar types of expenditures.

Chapter Nineteen discusses stocks, as well as bonds and other investments, in greater detail.

MANAGING THE FINANCES OF THE FIRM

Financial managers are responsible for maintaining the proper flow of funds. They help manage the uses of funds and find the appropriate sources of funds. They also invest excess cash to earn additional income for the company. In performing these duties, the financial manager has to manage the company's working capital, develop capital budgets, and develop appropriate financial controls.

Managing Working Capital

If a firm's current liabilities (obligations that must be paid within a year) are subtracted from its current assets, the result is the value of *working capital*. Working capital represents the amount of capital available for the day-to-day running of the firm. Sufficient working capital is obviously important to the effective management of a firm's operations.

In managing current assets, the financial manager needs to concentrate on three assets: cash, accounts receivable, and inventory. The primary concern with *cash* is that it should never be left idle; it should always be working. Funds not immediately needed should be invested and earning interest. At the very least, an interest-earning checking account should be used. Investment possibilities were discussed earlier in this chapter.

Float
The amount of money not yet withdrawn from the company's checking account even though checks have been written.

The **float** is the amount of money that has not yet been withdrawn from the company's checking account even though checks have been written. If you have a checking account, you may notice that when you balance it at the end of the month, some of the checks you have written have not yet cleared. Therefore the balance on your statement is greater than the balance in your checkbook. The difference is float. The same is true for businesses. In a large company such as General Motors, this may represent billions of dollars and significant potential earnings. Actions taken by the Federal Reserve System and advances in electronic payment systems have resulted in the float being less significant today than in the past. However, float still occurs, with three primary components (sources): mail float, processing float, and check clearing float.[15]

Accounts receivable are really promises of cash from customers of the firm. Until this cash is in hand, the firm has only the promise. One task of the financial manager is to speed up the collection of accounts receivable as much as possible. This, of course, must be done without offending customers and with the understanding that, in many cases, providing credit is necessary to sales.

In managing accounts receivable, the financial manager needs to date accounts receivable so that overdue accounts are flagged immediately and appropriate letters are sent or some other action is taken. The financial manager also wants to speed up the conversion of received payments into cash in the company's account. Once received at the office, they must be processed and then sent to the bank. This means that the cash may not be credited to the company's account for two more days. To speed this up, many companies have a *lockbox*, a post office box used as a mailing address. The bank collects payments directly from the lockbox several times a day and immediately starts to process and credit payments to the customer's account. The business receives a summary of payments and can then credit the customers' accounts.

Inventory is an investment in future sales. Until sold, however, it represents a cash use for the firm. The financial manager needs to continuously review inventory levels to pinpoint any excess inventory and work with production and marketing to alleviate the condition. Of course, understanding inventory's importance to sales, the financial manager will also work with production and marketing to make sure sufficient inventory is available to satisfy customer needs.[16]

Many inventory models use computer programs and company information to determine the best level of inventory for different levels of sales. These models also help determine the best time to order additional inventory and the amount of inventory to order. The auto industry has begun working more closely with its suppliers to reduce the lead time needed for deliveries. The goal is to achieve just-in-time (JIT) deliveries, or deliveries of materials that arrive at the plant just when they are actually needed for production (see discussion of JIT in Chapter Nine).[17]

The management of current liabilities was covered earlier in this chapter. As we discussed, taking advantage of cash discounts offered by suppliers generally makes sense.

Developing Capital Budgets

Capital budgets represent the funds allocated for future investments of the firm's cash. These may be plant expansion, equipment improvement, acquisitions, or other major expenditures. The process of **capital budgeting** involves comparing and evaluating alternative investments.

Capital investments are generally long-term investments and therefore involve long-term sources of funds. When evaluating different capital projects, the financial manager looks not only at the amount of money required to do the project but also at the incremental cash flow the project will produce. These cash flows are looked at to determine when the project will have paid for itself (generated sufficient cash to pay for the initial investment) and what the long-run rate of return will be.

Determining the long-term rate of return can be difficult because it depends on factors such as customer response, competitive reactions, the state of the

Capital Budgeting
The budgeting of funds for future, generally major, investments of the firm's cash; investments are generally ranked on the basis of the return potential.

The expansion of the University of Iowa Hospitals in Iowa City is part of a capital improvement. A capital improvement budget was prepared to describe the expansion costs.

Courtesy of The University of Iowa Hospitals and Clinics

economy, and other environmental factors. Therefore, future benefits are difficult to gauge in advance. Managers generally look at the most likely circumstances and try to estimate returns based on these. However, this does not always work. Case 18.2 at the end of this chapter shows how risky the future can be.

Developing Financial Controls

Financial controls mean that once cash flow projections, capital budgets, and so on are established, they must be reviewed to make sure that the actual results match projected results. Without review, there is little reason to do the budgeting in the first place. If you set a budget for a particular capital project—for example, building an extension onto the current plant—the estimated returns for that project are based on the budgeted costs. If the project comes in over cost, then the returns will be less, and some other project may have proved to be a better investment. When comparing actual and projected results, the financial manager must look for deviations. If they occur, the reasons must be found and corrective action taken. Financial planning is only worthwhile if financial controls are put in place that ensure that the financial plan is followed.

In this chapter, we have discussed the financial management of the firm. The next chapter looks at firms as investments and at your own personal financial management.

Companies Invest in Market Share

In the 21st century, business winners will beat the Japanese and Europeans at their own game—winning market share on a global scale. Managing for quick profits will give way to solid growth by increased investment in three key areas: (1) developing innovative, lower-cost manufacturing tools and processes for faster, better production; (2) focusing R&D on new applications and continuous improvement to bring newer, better, cheaper products to market; and (3) retraining workers for a high-tech, collaborative workplace. Xerox and other harbingers of this investment approach were successful in the 1990s, providing a worldwide demand for well-made, low-priced products.[18]

SUMMARY OF LEARNING OBJECTIVES

1. To define *finance* and explain its role within the firm.

   Finance is the study of money within the firm. It is also the functional area with responsibility for managing corporate funds. To function, the firm must have adequate funding, and the finance department manages these funds by developing and monitoring the firm's financial plan. This plan should include balancing the monthly inflows and outflows of funds, determining liquid investments for excess funds, finding efficient outside sources for funds, and properly monitoring and controlling the process.

2. To identify the reasons firms need cash and why financial management is important.

   Firms need cash to fund the cost of daily operations, to handle the cost of the firm's credit service, to handle the cost of the firm's inventory, to purchase major assets, to service the firm's debt, and to pay dividends. Financial management is important to this process because the financial manager not only determines the future uses of funds but also identifies the most efficient sources of these funds. The financial manager makes it possible for the firm to function uninterrupted and efficiently.

3. To discuss the different sources of funds available to a firm.

   The firm has several sources of funds. The most obvious is the revenue generated from daily operations. When additional cash is needed, the firm should use short-term sources for short-term needs and long-term sources for long-term needs. Short-term sources of funds include debt capital: trade credit; family and friends; commercial bank loans (secured and unsecured), lines of credit, factoring of accounts receivable, and floor planning; commercial paper; and internal funds management. Long-term sources include long-term loans, bonds, and equity financing. Equity capital includes retained earnings, additional contributions of current owners, the sale of partnerships, and the sale of public stock issues.

4. To compare the different types of short- and long-term financing.

For *short-term financing,* unsecured commercial bank loans may be preferred, but are often difficult to get. Many businesses must secure the loan with some form of collateral, a situation which ties up the property used as collateral until the loan is paid off. Loans from family and friends can be a problem, unless they are handled as a legal loan obligation complete with written and agreed-upon terms. Trade credit should always be used, since this is like an interest-free loan. Commercial paper will generally only be available as an option to large companies. Factoring accounts receivable poses a danger because it is expensive and negatively impacts the reputation of the firm.

For *long-term sources,* long-term loans are perhaps the easiest to execute, although they may require relatively high rates of interest. For small amounts, they make sense. Bonds are better for larger amounts, due to the more favorable terms, although only larger firms can issue these. The firm needs to prepare for the date the bonds come due. Long-term debt financing also provides leverage. Equity financing has the advantage of not requiring interest or repayment; however, it reduces the return of profits to current owners and may require some sharing of ownership responsibility.

5. To identify the specific duties of the financial manager.

The financial manager is responsible for maintaining the proper flow of funds. To accomplish this, he or she must manage uses of funds, help find sources of funds, find appropriate investments for excess cash, and manage the company's working capital and capital budgeting processes. The financial manager must also develop appropriate financial controls.

6. To explain the role of working capital management and capital budgeting in the ongoing success of the firm.

Working capital is the current assets minus the current liabilities of the firm. The current assets of cash, accounts receivable, and inventory must be managed. Cash must always be earning interest income, accounts receivable should be collected quickly, and inventory should be kept to the minimum needed to satisfy customer demand. Accounts payable should generally be paid in time to take advantage of cash discounts. Otherwise payment should not be made until the last possible day.

Capital budgets represent the funds allocated for future investments of the firm's cash. These investments include plant expansion, equipment improvement, or other major expenditures. The capital budget has limited funds, so all proposed capital expenditures must be evaluated to determine which will provide the best return.

KEY TERMS

Finance, p. 639

Treasury Bill, p. 647

Commercial Paper, p. 647

Certificate of Deposit (CD), p. 647

Debt Capital, p. 647

Equity Capital, p. 647

Trade Credit, p. 648

Unsecured Loan, p. 649

Secured Loan, p. 649

Line of Credit, p. 649

Revolving Credit Agreement, p. 650

Factoring, p. 650

Promissory Note, p. 652

Bond, p. 652

Junk Bond, p. 652

Leverage, p. 653

Venture Capital, p. 656

Float, p. 658

Capital Budgeting, p. 659

QUESTIONS FOR DISCUSSION AND REVIEW

1. Why does a manager need to understand the concept of cash flow?

2. What is the difference between short-term and long-term financing?

3. What sources of funds would a new-business owner count on to sustain the business?

4. If you were opening a new business, what should you consider relative to needed start-up capital? Be as specific as possible.

5. List the steps in the financial planning process. Explain why each of these steps is necessary.

6. Explain internal funds management. How can it be used to generate funds?

7. What is a corporate bond? What are the different types of bonds discussed in the text? Are there any concerns a firm should have when it issues bonds? If so, what are they?

8. What are the responsibilities of the financial manager of the firm?

9. Name the different types of equity financing. What are the advantages or disadvantages of each?

10. Why would a lender decide to offer unsecured loans rather than demand collateral?

CASE 18.1
HealthCorp's Financial Management Dilemma

Tom Williams is the new corporate finance officer for HealthCorp, Inc., a small company that produces a line of health foods to be sold in supermarkets and health food stores. The company, in business for about nine years, has made a profit in each of the last five years. Sales have grown at about a 20 percent pace. For the past two years, sales were $1,800,000 and $2,100,000, respectively. Tom now faces some significant problems.

1. Because HealthCorp is in the food business and depends on fresh-grown items for many of its products, the inventory needs of the company tend to be strongest in the fall when crops are coming in. For this reason, the company runs into considerable cash shortfalls in September, October, and November. Fall inventory needs have been running at about 50 percent of annual cost of goods sold. Cost of goods is 70 percent of total sales.

2. The two brothers who currently own the company have reinvested earnings in the firm. As a result, the firm's equity now is about $450,000, with cash reserves of about $50,000. The machinery in the firm is getting old, however, and needs to be replaced. The estimated cost of replacement is $185,000.

3. The demand for the firm's product is constantly increasing, and the company is now about at production capacity. The brothers want to expand, but Tom is not sure this is a good idea. The estimated cost of land, a building, and machinery for the expansion is $520,000.

Tom sees from the income statement that after-tax profit for the last two years was $90,000 and $102,000, respectively. Tom is now reviewing the above problems.

Questions for Discussion
1. What should Tom do to handle the cash flow needs in the fall?
2. What do you think are the best alternatives for replacing the machinery? Why?
3. Should the firm expand now? Why or why not? If so, what do you feel would be the best way to fund this expansion? Support your answer.

CASE 18.2
Small-Business Buyers Must Be Alert

When Ron Blackstone quit his corporate job four years ago to buy a Wendy's Restaurant on Chicago's south side, he had lofty dreams. The former sales manager envisioned making millions, creating jobs in the surrounding inner-city neighborhood, and branching into other lucrative businesses. But those dreams swiftly turned into an enduring nightmare that shows how easy it is to get burned when buying a business. Another Wendy's opened close to Blackstone's store. That competition and the loss of patrons when a nearby disco closed soured sales, he says, and losses have totaled $350,000 so far.

Purchasing a small business can be one of the most treacherous experiences in an entrepreneur's career. Financial flash fires such as Blackstone's misfortunes occur all the time. Buyers of small businesses also are more likely to make costly mistakes, because they frequently don't know where to get information or even what questions to ask. The result is often a rushed purchase and, more than likely, regret.

"It's horrible how buyers get so carried away following their dream that they'll drop their savings on any deal that promises to make them boss," says Wally Stabert, president of the Institute for Certified Business Counselors in Eugene, Oregon.

Bernard Liebowitz, a psychologist who counsels small-business owners, states, "Some get caught up in the aura of a business's success. They will believe anything the seller tells them. . . . Others, imbued with past successes, convince themselves they can work miracles with someone else's troubled concern."

Daniel Imasdounian bought a nameplate company eight years ago. He says he should have known the seller wasn't disclosing everything when the seller's wife refused to part with the firm's record of receivables. Disregarding his instincts, he signed the deal anyway. Ugly surprises followed: a $2,500 court claim from unpaid suppliers, overdue tax bills of $6,600, and $15,000 in bills from other suppliers the seller had promised to pay. He sued the sellers and eventually won in court, but the process sapped his energy for running the business.

Carolyn Draper ran into a problem with a manager that stayed after she bought a delivery service three years ago. When sales dropped several months later, she grew suspicious. Visiting the company unannounced one midnight, she discovered the manager running his own delivery service, shipping packages to customers the company had lost.

The Banawans invested $200,000 in a Charlotte, North Carolina, day-care center and discovered that you had better know both the laws and the bureaucracy. Just a few days after the purchase, a local welfare agency, which had contracted with the previous owners for the care of 22 children, pulled the children out. The Banawans had not obtained their own license to run a day-care center, and the previous agency's contract was not transferable. The center lost $31,000 before the Banawans could correct the situation.

Even the environment can be a problem, as Austin Fernandes discovered when he purchased a commercial lot for a real-estate development last year. Checking records in the local county assessor's office, he discovered two empty underground storage tanks left from a gas station that had been there years earlier. Federal and state laws require an owner to remove unused tanks and clean up any damage they caused. His bill could run anywhere from $25,000 to $50,000, possibly wiping out his initial investment. He has sued the sellers and brokers in a California state court but has no guarantee he will win.

Questions for Discussion

1. Should a person starting a business have help from a lawyer? Why?
2. What type of cash flow analysis should Ron Blackstone have conducted prior to purchasing his Wendy's?
3. What kind of financial controls are needed for any business?

INVESTMENTS AND PERSONAL FINANCE

LEARNING OBJECTIVES

1. To define *common stock* and *preferred stock.*

2. To identify the major types of investors.

3. To discuss five investment objectives and identify appropriate investments for each objective.

4. To explain various investment options.

5. To describe the investment exchanges.

6. To explain the investment process and the role of the stockbroker.

7. To identify the principal regulations dealing with investment markets.

8. To explain the need for budgeting and planning in personal finances.

To get the individual investor off the endangered species list, Wall Street might consider firing the traders and hiring a few Boy Scouts. The investing public distrusts the securities industry and knows little about what it sells, according to *The Wall Street Journal*'s "American Way of Buying" consumer survey. The small investor—effectively missing from

unethical, greedy broker is well embedded in investors' minds. Names such as Michael Milken, Ivan Boesky, and Dennis Levine have become all too familiar to the public.

The *Journal* survey also found that half of all consumers—including a fourth of those with incomes over $50,000—say they don't even know how to buy

advertising should emphasize the basic strengths of investing and try to expand the customer base.

According to the survey, the American public trusts brokers less than bankers and other financial intermediaries, including the shaky, scandal-ridden savings and loan industry. Carol Moog, a psychologist, suggests that because people's fears about volatility and dishonesty were reinforced by the 1987 crash and the insider trading scandals, a confessional approach to advertising could help restore credibility. She advises brokers to start with an apology. Truck driver James Hines says he thinks of the crash when he hears the word *stockbroker*. All his savings are in the bank. According to the survey results, he is not alone.

Doug Armand/TSW

the 1988–89 bull market—seems disillusioned and may not return until stockbrokers demonstrate more honesty, personal attention to the customer, and a willingness to clearly explain their investment strategies.

What the public wants is what brokers derisively refer to as handholding. But a face-lift could help. Insider trading scandals have pointed to brokers' ethical failures and greed. The stereotype of the

shares of stock. Roy Grace, a partner in the Grace & Rothschild advertising agency in New York, lays the blame for investment ignorance on the lack of information in Wall Street's marketing. "When you have an industry personified by bulls and a variety of other animals to communicate confidence, you know you are in trouble," says Mr. Grace, whose clients include Whittle Communications and Salomon Brothers. He suggests that rather than pitching to existing investors,

The top investment is certificates of deposit, held by two out of three Americans. They understand CDs and savings bonds, but they don't understand the workings of the stock market. Some think broker commissions are 10 percent instead of the 1 to 3 percent they really are. Many don't know that securities in customer accounts at brokerage houses are insured by federal insurance.

According to Michael Emmert, a Chicago business consultant, stockbrokers don't view themselves as long-term service providers. "I get called regularly by brokers who don't want to know anything about me or my goals," he says. "All they want is to sell me some hot stock. That approach just turns me off."[1]

hen people think of investments, they often think of the stock market. As the previous chapter pointed out, corporations use stocks and bonds and other securities as a means to finance long-term capital expenditures. Understanding the workings of financial markets is important to firms that may, at some point, depend on them for the very livelihood of the firm. These markets are equally important to individuals, who may improve their own financial security through careful investment.

Even the most casual observer has become somewhat more familiar with the stock market in the last couple of years. The insider trading scandals, federal investigations, the crash of 1987, and the movie *Wall Street* have helped make us more aware. But the details of the market often escape us. This chapter will familiarize you with the stock market and how it works, as well as with other investment markets.

We begin by reviewing the use of stocks and bonds as a source of long-term financing for corporations. Then we take a look at who invests in the market and the expanding role that institutional investors play. Next we discuss the objectives different investors may have. We examine the various investment options available, the exchanges on which investments take place, and the methods used to make investments. Then we identify the major regulations affecting the securities markets. Finally, we look at personal finances and some strategies individuals can follow.

USE OF SECURITIES FOR LONG-TERM FUNDING

In Chapter Eighteen, we discussed the use of **securities** (documents, such as stocks and bonds, that can be bought or sold and that reflect ownership or debt) as a means to provide long-term funding for the firm. A firm's use of securities for funding is generally referred to as either debt capital (bonds) or equity capital (stocks). Stocks (sharing of ownership) and bonds (leverage) as long-term fund-raising options were compared in Figure 18.3. In this chapter, we examine the use of securities markets in greater detail.

Firms can, of course, use the securities market to invest funds and thereby increase income by making money from the invested funds. However, companies also commonly use security markets as a means to get cash when funds are short.

Securities
Documents that can be bought or sold and that reflect ownership or debt.

Use of Bonds

Companies issue bonds to investors for several reasons. They may give the firm a favorable interest rate, permit a long period for payback, or allow a firm to borrow more than it could from traditional commercial sources. Regardless of the reasons, bonds are an extremely common method of long-term financing. Using bonds allows the firm to maintain complete management control, since bondholders have no vote in decision making. Also, interest paid to bondholders is a deductible expense. Managers must consider, however, that bonds increase a firm's debt, interest is a legal obligation, and the face value of the bonds must be repaid at maturity.

Use of Stocks

The sale of stock means a company has decided to create needed funds by selling some ownership in the firm itself. Offering stock has advantages: shareholders never have to be repaid, there is no legal obligation to pay dividends, and the sale of stock can improve the balance sheet. Of course, firms do give up some control to voting shareholders. They must pay dividends out of after-tax profits. And managers sometimes become so focused on shareholders that they change decisions to satisfy them.

A firm can issue two types of stock: preferred stock and common stock. In each case, the evidence of the purchase is called a stock certificate (see Figure 18.4 for an example of a stock certificate).

Preferred stock   The fact that it has preference over common stock in the payment of dividends and in any claim against the firm's assets gives this stock its name: **preferred stock.** Preferred stock dividends must be paid before any common stock dividends. And if the firm is liquidated, the holders of preferred stock will have to be paid out of the proceeds of the sale of the firm's assets before any holders of common stock would be paid. Payments would include both dividends owed and the value of the stock itself.

The dividend on preferred stock is generally fixed. It is typically based on some percentage of the par, or face, value of the preferred stock. For example, if a preferred stock has a par value of $50 and pays a 6 percent dividend, the annual dividend would be $3 (.06 × $50).

Some preferred stock is *cumulative*. It simply accumulates unpaid dividends until they are all paid. If a company decided not to pay dividends one year because of a cash crunch, preferred stock rights to dividends would accumulate until dividends were paid. If an individual had one share of 8 percent, $100 par value, cumulative preferred stock and the company did not pay dividends one year, the individual would be entitled to $16 the second year—assuming dividends were paid in the second year—and would be entitled to payment before any common stock dividends could be distributed. Preferred stock also is sometimes *convertible;* it can be converted to common stock at a price specified at the time the preferred stock is purchased.

Because preferred stock offers these extra benefits, holders of such stock are typically not entitled to vote for the board of directors or on other corporate matters.

Common stock   Why would anyone want to buy common stock when it offers no guarantees? Because **common stock** gives shareholders a vote in corporate matters, an opportunity to realize greater growth in the value of their investment, and the possibility of greater income return since the dividend rate is not fixed. Common stock does not guarantee any dividends or entitle holders to any share in the assets until all other creditors have been paid.

Common stock has two values: a market value and a book value. The **market value** of the stock is the price at which the stock is currently selling. The **book value** is the value of the stock relative to the value of the company. Book value is obtained by subtracting the value of all liabilities and preferred stock from the value of all assets, and dividing the result by the number of shares of common stock outstanding.

Preferred Stock
Stock that has preference over common stock in the payment of dividends and in claims against the assets of the firm, but does not confer voting rights.

Common Stock
Stock that confers voting rights but not preferential rights of dividends or claims against the assets of the firm.

Market Value
The price at which a share of common stock is currently selling.

Book Value
The value of common stock relative to the value of the company.

FIGURE 19.1

Stock and Bond Offerings

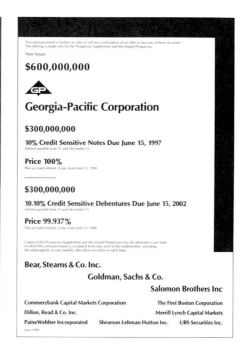

Courtesy of Bear, Stearns & Co. Inc.

Making a Stock or Bond Offering

Stock and bond offerings appear daily in the form of simple announcements in business newspapers such as *The Wall Street Journal* (see Figure 19.1). Potential investors can find a stock offering price per share and where to obtain a copy of the **prospectus**, a statement containing information about the firm, its management, its operations, the purpose for the stock issue, and other information that might be helpful to a potential buyer. The bond offering announcement gives similar information for bonds. It states the interest and due date and whether the bonds are convertible.

While a corporation can market its own bond or stock issue, investment bankers handle most large offerings. **Investment bankers** are financial specialists who handle the sale of new stock or bond offers. Some better-known investment bankers include Bear, Stearns & Co. Inc., Salomon Brothers, Oppenheimer, and the investment bank division of Merrill Lynch. The investment banker advises the issuer on the timing, pricing, and appropriate size of the offering, and purchases the total issue from the company at a discount. For example, an investment banker may purchase a $5 per share stock offering for

Prospectus
A statement used by potential investors that gives information about a firm, its management, its operations, the purpose for the stock issue, etc.

Investment Banker
A financial specialist who handles the sale of new stock or bond offers.

Those Bonds Are Plastic

Rock solid may be your style in securities, but don't be surprised if your broker suggests "plastic bonds." Such bonds get their nickname from being backed by what people owe on their credit cards. First issued by Citicorp and aimed at conservative investors, these securities boast a AAA rating.

The 19 percent interest that cardholders pay is not passed intact to holders of plastic bonds. The bank sets aside 4 points as a reserve against predictable defaults, 3 points against widespread economic trouble, and another 3 points to back up guarantees. That reduces what's left for investors to 9 percent, or 9.14 percent after compounding (computing interest on the principal and accrued interest).

Citicorp is happy with the concept. In recent years, banks have had to increase their reserves or shed assets. To help with the problem, Citicorp sold a $500 million portion of its $20 billion in Master-Card and Visa receivables to the public under the name Citi Credit Card Trust 1989–1. The trust is sliced into pieces as small as $1,000 and sold to investors by brokers. The monthly interest payments can be deposited directly into customers' cash management accounts at brokerage houses. The bonds mature on June 15, 1993.

Citicorp's plastic bonds pay a little more than CDs when issued; their 9.14 percent yield bested the 8.98 percent yield on its own four-year CD by 16 basis points (9.14 − 8.98 = 16). Although not FDIC-backed, the bonds are seen as extremely safe. Even if large numbers of credit card customers stopped making their payments, provisions exist to cover the trust.

Citicorp's issue was followed by many more. Retail giant Sears Roebuck issued $250 million of its own plastic bonds. A market for securities backed by consumer credit, from boat and car loans to home equity loans, is now blossoming. Evidently investors are as interested in investing in the plastic cards as they are in using them. Over $6 billion of credit card securities were issued in the first quarter of 1990 alone; the total for that year far surpassed 1989's volume of $10 billion.[2]

$4.50 per share. The investment banker may then sell the shares to other underwriters, who will sell them to the public.

Firms constantly devise new ways to fund operations. The Business Action describes one unique instrument being used.

WHO INVESTS IN THE SECURITIES MARKET?

The securities market sees two major types of investors: institutional and private. *Institutional investors* are professional investors who invest for large groups or organizations such as pension funds, insurance companies, mutual funds, and universities. Institutional investors have come to dominate the trading on Wall Street. They represent 75 to 80 percent of all trading, although private investors still hold approximately 60 percent of the stock.[3] Institutional traders have had far-reaching impacts on the nature of the market—for example, in the crash of October 1987, when institutional traders flooding the trade floor with orders made such a large drop occur so quickly.[4]

The securities market still has room for private investors, however, and many participate. About 40 million people own corporate shares of stock—but in a market much trickier than it used to be. In the early 1980s, the market was rising and making money in the market was relatively easy; now it takes greater care to make a profit.[5] Yet stocks remain a good investment. Since 1927, even including the crashes of 1929 and 1987 and the downturn of the mid-70s, the

Courtesy of Salomon Brothers Inc.

Professional investors like Salomon Brothers handle investments for a variety of organizations around the world.

securities market has returned investors an average of 6.6 percent after adjustment for inflation.[6]

The mix of investors is changing. Today, as many women as men participate in the securities market. The average age of traders has been constantly dropping, and the median age of shareholders is now 44, down from 53 in 1975.[7] Some amateur investors do quite well in the market. The National Association of Investors Corporation claims that 47 percent of the nation's 6,900 investment clubs equaled or surpassed the Standard & Poor's 500 stock index, while only about one fourth of investment professionals were able to perform as well.[8]

Many individuals invest in the market. What motivates them to purchase stocks and other securities? What are their reasons for making investments of any kind? The next section discusses some of the motivations individuals have for making investments.

WHY INDIVIDUALS INVEST IN SECURITIES

People's reasons for investing in the market can be quite diverse. Their objectives typically fall into one of five categories: growth, income, security, liquidity, and deferment of taxes.

Growth

Many people see the market as a way to greatly increase their personal wealth. They are interested in getting *capital gains*. Capital gains are the profit you make when you sell an investment for more than you paid for it. If you bought a stock for $5 and sold it a year later for $10, you would have realized a $5 profit, a $5 capital gain.

Investors who have gain as their objective will invest in growth stocks (young or rapidly expanding companies), real estate, precious metals, or, in some cases, collectibles. (Collectibles are items that increase in value because they are rare, such as stamps, coins, or baseball cards.) Growth stocks may not pay dividends since fast-growing companies prefer to plow money back into the company to finance the growth rather than pay dividends. An example of just how much growth can be realized is shown in Figure 19.2. However, because high-growth stocks represent young or rapidly expanding companies, they typically carry greater risk than other stocks. Such companies do not have the long record of success that more mature corporations have.

Income

Blue-Chip Stock
Stock issued by large, well-capitalized companies that consistently pay dividends.

Many individuals look to investments in securities as a means to produce additional income. They want to receive a steady, reasonably predictable flow of income. Investors desiring steady income may look at Treasury bills, corporate bonds, and some common stocks, such as utilities or blue-chip stocks. **Blue-chip stocks** are stocks issued by large, well-capitalized companies, such as IBM or Exxon, that have paid consistent dividends. These stocks return fairly high levels of income. Obviously the opportunities for income vary greatly; a savings account insured by the federal government may pay a guaranteed 5

FIGURE 19.2

High-Growth Stock at Wal-Mart

DID YOU KNOW? *Investors who bought Wal-Mart stock in 1973 have seen their investment grow 500 times.*

A $1,000 investment in 1973   = $500,000 in stock value today

percent interest, whereas some highly speculative corporate bonds (junk bonds) may return 15 percent or 18 percent interest. The factor that dictates the difference in return is the level of risk.

Security

The more concerned an individual is about losing an investment, the farther that person should stay from speculative investments. Typically the higher the risk, the higher the rate of return. The **rate of return** is the dollar value of the interest earned or dividend received from a security, divided by the market value of the security. This concept is sometimes referred to as the risk-return trade-off: investors must be willing to assume a certain level of risk in order to accomplish higher rates of return, either in growth or income. Those interested in security may invest in highly secure investments such as savings bonds, certificates of deposit, or Treasury bills.

Rate of Return
The dollar value of the interest earned or dividend received divided by the market value of the security.

Liquidity

Some investors need to keep their money as liquid as possible; that is, they need to be able to get the cash out of their investment at any time. Those who desire liquidity will not want to choose an investment with a value that fluctuates very much in the short run. If an investor who chose such a stock needs to get the money out when the stock's value is low, the unfortunate timing of the need means the loss of a great deal of money. For example, an individual investing $10,000 in a stock selling for $10 at the time of purchase would own 1,000 shares of stock. If the price of the stock dropped to $9 and the investor had to sell it to get cash, the sale would bring only $9,000, for a $1,000 loss.

People who want liquidity need to invest in stable investments, those with little fluctuation. As noted in Chapter Eighteen, marketable securities such as certificates of deposit and Treasury bills are excellent investments for liquidity and provide a reasonably high rate of return.

Tax Deferment or Avoidance

Investors may want to put off paying taxes on a portion of their income, and some investment vehicles do allow tax deferment. The last section of this chapter will discuss tax-deferred investments. Other people want some of their income to be tax free. Many municipal bonds and government securities are not taxed. Municipal bonds typically do not require the payment of any federal income tax on the income they provide. Some federal government securities do not require the payment of any state or local income tax on their income. However, the Supreme Court has given Congress the right to tax these if it chooses to do so. Because such securities are currently tax free, they typically have a slightly lower rate of return than fully taxable investments.

CHOICES FOR INVESTMENT

The principal investment choices are stocks, bonds, government securities, certificates of deposit, money market funds, mutual funds, and commodities. Real estate and collectibles also are options, but here we will concentrate on investing in the intangible property listed above.

Stocks

Although, as explained above, the two types of stocks are common stock and preferred stock, we will focus here only on common stock. Stock investments are typically made through the stock exchanges (discussed in the next section). As you know, stock prices change regularly. We hear daily and even hourly reports of how many points up or down the market is.

Bull Market
A market state in which stock values are generally rising and investors are generally optimistic.

Over time the market tends to rise and fall as the economy expands and contracts. During boom years, the market is usually bullish. In a **bull market,** share values are generally going up. During recessions the market typically becomes bearish. Share values generally decline in a **bear market.** Of course these are general trends. Some stocks may go down in a bull market either because of the nature of their industry, such as oil in the 1980s, or because the company's performance is questionable. Likewise some stocks can go up in price during a bear market. Investors must understand several terms referring to the purchase of stock; we will discuss these terms now.

Bear Market
A market state in which stock values are generally declining and investors are generally pessimistic.

Round Lot
A stock purchase of 100 shares.

Lot purchases   Stocks are typically purchased in quantities called **round lots,** which are 100-share lots of stock. An individual who wants to buy stock in a smaller quantity will be purchasing in **odd lots.** Odd lots are typically grouped together for sale to form round lots; that is, the odd-lot purchases are grouped into round lots to make actual market purchases and then distributed to the various odd-lot puchasers. Odd lots are generally more expensive to trade.

Odd Lot
A stock purchase of less than 100 shares.

Margin Trading
Purchasing more stock shares than a given amount of money would buy because a portion of the shares are bought on credit.

Margin trading   When buying stock, an investor can pay the full price for the stock at the time of purchase or can buy the stock on margin. **Margin trading** means that the investor does not pay the full price for the stock but rather puts down a portion of the price and borrows the remainder from the broker. The broker retains the stock as collateral and charges interest on the loan. *Margin rates*—the percentage of the purchase price required in cash—are under the

The Leverage Effect in Margin Trading   **FIGURE 19.3**

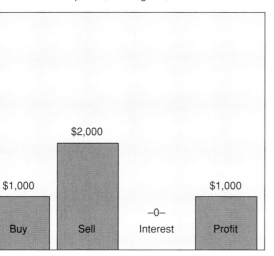

Investment: $1,000
Stock price: $10 bought $20 sold

Straight trade

Straight trade: Individual purchases 100 shares of stock. Sale of stock later at $20 represents $1,000 gain and $1,000 profit.

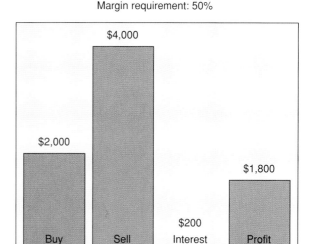

Loan interest: 10% annual
Margin requirement: 50%

Margin trade

Margin trade: Individual purchases 200 shares of stock using 50% margin requirement. Sale of stock at $20 represents a gain of $2,000, and this less the interest cost of $200 on the margin loan represents a profit of $1,800.

control of the Federal Reserve Board and can change; the current margin rate of 50 percent has been in effect for a number of years.

Margin trading enables an individual to leverage a purchase. For example, a person investing $1,000 could ordinarily buy 200 shares of a $5 stock. With a 50 percent margin, that same $1,000 investment can purchase 400 shares. If that person bought 400 shares on margin at $5 and the price went up to $6 after one year, he or she would make $400 profit minus the interest paid on the margin loan. If the investor had not bought on margin, the profit would have been $200 (see Figure 19.3). Investors must take care when buying on margin; if the stock value falls, the losses double.

Stock options   If you see a car you think you might want to buy and you want to make sure it is not sold to someone else, you might put a $100 deposit on the car. This deposit will give you the right to purchase the car at the specified price within some time period, say five days. If at the end of five days you decide you do want the car, you can get it for the price you originally offered, regardless of what other offers the dealer may have received or whether the price of identical cars has gone up. If after five days you decide not to purchase the car, you will lose the $100 deposit.

Stock options work in the same way. A **stock option** is the purchased right (similar to the deposit on a car) to buy or sell shares of a stock at a predetermined price, provided the purchaser does so within a specified time. If the

Stock Option
The purchased right to buy or sell shares of stock at a predetermined price within a specified time period.

FIGURE 19.4 **Reading Stock Quotations**

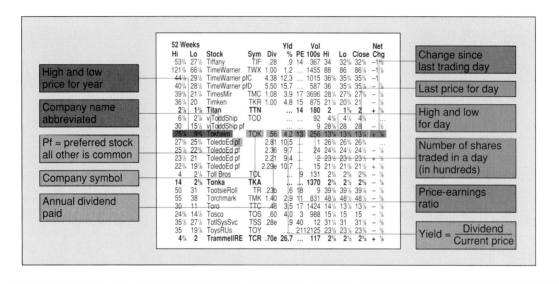

stock goes up in price, you may exercise your option and purchase the stock at the predetermined price and then immediately sell it at a profit. If the stock goes down in price, you may choose to let your option expire and forfeit the price you paid for the option.

Two types of options are available: put options and call options. A **put option** allows you to sell at a predetermined price (you purchase the stock at market price). A **call option** allows you to purchase a stock at a predetermined price and then sell it at market price. If you bought a put option for a stock at $10 and the stock went to $12, you would have to purchase the stock at $12 to exercise your put at $10, and you would lose $2 per share. On the other hand, if you had a call option for that same stock, you could buy the $12 stock at $10 and make $2 a share.

Options are cheaper than buying actual stocks, but they are riskier. If you choose not to exercise your option, you lose it and the money you paid for it. When you buy stock, you receive the stock and can wait for the market to shift.

Reading stock quotations Figure 19.4 will help you understand how to read stock quotations. It reproduces a stock quotation from *The Wall Street Journal*. Other sources of stock quotations include *USA Today* and most major daily newspapers.

Notice the shaded stock Tokheim, which manufactures gas pumps. Starting from the left column, we see that the highest price paid for this stock in the last 52 weeks was 25⅞, or $25.875, and the lowest price for the same period was 9¾, or $9.75. The symbol used on the stock tapes follows the name of the stock. The next column is the annual dividend; in this case, shareholders received 56 cents per share. This is followed by the yield percentage, the percentage of the closing stock price that the dividend represents. The next

Put Option
An option to buy stock shares at market price and sell at a specified price.

Call Option
An option to buy stock shares at a specified price and sell at market price.

column shows the **price-earnings ratio,** the closing stock price divided by the annual earnings per share (total earnings divided by the number of shares outstanding). The price-earnings ratio for Tokheim is 13. You can use this number to find the earnings per share by dividing the closing price of the stock by the price-earnings ratio (in this case, 13¼ ÷ 13 = $1.0192 per share). The remaining columns summarize the activity for that day. First the volume of shares traded is shown in 100s. Price information is next: the highest price paid that day for a share of stock was $13.625, the lowest was $13.25, and the closing (end of the trading day) price was $13.25. This was a drop of 12½ cents from the closing price of the previous day (net change).

Reading stock quotes seems difficult at first but gets easier after some time and practice. Pick a stock, make an imaginary investment in it, and see how you do for 30 days.

Bonds

As Chapter Eighteen explained, corporate bonds are debts owed by the corporation to purchasers of the bonds. They typically pay the holder a set rate of interest on a semiannual basis.

Bonds are initially offered and sold at a specified price, typically $1,000 or multiples of $1,000. However, once a bond is on the market, the actual selling price of the bond may vary. Bondholders do not have to keep their bonds until maturity; in fact very few do. As with stocks, bonds can be sold to other investors. The difference is that the selling price of a bond results primarily from changes in the interest rate and the value of the corporation.

Assume you bought a $1,000 bond that would return an annual interest of 10 percent, or $100. Assume also that the interest rate on similar bonds goes up to 12.5 percent. Obviously investors will not want to buy your bond for $1,000 to earn a return of 10 percent when they can get similar bonds for $1,000 that will return 12.5 percent. You may be able to sell your bond for a price that would enable the buyer to in effect earn 12.5 percent. In this case, paying $800 for the $1,000 bond that yields 10 percent interest ($100) would produce the equivalent yield ($100 ÷ $800 = 12.5 percent). Therefore, your bond might sell for approximately $800, a price determined by interest rate changes.

The value of the corporation also affects the price. Bonds are rated by rating services. The rating services give the bonds a grade based on the likelihood that the corporation is going to be able to pay the interest and the principal as indicated. Very high quality bonds are rated AAA, and very low quality bonds are rated C. The amount of interest a bond must earn for the person holding it is dictated by the rating of the bond as well as the market interest rate. In the example above, if the bond you held was rated as a B bond, it may have to return its holder a 15 percent rate to be acceptable. This means the bond would have to sell for $666.66 ($100 ÷ $666.66 = 15 percent).

Defaults on bonds   When a corporation fails to make an interest payment on a bond it has issued, it is said to have defaulted. Bonds in **default** are rated D, the lowest rating. Bonds in this rating are priced based on the likelihood that the company will be able to make future payments. If that is not likely, the price is based on the salvage value of the bond—its likely share from the sale of the firm's assets.

Price-Earnings Ratio
The current market price of a stock divided by the annual earnings per share.

Default
Failure to pay the interest on a debt instrument.

FIGURE 19.5

Reading Bond Quotations

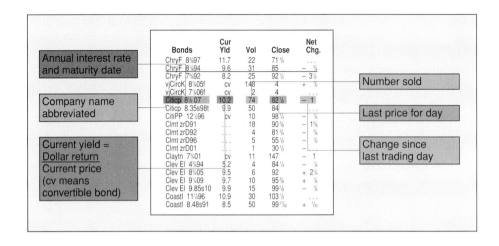

Reading bond quotes   Look at the bond quotation from *The Wall Street Journal* in Figure 19.5. Notice the shaded listing for Citicorp. The numbers next to "Citicp" read 8½ 07, which means that this bond was issued to pay an annual interest rate of 8½ percent and has a maturity date of 2007. The next number, 10.2, is the current yield of the bond. In this case, the bond is actually paying 10.2 percent of its current selling price in interest. The next number indicates the volume of trading: 74 of these bonds were traded on this day. The close number, 82½, represents the price these bonds were selling for at the end of the trading day. Bond prices are quoted in 100s, and bonds are issued in denominations of $1,000. Thus the actual selling price for each bond is 10 times the stated closing price; this bond was trading for $825 at the close of the day. The final entry tells us that the current price is unchanged from the previous day's price.

Government securities   The U.S. government finances its projects primarily through taxes. However, just as in business, these funds do not always come in when needed, so borrowing becomes necessary. Another reason for government borrowing is to finance the deficit.

The government finances most of its borrowing with Treasury bills (T bills). These mature in 91 to 364 days and do not pay interest but rather are sold at a discount and then redeemed at full face value at maturity. The buyer makes a profit equal to the difference between the full face value and the discounted selling price.

The government also issues Treasury bonds and U.S. government bonds. These finance long-term debt. Treasury bonds mature in 1 to 7 years, and U.S. government bonds mature in 7 to 30 years. These securities pay a fixed amount of interest, generally about 1 percent less than the rate of interest on high-quality corporate bonds. The interest is exempt from all state and local income taxes.

Many other agencies issue debt securities to finance their operations. Some of the better known include the Government National Mortgage Association (Ginnie Maes) and the Federal National Mortgage Association (Fannie Maes).

Take The First Step Toward Higher Education.
Buy U.S. Savings Bonds. Now Tax Free For College.

Some of the most important steps in any child's life are taken by the parents. Such as buying U.S. Savings Bonds. After all, it's never too early to start your tax free tuition fund, especially the way fees and tuitions are rising. For years, Bonds have been the smart, convenient way to save money for college. Now, Bonds can also be completely tax free.
Take the first step. Buy Bonds at your local bank, or ask about the Payroll Savings Plan at work.

A public service of this publication

U.S. Savings Bonds

The Great American Investment

Courtesy of U.S. Savings Bonds

U.S. Savings Bonds can be used to save money for a child's education.

Municipal bonds   **Municipal bonds** are issued by states, towns, and other municipalities to finance schools, hospitals, roads, and other civic projects. Municipal bonds currently are exempt from federal income tax (although a recent Supreme Court ruling makes it possible for Congress to tax these); in many cases, they are free from state and local income taxes. Because of their tax-exempt status, municipal bonds pay a lower rate of interest than many other securities do.

Municipal Bonds
Bonds issued by states, towns, and other municipalities to finance schools, hospitals, roads, and other civic projects.

Certificates of Deposit

A certificate of deposit (CD) is really a time deposit that pays a higher than average rate of interest to the investor (see Chapter Eighteen). CDs, insured by the federal government, are very secure. But an investor can suffer a substantial interest penalty if the certificate is not held until its maturity date. A person who purchases CDs through brokers can sometimes avoid an interest penalty for early withdrawal because the CDs can be resold to other investors. In this case, they are treated in much the same way as bonds.

Mutual Funds

Small investors sometimes find it difficult to participate in the market. The idea behind **mutual funds** is that a group of investors can pool their money and invest in securities. These funds are generally formal organizations, and the investments are usually handled by a professional investment manager. The fund may

Mutual Fund
A fund formed by a group of individuals, who pool their money to invest in securities, and usually handled by a professional investment manager.

Drought damage can cause the price of corn to fall dramatically.

John Patsch/Journalism Services

buy stock, bonds, government securities, commodities, or other investments. The share price of a mutual fund is calculated by adding up the value of all the shares held by the fund and dividing by the number of shares outstanding.

The Wall Street Journal reports that more than 2,600 mutual funds currently operate in the United States. Once heavily invested in equities (stocks), these funds have shifted more toward bonds and money markets since the stock market crash of 1987. Of course the blend of securities may change again as market conditions change and investors gain more confidence.

Mutual fund quotes are provided in *The Wall Street Journal* and many other newspapers. Figure 19.6 shows a portion of *The Wall Street Journal*'s mutual fund quotations. The first number is the net asset value per share. This represents the net asset value of the fund divided by the number of shares. For MichTx, the net asset value per share is $8.11. The second number represents the offer price and includes the maximum sales charge that would be paid at purchase; the offer price is $8.51. The third number is the change in the net asset value since the last trade day, down two cents.

Commodities

Commodities
Large-volume items, such as raw materials, precious metals, and agricultural products, in which individuals can invest.

Commodities are items, primarily raw materials, precious metals, and agricultural products such as wheat, corn, and cattle, that can be traded in large volume at a commodities exchange. The major exchange is located in Chicago. Two types of trading occur at the exchange. The first is *spot market trading,* where the actual merchandise is purchased at the time of the sale. The second is *futures market trading,* where the purchase is made for future delivery, sometimes up to a year or more later.

Reading Mutual Fund Quotations

FIGURE 19.6

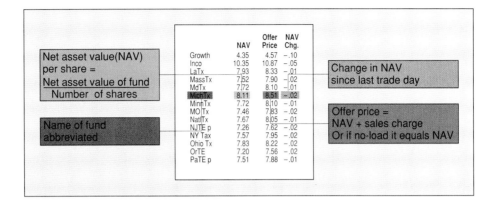

Reading Commodities Quotations

FIGURE 19.7

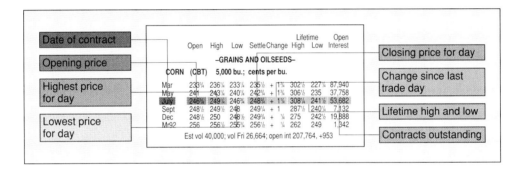

Commodities trading is highly speculative. The commodities market is driven by weather, rumor, political climate, the economy, and almost any other environmental condition you can think of. Because the market is volatile— changing rapidly—getting caught in a shifting market and losing a great deal of money is easy.

Figure 19.7 shows the quotation system for commodities from *The Wall Street Journal*. The pricing method used and the size of a contract appear at the top of the quotation. In the case of corn, the price is in cents per bushel, and the purchase contract represents 5,000 bushels.

The date of the contract, in the first column, states the date when the actual product will be delivered. Then the quotation shows the open, high, low, and closing (settle) prices for the day. The final columns show the change in price since the last trade day, the lifetime high and low, and the open interest in each contract—that is, the number of contracts outstanding. Notice that the closing price of corn for July was 248¾; because corn is priced in cents per bushel, that translates to $2.4875 per bushel. Thus the market value of a contract is $12,437.50, since each contract involves 5,000 bushels.

The Sting in the Pits

It sounds like a story out of a spy novel. For two tense years, FBI undercover agents worked Chicago's trading pits. Donning brightly colored trader's jackets, they roamed the Chicago Board of Trade and the Chicago Mercantile Exchange, where billions of dollars worth of commodity futures change hands every day. Tape-recording hundreds of conversations, the feds slowly accumulated evidence that dozens of dishonest traders were cheating customers out of millions by executing orders at fictitious prices. On the night the undercover agents started to move in, suspects received visits from men they knew as fellow traders and were served with grand jury subpoenas.

The sting, reportedly planned by U.S. Attorney Anton Valukas, was as bold as it was extensive. As the *Chicago Tribune* and other sources reported, several FBI agents penetrated the trading pits. One, known as Richard Carlsong, bought a Board of Trade seat (reportedly with several hundred thousand dollars of government money) and traded soybean futures. Others traded Treasury bond futures, Swiss francs, and Japanese yen. They followed the routines of successful traders, reportedly extracting information during meals and informal meetings.

The exchange of commodities is particularly open to fraud because of the way trades are conducted.

A trade called in to a broker at the commodity exchange is taken to a floor broker in a "pit" where the particular commodity or financial instrument is traded. The floor broker executes the trade through an "open outcry" system of trading, in which the broker uses hand signals and shouts to communicate his trade. Another broker or trader willing to make that trade signals or shouts back, and the deal is made.

The investigation uncovered evidence that crooked traders took advantage of the open-outcry system. "This system, more than most financial systems, relies on personal integrity," says Rep. Dan Glickman of the House Agriculture Committee. Essentially, customers were charged above-market prices when they sold. The traders pocketed the difference. They reportedly avoided detection by keeping their phony prices within the range of current market prices.

On July 9, 1990, in the first trial resulting from the sting, a federal jury delivered guilty verdicts on 8 out of 10 charges. Although the evidence appeared overwhelming, jurors interviewed after the trial indicated that many of the tapes proved inconclusive. But lawyers on both sides believe that upcoming trials may see more convictions. Even defense attorneys have acknowledged that the taped conversations are incriminatory.[9]

Financial Futures

Another avenue of trading is financial futures. Like commodity futures, **financial futures** require the purchaser to buy or sell a specific financial instrument, such as stocks or Treasury bonds, for a set price at a specific date. Most of these are purchased on margin, and since margin requirements on financial futures are lower than the margin requirements on stocks, the potential risk is magnified.

Financial Future
A future that requires the purchaser to buy or sell a specific financial instrument.

WHERE INVESTMENTS ARE HANDLED

For the most part, security transactions occur on or through an organized exchange. A **stock exchange** is simply an organization of individuals who buy and sell securities to the public. While this is usually a physical location, it does not have to be. The largest stock exchange in the United States is the New York Stock Exchange (NYSE). More than 75 percent of all trading is done at the NYSE. The American Stock Exchange (AMEX), also located in New York, is much smaller. Both are national exchanges that handle stocks for companies from all over the United States. Securities of international firms may be listed on foreign exchanges such as those in London and Tokyo.

Stock Exchange
An organization of individuals who buy and sell securities to the public.

In addition to the national and foreign exchanges, regional exchanges are located in Chicago, San Francisco, Philadelphia, Boston, Cincinnati, Spokane, and Salt Lake City. Regional exchanges primarily list the stocks of firms within their own market area, although some national firms also list on regional exchanges.

Many stocks are not listed on any of the major or regional exchanges. These stocks are traded through the **over-the-counter (OTC) market** and handled through an electronic network of several thousand brokers who communicate trades through the National Association of Securities Dealers Automated Quotation System (NASDAQ). Besides OTC stocks—some of which are very well known, such as Coors and Apple—the OTC market handles most corporate and U.S. government bonds as well as many city and state government bonds. NASDAQ quotes are given in *The Wall Street Journal* on a daily basis.

Over-the-Counter (OTC) Market
An electronic network of several thousand brokers who communicate trades through NASDAQ.

Commodity exchanges specialize in the buying and selling of commodities such as agricultural goods and precious metals. The Chicago Board of Trade is the largest commodity exchange; the Chicago Mercantile Exchange is the second largest. These exchanges operate similarly to stock exchanges.

Commodity Exchange
An organization that specializes in buying and selling commodities.

Commodities trading is extremely risky. It requires great expertise and should be conducted only by professionals. Most people who speculate in commodities lose money. More than just risky, commodities in recent years have been the object of several frauds on the exchange, as the Business Action reports.

THE INVESTMENT PROCESS

The investment process typically involves several steps. An investor usually works with a stockbroker to decide on which stock to buy, the broker places the order, and the investor follows the movement of the purchased stock and the market in general by reading market indicators.

Contacting a Broker

Stockbroker
An individual licensed to act on behalf of an investor in the buying and selling of securities.

The first step in investing in stocks or bonds is to contact a **stockbroker,** an individual licensed to act on an investor's behalf in buying and selling securities. Stockbrokers are listed in the Yellow Pages under Stock and Bond Brokers. The stockbroker acts as a financial intermediary and in many cases as an investments adviser. When dealing with stockbrokers, clients need to make their investment objectives known to the stockbroker. Your broker needs to know whether you are looking for growth or income, the risk you are willing to take, the level of liquidity you want to maintain, and whether you are looking for tax deferment or tax avoidance. With this understanding, the stockbroker can recommend the types of securities you should consider and, for stocks and bonds, recommend specific company securities.

Ordering

Market Order
An order that authorizes a broker to purchase stock at the current market price.

Limit Order
An order to purchase stock only if the price is at or below a specified limit.

Once you have decided to purchase a particular stock to meet your goals, your broker can place the order for you through the appropriate stock exchange. Let's say you want to purchase some Rockwell stock, which is trading at around 23½. You think the stock is going to go up, so you place a *market order* with your broker. A **market order** authorizes the broker to purchase at the current market price. If you want to make sure you do not pay more than a certain price, you can place a **limit order.** Under a limit order, the broker would purchase the stock only if the price were at or below the price you had specified as the limit. Of course you would typically place the order for round lots of 100 shares to minimize transaction costs.

To place the order, the stockbroker teletypes or calls the firm's member on the floor of the New York Stock Exchange (Rockwell is listed on the NYSE). The New York representative goes directly to the location on the floor of the

Stock exchanges in other countries such as Barcelona, Spain, can be used as market indicators.

The Image Works

exchange where Rockwell is traded and attempts to make the purchase, provided someone is offering (selling) at the time the purchase will be made; otherwise the order will be held to wait for someone to offer to sell. The same process is followed if you decide to sell, except that you would place a sell order.

Reading the Market Indicators

Several indicators provide information on the condition and direction of the stock market. As we noted previously, investors can get current information on certain stocks in the stock listings of local newspapers or national newspapers such as *The Wall Street Journal*. That paper features a number of good articles every day concerning the financial markets. Investors should also watch what is happening to the economy in the United States and in the world and be aware of any special activity in any industry. Most of all, investors should consult with their brokers, whose job it is to keep their customers informed.

Broad indicators of stock market activity are also available. The most well known of these is the Dow Jones Industrial Average, which is really three different indexes based on the market prices of 30 industrial, 20 transportation, and 15 utility stocks. The Dow Jones index indicates the total value of one share of each stock (adjusted by a factor that takes into account the effect of stock splits and the rare changes in the firms that make up the average). The "Dow," as it is commonly called, includes firms such as Sears Roebuck and McDonald's as well as General Motors and Boeing. Figure 19.8 lists the stocks that currently make up the Dow Jones Industrial Average. The Dow is the most widely reported index of the stock market's activities and can sometimes cause panic, as in October 1987 when it dropped over 500 points in a single day of trading. Many people believe the Dow is too narrowly defined since it represents a relatively small number of large blue-chip companies. Another index, Standard & Poor's, is more broadly based, developed from the market performance of 400 industrial, 40 financial, 40 utility, and 20 transportation stocks.

Dow Jones Industrial Average Companies as of January 1, 1990   **FIGURE 19.8**

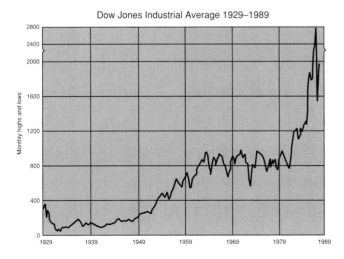

Dow Jones Industrial Average 1929–1989

30 firms used to compute the Dow Jones Industrial Average

Allied-Signal, Inc.	International Paper Co.
ALCOA	McDonald's Corporation
American Express Company	Merck & Co., Inc.
AT&T	Navistar
Bethlehem Steel Corporation	Philip Morris Incorporated
The Boeing Company	Primerica Corp.
Chevron Corporation	The Procter & Gamble Co.
The Coca-Cola Company	Sears Roebuck & Co.
Du Pont	Texaco, Inc.
Eastman Kodak Company	3M
Exxon Corporation	Union Carbide Corporation
General Electric Company	USX Corp.
General Motors Corporation	United Technologies Corp.
The Goodyear Tire & Rubber Company	Westinghouse Electric Corporation
IBM Corporation	F.W. Woolworth Co.

The original list published in 1896 had only 12 stocks, many of which no longer exist. The original list consisted of:

American Cotton Oil	Laclede Gas
American Sugar	National Lead
American Tobacco	North American
Chicago Gas	Tennessee Coal and Iron
Distilling and Cattle Feeding	U.S. Leather Preferred
General Electric	U.S. Rubber

REGULATION OF SECURITIES MARKETS AND TRANSACTIONS

Blue-Sky Laws
State laws that prevent corporations from issuing worthless securities; also require stockbrokers to be licensed and securities to be registered.

Both the issuance and trading of securities are regulated by state and federal laws. State laws, often called **blue-sky laws,** prevent corporations from issuing worthless securities to unsuspecting investors. These laws also require stockbrokers to be licensed and securities to be registered before they can be sold.

At the federal level, the most significant legislation is the *Securities Act of 1933.* This act protects the public from interstate sales of fraudulent securities. It requires a firm to provide full disclosure of information that might affect the value of its securities. This information is filed in a registration with the Securities and Exchange Commission (SEC). In addition, every prospective buyer of the securities must be given a prospectus. As we noted earlier, the prospectus is a summary of the registration statement filed with the SEC and contains information about the firm and any information that would be helpful to a potential investor. The SEC does not judge the merit of individual securities, however, so the buyer should pay careful attention to the information in the prospectus.

The SEC was established by the *Securities Exchange Act of 1934.* The SEC is a five-member commission appointed by the president with the consent of the Senate. Based on this act, all corporations whose securities are listed on national securities exchanges must file registration statements with the SEC. They must also update their registration statements with annual reports.

The National Association of Securities Dealers (NASD) was created by the *Maloney Act (1938),* an amendment to the Securities Exchange Act. The NASD was created as a private trade organization to regulate the OTC market. The SEC, however, does maintain final authority over the OTC market. Mutual funds were brought under the jurisdiction of the SEC by the *Investment Company Act of 1940.*

Investors receive some protection through regulation. But they are not protected against losses caused by the failure of a company. An investor who purchases a stock takes on the risk of company failure. The situation may differ, however, when funds are left with a brokerage house. The *Securities Investor Protection Act of 1970* established the Securities Investor Protection Insurance Corporation. The corporation, which is not a government agency, provides insurance protection for investors who suffer losses resulting from fraud or from a broker going out of business while still owing investors money. Investors are protected for up to $100,000 in cash losses and up to $400,000 in losses of securities.

PERSONAL FINANCE

Chapter Eighteen discussed the discipline organizations must develop if they hope to be successful. They must gain sufficient capital before success becomes a reasonable proposition. They must manage their working capital so that funds are always available for daily activities and funds not being used can be invested. They must determine their long-term funding needs and then develop sources for those funds either internally, through debt, or through equity. A company that wants to be successful has to know what is being spent and why and has to have control over spending.

Individuals have similar financial concerns and must develop comparable discipline. We need to save sufficient capital before making major purchases (car, home, boat), or we may find ourselves in cash flow trouble. We must manage current assets to make sure funds are available to pay ongoing household expenses and cover some unexpected expenses. And, like businesses, we need to plan for the future. To gain control of finances, each of us should become aware of our spending habits and determine how to adjust to provide adequate savings.

Role of a Budget

Understanding how and why we spend money is the first step to managing personal finances. To start, an individual needs to create a budget and then record all expenditures and the reasons for these expenditures. Keeping a daily log is one way. After some period of time, perhaps six months (so that quarterly, semi-annual, and even annual payments are included), this log should be critically reviewed to find possible adjustments in both the sources and uses of funds. The next step involves establishing a monthly cash flow budget that projects the expected expenses and income for each month. Review these to see where additional sources of cash will be needed and where excess funds may exist.

A workable budget must include all possible expenses. People frequently forget to include expenses such as:

- *Quarterly, semi-annual, and annual payments.* Because expenses such as insurance and property taxes do not occur every month, people often forget to put them in the budget.

- *Unexpected and emergency expenses.* Unexpected expenses obviously cannot be accurately predicted. But because they do occur, some amount should be set aside each month for this contingency.

- *Long-term replacement costs* of automobiles, major appliances, and other major purchase items. These should be budgeted so that the needed cash will be available.

- *Entertainment.* Many people do not put entertainment in their monthly budget, or they allow a ridiculously low amount. But budgets must be realistic. Look at your log to determine the actual cost and then either budget it or adjust it to a reasonable figure.

Use of Credit

Individuals, like corporations, often use credit to supplement their cash flow. Using credit is appropriate for necessary major purchases and as a temporary stopgap for those months when cash flow is low and additional cash is needed. But when credit is used to supplement cash flow, the loan should be paid off immediately. Any credit used for major purchases should be paid on time or early if possible to save interest charges.

Homes provide a good investment opportunity in the United States. Interest paid on home mortgages can also be deducted from federal income tax.

Courtesy of United Van Lines, Inc.

Each person should possess at least one major credit card because credit cards are important in our society. Using them occasionally establishes a credit rating, which is helpful when we want to make a major purchase. Many merchants ask for credit cards as identification for check writing. Renting a car becomes difficult if you have no credit card. They are convenient to use when traveling. They also help us keep track of purchases. The credit card statement contains an itemized list of purchases and enables the cardholder to pay for all purchases with one check at the end of the month.

Credit cards can be an important financial tool for careful financial planners. However, in the hands of individuals who do not exercise restraint, they pose a danger. They can spell financial disaster. Many people use credit cards to purchase items they really don't need and would not have purchased if credit were not available. And shoppers can easily pile up credit charges beyond their ability to pay.

Investing in a Home

Owning a home is a common goal for Americans. Home ownership offers several investment advantages. The value of the property is likely to increase over time, which increases financial worth. Home ownership costs remain relatively the same, even though other costs are inflating. At the same time, an individual's income often rises, and the house becomes less of a financial burden. Also, home ownership is a form of forced savings; every month you make payments toward something that will grow in value. Finally, since the Tax Reform Act of 1986, interest paid for home mortgages is the only type of interest that can be deducted on federal income tax returns.

Anyone deciding whether to buy a home or to rent needs to consider the interest deduction. The tax savings impact the decision. For example, if you bought a home and your monthly payment was $900, during the first few years almost the entire payment would be for interest. The interest portion of a house payment is tax deductible. If you are in a 28 percent income tax bracket, about $250 of your $900 payment (mostly interest) would be deducted on your federal income tax. Subtracting this savings from your house payment leaves roughly $650 a month as your real cost for the house for the first few years. This may compare favorably to rental costs. Because rent does not purchase any property, you gain no equity. Furthermore, rent will likely rise every year or so, while your basic house payment will stay the same (although insurance and taxes may rise).

Depending on a person's financial situation, career, and plans for the future, a home can be an excellent investment. Connections will give you an idea of whether home ownership would be feasible for you.

In addition to home ownership, we have discussed a number of investment opportunities in this chapter. The main thing, for individuals as well as for businesses, is to remember your objectives and work toward accomplishing them. A professional financial planner may be able to help you in this area.

Insurance Coverage

People often find that they need several types of insurance coverage. Wage earners with families need some form of *life insurance* to provide financial security in the case of their death. Of the many types of life insurance, term insurance is usually the best buy. It is pure insurance, since you pay only for coverage for a specified term. Other forms of insurance, such as whole life, return some cash value but cost more. Generally you can make more money by buying the less expensive term insurance and investing the premium savings in another vehicle.

Many insurers are developing new options in life insurance. You may want to learn about them. But most people find that term insurance provides the coverage they need, when they need it (such as during child-rearing years), at the least cost. Today, with most women earning wages, they as well as men need to carry some form of life insurance.

Casualty insurance, which protects against property losses resulting from fire, theft, and other perils, is necessary for cars, boats, and other property. Homeowners, of course, need to carry insurance protecting against losses and damages occurring at home and on their property; mortgage companies require insurance coverage before lending money for a home.

Health insurance is extremely important. A serious illness without proper health insurance can spell disaster for an individual or family. Employers frequently provide health insurance through group plans with insurers. Self-employed people or others with no employer health plan available can obtain individual insurance policies. Those purchasing individual health insurance often find health maintenance organizations (HMOs) an attractive alternative. Besides providing coverage for hospital and other major medical expenses, HMOs stress preventive health care and emphasize checkups. Because benefits vary greatly, anyone considering an HMO should investigate several plans.

Is Home Ownership Right for You?

Directions: Answer each of the questions below. If you do not own a home, this quiz will help you decide if you should.

1. How much has the price of a typical house in your area increased in the past five years? If less than 20 percent, score five points. _____

2. Do you plan to move within four years? If so, score five points. _____

3. Do you have ready assets for a down payment and closing expenses worth at least 25 percent of the price of a typical house in your neighborhood? If not, score three points. _____

4. Are you willing to devote enough time to repair the plumbing, care for the lawn, grout bathroom tiles, and handle similar homeowner headaches? If not, score one point. _____

5. Will you be in the 15 percent tax bracket in the current year? If yes, score two points. _____

6. Do you contribute at least 10 percent of your income each year to tax-deferred savings plans such as 401(k) and Keogh plans to compensate for the lack of a mortgage deduction? If yes, score one point. _____

Individuals also should consider carrying some form of *disability insurance*. This insurance pays part of the cost of a long-term illness or disability. In addition to increased hospital benefits, disability insurance provides some level of continuing income. Chapter Twenty discusses the various forms of insurance in more detail.

Retirement Planning

To ensure a reasonable standard of living later, retirement planning needs to start early. According to *Fortune* magazine, a 30-year-old American making $32,000 a year would need to have $1.8 million in available retirement funds at age 65 to maintain 70 percent of his or her preretirement income.[10]

Social security   When many Americans think of retirement benefits, they think of social security. But relying on social security as one's sole retirement income is unadvisable. The maximum annual social security benefit is slightly over $10,000, a small sum to live on.

Many social and political observers question the future of the U.S. social security program. The number of workers paying into the program will drop as the U.S. population ages. For example, by the time someone who is now 30 retires, only about two workers will be paying into social security for each individual collecting from it; the current ratio is 3.3 to 1.[11] Furthermore, benefits may not be

7. Are attractive, fairly inexpensive rentals available in your area? If yes, score two points. _____

8. Is your credit so good that you could borrow $20,000 without using a house as collateral? If yes, score one point. _____

9. Is your annual income less than 32 percent of the purchase price of the kind of house you want? If yes, score three points. _____

Total score = _____

Feedback: Add up your score. If you scored 9 or fewer points, it may be time to buy a home; 10 or more suggests that you should be renting. Some things to think about though: Don't overextend yourself. The total cost of owning shouldn't consume more than 40 percent of your monthly net income. Comparison shop. Even if you can afford to buy a house, you may come out ahead by renting. Think twice about buying if you plan to move to another city within a few years. By tying up money in a down payment and closing costs, you are forgoing interest that you could be earning on your savings. If a house is not likely to appreciate at least 10 to 15 percent over four years, you would be better off renting as long as your rent is no more than the monthly cost of owning.

available. The federal government is spending current social security surpluses and, in effect, is writing IOUs to the social security trust fund. Since government income comes from taxes, the bill for these IOUs will fall to the taxpayers, who can expect taxes to rise even higher.[12] Americans therefore will need some other retirement income sources, as Figure 19.9 illustrates.

Pension plans   U.S. workers often have pension plans through their employers. But as many industries restructure, they are eliminating pension plans in favor of contribution plans. In a **contribution plan**, you make contributions from your paycheck, and in many cases your employer matches your contribution. These programs, called 401(k) plans, defer taxes on earnings and usually allow you to decide how the money should be invested: in stocks, bonds, or (in some cases) real estate. Such plans can provide excellent savings opportunities, especially since your contributions are not taxed until used.

Contribution Plan
A pension plan where employees make contributions from paychecks, in many cases matched by the employer.

These plans present one potential problem. If you change jobs, you have to transfer the money into a new fund with your new employer. When this happens, many people spend the money rather than reinvesting it. They not only eliminate a significant portion of their retirement nest egg but also pay a heavy tax penalty.

Savings   When you plan how to save for retirement, look at tax-deferred savings programs. These benefit you in the present by lowering the amount of

FIGURE 19.9

Retirement Income: How Much? Where From?

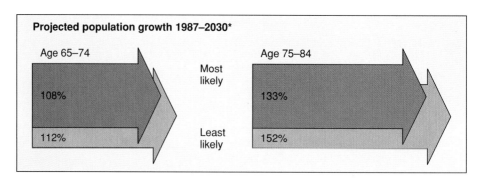

Projected population growth 1987–2030*

Age 65–74 — 108% / 112%
Most likely / Least likely
Age 75–84 — 133% / 152%

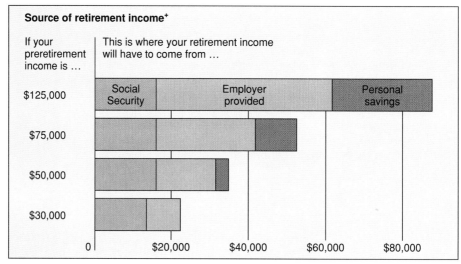

Source of retirement income†

If your preretirement income is …

This is where your retirement income will have to come from …

Social Security / Employer provided / Personal savings

$125,000
$75,000
$50,000
$30,000

0 | $20,000 | $40,000 | $60,000 | $80,000

*Source: Social Security Administration.
†Source: Noble Lowndes USA.
Source: FORTUNE, July 31, 1989. © 1989 The Time Magazine Company. All rights reserved.

your taxable income and in the future because they provide excellent retirement savings opportunities.

Individual Retirement Account (IRA)
A savings plan to which qualified individuals can contribute a certain amount yearly; IRA contributions are tax deductible.

IRAs   **Individual retirement accounts (IRAs)** are still a feasible means of saving for retirement although, under the 1986 Tax Reform Act, not everyone can qualify to deduct contributions to an IRA. Now, if you are not covered by another retirement plan (and neither is your spouse if you are married and both have incomes) or if your total adjusted gross income is less than $25,000 on an individual return (or $40,000 on a joint return), you can deduct up to $2,000 ($2,000 each for a working couple) for contributions to an IRA.

Keogh Plan
A retirement plan by which self-employed people can contribute 20 percent of net income on a tax-deferred basis.

Keogh plans   A **Keogh plan** is designed for self-employed people, who do not have the benefit of a corporate retirement system. Under a Keogh plan, you can contribute 20 percent of your net income earned from self-employment, up to a maximum of $30,000.[13] Taxes on amounts contributed to a Keogh plan are deferred, as are taxes on the fund's earnings.

Courtesy of the Xerox Corporation

Xerox Financial Services and a host of other companies help individuals plan for an enjoyable retirement.

Other tax-deferred plans exist for state and federal workers and for those who work in education. Anyone in these situations can check with the employer or with an accountant for further information.

You'll Know It's the **Century When . . .**

Career Paths Have Sidetracks

By 2000, dual incomes and forgiving employers will make it easier for skilled people to slip in and out of the work force. Many people will work part-time while going to school, raising a family, or after retiring from a lifelong career.

Higher education will be expensive but jobs will be plentiful, so many young people will work before they go to college. By 2000, half of all college students will be aged 25 or older. Adult education will continue to grow.

Early retirement may tempt executives who have topped out, but many 21st-century employers will have eliminated retirement incentives as they try to retain skilled workers. And the high cost of retirement will keep many workers on the job. One retiree in three will return to work within two years. To retire in 2030 on today's equivalent of $1,000 a month, workers will have to save $4,800 a year starting now.[14]

SUMMARY OF LEARNING OBJECTIVES

1. To define *common stock* and *preferred stock*.
   Preferred stock has preference over common stock in the payment of dividends and in claims against the firm's assets. Holders of preferred stock are generally not entitled to vote. *Common stock* is voting stock. The holders of common stock have no guarantees of return and their rights to assets of the firm are subordinate to the rights of creditors and holders of preferred stock. Common stock has greater income potential than preferred stock.

2. To identify the major types of investors.
   There are two major types of investors, institutional and private. Institutional investors are professionals who invest for large groups such as pension funds and insurance companies. Private investors are individuals who invest in the market on their own behalf.

3. To discuss five investment objectives and identify appropriate investments for each objective.
   Investor objectives include *growth,* which can be satisfied with high-growth stocks, real estate, precious metals, and collectibles; *income,* best gained with Treasury bills, bonds, utilities, and blue-chip stocks; *security,* best satisfied with nonspeculative investments such as savings bonds, certificates of deposit, or Treasury bills; *liquidity,* which requires the use of marketable securities such as T bills and certificates of deposit; and *tax deferment or avoidance,* which means using government or municipal bonds.

4. To explain various investment options.
   Investment choices include *stocks* (including stock options, the purchased right to buy or sell stock at a fixed price); *bonds,* loans to corporations and governments; *government securities,* secure loans to the government; *mutual funds,* pooled funds for investment by many investors; and *commodities,* items people will later purchase, such as gold, corn, and cattle.

5. To describe the investment exchanges.
   A *stock exchange* is an organization of individuals who buy and sell securities to the public. The largest is the New York Stock Exchange. Others include the American Stock Exchange and the regional exchanges at Chicago, San Francisco, Philadelphia, Boston, Cincinnati, Spokane, and Salt Lake City. *Over-the-counter (OTC) stocks* are traded on the NASDAQ. *Commodity exchanges* are similar to stock exchanges but deal in commodities.

6. To explain the investment process and the role of the stockbroker.
   Stockbrokers are individuals licensed to act on investors' behalf in the buying and selling of securities. The stockbroker not only places trades but also advises on trades. The process of making a securities trade involves the investor discussing the trade with the broker, placing a market order or a limit order, and the broker calling the order to the appropriate exchange. The broker's representative then goes to the appropriate area on the stock trading floor and places the order.

7. To identify the principal regulations dealing with investment markets.
   The states have *blue-sky laws* that prevent corporations from issuing worthless stocks. On the federal level, the most significant legislation is

the *Securities Act of 1933,* which requires full disclosure of information about the firm to prospective buyers. The *Securities Exchange Act of 1934* established the Securities and Exchange Commission (SEC) and requires any corporation whose securities are listed on the national exchanges to file registration statements with the SEC. The National Association of Securities Dealers (NASD) was created by the *Maloney Act* in 1938; mutual funds were brought under the SEC's jurisdiction by the *Investment Company Act of 1940.*

8. To explain the need for budgeting and planning in personal finances.
    As individuals we have many of the same financial concerns and responsibilities as organizations. Both short- and long-term sources and uses of funds have to be balanced and funds must be managed. Individuals need to know what they spend, to budget, to use credit wisely, to look into home investment and other forms of saving and investment, to cover possible losses with insurance, and to plan and be ready for retirement by developing a retirement savings program.

KEY TERMS

Securities, p. 669

Preferred Stock, p. 670

Common Stock, p. 670

Market Value, p. 670

Book Value, p. 670

Prospectus, p. 671

Investment Banker, p. 671

Blue-Chip Stock, p. 674

Rate of Return, p. 675

Bull Market, p. 676

Bear Market, p. 676

Round Lot, p. 676

Odd Lot, p. 676

Margin Trading, p. 676

Stock Option, p. 677

Put Option, p. 678

Call Option, p. 678

Price-Earnings Ratio, p. 679

Default, p. 679

Municipal Bond, p. 681

Mutual Fund, p. 681

Commodities, p. 682

Financial Futures, p. 685

Stock Exchange, p. 685

Over-the-Counter (OTC) Market, p. 685

Commodity Exchange, p. 685

Stockbroker, p. 686

Market Order, p. 686

Limit Order, p. 686

Blue-Sky Laws, p. 688

Contribution Plan, p. 693

Individual Retirement Account (IRA), p. 694

Keogh Plan, p. 694

QUESTIONS FOR DISCUSSION AND REVIEW

1. Why do companies use bonds to secure long-term financing? What are the advantages to using bonds as opposed to stock issues?

2. If you had $1,000 to invest in stock, would you invest it in preferred stock or common stock? Why?

3. If you had $10,000 to invest in any single investment or combination you wanted, what would you choose? Why? Would any conditions, environmental or economic, change your decision?

4. Do you think the stock market is still a healthy place for small investors, or have the large investors made it too treacherous? Explain your answer.

5. If you have $5,000 to purchase stock shares and you buy 100 shares of Acme at $50 a share, how much money will you make on the sale of the stock if the stock price goes up to $60 in one year? How much money would you make if you used margin trading to increase your potential investment, if the cost of the margin loan were 10 percent per year?

6. What are stock options? What is the difference between a put option and a call option? If you buy stock options on a stock that is currently trading for $10 and that you expected to go up in value, should you buy put options or call options? Why?

7. In the stock quotation in Figure 19.4, what was the final selling price for the day for Tonka? What was the price-earnings ratio for Tiffany? If you had to choose one of the stocks on that page to purchase, which one would you choose? Why?

8. Assume that you buy a $1,000 bond that will yield 8 percent. A year later, when you want to sell that bond, similar bonds are yielding 10 percent. How much will you have to sell your bond for? If similar bonds were yielding 6 percent, what would you have to sell the bond for?

9. Describe the process you would go through to invest in the stock market. If you invested, would you place a market order or a limit order? Why?

10. What is the role of a budget in your personal finances? Do you use one? Make out a budget of your personal expenses for the next month. Keep a log of all of your expenditures for that period, then assess how your spending compared to your budget.

CASE 19.1
Mutual Fund Fees

Mutual fund accounts can be purchased as load funds, which charge a sales fee at the time of purchase, and no-load funds, which charge no sales fee and are typically sold through ads and by mail. But mutual fund fees are not quite that simple.

Shortly before the 1987 stock market crash, Mary Rains, a retired schoolteacher in Golden, Colorado, put $18,000 into Shearson Lehman Hutton's Sector Analysis stock mutual fund. "Is there anything here I need to know before I sign?" she says she asked her broker, Craig Zeller. Zeller didn't tell her that she would have to pay a 5 percent "exit fee" to retrieve the money anytime soon. "Shearson really messed me up," says Rains, who wanted to withdraw the money when the fund's value slumped but, to avoid the exit fee, didn't. Zeller concedes that he feared mentioning the fee because it might kill the sale and says, "I was a wimp."

The SEC is investigating gripes from fund investors who say they were never told they would have to pay fees to get their money out. Nearly a fifth of the $487 billion of stock and bond funds use exit fees.

Mutual fund fees are, of course, listed in the prospectus. But the prospectus is not always available until the time of close, and many people count on a broker to explain the rather lengthy, small-print document. Few people protest the management fees that most funds charge—typically less than 0.6 percent of assets annually. On the other hand, they often complain of the upfront load fees that many funds charge. These fees rake off as much as 8.5 percent of the initial investment and pass along about 40 percent of this fee to the selling broker.

More and more brokers, increasingly desperate for business, are pushing mutual funds with less obvious charges, such as exit fees. They have been allowed by the SEC since 1982 and in many cases shrink from 5 percent the first year to zero after five years.

Questions for Discussion

1. Name some possible methods for charging fees on mutual funds. How do you think they should be charged?
2. Given the problems stated above, what if any new rules are necessary from the SEC?
3. How and where should fees charged on mutual funds be stated?
4. Do you think exit fees should be charged? Why or why not?

Adapted from Werner Renberg, "Unhappy Returns?" *Barron's,* May 14, 1990, pp. 29–30; Jon Friedman, "How the Fund Families Measure Up," *Business Week,* June 11, 1990, pp. 64–65; Michael Siconolfi, "Mutual Funds Use of 'Exit Fees' Stirs Investors' Complaints," *The Wall Street Journal,* March 13, 1989.

CASE 19.2
Credit for Sale

For Elmer Hedgpeth, love and credit proved a near-ruinous mix. Caught up in a whirlwind romance with a California woman, the 63-year-old Phoenix resident lived what he wistfully calls a "fantasy, the kind you dream about" for nearly three years. The once thrifty former postal worker and his friend frequently embarked on spur-of-the-moment trips to Los Angeles, Las Vegas, and Salt Lake City.

At first, paying the bills with his eight credit cards wasn't a problem because Hedgpeth regularly drew a cash advance on one card to make payments on another. But then he hit the credit ceilings on all eight cards. With $19,000 in charges, minimum monthly payments of $2,000, and an after-tax monthly income of $1,000, he couldn't meet the payments.

He had to sell his car to help whittle down the debt, and the companies settled for partial repayments. Perhaps worst of all, the romance quickly faded. "About the only way one of these gals will look at a guy is if you've got money," he laments.

But have credit card issuers deserted him? Hardly. "I keep getting solicitations in the mail for credit cards," he says with disbelief. "I've gotten about three or four, but I just threw them out."

The problem is that the institutions appear to be addicted to credit, just as addicted as some people are to using credit cards. They are attracted by the cards' profit potential: the 2½ to 3 percent that many issuers earn on their card debt outstanding is alluring to bankers who are doing well to chalk up a 1 percent return on total assets. And with the pool of potential new cardholders dwindling in the saturated market, some credit card executives believe that time is running out before a recession cuts consumer spending and boosts credit card defaults.

As a result, many card issuers are mailing out blanket solicitations and, except for the highest credit risks, are ignoring or easing their own credit standards. The issuers are simply hoping that the less creditworthy consumers they are wooing won't turn out to be deadbeats. Unfortunately the financial health of many card issuers and many new cardholders is increasingly at risk.

As one credit counselor states, "Most Americans over 25 are inundated with credit, and now the credit community is starting to go after high school seniors and college freshmen." The problem continues to grow. Deregulation has allowed a host of new competitors, including Sears, General Electric, and Merrill Lynch, to buy special-purpose credit card banks. The issuers of general-purpose cards have ballooned to about 2,500, and the average number of such cards rose to 3.3 per household. With an estimated 250 million Visa, Master-Card, American Express, and Discover cards in their pockets, Americans aren't lacking for credit. But only about 8 percent of the $3 trillion in annual

Adapted from John Meehan, "Picking a Path through the Plastic Jungle," *Business Week,* August 6, 1990, pp. 84–85; "How to Choose a Credit Card," *Consumer Reports,* May 1990, p. 315; Robert Guenther, "Credit-Card Issuers Ease Their Standards to Get New Accounts," *The Wall Street Journal,* May 22, 1989, p. 1A.

U.S. consumer spending involves a general-purpose card, leaving enormous potential for growth in charge volume.

Questions for Discussion
1. Do you think there is a problem with the way banks are issuing credit cards? Explain.
2. Whose responsibility do you think it is to protect consumers from debt problems?
3. Are constraints needed on who can have access to credit? If so, who should initiate them? What kind of constraints?

CHAPTER TWENTY

RISK MANAGEMENT AND INSURANCE

LEARNING OBJECTIVES

1. To define *risk* and explain the difference between speculative and pure risk.

2. To explain the strategies of risk avoidance and risk reduction.

3. To identify the strategies of risk coverage and explain the difference between assumption and transference of risk.

4. To explain how insurance works and how the law of large numbers affects it.

5. To identify the major sources of insurance.

6. To discuss the role of insurance for businesses and identify the major types of business insurance.

7. To discuss insurance programs provided by employers for their employees.

The insurance industry had suffered its worst losses in history in 1985, when claims ran just under $3 billion. Then came the fall of 1989, when Mother Nature wreaked havoc on both U.S. coasts. On September 22, monster Hurricane Hugo hit the South Carolina shore with winds in excess of 135 miles per hour. When

Michael Nichols/Magnum

Hugo slammed into Charleston, it destroyed 3,400 homes and damaged another 13,800. The storm was so strong that when it headed inland and north, it still held much of its power. Striking Charlotte, North Carolina, some 150 miles inland, it was still packing 100 mph–plus winds. The devastation was mind-boggling, the scene a true disaster.

But Mother Nature was not yet finished. Just as the residents of Charleston were digging themselves out, on the opposite coast some 3,000 miles away, a major earthquake struck south of San Francisco. Millions of television viewers from all over the United States knew of the quake almost immediately, since it struck during the warm-up for the third game of baseball's World Series. Candlestick Park shook, and a nation waited to see how bad San Francisco area damage was going to be.

The insurance industry, windswept by Hugo, was now rattled by the San Francisco earthquake. The estimated claims bill for the latter disaster exceeded $5 billion, bringing the total catastrophe losses to almost $7 billion. That figure more than doubled the previous high of $3 billion.

The bill would have been considerably higher, except that insurance coverage for the two types of disasters is quite different. As a wind storm, Hugo was considered a basic peril and was covered under property policies. The earthquake was not and therefore required separate insurance or a special provision (rider) on the normal property policy. The insurance companies will have to pay an estimated 75 percent of the total damage inflicted by Hugo; most people affected have some form of property insurance and are therefore covered. In contrast, only about one fourth of the people in the San Francisco Bay area were carrying earthquake coverage. Because of the 5 percent to 10 percent deductible that insurance companies apply to earthquake coverage and the strict policy size limits, the cost to insurance companies for damage from the earthquake is only about $1 billion of the total damage of about $10 billion.

The total bill of $6 billion to $7 billion from Hugo and the earthquake is somewhat catastrophic in itself. Insurance companies claim that there should be no major insurance rate hikes because of it, but time alone will tell.[1]

People who live and conduct business on the Atlantic Coast know a hurricane may hit their area at some point in their lives and that, if one does, damage to their property or injury to themselves is likely. People who live and conduct business in the bay area of California know that they may experience a serious earthquake at some time during their lives and that, if they do, damage to their property or injury to themselves is likely.

This chapter is about risk and how it affects business. We begin with a discussion of risk and the types of risk that businesses face. We then look at the various strategies one can follow to cope with risk. A discussion of insurance as a strategy for transferring risk follows. The chapter ends with a discussion of the types of insurance available to businesses and their employees.

THE NATURE OF RISK

Risk is simply the possibility of suffering an injury or loss. It is the direct result of uncertainty, the fact that in many cases we cannot know what the future holds. A large retailer who, after careful analysis, decides to purchase a piece of property and build a store cannot be certain what the future of that store will be. Perhaps the location will be perfect, and the store will do well. Perhaps traffic will be rerouted to a new superhighway, and business will be poor. For any number of reasons, the location may or may not work out. The retailer speculates that it will and that his choice is correct. This is called **speculative risk**—risk involving the chance of making a profit or taking a loss.

Speculative risk is necessary in business. Each time a businessperson makes a decision regarding a purchase, an advertisement, a promotional program, a new product, or any other business decision, the possibility exists that the decision will lead to additional profit. But there is also the possibility that the decision will lead to no profit or even to a loss.

Often managers face risks with no chance of profit; the best they can hope for is no loss. This is **pure risk**—the threat of a loss with no chance of profit. The residents and businesses in Charleston and San Francisco were facing pure risk with the possibility of a hurricane or earthquake. These are considered pure risks because if they do not occur, the firm does not make money; it gains nothing.

Risk
The possibility of suffering an injury or loss.

Speculative Risk
Risk involving the chance of making a profit or taking a loss.

Pure Risk
The threat of a loss with no chance of profit.

DEALING WITH RISK

Figure 20.1 summarizes the methods for dealing with risk. Good managers try to reduce speculative risk through careful study and planning. The more information that goes into making a decision, the less likely it is that the decision will lead to a loss—and the lower the speculative risk. A business can handle the presence of pure risk in two different ways. The company can *manage* risk, or it can *cover* risk.

FIGURE 20.1   **Methods for Dealing with Risk**

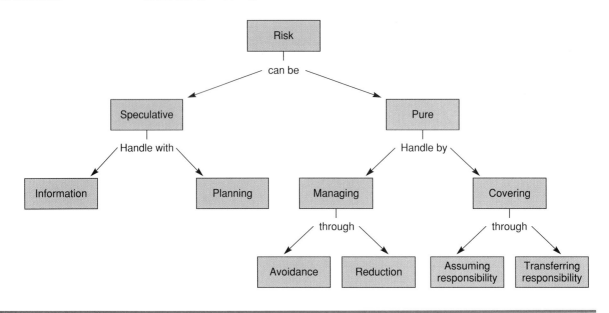

Managing Risk

Risk Management
Minimizing the amount and cost of pure risk a company will face.

In **risk management,** a firm tries to minimize the amount of pure risk it will face and the cost of that pure risk. To manage risk, a firm can follow one of two strategies: risk avoidance and risk reduction.

Risk Avoidance
A risk management strategy of not taking on or of getting out of risky ventures.

Risk avoidance   One way to handle risk is through **risk avoidance**—eliminating the source of it. An individual who thinks that the risk of a plane crash is too great may avoid that risk by never getting on an airplane. A student who hears that a particular professor grades very hard may avoid the risk of failure by not taking that professor's classes. Companies may decide to avoid risks by not developing new products that may be hazardous to some individuals or by dropping certain lines of business where the dangers are too great. For example, because of the high risk of lawsuits, all but one American drug company has stopped large-scale research into new kinds of contraception.[2]

Risk avoidance is not always possible. Many firms cannot afford to drop major lines or get out of certain businesses. Furthermore firms who do not develop and sell new products are rarely leaders in their industry.

Risk Reduction
A risk management strategy of using loss prevention programs and other management programs.

Risk reduction   If a firm cannot avoid risk, it should at least aim for **risk reduction,** or reducing the level of risk and the level of liability. Loss prevention programs can help accomplish this. A company needs to follow programs to lower the likelihood of fire, employee accidents, damage to company equipment, product liability suits, and other risks.

For example, to help reduce the chance of fire or the amount of fire damage, the company could install a sprinkler system, designate areas for employee smoking, and regularly inspect the plant for potential fire hazards. In order to avoid injury to employees, a company can require employees to wear protective gear, it can install safety shields on dangerous machinery, and it can provide

FIGURE 20.2

**The Shift to
Self-Insurance**

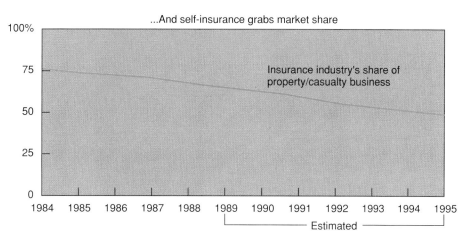

...And self-insurance grabs market share

Insurance industry's share of
property/casualty business

Source: Jan Schute, "Insurance the Lure of the Alternative Market," *Institutional Investor* 24 (May 1990),
p. 171; *Business Week*, August 21, 1989, p. 73.

nonskid floor surfaces. To avoid product liability suits, the company has to
carefully test all of its products and review products with consumer panels who
may see potential dangers the company might miss. For example, to reduce risk,
a toy manufacturer would want to avoid sharp edges on toys, pieces that young
children can swallow and choke on, plastic bags that could suffocate young ones,
and the use of potentially toxic substances. Retailers may reduce potential liability losses by reducing customer hazards such as glass displays, crowded
aisles, or overstocked shelves.

Covering Risk

Regardless of the success of its programs to avoid and reduce risk, the company
will still face financial risks. Eliminating all risk is impossible. Therefore companies must act to cover the chance of losses from accidents, fires, storms, and
other risk situations. In covering pure risk, a firm tries to make sure that it has
a sufficient cash reserve to pay for any losses without having to take funds away
from daily operations and thus possibly interrupt business. A company can
cover these risks by either assuming the risks itself or transferring the risk to an
insurance company.

Risk assumption   When a company assumes the risk itself, it sets aside a
portion of its own income to cover future losses. The company takes a certain
percentage of its earnings and creates an insurance cash reserve. The money is
invested in marketable securities so that it earns interest while still being available to cover pure risk losses. This method is referred to as **self-insurance**
because the company is insuring itself against large potential losses by saving
its own money to cover these.

Self-insurance has become increasingly popular, partly because insurance
companies will not provide coverage for high-risk ventures and partly because
the costs of insurance have risen so dramatically that companies are finding
self-insurance a less expensive alternative. Figure 20.2 shows this shift. Self-

Self-Insurance
Method by which companies
assume risk by putting aside
cash reserves to cover their
potential future losses.

Insurance cannot be purchased to protect against all risks such as the war in the Persian Gulf.

Bill Gentile/Sipa

insurance went from about 25 percent in 1984 to about 35 percent of the property and casualty insurance business in 1989 and is projected to go to 50 percent by 1995.

Generally self-insurance makes more sense for larger firms than for smaller ones. The larger company with many plants knows there is little likelihood of fires occurring in all of them at one time, and the risk of a fire in any one of the plants can be measured and protected against. The small company cannot afford to set aside the funds to cover such a large potential loss.

Transferring risk   When a company cannot afford to cover losses with its own funds, it must turn to an outside organization for protection. It transfers the responsibility for risk by purchasing insurance.

Insurance
A written contract that transfers the risk of loss from the insured to the insurer.

Insurance is a written contract, taken with the insuring company, that transfers the risk of loss to the insurer according to the terms of the contract. However, not all risks are insurable. If an insurance company would have difficulty calculating the likelihood that a loss would occur because of some risk, it is reluctant to insure against that risk. Risks of this type are generally referred to as *uninsurable risks*. For example, while insurance can be purchased from the federal government to protect against losses from floods, insurance cannot generally be purchased to protect against a drought, even though droughts can have devastating effects on farmers' livelihoods. Other things that cannot generally be insured against are political changes, changes in the economy, war or insurrection, strikes, or losses resulting from changes in the marketplace.

While these and many other risks are not generally insurable, many risks can be covered. An **insurable risk** is one for which likelihood of loss can be calculated and that meets the requirements set by most insurance underwriters to be insurable.

Insurable Risk
A risk for which an acceptable level of loss can be calculated and that meets the requirements set by the insurer.

To determine whether a loss is insurable or not, insurance companies generally use a specific set of guidelines.

1. *The individual policyholder must have an insurable interest.* This simply means you must actually suffer the loss to be the beneficiary of the insurance. You cannot insure your neighbor's car against theft and then collect if his car is stolen. However, you can insure the life of your spouse or a close friend and collect the benefits if he or she should die, because in this case you would have suffered a loss, even though not a financial one.

2. *The likelihood of loss needs to be predictable.* Insurance companies employ people called actuaries to predict the likelihood of losses. **Actuaries** predict the likelihood of future events, based on historical records. They can predict the likelihood of a particular plant in a particular city suffering a damaging fire, or the likelihood of a car being stolen, given the neighborhood the owner lives in. By knowing the likely number of such losses and their average size, insurance companies can calculate the amount of money that must be charged to insure such losses. Without this predictability, the insurance company would not know how much to charge for its services.

Actuary
An insurance employee who predicts the likelihood of future events, based on their occurrence in the past.

3. *The amount of loss must be financially measurable.* Some losses, like the loss of a life, are not easily measured. For such losses, insurance policies are written in specific amounts. For example, a life insurance policy may pay $100,000 to the spouse when the insured person dies. Other policies, where losses and the likelihood of losses are more easily measured, may pay for the amount of the loss. Most auto insurance, for example, pays for the repair of a damaged vehicle or the market value of the vehicle, whichever is less.

4. *The losses must be fortuitous (accidental).* Insurance companies will not pay for losses created by the policyholder. If you intentionally set fire to your home, for example, your property insurance will not cover the loss.

5. *The risk should be dispersed.* In order to cover risks and pay for the losses incurred, insurance companies count on collecting premiums from a great number of people who suffer no losses. This is called the *law of large numbers* (discussed in the next section). The idea is that if the risk is all in one area, all of the insured may suffer the same loss at the same time. Therefore, an insurer would not want to provide flood insurance in only one area, because a flood in that area could bankrupt the company.

6. *The insured must meet certain standards to qualify.* In recent years, insurance companies have started to charge smokers higher rates for life and

health insurance. When occupations, such as firefighting, are risky, some insurance companies will not insure people in those occupations; others charge a higher rate for insurance. Individuals with heart problems may not be insured. In all such cases, the insurance company has the right to set standards in order to limit the risk of loss.

HOW INSURANCE WORKS

Premium
A fee paid to the insurance company for protection.

Law of Large Numbers
Uses the probability of a specific loss occurring, the likely cost of that loss, and the number of individuals covered to calculate the premiums charged each insured individual.

When you purchase insurance, you buy an *insurance policy.* This is your contract with the insurance company. It states what losses the insurance company will cover. To get this coverage, you pay the insurance company a fee, called the **premium.** The amount of the premium is based on the **law of large numbers.** Insurers use the probability of a specific loss occurring, the likely cost of that loss, and the number of individuals covered to calculate the premiums charged to each individual insured. Of course the insurance company needs to include a charge to cover its operating expenses and provide a reasonable profit.

A simple example may help to explain this process. Say that an insurance company is going to insure automobiles against theft. In a particular city, they know that they will insure 30,000 automobiles. Furthermore they know from actuarial information that approximately 300 of these vehicles will be stolen and that the average loss will be $6,000. With this information, the company can calculate that it should expect to pay out $1.8 million dollars in claims (300 × $6,000). If the insurance company spreads these losses over all 30,000 policyholders, the premium for each policyholder would be $60 ($1.8 million ÷ 30,000). Of course the insurance company would also build in additional money to pay for operating expenses and allow for a reasonable profit, thus increasing the individual premium amounts.

The law of large numbers explains insurance premiums in part. But not all 30,000 individuals stand the same level of risk. One individual's car may be a foreign luxury car (a popular target of professional thieves), while another may contain a burglar alarm. Each owner is not at equal risk. To be fair, individuals seemingly should pay premiums based on their level of risk, not just the average level of risk. When insurance companies calculate premiums, they have to take level of risk into consideration. That is why older people pay higher premiums to take out a life insurance policy than do younger people. On the other hand, because they have more accidents, younger drivers pay higher car insurance premiums than older drivers.

Deductible
The amount of loss that the insured agrees to cover before insurance coverage begins.

In addition to charging certain policyholders higher premiums, insurance companies also use deductible clauses to help control their costs. A **deductible** in a policy is the amount of loss the insured assumes; the insurance company is responsible only for losses that exceed that specified amount. Therefore, if a person insures a car with a policy that includes a $150 deductible, that individual would have to pay the first $150 of each loss and then the insurance company would begin to pay. Deductibles can help reduce premiums, but insured individuals must also remember that they are not insured for the deductible portion of losses.

INSURANCE SOURCES

The size of the insurance industry shows the importance of insurance in managing risk. The industry controls more than $1 trillion in assets and receives more than $300 billion in premiums each year. However, the largest amount of insurance is provided not by private firms but by public sources.

Public Sources

The federal government and certain state agencies may provide insurance for individuals or businesses. Public insurance is available to cover such losses as unemployment, pension, and work-related accidents and injuries causing disability, among other things.

Social security   Initiated under the Social Security Act of 1935, social security is perhaps the best-known form of public insurance. The official title of the program is Old-Age, Survivors, Disability, and Health Insurance. Under this program, more than 90 percent of the U.S. working population and their dependents are eligible for retirement benefits, life insurance, health insurance, and disability income insurance.

As Chapter Five noted, social security is financed through a tax taken out of employees' paychecks. Employers pay an equal and matching amount of tax to the federal government to help cover benefits.

The benefits of Social Security include:

- Payments for death, including a small lump-sum payment and continuing payments to spouses with dependent children.
- Income payments for disability if the disability is expected to last at least 12 months and is total.
- Retirement benefits.
- Hospital and medical payments for eligible persons age 65 or over. This is the medicare program.

Unemployment insurance   Every state has some form of unemployment insurance. Benefits differ from state to state. But generally the program provides some weekly payments (usually for 26 to 39 weeks) to replace a portion of lost wages and offers job counseling, training, and placement services to help workers find new jobs. These insurance programs are funded by payroll taxes paid by employers.

Workers' compensation   Every state requires that employers provide some form of workers' compensation insurance. This insurance guarantees payment of wages and salaries (generally equal to about one half to two thirds of the employee's weekly salary) as well as medical costs and rehabilitation services to employees injured in the workplace. These programs also provide benefits to the worker's family in the event that the worker dies from a work-related injury, accident, or condition. The employer alone pays the premiums for workers' compensation insurance.

Workers' compensation insurance pays individuals wages and salaries, as well as medical and rehabilitation expenses, if they are injured on the job.

Courtesy of the Boise Cascade Corporation

In addition to the programs mentioned above, the federal and state governments and their agencies provide many other forms of insurance. For example, we learned in Chapter Seventeen that bank deposits, savings in thrift institutions, and accounts in credit unions are insured by government agencies. Other agencies, such as the Federal Housing Administration, provide insurance on mortgages and other government-insured loans. The National Flood Insurance Association offers flood insurance and federal crime insurance is provided in some high-crime areas, since private insurance coverage is unavailable or cost prohibitive.

Private Sources

Private insurance companies can be either stock companies or mutual companies. A *stock company* is a profit-making company. The shareholders own the company, and profits are returned to them in the form of dividends. A *mutual company* is a nonprofit cooperative; it is owned by its policyholders. Profits are returned to the policyholders in the form of dividends or reduced insurance premiums.

TYPES OF INSURANCE BUSINESSES NEED

A business can purchase many types of insurance to protect itself against losses. Insurance can be purchased to cover losses that arise from damage to property, injury to an individual, or damage to another's property. Insurance can also be purchased to protect a company from loss of income. Finally, insurance can be purchased to protect a company's employees. The most common types of insurance a company purchases for its employees are health and life insurance.

Property Insurance

Companies can experience losses from many different sources. Sometimes the cause is unusual, as in the case of the Sealtest truck full of ice cream headed from the Sealtest plant in Saginaw, Michigan, to Detroit. Driving down Interstate 75, the truck driver misjudged a bridge overpass and rammed the top of the semitrailer into it, peeling back the top of the trailer and wedging it under the bridge. By the time a wrecking crew was able to remove the truck three hours later, the ice cream had melted into a sweet, gooey lake in the middle of the road. Sealtest experienced losses from the damage to the trailer and the loss of the ice cream. The company has to insure itself against such losses of property.

Property insurance protects a company against financial losses resulting from physical damage to or destruction of property or property loss from theft. A business is subject to property losses as the result of wind, fire, flood, theft, vandalism, and accidents. Losses from these perils can be sizable; any of them might be sufficient to ruin a business without some form of insurance.

Property Insurance
Protection for losses due to physical damage to or destruction of property or for property loss due to theft.

A business can purchase property insurance under one of two options: replacement-cost coverage or depreciated-value coverage. A company that purchases *replacement-cost coverage* will pay higher premiums, but the insurance will pay for the replacement of the insured item with a new item. So, replacement-cost coverage on a truck would allow the insured company to purchase a new truck. *Depreciated-value coverage* assumes that property used for some period of time is worth less because the owner has received some use, thus reducing its value. Under this policy, if the owner's 1984 Dodge van was totaled in an accident, the owner would receive the fair market price of a 1984 Dodge van as settlement for the claim.

Besides damage to property, a business can sustain a financial loss because of dishonesty on the part of outsiders or employees or the nonperformance of contracted work. The potential hazards of employee theft and pilferage and shoplifting by outsiders are great. Pilferage represents an average loss to retail business of about 1.5 percent of total sales, a dollar loss in excess of $20 billion.[3] Insurance offers various ways of dealing with this problem. One way, a *fidelity bond,* protects an employer from losses resulting from employees' dishonest acts, such as embezzlement, forgery, or theft. Banks, loan companies, and other firms commonly use fidelity bonds to cover employees who handle company funds. Of course, in addition to insuring against this risk, wise businesses invest in a strong security program, which can pay big benefits in risk reduction.

A large construction firm contracts with a smaller subcontractor to complete some roof work on a new factory it is building. When the subcontractor starts the job but fails to finish, the large construction contractor loses $5,000 a day in late construction penalties and must pay a crew to complete the work subcontracted out. In order to insure against such losses, a firm can take out a *surety bond.* A surety bond is a contract written by a third party, usually an insurance company. It protects one party that has contracted to have work done, from loss due to nonperformance of the job by the contracted party. For example, all public construction projects must be covered with surety bonds that guarantee the performance of every contract. The insurance company holding the bond is then required to pay damages if the contracted work is not completed.

Businesses may also need title insurance and credit insurance. Purchasers of real estate often obtain *title insurance* to protect against losses that could occur because of a defect in the title to the property. With title insurance, they do not need to look through legal records to find the true owner of the property and any claims against it. *Credit insurance* offers firms protection against some losses from the insolvency of customers to whom they have extended credit. Credit insurance especially benefits firms who conduct business internationally, since it covers losses for nonpayment because of political reasons as well as bankruptcy of foreign firms.

Business firms also need to protect themselves against financial losses resulting from crime. Three types of crime insurance are available: *burglary insurance,* which covers losses due to the taking of property by forcible entry; *robbery insurance,* which covers losses from the unlawful taking of property from another person by force or threat of force; and *theft insurance,* which covers losses from theft of any kind.

Liability Insurance

Liability Insurance
Covers losses from injury to another individual or from damage to other people's property.

Liability insurance covers losses resulting from injury to another individual or from damage to other people's property. When the Sealtest truck in the above example hit the bridge, it not only damaged the truck and the ice cream but did structural damage to the bridge. State highway department officials inspected the bridge the next day and determined that the cost to repair it would be $40,000. A claim for this amount was then filed against Sealtest. This is a liability claim. Unlike property claims, liability claims are made to reimburse injured individuals or repair the damaged property of other people. The damage to the truck and the ice cream is a property claim, but the damage to the bridge (which belongs to the state) is a liability claim.

Liability claims can run quite high, in the millions of dollars; however, most liability policies place limits on the amount that will be covered for liability claims. For this reason, many homeowners and businesses purchase *umbrella liability insurance,* which extends the amount of coverage limits to $1 million or more. This additional coverage provides a larger umbrella of protection for the business should a claim be filed.

Malpractice Insurance
Protects professionals (doctors, lawyers, etc.) from losses due to injury caused by the improper handling of their responsibilities.

Malpractice insurance is a form of liability insurance that protects professionals from losses resulting from claims of malpractice, the improper handling of their responsibilities. Doctors, lawyers, accountants, market researchers, and even college professors find themselves the target of malpractice lawsuits. A malpractice suit claims that a party was injured in some way through the improper practicing of a professional. For example, a young boy goes into a doctor's office after suffering a severe cut on the wrist. The doctor administers an anesthetic and stitches the cut closed. Three days later, the boy loses all feeling in the hand, and the hand becomes paralyzed. The boy's parents, claiming that the doctor's failure to perform his duties properly (malpractice) led to the paralysis of the boy's hand, sue the doctor.

Malpractice suits have increased in recent years, presenting a problem to professionals in need of malpractice insurance. The premiums for malpractice insurance for obstetricians, for example, can run in excess of $50,000 a year. Many other medical specialists face similarly high rates.

Product Liability Insurance
Covers losses for injuries caused by the use of a company's products.

Firms are finding it increasingly necessary to carry **product liability insurance,** which protects against claims for damages resulting from the use of a

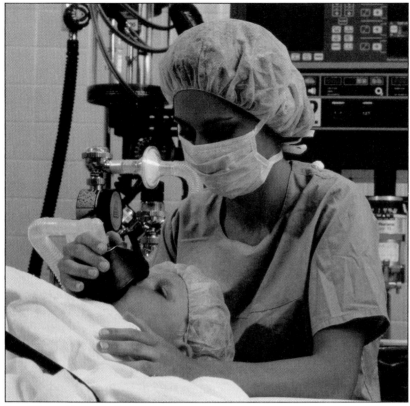

Anesthesiologists and other medical specialists carry large amounts of malpractice insurance.

Scott Kilbourne/Journalism Services

company's products. As with malpractice liability, in recent years product liability claims have increased in number, and the size of monetary awards to claimants has risen dramatically. Such claims can sometimes be carried to an extreme.

Product liability is a serious issue for firms. To stay competitive and successful, businesses must be innovative; yet innovative items are the ones most susceptible to liability claims. Companies who manufacture and market high-technology and medical products are especially vulnerable. Between 1965 and 1985, for instance, the number of vaccine manufacturers declined by more than half. Since 1986 only one manufacturer has produced vaccines against measles, mumps, rubella, and rabies. Some universities refuse to license patents to small companies, fearing suits will name them as codefendants, and product development in small aircraft and reproductive technologies has slowed dramatically.[4]

The number and amount of liability claims and the resulting skyrocketing of insurance premiums have brought about a major crisis in the insurance industry and in business in general. Many small businesses find it very hard to obtain any liability coverage. Areas having difficulty obtaining liability coverage include day-care centers, medical practices, commercial fishing boats, and municipalities.[5] Many companies have had to abandon products because they could not get insurance or the cost of coverage was too high. In fact, one survey

When Is Enough, Enough?

"Without benefit of legislation or the vote of the American people, a hidden tax is levied on virtually everything we buy, sell, and use. The tax costs American companies, individuals, and local governments at least $80 billion a year and some estimate as much as $300 billion. It accounts for 30 percent of the price of a stepladder and for over 95 percent of the price of childhood vaccines. One quarter of the price of a ticket on a Long Island, N.Y., tour bus and one third of the price of a small airplane go to pay this tax. Soon large cities will have to spend as much on this tax as they currently do on fire and sanitation. No legislature approved this highly regressive tax."

The "tax" spoken of in this quote from a 1988 *Forbes* article is called tort liability. It is the excessive punitive damages paid by companies in civil liability suits. Some examples:

- Two asbestos victims are awarded $150 million in punitive damages.
- A jury awards $986,000 to a woman who claims she lost her psychic powers after a CAT scan.
- An occupant of a telephone booth crashed into by a drunken driver collects from the booth manufacturer.

- A plaintiff is awarded $3.5 million in punitive damages from Aetna Life Insurance Co. when the company fails to pay a $1,650 insurance claim.

Peter Huber, author of *Liability: The Legal Revolution and Its Consequences,* says the problem is one of protection under the law. In the world of tort liability, according to Huber, old-fashioned notions of cause and fault and contracts have been tossed. Instead we find a system that seeks to compensate victims regardless of who is at fault and that allocates funds from those who have them to those who supposedly need them—and to their lawyers. This is sometimes called "deep pocket" liability, because judgments are often based on the ability rather than the responsibility to pay.

The issue is scheduled to go before the U.S. Supreme Court. Although they have considered it before, the justices have not thought the right case has been brought to settle the question.

The argument brought by lawyers against the current trend in punitive damages is that they violate the U.S. Constitution's Eighth Amendment prohibition against excessive fines. This principle has long been accepted in criminal cases but never in civil suits.

The questions dealing with tort liability are crucial for business. "Across the board," Huber states,

"modern tort law weighs heavily on the spirit of innovation and enterprise." Huber doubts whether, under present conditions of product liability, Henry Ford would ever have been able to bring out the Model T or the Wright brothers to get off the ground.

Meanwhile the costs mount. Damage claims against cities doubled between 1982 and 1986. The probability that a plaintiff will win a lawsuit has also increased dramatically, from 20 to 30 percent in the 1960s to more than 50 percent in the 1980s. The first jury verdict exceeding $1 million came in 1962; today there are more than 400 in that amount each year.

While companies hope for Supreme Court action, they are hedging their bets by aggressively lobbying in the state legislatures. Since the mid-1980s, some 41 states have curbed pain and suffering awards, raised the burden of proof for punitive damages, or curtailed the rights of plaintiffs to sue more than one company for the same injuries. And 12 states have capped product liability awards. Businesses are also pushing for exemptions for products that meet government standards.

What the Supreme Court will decide is unknown. But no matter the outcome, the area of liability will obviously continue to be controversial for some time to come.[6]

showed that a number of companies have canceled introductions of new products because they were concerned about the potential liability.[7] The problem threatens many forms of needed products and services, such as day care and certain types of medical services, and has forced huge increases in the prices of others, such as childhood vaccines, where 95 percent of the price is the result of liability insurance and claims.[8] The Business Action discusses some of the liability problems businesses and insurance companies face.

Protection against Income Losses

In addition to the common areas of property and liability, companies insure themselves against loss of income resulting from an uncontrollable interruption in business and, a related area, loss of the needed expertise of a key employee.

Many types of insurance protect a company against loss of income due to interruption of its business. A company that suffers a loss from fire loses more than property. A business not capable of functioning because of damage from the fire loses much more. Employee salaries, rent, utilities, and interest will likely still need to be paid, but with the business unable to function, where will the funds come from? If there is no source for these funds, the business could be forced into bankruptcy. Three common forms of insurance used to cover these losses are business-interruption insurance, extra-expense insurance, and contingent business–interruption insurance. **Business-interruption insurance** provides funds to cover the ongoing expenses of the business when a fire or some other disaster forces the business to shut down temporarily. The policy benefits pay for ongoing expenses and protect the business from further action by its creditors. *Extra-expense insurance* provides the funds to pay for extra expenses when the business has to reopen in temporary quarters, rent needed equipment, or subcontract some of its work to other firms. *Contingent business–interruption insurance* protects against losses caused by an interruption of needed supplies. This coverage is different from business-interruption insurance. It only applies when the insured's business is interrupted because of the interruption of a key source of supply, perhaps a major supplier who has experienced a fire.

Business-Interruption Insurance
Covers the ongoing expenses of a business forced by disaster to shut down temporarily.

In addition to protecting income, many firms protect themselves from losses of income resulting from the loss of important personnel. These policies, called *key-employee insurance,* can be purchased by a company to protect itself against the impact of the death of a key employee, one whose expertise or skills are necessary to the smooth and successful running of the business. The assumption is that the loss of the key employee will cause the policyholding firm to lose the income that the key employee would have produced until a suitable replacement can be found.

Employee Insurance Policies

Besides carrying various types of property and liability insurance, most companies purchase insurance for their employees. They do this partly to be good employers and provide benefits and partly to be competitive with other employers in securing the best personnel to fill positions in the company.

As we stated previously, employers pay for some forms of insurance coverage because the law requires it. Employers have to pay half the cost of social security benefits and must provide money to the state to pay for unemployment benefits. All 50 states also require employers to carry acceptable workers' compensation coverage. Beyond these required programs, most employers provide additional insurance for their employees. The two most popular types are health insurance and life insurance.

Health insurance   Health insurance provides coverage for losses due to sickness or accidents. Currently more than 160 million Americans have some form of employer-provided health insurance. Employer spending for health insurance exceeds the after-tax corporate profits of $140 billion.[9]

Recent developments may cause employer spending to increase even more. The state of Massachusetts has legislated universal health coverage for all of its residents. This plan is scheduled for implementation in 1992. A similar plan has been proposed by Sen. Edward Kennedy of Massachusetts to cover the entire country.

Health insurance sources   Most employers provide their employees with some form of health and accident insurance as part of a fringe benefit package. Employers make coverage available through group policies. Rather than having an individual policy, an employee is insured as a member of a particular group: employees of the firm. Besides such private group programs, most health care insurance providers also sell individual policies, though usually at a higher cost to the insured. The federal government also provides health insurance through

Companies like Wausau sell health insurance to business firms that provide this benefit to their employees.

Courtesy of the Wausau Insurance Companies

the medicare and medicaid programs. Some 3.2 million people are covered by medicare.

The costs of health care continue to rise, even as health insurance is being provided to a larger and larger portion of the population. Figure 20.3 charts the spiraling health care costs. One way to help reduce your personal cost of health care is to become more aware of your own health. Connections will help you check your awareness of certain foods that can cause health problems in the long run.

The primary sources of employee health insurance are private insurance companies, including Blue Cross/Blue Shield, health maintenance organizations, and preferred provider organizations. Numerous *private insurance companies,* such as the Travelers Insurance Group, write private health insurance policies, primarily on a group basis. *Blue Cross/Blue Shield,* a group of 78 nonprofit plans, also provides insurance coverage. Perhaps the best known of the health insurance programs, Blue Cross/Blue Shield currently covers about 31 percent of all U.S. households.

Health maintenance organizations (HMOs) provide extensive health services and benefits for members, based on a prepaid monthly fee. Employees do not pay for health care services as they are administered; instead these services are provided by the HMO. The HMO hires its own physicians and health care specialists on a salaried basis. Many HMOs own their own hospitals. Federal law requires employers to offer HMO plans to employees as an alternative to a group insurance plan when HMO plans are available in the area.

As HMOs have taken a larger portion of the health care business and health care costs have continued to rise, major insurers such as Blue Cross/Blue Shield have begun to develop special programs. The **preferred provider organization (PPO)** is a relatively new form of health care coverage. Negotiating lower prices with certain physicians and hospitals, the PPO develops an

Health Maintenance Organization (HMO)
An organization that provides extensive medical care and services for members, based on a prepaid monthly fee.

Preferred Provider Organization (PPO)
A form of health care coverage that offers employers reduced premiums; employees must choose physicians and hospitals from the PPO's list of approved providers.

The Rapid Rise of Health Care Costs   **FIGURE 20.3**

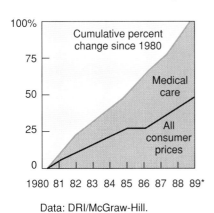
As health care costs shoot up...

Data: DRI/McGraw-Hill.

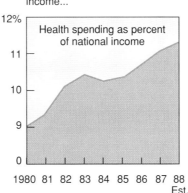
...They eat up more of national income...

Data: U.S.Health Care Financing Administration, BW.

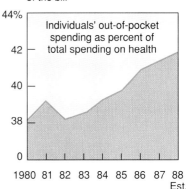
...And individuals foot more of the bill

Data: U.S.Health Care Financing Administration, BW.

*First nine months, annualized.

Source: Arnold J. Chassen, "One Solution to Rising Healthcare Costs," *Management Accounting* 72 (October 1990), pp. 28–29; *Business Week,* November 20, 1989, p. 112.

● C o n n e c t i o n s

Do You Know about Your Health?[10]

Directions: Answer the following questions about foods and health. Then compare your answers with those below.

1. Is cholesterol found in vegetables and vegetable oils, animal products, or all foods containing fats?

_____

2. Which is higher in calories: saturated fat or polyunsaturated fat? Or are they both the same?

_____

3. Is a food labeled cholesterol-free low in saturated fat or high in saturated fat? Could it be either?

_____

4. Is a product containing vegetable oil low in saturated fat, high in saturated fat, or either?

_____

---

approved list of providers—preferred providers. Thus it reduces the cost of premiums for health care packages offered to employers.

Types of health insurance   Health insurance covers a wide variety of medical expenses. Most health insurance programs can be grouped into one of five general categories:

1. *Hospitalization plans.* These plans—Blue Cross/Blue Shield is one—pay the major portion of the cost of a hospital stay. Most base fees on a semiprivate room. Usually the plan covers all drugs and services provided while the insured is in the hospital.

2. *Surgical and medical plans.* These plans specifically cover surgical expenses. They pay the cost of surgery, the fees of medical specialists, and the physician's care while the insured is in the hospital. Generally these policies have designated maximum benefit amounts.

3. *Major medical insurance plans.* Such plans protect against catastrophic loss from a serious injury or lengthy illness. They cover all medical expenses not covered under hospitalization insurance or surgical and medical insurance. The typical policy requires a deductible payment before medical expenses are covered. A typical policy deductible might be $150 per person or $450 per family. Many major medical policies pay 80 or 90 percent of the total medical expense up to a maximum, often $250,000.

4. *Dental and vision insurance plans.* These plans have become popular in recent years, after getting off to a slow start in the 1960s. The plans pay a fixed percentage of an insured's expenses for dental work, eyeglasses, and some contact lenses. A typical plan may pay 70 percent of all expenses up to a maximum of $1,000, after which all expenses are paid.

Feedback: Here are the correct answers to the questions. The percentages in parentheses indicate the number of people surveyed who answered each question wrong. These percentages are high, considering the amount of nutritional information available these days in a variety of sources.

1. Cholesterol is found in animal products only (53 percent).
2. Saturated and polyunsaturated fats have the same caloric content (40 percent).
3. Cholesterol-free food can be either high or low in saturated fat (49 percent).
4. Vegetable oils can be either high or low in saturated fat (42 percent).

5. *Mental health insurance plans.* These plans pay for psychiatric and/or psychological counseling. Once the deductible has been paid, the insured is eligible for benefit payments that generally range from 50 percent to 80 percent of the covered cost of treatment.

One other type of health insurance, *disability insurance,* protects against loss of income while an employee is disabled as a result of accident or illness. The policy usually pays the disabled worker weekly or monthly payments after a specified waiting period.

While many companies offer all of the above programs, others offer only parts of the coverage. The most popular plans combine the hospitalization, surgical and medical, and major medical plans.

Life insurance   In addition to health insurance coverage, many firms also provide their employees with life insurance. Unlike other forms of insurance, life insurance deals with a risk that is certain: the likelihood of dying is 100 percent. The uncertainty is when. Life insurance provides financial protection to the family of the policyholder. In the event of the policyholder's death, the family receives a benefit equal to the value of the policy. (Most policies are void, however, if the policyholder commits suicide within the first year the policy is in force.) The individual or individuals designated to receive the benefits of a life insurance policy are referred to as the *beneficiaries.*

The appropriate amount of life insurance to purchase is a matter of personal need, depending on family responsibility. Most life insurance experts recommend that an adult with a family purchase at least four to five times his or her annual salary. However, most people have insurance worth no more than two years' financial protection.

Life insurance provides financial protection for individuals and families should one of the family members die.

Courtesy of the John Hancock Mutual Life Insurance Company

Group policies   As with health insurance, life insurance policies can be purchased on a group or individual basis. These policies can be purchased for almost any amount. Typically the smallest policies are $1,000, while policies of some executives may be worth many millions of dollars. Life insurance policies are limited only by the amount of premiums individuals can or will pay. For larger policies, a physical examination is usually required to ensure the good health of the purchaser.

Group life insurance is frequently purchased by businesses as a benefit for their employees. Policies can be purchased on a participating basis—the employee contributes part of the cost—or a nonparticipating basis—the employer pays the full fee. Since group life insurance is written under a master policy, employees generally are not required to have a physical. Because group life insurance is usually more affordable than individual life insurance, taking advantage of it when it is available makes sense.

Earlier we described one unique form of life insurance, key-employee insurance. This insurance is purchased on the life of an executive of a company, with the company designated as beneficiary. Firms purchase such insurance to help make the transition when a key executive dies suddenly.

Types of life insurance   Life insurance protection for a specified number of years is called **term insurance.** It protects for the term of the policy but has no value at the end of the term. If the covered individual does not die before the end of the policy term, the policy simply expires. While policies can be written for any length of time, most terms range from 5 to 20 years. Policies generally have a renewal option. The premium increases with each higher age range, and most policies do not cover individuals past age 65. Term insurance often offers the most economical way for young families to obtain the insurance protection they need for a number of years while they develop financial security through investments and savings.

A special kind of term insurance, *credit life insurance,* pays off a loan or installment contract if the insured dies. Individuals buying a home often purchase credit life insurance, which protects both the family and the lender. The value of the insurance decreases as the loan is repaid.

Whole life insurance, more expensive than term insurance, provides a combination of insurance and savings. Whole life policies generally stay in force for the entire life of the insured, as long as premiums are paid. In whole life policies, the premium (based on the age of the insured) remains constant for the life of the policy unless the policy is changed.

Whole life policies accumulate value much like a savings account. The beneficiary receives the stated face value of the policy in the case of the insured's death. Because of the savings element of the whole life policy, a cash value for the policy is also stated. This cash value grows larger as the policy is in force longer. The policyholder can take out low-interest loans against this cash value or, at retirement, can take out the accumulated value either in one lump-sum payment or in annual payments.

Endowment insurance combines elements of term insurance and whole life insurance. Like a whole life policy, it provides both savings and insurance; like term insurance, it covers the insured only for a specified term. If the insured dies before the term expires, the insurance company pays the face value of the policy to the beneficiary. If the insured is still alive when the policy expires, the insurance company pays the full face value to the insured at that time.

With the high inflation rates of the 1970s and early 1980s and with the corresponding high interest rates, many people were avoiding insurance and investing their money in mutual funds, money market certificates, and other higher-paying investments. Faced with a decreasing customer base, insurance companies needed to devise alternative investment vehicles for their customers. One such vehicle is the variable life policy. Like whole life insurance, **variable life insurance** pays a death benefit and accumulates cash value over the life of the policy, but it differs in that the policyholder decides how any cash value should be invested: in bonds, stocks, money market funds, or any other form of investment. Whether the cash value accumulates quickly or slowly depends on the ability of the policyholder to invest the funds. Usually the death benefit is guaranteed.

Another type of policy that insurance companies created in response to the high interest and inflation rates of the late 70s and early 80s was the universal life policy. **Universal life insurance** combines term insurance and a savings account. The savings account, a tax-deferred account, earns interest at bond market rates. If the insured dies, the base policy amount plus any accumulated earnings are paid to the beneficiaries. Otherwise the accumulated earnings are paid directly to the policyholder. One advantage of universal life policies is

Term Insurance
Life insurance that covers an individual for a specified number of years but has no value when the term is over.

Whole Life Insurance
Provides a combination of insurance and savings and stays in force for the life of the insured.

Variable Life Insurance
Allows the policyholder to determine where the cash value of a policy should be invested.

Universal Life Insurance
Combines term insurance with a tax-deferred savings account earning interest at bond market rates.

Life Insurance that Pays Off While You're Still Alive

Heaven forbid that you should become terminally ill. But if you do, you may question the value of your life insurance policy. You have been paying on it for years, but you can't take it with you, and you can't spend it while you are here. Oh sure, the benefits are meant for the beneficiaries, but if you use up all the family savings and run the family into debt paying for care, not much may be left of the benefits anyway.

Is there an answer to this dilemma? Perhaps. More than a dozen insurance companies offer policies that let you get your hands on at least part of the so-called death benefit while you're still alive. Such policies already are available in about 35 states. They are the insurance industry's response to the heavy medical expenses that go hand in hand with the graying of America. As people live longer, the odds increase that they will need to pay for nursing home care or such costly procedures as dialysis, coronary bypass, and organ transplant.

While long-term policies exist to cover catastrophic illness and long-term nursing home stays, the premiums can be quite high. Most of these policies have met with considerable sales resistance, says Edward Murphy, an actuary at National Travelers Life in Des Moines, Iowa. Few people of advanced age want to bear the hefty premiums. So insurers have devised an alternative: "accelerated benefits" or "living benefits" coverage attached to a whole life or universal life policy.

How do these plans work? Jackson National Life in Lansing, Michigan, provides one example. On their policy, you may immediately collect a lump sum of the policy's face value—20, 25, or 30 percent—to pay for an expensive operation or treatment. Plans offered by First Penn and National Travelers allow you to collect 1 percent to 3 percent of the face value each month as long as you are in a nursing home. Of course the amount received reduces the sum your beneficiaries receive. Prudential will allow policyholders to claim their entire death benefit if doctors say they have less than six months to live. Other companies are considering similar plans.

The new plans are not expensive. As a rider on a standard life insurance contract, the accelerated-benefits feature raises premium costs only 3 to 5 percent. In most cases, notes Murphy, the extra cost is "less than you'd pay for an accidental-death rider." Some companies are even considering allowing current policyholders to purchase a low-cost accelerated benefit rider for their policies. For example, at Provident Life, an accelerated bene-

fits policy would cost a 45-year-old nonsmoker about $1,400 for each $100,000 worth of coverage. If a stroke, cancer, or some other specified emergency occurs, the policyholder can immediately collect up to $30,000 from a $100,000 policy, $300,000 from a $1 million policy. The lump-sum payment can be used for any purpose.

Once you collect, the death benefit drops to 70 percent of the original amount but so does the annual premium. And assuming that a serious health problem will adversely affect your income, premium payments are waived for the next two years.

A policy with First Penn might ease worry about a nursing home stay. After six months in a convalescent facility, the company pays out 2 percent of the death benefit each month. Other companies have similar policies.

Of course, no one is sure of Uncle Sam's reaction. Although the death benefit proceeds of life insurance policies are generally not taxable, these policies are too new to get a reading from the IRS. The insurance industry's position is that any predeath sum you receive does not constitute income. For that reason, they say, the money should have no adverse effect on anyone's social security or health insurance benefits.[11]

flexibility. The policyholder can adjust the amount of premium paid (as long as it covers the cost of the term insurance portion) as well as borrow from the policy, take out accumulated earnings, or leave the earnings with the policy to continue to accumulate for retirement.

As you can see, individuals have many life insurance options. (The Business Action explores one fairly new option: pay-now life insurance.) The question of what insurance is best is not easy to answer. Many investment experts recommend buying term insurance and investing the savings. With policies such as universal life paying money market rates, achieving a high level of earnings and security at the same time is possible. When choosing the type and amount of insurance to buy, people must consider their age, health, family size, children's ages, savings or investment plans already in place, the income your family would need in the event of your death, whether college educations will need to be funded, and the cost of insurance. A qualified insurance agent can help answer many of these questions. But since agents are paid on commission, consumers should have some knowledge of the types of policies and options available.

You'll Know It's the **Century When . . .**

• People Retire at 70

U.S. News & World Report called the 21st century the Retirement Century, but carefree retirement years may be only a dream for baby boomers who reach their 60s after the year 2000. By then about 5 million people will be 85 years old, double the number now; by 2025 an estimated 58 million workers will be retired—again, double the number in 1990. Couple those facts with a growing shortage of workers to support aging Americans, and many healthy "young seniors" may delay retirement, lured to stay on the job by extended health, dental, and life insurance. The soaring health costs that accompany a graying America may also pressure insurers into covering long-term home care and preventive programs, such as mammography.[12]

SUMMARY OF LEARNING OBJECTIVES

1. To define *risk* and explain the difference between speculative and pure risk.
   Risk is the possibility of suffering an injury or loss; it is the direct result of uncertainty. *Speculative risk* involves the chance of making a profit or taking a loss. Business owners take speculative risks when they decide to open a new store or run a promotion. *Pure risk* is the threat of a loss with no chance of profit, such as the risk of a natural disaster.

2. To explain the strategies of risk avoidance and risk reduction.
   Risk management can involve avoiding risk or reducing risk. A firm follows a strategy of *risk avoidance* by eliminating the source of risk, such as when it decides not to produce a new item because the risk of lawsuits is too high. A firm follows a strategy of *risk reduction* when it acts to

reduce the likelihood of loss. For example, it may put in sprinklers to lower the risk of fire and may conduct regular fire inspections.

3. To identify the strategies of risk coverage and explain the difference between assumption and transference of risk.

When a firm decides to cover risk, it finds a way to reserve sufficient funds to cover the financial losses that may occur, without interrupting the ongoing business. A firm can *assume risk* by setting aside a portion of the company's profits to cover future losses. Or it can *transfer risk* to an insurer, who will take the risk in exchange for a regular premium payment.

4. To explain how insurance works and how the law of large numbers affects it.

Insurance works on the basis that risks can be predicted by actuaries who use past data to predict future likelihoods. The law of large numbers is used to calculate the necessary premiums. With knowledge of the probability of loss, the likely cost of each loss, and the number of individuals covered, an insurance company can calculate its needed premiums.

5. To identify the major sources of insurance.

The major sources of insurance are public and private sources. The public sources include federal and state agencies that, through employers, provide coverage for retirement, disability and unemployment compensation, and some health insurance. *Private sources* can be either stock companies (profit-making) or mutual companies (nonprofit cooperatives).

6. To discuss the role of insurance for businesses and identify the major types of business insurance.

Insurance transfers some of the financial responsibility for risk to the insurance company, thus making it possible for a business to continue to function when a major loss occurs. Businesses will typically purchase insurance to cover property, liability, income, and personnel losses. In addition, most businesses purchase insurance to cover health and life benefits for employees.

7. To discuss insurance programs provided by employers for their employees.

Most companies provide two types of insurance for employees: health and life. *Health insurance* can be provided through a group plan administered by a private firm, a health maintenance organization (HMO), or a preferred provider organization (PPO). *Life insurance,* also usually provided through a group plan, is generally term insurance, although many other forms of life insurance are available.

KEY TERMS

Risk, p. 705

Speculative Risk, p. 705

Pure Risk, p. 705

Risk Management, p. 706

Risk Avoidance, p. 706

Risk Reduction, p. 706

Self-Insurance, p. 707

Insurance, p. 708

Insurable Risk, p. 709

Actuary, p. 709

Premium, p. 710

Law of Large Numbers, p. 710

Deductible, p. 710

Property Insurance, p. 713

QUESTIONS FOR DISCUSSION AND REVIEW

1. What is risk? Do you think companies face more speculative risk or more pure risk? What strategies can they follow to help control speculative risk?

2. Describe the strategies of risk management. Give specific examples of ways firms might be able to practice risk management.

3. What is the difference between risk assumption and risk transference? What kinds of firms should practice risk assumption? Risk transference?

4. Name some types of uninsurable risks. Why are these generally considered uninsurable?

5. What guidelines do insurance firms follow when they decide whether or not a risk is insurable? Why do you think they follow these?

6. Explain the law of large numbers. In a town of 50,000 homes with a single insurer, what will premiums be if there is a likelihood of 500 fires per year and the average loss from a fire is expected to be $30,000?

7. What insurance is provided through public sources? How are employers tied in to this responsibility?

8. What types of insurance do businesses need? What kinds of insurable losses can businesses suffer?

9. What kinds of health insurance might employers provide for employees? Name the sources of this insurance.

10. List the different types of life insurance. Briefly describe each. What type of life insurance would you prefer? Why?

CASE 20.1
Insuring the Potter Company

The Potter Company, a full-line men's shoe manufacturer, has experienced heavy liability losses over the last three years. In 1989 the company suffered a major fire that closed the plant for three weeks. Joe Potter, the owner, had no insurance coverage for this loss; the company was self-insured. In 1990 a major workers' compensation claim was filed; later a heavy liability loss resulted when three workers were seriously injured after they fell from an improperly secured scaffold. In 1991 the company suffered serious inventory losses, evidently caused by employee theft.

Joe is discussing the problem with his foreman. "Tom, I don't know how much more we can take," he says. "The self-insurance fund is nearly wiped out. I am really in trouble. Think about a plan to help us get this thing under control, and come back tomorrow with some specific recommendations."

Tom leaves Joe's office and goes home to think about the Potter Company's problem.

Questions for Discussion
1. What does Joe mean when he says the company is self-insured?
2. If you were Tom, what recommendations would you make to Joe? Be specific and complete in your recommendations.
3. Should Joe be carrying insurance? If so, what kinds?

CASE 20.2
The Risk of Computer Viruses

As the business sector, and indeed all of our society, becomes more dependent on computers, concern about computer security grows. According to *Business Week,* roughly $1 trillion is transferred every day via computer networks. Yet a knowledgeable person can, with relative ease, access a computer system and cause serious damage. Estimates of the annual cost of computer crime range from $1 billion to $2 billion.

One of the most recent computer problems firms face is called a "computer virus." A virus is a type of computer program that is intentionally hidden in

Adapted from John Mezzacappa and Karen M. Cooke, "Computer Viruses and the All Risk Policy," *Best's Review,* July 1990, pp. 80–82; Evan I. Schwartz, Jeffrey Rothfeder, and Mark Lewyn, "Viruses? Who You Gonna Call? 'Hackbusters,' " *Business Week,* August 6, 1990, pp. 71–72.

other computer programs. When a program with a virus comes into contact with other programs, the virus attacks the other programs. Some viruses can destroy every bit of information on a computer. Businesses also face the problem of losing highly confidential data to computer hackers. These individuals break into computer systems and steal information or damage programs.

Computer viruses and computer hackers present a huge potential risk to firms. They have shut down entire computer systems in some large companies.

Fortunately, business firms can now obtain insurance coverage for losses from computer crime. Although some policies specifically cover computer viruses, many others were drafted before computer viruses became a problem. These policies generally insure all risks of direct physical loss or damage, unless something is specifically excluded. The issue then becomes whether or not the damage caused by a computer virus is a physical loss. In some cases, insurance companies have maintained that information lost on a computer is not physical property and thus is not covered by a traditional all-risk policy.

Many insurance companies are beginning to use policy language that deals specifically with the loss of computer information. In this way, the insured understands what is covered, and the insurance company can avoid a large, unexpected loss. Courts have held that information stored on the computer is tangible property in tax cases. In property insurance cases, they may handle the destruction of computer information the same way. Destruction of valuable information, therefore, could result in a catastrophic loss that is covered under an all-risk policy unless there is limiting language.

Questions for Discussion

1. Why is computer crime a risk to businesses?
2. Why is there a problem in determining whether or not the destruction of information by a computer virus is covered under an all-risk policy?
3. How can insurance firms protect themselves against unexpected losses from computer viruses?

FINANCE

We have all handled money, with varying success, for most of our lives. But financial specialists are artists at managing money and getting the most for their investment dollars. They concern themselves with interest rates, inflation, stock prices, credit risks, real estate prices, and much, much more.

Career opportunities in finance are varied and offer exciting challenges. Financial institutions employ thousands of people at every level. These institutions may be commercial banks, savings and loan associations, or other organizations such as finance companies or credit unions. They provide a wide range of services: lending money, keeping savings, providing checking accounts, managing trust funds, advising individuals and companies on investments and business affairs, and so on. Investment banks, stock brokerage firms, and even insurance companies, also considered financial institutions, primarily provide such services as helping one firm buy another, brokering stocks and bonds, and providing financial advice.

Today's world of finance knows few boundaries. Government deregulation has reduced many restrictions so that banks, insurance companies, savings and loans, and brokerage houses cross over into one another's territories. People interested in a career in finance now have a wide choice. Opportunities in financial institutions and businesses are promising and include a number of alternatives.

BANKING

The old image of the staid banker who keeps "banker's hours" is a thing of the past. Today's bankers are aggressive marketers in a highly competitive business.

The field contains a number of specialities, but career opportunities generally fall into four functional areas: lending, trusts, systems, and operations. Regardless of the functional area, bank officers have two major areas of responsibility—making loans and selling services.

Loan officers work with customers seeking loans or credit. Officers generally specialize in either consumer loans, commercial loans, or mortgages. In consumer banking, the loan officer decides whether to recommend personal loans to individuals. In commercial banking, a loan officer evaluates the risk of granting a loan or line of credit to businesses. To determine if backing the applicant is a good loan risk, all loan officers analyze the applicant's financial status, creditworthiness, and overall ability to pay back the loan.

Trust officers are responsible for managing and investing money, property, or other assets entrusted to the bank. Trust officers must

---

Duties: Loan Officer

- Evaluating credit.
- Providing financial advice.
- Making decisions on loans.
- Appraising property.
- Coordinating work flow.

see that all terms and legal requirements of the trust agreements are properly executed. They must know probate and tax laws as well as investment strategies and financial planning.

Operations officers oversee internal operations for providing customers with all nonloan services: money transfers, letters of credit, foreign exchanges, financial planning, and credit cards. They are responsible for planning, coordinating, and controlling the bank's work flow, updating systems, and handling the paperwork between departments. They are responsible for the smooth and efficient operation of a particular area. Operations officers manage the clerical staff, make certain they comply with established procedures, and sometimes troubleshoot for customer problems.

Branch managers oversee the local branches of major banks. They are responsible for integrating the branch office into the neighborhood and generating local business. They must be aware of local business, economic, and so-

cial conditions. Responsibilities include supervision of bank employees, overseeing daily operations, making final decisions on loans, and generating ideas for new services, procedures, or security.

Additional Banking Resources

American Bankers Association
1120 Connecticut Avenue, N.W.
Washington, DC 20036

Consumers Bankers Association
1300 North 17th Street
Arlington, VA 22209

National Association of Bank Women
500 North Michigan Avenue
Chicago, IL 60611

National Association for Bank Cost
  Analysis and Management
  Accounting
P.O. Box 27448
San Francisco, CA 94127

CORPORATE FINANCE

Corporate finance includes accounting for expenditures, analyzing past and planned expenses, budgeting for the future, managing and investing capital, and financing expansion plans. An entry-level assignment might be in one of sev-

Finance/Accounting Departments

General accounting
Cost accounting
Capital budgeting
Financial planning
Pricing
Investments
Tax
Internal auditing
Accounting systems
Cost control

---

eral accounting or finance departments. Frequent movement occurs between departments so people can gain experience in a wide number of areas. The first assignment is typically in general accounting to gain familiarity with the company's record-keeping procedures.

A common entry-level position in corporate finance for an M.B.A. is that of financial analyst. The financial analyst analyzes financial operations, policies, or decisions and prepares reports to management making specific recommendations. The position usually is a steppingstone to a financial management assignment.

Promotions often occur every two to four years. As one advances, the time between promotions tends to become longer. Promotions normally bring sizable pay raises because of the great need for qualified financial managers and executives. Initial assignments are project oriented and require attention to detail. As one progresses up the corporate ladder, jobs require more management skills and the ability to supervise people.

Requirements: Banking

Personal skills:
• Interpersonal
• Analytical
• Decision-making

Education:
• Bachelor's degree in business administration
• Master's in business administration
• Major in finance
• Major in accounting

Requirements: Corporate Finance

Personal skills:
• Decision-making
• Communication
• Analytical
• Computer

Education:
• Master's in business administration
• Major in finance
• Major in accounting

Most corporate finance jobs do not involve extensive travel.

The top position in corporate finance is the chief financial officer (CFO), who frequently has the title of vice president of finance. The chief financial officer heads the treasury function—the acquisition, administration, and protection of funds. The CFO also manages the controller's function—accounting systems, financial planning, and compliance with tax and regulatory agencies.

Additional Corporate Finance Resources

Financial Management Association
College of Business Administration
University of South Florida
4202 Fowler Avenue
Tampa, FL 33620

Institute of Chartered Financial Analysts
Box 3668
Charlottesville, VA 22903

Institute of Cost Analysis
7111 Marlan Drive
Alexandria, VA 22307

CAREER PROFILE: Steve Prelosky

Marc Bolster

STEVE PRELOSKY

Age: 30
Hometown: Pittsburgh
Undergraduate degree: Pennsylvania State University
Graduate: Master's degree in business administration Carnegie Mellon University
Last job: Salesman for GE
Immediate plans: To be a financial planner for a small chemical company
Long-term goal: To own the company

SECURITIES

Millions of people and businesses invest in stocks and bonds every day. Nightly newscasts and daily newspapers routinely report the day's stock trading and averages. The nation regularly follows the stock market as a sign of the country's economic health.

The securities industry involves the buying and selling of stocks, bonds, or shares in mutual funds for investors. Careers in the industry generally fall into four basic functional areas: sales, trading, underwriting, and research.

The employment market for the industry tends to fluctuate with the economy. In the mid-1980s, demand was high, but a number of brokerage houses have merged or closed since then, leading to a reduced number of job opportunities.

Sales

Securities salesworkers act as agents for investors wanting to buy or sell securities. They must be registered as representatives of a brokerage firm and must pass a general security examination with the Securities and Exchange Com-

mission. They may also be called stockbrokers, account executives, or registered representatives.

Securities salespeople perform various services for clients, including providing advice on securities, supplying the latest stock and bond price quotations, and furnishing information on the financial positions of corporations. They may specialize in a particular type of security, such as stocks, government bonds, stock options, commodity futures, mutual funds, or annuities.

Newcomers participate in a

After graduating from Pennsylvania State University in 1979 with a degree in mechanical engineering, Steve Prelosky spent six years working for General Electric Co. There he did a variety of jobs, at one point even traveling to the Middle East to sell parts for gas turbine engines. The longer he worked, however, the more convinced he became that his future lay outside a large company. As markets matured, he saw his opportunities for advancement and—with them—the promise of job security dry up. Finally he decided to quit and go to school for his M.B.A. "With my wife working and no kids, I felt it was a good time to take a risk," he says.

During his second year in graduate school, Prelosky got wind of a part-time job with a young Pittsburgh-based company, a $5 million business that produces carbon dioxide for industrial uses. The founder, a friend of his family, was thinking about adding capacity and asked Prelosky to crunch some numbers. "I analyzed the profit and loss margins under several different scenarios, things I didn't even know how to do before going to business school." His findings convinced the company to proceed with expansion—and to offer Prelosky a full-time position on its finance staff.

Prelosky expects to have many new opportunities and challenges in his finance job. "Besides working on the financial end of the business, I plan to have some input into marketing and to bring in some business," he says. His salary is $4,000 to $5,000 less than the $40,000 he was making at GE. But he now has 10 percent of the equity of a growing company. "My goal is to help this company grow and to make sure that we stay lean, because that's our advantage."

bonds, or commodities. The work is extremely high paced and requires the ability to make quick decisions.

Underwriting

Investment bankers handle the financing of the sale of a corporation's securities to the public. Essentially the investment banking firm underwrites the sale by purchasing the securities of the corporation and then selling them to the public on the market. With billions of dollars at stake, this is considered one of the riskiest, most challenging areas of finance. Competition is extremely fierce for employment, and opportunities are limited to the very top M.B.A. graduates.

Requirements: Securities

Personal skills:
- Self-confidence
- Ability to work under pressure
- Analytical ability
- Drive

Education:
- Master's in business administration
- Major in finance

---

training program, usually for about six months. After meeting the licensing registration requirements, beginners start by building up a clientele from personal and telephone contacts. They start by handling the accounts of individual investors and may advance to handling the large accounts of large institutional investors.

During the training period, newcomers receive salaries. Once they complete training, earnings consist solely of commissions on the sale of securities. These commissions can be substantial. Earnings are limited only by the number and size of accounts served.

Opportunities exist to advance into management and to supervise the work of other salespeople. However, many people prefer to remain in sales because of the high earnings potential.

Trading

Traders do not deal with investors. They spend their time on the exchange trading floor actually filling the orders to buy and sell securities. Traders also specialize by type of security, such as stocks,

Research

Research and analysis are crucial to the sale, trading, and underwriting of securities. Analysts study stocks and bonds, assess their current value, and forecast their earning potential. Security analysts tend to specialize in an industry and become experts in their area, such as the automobile or retailing industry. Strong analytical skills as well as verbal and writing skills are

Agents

Agents sell insurance policies to individuals and businesses. Selling insurance involves prospecting for new clients, interviewing clients to determine their insurance needs, and providing service. Clients may be executives buying policies for their company or individuals buying personal protection policies. Agents spend most of their time discussing policies with potential and existing clients.

Requirements: Insurance

Personal skills:
- Analytical ability
- Patience
- Orientation to detail

Education:
- Bachelor's degree
- Open to any major
- Major in finance

An agent may be an employee of a single insurance company or a broker who acts as an independent agent representing several companies. Beginning agents usually receive a base salary for a year or two. Earnings are then based strictly on commissions and may become substantial within a short period of time.

Underwriters

After an agent or broker sells an insurance policy, the client fills out an insurance application. An underwriter then evaluates the application to determine whether the applicant is a good or bad risk. Underwriters assess the degree of risk to the insurance company and decide whether or not the company should issue a policy.

"Buy...sell...buy...sell...buy..."

Source: Joseph Farris, *Just a Cog in the Wheel* (Holbrook, Mass.: Bob Adams, 1989).

essential for success as a securities analyst.

Additional Securities Resources

Securities Industry Association
35th Floor
120 Broadway
New York, NY 10271

Society of Financial Examiners
1100 Raleigh Building
Box 2598
Raleigh, NC 27602

National Association of Security Dealers
2 World Trade Center
New York, NY 10048

INSURANCE

To protect themselves against financial loss from property damage, injuries, and illnesses, individuals and companies buy insurance policies.

The risk of loss is transferred from the policyholder to the insurance company. The insurance industry provides a variety of employment opportunities in several areas.

Most underwriters specialize in a type of insurance, such as fire, automobile, health, or life. Some may specialize in individual or group policies. Underwriters must be able to make personal judgments and assume responsibility; their decisions are crucial to the financial success of the insurance company.

Actuaries

Actuaries analyze the amount of risk and then recommend the premium or price to charge for insurance. They analyze and calculate the probability of loss due to death, fires, accidents, illnesses, theft, and other catastrophes and calculate the probable cost of the losses.

Additional Insurance Resources

American Institute for Property and
  Liability Underwriters
Insurance Institute of America
Providence and Sugartown Roads
Malvern, PA 19355

American Insurance Association
85 John Street
New York, NY 10038

Insurance Information Institute
110 William Street
New York, NY 10038

National Association of Life
  Underwriters
1922 F Street, N.W.
Washington, DC 20006

Professional Insurance Agents
400 North Washington Street
Alexandria, VA 22314

PART SEVEN

ACCOUNTING AND INFORMATION SYSTEMS

CHAPTER TWENTY-ONE

ACCOUNTING FUNDAMENTALS

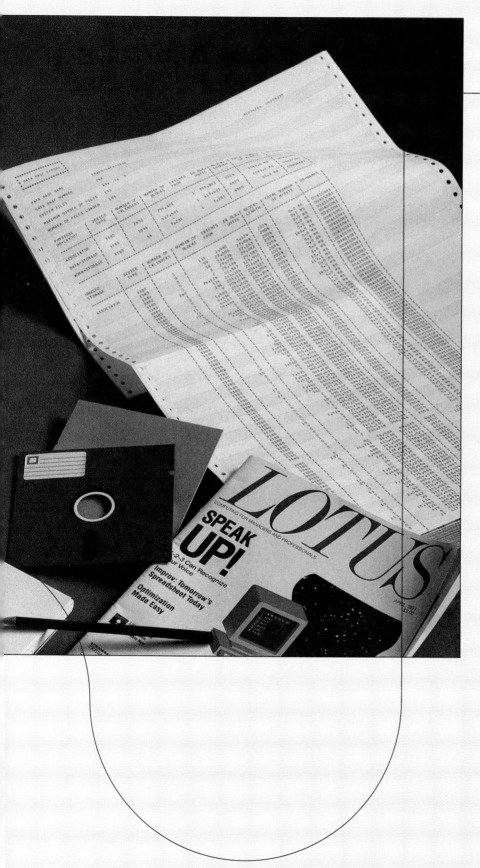

LEARNING OBJECTIVES

1. To explain the purpose of accounting and its importance to a firm's managers, creditors, and investors.

2. To describe the CPA and CMA designations and distinguish between public and private accountants.

3. To list the steps in the accounting cycle.

4. To state the accounting equation, define its elements, and describe its relationship to double-entry bookkeeping.

5. To explain the purpose of the balance sheet and identify its major elements.

6. To explain the purpose of the income statement and identify its major elements.

7. To describe common-size financial statements and how they are used.

8. To explain the purpose of ratio analysis and list the major financial ratios.

To Sea World visitors, Shamu looks like a killer whale. But to accountants at Anheuser-Busch, she looks like a depreciable asset. What does Shamu have to do with accounting? Here's the story.

In September 1989, Harcourt Brace Jovanovich (HBJ) announced it was selling several theme parks to Anheuser-Busch,

The Image Works

Inc. for $1.1 billion. They were the Boardwalk and Baseball parks and Cypress Gardens, all in central Florida, and the Sea World parks in Texas, Ohio, California, and Florida. Included in the deal were 15 whales—including Shamu, who lives at the Florida Sea World.

Attendance at the parks in 1988 totaled 14 million. For the 12-

month period ending June 1989, these parks earned income of $68.3 million on revenues of $382 million. These figures represented an increase from the previous 12-month period, which saw income of $52.8 million on revenues of $348 million.

Why would HBJ sell such valuable, revenue-generating properties? In 1987 Robert Maxwell, a British financier and the owner of Macmillan Publishing, attempted a takeover of HBJ. To the approval of Wall Street, HBJ fought off the takeover attempt by paying $40-a-share cash dividends and taking on heavy long-term debt totaling $2.8 billion.

This heavy debt burden required HBJ to pay interest to the tune of $340 million per year. The company's cash flow was too meager to cover this bill. Any money HBJ would earn from selling its assets

would have to go to pay off these loans—leaving the company still under the burden of $2 billion of costly junk bonds and preferred stock.

Along came Anheuser-Busch to the rescue. Anheuser-Busch offered to pay HBJ $1.1 billion to take the theme parks off its hands. This price was considerably lower than the $1.7 billion that HBJ had originally hoped to sell the parks for. The price was lower, in part, because great sums of money—up to $100 million by some estimates—were required to upgrade and maintain the facilities. With all of its financial problems, HBJ didn't have money to spend on cleaning aquariums, not even giant, revenue-producing ones.

Even though HBJ did not realize as much on the sale as it had hoped, the company still benefited. It improved cash flow, lowered its debt, and was able to increase its capital spending. But the company needs to sell even more assets, as its stock fell from $19 a share in 1989 to $3 in 1990.

What about Shamu and friends? HBJ accountants must have thought the parks' residents would live forever; they were being carried on the company's books at the same value year after year. Anheuser-Busch accountants, however, see the whales as depreciable assets. They have figured out a whale's life span. From now on, as the years wind down, so will Shamu's value.[1]

Accounting is an old profession. Business transactions have been recorded and analyzed for centuries. But only in the last 50 years or so has accounting been given the importance and respect accorded other professions.

Accounting is more than bean counting—or killer whale counting. Today accounting is the language of business; anyone who aspires to a business career must, to some degree, speak that language. Corporations run on their numbers, and accounting plays an increasingly important role in business decisions. And with the economic unification of Europe in 1992 and increasing opportunities in global business, international accounting will also gain in importance.[2]

In this chapter, we examine how businesses use accounting information. We first define accounting and discuss the various uses and users of accounting information. We describe the professional certifications that accountants may attain and differentiate between public and private accountants. We identify and briefly describe the accounting regulatory bodies. We then explain the accounting cycle, the accounting equation, and double-entry bookkeeping. Next we present the basic financial statements and their components. Finally we show how business firms interpret the financial statements through the use of common-size statements and ratio analysis.

WHAT IS ACCOUNTING?

The American Accounting Association defines **accounting** as "the process of identifying, measuring, and communicating economic information to permit informed judgments and decisions by users of the information."[3] Accounting information interests investors, creditors, managers, unions, and governmental organizations. Current investors use it to review the past performance of the company in which they invested and to determine whether to maintain, increase, or liquidate their investment. Potential investors use it to help them make investment decisions. Creditors use financial information to evaluate credit applicants.

Company managers are the largest users of accounting information. They must have reliable information to make decisions about allocating company resources. Accounting information can be used to predict each alternative's consequences. Managers also use accounting information to compare actual financial results with expectations. By reviewing financial data regularly, management can react swiftly when results deviate too much from expectations.

Unions review company financial information to help determine wage and benefit demands in salary negotiations. Governmental organizations rely on accounting information when establishing a company's tax liability. Table 21.1 lists the various users of accounting information and some of the purposes for which the information is used.

Accounting
The process of identifying, measuring, and communicating economic information to permit informed decisions by users of the information.

TYPES OF ACCOUNTANTS

In the United States today, more than a million people work as accountants and several million work in accounting-related careers. Accountants may be classified by the type of certification they achieve, as either a certified public accountant (CPA) or a certified management accountant (CMA). They are also classified as public or private accountants.

TABLE 21.1

Users and Uses of Accounting Information

User	Typical Uses
Current investors	Evaluate the income generated by a company and its components.
	Evaluate the cash flow generated by a company.
	Evaluate management's performance.
Potential investors	In addition to the above, determine a company's future growth potential and the risk of investing in the company.
Creditors	Evaluate a prospective borrower's ability to make principal and interest payments.
Managers	Make resource allocation decisions.
	Compare actual financial results with budgeted plans.
	Measure managerial performance.
Unions	Review a company's financial condition before negotiating wages and benefits.
Government agencies	Determine a company's tax liability.

TABLE 21.2

The Big 6 Accounting Firms

DID YOU KNOW? *Who are the "Big 6" accounting firms?*

Firm	Sample Clients
Arthur Andersen & Co.	United Air Lines, ITT
Coopers & Lybrand	Ford, AT&T
Deloitte & Touche	General Motors, Procter & Gamble
Ernst & Young	McDonald's, Coca-Cola
KPMG Peat Marwick	Xerox, General Electric
Price Waterhouse & Co.	Exxon, IBM

Certified Public Accountants

CPA
Designation for accountants who pass a rigorous examination, have accounting experience, and are licensed by the state; may be public or private accountants; qualified to conduct audits of companies' financial statements.

Certified public accountants (CPAs) are licensed by the state in which they practice. Licensing requirements vary by state, but generally a CPA must meet certain educational requirements and pass a rigorous, four-part examination developed by the American Institute of Certified Public Accountants (AICPA). In most states, two years of accounting experience are required. Today approximately 400,000 CPAs practice in the United States.[4]

Public Accountants

Public Accountant
Works for a firm that provides accounting services to companies, other organizations, and the general public on a fee-for-service basis; typical areas of service include auditing, tax consulting, and management consulting.

A **public accountant** works for an accounting firm that provides accounting services to companies, other organizations, and the general public on a fee-for-service basis. Public accounting firms vary in size from the very largest, known as the Big 6, to sole-practitioner firms. The Big 6 have thousands of employees and offices throughout the world. Table 21.2 lists these accounting

You get to the top
by getting
to the bottom.

In today's competitive world, you've got to know your
market and customers bottom to top, inside and out. You
need to understand how to combine technology
with the human factors in your operation, to put
both top quality and time-to-market on your
side. And you've always got to keep your eye on
the bottom line while reaching for that top
position in the industry.

Ernst & Young can help. We work
with leaders in every segment of high
technology, providing integrated ser-
vices and the hands-on experience you need in accounting, finance, tax, and consulting. As the market leader in serving high tech clients, we can use our in-depth
knowledge and understanding to help you get to the top.

For more information about our High Technology Industry Services, contact
G. Steven Burrill at (415) 981-8890, or Antonio M. Laliberte at (408) 947-5500.

≡J/ ERNST & YOUNG

Courtesy of Ernst & Young

Public accountants work for firms like Ernst & Young, providing accounting services on a fee-for-service basis.

firms and some of their major clients. CPAs in a public accounting firm typically provide three areas of service: auditing, tax consulting, and management consulting.

Auditing, the oldest area of practice, remains the largest for many firms. An **audit** is a CPA's examination of a company's financial statements in order to express an opinion about the fairness of those statements in accordance with generally accepted accounting principles. When a company wants to borrow funds from a bank or have its stock listed on a stock exchange, it must present statements regarding its financial affairs. Because these statements are prepared by independent auditors, those interested in the information know it has been presented fairly and accurately.

A rapidly growing area of practice is *tax consulting and compliance.* Public accounting firms help devise strategies to minimize the tax liabilities of their client companies. In many instances, the accounting firm will prepare or review the company's tax returns.

The third major area of practice for public accounting firms is *management consulting.* Activities in this area typically vary from one firm to another. Some examples include computer systems analysis, design, and implementation; employee benefits and compensation consulting; risk management services; and litigation support. The Business Action discusses how *perestroika* is bringing public accounting firms to the Soviet Union.

Audit
A CPA's examination of a company's financial statements to determine the fairness of the statements in accordance with generally accepted accounting principles.

Public Accounting Comes to the Soviet Union

One of the outcomes of *perestroika,* the new openness in the Soviet Union, is that public accounting firms are popping up in that country. For decades during the rule of the Communist party, the Soviet Union had no public accounting profession; there was no need for one. But times are changing rapidly as the Soviet Union attempts to understand the Western concept of profit.

One of the first U.S. accounting firms to do business in the Soviet Union was Ernst & Young. Late in 1989, the Big 6 firm and the Soviet consulting firm Uneshconsult, developed the first Western-Soviet accounting firm. It offers tax accounting, auditing, accounting for joint ventures in the Soviet Union, and other consulting services. One area of consulting in demand deals with market entry strategies.

Although the newly formed firm is not the first public accounting firm in the Soviet Union, there have been few others. None successfully established a viable practice; the demand simply did not

exist. Additionally, the Soviet Union has not been open to outside accounting firms doing business there. But Ernst & Young believes that a combined Western-Soviet firm will succeed.

Ernst & Young emphasizes that Ernst & Young/Uneshconsult will be regarded as a true partnership, not just a politically convenient vehicle to conduct business in the Soviet Union. Uneshconsult, well known in the Soviet Union, brings considerable resources to the partnership. By making the Soviet firm a full working partner and by providing the training and procedures, Ernst & Young hopes for a big success.[5]

Certified Management Accountants

Certified management accountants (CMAs) must meet educational and experience requirements similar to those for a CPA. They take a five-part examination developed by the National Association of Accountants. About 9,600 CMAs operate in the United States.[6] Both CPAs and CMAs are employed in public accounting; however, only a CPA can conduct an audit as to the fairness of a company's financial statements.

Private Accountants

The title **private accountant** includes all positions not in public accounting. Private accounting can be divided into management accounting, government accounting, and academia. Management accounting describes accounting positions within a company. The accountant is employed by a single business, as opposed to public accountants, who may have many clients. Government

CMA
Designation for accountants who pass a rigorous examination, have accounting experience, and are licensed by the state; may be public or private accountants but cannot conduct audits of corporate financial statements.

Private Accountant
Accountant in any position not included in public accounting; may work in management accounting, government accounting, or academia.

Some firms handle their own accounting needs with systems like Accounting Plus®.

Courtesy of Systems Plus Inc.

● **C o n n e c t i o n s**

Are You Up on Accounting?

Directions: Below are some statements about job opportunities in accounting and the different types of accountants. Circle the number that represents how strongly you agree or disagree with each statement.

	Strongly Disagree				Strongly Agree
1. Accountants tend to be employed in very boring jobs.	1	2	3	4	5
2. There is little opportunity to move out of accounting because other departments do not want "bean counters."	1	2	3	4	5
3. Accountants do not make enough money.	1	2	3	4	5
4. Because accountants deal primarily with numbers, they do not need good people skills.	1	2	3	4	5
5. The opportunities for women in accounting are not as good as those for men.	1	2	3	4	5
6. The only accountants with professional certifications are CPAs.	1	2	3	4	5
7. A CPA is independent with respect to his/her client.	1	2	3	4	5

---

accounting positions can be at the federal, state, or local level. Accountants in academia teach and conduct research at the college and university level.

In this discussion of the types of accountants, we mention only briefly some of the career opportunities available to those interested in accounting as a profession. For more information about jobs in the accounting field, see the Career Appendix at the end of this section of the book. How much do you know about the accounting field? Connections will help you assess your knowledge and perceptions of accounting.

ACCOUNTING REGULATORY AGENCIES

As mentioned previously, accounting—in particular the auditing practice of a public accounting firm—is intertwined with the public interest. For this reason, numerous regulatory bodies have been created over the years. The most important accounting regulatory agencies are described here.

8. A CMA is independent with respect to his/her client.   1   2   3   4   5

9. CPAs are limited to jobs in public accounting.   1   2   3   4   5

10. CMAs in public accounting can express an independent audit opinion on a company's financial statements.   1   2   3   4   5

Feedback: If you tended to agree with the first four statements, you need to learn some basic facts about the accounting profession. Whether it is auditing a multinational company such as IBM or working for the FBI as an agent, opportunities abound for accountants to move out of the accounting area and into other departments. Most departments view the financial training accountants receive as an excellent background for all areas of business. Also, opportunities for women within the accounting profession today are every bit as good as they are for men. Most larger CPA firms actively recruit, hire, and promote qualified accountants who happen to be women. Women make up more than 50 percent of the enrollment in many accounting programs in schools around the country.

The last five questions deal with types of accountants. CPAs are entrusted with the public welfare when they undertake audits of financial statements; the primary responsibility of CMAs is to their employers. CPAs are extensively employed outside of public accounting. More AICPA members are engaged in private practice than in public accounting. Another fundamental difference between CPAs and CMAs is that only a CPA can express an audit opinion on a company's financial statements.

American Institute of Certified Public Accountants

The American Institute of Certified Public Accountants (AICPA) is the primary association of accountants in the United States. Founded in 1887, it has grown from a handful of members to a membership exceeding 300,000. Prior to 1973, the AICPA's Committee on Accounting Procedure (and later the Accounting Principles Board) was primarily responsible for setting accounting standards. The committee issued numerous *Accounting Research Bulletins* recommending principles for accountants to follow. The board has issued *Opinions* regarding policies and procedures. Accountants are generally required to conform to these *Opinions* in practice.

Financial Accounting Standards Board

The Financial Accounting Standards Board (FASB) began in 1973 as an independent agency charged with setting accounting standards. The board consists of seven full-time members drawn from public and private accounting. So far the FASB has issued close to 100 *Statements of Financial Accounting Standards* for accounting and financial reporting. For instance, the FASB decreed that all companies must break out each line of business that constitutes over 10 percent of sales and must report revenues, profits, assets, depreciation expenses, and capital expenditures for each.[7]

Securities and Exchange Commission

The Securities and Exchange Commission (SEC), created by the Securities Exchange Act of 1934, oversees the financial reporting practices of all publicly held companies. A publicly held company's stock is traded on a recognized securities exchange or in the over-the-counter market. Although the SEC has the power to set accounting standards for those companies under its jurisdiction, it has rarely exercised this power. Instead, it works closely with the private sector (that is, the FASB) to develop accounting standards.

THE ACCOUNTING CYCLE

A primary purpose of accounting is to communicate the results of business transactions. The accounting cycle was developed to accomplish this goal. The steps in the **accounting cycle** include analyzing, recording, posting, and preparing financial statements.

Accounting Cycle
The steps—analyzing, recording, posting, and preparing reports—by which the results of business transactions are communicated.

The accountant first *analyzes* business transactions to determine which should be recorded and at what amount. Typically accountants only record transactions that can be measured and verified with some degree of precision. For example, the purchase of a truck can be accurately measured and easily verified. The resignation of a key company official, also a business transaction, would not be recorded. Although such an event may represent an economic loss to a company, it is difficult to determine whether a loss has occurred and, if so, what the amount of the loss would be.

Journal
A book or computer file in which business transactions are recorded chronologically.

Transactions are then *recorded* chronologically in a **journal**. A journal may be either a book (in a manual accounting system) or a file (in a computerized accounting system). Each entry contains the date of the transaction, its description, and debit and credit columns. Transactions are recorded in the firm's general journal or in specialized journals. A *general journal* is a book or file in which transactions are recorded in the order they occur. As businesses expand, they may adopt *specialized journals* to record particular types of business transactions (for example, credit sales or cash disbursements).

Account
Record of all transactions affecting a particular financial statement element.

Businesses need to know the balances in various financial statement elements (assets, liabilities, owners' equity, revenues, and expenses) at any point in time. **Accounts** are used to summarize all transactions that affect a particular financial statement element. A business maintains separate accounts for each of its assets, liabilities, equities, revenues, and expenses. All transactions affecting an account are *posted* (recorded) from the general journal or specialized journals to the account. All the accounts of a business are summarized in the **general ledger**.

General Ledger
A book or computer file summarizing all the accounts of a business.

Financial Statement
Document presenting a company's financial position, results of operations, and cash flow during a stated period of time.

The final step of the accounting process is *preparing* financial statements. **Financial statements** present a company's financial position, results of operations, and flow of cash during a particular period of time. They can be prepared for any time interval, but they are always prepared annually. Investors, creditors, company managers, and others interested in a firm's financial position all rely heavily on financial statements.

THE ACCOUNTING EQUATION

The **accounting equation** indicates a company's financial position at any point in time. On its framework rests the entire accounting process. According to the accounting equation, a company's assets equal its liabilities plus owners' equity, thus:

Assets = Liabilities + Owners' Equity

Any recorded business transaction can be analyzed in terms of its effect on the accounting equation. Also, business transactions must be recorded to maintain the equality of this equation. This equality is reflected in the balance sheet, one of the financial statements a firm is required to prepare.

Assets are anything of value owned by the business and used in conducting its operations. Examples include cash, investments, inventory, accounts receivable, and furniture and fixtures. **Liabilities** are amounts owed by the business to its creditors, including obligations to perform services in the future. Liabilities include accounts payable and notes payable (for example, when a firm uses credit to purchase machinery or inventory), wages payable to employees, and taxes payable. **Owners' equity** represents the claims of the owners, partners, and shareholders against the firm's assets. It is the owners' claim on the firm's assets, or the excess of assets over all liabilities.

Revenues are increases in assets or decreases in liabilities from the ongoing operation of a business. Businesses generate revenues by sales of goods and services, interest earned on investments, rents, royalties, and dividends. **Expenses** are decreases in assets or increases in liabilities from the ongoing

Accounting Equation
Assets = Liabilities + Owners' Equity, indicating a company's financial position at any point in time.

Asset
Anything of value owned by the business and used in its operation.

Liability
Amounts owed by a business to its creditors.

Owners' Equity
Claims of owners, partners, and shareholders against the firm's assets; the excess of assets over all liabilities.

Revenue
Increase in assets or decrease in liabilities from the ongoing operation of a business.

Expenses
Decreases in assets or increases in liabilities from the ongoing operation of a business.

Courtesy of Pier 1 Imports, Inc.

Pier 1 Imports maintains a large assortment of merchandise in its retail stores. The inventory, furnishings, and fixtures inside a store are assets.

operation of a business. Expenses include cost of goods sold (the cost of the goods or services that the firm used to generate revenues), salaries, utilities, taxes, advertising, and interest payments. **Net income**, or the bottom line, is the excess of revenues over expenses. Net income, a chief barometer of business performance, is closely watched by investors, creditors, and company managers.

Net Income
The excess of revenues over expenses; also called the bottom line.

Double-Entry Bookkeeping

Every business transaction is analyzed to determine whether it increases or decreases a firm's assets, liabilities, owners' equity, revenues, and expenses. Debits and credits are bookkeeping entries that reflect business transactions. **Debits** are used to record increases in assets, decreases in liabilities, or decreases in owners' equity. Debits are recorded on the left side of an entry in the journal or ledger. **Credits** are used to record decreases in assets, increases in liabilities, or increases in owners' equity. Credits are recorded on the right side of entries made in the journal and ledger.

The terms *debit* and *credit* can be confusing. Whether debits and credits *increase* or *decrease* accounts depends on the type of account being debited or credited. The important point to remember is that debit means left side of a journal or ledger entry, and credit means right side.

Double-entry bookkeeping enables the firm to keep the accounting equation in balance. In **double-entry bookkeeping**, each business transaction is recorded with two offsetting entries in which the total amount of debits equals the total amount of credits. Figure 21.1 shows an example of journal and ledger entries for the Music Box, a hypothetical retail establishment specializing in compact-disk players and other stereo equipment.

The Music Box's books are kept by Laura Baker, the owner. The accounts shown on the journal page in the upper portion of Figure 21.1 represent the company's sources and uses of funds. These accounts are then summarized in the ledger accounts, which are shown in the lower portion of the figure.

On September 1, Laura Baker contributed $40,000 cash in return for capital stock to get the company started. This transaction increased the firm's assets and the owners' equity. The Cash account is debited (to show an increase in assets), and the Capital Stock account is credited (to show an increase in owners' equity).

Debit
An entry that records an increase in assets, a decrease in liabilities, or a decrease in owners' equity; recorded on the left side of a journal or ledger entry.

Credit
An entry that records a decrease in an asset, an increase in a liability, or an increase in owners' equity; recorded on the right side of a journal or ledger entry.

Double-Entry Bookkeeping
A method of recording business transactions in which offsetting debits and credits keep the accounting equation in balance.

Assets   = Liabilities + Owners' equity
$40,000 = $0   + $40,000
(Cash)   (Capital Stock)

On October 2, Terry Jones paid $2,000 cash for a CD player/stereo system. The journal entry records a debit (to show the increase in cash) and a credit (sales increase equities, and credits are used to show increases in owners' equity).

Assets = Liabilities + Owners' equity
$2,000 = $0   + $2,000
(Cash)   (Sales Revenue)

As you can see, double-entry bookkeeping keeps the accounting equation in balance.

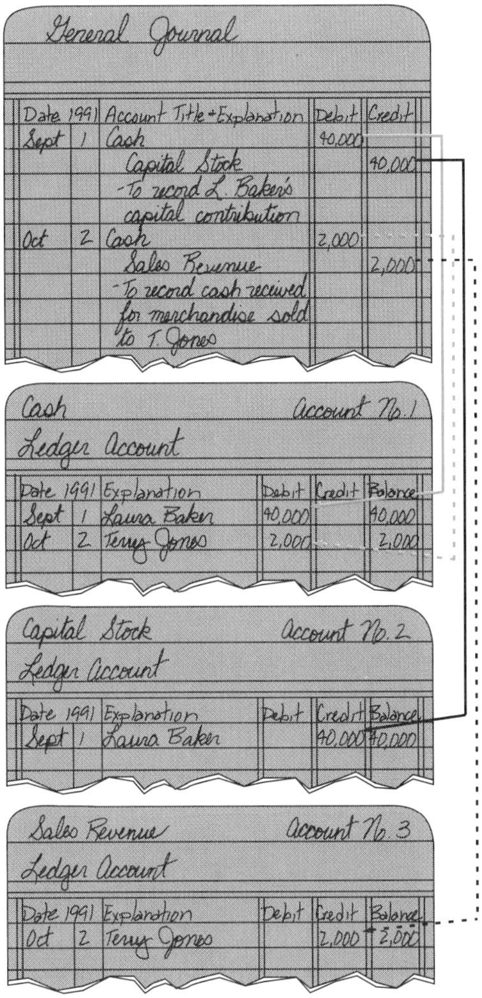

FIGURE 21.1

Sample Journal and Ledger Entries

FINANCIAL STATEMENTS

We already know that one accounting cycle step is to summarize a firm's transactions in various financial statements. Every business prepares a balance sheet and an income statement. Many businesses also prepare a statement of cash flows. A fourth financial statement, the statement of retained earnings, is beyond the scope of this chapter and is mentioned here only so you know it exists.

The numbers and accounts appearing in the financial statements are drawn from the general ledger. The elements of the accounting equation (assets, liabilities, and owners' equity) are reflected in the balance sheet. Revenues and expenses are shown on the income statement. These two statements indicate a

The Value of Brand Names

A new trend in accounting is recording brand names as assets on a firm's balance sheet. The practice is based on the assumption that customer loyalty to a particular brand is an asset to the corporation and can be valued.

Most businesspeople will agree that brand names are valuable. The Swiss food giant Nestlé paid $4.5 billion for Rowntree, a British confectioner; RJR Nabisco bought Winston and other cigarette brands for $25 billion. Because such brand names are recognizable and have a loyal following of consumers, firms believe the true value of these brands is not reflected in a typical balance sheet. The omission has led to the recent practice of listing brand names on the balance sheet as assets.

For several reasons, however, placing a value on brand names does not make much sense. First, it is difficult to separate the brand name from the product itself as an asset. For example, consider an IBM PC2. How much value comes from IBM, how much from the brand PC2, and how much from the physical product? Second, many companies play accounting games when placing a value on a brand. While firms may want to place a high value on brand names for investors to see, few want to divulge the true market value of their brands. Revealing too much information about the value of a brand could encourage a takeover attempt.

Some managers think the only way to resolve the issue is to establish accounting standards for placing a value on brands. One option would be to list the profits earned by each of a firm's brands. In this way, analysts could be more objective in assessing a firm's value. More profitable brands would increase the value of a company. Of course, if brands were less profitable than the value firms place on them, firms might prefer to record brands as an asset rather than showing their profits.[8]

firm's current financial position and give an analysis of the firm's income, expenses, and profits for those interested in such information both inside and outside the firm.

Balance Sheet

The **balance sheet,** or statement of financial position, lists the assets, liabilities, and owners' equity of the firm. A balance sheet indicates the firm's financial position at a particular moment in time (the date of the balance sheet). This financial statement reflects a firm's solvency, or its ability to pay debts as they come due. The balance sheet for the Music Box for the year ending December 31, 1990 is shown in Table 21.3.

Balance Sheet
A financial statement that indicates a firm's financial position at a particular moment in time; reflects a firm's solvency, or its ability to pay its debts as they come due. Also called statement of financial position.

Assets Assets (items of value to the company) can be classified on the basis of *liquidity,* or how quickly they can be turned into cash. Assets are usually listed on the balance sheet in the order of their liquidity. Commonly included are current and fixed assets. Some firms record brand names as assets on the balance sheet, as the Business Action illustrates.

TABLE 21.3

THE MUSIC BOX Balance Sheet At December 31, 1990			
Assets			
Current assets:			
Cash		$ 62,000	
Accounts receivable	$53,000		
Less: Allowance for doubtful accounts	3,000	50,000	
Inventory		85,000	
Total current assets			$197,000
Fixed assets:			
Store equipment	30,000		
Less: Accumulated depreciation	5,000	25,000	
Furniture and fixtures	70,000		
Less: Accumulated depreciation	10,000	60,000	
Total fixed assets			85,000
Total assets			$282,000
Liabilities			
Current liabilities:			
Accounts payable		$ 50,000	
Long-term liabilities:			
Notes payable in 1997		150,000	
Total liabilities			$200,000
Owners' Equity			
Capital stock		$ 40,000	
Retained earnings		42,000	
Total owners' equity			82,000
Total liabilities and owners' equity			$282,000

Current Assets
Cash plus items that can or will be converted to cash and used within one year.

Current assets   Usually listed first, **current assets** include cash and items that can or will be converted to cash and used within one year. These are the most liquid of a firm's assets. The Music Box's current assets are:

1. *Cash* ($62,000)—cash on hand and bank funds that management has immediate access to when needed.
2. *Accounts receivable* ($50,000)—amounts owed to the store by customers who made purchases on credit. Because the manager believes that not all of this amount will be collected, an allowance for doubtful accounts is included to reflect this possibility ($53,000 − $3,000).
3. *Inventory* ($85,000)—merchandise (CD players, stereos, speakers, etc.) on hand for sale to customers.

Fixed Assets
Relatively permanent assets that a firm expects to use for more than one year; also called plant assets.

Depreciation
Procedure for spreading the cost of a long-term asset over the course of its useful life.

Fixed assets   Relatively permanent assets that a firm expects to use for periods longer than one year are **fixed assets,** also called plant assets. Long-term assets include such items as land, buildings, machinery, vehicles, and furniture and fixtures. Except for land, all these assets are considered depreciable because they wear out and must be replaced. **Depreciation** divides the cost of a long-term asset over the course of its useful life. (Remember Shamu from this chapter's opening vignette?) This procedure gives a more accurate idea of the total cost involved in a firm's operations. The Music Box's fixed assets include:

1. Store equipment ($25,000)—office computers, display models. This amount was obtained by deducting accumulated depreciation from the assets' cost ($30,000 − $5,000).
2. Furniture and fixtures ($60,000)—office furniture, display cases, cabinetry, and lighting. Again, the cost of these items was reduced to reflect accumulated depreciation ($70,000 − $10,000).

Liabilities   As we have already noted, liabilities are amounts the business owes to its creditors. Businesses list liabilities on the balance sheet in the order in which they are due to be paid. Two types of liabilities show on the balance sheet: current and long term.

Current Liabilities
Financial obligations of a firm that will be repaid within one year.

Current liabilities   Financial obligations of the firm that will be repaid within one year are classed as **current liabilities.** Current liabilities for the Music Box include accounts payable ($50,000). These accounts reflect the portions of inventory and supplies that were purchased on credit.

Because current liabilities must be repaid within one year, they could create a financial crunch for a firm with inadequate cash reserves or other liquid assets. So firms pay close attention to the relationship between current assets and current liabilities. **Working capital,** the difference between current assets and current liabilities, reflects the firm's ability to meet its short-term obligations. For the Music Box, working capital amounts to $147,000 ($197,000 − $50,000).

Working Capital
Measure of a firm's ability to meet short-term obligations; computed as current assets minus current liabilities.

Long-Term Liabilities
Amounts owed by a business that must be repaid more than one year from the balance sheet date.

Long-term liabilities   Amounts owed that must be repaid more than one year from the balance sheet date are called **long-term liabilities.** For the Music Box, long-term liabilities include notes payable ($150,000) in 1997.

Owners' equity Owners' equity represents the claims of the owners, partners, and shareholders against the firm's assets. It is the excess of assets over liabilities and includes both capital stock and retained earnings.

Capital stock The owners' investment in the business is shown as capital stock. Laura Baker invested $40,000 to get the Music Box off and running, so this amount becomes the capital stock entry on the balance sheet.

Retained earnings A firm's profits can either be distributed as dividends to shareholders or retained and reinvested in the firm. **Retained earnings** are a firm's accumulated net income minus dividends to shareholders. They help a firm grow and expand by providing the means to invest in land or buildings or expand the items carried in inventory. The Music Box has retained earnings of $42,000.

Retained Earnings
A firm's accumulated net income minus dividends to shareholders.

As you can see in Table 21.3, the balance sheet illustrates the accounting equation in that assets ($282,000) equal liabilities ($200,000) plus owners' equity ($82,000).

Income Statement

The **income statement** (sometimes called an earnings statement or statement of profit and loss) lists a firm's revenue, expenses, and net income over some *period* of time, typically a year. (Recall that the balance sheet indicates the firm's financial position as of a particular *moment* in time, the balance sheet date.) The firm's profitability, its ability to generate income, is determined by comparing revenues to the expenses incurred in producing these revenues.

Income Statement
A financial statement showing a firm's revenues, expenses, and net income for some period of time; indicates profitability, the ability to generate income. Also called earnings statement or statement of profit and loss.

In addition to indicating a firm's profitability (or unprofitability), the income statement focuses on overall revenues and costs, giving managers the big picture of the firm's operations. It also provides data for the ratio analyses used by managers to get the little picture of day-to-day operations. (Ratio analysis is discussed later in the chapter.)

The income statement for the Music Box for the year ending December 31, 1990, appears in Table 21.4. On the income statement, all expenses are deducted from revenues to determine net profit (or loss), the net income. For the Music Box,

Revenues − Expenses = Net income
$720,000 − $712,000 = $8,000

Revenues As mentioned earlier, sales of products or services, interest, rents, royalties, and dividends generate revenues. The Music Box earned a gross revenue of $740,000 on the sale of compact-disk players, stereos, CDs, and other merchandise during the year. This figure minus returned and defective merchandise yielded a net revenue (also called net sales) of $720,000.

Cost of sales This section of the income statement itemizes the cost of the goods or services that generate revenues for the firm. Here's how the Music Box determines cost of sales. Inventory on hand at the beginning of the year was $70,000. To this amount is added the cost of new inventory purchased during the year ($605,000). This calculation results in the firm's cost of goods

TABLE 21.4

THE MUSIC BOX Income Statement For the Year Ended December 31, 1990			
Revenues:			
Gross revenue		$740,000	
Less: Sales returns and allowance		20,000	
Net revenue			$720,000
Cost of sales:			
Beginning inventory		70,000	
Purchases during year		605,000	
Cost of goods available for sale		675,000	
Less: Ending inventory		85,000	
Cost of sales			590,000
Gross profit			130,000
Operating expenses:			
Selling expenses:			
Sales salaries	$35,000		
Advertising	3,000		
Total selling expenses		38,000	
General and administrative expenses:			
Administrative salaries	35,000		
Rent	10,000		
Utilities	2,500		
Insurance	2,000		
Depreciation—equipment	15,000		
Total general expenses		64,500	
Total operating expenses			102,500
Income from operations			27,500
Interest expense			15,000
Income before taxes			12,500
Income tax expense (at 36 percent)			4,500
Net income			$ 8,000

available for sale, $675,000. From this figure deduct the ending (unsold) inventory amount ($85,000) as of the income statement date. The resulting amount, $590,000, represents the cost of sales for the Music Box.

Firms determine gross profit by subtracting the cost of sales from net revenue. The Music Box had a gross profit of $130,000 ($720,000 − $590,000).

Operating expenses   A firm's **operating expenses** include all the costs of doing business except the cost of sales.

Selling expenses are the costs incurred in marketing and distributing the firm's goods or services. For the Music Box, selling expenses include salespeoples' salaries ($35,000) and advertising ($3,000).

General and administrative expenses arise from the overall management of the business. For the Music Box, they include Laura Baker's salary ($35,000), rent ($10,000), utilities ($2,500), insurance ($2,000), and depreciation on equipment ($15,000), for a total of $64,500.

Operating Expenses
All the costs of doing business except the cost of sales.

Selling Expenses
Costs incurred in marketing and distributing a firm's goods and services.

General and Administrative Expenses
Costs incurred in the overall management of the business.

Cathlyn Melloan/TSW

Operating expenses include salespeople's salaries, rent for the store, utilities, and depreciation for equipment such as display cases.

Net income or loss Net income is the bottom line, the firm's profit or loss over a period of time. It is literally the bottom line of the income statement. Net income (or loss) is determined by subtracting all expenses from revenues.

Income from operations is determined by deducting total operating expense from gross profit. In our example, $130,000 minus $102,000 yields income from operations of $27,500. We must then deduct interest expense ($15,000) and income taxes ($4,500) to arrive at the bottom line, a net income of $8,000 for the Music Box.

Statement of Cash Flows

The last financial statement to be presented in this chapter is the statement of cash flows. In November 1987, the FASB made the statement of cash flows a requirement (as are the balance sheet and income statement) for all companies listed on an organized stock exchange. The statement of cash flows is the most complicated of the primary financial statements, and we will not give a detailed analysis here.

The **statement of cash flows** shows the flow of cash into and out of a business during a period of time. This statement indicates net cash flow (either inflow or outflow) from operating, investing, and financing activities. Cash flow from *operations* measures the cash results of the firm's primary revenue-generating activities. (In the case of the Music Box, cash flow from operations represents net cash flow from merchandising activities.) *Investing* activities include buying fixed assets, buying stock in other companies, and selling stock held as an investment in another company. *Financing* activities include issuing new stock, paying dividends to shareholders, borrowing from banks, and repaying

Statement of Cash Flows Financial statement showing the flow of cash into and out of a business during a period of time.

amounts borrowed. The statement of cash flows also shows the net change in cash for the period.

As a summary of the effects on cash of all the firm's operating, financing, and investing activities, the statement of cash flows allows managers to see the results of past decisions. The statement may, for example, indicate a great enough cash flow to allow the firm to finance all projected needs itself rather than borrow funds from a bank. Or management can examine the statement to determine why the firm has a cash shortage, if that is the case. Investors and creditors can use the statement of cash flows to assess the firm's abilities to generate future cash flows, to pay dividends, and to pay its debts when due, as well as its potential need to borrow funds.

ANALYZING FINANCIAL STATEMENTS

Once financial statements have been prepared, managers, creditors, and investors are interested in interpreting them. Managers' analyses of the financial statements primarily pertain to *parts* of the company, which allows them to plan, control, and evaluate company operations. Creditors and investors focus on the company as a *whole* to decide whether the company is a good credit or investment candidate.

Financial statement analysis compares (or finds relationships in) accounting information to make the data more useful or practical. For example, knowing that a company's net income was $50,000 is somewhat useful. Knowing also that the prior year's net income was $100,000 is more useful. Knowing the amounts of the company's assets and sales is better yet. To this end, several types of financial statement analysis have been developed. In this chapter, we will discuss the techniques of common-size financial statements and ratio analysis.

Common-Size Financial Statements

Common-Size Statements
Method of analyzing financial information by expressing various financial statement elements as a percentage of another element of the same statement.

Common-size statements express various elements of a financial statement as a percentage of some other element of the same statement. Only percentages appear, not dollar amounts. For example, all items on a common-size balance sheet are expressed as a percentage of *total assets*. Common-size income statement items are typically expressed as a percentage of *net revenue*. (Recall from our discussion of income statements that net revenue is gross revenue minus customer returns and allowances.)

A common-size analysis shows the makeup of a firm's assets—that is, does the firm maintain a large buffer of current assets, or are most of its assets of a long-term, productive nature? It also shows the relative importance of liabilities and owners' equity in financing the firm's assets. A common-size income statement provides information on the relative magnitudes of expense accounts.

Table 21.5 brings back the balance sheet for the Music Box, which we first saw in Table 21.3, and adds a common-size analysis of the data. Items on the balance sheet were compared with total assets. The income statement for the

TABLE 21.5

THE MUSIC BOX Common-Size Comparative Balance Sheets December 31, 1991 and 1990				
			Percentage of total assets	
	1991	1990	1991	1990
Assets				
Current assets:				
Cash	$ 40,000	$ 62,000	13.6%	22.0%
Accounts receivable	70,000	50,000	23.7	17.7
Inventory	110,000	85,000	37.3	30.1
Total current assets	220,000	197,000	74.6	69.8
Fixed assets:				
Store equipment (net of accumulated depreciation)	25,000	25,000	8.5	8.9
Furniture and fixtures (net of accumulated depreciation)	50,000	60,000	16.9	21.3
Total fixed assets	75,000	85,000	25.4	30.2
Total assets	$295,000	$282,000	100.0%	100.0%
Liabilities				
Current liabilities:				
Accounts payable	$ 55,000	$ 50,000	18.6%	17.7%
Long-term liabilities:				
Notes payable	150,000	150,000	50.8	53.2
Total liabilities	205,000	200,000	69.4	70.9
Owners' Equity				
Capital stock	40,000	40,000	13.6	14.2
Retained earnings	50,000	42,000	16.9	14.9
Total owners' equity	90,000	82,000	30.5	29.1
Total liabilities and owners' equity	$295,000	$282,000	100.0%	100.0%

Music Box (originally seen as Table 21.4) is reprised as Table 21.6, with the addition of a common-size analysis. Income statement items were compared with revenues.

We can reach a number of conclusions about the Music Box from its common-size statements. The company is heavily financed by long-term debt. Financing through the use of debt is referred to as *financial leverage*. Financial leverage typically increases earnings during an economic upswing. If the economy turns down, financial leverage increases the risk of bankruptcy because the company may not have enough cash to make required interest payments.

The common-size balance sheet also indicates that the composition of the firm's assets has changed during the two years. Cash declined as a percentage of assets while accounts receivable and inventory increased. If this deteriorating cash position continues, the company's future financial health is questionable.

TABLE 21.6

			Percentage of total assets	
	1991	1990	1991	1990
Net revenue	$800,000	$720,000	100.0%	100.0%
Cost of sales	640,000	590,000	80	82
Gross profit	160,000	130,000	20	18
Operating expenses:				
Selling expenses				
Sales salaries	39,500	35,000	4.9	4.9
Advertising	4,000	3,000	.5	.4
Total selling expenses	43,500	38,000	5.4	5.3
General and administrative expenses				
Administrative salaries	39,500	35,000	4.9	4.8
Rent	15,000	10,000	1.9	1.4
Utilities	6,000	2,500	.8	.3
Insurance	2,000	2,000	.2	.3
Depreciation	15,000	15,000	1.9	2.1
Total general expenses	77,500	64,500	9.7	8.9
Total operating expenses	121,000	102,500	15.1	14.2
Income from operations	39,000	27,500	4.9	3.8
Interest expense	15,000	15,000	1.9	2.1
Income before taxes	24,000	12,500	3.0	1.7
Income tax expense (at 36 percent)	8,640	4,500	1.1	.6
Net income	$ 15,360	$ 8,000	1.9%	1.1%

THE MUSIC BOX
Common-Size Comparative Income Statements
For the Years Ended December 31, 1991 and 1990

The composition of the income statement has not changed much, according to the common-size analysis. However, the Music Box does appear to operate on a very narrow profit margin. In other words, the company's profit on each dollar of sales is small. This means that management needs to keep a very close watch on expenses.

Ratio Analysis

Ratio Analysis
Method of analyzing financial information by comparing logical relationships between various financial statement items.

Another way to interpret financial information is by ratio analysis. **Ratio analysis** examines the logical relationships between various financial statement items. Items may come from the same financial statement or from different statements. The only requirement is that a logical relationship exist between the items.

The dollar amounts of the related items are set up as fractions and called *ratios*. Comparing company ratios to industry standards can indicate areas in which the company is successful—and those in which the company is below standard. Trends in a company's performance are also easily spotted by comparing ratios from the current period to ratios from earlier periods. Four kinds of ratios are commonly used: liquidity, activity, profitability, and debt.

Liquidity ratios   A firm's ability to pay its short-term debts as they come due is measured by **liquidity ratios.** (Recall that liquidity is a measure of how quickly an asset may be converted to cash.) Highly liquid firms can more easily convert assets to cash when needed to repay loans. Less liquid firms may have trouble meeting their obligations or obtaining loans at low cost. Two common liquidity ratios are the current ratio and the quick (acid-test) ratio.

> **Liquidity Ratio**
> Measure of a firm's ability to pay its short-term debts as they come due.

We have already said that working capital is the excess of current assets over current liabilities. The **current ratio,** which is current assets divided by current liabilities (two balance sheet items), indicates a firm's ability to pay its current liabilities from its current assets. Thus the ratio shows the strength of a company's working capital.

> **Current Ratio**
> The measure of a firm's ability to pay its current liabilities from its current assets; computed by dividing current assets by current liabilities.

$$\text{Current ratio} = \frac{\text{Current assets}}{\text{Current liabilities}}$$

Current ratios for the Music Box for 1990 and 1991 are computed as follows:

1990: $\dfrac{197{,}000}{50{,}000} = 3.94 \text{ to } 1$

1991: $\dfrac{220{,}000}{55{,}000} = 4 \text{ to } 1$

The current ratio is excellent in both years. Generally a ratio in excess of 2 to 1 is considered favorable. In 1991 the Music Box's current ratio increased slightly to 4 to 1, meaning it had $4 of current assets for every $1 of current liabilities.

The **quick ratio,** also called the acid-test ratio, divides *quick assets* by current liabilities. It measures more immediate liquidity by comparing two balance sheet items. Quick assets do not include inventory because to convert inventory to cash, merchandise must be sold and a receivable collected. Quick assets are cash or those assets the firm expects to convert to cash in the near future. For the Music Box, the quick ratio is computed as follows:

> **Quick Ratio**
> The measure of a firm's immediate liquidity; computed by dividing quick assets by current liabilities. Also called acid-test ratio.

$$\text{Quick ratio} = \frac{\text{Quick assets}}{\text{Current liabilities}}$$

1990: $\dfrac{112{,}000}{50{,}000} = 2.24 \text{ to } 1$

1991: $\dfrac{110{,}000}{55{,}000} = 2 \text{ to } 1$

Traditionally, quick ratios of 1 to 1 (quick assets equal current liabilities) have been considered adequate. Although the Music Box's quick ratio is more than adequate, it has deteriorated slightly.

> **Activity Ratio**
> Measure of how efficiently assets are being used to generate revenues.

Activity ratios   How efficiently the firm uses its assets to generate revenues is measured by **activity ratios.** These ratios indicate how efficiently a firm uses its resources. A common activity ratio is accounts receivable turnover. **Accounts receivable turnover** is the number of times per year that the average

> **Accounts Receivable Turnover**
> The number of times per year that the average accounts receivable is collected; computed by dividing net sales by average net accounts receivable.

accounts receivable is turned over (collected). An income statement item (net sales) is compared to a balance sheet item (accounts receivable). We calculate this ratio by dividing net sales by average net accounts receivable.

The allowance for doubtful accounts is first deducted to arrive at net accounts receivable. *Average* net accounts receivable is computed by adding the accounts receivable amounts at the beginning and end of the year, then dividing by two. For the Music Box, we determine this figure for 1991 by adding the beginning amount (which is 1990's ending amount, $50,000) to the ending amount ($70,000) and dividing by two to reach $60,000.

Accounts receivable turnover for the Music Box is computed as follows:

$$\frac{\text{Accounts receivable}}{\text{turnover}} = \frac{\text{Net sales}}{\text{Average net accounts receivable}}$$

$$1991: \frac{800,000}{60,000} = 13.3$$

The Music Box is, then, collecting its accounts receivable 13 times per year on average.

We can also look at accounts receivable turnover by computing the number of days it takes for each credit sale to be converted to cash. In other words, how many days does it take credit customers to pay their bills? This measure, referred to as the *number of days sales in receivables,* is computed as follows:

$$\text{Number of days sales in receivables} = \frac{\text{Number of days in year}}{\text{Accounts receivable turnover}}$$

$$1991: \frac{365}{13.3} = 27.4 \text{ days}$$

This means that the Music Box's accounts receivable are collected in 27 days on average. Because the Music Box's credit terms for its customers are for payment to be made within 30 days, this ratio indicates that customers are indeed paying for their credit purchases within the required time. Thus the company's accounts receivable are considered to be of good quality.

A larger ratio, say 50 or 60 days, would indicate that credit customers are slow in paying their bills; thus they would be using the Music Box as a source of interest-free credit (the company does not charge interest on past-due accounts).

Profitability ratios   A company's overall operating success—its financial performance—is measured by **profitability ratios.** These ratios measure a firm's success in terms of earnings compared to sales or investments. Over time these ratios can indicate how successfully or unsuccessfully management operates the business. Two common profitability ratios are return on sales and return on equity.

Profitability Ratio
Ratio that measures a firm's financial performance by comparing earnings to sales or investments.

Return on Sales
Measure of a firm's profitability, or its ability to generate income; computed by dividing net income by net sales.

Return on sales measures a firm's profitability by comparing net income and net sales, both income statement items. It is computed by dividing net income by net sales. For the Music Box,

$$\text{Return on sales} = \frac{\text{Net income}}{\text{Net sales}}$$

$$1990: \frac{8,000}{720,000} = 1.1 \text{ percent}$$

1991: $\dfrac{15,360}{800,000} = 1.9$ percent

These ratios show a quite low profit per dollar of sales. Retail establishments average around 5 percent. However, return on sales did increase from 1.1 percent in 1990 to 1.9 percent in 1991. This trend may mean the company is becoming more profitable.

Return on equity measures the return the company earns on every dollar of shareholders' (and owners') investment. Investors are very interested in this ratio; it indicates how well their investment is doing. We compute return on equity by dividing net income (an income statement item) by equity (a balance sheet item). For the Music Box,

Return on Equity
Measure of the return the company earns on every dollar of owners' and share-holers' investments; computed by dividing net income by equity.

$$\text{Return on equity} = \frac{\text{Net income}}{\text{Equity}}$$

1990: $\dfrac{8,000}{82,000} = 9.8$ percent

1991: $\dfrac{15,360}{90,000} = 17.1$ percent

Shareholders are interested in the return on equity—the return they are earning on their investments.

Frank Siteman/Stock Boston

For every dollar invested in 1990, the Music Box earned nearly 10 cents. This return on equity is not good. A return of 9.8 percent is not much better than what can be earned on a bank certificate of deposit. Stock investments carry more risk, so they should offer higher returns. The 17 percent return on equity in 1991, a substantial improvement, is a better return for the risk assumed by investing in stocks.

Debt ratios   We measure a company's ability to pay its long-term debts by **debt ratios.** These ratios try to answer questions such as (1) Is the company financed mainly by debt or equity? and (2) Does the company make enough to pay the interest on its loans when due? Potential investors and lenders are very interested in the answers to such questions. Two ways to answer them are the debt to total assets ratio and the times interest earned ratio.

Debt Ratio
Measure of a company's ability to pay its long-term debts.

The **debt to total assets ratio** measures a company's ability to carry long-term debt. It is calculated by dividing total liabilities by total assets, both balance sheet items. For the Music Box,

$$\text{Debt to total assets} = \frac{\text{Total liabilities}}{\text{Total assets}}$$

Debt to Total Assets Ratio
The measure of a company's ability to carry long-term debt; computed by dividing total liabilities by total assets.

$$1990: \quad \frac{200,000}{282,000} = 70.9$$

$$1991: \quad \frac{205,000}{295,000} = 69.5$$

In 1991 the Music Box carried 69.5 cents of debt for every dollar of assets, which means the firm is largely financed by debt. This high level of debt could be a problem if the company's revenues decline.

Creditors need to know whether a borrower can meet interest payments when they come due. The **times interest earned ratio** compares cash received from operations with cash paid for interest payments. It measures how many times the firm earns the amount of interest it must pay during the year. This ratio is calculated by dividing income before interest and taxes ("Income from operations" in Table 21.6) by interest expense, two items on the income statement. For the Music Box,

Times Interest Earned Ratio
The measure of how many times during the year a business earns the amount of interest it must pay; computed by dividing income before interest and taxes by interest expense.

$$\text{Times interest earned} = \frac{\text{Income before interest and taxes}}{\text{Interest expense}}$$

$$1990: \quad \frac{27,500}{15,000} = 1.83$$

$$1991: \quad \frac{39,000}{15,000} = 2.6$$

These ratios, although improving, are not high. The higher the ratio, the more likely that interest payments will be made. Low ratios mean a company may have trouble making its interest payments to its creditors. The Music Box's ratios would probably be considered unsatisfactory.

You'll Know It's the **Century When . . .**

↳ Accountants Are Sitting Pretty

According to the federal *Occupational Outlook Quarterly,* the 21st century looks promising for accountants and auditors: by then, 211,000 jobs will have been added to the economy, an increase of 22 percent. Opportunities will open up as the number of small businesses soars and the demand for better accounting procedures in both private and public sectors intensifies. The widest array of job options will go to tax accountants, CPAs with auditing skills, accountants with data processing capabilities—and any accountant with a master's degree. CPAs will also find a growing market in the booming over-65 population—people seeking help with estate and succession planning. Accountants will also find increasing opportunities in the international arena. Some will work primarily in the United States, jetting around the world as needed, while others will land temporary overseas assignments (18 months to three years).[9]

SUMMARY OF LEARNING OBJECTIVES

1. To explain the purpose of accounting and its importance to a firm's managers, creditors, and investors.

   Accounting identifies, measures, and communicates financial information about a company to its managers and outside parties to improve their decisions about allocating company resources and to evaluate the results of those decisions. Creditors examine a company's financial records to decide whether a firm is a good credit risk. Investors need to know whether a firm is a good investment candidate and, if so, how their investment is doing.

2. To describe the CPA and CMA positions and distinguish between public and private accountants.

   CPAs have passed a four-part examination conducted by the AICPA, generally have accounting experience, and are licensed by the state. They may be employed as *public accountants,* who provide accounting services for companies, other organizations, and the general public on a fee-for-service basis. These services include conducting audits of clients' financial records and providing management and tax consulting service.

   CMAs must meet educational and experience requirements similar to those for CPAs. They must also pass an examination by the National Association of Accountants. CMAs may be employed as public accountants, but they do not audit a company's financial statements.

   Private accountants work in areas outside the public accounting field. They may work as management accountants, providing accounting services for a single client. They also may work for government agencies at the local, state, and federal levels or teach and conduct research at universities.

3. To list the steps in the accounting cycle.

The accounting cycle is the way accountants communicate the results of financial transactions. First they *analyze* business transactions to determine which can be measured and verified with some precision. These transactions are then *recorded* chronologically in a journal. Next these journal entries are *posted* in the general ledger, which summarizes all the company's accounts. In the final step, the accountant *prepares* financial statements.

4. To state the accounting equation, define its elements, and describe its relationship to double-entry bookkeeping.

The accounting equation states that assets equal liabilities plus owners' equity. Assets are anything of value owned by the company and used in the process of conducting business. Liabilities are creditors' claims against a company's assets. Owners' equity is the owners' claim against the company's assets.

This equation is always kept in balance. Double-entry bookkeeping uses two entries (a debit and a credit) to record each transaction, thus keeping the accounting equation in balance.

5. To explain the purpose of the balance sheet and identify its major elements.

The balance sheet indicates a firm's financial position at a particular *moment* in time and reflects a firm's solvency, or its ability to pay debts as they come due. The major elements of the balance sheet are those of the accounting equation—assets, liabilities, and owners' equity.

6. To explain the purpose of the income statement and identify its major elements.

The income statement reflects a firm's profitability, or its ability to generate income. It indicates a firm's financial position over a *period* of time. All expenses are deducted from net revenue, thus giving the bottom line: the firm's profit or loss for the period of time covered by the income statement.

7. To describe common-size financial statements and how they are used.

Accountants can interpret a firm's financial information through use of common-size statements. Common-size financial statements express certain financial statement items as a percentage of other items. Items on a common-size balance sheet are expressed as a percentage of total assets. Common-size income statements indicate what percentage of net revenue each item is.

Such statements indicate the relative composition of the firm's assets (whether current or long-term) and the relative importance of liabilities and owners' equity in financing these assets.

8. To explain the purpose of ratio analysis and list the major financial ratios.

Accountants use ratio analysis as another method of interpreting a company's financial information. Ratio analysis examines the logical relationships between various financial statement items. Comparing a company's ratios to those of other companies in the same industry gives an indication of how well the firm is doing according to industry standards. Comparing the company's ratios for the current period to those of previous periods may indicate trends (positive or negative) in the company's performance. The major categories of financial ratios are liquidity, activity, profitability, and debt.

KEY TERMS

Accounting, p. 741

Certified Public Accountant
(CPA), p. 742

Public Accountant, p. 742

Audit, p. 743

Certified Management Accountant
(CMA), p. 745

Private Accountant, p. 745

Accounting Cycle, p. 748

Journal, p. 748

Account, p. 748

General Ledger, p. 748

Financial Statement, p. 748

Accounting Equation, p. 749

Asset, p. 749

Liability, p. 749

Owners' Equity, p. 749

Revenue, p. 749

Expenses, p. 749

Net Income, p. 750

Debit, p. 750

Credit, p. 750

Double-Entry Bookkeeping, p. 750

Balance Sheet, p. 753

Current Assets, p. 754

Fixed Assets, p. 754

Depreciation, p. 754

Current Liabilities, p. 754

Working Capital, p. 754

Long-Term Liabilities, p. 754

Retained Earnings, p. 755

Income Statement, p. 755

Operating Expenses, p. 756

Selling Expenses, p. 756

General and Administrative
Expenses, p. 756

Statement of Cash Flows, p. 757

Common-Size Statements, p. 758

Ratio Analysis, p. 760

Liquidity Ratio, p. 761

Current Ratio, p. 761

Quick Ratio, p. 761

Activity Ratio, p. 761

Accounts Receivable Turnover, p. 761

Profitability Ratio, p. 762

Return on Sales, p. 762

Return on Equity, p. 763

Debt Ratio, p. 764

Debt to Total Assets Ratio, p. 764

Times Interest Earned Ratio, p. 764

QUESTIONS FOR DISCUSSION AND REVIEW

1. What is accounting? How do managers, creditors, and investors use accounting information?

2. What is the difference between public and private accountants? What professional certifications may accountants attain?

3. Name the major accounting regulatory agencies.

4. What are the four steps in the accounting cycle?

5. What functions do journals and the general ledger serve?

6. What is the fundamental accounting equation?

7. Explain the role of double-entry bookkeeping in the accounting cycle.

8. Which accounting elements make up the balance sheet? How is it used?

9. Which accounting elements make up the income statement? How is it used?

10. What is the purpose of the statement of cash flows?

11. What are common-size financial statements? How are they used to analyze financial information?

12. How are liquidity ratios used in financial statement analysis? What are the common liquidity ratios?

13. How are activity ratios used in financial statement analysis? What is accounts receivable turnover?

14. How are profitability ratios used in financial statement analysis? Name two commonly used profitability ratios.

15. How are debt ratios used in financial statement analysis? Name two common debt ratios.

CASE 21.1
ICC's Income Statement

International Communication Corporation (ICC) is the largest and most recognized maker of communication systems and equipment in the world. ICC, one of the largest manufacturing companies in the United States, has also been one of the most profitable for the past several years.

ICC's financial results for 1991 showed continued success for the company. Net earnings increased 9.8 percent from 1990 to 1991; revenues also increased 9.8 percent. The following information on revenues and expenses was summarized from ICC's general ledger.

Revenues:	
Sales	$36,345,000,000
Maintenance services	7,691,000,000
Program products	6,836,000,000
Rentals and other services	3,345,000,000
Other	1,352,000,000
Expenses:	
Cost of sales	$17,332,000,000
Cost of maintenance services	3,417,000,000
Cost of program products	1,957,000,000
Cost of rentals and other services	1,904,000,000
Selling, general, and administrative expenses	16,431,000,000
Research, development, and engineering expenses	5,434,000,000
Interest expense	485,000,000
Income tax expense	3,351,000,000

ICC lists each revenue and expense account separately when preparing its income statement. The last six places in the above account balances are dropped off, and the statement is labeled to show that dollar amounts are in millions. The other revenue—primarily interest—is listed separately from operating revenues.

ICC's income statement follows a particular format. Revenues are listed first. The costs directly associated with generating the revenues (the first four expenses listed above) are presented next. The difference between revenues and the costs directly associated with them is *gross profit*. Gross profit appears separately on ICC's income statement.

Expenses incurred in generating revenues, other than those directly related to the sale of products, are deducted from gross profit to arrive at operating income. Both selling, general, and administrative expenses and research, development, and engineering expenses are considered operating expenses.

Interest expense is not an operating expense but rather is a financing expense. This expense resulted from management's decision about how to finance the level of operations. Interest expense is deducted and other income (primarily interest) is added in arriving at income before taxes. Income tax expense is deducted, thus leaving net income.

Earnings per share (EPS) is one of the most closely watched indicators of business performance. EPS expresses net income on a per share basis. In its simplest form, EPS is net income divided by the number of shares of stock. Rather than in millions of dollars, EPS is expressed in dollars. To calculate ICC's EPS, 602,961,631 shares of stock are used.

Questions for Discussion

1. What was ICC's gross profit in 1991?
2. What was ICC's operating income in 1991?
3. What was ICC's earnings per share in 1991?
4. Prepare an income statement for ICC, following the guidelines discussed in the case.

CASE 21.2
Creative Accounting in Hollywood

After Art Buchwald convinced a judge that the hit movie *Coming to America* was actually his idea used without his permission, he was awarded a percentage of the net profits. Little did Buchwald know that the real battle had only begun. The Paramount picture starring Eddie Murphy already had grossed $325 million, making it one of the top movies of the 1980s. But Paramount claims the film lost money. So Buchwald and his lawyer, Pierce O'Donnell, now must convince the court that the film was indeed profitable.

Buchwald and others are questioning Hollywood studios over "net profit" contracts. Such contracts, a long-standing tradition in Hollywood, entitle actors or writers to a percentage of a film's profits. Over the years, however, net profit contracts have resulted in little money for the profit participants, regardless of a movie's success. How do studios manage to avoid paying actors and writers their share of the profits? The secret lies in the way they define net profit.

The studio takes about 40 to 50 percent off the top; this is the studio's gross. In the case of *Coming to America,* Paramount took $151 million from the $325 million the film grossed. Then the deductions begin. First the studio deducts about 35 percent of its gross as a "distribution fee" for putting the movie in theaters. Paramount deducted $53 million for *Coming to America*. Next, the studio deducts "distribution expenses" for making prints, storing reels, advertising and marketing, and other direct costs of distribution. Paramount deducted $40 million for distribution expenses.

Adapted from Dana Wechsler, "Profits? What Profits?" *Forbes*, February 19, 1990, pp. 38–40; Robert Wolfe, "Counting the King's Gold," *American Film*, May 1990, pp. 13–14; "There's No Business like Show Business," *U.S. News & World Report*, January 22, 1990, p. 14.

These deductions still left Paramount with a hefty amount of money, about $58 million. From this amount, Paramount deducted the cut of the *gross players,* $22 million. The costs of producing the film, referred to in the film industry as *negative costs,* are deducted next. Paramount deducted $50 million, including 15 percent for the film's star, Eddie Murphy, and 22 percent for studio overhead. Finally, $6.5 million was deducted for "interest expense." According to the accountants, the film lost $20.5 million. Only at this point do net profits begin to accumulate.

Buchwald is not the only person to sue over a net profit contract. Jane Fonda sued Universal for a greater share of the profits from *On Golden Pond* and received an undisclosed settlement. James Garner received a settlement of about $12 million from Universal for the television series "The Rockford Files." Garner's contract entitled him to 37.5 percent of the net profits, but he had been paid less than $250,000. Universal paid Garner rather than tell a jury how his cut could be so low. According to the Los Angeles office of Laventhol & Horwath, an accounting firm that conducts many profit participation audits, nearly every audit it conducts leads to both additional claims and additional payment by the studios.

Attorney O'Donnell believes the only way to change the system is through litigation. O'Donnell plans to argue that Hollywood's net profit contracts are basically a monopoly against talent and that studios produce false accounting statements. By attacking the studios' books, O'Donnell thinks, he can prove there are indeed net profits to distribute.

Questions for Discussion
1. What is net profit?
2. How is net profit normally calculated?
3. How did Paramount determine that *Coming to America* was losing money?
4. Do you think that writers and actors who have signed net profit contracts have a legitimate complaint? Why or why not?

CHAPTER TWENTY-TWO

COMPUTERS AND MANAGEMENT INFORMATION SYSTEMS

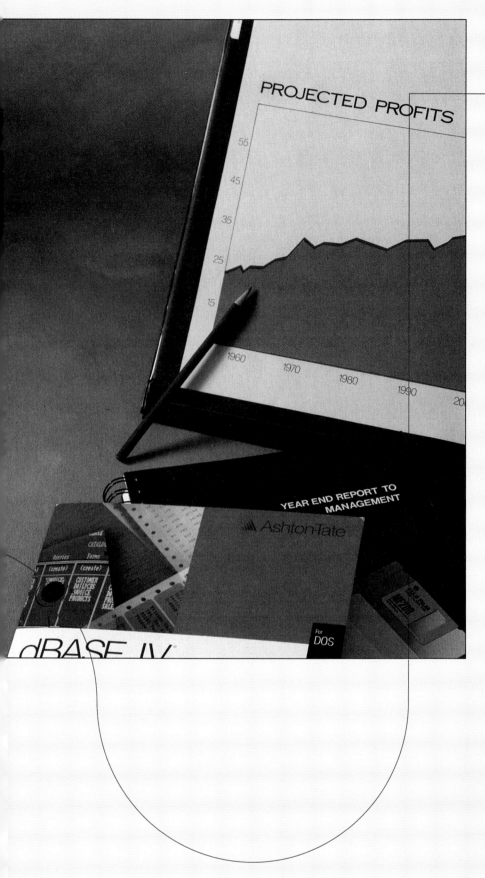

LEARNING OBJECTIVES

1. To explain why business managers need computers in this age of information.

2. To trace the evolution of computers.

3. To identify the different types of computers and the components common to all.

4. To outline the capabilities of computers.

5. To define *management information system (MIS)* and explain how an MIS is used.

6. To list trends in computer development and use and in management information systems.

Computers land airplanes, set baseball schedules, control inventory levels in stores and warehouses, and help tourists plan their vacation travels. They help doctors make faster and more accurate diagnoses. They also build cars in state-of-the-art automobile plants. Computers today can perform an astounding number and variety of

ver's restaurants, for example, feed information to a computer at the headquarters of its parent company, Jerrico, in Lexington, Kentucky. The computer there tells executives which restaurants are performing well and which poorly, and which meals are selling well in each advertising area. Eventually information gathered at Jerrico

on its paperwork. The Pentagon, for example, spends $5 billion each year to handle technical information for weapons. One 9,600-ton navy cruiser alone carries 26 tons of manuals explaining how to operate its complex weapons systems. Some navy officials are concerned that massive documentation is hindering performance. So the Defense Department has launched a $1 billion program called Computer-aided Acquisitions & Logistics Support (CALS) to help reduce the volume of paper handled by the Pentagon.

Computers are even changing *where* people work. Large companies such as J. C. Penney, Travelers Insurance, Pacific Bell, and IBM allow some employees to work at home and communicate with the office through computers. Telecommuting, as it is called, helps companies recruit and retain qualified employees as well as reduce the cost of office space. In large cities such as Los Angeles, where businesses are being held responsible for reducing the number of private vehicles used for commuting, some firms arrange for employees to work at home on computers. Although no statistics are available, experts estimate that from 1 million to 5 million people in the United States work at home via computers. Analysts expect this number to grow to 15 million by the mid-1990s.[1]

The Image Works

tasks, and their capabilities are doubling every two or three years. Over 70 percent of the people who work in finance, insurance, and real estate use a computer; nearly 40 percent of all American workers use a computer. Beyond a doubt, computers are significantly changing the way companies do business.

Computerized cash registers at more than 1,000 Long John Sil-

headquarters reaches personal computers at the restaurants and helps managers schedule workers and order supplies. If this system saves each manager one hour a week, Jerrico saves 52,000 hours a year—time managers can spend with employees or customers.

Computers have replaced paper in numerous industries. Banks, insurance companies, stockbrokers, and other firms offering financial services could not operate without computers. The federal government uses computers to cut down

Computers are firmly entrenched in our society, particularly in the workplace. They perform tasks from the most mundane to the most complex. They store libraries of information in a tiny space. By quickly transmitting and analyzing important information, computers help business managers make complicated decisions. And unlike humans, computers are available 24 hours a day, seven days a week. They never complain, take vacation, or ask for a raise (although they do break down occasionally).

In this chapter, we introduce computers and management information systems. First we look at how the information explosion has increased the importance of computers in business. Then we examine the evolution of computers, explain the different types of computers, and distinguish between hardware and software. Next we investigate the many uses of computers in business. A discussion of management information systems follows. Finally we examine the future of computers and management information systems.

THE AGE OF INFORMATION

Businesses today have access to more information than ever before. The abundance of newspapers, journals, magazines, television and radio programs, business and government reports, and seminars has led many commentators to label this the Age of Information. Information will be the main catalyst for growth in the global economy of the 1990s.[2] But the sheer volume of information available presents a real challenge to business managers. Obviously every manager cannot use all available information. The challenge is to collect, store, process, report, and use the most relevant information to make more effective decisions.

Computers help firms meet this challenge. They assist managers in converting **data**—unorganized facts, statistics, and predictions concerning people, objects, events, and ideas—into useful information. Thus **information** is data organized to meet certain needs. Firms are becoming increasingly dependent on computers to transform data into useful information. Computers are steadily becoming more available, affordable, portable, and easier to use. Figure 22.1 will give you an idea of the extent to which companies rely on computers.

Data
Unorganized facts, statistics, and predictions concerning people, objects, events, and ideas.

Information
Useful or relevant data.

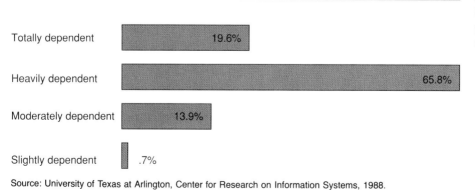

Totally dependent — 19.6%

Heavily dependent — 65.8%

Moderately dependent — 13.9%

Slightly dependent — .7%

Source: University of Texas at Arlington, Center for Research on Information Systems, 1988.

FIGURE 22.1

How Dependent on Computers Are Firms?

● C o n n e c t i o n s

Living in the Age of Information

Directions: Many of us have thought at times that computers complicate our lives. In some ways, perhaps they do. But computers are, of course, here to stay. Let's see how you react to that fact. For each statement, circle the number that shows your level of agreement.

	Strongly Disagree				Strongly Agree	
1. I think computers have helped businesses serve customers better.	1	2	3	4	5	6
2. I would like a job in which I use computers.	1	2	3	4	5	6
3. Computer courses are very helpful to students.	1	2	3	4	5	6

Are you ready to cope in the age of information? Choosing and using information through computers may seem complicated, but each one of us must be prepared. Even traditional manual jobs such as working on cars have been affected by computers.

Although workers and customers find computers frustrating at times, computers are truly friends to business. Of course, when computers are blamed for a late flight, an incorrect bill, or the wrong grade in a college course, human error is actually the cause. The next section traces the evolution of computers and provides an overview of the different types of computers as well as computer hardware and software. Before you read further about computers, complete Connections and assess your readiness to work in the Age of Information.

INTRODUCTION TO COMPUTERS

Computer
An electronic device used to input, store, and process data and to output them as useful information.

A **computer** is an electronic device used to input, store, and process data and to output data as useful information. Universities, for instance, can enter into a computer the grade reports on thousands of students from hundreds of courses, store the information, process grades in a matter of seconds, and print out individual student grade reports ready to mail. Students can receive their grades a few days after classes conclude. Before computers, the process could take weeks.

4. I like the idea of paying bills
through a computer.   1   2   3   4   5   6

5. Computers have helped im-
prove day-to-day life.   1   2   3   4   5   6

Feedback: If you strongly agree with the statements (circled 5 or 6 for most), you have accepted computers. You may realize they offer new challenges and can help businesses improve operations and service. If you circled 3 or 4 for most statements, you seem skeptical about computers. You may recognize their benefits but see the changes they've brought as too widespread or too quick. Finally, strong disagreement with the statements indicates a low tolerance for computers. You may prefer to avoid them if you can. If you are considering a career in business, avoiding them will be difficult if not impossible. We hope this chapter shows you that computers are essential and beneficial to business.

The Evolution of Computers

Electronic computers have evolved through five generations. The first generation (1946–1958) began with the introduction of the ENIAC (electronic numerical integrator and calculator). This massive computer, weighing over 30 tons, operated with 18,000 glass vacuum tubes. Primitive by today's standards, these tubes were extremely hot and burned out frequently—an average one every seven seconds. Computer operators stood by with baskets of replacement tubes.[3] During this period, computers were used primarily for scientific purposes. However, business firms also began to realize the value of computers in processing data. ENIAC, with all its limitations, was a major start for the electronic computer era.

The second generation of computers (1959–1964) was characterized by the use of the **transistor,** a small switch that controls electrical current. Transistors were much faster than vacuum tubes and produced less heat. With transistors, smaller, more powerful computers could be built at less cost than the first-generation computers. Businesses, even medium-sized and small ones, began using the computer to process an increasing number of business applications.

The third generation (1965–1977) began with the introduction of **integrated circuits,** small silicon chips containing dozens of tiny transistors and connections. Integrated circuitry resulted in much faster, smaller, and more reliable computers. Faster input and output methods and increased data storage facilities were developed during the third generation. More and more business firms began to rely heavily on computers. Remote terminals, typewriter-like machines located away from the computer but connected to it by telephone lines,

Transistor
A small switch that controls electrical current; characterized second-generation computers.

Integrated Circuit
Small silicon chip containing dozens of tiny transistors and connections; used in third-generation computers.

Mass production of super-chips made possible the development of personal computers at affordable prices. In this instance, the small superchip (bottom right) can perform the same functions as the large circuitboards in the background.

Courtesy of the General Instrument Corporation

Large-Scale Integrated (LSI) Circuit
Superchip that contains thousands of small transistors; fourth-generation innovation that made personal computers possible.

Very Large-Scale Integration (VLSI)
Superchip circuitry, resulting from extremely compact transistors and circuits assembled on a single silicon chip; marked start of fifth generation of computers.

Artificial Intelligence
A developing technology that allows computers to solve problems involving imagination, abstract reasoning, and common sense.

made access to the computer possible from separate offices or even distant cities.

The fourth generation (1971 to present) started with **large-scale integrated (LSI) circuits.** These *superchips,* a mere cubic inch in size, contain thousands of small transistors. LSI technology enabled the development of personal computers, which are so common and so valuable today. Mass production of computer chips led to lower prices for small home and business computers. Increased storage capabilities in these small computers gave business firms the means of storing vast amounts of data.

Computer technology now is entering a fifth generation, as a result of **very large-scale integration (VLSI).** VLSI circuitry consists of a superchip created from extremely compact transistors and circuits assembled on a single silicon chip. A developing technology called **artificial intelligence** allows computers to solve problems involving imagination, abstract reasoning, and common sense. Computer scientists are trying to empower computers to behave as though they could think, by perceiving and absorbing data, reasoning, and communicating in ways similar to human behavior. Although artificial intelligence has had limited impact on business to date, it will play a major role in business decisions during the next decade.[4]

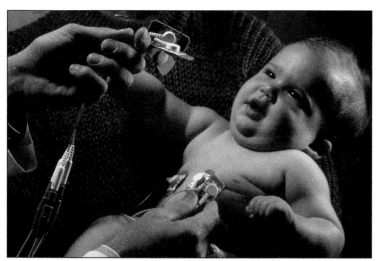

Courtesy of the Hewlett-Packard Company

Artificial intelligence is being used to diagnose electrocardiograms (ECGs) the way a doctor does.

Types of Computers

Depending on their needs and resources, organizations use one of three types of computers: mainframes, minicomputers, and microcomputers. The largest and fastest computer, with the greatest storage capacity, is the **mainframe.** Large businesses and government units use mainframes to process and store vast amounts of data. Most mainframes today can be used by many people in several different locations at the same time. Because of their incredible speed and capacity to serve many users, mainframe computers are very expensive. For instance, IBM's newest generation of mainframes is priced from $70,000 to more than $2 million.[5] Some large businesses and government agencies connect multiple mainframes together to form **supercomputers,** the fastest computers available. Some supercomputers can make billions of calculations in one second with 20-digit accuracy.[6]

A **minicomputer** is a smaller, slower version of the mainframe. Many smaller firms rely heavily on minicomputers because, priced at $10,000 or more, they cost much less than mainframes. Most minicomputers are the size of a desk, yet can perform most of the operations accomplished by mainframes.

A **microcomputer,** or personal computer, is smaller, less powerful, and less costly than a minicomputer. Microcomputers include a cathode ray tube (CRT), which is a visual display device that shows data on a television-like screen, or monitor, and a keyboard like that of a typewriter. Designed for use by one person, micros are self-contained units that usually fit on a desk or table and can be moved. They can be purchased for a few thousand dollars or less. *Laptop* computers are even smaller versions of microcomputers. As the name says, they fit on a person's lap and are convenient for use while traveling. Microcomputers are popular for use in homes and professional offices as well as in corporations of all sizes. A survey of manufacturing and service firms conducted by *Business Marketing* magazine reported that 6 of every 10 individuals responding used personal computers.[7]

Mainframe
The largest and fastest type of computer, with the greatest storage capacity.

Supercomputer
A computer formed by connecting multiple mainframes.

Minicomputer
A smaller, slower version of the mainframe computer.

Microcomputer
A personal computer, including a cathode ray tube and a keyboard.

Computers for the Disabled

In the early 1980s, a single talking computer existed. Less than a decade later, many computer programs could turn text into artificial speech and enable blind people to use computers. Personal computers are available with large-print screens; they also can change letters into braille for printing. Such advanced technology has made personal computers readily accessible to the roughly 36 million disabled people in the United States.

"If you can control a single muscle in your body, or a group of muscles, like moving your eyebrows up and down, you can operate a computer," says Mary Pat Radabaugh, manager of the National Support Center for Persons with Disabilities. For instance, some keyboards work through light pointers attached to a person's head. As the prices of such products come down, personal computers become easier for the disabled to acquire and use.

Perhaps the major benefit disabled individuals gain from computer use is greater control over their environment. With assistive devices, they can use personal computers to operate a radio, telephone, television, and other electronic equipment. Such devices also make it practical and economical for employers to hire disabled workers. Firms no longer have to purchase expensive computer systems for disabled workers, since personal computers can be adapted at much less cost.

In 1986 Congress passed a law (amending the Rehabilitation Act of 1973) that requires government offices to make computers accessible to employees with disabilities. The response of the computer industry has been mixed, but some firms are developing new products for the disabled. IBM introduced the Screen Reader to accompany its Personal System/2®. The device speaks the words and numbers displayed on the screen while giving a visually impaired person control over the speed of the voice. Apple Computer has introduced Sticky Keys, a keyboard that eliminates the need to press two keys at once to perform some of the computer functions. Hundreds of smaller companies are also designing computer accessories for the disabled. The National Rehabilitation Information Center in Washington, D.C., estimates that 1,000 computer accessories to aid the disabled (made by 400 companies) are available for a single personal computer system.[8]

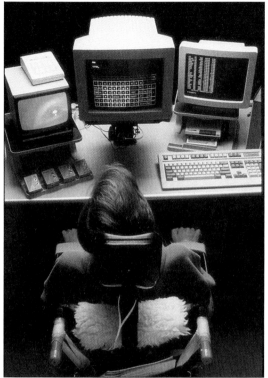

The Eyegage System is a personal computer that enables severely disabled people to do many things with their eyes that they would otherwise do with their hands.

Courtesy of L C Technologies Inc., Fairfax, Virginia

Microcomputers are capable of numerous functions, flexible for diverse situations, and affordable. The Business Action examines how personal computers are being developed for disabled people.

Computer Hardware

The physical devices that make up a computer system are called **hardware.** Figure 22.2 diagrams the basic hardware of a computer, including the input device, the central processing unit, and the output device.

Through an **input device,** a user enters data into a computer and makes requests of the computer. The most common input device is a keyboard for typing data or requests. Other input devices are disks, magnetic tapes, punch cards, optical scanners such as those that read universal product codes in supermarkets, the movable mouse, and voice recognition devices.

The **central processing unit (CPU),** the heart of the computer, controls the entire computer system. The CPU includes the electronic hardware that performs the computer operations and consists of three components. **Main memory** stores data, instructions, and other information the computer needs to operate. If something is not in a computer's main memory, the CPU cannot process it. Memory is measured in *bytes;* one byte is the same as one character—a numeral or letter of the alphabet. For example, computers containing 640KB (kilobytes) of main memory have the capacity to store 640,000

Hardware
The physical devices that make up a computer system.

Input Device
The hardware used to enter data into and make requests of the computer.

Central Processing Unit (CPU)
The electronic hardware that performs the computer operations and controls the entire system.

Main Memory
The part of the computer central processing unit that stores data and instructions.

FIGURE 22.2

Basic Computer Hardware

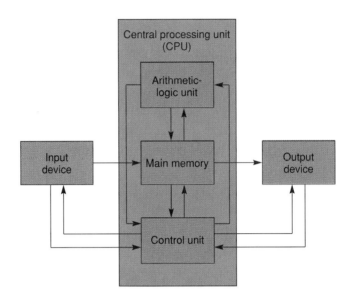

Arithmetic-Logic Unit
The part of a computer's central processing unit that performs computations.

Control Unit
The part of a computer's central processing unit that guides the operations of the computer.

Output Device
The hardware that displays the computer's requests or processed data.

characters. The **arithmetic-logic unit** performs the computations. Data that need to be added, subtracted, multiplied, or divided are moved from the main memory to the arithmetic-logic unit. After the calculations have been performed, the resulting data are moved back into main memory. The **control unit** guides the operations of a computer. It directs the sequence of operations, interprets coded instructions, and sends needed data and instructions to the other units.

The **output device** is the hardware that displays the computer's requests or processed data. The most commonly used output devices are the display screen and the printer, which produces a paper printout (called hard copy). Other output devices include disks, magnetic tapes, graphic plotters, and even the spoken word.

Computer Software

Software
A sequence of instructions that a computer can carry out.

Computer Program
A detailed set of instructions written in a computer language.

Computers cannot think. They can operate and perform calculations only by following precise instructions devised by people. **Software** is the term for the instructions that tell the computer hardware what to do. Software is a collection of **computer programs,** which are detailed sets of instructions written in a computer language such as BASIC, COBOL, FORTRAN, or Pascal. When the programs are in main memory, they can be carried out by the CPU. The act of performing these instructions is referred to as running the program. Computer programs instruct the computer to read data, process the data in some manner, and output the information in a specified format. Without software, computer hardware is useless.

Businesses sometimes develop their own computer software for specific tasks. For instance, many firms employ computer programmers to write special programs for payroll, billing, inventory control, and other functions. The programmer must analyze the problem and outline a series of logical steps that will provide a solution. Developing software can be both time-consuming and expensive, and often is not practical for small firms, which generally do not have programmers on staff. Therefore many firms purchase ready-made software, available from a multitude of companies. Ready-made software can handle a variety of business applications and often costs less than developing computer programs from scratch. Ready-made software is also instantly available, whereas developing a computer program could take months or even years.

Much of today's computer software is "user friendly," meaning that people can use it without a great deal of technical training. User-friendly software communicates in a conversational style. Complex computer programs used in the United States, for example, allow users to issue commands in English rather than a computer language. This breakthrough in software development brought computers into the daily lives of many more people at work, school, and home.

COMPUTERS AND BUSINESS

Computers are a valuable asset to and often a necessity for business firms. In this section, we examine various capabilities of computers and common business applications.

Computer Capabilities

Computers possess virtually unlimited capabilities. Computer technology changes so rapidly that new uses for computers are being discovered almost daily. Computer hardware and software today can satisfy almost any business need. Let's look at some of the ways firms commonly use computers.

Word processing   Computers, in particular the micro or personal computer (PC), have revolutionized **word processing,** which consists of creating documents such as letters, reports, newsletters, memos, and books. In fact, compared to computers, typewriters have become outdated office equipment. Through the computer keyboard, an individual enters documents and instructions into computer memory to be stored on magnetic disk. Material stored on disk can be accessed and altered easily and kept for later use. For instance, a manager can write memos, letters, and reports, store them on disk, and print them when needed. Many word-processing programs (e.g., WordStar®, WordPerfect®), perform functions such as checking spelling and grammar, suggesting alternate words, and inserting graphics such as lines, boxes, diagrams, and illustrations.

Word Processing
Creating written documents with a computer.

Spreadsheets   Many firms use computer software to generate electronic accounting ledgers as **spreadsheets.** A manager or accountant can use computerized spreadsheets to organize data into rows and columns and to perform mathematical calculations. Popular spreadsheet software such as Lotus® 1–2–3® is used to generate balance sheets, develop sales projections, and estimate profits.

Spreadsheets
Electronic accounting ledgers generated by computer software.

Computer graphics   Computer programs can also translate data into graphs or figures. Computer graphics are useful to display financial information and to make comparisons between companies or performance in different years. Graphics add clarity and emphasis and are extremely valuable in both written reports and oral presentations. Figure 22.3 illustrates some of the graphics capabilities of computers.

Desktop publishing   The computer can also be used to produce high-quality printed materials. With **desktop publishing** software, the user can design page layouts and formats comparable to magazines and books, and insert graphics, including illustrations, wherever needed. Desktop publishing enables individuals and firms of any size to produce high-quality reports, brochures, and newsletters at much less than the price charged by a printer. Desktop publishing typically requires the use of a powerful laser printer, now available for as little as $1,000.

Desktop Publishing
Producing printed materials using computer software that can do page layouts and formats, insert graphics, and print with high quality.

Business Applications

Firms use computers to perform a variety of tasks quickly, efficiently, and accurately. The most common business applications of computers are payroll, record-keeping, inventory control, scheduling, order processing, electronic mail, and relationship marketing.

Desktop publishing software can be used to produce professional-looking documents.

Courtesy of Logitech

FIGURE 22.3

Examples of Computer Graphics

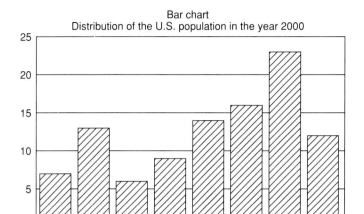

Bar chart
Distribution of the U.S. population in the year 2000

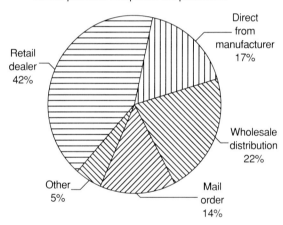

Pie chart
Where personal computers are purchased

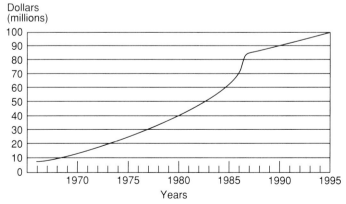

Graph
Total advertising expenditures

Payroll   Many companies generate their payroll with computers. For most, calculating employees' pay is complicated. They must make deductions for taxes, insurance, profit-sharing programs, and even parking fees and contributions to charity. Employee pay may be calculated in several ways, including salary, sales, bonus, commission, and hourly wages plus overtime. Computers can make the many calculations required to meet a payroll in a matter of seconds.

Record-keeping   Computers are valuable for maintaining and updating records such as personnel files, customer lists, accounts receivable, and accounts payable. Business owners and managers can easily maintain accounting and financial records on a computer. With computer record-keeping, firms can update records and generate financial statements on demand.

Inventory control   Another common application of computers in business is inventory control. Many firms use programs to keep track of inventory and place orders when inventory drops to a certain level. These programs can also tell a manager the quantity and dollar amount of inventory at any time.

Scheduling   Computers can be used to schedule a variety of activities. Managers rely on computers in scheduling production, traffic routes, delivery timetables, and sales calls. For example, some commercial vehicles use a computerized map called "Navigator" to tell drivers the most efficient routes and how to avoid traffic congestion.[9] Firms can also use computers to develop work schedules for employees.

Order processing   Firms of all types and sizes use computers to process orders. Supermarket checkout lanes have computerized registers. Large manufacturing firms use computers to place orders at a warehouse, check customer credit and inventory levels, and print invoices. Many catalog retailers use computers to fill mail and telephone orders. Arby's is testing a computer system that will enable customers to place orders by touching boxes on a screen on the front counter.[10]

Electronic Mail
A computer network used to relay messages from one user to another instantly.

Electronic mail   Computer networks can relay messages from one user to another instantly. Through **electronic mail,** a user can send a letter or memo to one other designated user or to several. Electronic mail software keeps track of all communications sent and alerts the sender that the message has been received. Replies can be routed to the sender.

Relationship marketing   One of the more recent uses of computers is to develop one-on-one relationships with customers. Computer software has been developed that allows data to be entered and retrieved from a touch-tone phone. Computers can respond to hundreds of thousands of calls per hour—to take orders, for example. Consumer products firms such as General Foods and RJR Nabisco see potential for connecting customers with computers to track their buying habits.[11] Eventually this technology will enable companies to have a direct relationship with their customers.

MANAGEMENT INFORMATION SYSTEMS

Because of the information explosion, managers making decisions must regularly confront an abundance of facts and figures and determine which information is most useful. Many organizations design management information systems to provide managers with the necessary information to make intelligent decisions. A **management information system (MIS)** combines computers and regular, organized procedures to provide the information managers use in making decisions.

Management Information System (MIS)
A combination of computers and procedures for providing information that managers use in making decisions.

MIS Functions

A management information system is used to collect data, store and process data, and present information to managers (see Figure 22.4). This section discusses each of these functions.

Collect data We have emphasized the massive amount of information available to organizations—personnel records, information about competitors, sales data, accounting data, information about customers, and so on. The first function of an MIS is to determine the information needed to make decisions and to organize it into a database. A **database** is an integrated collection of data stored in one place for efficient access and information processing.

Database
An integrated collection of data stored in one place for easy access and information processing.

Data can be obtained from sources within and outside the organization. Generally most data collected for an MIS come from internal sources such as company records or reports and information compiled by managers themselves. External sources include trade publications, customers, and consultants. The Business Action details Mastic Corporation's use of several sources of data for its MIS.

Store and process data Once created, a database must be stored and processed in a form useful to managers. Data are generally stored on magnetic tape or hard disks when mainframe computers are used and on hard disks or floppy

FIGURE 22.4

Functions of an MIS

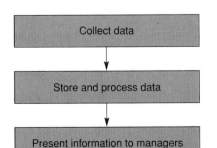

Mastic Corporation Stays Close to the Customer

Satisfying customers requires quick response to their needs. One way for firms to stay close to customers is through a management information system (MIS). Mastic Corporation is a leading supplier of vinyl siding, with a 16 percent share of industry sales. Competition is keen in this $500 million industry. To stay on top, Mastic developed a computer-based MIS to react more quickly to changing customer needs. Market research and planning manager Andrew P. Panelli says, "As the industry becomes competitive, you have to direct sales campaigns to where they're going to generate the most business and create the most impact. That becomes harder to do if you don't have a feel for what your customers want and need."

Mastic's managers developed an MIS to monitor market share and product sales performance by territory and to be able to determine the market potential for various territories. The MIS compiles information from several sources. It collects sales data from the county level up to the national level, then converts the information to the territory level. It gathers information on market trends, such as housing starts, ages of homes, changes in home styles, and acceptability of vinyl siding—all of which helps in estimating demand for vinyl siding.

The company surveys siding dealers to determine how much vinyl they sell, how much of it is made by Mastic, how much goes for new construction, and how much for remodeling. This information enables Mastic to rank competitor strength by territory and to keep track of where its vinyl is sold—at lumber yards, factory warehouses, or other outlets.

The MIS helps Mastic provide better sales coverage and set up new, more efficient sales territories. It provides sales managers with annual performance reports as well as monthly reports comparing current sales to the previous year's sales. Information in the MIS also led Mastic to become more aware of ethnic populations in the United States where siding dealers do not speak English, and to print promotional materials in other languages. Mastic officials, pleased with their MIS, are expanding the system to other divisions, which produce vinyl materials for windows, new construction, and mobile homes.[12]

Colin Chilvers prefers that his nightmares show up on the silver screen, not his computer screen.

SONY.

Courtesy of Sony Corporation of America

Data stored on floppy disks can be loaded into a computer in seconds.

(soft) disks when minicomputers or microcomputers are used. The data can be loaded into the computer in seconds for easy access by the user.

Data for an MIS must be current, which requires periodic updating of the database. A computer operator or programmer can update the database manually by loading the appropriate tape or disk into the computer, which locates the data to be changed and makes the necessary changes. Systems also are available to automatically update data. In this case, the database is permanently connected to the MIS, and the computer automatically makes changes as new data become available.

Once data are stored in the MIS, managers can use the data for decision making. Some data can be used in the form in which they are stored. But more often, data must be processed to meet specific information needs of managers. **Data processing** involves mechanically transferring raw data into some specific form of information. Business firms process both text, such as reports, and numerical data, such as sales figures.

A **database management system (DBMS)** is a computer software program that helps firms manage their data files. Such programs change information stored in data files, add new information, and delete information no longer needed. DBMS software can also be used to sort and merge files, process data, and print reports. Some database programs used frequently are dBASE III PLUS®, R:BASE®, Rapidfile, and PC–File.

Present information to managers   Processed data must be put in a form useful to managers. Verbal information can be presented in text format in the form of reports, outlines, lists, articles, or books. Numerical information can

Data Processing
Mechanically transferring raw data into some specific form of information.

Database Management System (DBMS)
Computer software that helps firms manage various data files.

FIGURE 22.5

**Hanna Industries'
Computer Network**

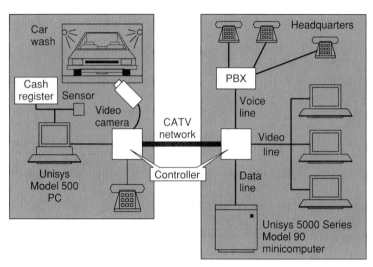

Source: Hanna Car Wash International, Portland, Oregon.

be presented in table or graph format. As noted earlier, computer programs can offer numerous graphic options.

The most commonly used computer graphics are bar charts, pie charts, and graphs (see Figure 22.3). A *bar chart* uses vertical or horizontal bars to represent values, with longer bars representing greater values. A *pie chart* is a circle divided into portions, or "slices," each representing a different item. The size of each slice shows the proportion of that item to the total. Bar charts and pie charts help visualize the relative size or importance of various information. A *graph* is used to plot data, illustrating how information changes over time.

Computer Networks

Computer Network
A collection of computers connected so that they can function individually and communicate with each other.

A management information system can include multiple computers connected to each other. A **computer network** is a collection of computers connected in a manner that allows them to function individually and communicate with each other. Computer networks usually include a mainframe or minicomputer as the foundation of the system. Other mainframes, minicomputers, or microcomputers can communicate with the mainframe or minicomputer or with each other. Networks link computers within an office, across the country, or even worldwide—in which case the computers are linked by telephone lines or satellites. Hanna Industries International, for example, uses a computer network to manage 30 car washes and to communicate with five branch offices (see Figure 22.5). By 1995 the company plans to link 5,000 car washes on the network.[13]

Local Area Network (LAN)
A system of telecommunications links that connects all computers in one firm directly, without telephone lines.

A **local area network (LAN)** is a system of telecommunications links that connects all computers in one company directly without telephone lines.[14] Because computers in the network can communicate with one another, members of a firm can send information back and forth instantly.

Decision Support Systems

A **decision support system (DSS)** is an interactive information system that enables managers to gain instant access to information in a less structured format than an MIS. DSS software combines corporate information on past performance with what is currently taking place; it allows managers to work with large amounts of data not available otherwise.[15] Through a DSS, managers can obtain information about the firm, competitors, and the business environment. Computer programs use the information to generate new facts or beliefs as a basis for decision making. For instance:[16]

> **Decision Support System (DSS)**
> A system that enables managers to instantly access information on past and current performance.

- Gillette uses a DSS to check market positions and daily sales activity in three divisions.
- One fast-food chain uses a DSS to tell how many customers ordered french fries with hamburgers on the previous day.
- Firestone Tire & Rubber uses a DSS to pinpoint lagging areas and to control costs.
- A manufacturing company uses a DSS to evaluate the numbers and assumptions that managers have used in forecasts.
- Phillips Petroleum uses a DSS to manage operations and monitor economic and political news influencing the oil business.

An **executive information system (EIS)** is a user-friendly DSS designed specifically for executives. An EIS is easy to use and requires no knowledge of the computer. By moving a mouse or merely touching the screen, the user directs the computer to provide information. Executive information systems use big-screen, high-quality monitors and produce full-color displays. An EIS allows top-level managers to ask questions and receive immediate answers in the form of graphs, charts, and reports.

> **Executive Information System (EIS)**
> A user-friendly decision support system designed for executives that requires little computer knowledge and provides instant high-quality displays.

TRENDS IN COMPUTERS AND MANAGEMENT INFORMATION SYSTEMS

The amount of information available to managers will continue to increase dramatically in the future. The ever growing volume of information will make computers even more crucial to firms. The business sector's use of computers to process information is expected to grow rapidly. Virtually no business firm, regardless of size, will be able to function efficiently without one. Some experts even point to a ''paperless'' society in which computers will be used for nearly all letters, memos, reports, and other business correspondence.

The amount of computer power a dollar can buy has grown a thousand times every two decades, and this rate shows no sign of slowing.[17] The trend toward smaller, faster, and less costly computers will also continue. Engineers are packing more and more functions onto a single computer chip without increasing the power the chip burns up.[18] This technology points to smaller computers. Notebook-size computers are already available, such as the Casio BOSS, weighing 5–9 ounces, and the Sharp Wizard, weighing 9 ounces.

One problem in making computers even smaller, however, is the keyboard. Some companies are developing computers that convert handwritten text into

Laptop computers can go nearly anywhere.

Courtesy of Kurt Strand

data and so eliminate the need for a keyboard.[19] The future will also bring computers with greater capabilities of recognizing the human voice.[20]

Smaller, portable computers such as laptops are changing the way people in business use computers. Laptop computers now are as essential as a briefcase or suitcase for many business travelers. Salespeople, reporters, writers, managers, and others use the small computers to work on airplanes and commuter trains and in hotels and to communicate with co-workers in other places. Salespeople often have computers in their cars for quick access to information from their managers. Computers in Federal Express vans and trucks help couriers keep track of letters and packages being shipped. As Figure 22.6 shows, even more people are expected to work from portable offices in homes, hotels, and vehicles in the future.

Because of the ever increasing power of computers, management information systems are also becoming more sophisticated. **Expert systems,** which actually make decisions, are computer programs that imitate human thinking and offer advice or solutions to complex problems in much the same way that a human expert does. For instance, people use expert systems to plan shipping schedules, provide financial advice to investors, and help managers respond to the actions of competing firms. Wendy's uses an expert system for solving food-ordering and cooking-equipment problems. The system has resulted in a smoother operation and increased productivity.[21]

Computers have increasing significance in our lives, not only for work but also for personal and family use and for play. Roughly 66 million personal computers have been sold, and 16 million more are sold each year.[22] Eventually they may be as common in homes as microwave ovens. The profusion of

Expert System
Computer software that imitates human thinking.

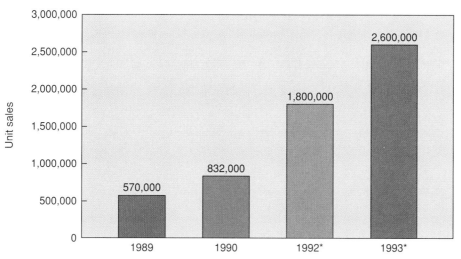

FIGURE 22.6

The Growth of Laptops

DID YOU KNOW? *By the mid-1990s, laptops will account for more than half of all personal computers sold in the United States.*

*Projected unit sales.

Source: From industry reports and Forrester Research, Inc.

computers will enable business firms to explore still more computer applications, such as placing orders, paying bills, and performing bank transactions through personal computers in homes or offices.

The growth of computer technology has drawbacks. Computer crime, for instance, has gained much attention in recent years. People have used access to computer records to steal money and tamper with records in business firms and government agencies. Another serious threat to computer users is the *computer virus,* a computer program that copies itself endlessly to other programs and destroys stored data in the process. One virus spread across a national computer network known as Internet and paralyzed about 6,000 computers in businesses, universities, and government laboratories. To defend against viruses, IBM has developed a program that identifies viruses, although it does not remove them.[23] Experts estimate that damage from computer crime in the United States runs anywhere from $500 million to $5 billion. Some suspect it is much higher because only a small percentage of computer crimes are reported, and fewer still are prosecuted.[24]

Improper use of the computer's tremendous capability to compile information can violate people's right to privacy. Some businesses have been accused of keeping large data files on individuals and then releasing the data unethically. For example, firms sometimes sell their customer database to others who may use it to solicit business. Selling customer lists has led to an increase in junk mail and telephone solicitations. In many cases, computers actually make telephone calls and play recordings to try to sell products or solicit donations.

Computers have become a major part of our lives. Without them, we would have fewer of the conveniences to which we have grown accustomed. When used properly, computers can increase business efficiency, assist managers in decision making, and even save lives. Computers will continue to play an ever increasing role in the world of business and in society.

You'll Know It's the **Century When . . .**

More People Read Computer Printouts Than Books

The children of the 21st century will be on intimate terms with computer chips. They will learn to use computers in grade school, and their homes will be filled with programmable VCRs, remote controls, and other computerized gadgets. Unlike many 20th-century adults, the new generation will be computer literate. And people with only a high school education will be just as likely as college-educated people to use personal computers in their daily lives.

Computer games will still be a favorite pastime in the 21st century, but a new product—"Virtual Reality"—will dominate the market. "Virtual Reality" allows users to see and experience places and events as though they were actually there. Most users will play for fun, but the product will also have educational and therapeutic uses.[25]

SUMMARY OF LEARNING OBJECTIVES

1. To explain why business managers need computers in this age of information.
   Managers today have access to more statistics, facts, and predictions than ever before. Computers enable businesses to convert all these data into useful information. With computers readily available and affordable, business firms are taking advantage of their capabilities and becoming increasingly dependent on them.

2. To trace the evolution of computers.
   Through an evolution of five generations, computers have become smaller, faster, less costly, and capable of more functions and greater storage. The first generation consisted of enormous computers operating with vacuum tubes. The second was marked by transistors. The third began with integrated circuits. The fourth generation resulted from large-scale integrated (LSI) circuits contained on tiny superchips. The fifth and current generation is developing through very large-scale integration (VLSI) and the study of artificial intelligence.

3. To identify the different types of computers and the components common to all.
   Three different types of computers can meet the needs and resources of firms. The largest and fastest, *mainframes* are also the most expensive. *Minicomputers* are smaller, somewhat slower, less costly versions of the mainframe. *Microcomputers,* which include a display screen and keyboard, are adaptable, affordable, and adequate for use in homes and businesses. All computers consist of physical devices called *hardware,* including an input device, central processing unit (CPU), and output device. *Software,* sets of instructions called computer programs, is needed to tell the computer exactly what to do.

4. To outline the capabilities of computers.
   Computers possess vast capabilities to help users perform many functions with accuracy, speed, and efficiency. Computers excel in word process-

ing, spreadsheets, graphics, and desktop publishing. Businesses commonly use computers for payroll, record-keeping, inventory control, scheduling, order processing, electronic mail, and relationship marketing.

5. To define *management information system (MIS)* and explain how an MIS is used.

A management information system is a combination of computers and procedures for providing regular, timely information that managers use in making decisions. Through an MIS, a firm can collect data from internal and external sources, store and process data, and present information in a form useful to managers.

6. To list trends in computer development and use and in management information systems.

The continuing information explosion will prompt business firms to make even greater use of computers and management information systems. Computers will become faster, smaller, and more portable; management information systems will become increasingly sophisticated to further aid decision making. As more and more personal computers enter homes, they will increase in importance for personal and family use as well as for work. Along with the growth of computers has come a trend toward more computer crime, including invasion of privacy.

KEY TERMS

Data, p. 775

Information, p. 775

Computer, p. 776

Transistor, p. 777

Integrated Circuit, p. 777

Large-Scale Integrated (LSI) Circuit, p. 778

Very Large-Scale Integration (VLSI), p. 778

Artificial Intelligence, p. 778

Mainframe, p. 779

Supercomputer, p. 779

Minicomputer, p. 779

Microcomputer, p. 779

Hardware, p. 781

Input Device, p. 781

Central Processing Unit (CPU), p. 781

Main Memory, p. 781

Arithmetic-Logic Unit, p. 782

Control Unit, p. 782

Output Device, p. 782

Software, p. 782

Computer Program, p. 782

Word Processing, p. 783

Spreadsheets, p. 783

Desktop Publishing, p. 784

Electronic Mail, p. 786

Management Information System (MIS), p. 787

Database, p. 787

Data Processing, p. 789

Database Management System (DBMS), p. 789

Computer Network, p. 790

Local Area Network (LAN), p. 790

Decision Support System (DSS), p. 791

Executive Information System (EIS), p. 791

Expert System, p. 792

QUESTIONS FOR DISCUSSION AND REVIEW

1. What does "Age of Information" mean? What is the role of computers in this era?
2. What is a computer?
3. Trace the evolution of electronic computers through the five generations.
4. Describe the three major types of computers.
5. Name the devices that make up the basic hardware of a computer system. How does each function in processing data?
6. What is the importance of computer software?
7. Why would a small communications firm prefer to use computers for word processing and desktop publishing, rather than typewriters and a printing company?
8. Describe three business applications for which a small firm would usually use a computer.
9. What does a management information system offer an organization? Describe the major functions of an MIS.
10. What is a computer network? What advantages does a firm gain with a computer network?
11. Why would a busy executive benefit from an executive information system?
12. Describe the developments computer technology is likely to bring in the future.
13. What are potential hazards of the computer's remarkable capabilities? Explain.

CASE 22.1
Software: Over-the-Counter or Tailor-Made?

An abundance of software has been developed in recent years for virtually all computers, ranging from large mainframes to desktop and laptop microcomputers. Such a wide choice presents a dilemma for business firms: which type is better for the business, over-the-counter products purchased through local computer stores or software specifically developed for the firm's needs? The answer to this difficult question depends on the firm's size, budget, computer knowledge, and needs.

According to the manufacturer of Marketbase, a database management system, over-the-counter products have several advantages. First, the product is available immediately, without the wait for custom software to be designed. In many instances, managers can solve problems right away rather than waiting until it may be too late. Second, ready-made software costs less than the custom-designed variety. While Marketbase costs $8,000, it took five years to create; similar software would cost a firm much more to develop.

Many companies have used commercial software successfully. Consumer products companies often use software developed by A. C. Nielsen. It tracks sales by regions and highlights important changes, analyzing data collected monthly from 3,000 supermarkets. For instance, it can provide data on how many 32-ounce jars of Prego spaghetti sauce with mushrooms were sold in a specific store during a given week. Information Resources has developed software that summarizes important trends in sales data collected monthly from 2,400 supermarkets. Firms in diverse industries find other software products such as Lotus® and dBASE® useful for a variety of business applications such as accounting and inventory control.

The major drawback to over-the-counter software is that these programs assume all businesses are basically the same. Some firms with unique requirements or problems will not find suitable software available. In other cases, firms use a less than ideal commercial software program and end up compromising some aspect of their business. Many firms, especially those with larger computer systems, prefer tailor-made software.

Questions for Discussion
1. What is the difference between over-the-counter and tailor-made software?
2. What are some of the advantages of over-the-counter software?
3. Why would a firm design its own software?

Adapted from Jeffrey Rothfeder, Jim Bartimo, Lois Therrien, and Richard Brandt, "How Software Is Making Food Sales a Piece of Cake," *Business Week,* July 2, 1990, pp. 54–55; Michael Finley, "Tailor-Made or Off-the-Shelf," *Marketing News,* April 24, 1989, pp. 1–2; Keith H. Hammonds, Deidre A. Depke, and Richard Brandt, "Software: It's a New Game," *Business Week,* June 4, 1990, pp. 102–6.

CASE 22.2
Computers Threaten Our Privacy

While the computer has helped businesses run more efficiently, many people believe computer use also threatens our right to privacy. Firms needing information about consumers will often pay for computer-generated lists of names, addresses, and information such as buying habits, income range, and education levels. Many companies that maintain large databases on customers will share them with other firms for a hefty fee.

The computer also helps businesses track down information concerning customers much more quickly. For instance, they can easily call credit bureaus to check on consumers and obtain information instantly without the individuals' knowledge. Anyone with a personal computer and the know-how can easily get information such as social security numbers and credit and driving histories on millions of people.

Firms also use computers to compile information on their own employees. Many major U.S. firms use computers to monitor employees on and off the job. They argue that such tracking is necessary to protect themselves against theft, loss of company secrets to other firms, and unacceptable behavior such as drug abuse. But being subjected to computer monitoring makes honest employees feel humiliated.

The public's growing concern about privacy poses a serious threat to firms. The Roper Organization reported that 60 percent of all Americans see lack of privacy as a serious problem. An American Express survey found that 80 percent of Americans do not think companies should share personal information on customers. The growing concern about privacy has led legislatures to consider hundreds of bills that could restrict the use of consumer information.

Four bills before the U.S. Congress would strengthen the Fair Credit Reporting Act by restricting access to credit companies' databases. Nearly every state in the country is also considering some type of privacy-related bill. A California bill passed in the state assembly (but still under consideration in the senate) would require companies to notify consumers each time their names are sold or rented. A New York law makes it illegal for businesses to require customers to put their address or phone number on a credit card receipt.

Such bills regulating the use of consumer information would have the greatest impact on database marketers such as credit bureaus. But they would also affect thousands of business firms that rely on consumer information for their daily operations. Some firms believe that public fears are overshadowing all the good that businesses can do if they have information about customers. They are trying to show the public how information can benefit the consumers who provide it. They think that being honest with consumers by telling them how information is used to serve them better will reduce the public's concern about invasion of privacy.

Adapted from Dan Fost, "Privacy Concerns Threaten Database Marketers," *American Demographics,* May 1990, pp. 18–21; Jeffrey Rothfeder, "The Scoop on Snooping: It's a Cinch," *Business Week,* September 4, 1989, p. 82; Martha Farnsworth Riche, "The Rising Tide of Privacy Laws," *American Demographics,* March 1990, p. 24; Jeffrey Rothfeder, Michele Galen, and Lisa Driscoll, "Is Your Boss Spying on You?" *Business Week,* January 15, 1990, pp. 74–75.

Questions for Discussion
1. What business trends have contributed to the threat to privacy, as some call it? How has the use of computers contributed?
2. Why do business firms need to collect information about consumers and employees?
3. Do you think firms violate consumers' rights to privacy by sharing information with others?
4. What impact would laws regulating the use of consumer information have on business?

ACCOUNTING / IS

Today's world is a computer world. We print bills by computer, check out groceries by computer, record grades by computer, issue tickets by computer, and calculate and print paychecks by computer. Computers have revolutionized the way we live our lives and the way businesses handle operations.

In business—even in the smallest enterprise—computerized accounting systems are now the norm. Record-keeping is no longer a tedious manual effort but rather a fast, efficient, computerized operation that provides timely information. Before the computer age, accountants spent hours making calculations that now take only seconds on the computer.

The Age of Information has created a new wave of job openings in the computer field and in accounting. Career opportunities in both fields are excellent. The demand for computer specialists and accountants continues to be higher than the supply of qualified candidates. Opportunities in the fields of accounting and information systems are tremendous and still growing.

ACCOUNTING

The days of accountants wearing green eyeshades and working in the back room are long gone. Today's accountants are distinguished professionals working with top management. Many chief executive officers (CEOs) of leading firms began their careers in the accounting department.

The accounting profession is a large one. Today over a million accountants work in about 30,000 firms. The field has a growing number of specialties, but most professionals work in one of three major areas: public accounting, management accounting, and government accounting.

Public Accounting

The biggest and best-known area in the field of accounting is public accounting. Organizations that provide accounting services for businesses or individuals for a fee are public accounting firms.

One of the major functions of public accounting firms is auditing the financial records of organizations. Government regulations require stock-issuing businesses to have their financial statements reviewed by an independent third party. Public accountants conduct these independent audits and issue unbiased opinions about the accuracy of the financial statements. Public accountants also provide many additional services, such as preparing tax returns, advising on tax matters and other financial concerns, setting up accounting and computer systems, and preparing financial reports.

Public accounting was long dominated by the "Big Eight" accounting firms. Mergers have now reduced the number to six dominant firms—the biggest and best known among accounting firms. Together these firms have revenues of more than $9 billion and employ thousands of accountants in the

REPORT OF INDEPENDENT PUBLIC ACCOUNTANTS

 Peat Marwick

The Board of Directors and Stockholders
Kemper Corporation:

We have audited the consolidated balance sheet of Kemper
Corporation and subsidiaries as of December 31, 1989 and 1988 and
the related consolidated statements of income, stockholders' equity
and cash flows for each of the years in the three-year period ended
December 31, 1989. These consolidated financial staements are the
responsibility of the Company's management. Our responsibility is to
express an opinion on these consolidated financial statements based
on our audits.

We conducted our audits in accordance with generally accepted
auditing standards. Those standards require that we plan and perform
the audit to obtain reasonable assurance about whether the financial
statements are free of material misstatement. An audit includes
examining, on a test basis, evidence supporting the amounts and
disclosures in the financial statements. An audit also includes
assessing the accounting principles used and significant estimates
made by the management, as well as evaluating the overall financial
statement presentation. We believe that our audits provide a
reasonable basis for our opinion.

In our opinion, the consolidated financial statements referred to
above present fairly, in all material respects, the financial position of
Kemper Corporation and subsidiaries at December 31, 1989 and
1988, and the results of their operations and their cash flows for each
of the years in the three-year period ended December 31, 1989, in
conformity with generally accepted accounting principles.

Chicago, Illinois
March 7, 1990

"Big Eight" → "Big Six" Accounting Firms

Arthur Andersen	Arthur Andersen
KPMG/Peat Marwick	KPMG/Peat Marwick
Coopers & Lybrand	Coopers & Lybrand
Price Waterhouse	Price Waterhouse
Deloitte, Haskins & Sells	Deloitte & Touche
Touche Ross	
Ernst & Whinney	Ernst & Young
Arthur Young	

United States and around the world.

Public accounting firms usually require their accountants to pursue certification as a certified public accountant (CPA). Certification is necessary for a firm to audit the books of companies. To become a CPA, one needs to pass a special qualifying exam as well as complete two years of work experience in public accounting. The CPA examination, developed by the American Institute of Certified Public Accountants (AICPA), is standardized throughout the country. The specific regulations for certification vary from state to state, but a minimum number of accounting courses (24–30 credit hours) and a four-year college degree are required to take the examination.

Entry into public accounting is competitive, particularly with the best-known firms. Most firms seek graduates in the top 25 percent of their classes and place a good deal of emphasis on classroom performance. CPA firms look for top students who are likely to pass the difficult CPA examination. As well, firms look for strong interpersonal and communication skills in their employees, who constantly meet with clients. Writing skills are also important for preparing reports to clients.

Public accountants have considerable pressure, particularly during tax preparation time. Then, and often at other times as well, they need to work more than 40 hours a week and more than five days a week. Most work is performed in the client's office, requiring a good deal of travel.

The number of people leaving public accounting firms tends to be quite high. Less than 20 percent of those who start with a public accounting firm remain for 10 years. Many leave because of attractive offers elsewhere; accountants with

Career Path: Public Accounting

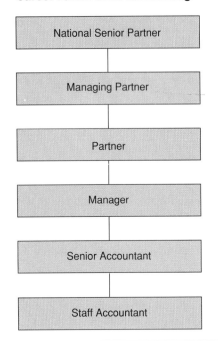

- National Senior Partner
- Managing Partner
- Partner
- Manager
- Senior Accountant
- Staff Accountant

New hires in public accounting usually begin in an entry-level assignment as a *staff accountant*. Most staff accountants begin in auditing and then may move into tax preparation or management advisory service (consulting). Occasionally a few people are hired directly into one of these specialties. Staff accountants receive training in formal classes and informal training from their supervisors. Assignments are with a variety of clients.

Supervisory responsibility comes at the *senior accountant* level, after 2–3 years' experience with the firm. Seniors deal with a variety of jobs and assume responsibility for several staff accountants. They perform more planning and budgeting tasks and review and evaluate the work of the staff accountants.

The *manager* level comes after 5–8 years of experience. Managers have more direct contact with the clients and have overall responsibility for managing the job. Managers assign the seniors and staff to the jobs and make recommendations to the client about ways to improve operations.

Only the most successful in the firm reach the *partner* level. Statistically only 2 out of 100 staff accountants reach this level, normally in 12 to 14 years. Final responsibility for the client rests with partners. Partners take part in policy formulation and decision making as well as developing new clients. Partnership brings substantial financial rewards; most earn six-figure salaries.

---

several years' experience in a major public accounting firm are highly sought after. Some leave because of the travel and long hours or because they cannot advance to a partner position within the firm. Nearly all who leave public accounting, however, stay in the accounting field.

Management Accounting

Management accountants are employed by businesses and manufacturers to manage internal financial record-keeping. Because they work full-time for one organization (unlike public accountants, who are hired for a fee by many different firms), they are known as private accountants. More than 60 percent of all accountants are in management accounting.

Management accountants are responsible for providing the firm

with accurate financial information needed to make decisions. They prepare financial statements as well as supervise the record-keeping staff.

Large firms frequently organize the financial function into several operating departments. Within each department, a staff performs the basic work activities. The staffs are managed by accounting managers, who usually report to the controller.

The *general accounting* department is responsible for maintaining the general ledger, which involves preparing the detailed journal entries to keep track of the firm's expenditures. Depending on the size of the firm, the general accounting department may also handle payroll, accounts receivable, accounts payable, and preparation of financial statements.

Cost accounting departments determine the exact cost of producing goods and services. Assignments might involve estimating the costs for a new product, setting cost standards for products, analysis of operating variances, or preparing a cost analysis on an operating facility. Cost accountants also try to identify ways to control costs to keep them as low as possible.

Tax accounting departments prepare federal, state, and local tax returns and see that thorough records are kept for tax records. Tax accountants also provide guidance on tax planning, new legislation, and interpretations of tax laws. A good tax department can save substantial sums of money for the firm by careful planning and taking advantage of legally allowed deductions.

The *internal auditing* department performs studies of the financial and operational systems. The internal auditor reports on ways to improve efficiency and to minimize waste within the organization. Internal auditors also check bookkeeping records to ensure that they are accurate and that correct procedures are being followed.

Many firms require professional certification for the top positions. Individuals can earn a certificate in management accounting (CMA) or qualify as a certified internal auditor (CIA). The CMA exam is sponsored by the National Association of Accountants, and the CIA exam is sponsored by the Institute of Internal Auditors. Work experience is also required for certification.

Requirements: Accounting

Personal skills:
- Orientation to detail
- Ability to work independently
- Communications skills
- Mathematical ability

Education:
- Business administration degree
- Major in accounting

Government Accounting

Government and nonprofit accounting serves the public and not-for-profit sectors. Government accountants review the financial records of government agencies and help perform financial planning.

The single largest employer of accountants in the United States is the Internal Revenue Service. Revenue agents examine selected income tax returns. When necessary, they conduct field audits and investigations to verify the information

---

CAREER PROFILE: Alicia Verdun

Courtesy of Alicia Verdun

ALICIA VERDUN

Undergraduate degree: Pace University, New York
Major: Business and computer science
First job: Applications programmer
Current job: Information systems officer

Alicia Verdun was one of those fortunate students who took charge of her future by actively planning her career. After her third course in accounting, Verdun decided she needed to get work experience to determine whether or not she wanted to be a certified public accountant.

"I landed a part-time position at the NYC Transit Authority in the controller's office. My assignment was to reconcile their token control book. I was a little bored with that assignment, so I nosed my way into the data processing department. From that experience, I decided to change my curriculum to computers," she explains.

Combining a double major in business and computer science with her accounting courses and work experience, Verdun says, gave her an edge over other graduates seeking entry-level jobs.

Her first position was as applications programmer for a small consulting firm. With a promotion to senior programmer came a 20 percent salary increase. After three years at the firm, she decided it was time to make a change. For the next year and a half, Verdun felt challenged as senior programmer analyst at Bankers Trust, but she then realized that her programming days were numbered.

"I'm more of a people person, so I created a liaison position between the systems data center and user area," she says. "I resolved discrepancies in systems applications, expediting problems and offering resolutions. I found it challenging. Once you start dealing with different personalities, it becomes a whole different ball game."

She moved to Chase Manhattan Bank a little over four years ago and switched from applications to data center work. After only a year, she was promoted to data center manager of the area.

"I wanted to become an officer. The opportunity didn't present itself, but I continued looking for two years to see what the bank could offer me globally," Verdun says. She found it. Chase started a new department, a data center management program, under its corporate systems division.

Now Verdun is second vice president in charge of information systems. "My career is just where I want it to be, but I'm still looking to what's next," she says.

Source: Adapted from Patricia Cinelli, "Five People, Five Career Paths," *Computerworld,* Campus edition, October 28, 1988, pp. 22–24.

Career Path: Information Systems

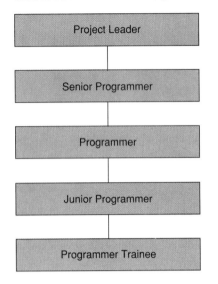

The *programmer trainee* usually has very limited experience in programming. The trainee is closely supervised and gets training in programming, coding, and flowcharting.

Junior programmers generally have less than two years of experience in programming. They usually work as members of a team. Some programming projects may take two or three years to complete the full installation. Responsibilities may include writing the program code, preparing test data, testing and debugging the program, writing documentation, and updating existing programs.

A *programmer* usually has two or more years' experience and is expected to be able to work independently or in groups. Programmers may continue to work as a part of a team under supervision because of the need to coordinate the work of several people working on the same project. They may work on designing new computer applications or modifying existing programs.

The *senior programmer,* or *lead programmer,* works without supervision and has about five years' experience. The senior programmer acts as a liaison with other technical departments and works closely with systems analysts. Senior and lead programmers have dual responsibilities in programming and supervising other programmers.

The *project leader* heads the team of programmers on large projects. Responsibilities include planning and coordinating the work of the team and assigning and monitoring the work. The project leader estimates and monitors the amount of time needed to complete the project and maintains the budget.

---

reported. The IRS provides extensive classroom training in aspects of tax law, fraud examination, and research techniques.

Additional Accounting Resources

American Accounting Association
5717 Bessie Drive
Sarasota, FL 33583

American Institute of Certified Public
  Accountants
1211 Avenue of the Americas
New York, NY 10036

American Society of Women
  Accountants
Suite 1036
35 E. Wacker Drive
Chicago, IL 60601

Association of Government Accountants
Suite 120
727 South 23rd Street
Arlington, VA 22202

Institute of Internal Auditors, Inc.
249 Maitland Avenue
Altamonte Springs, FL 32701

National Association of Accountants
919 Third Avenue
New York, NY 10022

INFORMATION SYSTEMS

The computer industry is a fast-paced, rapidly changing business. You don't have to be a technical whiz kid to be successful in the computer industry, but you do have to be excited about the world of computers.

Career opportunities in the computer field have skyrocketed. Computer-based occupations are among the fastest growing in the job market. Businesses across all industries employ computer personnel. Almost 2 million computer-related jobs exist today.

The strong demand for experienced, skilled people is expected to continue. Building a strong base of experience and keeping up on the latest developments are very important to a successful career. Most beginning opportunities for

Requirements: Information Systems

Personal skills:
• Analytical
• Communications
• Mathematical

Education:
• Bachelor's degree
• Master's degree
• Major in information systems

---

college graduates are in programming and systems analysis.

Programmers

Computer programmers prepare specific instructions for a computer to make it perform the desired operation. Broadly speaking, there are two types of computer programmers: systems programmers and applications programmers. *Systems programmers* work with the operating systems software that

Information System Titles

Project leader	EDP auditor
Systems analyst	Data security specialist
Programmer Analyst	Training specialist
Junior programmer	Systems consultant
Database administrator	Marketing representative

runs the entire computer system—the computer itself, the terminals, printers, and disk drives. *Applications programmers* write the series of logical steps to accomplish a certain task—the application. In a business setting, an application might be to pay the company's bills or to calculate and issue the company's monthly payroll.

In the field of information systems, initial assignments for new hires are typically in programming. Because programming is the basic building block for all computer systems, experience in programming is important to a career in information systems. Programmers may move into systems analysis after 1 to 2 years of programming experience and then into management responsibilities later. However, many choose to remain in applications programming and advance to senior or lead programmer. The lead programmer usually supervises several other programmers and directs a programming project.

Systems Analysts

Systems analysts are essential in shifting from manual methods of doing business to computerized methods. They help define the exact nature of an information problem and then design a more efficient computerized solution.

Systems analysts work to define information needs and develop systems to solve information problems. They analyze the way a company uses and stores information and then plan, schedule, and coordinate the activities necessary to process data into useful information.

Systems analysts may operate in teams or alone. They work with both the end user of the information and the programmers who program the computer. Analysts must be able to understand the overall business operations and have a good understanding of the goals and problems of the information user. They also must be familiar with current data processing methods and computers. A background in programming is very helpful, and many employers require it.

Additional Specialties

As computers became increasingly important and spread throughout businesses, more and more specialties developed within the field. Opportunities have grown in a variety of areas beyond programming and systems analysis. New jobs have emerged for experienced, knowledgeable people in distinctive areas such as data communications, technical writing, telecommunications, database administration, and data security.

Additional Information Systems Resources

American Federation of Information
  Processing Societies
1899 Preston White Drive
Reston, VA 22091

American Society for Information
  Science
1010 16th Street, N.W.
Washington, DC 20036

Association for Systems Management
24587 Bagley Road
Cleveland, OH 44138

Association of Computer Programmers
  and Analysts
P.O. Box 95
Kensington, MD 20795

Data Processing Management
  Association
505 Busse Highway
Park Ridge, IL 60068

Glossary

Absolute Advantage   The advantage held by a nation that can produce a product more efficiently than any other nation.

Account   Record of all transactions affecting a particular financial statement element. Separate accounts are maintained for each asset, liability, equity, revenue, and expense.

Accounting   The process of identifying, measuring, and communicating economic information to permit informed judgments and decisions by users of the information.

Accounting Cycle   The steps— analyzing, recording, posting, and preparing reports—by which the results of business transactions are communicated.

Accounting Equation   Assets = Liabilities + Owners' equity; indicates a company's financial position at any point in time and is the framework of the entire accounting process.

Accounts Receivable Turnover   An activity ratio that tells the number of times per year that the average accounts receivable is collected; computed by dividing net sales by average net accounts receivable.

ACH   See **Automated Clearinghouse.**

Acid-Test Ratio   See **Quick Ratio**.

Activity Ratio   Measure (e.g., accounts receivable turnover) of how efficiently assets are being used to generate revenues.

Actuary   An insurance employee who predicts the likelihood of future events, based on their occurrence in the past.

ADA   See **Americans with Disabilities Act.**

Administered VMS   A marketing channel in which independent organizations use informal

coordination, generally dominated by one large and powerful channel organization.

Administrative Law   Regulation affecting business, passed by state and federal administrative agencies.

Advertising   A paid form of nonpersonal communication to a target audience through a mass medium such as television, newspapers, or magazines.

Advertising Media   Advertising outlets, including newspapers, television, direct mail, radio, magazines, and outdoor displays.

Affirmative Action Program Program begun and carried out by a business to increase the number of women, minorities, and handicapped individuals throughout the organization.

AFL–CIO   The merged body of the American Federation of Labor and the Congress of Industrial Organizations.

Agency   A legal relationship between two parties who agree that the agent will act on behalf of the principal.

Agency Shop   A company where all employees pay union dues, whether or not they are union members.

Agent   A wholesaler hired by a buyer or seller on a permanent basis and paid commissions.

Allocation   The process of choosing how resources will be used to meet a society's needs and wants; includes the distribution of products to consumers.

Americans with Disabilities Act (ADA)   A comprehensive antidiscrimination law, passed in 1990, aimed at integrating the disabled into the American work force; prohibits all employers from discriminating against disabled employees or applicants.

Anti-Injunction Act   See **Norris-LaGuardia Act.**

Arbitrator   Third party to a labor dispute who makes the final, binding decision about some disputed issue.

Arithmetic-Logic Unit   The part of a computer's central processing unit that performs computations.

Artificial Intelligence   A developing technology that allows computers to solve problems involving imagination, abstract reasoning, and common sense.

Assembly Line   A production line made up of workers who each perform one specific task as the product moves past, toward completion. Also, a moving conveyor belt that carries work from one workstation to the next.

Asset   Anything of value owned by the business and used in its operation.

ATM   See **Automated Teller Machine.**

Atmosphere   The design of a store's physical space.

Audit   A CPA's examination of a company's financial statements in order to express an opinion about the fairness of the statements in accordance with generally accepted accounting principles.

Autocratic Leadership   A type of close supervision in which the manager delegates as little authority as possible.

Automated Clearinghouse (ACH)   A system that allows payments or withdrawals to and from a bank account by magnetic computer tape. Expensive to implement, ACH systems are only efficient for large batch processing.

Automated Teller Machine (ATM)   Machine that dispenses cash from a customer's account, accepts deposits to the account, or performs other banking functions 24 hours a day, either at the bank or from remote sites.

Balance of Payments   The total flow of money into and out of a country; determined by a country's balance of

trade, foreign aid, foreign investments, military spending, and money spent by tourists in other countries.

Balance of Trade   The difference (expressed in monetary terms) between the amount a country exports and the amount it imports. A nation that exports more than it imports has a *trade surplus*; one that imports more than it exports has a *trade deficit*.

Balance Sheet   A financial statement that indicates a firm's financial position at a particular moment in time; reflects a firm's solvency or its ability to pay its debts as they come due. Also called a statement of financial position.

Bankruptcy   The legal procedure for individuals and businesses that cannot pay their debts.

Barter   The exchange of goods without using money.

Bear Market   A market state in which stock values are generally declining and investors are generally pessimistic.

Behavior Modification   The application of a set of learning principles, called operant conditioning, developed by psychologist B. F. Skinner; based on the concept that behavior depends on its consequences: if consequences are favorable, the behavior will probably be repeated.

Benefits   Forms of indirect compensation that are financial in nature; examples include health insurance and pension fund contributions.

Blue-Chip Stock   Stock issued by a large, well-capitalized company that consistently pays dividends.

Blue-Sky Law   State law that prevents corporations from issuing worthless securities to unsuspecting investors and requires stockbrokers to be licensed and securities to be registered prior to their sale.

Bond   A form of long-term debt financing that is an agreement between a firm and an investor, with specific terms spelled out in an indenture.

Book Value   Pertaining to stocks, the value of the stock relative to the value of the company: the value of all assets minus the value of all liabilities and preferred stock, divided by the number of shares of common stock outstanding.

Boycott   A bargaining tactic in which the union refuses to do business with a firm or attempts to get people or other organizations to refuse to deal with the firm.

Brand   A name, sign, symbol, or design a company uses to distinguish its product from those of competitors.

Brand Name   The part of the brand of a product that can be spoken.

Breach of Contract   The failure of one party to live up to a contractual agreement.

Breakeven Analysis   A determination of how many product units must be sold at various prices for a firm to recover costs and begin making a profit.

Breakeven Quantity   The point (the number of product units) at which the total revenue for all units sold is equal to the total cost of all units sold.

Broker   A wholesaler who brings together buyers and sellers on a temporary basis.

Bull Market   A market state in which stock values are generally rising and investors are generally optimistic.

Business   The exchange of goods, services, or money for mutual benefit or profit.

Business Enterprise   An organization involved in exchanging goods, services, or money to earn a profit.

Business Ethics   The evaluation of business activities and behavior as right or wrong.

Business Plan   A written document that describes the business, product, customers, competition, financing, and all activities necessary to enter business and make or sell a product.

Business Profit   The difference between business income (revenue) and business expenses (costs); the selling price of a product minus all costs of making and selling it, including taxes.

Business Representative   A union official who negotiates and administers the labor agreement and settles contract problems; also collects dues, recruits new members, coordinates social activities, and arranges union meetings.

Business Trust   A business used to hold securities for investors; allows the transfer of legal title to a property of one person for the use and benefit of another.

Business-Interruption Insurance   Coverage that provides funds for the ongoing expenses of a business forced by disaster to shut down temporarily.

CAD   See **Computer-Aided Design**.

CAE   See **Computer-Aided Engineering**.

Call Option   An option to buy stock shares at a specified price and sell them at market price.

CAM   See **Computer-Aided Manufacturing.**

Cancellation Provision   The contract provision giving a franchisor the power to cancel an arrangement with a franchisee.

Capital Budgeting   The process of comparing and evaluating alternatives in order to budget funds for future, generally major, investments that are usually ranked on the basis of their return potential.

Capital Resources   Goods produced for the purpose of making other types of goods and services; includes current assets (short-lived) and fixed capital (long-lived).

Capitalism   A type of economic system characterized by private ownership of capital, competition

among businesses seeking a profit, and consumers' freedom of choice.

Cascade Approach   A procedure for setting objectives in which the objectives are set from the top level of management down.

Catalog Showroom   A showroom, similar to a warehouse showroom, that also has catalogs available to customers in the store, as well as in the home.

CD   See **Certificate of Deposit.**

Central Processing Unit (CPU)   The electronic hardware that performs the computer operations and controls the entire system.

Centralized Business   An organization in which all, or nearly all, authority to make decisions is retained by a small group of managers.

Certificate of Deposit (CD)   An interest-bearing note issued by a commercial bank or brokerage firm; a time deposit that pays a higher than average rate of interest to the investor.

Certified Management Accountant (CMA)   Designation for an accountant who passes a rigorous examination, has several years of accounting experience, and is licensed by the state; cannot conduct audits of corporate financial statements. May be a public or private accountant.

Certified Public Accountant (CPA)   Designation for an accountant who passes a rigorous examination, has several years of accounting experience, and is licensed by the state; qualified to conduct audits of companies' financial statements. May be a public or private accountant.

Chain of Command   The channel in which communication, coordination, and control flow through the various levels of management to subordinates.

Channel of Distribution   See **Marketing Channel.**

Charter   A state-issued document giving a corporation the right to operate as a business.

Civil Rights Act of 1964   An act that makes various forms of discrimination illegal. Title VII of the act spells out the forms of illegal discrimination.

Closed Shop   A company that hires only workers who are members of the union; illegal under the Taft-Hartley Act.

CMA   See **Certified Management Accountant.**

Code of Ethics   A statement spelling out exactly what an organization considers ethical behavior.

Collective Bargaining   The process by which representatives of management and the union negotiate a labor contract; steps include prenegotiation, selecting negotiators, developing a strategy, using negotiation tactics, and reaching a formal agreement.

Commercial Bank   A profit-making institution that holds the deposits of individuals and businesses in checking and savings accounts and then uses these funds to make loans to individuals, businesses, and the government.

Commercial Paper   A short-term note that represents a loan to a major corporation with a high credit standing.

Commodities   Items, such as raw materials, precious metals, and agricultural products, that can be traded in large volume at a commodities exchange, either in spot market trading or in futures market trading.

Commodity Exchange   An organization that specializes in buying and selling commodities.

Common Law   The body of law created by judges through their court decisions; such decisions establish precedents that later are used in similar cases.

Common Stock   Stock that confers voting rights but does not grant preferential rights of dividends or claims against the assets of the firm.

Common-Size Statements Method of analyzing financial information by expressing various financial statement elements as a percentage of another element of the same statement. All items on a common-size balance sheet are expressed as a percentage of total assets; all common-size income statement items are expressed as a percentage of net revenue.

Comparable Worth The concept of equal pay for jobs that require similar levels of skills, training, and experience.

Comparative Advantage The advantage held by a country that can produce one product more efficiently than other products, in comparison to other nations.

Competition-Oriented Pricing A pricing method whereby a firm sets prices on the basis of its competitors' prices rather than its own costs and revenues.

Computer An electronic device used to input, store, and process data and to output them as useful information.

Computer Network A collection of computers connected so that they can function individually and communicate with each other.

Computer Program A detailed set of instructions written in a computer language.

Computer-Aided Design (CAD) The use of computers to draw plans for a product.

Computer-Aided Engineering (CAE) The use of computers to plan engineering processes and test designs.

Computer-Aided Manufacturing (CAM) The use of computers to guide or control the actual production of goods.

Conceptual Skills The ability to organize and integrate information to better understand the organization as a whole.

Conglomerate Merger A merger involving firms selling goods in unrelated markets.

Consumer A person who purchases a good or service for personal use.

Consumer Buying Behavior The actions and decisions of individuals who purchase products for personal use; choosing can involve routine, limited, or extensive decision making.

Consumer Market People who purchase products for personal use.

Consumer Product A good or service used for personal or family consumption.

Consumer Sales Promotion Activities—including coupons, rebates, samples, gifts, premiums, trading stamps, contests, and sweepstakes—directed at consumers to encourage them to buy certain brands or shop at a particular store.

Consumerism Activities of individuals, groups, and organizations aimed at protecting consumer rights.

Contest Competition in which consumers compete for prizes based on some skill.

Contract A legally enforceable, voluntary agreement between two or more parties.

Contractual VMS A marketing channel in which the member organizations' relationships are formalized through legal agreements.

Contribution Plan Savings and investment plan in which the employee makes contributions (deductions from paychecks), in many cases matched by the employer; such plans, called 401(k) plans, frequently replace pension plans eliminated in industry or corporate restructuring.

Control Unit The part of a computer's central processing unit that guides the operations of the computer.

Controlling The management function of checking to determine whether employees are following plans and progress is being made, and of taking action to reduce discrepancies between performance and plans.

Convenience Product A frequently purchased, inexpensive item that

buyers spend little effort to find and purchase.

Convenience Store A small retail store in a convenient location and open for long hours; carries limited number of items, usually at prices higher than supermarkets.

Cooperative (Co-op) An organization in which people collectively own and operate a business in order to compete with larger businesses.

Copyright Protection of a creator's exclusive right to publish and sell original written materials; filed with the U.S. Copyright Office.

Corporate VMS A marketing channel in which one organization owns all stages of the channel.

Corporation A business that is a legal entity separate from its owners, having the rights of a legal person to own property, purchase goods and services, and sue other persons or corporations.

Cost-Oriented Pricing A pricing method whereby a firm determines a product's total cost, then adds a markup to that cost to achieve the desired profit margin.

Countertrading Bartering agreements between two or more countries.

Coupon Certificate providing a price reduction for consumers who buy a specific product; distributed by manufacturers and retailers.

CPA See **Certified Public Accountant.**

CPU See **Central Processing Unit.**

Craft Union A union in which all members belong to one craft or to a closely related group of occupations.

Credit An entry that records a decrease in an asset, an increase in liability, or an increase in owners' equity; recorded on the right side of a journal or ledger entry.

Credit Unions Member-owned savings cooperatives, normally sponsored by a union, company, or professional or religious group. Typically they concentrate on savings accounts and short-term consumer loans, although with deregulation some now offer share draft accounts and some long-term mortgages.

Currency   The coins and paper money spent to purchase things; represents about 20–25 percent of the total M_1 money supply. Cashier's checks, money orders, and traveler's checks are also considered currency.

Current Assets   Cash plus items that can or will be converted to cash and used within one year; the most liquid of a firm's assets.

Current Liabilities   Financial obligations of a firm that will be repaid within one year.

Current Ratio   A liquidity ratio that measures a firm's ability to pay its current liabilities from its current assets; computed by dividing current assets by current liabilities.

Data   Unorganized facts, statistics, and predictions concerning people, objects, events, and ideas.

Data Processing   Mechanically transferring raw data into some specific form of information.

Database   An integrated collection of data stored in one place for easy access and information processing.

Database Management System (DBMS)   Computer software that helps firms manage various data files. Examples include dBASE III PLUS®, R:BASE®, Rapidfile, and PC–File.

DBMS   See **Database Management System.**

Debit   An entry that records an increase in assets, a decrease in liabilities, or a decrease in owners' equity; recorded on the left side of a journal or ledger entry.

Debit Card   A plastic card, similar to a credit card, that transfers funds directly from the customer's account to the seller's rather than creating a loan.

Debt Capital   Funds obtained through borrowing.

Debt Ratio   Measure of a company's ability to pay its long-term debts. Two such ratios are the debt to total assets ratio and the times interest earned ratio.

Debt to Total Assets Ratio   A debt ratio that measures a company's ability to carry long-term debt; computed by dividing total liabilities by total assets.

Decentralized Business   An organization in which a significant amount of the authority to make decisions is delegated to lower-level managers.

Decertification   The process, guided by the National Labor Relations Board, that results in voting out a union that has been representing employees.

Decision Support System (DSS)   A system that enables managers to instantly access information on past and current performance; less structured format than in a management information system.

Deductible   The amount of loss that the insured agrees to cover before insurance coverage begins.

Default   The failure to pay the interest on a debt instrument.

Delegation   The process by which authority is distributed or pushed downward in an organization; giving an employee at a lower level in the organization the responsibility for a given task as well as the authority to carry it out.

Demand   The quantity of a product that consumers will purchase at various prices.

Demand Deposit   Deposit at a bank against which an account holder can write checks, withdrawing money immediately and without prior notice.

Demand-Oriented Pricing   A pricing method based on the level of demand for the product.

Democratic Leadership   A type of general supervision in which the manager consults with subordinates about job-related issues; also referred to as participative leadership.

Department Store   A large retailer organized into separate departments and offering a full line of services and a wide product mix.

Depreciation   The procedure for speading the cost of a long-term asset over the course of its useful life.

Depression   A period of drastic economic decline, characterized by decreasing business transactions, falling prices, and high rates of unemployment.

Deregulation   The process of reducing government involvement in the regulation of business by eliminating legal restraints on competition.

Desktop Publishing   Producing printed materials using computer software that can do page layouts and formats, insert graphics, and print with high quality.

Direct Compensation   An employee's base pay (wages and salary) and performance-based pay (incentives).

Direct Marketing   Nonstore retailing activities that use nonpersonal media to introduce products to consumers, who then purchase the products by mail, telephone, or computer.

Direct Ownership   The purchase of one or more business operations in a foreign country.

Directing   The management function of initiating action: issuing directives, assignments, and instructions.

Discount Rate   The rate of interest charged to member banks when they borrow money from the Federal Reserve.

Discount Store   A retailer offering a wide variety of general merchandise at low prices and with minimum services.

Division of Labor The principle of organization that a job can be performed more efficiently if the jobholder is allowed to specialize; involves dividing a major task into separate smaller tasks.

Domestic Corporation A corporation that conducts business in the state or country in which it is chartered.

Double Taxation The practice of taxing both corporate income and the dividends the corporation issues to individual owners.

Double-Entry Bookkeeping A method of recording business transactions in which offsetting debits and credits keep the accounting equation in balance.

Downsizing Cutting out entire layers of management in the organization.

DSS See **Decision Support System.**

Dumping The practice of selling surplus products in a foreign country at a lower price than in the country of origin.

Earnings Statement See **Income Statement.**

Economic Community An organization that facilitates the movement of products among member nations through the creation of common economic policies.

Economic Profit What remains after both actual expenses and opportunity costs are subtracted from revenue earned.

Economic System The accepted process by which labor, capital, and natural resources are organized to produce and distribute goods and services in a society.

Economics The study of how a society chooses to use scarce resources to produce goods and services and to distribute them to people for consumption.

EEOC See **Equal Employment Opportunity Commission.**

EFT See **Electronic Funds Transfer.**

EIS See **Executive Information System**.

Electronic Funds Transfer (EFT) The transfer of funds by means of an electronic terminal, telephone, computer, or magnetic tape that orders a bank or other financial institution to debit (reduce) or credit (increase) an account.

Electronic Mail A computer network used to relay messages from one user to another instantly.

Embargo A total ban on certain imports and exports.

Endorsement A person's signature on the back of a negotiable instrument, making it transferable.

Entrepreneur A person who takes the risks necessary to organize and manage a business and receives the financial profits and nonmonetary rewards.

Equal Employment Opportunity Act of 1972 A law that has specific provisions about equal opportunities for employment; provided for the establishment of the Equal Employment Opportunity Commission.

Equal Employment Opportunity Commission (EEOC) A federal agency whose purpose is to increase job opportunities for women and minorities; empowered to take legal action against companies that discriminate in their employment policies.

Equity Capital Funds obtained in exchange for some ownership in the firm.

Esteem Need The need for self-respect and for respect from others; the fourth level of needs in Maslow's needs hierarchy.

Ethics The principles of behavior that distinguish between right and wrong.

Exchange The process by which one or more parties provide something of value to one another to satisfy the needs of each.

Exchange Controls Restrictions on the amount of a certain currency that can be bought or sold in a nation.

Exchange Rate The rate at which one country's currency can be exchanged for that of another country.

Exclusive Distribution Market coverage in which only one outlet is used in a specific geographic area for distributing a product.

Exclusive Handling A form of control in which a franchisor requires the franchisee to purchase only supplies approved by the franchisor.

Executive Information System (EIS) A user-friendly decision support system designed for executives that requires little computer knowledge and provides instant high-quality displays.

Expenses Decreases in assets or increases in liabilities from the ongoing operation of a business.

Expert System Computer software that imitates human thinking and offers advice on or solutions to complex problems.

Exporting Selling domestic-made goods in another country.

Express Warranty Oral or written assurances made by the seller regarding a product.

Extrinsic Reward Reward external to the work itself and administered by someone else, such as a manager; examples include pay, fringe benefits, recognition, and praise.

Factoring The sale of accounts receivable to a bank or other lender, generally at a considerable discount.

Fed See **Federal Reserve System.**

Federal Reserve System (Fed) Term used to refer to the Federal Reserve Bank, the central bank of the United States. Established by Congress in the Federal Reserve Act of 1913 to control the nation's money supply.

Finance The study of money within the firm; the business function responsible for finding funds, managing them, and determining their best use.

Finance Companies　Institutions that acquire funds by issuing commercial paper or stocks and bonds and use those funds to make short-term loans to individuals and businesses unable to obtain loans elsewhere; typically charge a higher interest rate to cover higher risk.

Financial Future　A future that requires the purchaser to buy or sell a specific financial instrument, such as stocks or Treasury bonds, for a set price at a specific date.

Financial Statement　Document presenting a company's financial position, results of operations, and cash flow during a stated period of time.

Fixed Assets　Relatively permanent assets that a firm expects to use for more than one year; also called plant assets.

Fixed Exchange Rate　An unvarying exchange rate set by government policy.

Flexible Manufacturing Systems (FMS)　The use of computers to change from one production process to another in order to produce different goods.

Float　The amount of money not yet withdrawn from the company's checking account even though checks have been written.

Floating Exchange Rate　An exchange rate that fluctuates with market conditions.

FMS　See **Flexible Manufacturing Systems.**

Foreign Corporation　A corporation that conducts business in a state or country other than the one in which it is chartered.

Form Utility　The value added to materials by changing them into products, giving them useful form.

Formal Authority　The right to give orders.

Formal Organization　The management-designed, official structure of the business.

401(k) Plan　See **Contribution Plan.**

Franchise　The right to use a specific business name (e.g., Pizza Hut, Subway, H & R Block, Blockbuster, Masterworks International) and sell its goods or services in a specific city, region, or country.

Franchisee　The independent owner of a franchise outlet who enters into an agreement with a franchisor.

Franchising　A system for selective distribution of goods and/or services under a brand name through outlets owned by independent business owners; offering a product through use of a contractual agreement in which a supplier (the franchisor) grants a dealer (the franchisee) the right to sell the product(s).

Franchisor　The licensing company in the franchise arrangement.

Free Enterprise　A system in which private businesses are able to start and do business competitively to earn profits, with a minimal degree of government regulation.

Functional Structure　A structure in which each unit or department has a different set of activities and responsibilities.

GATT　See **General Agreement on Tariffs and Trade.**

General Agreement on Tariffs and Trade (GATT)　An agreement, signed in 1947, that formed an international organization to work to reduce or eliminate tariffs and other barriers to international trade.

General and Administrative Expenses　Costs incurred in the overall management of the business.

General Ledger　A book or computer file summarizing all the accounts of a business.

General Partnership　A partnership in which at least one partner has

unlimited liability for the debts of the business and has authority to act and make binding decisions in the business.

Global Market　The worldwide economic marketplace in which business operates today, buying and selling both finished products and labor, material, and energy resources.

GNP　See **Gross National Product.**

Goal　A broadly stated general guideline that an organization or individual is attempting to achieve.

Goal Setting　The process of identifying specific levels of performance to be achieved in a certain time frame.

Golden Handcuffs　A benefit program that makes it too costly for an executive to leave a company, because of benefits that would be forfeited.

Golden Parachute　An executive termination package that provides financial protection by guaranteeing employment or severance pay even when another firm takes over.

Grievance　Complaint made by an employee or the union about a job, person, or condition that creates dissatisfaction or discomfort.

Gross National Product (GNP)　The market value of all final goods and services produced over a one-year period.

Hardware　The physical devices that make up a computer system.

Hawthorne Studies　A series of experiments at a Western Electric plant, conducted from 1927 to 1932, that found that work groups significantly affected the way workers behave and perform.

Health Maintenance Organization (HMO)　An organization that provides extensive medical care and services for members, based on a prepaid monthly fee.

HMO　See **Health Maintenance Organization.**

Home-Based Business   Business in which individual(s) works or conducts activities based in the home.

Horizontal Merger   A merger involving competitive firms in the same market.

Hot-Cargo Agreement   A boycott agreement between management and union that workers may avoid working with materials that come from employers that have been struck by a union; illegal except in the construction and clothing industries.

Human Relations Skills   The ability to relate and interact with subordinates, peers, superiors, and customers or clients.

Human Resource Management (HRM)   The process of acquiring, retaining, terminating, developing, and properly using the human resources in an organization.

Human Resource Planning   The steps taken in estimating the size and makeup of the future work force.

Humanistic Philosophy   A set of moral principles focusing on individual rights and values.

Hygiene Factor   In Herzberg's work motivation model, an external characteristic essential to avoiding job dissatisfaction; factors include pay, job security, personal life, working conditions, status, interpersonal relations, technical supervision, and company policies.

IMF   See **International Monetary Fund.**

Immigration Reform and Control Act (IRCA)   A law, passed in 1986, that places on employers a major responsibility to stop the flow of illegal immigrants into the United States by not employing unauthorized aliens.

Implied Warranty   Warranty legally imposed on the seller; ensures that the seller owns the products and that they will serve the purpose for which they are sold.

Import Tariff   A duty, or tax, levied against goods brought into a country.

Importing   Purchasing goods made in another country.

Income Statement   A financial statement showing a firm's revenues, expenses, and net income for some period of time; indicates profitability, the ability to generate income. Also called earnings statement or statement of profit and loss.

Incubator   A facility, office, shop, or location in which fledgling businesses can share space, costs, services, and information while their firms grow and become strong enough to leave and operate independently.

Indirect Compensation   Federally required and state-mandated protection programs, private protection programs, paid leave, and miscellaneous benefits.

Individual Retirement Account (IRA)   Retirement savings plan for individuals that are not covered by another retirement plan or that meet certain requirements for adjusted gross income.

Industrial Buying Behavior   The actions and decisions of buyers in organizations, such as producers, resellers, and government agencies.

Industrial Market   Individuals or organizations that purchase products to use in the production of other products or to resell.

Industrial Product   A good or service used by an organization in producing other goods or services or in carrying out its operations.

Industrial Revolution   The development of modern technology and production processes; began in England about 1769 and in America about 1790.

Industrial Union   A union in which all members are employed in a company or industry, regardless of occupation.

Inflation   The rise in the average level of prices for all goods and services in a particular time period, with a corresponding decline in the purchasing power of the dollar.

Informal Organization   The network of personal and social relationships that emerges when people work together.

Information   Useful or relevant data; data organized to meet certain needs.

In-Home Selling   Nonstore retailing activities that involve personal contact with consumers in their homes.

Injunction   Court order that prohibits the defendant from engaging in certain activities, such as strikes.

Input Device   The hardware used to enter data into and make requests of the computer.

Insider Trading   The illegal practice of buying and selling stock on the basis of information gained through positions or through contacts with others that is not available to other investors or the general public.

Institutional Advertising   Advertising used to build goodwill and create a favorable public image.

Insurable Risk   A risk for which an acceptable level of loss can be calculated and that meets the requirements set by the insurer.

Insurance   A written contract that transfers the risk of loss from the insured to the insurer, according to the terms specified in the contract.

Intangible Personal Property   Property represented by a document or other written statement.

Integrated Circuit   Small silicon chip containing dozens of tiny transistors and connections; used in third-generation computers.

Intensive Distribution   Market coverage in which all available outlets are used for distributing a product.

International Business   The performance of business activities across national boundaries.

International Monetary Fund (IMF)   An international financial organization, founded in 1944, that lends money to countries to conduct international trade.

Intrapreneur An entrepreneurial person employed by a corporation and encouraged to be innovative and creative.

Intrinsic Reward A sense of gratification directly related to performing the job; often described as self-administered.

Inventory Management The process of developing and maintaining stocks of products that customers want and need.

Investment Banker Financial expert who handles the sale of new stock or bond offers; advises issuers on timing, pricing, and appropriate size of offerings.

IRA See **Individual Retirement Account.**

IRCA See **Immigration and Reform Control Act.**

JIT See **Just-in-Time.**

Job Analysis The process of determining the tasks that make up a job and the skills, abilities, and responsibilities needed to perform the job.

Job Description A written statement that furnishes information about a job's duties, technology, conditions, and hazards; based on data from the job analysis.

Job Enrichment A motivational technique that involves designing or redesigning a job by incorporating variety, feedback, and autonomy in the job in order to increase the satisfaction and motivation of workers.

Job Evaluation System A process by which the relative values of jobs within the organization are determined.

Job Specification A written statement of the human qualifications, education, and experience needed to perform a job.

Joint Venture Special type of partnership characterized by formal cooperation between two or more businesses to share business decision making, investment risks, and profits in a business venture for a specific time period; may be a partnership between a domestic firm and a firm in a foreign country.

Journal A book or computer file in which business transactions are recorded chronologically.

Junk Bond A low-grade bond that carries a very high risk because it is issued by financially weak companies with no solid collateral, to fund internal expansion or corporate acquisitions and buyouts.

Jurisdiction The right and power of a court to interpret and apply laws and make binding decisions.

Just-in-Time (JIT) An inventory control system that keeps the inventory of parts and materials at the lowest possible level by using suppliers who deliver the fewest possible items at the latest possible moment, just in time to keep production moving smoothly.

Keogh Plan A retirement savings plan for self-employed individuals, who do not have the benefit of a corporate retirement system; entitles individual to contribute up to 20 percent of net income earned from self-employment, up to a maximum of $30,000.

Knights of Labor The first union federation to achieve significant size and influence, attracting members from local unions from all crafts and occupational areas.

Labeling The display of important information on a product package.

Labor-Management Relations Act See **Taft-Hartley Act.**

Labor-Management Reporting and Disclosure Act See **Landrum-Griffin Act.**

Labor Resources The human talent, skills, and competence available in a nation.

Labor Union An organization of employees who join together to protect, maintain, and improve their economic, social, and political power and well-being.

Laissez-Faire Leadership A type of supervision in which the manager avoids power and responsibility by giving assignments and support but staying out of the group's way.

LAN See **Local Area Network System.**

Landrum-Griffin Act A law, passed in 1959, that requires unions and employees to file financial reports with the secretary of labor and that specifies certain activities to ensure democratic operation of the union; also called the Labor-Management Reporting and Disclosure Act.

Large-Scale Integrated (LSI) Circuit Superchip that contains thousands of small transistors; fourth-generation innovation that made personal computers possible.

Law A standard or rule established by a society to govern the behavior of its members.

Law of Large Numbers Mathematical principle involved when insurers use the probability of a specific loss occurring, the likely cost of that loss, and the number of individuals covered to calculate the premiums charged to each insured individual.

Leadership The process of influencing the activities of an individual or group toward accomplishing objectives; may be autocratic, democratic, or laissez-faire.

Leverage The use of long-term debt to raise needed cash.

Liability Amounts owed by a business to its creditors.

Liability Insurance Protection for losses from injury to another individual or from damage to other people's property.

Licensing An agreement in which one firm (the licensor) allows another firm (the licensee) to sell its product and use its brand name in return for a commission or royalty.

Limit Order   A market order in which the broker is authorized to purchase the stock only if the price is at or below a specified price.

Limited Partnership   A partnership in which at least one owner is a general partner and one or more are limited partners, who are liable for loss only up to the amount of their investment.

Line Authority   Unquestioned, direct authority over lower positions in the hierarchy.

Line of Credit   A preapproved amount of money the holder may borrow, in whole or in part, provided the bank has funds available.

Liquidity   The ease (speed) with which an asset can be converted into cash.

Liquidity Ratio   Measure of a firm's ability to pay its short-term debts as they come due. Two common liquidity ratios are the current ratio and the quick (acid-test) ratio.

Local Area Network (LAN) System   A system of telecommunications links that connects all computers in one firm directly, without telephone lines.

Lockout   Management pressure tactic that involves denying employees access to their jobs.

Long-Term Liabilities   Amounts owed by a business that must be repaid more than one year from the balance sheet date.

LSI Circuit   See **Large-Scale Integrated Circuit.**

M₁ The first level of money supply measurement; includes the most highly liquid forms of money: currency and demand deposits.

M₂ The second level of money supply measurement; includes time deposits and money market accounts in addition to currency and demand deposits.

Main Memory   The part of the computer's central processing unit that stores data and instructions.

Mainframe   The largest and fastest type of computer, with the greatest storage capacity.

Maintenance of Membership Agreement   Agreement that, although employees do not have to join a union, union members must maintain membership in the union over the length of the contract.

Malpractice Insurance   Coverage that protects professionals (doctors, lawyers, etc.) from losses due to injury caused by the improper handling of their responsibilities.

Management   The application of planning, organizing, staffing, directing, and controlling functions in the most efficient manner possible to accomplish organizational objectives.

Management Development   The process of educating and developing selected personnel so that they have the knowledge, skills, attitudes, and understanding needed to manage in future positions.

Management Information System (MIS)   A combination of computers and procedures for providing information that managers use in making decisions.

Management Skills   The ability to use knowledge, behaviors, and aptitudes to perform a task; classified as technical, human relations, and conceptual skills.

Managerial Hierarchy   The levels of management in an organization, typically three distinct levels: executive, middle, and first line; usually portrayed as a pyramid.

Manufacturing   The actual processes of making products out of materials and parts: literally, creating something by the work of one's hands.

Margin Trading   Purchasing more stock shares than a given amount of money would buy because a portion of the shares are bought on credit.

Market   A group of people who need and want a product and have the ability, willingness, and authority to purchase it; may be consumer market or industrial market.

Market Coverage   The number of outlets in which a product is sold.

Market Order   An investor's order that authorizes the broker to purchase stock at the current market price.

Market Segment   A group of individuals or organizations with one or more similar product needs.

Market Segmentation Approach   The division of the total market into segments, with a marketing mix directed to one of the segments.

Market Value   Pertaining to stocks, the price at which the stock is currently selling.

Marketing   The process of planning and executing the conception, pricing, promotion, and distribution of ideas, goods, and services to create exchanges that satisfy individual and organizational objectives.

Marketing Channel   A group of interrelated organizations that directs the flow of products from producers to ultimate consumers; also called channel of distribution.

Marketing Concept   A management philosophy of striving to satisfy customers' needs through a coordinated set of activities that also allows the organization to achieve its objectives and long-term success.

Marketing Environment   All the forces outside an organization that directly or indirectly influence its marketing activities; forces include competition, government and industry regulation, politics, society, economic conditions, and technology.

Marketing Intermediary   An individual or organization in a marketing channel that provides a link between producers, other channel members, and final consumers.

Marketing Mix   The combination of four elements—product, price, promotion, and distribution—used to satisfy the needs of the target market.

Marketing Research The systematic gathering, recording, and analyzing of information for guiding marketing decisions.

Marketing Research Process Series of steps involved in marketing research; steps include problem definition, research design, data collection, data analysis, interpretation, and conclusions.

Marketing Strategy An overall plan for conducting marketing activities to enable the organization to use its resources and strengths to meet the needs of the marketplace; includes two steps: (1) select and analyze a target market and (2) design and maintain a marketing mix that will satisfy the target market.

Markup In cost-oriented pricing, a percentage added to the total cost of the product to cover marketing expenses and allow a profit.

Mass Production Rapid manufacture of large quantities of goods accomplished through division of labor, specialization, and standardization.

Master Limited Partnership (MLP) A partnership that sells units traded on a recognized stock exchange; has many advantages of a corporation but does not pay corporate taxes.

Materials Handling The physical handling of products during transportation and warehousing.

Materials Requirements Planning (MRP) A computerized forecasting system used to plan the ordering of parts and materials for manufacturing.

Matrix Structure A functional structure combined with either a product or a project structural arrangement.

Mediator Third party to a labor dispute who tries to get union and management to reason and works at improving communication between them; typically full-time employees of the Federal Mediation and Conciliation Service.

Mentor A role model who provides orientation, emotional support,

coaching, and insight to new employees.

Mercantilism A system of state power, with public authority controlling and directing the nation's economic life.

Merchant Wholesaler A marketing intermediary that takes ownership of goods and the risks associated with ownership, then sells the goods to retailers, other wholesalers, or industrial users.

Merger The combination of two or more business enterprises into a single entity.

MESBIC See **Minority-Enterprise Small-Business Investment Company.**

Microcomputer A personal, self-contained computer, including a cathode ray tube (monitor) and a keyboard, that is movable and usually fits on a desk or table.

Minicomputer A smaller, slower version of the mainframe computer.

Minority-Enterprise Small-Business Investment Company (MESBIC) A small-business investment company owned and operated by minority-group members: established industrial or financial concerns, private investors, or business-oriented economic development organizations.

MIS See **Management Information System.**

Mixed Economy An economy in which both the government and private business enterprises produce and distribute goods and services.

MLP See **Master Limited Partnership.**

Money Anything commonly accepted as a means of paying for the goods and services individuals need and want.

Money Market Accounts Deposits that earn interest rates very competitive with those paid on other short-term investments; some allow account holder to write a limited number of checks in amounts over $500.

Moral Philosophy The set of principles that dictate acceptable behavior; learned from family, friends, co-workers, and other social groups and through formal education.

Motivation The way drives or needs direct a person's behavior toward a specific goal; involves the level of effort put forth to pursue the goal.

Motivator In Herzberg's work motivation model, a content-oriented characteristic that contributes to job satisfaction; motivators include achievement, recognition, advancement, the job itself, growth opportunities, and responsibility.

MRP See **Materials Requirements Planning.**

Multinational Corporation A firm that operates on a global basis, as if the entire world were a single market.

Municipal Bonds Bonds issued by states, towns, and other municipalities to finance schools, hospitals, roads, and other civic projects.

Mutual Fund A fund formed by a group of individual investors, who pool their money to invest in securities, and usually handled by a professional investment manager.

NASDAQ National Association of Securities Dealers Automated Quotation System.

National Labor Relations Act See **Wagner Act.**

National Labor Relations Board (NLRB) A board that investigates cases of alleged unfair labor practices by employers and unions and holds elections to determine whether groups of employees want to be unionized.

Natural Resources Resources that nature provides in limited amounts, including crude oil, natural gas, minerals, timber, and water.

Need for Achievement A strong desire to succeed, to grow, to accomplish challenging tasks.

Needs Hierarchy Psychologist Abraham Maslow's motivational theory that people have five basic needs arranged in a hierarchy:

physiological, safety, social, esteem, and self-actualization. Each higher-order need has the power to motivate behavior only when lower-level needs have been fulfilled.

Negative Reinforcer   A consequence of behavior, such as a reprimand, that when administered encourages employees to adopt more desirable behavior to avoid the unpleasant consequence.

Negotiable Instrument   A written promise (e.g., check, draft, certificate of deposit) to pay a specified sum of money; may be transferred from one person or business to another.

Net Income   The excess of revenues over expenses; also called the bottom line.

NLRB   See **National Labor Relations Board.**

Nonprice Competition   The emphasis on aspects other than price, such as quality, service, and promotion, to differentiate products in the marketplace.

Nonprofit Corporation   An incorporated enterprise (e.g., university, charity, church) that is not driven by a profit-seeking motive.

Nonstore Retailing   Retailing that takes place outside of stores; can be in-home selling, direct marketing, or vending machines.

Norris-LaGuardia Act   A 1932 law that limited the power of federal courts to stop union picketing, boycotts, and strikes and that made the yellow-dog contract unenforceable; also called the Anti-Injunction Act.

Objectives   Specific, desired results to be reached by a certain time.

Occupational Safety and Health Act (OSHA)   Law, passed in 1970, that mandates safety and health standards for U.S. businesses. Provided for the establishment of the Occupational Safety and Health Administration.

Occupational Safety and Health Administration (OSHA)   A federal agency with the primary purpose of ensuring safe working conditions.

Establishes and enforces safety standards in the workplace, covering all employees except government workers and those protected under specific employment acts.

Odd Lot   A stock purchase of less than 100 shares; generally more expensive to trade than round lots.

Open Shop   A company in which employees do not have to join a union or pay dues but can decide without pressure whether to become union members.

Operating Employees   The nonmanagers in an organization, who perform specific tasks and usually manufacture a product or provide a service for customers.

Operating Expenses   All the costs of doing business except the cost of sales.

Operations   Any function(s) needed to carry out a strategic plan, to keep the company producing.

Opportunity Cost   The cost of choosing to use resources for one purpose while sacrificing the next-best alternative for the use of those resources.

Order Getter   A salesperson who recruits new customers and increases sales to current customers.

Order Processing   The receipt and preparation of an order for shipment.

Order Taker   A salesperson who processes repeat sales and maintains positive relationships with customers.

Organization Chart   A graphic blueprint, or map, of positions, people, and formal authority relationships in the organization; the formal structure of the business.

Organization Structure   The arrangement of work to be done in a business.

Organizing   The management function of grouping people and assignments to properly carry out job tasks and the organization's mission.

OSHA   See **Occupational Safety and Health Act** and **Occupational Safety and Health Administration.**

OTC   See **Over-the-Counter Market.**

Output Device   The hardware that displays the computer's requests or processed data. The most commonly used are the display screen and the printer; others include disks, magnetic tapes, graphic plotters, and even the spoken word.

Over-the-Counter (OTC) Market   An electronic network of several thousand brokers who communicate trades through the National Association of Securities Dealers Automated Quotation System (NASDAQ).

Owners' Equity   Claims of owners, partners, and shareholders against the firm's assets; the excess of assets over all liabilities.

Packaging   The development of a container and a graphic design that will identify, protect, and attract attention to a product.

Partnership   The association of two or more people as co-owners of a business for profit.

Patent   The exclusive right, granted by the U.S. Patent and Trademark Office, of an inventor to make, use, or sell the registered product for 17 years; not renewable.

Personal Selling   Person-to-person communication with one or more prospective customers in order to make a sale.

PERT   See **Program Evaluation and Review Technique.**

Physical Distribution   Activities that involve the movement of products through marketing channels from manufacturer to consumer: establishing customer service standards, selecting transportation modes, designing and operating warehouse facilities, handling products, and managing inventory.

Physiological Need   Biological need, such as for food, air, and water; the first level of needs in Maslow's needs hierarchy.

Pioneer Pricing   The new-product pricing strategies of charging the highest possible price to regain costs quickly (price skimming) or setting the price below competitors' prices to build sales quickly (penetration pricing).

Planned Economy   An economy in which the government owns the productive resources, financial enterprises, retail stores, and banks.

Planning   The management function of establishing objectives and developing plans to accomplish them.

Plant Closing Bill   See **Worker Adjustment and Retraining Notification Act.**

Point-of-Purchase Displays Promotional displays, such as signs, posters, freestanding shelves, and video displays, used in retail stores.

Point-of-Sale (POS) System   Along with electronic funds transfer, allows merchants to draw money directly from a customer's bank account at the time a purchase is made.

Pollution   The contamination of air, water, and land.

Positive Reinforcer   A consequence of behavior, such as praise or other rewards, that when administered increases the chances that the behavior will be repeated.

Power of Attorney   A legal document authorizing an agent to act on behalf of the principal.

PPO   See **Preferred Provider Organization.**

Preferred Provider Organization (PPO)   A relatively new form of health care coverage in which the provider negotiates lower prices with certain physicians and hospitals and thereby reduces insurance costs.

Preferred Stock   Stock that has preference over common stock in the payment of dividends and in claims against the assets of the firm, but does not confer voting rights.

Premium   In insurance, a fee paid to the insurance company for protection against loss; in consumer sales promotion, a gift given to a customer for buying a certain product.

Premium or Push Money Additional compensation provided to salespeople to encourage them to sell a product.

Price   The value that buyers exchange for a product in the marketing transaction.

Price Competition   The use of price to differentiate a product in the marketplace.

Price Discounting   A pricing policy of offering buyers deductions from the price of a product.

Price-Earnings Ratio   The current market price of a stock divided by the annual earnings per share.

Pricing Method   A systematic procedure for determining prices on a regular basis; considers costs, product demand, or competitors' prices.

Primary-Demand Advertising Advertising used to create or increase demand for all products in a product group.

Principle   A guideline that managers can use in making decisions.

Private Accountant   An accountant working in any position not included in public accounting; may work in management accounting, government accounting, or academia.

Product   A good, service, or idea, including all the tangible and intangible characteristics provided in an exchange between buyer and seller.

Product Differentiation   The use of advertising, packaging, or other product characteristics to distinguish and establish the superiority of a product.

Product Liability   Area of tort law that holds business firms responsible for negligence in design, manufacture, sale, and operation of their products.

Product Liability Insurance Coverage for losses for injuries caused by the use of a company's products.

Product Life Cycle   The theoretical life of a product, consisting of four stages: introduction, growth, maturity, and decline.

Product Line   A group of related products considered a unit because of marketing, technical, or use similarities and marketed by a firm.

Product Mix   The total group of products a firm offers for sale, or all of the firm's product lines.

Product Modification   The changing of one or more of a product's characteristics as a strategy to extend its life cycle.

Product Structure   An organization structure in which a manager is placed in charge of and has responsibility for a product or product line.

Production   The total process by which a company produces finished goods or services; also, the total amount of product brought forth.

Productivity   The rate at which goods and services are created.

Professional Pricing   A pricing policy—practiced by doctors, lawyers, and others with skills or experience in a particular field—of charging a standard fee for a particular service.

Professional Service Organization An organization of professional people, organized under professional association laws and treated as a corporation for tax purposes.

Profit Motive   Expected or actual returns (profits) that motivate business leaders to do what must be done in a business venture.

Profitability Ratio   Measure of a firm's financial performance that compares earnings to sales or investments. Two common profitability ratios are return on sales and return on equity.

Program Evaluation and Review Technique (PERT)   A production planning technique that tracks a project's progress and enables management to make the best allocation of resources to the activities required to complete the project.

Progressive Tax   Form of taxation in which the percentage of income paid in taxes increases as income increases.

Promissory Note   A legally binding promise of payment that spells out the terms of a loan agreement.

Promotion   The communication of favorable, persuasive information about a firm or product in order to influence potential buyers.

Promotion Mix   The combination of advertising, personal selling, sales promotion, and publicity used to promote a specific product.

Property Insurance   Protection for losses due to physical damage to or destruction of property or for property loss due to theft; includes two options: replacement-cost coverage or depreciated-value coverage.

Prospectus   A statement containing information about a firm, its management, its operations, the purpose for a stock issue, and other information that might be helpful to a potential buyer of securities.

Protection Programs   Programs that assist employees and families when direct compensation is terminated and with health care expenses.

Proxy   A written statement, signed by a shareholder of a corporation, allowing someone else to cast his or her number of votes.

Psychological Pricing   A pricing policy that encourages purchase decisions based on emotion rather than reason; includes odd-even pricing, customary pricing, prestige pricing, and price lining.

Public Accountant   An accountant who works for a firm that provides accounting services to companies, other organizations, and the general public on a fee-for-service basis; typical areas of service include auditing, tax consulting, and management consulting.

Public Relations   A set of communications activities designed to create and maintain a favorable public image for a firm.

Publicity   A nonpersonal form of communication transmitted in news story form and not paid for directly by a sponsor; a part of public relations.

Pull Strategy   Promotion of a product directly to consumers to stimulate strong consumer demand, which "pulls" the product into stores.

Punishment   An undesirable consequence of a particular behavior; one example would be docking the pay of a frequently tardy worker.

Pure Risk   The threat of loss with no chance of profit.

Push Strategy   Promotion of a product to wholesalers or retailers in the marketing channel, who in turn promote, or "push," the product to consumers.

Put Option   An option to buy stock shares at market price and sell them at a specified price.

Quality Circles   A method of grouping employees in small units that work together to improve quality and processes to further the company's goals; usually consists of 7 to 11 people working in a related area.

Quality of Work Life (QWL) Managerial programs designed to improve the quality of human experience in the workplace. They increase outcomes such as productivity or performance by better management of jobs, people, and working conditions.

Quick Ratio   A liquidity ratio that measures a firm's immediate liquidity; computed by dividing quick assets by current liabilities. Also called acid-test ratio.

Quota   A limit on the amount of a product that can leave or enter a country.

QWL   See **Quality of Work Life**.

Railway Labor Act   The first labor legislation passed by Congress, in 1926, since the Clayton Act; established the process of collective bargaining as a means for resolving labor-management disputes.

Rate of Return   The dollar value of the interest earned or dividend received divided by the market value of the security; sometimes referred to as the risk-return trade-off.

Ratio Analysis   Method of analyzing financial information by comparing logical relationships between various financial statement items.

Real Property   Real estate (land and anything permanently attached to it, such as houses, buildings, and parking lots).

Rebate   A discount given to a consumer who buys a product and sends in proof of purchase; ranges from a small percentage of the purchase price to the full purchase price.

Recession   A period or cycle in which the level of economic activity declines for at least six months.

Recruitment   Steps taken to staff an organization with the best-qualified people.

Recycling   Reusing materials such as paper, plastic, glass, and aluminum to make other products in order to conserve natural resources and reduce the amount of waste.

Reinforcer   A consequence of behavior that improves the chances it will (positive reinforcer) or will not (negative reinforcer) reoccur.

Reserve   The prescribed amount of funds—a percentage of deposits set by the Federal Reserve—that a bank must keep on hand or on deposit in the Federal Reserve Bank.

Retailing   The marketing activities involved in selling products to final consumers for personal or household use.

Retained Earnings   A firm's accumulated net income minus dividends to shareholders.

Return on Equity   A profitability ratio that measures the return the company earns on every dollar of owners' and shareholders' investments; computed by dividing net income by equity.

Return on Sales   A profitability ratio that measures a firm's ability to generate income; computed by dividing net income by net sales.

Revenue   Increase in assets or decrease in liabilities from the ongoing operation of a business.

Revolving Credit Agreement   An agreement that the bank will honor the holder's line of credit up to the stated amount; usually requires payment of a fee.

Right-to-Work Laws   State laws, permitted under the Taft-Hartley Act, requiring that two people doing the same job be paid the same wages, whether or not they belong to the union.

Risk   In insurance, the possibility of suffering an injury or loss; a direct result of uncertainty.

Risk Avoidance   A risk management strategy of not taking on or of getting out of risky ventures.

Risk Management   Minimizing the amount and cost of pure risk a company will face; involves either risk reduction or risk avoidance.

Risk Reduction   A risk management strategy of using loss prevention programs and other management programs to lower the level of risk and the level of liability.

Robot   A computerized, reprogrammable, and multifunctional machine that can manipulate materials and objects in the performance of particular tasks.

Role   A set of expected behaviors.

Round Lot   A stock purchase of 100 shares. Stocks are typically purchased in round lots.

S Corporation   A corporation with 35 or fewer owners that files an income tax return as a partnership to take advantage of lower tax rates.

S&L   See **Savings and Loan**.

Safety Need   Security need, such as the need to be financially secure and protected against job loss; the second level of needs in Maslow's needs hierarchy.

Salaries   Compensation based on a longer time period: a week, a month, or longer.

Sales Branch   A manufacturer-owned wholesaler that takes title to products, assumes the risks of ownership, resells the products, and provides services.

Sales Contest   A competition designed to stimulate sales efforts by offering prizes to salespeople, distributors, or retailers who meet certain sales goals in a specific time period.

Sales Law   Body of law involving the sale of products for money or on credit.

Sales Office   A manufacturer-owned sales force that sells products without maintaining an inventory.

Sales Promotion   A paid form of nonpersonal selling that offers customers, salespeople, or marketing intermediaries direct incentives for purchasing a product.

Sample   A free package or container of a product given to consumers to encourage them to try the product.

Savings and Loan Association (S&L)   Corporation that traditionally offered savings accounts with interest rates higher than banks'. Since deregulation, an S&L offers both checking and savings accounts but still uses the majority of funds to finance home mortgages. Along with savings banks, sometimes called a thrift.

Savings Banks   Depositor-owned, banklike institutions chartered by individual states and almost identical to savings and loans in operation. They began in New England in the early 19th century for the purpose of paying interest on deposits.

SBA   See **Small Business Administration**.

SBIC   See **Small-Business Investment Company**.

Scab   The union label for a strike replacement hired by management.

Scalar Principle   The principle of organization that authority and

responsibility should flow in a clear, unbroken line from the highest to the lowest manager.

Scientific Management   The scientific study and breakdown of work into its smallest mechanical elements, and then rearrangement into their most efficient combination.

Scrambled Merchandising   Adding unrelated products to a firm's existing product mix.

Secured Loan   A loan backed with some form of collateral: property, equipment, inventory, or accounts receivable.

Securities   Documents, such as stocks and bonds, that can be bought or sold and that reflect ownership or debt.

Segmentation Base   The individual or group characteristics that marketing managers use to divide a total market into segments; common bases are geographic, demographic, psychographic, and product-related.

Selection   In employment, a series of steps that starts with the initial screening and ends with a hiring decision.

Selective (Brand) Advertising   Advertising used to sell a specific product or brand.

Selective Distribution   Market coverage in which only some of the available outlets are used for distributing a product.

Self-Actualization Need   The need to use and display one's full range of skills and competence; the fifth and highest level of needs in Maslow's needs hierarchy.

Self-Insurance   A method by which companies assume risk by putting aside cash reserves to cover their potential future losses.

Selling Expenses   Costs incurred in marketing and distributing a firm's goods and services.

Selling Process   A series of steps salespeople perform, consisting of prospecting, preparing, approaching, presenting, answering objections, closing, and following up.

Service Standard   A specific, measurable goal (e.g., on-time delivery) relating to physical distribution activities.

Services   In business, intangible products that cannot be physically possessed and that involve performance or effort; examples include teaching, nursing, air travel, tailoring, accounting, and the opera. In employee compensation, indirect compensation in the form of programs, facilities, or activities supplied by employers for employees' use.

Shopping Product   A good or service that buyers will expend time and effort to find and purchase.

Small Business   A business that is independently owned and operated, is not dominant in its field of operation, and can be started with a moderate investment for that industry.

Small Business Administration (SBA)   An independent agency of the federal government, created in 1953 for the purpose of protecting the interests of small-business owners.

Small-Business Investment Company (SBIC)   A privately owned and operated company licensed by the Small Business Administration to furnish loans to small firms.

Social Audit   An organization's systematic review of its performance in the area of social responsibility activities; assesses the firm's short- and long-run contributions to society.

Social Need   The need to belong and to interact with other people; the third level of needs in Maslow's needs hierarchy.

Social Responsibility   The awareness that business activities have an impact on society, and the consideration of that impact by firms in decision making; making deliberate regular efforts to have an increasingly positive impact on society while reducing negative impact.

Software   A sequence of instructions that a computer can carry out.

Sole Proprietorship   A business owned and managed by one individual.

Span of Control   The principle of organization that limits the number of subordinates reporting to a supervisor.

Specialty Product   A good or service with one or more unique characteristics that a group of buyers will spend considerable time and effort to purchase; not easily substituted.

Specialty Store   A retailer that carries a narrow mix of products with deep product lines.

Speculative Risk   Risk involving the chance of making a profit or taking a loss.

Spreadsheets   Electronic accounting ledgers generated by computer software.

Staff Authority   An advisory authority in which a person studies a situation and makes recommendations but has no authority to take action.

Staffing   The management function of selecting, placing, training, developing, and compensating subordinates.

Stagflation   A stalled economy (stagnation) faced with rising prices (inflation) for goods and services.

Standard of Living   A measure of how well a person or family is doing in terms of satisfying needs and wants with goods and services.

Statement of Cash Flows   Financial statement showing the flow of cash into and out of a business during a period of time.

Statement of Financial Position   See **Balance Sheet**.

Statement of Profit and Loss   See **Income Statement.**

Statute   A law created by a federal, state, or local legislature, treaty, or constitution.

Statutory Law   As a body, the laws enacted by federal, state, and local governments, constitutions, or treaties.

Stock Exchange   An organization of individuals who buy and sell securities to the public.

Stock Option   The purchased right to buy or sell shares of stock at a predetermined price within a specified time period. If the stock price goes up, exercising the option will produce a profit; if the stock price goes down and the option expires, the price paid is forfeited.

Stockbroker   An individual licensed to act on behalf of an investor in the buying and selling of securities.

Strict Product Liability   Legal concept that holds manufacturers responsible for injuries caused by products, regardless of whether negligence was involved.

Strike   A union weapon that involves withholding employees' services to get management to make concessions.

Supercomputer   A computer formed by connecting multiple mainframes.

Supermarket   A large, self-service retailer that stocks a wide variety of groceries and a limited assortment of nonfood products.

Superstore   A giant retail outlet that stocks food and nonfood items as well as most other routinely purchased products.

Supply   The quantity of a product that producers will sell at various prices.

Supply-Side Economics   The theory that reducing the government's role in business by decreasing taxes and limiting government rules and regulations will raise the total amount of goods and services produced.

Support Salespeople   Salespeople who assist in selling by locating potential customers, educating them about products, building goodwill, and providing after-sale service.

Sweepstakes   A sales promotion method in which consumers send in their names to be entered in a drawing for prizes.

Sweetheart Contract   Agreement between union leaders and management to terms that works to their mutual benefit but maintains poor working conditions for other employees.

Syndicate   The joining together of two or more businesses to accomplish specific business goals, usually financial transactions; a form often used in underwriting large amounts of corporation stocks.

Taft-Hartley Act   A law, passed in 1947, that prohibits the closed shop, requires unions to bargain in good faith, and makes it illegal for a union to discriminate against employees who do not join the union; also called the Labor-Management Relations Act.

Tangible Personal Property   Physical items, such as goods and equipment.

Target Market   The market segment to which a firm directs its marketing activities.

Tax   A payment for the support of government activities, required of organizations and individuals within the domain of the government.

T-Bill   See **Treasury Bill.**

Technical Skills   Skills involved in making a product or providing a service.

Term Insurance   Life insurance that covers an individual for a specified number of years but has no value when the term is over.

Territorial Structure   An organization structure in which units are divided on the basis of territory or geographical region.

Theory X   In Douglas McGregor's theory of managerial style, the managerial assumptions that employees dislike work, responsibility, and accountability and must be closely directed and controlled to be motivated to perform.

Theory Y   In Douglas McGregor's theory of managerial style, the managerial assumptions that

employees want to be challenged, like to display creativity, and can be highly motivated to perform well if given some freedom to direct or manage their own behavior.

Theory Z   Management researcher William Ouchi's management theory that emphasizes consensus management practices; draws on the characteristics of successful Japanese and American managers.

Time Deposit   Savings account that allows the financial institution to require notice before withdrawal or to assess a penalty for early withdrawal.

Times Interest Earned Ratio   A debt ratio that measures how many times during the year a business earns the amount of interest it must pay; computed by dividing income before interest and taxes by interest expense.

Title VII   Part of the Civil Service Reform Act of 1978; outlawed certain unfair labor practices and created the Federal Labor Relations Authority (FLRA); granted employees the right to form, join, or assist any labor organization or to refrain from such activity, freely and without reprisals.

Tort   A noncriminal (civil) injury to other persons, their property, or their reputations; results from intentional acts or negligence.

Trade Allowance   A discount a manufacturer gives retailers and wholesalers for performing certain functions or making purchases during a specified time period.

Trade Credit   Credit given to a firm by suppliers for purchases the firm makes.

Trade Sales Promotion   Activities a firm directs to wholesalers, retailers, or salespeople to encourage them to stock or sell its products; includes point-of-purchase displays, trade shows, trade allowances, premium or push money, and sales contests.

Trade Show   A temporary exhibit where manufacturers display and demonstrate products to potential customers and gather names for a list of prospects.

Trademark   A name or symbol registered with the U.S. Patent and Trademark Office, which guarantees the owner exclusive rights to its use for 20 years; such rights are renewable.

Trading Company   A firm that buys products in one country and sells in another without being involved in manufacturing.

Trading Stamps   Stamps given by retailers to customers based on the dollar amount spent; can be saved and redeemed for merchandise.

Training   A continual process of helping employees to perform at a high level.

Transistor   A small switch that controls electrical current; characterized second-generation computers.

Transportation   Shipping goods to customers by rail, air, truck, water, and pipeline.

Treasury Bill   A loan to the U.S. Treasury, typically with a maturity date of three or six months. Often called a T-bill.

Trust   A legal entity set up to hold and manage assets for a designated beneficiary. Funds in a trust are typically invested in stocks, bonds, real estate, and other investments.

UCC   See **Uniform Commercial Code.**

Undifferentiated Approach   The tactic of developing one marketing mix for the total market for a product.

Uniform Commercial Code (UCC)   Comprehensive statutory laws designed to eliminate differences between state laws governing business, thereby simplifying interstate commerce.

Union Shop   A company that requires employees to join the union after being hired.

Union Steward   A person who represents the interests of local union members in their on-the-job relations with managers.

Unity of Command   The principle of organization that no employee should report to more than one superior.

Universal Life Insurance   Life insurance that combines term insurance with a tax-deferred savings account earning interest at bond market rates.

Unlimited Liability   The obligation of investors to use personal assets, when necessary, to pay off debts to business creditors; a disadvantage of sole proprietorships and partnerships.

Unsecured Loan   A loan issued on the good credit of the borrower and not requiring collateral.

Utilitarian Philosophy   A set of moral principles focusing on the greatest good for the largest number of people.

Utility   The ability of a product to satisfy consumers' needs.

Variable Life Insurance   Life insurance that allows the policyholder to determine where the cash value of a policy should be invested.

Venture Capital   Funds provided by individuals or organizations to firms with high potential for growth. The investor receives a share of ownership and frequently some control. Popular with new, small, or struggling businesses.

Vertical Integration   The combining of two or more functions of a marketing channel under one management: one organization in the marketing channel assuming control of another.

Vertical Marking System (VMS)   A planned marketing channel in which all intermediaries are under one manager (a single channel member) to improve distribution.

Vertical Merger   A merger in which a firm joins with its supplier.

Very Large-Scale Integration (VLSI)   Superchip circuitry, resulting from extremely compact transistors and circuits assembled on a single silicon chip; marked start of fifth generation of computers.

VLSI   See **Very-Large Scale Integration.**

VMS   See **Vertical Marketing System.**

Wages   Compensation based on time worked or number of units produced.

Wagner Act   The 1935 law that made collective bargaining legal and required employers to bargain with the representatives of the employees; also referred to as the National Labor Relations Act. Established the National Labor Relations Board.

Warehouse Club   A large discount retail store offering members a broad range of name-brand merchandise at low prices.

Warehouse Showroom   Retail stores with sizable inventories housed in large buildings and dealing in volume while providing limited service.

Warehousing   The receiving, storing, and shipping activities involved in the physical distribution of goods.

WARN   See **Worker Adjustment and Retraining Notification Act.**

Wheel of Retailing   A depiction of the cycle retailers go through as they enter the market, evolve, and become vulnerable to new competitors.

Whistle-Blower   An employee who informs superiors, the media, or a government regulatory agency about unethical behavior within an

organization, often risking great professional and personal danger.

White Knight   A buyer (person or company) considered more favorable by a target firm than the takeover it is facing.

Whole Life Insurance   Life insurance that provides a combination of insurance and savings and stays in force for the life of the insured.

Wholesaling   The marketing activities of intermediaries that sell to retailers, industrial users, and other wholesalers.

Word Processing   Creating written documents with a computer.

Work Motivation Model   Psychologist and consultant Frederick Herzberg's explanation of motivation that defines hygiene factors and motivator factors, and their effect on job satisfaction and dissatisfaction.

Worker Adjustment and Retraining Notification Act (WARN)   The 1989 law that requires employers with 100 or more full-time employees to give affected employees 60 days' written notice of a plant or office closing or other mass layoffs; covers nonprofit businesses but not federal, state, and local governments. Also called the Plant Closing Bill.

Working Capital   Measure of a firm's ability to meet short-term obligations; computed as current assets minus current liabilities.

World Bank   An international organization that lends money to underdeveloped and developing countries to fund the development of roads, factories, and medical facilities.

Yellow-Dog Contract   A statement signed by an employee promising not to form or join a union.

End Notes

Chapter 1

1. Adapted from Jenny C. McCune and Don Wallace, "Never Say Die," *Success,* July–August 1990, pp. 33–36; Michael Selz, "Hold-outs Vow to Remain All-American," *The Wall Street Journal,* July 27, 1990, p. B1; Tim W. Ferguson, "Motorola Aims High, So Motorolas Won't Be Getting High," *The Wall Street Journal,* June 26, 1990, p. A19; John Hill-kirk, "Top Quality Is Behind Comeback," *The Wall Street Journal,* July 27, 1990, p. B1; Jack Fulvey, "How the King Maintains the Edge," *The Wall Street Journal,* April 23, 1990, p. A12.

2. Peter Nulty, "How the World Will Change," *Fortune,* January 15, 1990, pp. 40–54.

3. *Statistical Abstract of the United States,* 1990 (Washington, D.C.: U.S. Department of Commerce), p. 522.

4. Lee Smith, "Fear and Loathing of Japan," *Fortune,* February 26, 1990, pp. 50–60.

5. Ruth Simon and Graham Button, "What I Learned in the Eighties," *Forbes,* January 8, 1990, pp. 100–114.

6. Joseph Schumpeter, *Can Capitalism Survive?* (New York: Harper & Row, 1952), p. 72.

7. David H. Hyman, *Economics* (Homewood, Ill.: Richard D. Irwin, 1989).

8. Paul R. Gregory, *Restructuring the Soviet Economic Bureaucracy* (New York: Cambridge University Press, 1990).

9. Adapted from "A Month Later, Moscow and McDonald's Is Still Drawing Long and Hungry Lines," *Houston Post,* March 1, 1990, p. C4; Marshall I. Goldman, Kevin Maney, and Diane Rinehart, "McDonald's in Moscow Opens Today," *USA Today,* January 31, 1990, pp. 18–28; Steven R. Reed, "A Taste of Capitalism," *Houston Chronicle,* February 1, 1990, pp. 1–2; "Joint Ventures Return to Communist China and the Soviet Union," *Business in the Contemporary World,* Winter 1989, pp. 84–92.

10. Robert L. Heilbroner and Lester C. Thurrow, *Economics Explained* (New York: Simon & Schuster, 1987).

11. Charles C. Man, "The Man with All the Answers," *Atlantic Monthly,* January 1990, pp. 45–62.

12. Eugene N. White, ed., *Crashes and Panics: The Lessons from History* (Homewood, Ill.: Business One Irwin, 1990), p. 145.

13. Adapted from Carla Rapoport, "The Big Split," *Fortune,* May 6, 1991, pp. 38–48; Lorraine Dusky, "Bright Ideas," *Working Woman,* July 1990, pp. 58–63; and Christopher Byron, "Riding on Air," *The Bottom Line,* January 14, 1991, pp. 12–13.

14. David Kirkpatrick, "Environmentalism: The New Decade," *Fortune,* February 12, 1990, pp. 44–56.

15. "You'll Know It's the 21st Century When. . .," *American Demographics*, December 1990, pp. 26–27.

Chapter 2

1. John Case, "With a Little Help from His Friends," *Inc.,* April 1989, pp. 131–44.

2. Louis Rukeyser, *Business Almanac* (New York: Simon & Schuster, 1988), pp. 247–63.

3. Adapted from Jolie Solomon, "Management Secrets," *Working Woman,* June 1990, pp. 53–54, 98–99; "The Best Advice I Ever Got," *Entrepreneur,* February 1989, pp. 102–16.

4. Burt A. Leete, *Business Law: Text and Cases* (New York: Macmillan, 1982), pp. 720–22.

5. *Statistical Abstract of the United States, 1990* (Washington, D.C.: U.S. Department of Commerce), p. 521.

6. G. Christian Hill, "HP Joins Forces with Samsung in Workstations," *The Wall Street Journal,* August 8, 1989, pp. B1–B4.

7. Alexei Badanov and Valery Sumarakov, *JV Archipelago,* October 1990, pp. 30–31.

8. Charalambos Vlachoutsikos, "How Small- to Mid-Sized U.S. Firms Can Profit from Perestroika," *California Management Review,* Spring 1989, pp. 91–112.

9. Gail Rutman, "Should You Incorporate?" *Nation's Business,* May 1990, pp. 46–48.

10. "The Fortune 500," *Fortune,* April 23, 1990, pp. 340–68.

11. Adapted from Working Group On Corporate Governance, "A New Compact for Owners and Directors," *Harvard Business Review,* July–August 1991, pp. 141–43; Elmer W. Johnson, "An Insider's Call For Outside Directors," *Harvard Business Review,* March–April 1990, pp. 46–48, 52–56; "Who's In Charge Here?" *Business Week,* March 19, 1990, pp. 38–39; and "A Seat on the Board Is Getting Hotter," *Business Week,* July 3, 1989, pp. 72–73.

12. "The Best and Worst Deals of the '80s," *Business Week,* January 15, 1990, pp. 52–57.

13. Gary Brenner, Joel Evan, and Henry Custer, *The Complete Handbook For the Entrepreneur* (Englewood Cliffs, N.J.: Prentice Hall, 1990), pp. 94–96.

14. John H. Taylor, "Niche Player," *Forbes,* April 1, 1991, p. 70.

15. Joe Cappo, *Future Scope: Success Strategies for the 1990s and Beyond* (Chicago: Longman Financial Services Institute, 1990), p. 9; John Naisbitt and Patricia Aburdene, *Reinventing the Corporation: Transforming Your Job and Your Company for the New Information Society* (New York: Warner Books, 1985), pp. 251–52; Marvin Cetron and Owen Davies, *American Renaissance* (New York: St. Martin's Press, 1989), pp. 361–62.

Chapter 3

1. Adapted from John Reynolds, "Franchising Explodes into the '90s," *Franchising Opportunities,* February 1990, pp. 13–18; "Chicken on Broker's Menu," *The Houston Post,* August 2, 1991, p. B-1.

2. Robert D. Hisrich and Michael P. Peters, *Entrepreneurship* (Homewood, Ill.: Richard D. Irwin, 1989), p. 9.

3. John R. McLaurin and James A. Johnson, "Entrepreneurism: A New Model for the Coming Decade," *Business Perspectives,* Spring 1989, pp. 47–49.

4. Gary Brenner, Joel Evan, and Henry Custer, *The Complete Handbook For the Entrepreneur* (Englewood Cliffs, N.J.: Prentice Hall, 1990).

5. Gregory Matusky, "The Competitive Edge," *Success,* September 1990, p. 59.

6. Robert M. Rosenberg and Madelon Redell, *Profits from Franchising* (New York: McGraw-Hill, 1969), p. 41.

7. Meg Whittemore, "Changes Ahead for Franchising," *Nation's Business,* June 1990, pp. 49–58.

8. Rosenberg and Redell, *Profits,* p. 12.

9. Adapted from Kevin McLaughlin and Scott Matulis, *Entrepreneur,* January 1989, pp. 132–37.

10. Robert E. Johnson, "E. and G. Graves and Earvin 'Magic' Johnson Buy $60 million Pepsi Franchise," *Jet,* August 20, 1990, pp. 8–10.

11. Rosenberg and Redell, *Profits,* p. 12.

12. Adapted from Jeremy Main, "Why Franchising Is Taking Off," *Fortune,* February 12, 1990, p. 124; Barbara Marsh, "Going for the Golden Arches," *The Wall Street Journal,* May 1, 1989, p. B1; Leon E. Wynter, "How Two Black Franchisees Owe Success to McDonald's," *The Wall Street Journal,* July 25, 1989, p. B1; Mike Connelly, "Corporate Giants Drawn to Franchising," *The Wall Street Journal,* December 30, 1988, p. B1; Ronaleen R. Roha and Adrianne Blum, "The Elusive Affordable Franchise," *Changing Times,* October 1989, pp. 60–68; Elizabeth Birkelund, "The Start-Up: Treading Water until Your Ship Comes In," *Working Woman,* April 1990, pp. 41–44.

13. Carol Steinberg, "Franchise Boom Still in High Gear," *USA Today,* May 8, 1989, p. 8E.

14. Karl H. Vesper, *New Venture Strategies* (Englewood Cliffs, N.J.: Prentice Hall, 1990).

15. Adapted from Suzanne Woolley, "Feathered Nests for Your Fledgling Business," *Business Week,* February 19, 1990, pp. 139–40; Iris Lorenz-Fife, "Incubators Come of Age," *Entrepreneur,* January 1989, pp. 89–98.

16. Jeffrey A. Timmons, *New Venture Creation: Entrepreneurship in the 1990s* (Homewood, Ill.: Business One Irwin, 1990).

17. Martha E. Manglesdorf, "Hotline," *Inc.,* February 1989, p. 20.

18. "Biggest Black Firms Hampered by Economy Slowed by Unemployment," *Jet,* May 28, 1990, p. 27.

19. "Masters of Innovation," *Business Week,* April 10, 1989, p. 58.

20. Stephen Wagner, "25 Best Home-Based Businesses to Start

Right Now," *Increase Opportunities,* March 1990, pp. 47–50, 72, 79; Lynie Arden, "Home-Based Franchises," *Income Opportunities,* March 1990, pp. 51–52, 66, 68, 70.

21. Ray Bard and Sheila Henderson, *Own Your Own Franchise: Everything You Need to Know about the Best Opportunities in America* (Reading, Mass.: Addison-Wesley Publishing, 1987), p. 1; Marvin Cetron with Alicia Pagano and Otis Port, *The Future of American Business: The U.S. in World Competition* (New York: McGraw-Hill, 1985), pp. 146–47.

Chapter 4

1. Michele Galen, "Turn Exxon into Model Environmental Citizen," *Business Week,* May 20, 1991, p. 44; Michele Galen and Vicky Cahan, "The Legal Reef Ahead for Exxon," *Business Week,* March 12, 1990, p. 39; Ken Wells and Charles McCoy, "How Unpreparedness Turned the Alaska Spill into Ecological Debacle," *The Wall Street Journal,* April 3, 1989, pp. A1, A4; Allanna Sullivan and Amanda Bennett, "Critics Fault Chief Executive of Exxon on Handling of Recent Alaskan Oil Spill," *The Wall Street Journal,* March 31, 1989, p. B1; Randy Lee Loftis, "One Year Later, Effects of Alaskan Oil Spill Still Unclear," *Herald-Leader* (Lexington, Ky.), March 24, 1990, p. A2.

2. Ann M. Morrison, "Saving Our Schools," *Fortune,* Spring 1990 (special issue), pp. 8–10.

3. "Newman Has Good Year," *Herald-Leader* (Lexington, Ky.), January 17, 1990, p. A14.

4. *McDonald's and the Environment* (McDonald's Corporation, 1990), pamphlet.

5. "Shopping Guide Rates Companies on Basis of Social Responsibility," *Herald-Leader* (Lexington, Ky.), January 22, 1990, p. D11.

6. William Mueller, "Who's Afraid?" *American Demographics,* September 1990, pp. 40–43.

7. Adapted from Philip Shabecoft, New York Times News Service, "As Sales Fall, Apple Growers Say They Will Stop Using Alar," *Herald-Leader* (Lexington, Ky.), May 16, 1989, pp. A1, A6; Barbara Rosewicz, "Study Finds Alar Residue Even in 'Alar-Free' Produce," *The Wall Street Journal,* March 30, 1989, p. B1.

8. "Dangerous Cars that Are Still on the Road," *Bottom Line Personal,* August 30, 1988, p. 14.

9. "Honest Lee's Used Cars," *Time,* September 5, 1988, p. 53.

10. Sue Shellenbarger, "A Movement to Farm without Chemicals Makes Surprising Gains," *The Wall Street Journal,* May 11, 1989, pp. A1–A9.

11. Associated Press, "Call Blocking May Curb Phone-Service Abuses," *Herald-Leader* (Lexington, Ky.), February 6, 1988, p. A3.

12. Paul Prather, "Company Works to Cut Injury Rate," *Herald-Leader* (Lexington, Ky.), April 2, 1990, pp. A1, A6.

13. "State Farm Is Stuck with a Colossal Claim," *U.S. News & World Report,* February 1, 1988, p. 10.

14. Adapted from Louisiana Land and Exploration Company, "Loss of Louisiana Wetlands," April 1990, pp. 1–24; LL&E, "Louisiana's National Treasure," April 1990; W. L. Berry and G. J. Voisin, "One Company's Experiences with Wetlands Conservation" (Paper presented at the 43rd Annual Convention of the National Association of Conservation Districts, Salt Lake City, Utah, February 1989).

15. Sonia L. Nazario, "Pesticide Regulation, Mainly the States' Job, Is Spotty and Weak," *The Wall Street Journal,* January 18, 1989, pp. A1, A9.

16. Paul Ingrassia and Joseph B. White, "Debate over Pollution and Global Warming Has Detroit Sweating," *The Wall Street Journal,* May 4, 1989, pp. A1, A6.

17. Peter Nulty, "Global Warming: What We Know," *Fortune,* April 9, 1990, pp. 101–5.

18. Vicky Cahan, "Fixing the Hole Where the Rays Come In," *Business Week,* July 2, 1990, p. 58.

19. Rose Gutfeld, "Even Environmentalists Still Use Disposable Diapers," *The Wall Street Journal,* December 26, 1989, p. B1.

20. "Americans Push Aluminum Can Recycling Rate to Record 61%," *USA Today,* August 7, 1990, p. 5D.

21. "Diapers and the Environment" (Procter & Gamble), undated pamphlet.

22. Royce Flippen, "Can Do," *American Health,* September 1989, p. 70.

23. Pete Engardio, Gail DeGeorge, and Jeffrey M. Loderman, "The Penny Stock Scandal," *Business Week,* January 23, 1989, pp. 74–81.

24. Chuck Hawkins, Jon Friedman, and David Greising, "How Pushing Real Estate Backfired on Pru-Bache," *Business Week,* February 26, 1990, pp. 88–91.

25. "To You . . . and Your Money," *Bottom Line Personal,* February 26, 1990, p. 15.

26. Chris Welles and Michele Galen, "Milken Is Taking the Fall for a 'Decade of Greed,'" *Business Week,* December 10, 1990, p. 30.

27. John A. Byrne, Ronald Glover, and Todd Vogel, "Is the Boss Getting Paid Too Much?" *Business Week,* May 1, 1989, pp. 46–52.

28. John A. Byrne, "The Flap Over Executive Pay," *Business Week,* May 6, 1991, pp. 90–96.

29. Byrne, Glover, and Vogel, "Is the Boss Getting Paid Too Much?" p. 48.

30. Todd Vogel, Wendy Zelner, and Monica Roman, "The List Nobody Wants to Be On," *Business Week,* May 1, 1989, p. 50.

31. Monica Roman and Keith H. Hammonds, "Some Bosses Are Worth Their Salt—And Others. . . ," *Business Week,* May 7, 1990, p. 58.

32. Brenda Rios, "Drug Company to Start Health Care Plan for Homeless," *Herald-Leader* (Lexington, Ky.), February 22, 1990, p. A6.

33. Ted Gup, "Foul!" *Time,* April 3, 1989, pp. 54–60.

34. Charles J. Sykes, *ProfScam* (Washington, D.C.: Regnery Gateway, 1988), pp. 5–7.

35. "Spread the Word: Gossip Is Good," *The Wall Street Journal,* October 4, 1988, p. B1.

36. Alix M. Freedman, "Absolut Importer Sues Brown-Forman over Ad It Complains Copied Its Style," *The Wall Street Journal,* April 10, 1989, p. B4.

37. Pamela Sebastian, "Vendors' Gifts Pose Problems for Purchasers," *The Wall Street Journal,* June 26, 1989, p. B1.

38. Neal Templin, "Hertz to Pay Fine, Refund Overbillings," *USA Today,* August 5, 1988, p. 1B.

39. New York Times News Service, "Study Clears Whooping Cough Vaccine," *Herald-Leader* (Lexington, Ky.), March 23, 1990, p. D12.

40. John A. Byrne, "Businesses Are Signing Up for Ethics 101," *Business Week,* February 15, 1988, pp. 56–57.

41. "You'll Know It's the 21st Century When. . .," *American Demographics*, December 1990, pp. 26–27.

Chapter 5

1. "Sunscreen Ingredient May Promote Cancer," *Herald-Leader* (Lexington, Ky.), March 12, 1991, p. A3; "Study Applauds Oat Bran Again for Reducing Cholesterol Levels," *Herald-Leader* (Lexington, Ky.), April 10, 1991, p. C1; Joan O. C. Hamilton, "Sun Protection? There's a Rub," *Business Week,* June 11, 1990, pp. 22–23; Joanne Lipman, "Some Food Marketers May Shelve Outlandish Health Claims," *The Wall Street Journal,* January 29, 1990, p. B1; Jennifer Lawrence and Janet Meyers, "States Urge FDA Crackdown, *Advertising Age,* January 8, 1990, pp. 1, 42.

2. John R. Emshwiller, "Vons Stores Remove Tobacco Products that Lack Health-Warning Labels," *The Wall Street Journal,* October 5, 1988, p. B6.

3. Richard B. Schmitt, "Singers Get Green Light to Sue Imitators," *The Wall Street Journal,* August 19, 1988, p. 17.

4. Jay Lewis, "Sweet-Sounding Victory," *Herald-Leader* (Lexington, Ky.), October 31, 1989, p. A12.

5. Christopher Elias, "More and More Disputants See Court as a Last Resort," *Insight,* April 23, 1990, pp. 38–39.

6. Jethro K. Lieberman and George J. Siedel, *The Legal Environment of Business* (San Diego: Harcourt Brace Jovanovich, 1989), p. 102.

7. Adapted from "High Court to Decide Whether Labels Protect Cigarette Makers from Suits," *Herald-Leader* (Lexington, Ky.),

March 26, 1991, pp. A1, A5; Tim Smart, "The Liability Battle: Business Becomes a Road Warrier," *Business Week,* April 9, 1990, p. 25; Scott Ticer and Lawrence J. Tell, "This Tobacco Case Hardly Clears the Air," *Business Week,* March 7, 1988, pp. 76–78; Laurie P. Cohen and Alix M. Freedman, "Cracks Seen in Tobacco's Liability Dam," *The Wall Street Journal,* June 15, 1988, p. 25.

8. Kathryn Hudson, "Warnings on Noise for Rock Concerts?" *Insight,* January 30, 1989, p. 51.

9. James Lyons, "Smash the Competition," *Forbes,* September 3, 1990, p. 46.

10. Harris Collingwood, "It's Songwriters against Sony," *Business Week,* July 23, 1990, p. 36.

11. "Two Watchdogs for the Price of One, 1914," *The Wall Street Journal,* March 14, 1989, p. B1.

12. Julia Flynn Siler, Susan B. Garland, Catherine Yang, and Dean Foust, "Pressure on Professionals," *Business Week,* July 23, 1990, pp. 24–25.

13. Stephen Barlas, "FTC Steps Up Battle against Fraud," *Marketing News,* June 25, 1990, pp. 1, 13.

14. Joseph Weber, "Mom and Pop Move out of Wholesaling," *Business Week,* January 9, 1989, p. 91.

15. Adapted from Larry Marty and Rich Thomas, "The Corporate Shell Game," *Newsweek,* April 15, 1991, pp. 218–49; adapted from Jeff Shear, "Profits Elude Internal Revenue at Foreign-Owned Companies," reprinted by permission from Insight. Copyright 1990 Insight. All rights reserved.

16. Dick Janssen, "Taking the Fangs Out of This Year's Tax Bite," *Business Week,* March 11, 1991, pp. 108–9.

17. Alix M. Freedman, "Koop Urges an Excise-Tax Increase, Ad

Restrictions on Alcoholic Beverages," *The Wall Street Journal,* June 1, 1989, p. B6.

18. "You'll Know It's the 21st Century When. . .," *American Demographics*, December 1990, pp. 26–27.

Chapter 6

1. Norm Alster, "Hoops Go Global," *Forbes,* October 15, 1990, pp. 124–25; "Tracking Shares," *Advertsising Age,* May 7, 1990, p. 49; Jeffrey A. Trachtenberg, "Playing the Global Game," *Forbes,* January 23, 1989, pp. 90–91; Jack McCallum, "Tomorrow the World," *Sports Illustrated,* November 7, 1988, pp. 58–63.

2. Jeff Shear, "Foreign Investment Is Making a Borderless Corporate World," *Insight,* July 2, 1990, pp. 40–42.

3. Jack Anderson, "Who Owns America?" *Parade,* April 16, 1989, pp. 4–8.

4. Rose Brady, Peter Galuszka, Igor Reichlin, Paul Magnusson, and Bill Janetski, "Three Days that Shook the Kremlin," *Business Week,* February 19, 1990, pp. 30–33.

5. Kari Seppala and Mark A. Meyer, "Time Ripe for U.S. Firms to Enter Soviet Market," *Marketing News,* February 5, 1990, pp. 6, 9.

6. Blanca Riemer and Igor Reichlin, "On Your Mark, Get Set . . . Sell to Germany," *Business Week,* July 16, 1990, pp. 41–44.

7. Louis Kraar, "The Rising Power of the Pacific," *Fortune,* Fall 1990, pp. 8–12.

8. Amanda Bennett, "The Chief Executives in Year 2000 Will Be Experienced Abroad," *The Wall Street Journal,* February 28, 1989, pp. A1, A7.

9. Vern Terpstra, *International Dimensions of Marketing,* 2nd

ed. (Boston: Kent Publishing, 1988), p. 3.

10. Commerce Department, Electronic Industries Association, in John Hillkirk, "Zenith Tries to Keep from Fading Out," *USA Today,* December 9, 1987, pp. 1B, 2B.

11. William J. Holstein, Steven J. Dryden, Gail Schares, Ted Holden, and Jonathon B. Levine, "Made in the U.S.A.," *Business Week,* February 29, 1988, pp. 60–62.

12. Gene Koretz, "Japan's Trade Surplus May Still Be Headed Down," *Business Week,* May 21, 1990, p. 32.

13. *Economic Indicators* (Washington, D.C.: U.S. Government Printing Office, July 1990), p. 36.

14. Michael Rogers, "Fast-Food Quiz: Will Takeout Sell in China?" *Fortune,* September 15, 1986, p. 116.

15. Marcus W. Brauchli, "Japanese Consumers, Long Known as Savers, Catch On to Credit," *The Wall Street Journal,* April 10, 1989, pp. A1, A8.

16. Maria Shao, "Laying the Foundation for the Great Mall of China," *Business Week,* January 25, 1988, pp. 68–69.

17. Ted Holden and Suzanne Woolley, "The Delicate Art of Doing Business in Japan," *Business Week,* October 2, 1989, p. 120.

18. Carolyn Lochhead, "Japan Surrenders to Yankee Beefs," *Insight,* August 1, 1988, pp. 44–46.

19. Robert Neff, William J. Holstein, and Pal Magnusson, "Is Japan Cracking? Hardly," *Business Week,* April 16, 1990, pp. 22–23.

20. Mark M. Nelson, "GATT Nations Settle Dispute Imperiling Talks," *The Wall Street Journal,* April 10, 1989, pp. A3, A5.

21. Adapted from Eckart E. Goette, "Europe 1992: Update for Business Planners," *Journal of Business Strategy,* March–April 1990, pp. 10–13; Igor Reichlin and Thane Peterson, "German Unity: A Threat to Europe 1992," *Business Week,* January 22, 1990, pp. 40–42; Bryan Iwamoto, "1992: A Wake Up Call," *Express Magazine,* September 1989, pp. 2–5.

22. John S. McClenahen, "How U.S. Entrepreneurs Succeed in World Markets," *Industry Week,* May 2, 1988, pp. 47–49.

23. Damon Darlin, "Myth and Marketing in Japan," *The Wall Street Journal,* April 6, 1989, p. B1.

24. Monci Jo Williams, "Rewriting the Export Rules," *Fortune,* April 23, 1990, pp. 89–96.

25. Scott Hume, "How Big Mac Made It to Moscow," *Advertising Age,* January 22, 1990, pp. 16, 51.

26. Sheila Tefft, Cheryl Debes, and Dean Foust, "The Mouse that Roared at Pepsi," *Business Week,* September 7, 1987, p. 42.

27. Bart Ziegler, "Light in the East," *Herald-Leader* (Lexington, Ky.), September 23, 1990, pp. D1, D5.

28. Adapted from Andrew Kupfer, "How to Be a Global Manager," *Fortune,* March 14, 1988, pp. 52–56; Dori Jones Yang, Michael Oneal, Stewart Toy, Mark Maremont, and Robert Neff, "How Boeing Does It," *Business Week,* July 9, 1990, pp. 46–50; Gene G. Marcial, "A Beleaguered Boeing May Be on Lockheed's Tail," *Business Week,* March 13, 1989, p. 130.

29. "Coke Spins Same Sell All Around the World," *USA Today,* December 28, 1988, p. 6B.

30. Mauricio Lorence, "They're Cheap, They're Late . . . They're American Products," *Business Marketing,* September 1987, pp. 94, 96.

31. Carolyn Lochhead, "A Fight with Foreign Petal Pushers," *Insight,* April 10, 1989, pp. 42–43.

32. Shao, "Laying the Foundation," pp. 68–69.

33. Damon Darlin, "Commonplace Sexist Ads Raise Only a Few Eyebrows in Japan," *The Wall Street Journal,* April 19, 1989, p. B10.

34. Louis Rukeyser with John Cooney and George Winslow, eds., *Louis Rukeyser's Business Almanac* (New York: Simon & Schuster, 1988), pp. 24–27; Joel Kotkin and Yoriko Kishimoto, *The Third Century: America's Resurgence in the Asian Era* (New York: Crown Publishers, 1988), pp. 72–73, 202–3, 211; Joseph E. Pattison, *America's Survival and Success in the Global Economy* (Homewood, Ill.: Dow Jones-Irwin, 1990), pp. 20–21, 240–41.

Chapter 7

1. "Keep Our Powder Dry," *Forbes,* January 8, 1990, p. 128. Books listed include Thomas J. Peters and Robert H. Waterman, Jr., *In Search of Excellence* (New York: Harper & Row, 1982); Thomas J. Peters and Nancy Austin, *A Passion for Excellence* (New York: Random House, 1985); Tom Peters, *Thriving on Chaos* (New York: Alfred A. Knopf, 1987); Robert H. Waterman, Jr., *The Renewal Factor* (New York: Bantam Books, 1987); Harvey Mackay, *Swim with the Sharks without Being Eaten Alive* (New York: Morrow, 1988); Kenneth Blanchard and Spencer Johnson, *The One-Minute Manager* (New York: Morrow, 1982).

2. Based on "The Ideal Hunter," *Success,* January–February 1988, p. 61.

3. Gary Hoover, Alta Campbell, and Patrick J. Spain, *Profiles of Over 500 Major Corporations*

(Emeryville, Calif.: Publishers Group West, 1990), p. 243.

4. Adapted from Peters, *Thriving on Chaos,* pp. 167–69; Richard T. Jaffe, "Chapparal Steel Company: A Winner in a Market Dominated by Imports," *Planning Review,* July 1986, pp. 20–27.

5. Mary Parker Follett, *Creative Experience* (London: Longmans, Green, 1924).

6. William J. Broad, "Critics Say NASA Decline Threatens Agency's Goals," *New York Times,* September 9, 1990, pp. 1, 22.

7. "Now Japan Is Getting Jumpy about Quality," *Business Week,* March 5, 1990, pp. 40–42.

8. Peter Drucker, "Making Managers of Communist Bureaucrats," *The Wall Street Journal,* August 15, 1990, p. A8.

9. Henry J. Mintzberg, *The Nature of Managerial Work* (New York: Harper & Row, 1973).

10. J. Horne and T. Lupton, "The Work Activities of Middle Managers: An Exploratory Study," *Journal of Management Studies,* January 1965, pp. 14–33.

11. Adapted from Sarah Stiansen, "Making Time," *Success,* April 1990, p. 18; "What Do You Do on an Airplane?" *Fortune,* June 4, 1990, p. 254; Ford S. Worthy, "How CEOs Manage Their Time," *Fortune,* January 18, 1988, pp. 88–97.

12. Robert L. Katz, "Skills of an Effective Administrator," *Harvard Business Review,* September–October 1974, pp. 90–102.

13. V. R. Boehm, "What Do Managers Really Do?" (Paper presented at the Annual Meeting of the AACSB Graduate Management Admissions Council, Toronto, June 1981).

14. R. Burnaska, "Early Careers and Assessment Centers" (Paper

presented at the Annual Meeting of the AACSB Graduate Management Admissions Council, Toronto, June 1981).

15. Theresa R. Walter, "Readin', Writin', and . . . ," *Industry Week,* January 16, 1989, pp. 33–34.

16. M. Burley-Allen, *Listening: The Forgotten Skill* (New York: John Wiley & Sons, 1982).

17. James H. Donnelly, Jr., James L. Gibson, and John M. Ivancevich, *Fundamentals of Management,* 7th ed. (Homewood, Ill.: Richard D. Irwin, 1990), p. 432.

18. Patrick Houston, "48 Hours on the Job," *Business Month,* September 1990, pp. 42–49.

19. "You'll Know It's the 21st Century When. . .," *American Demographics,* December 1990, pp. 24–25.

Chapter 8

1. Adapted from "Eeeeeyyyooow!!!!" *Time,* August 6, 1990, pp. 60–62; "Arrow Presents Suspended Coaster" (Clearfield, Vt.: Arrow Dynamics, Inc., 1990); Melree Zamorino, marketing coordinator at Arrow Dynamics, telephone conversation, August 30, 1990; Joe McDonald, "Risking High Again," *Southtown Economist,* August 10, 1990, pp. B1, B2.

2. Sally Bell, "Surviving and Thriving," *Nation's Business,* March 1990, p. 98.

3. Lee Tom Perry, *Offensive Strategy* (New York: Harper & Row, 1990), p. 13.

4. Lis Buyer, "EuroDisney: As Close to Risk Free as a Deal Can Get," *The Journal of European Business,* March–April 1990, pp. 26–28, 41.

5. Susan Lee and Christie Brown, "The Proteam Corporation," *Forbes,* August 24, 1987, pp. 76–79.

6. Adapted from Alfred D. Chandler, Jr., "Origins of the

Organization Chart," *Harvard Business Review,* March–April 1988, pp. 156–57.

7. Adapted from Ronald Henkoff, "Cost Cutting: How to Do It Right," *Fortune,* April 9, 1990, pp. 40–49; Mark Ivey, "Baker Hughes: It Pays to Be a Big Spender," *Business Week,* March 12, 1990, p. 81; Chet Borucki and Carole K. Barnett, "Restructuring for Self-Renewal: Navistar International Corporation," *Academy of Management Executive,* February 1990, pp. 36–49; Thomas Moore, "Goodbye, Corporate Staff," *Fortune,* December 21, 1987, pp. 65–67.

8. Peter F. Drucker, "The Coming of the New Organization," *Harvard Business Review,* January–February 1988, pp. 45–53.

9. James H. Donnelly, Jr., James L. Gibson, and John M. Ivancevich, *Fundamentals of Management,* 7th ed. (Homewood, Ill.: Richard D. Irwin, 1990), pp. 104–5.

10. Chris Argyris, *Overcoming Organizational Defenses* (Englewood Cliffs, N.J.: Prentice Hall, 1990).

11. Arthur H. Walker and Jay Lorsch, "Organizational Choice: Product versus Function," *Harvard Business Review,* November–December 1968, pp. 129–38.

12. E. Raymond Corey and Steven H. Star, *Organization Strategy: A Marketing Approach* (Cambridge, Mass.: Division of Research, Graduate School of Business Administration, Harvard University, 1970).

13. "Greyhound Splitting into Four to Go after Short Haul Trade," *Chicago Tribune,* April 30, 1986, sec. 3, p. 8.

14. John M. Ivancevich, James H. Donnelly, Jr., and James L. Gibson, *Management: Principles and Functions* (Plano, Tex.:

Business Publications, 1989), p. 101.

15. Charles Hampden Turner, *Charting the Corporate Mind: Graphic Solutions to Business Conflicts* (New York: Free Press, 1990).

16. "You'll Know It's the 21st Century When. . .," *American Demographics,* December 1990, pp. 24–25.

Chapter 9

1. Mark Albert, "The Ultimate Computer Factory," *Fortune,* February 26, 1990, pp. 75–79.

2. Alicia Swasey and Carol Hymowitz, "The Workplace Revolution," *Wall Street Journal Reports,* February 9, 1990, p. R6.

3. Samuel Huber, *Efficiency and Uplift* (Chicago: University of Chicago Press, 1964).

4. Richard B. Chase and Nicholas J. Aquilano, *Production and Operations Management: A Life Cycle Approach* (Homewood, Ill.: Richard D. Irwin, 1989), pp. 19–20.

5. Erwin S. Stanton, *Reality-Centered People Management: Key to Improved Productivity* (New York: AMACOM, 1982).

6. Joseph H. Boyett and Henry P. Conn, *Workplace 2000* (New York: E. P. Dutton, 1991), pp. 23–27.

7. Gary Reiner, "Lessons from the World's Best Product Developers," *The Wall Street Journal,* August 6, 1990, p. A12.

8. Gary Slutsker, "Struggling against the Tide," *Forbes,* November 12, 1990, pp. 312–14.

9. Soltan Dzarosov, "The Chervonets Again?" *Business in the USSR,* September 1990, p. 21; *Marketwise: A Financial Overview from Prudential-Bache*

Securities (New York: Prudential-Bache Securities, February 1990), p. 2.

10. William J. Stevenson, *Production and Operations Management* (Homewood, Ill.: Richard D. Irwin, 1990), p. 624.

11. Urban C. Lehner, "The Nuts and Bolts of Japan's Factories," *The Wall Street Journal,* March 31, 1981.

12. Chase and Aquilano, *Production and Operations Management,* p. 55.

13. Mark Hornung and Richard A. Moran, *Opportunities in Microelectronic Careers* (Lincolnwood, Ill.: NTC Group, 1985), pp. 27–28.

14. Susan Moffat, "Personalized Production," *Fortune,* October 22, 1990, pp. 132–35.

15. David Woodruff, "A New Era for Auto Quality," *Business Week,* October 23, 1990, pp. 84–96.

16. "Epidemic of Recalls Embarrasses Japanese Electronics Industry," *Houston Post,* March 29, 1990, p. A–10.

17. Sherie Posesorski, "Here's How to Put Statistical Process Control to Work for You," *Canadian Business,* December 1985, p. 163.

18. Allen E. Puckett, "People Are the Key to Productivity," *Industrial Management,* September–October 1985, pp. 12–15; Philip E. Atkinson and Brian W. Murray, "Managing Total Quality," *Management Services,* October 1985, pp. 18–21.

19. "Quality Circles: A Worthy Tool to Use under the QIP Umbrella," *Quality Update,* Fall 1990, pp. 26–29.

20. Anatoly Brylov, "Aeroflot Taking the Dollar under Its Wing," *Business in the USSR,* September 1990, pp. 38–39.

21. Thomas J. Peters and Robert H. Waterman, Jr., *In Search of*

Excellence: Lessons from America's Best-Run Companies (New York: Harper & Row, 1982), p. 249.

22. Ibid., p. 239.

23. Ibid.

24. Albert R. Karr, "The Corporate Race Belongs to the Safest," *The Wall Street Journal*, July 5, 1990, pp. B1, B5.

25. Tom W. Ferguson, "Job Injury Burden Could Disable Some Companies," *The Wall Street Journal*, July 10, 1990, p. A17.

26. "Manufacturing for the 1990s: Volvo Revamps the Plant," *Business International*, October 22, 1990, pp. 349–50; Richard A. Melcher, "Rolls-Royce Sees the Future—and It's Still Handmade," *Fortune*, October 22, 1990, p. 96.

27. *Time*, October 23, 1989, pp. 60–62.

28. "You'll Know It's the 21st Century When. . .," *American Demographics*, December 1990, p. 24.

Chapter 10

1. Richard Poe, "The Motivation Generation," *Success*, September 1990, p. 80; Kurt Eichenwald, "Wall Street in Search of Itself on the Yampa," *New York Times*, June 24, 1990, pp. 4–5; Ken Wells, "The Athletic Approach," *The Wall Street Journal*, February 26, 1988, pp. 9D–10D.

2. Gilbert Fuchsberg and Amanda Bennett, "Need a Motivator for Weary Workers? Try a Congratulator," *The Wall Street Journal*, May 4, 1990, pp. A1, A7.

3. Walter C. Clemens, Jr., "Perestroika Needs a Work Ethic to Work," *The Wall Street Journal*, December 5, 1989, p. A18.

4. Adapted from "How to Make the U.S. Bulletproof," *Fortune*, March 26, 1990, pp. 31–32;

Todd Mason, *Perot: An Unauthorized Biography* (Homewood, Ill.: Business One Irwin, 1990); Ross Perot, "How I Would Turn Around GM," *Fortune*, February 15, 1988, pp. 44–48.

5. "Hawthorne Revisited: The Legend and the Legacy," *Organizational Dynamics*, Winter 1975, pp. 66–80.

6. Ibid.

7. Peter Drucker, *Management: Tasks, Responsibilities, Practices* (New York: Harper & Row, 1974), p. 504.

8. Abraham H. Maslow, ed., *Motivation and Personality* (New York: Harper & Row, 1954).

9. Amanda Bennett, "White-Collar Guide to Job Security," *The Wall Street Journal*, September 11, 1990, pp. B1, B10.

10. Douglas McGregor, *The Human Side of Enterprise* (New York: McGraw-Hill, 1960).

11. Adapted from "P&G Gives Itself a Makeover," *Sales & Marketing Management*, June 1990, pp. 66–67; John P. Kotter, "What Leaders Really Do," *Harvard Business Review*, May–June 1990, p. 110.

12. William Ouchi, *Theory Z* (Reading, Mass.: Addison-Wesley Publishing, 1981).

13. Frederick Herzberg, Bernard Mausner, and Barbara Snyderman, *The Motivation to Work* (New York: John Wiley & Sons, 1959).

14. Ronald Whipple, "Rewards Have Value," *Personnel Journal*, September 1990, pp. 92–93.

15. Abraham H. Maslow, "Self-Actualizing People: A Study of Psychological Health," in *Motivation and Personality*, ed. Abraham H. Maslow (New York: Harper & Row, 1954).

16. Edwin Locke and Gary Latham, *A Theory of Goal Setting*

(Englewood Cliffs, N.J.: Prentice Hall, 1991).

17. Robert J. Vance and Adrienne Colella, "Effects of Two Types of Feedback on Goal Acceptance and Personal Goals," *Journal of Applied Psychology*, February 1990, pp. 68–76.

18. R. D. Pritchard, S. D. Jones, P. L. Roth, K. K. Stuebing, and S. E. Ekeberg, "Effects of Group Feedback, Goal Setting, and Incentives on Productivity," *Journal of Applied Psychology*, April 1988, pp. 337–58.

19. "The Science of Success: How to Develop New Performance Habits," *Success*, September 1990, pp. 48–49.

20. J. R. Hackman and J. E. Suttle, eds., *Improving Life at Work: Behavioral Science Approaches to Organizational Change* (Santa Monica, Calif.: Goodyear Publishing, 1977).

21. Richard E. Walton, "Quality of Working Life: What Is It?" *Sloan Management Review*, 1973, pp. 11–21.

22. B. F. Skinner, *About Behaviorism* (New York: Alfred A. Knopf, 1974).

23. Charles Storch, "A New Spin on Job Motivation," *Chicago Tribune*, September 23, 1990, p. 9E.

24. "You'll Know It's the 21st Century When. . .," *American Demographics*, December 1990, p. 24.

Chapter 11

1. "Leaders of the Most Admired," *Fortune*, January 21, 1990, pp. 40–54; "Merck & Co.," *Changing Times*, July 1990, p. 32.

2. Based on Robert Levering, *A Great Place to Work* (New York: Random House, 1988), pp. 143–61.

3. Morton E. Grossman and Margaret Magnus, "Hire

Spending,'' *Personnel Journal,* February 1989, pp. 73–76.

4. Adapted from Sharon Nelton, ''Men, Women, and Leadership,'' *Nation's Business,* May 1991, pp. 16–22; Larry Reynolds, ''Civil Rights Proposals: Focus on Workplace Issues,'' *HR Focus,* June 1991, p. 12.

5. See John M. Ivancevich and William G. Glueck, *Human Resource Management: Foundations of Personnel,* 4th ed. (Homewood, Ill.: Business One Irwin, 1989), p. 226.

6. Philip R. Voluck, ''Recruiting, Interviewing, and Hiring: Staying within the Boundaries,'' *Personnel Administrator,* May 1987, pp. 45–52.

7. J. Freedley Hunsecker, Jr., ''Ready or Not: The ADA,'' *Personnel Journal,* August 1990, pp. 80–86.

8. Deborah L. Jacobs, ''Japanese-American Cultural Clash,'' *New York Times,* September 9, 1990, part 3, p. 1.

9. Derek T. Dingle, ''Managing the War on Drugs,'' *Black Enterprise,* July 1990, pp. 43–49.

10. Robert M. Stutman, ''Can We Stop Drug Abuse in the Workplace?'' *USA Today,* July 1990, pp. 18–20.

11. National Report on Substance Abuse, Bureau of National Affairs, February 4, 1987, pp. 1–2.

12. Adapted from ''The Impact of AIDS on Benefit Plans,'' *Nation's Business,* March 1989, pp. 60–61.

13. Telephone conversation with the National AIDS Information Clearing House, Rockville, MD (1-800-458-5231), on May 15, 1991.

14. Martin Levy, ''Almost Perfect Performance Appraisals,'' *Personnel Journal,* April 1989, pp. 76–83.

15. Adapted from ''How You'll Be Paid in the 1990s,'' FORTUNE, April 9, 1990, p. 11; Brian Dumaine, ''Those Highflying PepsiCo Managers,'' FORTUNE, April 10, 1989, pp. 78–86. © 1989, 1990 The Time Magazine Company. All rights reserved.

16. Cindy Skrzycki, ''Employee Bonuses Spur Productivity,'' *Houston Chronicle,* February 18, 1990, p. 4C.

17. Ira Kay, ''Do Your Workers Really Merit a Raise?'' *The Wall Street Journal,* March 26, 1990, p. A10.

18. Richard I. Henderson, *Compensation Management: Rewarding Performance* (Reston, Va.: Reston, 1989), p. 231.

19. U.S. Department of Labor, Bureau of Labor Statistics, ''Employee Benefits in Medium and Large Firms, 1988,'' August 1989, p. 406.

20. Based on ''Inspire Your Team,'' *Managing,* October 1989; ''Incentive . . . the Key to Quality,'' *Recognition '83,* August 1983, pp. 14–15.

21. Barbara Berish Brown, ''Federal Legislative Law Update,'' *National Employment Discrimination Law Update* (Washington, D.C., August 1989).

22. James T. Brinks, ''The Comparable Worth Issue: A Salary Administration Bombshell,'' *Personnel Administrator,* November 1981, pp. 37–40.

23. Michael F. Carte, ''Comparable Worth: An Idea Whose Time Has Come?'' *Personnel Journal,* October 1981, pp. 792–94.

24. Lynne Kirkpatrick, ''In Ontario, 'Equal Pay for Equal Work' Becomes a Reality, but Not Very Easily,'' *The Wall Street Journal,* March 9, 1990, pp. B, B4.

25. Steve Pomper, ''Health Care Choices of a New Generation,'' *Business Week,* April 1990, pp. 68–69.

26. W. H. Wagel, ''Eldercare Assistance for Employees at the Travelers,'' *Personnel,* October 1987, pp. 4–6.

27. Allan Tran, ''HR Economics,'' *HR Focus,* January 1991, p. 23.

28. Earl Ubell, ''Is Your Job Killing You?'' *Parade,* January 9, 1989, pp. 4–7.

29. Ibid.

30. ''It's About Time,'' *HR Focus,* February 1991, p. 87.

31. ''You'll Know It's the 21st Century When. . .,'' *American Demographics,* December 1990, p. 24.

Chapter 12

1. ''More Picket Lines, for Rank-and-Filers,'' *Business Week,* May 7, 1990, p. 7; Dianne Solis and Jose De Cordoba, ''Eastern Strike Carries Long-Festering Anger over Sense of Betrayal,'' *The Wall Street Journal,* March 17, 1989, pp. A1, A8; Jill Abramson, ''Texas Air's Lorenzo May Be Union's No. 1 Foe, yet His Allies Include Some Powerful Democrats,'' *The Wall Street Journal,* March 17, 1989, p. A12; John Schwartz and Peter Katel, ''Frank Lorenzo Is Grounded,'' *Newsweek,* April 30, 1990, p. 40.

2. Craig Hukill, ''Labor and the Supreme Court: Significant Issues of 1990–1991,'' *Monthly Labor Review,* January 1991, pp. 34–40.

3. Based on Robert Hamrin, *America's New Economy: The Basic Guide* (New York: Franklin Watts, 1988), p. 442.

4. Lindley H. Clark, Jr., ''U.S. Unions Did Too Well for Themselves,'' *The Wall Street Journal,* June 13, 1990, p. A14.

5. Thomas Karier, "Unions and the U.S. Comparative Advantage," *Industrial Relations,* Winter 1991, p. 4.

6. W. C. Hammer and F. J. Smith, "Work Activities as Predictors of Unionization Activity," *Journal of Applied Psychology,* August 1978, pp. 414–21.

7. Charlene Marmer Solomon, "Nightmare at Nordstrom," *Personnel Journal,* September 1990, pp. 76–83.

8. Francine Schwadel, "Irate Nordstrom Straining in Labor Fight," *The Wall Street Journal,* April 6, 1990, p. B1.

9. Betty S. Murphy, Wayne E. Barlow, and D. Diane Hatch, "Final Plant Closing Regulations Issued," *Personnel Journal,* June 1989, pp. 28, 31; Paul D. Staudohar, "New Plant Closing Law," *Personnel Journal,* January 1989, pp. 87–90.

10. Based on a telephone conversation with the National Labor Relations Board in Washington, D.C., on June 12, 1991.

11. "Right or Wrong in Employee Relations," *Office,* May 1990, p. 83.

12. From JACK LONDON: AMERICAN REBEL. Edited by Philip S. Foner. Copyright © 1947 by The Citadel Press. Published by arrangement with Carol Publishing Group.

13. Robert Tomsho, "Employers Add RICO Suits to Arsenal for Labor Battles, and Unions Fire Back," *The Wall Street Journal,* April 12, 1990, pp. B1, B6.

14. Adapted from "The Union's Role as Co-Manager," *Fortune,* March 26, 1990, p. 37; "The Boardroom's Revenge," *Economist,* May 12, 1990, p. 72; Gregory A. Patterson, "UAW Hotly Debates Whether It Is Too Cozy with Car Companies," *The Wall Street Journal,* June 15,

1989, pp. A1, A8; "Suddenly, USX Is Playing Mr. Nice Guy," *Business Week,* June 26, 1989, pp. 151–52; "The UAW Rebels Teaming Up against Teamwork," *Business Week,* March 27, 1989, pp. 110–14.

15. Micheline Maynard, "Enthusiasm Drives Saturn Workers," *USA Today,* August 31, 1990, p. 2B.

16. Kenneth R. Sheets, "Labor's Agenda for the '90s," *U.S. News & World Report,* March 19, 1990, pp. 37–39.

17. Fred K. Foulkes, *Personnel Policies in Large Non-Union Companies* (Englewood Cliffs, N.J.: Prentice Hall, 1980), pp. 45–57.

18. Louis Rukeyser with John Cooney and George Winslow, eds., *Louis Rukeyser's Business Almanac* (New York: Simon & Schuster, 1988), p. 61; "Today's Leaders Talk about Tomorrow," *Fortune,* March 26, 1990, p. 37; Joe Cappo, *Future Scope: Success Strategies for the 1990s and Beyond* (Chicago: Longman Financial Services Institute, 1990), pp. 131–32.

Chapter 13

1. Ronald Henkoff, "Bic Mac Attacks with Pizza," *Fortune,* February 26, 1990, pp. 87–89; Richard Gibson and Robert Johnson, "Big Mac, Cooling Off, Loses Its Sizzle," *The Wall Street Journal,* September 29, 1989, pp. B1, B5; Richard Gibson, "McDonald's Makes a Fast Pitch to Pizza Buffs Who Hate to Wait," *The Wall Street Journal,* August 28, 1989, p. B3; Scott Hume, "McDonald's Fred Turner: Making All the Right Moves," *Advertising Age,* January 1, 1990, pp. 6, 17; Phil West, "Mac to the Future," *Herald-Leader* (Lexington, Ky.), August 30, 1990, p. A1.

2. "AMA Board Approves New Marketing Definition," *Marketing News,* March 1, 1985, p. 1.

3. Gifford Claiborne, "How Marketing Rescued an L.A. Rescue Mission," *Marketing News,* December 8, 1989, p. 13.

4. Philip Kotler, *Marketing Management: Analysis, Planning and Control,* 5th ed. (Englewood Cliffs, N.J.: Prentice Hall, 1984), p. 8.

5. Susan Dillingham, "New Milk Lines Are Moo-ving Fast," *Insight,* February 26, 1990, pp. 42–43.

6. Lynn W. McGee and Rosann L. Spiro, "The Marketing Concept in Perspective," *Business Horizons,* May–June 1988, pp. 40–45.

7. Sharyn Hunt and Ernest F. Cooke, "It's Basic but Necessary: Listen to the Customer," *Marketing News,* March 5, 1990, pp. 22–23.

8. Adapted from Patricia Sellers, "What Customers Really Want," *Fortune,* June 4, 1990, pp. 58–68; Stephen Phillips, Amy Dunkin, and others, "King Customer," *Business Week,* March 12, 1990, pp. 88–91, 94; Hunt and Cooke, "It's Basic but Necessary," pp. 22–23.

9. Tim Smart and Dean Foust, "Has Alcoa Found a Way to Foil the Aluminum Cycle?" *Business Week,* January 8, 1990, pp. 36–37.

10. Pat Sloan, "Shades of Summer," *Advertising Age,* March 26, 1990, p. 44.

11. Mark Lewyn, "PC Makers, Palms Sweating, Try Talking to Women," *Business Week,* January 15, 1990, p. 48.

12. Judith Waldrop and Thomas Exter, "What the 1990 Census Will Show," *American Demographics,* January 1990, pp. 20–30.

13. Howard Schlossberg, "Hispanic Market Strong, but Often Ignored," *Marketing News,* February 19, 1990, pp. 1, 12.

14. *Advertising Age,* February 26, 1990, p. 45.

15. Carol Pugh, "Estefan's Return to Roots Turns a Nice Gesture into Smart Business," *Herald-Leader* (Lexington, Ky.), October 27, 1989, p. B–10.

16. Jennfier Lawrence and Janet Meyers, "States Urge FDA Crackdown," *Advertising Age,* January 8, 1990, pp. 1, 42.

17. James F. Engel, Roger D. Blackwell, and Paul W. Miniard, *Consumer Behavior* (Hinsdale, Ill.: Dryden Press, 1990), p. 3.

18. Adapted from Joshua Levine, "Cluck, Cluck, Oink," *Forbes,* April 16, 1990, pp. 126, 128; "Pork Claims Raise Squeals in D.C.," *Chicago Tribune,* March 25, 1990, sec. 7, p. 6; Alix M. Freedman, "Pig Producers Try to Hog a New Perch in the Chicken Coop," *The Wall Street Journal,* December 30, 1987, pp. 1, 9; Steve Weiner, "Beef Is a Four-Letter Word," *Forbes,* February 19, 1990, pp. 124, 128.

19. *Report of the Definitions Committee of the American Marketing Association* (Chicago: American Marketing Association, 1961).

20. Jennifer Lawrence, "Frito's Micro Move," *Advertising Age,* February 12, 1990, p. 44.

21. James Cox, "Firms Go Toe-to-Toe on Marketing," *USA Today,* September 9, 1989, pp. 1B–2B.

22. Joshua Levine, "The Orange Juice War," *Forbes,* May 28, 1990, pp. 338–40.

23. Christopher Elias, "Goodyear Race with Michelin: Burning Rubber to Be No. 1," *Insight,* May 7, 1990, pp. 36–39.

24. "You'll Know It's the 21st Century When. . .," *American Demographics,* December 1990, p. 26.

Chapter 14

1. John Huey, "The New Power in Black & Decker," *Fortune,* January 2, 1989, pp. 89–94; Peter Coy, "Inventions of Star Engineer Mean Profits for Black & Decker," *Herald-Leader* (Lexington, Ky.), December 27, 1987, p. B1.

2. Yoram J. Wind, *Product Policy: Concepts, Methods, and Strategy* (Reading, Mass.: Addison-Wesley Publishing, 1982), p. 67.

3. Betsy Pisik, "For 10 Years, Post-its Stick Around," *Insight,* January 29, 1990, p. 41.

4. Jim Betts, *The Million Dollar Idea* (Point Pleasant, N.J.: Point Publishing, 1985), p. 7.

5. Merle Crawford, *New Product Management* (Homewood, Ill.: Richard D. Irwin, 1987), p. 21.

6. Howard Schlossberg, "Fear of Failure Stifles Product Development," *Marketing News,* May 14, 1990, pp. 1, 16.

7. Robert D. Hisrich and Michael P. Peters, *Marketing Decisions for New and Mature Products* (Columbus, Ohio: Charles E. Merrill, 1984), p. 15.

8. Ibid.

9. George Stalk, Jr., "Time—The Next Source of Competitive Advantage," *Harvard Business Review,* July–August 1988, pp. 41–51.

10. Glen L. Urban, John R. Hauser, and Nikhilesh Dholakia, *Essentials of New Product Management* (Englewood Cliffs, N.J.: Prentice Hall, 1987), pp. 6–7.

11. Laurie Freeman, "Dow Brands Cleans Up with Spiffits," *Advertising Age,* February 19, 1990, pp. 4, 73.

12. Adapted from Robert Johnson, "Naming a Product Is Tough When the Best Names Are Taken," *The Wall Street Journal,* January 19, 1988, p. 33; Joshua Levine, "No Brand like an Old Brand," *Forbes,* June 11, 1990, pp. 179–80.

13. Robert D. Hof, "A Washout for Clorox," *Business Week,* July 9, 1990, pp. 32–33.

14. Crawford, *New Product Management,* p. 423.

15. Tim Friend, "Cost per Treatment: 1–5 Cents," *USA Today,* January 28, 1988, p. A1.

16. "Fresh Packaging Idea Wins Kudos for Armour Meats," *Marketing News,* January 18, 1988, p. 8.

17. "Wella Shampoo Container Employs High-Tech, Self-Pressurized System," *Marketing News,* February 1, 1988, p. 18.

18. Susan Dillingham, "Hawking Consumer Goods with the Environmental Pitch," *Insight,* March 26, 1990, pp. 40–42.

19. Stephan Barlas, "Congress Mulls Strict Nutrition Labeling Law," *Marketing News,* January 22, 1990, pp. 1, 11.

20. Christie Brown, "Where the Beatles Outsell Elvis," *Forbes,* March 5, 1990, pp. 146–47.

21. Adapted from Claire Poole, "Born to Hustle," *Forbes,* May 28, 1990, pp. 190, 194; Ira Teinowitz, "Alamo's Fighting Mad on Mileage," *Advertising Age,* March 26, 1990, p. 46.

22. Joseph P. Guiltinan, "The Price Bundling of Services: A Normative Framework," *Journal of Marketing,* April 1987, pp. 74–85.

23. "You'll Know It's the 21st Century When. . .," *American Demographics,* December 1990, p. 25.

Chapter 15

1. Peter Drucker, "Manage by Walking Around—Outside," *The Wall Street Journal*, May 11, 1990, p. B1; Amy Dunkin, "Slugging It Out for Survival," *Business Week*, January 8, 1990, pp. 32–33, 85; James Morgan, "Distribution in the 1990s," *Purchasing*, May 17, 1990, pp. 70–75.

2. Louis W. Stern and Adel I. El-Ansary, *Marketing Channels*, 3rd ed. (Englewood Cliffs, N.J.: Prentice Hall, 1988), p. 3.

3. Associated Press, "Home on the U.S. Range, Japanese Style," *Herald-Leader* (Lexington, Ky.), January 7, 1990, pp. E1, E3.

4. David E. Gumpert, "They Can Get It for You Wholesale," *Working Woman*, August 1990, pp. 33–36, 94.

5. Adapted from Gumpert, "They Can Get It for You Wholesale." Reprinted with permission from WORKING WOMAN magazine. Copyright © 1990 by WWT Partnership.

6. *Census of Wholesale Trade* (1985), pp. 1–3.

7. J. Barry Mason and Morris L. Mayer, *Modern Retailing: Theory and Practice*, 5th ed. (Homewood, Ill.: Richard D. Irwin, 1990), p. 5.

8. U.S. Department of Labor, *Employment Projections for the 1980s* (Washington, D.C.: Government Printing Office).

9. Chuck Hawkins, "Will Home Depot Be the Wal-Mart of the '90s?" *Business Week*, March 18, 1990, pp. 124–26.

10. "Supermarkets Quickly Becoming One-Stop Minimalls," *Marketing News*, February 14, 1988, p. 11.

11. Kevin Kelly and Amy Dunkin, "Wal-Mart Gets Lost in the Vegetable Aisle," *Business Week*, May 28, 1990, p. 48.

12. Ibid.; Alison L. Sprout, "America's Most Admired Corporations," *Fortune*, February 11, 1991, pp. 52–60; John Huey, "Wal-Mart: Will It Take Over the World?" *Fortune*, January 30, 1989, pp. 52–61.

13. "Membership Warehouse Club Report" (Santa Barbara, Calif.: James M. Degen & Company).

14. Howard Schlossberg, "Picture Still Looks Bright for TV Shopping Networks," *Marketing News*, October 23, 1989, p. 8.

15. Brian Bremner and Keith H. Hammonds, "Lands' End Looks a Bit Frayed at the Edges," *Business Week*, March 19, 1990, p. 42.

16. Susan Dillingham, "Vending Machine Plan Is on Hold in Japan," *Insight*, July 2, 1990, p. 43.

17. Carolyn Lochhead, "Taking a Tip from Retailing, Branch Banks Get Gussied Up," *Insight*, July 16, 1990, pp. 38–39.

18. Alison Fahey, "Off-Price Chains Strike Back at Price Cutters," *Advertising Age*, July 16, 1990, p. 28.

19. Marge Meeh, "Poll Shows Shift toward Customer Service," *Chain-Store Age Executive*, May 1990, pp. 286–92.

20. Mark Stevens, "How to Take a Good Business and Make It Better," *Working Woman*, March 1990, pp. 38–46.

21. Cyndee Miller, "Hanes Takes the Snags out of Maintaining Hosiery Inventories," *Marketing News*, May 14, 1990, p. 23.

22. Steven P. Galante, "Small Manufacturers Shifting to 'Just-in-Time' Techniques," *The Wall Street Journal*, December 21, 1987, p. 21.

23. Joe Cappo, *Future Scope: Success Strategies for the 1990s and Beyond* (Chicago: Longman Financial Services Institute, 1990), pp. 69–72.

Chapter 16

1. Donna DeMayo, "Tuna Marketers Using Promotion to Ride the 'Dolphin Safe' Wave," *PROMO*, August 1990, pp. 24, 47; "Swim with the Dolphins: Tuna Fishing Will Change," *Newsweek*, April 23, 1990, p. 76; August Felando, "Dolphin-Safe Tuna: No Real Gain," *The Wall Street Journal*, June 12, 1990, p. A15.

2. William P. Dommormuth, *Promotion: Analysis, Creativity, and Strategy* (Boston: Kent Publishing, 1984), p. 4.

3. Robert J. Coen, "Tough Times for Ad Spending," *Advertising Age*, May 14, 1990, pp. 12, 59.

4. "Millionaire Mounts Big Mac Attack," *Herald-Leader* (Lexington, Ky.), April 5, 1990, p. A14.

5. *Advertising Age*, February 26, 1990, p. S–1.

6. *The Wall Street Journal*, March 16, 1988, p. 33.

7. Ibid., March 10, 1988, p. 23.

8. Wayne Walley, "Automakers, Sears Fuel Gain in TV Spending," *Advertising Age*, March 12, 1990, p. 4.

9. John McManus, "Super Bowl Rate Up 17%," *Advertising Age*, April 16, 1990, pp. 3, 65.

10. Dennis Kneale, " 'Zapping' of TV Ads Appears Pervasive," *The Wall Street Journal*, April 25, 1988, p. 21.

11. Roper report published in *USA Today*, June 28, 1990, p. D1.

12. Joshua Levine, "Drive Time," *Forbes*, March 19, 1990, pp. 144–46.

13. Elizabeth Snead, "Information Deluge a Strain on the Brain," *Herald-Leader* (Lexington, Ky.), February 6, 1990, p. D1.

14. "Ad Age 300," *Advertising Age*, June 18, 1990, pp. 5–12.

15. Adapted from Nancy L. Croft, "Spiels on Wheels," *Nation's*

Business, February 1987, p. 14; James Cox, "Ad Attack: No Place to Escape," *USA Today,* March 22, 1988, p. 1B; James Cox, "In-Air Ads Enjoy Flush of Success," *USA Today,* February 9, 1988, p. 1B; Scott Hume, "Bounty in Most Unusual Places," *Advertising Age,* August 27, 1990, pp. S–1, S–14.

16. Carlton A. Pederson, Milburn D. Wright, and Burton A. Weitz, *Selling: Principles and Methods,* 9th ed. (Homewood, Ill.: Richard D. Irwin, 1988), p. 11.

17. Ibid., p. 15.

18. "Survey Finds Companies Spending More on Consumer Promotions," *Marketing News,* March 28, 1988, pp. 10–11.

19. Joanne Lipman, "Too Many Coupons in the Paper? Advertisers Rethink Promotion," *The Wall Street Journal,* June 26, 1989, p. B4.

20. "Troubled Green-Stamp Firm Says It's Not Licked Yet," *Herald-Leader* (Lexington, Ky.), May 29, 1989, p. D7.

21. Michael Oneal and Peter Finch, "Nothing Sells like Sports," *Business Week,* August 31, 1987, pp. 48–53; Kevin Maney, "Big Events Can Boost Bottom Line," *USA Today,* January 29, 1988, p. B1; Maureen McFadden, "Spring's Commercial Break," *USA Today,* March 17, 1988, p. 2B; Bruce Britt, "Paul McCartney's Tour Gets a Charge from Visa," *Herald-Leader* (Lexington, Ky.), December 3, 1989; Jeffrey A. Trachtenberg, "Does Sports Marketing Make Sense?" *The Wall Street Journal,* April 19, 1989, p. B1.

22. Betsy D. Gelb, "How Marketers of Intangibles Can Raise the Odds for Customer Satisfaction," *Journal of Services Marketing,* Summer 1987, pp. 11–18.

23. "You'll Know It's the 21st Century When . . . ," *American Demographics,* December 1990, p. 24.

Chapter 17

1. Joan O. C. Hamilton, "Will BankAmerica Have the Last Laugh?" *Business Week,* November 26, 1990, pp. 148–49; Charles McCoy, "Combat Banking: A Slashing Pursuit of Retail Trade Brings BankAmerica Back," *The Wall Street Journal,* October 2, 1989, pp. A1, C6.

2. Matt Schaeffer, *Winning the Countertrade War* (New York: John Wiley & Sons, 1989), pp. 139–54.

3. Frederick S. Mishkin, *The Economics of Money, Banking, and Financial Markets* (Glenview, Ill.: Scott, Foresman, 1989), pp. 245–46.

4. Bill Saporito, "Who's Winning the Credit Card War?" *Fortune,* July 2, 1990, pp. 66–71.

5. Mishkin, *Economics of Money,* p. 186.

6. Adapted from Jersy Gilbert, "Credit Cards R Us," *Money,* January 1990, p. 38; Terri Thompson, "How Tykes Can Be Tycoons," *U.S. News & World Report,* February 19, 1990, pp. 68–69; "Seed Money for Small Fry," *Newsweek,* March 28, 1988, p. 50.

7. "Plodding Along in Financial Services," *Fortune,* April 25, 1988, pp. 108–9.

8. Steven Schwartz and Steve Weiner, "Many Firms Back Off from Offering Arrays of Financial Services," *The Wall Street Journal,* November 12, 1986, p. 1.

9. "Ten Money Saving Questions for Your Banker," *Money,* March 1988, p. 100. Reprinted from MONEY Magazine by special permission; copyright 1988 The Time Inc. Magazine Company.

10. "Governor Orders Banks to Close in Rhode Island," *Houston Post,* January 2, 1991, p. A4.

11. Gary Hector, "S&Ls: Where Did All Those Billions Go?" *Fortune,* September 10, 1990, pp. 82–88.

12. Catherine Yang, "Why Silverado Bought the Ranch," *Business Week,* December 3, 1990, pp. 146–47.

13. "A Small Success," *Economist,* November 10, 1990, pp. 101–2.

14. "When a Bank Collapses," *USA Today,* May 29, 1990, p. 2B.

15. "Accounting for Bank Problems," *USA Today,* May 29, 1990, p. 3B.

16. E. V. Bowen, *Money, Banking, and the Financial System* (St. Paul, Minn.: West Publishing, 1989), pp. 161–63.

17. "Putting Keynes' Head on Milton Friedman's Body," *Business Week,* July 31, 1989.

18. Manuel Shiffres, "The Federal Reserve Walks Quietly, but It Affects the Economy with a Big Stick," *Changing Times,* December 1988, p. 16.

19. "One Hole for All," *Economist,* September 8, 1990, p. 93.

20. "Spreading Financial Network," *Nation's Business,* June 1985, p. 42.

21. "Home Banking Is Here—If You Want It," *Business Week,* February 29, 1988, pp. 108–9.

22. "Banc One Branches Out for Future," *USA Today,* May 31, 1990, p. 1B.

23. Adapted from Gary Hector, "The Brash Banker Who Bought Texas," FORTUNE, August 27, 1990, pp. 53–62. © 1990 The Time Magazine Company. All rights reserved.

24. Sarah Bartlett, "Are Banks Obsolete?" *Business Week,* April 6, 1987, p. 76.

25. Terence P. Pare, "Banks Discover the Consumer,"

Fortune, February 12, 1990, pp. 96–104.

26. "Today's Leaders Talk about Tomorrow," *Fortune*, March 26, 1990, pp. 108–9; "A Brave New World for America's Banks," *The Economist*, January 12–18, 1991, pp. 69–70.

Chapter 18

1. "Risky Business," *Inc.*, March 1990, pp. 29–37; Elizabeth Conlin, "Adventure Capital," *Inc.*, September 1989, pp. 32–48.

2. Asra Nomani and Bridget O'Brian, "Winging It: A Braniff 'Consultant,' Age 24, Helped Run Airline into Ground," *The Wall Street Journal*, November 22, 1989, pp. 1A, 10A.

3. Roger Ricklefs, "Success Comes Too Late for Small Firm," *The Wall Street Journal*, June 12, 1989, p. 1B. Reprinted by permission of THE WALL STREET JOURNAL, © 1989 Dow Jones & Company, Inc. All Rights Reserved Worldwide.

4. David Ignatius, "U.S. Steel Makers Fail to Modernize, Quickly Fall behind Japanese," *The Wall Street Journal*, August 5, 1977, p. 1.

5. Scott Ticer, "Tobacco Company Profits Just Won't Quit," *Business Week*, December 22, 1986, p. 66.

6. Betsy Morris, "Philip Morris Jabs at Its Weakened Rival," *The Wall Street Journal*, July 21, 1989, p. 1B.

7. Daniel Timm, "LBO's Issues for Today, Concerns for Tomorrow," *Business Credit*, October 1989, pp. 18–19.

8. Ellyne E. Spragins, "Courting Your Banker," *Inc.*, May 1989, p. 129.

9. "Ain't Too Proud to Beg," *Business Month*, September 1990, p. 72.

10. John Huey, "Wal-Mart: Will It Take Over the World?" *Fortune*, January 30, 1989, p. 52.

11. Francine Schwadel, "Little Touches Spur Wal-Mart's Rise," *The Wall Street Journal*, September 22, 1989, p. 1B.

12. "It's Time to Be Cautious with Bonds," *Fortune: 1991 Investor Guide*, Fall 1990, p. 21.

13. Adapted from "Seven Deadly Sins of Debt," *Newsweek*, January 29, 1990; John Greenwald, "Predators Fall," *Time*, February 26, 1990, pp. 46; John Greenwald, "How Do You Spell Relief?" *Time*, January 22, 1990, pp. 48–49; "Crumbling Dream: Deep in Debt, Campeau Sees His Retail Empire Beginning to Slip Away," *The Wall Street Journal*, September 14, 1989, p. 1A; Francine Schwadel and Teri Agins, "Campeau's Woes May Mean Merrier Christmas Shopping," *The Wall Street Journal*, September 21, 1989, p. 1B.

14. Joann S. Lublin, "Walt Disney Co. Is Planning to Slip European Investors a Mickey," *The Wall Street Journal*, September 13, 1989, p. 1C; "EuroDisney: The Heart of Make Believe," Disney Productions, 1991.

15. Charles Moyer, James R. McGuigan, and William J. Kretlow, *Contemporary Financial Management* (St. Paul, Minn.: West Publishing, 1990), pp. 618–19.

16. "White Elephant to the Rescue," *Business Month*, September 1990, p. 80.

17. Richard J. Schonberger, "Just-in-Time Systems Focus on Simplicity," *Industrial Engineering*, October 1984, pp. 52–63.

18. Thomas A. Stewart, "The New American Century: Where We Stand," *Fortune*, Spring–Summer 1991 (Special Issue), pp. 14–23; Joseph E. Pattison, *Acquiring the Future: America's Survival and Success in the Global Economy* (Homewood, Ill.: Dow Jones-Irwin, 1990), pp. 224–26; Raynor Cannastra Associates, eds., *Career Sourcebook II: A Guide to Living and Working in the 21st Century*, 2nd ed. (Washington, D.C.: Edison Electric Institute), p. 12.

Chapter 19

1. Gary Putka, "People Invest Little Faith in Wall Street," *The Wall Street Journal*, September 25, 1989, p. 1B; Doug Bandow, "Insider Trading—Where's the Crime?" *National Review*, April 16, 1990, pp. 37–38; George Russell, "Trashing Wall Street," *Commentary*, July 1990, pp. 48–51.

2. Adapted from "Betting on the Value of Regional Banks' Plastic Portfolio," *Money*, January 1990, pp. 57–59; "You Love Plastic. Are You Ready for Plastic Bonds?" *Business Week*, July 17, 1989, p. 182; "Banks Pour Money into Bonds Backed by Credit Card Loans," *The Wall Street Journal*, March 26, 1990, p. C–1.

3. John Paul Newport, Jr., "Little Guys Face a New Market Era," *Fortune*, September 26, 1988, p. 117.

4. Ibid., p. 120.

5. Ibid., p. 117.

6. Ibid., p. 120.

7. *Fact Book* (New York: New York Stock Exchange, 1989).

8. "Yes, It's True: Amateur Investors Do Regularly Beat Wall Street," *The Wall Street Journal*, January 2, 1990, p. C–1.

9. Adapted from David Greising, "Was the Scandal in the Pits Mostly Small Potatoes?" *Business Week*, July 23, 1990, p. 27; "The Sting in the Pits," *Newsweek*, January 30, 1989, p. 54.

10. David Kirkpatrick, "Will You Be Able to Retire?" *Fortune*, July 31, 1989, p. 56.

11. Ibid.

12. Ibid., p. 59.

13. *Tax Guide for College Teachers* (College Park, Md.: Academic Information Services, 1987).

14. "You'll Know It's the 21st Century When. . .," *American Demographics*, December 1990, p. 25.

Chapter 20

1. Adapted from Joyce Price, "Debris Lingers Long after Hugo," *Insight*, April 2, 1990, p. 26; Thomas Jaffe, "The Morning After," *Forbes*, January 22, 1990, pp. 156–57; Michael Bradford and Louise Kertesz, "Quake's Insured Losses Estimated at $1 Billion," *Business Insurance*, October 30, 1989; "Hugo's Wrath Hits Insurers," *Business Insurance*, September 23, 1989; "After Shocks: The Bay Area Reeling, Plans a Fast Comeback from Ferocious Quake," *The Wall Street Journal*, October 19, 1989.

2. Michael M. Phillips, "Contraception R&D Falls out of Favor," *Los Angeles Times*, February 6, 1983, part 4, p. 3.

3. Barry Berman and Joel R. Evans, *Retail Management: A Strategic Approach*, 4th ed. (New York: Macmillan, 1989).

4. Ronald Bailey, "Legal Mayhem," *Forbes*, November 14, 1988, pp. 97–98.

5. David B. Hilder, "Small Firms Face Sharp Cost Hikes for Insurance—If They Can Get It," *The Wall Street Journal*, August 8, 1985.

6. Adapted from Bailey, "Legal Mayhem," pp. 97–98; Tim Smart, "A Shot at Shooting Down Punitive Damages," *Business Week*, July 16, 1990, pp. 62–63; "Punitive Damages: How Much Is Too Much?" *Business Week*, March 27, 1989, pp. 54, 56; David R. Strawbridge, "Does Punishment Fit the Civil Crime?" *Risk Management*, August 1988, pp. 44, 46–47; Peter W. Huber, *Liability: The Legal Revolution and Its Consequences* (New York: Basic Books, 1989).

7. Carolyn Lochhead, "Strict Liability Causing Some Firms to Give Up on Promising Ideas," *Washington Times*, August 22, 1988, pp. 46–47.

8. Bailey, "Legal Mayhem," p. 97.

9. "Corporate Profits Larger than Expected," *New York Times*, February 21, 1989, p. D1.

10. *Business Week*, October 9, 1989, p. 120.

11. Adapted from Don Dunn, "Putting More Life into Death Benefits," *Business Week*, February 19, 1990, p. 140; Leslie N. Vreeland, "Life Insurance for the Living," *Money*, March 1990, pp. 33–34; "You Can't Take It with You," *Newsweek*, May 8, 1989, p. 45; "Life Insurance that Pays Off While You're Still Around," *Business Week*, July 31, 1989, p. 100.

12. "How We Will Live," *U.S. News & World Report*, December 25, 1989–January 1, 1990, p. 62; "21st Century Health Solutions," *Prevention*, January 1990, p. 36; Marvin Cetron and Owen Davies, *American Renaissance: Our Life at the Turn of the 21st Century* (New York: St. Martin's Press, 1989), pp. 34, 39.

Chapter 21

1. Shirley A. Lazo, "Speaking of Dividends," *Barron's*, July 30, 1990, p. 52; Richard Behar, "Debt Topples a Tycoon," *Time*, June 11, 1990, p. 42; Stuart Flack, "Some Victory," *Forbes*, October 30, 1989, p. 10; "Accounting for Shamu," *New York Times*, February 11, 1990, sec. 3, p. 2; Calvin Reid, "HBJ Sells Theme Parks to Anheuser for $1.1 Billion," *Publishers Weekly*, October 13, 1989, p. 11.

2. "Best Moves 1990," *Changing Times*, January 1990, p. 46.

3. American Accounting Association, *A Statement of Basic Accounting Theory* (Evanston, Ill.: American Accounting Association, 1966), p. 1.

4. *Journal of Accountancy*, August 1990, p. 61.

5. Adapted from Joseph F. McKenna, "To Russia with Ledgers," *Industry Week*, January 22, 1990, p. 57. Reprinted with permission from INDUSTRY WEEK, January 22, 1990. Copyright Penton Publishing, Inc., Cleveland, Ohio.

6. Institute of Certificate Management Accountants.

7. Dana Wechsler and Wandycz Katarzyna, "In Inate Fear of Disclosure," *Forbes*, February 5, 1990, pp. 127–28.

8. Adapted from "On the Bandwagon," *Economist*, January 20, 1990, pp. 17–18; Howard Schlossberg, "Slashing through Market Clutter: Brand Equity Seen as a Major New Face for the 90s," *Marketing News*, March 5, 1990, pp. 1, 6.

9. Carol Klaiman, "In Accounting Jobs, Master's a Real Plus" (Jobs Column) *The Chicago Tribune*, June 2, 1991, sec. 8, p. 1; *Administration, Business, and Office*, in the Career Information Center Series, 4th ed. (Mission Hills, Calif.: Glencoe/Macmillan, 1990), pp. 106–8; Marvin Cetron and Owen Davies, *American Renaissance: Our Life at the Turn*

of the 21st Century (New York: St. Martin's Press, 1989), p. 235; "The Growth Careers," *Working Woman*, July 1991, p. 58.

Chapter 22

1. "Periscope," *Newsweek*, April 8, 1991; Kathleen E. Christensen, "Taking the Office outside Corporate Walls," *Working Woman*, May 1990, pp. 65–75; Frances Seghers, "A Search-and-Destroy Mission—against Paper," *Business Week*, February 6, 1989, pp. 91–95; Susan Dillingham, "Employers Find Advantages in Sending Workers Home," *Insight*, December 5, 1988, pp. 40–41.

2. Floyd Kemske, "Brains Will Replace BTUs," *Information Center*, June 1990, pp. 22–24.

3. "Soldiering into the Modern Computer Era, 1943," *The Wall Street Journal*, June 16, 1989, p. B1.

4. Clyde W. Holsapple and Andrew B. Whinston, *The Information Jungle* (Homewood, Ill.: Dow Jones-Irwin, 1988), p. 26.

5. "IBM Shows Off Upgraded Mainframes," *Herald-Leader* (Lexington, Ky.), September 6, 1990, p. C5.

6. John W. Verity, "Supercomputers: Brute Strength—and a Sensitive Issue," *Business Week*, April 30, 1990, p. 83.

7. Bob Donath, "Business Marketers and Their Micros," *Business Marketing*, May 1988, pp. 68–76.

8. Adapted from Richard E. Ladner, "Computer Accessibility for Federal Workers with Disabilities: It's the Law," *Communications of the ACM*, August 1989, pp. 952–56; Susan Kerr, "For People with Handicaps, Computers = Independence," *Datamation*, May 1, 1988, pp. 39–42; Kathryn Hudson, "The Disabled Get Computer Ability," *Insight*, May 23, 1988, pp. 42–43.

9. Robert S. Boyd, "Computer Guidance," *Herald-Leader* (Lexington, Ky.), March 12, 1989, pp. A1, A7.

10. "Speaking of Fast Food," *Herald-Leader* (Lexington, Ky.), January 29, 1990, p. D2.

11. Gary Slutsker, "Relationship Marketing," *Forbes*, April 3, 1989, pp. 145–47.

12. Adapted from Tom Eisenhart, "Faced with Limited Resources, the Computer Is Becoming a Key Tool in Staying Close to the Customer." Reprinted with permission from *Business Marketing*, May 1988, pp. 49–52. Copyright Crain Communications, Inc. All Rights Reserved.

13. Paul Desmond, "Car Wash King Oversees Empire via Integrated Network," *Network World*, November 14, 1988, pp. 1, 87.

14. G. Michael Ashmore, "Telecommunications Opens New Strategic Vistas," *Journal of Business Strategy*, March–April 1990, pp. 58–61.

15. Jeffrey P. Stamen, "Decision Support Systems Help Planners Hit Their Targets," *Journal of Business Strategy*, March–April 1990, pp. 30–33.

16. Christopher Elias, "An 'Executive' Newcomer Takes Its Place in the Office," *Insight*, July 11, 1988, pp. 38–40.

17. Michael W. Miller, "Computers May Get Vast Ability to Blend Data, Images, Sound," *The Wall Street Journal*, June 7, 1989, pp. A1, A4.

18. Kathleen K. Wiegner, "Speed Demons," *Forbes*, January 9, 1989, pp. 302–3.

19. Maria Shao, "Beyond the Laptop: The Incredible Shrinking Computer," *Business Week*, May 15, 1989, pp. 134–37.

20. James Fischer, "Predictions," *Information Center*, August 1990, p. 6.

21. James Daly, "Wendy's System Finds the Beefs," *Computerworld*, September 25, 1989, p. 39.

22. Geoff Lewis, "Computers Are Getting More Personal than Ever," *Business Week*, January 9, 1989, p. 93.

23. David C. Rudd, "IBM Prepares 'Vaccine' for Computer Virus," *Chicago Tribune*, October 6, 1989, pp. 1–2.

24. Gayle Hanson, "Computer Users Pack a Keypunch in a Hightech World of Crime," *Insight*, April 15, 1991, pp. 8–16.

25. "You'll Know It's the 21st Century When. . .," *American Demographics*, December 1990, p. 26.

S ubject Index